MW01091721

Tax Formula for Individi

Income (broadly defined)	$xx,xxx
Less: Exclusions	(x,xxx)
Gross income	$xx,xxx
Less: Deductions *for* adjusted gross income	(x,xxx)
Adjusted gross income	$xx,xxx
Less: The greater of— Total itemized deductions *or* standard deduction	(x,xxx)
Less: Personal and dependency exemptions*	(x,xxx)
Deduction for qualified business income**	(x,xxx)
Taxable income	$xx,xxx
Tax on taxable income	$ x,xxx
Less: Tax credits (including Federal income tax withheld and prepaid)	(xxx)
Tax due (or refund)	$ xxx

*Exemption deductions are not allowed from 2018 through 2025.
**Only applies from 2018 through 2025.

Note: For 2021, individuals using the standard deduction may also subtract *from* adjusted gross income, cash charitable contributions of up to $300 ($600 if married, filing jointly).

Basic Standard Deduction Amounts

Filing Status	2021	2022
Single	$12,550	$12,950
Married, filing jointly	25,100	25,900
Surviving spouse	25,100	25,900
Head of household	18,800	19,400
Married, filing separately	12,550	12,950

Amount of Each Additional Standard Deduction

Filing Status	2021	2022
Single	$1,700	$1,750
Married, filing jointly	1,350	1,400
Surviving spouse	1,350	1,400
Head of household	1,700	1,750
Married, filing separately	1,350	1,400

Personal and Dependency Exemption

2021	2022
$4,300	$4,400

Note: Exemption deductions have been suspended from 2018 through 2025. However, the personal and dependency exemption amount is used for other purposes (including determining whether a "qualifying relative" is a taxpayer's dependent).

Essentials of Taxation: Individuals and Business Entities

2023

General Editors

Annette Nellen
J.D., CPA, CGMA

Andrew D. Cuccia
Ph.D., CPA

Mark B. Persellin
Ph.D., CPA, CFP®

James C. Young
Ph.D., CPA

Contributing Authors

Andrew D. Cuccia
Ph.D., CPA
University of Oklahoma

Annette Nellen
J.D., CPA, CGMA
San Jose State University

Mark B. Persellin
Ph.D., CPA, CFP®
St. Mary's University

William A. Raabe
Ph.D., CPA
Philadelphia, Pennsylvania

Miles Romney
Ph.D.
Florida State University

Toby Stock
Ph.D., CPA
Ohio University

Donald R. Trippeer
Ph.D., CPA
State University of New York College at Oneonta

Kristina Zvinakis
Ph.D.
The University of Texas at Austin

SWFT Series Authors

James H. Boyd
Ph.D., CPA
Arizona State University

Bradrick M. Cripe
Ph.D., CPA
Northern Illinois University

D. Larry Crumbley
Ph.D., CPA
Texas A&M University – Corpus Christi

Andrew D. Cuccia
Ph.D., CPA
University of Oklahoma

Steven C. Dilley
J.D., Ph.D., CPA
Michigan State University

Sharon S. Lassar
Ph.D., CPA
University of Denver

David M. Maloney
Ph.D., CPA
University of Virginia

Annette Nellen
J.D., CPA, CGMA
San Jose State University

Mark B. Persellin
Ph.D., CPA, CFP®
St. Mary's University

William A. Raabe
Ph.D., CPA
Philadelphia, Pennsylvania

Toby Stock
Ph.D., CPA
Ohio University

James C. Young
Ph.D., CPA
Northern Illinois University

Kristina Zvinakis
Ph.D.
The University of Texas at Austin

Australia • Brazil • Canada • Mexico • Singapore • United Kingdom • United States

***South-Western Federal Taxation: Essentials of Taxation: Individuals and Business Entities,* 2023 Edition**

Annette Nellen, Andrew D. Cuccia, Mark B. Persellin, James C. Young

SVP, Product: Erin Joyner

VP, Product: Thais Alencar

Product Director: Joe Sabatino

Product Manager: Jonathan Gross

Product Assistant: Flannery Cowan

Learning Designer: Kristen Meere

Sr. Content Manager: Nadia Saloom

Digital Project Manager: Steven McMillan

VP, Product Marketing: Jason Sakos

Director, Product Marketing: Danae April

Product Marketing Manager: Colin M. Kramer

IP Analyst: Ashley Maynard

IP Project Manager: Nick Barrows

Production Service: Straive

Designer: Chris Doughman

Cover Image Source: Pgiam/E+/Getty Images

Interior Image Source:
Concept Summary: iStock.com/enot-poloskun
Global Tax Issues: Enot-Poloskun/E+/Getty Images
Ethics & Equity: iStock.com/LdF
Comprehensive Tax Return Problems: iStock.com/peepo
Financial Disclosure Insights: Vyaseleva Elena/Shutterstock.com
Framework 1040: Concept Photo/Shutterstock.com

ISSN: 1544-3590
2023 Annual Edition

Student Edition ISBN: 978-0-357-72010-3
Looseleaf Edition ISBN: 978-0-357-72012-7

Cengage
200 Pier 4 Boulevard
Boston, MA 02210
USA

Cengage is a leading provider of customized learning solutions with employees residing in nearly 40 different countries and sales in more than 125 countries around the world. Find your local representative at **www.cengage.com**.

To learn more about Cengage platforms and services, register or access your online learning solution, or purchase materials for your course, visit **www.cengage.com**.

Printed in the United States of America
Print Number: 01   Print Year: 2022

Preface

Committed to Educational Success

South-Western Federal Taxation (SWFT) is the most trusted and best-selling taxation series used by colleges and universities. We are focused exclusively on providing the most useful, comprehensive, and up-to-date tax texts, online study aids, tax preparation tools, and research tools to help instructors and students succeed in their tax courses and beyond.

SWFT is a comprehensive package of teaching and learning materials, significantly enhanced with each edition to meet instructor and student needs and to add overall value to learning taxation.

Essentials of Taxation: Individuals and Business Entities, 2023 Edition provides a dynamic learning experience inside and outside of the classroom. Built with resources and tools that have been identified as the most important, our complete learning system provides options for students to achieve success.

In addition, *Essentials of Taxation: Individuals and Business Entities*, 2023 Edition provides accessible, comprehensive, and authoritative coverage of the relevant tax code and regulations as they pertain to the individual or business taxpayer, as well as coverage of all major developments in Federal income taxation.

In revising the 2023 Edition, we focused on:

- ***Accessibility. Clarity. Substance.*** The authors and editors made this their focus as they revised the 2023 edition. Coverage has been streamlined to make it more accessible to students, and difficult concepts have been clarified, all without losing the substance that makes up the *South-Western Federal Taxation* series.
- ***Developing professional skills.*** SWFT excels in bringing students to a professional level in their tax knowledge and skills, to prepare them for immediate success in their careers. In addition to exposing students to tax policy and law, our materials include opportunities for students to further develop communication skills, to use tax preparation and research software, to apply net present value concepts to the tax planning process, to enhance their spreadsheet and data analytics capabilities, and to familiarize themselves with the format and content of the CPA Exam (including the upcoming CPA Evolution version of the exam).
- ***CNOWv2 as a complete learning system.*** Cengage Learning understands that digital learning solutions are central to the classroom. Through sustained research, we continually refine our learning solutions in CNOWv2 to meet evolving student and instructor needs. CNOWv2 fulfills learning and course management needs by offering a personalized study plan, video lectures, auto-graded homework, auto-graded tests, and a full eBook with features and advantages that address common challenges.

Learning Tools and Features to Help Students Make the Connection

Full-Color Design: We understand that students struggle with learning difficult tax law concepts and applying them to real-world scenarios. The 2023 edition uses color to bring the text to life, capture student attention, and present the tax law in an understandable and logical format.

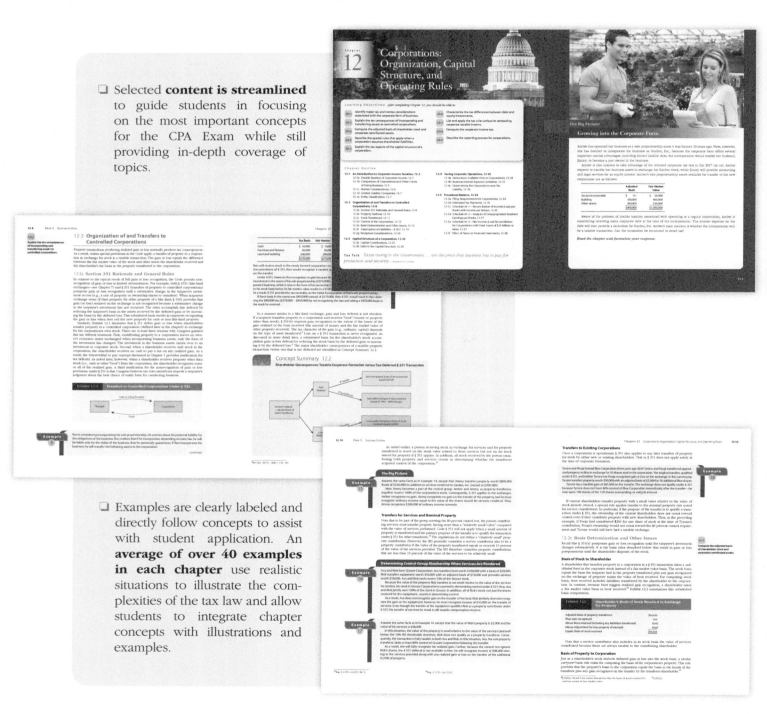

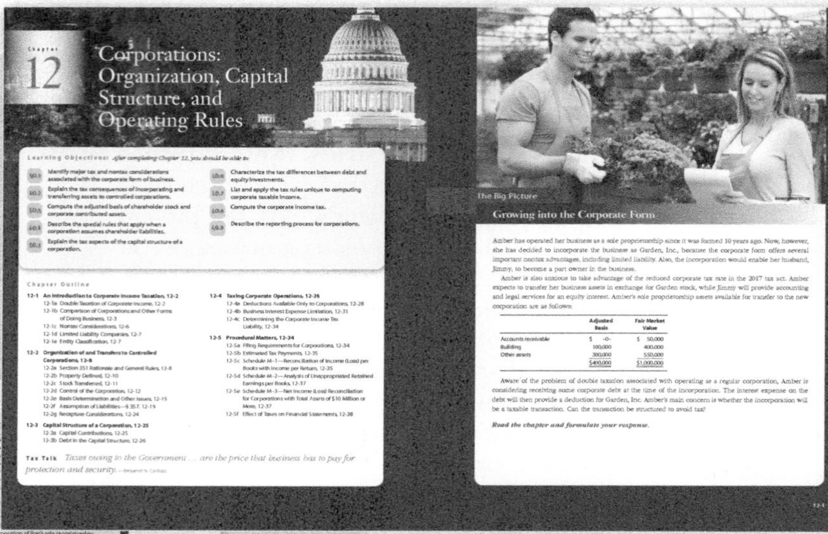

- Selected **content is streamlined** to guide students in focusing on the most important concepts for the CPA Exam while still providing in-depth coverage of topics.

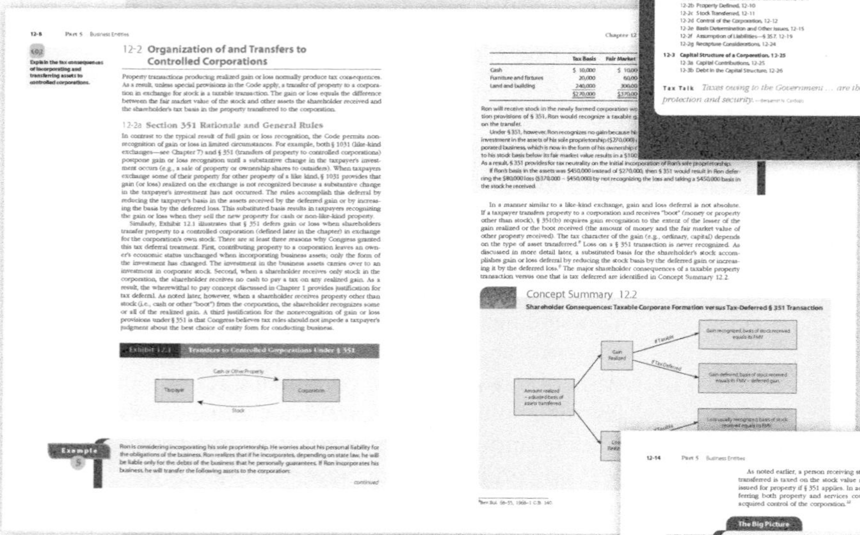

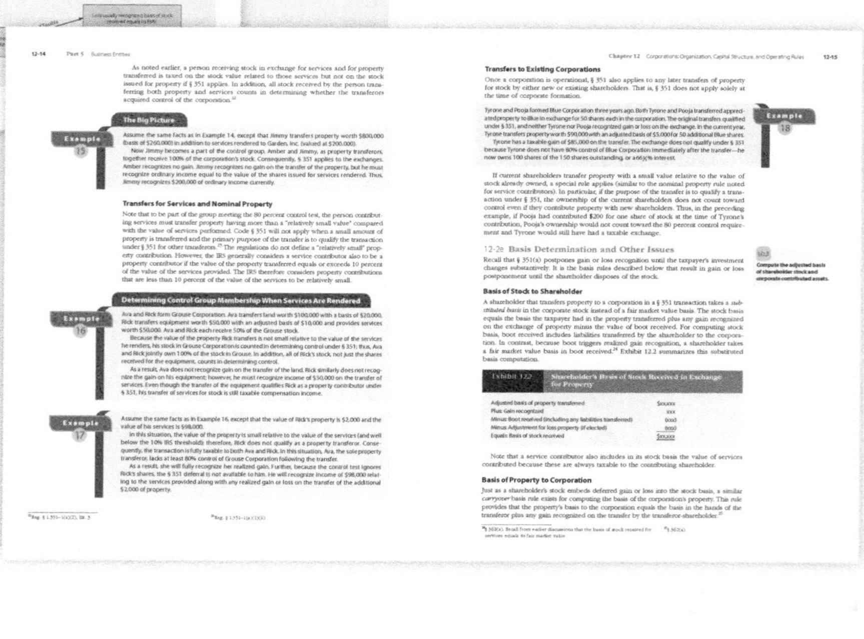

- Examples are clearly labeled and directly follow concepts to assist with student application. An **average of over 40 examples in each chapter** use realistic situations to illustrate the complexities of the tax law and allow students to integrate chapter concepts with illustrations and examples.

Computational Exercises: Students need to learn to apply the rules and concepts covered in each chapter to truly understand them. These exercises, many of which mirror text examples, allow students to practice and apply what they are learning.

- ❑ Found in the end-of-chapter sections of the textbook
- ❑ CNOWv2 provides algorithmic versions of these problems

Computational Exercises

1. **LO.4** Enerico contributes $100,000 cash in exchange for a 40% interest in the calendar year ABC LLC. This year ABC generates $80,000 of ordinary taxable income and has no separately stated items. Enerico withdraws $10,000 cash from the partnership at the end of the tax year.
   a. Compute Enerico's gross income from ABC's ordinary income for the tax year.
   b. Compute Enerico's gross income from the LLC's cash distribution.
2. **LO.2** Henrietta transfers cash of $75,000 and equipment with a fair market value of $25,000 (basis to her as a sole proprietor, $10,000) in exchange for a 40% profit and loss interest worth $100,000 in the XYZ Partnership.
   a. Compute Henrietta's realized and recognized gains from the asset transfers.
   b. Compute Henrietta's basis in her interest in XYZ.
   c. What is XYZ's basis in the equipment that it now holds?

Research and Data Analytics Problems:

- ❑ Research Problems provide students with vital practice in an increasingly demanded skill area. These end-of-chapter items ask students to find and analyze tax documents, helping them to understand the application of this information in various scenarios. These essential features prepare students for professional tax environments.

Becker Professional Education Review Questions: End-of-chapter CPA Review Questions from Becker PREPARE STUDENTS FOR SUCCESS. Students review key concepts using proven questions from Becker Professional Education®—one of the industry's most effective tools to prepare for the CPA Exam.

- ❑ Located in select end-of-chapter sections
- ❑ Tagged by concept in CNOWv2
- ❑ Questions similar to what students would actually find on the CPA Exam

Becker

Becker CPA Review Questions

Becker

1. On January 1, year 5, Olinto Corp., an accrual basis, calendar year C corporation, had $35,000 in accumulated earnings and profits. For year 5, Olinto had current earnings and profits of $15,000 and made two $40,000 cash distributions to its shareholders, one in April and one in September of year 5. What amount of the year 5 distributions is classified as dividend income to Olinto's shareholders?
   a. $15,000 c. $50,000
   b. $35,000 d. $80,000
2. Fox Corp. owned 2,000 shares of Duffy Corp. stock that it bought in year 0 for $9 per share. In year 8, when the fair market value of the Duffy stock was $20 per share, Fox distributed this stock to a noncorporate shareholder. Fox's recognized gain on this distribution was:
   a. $40,000 c. $18,000
   b. $22,000 d. $0

See how the SWFT series helps students understand the big picture and the relevancy behind what they are learning.

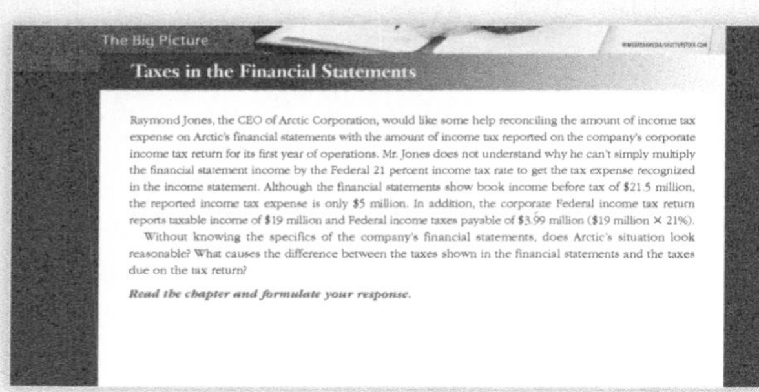

The Big Picture

Taxes in the Financial Statements

Raymond Jones, the CEO of Arctic Corporation, would like some help reconciling the amount of income tax expense on Arctic's financial statements with the amount of income tax reported on the company's corporate income tax return for its first year of operations. Mr. Jones does not understand why he can't simply multiply the financial statement income by the Federal 21 percent income tax rate to get the tax expense recognized in the income statement. Although the financial statements show book income before tax of $21.5 million, the reported income tax expense is only $5 million. In addition, the corporate Federal income tax return reports taxable income of $19 million and Federal income taxes payable of $3.99 million ($19 million × 21%).

Without knowing the specifics of the company's financial statements, does Arctic's situation look reasonable? What causes the difference between the taxes shown in the financial statements and the taxes due on the tax return?

Read the chapter and formulate your response.

The Big Picture: **Tax Solutions for the Real World.**

Taxation comes alive at the start of each chapter as The Big Picture examples provide a glimpse into the lives, families, careers, and tax situations of typical individual or business taxpayers. Students will follow a family, individual, or other taxpayer throughout the chapter, to discover how the concepts they are learning apply in the real world.

Finally, to solidify student comprehension, each chapter concludes with a **Refocus on The Big Picture** summary and tax planning scenario. These scenarios re-emphasize the concepts and topics from the chapter and allow students to confirm their understanding of the material.

Bridge Discipline Boxes and End-of-Chapter Questions:

Bridge Discipline boxes throughout the text present material and concepts from other disciplines such as economics, financial accounting, law, and finance. They help to bridge the gap between taxation issues and topics raised in other business courses. **Bridge Discipline questions**, in the end-of-chapter material, help test these concepts and give students the chance to apply concepts they've learned in the Bridge Discipline boxes.

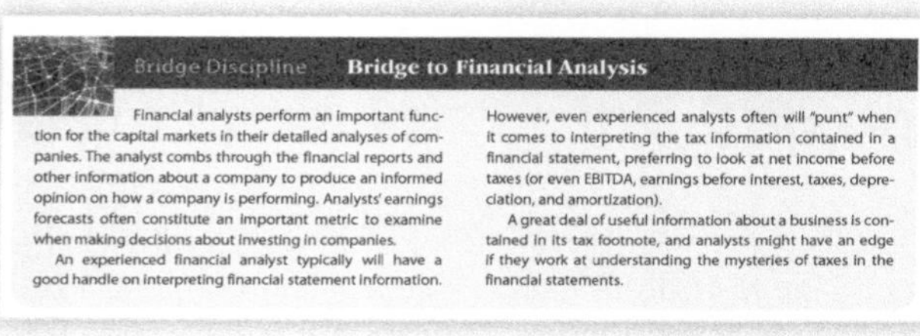

Bridge Discipline **Bridge to Financial Analysis**

Financial analysts perform an important function for the capital markets in their detailed analyses of companies. The analyst combs through the financial reports and other information about a company to produce an informed opinion on how a company is performing. Analysts' earnings forecasts often constitute an important metric to examine when making decisions about investing in companies.

An experienced financial analyst typically will have a good handle on interpreting financial statement information. However, even experienced analysts often will "punt" when it comes to interpreting the tax information contained in a financial statement, preferring to look at net income before taxes (or even EBITDA, earnings before interest, taxes, depreciation, and amortization).

A great deal of useful information about a business is contained in its tax footnote, and analysts might have an edge if they work at understanding the mysteries of taxes in the financial statements.

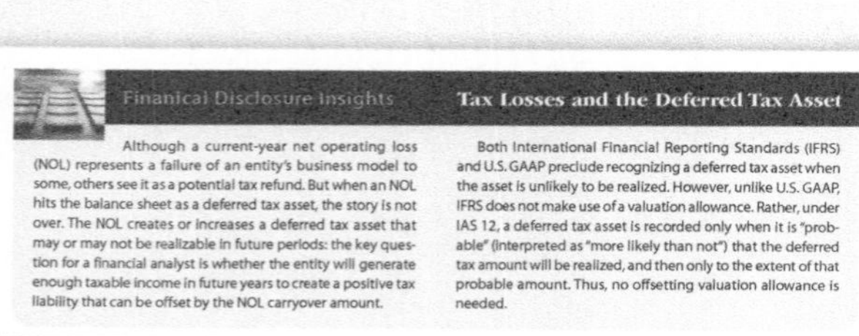

Finanical Disclosure Insights **Tax Losses and the Deferred Tax Asset**

Although a current-year net operating loss (NOL) represents a failure of an entity's business model to some, others see it as a potential tax refund. But when an NOL hits the balance sheet as a deferred tax asset, the story is not over. The NOL creates or increases a deferred tax asset that may or may not be realizable in future periods: the key question for a financial analyst is whether the entity will generate enough taxable income in future years to create a positive tax liability that can be offset by the NOL carryover amount.

Both International Financial Reporting Standards (IFRS) and U.S. GAAP preclude recognizing a deferred tax asset when the asset is unlikely to be realized. However, unlike U.S. GAAP, IFRS does not make use of a valuation allowance. Rather, under IAS 12, a deferred tax asset is recorded only when it is "probable" (interpreted as "more likely than not") that the deferred tax amount will be realized, and then only to the extent of that probable amount. Thus, no offsetting valuation allowance is needed.

Financial Disclosure Insights:

Tax professionals need to understand how taxes affect financial statements. **Financial Disclosure Insights**, appearing throughout the text, use current information about existing taxpayers to highlight book-tax reporting differences, effective tax rates, and trends in reporting conventions.

Digging Deeper:

Designed to help students go further in their knowledge of certain topics, **Digging Deeper** links within the text provide more in-depth coverage than the text provides. Digging Deeper materials can be found on the book's website at **www.cengage.com**. Some of the end-of-chapter exercises are labeled "Digging Deeper" to indicate that students should use those materials to help answer the question.

Information on criteria used in designing a tax structure can be found on this book's companion website: www.cengage.com | 1 Digging Deeper

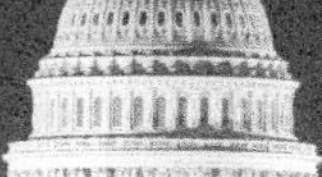

Tax Planning Framework: To demonstrate the relevance of tax planning for business and individual taxpayers, ***Essentials of Taxation: Individuals and Business Entities*** presents a **tax planning framework** like one used by tax practitioners. Introduced in Chapter 1, this framework extends to a series of **Tax Planning Strategies** incorporated throughout the remainder of the text. The inclusion of the tax planning framework, and the planning strategies in each chapter, makes it easier than ever to understand the effects that careful tax planning can have in today's world.

Exhibit 1.3 General Framework for Income Tax Planning

Tax Formula	Tax Planning Strategy	Tax Planning Examples
Income and exclusions	➢ **Avoid income recognition.**	Compensate employees with nontaxable fringe benefits (see Example 19).
	➢ **Postpone recognition of income to achieve tax deferral.**	Postpone sale of assets (see Example 20).
− Deductions	➢ **Maximize deductible amounts.**	Invest in stock of another corporation (see Example 21).
	➢ **Accelerate recognition of deductions to achieve tax deferral.**	Elect to deduct charitable contribution in year of pledge rather than in year of payment (see Example 22).

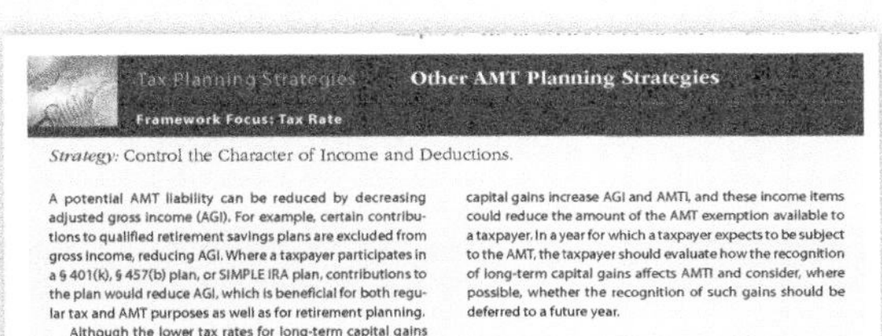
Tax Planning Strategies **Other AMT Planning Strategies**

Framework Focus: Tax Rate

Strategy: Control the Character of Income and Deductions.

A potential AMT liability can be reduced by decreasing adjusted gross income (AGI). For example, certain contributions to qualified retirement savings plans are excluded from gross income, reducing AGI. Where a taxpayer participates in a § 401(k), § 457(b) plan, or SIMPLE IRA plan, contributions to the plan would reduce AGI, which is beneficial for both regular tax and AMT purposes as well as for retirement planning.

Although the lower tax rates for long-term capital gains apply for both regular tax and AMT purposes, such long-term capital gains increase AGI and AMTI, and these income items could reduce the amount of the AMT exemption available to a taxpayer. In a year for which a taxpayer expects to be subject to the AMT, the taxpayer should evaluate how the recognition of long-term capital gains affects AMTI and consider, where possible, whether the recognition of such gains should be deferred to a future year.

Tax Planning Strategies: The tax planning framework extends to subsequent chapters as **Tax Planning Strategies boxes** that are tied to the topical coverage of the chapters. Planning Strategies often contain examples to further illustrate the concept for students.

Global Tax Issues: The **Global Tax Issues** feature gives insight into the ways in which taxation is affected by international concerns and illustrates the effects of various events on tax liabilities across the globe.

Global Tax Issues **Filing a Joint Return**

John is a U.S. citizen and resident, but he spends much of his time in London, where his employer sends him on frequent assignments. John is married to Victoria, a citizen and resident of the United Kingdom.

Can John and Victoria file a joint return for U.S. Federal income tax purposes? Although § 6013(a)(1) specifically precludes the filing of a joint return if one spouse is a nonresident alien, another Code provision permits an exception. Under § 6013(g), the parties can elect to treat the nonqualifying spouse as a "resident" of the United States. This election would allow John and Victoria to file jointly.

But should John and Victoria make this election? If Victoria has considerable income of her own (from non-U.S. sources), the election could be ill-advised. As a nonresident alien, Victoria's non-U.S. source income ordinarily *would not* be subject to the U.S. income tax. If she is treated as a U.S. resident, however, her non-U.S. source income *will be subject to U.S. tax*. Under the U.S. worldwide approach to taxation, all income (regardless of where earned) of anyone who is a *resident* or *citizen* of the United States is subject to tax.

Take your students from Motivation to Mastery with CNOWv2

CNOWv2 is a powerful course management tool and online homework resource that elevates student thinking by providing superior content designed with the entire student workflow in mind.

- **Motivation:** engage students and better prepare them for class
- **Application:** help students learn problem-solving behavior and skills to guide them to complete taxation problems on their own
- **Mastery:** help students make the leap from memorizing concepts to actual critical thinking

Motivation —

To help with student engagement and preparedness, CNOWv2 for SWFT offers:

- **"Tax Drills" test students on key concepts and applications.** With three to five questions per learning objective, these "quick-hit" questions help students prepare for class lectures or review prior to an exam.

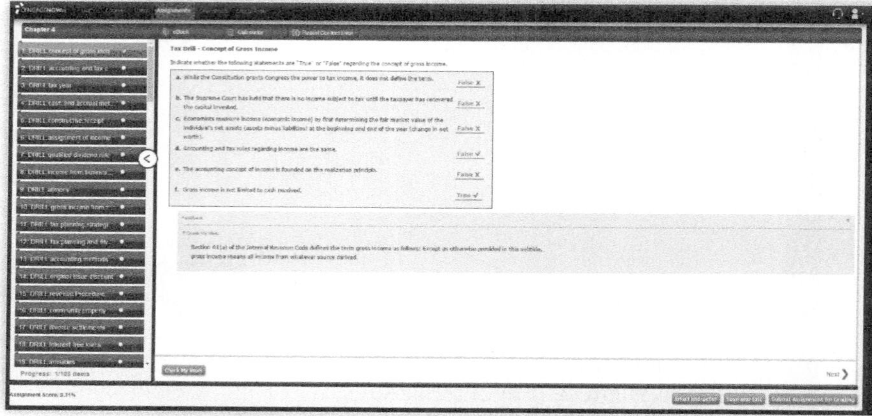

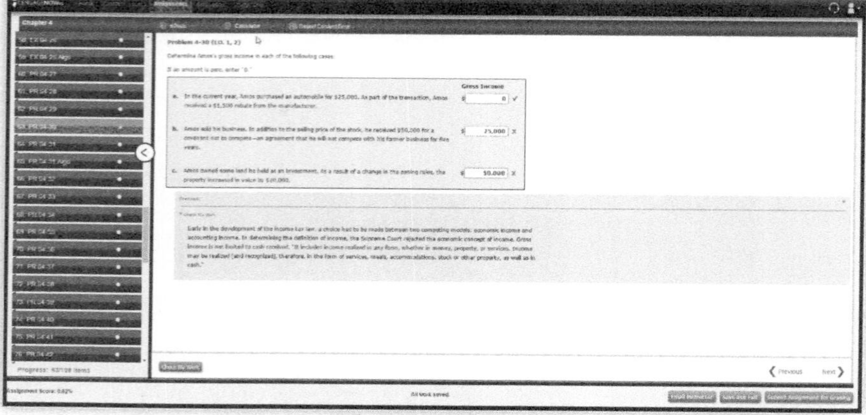

Application —

Students need to learn problem-solving behavior and skills, to guide them to complete taxation problems on their own. However, as students try to work through homework problems, sometimes they become stuck and need extra help. To reinforce concepts and keep students on the right track, CNOWv2 for SWFT offers the following:

- **End-of-chapter homework from the text** is expanded and enhanced to follow the workflow a professional would use to solve various client scenarios. These enhancements better engage students and encourage them to think like a tax professional.

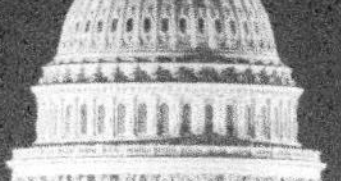

- **Algorithmic versions** of end-of-chapter homework are available for computational exercises and at least 15 problems per chapter.
- **"Check My Work" Feedback.** Homework questions include immediate feedback so students can learn as they go. Levels of feedback include an option for "check my work" prior to submission of an assignment.
- **Post-Submission Feedback.** After submitting an assignment, students receive even more extensive feedback explaining why their answers were incorrect. Instructors can decide how much feedback their students receive and when, including the full solution.
- **Built-in Test Bank** for online assessment.

Mastery —

- **Tax Form Problems** give students the option to complete the Cumulative Intuit ProConnect Tax problems and other homework items found in the end-of-chapter manually or in a digital environment.
- **An Adaptive Study Plan** comes complete with an eBook, practice quizzes, glossary, and flashcards. It is designed to help give students additional support and prepare them for the exam.

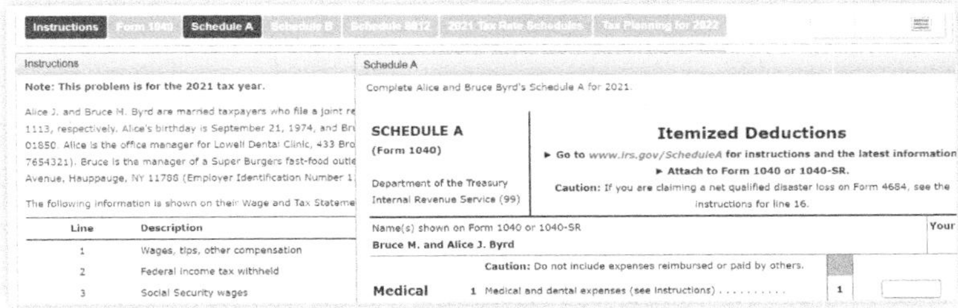

CNOWv2 Instant Access Code ISBN:
978-0-357-72015-8

Contact your Cengage Learning Consultant about different bundle options.

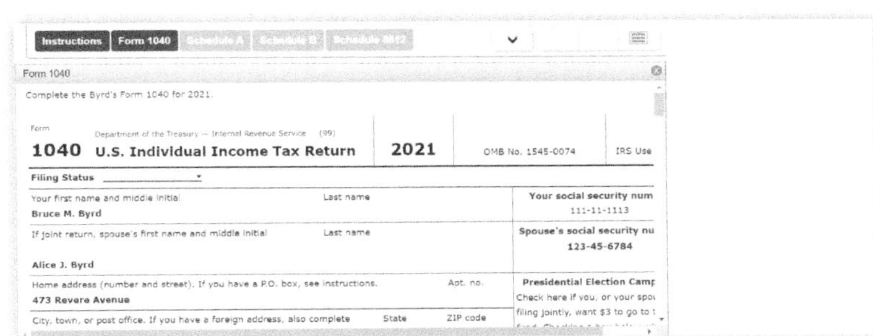

Extensively Revised. Definitively Up to Date.

Each year the ***South-Western Federal Taxation*** series is updated with thousands of changes to each text. Some of these changes result from the feedback we receive from instructors and students in the form of reviews, focus groups, web surveys, and personal e-mail correspondence to our authors and team members. Other changes come from our careful analysis of the evolving tax environment. **We make sure that every tax law change relevant to the introductory taxation course was considered, summarized, and fully integrated into the revision of text and supplementary materials.**

The ***South-Western Federal Taxation*** authors have made every effort to keep all materials up to date and accurate. All chapters contain the following general changes for the 2023 edition:

- Updated materials to reflect changes made through legislative action, new administrative rulings, and court decisions.
- Streamlined chapter content (where applicable) to clarify material and make it easier for students to understand.
- Revised numerous materials as the result of changes caused by indexing of statutory amounts.
- Revised Problem Materials, Computational Exercises, and CPA Exam problems.
- Updated Chapter Outlines to provide an overview of the material and to make it easier to locate specific topics.
- Revised *Financial Disclosure Insights* and *Global Tax Issues* for current developments.
- Added a "Planning" icon to end-of-chapter questions requiring tax planning considerations.

In addition, the following materials are available online:

- An appendix that helps instructors broaden and customize coverage of important tax provisions of the Affordable Care Act. (Instructor Companion Website at **www.cengage.com/login**)
- An appendix that covers depreciation and the Accelerated Cost Recovery System (ACRS). (Instructor Companion Website at **www.cengage.com/login**)

Chapter 1

- Expanded discussion on the relevance of taxation to accounting and finance professionals to include the role of a corporate tax director in global growth strategy (added to the planning function), ESG reporting (likely covered in other accounting and business courses and now part of AACSB accreditation standards), and tax advocacy.
- Added information on space travel tax proposals to Digging Deeper #3.
- Added information (and a related example involving a college student intern) on Preparer Tax Identification Numbers (PTINs).
- Updated figures based on revised IRS data and inflation adjustments.
- Added Research Problem 5 on the data security question tied to the "Safeguards Rule" that is on Form W–12 to obtain or renew a PTIN (ties to the CPA Evolution Model Curriculum).

Chapter 2

- Added information on IRS FAQs to Digging Deeper #1 [covering new IRS procedures identified in IR-2021-202 (October 15, 2021)].
- Added Problem 31 asking students to gather information about the House Ways and Means Committee.

Chapter 3

- Updated a Financial Disclosure Insights feature to discuss profitable corporations paying no income tax in 2020.
- Deleted the discussion of the corporate alternative minimum tax and the deferred tax asset it created.
- Added an end-of-chapter problem regarding the effect of tax rate changes on reported tax expense.
- Added an end-of-chapter problem requiring the creation of an Excel workbook to perform a provision.

Chapter 4

- Made minor updates such as for inflation-adjusted amounts.

Chapter 5

- Revised and clarified the discussion of research and experimental expenditures.
- Updated chapter materials as needed to reflect changes to § 179 limits (including SUVs) and luxury automobile limits.
- Added discussion regarding the impact of the § 179 expense on the requirement to use the mid-quarter convention.
- Added the depletion rates for several minerals.
- Added four new Becker CPA Review Questions.

Chapter 6

- Added new Digging Deeper topic on individual taxpayer net operating losses.

Chapter 7

- Revised and clarified discussion of cost basis identification problems.
- Revised Concept Summary 7.3 to clarify the replacement property tests applicable to involuntary conversions.

Chapter 8

- Revised and clarified discussion of special holding period rules.
- Revised Concept Summary 8.4 to clarify the capital gain tax rates applicable to noncorporate taxpayers.
- Updated Tax Fact illustrating the proportion of AGI comprised of capital gain and qualified dividend income.
- Revised and clarified discussion of § 1250 recapture, including § 291 for corporations, as well as related Example 51.

Chapter 9

- Updated chapter materials to reflect 2021 tax legislation and 2022 inflation adjustments.

Chapter 10

- Streamlined discussion on prizes and award.
- Streamlined discussion on tax credits.
- Moved brief discussion of premium tax credit to Digging Deeper and online ACA appendix.

Chapter 11

- Updated discussion on retirement plans for sole proprietors.

Chapter 12

- Streamlined and clarified chapter materials as needed.

Chapter 13

- No significant changes needed or made.

Chapter 14

- Updated inflation-adjusted amounts.
- Updated Tax Fact features for most recent IRS statistics on business returns filed.

Chapter 15

- Expanded Bridge Discipline Problem 1 to also have students check if their state imposes an entity level tax on S corporations.
- Added Research Problem 3 for students to review and summarize an IRS FSA on stock basis and losses for an S corporation shareholder.

Chapter 16

- Updated and added statistics about the global economy and worldwide tax rates.
- Added a new Digging Deeper on recent modernization by the Multistate Tax Commission of the authority for states to impose income tax obligations within P.L. 86–272.
- Added one new Becker CPA Review Question.

Chapter 17

- Updated Tax Fact illustrating the amount of various credits claimed by corporations.
- Updated text and end-of-chapter problems for numerous inflation adjustments.
- Added a new research problem that directs students to examine the number of taxpayers with an AMT liability and how much AMT was paid in the years surrounding the TCJA of 2017.
- Removed discussion of premium tax credit, which is covered in the online appendix on the Affordable Care Act.

Chapter 18

- Updated Tax Fact and related Exhibit 18.1 regarding the number and proportion of businesses conducted in various legal forms.
- Added a new problem requiring the review of a semi-complete Schedule K–1 (1065) and the computation of self-employment earnings for a partner.

Tax Law Outlook

From your SWFT Series Editors:
Legislation related to the COVID-19 pandemic was a vehicle for tax changes in 2021, including a wide variety of tax changes incorporated into the American Rescue Plan Act of 2021. The Biden administration and Congress continue to discuss a wide variety of tax law changes. Although the Build Back Better plan was not enacted, pieces of that proposal are likely to be debated (and possibly adopted) before the end of 2022. In addition, it is likely that Congress will return to its pattern of extending expired and expiring tax provisions sometime in 2022.

Annually, the Joint Committee on Taxation publishes a report of all expired and expiring provisions in the tax law. The report released in January 2022 lists 40 provisions that expired in 2021 (**jct.gov/publications/2022/jcx-1-22/**). This list does not include the change to § 174 for R&D expenditures to be capitalized and amortized (rather than currently expensed) for tax years beginning after 2021. The Build Back Better Act passed by the House in November 2021 extended that date by four years. If that act does not become law, it is likely that Congress will find another way to extend the effective date of this change that originated with the Tax Cuts and Jobs Act of 2017.

Taxpayers and their advisers will need to evaluate how these changes affect their financial planning strategies and adjust their plans appropriately. The SWFT editors will be monitoring these activities and provide updates to adopters as needed.

Supplements Support Students and Instructors

Built around the areas students and instructors have identified as the most important, our integrated supplements package offers more flexibility than ever before to suit the way instructors teach and students learn.

Online and Digital Resources for Students

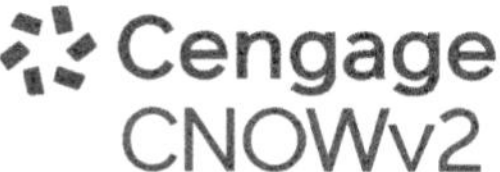

CNOWv2 is a powerful course management and online homework tool that provides robust instructor control and customization to optimize the student learning experience and meet desired outcomes.

CNOWv2 Instant Access Code ISBN:
978-0-357-72015-8

Contact your Cengage Learning Consultant about different bundle options.

Thomson Reuters Checkpoint™ is the leading online tax research database used by professionals. Checkpoint™ helps introduce students to tax research in three simple ways:

- Intuitive web-based design makes it fast and simple to find what you need.
- Checkpoint™ provides a comprehensive collection of primary tax law, cases, and rulings along with analytical insight you simply can't find anywhere else.
- Checkpoint™ has built-in productivity tools such as calculators to make research more efficient—a resource more tax pros use than any other.

Six months' access to Checkpoint™ (after activation) is packaged automatically with every NEW copy of the textbook.*

ProConnect™ Tax More than software: Put the experience of ProConnect™ Tax on your side.

- Get returns done right the first time with access to all the forms you need, backed by industry-leading calculations and diagnostics.
- Save time with logical data-entry worksheets instead of traditional forms-based methods.
- It's all online, so there's nothing to install or maintain.

Online access to ProConnect™ Tax software is offered with each NEW copy of the textbook—at no additional cost to students.*

www.cengage.com Students can use **www.cengage.com** to select this textbook and access Cengage Learning content, empowering them to choose the most suitable format and giving them a better chance of success in the course. Buy printed materials, eBooks, and digital resources directly through Cengage Learning and save at **www.cengage.com**.

Online Student Resources

Students can go to **www.cengage.com** for free resources to help them study as well as the opportunity to purchase additional study aids. These valuable free study resources will help students earn a better grade:

- Flashcards use chapter terms and definitions to aid students in learning tax terminology for each chapter.
- Online glossary for each chapter provides terms and definitions from the text in alphabetical order for easy reference.
- Learning objectives can be downloaded for each chapter to help keep students on track.
- Tax tables used in the textbook are downloadable for reference.

Cengage Unlimited The first-of-its-kind digital subscription designed specially to lower costs.

Students get total access to everything Cengage has to offer on demand—in one place. That's 20,000 eBooks, 2,300 digital learning products, and dozens of study tools across 70 disciplines and over 675 courses. **www.cengage.com/unlimited**

Printed Resources for Students

Looseleaf Edition (978-0-357-72012-7)

This version provides all the pages of the text in an unbound, three-hole-punched format for portability and ease of use. Online access to ProConnect™ Tax software is included with every NEW textbook as well as Checkpoint™ from Thomson Reuters.*

*NEW printed copies of the textbook are automatically packaged with access to Checkpoint™ and ProConnect™ Tax software. If students purchase the eBook, they will not automatically receive access to Checkpoint™ and ProConnect™ Tax software.

Comprehensive Supplements Support Instructors' Needs

Cengage CNOWv2

CNOWv2 is a powerful course management and online homework tool that provides robust instructor control and customization to optimize the student learning experience and meet desired outcomes. In addition to the features and benefits mentioned earlier for students, CNOWv2 includes these features for instructors.

- **Learning Outcomes Reporting** and the ability to analyze student work from the gradebook. Each exercise and problem is tagged by topic, learning objective, level of difficulty, estimated completion time, and business program standards to allow greater guidance in developing assessments and evaluating student progress.
- **Built-in Test Bank for online assessment.** The Test Bank files are included in CNOWv2 so that they may be used as additional homework or tests.

Solutions Manual

Written by the ***South-Western Federal Taxation*** editors and authors, the Solutions Manual features solutions arranged in accordance with the sequence of chapter material.

Solutions to all homework items are tagged with their Estimated Time to Complete, Level of Difficulty, and Learning Objective(s), as well as the AACSB's and AICPA's core competencies—giving instructors more control than ever in selecting homework to match the topics covered. The Solutions Manual also contains the answers with explanations to the end-of-chapter Becker CPA Review Questions. **Available on the Instructor Companion Website at www.cengage.com/login.**

PowerPoint® Lectures with Notes

The Instructor PowerPoint® Lectures contain more than 30 slides per chapter, including outlines and instructor guides, concept definitions, and key points. **Available on the Instructor Companion Website at www. cengage .com/login.**

Test Bank

Written by the ***South-Western Federal Taxation*** editors and authors, the Test Bank contains approximately 2,200 items and solutions arranged in accordance with the sequence of chapter material.

Each test item is tagged with its Estimated Time to Complete, Level of Difficulty, and Learning Objective(s), as well as the AACSB's and AICPA's core competencies—for easier instructor planning and test item selection. The 2023 Test Bank is available in Cengage's test generator software, Cognero.

Cengage Learning Testing Powered by Cognero is a flexible, online system that allows you to:

- author, edit, and manage Test Bank content from multiple Cengage Learning solutions
- create multiple test versions in an instant
- deliver tests from your LMS, your classroom, or wherever you want
- create tests from school, home, the coffee shop—anywhere with Internet access (No special installs or downloads needed.)

Test Bank files in Word format as well as versions to import into your LMS are available on the Instructor Companion Website. **Cognero Test Banks are available via single sign-on (SSO) account at www.cengage .com/login.**

Other Instructor Resources

All of the following instructor course materials are available online at www.cengage.com/login. Once logged into the site, instructors should select this textbook to access the online Instructor Resources.

- Instructor Guide
- Edition-to-edition correlation grids by chapter
- An appendix that helps instructors broaden and customize coverage of important tax provisions of the Affordable Care Act
- Depreciation and the Accelerated Cost Recovery System (ACRS) appendix

Custom Solutions

Cengage Learning Custom Solutions develops personalized solutions to meet your taxation education needs. Consider the following for your adoption of ***South-Western Federal Taxation 2023 Edition***.

- Remove chapters you do not cover or rearrange their order to create a streamlined and efficient text.
- Add your own material to cover additional topics or information.
- Add relevance by including sections from Sawyers/Gill's *Federal Tax Research* or your state's tax laws and regulations.

Acknowledgments

We want to thank all the adopters and others who participated in numerous online surveys as well as the following individuals who provided content reviews and feedback in the development of the ***South-Western Federal Taxation 2023 titles***.

Annette Nellen / Andrew D. Cuccia / Mark B. Persellin / James C. Young

Ken Abramowicz, *University of Alaska Fairbanks*
Lindsay G. Acker, *University of Wisconsin – Madison*
Deborah S. Adkins, *Nperspective, LLC*
Mark P. Altieri, *Kent State University*
Susan E. Anderson, *Elon University*
Henry M. Anding, *Woodbury University*
Jennifer A. Bagwell, *Ohio University*
George Barbi, *Lanier Technical College*
Terry W. Bechtel, *Texas A&M University – Texarkana*
Chris Becker, *LeMoyne College*
Tamara Berges, *UCLA*
Ellen Best, *University of North Georgia*
Tim Biggart, *Berry College*
Rachel Birkey, *Illinois State University*
Israel Blumenfrecht, *Queens College*
Patrick M. Borja, *Citrus College / California State University, Los Angeles*
Dianne H. Boseman, *Nash Community College*
Cathalene Bowler, *University of Northern Iowa*
Madeline Brogan, *Lone Star College – Montgomery*
Darryl L. Brown, *Illinois Wesleyan University*
Timothy G. Bryan, *University of Southern Indiana*
Robert S. Burdette, *Salt Lake Community College*
Ryan L. Burger, *Concordia University Nebraska*
Lisa Busto, *William Rainey Harper College*
Julia M. Camp, *Providence College*
Al Case, *Southern Oregon University*
Machiavelli W. Chao, *Merage School of Business, University of California, Irvine*
Eric Chen, *University of Saint Joseph*
Christine Cheng, *Louisiana State University*
James Milton Christianson, *Southwestern University and Austin Community College*
Wayne Clark, *Southwest Baptist University*
Ann Burstein Cohen, *University at Buffalo, The State University of New York*
Ciril Cohen, *Fairleigh Dickinson University*
Seth Colwell, *University of Texas – Rio Grande Valley*
Dixon H. Cooper, *University of Arkansas*
John P. Crowley, *Castleton University*
Susan E. M. Davis, *South University*
Dwight E. Denman, *Newman University*
James M. DeSimpelare, *Ross School of Business at the University of Michigan*
John Dexter, *Northwood University*
James Doering, *University of Wisconsin – Green Bay*
Michael P. Donohoe, *University of Illinois at Urbana Champaign*
Deborah A. Doonan, *Johnson & Wales University*
Monique O. Durant, *Central Connecticut State University*
Wayne L. Edmunds, *Virginia Commonwealth University*
Rafi Efrat, *California State University, Northridge*
Frank J. Faber, *St. Joseph's College*
A. Anthony Falgiani, *University of South Carolina, Beaufort*
Jason Fiske, *Thomas Jefferson School of Law*
John Forsythe, *Eagle Gate College*
Alexander L. Frazin, *University of Redlands*
Carl J. Gabrini, *College of Coastal Georgia*
Kenneth W. Gaines, *East-West University, Chicago, Illinois*
Carolyn Galantine, *Pepperdine University*
Sheri Geddes, *Hope College*
Alexander Gelardi, *University of St. Thomas*
Joel Gelb, *Farleigh Dickinson University*
Daniel J. Gibbons, *Waubonsee Community College*
Martie Gillen, *University of Florida*
Charles Gnizak, *Fort Hays State University*
J. David Golub, *Northeastern University*
George G. Goodrich, *John Carroll University*
Marina Grau, *Houston Community College – Houston, TX*
Vicki Greshik, *University of Jamestown College*
Jeffrey S. Haig, *Santa Monica College*
Marcye S. Hampton, *University of Central Florida*
June Hanson, *Upper Iowa University*
Donald Henschel, *Benedictine University*
Kenneth W. Hodges, *Sinclair Community College*
Susanne Holloway, *Salisbury University*
Susan A. Honig, *Herbert H. Lehman College*
Jeffrey Hoopes, *University of North Carolina*
Christopher R. Hoyt, *University of Missouri (Kansas City) School of Law*
Marsha M. Huber, *Youngstown State University*
Carol Hughes, *Asheville-Buncombe Technical Community College*
Helen Hurwitz, *Saint Louis University*
Richard R. Hutaff, *Wingate University*
Zite Hutton, *Western Washington University*
Steven L. Jager, *Cal State Northridge*
Janeé M. Johnson, *University of Arizona*
Brad Van Kalsbeek, *University of Sioux Falls*
Carl Keller, *Missouri State University*
Cynthia Khanlarian, *Concord University*
Bob G. Kilpatrick, *Northern Arizona University*
Gordon Klein, *UCLA Anderson School*
Taylor Klett, *Sam Houston State University*
Aaron P. Knape, *Peru State College*
Cedric Knott, *Colorado State University – Global Campus*
Ausher M. B. Kofsky, *Western New England University*
Emil Koren, *Saint Leo University*
Jack Lachman, *Brooklyn College – CUNY*
Adena LeJeune, *Louisiana College*
Gene Levitt, *Mayville State University*
Teresa Lightner, *University of North Texas*
Sara Linton, *Roosevelt University*
Roger Lirely, *The University of Texas at Tyler*
Jane Livingstone, *Western Carolina University*
Heather Lynch, *Northeast Iowa Community College*
Mabel Machin, *Florida Institute of Technology*
Maria Alaina Mackin, *ECPI University*
Anne M. Magro, *George Mason University*
Richard B. Malamud, *California State University, Dominguez Hills*
Harold J. Manasa, *Winthrop University*
Barry R. Marks, *University of Houston – Clear Lake*
Dewey Martin, *Husson University*
Anthony Masino, *East Tennessee State University*
Norman Massel, *Louisiana State University*
Bruce W. McClain, *Cleveland State University*
Jeff McGowan, *Trine University*
Allison M. McLeod, *University of North Texas*
Meredith A. Menden, *Southern New Hampshire University*
Robert H. Meyers, *University of Wisconsin-Whitewater*
John G. Miller, *Skyline College*
Tracie L. Miller-Nobles, *Austin Community College*

Jonathan G. Mitchell, *Stark State College*
Richard Mole, *Hiram College*
David Morack, *Lakeland University*
Lisa Nash, *University of North Georgia*
Mary E. Netzler, *Eastern Florida State College*
Joseph Malino Nicassio, *Westmoreland County Community College*
Mark R. Nixon, *Bentley University*
Garth Novack, *Pantheon Heavy Industries & Foundry*
Claude R. Oakley, *DeVry University, Georgia*
Al Oddo, *Niagara University*
Sandra Owen, *Indiana University – Bloomington*
Vivian J. Paige, *Old Dominion University*
Carolyn Payne, *University of La Verne*
Ronald Pearson, *Bay College*
Thomas Pearson, *University of Hawaii at Manoa*
Nichole L. Pendleton, *Friends University*
Chuck Pier, *Angelo State University*
Lincoln M. Pinto, *DeVry University*
Sonja Pippin, *University of Nevada – Reno*
Steve Platau, *The University of Tampa*
Elizabeth Plummer, *TCU*
Walfyette Powell, *Strayer University*
Darlene Pulliam, *West Texas A&M University*
Thomas J. Purcell, *Creighton University*
John S. Repsis, *University of Texas at Arlington*
Jennifer Hardwick Robinson, *Trident Technical College*
Shani N. Robinson, *Sam Houston State University*
Donald Roth, *Dordt College*
Richard L. Russell, *Jackson State University*
Robert L. Salyer, *Northern Kentucky University*
Rhoda Sautner, *University of Mary*
Bunney L. Schmidt, *Keiser University*
Allen Schuldenfrei, *University of Maryland – Baltimore County*
Eric D. Schwartz, *LaRoche College*
Tony L. Scott, *Norwalk Community College*
Randy Serrett, *University of Houston – Downtown*
Wayne Shaw, *Southern Methodist University*
Paul A. Shoemaker, *University of Nebraska – Lincoln*
Kimberly Sipes, *Kentucky State University*
Georgi Smatrakalev, *Florida Atlantic University*
Randy Smit, *Dordt College*
Leslie S. Sobol, *California State University Northridge*
Eric J. Sommermeyer, *Wartburg College*
Marc Spiegel, *University of California, Irvine*
Teresa Stephenson, *University of Alaska Anchorage*
Beth Stetson, *Oklahoma City University*
Debra Stone, *Eastern New Mexico University*
Frances A. Stott, *Bowling Green State University*
Todd S. Stowe, *Southwest Florida College*
Julie Straus, *Culver-Stockton College*
Martin Stub, *DeVry University*
James Sundberg, *Eastern Michigan University*
Kent Swift, *University of Montana*
Robert L. Taylor, *Lees-McRae College*
Francis C. Thomas, *Richard Stockton College of New Jersey*
Randall R. Thomas, *Upper Iowa University*
Ronald R. Tidd, *Central Washington University*
MaryBeth Tobin, *Bridgewater State University*
James P. Trebby, *Marquette University*
Heidi Tribunella, *University of Rochester*
James M. Turner, *Georgia Institute of Technology*
Anthony W. Varnon, *Southeast Missouri State University*
Adria Palacios Vasquez, *Texas A&M University – Kingsville*
Stanley Veliotis, *Fordham University*
Terri Walsh, *Seminole State College of Florida*
Natasha R. Ware, *Southeastern University*
Mark Washburn, *Sam Houston State University*
Bill Weispfenning, *University of Jamestown (ND)*
Kent Williams, *Indiana Wesleyan University*
Candace Witherspoon, *Valdosta State University*
Sheila Woods, *DeVry University, Houston, TX*
Xinmei Xie, *Woodbury University*
Thomas Young, *Lone Star College – Tomball*

Special Thanks

We are grateful to the faculty members who have diligently worked through the problems and test questions to ensure the accuracy of the ***South-Western Federal Taxation*** homework, solutions manuals, test banks, and comprehensive tax form problems. Their comments and corrections helped us focus on clarity as well as accuracy and tax law currency. We also thank Thomson Reuters for its permission to use Checkpoint™ with the text.

Sandra A. Augustine, (retired) *Hilbert College*
Robyn Dawn Jarnagin, *University of Arkansas*
Kate Mantzke, *Northern Illinois University*
Ray Rodriguez, *Murray State University*
Miles Romney, *Florida State University*
George R. Starbuck, *McMurry University*
Donald R. Trippeer, *State University of New York College at Oneonta*
Raymond Wacker, *Southern Illinois University, Carbondale*
Michael Weissenfluh, *Tillamook Bay Community College*
Marvin Williams, *University of Houston – Downtown*

The South-Western Federal Taxation Series

To find out more about these books, go to www.cengage.com.

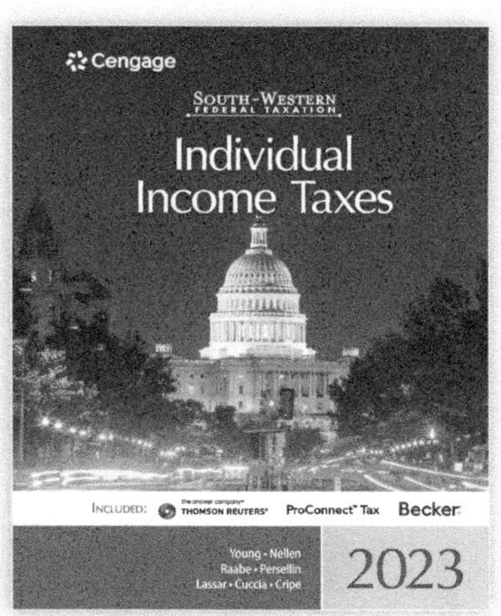

Individual Income Taxes, 2023 Edition

(Young, Nellen, Raabe, Persellin, Lassar, Cuccia, Cripe, Editors) provides accessible, comprehensive, and authoritative coverage of the relevant tax code and regulations as they pertain to the individual taxpayer, as well as coverage of all major developments in Federal taxation.

(ISBN 978-0-357-71982-4)

Corporations, Partnerships, Estates & Trusts, 2023 Edition

(Raabe, Young, Nellen, Cripe, Lassar, Persellin, Cuccia, Editors) covers tax concepts as they affect corporations, partnerships, estates, and trusts. The authors provide accessible, comprehensive, and authoritative coverage of relevant tax code and regulations, as well as all major developments in Federal income taxation. This market-leading text is intended for students who have had a previous course in tax.

(ISBN 978-0-357-71996-1)

Comprehensive Volume, 2023 Edition

(Young, Nellen, Maloney, Persellin, Cuccia, Lassar, Cripe, Editors) Combining the number one individual tax text with the number one corporations text, *Comprehensive Volume, 2023 Edition* is a true winner. An edited version of the first two ***South-Western Federal Taxation*** textbooks, this book is ideal for undergraduate or graduate levels. This text works for either a one-semester course in which an instructor wants to integrate coverage of individual and corporate taxation or for a two-semester sequence in which the use of only one book is desired.

(ISBN 978-0-357-71968-8)

Essentials of Taxation: Individuals and Business Entities, 2023 Edition

(Nellen, Cuccia, Persellin, Young, Editors) emphasizes tax planning and the multidisciplinary aspects of taxation. This text is designed with the AICPA Model Tax Curriculum in mind, presenting the introductory Federal taxation course from a business entity perspective. Its **Tax Planning Framework** helps users fit tax planning strategies into an innovative pedagogical framework. The text is an ideal fit for programs that offer only one course in taxation where users need to be exposed to individual taxation, as well as corporate and other business entity taxation. This text assumes no prior course in taxation has been taken.

(ISBN 978-0-357-72010-3)

Federal Tax Research, 12E

(Sawyers and Gill) *Federal Tax Research*, Twelfth Edition, offers hands-on tax research analysis and fully covers computer-oriented tax research tools. Also included in this edition is coverage on international tax research, a review of tax ethics, and many new real-life cases to help foster a true understanding of Federal tax law.

(ISBN 978-0-357-36638-7)

About the Editors

Annette Nellen, J.D., CPA, CGMA, directs San José State University's graduate tax program (MST) and teaches courses in tax research, tax fundamentals, accounting methods, property transactions, employment tax, ethics, leadership, and tax policy. Professor Nellen is a graduate of CSU Northridge, Pepperdine (MBA), and Loyola Law School. Prior to joining SJSU in 1990, she was with a Big 4 firm and the IRS. At SJSU, Professor Nellen is a recipient of the Outstanding Professor and Distinguished Service Awards. Professor Nellen is an active member of the tax sections of the AICPA and American Bar Association. In 2013, she received the AICPA Arthur J. Dixon Memorial Award, the highest award given by the accounting profession in the area of taxation. Professor Nellen is the author of BloombergBNA Tax Portfolio, *Amortization of Intangibles*. She has published numerous articles in the *AICPA Tax Insider*, *Tax Adviser*, *Tax Notes State*, and *The Journal of Accountancy*. She has testified before the House Ways & Means and Senate Finance Committees and other committees on Federal and state tax reform. Professor Nellen maintains the 21st Century Taxation Website and blog (21stcenturytaxation.com) as well as Websites on tax policy and reform, virtual currency, and state tax issues (sjsu.edu/people/annette.nellen/).

Andrew D. Cuccia, Ph.D., CPA, is the Steed Professor of Accounting at the University of Oklahoma. He is a graduate of Loyola University, New Orleans (B.B.A.), and the University of Florida (Ph.D.). Prior to entering academia, Andy practiced as a CPA with a Big 4 accounting firm. Before joining the University of Oklahoma, he was on the faculty at Louisiana State University and the University of Illinois. His research focuses on taxpayer and tax professional judgment and decision making and has been published in several journals, including *The Accounting Review*, *Journal of Accounting Research*, *The Journal of the American Taxation Association*, and *Tax Notes*. He has taught undergraduate and graduate courses in income tax fundamentals as well as graduate courses in corporate tax, tax policy, and tax research. Andy is a past president of the American Taxation Association and a member of the American Accounting Association and the AICPA.

Mark B. Persellin, Ph.D., CPA, CFP®, is the Ray and Dorothy Berend Professor of Accounting at St. Mary's University. He is a graduate of the University of Arizona (B.S.), the University of Texas at Austin (M.P.A. in Taxation), and the University of Houston (Ph.D.). He teaches Personal Income Tax, Business Income Tax, and Research in Federal Taxation. Prior to joining St. Mary's University in 1991, Professor Persellin taught at Florida Atlantic University and Southwest Texas University (Texas State University) and worked on the tax staff of a Big 4 firm. His research has been published in numerous academic and professional journals including *The Journal of the American Taxation Association*, *The Accounting Educators' Journal*, *The Tax Adviser*, *The CPA Journal*, *Journal of Taxation*, *Corporate Taxation*, *The Tax Executive*, *TAXES—The Tax Magazine*, *Journal of International Taxation*, and *Practical Tax Strategies*. In 2003, Professor Persellin established the St. Mary's University Volunteer Income Tax Assistance (VITA) site, and he continues to serve as a trainer and reviewer at the site.

James C. Young is the PwC Professor of Accountancy at Northern Illinois University. A graduate of Ferris State University (B.S.) and Michigan State University (M.B.A. and Ph.D.), Jim's research focuses on taxpayer responses to the income tax using archival data. His dissertation received the PricewaterhouseCoopers/American Taxation Association Dissertation Award, and his subsequent research has received funding from a number of organizations, including the Ernst & Young Foundation Tax Research Grant Program. His work has been published in a variety of academic and professional journals, including the *National Tax Journal, The Journal of the American Taxation Association*, and *Tax Notes*. Jim is a Northern Illinois University Distinguished Professor, received the Illinois CPA Society Outstanding Accounting Educator Award in 2012, and has received university teaching awards from Northern Illinois University, George Mason University, and Michigan State University.

Brief Contents

Part 5: Business Entities

Part 6: Special Business Topics

Contents

Part 1: The World of Taxation

Part 3: Property Transactions

Chapter 7 Property Transactions: Basis, Gain and Loss, and Nontaxable Exchanges 7-1

Chapter 8 Property Transactions: Capital Gains and Losses, Section 1231, and Recapture Provisions 8-1

Part 4: Taxation of Individuals

Part 6: Special Business Topics

Appendices

Online Appendices

Digging Deeper

Each chapter has additional content that is described and highlighted throughout the text. This can be found at **www.cengage.com**.

The World of Taxation

Chapter 1
Introduction to Taxation

Chapter 2
Working with the Tax Law

Chapter 3
Taxes in the Financial Statements

Part 1 provides an introduction to taxation in the United States. Taxes imposed by Federal, state, and local governments are discussed. A unique tax planning framework is introduced that is applied throughout the text in developing tax planning strategies for both business entities and individual taxpayers. The tax research process, including the role played by the legislative, administrative, and judicial branches in shaping our tax laws and providing guidance for tax compliance and planning, is introduced. Part 1 concludes with a chapter on accounting for income taxes in financial statements, as a bridge to topics covered in other accounting courses.

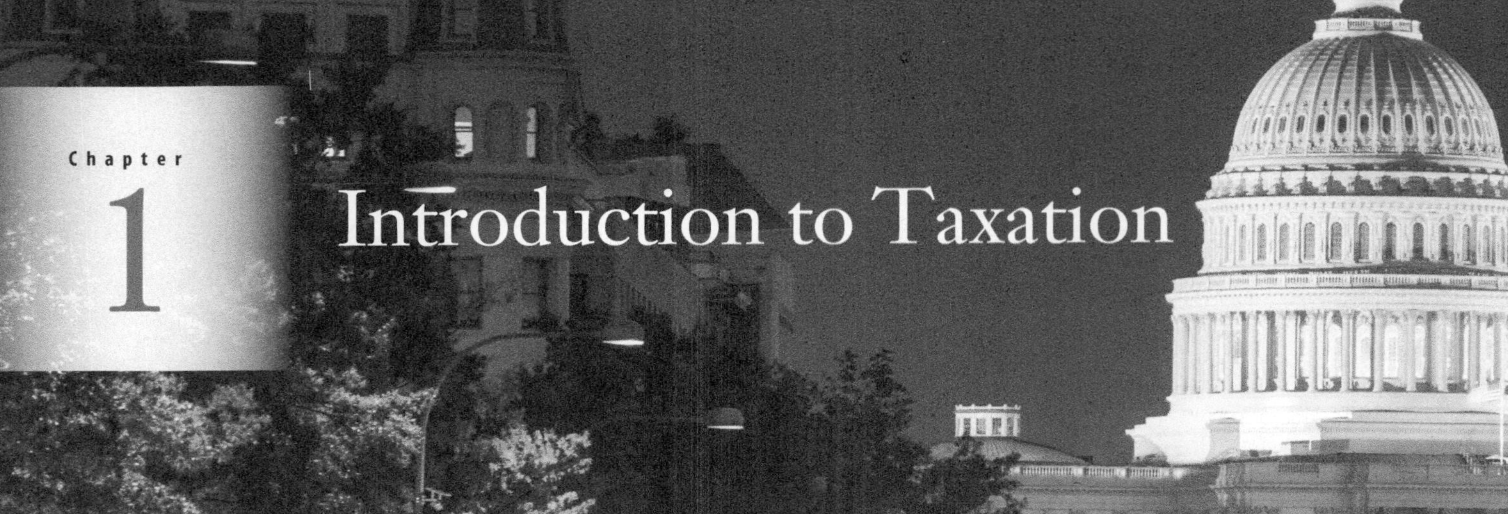

Chapter 1

Introduction to Taxation

Learning Objectives: *After completing Chapter 1, you should be able to:*

LO.1 Explain the importance of taxes, how to study taxes, and how tax and finance professionals work with taxes.

LO.2 Explain the components of a tax.

LO.3 Identify the various taxes affecting business entities and individuals.

LO.4 Describe the basic tax formula for individuals and business entities.

LO.5 Explain the tax systems that apply to business entities and their owners.

LO.6 Identify tax planning opportunities using a general framework for tax planning.

LO.7 Explain the economic, social, equity, political, and compliance considerations that underlie the tax law.

LO.8 Describe the influence of the IRS and the courts on the Federal tax system.

Chapter Outline

Tax Talk *How many people were taxed, who was taxed, and what was taxed tell more about a society than anything else.* —Charles Adams

The Big Picture

A Typical Tax Year for A Modern Family

Travis and Amy Carter are married and live in a state that imposes both a sales tax and an income tax. They have two children, April (age 17) and Martin (age 18). Travis is a mining engineer who specializes in land reclamation. After several years with a mining corporation, Travis established a consulting practice that involves a considerable amount of travel due to work he performs in other states.

Amy is a registered nurse who, until recently, was a homemaker. In November of the current year, she decided to reenter the job market and accepted a position with a medical clinic.

The Carters live only a few blocks from Ernest and Mary Walker, Amy Carter's parents. The Walkers are retired and live on interest, dividends, and Social Security benefits.

The following activities with current year and possible future tax ramifications occurred.

- The ad valorem property taxes on the Carters' residence increased, while those on the Walkers' residence decreased.
- When Travis registered an automobile that was purchased last year in another state, he paid a sales tax to his home state.
- As an anniversary present, the Carters gave the Walkers a recreational vehicle (RV).
- Travis employed his children to draft blueprints and prepare scale models for use in his work. Both April and Martin have had training in drafting and topography.
- Early in the year, the Carters were audited by the state on an income tax return filed a few years ago. Later in the year, they were audited by the IRS on a Form 1040 they filed for the same year. In each case, a tax deficiency and interest were assessed.
- The Walkers were audited by the IRS. Unlike the Carters, they did not have to deal with a revenue agent, but settled the matter by mail.

Explain these developments and resolve any tax issues raised.

Read the chapter and formulate your response.

Explain the importance of taxes, how to study taxes, and how tax and finance professionals work with taxes.

1-1 Taxes in Our Lives

"Taxes are what we pay for civilized society."

This is a famous quote from U.S. Supreme Court Justice Oliver Wendell Holmes, Jr. It is engraved on the government building at 1111 Constitution Avenue in Washington, D.C.—headquarters of the Internal Revenue Service (IRS). This quote eloquently sums up the primary purpose of taxation—to raise revenue for government operations. Governments at all levels—national, state, and local—require funds for defense, protection (police and fire), education, transportation, the court system, social services, and more. Various types of taxes provide the resources to pay for government services.

In addition, taxation often is used as a tool to influence the behavior of individuals and businesses. For example, an income tax credit (which reduces a taxpayer's tax bill) may be designed to *encourage* people to purchase a fuel-efficient car. A tobacco excise tax may *discourage* individuals from smoking by increasing the cost of tobacco products. The tax system can also be used to provide direct benefits to taxpayers (e.g., to help pay for health insurance) and indirect benefits (in the form of exclusions, deductions, and credits that reduce a taxpayer's tax liability).

Taxes permeate our society. Various types of taxes, such as income, sales, property, and excise taxes, come into play in many of the activities of individuals, businesses, nonprofit entities (like charities), and governments themselves.

Most directly, individuals are affected by taxes by paying them. Taxes may be paid directly or indirectly. A direct tax is paid to the government by the person who owes the tax. Examples include the personal income tax, which is paid by filing a personal income tax return (Form 1040 at the federal level), and property taxes on one's home (paid to the local government). Individuals also pay many taxes indirectly. For example, when you buy gasoline for your car, the price you pay likely includes some of the income taxes and the gasoline excise taxes owed by the oil company. And a renter indirectly pays property taxes assessed on the landlord (who will consider that cost when determining how much rent to charge).

Ultimately, all taxes are paid by individuals. The corporate income tax, for example, is paid directly by the corporation, but it really is paid indirectly by individuals in their capacity as customers, investors (owners), or employees; the taxes are passed along to individuals through higher prices for products and services, lower dividends, and/or lower wages.

Taxes also affect the lives of individuals via the ballot box. Federal, state, and local elections often include initiatives that deal with taxation, such as whether Federal income taxes should be raised (or lowered), whether a new tax should be imposed on soda, or whether the sales tax rate should be increased. Candidates running for office often have ideas on tax changes they would like to make if they are elected.

1-1a The Relevance of Taxation to Accounting and Finance Professionals

The Federal corporate income tax rate is 21 percent. State income taxes constitute, on average, an additional 5 percent. So a large corporation may devote about 25 percent of its net income to pay income taxes. In addition, businesses are subject to employment taxes, property taxes, sales taxes, and various excise taxes. Corporations with international operations are subject to taxation in other countries. Small businesses also pay a variety of taxes that affect profits and cash flows.

Given its significance, taxation is a crucial topic for accounting and finance professionals. They must understand the various types of business taxes to assist effectively with:

- *Compliance:* Ensure that the business files all tax returns and makes all tax payments on time. Mistakes and missed due dates will lead to penalties and interest expense.
- *Planning:* Help a business to apply favorable tax rules, like deferring income and obtaining tax credits, to minimize tax liability (and maximize owner wealth). The time value of money concept also is important here, as is coordinating tax planning with other business goals to maximize earnings per share.[1]

[1] A corporate tax director or vice president of tax is typically involved in the strategic planning and growth of the company due to the significance of tax liabilities and planning opportunities to the business. For example, a recent position announcement for a Tax Director at Roblox stated that the director would "lead initiatives to support global growth of the company."

- *Financial reporting:* Financial statements include a variety of tax information, including income tax expense on the income statement and deferred tax assets and liabilities on the balance sheet. Footnotes to the financial statements report various tax details, including the company's effective tax rate. Computation and proper reporting of this information requires knowledge of both tax and the financial reporting rules [including the Financial Accounting Standards Board's Accounting Standards Codification (ASC) 740, *Income Taxes*].
- *Environmental, Social, and Governance (ESG) reporting:* A growing trend in corporate reporting is to address various business sustainability and responsibility matters and report environmental, social, and governance activities and impact. Standard reporting frameworks might include tax metrics, such as the Global Reporting Initiative (GRI) Standards or ones generated by the World Economic Forum.[2] This reporting can include taxes paid in each country (part of "country-by-country reporting"), reconciliation between taxes paid and the statutory tax rate on financial statement profits, financial assistance received from governments via tax deductions and credits, and an explanation of the corporation's tax policy and strategy.[3]
- *Controversy:* Assist when the taxpayer interacts with a tax agency (like the IRS). The IRS and state and local tax agencies regularly audit tax returns to verify that taxes were properly computed and paid.
- *Cash management:* Taxes must be paid on time to avoid penalties and interest. Income taxes must be estimated and paid quarterly and reconciled on the annual return. Other taxes may be due weekly, monthly, quarterly, or semiannually. Businesses must be sure they have the funds ready when the taxes are due and have procedures to track due dates.
- *Data analysis:* With a majority, if not all, of a company's records maintained in digital form, there are opportunities to use this information to enhance profits, better understand the customer base, and improve and understand the information from a tax perspective. Tax practitioners often need skills in data analysis and visualization to identify samples for both internal and external audits, find ways to identify the products and services subject to sales tax in different states, and extract tax data to help inform other business functions, such as where to locate a new sales office. The IRS and state tax agencies also use data analysis to help identify potential audit issues.
- *Tax advocacy:* Taxpayers and tax practitioners can add tremendous value to the improvement and evolution of our tax laws by sharing their knowledge, experiences, and ideas with lawmakers and tax agencies. Some of this work is performed by professional organizations [e.g., the American Institute of CPAs (AICPA)], industry associations, and various policy organizations. This input might take the form of comment letters, testimony before legislative committees (delivered in person or submitted for the record), or individual correspondence and meetings.[4]

The level and depth of tax knowledge needed for any accounting or tax professional depends on his or her specific job. The vice president of tax for a company clearly needs thorough knowledge in all areas of taxation; the same is true of a partner in a CPA firm. In contrast, the corporate treasurer likely focuses more on cash management, working closely with the company's tax advisers, so needs only a basic understanding of taxes.

[2]For example, see World Economic Forum, *Toward Common Metrics and Consistent Reporting of Sustainable Value Creation*, January 2020; **www3.weforum.org/docs/WEF_IBC_ESG_Metrics_Discussion_Paper.pdf.**

[3]For examples, see Intel Corporation's 2020–21 Corporate Responsibility Report; **csrreportbuilder.intel.com/pdfbuilder/pdfs/CSR-2020-21-Full-Report.pdf;** and The Walt Disney Company's 2020 Corporate Social Responsibility Report; **thewaltdisneycompany.com/app/uploads/2021/02/2020-CSR-Report.pdf.**

[4]For examples of such advocacy, see formal letters submitted by the AICPA (**aicpa.org/advocacy/tax.html**); testimony delivered at tax reform hearings in Congress (**sjsu.edu/people/annette.nellen/website/117th-hearings.htm**); and tax policy activities and reports of various industry and policy organizations such as the U.S. Chamber of Commerce (**uschamber.com/taxes**) and the Center on Budget and Policy Priorities (**cbpp.org/research/topics/federal-tax**).

It is essential to maintain a balanced perspective when working with tax systems. A corporation that is deciding where to locate a new factory does not automatically select the city or state that offers the most generous tax benefits. Nor does the person who is retiring to a warmer climate pick Belize over Arizona because Belize has no income tax while Arizona does. Tax considerations should not control decisions, but they are one of many factors to be considered.

1-1b **How to Study Taxation**

The goal of studying taxation is to be able to recognize issues (or transactions) that have tax implications and to try to understand the justification for the related tax rules.

You may have heard that tax is a difficult subject because of the many rules, exceptions, and definitions, as well as frequent changes to tax rules. You even may have heard that taxation is boring. Taxation *is* a challenging topic, but it is certainly *not* boring. Taxation is an important and exciting topic due to constant changes made by the three branches of our Federal government (as well as by state and local jurisdictions), the significance of taxes to the bottom line of a company and an individual's finances, and the effects of taxes on our economy and society.

Tax professionals tend to find enjoyment in their chosen field due to the intellectual challenge of dealing with tax rules for compliance and planning purposes, the opportunity to interact with colleagues or clients to help them understand the effects brought about by taxes, and the knowledge that their work affects the financial well-being of individuals and businesses.

For tax professionals, the study of taxation is an ongoing and intriguing process. When Congress changes the tax law, tax professionals must review the new rules to understand how they affect clients or their employer. In addition, decisions rendered by the courts in tax disputes and guidance issued by the Treasury Department and Internal Revenue Service must be understood to ensure correct compliance with the law and to identify updated tax planning ideas.

In studying taxation, one should focus on understanding the rules and the why(s) behind them rather than memorizing numerous rules and terms. The rules become more meaningful by thinking about why the rule exists for the particular type of tax. For example, why do Federal income tax rules allow for a child care credit? Why is tax depreciation different from that used for financial reporting? Aiming for understanding, rather than memorization, will make your journey into the world of taxation interesting and meaningful, and it will prepare you well for dealing with taxation in your accounting or finance career.

1-1c **Individuals and Taxes**

The following diagram illustrates the many ways individuals interact with taxes. For example, as shown in the outer circle, individuals pay taxes and file tax returns (tax compliance). They also engage in tax planning as part of their desire to maximize the present value of after-tax wealth. If their tax return is audited or they do not pay their taxes, taxpayers will deal with the IRS or a state/local tax agency (tax controversy). Individuals deal with tax rules and planning in their roles as consumers, employees, investors, and business owners. Tax law is designed around these various taxpayer activities. Finally, as shown by the inner circle, individuals have a personal responsibility to comply with tax laws and pay any taxes due. Individuals also have a civic responsibility to understand taxes in their role as citizens and voters. Moreover, individuals need to understand how taxes affect their personal cash flows, consumption, and savings.

Use this diagram as you study the materials in this text, considering where in the circle various rules fit.

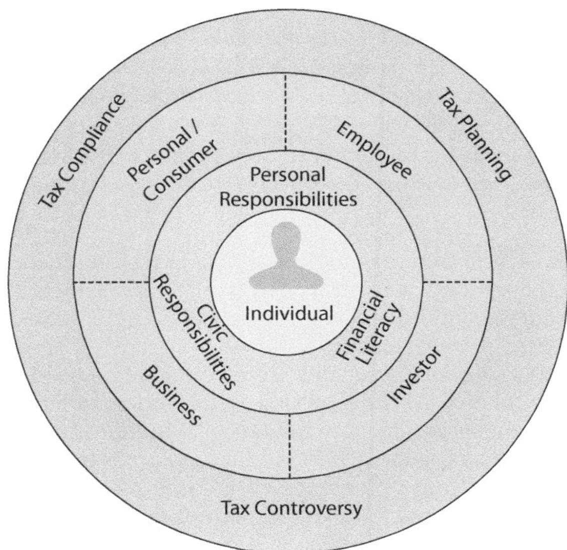

1-2 The Structure of Tax Systems

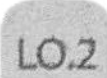

Explain the components of a tax.

Most taxes have two components: a tax rate and a tax base (such as income, wages, value, or sales price). Tax liability is computed by multiplying these two components. Taxes vary by the structure of their rates, the base subject to tax, and whether reductions to the tax liability are allowed (e.g., credits). The tax formula (below) is helpful in both calculating a taxpayer's tax liability for any type of tax and understanding the effect of proposals to change the tax laws.

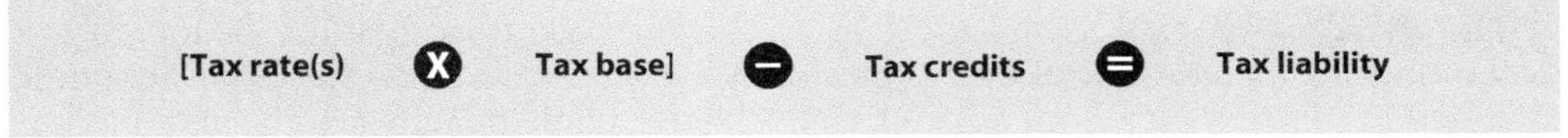

1-2a Tax Rates

Tax rates can be progressive, proportional, or regressive. A tax rate is *progressive* if the rate increases as the tax base increases. The Federal income tax imposed on individuals is a progressive tax as indicated by the Tax Rate Schedules you can find inside the front cover of this text. Currently, the tax rates increase from 10 percent to 37 percent as taxable income (the tax base) increases.

A tax is *proportional* if the rate of tax is constant, regardless of the size of the tax base. State retail **sales taxes** are proportional.

Bob purchases an automobile for $6,000. If the sales tax on automobiles is 7% in Bob's state, he will pay a $420 tax. Alternatively, if Bob pays $20,000 for a car, his sales tax will be $1,400 (still 7% of the sales price). Because the average tax rate does not change with the tax base (sales price), the sales tax rate is *proportional*.

Finally, *regressive* tax rates decrease as the tax base increases. Federal **employment taxes**, such as FICA and FUTA, can be termed regressive. When the tax base and the taxpayer's ability to pay generally are positively correlated (i.e., when they move in the same direction), many tax pundits view regressive tax rates as unfair. This is because the tax burden decreases as a *percentage* of the taxpayer's ability to pay.

Example 2

In 2022, the combined Social Security and Medicare tax rate levied on the wages of employees is 7.65% up to a maximum of $147,000 and 1.45% on all wages over $147,000. Pooja earns a salary of $30,000. She pays FICA taxes of $2,295, an average tax rate of 7.65%. Alternatively, if Pooja earns $160,000, she pays $11,434 {(7.65% × $147,000) + [1.45% × ($160,000 − $147,000)]}, an average tax rate of 7.15%.

Once the FICA base exceeds the maximum amount subject to the Social Security part of FICA, the FICA tax rate becomes *regressive* because the tax rate decreases as the tax base increases.

Under all three tax rate structures, the *amount* of taxes due increases as the tax base increases. The structure of tax rates only affects the *rate* of increase (i.e., progressive taxes increase at an increasing rate, proportional taxes increase at a constant rate, and regressive taxes increase at a decreasing rate).

The terms *progressive*, *proportional*, and *regressive* are also used to describe the *effect* of a tax on taxpayers relative to their income. The Federal income tax is *progressive* because the tax represents a greater percentage of a higher-income taxpayer's income relative to a lower-income taxpayer. A flat rate income tax is *proportional* (or flat) since each taxpayer devotes the same percentage of income to pay the tax. Finally, a tax is *regressive* if lower-income taxpayers devote a greater percentage of income to pay the tax relative to higher-income individuals. For example, if two individuals, one with $10,000 of income and the other with $200,000 of income, both buy the same number of gallons of gasoline during the year, the excise tax paid represents a larger percentage of the lower-income individual's income compared to the higher-income individual. See further discussion in text Section 1-6d on equity considerations of tax systems.

The terms *progressive, proportional,* and *regressive* are most often used to describe tax rates in the design of tax systems or to describe the economic effect of taxes on individuals. *Effective tax rates* (described below) are also used for this purpose. For tax compliance and planning purposes, a taxpayer's *statutory, marginal,* and *average* tax rates are determined and used.

The **statutory tax rate** is the tax rate (or rates) specified in the law. For example, Code § 11 provides that the income tax rate for corporations is 21 percent. Code § 1 provides that the top income tax rate applicable to individuals is 37 percent.

The **marginal tax rate** is the tax rate applicable to the next dollar of income (if describing an income tax effect). For example, using the 2022 Tax Rate Schedule included in this text (see Appendix A), notice that a single person with taxable income of $25,000 has a marginal tax rate of 12 percent. This rate is relevant to let a taxpayer know the tax effect of, for example, earning a $1,000 bonus from one's employer (in this case, the taxpayer's income tax would increase by $120; note that employment taxes would also be owed on such income).

The **average tax rate** is equal to the tax liability divided by taxable income. This rate can be useful in comparing taxpayers or a taxpayer's changed tax picture from one year to another.

The **effective tax rate** is equal to taxes paid (often the tax liability) divided by the taxpayer's ability to pay (some income measure, like adjusted gross income or disposable income). This rate is often used by policy makers to measure the progressivity of a tax system. For financial reporting purposes, effective tax rate generally refers to total tax expense as a percentage of pretax book income (see text Section 3-3c).

Example 3

In 2022, Jasmine, who is single, has adjusted gross income of $77,950, uses the standard deduction of $12,950, and has $65,000 of taxable income. Her Federal income tax computed using the Tax Rate Schedule is $9,917, determined as follows (using the Tax Rate Schedule for single taxpayers in Appendix A):

10% × $10,275	$1,027
12% × ($41,775 – $10,275)	3,780
22% × ($65,000 – $41,775)	5,110
Total Federal income tax	$9,917

- Jasmine's *statutory tax rates* are 10%, 12%, and 22%.
- Jasmine's *marginal tax rate* is 22%. Her next dollar of income is taxed at this rate (and this tax rate will be applied until she reaches $89,076 of taxable income, at which point her marginal tax rate becomes 24%).
- Jasmine's *average tax rate* is 15.26% ($9,917 ÷ $65,000).
- Jasmine's *effective tax rate* (using her AGI) is 12.72% ($9,917 ÷ $77,950).

In the example above, the statutory, marginal, average, and effective tax rates differ because they were determined using the *progressive* Federal income tax for individuals. If instead, the taxpayer was a corporation, all the tax rates would be 21 percent because the Federal corporate income tax is *proportional.*

1-2b Tax Bases

Most taxes are levied on one of four kinds of tax bases.

- Transactions [including sales or purchases of goods and services and transfers of wealth (e.g., by gift or at death)].
- Property or wealth (including ownership of specific kinds of property).

Information on criteria used in designing a tax structure can be found on this book's companion website: www.cengage.com

1 Digging Deeper

- Privileges and rights (including the ability to do business as a corporation, the right to work in a certain profession, and the ability to move goods between countries).
- Income on a gross or net-of-expenses basis.

Because the Federal income tax usually has the most significant influence when decisions are made, it is the principal focus of this text.

1-2c Incidence of Taxation

We most often think of our tax burden as including only the taxes we pay *directly* (like income taxes). But we also pay many taxes *indirectly.* Often, the *incidence* of various taxes directly paid by businesses is on the final consumer of goods and services. Similarly, the incidence of property taxes on an apartment building is primarily on the tenant rather than the owner, since the owner factors this tax into the rental rate. Individuals also bear the incidence of the corporate income tax in their capacities as employees and investor/owners.

In evaluating tax systems, it is important to consider taxes paid both directly and indirectly in order to understand the effect of taxes on individuals. Determining the incidence of all taxes, though, is not easy due to the influence of economic factors, like the effect of supply and demand on the pricing of goods and services at any point in time.

1-3 Types of Taxes

LO.3

Identify the various taxes affecting business entities and individual.

In many countries, transaction taxes are more important than income taxes. We will discuss three types of transaction taxes: sales and certain **excise taxes**, employment taxes, and taxes on the transfer of wealth (as gifts and at death).[5]

1-3a Taxes on the Production and Sale of Goods

Sales tax and some excise taxes are imposed on the production, sale, or consumption of commodities or the use of services. Excise taxes and general sales taxes differ by the breadth of their bases. An excise tax base is limited to a specific kind of good or service, but a general sales tax is broad-based (e.g., it might be levied on all retail sales). All levels of government impose excise taxes, while state and local governments (but not the U.S. Federal government) make heavy use of the general sales tax.

Federal Excise Taxes

Together with customs duties, excise taxes served as the principal source of revenue for the United States during its first 150 years of existence. Since World War II, the role of excise taxes in financing the Federal government has decined steadily, falling from about 30 to 40 percent of revenues just prior to the war to about 2 percent now. During this time, the Federal government came to rely upon income and employment taxes as its principal sources of funds.

[5]Employment taxes are imposed on wages and self-employment income with some limits and so can also be categorized as income taxes. The estate tax uses value as the tax base and so can also be categorized as a wealth tax.

Despite the decreasing contribution of excise taxes to the Federal government, they continue to have a significant impact on specific industries. Currently, trucks, trailers, tires, liquor, tobacco, firearms, certain sporting equipment, medical devices, and air travel all are subject to Federal excise taxes. Excise taxes extend beyond sales transactions. They also are levied on privileges and rights, as discussed below.

The bases used for Federal excise taxes are as diverse as the goods that are taxed. Fuels are taxed by the gallon, vaccines by the dose, air travel by the price paid for the ticket, water travel by the passenger, coal by the ton extracted or by the sales price, insurance by the premiums paid, and the gas guzzler tax by the mileage rating on the automobile produced. Some of these taxes are levied on producers, some on resellers, and some on consumers. In almost every circumstance, the tax rate structure is proportional.

With the exception of Federal excise taxes on alcohol, tobacco, and firearms, Federal excise taxes are due at least quarterly, when the Federal excise tax return (Form 720) is filed.

State Excise Taxes

Many states levy excise taxes on the same items taxed by the Federal government. For example, most states have excise taxes on gasoline, liquor, and tobacco. However, the tax on specific goods can vary dramatically among states. Compare New York's $4.35 tax on each pack of 20 cigarettes to Missouri's $0.17 per pack.[6]

Other goods and services subject to state and local excise taxes include admission to amusement facilities; hotel occupancy; rental of other facilities; and sales of playing cards and prepared foods. Some counties impose a tax on transfers of property that require recording of documents (such as real estate sales and sales of stock and securities).

Local Excise Taxes

Over the last few years, two types of excise taxes imposed at the local level have become increasingly popular. These are the hotel occupancy tax and the rental car "surcharge." Because they tax the visitor who cannot vote, they are a political windfall and serve as a means of financing special projects that generate civic pride (e.g., convention centers and state-of-the-art sports arenas). A few cities have created excise taxes that apply to digital transactions, like fees for streaming music and movies, app downloads, Uber and Lyft fares, and Airbnb rentals.

General Sales Tax

The broad-based general sales tax is a major source of revenue for most state and local governments. It is used in all but five states (Alaska, Delaware, Montana, New Hampshire, and Oregon). The U.S. Federal government does not levy a general sales tax.

Although specific rules vary from state to state, the sales tax typically employs a proportional tax rate and includes retail sales of tangible personal property (and occasionally personal services) in the base. Some states exempt medicine and groceries from the base (or tax these items at a lower rate), and sometimes tax rates vary with the good being sold (e.g., the sales tax rate for food may differ from the rate on other goods). The sales tax is collected by the retailer and then paid to the state government.

Local general sales taxes, over and above those levied by the state, are common. It is not unusual to find taxpayers living in the same state who pay different general sales tax rates based on the city or county in which they make their purchases.

For various reasons, some jurisdictions temporarily suspend the application of a general sales tax. The prevalent justification for these sales tax holidays is to reduce the cost of certain necessities, such as back-to-school items or hurricane preparedness items.

Use Taxes

One obvious approach to avoiding state and local sales taxes is to purchase goods in a state that has little or no sales tax and then transport the goods back to one's home state. Another alternative is to purchase goods from a small out-of-state internet-based vendor that then ships the goods directly to the purchaser. **Use taxes** exist to prevent this tax reduction ploy. The use tax is a transaction tax imposed at the same rate as the sales tax on the use, consumption, or storage of tangible property. Every state that imposes a general sales tax levied on the consumer also applies a use tax.

[6] Some excise taxes are referred to as "sin" taxes (because goods such as liquor, marijuana, and tobacco are subject to the tax). Although it is commonly believed that these taxes are imposed for the purpose of discouraging consumption of the taxed item, evidence frequently fails to show this effect among all age groups.

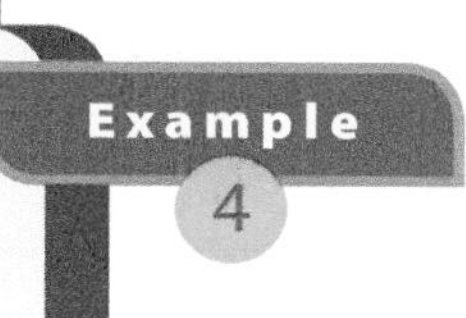

Return to the facts of *The Big Picture* on p. 1-1. The payment Travis made when he registered the car is probably a use tax. When the car was purchased in another state, likely no sales tax (or a lower amount) was levied. The current payment makes up for the amount of sales tax he would have paid had the car been purchased in his home state.

The use tax is difficult to enforce for many purchases since many consumers are not aware of the tax. Most states have measures to curtail the loss of this revenue (e.g., by requiring consumers to report and pay the tax when they file their state income tax return).

Value Added Tax

The **value added tax (VAT)** is a variation of a sales tax and is levied at each stage of production on the value added by the producer. A VAT is used by almost all countries around the world; the United States is one of the few countries that does not use a VAT. The tax typically serves as a major source of revenue for governments that use it.[7]

The most commonly used form of VAT is the *credit invoice* VAT. In its basic form, sellers charge a VAT on everything they sell, and all buyers pay the VAT. Business buyers, though, get the VAT they pay refunded (or *credited*) against the VAT they collect and have to remit to the government. As a result, the final consumer pays the VAT, but it is assessed and collected throughout the production and distribution of the goods or services (in contrast, the sales tax is paid by the final consumer only). A credit invoice VAT system can be fairly simple, although many countries add complexities (e.g., special rates on certain goods or services, or exemptions for small businesses).

Country X imposes a VAT at a 10% rate and uses the credit invoice VAT system. Farmer Jane grows wheat and sells it to ABC Mill for $110 [$100 plus VAT of $10 (10% × $100)]. ABC Mill sells refined wheat flour to Birch Bakery for $154 [$140 plus VAT of $14 (10% × $140)]. Finally, Birch Bakery uses the flour to sell cupcakes to consumers for $187 [$170 plus VAT of $17 (10% × $170)]. Along the way, the parties involved pay, collect, and remit the following VAT, resulting in total VAT paid to the government of $17.

Farmer Jane	$10 collected and remitted to the government
ABC Mill	4 remitted to the government ($14 collected less $10 paid)
Birch Bakery	3 remitted to the government ($17 collected less $14 paid)
Total VAT	$17

If Country X instead used a sales tax, the sales from Farmer Jane to ABC Mill to Birch Bakery would be exempt from tax because the goods were purchased for resale. The buyers of the final cupcakes would pay sales tax of $17, the same amount collected under the credit invoice VAT.

1-3b Employment Taxes

Both Federal and state governments tax the salaries and wages paid to employees. On the Federal side, employment taxes represent a major source of funds. For example, the **FICA tax** accounts for more than one-third of revenues in the Federal budget, second only to the income tax in its contribution.

The Federal government imposes two kinds of employment tax. The Federal Insurance Contributions Act (FICA) imposes a tax on self-employed individuals, employees, and employers. The proceeds of the tax are used to finance Social Security and Medicare benefits. The Federal Unemployment Tax Act (FUTA) imposes a tax on employers only. The **FUTA tax** provides funds to state unemployment benefit programs. Most state employment taxes are similar to the FUTA tax, with proceeds used to finance state unemployment benefit payments.

[7]Some proposals to reduce the Federal government's reliance on the employment and income taxes or help reduce the national debt have focused on VAT as an alternative tax system.

FICA Taxes

The FICA tax has two components: old age, survivors, and disability insurance payments (commonly referred to as Social Security) and Medicare health insurance payments. The Social Security tax rate is 6.2 percent for the employee and 6.2 percent for the employer, and the Medicare tax rate is 1.45 percent for both the employer and the employee. The maximum base for the Social Security tax is $147,000 for 2022 and $142,800 for 2021. There is no ceiling on the base amount for the Medicare tax. The employer withholds the FICA tax from an employee's wages.

Payments usually are made through weekly or monthly electronic payments or deposits to a Federal depository. Employers also file Form 941, Employer's Quarterly Federal Tax Return, by the end of the first month following each quarter of the calendar year (e.g., by July 31 for the quarter ending on June 30) and pay any remaining amount of employment taxes due for the previous quarter. Failure to pay can result in large penalties.

FICA tax is not assessed on all wages paid. For example, wages paid to children under the age of 18 who are employed in a parent's trade or business are exempt from the tax.

The Big Picture

Example 6

Return to the facts of *The Big Picture* on p. 1-1. Presuming that April and Martin perform meaningful services for Travis (which the facts seem to imply), they are legitimate employees. April is not subject to Social Security tax because she is under the age of 18. However, Martin is 18, and Travis needs to collect and pay FICA taxes for him.

Furthermore, recall that Amy Carter now is working and is subject to the Social Security and Medicare taxes. Travis, as an independent contractor, is subject to self-employment tax, discussed in the next section.

An additional 0.9 percent Medicare tax is imposed on earned income (including self-employment income) *above* $200,000 (single filers) or $250,000 (married filing jointly). Unlike the Social Security tax of 6.2 percent and the regular Medicare portion of 1.45 percent, an employer does not match the employees' 0.9 percent additional Medicare tax.

Similarly, an additional 3.8 percent Medicare tax is assessed on the investment income of individuals whose modified adjusted gross income exceeds $200,000 or $250,000. For this purpose, investment income includes interest, dividends, net capital gains, and income for similar portfolio items.

The Big Picture

Return to the facts of *The Big Picture* on p. 1-1. The combined income of Travis and Amy Carter may be large enough to trigger one or both of the additional Medicare taxes. The marginal tax rate of "upper-income" taxpayers is higher than that of other individuals because of these taxes. Congress has designated these taxes to cover a portion of Federal health care costs. Betty would have considered these taxes when making her decision to reenter the workforce.

Self-Employment Tax

Self-employed individuals also pay into the FICA system in the form of a self-employment (SE) tax (determined on Schedule SE, filed with Form 1040, U.S. Individual Income Tax Return). Self-employed individuals are required to pay both the employer and the employee portion of the FICA taxes. The 2022 SE tax rate is 15.3 percent on self-employment income up to $147,000 and 2.9 percent on all additional self-employment income. Self-employed individuals deduct half of the SE tax—the amount normally deductible by an employer as a business expense. Self-employment income is discussed in more detail in text Section 11-4b.

Unemployment Taxes

For 2022, FUTA applies at a rate of 6.0 percent on the first $7,000 of covered wages paid during the year to each employee. As with FICA, this represents a regressive rate structure. The Federal government allows a credit for unemployment tax paid (or allowed under a merit rating system)[8] to the state. The credit cannot exceed 5.4 percent of the covered wages. As a result, the amount required to be paid to the U.S. Treasury could be as low as 0.6 percent (6.0% − 5.4%) of an employee's wages.

FUTA and state unemployment taxes differ from FICA in that the tax is imposed only on the employer.

1-3c Taxes at Death

The transfer of property upon the death of the owner may be a taxable event. If the tax is imposed on the transferor at death, it is called an **estate tax**. If the law taxes the recipient of the property, it is termed an **inheritance tax**. As is typical of other types of transaction taxes, the value of the property transferred provides the base for determining the amount of the tax at death.

The Federal government imposes an estate tax. Only a few state governments levy their own additional inheritance taxes, estate taxes, or both.

In a typical year, about 3 million U.S. individuals die. At the same time, less than 3,000 estates file a Federal estate tax return showing an estate tax liability. Total collections of Federal estate and gift tax revenues in 2020 were about $18 billion. This represents less than one percent of total Federal tax collections.

At the time of her death, Wilma lived in a state that imposes an inheritance tax but not an estate tax. Mary, one of Wilma's heirs, lives in the same state. Wilma's estate is subject to the Federal estate tax, and Mary is subject to the state inheritance tax.

The Federal Estate Tax

Never designed to generate a large amount of revenue, the Federal estate tax was intended to prevent large concentrations of wealth from being kept within a family for many generations. Whether this objective has been accomplished is debatable, because estate taxes can be substantially reduced (or deferred for decades) through careful tax planning activities.

Determination of the estate tax base begins with the *gross estate*, which includes property the decedent owned at the time of death. It also includes property interests, such as life insurance proceeds paid to the estate or to a beneficiary other than the estate if the deceased-insured had any ownership rights in the policy. Most property included in the gross estate is valued at fair market value as of the date of death.

Deductions from the gross estate in arriving at the *taxable estate* include funeral and administration expenses, certain taxes, debts of the decedent, and transfers to charitable organizations. A *marital deduction* is available for amounts passing to a surviving spouse (a widow or widower).

When Luis died, he owned $30,000,000 in various securities, real estate, and personal effects. Under his will, Luis gave $1,000,000 to the local art museum and provided $12,000,000 to his surviving wife Angelina. Luis's executor computes a Federal estate tax on the $17,000,000 taxable estate.

Once the taxable estate has been determined and certain taxable gifts have been added to it, one must determine a tentative tax liability. The tentative liability is reduced by a variety of credits to arrive at the amount due.

In 2022, $12,060,000 of a U.S. decedent's estate effectively is excluded from the estate tax, with a maximum 40 percent tax rate on any excess. Spouses can share a $24,120,000 estate tax exclusion. These amounts are indexed annually for inflation.[9]

State Taxes at Death

States usually levy an inheritance tax, an estate tax, or both. The two forms of tax differ according to whether the liability is imposed on the heirs or on the estate.

[8]States follow a policy of reducing unemployment tax on employers with stable employment. Thus, an employer with no employee turnover might face state unemployment tax rates as low as 0.1% or, in some cases, zero. This *merit rating system* explicitly accounts for the savings generated by steady employment.

[9]§ 2010; in 2021, the exemption amount was $11.7 million.

Typically, an inheritance tax divides the heirs into classes based on their relationship to the decedent. The more closely related the heir, the lower the rates imposed and the greater the exemption allowed. Some states allow a zero rate of tax on amounts passing to a surviving spouse.

1-3d Gift Tax

Like estate and inheritance taxes, the Federal **gift tax** is an excise tax levied on the right to transfer property. In this case, however, the tax is imposed on transfers made during the owner's life rather than at death. The tax applies only to transferred amounts that are not supported by full and adequate consideration (i.e., gifts).

Carl sells property worth $20,000 to his daughter, Bryce, for $1,000. Carl has made a $19,000 gift to Bryce.

The Federal gift tax is intended to complement the estate tax. The gift tax base is the sum of all taxable gifts made *during one's lifetime*. Gifts are valued at the fair market value of the property on the date of the gift. To compute the tax due in a year, the tax rate schedule is applied to the sum of all lifetime taxable gifts. The resulting tax is then reduced by gift taxes paid in prior years.

The Federal gift tax and the Federal estate tax are *unified*.[10] The transfer of assets by a decedent at death effectively is treated as a final gift under the tax law. As a result, the 2022 $12,060,000 exclusion and the 40 percent top tax rate for the estate tax also is available to calculate the tax liability generated by lifetime gifts. If the exclusion is exhausted during one's lifetime against taxable gifts, it is not available to reduce the estate tax liability. The same tax rate schedule applies to both lifetime gifts and the estate tax.

Before his death, Ben makes taxable gifts exceeding the exclusion amount. Because the unified transfer tax exclusion was used up during his life to offset the tax due on these gifts, no further amount is left to reduce Ben's estate tax liability.

Annual taxable gifts are determined by reducing the fair market value of gifts given by an *annual exclusion* of $16,000 per donee ($15,000 for 2021); this amount does not use up any of the lifetime exclusion. A married couple can elect *gift splitting*, which enables them to transfer twice the annual exclusion ($32,000) per donee per year, before eroding the lifetime exclusion amount.

Taxable gifts are reduced by deductions for gifts to charity and to one's spouse (the *marital deduction*). Gifts for medical and educational purposes may be exempt from the gift tax as well.

Gift Tax Exclusion and Deductions

Marco made the following gifts: $500,000 to his wife Irena, $100,000 to their daughter Anita, and $100,000 to the San Mateo Church.

The marital and charitable deductions offset the gifts to Irena and the church. The $16,000 per donee annual exclusion reduces the taxable gift to Anita. Another $16,000 of the taxable gift could be eliminated if Irena agrees to a gift-splitting election.

On December 31, Vera gives $16,000 to each of her four married children, their spouses, and her eight grandchildren. On January 3 of the following year, she repeats the procedure.

Due to the annual exclusion, Vera has *not* made a taxable gift, although she transferred $256,000 [$16,000 × 16 (the number of donees)] twice, in a matter of days, for a total of $512,000.

If Vera had been married, she could have given twice as much ($1,024,000) tax-free, by electing gift splitting with her spouse.

[10] §§ 2010 and 2505.

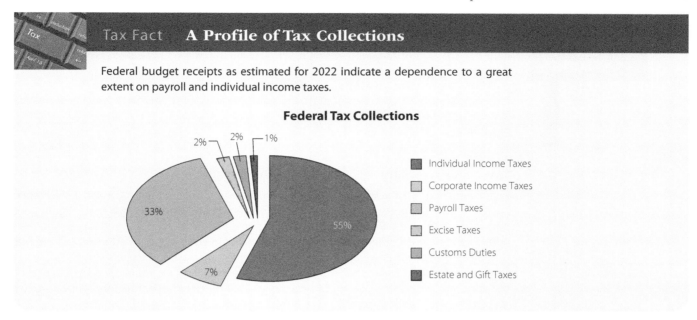

Tax Fact A Profile of Tax Collections

Federal budget receipts as estimated for 2022 indicate a dependence to a great extent on payroll and individual income taxes.

Federal Tax Collections

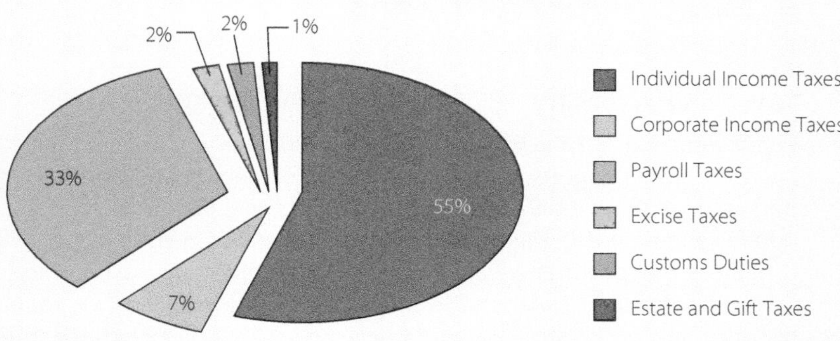

Unlike death, the timing of which usually is involuntary, the making of a gift is a voluntary parting of ownership. As a result, the ownership of a business or a plot of land can be transferred gradually without incurring drastic and immediate tax consequences.

1-3e Property Taxes

A property tax can be a tax on the ownership of property or a tax on wealth depending on the base used. Any measurable characteristic of the property being taxed can be used as a base (e.g., weight, size, number, or value). Most property taxes in the United States are taxes on wealth; they use value as a base. These value-based property taxes are known as **ad valorem taxes**. Property taxes generally are administered by state and local governments, where they serve as a significant source of revenue.

Taxes on Realty

Property taxes on real property, or **realty**, are used exclusively by states and their local political subdivisions such as cities, counties, and school districts. They represent a major source of revenue for local governments, but their importance at the state level is limited.

How realty is defined can have an important bearing on which assets are subject to tax. This is especially true in jurisdictions that do not impose ad valorem taxes on **personalty** (all assets that are not realty, discussed in the next section). Realty generally includes real estate and any capital improvements that are classified as fixtures. A fixture is something so permanently attached to the real estate that its removal will cause irreparable damage. A built-in bookcase might be a fixture, whereas a movable bookcase is not. Certain items such as electrical wiring and plumbing change from personalty to realty when installed in a building.

The following are some of the characteristics of ad valorem taxes on realty.

- States may have a homestead exemption, which makes some portion of the value of a personal residence exempt from tax.
- Lower taxes may apply to a residence owned by a taxpayer age 65 or older.
- Some jurisdictions extend immunity from tax for a specified period of time (a tax holiday) to new or relocated businesses.
- Some states provide for lower valuations on property dedicated to agricultural use or other special uses (e.g., wildlife sanctuaries).

The Big Picture

Example 14

Return to the facts of *The Big Picture* on p. 1-1. Why did the Walkers' taxes decrease while those of the Carters increased?

A likely explanation is that one (or both) of the Walkers achieved senior citizen status, leading to lower tax rates. In the case of the Carters, the assessed value of their property probably increased. Perhaps they made significant home improvements (e.g., kitchen/bathroom renovation, addition of a sundeck).

Taxes on Personalty

Personal property, or personalty, includes all assets that are not realty. There is a difference between how property is *classified* (realty or personalty) and how it is *used*. Realty and personalty can be either business use or personal use property. Examples include a residence (personal use realty), an office building (business use realty), surgical instruments (business use personalty), and the family car (personal use personalty).

Personalty also can be classified as tangible property or intangible property. For property tax purposes, intangible personalty includes stocks, bonds, and various other securities (e.g., bank shares).

The following generalizations may be made concerning the property taxes on personalty.

- Generally, for individuals, vehicles (cars and boats, for example) are the only nonrealty personal use assets subject to property tax. The value of a vehicle typically is established by a schedule based on the vehicle's age and make/model. Usually, any vehicle property tax is assessed and collected along with vehicle license or registration fees.
- Generally, businesses are assessed property taxes on equipment and other tangible property, although many states do not tax inventory.
- Some jurisdictions impose an ad valorem property tax on intangibles, like stocks and bonds.

Digging Deeper 2

Additional information on real property valuation can be found on this book's companion website: www.cengage.com

1-3f Other U.S. Taxes

Federal Customs Duties

Customs duties or tariffs can be characterized as a tax on the right to move goods across national borders. These taxes, together with selective excise taxes, provided most of the revenues needed by the Federal government during the nineteenth century. For example, tariffs and excise taxes alone paid off the national debt in 1835 and enabled the U.S. Treasury to pay a surplus of $28 million to the states. Today, however, customs duties account for only 1 percent of revenues in the Federal budget.

In recent years, tariffs have acted more as an instrument for carrying out protectionist policies and to generate revenue. As a result, a particular U.S. industry might be saved from economic disaster, so the argument goes, by placing customs duties on the importation of foreign goods that can be sold at lower prices. Protectionists contend that the tariff therefore neutralizes the competitive edge held by the offshore producer of the goods. But tariffs often lead to retaliatory action on the part of the nation or nations affected.

Miscellaneous State and Local Taxes

A **franchise tax** is a tax on the privilege of doing business in a state or local jurisdiction. Typically, the tax is imposed by states on corporations, but the tax base varies from state to state. Although some states use a measure of corporate net income as part of the base, most states base the tax on the capitalization of the corporation (with or without certain long-term debt).

Closely akin to the franchise tax are **occupational taxes** applicable to various trades or businesses, such as a liquor store license, a taxicab or shared-ride permit, or a fee to practice a profession such as law, medicine, or accounting. Most of these are not significant revenue producers and fall more into the category of licenses than taxes. The revenue derived is used to defray the cost incurred by the jurisdiction to regulate the business or profession for the public good.

The Big Picture

Return to the facts of *The Big Picture* on p. 1-1. Although the facts do not mention the matter, both Travis and Amy will almost certainly pay occupational fees—Travis for engineering and Amy for nursing.

Severance Taxes

Severance taxes are based on the extraction of natural resources (e.g., oil, gas, iron ore, and coal). They are an important source of revenue for many states; Alaska does not levy either a state-level income or sales/use tax, because the collections from its severance taxes typically are quite large.

1-3g Income Taxes

Income taxes are levied by the Federal government, most states, and some local governments. In recent years, the trend in the United States has been to place greater reliance on this method of taxation, while other countries are relying more heavily on transactions taxes such as the VAT.

Income taxes generally are imposed on individuals, corporations, and certain fiduciaries (estates and trusts). Most jurisdictions attempt to ensure the collection of income taxes by requiring certain pay-as-you-go procedures, including withholding requirements for employees and estimated tax prepayments for all taxpayers.

The Structure of the Federal Income Tax

Describe the basic tax formula for individuals and business entities.

Although some variations exist, the basic Federal income tax formula is similar for all taxable entities. This formula is shown in Exhibit 1.1.

The income tax is based on the doctrine known as *legislative grace*: all income is subject to tax, and no deductions are allowed unless specifically provided for in the law. Some types of income are excluded on the basis of various economic, social, equity, and political considerations. Examples of such exclusions from the income tax base include gifts, inheritances, life insurance proceeds received by reason of death, and interest income from state and local bonds.

All entities are allowed to deduct business expenses from gross income, but a number of limitations and exceptions are applied. A variety of credits against the tax are also allowed, again on the basis of economic, social, equity, or political goals of Congress.

Individual rates range from 10 percent to 37 percent. Estates and trusts are also subject to income taxation, with rates ranging from 10 percent to 37 percent. Additional Medicare taxes (discussed previously) apply on top of these rates for certain upper-income taxpayers.

Exhibit 1.1 Basic Formula for Federal Income Tax

Income (broadly defined)	$xxx,xxx
Less: Exclusions (income that is not subject to tax)	(xx,xxx)
Gross income (income that is subject to tax)	$xxx,xxx
Less: Deductions	(xx,xxx)
Taxable income	$xxx,xxx
Federal income tax on taxable income (see Tax Rate Schedules in the endsheets of text)	$ xx,xxx
Less: Tax credits (including Federal income tax withheld and other prepayments of Federal income taxes)	(x,xxx)
Tax due (or refund)	$ xxx

Partnerships, qualifying small business corporations, and some limited liability companies are not taxable entities but must file information returns. Owners of these business entities then are taxed on the net taxable income of the enterprise, proportionate to their holdings. See text Sections 1-4c through 1-4e.

For individuals, deductions are separated into two categories—deductions *for* adjusted gross income (AGI) and deductions *from* AGI. Generally, deductions *for* AGI are related to business activities, while deductions *from* AGI often are personal in nature (e.g., medical expenses, mortgage interest and property taxes on a personal residence, charitable contributions, and personal casualty losses stemming from a Federally declared disaster). Deductions *from* AGI take the form of *itemized deductions* and the deduction for qualified business income. Individuals may take a *standard deduction* (a specified amount based on filing status) rather than itemize actual deductions. An overview of the individual income tax formula is provided in Exhibit 1.2.

Exhibit 1.2 Federal Income Tax Formula for Individuals

Income (broadly defined)	$xx,xxx
Less: Exclusions (income that is not subject to tax)	(x,xxx)
Gross income (income that is subject to tax)	$xx,xxx
Less: Certain deductions (usually referred to as deductions *for* adjusted gross income)	(x,xxx)
Adjusted gross income	$xx,xxx
Less: The greater of:	
Certain personal deductions (usually referred to as *itemized deductions*)	
or	
The standard deduction (including any *additional* standard deduction)	(x,xxx)
Less: Deduction for qualified business income	(x,xxx)
Taxable income	$xx,xxx
Federal income tax on taxable income (see the Tax Tables and Tax Rate Schedules in Appendix A)	$ x,xxx
Less: Tax credits (including Federal income tax withheld and other prepayments of Federal income taxes)	(xxx)
Tax owed (or refund)	$ xxx

State Income Taxes

Most states (except Alaska, Florida, Nevada, South Dakota, Tennessee, Texas, Washington, and Wyoming) impose a traditional income tax on individuals. New Hampshire imposes an individual income tax only on dividend and interest income. Most states also impose either a corporate income tax or a franchise tax based in part on corporate income. The following additional points can be made about state income taxes. See also text Section 16-3.

- State income tax laws usually rely on Federal income tax laws to some degree—the states use Federal taxable income (or Federal adjusted gross income) as a base, with a few adjustments (e.g., a few states allow an exclusion for interest income earned on Federal securities).
- Most states require withholding of state income tax from salaries and wages and estimated tax payments by corporations and self-employed individuals.
- Most states have their own set of rates, exemptions, and credits.
- Many states allow a credit for taxes paid to other states.
- Virtually all state income tax returns provide checkoff boxes for donations to various causes. Many are dedicated to medical research and wildlife programs, but special projects are not uncommon. For example, Wisconsin uses one for the maintenance and operating costs of Lambeau Field (home of the Green Bay Packers). These checkoff boxes have been criticized as adding complexity to the returns and misleading taxpayers.

Local Income Taxes

Cities imposing an income tax include Baltimore, Cincinnati, Cleveland, Detroit, Kansas City (Missouri), New York, Philadelphia, and St. Louis, among others. City income taxes usually apply to anyone who earns income in a city, including those who live in close-by suburbs but work in the city.

Concept Summary 1.1 provides an overview of the major taxes existing in the United States and specifies which political jurisdiction imposes them.

Information on major tax reform proposals can be found on this book's companion website: www.cengage.com

3 Digging Deeper

Bridge Discipline Bridge to Political Science and Sociology

The tax law and its effects on citizens and businesses of the United States are included in many other academic disciplines. Tax burdens are part of American fiction, family studies, and minority issues as well as economics, finance, and management courses.

In the Bridge feature found in most chapters of this text, we relate the concerns of other disciplines to a more specific review of tax law, as presented here. With the topical knowledge obtained in this text, the reader can better understand the issues raised by other disciplines, sometimes to support beliefs held by others and sometimes to refute them.

For instance, the structure of the U.S. tax system raises many issues of equity and fairness. Politicians and journalists discuss these issues freely, often without the requisite tax knowledge to draw proper conclusions.

- Should the property tax on real estate be used to finance the local public education system? Why should elderly taxpayers with grown children or parents who send their children to private schools continue to pay for public schools through these taxes?
- Would the lack of a charitable contribution deduction impair the ability of charities to raise operating and capital funds?
- Does the real property tax impose a greater burden on low-income renters who pay this tax indirectly as part of rent?
- Is the tax law "friendly" to marriage and to families with children?
- Should the tax law be used to encourage investments in "green" energy products? In improving access speeds for the internet?

Concept Summary 1.1

Overview of Taxes in the United States

Type of Tax	Imposed by Jurisdiction		
	Federal	**State**	**Local**
Property taxes:			
Ad valorem on realty	No	Yes	Yes
Ad valorem on personalty	No	Yes	Yes
Transaction taxes:			
Excise	Yes	Yes	Few
General sales	No	Most	Some
Severance	Yes	Some	No
Estate	Yes	Few	No
Inheritance	No	Few	Few
Gift	Yes	Few	No
Income taxes:			
Corporations	Yes	Most	Few
Individuals	Yes	Most	Few
Employment taxes:			
FICA	Yes	No	No
FUTA	Yes	Yes	No
Other taxes			
Customs duties	Yes	No	No
Franchise taxes	No	Yes	No
Occupational taxes or fees	Yes	Yes	Yes

Financial Disclosure Insights: What Do You Mean by "Income" Anyway?

Most business taxpayers keep at least "two sets of books," in that they report one amount of "income" for financial accounting purposes and another amount of "taxable income" as required by various taxing jurisdictions—the definition that will be used throughout this book. In fact, "income" might be defined in many different ways depending on the recipient of the income reports of the enterprise. For instance, a business entity might prepare different income reports for lenders, employee unions, managers in operating divisions, and international agencies.

Financial accounting income guidance is provided for U.S. businesses by the **Financial Accounting Standards Board (FASB)**, using the accumulated **Generally Accepted Accounting Principles (GAAP)** for the reporting period. When an entity conducts business outside the United States, the **International Financial Reporting Standards (IFRS)** of the **International Accounting Standards Board (IASB)** also may apply.

Throughout this book, we point out some of the effects that Federal income tax provisions can have on the taxpayer's financial accounting results for the tax year. The vast majority of an entity's business transactions receive identical treatment under GAAP, IFRS, and the Federal tax law. But when the applicable provisions differ, "income" can be reported as different amounts—accounting professionals often refer to these as "book-tax differences."

A tax professional must be able to identify and explain the various constructs of "income" so that the business entity's operating results will be accurately reflected in its stock price, loan covenants, and cash-flow demands.

1-4 Income Taxation of Business Entities

LO.5

Explain the tax systems that apply to business entities and their owners.

1-4a Proprietorships

The simplest form of business entity is a **proprietorship**, which is not a separate taxable entity. Instead, the proprietor reports the net profit of the business on his or her own individual income tax return.

Individuals who own proprietorships (e.g., "Jenny's Fruit Stand") often have specific tax goals with regard to their financial interactions with the business. Because a proprietorship is, by definition, owned by an individual, the individual has great flexibility in structuring the entity's transactions in a way that will minimize his or her marginal income tax rate (or, in some cases, the marginal income tax rates of the family unit). For example, a cash method sole proprietor might push income into the next year by delaying year-end billing.

A proprietorship itself is not a taxpaying entity. The owner of the proprietorship reports the income and deductions of the business on a Schedule C (Profit or Loss from Business) and the net profit (or loss) of the proprietorship on his or her Form 1040 (U.S. Individual Income Tax Return). Taxation of sole proprietorships is covered in Chapter 11.

1-4b C Corporations

Some corporations pay tax on corporate taxable income, while others pay no tax at the corporate level. Corporations that are separate taxable entities are referred to as **C corporations**, because they are governed by Subchapter C of the Internal Revenue Code (Code), the statute that provides the Federal tax law. Chapters 12 and 13 are devoted to C corporation taxation.

A C corporation files its own tax return (Form 1120) and is subject to the Federal income tax. The shareholders then pay income tax on the dividends they receive when the corporation distributes its profits. As a result, the profits of the corporation can be seen as subject to *double taxation*, first at the corporate level and then at the shareholder level.

Joseph is the president and sole shareholder of Falcon Corporation. Falcon's taxable income is $50,000, and its tax liability is $10,500 ($50,000 × 21%).

If Joseph has the corporation pay all of its after-tax income to him as a dividend, he will receive $39,500 ($50,000 − $10,500) and pay Federal income tax on that amount as an individual taxpayer. In this case, a large portion of Falcon's $50,000 income has been subjected to Federal income tax twice.

1-4c Partnerships

A partnership is not a separate taxable entity. The partnership files a tax return (Form 1065) on which it summarizes the financial results of the business. Each partner then reports his or her share of the net income or loss and other special items that were reported on the partnership return. In Chapter 14, we discuss the tax rules that apply to partnerships and similar entities.

Cameron and Connor form a partnership in which they are equal partners. The partnership reports a $100,000 net profit on its tax return but is not subject to the Federal income tax. Instead, Cameron and Connor each report $50,000 net income from the partnership on their separate individual income tax returns.

1-4d S Corporations

Corporations that meet certain requirements and pay no Federal income tax at the corporate level are referred to as **S corporations**, because they are governed by Subchapter S of the Code. We discuss the taxation of S corporations in Chapter 15.

An S corporation is treated like a C corporation for all nontax purposes as both are entities formed under a particular state's corporate law. Shareholders have limited liability, shares are freely transferable, the entity uses centralized management (vested in the board of directors), and there can be an unlimited continuity of life (i.e., the corporation continues to exist after the withdrawal or death of a shareholder).

With regard to tax factors, however, an S corporation is more like a partnership. The S corporation is not subject to the Federal *income tax*. Like a partnership, it does file a tax return (Form 1120S), but the shareholders report their share of net income or loss and other special items on their own tax returns.

Kay and Dawn form a corporation and elect to treat it as an S corporation. Kay owns 60% of the stock of the corporation, and Dawn owns 40%. The S corporation reports a $100,000 net profit on its tax return. Kay reports $60,000 net income from the S corporation on her individual income tax return, and Dawn reports $40,000 on her tax return.

1-4e Limited Liability Companies and Limited Liability Partnerships

Limited liability companies (LLCs) and limited liability partnerships (LLPs) offer limited liability and some (but not all) of the other nontax features of corporations. Both forms usually are treated as partnerships for tax purposes.

The S corporation, limited liability company, and partnership forms of organization, which are referred to as *flow-through* entities, avoid the double taxation problem associated with the C corporation.

1-4f Dealings between Individuals and Their Business Entities

Many of the provisions in the tax law deal with the relationships between owners and the business entities they own. The following are some of the major interactions between owners and business entities.

- Owners put assets into a business when they create a business entity (e.g., a proprietorship, partnership, or corporation).
- Owners take assets out of the business during its existence in the form of salary, dividends, withdrawals, redemptions of stock, etc.
- Through their entities, owner-employees set up retirement plans for themselves, including IRAs and qualified retirement and pension plans.
- Owners dispose of all or part of a business entity.

Every major transaction that occurs between an owner and a business entity has important tax ramifications. The following are a few of the many tax issues that arise.

- How the tax law applies at both the owner level and the entity level (i.e., the multiple taxation problem) and what effective tax rate is assessed on such income.
- How to move assets into the business with the least adverse tax consequences.
- How to pull assets and accumulated profits out of the business with the least adverse tax consequences.
- How to dispose of the business entity with the least adverse tax consequences.
- Whether certain tax rules will apply less favorably because the business and owner(s) are related parties.

Financial Disclosure Insights **Book-Tax Differences**

"Income" is defined differently for Federal income tax and financial accounting purposes. Financial accounting income (FAI) is designed to indicate the profitability of the business entity for the reporting period, in a fair and understandable way, to shareholders, creditors, and other parties who are interested in the results. Taxable income is a device used by Congress to raise revenue; stimulate or stabilize the economy; and accomplish other economic, social, and political goals in an equitable manner. In general, FAI recognizes *revenue* and *expenses*, while taxable income includes *gross income* and *deductions*.

The taxable income of a business taxpayer is not identical to FAI to the extent that *temporary* and *permanent* book-tax differences exist. Broadly, book-tax differences result when:

- Tax benefits are accelerated or deferred relative to their recognition for book purposes, for example, when cost recovery deductions are claimed earlier than depreciation expenses are allowed.
- Tax benefits are not recognized at all for book purposes (e.g., there is no book expense item corresponding to the domestic production activities deduction).

As a result of temporary book-tax differences, income tax payable (the amount due on the tax return, referred to by many tax professionals as the "cash tax") differs from the income tax expense on the book income statement. The income statement reflects the full income tax burden for the FAI of the reporting period, under the GAAP matching principle, but it is broken into the components *current income tax expense* and *deferred income tax expense*.

When a tax benefit is delayed for book purposes, such as for accelerated cost recovery deductions, a **deferred tax liability** is created on the entity's balance sheet. Taxable income will be greater than FAI in a subsequent year.

When a tax benefit is delayed for tax purposes, such as when a bad debt allowance is used for accounts receivable but is not permissible on the tax return, a **deferred tax asset** is created on the balance sheet. Taxable income will be less than FAI in a subsequent year.

Permanent book-tax differences, such as the exclusion for interest income from a state bond, do not affect the balance sheet. But because FAI and taxable income differ in this amount, the effective tax rate of the taxpayer is higher or lower than might be expected. The financial statement footnotes reconcile the statutory and effective tax rates of the entity in dollar and/or percentage amounts.

The balance sheet accounts for deferred taxes can be sizable. For instance, in most years, Citigroup's deferred tax assets make up about one-third of its tangible equity capital.

1-5 Tax Planning Fundamentals

Identify tax planning opportunities using a general framework for tax planning.

1-5a Overview of Tax Planning and Ethics

Taxpayers generally attempt to minimize their tax liabilities, and it is perfectly acceptable to do so using legal means. It is a long-standing principle that taxpayers have no obligation to pay more than their fair share of taxes. As noted by Judge Learned Hand in *Commissioner v. Newman*:

> Over and over again courts have said that there is nothing sinister in so arranging one's affairs as to keep taxes as low as possible. Everybody does so, rich or poor; and all do right, for nobody owes any public duty to pay more than the law demands; taxes are enforced exactions, not voluntary contributions. To demand more in the name of morals is mere cant.[11]

Tax Planning: Avoidance Versus Evasion

Minimizing taxes legally is referred to as **tax avoidance**. On the other hand, some taxpayers attempt to *evade* income taxes through illegal actions. There is a major distinction between tax avoidance and **tax evasion**. Although eliminating or reducing taxes is also a goal of tax evasion, the term *evasion* implies the use of subterfuge and fraud as a means to this end. Tax avoidance is legal, but tax evasion subjects the taxpayer to numerous civil and criminal penalties, including possible prison sentence.

[11] 47–1 USTC ¶9175, 35 AFTR 857, 159 F.2d 848 (CA–2, 1947).

Clients expect tax professionals to provide advice to help them minimize their tax costs. This part of the tax practitioner's practice is referred to as *tax planning*. To structure a sound tax plan, a practitioner first must have a thorough knowledge of the tax law. Tax planning skill is based on knowledge of tax saving provisions in the tax law as well as provisions that contain costly pitfalls for the unwary.

Thorough study of the remainder of this text will provide a solid base of the knowledge required to recognize opportunities and avoid pitfalls. Tax planning requires the practitioner to have in mind both a framework for planning and an understanding of the tax planning implications of a client's situation.

The Ethics of Tax Planning

Tax planning (avoidance) is a fully ethical activity by the taxpayer and the tax professional, but tax evasion (fraud) is not. The tax adviser's actions are limited by the codes of conduct of various professional organizations, such as the American Institute of CPAs (AICPA) or the pertinent state bar association.

Other formal restrictions and directives concerning the conduct of the tax professional can be found in two broad forms.

- Penalties and interest may apply to the taxpayer when a tax liability is understated. Examples include penalties for filing a tax return after its due date, understating gross income amounts, and underpaying withholding or estimated taxes that are due.
- Sanctions are used for tax preparers who disregard the tax law. The Treasury issues a regulation known as *Circular 230* to provide guidance to tax return preparers. Tax penalties also apply when the tax preparer fails to sign a tax return that he or she has worked on or takes an improper filing position on a tax return.

★ Tax Planning Framework

1-5b A General Framework for Income Tax Planning

The primary goal of tax planning is to design a transaction so as to minimize its tax costs while meeting the other nontax objectives of the client. Generally, this means that the client attempts to maximize the present value of its after-tax income and assets. Selecting a specific form of transaction solely for the sake of tax minimization often leads to a poor business decision. Effective tax planning requires careful consideration of the nontax issues involved in addition to the tax consequences.

Careful analysis of the tax formula (refer to Exhibit 1.1) reveals a series of tax minimization strategies. Through tax planning that also takes into consideration a client's nontax concerns, many components of the tax formula can be structured in a way that will help to minimize the client's tax liability. The General Framework for Income Tax Planning in Exhibit 1.3 lists each element in the income tax formula, develops tax planning strategies designed to minimize taxes, and provides brief summaries of specific examples of tax planning. The framework is followed by a discussion of the tax planning strategies, along with detailed examples of how the strategies can be applied. In Chapters 4 through 18 of this book, these strategies and their tax formula components provide the framework for Tax Planning Strategies features.

Exhibit 1.3 General Framework for Income Tax Planning

Tax Formula	Tax Planning Strategy	Tax Planning Examples
Income and exclusions	➢ **Avoid income recognition.**	Compensate employees with nontaxable fringe benefits (see Example 19).
	➢ **Postpone recognition of income to achieve tax deferral.**	Postpone sale of assets (see Example 20).
− Deductions	➢ **Maximize deductible amounts.**	Invest in stock of another corporation (see Example 21).
	➢ **Accelerate recognition of deductions to achieve tax deferral.**	Elect to deduct charitable contribution in year of pledge rather than in year of payment (see Example 22).
= Taxable income		
× Tax rate	➢ **Shift net income from high-bracket years to low-bracket years.**	Postpone recognition of income to a low-bracket year (see Example 23).
		Postpone recognition of deductions to a high-bracket year (see Example 24).
	➢ **Shift net income from high-bracket taxpayers to low-bracket taxpayers.**	Pay children to work in the family business (see Example 25).
	➢ **Shift net income from high-tax jurisdictions to low-tax jurisdictions.**	Establish subsidiary operations in countries with low tax rates (see Examples 26 and 27).
	➢ **Control the character of income and deductions.**	Hold assets long enough to qualify for long-term capital gain rates before selling them (see Example 28).
	➢ **Avoid double taxation.**	Operate as a flow-through entity rather than a C corporation (see Example 29).
		Maximize deductible expenses paid by a C corporation to a shareholder/employee (see Example 30).
= Federal income tax		
− Tax credits	➢ **Maximize tax credits.**	Make structural changes to a building where the expenditures qualify for the rehabilitation tax credit (see Example 31).
= Tax owed (or refund)		

In addition to a planning framework focused on the tax formula, another planning framework is focused on four questions: when?/what?/who?/where?

- **When:** How do tax accounting method rules affect *when* income and deductions are reported? See text Sections 4-3 and 5-2.
- **What:** What exclusions, deductions and tax credits can be applied to reduce taxable income and tax liability? See Chapters 4, 5, 10, and 17.
- **Who:** Which party to a transaction will report income? See text Section 9-5e and Chapters 12 through 15.
- **Where:** In which state or states (or foreign country) can the income be generated or taxed? See Chapter 16.

1-5c Tax Minimization Strategies Related to Income

★ **Framework Focus: Income**

➢ ***Tax Planning Strategy***

➢ *Avoid Income Recognition.* Code § 61(a) defines gross income as "all income from whatever source derived." However, the Code contains provisions that allow various types of income to be excluded from the tax base. Numerous exclusions are available for individuals (including a number that are available to employees), but very few are available for corporations.

The average employee of Penguin Corporation is a 25% bracket taxpayer, considering Federal, state, and local income taxes. In negotiations with the employees' union, Penguin proposes that it will increase the amount it spends on nontaxable fringe benefits by an average of $3,000 per employee in lieu of granting a $3,000 average salary increase; the benefits provided would be fully deductible by Penguin. The average employee will be better off by $750 if the union accepts Penguin's offer.

	Salary Increase	Fringe Benefit Increase
Value of compensation received	$3,000	$3,000
Tax on employee's compensation	(750)	(–0–)
After-tax increase in compensation	$2,250	$3,000

Although the average employee receives a $750 benefit, there is no tax cost to Penguin because both the fringe benefits and salaries are deductible by Penguin.

➤ *Tax Planning Strategy*

➤ ***Postpone Recognition of Income to Achieve Tax Deferral.*** The tax law requires that both income and expenses be reported in the proper tax year. If not for this requirement, taxpayers could freely shift income and expenses from year to year to take advantage of tax rate differentials, or they could defer tax liabilities indefinitely, thereby achieving a time value of money advantage. Although various rules limit the shifting of income and deductions across time periods, some opportunities still exist.

In 2014, Turquoise Corporation acquired land for investment purposes at a cost of $500,000. In November 2022, Turquoise is negotiating to sell the land to Aqua Corporation for $800,000. Aqua insists that the transaction be completed in 2022, but Turquoise wants to delay the sale until 2023 to defer the tax on the gain. In an effort to compromise, Turquoise agrees to sell the land in November 2022 and asks Aqua to pay for the land in two installments, $400,000 in December 2022 and $400,000 in January 2023. This enables Turquoise to use the installment method for recognizing the gain, under which Turquoise will report $150,000 of the gain in 2022 and the remaining $150,000 in 2023.

By electing the installment method, Turquoise defers the payment of tax on $150,000 of the gain for one year. If the marginal tax rate for Turquoise is 21%, this tax deferral strategy provides $31,500 ($150,000 × 21%) to be invested or used in the business for another year.

★ **Framework Focus: Deductions**

➤ *Tax Planning Strategy*

1-5d Tax Minimization Strategies Related to Deductions

➤ ***Maximize Deductible Amounts.*** A corporation that owns stock in another corporation is eligible for a *dividends received deduction (DRD)*. The DRD is equal to a specified percentage of the dividends received. The percentage is based on the amount of stock that the investor corporation owns in the investee corporation.

- 50 percent deduction for ownership of less than 20 percent.
- 65 percent deduction for ownership of 20 percent or more but less than 80 percent.
- 100 percent deduction for ownership of 80 percent or more.

Falcon Corporation invests in bonds of Sparrow Corporation and receives interest of $20,000. Red Hawk Corporation acquires 15% of the stock of Pheasant Corporation and receives a $20,000 dividend.

Falcon's taxable income is increased by $20,000 for the interest received. Red Hawk's income is increased by $20,000 in dividend income, but it is allowed a $10,000 dividends received deduction, thus increasing taxable income by only $10,000 for that type of income.

Example 21 demonstrates the *tax* advantage of dividend income versus interest income. However, it is also important to consider *nontax* factors. Is the investment in bonds safer than the investment in stock? Does the potential growth in the value of stock outweigh the possible risk of investing in stock versus bonds?

➤ ***Tax Planning Strategy***

➤ ***Accelerate Recognition of Deductions to Achieve Tax Deferral.*** Both corporate and noncorporate taxpayers may deduct charitable contributions if the recipient is a qualified charitable organization. Generally, a deduction is allowed only for the year in which the payment is made. However, an important exception is available for *accrual basis C corporations.* They may claim the deduction in the year *preceding* payment if two requirements are met. First, the contribution must be authorized by the board of directors by the end of that year. Second, the contribution must be paid on or before the fifteenth day of the fourth month of the next year.

Blue, Inc., a calendar year, accrual basis corporation, wants to make a $10,000 donation to the Atlanta Symphony Association (a qualified charitable organization) but does not have adequate funds to make the contribution in 2022. On December 28, 2022, Blue's board of directors *authorizes* a $10,000 contribution to the Association. The donation is made on April 14, 2023. Because Blue is an accrual basis corporation, it may claim the $10,000 donation as a deduction for tax year 2022 even though payment is not made until 2023.

Blue was able to take advantage of a tax provision and reduce 2022 taxable income by $10,000. Blue is in the 21% marginal bracket, so the corporation defers payment of $2,100 in Federal income tax. The $2,100 can be invested or used in the business for another tax year.

1-5e Tax Minimization Strategies Related to Tax Rates

★ **Framework Focus: Tax Rates**

➤ ***Tax Planning Strategy***

➤ ***Shift Net Income from High-Bracket Years to Low-Bracket Years.*** One objective of shifting income is to defer the payment of income tax (refer to Example 20). A second time-shifting strategy is to shift *net* income from high-tax to low-tax years. This can be accomplished by shifting income from high-bracket years to low-bracket years and by shifting deductions from low-bracket years to high-bracket years.

Shift Income to Low-Bracket Years

Example 23

Allie Singh, a calendar year taxpayer, is in the 35% bracket in 2022 but expects to be in the 24% bracket in 2023. Allie is negotiating a $10,000 service contract with a client, and she decides to wait until 2023 to sign the contract and perform the services. The client is indifferent as to when the contract is completed. As a result, Allie saves $1,100 in income tax by deferring the service contract income to 2023, when she will be taxed at the lower Federal income tax rate.

In this case, the income-shifting strategy is used to accomplish two tax planning objectives. First, shifting the income defers the payment of income tax from 2022 to 2023. Second, the shifting strategy results in the income being taxed at a rate of 24% rather than 35%.

Example 24

Ken, a single individual, has been sued for $125,000 damages by a customer, and the parties decided to settle out of court for $100,000. Ken expects to be in the 24% bracket in 2022 and the 35% bracket in 2023. Ken will save $11,000 in income tax if he finalizes the agreement in January 2023 rather than December 2022 [$100,000 × (35% − 24%)].

➤ ***Tax Planning Strategy***

➤ ***Shift Net Income from High-Bracket Taxpayers to Low-Bracket Taxpayers.*** Individual income tax rates range from 10 percent to 37 percent (before considering the additional Medicare taxes on certain high-income individuals). Although several provisions in the tax law prevent shifting income from high-bracket taxpayers to low-bracket taxpayers, some opportunities to do so remain. Business entities can be effective vehicles for shifting income to low-bracket taxpayers.

Jill Gregory is the president and sole shareholder of Grayhawk, Inc., an S corporation. She projects that Grayhawk will earn $400,000 this year. Jill is taxed on this income at a 35% marginal rate. Jill and her spouse have four teenage children. The Gregorys record no other taxable income; they file a joint return.

Jill employs the children as part-time workers throughout the year and pays them $11,000 each. This reduces Jill's income from Grayhawk by $44,000 and reduces her Federal income tax by $15,400 ($44,000 × 35%).

The salaries paid to the children will be subject to their lower Federal income tax rates. The salaries also might be exempt from the FICA and other payroll taxes, so the family unit's total tax liability has been reduced by shifting taxable income to the children.

➤ ***Tax Planning Strategy***

➤ ***Shift Net Income from High-Tax Jurisdictions to Low-Tax Jurisdictions.*** A choice of the state or country where income is earned (or where a deduction is incurred) can have a large effect on an entity's overall tax liability. Hence, shifting income from high-tax jurisdictions to low-tax jurisdictions or shifting deductions from low-tax jurisdictions to high-tax jurisdictions is an important tax planning strategy.

Shifting Tax Jurisdictions

Patti moves from Utah to Texas to be closer to the clients she services in her data analysis sole proprietorship. Marginal income tax rates for Patti are 5% in Utah and zero in Texas. Her business generates a $100,000 profit this year, so Patti's state income tax liability is reduced from $5,000 to zero (assuming all of the income is generated in Texas).

Stefano operates his health care management sole proprietorship in several U.S. states. His $50,000 deduction for office supplies is worth $2,875 more to him if it is incurred in North Carolina, where his marginal income tax rate is 5.75%, than it is in Florida, where the tax rate is zero.

➤ ***Tax Planning Strategy***

➤ ***Control the Character of Income and Deductions.*** For various policy reasons, Congress has chosen to treat certain categories of income and losses more favorably than others. For instance, the provisions that apply to most individuals and tax long-term capital gains at a maximum rate of 20 percent, compared with a top 37 percent rate on ordinary income, were enacted to encourage individuals to make long-term investments of capital in the economy.

Lisa is the proprietor of Designer Enterprises. Because a proprietorship is a flow-through entity, Lisa reports all of Designer's transactions on her individual income tax return. On October 9, 2022, Lisa invested $25,000 of Designer's excess cash in Innovation Corporation stock. On October 1, 2023, the stock was worth $35,000.

Lisa's marginal tax rate is 34% for ordinary income and 15% for long-term capital gain. She has decided to sell the stock and use the cash to increase Designer's inventory. She must hold the stock until October 10, 2023, for the gain to qualify as long term (held more than a year). If Lisa sells the stock before October 10, 2023, the gain is taxed as short term and she pays 34% tax on the gain. If she sells the stock after October 9, 2023, the gain is long term and she will pay 15% tax on the gain.

➤ ***Tax Planning Strategy***

➤ ***Avoid Double Taxation.*** The owners of a corporation can choose between two entity forms. A C corporation is a taxable entity that pays tax on corporate profits. Shareholders also pay tax on dividends received from a C corporation, resulting in what is commonly referred to as *double taxation* (refer to Example 16). Note, however, as discussed in Chapter 4, that the dividends may be eligible for a beneficial tax rate.

Tax Fact The U.S. Federal Income Tax

The Federal income tax is pervasive throughout our lives, but how much do we know about where it came from and how it works?

- The current version of the Internal Revenue Code has surpassed its 100th birthday; it was first effective on March 1, 1913.
- A temporary Federal income tax was used to finance the Civil War and the Spanish-American War. The current Federal tax code was adopted after Britain, Germany, France, and other countries in Europe had adopted similar taxing systems.
- The first Form 1040 was four pages long.
- The individual tax return became Form 1040 because that was the next number sequentially in issued Federal forms.
- The first Form 1040 was due on March 1, 1914. The unextended due date became March 15 for calendar year 1918 returns and April 15 for calendar year 1954 returns.
- Taxes largely are paid today using a withholding system, a creation made necessary with the increased taxes used to pay for World War II. But at first, no money was sent with the return. A field auditor checked every return and sent a bill to the taxpayer by June 1, payable by June 30.
- A majority of taxpayers at every income level today engage paid tax professionals for assistance in preparing Federal income tax returns.
- About 90 percent of all Forms 1040 are filed electronically. About 70 percent of Forms 1040 show a refund due to the taxpayer; the average annual refund is about $2,900.

Shareholders can avoid double taxation by electing that a corporate entity become an S corporation. Unlike a C corporation, an S corporation is not a taxable entity. Instead, the profits and losses of the S corporation flow through to the shareholders and are reported on their tax returns (see Chapter 15).

Champ, Inc., a C corporation with net income of $100,000, pays Jermaine, its sole shareholder, a $79,000 dividend. Champ must pay corporate income tax of $21,000 on the net income of $100,000, and Jermaine must pay Federal income tax on the $79,000 dividend.

Sparrow, Inc., an S corporation, also earns $100,000. Sparrow is not a taxable entity, so it pays no income tax on the $100,000 net income. Kayla, who is the sole shareholder of Sparrow, includes $100,000 from the S corporation in computing her taxable income.

Other entity choices can be used to avoid double taxation, including partnerships and limited liability companies. Partnerships and limited liability companies, like S corporations, are flow-through entities rather than taxable entities (see Chapter 14).

Choosing to operate as a **flow-through entity** is not the only way to avoid double taxation. Double taxation can be avoided or minimized by having the corporation make tax-deductible payments, such as salaries, rent, and interest to the shareholders.

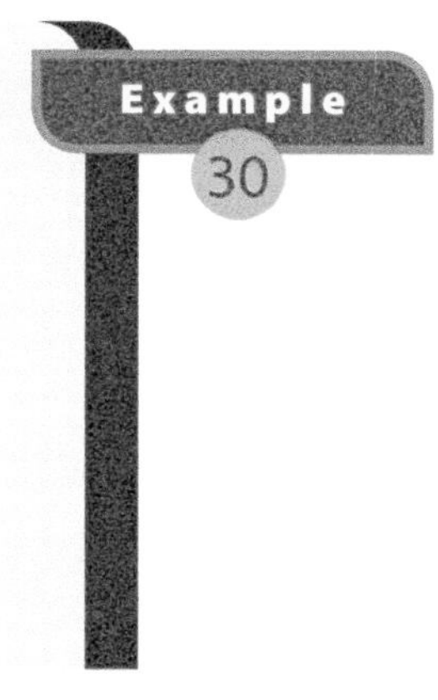

Walt is the president and sole shareholder of Meadowlark, Inc., a C corporation. Meadowlark's taxable income before any payment to Walt is $600,000. Walt, a skilled manager, is primarily responsible for the profitability of the corporation. If Meadowlark pays Walt a dividend of $400,000, the corporation must pay Federal income tax on $600,000 and Walt must include the $400,000 dividend in gross income. However, if Meadowlark pays Walt a salary of $400,000, the salary is deductible and the corporation has only $200,000 of taxable income. Walt must include the $400,000 salary in gross income.

In either case, Walt includes $400,000 in gross income (the dividends may be eligible for a beneficial tax rate). Meadowlark, on the other hand, reports $400,000 less taxable income if the payment to Walt is a salary payment rather than a dividend payment.

In considering this plan, Meadowlark should examine the effects of employment taxes on Walt and the corporation as well.

★ **Framework Focus: Tax Rates**

➤ ***Tax Planning Strategy***

1-5f Tax Minimization Strategies Related to Tax Credits

➤ ***Maximize Tax Credits.*** Congress uses the tax credit provisions of the Code liberally in implementing tax policy. It is important to understand the difference between a credit and a deduction, both of which reduce a taxpayer's tax liability. A deduction reduces taxable income, which results in a reduction of the tax paid. The tax benefit of the deduction depends on the amount of the qualifying expenditure and the taxpayer's tax rate. A tax credit reduces the tax liability dollar for dollar and is not affected by the taxpayer's tax rate.

Oriole Corporation, which is in the 21% marginal Federal income tax bracket, has a $6,000 deduction for expenditures made to repair a machine. The deduction reduces taxable income by $6,000 and results in a tax liability reduction of $1,260 ($6,000 deduction × 21% marginal rate).

Oriole also incurred expenditures of $6,000 to rehabilitate a building, which qualifies the corporation for a tax credit of $600 ($6,000 rehabilitation expenditures × 10% rate for the credit). The rehabilitation expenditures credit results in a $600 reduction of Oriole's tax liability.

The tax benefit related to the $6,000 expenditure affects Oriole's tax liability in different ways depending on whether the expenditure is treated as a deduction or a credit.

Global Tax Issues — Outsourcing of Tax Return Preparation

The use of foreign nationals to carry out certain job assignments for U.S. businesses is an increasingly popular practice. Outsourcing such activities as telemarketing to India, for example, usually produces the same satisfactory result at a much lower cost.

Outsourcing also is used in the preparation of tax returns. This practice likely will continue (and probably increase in volume). Outsourcing tax return preparation does not violate Federal law, and the practice is compatible with accounting ethical guidelines as long as three safeguards are followed: First, the practitioner must make sure that client confidentiality is maintained. Second, the practitioner must verify the accuracy of the work that has been outsourced. Third, the practitioner must gain the consent of clients when any offshore third-party contractor is used to provide professional services.

Tax professionals justify tax preparation outsourcing as a means of conserving time and effort that can be applied toward more meaningful tax planning on behalf of their clients.

Sources: Reg. § 301.7216–2(c)(2); AICPA Ethics Interpretation 1.700.040.

1-6 Understanding the Federal Tax Law

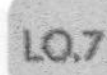

Explain the economic, social, equity, political, and compliance considerations that underlie the tax law.

The Federal tax law reflects the three branches of our Federal government. It is a mixture of laws passed by Congress, explanations provided by the Treasury Department and the Internal Revenue Service (IRS), and court decisions. For the person who analyzes this information to find the solution to a tax problem, it is good to know that there are reasons behind the law. Recognizing the "whys" of the various rules is helpful in understanding the tax law.

1-6a Revenue Needs

Raising revenues to fund the cost of government operations is the primary function of a tax system. In an ideal world, taxes raised by the government would equal the expenses incurred by government operations. However, this goal has not been achieved at the Federal level. Many states have achieved this objective by passing laws or constitutional amendments precluding deficit spending (i.e., balanced budgets are required).

The U.S. Constitution allows deficit spending, and politicians often find it hard to resist the temptation to spend more than the tax system collects currently. Congress uses several approaches to reduce a tax bill's net revenue loss. When tax reductions are involved, the full effect of the legislation can be phased in over a period of years. As an alternative, the tax reduction can be limited to a specified time period. When that period expires, Congress can then renew, modify, or repeal the provision in light of budget considerations.

1-6b Economic Considerations

Sometimes tax legislation is designed to help control the economy in some manner or encourage certain activities, industries, or businesses.

Encouragement of Certain Activities

Congress often uses the tax law to encourage certain types of economic activity or segments of the economy. For example, to encourage investment in certain business assets, such as equipment, the tax law may allow for extra ("bonus") depreciation in the year of acquisition. Given the time value of money, the tax savings from a current deduction is usually preferable to capitalizing the cost with a write-off over the estimated useful life of the asset created.

Ecological considerations justify a tax provision that permits a more rapid expensing of the costs of installing pollution control facilities or tax credits for the use of alternative energy. Since these provisions may aid in maintaining a clean air environment and conserving energy resources, these provisions can also be justified under social considerations (helping our environment).

Is it wise to stimulate U.S. exports of goods and services? Considering the pressing and continuing problem of a deficit in the U.S. balance of payments, Congress has established incentives for U.S. citizens who accept employment overseas and for business entities that operate in countries outside the United States.

Is saving desirable for the economy? Saving can lead to capital formation, making funds available to finance home construction and industrial expansion. The tax law encourages saving by according preferential treatment to private retirement plans. Besides deductions being allowed for contributions to certain retirement plans and Individual Retirement Accounts (IRAs), income on the contributions might not be taxed until withdrawn.

Encouragement of Certain Industries

Historically, agricultural activities have been favored under Federal tax law. Among the tax benefits are the election to expense rather than capitalize certain soil and water conservation expenditures and fertilizers and the election to defer the recognition of gain on the receipt of crop insurance proceeds.

To stimulate research and production of alternative fuel sources, tax incentives are allowed with respect to operations and sales of certain solar and wind energy devices and of autos that do not consume petroleum products.

Encouragement of Small Business

A consensus exists in the United States that what is good for small business is good for the economy as a whole. This belief has led to special provisions in the tax law that favor small business. Several income tax provisions can be explained by the desire to benefit small business, including use of the cash method of accounting rather than the accrual method.

1-6c Social Considerations

Some provisions of the Federal tax law, particularly those dealing with individuals, can be explained by a desire to encourage certain social results.

- Certain benefits provided to employees through accident and health insurance plans financed by employers are nontaxable to employees. It is socially desirable to encourage these plans because they provide medical benefits in the event of an employee's illness or injury.
- A contribution made by an employer to a qualified pension or profit sharing plan for an employee may receive special treatment. The contribution and any income it generates are not taxed to the employee until the funds are distributed. This arrangement also benefits the employer by allowing a tax deduction for its contribution to the qualified plan. Various types of retirement plans are encouraged to supplement the subsistence income level the employee otherwise would obtain under the Social Security system.

- A deduction is allowed for contributions to qualified charities. The deduction shifts some of the financial and administrative burden of socially desirable programs from the public (government) to the private (citizens) sector.
- Various tax incentives are designed to encourage taxpayers to obtain or extend their level of education.
- A tax credit is allowed for amounts spent to furnish care for certain minor or disabled dependents to enable the taxpayer to seek or maintain gainful employment.
- A tax deduction is denied for certain expenditures deemed to be contrary to public policy. Deductions are not allowed for fines, penalties, illegal kickbacks, bribes to government officials, and gambling losses in excess of gains. Social considerations dictate that the tax law should not encourage these activities by permitting a deduction.

1-6d Equity Considerations

The concept of equity (or fairness) is relative. One measure of equity is whether a tax is *progressive* or *regressive*. The determination is made by calculating the percentage of a taxpayer's income that is used to pay a tax. As noted earlier, the Federal income tax is progressive. In contrast, the gasoline excise tax is regressive.

Hanna and Lori are single taxpayers living in the same state. Hanna has income of $100,000, and Lori has income of $10,000. Assume that Hanna pays $5,000 in state income taxes while Lori pays $100. The state income tax represents 5% of Hanna's income, but only 1% of Lori's income. Because the higher-income taxpayer (Hanna) devotes a larger percentage of her income to pay the tax relative to a lower-income taxpayer (Lori), this state income tax is *progressive* in its effect on taxpayers.

Alternatively, assume that Hanna and Lori each purchase the same quantity of gasoline during the year and each pays gasoline excise taxes of $200. This tax represents less than 0.1% of Hanna's income, but 2% of Lori's income. Because the lower-income taxpayer (Lori) devotes a larger percentage of her income to pay the tax relative to a higher-income taxpayer (Hanna), the gasoline excise tax is *regressive* in its effect on taxpayers.

Lawmakers and others often consider whether a tax change is progressive or regressive to understand its impact on taxpayers and whether the change should be made. If a tax represents the same percentage of the income of all taxpayers, it is a *proportional* tax.

Eduardo and Sanjay are single taxpayers living in the same state. Eduardo has income of $50,000 and pays $1,500 in state taxes. Sanjay has income of $20,000 and pays $600 in state taxes. In this case, Eduardo and Sanjay are devoting the same percentage of their income to the state tax (3%), making the tax *proportional* in terms of the effect it has on taxpayers.

The concept of equity also appears in tax provisions that alleviate the effect of multiple taxation and postpone the recognition of gain when the taxpayer lacks the ability or wherewithal to pay the tax. Provisions that mitigate the effect of the application of the annual accounting period concept or help taxpayers cope with the impact of inflation on taxable income also reflect equity considerations.

The Wherewithal to Pay Concept

The **wherewithal to pay** concept recognizes the inequity of taxing a transaction when the taxpayer lacks the means (i.e., funds) to pay the tax when an otherwise taxable transaction has been completed. The wherewithal to pay concept underlies a provision in the tax law dealing with the treatment of gain resulting from an involuntary conversion. An involuntary conversion occurs when property is destroyed by casualty or taken by a public authority through condemnation. If gain results from the conversion, it need not be recognized immediately if the taxpayer replaces the property within a specified time period.

Ron, a rancher, owns some pasture land that is condemned by the state for use as a game preserve. The condemned pasture land cost Ron $120,000, but the state pays him $150,000 (its fair market value). Shortly thereafter, Ron buys more pasture land for $150,000.

Ron has a realized gain of $30,000 [$150,000 (condemnation award) − $120,000 (cost of land)]. It would be inequitable to require Ron to pay a tax on this gain: without selling the new land, Ron would find it difficult to pay the tax (Ron used the condemnation proceeds to purchase more land).

What if Ron reinvests only $140,000 of the award in new pasture land? Now Ron recognizes a $10,000 taxable gain in the current year. Instead of ending up with only replacement property, Ron now holds the new land and $10,000 in cash.

Mitigating the Effect of the Annual Accounting Period Concept

Federal income tax returns are due for every tax year of the taxpayer. The application of this annual accounting period concept can lead to dissimilar tax treatment for taxpayers who are, from a long-range standpoint, in the same economic position.

José and Alicia, both unmarried sole proprietors, experienced the following results during the indicated tax years.

	Profit (or Loss)	
Year	**José**	**Alicia**
2020	$50,000	$150,000
2021	60,000	60,000
2022	60,000	(40,000)

Although José and Alicia have the same total profit of $170,000 over the three-year period, the annual accounting period concept places Alicia at a disadvantage for tax purposes, both in terms of the time value of money and due to the higher tax rates that will apply to Alicia under the progressive rate structure.

However, the net operating loss deduction generated in 2022 offers Alicia some relief. She can "carry forward" the loss and use it to offset profits in a future tax year. Taxable income cannot be less than zero in a tax year, so the loss is of no immediate use to Alicia.

1-6e Political Considerations

A large segment of the Federal tax law is made up of statutory provisions. Because these statutes are enacted by Congress, political considerations often influence tax law. The effect of political considerations on the tax law includes special interest legislation and state and local government influences.

Special Interest Legislation

Certain provisions of the tax law largely can be explained by the political influence some groups have had on Congress. For example, prepaid subscription and dues income is not taxed until earned, but prepaid rents are taxed to the landlord in the year received. This exception was created because certain organizations (e.g., the American Automobile Association) convinced Congress that special tax treatment was needed for multi-year dues and subscriptions.

State and Local Government Influences

State law has had an influence in shaping our present Federal tax law. One example of this effect is the evolution of Federal tax law in response to states with community property systems. The states with community property systems are Arizona, California, Idaho, Louisiana, Nevada, New Mexico, Texas, Washington, and Wisconsin. Spouses in Alaska can elect community property treatment. The rest of the states are common law jurisdictions.

The difference between common law and community property systems centers around the property rights held by married persons. In a common law system, each spouse owns whatever he or she earns. Under a community property system, one-half of the earnings of each spouse is considered owned by the other spouse.

Al and Fran are married, and their only income is the $80,000 annual salary Al receives. If they live in New Jersey (a common law state), the $80,000 salary belongs to Al.

If, however, they live in Arizona (a community property state), the $80,000 is divided equally, in terms of ownership, between Al and Fran.

At one time, the tax position of the residents of community property states was so advantageous that many common law states adopted community property systems. Political pressure placed on Congress to correct the disparity in tax treatment was considerable.

To a large extent, this was accomplished when Congress changed the law to extend many of the community property tax advantages to residents of common law jurisdictions. The law change allowed married taxpayers to file joint returns and compute the tax liability as if one-half of the income had been earned by each spouse. This result is automatic in a community property state because half of the income earned by one spouse belongs to the other spouse. The income-splitting benefits of a joint return are incorporated as part of the tax rates applicable to married taxpayers. A similar motivation can be seen for the gift-splitting provisions of the Federal gift tax and the marital deduction of the Federal estate and gift taxes.

1-6f **Compliance Considerations**

A tax system generally includes rules to ensure proper compliance by taxpayers. For example, due dates for returns and tax payments are specified in the tax law. Interest accrues on past due tax liabilities. Procedures for examination (i.e., an audit) and collection activities of the IRS (or state tax agency) are also detailed in the law. The possibility of an audit can help improve voluntary compliance by taxpayers.

Numerous penalties also exist in the tax law to encourage proper compliance by taxpayers, as well as by their paid preparers. Penalties can be assessed on taxpayers for failing to pay their taxes (or failing to pay on time), claiming improper deductions or misstating income, or not having substantial legal authority for claiming a deduction or credit. Examples of penalties imposed on return preparers include failing to furnish the taxpayer with a copy of the return, failing to sign the return as a preparer, failing to furnish an identification number, and failing to keep copies of returns or maintain a client list. The identification number required of preparers of most Federal tax returns is the **Preparer Tax Identification Number (PTIN)**. A PTIN is required by anyone who is paid for preparing a Federal tax return (or assisting in a substantial portion of the return's preparation).[12]

In a few months, Jaden, an accounting major at State University, will start an internship at Nguyen & Associates, CPAs. He will assist other employees by organizing and analyzing client data for completeness, entering client information into the tax preparation software program used by the firm, and comparing results to the prior year's return. Jaden will not sign any tax returns.

Jaden will need to obtain a PTIN from the IRS because he is assisting in the preparation of the returns. If, instead, Jaden were only entering data provided by his colleagues and making copies, and not exercising any discretion or independent judgment regarding client tax information, he would not need a PTIN.[13]

[12]§ 6109(a)(4). Also see IRS website on PTINs that includes an online tool to obtain or annually renew a PTIN (**rpr.irs.gov/datamart/mainMenuUSIRS.do**), or Form W-12, IRS Paid Preparer Tax Identification Number (PTIN) Application and Renewal can be used.

[13]§ 6109(a)(4) and Reg. §§ 1.6109-2(d) and (g).

1-6g Influence of the Internal Revenue Service

Describe the influence of the IRS and the courts on the Federal tax system.

One of the keys to an effective administration of our tax system is the audit process conducted by the IRS. To facilitate the audit process, the IRS is aided by provisions that reduce the chance of taxpayer errors. For example, by increasing the standard deduction amount, the audit function is simplified because there are fewer returns claiming itemized deductions.

The IRS influences laws by suggesting changes to Congress based on compliance problems it discovers (e.g., during audits of tax returns). The U.S. Treasury Department and the IRS also affect tax laws via the Regulations and rulings they issue that explain and interpret Code provisions. Congress sometimes uses Code provisions to direct the Treasury Department to write particular rules within broad guidelines suggested by Congress.

Information on the IRS audit process can be found on this book's companion website: www.cengage.com

4 Digging Deeper

1-6h Influence of the Courts

In addition to interpreting statutory provisions and the administrative pronouncements issued by the Treasury Department and the IRS, the Federal courts have influenced tax law in two other ways. First, the courts have developed a number of judicial concepts and doctrines that help guide the application of various tax provisions, going beyond the strict language of the Code and Treasury Regulations. Second, certain key court decisions have led to changes in the Code and other sources of tax law.

Judicial Concepts and Doctrines Relating to Tax

Particularly in dealings between related parties, the courts test transactions by looking to whether the taxpayers acted in an arm's length manner. The question to be asked is: Would unrelated parties have handled the transaction in the same way?

Rex, the sole shareholder of Silver Corporation, leases property to the corporation for a yearly rent of $6,000. To test whether the corporation should be allowed a rent deduction for this amount, the IRS and the courts will apply the arm's length concept. Would Silver have paid $6,000 a year in rent if it had leased the same property from an unrelated party (rather than from Rex)?

Suppose it is determined that an unrelated third party would have charged an annual rent for the property of only $5,000. Under these circumstances, Silver can deduct only $5,000. The other $1,000 it paid for the use of the property represents a *nondeductible dividend*. Rex is treated as having received rent income of $5,000 and dividend income of $1,000.

An example of a judicial doctrine that must be considered in some transactions is the *substance over form* doctrine. This means that regardless of how a transaction is structured, the actual substance of how the transaction is carried out controls the tax implications of the transaction.

Gold Corporation hired Adam to work as its bookkeeper for six months while the regular bookkeeper is on sick leave. This is a full-time position, and Adam reports to Gold's CFO who directs his assignments. Gold gave Adam a contract that states he is not an employee of Gold but is instead an independent contractor. Despite the form saying Adam is not an employee, the substance of what he does and the relationship between Gold and Adam will control Adam's employment designation for tax purposes. Given these facts, Adam is an employee for tax purposes.

Judicial Influence on Statutory Provisions

Some court decisions have been of such consequence that Congress has incorporated them into statutory tax law. For example, many years ago, the courts found that stock dividends distributed to the shareholders of a corporation were not gross income and therefore were not subject to tax. This result largely was accepted by Congress, and a provision in the tax statutes now addresses the issue.

1-7 **Summary**

Tax laws are pervasive in today's global economy. Individuals and businesses must contend with complex rules in planning their personal and professional activities. Taxes can fall on income, wealth, asset transfers, consumer expenditures, and other events.

Tax professionals must be adept in various skills to deliver expected levels of service to clients and the government.

- Knowledge of technical tax law.
- Productive with technology and data analytics.
- Strengths in business acumen and so-called soft skills, like listening and motivation.
- Functional in problem solving and process improvement.
- Valued contributor in project management and cost-benefit analysis.
- Excellent verbal and written communication skills.

Tax planning is a means by which to manage the amount and timing of tax liabilities to accomplish one's long-term objectives. The conduct of tax practitioners is regulated by professional associations, lawmakers, and the taxing agencies.

Taxing systems are designed to provide revenues for governments to accomplish the common goals of citizens. In addition to its necessary revenue-raising objective, the Federal tax law has developed in response to several other factors.

- *Economic considerations.* Tax provisions can help to regulate the economy and encourage certain activities and types of businesses.
- *Social considerations.* Some tax provisions are designed to encourage (or discourage) socially desirable (or undesirable) practices.
- *Equity considerations.* Tax provisions can alleviate the effect of multiple taxation, recognize the wherewithal to pay concept, and mitigate the effect of the annual accounting period concept.
- *Compliance considerations.* Tax rules provide for examinations, penalties and interest to help ensure proper compliance (timely filing of returns and payment of taxes) by taxpayers.
- *Political considerations.* Tax provisions can carry out the desires of special interest groups or reflect the effect of state and local law.
- *Influence of the IRS.* Many tax provisions are intended to aid the IRS in the collection of revenue and the administration of the tax law.
- *Influence of the courts.* Court decisions have established a body of judicial concepts relating to tax law and have, on occasion, led Congress to enact statutory provisions to either clarify or negate their effect.

Refocus on The Big Picture

A Typical Tax Year for a Modern Family

CORBIS/SUPERSTOCK

The explanation given for the difference in the ad valorem property taxes—the Carters' increase and the Walkers' decrease—seems reasonable. It is not likely that the Carters' increase was due to a *general* upward assessment in valuation since the Walkers' taxes on their residence (located nearby) dropped. More business use of the Carters' residence (presuming that Travis conducts his consulting practice from his home) might be responsible for the increase, but capital improvements appear to be a more likely cause.

continued

The imposition of the use tax when Travis registered the new automobile illustrates one of the means by which a state can preclude the avoidance of its sales tax (see Example 4).

When gifts between family members are material in amount (e.g., an RV) and exceed the annual exclusion, a gift tax return needs to be filed. Even though no gift tax may be due because of the availability of the unified transfer tax exclusion ($12,060,000 for 2022, as indexed), the filing of a return starts the running of the statute of limitations.

The Carters must recognize that some of their income is subject to income taxes in more than one state and take advantage of whatever relief is available to mitigate the result of double taxation.

Significant Federal income tax savings might be available if Travis were to hire the children to work in the consulting practice.

What If?

Because of the double audit (i.e., both state and Federal) and the deficiency assessed, the Carters need to make sure that future returns do not contain similar errors. As the text suggests, taxpayers with prior deficiencies are among those whose returns may be selected for audit.

Suggested Readings

Amy J. N. Yurko, Christine Cheng, and Cheryl T. Metrejean, "The marriage tax penalty post-TCJA," *The Tax Adviser*, June 2019.

Ellen Cook, Troy Lewis, and Annette Nellen, "Tax Principles for the Digital Age," *Journal of Accountancy*, May 2017.

Janelle Cammenga "Does Your State Have a Sales Tax Holiday?" July 21, 2021, **taxfoundation.org/2021-sales-tax-holiday/**.

Key Terms

Problems

1. **LO.1** This textbook includes many features beyond the text materials in each chapter. For example, there is a glossary in the appendices and a list of suggested readings and a list of key terms at the end of each chapter. Throughout each chapter "Digging Deeper" notations highlight additional online information and examples to help deepen your understanding of chapter materials. Skim through the chapters, appendices, and any other supplemental materials required for your course, and identify two special features. For each, explain what it is and how it can help you in understanding taxation in this tax course.

Critical Thinking
Planning

2. **LO.3, 5, 6** James Corporation believes that it will have a better distribution location for its product if it relocates the corporation to another state. What considerations (both tax and nontax) should James weigh before making a decision on whether to make the move?

3. **LO.1, 2, 3** Distinguish between taxes that are *regressive* and those that are *progressive*.

Critical Thinking

4. **LO.3** Several years ago, Ethan purchased the former parsonage of St. James Church to use as a personal residence. To date, Ethan has not received any ad valorem property tax bills from either the city or the county tax authorities.
   a. What is a reasonable explanation for this oversight?
   b. What should Ethan do?

Digging Deeper

5. **LO.1, 6** In terms of Adam Smith's canon of *economy in collection*, how does the Federal income tax fare?

Critical Thinking

6. **LO.3** Jang, a resident of Washington (which imposes a general sales tax), goes to Oregon (which does not impose a general sales tax) to purchase his automobile. Will Jang successfully avoid the Washington sales tax? Explain.

Critical Thinking
Planning

7. **LO.3** The Adams Independent School District wants to sell a parcel of unimproved land that it does not need. Its three best offers are as follows: from the State Department of Public Safety (DPS), $2,300,000; from Second Baptist Church, $2,200,000; and from Baker Motors, $2,100,000. DPS would use the property for a new state highway patrol barracks, Second Baptist would start a church school, and Baker would open a car dealership. As the financial adviser for the school district, which offer would you prefer? Why?

Critical Thinking

8. **LO.3, 4** Sophia lives several blocks from her parents in the same residential subdivision. Sophia is surprised to learn that her ad valorem property taxes for the year were raised but those of her parents were lowered. What is a possible explanation for the difference?

Communications
Decision Making
Planning

9. **LO.5, 6** Marco and Cynthia have decided to go into business together. They will operate a food delivery business. They expect to generate a loss in the first and second years of the business and then to make a substantial profit.

   Marco and Cynthia are concerned about potential liability if a customer ever gets sick after eating one of their products. They have called your office and asked for advice about whether they should run their business as a partnership or as a corporation. Write a letter to Cynthia Clay, at 1206 Seventh Avenue, Fort Worth, TX 76101, describing the alternative forms of business they can select. In your letter, explain what form or forms of business you recommend and why.

Decision Making
Planning

10. **LO.5, 6** Ashley runs a small business that makes snow skis. She expects the business to grow substantially over the next three years. Because she is concerned about product liability and is planning to take the company public in year 2, she

currently is considering incorporating the business. Pertinent financial data are as follows.

	Year 1	Year 2	Year 3
Sales revenue	$150,000	$320,000	$600,000
Tax-free interest income	5,000	8,000	15,000
Deductible cash expenses	30,000	58,000	95,000
Tax depreciation	25,000	20,000	40,000

Ashley expects her combined Federal and state marginal income tax rate to be 25% over the three years before any profits from the business are considered. Assume that the corporation will face a flat 21% Federal corporate income tax and no state income tax. Ashley's after-tax cost of capital is 12%.

a. Considering only these data, construct a spreadsheet to compute the present value of the future cash flows for the three-year period, assuming Ashley incorporates the business and pays all after-tax income as dividends (for Ashley's dividends that qualify for the 15% rate).

b. Considering only these data, compute the present value of the future cash flows for the period, assuming that Ashley continues to operate the business as a sole proprietorship.

c. Should Ashley incorporate the business in year 1? Why or why not?

11. **LO.1** A disproportionate amount of the Federal income tax is paid by individuals at upper income levels. Is this a desirable condition? Defend your position in no more than three PowerPoint slides to be presented to your classmates. Communications

12. **LO.3** Franklin County is in dire financial straits and is considering a number of sources for additional revenue. Evaluate the following possibilities in terms of anticipated taxpayer compliance. Critical Thinking

a. A property tax on business inventories.

b. A tax on intangibles (i.e., stocks and bonds) held as investments.

c. A property tax on boats used for recreational purposes.

13. **LO.2, 7** Discuss the probable non-revenue justifications for each of the following provisions of the tax law.

a. A tax credit allowed for electricity produced from renewable sources.

b. A tax credit allowed for the purchase of a motor vehicle that operates on alternative energy sources (e.g., nonfossil fuels).

c. Favorable treatment accorded to research and development expenditures.

d. The deduction allowed for contributions to qualified charitable organizations.

e. An election that allows certain corporations to avoid the corporate level income tax and pass losses through to their shareholders.

14. **LO.4, 7** Discuss the probable justification for each of the following aspects of the tax law. Be sure to use concepts and terminology covered in this chapter.

a. A tax credit is allowed for amounts spent to furnish care for minor children while the parent works.

b. Deductions for interest on home mortgage and property taxes on a personal residence.

c. The income-splitting benefits of filing a joint return.

d. Fines and penalties are not deductible.

e. Net operating losses of a current year can be carried forward to profitable years.

f. A taxpayer who sells property on an installment basis can recognize gain on the sale over the period the payments are received.

g. The exclusion from Federal tax of certain interest income from state and local bonds.

h. Prepaid income is taxed to the recipient in the year it is received and not in the year it is earned.

Digging Deeper 15. **LO.3** Contrast a value added tax (VAT) with a national sales tax in terms of anticipated taxpayer compliance.

16. **LO.3** Distinguish between an estate tax and an inheritance tax.

a. Do some states impose both? Neither?

b. Which, if either, does the Federal government impose?

Communications 17. **LO.2, 7** Although the Federal income tax law is complex, most individual taxpayers are able to complete their tax returns without outside assistance. Gather data as to the accuracy of this statement. Summarize your comments in an e-mail to your instructor.

18. **LO.2, 7** In 2022, Madden, who is single, has adjusted gross income of $145,600, uses the standard deduction of $12,950, and has $132,650 of taxable income. Compute the following for Madden.

a. Federal income tax liability using the appropriate Tax Rate Schedule.

b. Statutory tax rate(s).

c. Marginal tax rate.

d. Average tax rate.

e. Effective tax rate, using adjusted gross income.

Critical Thinking 19. **LO.3, 4, 6** Mike Barr was an outstanding football player in college and expects to be drafted by the NFL in the first few rounds. Mike has let it be known that he would prefer to sign with an NFL team located in Florida, Texas, or Washington. Is Mike undertaking good income tax planning? Explain.

Ethics and Equity 20. **LO.2, 7** Many state income tax returns contain checkoff boxes that allow taxpayers to make donations to a multitude of local charitable causes. On what grounds can such provisions be criticized?

Bridge Discipline

1. Discuss with respect to the Federal policy for reducing poverty:

a. The individual income tax.

b. The Social Security tax.

Communications 2. Prepare a two-page paper titled "How I Would Apply the Tax Laws to Reduce Plastic and Paper Waste" to submit to your economics professor.

Communications 3. Prepare an outline for a 10-minute speech to give to your government class. The speech is titled "Why Basic Taxation Should be a Required High School Course."

4. When taxes are "too high," taxpayers start to cheat on their taxes and dangerous consequences can result. Evaluate this statement. Give at least two examples to illustrate your conclusions.

continued

5. Some tax rules can be justified on multiple grounds (e.g., economic or social). In this connection, comment on the possible justification for the rules governing the following.
   c. Pension plans.
   d. Education.
   e. Home ownership.

Research Problems

Use internet tax resources to address the following questions. Look for reliable websites and blogs of the IRS and other government agencies, media outlets, businesses, tax professionals, academics, think tanks, and political outlets.

Research Problem 1. Find a Federal or state proposal for a soda tax or sweetened beverage tax. Apply the AICPA's *Principles of Good Tax Policy* to support your recommendation for or against the bill.

Critical Thinking
Digging Deeper

Research Problem 2. Visit the websites of a few public accounting firms to learn how they are using data analytics and visualization in the tax function. In an e-mail to your instructor, explain what you found, provide the source(s) you used, and explain how you think the data analysis helps businesses engage in tax planning.

Communications
Data Analytics

Research Problem 3. Use the IRS website to find Form W-12 (IRS Paid Preparer Tax Identification Number (PTIN) Application and Renewal) and its instructions. Review these documents and specifically focus on question 11 (related to the data security responsibilities of the paid preparer). One purpose of this question is to remind preparers of their obligations to comply with the "Safeguards Rule" overseen by the Federal Trade Commission. Use IRS Publication 4557, Safeguarding Taxpayer Data, to find information on this rule. Prepare an email to your instructor that briefly describes this rule and lists three actions a preparer could take to help meet this rule.

Communications

Chapter 2

Working with the Tax Law

Learning Objectives: *After completing Chapter 2, you should be able to:*

LO.1 Describe the statutory, administrative, and judicial sources of the tax law and the purpose of each source.

LO.2 Locate and work with the tax law and explain the tax research process.

LO.3 Communicate the results of the tax research process in a client letter and a tax file memorandum.

LO.4 Employ a strategy for applying tax research skills in taking the CPA exam.

Chapter Outline

Tax Talk *The less people know about how sausages and laws are made, the better they'll sleep at night.* —Otto von Bismarck

MONKEY BUSINESS IMAGES/SHUTTERSTOCK.COM

The Big Picture

Researching Tax Questions

Early in November 2022, Fred and Megan Martel scheduled a meeting with you to discuss a potential tax problem. Fred and Megan purchased a 40-acre parcel of property in 2017 for $195,000. On it, they built their "dream home" in 2018. In March 2022, while walking on a remote part of their property, they spotted something shiny on the ground. They started digging and eventually unearthed eight metal cans containing more than 1,400 rare gold coins in $5, $10, and $20 denominations dated from 1846 to 1895. The face value of the gold coins is about $28,000, and many of the coins are in mint condition.

The Martels' delay in coming to you for tax advice was due to state law that required their discovery to be turned over to the state for disposition. The state, for a period of six months, was required to publicize the find and ask if anyone could prove ownership. When no one came forward, the coins were returned to the Martels in October 2022. They are now the rightful owners of the coins, so they want to know the income tax implications (if any) of their discovery.

Read the chapter and formulate your responses.

Federal tax law reflects work performed by the three branches of our Federal government. It is a mixture of laws passed by Congress, explanations provided by the Treasury Department and the Internal Revenue Service (IRS), and court decisions. The tax research process allows us to understand, evaluate, and apply these sources of tax law to questions that are raised by taxpayers and tax practitioners.

As part of knowing how to locate, interpret, and apply the tax law, a tax professional must understand the relative weight of authority that each source carries. The tax law is of little significance, however, until it is applied to a specific set of facts and circumstances. The *tax compliance process* involves research into past facts and circumstances. The *tax planning process* involves research into planned (future) transactions.

This chapter introduces the statutory, administrative, and judicial sources of the tax law *and* explains how the law is applied to business and individual transactions. It further explains how to apply tax research techniques effectively.

Tax research is necessary because the application of the law to a specific situation sometimes is not clear. As complicated as the tax rules are, they cannot clearly address every conceivable situation. As a result, the tax professional must determine the most likely tax treatment of a transaction through the research process. A strong foundation of knowledge of the tax system and rules helps in this process.

Working with knowledge gained from the study of taxation, regularly updating that knowledge for changes in the tax rules, and applying the tax research process, a tax professional can advise a client about the tax consequences of a variety of fact patterns. Tax research is of critical importance in properly characterizing completed events as well as in planning proposed transactions.

LO.1

Describe the statutory, administrative, and judicial sources of the tax law and the purpose of each source.

2-1 Tax Law Sources

Understanding taxation requires a strong understanding of the sources of the tax law. These sources include laws passed by Congress, which are accumulated in the Internal Revenue Code, and congressional Committee Reports, as well as Treasury Department Regulations, other Treasury Department and IRS pronouncements, and court decisions. So the *primary sources* of tax law come from all three branches of the Federal government: legislative (statutory), executive, and judicial. To be a *primary authority*, an item must be issued with the intent that taxpayers can rely on the item in applying the tax law. A Regulation issued by the Treasury Department is a primary source, but a publication released by the Internal Revenue Service (IRS) is not. The IRS publication is a secondary source because it is a summary of primary sources (see text Section 2-2d).

2-1a Statutory Sources of the Tax Law

Statutory sources of law include the Constitution (Article I, Sections 7, 8, and 10), tax treaties (agreements between countries to mitigate the double taxation of taxpayers subject to the tax laws of those countries), and the Internal Revenue Code. The Constitution grants Congress the power to impose and collect taxes, and it authorizes the creation of treaties with other countries. The Internal Revenue Code is the statutory basis for arriving at solutions to all tax questions.

Origin of the Internal Revenue Code

Before 1939, the statutory provisions relating to taxation were contained in the individual revenue acts enacted by Congress every year or two. The inconvenience and uncertainty of dealing with many separate acts led Congress to codify all of the Federal tax laws in 1939. Known as the Internal Revenue Code of 1939, this codification arranged all Federal tax provisions in a logical sequence and placed them in a separate part of the Federal statutes (Title 26 of the U.S. Code). Major amendments to this codification took place in 1954, 1986, and 2017.[1]

[1]The 1986 amendments were so extensive that the document was renamed the Internal Revenue Code of 1986, replacing the long-standing Internal Revenue Code of 1954. The 1954 Code largely was a reorganization of the provisions of the 1939 Code, whereas the 1986 and 2017 legislation both brought about significant tax policy and operational changes from Congress.

Tax Fact Scope of the U.S. Tax System

Although it started out in 1913 as a tax on only the uppermost-income individuals, the tax system today is pervasive in the lives of all U.S. citizens and residents.

- In the typical tax year, the IRS receives about 150 million individual income tax returns.
- The IRS estimates that the average time to prepare Form 1040 is about 12 hours. This includes time to gather records, assemble the return, and prepare the form and attachments. The estimated time is longer for returns reporting business activity.
- The IRS collects approximately $3.4 trillion in tax revenue annually, with a workforce of about 74,000 people and a budget of $12 billion.

Enacted statutory amendments to the tax law are integrated into the existing Code. Congress usually passes one or more laws each year that have tax provisions and become part of the Internal Revenue Code of 1986. This accumulative process is similar to the methods used by the Financial Accounting Standards Board with respect to its reporting rules.

The Legislative Process

Exhibit 2.1 illustrates the usual legislative process for enacting changes to the Internal Revenue Code. Federal tax legislation generally originates in the House of Representatives, where it first is considered by the House Ways and Means Committee.

Exhibit 2.1 Legislative Process for Tax Bills

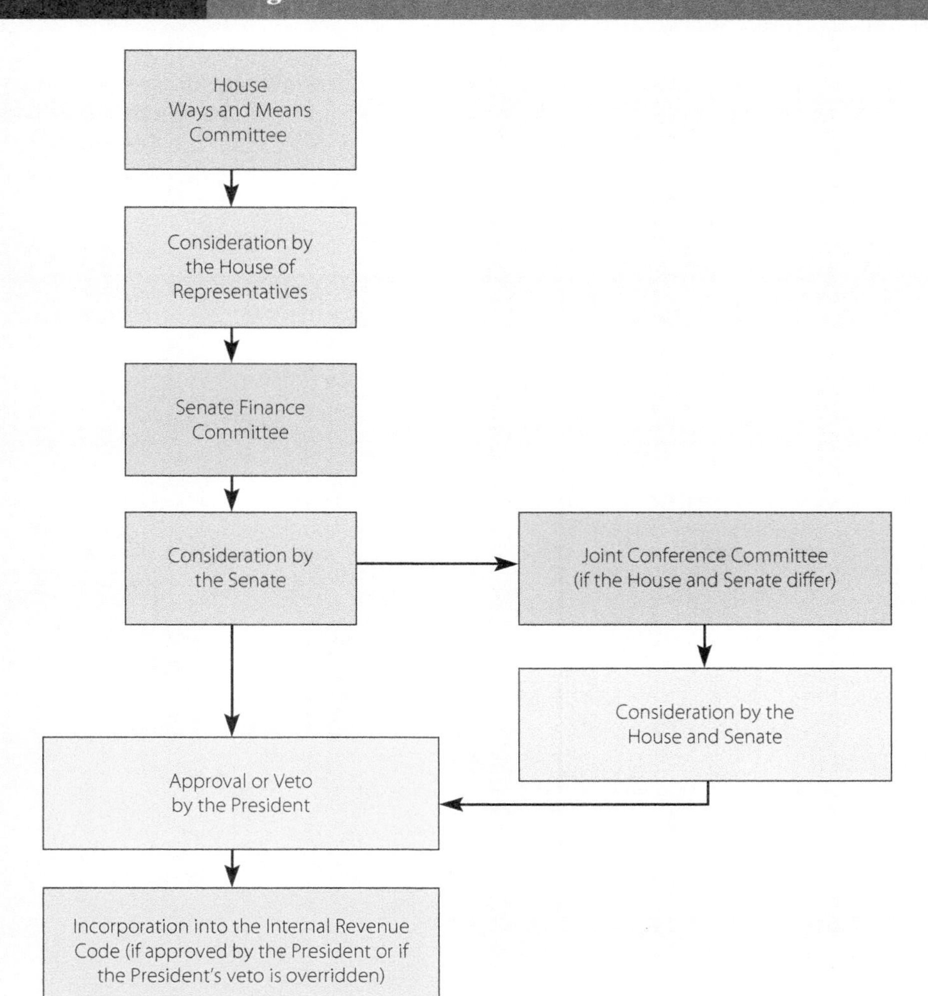

(Tax bills also can originate in the Senate if they are attached as riders to other legislative proposals.) Once approved by the Ways and Means Committee, the proposed bill is referred to the entire House of Representatives for a vote. Approved bills are sent to the Senate, where they initially are considered by the Senate Finance Committee.

After approval by the Finance Committee, the bill is sent to the entire Senate. Assuming no disagreement between the House and Senate, passage by the Senate means referral to the President for approval or veto. If the bill is approved or if the President's veto is overridden, the bill becomes law and part of the Internal Revenue Code.

When the Senate version of the bill differs from that passed by the House, the Conference Committee, which includes members of both the House Ways and Means Committee and the Senate Finance Committee, resolves the differences.

House and Senate versions of major tax bills frequently differ. One reason bills often are changed in the Senate is that under the usual rules of Congress, each senator has considerable latitude to make amendments when the Senate as a whole is voting on a bill referred to it by the Senate Finance Committee. On the contrary, under the rules in most years, the entire House of Representatives either accepts or rejects what is proposed by the House Ways and Means Committee, and changes from the floor are rare.

The deliberations of the Conference Committee usually produce a compromise between the two versions, which then is voted on by both the House and the Senate. If both bodies accept the revised bill, it is referred to the President for approval or veto.

The role of the Conference Committee indicates the importance of compromise in the legislative process. Exhibit 2.2 illustrates what happened with amendments to the child tax credit in the drafting of the Tax Cuts and Jobs Act of 2017.

The House Ways and Means Committee, the Senate Finance Committee, and the Conference Committee each typically produce a *Committee Report* for a tax bill. These Committee Reports often explain the provisions of the proposed legislation and are a valuable source for ascertaining the *intent of Congress*. What Congress had in mind when it considered and enacted tax legislation can be a key to interpreting legislation. Because it takes time to develop other primary authority (e.g., from the Treasury Department, the IRS, and the courts), tax researchers rely heavily on Committee Reports to interpret and apply new tax laws.

Exhibit 2.2 Example of Compromise in the Conference Committee

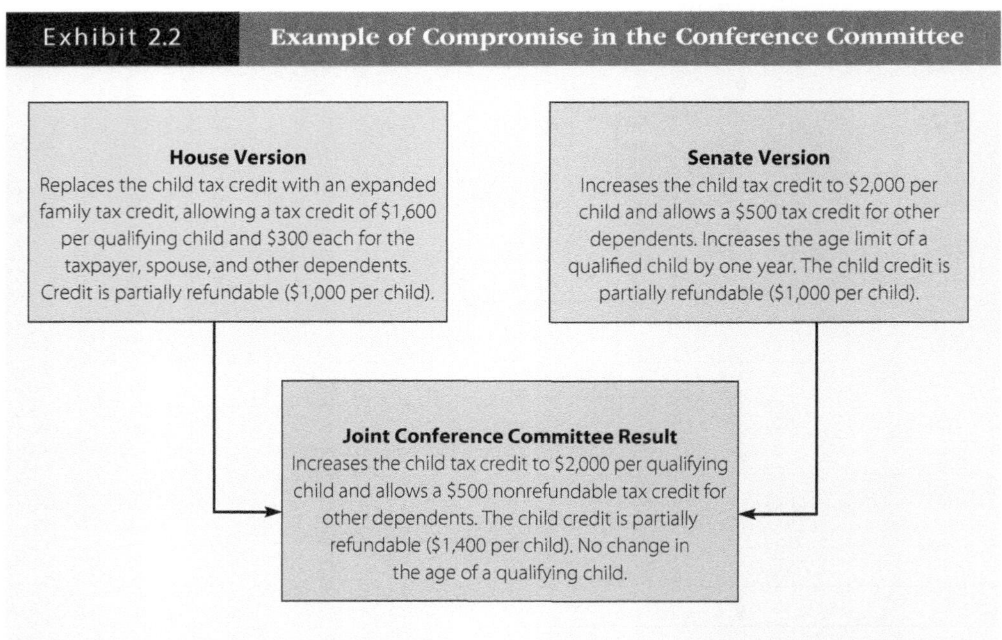

House Version
Replaces the child tax credit with an expanded family tax credit, allowing a tax credit of $1,600 per qualifying child and $300 each for the taxpayer, spouse, and other dependents. Credit is partially refundable ($1,000 per child).
Senate Version
Increases the child tax credit to $2,000 per child and allows a $500 tax credit for other dependents. Increases the age limit of a qualified child by one year. The child credit is partially refundable ($1,000 per child).
Joint Conference Committee Result
Increases the child tax credit to $2,000 per qualifying child and allows a $500 nonrefundable tax credit for other dependents. The child credit is partially refundable ($1,400 per child). No change in the age of a qualifying child.

Arrangement of the Internal Revenue Code

The Internal Revenue Code is found in Title 26 of the U.S. Code. The Code is organized by type of tax and by specific topics; it deals with all Federal taxes, not just income taxes. It also includes procedural rules, such as on due dates and penalties for noncompliance. Here is a partial table of contents.

Subtitle A. Income Taxes
  Chapter 1. Normal Taxes and Surtaxes
    Subchapter A. Determination of Tax Liability
      Part I. Tax on Individuals
        Sections 1–5
      Part II. Tax on Corporations
        Sections 11–12

In referring to a provision of the Code, the tax professional usually cites the Section number. In referring to § 2(a) (dealing with the status of a surviving spouse), for example, it is unnecessary to include Subtitle A, Chapter 1, Subchapter A, and Part I. Merely mentioning § 2(a) suffices, because the Section numbers run consecutively and do not begin again with each new Subtitle, Chapter, Subchapter, or Part. Not all Code Section numbers are used, however. Part I ends with § 5, and Part II starts with § 11 (at present, there are no §§ 6, 7, 8, 9, and 10).[2]

Tax professionals commonly refer to certain areas of income tax law by Subchapter designation. Some of the more common Subchapter designations include Subchapter C ("Corporate Distributions and Adjustments"), Subchapter K ("Partners and Partnerships"), and Subchapter S ("Tax Treatment of S Corporations and Their Shareholders").

Citing the Code

Code Sections often are broken down into subparts.[3] Code § 2(a)(1)(A) serves as an example.

Broken down by content, a citation for Code § 2(a)(1)(A) appears as follows.

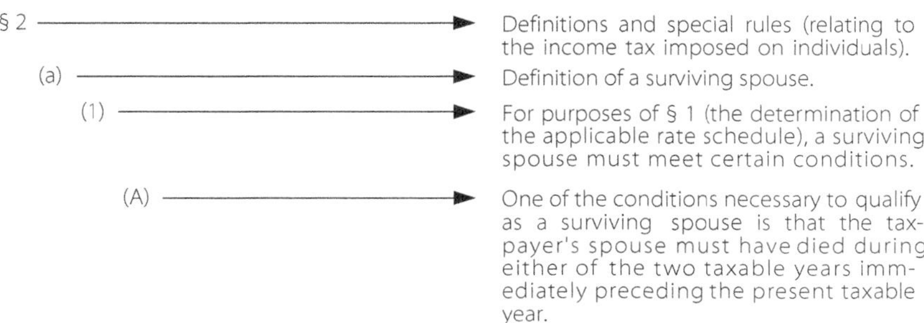

[2] When the Code was drafted, some Section numbers intentionally were unassigned so that later changes could be incorporated into the Code without disrupting its topical organization. When Congress does not leave enough space to accommodate new provisions, subsequent Code Sections are given A, B, C, etc., designations. A good example is the treatment of §§ 280A through 280H.

[3] Some Code Sections do not have subsections. See, for example, §§ 211 and 241.

[4] Some Code Sections omit the subsection designation and use, instead, the paragraph designation as the first subpart. See, for example, §§ 212(1).

Throughout this text, references to the Code Sections are in the form shown previously. The symbols "§" and "§§" are used in place of "Section" and "Sections," respectively. The following table illustrates the format used in the text.

Complete Reference	Text Reference
Section 2(a)(1)(A) of the Internal Revenue Code of 1986	§ 2(a)(1)(A)
Sections 1 and 2 of the Internal Revenue Code of 1986	§§ 1 and 2
Section 2 of the Internal Revenue Code of 1954	§ 2 of the Internal Revenue Code of 1954
Section 12(d) of the Internal Revenue Code of 1939[5]	§ 12(d) of the Internal Revenue Code of 1939

Effect of Treaties

The United States signs certain tax treaties (sometimes called tax conventions) with foreign countries to render mutual assistance in tax enforcement and to avoid double taxation. These treaties affect transactions involving U.S. persons and entities operating or investing in a foreign country, as well as persons and entities of a foreign country operating or investing in the United States. Although these bilateral agreements are not codified in any one source, they are available from the IRS at **tinyurl.com/taxtreaties**, as well as in various commercial tax services.

Neither a tax law nor a tax treaty automatically takes legal precedence.[6] When there is a direct conflict between the Code and a treaty, the most recently adopted item prevails. With certain exceptions, a taxpayer must disclose on the tax return any filing position for which a treaty overrides a tax law. There is a $1,000 per *failure to disclose* penalty for individuals and a $10,000 per failure to disclose penalty for C corporations.[7]

2-1b Administrative Sources of the Tax Law

The administrative sources of the Federal tax law include Treasury Department Regulations, Revenue Rulings and Revenue Procedures, and various other administrative pronouncements (see Exhibit 2.3). All are issued by either the U.S. Treasury Department or its subsidiary agency, the IRS.

Treasury Department Regulations

Regulations are issued by the U.S. Treasury Department under authority granted by Congress.[8] Usually interpretive by nature, they provide taxpayers with considerable guidance on the meaning and application of the Code and often include examples. Regulations carry considerable authority as the official interpretation of tax statutes.

Treasury Regulations are arranged in the same sequence as the Code. A number is added at the beginning, however, to indicate the type of tax or other matter to which they relate. For example, the prefix 1 designates the Regulations under the income tax law. As a result, the Regulations under Code § 2 are cited as Reg. § 1.2, with subparts added for further identification. The numbering pattern of these subparts often has no correlation with the Code subsections. Reg. § 1.351–1(a)(2) is an example of such a citation.

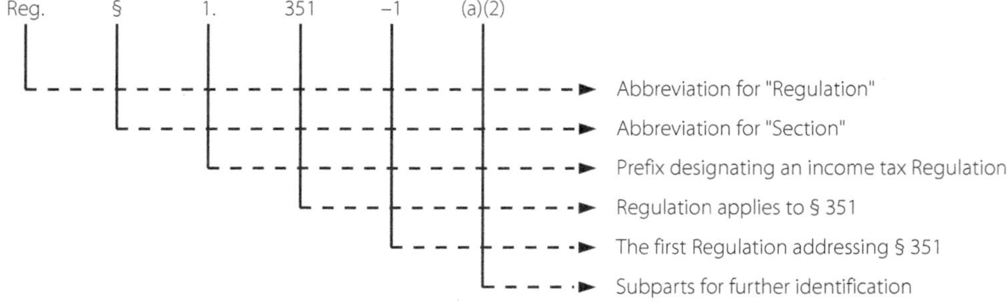

[5]Code § 12(d) of the Internal Revenue Code of 1939 is the predecessor to § 2 of the Internal Revenue Codes of 1954 and 1986.

[6]§ 7852(d)(1).

[7]§§ 6114, 6712(a).

[8]§ 7805.

Exhibit 2.3 Administrative Sources

Source	Location	Authority
Regulations	*Federal Register*	Force and effect of law.
Temporary Regulations	*Federal Register* *Internal Revenue Bulletin (IRB)* *Cumulative Bulletin**	May be cited as a precedent.
Proposed Regulations	*Federal Register* *Internal Revenue Bulletin* *Cumulative Bulletin**	Preview of Final Regulations. Not yet a precedent.
Revenue Rulings	*Internal Revenue Bulletin* *Cumulative Bulletin**	IRS interpretation only. Items published in the IRB are binding on the IRS. Taxpayers can rely on these items. ** Weak precedent.
Revenue Procedures Notices	*Internal Revenue Bulletin* *Cumulative Bulletin**	
Chief Counsel Advice Technical Advice Memoranda Actions on Decisions	Tax Analysts' *Tax Notes;* Thomson Reuters *Checkpoint***;* CCH *IntelliConnect;* IRS website	May not be cited as a precedent.
Letter Rulings	Tax services from Thomson Reuters, CCH Wolters Kluwer, and Bloomberg Law; IRS website	Applicable only to taxpayer addressed. May not be cited as precedent by others, but can be used as authority to avoid certain tax penalties on audit.

Note: All Administrative Sources can be accessed electronically through Thomson Reuters *Checkpoint* (and other commercial tax services).

*Through 2008, the contents of Internal Revenue Bulletins were consolidated semiannually into a Cumulative Bulletin. The IRS no longer produces a Cumulative Bulletin because Internal Revenue Bulletins from mid-2003 are available electronically on the IRS website (**irs.gov/irb**).

**Internal Revenue Manual (IRM) 4.10.7.2.4 (01-10-2018).

***Thomson Reuters *Checkpoint* includes a wide variety of tax resources. The most significant are materials produced by the Research Institute of America (RIA), including the *Federal Tax Coordinator 2d*.

Generally, the prefix 20 designates estate tax Regulations, 25 addresses gift tax Regulations, 31 relates to employment taxes, and 301 refers to procedure and administration. This list is not all-inclusive.

New Regulations and changes in existing Regulations usually are issued in proposed form before they are finalized. The interval between the proposal of a Regulation and its finalization permits taxpayers and other interested parties to comment on the propriety of the proposal. These comments usually are provided in writing, but oral comments can be offered at hearings held by the IRS on the Regulations in question pursuant to a public notice. This practice of notice-and-comment is a major distinction between Regulations and other forms of Treasury guidance such as Revenue Rulings, Revenue Procedures, and the like.

Proposed Regulations under Code § 2, for example, are cited as Prop.Reg. § 1.2. The U.S. Tax Court indicates that Proposed Regulations carry little weight in the litigation process.[9]

The Treasury Department issues **Temporary Regulations** relating to matters where immediate guidance is important. These Regulations are issued without the comment period required for Proposed Regulations. Temporary Regulations have the same authoritative value as final Regulations and may be cited as precedents. However, Temporary Regulations must also be issued as Proposed Regulations and automatically expire within three years after the date of their issuance.[10]

Proposed, Temporary, and **Final Regulations** are published in the *Federal Register*, the *Internal Revenue Bulletin*, and major tax services.

Regulations also may be classified as *legislative, interpretive*, or *procedural*. These terms are discussed in more detail in text Section 2-2d.

[9] *F. W. Woolworth Co.*, 54 T.C. 1233 (1970); *Harris M. Miller*, 70 T.C. 448 (1978); and *James O. Tomerlin Trust*, 87 T.C. 876 (1986).

[10] § 7805(e).

Revenue Rulings, Revenue Procedures, and Notices

Revenue Rulings are official pronouncements of the National Office of the IRS.[11] Like Regulations, they are designed to provide interpretation of the tax law. However, they do not carry the same legal force and effect as Regulations, but because Rulings are focused on a specific fact pattern, they may provide a more detailed analysis of the law.

Both Revenue Rulings and Revenue Procedures serve an important function in providing *guidance* to IRS personnel and taxpayers in handling routine tax matters. Revenue Rulings and Revenue Procedures generally apply retroactively and may be revoked or modified by subsequent rulings or procedures, Regulations, legislation, or court decisions.

Revenue Rulings typically provide one or more examples of how the IRS would apply a law to specific fact situations. Revenue Rulings may arise from other pronouncements by the IRS, court decisions, suggestions from tax practitioner groups, and various tax publications. A Revenue Ruling also may arise from a specific taxpayer's request for a letter ruling (discussed below). If the IRS believes that a taxpayer's request for a letter ruling deserves official publication due to its widespread effect, the letter ruling is converted into a Revenue Ruling and issued for a broader audience.

Revenue Procedures are issued in the same manner as Revenue Rulings, but they deal with the internal management practices and procedures of the IRS. Familiarity with these procedures increases taxpayer compliance and helps make the administration of the tax laws more efficient.

Some recent Revenue Procedures dealt with the following matters.

- A safe harbor procedure for claiming a qualified business income deduction for certain rental real estate.
- Inflation-adjusted amounts for various Code provisions.

Notices are issued when immediate guidance is needed by taxpayers. Typically, this guidance is transitional while the IRS works on permanent guidance on the particular topic. For example, Notice 2020–75 announced that the IRS would issue proposed regulations on the treatment of state and local income taxes paid by a partnership or an S corporation. This relates to a change made by the Tax Cuts and Jobs Act of 2017.

Revenue Rulings, Revenue Procedures, and Notices are published weekly by the U.S. Government in the *Internal Revenue Bulletin* (I.R.B.).

The proper form for citing Revenue Rulings is shown below. Revenue Procedures and Notices are cited in the same manner, except that "Rev.Proc." or "Notice" is substituted for "Rev.Rul."

Rev.Rul. 2021–2, 2021–4 I.R.B. 495.

Explanation: Revenue Ruling Number 2, beginning at page 495 of the 4th weekly issue of the *Internal Revenue Bulletin* for 2021.

Internal Revenue Bulletins are listed at **irs.gov/irb**.[12]

Letter Rulings

Letter rulings are issued by the IRS National Office for a fee upon a taxpayer's request. They describe how the IRS will treat a *proposed* transaction for tax purposes. Letter rulings can be useful for taxpayers who want to be certain of how a transaction will be taxed before proceeding with it. Letter rulings allow taxpayers to avoid unexpected tax costs.

Requesting a ruling can be quite time-consuming due to the required research and format, yet it sometimes is the most effective way to carry out tax planning. The IRS limits the issuance of letter rulings to restricted, pre-announced areas of taxation; it generally will not rule on situations that are fact-intensive.[13]

[11] Reg. §§ 601.201(a), 601.601(d)(2).

[12] Commercial sources for Revenue Rulings and Revenue Procedures are available for a subscription fee. Older Revenue Rulings and Revenue Procedures usually were cited as being published in the *Cumulative Bulletin* (C.B.) rather than the *Internal Revenue Bulletin* (I.R.B.).

[13] An *Internal Revenue Bulletin* issued early each year includes a list of areas in which the IRS will not issue rulings. This list may be modified throughout the year. See, for example, Rev.Proc. 2022–3.

The IRS makes letter rulings available for public inspection after identifying details are deleted.[14] Published digests of private letter rulings are found in Bloomberg BNA's *Daily Tax Reports* and Tax Analysts' *Tax Notes. IRS Letter Rulings Reports* (published by CCH) contains both digests and full texts of all letter rulings. In addition, letter rulings are available in electronic, searchable form through several commercial publishers.

Letter rulings are issued multidigit file numbers that indicate the year and week of issuance as well as the number of the ruling during that week. Consider, for example, Ltr.Rul. 202129001 holds that contractually obligated payments for part of the cost of acquiring water rights was deductible as an ordinary expense.

2021	**29**	**001**
Year 2021	29th week of 2021	1st ruling issued during the 29th week

Other Administrative Pronouncements

Treasury Decisions (TDs) are issued by the Treasury Department to announce new Regulations, amend or change existing Regulations, or announce the position of the Government on selected court decisions. Like Revenue Rulings, Revenue Procedures, and Notices, TDs are published in the *Internal Revenue Bulletin* (IRB).

The IRS also publishes various administrative communications on its website, such as IRs (News Releases), Chief Counsel Advice (CCA), Chief Counsel Notices (CCN), and frequently asked questions (FAQs).

Like letter rulings, **determination letters** are issued at the request of taxpayers and provide guidance on the application of the tax law. They differ from letter rulings in that the issuing source is an IRS director rather than the National Office of the IRS. Further, determination letters usually involve *completed* (as opposed to proposed) transactions. Determination letters are not published by the IRS, and they are released officially only to the party making the request.

The following examples illustrate the distinction between letter rulings and determination letters.

Difference between Letter Rulings and Determination Letters

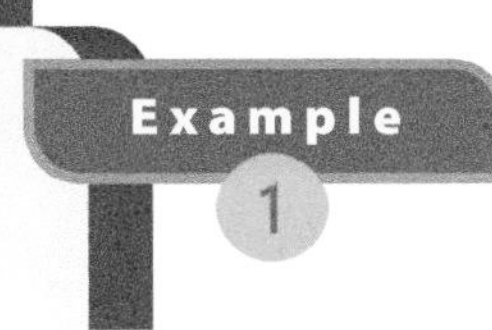

The shareholders of Red Corporation and Green Corporation want assurance that the consolidation of their corporations into Blue Corporation will be a nontaxable reorganization. The proper approach is to ask the National Office of the IRS to issue a letter ruling concerning the income tax effect of the proposed transaction.

The tax director of Bends Corporation wants confirmation that its retirement plan meets all requirements for optimal tax treatment for the employer and employees. The proper procedure is to request a determination letter from the IRS.

The National Office of the IRS provides **Technical Advice Memoranda (TAMs)** as needed. TAMs resemble letter rulings in that they give the IRS's determination of an issue. Letter rulings, however, are responses to requests by taxpayers, whereas TAMs are issued in response to questions raised by IRS field personnel during audits. TAMs deal with completed rather than proposed transactions and are numbered in the same manner as a letter ruling.

Information on Chief Counsel Advice and Frequently Asked Questions (FAQs) and their relevance to tax research can be found on this book's companion website: www.cengage.com

1 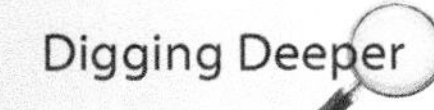

[14]§ 6110(c).

Exhibit 2.4 Federal Judicial System

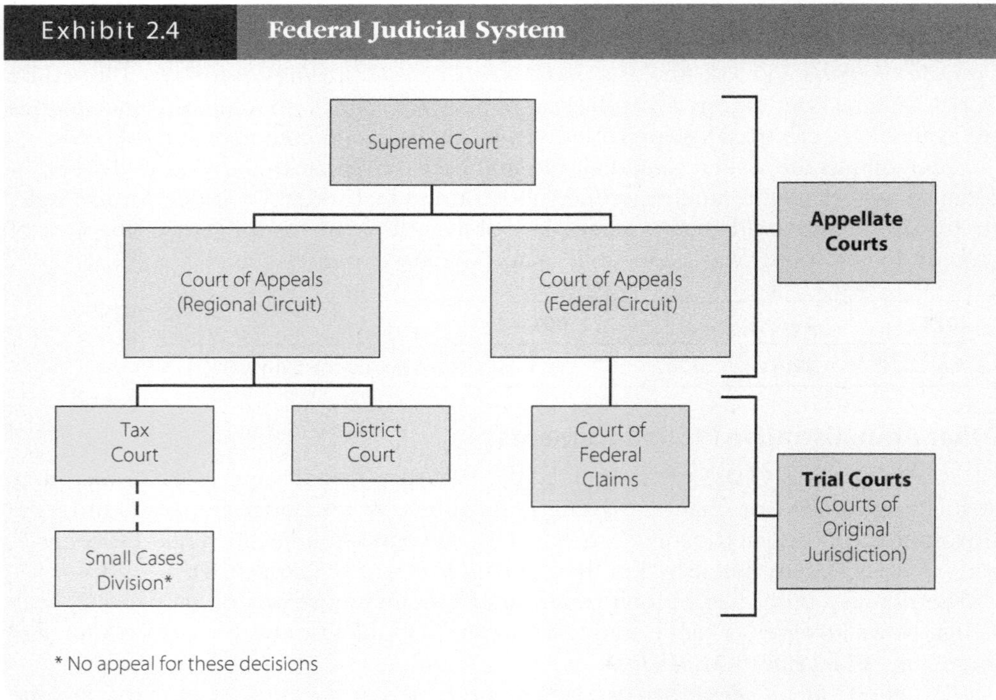

2-1c Judicial Sources of the Tax Law

Once a taxpayer has exhausted the remedies available within the IRS (i.e., no satisfactory settlement has been reached at the agent level or at the Appeals Division level), a dispute can be taken to the Federal courts. The court system for Federal tax litigation is illustrated in Exhibit 2.4. The dispute first is considered by a **court of original jurisdiction** (also known as a trial court). Appeals (either by the taxpayer or the IRS) then are taken to the appropriate appellate court. To commence litigation, the taxpayer chooses among the pertinent **U.S. District Court**, the **U.S. Court of Federal Claims**, the **U.S. Tax Court**, or the **Small Cases Division** of the U.S. Tax Court.

A court decision creates a *precedent*, such that future holdings will be followed in cases with similar facts and applicable law and in the same jurisdiction. For example, the decisions of an appellate court are binding only on the trial courts within its jurisdiction and not on other trial or appelate courts. Different appellate courts may reach different opinions about the same issue.

The jurisdiction of the Small Cases Division is limited to cases involving tax, interest, and penalty amounts totaling $50,000 or less. The broken line in Exhibit 2.4 between the U.S. Tax Court and the Small Cases Division indicates that there is no appeal from the Small Cases Division by either party to the case. Decisions from the Small Cases Division have no precedential value. They may not be relied upon by other taxpayers or even by the taxpayer itself in subsequent years.

Digging Deeper 2

Additional information on the judicial process can be found on this book's companion website: www.cengage.com

Here are several terms that are important for the tax professional who is working with court decisions. The *plaintiff* is the party requesting action in a court, and the *defendant* is the party against whom the suit is brought. Sometimes a court uses the terms *petitioner* and *respondent*. In general, *petitioner* is a synonym for *plaintiff*, and *respondent* is a synonym for *defendant*. At the trial court level, a taxpayer usually is the petitioner, and the government is the respondent. If the taxpayer wins and the Government appeals as the new petitioner (or appellant), the taxpayer now is the respondent.

Trial Courts

The differences among the various trial courts (courts of original jurisdiction) can be summarized as follows. Concept Summary 2.1 summarizes the characteristics of the Federal trial-level courts with respect to tax cases. A discussion of the differences among the courts then follows. Exhibit 2.5 shows the locations of the various U.S. District Courts.

Concept Summary 2.1

Federal Judicial System: Trial Courts

Issue	U.S. Tax Court	U.S. District Court	U.S. Court of Federal Claims
Number of judges per court	19*	1 per case	16
Payment of deficiency before trial	No	Yes	Yes
Jury trial available	No	Yes	No
Small Cases Division	Yes	No	No
Types of dispute	Tax cases only	Mostly criminal and civil issues	Claims against the United States
Jurisdiction	Nationwide	Location of taxpayer	Nationwide
IRS acquiescence policy	Yes	Yes	Yes
Appeal is to	U.S. Court of Appeals	U.S. Court of Appeals	U.S. Court of Appeals for the Federal Circuit

*Some positions may be unfilled at any time. Senior judges and special trial judges may be used to manage the caseload.

- *Number of courts.* There is only one Court of Federal Claims and only one Tax Court, but there are many District Courts. The taxpayer does not select the District Court that will hear the dispute, but must sue in the one that has jurisdiction for the taxpayer and the dispute.
- *Number of judges.* A case tried in a District Court is heard before only 1 judge. The Court of Federal Claims has 16 judges, and the Tax Court has 19 regular judges. The entire Tax Court, however, reviews a case (the case is heard *en banc*), thereby taking on a more compelling authority, when important or novel tax issues are involved. Most cases, though, are heard and decided by only 1 of the 19 regular judges.
- *Location.* The Court of Federal Claims meets most often in Washington, D.C., while a District Court meets at a prescribed seat for the pertinent location. Each state has at least one District Court, and the more populous states have more than one. Choosing the District Court usually minimizes the inconvenience and expense of traveling for taxpayers and their counsel. The Tax Court is based in Washington, D.C., but its judges regularly travel to different parts of the country and hear cases at predetermined locations and dates.
- *Jurisdiction of the Court of Federal Claims.* The Court of Federal Claims has jurisdiction over any claim against the U.S. government. So the Court of Federal Claims hears nontax litigation as well as tax cases.
- *Jurisdiction of the Tax Court and District Courts.* The Tax Court hears only Federal tax cases and is the most frequently used forum for tax cases. The District Courts hear a wide variety of nontax cases, including drug crimes and other Federal violations, as well as tax cases. For this reason, some suggest that the Tax Court has more expertise in tax matters, while the District Courts can be classified as generalists with respect to the tax law.
- *Jury trial.* A jury trial is available only in a District Court. Juries can decide only questions of fact and not questions of law. If a jury trial is not elected or available, the judge decides all issues. A District Court decision carries precedential value only in the district where it was issued.
- *Payment of deficiency.* Before the Court of Federal Claims or a District Court can have jurisdiction, the taxpayer must pay the tax deficiency assessed by the IRS and then sue for a refund. If the taxpayer wins (assuming no successful appeal by

the Government), the tax paid plus appropriate interest is recovered. Jurisdiction in the Tax Court, however, usually is obtained without first paying the assessed tax deficiency. As a result, whether to pay the tax in advance becomes part of the decision-making process of the taxpayer in selecting a trial court.

Digging Deeper 3

Additional information on the payment of tax and interest when litigating in the Tax Court can be found on this book's companion website: www.cengage.com

- *Appeals.* Appeals from a District Court or a Tax Court decision go to the Court of Appeals for the circuit in which the taxpayer resides. Appeals from the Court of Federal Claims go to the Court of Appeals for the Federal Circuit.
- *Bankruptcy.* When a taxpayer files a bankruptcy petition, the IRS, like other creditors, is prevented from taking action against the taxpayer. Sometimes a bankruptcy court settles a tax claim.
- *Gray areas.* Because there are "gray areas" in the tax laws, courts may disagree as to the proper tax treatment of an item. With these differences in possible outcome, the taxpayer must consider how a specific court might rule in choosing the most favorable forum to hear the case.

Appellate Courts

The losing party can appeal a trial court decision to the appropriate **Circuit Court of Appeals**. The 11 geographic circuits, the circuit for the District of Columbia, and the Federal Circuit are shown in Exhibit 2.5. The Court of Appeals for the Federal Circuit hears decisions appealed from the Court of Federal Claims.

Process and Outcomes If the government loses at the trial court level (District Court, Tax Court, or Court of Federal Claims), it need not (and frequently does not) appeal. The fact that an appeal is not made, however, does not indicate that the IRS agrees with the result and will not litigate similar issues in the future.

Exhibit 2.5 The Federal District Courts and Circuit Courts of Appeals

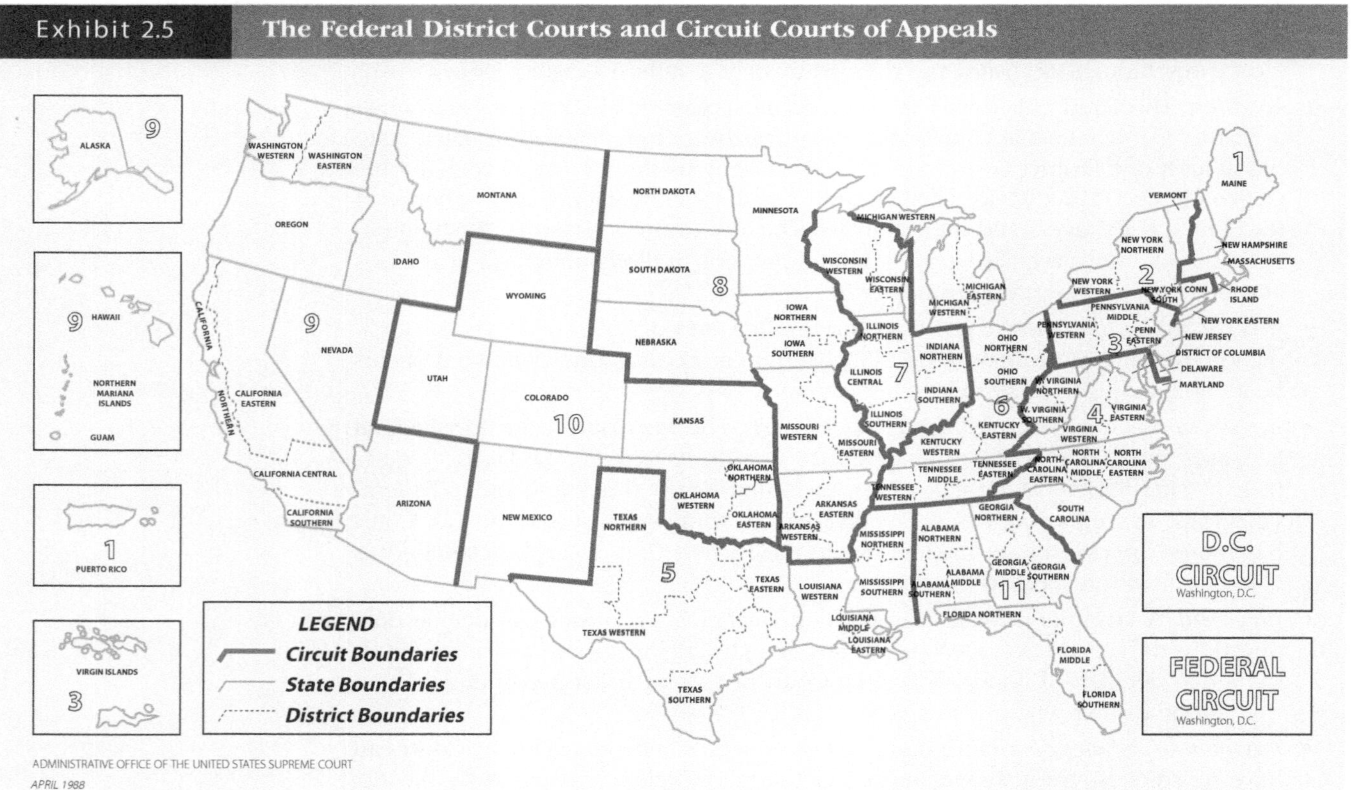

The IRS may decide not to appeal for a number of reasons. First, its current litigation load may be heavy. As a consequence, the IRS may decide that available personnel should be assigned to other cases. Second, the IRS may not appeal for strategic reasons. For example, the taxpayer may be in a sympathetic position, or the facts may be particularly strong in their favor. In that event, the IRS may wait for a different case to test the legal issues involved. Third, if the appeal is from a District Court or the Tax Court, the Court of Appeals of jurisdiction could have some bearing on whether the IRS decides to pursue an appeal. Based on past experience and precedent, the IRS may conclude that the chance for success on a particular issue might be more promising in a different Court of Appeals.

The role of appellate courts is limited to a review of the record of the case that was compiled by the trial courts. As a result, the appellate process usually involves a determination of whether the trial court applied the proper law in arriving at its decision, rather than a consideration of the trial court's factual findings.

An appeal can have a number of possible outcomes. The appellate court may let stand (affirm) or overturn (reverse) the lower court's finding, or it may send the case back to the trial court for further consideration (remand). When many issues are involved, a mixed result is not unusual. As a result, the lower court may be affirmed (*aff'd.*) on Issue A and reversed (*rev'd.*) on Issue B, with the appeals court remanding Issue C (*rem'd.*) back to the lower court for additional fact finding.

When more than one judge is involved in the decision-making process, disagreements are not uncommon. In addition to the majority view, one or more judges may concur (agree with the result reached but not with some or all of the reasoning) or dissent (disagree with the result). In any decision, the majority view controls. But concurring and dissenting views can influence other courts or, at some subsequent date when the composition of the court has changed, even when involving the same court.

Other Rules and Strategies The Federal Circuit at the appellate level provides taxpayers with an alternative forum to the Court of Appeals of their home circuit. When a particular circuit has issued an adverse decision for a case that is similar in facts, the taxpayer may prefer the Court of Federal Claims, because any appeal will be to the Court of Appeals for the Federal Circuit.

District Courts, the Tax Court, and the Court of Federal Claims must abide by the **precedents** set by the Court of Appeals of their jurisdiction. A particular Court of Appeals need not follow the decisions of another Court of Appeals. All courts, however, must follow decisions of the **U.S. Supreme Court**.

This pattern of appellate precedents raises an issue for the Tax Court. Because the Tax Court is a national court, it decides cases from all parts of the country. Appeals from its decisions, however, go to all of the Courts of Appeals except the Court of Appeals for the Federal Circuit. Accordingly, identical Tax Court cases might be appealed to different circuits with different results. As a result of *Golsen*,[15] the Tax Court will not follow its own precedents in a subsequent case if the Court of Appeals with jurisdiction over the taxpayer previously reversed the Tax Court on the issue at hand.

Example 3

Emily lives in Texas and sues in the Tax Court on Issue A. The Fifth Circuit Court of Appeals is the appellate court with jurisdiction. The Fifth Circuit already has decided, in a case involving similar facts but a different taxpayer, that Issue A should be resolved in favor of the taxpayer. Although the Tax Court maintains that the Fifth Circuit is wrong, under its *Golsen* policy, the Tax Court will hold for Emily.

Shortly thereafter, in a comparable case, Rashad, a resident of New York, sues in the Tax Court on Issue A. The Second Circuit Court of Appeals, the appellate court with jurisdiction in New York, never has expressed itself on Issue A. Presuming that the Tax Court has not reconsidered its position on Issue A, it will decide against Rashad.

As a result, it is possible for two taxpayers suing in the same court to end up with opposite results merely because they live in different parts of the country.

[15] *Jack E. Golsen*, 54 T.C. 742 (1970).

U.S. Supreme Court

Appeal to the Supreme Court is not automatic. One applies to be heard via a **Writ of Certiorari**. If the Court agrees to hear the case, needing at least four justices to do so, it will grant the Writ (*Cert. granted*). Most often, it declines to hear the case (*Cert. denied*). In fact, the Supreme Court rarely hears tax cases.

The Court usually grants certiorari to resolve a conflict among the Courts of Appeals (e.g., two or more appellate courts have opposing positions on a particular issue) or where the tax issue is extremely important. The granting of a *Writ of Certiorari* indicates that at least four of the nine members of the Supreme Court believe that the issue is of sufficient importance to be heard by the full Court.

Judicial Citations

Court decisions are an important source of tax law. The ability to locate a case, and to cite it in a proper manner, is a must in working with the tax law. Judicial citations usually follow a standard pattern: case name, volume number, reporter series, page or paragraph number, court (where necessary), and year of decision (if needed). These conventions are based on the legacy of publishing court decisions in hard copy books, but they carry on even in today's electronic research environment.

Judicial Citations—The Tax Court The Tax Court issues two types of decisions: Regular and Memorandum. The Chief Judge decides whether the opinion is issued as a Regular or Memorandum decision. The distinction between the two involves both substance and form. In terms of substance, *Memorandum* decisions deal with situations necessitating only the application of already established principles of law. *Regular* decisions involve novel issues of the tax law that have not previously been resolved by the court. In actual practice, however, this distinction is not always so clear. In any event, both Regular and Memorandum decisions represent the position of the Tax Court and, as such, carry precedential value for others.

Regular and Memorandum decisions issued by the Tax Court also differ in form. Memorandum decisions are not published officially, while Regular decisions are published by the U.S. Government as the *Tax Court of the United States Reports* (T.C.). Each volume of these *Reports* covers a six-month period (January 1 through June 30 and July 1 through December 31) and is given a succeeding volume number. But there is usually a time lag between the date a decision is rendered and the date it appears in official form. A temporary citation often is used to help the researcher locate a recent Regular decision. Consider, for example, the temporary and permanent citations for *Wiley Ramey*, a decision filed on January 14, 2021.

Temporary Citation	*Wiley Ramey*, 156 T.C. _____, No. 1 (2021). *Explanation:* Page number left blank because not yet known.
Permanent Citation	*Wiley Ramey*, 156 T.C. 1 (2021). *Explanation:* Page number now available.

The temporary citation tells us that the case ultimately will appear in Volume 156 of the *Tax Court of the United States Reports*. Until this volume becomes available to the general public, however, the page number is left blank. Instead, the temporary citation identifies the case as being the 1st Regular decision issued by the Tax Court since Volume 155 was closed. With this information, the decision easily can be located at the Tax Court website or in the Tax Court services published by Commerce Clearing House (CCH) and Thomson Reuters *Checkpoint*. Once Volume 156 is released, the permanent citation is substituted, and the number of the case is dropped. Regular decisions and Memorandum decisions are published and searchable at **ustaxcourt.gov**.

Before 1943, the Tax Court was called the Board of Tax Appeals, and its decisions were published as the *United States Board of Tax Appeals Reports* (B.T.A.). These 47 volumes cover the period from 1924 to 1942. For example, the citation *Karl Pauli*, 11 B.T.A. 784 (1928) refers to the 11th volume of the *Board of Tax Appeals Reports*, page 784, issued in 1928.

If the IRS loses a decision (other than at the U.S. Supreme Court), it may indicate whether it agrees or disagrees with the results reached by the court by publishing an **acquiescence** ("A" or "*acq.*") or **nonacquiescence** ("NA" or "*nonacq.*"), respectively.

The acquiescence or nonacquiescence result is published in the *Internal Revenue Bulletin* as an *Action on Decision*. An explanation of the IRS's decision is posted on the IRS website and by commercial tax publishers. After the announcement is made by the IRS, the result is added to the citation for the decision. For example, *TriNet Group, Inc. v. United States*, 979 F.3d 1311 (11th Cir. 2020), *nonacq.*, 2021–24 I.R.B. 1199. The IRS can revoke an acquiescence or nonacquiescence retroactively.

For more on the IRS acquiescence policy, see this book's companion website: www.cengage.com **4 Digging Deeper**

Tax Court Memorandum decisions are found at **ustaxcourt.gov**. Such decisions also are published by CCH and Thomson Reuters. Consider, for example, the ways that a Tax Court Memorandum case can be cited.

Nick R. Hughes, T.C.Memo. 2009–94.
Explanation: The 94th Memorandum decision issued by the Tax Court in 2009.

Nick R. Hughes, 97 TCM 1488 (2009).
Explanation: Page 1488 of Volume 97 of the CCH *Tax Court Memorandum Decisions*.

The second citation requires a parenthetical reference to the year in which the case was published. The first citation does not need this reference, because the publication date is included elsewhere in the citation.

U.S. Tax Court Summary Opinions relate to decisions of the Tax Court's Small Cases Division. These opinions are published commercially, and on the U.S. Tax Court website, with the warning that they may not be treated as precedent for any other case. For example, a Small Cases decision can be cited as follows.

Friday O. James, T.C. Summary Opinion 2020–11.

Judicial Citations—The District Courts, Court of Federal Claims, and Courts of Appeals District Court, Court of Federal Claims, and Court of Appeals decisions dealing with Federal tax matters are reported in both the *U.S. Tax Cases* (USTC) and the *American Federal Tax Reports* (AFTR) series.

District Court decisions, dealing with *both* tax and nontax issues, are also published in the *Federal Supplement Series* (F.Supp.). Volume 999, published in 1998, was the last volume of the Federal Supplement Series. The *Federal Supplement Second Series* (F.Supp.2d) is used for currently issued cases. A District Court case can be cited in three different formats.

Turner v. U.S., 2004–1 USTC ¶60,478 (D.Ct. N.Tex.).

Explanation: Reported in the first volume of the *U.S. Tax Cases* (USTC) for calendar year 2004 (2004–1) and located at paragraph 60,478 (¶60,478).

Turner v. U.S., 93 AFTR 2d 2004–686 (D.Ct. N.Tex.).

Explanation: Reported in the 93rd volume of the second series of the *American Federal Tax Reports* (AFTR 2d) beginning on page 686.

Turner v. U.S., 306 F.Supp.2d 668 (D.Ct. N.Tex., 2004).

Explanation: Reported in the 306th volume of the *Federal Supplement Second Series* (F.Supp.2d) beginning on page 668. The date reference is needed, because it is not found elsewhere in the citation.

Bridge Discipline **Bridge to Public Policy**

Sources of the Federal tax law reflect the general construct of the Federal government. The legislative branch issues the statutory tax law sources. The executive branch controls the administrative sources of the tax law, for the most part using the Department of the Treasury. The judicial branch issues various court decisions interpreting the tax law.

Access to the judicial sources of the Federal tax law is prohibitively expensive for most taxpayers. And although the tendency to settle most litigation outside the court system may be cost-effective for all parties, it inhibits the abilities of tax researchers to identify trends in the evolution of the law. Further, the Supreme Court grants certiorari for tax cases so few times each year that the judicial system effectively includes only one trial court and then one appellate opportunity for the taxpayer.

Finally, the political process dictates that wide swings in enforcement initiatives and budgets can occur from year to year. Taxpayers must be able to predict how the law will be administered as they craft and execute their tax plans, but that becomes especially difficult in politically charged times.

In all of the preceding citations, the names of both of the parties to the case are listed. This is a common practice in virtually all legal citations, with the name of the plaintiff or petitioner listed first. But in a Tax Court citation, because virtually all of the cases are brought by the taxpayer, no reference to the government is needed (i.e., "*v. Commissioner*" is omitted).

Decisions of the Courts of Appeals are published in the USTCs, the AFTRs, and the *Federal Second Series* (F.2d). Volume 999, published in 1993, was the last volume of the *Federal Second Series*. The *Federal Third Series* (F.3d) is used for currently issued cases. Decisions of the Court of Federal Claims are published in the USTCs, the AFTRs, and the *Claims Court Reporter* (abbreviated as Cl.Ct.).

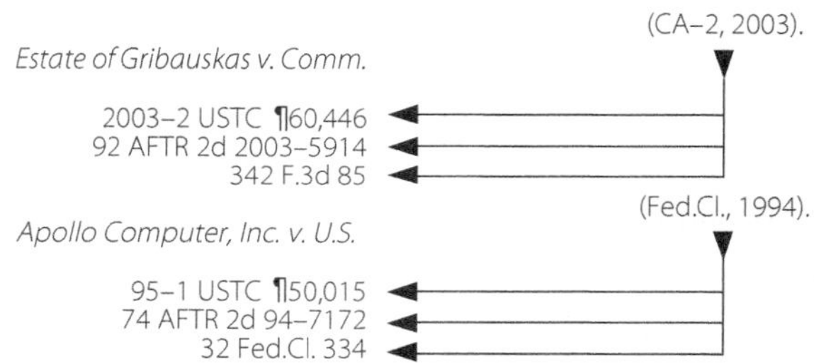

Gribauskas is a decision rendered by the Second Circuit Court of Appeals in 2003 (CA–2, 2003). *Apollo Computer, Inc.*, was issued by the Court of Federal Claims in 1994 (Fed.Cl., 1994), but it was not published in the USTC until 1995.

Digging Deeper 5

Additional information on the Court of Federal Claims can be found on this book's companion website: www.cengage.com

Judicial Citations—Supreme Court U.S. Supreme Court decisions dealing with Federal tax matters are published in the USTCs and in the AFTRs. The U.S. Government Printing Office publishes all Supreme Court decisions in the *United States Supreme Court Reports* (U.S.). Such decisions also are found in the *Supreme Court Reporter* (S.Ct.) and the *United States Reports, Lawyer's Edition* (L.Ed.).

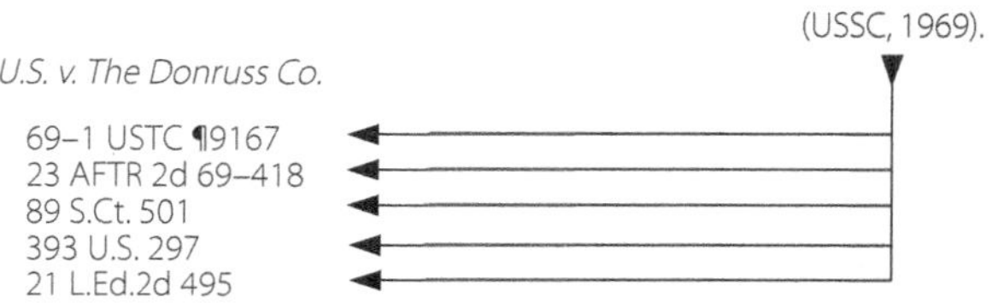

The parenthetical reference (USSC, 1969) identifies the decision as having been rendered by the U.S. Supreme Court in 1969.

2-2 Working with the Tax Law—Tax Research

LO.2

Locate and work with the tax law and explain the tax research process.

Tax research is undertaken to determine the best available solution to a situation that has tax consequences. In the case of a completed transaction, the objective of the research is to determine the tax result of what has already taken place. For example, is the expenditure incurred by the taxpayer deductible or not deductible for tax purposes? When dealing with proposed transactions, tax research has a different objective: effective tax planning by determining the tax consequences of various alternatives.

Tax research involves the following procedures.

- Identifying and refining the problem.
- Locating the appropriate tax law sources.
- Assessing the tax law sources.
- Arriving at the solution or at alternative solutions, including consideration of nontax factors.
- Effectively communicating the solution to the taxpayer or the taxpayer's representative.
- Updating the solution (where appropriate) in light of new developments.

This process is illustrated in Exhibit 2.6. The broken lines indicate steps of particular interest when tax research is directed toward proposed, rather than completed, transactions.

Exhibit 2.6 Tax Research Process

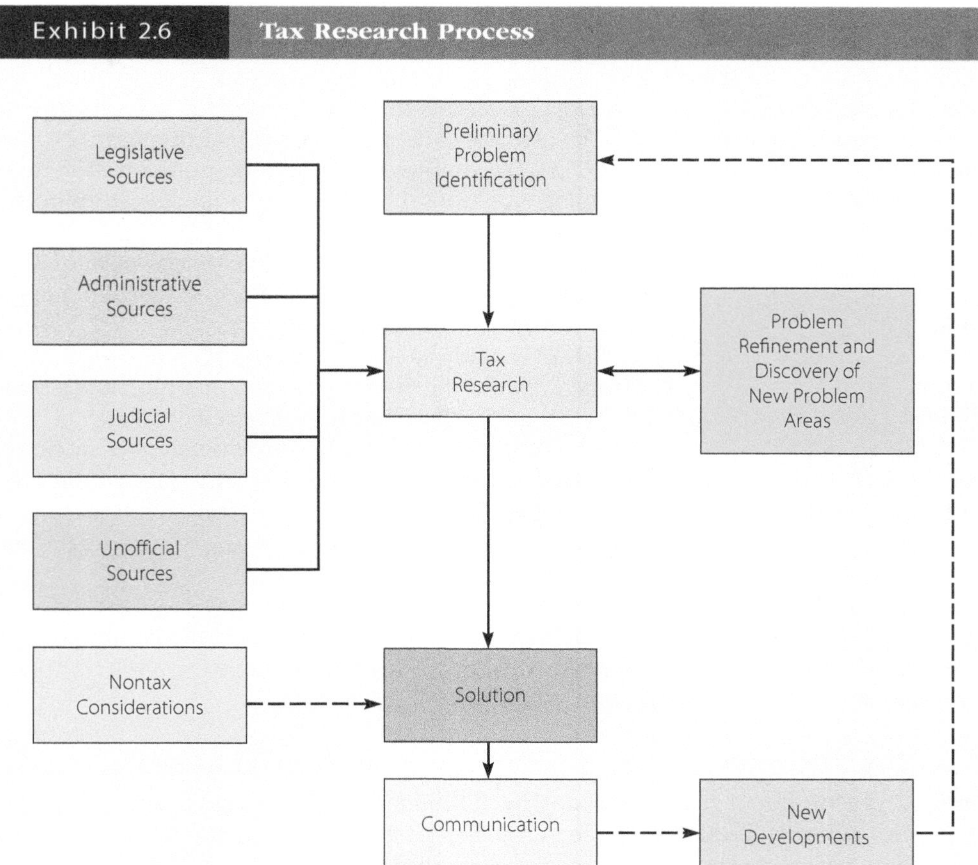

2-2a Identifying the Problem

Problem identification starts with a compilation of the relevant facts involved. In this regard, *all* of the facts that may have a bearing on the problem must be gathered; any omission could modify the solution reached. To illustrate, consider what appears to be a very simple problem.

In reviewing their tax and financial situation, Joan and Richard, a married couple, notice that Joan's investment in Airways stock has declined from its purchase price of $8,000 to a current market value of $5,500. Joan wants to sell this stock now and claim the $2,500 loss ($5,500 value − $8,000 cost) as a deduction this year. Richard, however, believes that Airways will yet prosper and does not want to part with the stock. Their daughter Margaret suggests that they sell the Airways stock to Maple, Inc., a corporation owned equally by Joan and Richard. That way, they can claim the deduction this year but still hold the stock through their corporation. Will this suggestion work?

2-2b Refining the Problem

Joan and Richard in Example 4 face three choices.

1. Sell the Airways stock through their regular investment broker and get a deduction in the current year (Joan's plan).
2. Continue to hold the Airways stock (Richard's plan).
3. Sell the Airways stock to a corporation owned 50–50 by Joan and Richard (Margaret's suggestion).

The tax consequences of plans (1) and (2) are clear, but the question that Joan and Richard want to resolve is whether plan (3) will work as anticipated. Refining the problem further, can shareholders deduct a loss from the sale of an asset to a corporation that they control? Code § 267(a)(1) indicates that losses from the sale of property between persons specified in § 267(b) are not deductible. This subsection lists 12 different relationships, including in § 267(b)(2): "an individual and a corporation more than 50 percent in value of the outstanding stock of which is owned, directly or indirectly, by or for such individual."

As a result, if Joan and Richard each own 50 percent of Maple, neither owns *more than* 50 percent, as § 267(b) requires. Accordingly, the loss disallowance rule would not apply to Joan, and Margaret's suggestion would appear to be sound.

The language of the statute, however, indicates that any stock owned *directly or indirectly* by an individual is counted toward the 50 percent test. Might Richard's stock be considered owned "indirectly" by Joan? Further research is necessary.

Code § 267(c) contains rules for determining "constructive ownership of stock," or when stock owned by one person will be attributed to someone else. One of the rules in this subsection declares that an individual is considered to own any stock that is owned by that person's *family*, and family is defined in § 267(c)(4) as including a person's spouse, among others.

Therefore, Richard's Maple stock will be attributed to Joan, and Joan is treated as owning all of the stock of Maple, Inc. As a result, § 267(a) would indeed apply, and no loss would be deductible if Joan sells the Airways stock to Maple. In short, we must conclude that Margaret's suggestion will not work.

2-2c Locating the Appropriate Tax Law Sources

Once a tax research problem is clearly defined, what is the next step? Most tax research begins with a keyword search using an electronic tax service. If the problem is not complex, the researcher may turn directly to the Internal Revenue Code and the Treasury Regulations. For the beginner, the latter procedure saves time and solves many of the more basic problems. If the researcher does not have a personal copy of the Code or Regulations, access to the appropriate volume(s) of a

Bridge Discipline **Bridge to Business Law**

U.S. income tax laws change daily by the action of Congress, tax administrators, and the courts. This process matches the three-branch structure of the rest of the government, with the legislative, executive, and judicial branches each having a say in making tax law.

Under the U.S. Constitution, legislation involving government revenues must start in the House of Representatives. This provision likely was included so that the public would have greater control over those who want greater access to their money. Several recent pieces of tax legislation, though, have been initiated as bills in the Senate. And most bills introduced in both houses of Congress are required to be "revenue-neutral" (i.e., they must include provisions by which the legislation's new programs will be paid for). In both houses, this has resulted in amendments to the Internal Revenue Code being attached to legislation involving clean air and water standards, child care programs, and product import and export limitations.

In a few cases, the courts considered a taxpayer challenge to the way that specific tax legislation was crafted. But so far the courts have failed to overturn any tax provisions solely because they were initiated outside of the House and its committee processes. In *Armstrong v. U.S.*, 759 F.2d 1378 (9th Cir., 1985), the court held that once a bill dealing with revenue starts in the House, the Senate is "fully empowered to propose amendments, even if their effect will be to transform a proposal lowering taxes into one raising taxes."

tax service is necessary.[16] A partial list of the major tax services and their publishers includes:

Thomson Reuters Checkpoint, Research Institute of America. Includes *Federal Tax Coordinator 2d.*

CCH IntelliConnect and *CCH AnswerConnect*, Commerce Clearing House. Includes the *Standard Federal Tax Reporter.*

Parker Tax Pro Library.

Tax Management Portfolios, Bloomberg BNA.

Westlaw services, Thomson Reuters. Includes access to *Federal Tax Coordinator 2d.*

Tax Center, LexisNexis. Mostly primary law sources.

Tax Services

In this text, it is not feasible to explain the use of any particular tax service—this ability can be obtained with further study (such as in a graduate tax program) and professional experience. However, several important observations about the use of tax services cannot be overemphasized. First, always check for current developments. Tax services are updated several times a day, and tax newsletters often feature highlights of recent tax law developments. Second, there is no substitute for the original source. Do not base a conclusion solely on a tax service's commentary. If a Code Section, Regulation, or case is vital to the research, read it.

Tax Commentary

Various tax publications are another source of relevant information. The use of tax editorial commentary in these publications often can shorten the research time needed to resolve a tax issue. If an article or a posting is relevant to the issue at hand, it may provide the references needed to locate the primary sources of the tax law that apply (e.g., citations to judicial decisions, Regulations, and other IRS pronouncements). As a result, the researcher obtains a "running start" in arriving at a solution to the problem.

[16] Several of the major tax services publish paperback editions of the Code and Treasury Regulations that can be purchased at modest prices. See also the IRS resource at **tinyurl.com/code-regs**.

The following are some of the more useful tax publications.

Journal of Taxation
Journal of International Taxation
Practical Tax Strategies
Estate Planning
Corporate Taxation
Taxation of Exempts
Real Estate Taxation
Journal of Multistate Taxation and Incentives
store.tax.thomsonreuters.com/accounting/Brand/WGL/c/3700

Tax Executive
tei.org

The Tax Adviser (AICPA)
thetaxadviser.com

The ATA Journal of Legal Tax Research
aaajournals.org/loi/jltr

Tax Notes
Tax Notes State
Tax Notes International
taxnotes.com

2-2d **Assessing Tax Law Sources**

Once a source has been located, the next step is to assess it in light of the problem at hand. Proper assessment involves careful interpretation of the tax law and consideration of its relevance and significance.

Interpreting the Internal Revenue Code

The language of the Code often is difficult to comprehend fully. The Code is intended to apply to more than 325 million citizens, most of whom are willing to exploit any linguistic imprecision to their benefit—to find a "loophole," in popular parlance. Moreover, many of the Code's provisions are limitations or restrictions involving two or more variables. Expressing such concepts algebraically would be more direct; using words to accomplish this task instead is often quite cumbersome.

Nevertheless, the Code should be the first source to be consulted by the tax researcher, and often it is the only source needed.

Assessing the Significance of a Treasury Regulation

Treasury Regulations are the official interpretation of the Code and are entitled to great deference. Occasionally, however, a court will invalidate a Regulation or a portion thereof on the grounds that the Regulation is contrary to the intent of Congress. Usually, courts do not question the validity of Regulations. Courts believe that "the first administrative interpretation of a provision as it appears in a new act often expresses the general understanding of the times or the actual understanding of those who played an important part when the statute was drafted."[17]

Keep in mind the following observations when you assess the significance of a Regulation.

- IRS examiners *must* give the Code and any related Regulations equal weight when dealing with taxpayers and their representatives.
- Proposed Regulations provide a preview of future final Regulations, but they are not binding on the IRS or taxpayers.
- Taxpayers have the burden of proof to show that a Regulation varies from the language of the statute and is not supported by the related Committee Reports.
- Final Regulations can be classified as procedural, interpretive, or legislative. **Procedural Regulations** often include procedural instructions, indicating information that taxpayers should provide the IRS, as well as information about the internal management and conduct of the IRS itself.

[17] *Augustus v. Comm.*, 41–1 USTC ¶9255, 26 AFTR 612, 118 F.2d 38 (CA–6).

- **Interpretive Regulations** rephrase or elaborate what Congress stated in the Committee Reports that were issued when the tax legislation was enacted. If the language has gone through the public notice and comment procedures discussed earlier in the chapter, interpretive Regulations are *hard and solid* and almost impossible to overturn unless they do not clearly reflect the intent of Congress.
- In some Code Sections, Congress has given the *Treasury Secretary or a delegate* the specific authority to prescribe Regulations to carry out the details of administration or to otherwise create rules not included in the Code. Here, Congress effectively is delegating its legislative powers to the Treasury. Regulations issued under this type of authority possess the force and effect of law and often are called **Legislative Regulations** (e.g., consolidated return Regulations).

The Big Picture

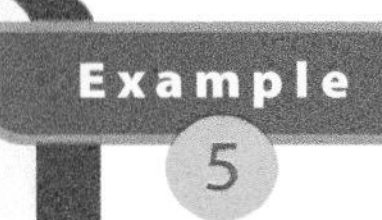

Return to the facts of *The Big Picture* on p. 2-1. Tax law involving the money found by the Martels is found largely in the Internal Revenue Code and Regulations.

Additional information on regulations can be found on this book's companion website:
www.cengage.com

6 Digging Deeper

Assessing the Significance of Other Administrative Sources of the Tax Law

Revenue Rulings issued by the IRS carry much less weight than Treasury Department Regulations. Revenue Rulings are important for the researcher, however, in that they reflect the position of the IRS on tax matters for specified fact patterns. IRS agents will follow the results reached in applicable Revenue Rulings.

Assessing the Significance of Judicial Sources of the Tax Law

A tax researcher may find that several court cases appear to be relevant for the issue at hand. How much reliance can be placed on a particular decision depends on the following factors.

- *The level of the court.* A decision rendered by a trial court (e.g., a District Court) carries less weight than one issued by an appellate court (e.g., the Fifth Circuit Court of Appeals). Until Congress changes the Code, decisions by the U.S. Supreme Court represent the last word on any tax issue.
- *The legal residence of the taxpayer.* If, for example, a taxpayer lives in Texas, a decision of the Fifth Circuit Court of Appeals means more than one rendered by the Second Circuit Court of Appeals. This is the case because any appeal from a District Court or the Tax Court would be to the Fifth Circuit and not to the Second Circuit.
- *The type of decision.* A Tax Court Regular decision carries more weight than a Memorandum decision; the Tax Court does not consider Memorandum decisions to have precedential value.[18]
- *The weight of the decision.* A decision that is supported by cases from other courts carries more weight than a decision that is not supported by other cases.
- *Subsequent events.* Was the decision affirmed or overruled on appeal?

[18]*Severino R. Nico, Jr.*, 67 T.C. 647 (1977).

In connection with the last two factors, a **citator** is helpful to the tax researcher.[19] A citator provides the history of a case to show how it progressed through the court system. Reviewing the references listed in the citator discloses whether the decision was appealed and, if so, with what result (e.g., affirmed, reversed, remanded). It also lists subsequent cases that referred to the earlier case and may indicate how they used that case. If the IRS lost the case, the citator will likely state whether the IRS issued an Action on Decision. In this way, a citator reflects on the currency and validity of a case and may lead to other relevant judicial material. If one plans to rely on a judicial decision to any significant degree, "running" the case through a citator is imperative.

The Big Picture

Example 6

Return to the facts of *The Big Picture* on p. 2-1. The Martels need to know if the gold coins are considered taxable income for them. If yes, they also need to know when to report that income and the amount. They share the story with their tax adviser, Jane, a CPA. Jane researches the Martels' questions.

- What if an appellate court ruling issued by the Federal circuit in which they live supports treatment as $28,000 of income in 2022? Is that decision controlling law? If not and the Martels' circuit has not ruled to the contrary on the issue but another circuit has ruled in their favor in a parallel case, the taxpayers could use that decision as support for their side of the argument.
- Assume that a Revenue Ruling also is found that supports treating the coins as income in 2022. How long ago were the Revenue Ruling and appellate decision issued? A legal precedent generally is stronger if it was issued more recently.
- If the Martels' circuit has ruled favorably, have other courts discussed the appellate court holding? What did these courts hold? The more courts that follow a holding and cite it favorably, the stronger the legal precedent of the holding. Information of this sort can be found by reviewing the case history of the decision or by consulting a citator.

Understanding Judicial Opinions

Reading judicial opinions can be more productive if certain conventions of usage are understood. Some courts, including the Tax Court, apply the terms *petitioner* and *respondent* to the plaintiff and defendant, respectively, particularly when the case does not involve an appellate proceeding. Appellate courts often use the terms *appellant* and *appellee* instead.

It also is important to distinguish between a court's final determination, or *holding*, and passing comments made in the course of its opinion. These latter remarks, examples, and analogies, often collectively termed *dicta*, are not part of the court's conclusion and do not have precedential value. Nevertheless, they often facilitate one's understanding of the court's reasoning and can enable a tax adviser to better predict how the court might resolve some future tax case.

Assessing the Significance of Other Sources

Primary sources of tax law include the Constitution, legislative history materials (e.g., Committee Reports), statutes, treaties, Treasury Regulations, IRS pronouncements, and judicial decisions. In general, the IRS regards only primary sources as substantial authority. However, reference to *secondary materials* such as tax publications, treatises, legal opinions, and written determinations may be useful. In general, secondary sources do not constitute tax authority.

[19]The major citators are published by CCH; Thomson Reuters Checkpoint™; WESTLAW; and Shepard's Citations, Inc.

Although the statement that the IRS regards only primary sources published in the Internal Revenue Bulletin as substantial authority is generally true, there is one exception. Substantial authority *for purposes of* the accuracy-related penalty includes a number of other items (e.g., letter rulings and proposed regulations).[20] "Authority" does not include conclusions reached in treatises, textbooks, and Web postings by tax commentators and written opinions rendered for compensation by tax professionals.

2-2e Arriving at the Solution or at Alternative Solutions

Example 4 raises the question of whether taxpayers would be denied a loss deduction from the sale of stock to a corporation that they own. The solution depends, in part, on the relationship of the corporation's shareholders to each other. Because Richard and Joan are married to each other, § 267(c)(2) attributes Richard's Maple stock to Joan in applying the "more than 50 percent" test of § 267(b)(2). Accordingly, Joan and Maple, Inc., are considered related parties under § 267(a), and a sale between them does not produce a deductible loss. If Richard and Joan were not related to each other, the constructive stock ownership rules would not apply and a loss could be deducted on a sale by Joan to Maple.

If Maple, Inc., were a *partnership* instead of a corporation, § 267 would not apply.[21] However, a different Code Section, namely § 707, produces the same result: no deduction is allowed for the loss from a sale between a "more than 50 percent" partner and the partnership. This additional research prevents the couple from erroneously selling their Airways stock to a related partnership in hopes of obtaining a loss deduction from the sale. Accordingly, Joan still must sell the Airways stock to an unrelated party to deduct the loss.

Because Richard still wants to own Airways stock, he might consider purchasing new Airways Co. stock to replace the stock that Joan sells to the unrelated party. Additional research reveals that for the loss on the sale to be deductible, the "wash sale" rule requires that more than 30 days elapse between the purchase of the new stock and the sale of the old stock.[22] This rule applies to purchases and sales of *substantially identical stock or securities*. As a result, to deduct the loss on the Airways stock, Richard either must wait more than 30 days after Joan sells the shares to buy new Airways stock or acquire stock in a different company at any time. This new company can even be in the same general business as Airways.[23]

2-2f Communicating Tax Research

Communicate the results of the tax research process in a client letter and a tax file memorandum.

Once a tax issue has been researched adequately, a memorandum, a letter, or a speech detailing the result may need to be prepared. The form the communication takes could depend on a number of considerations. For example, does an employer or instructor recommend a particular procedure or format for tax research memos? Is the memo to be given directly to the client, or will it first go to the preparer's employer? Whatever form it takes, a good research communication should contain the following elements.

- A clear statement of the issue.
- In more complex situations, a short review of the fact pattern that raised the issue.
- A review of the pertinent tax law sources (e.g., Code, Regulations, Revenue Rulings, Revenue Procedures, Notices, and judicial authority).
- Any assumptions made in arriving at the solution.
- The solution recommended and the logic or reasoning supporting it.
- The references consulted in the research process.

[20] § 6662; Reg. § 1.6662–4(d).

[21] Reg. § 1.267(b)–1(b)(1).

[22] § 1091.

[23] Rev.Rul. 59–44.

A memo to the tax file documents the findings, analysis (including summaries of relevant tax laws), and conclusion reached for a current tax research project. It is shared with others who have access to the research files so that they do not need to duplicate the current work at a later date. The file memo is written by a tax professional to be read by another tax professional, so it features citations in good form to the Code, Regulations, and other sources of the law, often hyperlinking directly to the underlying document. A file memo is organized so as to list the pertinent facts, open tax issues, a brief conclusion, and a discussion of the research findings and underlying tax logic.

A letter to the client is written to convey the results of a research engagement and to identify the next steps for the taxpayer to consider. Because most clients have little knowledge or experience in working with tax source documents, citations typically are not used. If the recipient of the letter is a tax executive or other colleague, a more technical approach is taken in the letter. The letter typically does not exceed a page or two, and it sometimes is supplemented with an attached spreadsheet or chart. The letter follows business letter formatting and often serves to document what may have already been conveyed to the client verbally.

Illustrations of the memo for the tax file and the client letter associated with Example 4 appear in Exhibits 2.7 and 2.8.

Exhibit 2.7 Tax File Memorandum

August 26, 2023

TAX FILE MEMORANDUM

FROM Gillian J. Jones

SUBJECT Joan and Richard Taxpayer Engagement

Today I spoke with Joan concerning her August 14, 2023 letter requesting tax assistance. Joan wants to know if she can sell some stock in Airways Co. to Maple, Inc., and deduct the $2,500 loss realized.

FACTS Maple, Inc., is owned 50% by Richard and 50% by Joan. Richard wants to continue holding Airways stock in anticipation of a rebound in its value, but Joan wants to sell her shares and deduct the realized loss. They have asked about a proposed sale of this stock to Maple.

ISSUE Can shareholders deduct a loss on the sale of an asset to a corporation, all of whose stock they own?

CONCLUSION Joan should *not* sell the Airways stock to Maple if the couple wants to deduct the realized loss in the current tax year. Instead, Joan should sell this stock to a third party. Then the couple should either acquire new Airways stock more than 30 days before or after the date of sale or acquire stock of a similar company.

ANALYSIS Code § 267(a) provides that no loss is deductible on a sale or exchange between certain related parties. One of these relationships involves a corporation and a shareholder who owns "more than 50 percent" of that corporation's stock [see § 267(b)(2)]. Although Richard owns only 50% of Maple, Inc., his wife, Joan, owns the other 50%. The constructive ownership rule of § 267(c)(2) attributes stock held by family members, and a spouse is part of a taxpayer's family for this purpose, according to § 267(c)(4). Consequently, Richard's Maple stock is attributed to Joan, who is then treated as owning 100% of Maple, Inc. The related-party disallowance rule then applies to the loss from Joan's selling the Airways stock to Maple. Accordingly, Joan must sell this stock to an unrelated party to make the realized loss deductible.

Because Richard wants to retain an investment in Airways, he can purchase replacement stock either before or after Joan sells the original Airways stock. Code § 1091(a), however, requires that more than 30 days elapse between the purchase and the sale or the sale and the purchase, as the case may be. Moreover, for this purpose, an option to buy the stock is treated as equivalent to the stock itself. As a result, Richard must wait more than 30 days between transactions and cannot utilize stock options in the interim to minimize his stock price exposure.

A final alternative might be to replace the Airways stock with securities of a comparable company in the same industry. Although no two companies are exactly alike, there may be another company whose management philosophy, marketing strategy, and financial data are sufficiently similar to Airways to provide an equivalent return on investment. Under this alternative, Richard could acquire the new company's shares immediately, without waiting the 30 days mandated by § 1091(a). Despite the two companies' investment similarity, they would not be treated as "substantially identical" for this purpose (see Rev.Rul. 59–44), and the Airways realized loss could be recognized.

Exhibit 2.8 Client Letter

SWFT, LLP
5191 Natorp Boulevard
Mason, OH 45040

August 30, 2023

Mr. and Ms. Richard Taxpayer
111 Tragg Boulevard
Williamsburg, VA 23185

Dear Joan and Richard:

It was good to see you last week at our firm's golf outing. I'm glad that your children are doing so well in college and that our work to build up their education funds was so effective in providing the needed cash flow!

I am responding to your request to review your family's financial and tax situation. Our conclusions are based upon the facts as outlined in your August 14 letter. Any change in the facts may affect our conclusions.

Joan owns stock in Airways Co. that has declined in value, but Richard would like to retain this stock in anticipation of a rebound in its value. You have proposed a sale of this stock at its current market value to Maple, Inc., a corporation owned 50–50 by the two of you. Such a sale, however, would not permit the loss to be deducted.

A better approach would be to sell the Airways stock to a third party before year-end and repurchase this stock in the market. Please understand that the loss will not be deductible unless more than 30 days elapse between the sale and the repurchase of the stock. You can sell the old stock first and then buy the new stock, or you can buy the new stock first and then sell the old stock; the ordering of the transactions does not change the result. However, it is essential that more than 30 days elapse between the sale and purchase transactions. Using options during this 30-day period is ineffective and also will prevent the loss from being deducted in the current taxable year.

If the 30-day requirement is unacceptable, you might consider replacing the Airways stock with securities of some other company, perhaps even a company in the same general business as Airways. In that situation, your loss on the Airways stock can be deducted without regard to when you buy the new stock.

Let's meet to discuss this some more—and to allow me to show you our new office. Please e-mail me if I can clarify any of these points or if you have more information for me to consider.

Sincerely yours,

Gillian J. Jones, CPA
Partner

2-2g Updates

Because tax research may involve a proposed (as opposed to a completed) transaction, a change in the tax law (legislative, administrative, or judicial) could alter the original conclusion. Additional research may be necessary to test the solution in light of current developments (refer to the broken lines at the right in Exhibit 2.6) or to account for additional information that may arise during the research process itself. To the extent that a client has engaged the tax researcher to provide updates to an initial report, new information should be presented in a concise manner.

2-2h Tax Research Best Practices

One's research skills developed in using browsers and apps may not transfer into the tax research setting. The researcher must use the document list that results from a search procedure in a professional manner. Most electronic tax services allow a user to retrieve documents in order of relevance or in the order listed by database sources. Such a listing seldom will account for the applicability and precedential value of the documents that are found. Reading the primary sources, validating their authority, and checking a citator are essential in reaching a correct answer.

Finding Relevant Materials Effectively

Usually, tax professionals use one of the following strategies when performing computer-based tax research.

- *Search* various databases using keywords that are likely to be found in the underlying documents, as written by Congress, the judiciary, or administrative sources.
- *Link* to tax documents for which all or part of the proper citation is known.
- *Browse* the tax databases, examining various tables of contents and indexes in a traditional manner or using cross-references in the documents to jump from one tax law source to another.

Sometimes a researcher can begin a search process using materials that are available at no direct cost. Such sources include the following.

- *The Web* provides access to a number of sites maintained by accounting and law firms, publishers, tax academics and libraries, and governmental bodies. The best sites offer links to primary authority. Exhibit 2.9 lists some of the websites that may be most useful to tax researchers and their internet addresses.
- *Blogs and RSS feeds* provide a means by which information related to the tax law can be exchanged among taxpayers, tax professionals, and others who subscribe to the group's services. The tax professional can read the exchanges among other members and offer replies and suggestions to inquiries as desired. Discussions address the interpretation and application of existing law, analysis of proposals and new pronouncements, and reviews of tax software.

Although tax information on the internet is plentiful, public domain information never should be relied upon without referring to other, more reliable sources. Always remember that anyone can set up a website and that quality control can be difficult for the tax professional to ascertain.

Exhibit 2.9 Tax-Related Websites

Website	Web Address at Press Date	Description
Internal Revenue Service	**irs.gov**	News releases, downloadable forms and instructions, tables, Circular 230, and filing advice.
Tax Analysts	**taxnotes.com**	Policy-oriented readings on tax laws and proposals to change the law; moderated bulletins on various tax subjects.
Tax laws online	**law.cornell.edu/cfr**	Treasury Regulations.
	law.cornell.edu/uscode	Internal Revenue Code.
	uscode.house.gov	
Commercial tax publishers	For example, **cch.com** and **tax.thomsonreuters.com**	Information about products and services available by subscription and newsletter excerpts.
Accounting firms and professional organizations	For example, the AICPA's page is at **aicpa.org**, Ernst & Young is at **ey.com**, and KPMG is at **kpmg.com**	Tax planning newsletters, descriptions of services offered and career opportunities, and exchange of data with clients and subscribers.
Cengage Learning	**cengage.com**	Informational updates, newsletters, support materials for students and adopters, and continuing education.

Caution: Web addresses change frequently.

Financial Disclosure Insights — Where Does GAAP Come From?

Tax law is developed by many entities, including Congress, the legislators of other countries, the courts, the U.S. states, and the IRS. Accounting principles also have many sources. Consequently, in reconciling the tax and financial accounting reporting of a transaction, the tax professional needs to know the hierarchy of authority of accounting principles—in particular, the level of importance to assign to a specific GAAP document. The diagram below presents the sources of GAAP arranged in a general order of authority from highest to lowest. Note how many of these GAAP sources parallel those that have been discussed with respect to the tax law.

Professional research is conducted to find and analyze the sources of accounting reporting standards in much the same way a tax professional conducts research concerning an open tax question. In fact, many of the publishers that provide tax research materials also can be used to find GAAP and IFRS documents. The Financial Accounting Standards Board (FASB) also makes its standards and interpretations available by subscription.

Highest Authority

- Financial Accounting Standards and Interpretations of the FASB.
- Pronouncements of bodies that preceded the FASB, such as the Accounting Principles Board (APB).

- FASB Technical Bulletins.
- Audit and Accounting Guides, prepared by the American Institute of CPAs (AICPA) and cleared by the FASB.
- Practice Bulletins, prepared by the American Institute of CPAs (AICPA) and cleared by the FASB.

- Interpretation Guides of the FASB Staff.
- Accounting Interpretations of the AICPA.
- ASB Accounting Standards.
- FASB Concepts Standards.
- Widely accepted accounting practices, professional journals, accounting textbooks, and treatises.

2-3 Tax Research on the CPA Examination

LO.4

Employ a strategy for applying tax research skills in taking the CPA exam.

The CPA examination includes tax-oriented questions in the following topical areas. Questions address issues involving tax compliance and tax planning matters.

- Federal tax procedures, ethics, and accounting issues.
- Federal taxation of property transactions.
- Federal taxation—individuals.
- Federal taxation—entities.

Each exam section includes multiple-choice questions and case studies called task-based simulations (TBSs). The Regulation section of the exam has 76 multiple choice questions and 8 TBSs. TBSs are small case studies designed to test a candidate's tax knowledge and skills using real-life work-related situations. Simulations make available access to certain authoritative literature for the candidate to research in completing the tax items (e.g., Internal Revenue Code, Regulations, IRS publications, and Federal tax forms).

Bridge Discipline — Bridge to Regulation and Oversight

The interests of the public are represented by Federal, state, and local governments as they oversee the various economic transactions carried out by individuals and businesses. Control of the financial sector is assigned to the Treasury Department and the Securities and Exchange Commission, among other agencies.

Most citizens assume that attorneys and CPAs hold broad high-level skills in working with the tax laws. But the nature of today's economy dictates that professionals working in law and accounting instead develop narrower specialties that clients will find valuable in the marketplace. Only a subset of CPAs and attorneys practice regularly with the tax law, but all such professionals must hold and maintain broad-based skills in taxation.

Tax law is the subject of only one of the sections of the CPA exam, and only a portion of those questions relate to specific provisions of the tax law. The exam also tests the candidate's research and communication skills, and because it is administered with computer software, the candidate must have some technological facility as well.

The depth and variety of the skills that are required of an effective tax professional almost certainly are not measured well by the CPA or bar examinations. The integrity of the taxing system may be at risk when one can attain credible professional certification with only entry-level skills. Many observers would prefer that further levels of specialty certifications and rigorous, lifelong knowledge and skill improvement be required of tax professionals.

The typical TBS requires 15 to 20 minutes to complete. A simulation requires that the candidate determine which of the provided information is relevant to the task and then complete an analysis that a new CPA is expected to be able to complete. Examples of such simulations follow.

CPA Exam Simulation Example

Example 7

The tax *citation type* simulation requires the candidate to research the Internal Revenue Code and enter a Code Section and subsection citation. For example, Amber Company is considering using the simplified dollar-value method of pricing its inventory for purposes of the LIFO method that is available to certain small businesses. What Internal Revenue Code Section is the relevant authority to which you should turn to determine whether the taxpayer is eligible to use this method? To be successful, the candidate must find § 474.

A *tax form completion* simulation requires the candidate to fill out a portion of a tax form. For example, Red is a limited liability company (LLC). Complete the income section of the Form 1065 for Red Company using the values found and calculated on previous tabs along with the following data.

Ordinary income from other partnerships	$ 5,200
Net gain (loss) from Form 4797	2,400
Management fee income	12,000

The candidate is provided with page 1 of Form 1065 on which to record the appropriate amounts.

Candidates can learn more about the CPA examination at **aicpa.org/becomeacpa/cpaexam.html**. This site reviews the exam's format, navigation functions, and tools. A collection of study materials is available, and a 30- to 60-minute sample exam will familiarize a candidate with the types of questions on the examination. Information also is provided as to how the exam is graded and what each jurisdiction's requirements are to sit for the exam.

In 2020, the AICPA and the National Association of State Boards of Accountancy (NASBA) announced the start of a modification to the CPA exam expected for 2024 (see **evolutionofcpa.org**). The change aims to ensure the CPA designation reflects the knowledge and skills expected of a CPA today. The new approach to the CPA exam (and licensure) is to test core knowledge plus a discipline. The core includes accounting, auditing, tax, and technology; all candidates take this part of the CPA exam. The three disciplines are business analysis and reporting, information systems and controls, and tax compliance and planning, with candidates taking an exam in *one* of these areas. Regardless of the chosen discipline, this model leads to full CPA licensure, and the CPA is not limited to practice only in the discipline selected for testing on the CPA exam.

Refocus on The Big Picture

Researching Tax Questions

In general, the fair market value of the coins that the Martels discovered must be included in their 2022 gross income. This conclusion is based on tax research that you conducted, indicating that the taxpayers having "undisputed possession" of the coins (as of October 2022) creates gross income, under § 61 of the Code, and opinions expressed in U.S. Treasury Department regulations and court cases.

Does it make any difference that the couple paid $195,000 for the land where the coins were buried? Since the couple found the gold coins on their own property, the taxpayers could argue that they purchased the coins when they purchased the land. This argument is similar to an individual discovering oil or natural gas on her property. And with natural resources, there must be a realization event (e.g., a sale or exchange) before there is income. Would this notion work for this couple? Unfortunately, no. A decision affirmed by the Sixth Circuit Court of Appeals indicates that the entire value of the couple's discovery would be included in their income in the year of discovery.

Moreover, the "value" of the assets under the tax law is not the $28,000 face value of the coins. Rather, it is the fair market value of the coins.

Given the potential value of this discovery, your letter to the clients would encourage them to seek out a competent appraiser. Once a determination of the value of the assets is made, you then would work with the clients on a plan to pay the related Federal and state income taxes related to this discovery.

What If?

It is not uncommon that you later receive additional information from Fred and Megan about their discovery. This may occur if additional facts occur to them, if Fred and Megan gave you incomplete information because they did not understand which of the facts were relevant in determining the tax outcome, or if your original interviews and data collection from them were incomplete.

If this new information changes the conclusions and recommendations that you already had developed, you should make certain that the clients understand that your original work no longer is valid and that they should not depend on it.

Suggested Readings

Annette Nellen, "Government Tax Treasures," *The Tax Adviser*, August 2015, **thetaxadviser.com/issues/2015/aug/government-tax-treasures.html**.

IRS, IRM Part 4, Chapter 10, Section 7, Issue Resolution on tax research information for IRS examiners, **irs.gov/irm/part4/irm_04-010-007**.

"Ten Steps to Tax Research," *Tax Research Tutorial*, **businesslibrary.uflib.ufl.edu/taxresearch**.

Key Terms

Acquiescence, 2-15
Circuit Court of Appeals, 2-12
Citator, 2-22
Court of original jurisdiction, 2-10
Determination letters, 2-9
Final Regulations, 2-7
Interpretive Regulations, 2-21
Legislative Regulations, 2-21
Letter rulings, 2-8
Nonacquiescence, 2-15
Notices, 2-8
Precedents, 2-13
Procedural Regulations, 2-20
Proposed Regulations, 2-7
Revenue Procedures, 2-8
Revenue Rulings, 2-8
Small Cases Division, 2-10
Tax research, 2-17
Technical Advice Memoranda (TAMs), 2-9
Temporary Regulations, 2-7
U.S. Court of Federal Claims, 2-10
U.S. District Court, 2-10
U.S. Supreme Court, 2-13
U.S. Tax Court, 2-10
Writ of Certiorari, 2-14

Problems

1. **LO.1** What precedents must each of these courts follow?
   a. U.S. Tax Court.
   b. U.S. Court of Federal Claims.
   c. U.S. District Court.

2. Communications **LO.1, 3** Sonja Bishop operates a small international firm named Tile, Inc. A new treaty between the United States and Spain conflicts with a Section of the Internal Revenue Code. Sonja asks you for advice. If she follows the treaty position, does she need to disclose this on this year's tax return? If she is required to disclose, are there any penalties for failure to disclose? Prepare a letter in which you respond to Sonja. Tile's address is 100 International Drive, Tampa, FL 33620.

3. **LO.1** Distinguish between the following.
   a. Treasury Regulations and Revenue Rulings.
   b. Revenue Rulings and Revenue Procedures.
   c. Revenue Rulings and letter rulings.
   d. Letter rulings and determination letters.

4. **LO.1, 2** Rank the following items from the lowest to highest authority in the Federal tax law system.
   a. Interpretive Regulation.
   b. Legislative Regulation.
   c. Letter ruling.
   d. Revenue Ruling.
   e. Internal Revenue Code.
   f. Proposed Regulation.

5. **LO.1** Interpret each of the following citations.
   a. Temp.Reg. § 1.956–2T.
   b. Rev.Rul. 2012–15, 2012–23 I.R.B. 975.
   c. Ltr.Rul. 200204051.

6. **LO.1** List an advantage and a disadvantage of using the U.S. Court of Federal Claims as the trial court for Federal tax litigation.

7. Communications **LO.1, 3** Eddy Falls is considering litigating a tax deficiency of approximately $229,030 in the court system. He asks you to provide him with a short

description of his litigation alternatives, indicating the advantages and disadvantages of each. Prepare your response to Eddy in the form of a letter. His address is 200 Mesa Drive, Tucson, AZ 85714.

8. **LO.1** A taxpayer lives in Michigan. In a controversy with the IRS, the taxpayer loses at the trial court level. Describe the appeal procedure for each of the following trial courts.
   a. Small Cases Division of the U.S. Tax Court.
   b. U.S. Tax Court.
   c. U.S. District Court.
   d. U.S. Court of Federal Claims.

9. **LO.1** For the U.S. Tax Court, the U.S. District Court, and the U.S. Court of Federal Claims, indicate the following.
   a. Number of regular judges per court.
   b. Availability of a jury trial.
   c. Whether the deficiency must be paid before the trial.

10. **LO.1** A taxpayer living in the following states would appeal a decision of the U.S. District Court to which Court of Appeals?
    a. Wyoming.
    b. Nebraska.
    c. Idaho.
    d. Louisiana.
    e. Illinois.

11. **LO.1** What is meant by the term *petitioner*?

12. **LO.1, 2** In assessing the validity of a prior court decision, discuss the significance of the following on the taxpayer's issue.
    a. The decision was rendered by the U.S. District Court of Wyoming. Taxpayer lives in Wyoming.
    b. The decision was rendered by the U.S. Court of Federal Claims. Taxpayer lives in Wyoming.
    c. The decision was rendered by the U.S. Second Circuit Court of Appeals. Taxpayer lives in California.
    d. The decision was rendered by the U.S. Supreme Court.
    e. The decision was rendered by the U.S. Tax Court. The IRS has acquiesced in the result.
    f. Same as part (e), except that the IRS has nonacquiesced in the result.

13. **LO.1** What is the difference between a Regular decision, a Memorandum decision, and a Summary Opinion of the U.S. Tax Court?

14. **LO.1** Explain the following abbreviations.
    a. CA–2.
    b. Fed.Cl.
    c. *aff'd.*
    d. *rev'd.*
    e. *rem'd.*
    f. *Cert. denied.*
    g. *acq.*
    h. B.T.A.
    i. USTC.
    j. AFTR.
    k. F.3d.
    l. F.Supp.
    m. USSC.
    n. S.Ct.
    o. D.Ct.

15. **LO.2** Referring to the citation only, determine which court issued these rulings.
    a. 716 F.2d 693 (CA–9, 1983).
    b. 20 T.C 734 (1953).
    c. 348 U.S. 426 (1955).
    d. 3 B.T.A. 1042 (1926).
    e. T.C.Memo. 1957–169.
    f. 50 AFTR 2d 92–6000 (Cl.Ct., 1992).
    g. Ltr.Rul. 9046036.
    h. 111 F.Supp.2d 1294 (S.D.N.Y., 2000).
    i. 98–50, 1998–1 C.B. 10.

16. **LO.2** Interpret each of the following citations.
    a. 14 T.C. 74 (1950).
    b. 592 F.2d 1251 (CA–5, 1979).
    c. 95–1 USTC ¶50,104 (CA–6, 1995).
    d. 75 AFTR 2d 95–110 (CA–6, 1995).
    e. 223 F.Supp. 663 (W.D. Tex., 1963).
    f. 491 F.3d 53 (CA–1, 2007).
    g. 775 F.Supp.2d 765 (D.Ct. V.I., 2011).

17. **LO.2** Which of the following items may be found in the *Internal Revenue Bulletin*?
    a. Action on Decision.
    b. Small Cases Division of the U.S. Tax Court decision.
    c. Letter ruling.
    d. Revenue Procedure.
    e. Final Regulation.
    f. Court of Federal Claims decision.
    g. Acquiescences to U.S. Tax Court decisions.
    h. U.S. Circuit Court of Appeals decision.

18. **LO.2** Answer the following questions based upon this citation: *United Draperies, Inc. v. Comm.*, 340 F.2d 936 (CA–7, 1964), *aff'g* 41 T.C. 457 (1963), *cert. denied* 382 U.S. 813 (1965).
    a. In which court did this case first appear?
    b. Did the appellate court uphold the trial court?
    c. Who was the plaintiff?
    d. Did the U.S. Supreme Court uphold the appellate court decision?

Critical Thinking

19. **LO.2, 4** For her tax class, Yvonne is preparing a research paper discussing the tax aspects of qualified stock options. Explain to Yvonne how she can research the provisions on this topic.

20. **LO.1, 2** Tom, an individual taxpayer, has been audited by the IRS and, as a result, has been assessed a substantial deficiency in additional income taxes (which has not yet been paid). In preparing his defense, Tom advances the following possibilities.
    a. Although a resident of Kentucky, Tom plans to sue in a U.S. District Court in Oregon that appears to be more favorably inclined toward taxpayers.
    b. If part (a) is not possible, Tom plans to take his case to a Kentucky state court where an uncle is the presiding judge.
    c. Because Tom has found a B.T.A. decision that seems to help his case, he plans to rely on it under alternative (a) or (b).
    d. If he loses at the trial court level, Tom plans to appeal either to the U.S. Court of Federal Claims or to the U.S. Second Circuit Court of Appeals because he has relatives in both Washington, D.C., and New York. Staying with these relatives could save Tom lodging expense while his appeal is being heard by the court selected.
    e. Whether or not Tom wins at the trial court or appeals court level, he feels certain of success on an appeal to the U.S. Supreme Court.

    Evaluate Tom's notions concerning the judicial process as it applies to Federal income tax controversies.

21. **LO.1** Using the legend provided, classify each of the following statements (more than one answer per statement may be appropriate).

Legend
D = Applies to the District Court
T = Applies to the Tax Court
C = Applies to the Court of Federal Claims
A = Applies to the Circuit Court of Appeals
U = Applies to the Supreme Court
N = Applies to none of the above

a. Decides only Federal tax matters.
b. Decisions are reported in the F.3d Series.
c. Decisions are reported in the USTCs.
d. Decisions are reported in the AFTRs.
e. Appeal is by *Writ of Certiorari*.
f. Court meets most often in Washington, D.C.
g. Offers the choice of a jury trial.
h. Is a trial court.
i. Is an appellate court.
j. Allows appeal to the Court of Appeals for the Federal Circuit and bypasses the taxpayer's own Circuit Court of Appeals.
k. Has a Small Cases Division.
l. Is the only trial court where the taxpayer does not have to first pay the tax assessed by the IRS.

22. **LO.1, 2** Using the legend provided, classify each of the following citations as to the type of court.

Legend
D = District Court
T = Tax Court
C = Court of Federal Claims
A = Circuit Court of Appeals
U = Supreme Court
N = None of the above

a. Rev.Rul. 2009–34, 2009–42 I.R.B. 502.
b. *Joseph R. Bolker*, 81 T.C. 782 (1983).
c. *Magneson*, 753 F.2d 1490 (CA–9, 1985).
d. *Lucas v. Ox Fibre Brush Co.*, 281 U.S. 115 (1930).
e. *Ashtabula Bow Socket Co.*, 2 B.T.A. 306 (1925).
f. *BB&T Corp.*, 97 AFTR 2d 2006–873 (D.Ct. Mid.N.Car., 2006).
g. *Choate Construction Co.*, T.C.Memo. 1997–495.
h. Ltr.Rul. 200940021.
i. *John and Rochelle Ray*, T.C. Summary Opinion 2006–110.

23. **LO.1, 2** Using the legend provided, classify each of the following tax sources.

Legend
P = Primary tax source
S = Secondary tax source
B = Both
N = Neither

a. Sixteenth Amendment to the U.S. Constitution.
b. Tax treaty between the United States and India.
c. Revenue Procedure.
d. An IRS publication.
e. U.S. District Court decision.
f. *Yale Law Journal* article.
g. Temporary Regulations (issued 2019).
h. U.S. Tax Court Memorandum decision.
i. Small Cases Division of the U.S. Tax Court decision.
j. House Ways and Means Committee report.
k. Notice.

24. **LO.1** In which Subchapter of the Internal Revenue Code would one find information about corporate distributions?

a. Subchapter S.
b. Subchapter C.
c. Subchapter P.
d. Subchapter K.
e. Subchapter M.

25. **LO.1, 2** To locate an IRS Revenue Procedure that was issued during the past month, which source would you consult?

a. *Federal Register*.
b. *Internal Revenue Bulletin*.
c. Internal Revenue Code.
d. Some other source.

26. **LO.1, 2** In the citation *Schuster's Express, Inc.*, 66 T.C. 588 (1976), *aff'd* 562 F.2d 39 (CA–2, 1977), *nonacq.*, to what do the 66, 39, and *nonacq.* refer?

27. **LO.1** Is there an automatic right to appeal to the U.S. Supreme Court? If so, what is the process?

Ethics and Equity

28. **LO.2** An accountant friend of yours tells you that he "almost never" does any tax research because he believes that "research usually reveals that some tax planning idea has already been thought up and shot down." Besides, he points out, most tax returns are never audited by the IRS. Can a tax adviser who is dedicated to reducing his client's tax liability justify the effort to engage in tax research? Do professional ethics *demand* such efforts? Which approach would a client probably prefer?

Communications

29. **LO.1** Go to the U.S. Tax Court website (**ustaxcourt.gov**).

a. What different types of cases can be found on the site?
b. What is a Summary Opinion? Find one.
c. What is a Memorandum decision? Find one.
d. Find the court's Rules of Practice and Procedures, and summarize one and its citation.
e. Is the site user-friendly? E-mail suggested improvements to your instructor.

30. **LO.1, 2** Locate the following Code provisions, and give a brief description of each in an e-mail to your instructor. Communications
    a. § 61(a)(12).
    b. § 643(a)(2).
    c. § 2503(g)(2)(A).

31. **LO.1** Log on to **waysandmeans.house.gov** (the website for the House Ways and Means Committee of the U.S. House of Representatives), and answer the following questions:
    a. Who is the Chair of the committee? What district does he or she represent?
    b. What is the total number of members on the committee? How many are representatives of each party (Democratic and Republican)?
    c. Locate and summarize the history of the committee.
    d. The Ways and Means Committee has several subcommittees. Identify three of these subcommittees.

Bridge Discipline

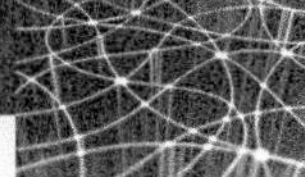

1. Comment on these statements.
    a. The tax law is created and administered in the same way as other Federal laws.
    b. Most taxpayers find it too expensive and time-consuming to sue the government in a tax dispute.
2. Using the title "The Future of Tax Research in the Era of Artificial Intelligence," write a two-page paper to submit in your accounting information systems or data analytics course. Find examples of AI uses that might be suitable for tax research, address issues and opportunities of this approach to research, and describe any changes needed to the skills and knowledge of a tax adviser when AI is used in the tax research process. Communications Data Analytics
3. Develop an outline from which you will deliver a 10-minute talk to the local Chamber of Commerce, with the title "Regulation of the Tax Profession in the 21st Century." Use no more than four PowerPoint slides for your talk, and discuss what the business community now needs with respect to oversight of a stable, yet productive revenue-raising system. Include administrative developments of the last two years in your research. Communications
4. A friend of yours, who is a philosophy major, observed you reading this chapter and declares that all tax research is "immoral." She says that tax research enables people with substantial assets to shift the burden of financing public expenditures to those who "get up every morning, go to work, play by the rules, and pay their bills." How do you respond? Ethics and Equity

Research Problems

Note: Solutions to the Research Problems can be prepared by using the Thomson Reuters Checkpoint™ online tax research database, which accompanies this textbook. Solutions can also be prepared by using research materials found in a typical tax library.

Research Problem 1. Locate the following items, and e-mail to your professor a brief summary of the results. Communications
    a. *Terrell*, T.C.Memo. 2016–85.
    b. Ltr.Rul. 200231003.
    c. Action on Decision 2019–01, February 19, 2019.

Research Problem 2. Locate the following Code citations, and list the subchapter and part in which it is located. Then give a brief description of each.

a. § 708(a).

b. § 1371(a).

c. § 2503(a).

Communications

Research Problem 3. Locate the following Regulations, and give a brief topical description of each. Summarize your comments in an e-mail to your instructor.

a. Reg. § 1.170A–4A(b)(2)(ii)(C).

b. Reg. § 1.672(b)–1.

c. Reg. § 1.1031(a)–3(a).

Research Problem 4. Determine the missing data in these court decisions and rulings.

a. *Higgins v. Comm.*, 312 U.S. __________ (1941).

b. *Talen v. U.S.*, 355 F.Supp.2d 22 (D.Ct. D.C., __________).

c. Rev.Rul. 2008–18, 2008–13 I.R.B.__________.

d. *Pahl v. Comm.*, 150 F.3d 1124 (CA–9, __________).

e. *Veterinary Surgical Consultants PC*, 117 T.C.__________ (2001).

f. *Yeagle Drywall Co.*, T.C.Memo. 2001__________.

Research Problem 5. Locate the following U.S. Tax Court case: *Thomas J. Green, Jr.*, 59 T.C. 456 (1972). Briefly describe the issue in the case, and explain what the U.S. Tax Court said about using IRS publications to support a research conclusion.

Research Problem 6. Can a U.S. Tax Court Small Cases decision be treated as a precedent by other taxpayers? Explain.

Partial list of research aids:
§ 7463(b).
Maria Antionette Walton Mitchell, T.C. Summary Opinion 2004–160.

Research Problem 7. Find *Kathryn Bernal*, 120 T.C. 102 (2003), and answer the following questions.

a. What was the docket number?

b. When was the dispute filed?

c. Who is the respondent?

d. Who was the attorney for the taxpayers?

e. Who was the judge who wrote the opinion?

f. What was the disposition of the dispute?

Communications

Research Problem 8. Find three blogs related to tax practice. In a one-page document, list the URLs for each blog and the general topical areas addressed at each. Pick one posting from one of the blogs, and summarize it. Then assess the quality of the blog from the standpoint of how easy it is to find and use. Send your document to the others in your course.

Communications

Research Problem 9. Find one instance of each of the following using a nonsubscription internet site or an online library at your school. In an e-mail to your professor, give a full citation for the document and describe how you found it.

a. Letter Ruling.

b. Action on Decision.

c. IRS Notice.

d. Revenue Ruling.

e. Revenue Procedure.

f. Code Section.

g. Tax Regulation.

h. Tax treaty.

i. U.S. Tax Court Summary Opinion.

j. U.S. Tax Court Regular decision.

Chapter 3

Taxes in the Financial Statements

Learning Objectives: *After completing Chapter 3, you should be able to:*

- **LO.1** Identify and characterize common book-tax differences.
- **LO.2** Explain the basic principles of Accounting Standards Codification (ASC) 740.
- **LO.3** Determine current tax expense.
- **LO.4** Determine deferred tax expense.
- **LO.5** Describe the purpose of the valuation allowance, when it is used, and its impact on tax expense.
- **LO.6** Identify and interpret the tax-related information disclosed in the financial statement footnotes.
- **LO.7** Apply the GAAP standards concerning tax uncertainties and tax law changes.
- **LO.8** Use financial statement income tax information to benchmark a company's tax position.

Chapter Outline

Tax Talk *Truth is, figuring out how much tax a company actually pays is impossible.... Tax disclosure is just inscrutable.* —Robert Willens

The Big Picture

Taxes in the Financial Statements

Raymond Jones, the CEO of Arctic Corporation, would like some help reconciling the amount of income tax expense on Arctic's financial statements with the amount of income tax reported on the company's corporate income tax return for its first year of operations. Mr. Jones does not understand why he can't simply multiply the financial statement income by the Federal 21 percent income tax rate to get the tax expense recognized in the income statement. Although the financial statements show book income before tax of $21.5 million, the reported income tax expense is only $5 million. In addition, the corporate Federal income tax return reports taxable income of $19 million and Federal income taxes payable of $3.99 million ($19 million × 21%).

Without knowing the specifics of the company's financial statements, does Arctic's situation look reasonable? What causes the difference between the taxes shown in the financial statements and the taxes due on the tax return?

Read the chapter and formulate your response.

Taxes are not a direct operating cost of producing the goods or services sold by a business enterprise. Nonetheless, taxes can significantly affect the income available to the owners of a business, and businesses may engage in significant tax planning activities to minimize the taxes owed. In addition, an entity's tax liability can convey much more to interested parties than simply the tax costs of conducting its business. For example, depending on one's perspective, a corporation's tax expense may indicate the extent to which the corporation engages in activities Congress has chosen to encourage through the tax law, how much effort they have devoted to aggressive tax planning, how good a corporate citizen they are, or how efficiently the business is managed. As a result, a number of parties (including investors and policymakers) are interested in the amount of income taxes incurred by corporations. However, because tax returns are not available to the general public, the primary source of information about a corporation's income tax liability is its financial statements. Because of their nature and significance, income taxes are separately reported in a corporation's income statement immediately following operating income.

However, due to the different goals underlying financial reporting and the tax law, the income tax expense reported in a corporation's financial statements will seldom equal the income tax liability reported on its tax return for the same reporting period. Interpreting the expense reported in the financial statements can be difficult for those not well versed in both financial accounting and tax law. Further, because of the complexities that arise in trying to provide tax-related information that achieves the goals of financial reporting and the limited number of professionals well versed in both financial accounting and tax law, the income tax expense reported in the financial statements may not always be reliable. Misreported income tax expense regularly accounts for a significant portion of financial statement restatements. In addition, the process of determining the reported income tax expense is among the top sources of material weaknesses in financial reporting systems. An understanding of the income tax expense reported in financial statements is important for financial statement preparers as well as users. Because accounting for income taxes requires an understanding of both financial reporting and tax law, those with a deep understanding of tax accounting are in great demand. This chapter covers the basics of income tax accounting that should be relevant for most accounting professionals, including those engaged in financial reporting, auditing, and tax planning, as well as for finance professionals, investors, and policymakers who must interpret the income tax expense reported in financial statements.

3-1 Accounting for Income Taxes—Basic Principles

Although both the financial reporting and tax systems focus heavily on the measurement of income, the systems serve very different purposes. Financial statements, prepared using **generally accepted accounting principles (GAAP)**, are intended to provide its readers with information regarding the future cash flows expected to be generated by a business. Alternatively, the taxable income and tax liability reported by taxpayers, as determined by the tax law, are primarily intended to capture taxpayers' relative abilities to pay tax based on their current and past financial activities within the context of economic and social goals established by Congress. As a result, it is not unreasonable for the income tax expense reported in an entity's financial statements to differ from the income tax liability reported to the Federal government for the same time period covered by those financial statements.

LO.1

Identify and characterize common book-tax differences.

3-1a Book-Tax Differences

As a general rule, taxable income and pretax income reported in the financial statements (i.e., pretax "book income") are determined in a similar manner. However, recall that the concept of income serves different purposes for tax and financial reporting purposes. Because of these different purposes, many items impact taxable income and pretax book income differently. From a tax perspective, these differences may be viewed as either *favorable* or *unfavorable*. Favorable book-tax differences cause taxable income to be lower than book income, reducing a corporation's current tax liability. Conversely, unfavorable book-tax differences cause taxable income to be greater than book income, increasing a corporation's current tax liability.

In addition to their impact on current taxable income, book-tax differences also can be considered in terms of their impact on future taxable income. Some items included in the determination of book income are never included in the determination of taxable income and vice versa. For example, although interest income on state and municipal bonds and fines and penalties are included in the determination of book income, they are neither taxable (state and municipal bond interest) nor deductible (fines and penalties) for tax purposes. These differences in the determination of financial accounting and taxable income are referred to as book-tax **permanent differences**.

Other items are included in both financial and taxable income, but because they are accounted for using different accounting methods or by different applications of the accrual method of accounting, they are taken into account in different accounting periods. Although these items cause differences in current book and taxable income, over time, these differences will *reverse*, resulting in the same amount of cumulative income being recognized for both book and taxable income purposes. These differences are referred to as book-tax **temporary differences**. Sources of temporary differences include the use of different accounting methods required for specific items (e.g., using MACRS for tax purposes versus straight-line depreciation for books and using the direct write-off method for tax purposes versus the allowance method for book) as well as differences in the general application of the accrual method for book and tax (e.g., the economic performance requirement that must be met for expenses to be deductible for tax purposes).

1

Diff, Inc., has $1,000,000 of pretax book income in both 2022 and 2023 before considering the following:

- $2,000 of nondeductible lobbying expenses incurred in 2022.
- A $10,000 lawsuit filed against it in 2022. The company's attorneys decided in 2022 that the company would probably be found liable for the full $10,000, but the suit was not settled and the $10,000 not paid until 2023. Although the settlement reduced book income in 2022, it is not deductible until 2023.

Diff's 2022 and 2023 book and taxable income would be computed as follows.

2022

	Book Income	Taxable Income	Book-Tax Difference Favorable/(Unfavorable)
Preliminary pretax book income	$1,000,000	$1,000,000	$ -0-
Lobbying expenses	(2,000)	-0-	(2,000)
Lawsuit settlement	(10,000)	-0-	(10,000)
Net income	$ 988,000	$1,000,000	($12,000)

2023

	Book Income	Taxable Income	Book-Tax Difference Favorable/(Unfavorable)
Preliminary pretax book income	$1,000,000	$1,000,000	$ -0-
Lobbying expenses	-0-	-0-	-0-
Lawsuit settlement	-0-	(10,000)	10,000
Net income	$1,000,000	$ 990,000	$10,000

continued

The lobbying expenses represent a permanent, unfavorable book-tax difference, increasing Diff's 2022 taxable income relative to its book income but having no future impact on either. The lawsuit settlement also represents an unfavorable book-tax difference in 2022, increasing taxable income relative to book income. However, it is a temporary difference since it reverses in 2023 when the payment is deducted, creating a favorable book-tax difference in 2023.

The Big Picture

Example 2

Return to the facts of *The Big Picture* on p. 3-1. Arctic, Inc., has pretax book income of $25,000,000, but it reports taxable income of only $19,000,000 on its tax return. Arctic has net positive book-tax differences of $6,000,000 for the year. Such a difference should not be a surprise given the different purposes for which book income and taxable income are used.

Given the differing goals of financial reporting and income taxation, many book-tax differences exist. A few of the more prominent differences, examined more closely later in this text, are described below. Temporary differences include the following:

- *Accrued income and expenses.* Although most income and expense items are recognized for tax and book purposes in the same period, a number of items may be accounted for in different tax years or accounting periods. In general, the tax law does not allow the use of estimates or reserves, as is common under GAAP. For example, for book purposes, the costs of honoring warranties on products sold by a taxpayer are estimated and expensed in the year the product is sold. However, due to the economic performance test, they are not deductible for tax purposes until the services are provided. The same is true of bad debts, which are expensed using the reserve method for financial reporting purposes but cannot be deducted for tax purposes until actually written off. Similarly, different methods regarding the timing of income recognition may create temporary differences. For instance, changes in the value of investments (i.e., unrealized gains and losses) are often recognized in the financial statements in the year of the change, whereas they are only recognized for tax purposes upon the sale or other disposition of the investments.
- *Depreciation on fixed assets.* Taxpayers may use an accelerated depreciation method for tax purposes [e.g., the modified accelerated cost recovery system (MACRS)] but adopt the straight-line method for book purposes. Even if identical methods are used, the period over which the asset is depreciated is likely to differ between book and tax (with tax recovery periods often shorter than an asset's estimated useful live used to calculate book depreciation). As a result, tax rules can allow the acceleration of the deductions over the asset's life.
- *Net operating losses.* Taxable income for the year cannot be less than zero, but operating losses from one tax year may be "carried over" (i.e., used to offset taxable income in another tax year). No such loss carryovers are used under GAAP; GAAP losses are reported as negative income amounts in the year incurred. As a result, the losses incurred in one year for book purposes may be used as a deduction for tax purposes in a different year.
- *Intangible assets.* Goodwill and some other intangibles are not amortizable for book purposes. Instead, GAAP requires an annual determination of whether the intangible asset has suffered a reduction in value (i.e., impairment).[1] If an intangible has suffered an impairment, a current expense is required to reduce the asset's book value to its economic value. For tax purposes, many intangibles (including goodwill) can be amortized over 15 years.[2]

[1] *Intangibles—Goodwill and Other*, ASC 350.

[2] § 197.

Permanent differences include the following:

- *Nontaxable income.* Due to social or economic reasons, some types of income are never included in gross income. A common example is municipal bond interest, which is included in income for book purposes even though it is nontaxable.
- *Nondeductible expenses.* Due to various policy or political concerns, some expenses are never deductible. For example, a portion of business meals, all entertainment expenses (with limited exceptions), and certain penalties are not deductible for tax purposes, but they are fully expensed in arriving at book income.
- *Tax credits.* Although credits such as the research activities credit do not reduce taxable income, they do reduce a company's tax liability directly. Because they have no corresponding impact on pre-tax book income, they are considered permanent book-tax differences.

Concept Summary 3.1 summarizes the sources of typical corporate book-tax differences.

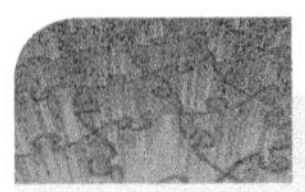

Concept Summary 3.1

Common Book-Tax Differences

Temporary Differences	Permanent Differences

• Accelerated recognition of unearned revenues.
• Expenses failing the *all events* or *economic performance* tests.
• Accelerated depreciation of fixed assets.
• Amortization of goodwill.
	• Nontaxable income (e.g., state/municipal bond interest; life insurance proceeds).
	• Nondeductible expenses:
	  ○ Meals and entertainment.
	  ○ Fines and penalties.
	  ○ Certain executive compensation.
	• Credits:
	  ○ Research and development credit.

A discussion of the book-tax differences related to goodwill can be found on this book's companion website: www.cengage.com

1 Digging Deeper 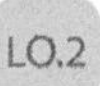

3-1b Generally Accepted Accounting Principles and ASC 740

LO.2

Explain the basic principles of Accounting Standards Codification (ASC) 740.

Accounting for income taxes under GAAP is governed by Accounting Standards Codification (ASC) 740. Consistent with most financial accounting principles, **ASC 740** emphasizes the balance sheet, taking a **balance sheet approach** to the accounting for income taxes. Specifically, it requires that the balance sheet reflect both a current liability related to all income taxes (Federal, state and local, and foreign) reflected on its tax returns for the year as well as a **deferred tax liability** or **deferred tax asset** for the future tax effects of items included in its current and prior financial statements but not in taxable income (i.e., temporary book-tax differences). That is, ASC 740 adopts a comprehensive inter-period allocation approach to income taxes, requiring that all income taxes that relate to the income reported in the current financial statements be reported in those same financial statements regardless of when they might be legally due under the tax law. The sum of the liabilities reflected on the current tax returns represents a corporation's **current tax expense** while the future tax effects related to its temporary book-tax differences lead to the recognition of either a **deferred tax expense** or **deferred tax benefit**.

Example 3

In 2022, PanCo, Inc., earns $100,000 in pretax book income before considering a $30,000 gain realized on an installment sale. This gain represents a favorable, temporary book-tax difference. For financial reporting purposes, the entire $30,000 gain is recognized in current-year income. However, for tax purposes, the gain can be recognized over the periods in which the sales proceeds are collected. Assuming that the proceeds will be collected evenly over three years, beginning in 2022, PanCo will report the installment sale gain as follows.

	Book Income	Taxable Income
2022	$30,000	$10,000
2023	–0–	10,000
2024	–0–	10,000
	$30,000	$30,000

In 2022, PanCo will report $130,000 ($100,000 + $30,000 gain) of pretax book income. However, it will report only $110,000 ($100,000 + $10,000 gain) of taxable income and pay $23,100 ($110,000 × 21%) of income taxes for the year. Therefore, its financial statements will reflect a current tax liability, and current tax expense, of $23,100.

However, PanCo also will report a deferred tax liability, and deferred tax expense, of $4,200 ($20,000 deferred gain × 21%). The total tax expense reported in the financial statements, $27,300 ($23,100 current tax expense + $4,200 deferred tax expense), captures the total income tax that will be paid on the $130,000 of pretax book income even though some of that tax expense is not yet due.

Note that in Example 3, the total tax expense reported in the financial statements is equal to the tax related to pretax book income. This is the intended result of ASC 740, which requires the recognition of the deferred tax liability and related expense. Due to the recording of the deferred tax expense, temporary differences will never cause the tax expense reported on the books to differ from what might be expected based on pretax book income. Even with a temporary difference, the total tax expense in the financial statements reflects taxes on the entire pretax book income, although some of that tax is deferred.

However, the same is not true for permanent book-tax differences. As a result, if there are permanent book-tax differences, tax expense cannot be determined simply by multiplying pretax book income by the tax rate.

Example 4

Referring back to Example 3, assume that PanCo's pretax book income included a $5,000 nondeductible fine. Its pretax book income would remain $130,000. However, its taxable income and related tax expense would be calculated as follows:

Pretax book income	$130,000
Book-tax permanent differences:	
Fines	5,000
Book-tax temporary differences:	
Gain deferred on installment sale	(20,000)
Taxable income	$115,000
Tax rate	× 21%
Current tax payable/expense	$ 24,150
Deferred tax expense (from Example 3)	4,200
Total tax expense	$ 28,350

Notice that in Example 4, total tax expense ($28,350) is greater than one might have expected based on pretax book income [$27,300 ($130,000 × 21%)]. This is due to the unfavorable, permanent book-tax difference ($5,000 × 21% = $1,050).

The Big Picture

Return to the facts of *The Big Picture* on p. 3-1. Mr. Jones is using Arctic's Federal tax rate to try to understand Arctic's tax expense. However, if Arctic operates in a state that imposes an income tax, the reported income tax expense will reflect state taxes as well.

The Big Picture

Return to the facts of *The Big Picture* on p. 3-1. Assume that Arctic's combined Federal and state tax rate is 25%. The tax expense reported in Arctic's income statement includes both current and deferred tax expense. Arctic's current tax expense is likely equal to the amount reported on both its Federal and state tax returns, or $4,750,000 ($19,000,000 × 25%). The remaining $250,000 of tax expense must be due to deferred taxes that relate to current-year pretax book income that is not yet includible in Federal taxable income. Mr. Jones should find a liability on the balance sheet for these deferred taxes.

The Big Picture

Return to the facts of *The Big Picture* on p. 3-1. If the difference between Arctic's pretax book income and taxable income were due only to temporary book-tax differences, one might expect its total reported tax expense to be $5,375,000 ($21,500,000 pretax book income × 25%). Given that total reported income tax expense is only $5,000,000, some of Arctic's book-tax differences must be permanent differences.

3-2 Capturing, Measuring, and Recording Tax Expense—The Provision Process

The process used to capture, measure, and record the tax expense reported in the financial statements, as well as the expense itself, is often referred to as the *tax provision*. As discussed previously, ASC 740 requires the reporting on the balance sheet of both a current tax liability (related to the liability reflected in a corporation's current tax returns) and a deferred asset or liability (related to the future tax consequences of items reported in the current or prior financial statements). However, while a corporation may have to issue its financial statements, including the tax provision, soon after year end, its tax returns may not be filed until much later.[3] In this case, estimates of book-tax differences and the current and deferred tax liabilities must be made as part of the tax provision process before the tax return is filed.

[3]Although the due date for a Federal corporate income tax return is three and one-half months after year-end (April 15 for a calendar year corporation), many corporations request an extension of time to file the tax return (using Form 7004). This six-month extension request is automatically approved by the IRS. While the due date for filing the tax return is extended, any taxes due must be paid by the original due date of the return.

LO.3

Determine current tax expense.

3-2a Current Tax Expense

Determining current tax expense begins with estimating the current tax liabilities to be reflected on the corporation's tax returns. This includes three steps:

1. Identifying (and adjusting pretax book income for) all permanent and temporary book-tax differences related to items included in current pretax book income.
2. Identifying (and adjusting pretax book income for) any tax carryovers that may impact current taxable income (e.g., capital losses, charitable contributions, NOLs).
3. Identifying (and reducing the current tax liability for) any tax credits that may be available but have no impact on either book or taxable income.

Exhibit 3.1 illustrates the process for determining current tax expense. Note that the book-tax differences captured in steps 1 and 2 above (with the exception of an NOL carryover) are the same items that are expected to appear in Schedule M–1 (see Exhibit 3.2) or Schedule M–3 (reproduced in Appendix B) of the corporation's Federal tax return when it is eventually filed.

Exhibit 3.1 Current Tax Expense (Simplified)

	Pretax book income
±	Schedule M–1/M–3 adjustments
	Taxable income before NOLs
–	NOL carryforwards
	Taxable income
×	Applicable tax rate
	Current tax expense (provision) before tax credits
–	Tax credits
	Current tax expense (provision)

Exhibit 3.2 Schedule M–1

Schedule M-1 Reconciliation of Income (Loss) per Books With Income per Return

Note: The corporation may be required to file Schedule M-3. See instructions.

1	Net income (loss) per books		7	Income recorded on books this year not included on this return (itemize): Tax-exempt interest $ ________	
2	Federal income tax per books				
3	Excess of capital losses over capital gains .				
4	Income subject to tax not recorded on books this year (itemize): ________		8	Deductions on this return not charged against book income this year (itemize):	
5	Expenses recorded on books this year not deducted on this return (itemize):		a	Depreciation . . $ ________	
a	Depreciation . . . . $ ________		b	Charitable contributions $ ________	
b	Charitable contributions . $ ________				
c	Travel and entertainment . $ ________				
			9	Add lines 7 and 8	
6	Add lines 1 through 5		10	Income (page 1, line 28)—line 6 less line 9	

Digging Deeper 2 **A discussion of Schedule M–3 can be found on this book's companion website:** www.cengage.com

Global Tax Issues — Accounting for Income Taxes in International Standards

The Financial Accounting Standards Board (FASB) and international accounting standard setters have worked for decades to enhance the comparability of financial statements prepared under U.S. GAAP and those prepared under international accounting standards. Currently, the FASB is a member of the Accounting Standards Advisory Forum (ASAF), which advises the International Accounting Standards Board (IASB) as it sets international standards.

Over time, accounting for income taxes under U.S. GAAP and International Financial Reporting Standards (IFRS) have converged. Nevertheless, several significant differences exist between ASC 740 and International Accounting Standards (IAS) 12. These include the thresholds for recognition and approach to valuation allowances and the measurement of uncertain tax positions.

The Big Picture

Return to the facts of *The Big Picture* on p. 3-1. To better understand Arctic's current tax expense, Mr. Jones should refer to Arctic's state tax return as well as its Federal return. To learn why the taxes reported on those returns are not equal to Arctic's pretax book income times 25% (Arctic's combined Federal and state tax rate), Mr. Jones can refer to Schedule M–1 or Schedule M–3 of Form 1120 to find the temporary and permanent book-tax differences. Any tax credits claimed by Arctic also will have to be factored into his analysis.

3-2b Deferred Tax Expense

Determine deferred tax expense.

Companies may report either a deferred tax expense or a deferred tax benefit in their income statement. A deferred tax expense is the result of a deferred tax liability (a future tax liability related to transactions already reflected in the financial statements). Similarly, a deferred tax benefit is the result of a deferred tax asset (future tax savings related to transactions already reflected in the financial statements).

Financial Disclosure Insights — The Book-Tax Income Gap

According to a recent study by the Institute on Taxation and Economic Policy, 55 Fortune 500 companies reported profits to their shareholders in 2020 yet paid zero or negative Federal corporate income taxes over the same period. These companies include FedEx, Nike, and Dish Network. Thirty-nine profitable Fortune 500 companies paid no taxes from 2018–2020, the first three years following the Tax Cuts and Jobs Act of 2017. Another 73 reported effective tax rates less than half that of the 21 percent U.S. statutory rate.

The study concluded that the companies were using a diverse array of legal means to eliminate their tax liabilities, including the following:

- Various forms of accelerated depreciation.
- Stock options.
- Alternative energy subsidies (e.g., subsidies for pursuing renewable energy).
- The research and development tax credit.

Source: *Corporate Tax Avoidance Under the Tax Cuts and Jobs Act* (**itep.org/corporate-tax-avoidance-under-the-tax-cuts-and-jobs-act/**).

Deferred tax assets and liabilities can be generated in several ways. The most common way is the use of different accounting methods for financial reporting and taxable income. For most large corporations, the accrual method generally is required for both financial reporting and tax purposes. However, in several situations, the accrual method is applied differently in determining book and taxable income. Further, different accounting methods may be used for specific transactions (e.g., the installment method is available for tax purposes in certain situations).

Generally, a *deferred tax asset* is produced when:

- The recognition of revenue is accelerated for tax purposes relative to book (e.g., the recognition of unearned revenues for tax earlier than book), or
- The deductibility of an expense reported in the financial statements is deferred for tax purposes (e.g., an expense reported in the financial statements has not yet met the economic performance test for tax).

Generally, a *deferred tax liability* is produced when:

- The recognition of revenue is deferred for tax purposes relative to book (e.g., when installment sale treatment is available for tax purposes but not for book), or
- The deductibility of an expense reported in the financial statements is accelerated for tax purposes (e.g., the use of accelerated cost recovery methods for tax purposes).

Identifying and Measuring Deferred Tax Assets and Liabilities

As discussed above, an accounting method difference that causes current book and taxable income to differ will produce both a deferred tax asset or liability on the balance sheet and a deferred tax benefit or expense on the income statement. Recall that a deferred tax benefit or expense relates to the *future* tax consequences attributable to events reported in the current or prior financial statements, not the current consequences of book-tax differences. As you will see, not all future tax benefits and expenses related to transactions already recorded in the financial statements are the result of accounting method differences. As a result, successfully identifying all deferred tax assets and liabilities requires more than the identification of current differences in book and taxable income.

A review of financial accounting principles may help at this point. Recall the basic accounting equation:

Assets = Liabilities + Owners' Equity

The equation suggests that income (which represents a change in owners' equity) must be accompanied by a similar change in assets or liabilities.

Imagine that we simultaneously maintain an accounting equation (or a set of double-entry books and records) for tax purposes using tax accounting methods rather than GAAP. In this system, assets and liabilities would be measured by their tax adjusted bases (AB) rather than their net book value (NBV). Any taxable income would similarly correspond to a change in the bases of assets and liabilities.[4] If the same accounting methods were used for financial reporting and tax purposes, assets, liabilities, and income would be the same in both equations (i.e., there would be no book-tax differences). However, the use of different methods results in not only book-tax differences in income but also differences in the tax ABs and the NBVs of assets and liabilities. Since it is the use of assets and the incurrence of liabilities that produce future income, it is these differences in the current NBV and tax ABs of assets and liabilities that will cause differences in future financial reporting and taxable income and, therefore, related deferred tax assets and liabilities.

[4]Note that although we typically do not consider a liability to have a tax basis, the idea is to capture what would be on the balance sheet if the taxpayer were using a double-entry accounting system for tax purposes.

Deferred Tax Assets and Liabilities

Orange, Inc., acquired an asset during the current year. Current-year book depreciation, using the straight-line method over the asset's useful life, is $100. However, MACRS produces a $500 cost recovery deduction for tax purposes. The impact of the asset's depreciation for book and tax purposes would be reflected in journal entries as follows:

	Debit	Credit
Book		
Depreciation expense	$100	
Net book value (NBV) of asset		$100
Tax		
Cost recovery deduction	$500	
Tax adjusted basis (AB) of asset		$500
Difference between NBV and AB of asset		$400

The $400 difference in the current net book value and tax adjusted basis of the asset will result in future taxable income being $400 higher than future book income. This will lead to a tax liability higher than what would relate to future book income, creating a *deferred tax liability*.

Blue, Inc., sells products subject to a two-year warranty. Blue estimates that it will spend $10,000 in the future to make repairs pursuant to warranties on products it sold in the current year. For book purposes, it accrues this $10,000 as a current-year expense. However, because there has been no economic performance, the estimated expenses are not currently deductible. This would be reflected in book and tax journal entries as follows:

	Debit	Credit
Book		
Warranty expense	$10,000	
Warranty liability (NBV)		$10,000
Tax		
Warranty expense	$ 0	
Warranty liability (AB)		$ 0
Difference between NBV and AB of liability		$10,000

The $10,000 difference in the net book value and tax adjusted basis of the liability reflects the $10,000 tax deduction available to Blue in the future for the expense reflected on the books currently. This future deduction represents a *deferred tax asset*.

Although accounting method differences produce NBV-AB differences (and, as a result, deferred tax assets and liabilities), not all deferred tax assets and liabilities are the result of accounting method differences. As a result, ASC 740 defines *temporary differences*, to which deferred tax assets and liabilities relate, as differences in the net book value and tax adjusted basis of a corporation's assets and liabilities (not as differences in current book and taxable income and expenses). Accordingly, the tax provision process requires the identification and measurement of these differences between net book value and tax adjusted basis. ASC 740 refers to temporary differences that lead to deferred tax assets as *deductible differences* while those that lead to deferred tax liabilities are referred to as *taxable differences*.

Of course, although the differences in the net book value and tax adjusted bases of a company's assets and liabilities lead to deferred tax assets and liabilities, these temporary differences do not accurately capture those deferred tax assets and liabilities. Rather, we are interested in the future tax consequences of these differences. As a result, these differences must be multiplied by the appropriate tax rate to capture a corporation's deferred tax assets and liabilities.

The appropriate tax rate is the one that, based on current tax law at the balance sheet date, is expected to apply when the tax consequences will be realized or when the temporary difference reverses. If no future changes in tax rates have been enacted as of the balance sheet date, this is the tax rate currently in effect. If, however, on the balance sheet date, legislation has been adopted that will modify the tax rate that is in effect when a deferred tax asset or liability is realized, then the modified future tax rate should be used in measuring deferred tax assets and liabilities.

Assume that in November 2023, Congress passes a law that increases the Federal corporate income tax rate from 21% to 25% for all taxable years beginning after December 31, 2023. AM, Inc., uses a calendar year for tax and financial reporting purposes. It will apply a tax rate of 21% to its 2023 taxable income to determine its 2023 tax liability, which will be reported as its current tax expense in its financial statements.

However, it will use a 25% rate to measure any deferred tax assets and liabilities reported in its 2023 financial statements, since that will be the rate applied to its temporary book-tax differences when they are eventually realized.

Finally, realize the deferred tax asset or liability that is identified exists as of the current balance sheet date. Recall that income and expenses are the result of changes in assets and liabilities during the year. As a result, a company's deferred tax benefit or expense for the year is the *change* in its deferred tax assets and liabilities from the beginning of the year to the end of the year. Examples 12 and 13 illustrate the determination of deferred tax expense.

Deferred Tax Expense

Example 12

PJ Enterprises began operations in 2022 and earned pretax book income of $500,000 in its first year of operations. In performing its 2022 tax provision, PJ noted the following temporary differences.

- In January 2022, PJ purchased equipment at a cost of $800,000. For book purposes, PJ depreciated the asset on a straight-line basis over 10 years, resulting in $80,000 of depreciation expense in 2022. For tax purposes, PJ was able to use a combination of accelerated cost recovery methods and deducted $720,000 in 2022.
- Most of PJ's sales are on account. At the end of 2022, it had established an allowance for uncollectible accounts of $30,000. For tax purposes, PJ must use the direct write-off method to account for uncollectible accounts, and no write-offs occurred during 2022.

PJ operates in a state with an income tax, making its combined Federal and state tax rate equal to 25%. No laws have been passed that will change the tax rates faced by PJ in the future. The provision for PJ's 2022 deferred tax expense was determined as follows.

Partial Balance Sheet (December 31, 2022)

	Net Book Value	Tax Adjusted Basis	Temporary Difference	Combined Tax Rate	Deferred Tax Asset/(Liability)
Accounts receivable (net of allowance for uncollectible accounts)	$100,000	$130,000	$ 30,000	25%	$ 7,500
Equipment	720,000	80,000	640,000	25%	(160,000)
Net deferred tax liability					($152,500)

At the end of 2022, PJ had a net deferred tax liability of $152,500, consisting of a $7,500 deferred tax asset (for the NBV–AB difference related to the accounts receivable) and a $160,000 deferred tax liability (for the NBV–AB difference related to the equipment). PJ made the following journal entry to record its 2022 deferred tax expense.

Deferred tax expense (income statement)	$152,500	
Deferred tax liability (balance sheet)		$152,500

Deferred Tax Expense

PJ Enterprises, from Example 12, earned pretax book income of $600,000 in 2023. PJ continues to use the equipment it acquired in 2022 and to depreciate it on a straight-line basis over 10 years. For tax purposes, PJ can recover $32,000 of the equipment's cost in 2023. At the end of 2023, it estimates that $45,000 of its accounts receivable will be uncollectible. The provision for PJ's 2023 deferred income tax expense is determined as follows.

Partial Balance Sheet (December 31, 2023)

	Net Book Value	Tax Adjusted Basis	Temporary Difference	Combined Tax Rate	Deferred Tax Asset/(Liability)
Accounts receivable (net of allowance for uncollectible accounts)	$150,000	$195,000	$ 45,000	25%	$ 11,250
Equipment	640,000	48,000	592,000	25%	(148,000)
Net deferred tax liability					($136,750)

At the end of 2023, PJ has a net deferred tax liability of $136,750, consisting of an $11,250 deferred tax asset (for the NBV–AB difference related to the accounts receivable) and a $148,000 deferred tax liability (for the NBV–AB difference related to the equipment).

PJ must reduce the $152,500 deferred tax liability recorded in 2022 to $136,750, with the $15,750 liability reduction representing a deferred tax benefit. PJ would make the following journal entry to record its 2022 deferred taxes.

Deferred tax liability (balance sheet)	$15,750	
Deferred tax benefit (income statement)		$15,750

After the above journal entry, PJ's 2023 balance sheet will reflect a deferred tax liability of $136,750.

There are those who would argue that recognizing deferred taxes makes little sense. After all, unlike most liabilities recorded in the financial statements, they are not legally enforceable. Should a corporation discontinue its operations, it would not be required to pay its deferred tax liability. Similarly, even if the business continues, the liability may never be settled. For example, a deferred tax liability related to accelerated cost recovery will continue to grow as long as a company continues to grow or its costs continue to rise.

However, failure to recognize deferred taxes can be misleading for financial statement users for at least two reasons. First, it would overstate a corporation's net assets. Recall that a basic premise of financial accounting is that an entity is a going concern and that its assets represent benefits that will be realized at some time in the future. If the adjusted basis of those assets is lower than their net book value, the benefit ultimately realized will be lower than what is reflected on the books.

Assume that Living the Life (LtL), Inc.'s only noncash asset is an apartment building. The fair market value and net book value of the building is $1,000,000. LtL has no liabilities. LtL faces a combined Federal and state tax rate of 25%. Its balance sheet reflects the following:

Assets		Liabilities and Owners' Equity	
Cash	$ 250,000	Liabilities	$ -0-
Real estate	1,000,000	Owners' equity	1,250,000
Total assets	$1,250,000	Total liabilities and owners' equity	$1,250,000

continued

A private investment group purchases all of the stock of LtL for $1,250,000 (the fair market value of its assets). When the building is sold, they learn that its tax adjusted basis is $0, resulting in a $1,000,000 taxable gain. After paying Federal and state taxes on the sale at a combined rate of 25%, LtL is left with only $1,000,000 of cash (rather than the $1,250,000 value expected based on the fair market value of the assets). The failure to record the deferred tax liability related to the property resulted in an overstatement of LtL's assets.

The failure to record deferred taxes also will provide an unreliable depiction of a corporation's current income and, therefore, its future income and cash flows.

Current, Inc., reported $1,000,000 of pretax operating income in 2022, its first year of operations. Current operated in a state with a 4% income tax, making its combined Federal and state tax rate 25%. However, because of several tax incentives available to businesses in its industry (all temporary book-tax differences), Current was able to reduce its 2022 taxable income to $600,000 and its combined Federal and state tax liability to $150,000. Ignoring deferred taxes, Current reported $850,000 of net income in its financial statements ($1,000,000 book income − $150,000 current tax expense).

This was higher than potential investors had anticipated, and several purchased Current stock. In 2023, Current's business grew 25% and it earned $1,250,000 of pretax operating income. However, the $400,000 of temporary book-tax differences that had reduced its 2022 tax liability reversed in 2023. As a result, Current paid taxes of $412,500 [($1,250,000 2023 pretax book income + $400,000) × 25%], much more than investors had anticipated. Investors were surprised and disappointed when Current's net income fell to $837,500 ($1,250,000 − $412,500 current tax expense).

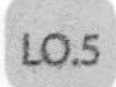

Describe the purpose of the valuation allowance, when it is used, and its impact on tax expense.

3-2c The Valuation Allowance

As discussed previously, a corporation may have deferred tax assets as well as deferred tax liabilities. Assets generally are considered to be probable future economic benefits available to an entity that result from past transactions or events.[5] Although a future benefit need not be certain for it to be recognized as an asset in the financial statements, recognition requires a reasonable expectation that a future benefit will be realized. ASC 740 specifically requires that a deferred tax asset not be recognized unless it is *more likely than not* (a greater than 50 percent likelihood) that a future tax benefit will eventually be realized.[6]

Recognizing Deferred Tax Assets

Pear, Inc., reported pretax book income and taxable income of $2,000,000 in 2022 (i.e., there are no temporary or permanent differences) and a current Federal income tax liability for the year of $420,000 before tax credits ($2,000,000 × 21%). During the year, Pear earned $100,000 in general business credits that it is not able to use on its 2022 tax return.

Pear's management believes it is *more likely than not* that Pear will be able to use the $100,000 of tax credits within the next 20 years (i.e., before they expire). Consequently, the future tax benefit of the tax credits is accounted for in the current-year book tax expense as a $100,000 deferred tax benefit.

The current and deferred tax expense are calculated as follows.

	Book	Tax
Current income tax expense/payable	$420,000	$420,000
Deferred tax expense (benefit)	(100,000)	
Total tax expense	$320,000	

[5] Statement of Financial Accounting Concepts No. 6.

[6] ASC 740-10-30-5(e).

Recognizing Deferred Tax Assets

Continue with the facts of Example 16. Pear records the following journal entry for the book income tax expense and deferred tax asset related to the expected use of the credits.

Income tax expense (provision)	$320,000	
Deferred tax asset	100,000	
Income tax payable		$420,000

Because the future benefits of the tax credit carryovers are considered more likely than not to be realized, they are recognized as a deferred tax asset and reduce Pear's current-year tax expense.

When a deferred tax asset does not meet the *more likely than not* threshold for recognition, ASC 740 requires that a valuation allowance be created. The **valuation allowance** is a contra-asset account that offsets all or a portion of the deferred tax asset (similar to the way an allowance for uncollectible accounts is used to reflect the net realizable value of accounts receivable).

Returning to Example 16, assume that Pear's management believes it is more likely than not that Pear will be able to use only $40,000 of the 2022 general business credits in any tax year, with the remaining $60,000 expiring unused. Pear will use a valuation allowance to reflect the realizability of the deferred tax asset, making the following journal entry in addition to the one made in Example 17.

Deferred tax expense	$60,000	
Valuation allowance		$60,000

As a result of recording the valuation allowance, Orange's tax expense will be increased to $380,000 as follows.

	Book		Tax
Current tax expense/payable		$420,000	$420,000
Deferred tax expense (benefit)			
Deferred tax asset	($100,000)		
Less: Valuation allowance	60,000	(40,000)	
Total tax expense		$380,000	

Finanical Disclosure Insights — Tax Losses and the Deferred Tax Asset

Although a current-year net operating loss (NOL) represents a failure of an entity's business model to some, others see it as a potential tax refund. But when an NOL hits the balance sheet as a deferred tax asset, the story is not over. The NOL creates or increases a deferred tax asset that may or may not be realizable in future periods: the key question for a financial analyst is whether the entity will generate enough taxable income in future years to create a positive tax liability that can be offset by the NOL carryover amount.

Both International Financial Reporting Standards (IFRS) and U.S. GAAP preclude recognizing a deferred tax asset when the asset is unlikely to be realized. However, unlike U.S. GAAP, IFRS does not make use of a valuation allowance. Rather, under IAS 12, a deferred tax asset is recorded only when it is "probable" (interpreted as "more likely than not") that the deferred tax amount will be realized, and then only to the extent of that probable amount. Thus, no offsetting valuation allowance is needed.

When evaluating the realizability of a deferred tax asset and the need for a valuation allowance, all relevant negative and positive evidence must be considered. Negative evidence (i.e., evidence suggesting that the deferred tax asset will not be realized) includes the following:[7]

- Cumulative losses in recent years.
- A history of loss or credit carryovers expiring unused.
- A carryback or carryforward period so brief as to practically preclude realization.
- An expectation of losses in upcoming years.
- Uncertainties that could adversely affect future profits on a continuing basis.

Given the existence of any negative evidence, offsetting positive evidence should be considered. Positive evidence (i.e., evidence that supports the realizability of the deferred tax asset) includes the following:[8]

- Existing contracts that will produce sufficient taxable income to allow realization of the deferred tax asset.
- Unrealized appreciation of assets.
- A strong earnings history exclusive of the loss that created the deferred tax asset.

ASC 740 requires that deferred tax assets be evaluated for realizability even if an entity reports an overall net deferred tax liability. In other words, although deferred tax assets and liabilities from different temporary differences may result in an overall net deferred tax liability, *the realizability of the deferred tax asset resulting from each temporary difference must be evaluated separately.*

The need for a valuation allowance is considered at each balance sheet date, including the one at the end of the period in which the deferred tax asset is first created as well as each subsequent period. An allowance is established whenever the deferred tax asset fails to meet the more likely than not test. Conversely, the allowance may be reduced or released when a deferred tax asset that had formerly failed to meet the recognition requirement is subsequently judged more likely than not to be realized.

Example 19

Referring back to Example 18, assume that in 2025, Pear signs sales contracts with several new customers. Based on the profits expected from the new contracts, Pear determines that it will generate enough income to fully utilize its general business credit carryforward before the end of the carryover period (i.e., Pear determines that it is *more likely than not*—a greater than 50% likelihood—that the general business credit carryforward will be used before it expires).

As a result, in 2025, Pear will release the valuation allowance it created in 2022, increasing its deferred tax assets and reducing its tax expense.

Valuation allowance	$60,000	
Deferred tax expense		$60,000

Notice that Pear is decreasing its tax expense in 2025 for tax credits that relate to transactions that occurred and were reported in the financial statements in 2022.

See Exhibit 3.3 for a summary of the calculation of the deferred tax expense (benefit).

Exhibit 3.3 Deferred Tax Expense (Benefit)

	NBV in excess of A.B. of assets at the balance sheet date
+	A.B. in excess of NBV of liabilities at the balance sheet date
	Cumulative net temporary book-tax differences
×	Applicable tax rate
	Net deferred tax liability (asset) at balance sheet date
−	Net deferred tax liability (asset) at prior balance sheet date
	Tentative deferred tax expense (benefit)
±	Change in valuation allowance
	Deferred tax expense (benefit)

[7]ASC 740-10-30-21.

[8]ASC 740-10-30-22.

Finanical Disclosure Insights — Releasing Valuation Allowances

If it is not *more likely than not* that a corporation will realize the benefits of a deferred tax asset, it must establish a valuation allowance. The result is to indirectly de-recognize the asset and increase reported tax expense. For example, if a taxpayer generates an NOL, it records a deferred tax asset for the future tax savings related to using the NOL. However, if the evidence suggests that it is *more likely than not* that all or a portion of the NOL never will be used, a valuation allowance must be recorded.

However, the valuation allowance may be subsequently reduced or eliminated, reducing reported tax expense and increasing book income, in a future period. To reduce the valuation allowance, the corporation's management must demonstrate that the facts and circumstances leading to the establishment of the valuation allowance have changed and there will be enough future taxable income to absorb the NOL in the future. Sources of future taxable income include reversals of temporary differences that will produce future taxable income, demonstrated efficiencies that will reduce future expenses, documented expected increases in sales (and capacity), and any other sources of future profits.

Taxpayers also may demonstrate that the adoption of new tax planning strategies will allow the use of deferred tax assets. The proposed tax strategies must be prudent and feasible in their execution, and the taxpayer must be willing to execute the strategy in a manner that will use the deferred tax assets. Such strategies might include the following:

- Slow down cost recovery deductions (e.g., by using straight-line methods or electing to capitalize expenditures).
- Sell off appreciated assets.
- Convert tax-exempt investments into taxable holdings.
- Change tax accounting methods (e.g., moving from LIFO to FIFO for inventories).

For example, assume that Pear, Inc., from Example 18, adopts new planning strategies in 2023 that will allow it ultimately to use all $100,000 of its general business credit carryforward. Pear earns $2,300,000 in book income before tax and reports $2,300,000 in taxable income in 2023 (i.e., there are no permanent or temporary differences). The current Federal income tax expense is $483,000 ($2,300,000 × 21%).

Based on new evidence (implementation of tax planning strategies), Pear's management determines that the entire $100,000 in credits will be used in the future before they expire. Accordingly, the $60,000 valuation allowance from 2022 is "released," and the tax benefit of this release affects the 2023 financial results as follows.

	Book	Tax
Income tax expense/payable	$423,000	$483,000
Current tax expense	$483,000	
Deferred tax expense	($ 60,000)	

Pear makes the following 2023 journal entry to record the book income tax expense and valuation allowance release related to the expected use of the credits.

Income tax expense (provision)	$423,000	
Valuation allowance	60,000	
Income tax payable		$483,000

Pear's effective tax rate for 2023 is 18.4% ($423,000/$2,300,000). Without the valuation allowance release, Pear's effective tax rate would have been 21% ($483,000/$2,300,000). This tax rate benefit is realized even though the $100,000 in credit carryforwards has yet to be used in Pear's tax return.

The Big Picture

Example 20

Return to the facts of *The Big Picture* on p. 3-1. Arctic Corporation's $3,000,000 deferred tax asset for an NOL carryforward has been offset by a $1,000,000 valuation allowance due to doubts over the levels of future sales and profitability.

But this year Arctic completed improvements to its inventory management system that are likely to increase the contribution margin of every product that Arctic sells. In addition, two of Arctic's largest customers have secured financing that will relieve the financial difficulties that have restricted them. In fact, Arctic just received purchase orders from those customers that will increase unit sales by 20% over the next 18 months. As a result, Arctic's management determines that a release of $200,000 of the valuation allowance in the current quarter can be supported.

Identify and interpret the tax-related information disclosed in the financial statement footnotes.

3-3 Tax Disclosures in the Financial Statements

As discussed previously, several tax-related items are recognized throughout the financial statements. Additional details regarding these items must be disclosed in the footnotes to those financial statements.

3-3a Presentation of Amounts Recognized in the Financial Statements

Deferred tax asset and liability accounts are treated as noncurrent items on the GAAP balance sheet.[9] A corporation may have both deferred tax assets and liabilities. The corporation should report the *net* deferred tax assets or liabilities related to any particular tax jurisdiction [e.g., the United States, state(s), and foreign jurisdiction(s)]. However, it should not offset assets and liabilities that relate to different jurisdictions. Therefore, a corporation operating in multiple taxing jurisdictions may report both a deferred tax asset and a deferred tax liability on its balance sheet.[10]

In its GAAP income statement, a corporation reports its total income tax expense that consists of both its current tax expense (or benefit) and the deferred tax expense (or benefit). The tax expense is further allocated among income from continuing operations, discontinued operations, other comprehensive income, and items directly impacting shareholders' equity. Amounts other than those relating to continuing operations generally are presented in the financial statements net of tax (i.e., without the related tax expense or benefit stated separately).

The Big Picture

Example 21

Return to the facts of The Big Picture on p 3-1. Even if Arctic has no permanent book-tax differences, the tax expense reported on its income statement may not equal 25% (its combined tax rate) of its pretax book income because part of that expense, or benefit, is netted with other items. Mr. Jones should determine whether Arctic is reporting sources of comprehensive income that appear below net income from continuing operations in the income statement (e.g., income from discontinued operations or other comprehensive income) or other items that directly impact shareholders' equity. If so, the tax attributed to these items should be disclosed in the related footnotes.

3-3b The Financial Statement Footnotes

The income tax footnote contains a wealth of information, including the following:[11]

- A breakdown of income between domestic and foreign sources.
- A breakdown of total tax expense by its current and deferred components.
- The deferred tax asset and liability associated with each source of temporary difference.
- The total valuation allowance applied against the deferred tax assets.
- A reconciliation of the reported tax expense (or effective tax rate) to the amount that would be expected based on pretax book income and the Federal statutory rate.
- A discussion of significant tax matters.

[9]ASC 740-10-45-4.

[10]ASC 740-10-45-6.

[11]The disclosures listed here apply to public entities. Nonpublic entities sometimes have fewer disclosure requirements.

3-3c The Effective Tax Rate Reconciliation

To provide readers of the financial statements more information about the reported tax expense, companies are required to disclose a reconciliation of the taxes reported in the income statement to what might be expected by a reader. Although this is often described as the tax **rate reconciliation**, a company may present a reconciliation of either:[12]

1. The tax expense it reports to the expense that would be expected based on its pretax income and the statutory rate of the country in which it is located, or
2. Its effective tax rate to its home country statutory rate.

For financial statement purposes, the *effective tax rate* refers to the total tax expense reported in the financial statements, whether currently payable or not, as a percentage of pretax book income. Reporting the deferred tax expense and deferred tax assets and liabilities ensures that the tax related to all income reported in the financial statements is included in tax expense. Since temporary book-tax differences will not cause the reported tax expense to differ from what might otherwise be expected, these items will not be included in the rate reconciliation. In addition to permanent book-tax differences, items that will cause the reported tax expense to differ from the expected tax expense, and the effective tax rate to differ from the statutory rate, include the following:

- Any change in the valuation allowance,
- Any change in deferred tax assets and liabilities due to a tax rate change,
- Any tax benefits resulting from available credits, and
- Any non-U.S. income tax expense or benefit (e.g., foreign and state income taxes).

Example 22

BoxCo, Inc., a domestic corporation, owns 100% of PaperCo, Ltd., a Macedonian corporation. The U.S. corporate tax rate is 21%; the Macedonian corporate tax rate is 10%. Book income, permanent and temporary differences, and current tax expense are computed as follows:

	BoxCo	PaperCo
Book income before tax	$300,000	$200,000
Permanent differences:		
Business meals expense	20,000	—
Municipal bond interest income	(50,000)	—
Book income after permanent differences	$270,000	$200,000
Temporary differences:		
Tax > book depreciation	(50,000)	—
Book > tax bad debt expense	10,000	—
Taxable income	$230,000	$200,000
Tax rate	× 21%	× 10%
Current tax expense	$ 48,300	$ 20,000

BoxCo will report current tax expense of $68,300 ($48,300 + $20,000).

BoxCo's deferred tax expense is determined by evaluating the change in its net deferred tax asset/liability during the year. To determine its deferred tax assets and liabilities, it identifies its temporary book-tax differences and determines the tax consequences of each. At the beginning of the year, BoxCo's deferred tax assets and liabilities were as follows:

	Net Book Value	Tax Adjusted Basis	Temporary Difference	Combined Tax Rate	Deferred Tax Asset/ (Liability)
Depreciable assets	$900,000	$750,000	($150,000)	21%	($31,500)
Accounts receivable	800,000	850,000	50,000	21%	10,500
Net deferred tax liability					($21,000)

continued

[12] ASC 740-10-50-12.

At the end of the year, BoxCo's deferred tax asset and liabilities are as follows.

	Net Book Value	Tax Adjusted Basis	Temporary Difference	Combined Tax Rate	Deferred Tax Asset/ (Liability)
Depreciable assets	$860,000	$660,000	($200,000)	21%	($42,000)
Accounts receivable	785,000	845,000	60,000	21%	12,600
Net deferred tax liability					($29,400)

BoxCo's deferred tax expense for the year is the $8,400 increase in its deferred tax liability ($29,400 − $21,000). Its total tax expense of $76,700 ($68,300 + $8,400) would be recognized in its income statement. The following details would be disclosed in its footnotes.

	Total Income
Domestic	$300,000
Foreign	200,000
	$500,000

	Tax Expense		
	Domestic	Foreign	Total
Current	$48,300	$20,000	$68,300
Deferred	8,400	–0–	8,400
	$56,700	$20,000	$76,700

	Deferred Tax Assets and Liabilities		
	Beginning of Year	End of Year	Change
Depreciable assets	($31,500)	($42,000)	($10,500)
Accounts receivable	10,500	12,600	2,100
Less: Valuation allowance	–0–	–0–	–0–
	($21,000)	($29,400)	($ 8,400)

	Effective Tax Rate Reconciliation	
	$	%**
Expected tax at U.S. statutory tax rate	$105,000	21.0%
Disallowed meals expense	4,200	0.8
Municipal bond interest	(10,500)	(2.1)
Foreign income taxed at less than U.S. rate	(22,000)*	(4.4)
Income tax expense (provision)	$ 76,700	15.3%

*$200,000 × (21% − 10%).

**The expected effective tax rate, rate changes attributable to permanent differences, and the actual effective tax rate are all determined by dividing the amount of tax shown by book income of $500,000.

Only permanent differences appear in the rate reconciliation. Temporary differences do not affect the *total* book income tax expense; they simply affect the amount of the tax expense that is current versus deferred.

The Big Picture

Example 23

Return to the facts of *The Big Picture* on p. 3-1. Arctic's total reported tax expense, $5,000,000, is not equal to what might be expected by applying the Federal tax rate of 21% to its pretax book income, or $4,515,000 ($21,500,000 × 21%). And given that Arctic's combined Federal and state income tax rate is 25%, one might expect to find book tax expense of $5,375,000.

Arctic's effective tax rate of 23.26% ($5,000,000 total tax expense ÷ $21,500,000 pretax book income) does not equal the Federal statutory rate of 21% or the combined Federal and state tax rate of 25%. This suggests that Arctic has some combination of permanent book-tax differences and/or available credits. Mr. Jones should be able to find these in Arctic's tax rate reconciliation in its tax footnote.

Because Arctic operates in a state that imposes an income tax, Mr. Jones should expect to find state taxes in the reconciliation as an item that increases Arctic's effective tax rate relative to the Federal statutory rate of 21% and its tax expense over what would be expected based on multiplying its pretax book income by the statutory rate. Because state income taxes increase Arctic's effective tax rate, Mr. Jones should expect to find other reconciling items that reduce Arctic's effective tax rate.

Bridge Discipline **Bridge to Financial Analysis**

Financial analysts perform an important function for the capital markets in their detailed analyses of companies. The analyst combs through the financial reports and other information about a company to produce an informed opinion on how a company is performing. Analysts' earnings forecasts often constitute an important metric to examine when making decisions about investing in companies.

An experienced financial analyst typically will have a good handle on interpreting financial statement information. However, even experienced analysts often will "punt" when it comes to interpreting the tax information contained in a financial statement, preferring to look at net income before taxes (or even EBITDA, earnings before interest, taxes, depreciation, and amortization).

A great deal of useful information about a business is contained in its tax footnote, and analysts might have an edge if they work at understanding the mysteries of taxes in the financial statements.

3-4 Special Issues

LO.7

Apply the GAAP standards concerning tax uncertainties and tax law changes.

3-4a The Financial Accounting for Tax Uncertainties

Given the complexity of business transactions, as well as the related tax laws, how tax law applies to a given transaction may sometimes be uncertain. Financial Accounting Standards Interpretation (FIN) 48, incorporated into ASC 740-10,[13] addresses how this uncertainty should impact the accounting for income taxes. As explained in more depth below, FIN 48 requires a two-step analysis to determine whether, and how much of, the tax savings (or tax benefits) related to an uncertain tax position taken by a taxpayer may reduce the tax expense reported in the taxpayer's financial statements. The two-step analysis, requiring consideration of whether the recognizable benefits are recognizable at all and, if so, the measurement of those recognizable benefits, is described below (see Concept Summary 3.2). Technically, FIN 48 requires this analysis of all tax positions taken by a company, although materiality typically limits the number of tax positions considered as part of this analysis.

Initial Recognition

Whether the tax benefits of an uncertain position may be *recognized* at all depends on the strength of the tax authority supporting the position. For tax purposes, taxpayers may take a tax position as long as there is *substantial authority* for the position.

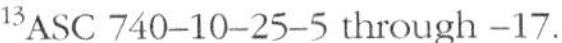

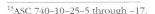

[13]ASC 740-10-25-5 through -17.

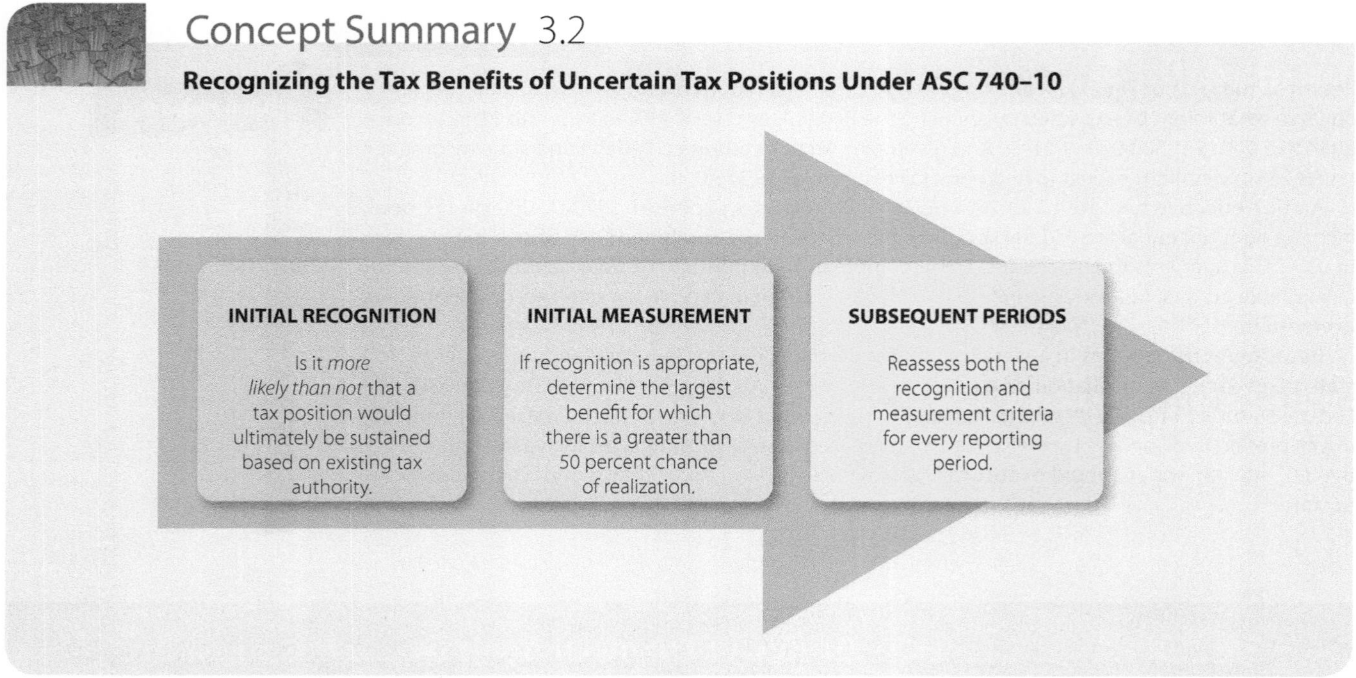

Concept Summary 3.2
Recognizing the Tax Benefits of Uncertain Tax Positions Under ASC 740-10
INITIAL RECOGNITION
Is it more likely than not that a tax position would ultimately be sustained based on existing tax authority.
INITIAL MEASUREMENT
If recognition is appropriate, determine the largest benefit for which there is a greater than 50 percent chance of realization.
SUBSEQUENT PERIODS
Reassess both the recognition and measurement criteria for every reporting period.

Although the substantial authority standard can be challenging to interpret and apply, the Regulations provide that a position may meet the standard even if its probability of being upheld (if challenged by the IRS) fails to exceed 50 percent.[14] Positions with much lower probabilities of success may be taken if a taxpayer discloses on the tax return the relevant facts surrounding the position.[15]

For financial reporting purposes, however, ASC 740 prohibits the recognition of any tax benefits related to an uncertain tax position unless it is *more likely than not* (i.e., a greater than 50 percent likelihood) that the position would ultimately be sustained based only on existing tax authority.[16] When applying this test, it must be assumed that the position is identified by the relevant tax enforcement agency; the possibility that the position is not detected by the authorities is irrelevant. As a result, it is possible that a corporation may legally take an uncertain tax position, and reduce its tax liability, but be unable to reduce the tax expense reported in its financial statements.

Assuming that the taxpayer has recorded its tax provision based on the position taken in its tax return, failure to meet the recognition criteria or the inability to recognize the full benefit of the position due to the measurement criteria will require the recognition of additional tax expense as well as a liability.

Initial Measurement

If the uncertain tax position meets the *more likely than not* threshold, the second step is to determine the amount of the tax benefit that may be recognized (the *measurement* process). The amount of the benefit that may be recognized is limited to the amount the taxpayer is likely to actually realize taking into account all relevant factors, including the probability the position is detected and the possible outcomes of any negotiated settlements between the taxpayer and the enforcement agency.

One way to measure the benefit to be recognized is to use a probability table that considers all of the possible post-audit and post-settlement outcomes that might result from taking the uncertain position and the probability of each. The benefit recognized is the largest amount for which it is *more likely than not* (a greater than 50 percent probability) to be realized, assuming that the taxing authority has full knowledge of all relevant information.[17]

---

[14] Reg. § 1.6662–4(d)(2).

[15] § 6662(d)(2)(B).

[16] ASC 740–10–25–5 through –7.

[17] ASC 740-10-30-7.

Example 24

StarksCo has adopted certain **transfer pricing** strategies with related parties overseas. These strategies reduce StarksCo's Federal income tax liability by $100,000. However, the IRS is likely to challenge the pricing structure in an audit. StarksCo estimates that although it is more likely than not that these positions will be upheld if taken to court after an IRS audit, the tax benefit may be reduced as a result of compromises it may make with the IRS to avoid the costs of going to court. StarksCo constructs a table of the potential outcomes from this negotiation process and their probabilities.

Resulting Estimated Tax Benefit	Probability of Realizing Tax Benefit	Cumulative Probability of Realization
$100,000	40%	40%
80,000	35%	75%
45,000	20%	95%
-0-	5%	100%

Assume that StarksCo recorded a book tax provision of $250,000, *including* the $100,000 tax benefit from the transfer pricing positions. In light of the requirements of ASC 740-10, StarksCo instead should recognize only an $80,000 tax benefit for this item, the largest amount for which there is at least a 50% cumulative probability of being realized (here, a 75% chance of acceptance exists).

As a result, StarksCo should increase its current tax expense, and recognize a related liability, for $20,000 ($100,000 − $80,000). The journal entry to record the unrecognizable tax benefit would be as follows.

Current income tax expense (provision)	$20,000	
ASC 740-10 liability		$20,000

Subsequent Events

Once an entity takes an uncertain tax position, the reporting for that position must be monitored for subsequent events that may impact its reporting. For example, the recognition and measurement of uncertain tax positions must be reassessed at each reporting date.[18] If the tax authority on which the initial recognition judgment was based changes (e.g., a new Regulation is issued related to the tax position), a previously unrecognized tax benefit may become recognizable. Conversely, a previously recognized benefit may need to be derecognized.

Example 25

Revisit the facts in Example 24. Starks previously recognized an $80,000 tax benefit related to its transfer pricing strategies. Assume in the subsequent year, the tax court rejects the use of a strategy that is similar to the one used by Starks. As a result, Starks reduces its belief that its strategy would be upheld in court to 45%. Starks is no longer allowed to recognize any tax benefit from its transfer pricing strategy. In the year the court case is settled, Starks must recognize $80,000 of additional tax expense as follows:

Tax Expense	$80,000	
ASC 740-10 liability		$80,000

Similarly, any change in the facts surrounding the initial measurement of a tax benefit will result in the recognition of a tax expense or benefit in the year of the change.

Finally, the ultimate resolution of the tax position must also be accounted for. Eventually, the position will be examined by the taxing authority and resolved or the statute of limitations will expire without the position every being examined. If the position is examined, any amounts to be paid to the taxing authority are considered first to be payments on the existing liability with no impact on current year tax expense or net income. Any payments less than or greater than the previously established liability will impact tax expense in the year the position is settled

[18]ASC 740-10-35.

Revisit the facts in Example 24. Two years after recognizing the $20,000 liability for uncertain tax positions, Starks is audited by the IRS. Starks agrees to pay $25,000 in additional taxes to settle the matter. As a result, Starks records the following:

Tax expense	$ 5,000	
ASC 740-10 liability	$20,000	
Cash		$25,000

Notice that Starks is recognizing $5,000 in tax expense related to income it included in its financial statements two years ago.

If the statute of limitations expires without the position being examined, the liability for unrecognized tax benefits as well as the tax expense are both reduced by the amount of the previously unrecognized benefit in the year in which the statute lapses.

Return to the facts of Example 24. Assume that the statute of limitations for the year in which Starks took the uncertain tax position lapses and the taxing authority can no longer challenge the position. Starks will reduce its liability and its tax expense as follows:

ASC 740-10 liability	$20,000	
Tax expense		$20,000

Again, notice that Starks is recognizing a tax benefit in the current year related to income it reported three years ago.

ASC 740 requires public companies to provide in its footnotes a reconciliation of its unrecognized tax benefits at the beginning and end of the year. The reconciliation must include the following:

- Any increase or decrease related to tax positions taken in prior years;
- Any increase related to tax positions taken during the current year;
- Any decreases related to settlements with the taxing authorities; and
- Any decreases due to the lapse of the applicable statute of limitations.

Companies also are required to provide a discussion of potential changes in unrecognized tax benefits that might occur over the 12 months following the date of the financial statements.

3-4b **Effects of Statutory Tax Rate Changes**

As discussed earlier, deferred tax expense is the change in an entity's deferred tax assets and deferred tax liabilities from the beginning to the end of the year. Usually, that change is due to changes in cumulative book-tax differences. However, even with no changes in cumulative book-tax differences, deferred tax assets and liabilities will change if there is a change during the year in the tax rate that will apply when those differences are expected to reverse.

For example, if future tax rates increase from 21 percent to 25 percent, the tax benefit of deferred tax assets generated by temporary differences also will increase since, when they are realized, they will reduce income taxed at 25 percent (rather than 21 percent). Conversely, an increase in future tax rates from 21 percent to 25 percent will increase the tax cost of deferred tax liabilities as they will generate taxable income taxed at 25 percent (rather than 21 percent when they are realized).

Although tax rate changes are uncommon, they can be significant when they do occur. For example, the Tax Cuts and Jobs Act (TCJA) of 2017 reduced Federal corporate tax rates from as much as 35 percent to 21 percent—significantly reducing the value of deferred tax assets but also reducing the cost of deferred tax liabilities (and impacting the financial statements of many corporations).

Effects of Change in Corporate Tax Rate

Alpha Corporation had accumulated a net temporary book-tax difference of $1,000,000 as of January 1, 2017, due primarily to the use of accelerated cost recovery. Accordingly, its deferred tax liability account on January 1, 2017, was $350,000 ($1,000,000 × 35%).

When the TCJA of 2017 reduced the applicable Federal corporate income tax rate to 21%, the balance of the deferred tax liability account was adjusted to $210,000 ($1,000,000 × 21%), reducing its deferred tax expense and increasing its 2017 book income by $140,000.

Beta Corporation had accumulated a net temporary book-tax difference of $1,000,000 as of January 1, 2017, due primarily to a net operating loss. Accordingly, its deferred tax asset account on January 1, 2017, was $350,000.

When the TCJA of 2017 reduced the applicable Federal corporate income tax rate to 21%, the balance of the deferred tax asset account was adjusted to $210,000 ($1,000,000 × 21%), reducing its deferred tax asset and decreasing its 2017 book income by $140,000.

3-4c The Corporate Tax Department

The corporate tax department often is charged with shaping and implementing the entity's tax strategies (*tax planning*) and filing all required tax returns (*tax compliance*) while preparing for subsequent audit and litigation activity (*tax controversy*). Tax professionals often work closely with those who prepare the entity's financial statements, especially concerning the tax footnote, tax deferral accounts, and tax rate reconciliations. Professional tax and accounting research underlies all of this work.

The functions of a modern tax department are illustrated in Exhibit 3.4. Tax professionals must be proficient in all of the indicated areas to meet the demands of the entity and its shareholders, regulators, and taxing agencies.

Exhibit 3.4 Functions of a Tax Department (by Percent of Time Spent)

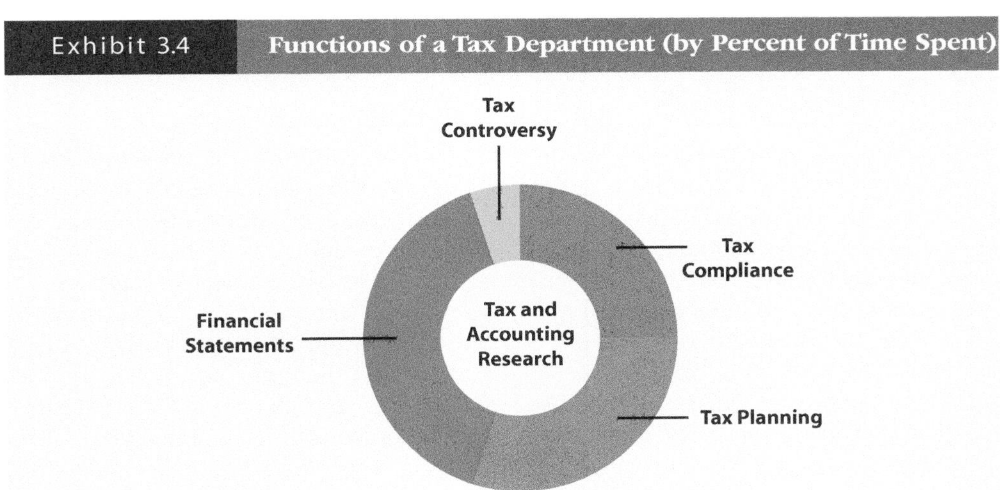

Information related to tax expense and its related balance sheet effects is required for SEC taxpayers long before the corporate income tax return is due. Tax professionals must work with those charged with completing financial reporting requirements so that these SEC deadlines are met (e.g., in filing a Form 10–K for a calendar year corporation in February or March of the following year, even though the extended due date of the Form 1120 is not until mid-October).

If the tax professional grasps both the tax and financial statement effects of various tax planning and compliance activities, the tax professional brings great value to the entity through the tax department.

A brief discussion of the evolution of accounting for income taxes can be found on this book's companion website: www.cengage.com

3 Digging Deeper

The steps in determining a corporation's income tax expense for book purposes are summarized in Concept Summary 3.3.

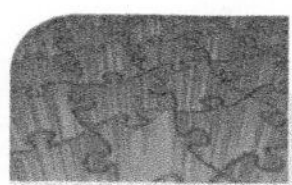

Concept Summary 3.3

The Income Tax Provision Process

Expense (Benefit) Recognized in the Financial Statements

Current Tax Expense (Benefit)

Sum of all liabilities expected to be reported on all (Federal, state, and foreign) current-year tax returns
± Change in unrecognized tax benefits
± Amounts attributable to items not included in income from continuing operations
Current tax expense (benefit)

+

Deferred Tax Expense (Benefit)

Change in deferred tax assets and liabilities during the reporting period (including that due to tax rate changes)
± Change in valuation allowance
± Change in unrecognized tax benefits
± Amounts attributable to items not included in income from continuing operations
Deferred tax expense (benefit)

Footnote Disclosures

- Breakdown of income between domestic and foreign sources
- Breakdown of tax expense between current and deferred
- Tax assets and liabilities attributable to individual temporary book-tax differences
- Amount of any valuation allowance
- Tax rate reconciliation
- Breakdown of changes in unrecognized tax benefits during the year

LO.8

Use financial statement income tax information to benchmark a company's tax position.

3-5 Benchmarking

As discussed earlier, an entity's tax expense can convey many things about the entity to a wide array of interested parties (e.g., shareholders, creditors, policymakers, and potential investors). A company's income tax expense is one of the single largest expense items on its income statement, and understanding the components of this expense is a critical activity for tax professionals, as well as for readers of the financial statements.

Consider a typical baseball game. Two teams meet, interact following a specific set of rules, and ultimately complete the game, generating a final score. Of course, the final score is of immediate interest to the teams and the fans, but once the game is over, the score and associated statistics (runs, hits, and errors) are relegated to the history books. Yet these statistics still can be quite useful. A team coach may use the game statistics to evaluate the strengths and weaknesses of the players to assist in improving performance. Other teams may use the data to develop strategies for upcoming games. Players can use this information to "benchmark" themselves against their own performance in prior games or against players on other teams. In short, there is a wealth of analytical possibilities in these historical data.

A taxpayer's reported income tax expense also is a valuable source of information for the company, its tax advisers, and its competitors. The reported information provides clues about a company's operational and tax planning strategies.

Companies may benchmark their tax situation to other years' results or to other companies in the same industry. The starting point for a **benchmarking** exercise usually is the data from the income tax note rate reconciliation.

3-5a Methods of Analysis

In addition to comparing effective tax rates, one can analyze entities' levels of deferred tax assets and liabilities.

Example 30

Akiko Enterprises reports a net deferred tax liability of $280,000. Erde, Inc., a company in the same industry, reports a net deferred tax liability of $860,000. The presence of deferred tax liabilities on the balance sheet indicates that both companies are benefiting from deferring actual tax payments (essentially, an interest-free loan from the government).

At first glance, it may appear that Erde is doing better in this regard. However, what if Akiko holds total assets of $2,600,000 and Erde's assets total $19,200,000? This information indicates that Akiko has 10.8% ($280,000/$2,600,000) of its total assets "financed" with an interest-free loan from the government; Erde has only 4.5% ($860,000/$19,200,000) of its assets "financed" with its deferred tax liabilities.

One may do a more refined benchmarking analysis by examining each component of an entity's deferred tax assets and liabilities as a percentage of total assets. For example, an observer can examine how the deferred tax assets or liabilities related to property, plant, and equipment compare with those of its competitors. The nature of the components of deferred tax liabilities and deferred tax assets becomes important in a benchmarking analysis.

Benchmarking Financial Results

Example 31

LinCo reports total book income before taxes of $10,000,000 and a total tax provision of $1,600,000, producing a 16% effective tax rate. TuckCo also reports book income before taxes of $10,000,000. TuckCo's total tax expense is $1,500,000, producing an effective tax rate of 15%. At first glance, it appears that the entities are similar based on their effective tax rates. The total tax expense divided between current and deferred is as follows.

	LinCo	TuckCo
Current tax expense	$2,500,000	$2,600,000
Deferred tax benefit	(900,000)	(1,100,000)
Total tax expense	$1,600,000	$1,500,000

Again, it appears that both companies have created deferred tax assets in the current year that are expected to produce tax savings in the future. Knowing the nature of the underlying deferred tax assets will add greatly to one's interpretation of the effective tax rates.

With additional investigation, you determine that the deferred tax asset generating LinCo's expected future tax savings is due to an NOL carryover. The deferred tax asset generating TuckCo's expected future tax savings is generated by the use of different book and tax methods in accounting for warranty expense. This additional information reveals that LinCo previously has incurred losses; to use the NOLs in the coming years, it will be critical for LinCo to generate future taxable income.

This is quite different from TuckCo's situation, which reveals only that common differences in accounting methods exist and that the future deductions likely will be used fully. Although the tax positions of LinCo and TuckCo seem very similar on the surface, a closer look reveals a striking difference.

Example 32

WageCo and SalaryCo operate in the same industry. Their book income and current, deferred, and total tax expense were reported as follows:

	WageCo	SalaryCo
Book income before tax	$1,500,000	$2,300,000
Current tax expense	$ 680,000	$ 24,000
Deferred tax expense (benefit)	(410,000)	390,000
Total tax expense	$ 270,000	$ 414,000
Effective tax rate	18%	18%

Although the companies have the same effective tax rate, WageCo is paying a significant amount of taxes currently, with a large portion of the tax benefits related to its operations deferred. SalaryCo appears to be deferring a substantial portion of its tax expense to future years. Although both companies report the same effective tax rate, the details indicate that the two companies face very different tax situations. By looking more closely at the financial statements, an analyst should be able to determine why these differences exist.

3-5b Tax Rate Sustainability

It is important in benchmarking exercises to remove the effect of nonrecurring items to evaluate the sustainability of effective tax rates across time or companies. Examples of nonrecurring items include restructuring costs, legal settlements, and IRS or other tax liability settlements. A nonrecurring item may significantly impact a company's current year effective tax rate. However, the very nature of this item implies that it has little to do with the company's *long-term* sustainable tax costs.

MetalCo and IronCo operate in the same industry, and they report the following tax rate reconciliations in their tax footnotes.

	MetalCo	IronCo
Hypothetical tax at U.S. statutory tax rate	21.0%	21.0%
State and local taxes	2.2	2.1
Foreign income taxed at less than U.S. rate	(6.2)	(6.1)
Tax Court settlement on disputed tax issue	(18.6)	—
Effective tax rate	(1.6)%	17.0%

Although it appears that MetalCo has a significantly lower effective tax rate than IronCo's effective tax rate, removing MetalCo's tax court settlement, a nonrecurring item, indicates that both companies may regularly face a similar 17% effective tax rate [(1.6)% + 18.6% = 17%].

3-5c Uses of Benchmarking Analysis

Benchmarking is part science and part art. A useful analysis requires both an accountant's knowledge of how the underlying financial statements are constructed, including arriving at the appropriate tax expense, and a detective's sense of where to look and what questions to ask.

In addition to benchmarking, financial analysts perform an important function for the capital markets in their detailed analyses of companies. The analyst combs through both the financial reports and other information about a company to produce an informed opinion on how a company is performing. Analysts' earnings forecasts often constitute an important metric to examine when making decisions about investing in companies.

An experienced financial analyst typically will have a good handle on interpreting financial statement information. However, even experienced analysts will often "punt" when it comes to interpreting the tax information contained in a financial statement, preferring to look at net income before taxes (or even EBITDA, earnings before interest, taxes, depreciation, and amortization). A great deal of useful information about a business is contained in its tax footnote, and analysts might have an edge if they work at understanding the mysteries of taxes in the financial statements. Some typical uses of benchmarking in an analysis of an entity's financial results are summarized in Concept Summary 3.4.

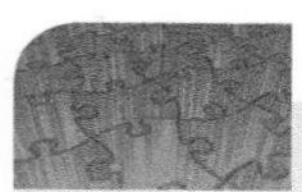

Concept Summary 3.4

Benchmarking Analysis

A benchmarking analysis can be helpful in comparing the tax positions of two or more business entities. One might consider the following aspects of the taxpayers' financial disclosures in this regard. This list is not all-inclusive; benchmarking also includes the judgment and experience of the parties conducting the analysis.

- Compare the effective tax rates of the entities.
- Explain the differences in effective rates. Are these differences sustainable over time?
- Apply the analysis to both the tax dollars involved and the underlying net assets of the entities.
- Discount (but do not ignore) any one-time tax benefits/detriments that are observed.
- Include in your analysis any knowledge of the nontax, competitive strategy and tactics employed and planned by the entity.

Refocus on The Big Picture

Taxes in the Financial Statements

Raymond Jones should understand that the tax expense reported on the company's financial statements and the tax payable on the company's income tax returns often differ as a result of both temporary and permanent differences in financial statement income and taxable income. Examples of permanent differences include nontaxable income such as municipal bond interest and tax credits. Temporary differences include depreciation differences and other amounts that are affected by the timing of a deduction or an inclusion, but they ultimately result in the same amount being reflected in the financial statements and income tax returns.

Temporary differences will cause pretax book income to differ from taxable income. However, because a corporation must report its deferred as well as its current tax expense, temporary differences will not cause the tax expense, or the effective tax rate, reported in the financial statements to differ from what might be expected given the corporation's pretax book income and the statutory tax rate. However, permanent differences will impact both a corporation's reported tax expense and effective tax rate.

In this case, Arctic's income tax expense of $5 million is higher than the current Federal income tax payable. This results from timing differences that lead to the recognition of a deferred tax liability as well as permanent differences that do not.

What If?

Mr. Jones is concerned about a newspaper article that said that companies reporting less tax on their tax returns than on their financial statements were cheating the IRS. Is this an accurate assessment?

Although differences in income taxes payable to the IRS and financial tax expense can result from aggressive and illegal tax shelters, differences also result from different methods of accounting that are required for financial statement reporting using GAAP and tax laws enacted by Congress.

Suggested Readings

Center on Budget and Policy Priorities, "Actual U.S. Corporate Tax Rates Are in Line with Comparable Countries," October 2017.

Rick C. Lau, The Association between Deferred Tax Assets and Liabilities and Future Tax Payments, *The Accounting Review*, Vol. 88 (4), p 1357–1383.

Key Terms

ASC 740, 3-5
Balance sheet approach, 3-5
Benchmarking, 3-26
Current tax expense, 3-5
Deferred tax asset, 3-5
Deferred tax benefit 3-5
Deferred tax expense 3-5
Deferred tax liability, 3-5
Generally accepted accounting principles (GAAP), 3-2
Permanent differences, 3-3
Rate reconciliation, 3-19
Temporary differences, 3-3
Transfer pricing, 3-23
Valuation allowance, 3-15

Problems

1. **LO.1** Evaluate the following statement: For most business entities, book income differs from taxable income because "income" is meant to capture different constructs for book and tax purposes.

Critical Thinking

2. **LO.1** Define the terms *temporary difference* and *permanent difference* as they pertain to the financial reporting of income tax expenses. Describe how these two book-tax differences affect the gap between book and taxable income. How are permanent and temporary differences alike? How are they different?

Communications

3. **LO.1** In no more than three PowerPoint slides, list several commonly encountered temporary and permanent book-tax differences. The slides will be used in your presentation next week to your school's Future CPAs Club.

Communications

4. **LO.1, 2** Marcellus Jackson, the CFO of Mac, Inc., notices that the tax liability reported on Mac's tax return is less than the tax expense reported on Mac's financial statements. Provide a letter to Marcellus outlining why these two tax expense numbers differ. Mac's address is 482 Linden Road, Paris, KY 40362.

5. **LO.5** While viewing the Business News Channel, you heard that YoungCo has "released one-third of its valuation allowances because of an upbeat forecast for sales of its tablet computers over the next 30 months." What effect does such a release likely have on YoungCo's current-year book effective tax rate? Be specific.

6. **LO.6, 7** While auditing a client, you notice its current tax expense does not equal the tax liability that is reflected on the client's tax return for the year. Provide at least two possible explanations for the difference and where you might look to see if those explanations are relevant.

7. **LO.7** DraftJacks, Inc., took an uncertain tax position in 2020, recording an unrecognized tax benefit of $100,000. In 2022, the IRS challenged the position and DraftJacks agreed to pay $120,000 to settle it. What impact does the settlement have on DraftJacks's 2022 book tax expense and book income? Explain.

Decision Making

8. **LO.8** Jill is the CFO of Portech, Inc. Portech's tax advisers have recommended two tax planning ideas. Each will provide $5,000,000 of current-year cash tax savings. One idea is based on a timing difference and is expected to reverse in full 10 years in the future. The other idea creates a permanent difference that never will reverse.

   Determine whether these ideas will allow Portech to reduce its reported book income tax expense for the current year. Illustrate in a table or timeline your preference for one planning strategy over the other. Which idea will you recommend to Jill?

9. **LO.8** RoofCo reports total book income before taxes of $32,000,000 and a total tax expense of $8,000,000. FloorCo reports book income before taxes of $48,000,000 and a total tax expense of $12,000,000. The companies' breakdown between current and deferred tax expense (benefit) is as follows.

	RoofCo	FloorCo
Current tax expense	$10.0	$13.0
Deferred tax benefit	(2.0)	(1.0)
Total tax expense	$ 8.0	$12.0

RoofCo's deferred tax benefit is created by the expected future use of a capital loss carryforward. FloorCo's deferred tax benefit is related to a lawsuit that will not be settled until early next year. FloorCo's lawyers predict that the company will probably lose the lawsuit. Compare and contrast these two companies' effective tax rates. How are they similar? How are they different?

10. **LO.8** LawnCo and TreeCo operate in the same industry, and both report a 25% effective tax rate (combined Federal, state, and global). Their book income and current, deferred, and total tax expense are reported below.

Critical Thinking
Communications

	LawnCo	TreeCo
Book income before tax	$600,000	$780,000
Current tax expense	$200,000	$ 20,000
Deferred tax expense (benefit)	(50,000)	175,000
Total Federal, state, and global tax expense	$150,000	$195,000
Effective tax rate	25%	25%

ShrubCo is a competitor of both of these companies. Prepare a letter to Laura Collins, VP-Taxation of ShrubCo, outlining your analysis of the other two companies' effective tax rates, using only the preceding information. ShrubCo's address is 9979 West Third Street, Peru, IN 46970.

11. **LO.8** HippCo and HoppCo operate in the same industry and report the following tax rate reconciliations in their tax footnotes.

	HippCo	HoppCo
Hypothetical tax at U.S. statutory tax rate	21.0%	21.0%
State and local taxes	2.7	3.9
Municipal bond interest	(12.5)	(7.8)
Tax Court settlement on disputed tax issue	6.0	—
Effective tax rate	17.2%	17.1%

Compare and contrast the effective tax rates of these two companies.

12. **LO.6, 7** In the current year, Dickinson, Inc., reports an effective tax rate of 36%, and Badger, Inc., reports an effective tax rate of 21%. Both companies are domestic and operate in the same industry. Your initial examination of the financial statements of the two companies indicates that Badger apparently is doing a better job with its tax planning, explaining the difference in effective tax rates. Consequently, all else being equal, you decide to invest in Badger.

Ethics and Equity

In a subsequent year, it comes to light that Badger had used some very aggressive tax planning techniques to reduce its reported tax expense. After an examination by the IRS, Badger loses the tax benefits and reports a very large tax expense in that year. Over this multiple-year period, it turns out that Dickinson had the lower effective tax rate after all.

Do you believe Badger was unethical in not fully disclosing the aggressiveness of its tax positions in its current financial statements? How does ASC 740-10 (FIN 48) affect Badger's disclosure requirement? Does ASC 740-10 (FIN 48) still leave room for ethical decision making by management in determining how to report uncertain tax positions? Explain.

13. **LO.1, 3** Prance, Inc., earned pretax book net income of $800,000 in 2021. Prance acquired a depreciable asset that year, and first-year tax depreciation exceeded book depreciation by $80,000. Prance reported no other temporary or permanent book-tax differences. The pertinent U.S. tax rate is 21%, and Prance earned an after-tax rate of return on capital of 4%. Compute Prance's current income tax benefit or expense for the year.

14. **LO.1, 4** Using the facts of Problem 13, determine Prance's 2021 deferred tax benefit or expense and any deferred tax asset or liability.

15. **LO.1, 3** Continuing with the facts from Problem 14, Prance reports $600,000 of pretax book net income in 2022. Prance's book depreciation exceeds tax depreciation that year by $20,000. Prance reports no other temporary or permanent book-tax differences. Assuming that the pertinent U.S. tax rate is 21%, compute Prance's current income tax benefit or expense for the year.

16. **LO.1, 4** Using the facts of Problem 15, determine Prance's 2022 deferred tax benefit or expense and any deferred tax asset or liability. In net present value terms, what has been the value to Prance of accelerating $20,000 of 2022 book depreciation to 2021? Use text Appendix E to calculate your answer.

17. **LO.1, 3** Mini, Inc., earns pretax book net income of $750,000 in 2021. Mini recognized $20,000 in bad debt expense for book purposes. This expense is not yet deductible for tax purposes. Mini reports no other temporary or permanent book-tax differences. The applicable U.S. tax rate is 21%, and Mini earns an after-tax rate of return on capital of 4%. Compute Mini's current income tax benefit or expense.

18. **LO.1, 4** Using the facts of Problem 17, determine Mini's 2021 deferred tax assets and liabilities, deferred tax benefit or expense, and total tax benefit or expense.

19. **LO.1, 3** Mini, in Problem 17, reports $800,000 of pretax book net income in 2022. For that year, Mini did not recognize any bad debt expense for book purposes but did deduct $15,000 in bad debt expense for tax purposes. Mini reports no other temporary or permanent differences. Assuming that the U.S. tax rate is 21%, compute Mini's current income tax benefit or expense.

20. **LO.1, 4** Using the facts of Problem 19, determine Mini's 2022 deferred tax assets and liabilities, deferred tax benefit or expense, and total tax benefit or expense. In net present value terms, what has been the cost to Mini of the deferred tax deduction for bad debts? Use text Appendix E to calculate your answer.

21. **LO.1, 4** Ovate, Inc., earns $140,000 in book income before tax and is subject to a 21% marginal Federal income tax rate in its first year of operations. Ovate estimates it will incur $6,000 over the next two years to honor warranties on products it sold during the current year and recorded the appropriate liability on its balance sheet at the end of the year.

    a. Determine the amount of Ovate's deferred tax assets and liabilities, if any, as of the end of the year.
    b. Express your computation as a Microsoft Excel formula.

22. **LO.4, 6** Facegram, Inc., reported net cumulative favorable book-tax temporary differences of $1,000,000 at the end of 2021. During 2022, legislation was enacted that will increase Facegram's tax rate from 21% to 25% beginning in 2023. Facegram expects to report $500,000 of 2022 pre-tax book and taxable income with no change to its net cumulative book-tax temporary differences.

    a. What will Facegram report as its deferred tax benefit or expense for 2022?
    b. What, if any, effect will the above information have on Facegram's 2022 tax rate reconciliation?
    c. (How) would the answers to parts (a) and (b) change if Facegram's $1,000,000 net cumulative book-tax temporary difference at the end of 2021 had been unfavorable rather than favorable?

23. **LO.5** In its books, Ion Corporation reports income tax expense and income tax payable of $200,000 and $250,000, respectively. Assume that Ion will be able to use only $30,000 of any deferred tax asset, with the balance expiring unused. Determine the amount of Ion's deferred tax asset and any necessary valuation allowance, and construct the appropriate journal entry that Ion would record.

24. **LO.5, 6** RadioCo, a domestic corporation, reports a deferred tax asset relating to receivables of $100,000 and a deferred tax liability relating to cost recovery of $165,000. How and where on the GAAP financial statement will RadioCo report these items?

25. **LO.1, 3, 4** Britton, Inc., an accrual basis C corporation, sells widgets on credit. Its pretax book income in its first year of operations is $50,000. Britton's book allowance for uncollectible accounts at the end of the year is $10,000. The applicable income tax rate (combined Federal, state, and global) for year 1 and thereafter is 30%. Compute Britton's year 1 current and deferred income tax benefit or expense.

26. **LO.1, 3, 4** Continue with the results of Problem 25. Prepare the GAAP journal entries for Britton's year 1 income tax expense.

27. **LO.1, 3** Rubio, Inc., an accrual basis C corporation, reports the following amounts for the tax year. The applicable income tax rate is 30% (combined Federal, state, and global). Compute Rubio's current income tax benefit or expense.

Book income, including the items below	$80,000
Interest income from City of Westerville bonds	10,000
Bribes paid to Federal inspectors	17,000
Liability for anticipated warranty costs (beginning of year)	20,000
Liability for anticipated warranty costs (end of year)	25,000

28. **LO.1, 4** Continue with the results of Problem 27.

a. Determine Rubio's deferred income tax benefit or expense and GAAP income for the year.

b. Express your calculation of Rubio's tax provision using Microsoft Excel commands.

29. **LO.1, 3, 4** Willingham, Inc., an accrual basis C corporation, reports pretax book income of $1,600,000. At the beginning of the year, Willingham reported no deferred tax assets or liabilities on its balance sheet. At the end of the year, Willingham's depreciable assets had a net book value of $15,000,000. It is subject to a 21% U.S. income tax rate in the current year and for the foreseeable future.

Willingham's book-tax differences include the following. Compute the entity's current and deferred Federal income tax benefit or expense for the year.

Estimate of uncollectible accounts at year end	$4,000,000
Tax depreciation in excess of book	3,000,000
Book gain from installment sale of nonbusiness asset, deferred for tax	2,000,000
Interest income from school district bonds	200,000

30. **LO.1, 3, 4** Continue with the results of Problem 29. Prepare the GAAP journal entries for Willingham's income tax benefit or expense.

31. **LO.1, 4** Relix, Inc., is a domestic corporation with the following balance sheet for book and tax purposes at the end of the year. Based on this information, determine Relix's Federal net deferred tax asset or net deferred tax liability at year-end. Assume a 21% Federal corporate tax rate, no state or foreign taxes, and no need for a valuation allowance.

	Tax Debit/ (Credit)	Book Debit/ (Credit)
Assets		
Cash	$ 500	$ 500
Accounts receivable	8,000	8,000
Buildings	750,000	750,000
Accumulated depreciation	(450,000)	(380,000)
Furniture & fixtures	70,000	70,000
Accumulated depreciation	(46,000)	(38,000)
Total assets	$332,500	$410,500

	Tax Debit/ (Credit)	Book Debit/ (Credit)
Liabilities		
Accrued litigation expense	$ -0-	($ 50,000)
Note payable	(78,000)	(78,000)
Total liabilities	($ 78,000)	($128,000)
Stockholders' Equity		
Paid-in capital	($ 10,000)	($ 10,000)
Retained earnings	(244,500)	(272,500)
Total liabilities and stockholders' equity	($332,500)	($410,500)

32. **LO.1, 4** Based on the facts and results of Problem 31 and the partial beginning-of-the-year tax and book balance sheet information below, determine Relix's deferred tax benefit or expense for the year. Provide the journal entry necessary to record this amount.

	Tax Debit/ (Credit)	Book Debit/ (Credit)
Assets		
Accumulated depreciation—Buildings	($417,000)	($360,000)
Accumulated depreciation—Furniture & fixtures	(35,200)	(31,000)
Liabilities		
Accrued litigation expense	$ -0-	$ 34,000

33. **LO.1, 3** In addition to the temporary differences identified in Problems 31 and 32, Relix, Inc., reported two permanent differences between book and taxable income. It earned $2,375 in tax-exempt municipal bond interest, and it incurred $780 in nondeductible business meals expense. Relix's book income before tax is $4,800. With this additional information, calculate Relix's current tax benefit or expense.

34. **LO.1, 3** Provide the journal entry to record Relix's current tax benefit or expense as determined in Problem 33.

35. **LO.1, 3, 4** Based on the facts and results of Problems 31–34, calculate Relix's total provision for income tax reported in its financial statements, and determine its book net income after tax.

36. **LO.6** Based on the facts and results of Problems 31–35, prepare the rate reconciliation, using both tax amounts and rates, Relix must include in its financial statement footnotes. Round calculations off to the nearest dollar or one tenth of one percent (e.g., 13.9 percent) as appropriate.

37. **LO.1, 4** Kantner, Inc., is a domestic corporation with the following balance sheet for book and tax purposes at the end of the year. Based on this information, determine Kantner's net Federal deferred tax asset or net deferred tax liability at year-end. Assume a 21% Federal corporate tax rate, no state or foreign taxes, and no need for a valuation allowance.

	Tax Debit/ (Credit)	Book Debit/ (Credit)
Assets		
Cash	$ 1,000	$ 1,000
Accounts receivable	9,000	9,000
Buildings	850,000	850,000
Accumulated depreciation	(685,000)	(620,000)
Furniture & fixtures	40,000	40,000
Accumulated depreciation	(10,000)	(8,000)
Total assets	$205,000	$272,000
Liabilities		
Accrued warranty expense	$ -0-	($ 40,000)
Note payable	(16,000)	(16,000)
Total liabilities	($ 16,000)	($ 56,000)
Stockholders' Equity		
Paid-in capital	($ 50,000)	($ 50,000)
Retained earnings	(139,000)	(166,000)
Total liabilities and stockholders' equity	($205,000)	($272,000)

38. **LO.1, 4** Based on the facts and results of Problem 37 and the partial beginning-of-the-year tax and book balance sheet information below, determine Kantner's deferred tax benefit or expense for the current year. Provide the journal entry necessary to record this amount.

	Tax Debit/ (Credit)	Book Debit/ (Credit)
Assets		
Accumulated depreciation—Buildings	($662,000)	($600,000)
Accumulated depreciation—Furniture & fixtures	(4,400)	(4,000)
Liabilities		
Accrued warranty expense	$ -0-	($ 30,000)

39. **LO.1, 3** In addition to the temporary differences identified in Problems 37 and 38, Kantner reported two permanent differences between book and taxable income. It earned $7,800 in tax-exempt municipal bond interest, and it reported $1,700 of business meals expense. Kantner's book income before tax is $50,000. With this additional information, calculate Kantner's current tax benefit or expense.

40. **LO.3** Provide the journal entry to record Kantner's current tax benefit or expense as determined in Problem 39.

41. **LO.1, 3, 4** Based on the facts and results of Problems 37–40, calculate Kantner's total provision for income tax expense reported on its financial statement and its book net income after tax.

42. **LO.6** Based on the facts and results of Problems 37–41, provide the income tax footnote rate reconciliation for Kantner. Round calculations off to the nearest dollar or one tenth of one percent (e.g., 13.9 percent) as appropriate.

43. **LO.1, 3, 4, 6** Refer back to Problems 37 through 42. Assume that you are a tax accountant with Kantner, Inc. Your supervisor has asked you to develop a Microsoft Excel workbook to automate as much as possible the current-year provision. She would also like the workbook to be structured so that it can be used for the provision every year going forward with minimal input required. She has suggested using separate worksheets to determine current tax expense, deferred tax expense, and the rate reconciliation. The worksheets should require as little numerical input as possible and be linked to avoid requiring the entry of the same information more than once. Create the workbook including this year's provision, and e-mail it to your instructor.

44. **LO.5** Does the taxpayer's effective tax rate increase or decrease when:
    a. It creates a valuation allowance against the deferred tax asset for a net operating loss?
    b. It releases a valuation allowance against the deferred tax asset for a net operating loss?

45. **LO.5** Identify whether each of the following items typically constitutes *positive* or *negative* evidence when a manufacturing entity assesses whether a valuation allowance is required or should be adjusted for its net operating losses.
    a. Product orders are increasing.
    b. Book income for the past three years totals to a negative amount.
    c. Investment assets held by the taxpayer show an unrealized gain.
    d. The industry in which the taxpayer operates is in a down cycle.
    e. The entity's tax plan includes a switch from MACRS accelerated depreciation to straight-line for future equipment purchases.

46. **LO.5** GinnyCo has pretax book and taxable income of $400,000 and reports a $100,000 income tax payable in the current year. GinnyCo has engaged in activities that it believes qualify for the research activities credit a general business tax credit of $40,000 that it cannot use this year, and its management believes that it is more likely than not that one-fourth of the credit carryforward will expire unused.
    a. Compute GinnyCo's income tax provision for the year, expressed as a Microsoft Excel formula.
    b. Construct the journal entry to report these items.

47. **LO.7** In 2019, LaceCo engaged in activities that it believes qualified for the research activities credit. The credit reduced its 2019 Federal income tax liability by $400,000, but LaceCo believed that the IRS would likely challenge the credit in an audit.

    LaceCo estimated that the tax benefit ultimately realized would be less than the immediate tax savings. The estimated potential benefits and related probabilities are presented in the following table.

Resulting Estimated Tax Benefit	Probability of Realizing Tax Benefit	Cumulative Probability of Realization
$400,000	10%	10%
300,000	35%	45%
250,000	40%	85%
-0-	15%	100%

LaceCo recorded a book tax provision of $600,000, *including* the $400,000 tax benefit from this tax uncertainty.
    a. Determine the amount that LaceCo should have recorded in 2019 for the tax benefit from this item under GAAP rules and ASC 740-10.
    b. Provide the journal entry that LaceCo should have recorded to account for the uncertainty surrounding the research activities credit.
    c. By the end of 2022, LaceCo has not been audited and the statute of limitations regarding its 2019 research activities credit expired. What, if anything, should the company recognize in 2022 related to the research credit taken in 2019?

48. **LO.7** Jazz, Inc., claimed $100,000 of rehabilitation credits on its 2022 tax return. There was sufficient tax authority to take the credits. However, due to uncertainty regarding the eligibility of some of the expenditures, Jazz only recognized $70,000 of the benefits in its 2022 financial statements. When its tax return was audited in 2023, the IRS challenged the eligibility of some of the expenditures and Jazz agreed to pay $20,000 additional tax to settle the dispute.
    a. By how much does the settlement impact Jazz's 2023 book tax expense?
    b. Provide the journal entry necessary to record the 2023 tax payment.

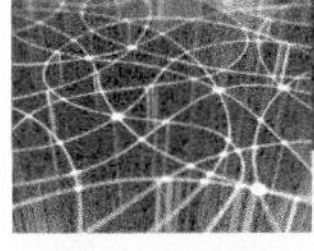

Bridge Discipline

1. Locate summary financial information for two companies in the same industry. Compare and contrast the following items across the two companies: debt-to-equity ratio, return on assets, return on equity, inventory turnover ratio, and effective tax rate.
2. Locate news or other items reporting financial analysts' forecasts or other information regarding two different companies. Determine whether the analyst appears to use any tax information in the report. For example, does the analyst use pretax or after-tax earnings in the analysis? Draft an e-mail to your instructor describing your findings. Communications
3. Using the annual reports or 10-Ks of two different public companies in the same industry, locate information regarding the compensation paid to their executives. Prepare a table comparing the compensation levels (cash and noncash) of top executives across the two companies, and send the table to your instructor. Illustrate graphically the relationship between executive compensation and company performance by comparing the compensation to other company information such as net income. Communications

Research Problems

Use internet tax resources to address the following questions. Look for reliable websites and blogs of the IRS and other government agencies, media outlets, businesses, tax professionals, academics, think tanks, and political outlets.

Research Problem 1. Locate the most recent financial statements of two companies in the same industry using the companies' websites or the SEC's website (**sec.gov**). Perform a benchmarking analysis of the two companies' effective tax rates using the effective tax rate reconciliation, levels of deferred tax assets and liabilities, and other relevant data. Summarize this information in an e-mail to your instructor. Communications

Research Problem 2. Metro builds and operates traditional shopping malls. It holds a $25,000,000 deferred tax asset relating to credit carryforwards at the state, local, and Federal levels. No valuation allowances exist. Communications, Critical Thinking

The shopping mall industry finds itself in hard times due to the loss of anchor stores and the increase in online shopping activity by consumers. Review various sources in the press that discuss how these problems arose and what some proposed solutions might be.

Metro's business plan for the next three years includes:

- The conversion of store space by new tenants (e.g., theaters, gyms, religious groups), none of which are likely to produce the profit levels lost from the stores they replace, and
- The sale of several malls at depressed prices.

In no more than three PowerPoint slides, summarize your thoughts as to the need for Metro to establish a valuation allowance against its deferred tax assets. Be specific in listing the indicators of future activity that support your conclusions.

Research Problem 3. Locate the financial statements of three different companies that report information in the income tax footnote regarding uncertain tax positions under ASC 740-10. Create a schedule that identifies the changes reported, and then compare and contrast the apparent tax strategies employed by the three companies. E-mail the schedule and analysis to your instructor. Communications

Communications
Critical Thinking

Research Problem 4. Locate summary financial information for two companies in the same industry. Compare and contrast the following items across the two companies: debt-to-equity ratio, return on assets, shareholder yield, return on equity, inventory turnover ratio, and effective tax rate. In your comparison, include the Federal, state/local, and international effective rates for the entities. Summarize in one paragraph the key reasons that make you believe the effective tax rates are so similar (or different).

Communications

Research Problem 5. Choose one of the so-called FAANG stocks (i.e., Facebook, Apple, Amazon, Netflix, Google/Alphabet). Using data that you find at EDGAR or the company website, provide the following information for the latest full reporting year, and indicate where in the financial statements you found this data. E-mail your findings to your instructor.

- Effective tax rate.
- Tax rate on international income.
- Total deferred tax assets.
- The largest single deferred tax asset.
- Total deferred tax liabilities.
- The largest single deferred tax liability.

What is your best estimate of the total tax reported by the company on its tax returns for the period?

Becker CPA Review Questions

Becker

1. Two independent situations are described below. Each involves future deductible amounts and/or future taxable amounts produced by temporary differences.

Situation	1	2
Taxable income	$40,000	$80,000
Amounts at year-end:		
Future deductible amounts	5,000	10,000
Future taxable amounts	–0–	5,000
Balances at beginning of year:		
Deferred tax asset	1,000	4,000
Deferred tax liability	–0–	1,000

The enacted state and Federal tax rate is 25% for both situations. Determine the change in the deferred tax asset balance for the year.

	Situation 1	Situation 2
a.	$5,000	$10,000
b.	$250	$1,500
c.	$1,250	$2,500
d.	$0	$0

2. Two independent situations are described below. Each situation has future deductible amounts and/or future taxable amounts produced by temporary differences.

Situation	1	2
Taxable income	$40,000	$80,000
Amounts at year-end:		
Future deductible amounts	5,000	10,000
Future taxable amounts	–0–	5,000
Balances at beginning of year:		
Deferred tax asset	1,000	4,000
Deferred tax liability	–0–	1,000

The enacted state and Federal tax rate is 25% for both situations. Determine the income tax expense for the year.

	Situation 1	Situation 2
a.	$10,000	$20,000
b.	$9,750	$21,750
c.	$250	$500
d.	$0	$0

3. At the end of year 6, the tax effects of temporary differences reported in Tortoise Company's year-end financial statements were as follows:

	Deferred Tax Assets (Liabilites)
Accelerated tax depreciation	($120,000)
Warranty expense	80,000
NOL carryforward	200,000
Total	$160,000

A valuation allowance was not considered necessary. Tortoise anticipates that $40,000 of the deferred tax liability will reverse in year 7, that actual warranty costs will be incurred evenly in year 8 and year 9, and that the NOL carryforward will be used in year 7. On Tortoise's December 31, year 6 balance sheet, what amount should be reported as a deferred tax asset under U.S. GAAP?

a. $160,000
b. $200,000
c. $240,000
d. $280,000

4. Cavan Company prepared the following reconciliation between book income and taxable income for the current year ended December 31, year 1.

Pretax accounting income	$1,000,000
Taxable income	(600,000)
Difference	$ 400,000
Book-tax differences:	
Interest on municipal income	$ 100,000
Tax depreciation in excess of book	300,000
Total	$ 400,000

Cavan's effective Federal and state income tax rate for year 1 is 30%. The depreciation difference will reverse equally over the next three years at enacted tax rates as follows:

Year	Tax Rate
Year 2	30%
Year 3	25%
Year 4	25%

In Cavan's year 1 income statement, the deferred portion of its provision for income taxes should be:

a. $120,000
b. $80,000
c. $100,000
d. $90,000

Structure of the Federal Income Tax

Part 2 introduces the components of the Federal income tax model. It begins with the gross income component, including the effect of exclusions, the accounting period, and accounting methods. This is followed by an analysis of business deductions, including amounts allowed and disallowed and the proper timing for deductions. Next, types of losses are explained, including how the tax treatment compares to financial accounting reporting procedures. Key rules that limit or postpone the use of losses and the reasons for these rules are also explained.

Chapter 4

Gross Income

Learning Objectives: *After completing Chapter 4, you should be able to:*

- **LO.1** Explain the differences between the economic, accounting, and tax concepts of gross income.
- **LO.2** Describe the taxable years and tax accounting methods generally available to taxpayers and other tax reporting entities.
- **LO.3** Identify the general sources of income and to whom they are taxed.
- **LO.4** Apply the statutory authority as to when to exclude an item from gross income.
- **LO.5** Describe the general tax consequences of property transactions.
- **LO.6** Explain the tax provision that excludes interest on state and local government obligations from gross income.
- **LO.7** Determine the extent to which life insurance proceeds are excluded from gross income.
- **LO.8** Describe when income must be reported from the discharge of indebtedness.
- **LO.9** Determine the extent to which receipts can be excluded under the tax benefit rule.
- **LO.10** Apply the tax provisions on loans made at below-market interest rates.
- **LO.11** Use the tax rules concerning the exclusion of leasehold improvements from gross income.

Chapter Outline

Tax Talk *The first nine pages of the Internal Revenue Code define income. The remaining 1,100 pages spin the web of exceptions and preferences.* —Warren G. Magnuson

TYLER OLSON/SHUTTERSTOCK.COM

Just What Is Included in Gross Income?

At the beginning of the year, Dr. Cliff Payne, age 27, opened his new dental practice as a personal service corporation. The entity uses a December 31 year-end and the accrual method of accounting. During the year, the corporation billed patients and insurance companies for $385,000 of dental services. At the end of the year, $52,000 of this amount had not been collected. The entity earned $500 interest on a money market account held at the local bank and another $500 interest on an investment in bonds issued by the Whitehall School District.

Dr. Payne's salary from his corporation is $10,000 per month. However, he did not cash his December payroll check until January. To help provide funds to invest in the new business, Dr. Payne's parents loaned him $150,000 and did not charge him any interest. He also owns stock in an unrelated corporation that has increased in value from $7,000 at the beginning of the year to more than $25,000 at the end of the year.

Although Dr. Payne took several accounting classes in college, he would like your help in calculating the correct amounts of his own gross income and the gross income of the corporation.

Read the chapter and formulate your response.

The first step in computing an income tax liability is the determination of the amount of income that is subject to tax. In completing that step, some of the following questions must be answered. We will address these and other concerns in this chapter.

- *What:* What is income?
- *When:* In which tax period is the income recognized?
- *Who:* To whom is the income taxable?

4-1 The Tax Formula

The basic income tax formula was introduced in Chapter 1 and summarized in Exhibit 1.1. This chapter, together with Chapters 5 through 8, examines the elements of this formula in detail. However, before embarking on a detailed study of the income tax, a brief introduction of each component of the tax formula, which follows, is provided as an overview.

4-1a Components of the Tax Formula

Income (Broadly Defined)

This includes all of the taxpayer's income, both taxable and nontaxable. Although it essentially is equivalent to gross receipts, it does not include a return of capital or borrowed funds.

Exclusions

For various reasons, Congress has chosen to exclude certain types of income from the income tax base. The principal income exclusions that apply to all entities (e.g., life insurance proceeds received by reason of death of the insured and state and local bond interest) are discussed later in this chapter, while exclusions that are unique to individuals are addressed in Chapters 9 through 11.

Gross Income

Code § 61(a) provides the following definition of **gross income**.

> Except as otherwise provided in this subtitle, gross income means all income from whatever source derived.

This language is taken from the Sixteenth Amendment to the Constitution. Supreme Court decisions have made it clear that *all* sources of income are subject to tax unless the income is explicitly excluded elsewhere in the Code.

> The starting point in all cases dealing with the question of the scope of what is included in "gross income" begins with the basic premise that the purpose of Congress was to use the full measure of its taxing power.[1]

Code § 61 provides perhaps the broadest definition of gross income possible. All income is taxable unless the Code says it is not. However, neither the Sixteenth Amendment nor the Code provide a definition of income itself. Rather, Congress left it to the judicial and administrative branches to determine the meaning of *income.*

A small set of items is specified as included in income, including:

- Compensation for services.
- Business income.

[1] *James v. U.S.*, 61–1 USTC ¶9449, 7 AFTR 2d 1361, 81 S.Ct. 1052.

- Gains from sales and other disposition of property.
- Interest.
- Dividends.
- Rents and royalties.
- Certain income arising from discharge of indebtedness.
- Income from partnerships.

Deductions

Generally, all ordinary and necessary trade or business expenses are deductible by taxpaying entities. Such expenses include the cost of goods sold, salaries, wages, operating expenses (such as rent and utilities), research and development expenditures, interest, taxes, depreciation, amortization, and depletion.

As noted in text Section 1-3g, individuals can use two categories of deductions—deductions *for* AGI and deductions *from* AGI. In addition, individuals are unique among taxpaying entities in that they are permitted to deduct a variety of personal expenses (i.e., expenses unrelated to business or investment), and they are allowed a standard deduction if this amount exceeds the deductible personal expenses.

Determining the Tax

Taxable income is determined by subtracting deductions (reflecting applicable limitations) from gross income. The tax rates (located on the inside front cover of this text) then are applied to determine the tax. Finally, tax prepayments (such as Federal income tax withholding on salaries and estimated tax payments) and a wide variety of credits are subtracted from the tax to determine the amount due to the Federal government or the refund due to the taxpayer. This formula is summarized on the inside back cover of this text and in text Exhibits 1.1 and 1.2.

4-2 Gross Income

4-2a Concepts of Income

Explain the differences between the economic, accounting, and tax concepts of gross income.

As noted above, Congress mostly left it to the judicial and administrative branches of government to determine the meaning of the term *income*. As the income tax law developed, two competing models of income were considered by these branches: economic income and accounting income.

The term **income** is used in the Code and defined broadly. Early in the history of our tax laws, the courts were required to interpret "the commonly understood meaning of the term which must have been in the minds of the people when they adopted the Sixteenth Amendment."[2]

Economists measure income (**economic income**) as the sum of (1) the value of goods and services consumed during a period and (2) the change in the value of net assets (assets minus liabilities) from the beginning to the end of the period. Note that the change in the value of net assets is not dependent on the sale or exchange of those assets: economic income can be derived by a mere change in the value of assets held. Similarly, economic income includes in consumption the imputed value of personal items, such as as the rental value of an owner-occupied home and the value of food grown for personal consumption.[3]

[2] *Merchants Loan and Trust Co. v. Smietanka*, 1 USTC ¶42, 3 AFTR 3102, 41 S.Ct. 386 (1921).

[3] See Henry C. Simons, *Personal Income Taxation* (Chicago: University of Chicago Press, 1933), Chapters 2–3.

Financial Disclosure Insights — What Does "Income" Mean to You?

Accountants use a definition of income that relies on the realization principle.[4] **Accounting income** is not recognized until it is realized. For realization to occur:

- An exchange of goods or services must take place between the entity and some independent, external party, and
- The goods or services received by the entity must be capable of being objectively valued.[5]

Thus, an increase in the fair market value of an asset before its sale or other disposition is not sufficient to trigger the recognition of accounting income. Similarly, the imputed savings that arise when an entity creates assets for its own use (e.g., feed grown by a farmer for his or her livestock) do not constitute accounting income because no exchange has occurred.

Business taxpayers often reconcile their annual income computations for financial accounting and tax law purposes. Taxpayers required to prepare audited financial statements must explain in the footnotes to the statements (1) the most important accounting principles used in computing book income and (2) the most important tax elections and other consequences of the tax law on earnings per share.

Example 1

Sharon's economic income is calculated by comparing her net worth at the end of the year (December 31) with her net worth at the beginning of the year (January 1) and adding the amount of her personal consumption.

Fair market value of Sharon's assets on December 31	$220,000	
Less liabilities on December 31	(40,000)	
Net worth on December 31		$ 180,000
Fair market value of Sharon's assets on January 1	$200,000	
Less liabilities on January 1	(80,000)	
Net worth on January 1		(120,000)
Increase in net worth		$ 60,000
Food, clothing, and other personal expenditures	$ 25,000	
Imputed rental value of the home Sharon owns and occupies	12,000	
Total consumption		37,000
Economic income		$ 97,000

The tax law relies to some extent on net worth as a measure of income.[6] Potentially, anything that increases net worth is income, and anything that decreases net worth is deductible (if permitted by statute). Thus, *windfall income* such as buried treasure found in one's backyard is taxable under the theory that net worth has increased.[7] Likewise, a lender does *not* recognize gross income on receipt of loan principal repayments. The lender's investment simply changes from a loan receivable to cash, so net worth does not change.

Because the strict application of a tax based on economic income would require taxpayers to determine the value of their assets annually, compliance would be burdensome. Controversies between taxpayers and the IRS inevitably would arise under an economic approach to income determination because of the subjective nature of valuation in many circumstances. In addition, using market values to determine income for tax purposes could result in liquidity problems. That is, a taxpayer's assets could increase

[4]See the American Accounting Association Committee Report on the "Realization Concept," *The Accounting Review* (April 1965): 312–322.

[5]Valuation is carried out in the local currency of the reporting entity.

[6]*Comm. v. Glenshaw Glass Co.*, 55–1 USTC ¶9308, 47 AFTR 162, 348 U.S. 426.

[7]*Cesarini v. U.S.*, 69–1 USTC ¶9270, 23 AFTR 2d 69–997, 296 F.Supp. 3 (D.Ct. N.Oh.), *aff'd* 70–2 USTC ¶9509, 26 AFTR 2d 70–5107, 428 F.2d 812 (CA–6); Reg. § 1.61–14.

in value but not be easily converted into the cash needed to pay the resulting tax (e.g., increases in the value of commercial real estate).[8] Thus, the IRS, Congress, and the courts have rejected the economic concept of income as impractical.

The Big Picture

Example 2

Return to the facts of *The Big Picture* on p. 4-1. Dr. Payne's portfolio has increased in value by more than 250% during the tax year, and that additional value constitutes economic income to him. But the Federal income tax law does not include the value increase in Dr. Payne's gross income, even though he could convert some of those gains to cash by selling the stock.

4-2b Comparing Accounting and Tax Concepts of Income

Although income tax rules frequently parallel financial accounting measurement concepts, differences do exist. Of major significance, for example, is that the unrealized increase in the value of marketable securities is included in financial accounting income but not in taxable income. Because of this and other differences, many corporations report financial accounting income that is substantially different from the amounts reported for tax purposes; these differences were the subject of much of Chapter 3.

The Supreme Court provided an explanation for some of the variations between accounting and taxable income.

> The primary goal of financial accounting is to provide useful information to management, shareholders, creditors, and others properly interested; the major responsibility of the accountant is to protect these parties from being misled. The primary goal of the income tax system, in contrast, is the equitable collection of revenue.... Consistently with its goals and responsibilities, financial accounting has as its foundation the principle of conservatism, with its corollary that "possible errors in measurement [should] be in the direction of understatement rather than overstatement of net income and net assets." In view of the Treasury's markedly different goals and responsibilities, understatement of income is not destined to be its guiding light....
>
> Financial accounting, in short, is hospitable to estimates, probabilities, and reasonable certainties; the tax law, with its mandate to preserve the revenue, can give no quarter to uncertainty.[9]

4-2c Form of Receipt

Income is not taxable until it is realized. Realization, however, does not require the receipt of cash. "Gross income includes income realized in any form, whether in money, property, or services. Income may be realized [and recognized], therefore, in the form of services, meals, accommodations, stock or other property, as well as in cash."[10]

Form of Receipt

Example 3

Ostrich Corporation allows Cameron, an employee, to use a company car for his vacation. Cameron realizes income equal to the rental value of the car for the time and mileage.

[8]In text Section 1-6d, this was identified as a justification of the wherewithal to pay concept.

[9]*Thor Power Tool Co. v. Comm.*, 79–1 USTC ¶9139, 43 AFTR 2d 79–362, 99 S.Ct. 773.

[10]Reg. § 1.61–1(a).

Form of Receipt

Example 4

Donna is a CPA specializing in individual tax return preparation. Her neighbor, Khalil, is a dentist. Each year, Donna prepares Khalil's tax return in exchange for two dental checkups. Khalil and Donna both have gross income equal to the fair market value of the services they receive.

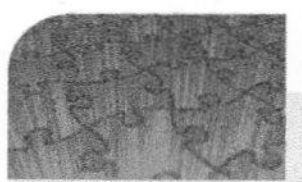

Concept Summary 4.1

Gross Income Concepts

Taxable income is computed using a specific form of income statement (i.e., one created by Congress). Taxable income can be seen as similar but not identical to both economic income and the income computation that is required by generally accepted accounting principles (GAAP).

1. Economic income is not appropriate for computing taxable income. Economic income depends on annual measures of market value and consumption, both of which would be difficult to apply on a short tax-filing deadline.
2. Many of the same accounting methods that are allowed by GAAP also can be used in computing gross income and tax deductions, since the tax law largely follows the realization principle of financial accounting.

4-3 Timing of Income Recognition

4-3a Taxable Year

The annual accounting period or **taxable year** is a basic component of our tax system. For the most part, a taxable year entails a period of 12 months ending on the last day of a calendar month.

Generally, a taxpayer uses the *calendar year* to report gross income. However, a *fiscal year* (a period of 12 months ending on the last day of any month other than December) can be adopted if the taxpayer maintains adequate books and records to make such computations.[11] In most cases, a fiscal year is not available to partnerships, S corporations, and personal service corporations (i.e., one performing services in health, law, engineering, architecture, accounting, actuarial science, performing arts, or consulting). Although it is not required, most individuals use a calendar tax year, and a business usually desires a tax year that corresponds with its year-end for financial accounting purposes.

It is important that income be recognized in the proper tax year for several reasons.

- With a progressive tax rate system, a taxpayer's marginal tax rate can change from year to year.
- Congress may change the tax rates.
- The relevant rates may change because of a change in the taxpayer's legal form (e.g., a proprietorship may incorporate or an individual could marry).
- Several provisions in the Code require computations using the taxpayer's income for the year (e.g., the charitable contribution deduction).
- The taxpayer wants to reduce the present value of any tax that is owed. In this regard, income recognition in a later year is preferred; the longer payment of the tax can be postponed, the lower the present value of the tax.

LO.2

Describe the taxable years and tax accounting methods generally available to taxpayers and other tax reporting entities.

4-3b Accounting Methods

The year an item of income is recognized depends on the **accounting method** the taxpayer employs. The three primary methods of accounting are (1) the cash receipts and disbursements method, (2) the accrual method, and (3) the hybrid method. Most individuals and many small businesses use the cash receipts and disbursements method of accounting, while

[11] § 441; Reg. § 1.441–1.

most larger businesses use the accrual method. Generally, the tax law requires the use of the accrual method for determining purchases and sales when inventory is an income-producing factor.[12] Some businesses employ a hybrid method that is a combination of the cash and accrual methods (e.g., using the accrual method for sales and inventories and the cash method for everything else).

In addition to these overall accounting methods, specialized tax accounting methods are available for certain items or transactions. For instance, a taxpayer may spread the gain from a sale of eligible property over the collection period by using the *installment method* of income recognition. Contractors may either spread profits from contracts over the period in which the work is done (the *percentage of completion method*) or defer all profit until the year in which the project is completed (the *completed contract method*, which can be used only in limited circumstances).[13]

The IRS holds broad powers to determine whether the taxpayer's accounting method is appropriate, and to have the taxpayer change the method if it does not *clearly reflect income*.

> If no method of accounting has been regularly used by the taxpayer, or if the method used does not clearly reflect income, the computation of taxable income shall be made under such method as, in the opinion of the Secretary . . . does clearly reflect income.[14]

Cash Receipts Method

Under the **cash receipts method**, income is recognized in the year of actual or constructive receipt by the taxpayer, regardless of whether the income was earned in that year.[15] Despite the method's name, the taxpayer need not receive cash to be required to recognize income under the cash receipts method. Rather, the receipt of anything that can be valued in terms of money, or that has a cash equivalent, is includible in income under the cash receipts method.[16]

As a result, a cash basis taxpayer that receives a note in payment for services recognizes gross income equal to the fair market value of the note in the year the note is received. However, a creditor's mere promise to pay (e.g., an account receivable), with no supporting note, usually is not considered to have a fair market value; it is not a cash equivalent.[17] Thus, a cash basis taxpayer who receives an account receivable in return for goods or services defers income recognition until the receivable is collected.

Example 5

Finch & Thrush, a CPA firm, uses the cash receipts method of accounting. In 2022, the firm performs an audit for Orange Corporation and bills the client for $5,000, which is collected in 2023. In 2022, the firm also performs an audit for Blue Corporation. Because of Blue's precarious financial position, Finch & Thrush requires Blue to issue an $8,000 secured negotiable note in payment of the fee. The note has a fair market value of $6,000. The firm collects $8,000 on the note in 2023. Finch & Thrush reports the following gross income for the two years.

	2022	2023
Fair market value of note received from Blue	$6,000	
Cash received		
From Orange on account receivable		$ 5,000
From Blue on note receivable		8,000
Less: Recovery of capital	–0–	(6,000)
Total gross income	$6,000	$ 7,000

[12] Reg. § 1.446–1(c)(2)(i); IRC § 471(c) though allows small businesses to use the cash method even though they have inventory.

[13] §§ 453 and 460.

[14] § 446(b).

[15] *Julia A. Strauss*, 2 B.T.A. 598 (1925). The doctrine of *constructive receipt* holds that if income is unqualifiedly available although not physically in the taxpayer's possession, it is included in gross income. An example is accrued interest on a savings account. Under the doctrine of constructive receipt, the interest is taxed to a depositor in the year available rather than the year actually withdrawn. The fact that the depositor uses the cash basis of accounting for tax purposes is irrelevant. Reg. § 1.451–2.

[16] Reg. §§ 1.446–1(a)(3) and (c)(1)(i).

[17] *Bedell v. Comm.*, 1 USTC ¶359, 7 AFTR 8469, 30 F.2d 622 (CA–2, 1929).

Generally, a cash basis taxpayer recognizes gross income when a check is received in payment for goods or services rendered in a business setting. This is true even if the taxpayer receives the check after banking hours. But if the person paying with the check requests that the check not be cashed until a subsequent date, the cash basis income is deferred until the date the check can be cashed.[18]

The tax law restricts the availability of the cash receipts method for several reasons. For example, the cash receipts method could distort taxable income since income and expenses from the same activity may be recognized in different tax years. Moreover, a taxpayer using the cash receipts method has some degree of control over when income is recognized (e.g., by delaying the sending of invoices to customers). One important restriction requires most corporations with average annual gross receipts greater than $27 million, computed over the preceding three-year period, to use the accrual method. Also, businesses with average annual gross receipts in excess of $27 million, whether or not they are corporations, are required to account for their inventory under the accrual method.[19]

Accrual Method

Under the **accrual method**, an item generally is included in gross income in the year in which it is earned, regardless of when the income is collected.[20] Gross income is earned when (1) all the events have occurred that fix the right to receive the income and (2) the amount to be received can be determined with reasonable accuracy. However, regardless of when these tests are actually met, they are generally treated as satisfied no later than when the revenue is included in the taxpayer's *applicable financial statement*.[21]

Generally, a taxpayer's right to income accrues when title to property being sold passes to the buyer or the services are performed for the customer or client.[22] If the rights to income have accrued but are subject to a potential refund claim (e.g., under a product warranty), the income is reported in the year of sale and a deduction is allowed in subsequent years when actual claims accrue.[23]

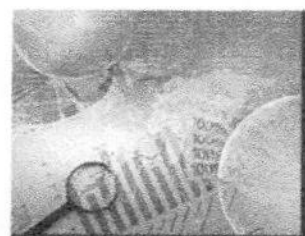

Tax Planning Strategies **Cash Receipts Method**

Framework Focus: Income

Strategy: Postpone Recognition of Income to Achieve Tax Deferral.

Framework Focus: Tax Rate

Strategy: Shift Net Income from High-Bracket Years to Low-Bracket Years.

The timing of income from services often can be controlled through the cash method of accounting. The usual lag between billings and collections (e.g., December's billings collected in January) can result in a deferral of some income until the next year.

As another example, before rendering services, a corporate officer approaching retirement may contract with the corporation to defer a portion of their compensation to the lower tax bracket retirement years.

[18] *Charles F. Kahler*, 18 T.C. 31 (1952); *Bright v. U.S.*, 91–1 USTC ¶50,142, 67 AFTR 2d 91–673, 926 F.2d 383 (CA–5).

[19] §§ 448, 471(c), and 263A(i). The $27 million amount is indexed for inflation. The accrual method requirement does not apply to individuals, partnerships without a C corporation partner, S corporations, estates, and trusts. In general, these taxpayers may use the cash receipts method regardless of their gross receipts [unless the taxpayer meets the definition at § 448(d)(3) of a tax shelter]. If such entity has inventory and average annual gross receipts in the prior three-year period in excess of $27 million, it uses either the accrual method or the hybrid method.

[20] These rules differ from those used for financial accounting purposes.

[21] IRC § 451(b), Reg. § 1.451–1(a). Generally, an applicable financial statement is a GAAP certified statement.

[22] *Lucas v. North Texas Lumber Co.*, 2 USTC ¶484, 8 AFTR 10276, 50 S.Ct. 184 (1930).

[23] *Brown v. Helvering*, 4 USTC ¶1222, 13 AFTR 851, 54 S.Ct. 356 (1933).

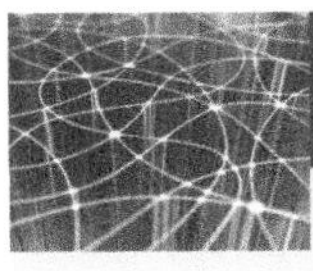

Bridge Discipline Bridge to Economics and Finance

Nontaxable Economic Benefits

Home ownership is the prime example of economic income from capital that is not subject to tax. If the taxpayer uses their capital to purchase investments but pays rent on a personal residence, they pay tax on the income from the investments but cannot deduct the rent payment.

However, if the taxpayer purchases a personal residence instead of the investments, they remove the investment income from the tax return but incur no other form of gross income. A homeowner "pays rent to himself," but such rent is not subject to income tax. Thus, the homeowner has substituted nontaxable for taxable income. This nontaxable income is sometimes referred to as imputed rental income.

Tax Deferral

Because deferred taxes are tantamount to interest-free loans to the taxpayer from the government, the deferral of taxes is a worthy goal of the tax planner. However, the tax planner also must consider the tax rates for the years the income is shifted from and to. For example, a one-year deferral of income from a year in which the taxpayer's tax rate was 24 percent to a year in which the tax rate will be 32 percent would not be advisable if the taxpayer expects to earn less than an 8 percent after-tax return on the deferred tax dollars. Text Appendix E provides tables to compute the present and future values of gross income, deductions, and tax liabilities.

The taxpayer often can defer the recognition of income from appreciated property by postponing the event triggering realization (e.g., the final closing on a sale or exchange of property). If the taxpayer needs cash, obtaining a loan by using the appreciated property as collateral may be the least costly alternative. When the taxpayer anticipates reinvesting the proceeds, a sale may be inadvisable.

Ira owns 100 shares of Pigeon Company common stock with a cost of $20,000 and a fair market value of $50,000. Although the stock's value has increased substantially in the past three years, Ira thinks the growth cycle for the stock is over. If he sells the Pigeon stock, Ira will invest the proceeds from the sale in other common stock. Assuming that Ira's marginal tax rate on the sale is 20%, he keeps only $44,000 [$50,000 − .20($50,000 − $20,000)] to reinvest. The alternative investment must substantially outperform Pigeon in the future for the sale to be beneficial.

Where a taxpayer's right to income is contested (e.g., when a customer claims that a contractor has failed to meet the specifications of a construction contract), gross income is recognized only when payment has been received.[24] If the payment is received before the dispute is settled, however, the court-made **claim of right doctrine** requires the taxpayer to recognize the income in the year of receipt.[25]

If Finch & Thrush in Example 5 uses the accrual basis of accounting, it recognizes $13,000 ($8,000 + $5,000) income in 2022, the year its rights to the income accrue.

Tangerine Construction, Inc., completes construction of a building at the end of the year and presents a bill to the customer. The customer refuses to pay the bill and claims that Tangerine has not met specifications. A settlement with the customer is not reached until the next year.

Under the accrual method of tax accounting, no gross income accrues to Tangerine until the second year.

[24] *Burnet v. Sanford and Brooks*, 2 USTC ¶636, 9 AFTR 603, 51 S.Ct. 150 (1931).

[25] *North American Oil Consolidated Co. v. Burnet*, 3 USTC ¶943, 11 AFTR 16, 52 S.Ct. 613 (1932).

Hybrid Method

The **hybrid method** is a combination of the accrual and cash methods. Generally, a taxpayer using the hybrid method is in the business of buying and selling inventory but not otherwise required to use the accrual method. As a result, the taxpayer using the hybrid method accounts for sales of goods and cost of goods sold using the accrual method, and the cash method is used for all other income and expense items (e.g., services and interest income). Because most small businesses can use the cash method for sales and cost of goods sold, the hybrid method is not commonly used.

4-3c Special Rules for Cash Basis Taxpayers

Constructive Receipt

Income that has not actually been received by the taxpayer is taxed as though it had been received—the income is considered constructively received if the amount is made readily available to the taxpayer and not subject to substantial limitations or restrictions.[26] For example, if an employee receives a paycheck on December 31 that is dated for January 8, it is not constructively received in December due to the date limitation. It would be considered taxable income in January.

The purpose of the **constructive receipt** doctrine is to prevent a cash basis taxpayer from deferring the recognition of income that, although not yet received, has been made practically available to them. For instance, a taxpayer is not permitted to defer income earned in December simply by refusing to accept payment until January.

Constructive Receipt

Rob, a physician, conducts his medical practice as a sole proprietorship. Rob also is a member of a barter club. This year, Rob provided medical care for other club members and earned 3,000 points. Each point entitles him to $1 in goods and services sold by other members of the club; the points can be used at any time. Rob exchanged his points for a new high-definition TV in the next year, but he recognizes $3,000 gross income in the first year (i.e., when the 3,000 points were credited to his account).[27]

On December 31, an employer issued a bonus check to an employee but asked her to hold it for a few days until the company could make deposits to cover the check. The income was not constructively received on December 31 because the issuer did not have sufficient funds in its account to pay the amount owed.[28]

Mauve, Inc., an S corporation, owned interest coupons that matured on December 31. The coupons can be converted to cash at any bank at maturity. Thus, the income was constructively received on December 31, even though Mauve failed to cash in the coupons until the following year.[29]

Flamingo Company mails dividend checks on December 31. The checks will not be received by the shareholders until January. The shareholders do not realize gross income until January.[30]

The constructive receipt doctrine does not apply to income the taxpayer is not yet entitled to receive, even though the taxpayer could have contracted to receive the income at an earlier date.

[26] Reg. § 1.451–2(a).

[27] Rev.Rul. 80–52.

[28] *L. M. Fischer*, 14 T.C. 792 (1950).

[29] Reg. § 1.451–2(b).

[30] Reg. § 1.451–2(b).

Murphy offers to pay Peach Corporation (a cash basis taxpayer) $100,000 for land in December of year 1. Peach Corporation refuses, but offers to sell the land to Murphy on January 1 of year 2, when the corporation will be in a lower tax bracket. If Murphy accepts Peach's offer, the gain is taxed to Peach in year 2, when the sale is completed.[31]

Additional information on constructive receipt can be found on this book's companion website: www.cengage.com

1 Digging Deeper

Original Issue Discount

Lenders frequently make loans that require a payment at maturity of more than the amount of the original loan. The difference between the amount due at maturity and the amount of the original loan, or the **original issue discount**, is actually interest. In these circumstances, the original issue discount must be reported as it is earned, regardless of the taxpayer's accounting method.[32] The *interest earned* is calculated using the effective interest rate method.

On January 1, year 1, Blue and White, a cash basis partnership, pays $90,703 for a 24-month certificate of deposit. The certificate is priced to yield 5% (the effective interest rate) with interest compounded annually. No interest is paid until maturity, when Blue and White receives $100,000.

The partnership's gross income from the certificate is $9,297 ($100,000 − $90,703). Blue and White calculates income earned each year as follows.

Year 1 (0.05 × $90,703) =	$4,535
Year 2 [0.05 × ($90,703 + $4,535)] =	4,762
	$9,297

The original issue discount rules do not apply to U.S. savings bonds or to obligations with a maturity date of one year or less from the date of issue.[33]

Amounts Received under an Obligation to Repay

The receipt of funds with an obligation to repay those funds in the future is the essence of borrowing. The taxpayer's assets and liabilities increase by the same amount, and no gross income is realized when the borrowed funds are received.

A landlord receives a damage deposit from a tenant. The landlord does not recognize income until the deposit is forfeited because the landlord has an obligation to repay the deposit if no damage occurs.[34] However, if the deposit is in fact a prepayment of rent, it is taxed in the year of receipt.

4-3d Special Rules for Accrual Basis Taxpayers

Unearned Income

For financial reporting purposes, advance payments received from customers are initially reflected in the financial statements of the seller as a liability and recognized as income over the period in which the income is earned. However, for tax purposes, unearned income generally is taxed in the year of receipt.

[31] *Cowden v. Comm.*, 61–1 USTC ¶9382, 7 AFTR 2d 1160, 289 F.2d 20 (CA–5).

[32] §§ 1272(a)(3) and 1273(a).

[33] § 1272(a)(2).

[34] *John Mantell*, 17 T.C. 1143 (1952).

In December 2022, Jared's sole proprietorship pays its January 2023 rent of $1,000. Jared's calendar year, accrual basis landlord includes the $1,000 in 2022 gross income for tax purposes, although $1,000 unearned rent income is reported as a liability on the landlord's financial accounting balance sheet for December 31, 2022.

Accrual basis taxpayers who receive advance payments for the sale of goods or services may elect to include in gross income in the year of receipt only the amount of any advance payment that is reported as income in their financial statements, with the remaining amount reported in the subsequent tax year.[35] This method of tax accounting also may be used for advance payments received for the licensing of intellectual property and the sale, lease, or license of software. When an accrual basis taxpayer elects to use the deferral rule for advance payments that span more than one year, book-tax differences result, as illustrated in Example 16.

Advance payments for prepaid rent or prepaid interest, however, always are taxed in the year of receipt, as illustrated in Example 15.

Yellow Corporation, an accrual basis calendar year taxpayer, sells its computer consulting services under 12-month, 24-month, and 36-month contracts. The corporation provides services to each customer every month. On May 1, year 1, Yellow sold the following contracts.

Length of Contract	Total Proceeds
12 months	$3,000
24 months	4,800
36 months	7,200

Yellow may defer until year 2 all of the income that will be reported on its financial statements after year 1.

Length of Contract	Income Recorded in Year 1	Income Recorded in Year 2
12 months	$2,000 ($3,000 × 8/12)	$1,000 ($3,000 × 4/12)
24 months	1,600 ($4,800 × 8/24)	3,200 ($4,800 × 16/24)
36 months	1,600 ($7,200 × 8/36)	5,600 ($7,200 × 28/36)

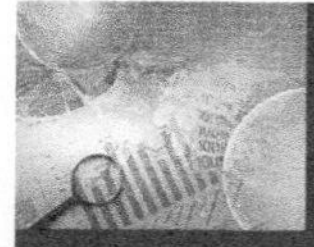

Tax Planning Strategies **Prepaid Income**

Framework Focus: Income

Strategy: Postpone Recognition of Income to Achieve Tax Deferral.

The accrual basis taxpayer who receives advance payments from customers should adopt the available tax accounting income deferral methods. It then should structure the transactions using those rules, so as to avoid a payment of tax on income before the time the income actually is earned.

In addition, both cash and accrual basis taxpayers sometimes can defer income by structuring the payments as deposits rather than prepaid income. For example, a tax-savvy landlord might consider requiring an equivalent damage deposit rather than prepayment of the last month's rent.

[35] § 451(c) and Reg. § 1.451–8.

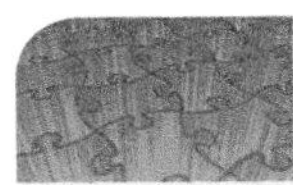

Concept Summary 4.2

Income Tax Accounting

Tax accounting methods often parallel those used for financial accounting, especially those that affect the timing of the tax recognition of income and deduction items. Certain exceptions do exist, however.

1. Businesses can adopt the cash, accrual, or hybrid method of accounting. The tax law allows certain businesses to use either the cash or hybrid method, while others may be required to use the accrual method. For instance, the accrual method typically is required if the taxpayer holds inventories or is a C corporation with over $26 million of gross receipts (other than a qualified personal service corporation).
2. Other tax accounting methods parallel those of financial accounting, such as the installment method and the treatment of long-term contracts.
3. Special rules apply when the taxpayer has control, but not possession, of funds that have been earned.
4. Tax accounting method rules allow a limited deferral of income recognition concerning advance payments for the sale of goods and services for accrual basis taxpayers.

4-4 General Sources of Income

LO.3

Identify the general sources of income and to whom they are taxed.

4-4a Income from Personal Services

It is a well-established principle of taxation that income from personal services are included in the gross income of the person who performs the services. This principle was first established in a Supreme Court decision, *Lucas v. Earl.*[36] Mr. Earl entered into a binding agreement with his spouse under which Mrs. Earl was to receive one-half of Mr. Earl's salary. Justice Holmes used the celebrated **fruit and tree metaphor** to explain that the fruit (income) must be attributed to the tree from which it came (Mr. Earl's services). A mere **assignment of income** to another party does not shift the liability for the tax.

Services of an Employee

As discussed above, the income from personal services generally is taxable to the person performing the services. However, services performed by an employee for an employer's customers are considered performed by the employer. Thus, the employer is taxed on the income from the services provided, and the employee is taxed on any compensation received from the employer.[37]

The Big Picture

Return to the facts of *The Big Picture* on p. 4-1. Dr. Payne has entered into an employment contract with his corporation and receives a salary. All patients contract to receive their dental services from the corporation, and those services are provided by the corporation's employee, Dr. Payne.

Thus, the corporation earned the income from patients' services and must include the patients' fees in its gross income. Payne includes his salary in his own gross income. The corporation claims a deduction for the reasonable salary paid to Payne.

Is there a minimum age for reporting income? Find out at this book's companion website: **www.cengage.com**

2 Digging Deeper

4-4b Income from Property

Income earned from property (e.g., interest, dividends, rent) is included in the gross income of the owner of the property. For example, if a father gives his daughter the

[36] 2 USTC ¶496, 8 AFTR 10287, 50 S.Ct. 241 (1930).

[37] *Sargent v. Comm.*, 91–1 USTC ¶50,168, 67 AFTR 2d 91–718, 929 F.2d 1252 (CA–8).

Tax Fact **How Much and What Type of Income?**

Of the more than 150 million individual income tax returns filed for the 2018 tax year, 83 percent included wage or salary income, and about 30 percent included taxable interest income. Except for these two categories, no other type of income was found in even a quarter of the returns filed. Sales of business assets were found on fewer than 2 percent of the returns, and about 6 percent of the returns included flow-through income or loss from partnerships and S corporations. Capital gains showed up on about 17 percent of the returns, but only when distributions from mutual fund investments were included.

right to collect the rent from his rental property (the "fruit"), the father will nonetheless be taxed on the rent because he retains ownership of the property (the "tree").[38]

Often income-producing property is transferred after income from the property has accrued but before the income is recognized under the transferor's method of accounting. The IRS and the courts have developed rules to allocate the income between the transferor and the transferee. These allocation rules are addressed below. Other allocation rules address income in community property states.

Digging Deeper 3

Information on income in community property states can be found on this book's companion website: www.cengage.com

Interest

Interest is considered to accrue daily. Therefore, the interest on an obligation for the period that includes a transfer of ownership is allocated between the transferor and the transferee based on the number of days during the period that each owned the obligation.

Example 18

Floyd, a cash basis taxpayer, gives his son, Seth, corporate bonds with a face amount of $12,000 and a 5% stated annual interest rate. The interest is payable on the last day of each quarter. Floyd makes the gift to Seth on February 28. Floyd recognizes $100 interest income at the time of the gift ($12,000 × 5% × 3/12 interest for the quarter × 2/3 months in the quarter earned before the gift).

For the transferor, the timing of the recognition of gross income from the property depends on the pertinent accounting method and the manner in which the property was transferred. In the case of a gift of income-producing property, the donor's share of the accrued income is recognized at the time it would have been recognized had the donor continued to own the property.[39] If the transfer is a sale, however, the transferor recognizes the accrued income at the time of the sale, because the accrued amount is included in the sales proceeds.

Example 19

Mia purchased a corporate bond at its face amount on July 1 for $10,000. The bond paid 5% interest each June 30. On September 30, Mia sold the bond for $10,600. Mia recognizes $125 interest income, accrued as of the date of the sale (5% × $10,000 × 3/12 months before the sale). She also recognizes a $475 capital gain from the sale of the bond, computed as follows.

Amount received from sale	$ 10,600
Accrued interest income already recognized	(125)
Selling price of bond, less interest	$ 10,475
Less cost of the bond	(10,000)
Capital gain recognized on sale	$ 475

[38] *Helvering v. Horst*, 40–2 USTC ¶9787, 24 AFTR 1058, 61 S.Ct. 144.

[39] Rev.Rul. 72–312.

Global Tax Issues Which Foreign Dividends Get the Discounted Rate?

A dividend from a non-U.S. corporation is eligible for qualified dividend status only if one of the following requirements is met: (1) the foreign corporation's stock is traded on an established U.S. securities market or (2) the foreign corporation is eligible for the benefits of a comprehensive income tax treaty or information-sharing agreement between its country of incorporation and the United States.[40]

FBAR information for reporting certain foreign bank and financial accounts can be found on this book's companion website: www.cengage.com

4 Digging Deeper

Dividends

As a separate taxable entity, a corporation is taxed on its earnings, with those earnings taxed again as dividends when distributed to shareholders. Therefore, corporate earnings distributed as dividends are subject to double taxation.

Partial relief from the double taxation of dividends has been provided to noncorporate taxpayers in that *qualified dividends* are taxed at the same marginal rate that is applicable to a net capital gain. Generally, net capital gains are subject to a 15 percent rate of Federal income tax. The rate is 0 percent for taxpayers with low taxable income and 20 percent for upper-income taxpayers. Distributions that are not qualified dividends are taxed at the rates that apply to ordinary income.[41]

Because the beneficial tax rate is intended to mitigate double taxation, only certain dividends are eligible for the beneficial treatment. Excluded are certain dividends from non-U.S. corporations, dividends from tax-exempt entities, and dividends that do not satisfy the holding period requirement.

Corporations that are shareholders (i.e., they own stock in another corporation) may be allowed a deduction to offset some or all of their dividend income. See text Section 12-4a.

A holding period requirement must be satisfied for the lower tax rates to apply: the stock that paid the dividend must have been held for more than 60 days during the 121-day period beginning 60 days before the ex-dividend date.[42] The purpose of this requirement is to prevent the taxpayer from buying the stock shortly before the dividend is paid, receiving the dividend, and then selling the stock at a short-term capital loss after the stock goes ex-dividend. A stock's price often declines after the stock goes ex-dividend.

Qualified Dividends

Green Corporation pays a dividend of $1.50 on each share of its common stock. Madison and Daniel, two unrelated shareholders, each own 1,000 shares of the stock. Consequently, each receives a dividend of $1,500 (1,000 shares × $1.50). Assume that Daniel satisfies the 60/120-day holding period rule, but Madison does not.

The $1,500 that Daniel receives is subject to the lower rates on qualified dividends. The $1,500 that Madison receives, however, is not. Because Madison did not comply with the holding period rule, her dividend is not a *qualified dividend*; it is taxed at ordinary income rates.

---

[40] §§ 1(h)(11)(C)(i), (ii).

[41] § 1(h)(11). Note that qualified dividends are *not* capital gains; thus, they are *not* reduced by capital losses. For certain high-income individuals, the additional Medicare tax on net investment income also may apply to dividends, interest, net capital gains, and the like. See text Section 9-5e.

[42] The ex-dividend date is the date before the record date on which the corporation finalizes the list of shareholders who will receive the dividends.

Qualified Dividends

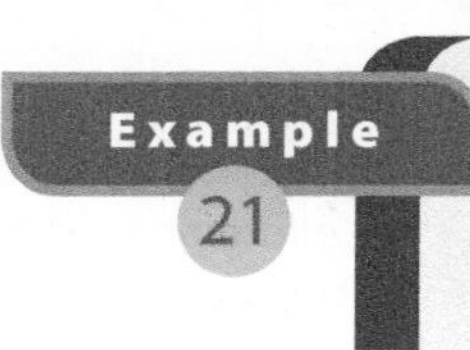

Assume that both Madison and Daniel in Example 20 are in the 32% Federal income tax bracket. Consequently, Madison pays a tax of $480 (32% × $1,500) on her dividend, whereas Daniel pays a tax of $225 (15% × $1,500) on his. The $255 saving that Daniel enjoys underscores the advantages of receiving a qualified dividend.

A distribution by a corporation to its shareholders is classified as a dividend only if it is paid from the entity's *earnings and profits* (E & P). If the distribution is not made from E & P, it is treated as a return of the shareholder's investment and generally is not taxed at the time of the distribution. See text Section 13-2c.

Interest generally accrues on a daily basis, but the declaration of a dividend is at the discretion of the corporation's board of directors. Generally, dividends are taxed to the person who is entitled to receive them—the shareholder of record as of the corporation's record date.[43] Thus, if a taxpayer sells stock after a dividend has been declared but before the record date, the dividend generally is taxed to the purchaser.

If a donor makes a gift of stock to someone (e.g., a family member) after the declaration date but before the record date, the donor does not shift the dividend income to the donee. The *fruit* has ripened sufficiently as of the declaration date to tax the dividend income to the donor of the stock.[44]

On June 20, the board of directors of Black Corporation declares a $10 per share dividend. The dividend is payable on June 30 to shareholders of record on June 25. As of June 20, Maria owns 200 shares of Black stock. On June 21, Maria sells 100 of the shares to Jon for their fair market value and gives 100 of the shares to Andrew (her son). Both Jon and Andrew are shareholders of record as of June 25.

Jon (the purchaser) is taxed on $1,000 because he is entitled to receive the dividend. However, Maria (the donor) is taxed on the $1,000 received by Andrew (the donee) because the gift was made after the declaration date but before the record date of the dividend.

Digging Deeper 5

Additional information on dividends can be found on this book's companion website: www.cengage.com

4-4c Income Received by an Agent

Income received by the taxpayer's agent is considered to be received by the taxpayer. Therefore, a cash basis principal recognizes the income at the time it is received by the agent.[45]

Longhorn, Inc., a cash basis corporation, delivers cattle to the auction barn in late December. The auctioneer, acting as the corporation's agent, sells the cattle and collects the proceeds in December. The auctioneer does not pay Longhorn until the following January. Longhorn includes the sales proceeds in its gross income in the year the auctioneer received the funds.

[43] Reg. § 1.61–9(c). The record date is the cutoff for determining the shareholders who are entitled to receive the dividend.

[44] *M. G. Anton*, 34 T.C. 842 (1960).

[45] Rev.Rul. 79–379.

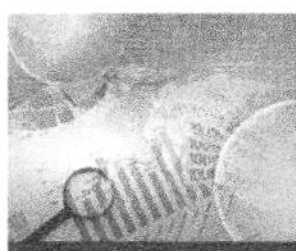

Tax Planning Strategies — Techniques for Reducing Investment Income

Framework Focus: Income

Strategy: Postpone Recognition of Income to Achieve Tax Deferral.

Framework Focus: Tax Rate

Strategy: Control the Character of Income

Because no tax is due until a gain has been recognized, the law favors investments that yield appreciation rather than annual income, and it favors capital gains over interest income.

Example 24

Chandra can buy a low-rated corporate bond or an acre of land for $10,000. The bond pays $600 of interest (6%) each year, and Chandra expects the land to increase in value 8% each year for the next 10 years. She is in the 40% (combined Federal and state) tax bracket for ordinary income and 26% for qualifying capital gains. If the bond would mature or the land would be sold in 10 years and Chandra would reinvest the interest at a 6% pretax return, she would accumulate the following amounts at the end of 10 years. See text Appendix E for any time value of money factors needed.

		Bond	Land
Original investment		$10,000	$10,000
Annual interest income	$ 600		
Less tax	(240)		
After-tax return	$ 360		
Compound amount reinvested for 10 years at 3.6% after-tax	× 11.79	4,244	
Future value		$14,244	
Future value, 10 years at 6%			× 1.79
			$17,900
Less tax on sale 26%($17,900 sale price – $10,000 original cost)			(2,054)
Future value			$15,846

Therefore, the value of the deferral that results from investing in the land rather than in the bond is $1,602 ($15,846 – $14,244).

4-5 Specific Items of Gross Income

LO.4 **Apply the statutory authority as to when to exclude an item from gross income.**

The all-inclusive principles of gross income determination as applied by the IRS and the courts have, on occasion, been expanded or modified by Congress through legislation. This legislation generally provides more specific rules for determining gross income from certain sources. Most of these special rules appear in §§ 71–91 of the Code.

In addition to provisions describing how specific sources of gross income are to be taxed, several specific rules *exclude* items from gross income. Authority for excluding specific items is provided in §§ 101–140 and in various other provisions in the Code.

Many statutory exclusions are unique to *individual taxpayers* (e.g., gifts and inheritances,[46] scholarships,[47] and a variety of fringe benefits paid to *employees*). These exclusions are discussed in Chapters 9 through 11. Other exclusions are broader and apply to all entities. These exclusions include interest on state and local bonds (§ 103), life

[46] § 102.

[47] § 117.

insurance proceeds received by reason of death of the insured (§ 101), the fair market value of leasehold improvements received by the lessor when a lease is terminated (§ 109),[48] and income from discharge of indebtedness (§ 108).

Taxpayers can recognize gross income when there is a sale or other disposition of a nonbusiness asset. These transactions are discussed in more detail in Chapters 7 and 8, but this section includes an introduction to the tax rules that apply in the most common situations. Some of the broadly applied statutory rules describing inclusions and exclusions are discussed next.

LO.5

Describe the general tax consequences of property transactions.

4-5a Gains and Losses from Property Transactions

When property is sold or otherwise disposed of, gain or loss may result. Such gain or loss has an effect on the gross income of the party making the sale or other disposition when the gain or loss is *realized* and *recognized* for tax purposes. The concept of realized gain or loss is expressed as follows.

Amount realized from the sale − **Adjusted basis of the property** = **Realized gain (or loss)**

The *amount realized* is the selling price of the property less any costs of disposition (e.g., brokerage commissions) incurred by the seller. The *adjusted basis* of the property is determined as follows.

Cost (or other original basis) at date of acquisition[49]	
Add:	**Capital additions**
Subtract:	**Depreciation (if appropriate) and other capital recoveries (see Chapter 5)**
Equals:	**Adjusted basis at date of sale or other disposition**

Without realized gain or loss, generally, there can be no recognized (taxable) gain or loss. All realized gains are recognized unless some specific part of the tax law provides otherwise. Realized losses may or may not be recognized (deductible) for tax purposes, depending on the circumstances involved. For example, losses realized from the disposition of personal use property (property held by individuals and not used for business or investment purposes) are not recognized.

During the current year, Ted sells his sailboat (adjusted basis of $4,000) for $5,500. Ted also sells one of his personal automobiles (adjusted basis of $8,000) for $5,000. Ted's realized gain of $1,500 from the sale of the sailboat is recognized. The $3,000 realized loss on the sale of the automobile, however, is not recognized. Thus, the gain is taxable, but the loss is not deductible.

Once it has been determined that the disposition of property results in a recognized gain or loss, that amount is included in adjusted gross income. The next step is to classify the gain or loss as capital or ordinary. Although ordinary gain is fully taxable and ordinary loss is fully deductible, the same is not true for capital gains and capital losses.

Capital Gains and Losses

Gains and losses from the disposition of capital assets receive special tax treatment. Capital assets are defined in the Code as any property held by the taxpayer *other than*, among other things, inventory, accounts receivable, and depreciable property or real estate used in a business. The sale or exchange of assets in these categories usually results in ordinary income or loss treatment (see text Section 8-2). The sale of any other asset generally creates a capital gain or loss.

[48] If the tenant made the improvements in lieu of rent payments, the value of the improvements is included in the landlord's gross income.

[49] Cost usually means purchase price plus expenses related to the acquisition of the property and incurred by the purchaser (e.g., brokerage commissions). For the basis of property acquired by gift or inheritance and other basis rules, see text Sections 7-2b and 7-2c.

Cardinal, Inc., owns a pizza parlor. During the current year, Cardinal sells an automobile. The automobile, which had been used as a pizza delivery car for three years, was sold at a loss of $1,000. Because this automobile was a depreciable asset used in its business, Cardinal reports an ordinary loss of $1,000 rather than a capital loss. Cardinal also sold securities held for investment during the current year. The securities were sold for a gain of $800. The securities are capital assets. Therefore, Cardinal reports a capital gain of $800.

Computing the Net Capital Gain/Loss To ascertain the appropriate tax treatment of capital gains and losses, a netting process first is applied.

1. Capital gains and losses are classified as:
   a. short term if the sold asset was held for one year or less, or
   b. long term if the sold asset was held for more than one year.
   In counting the time period an asset is held, the day of acquisition is ignored but the day of disposition is counted.
2. Capital gains and losses then are netted within these two classifications. Specifically, short-term capital losses (STCL) are offset against short-term capital gains (STCG), resulting in either a net short-term capital loss (NSTCL) or a net short-term capital gain (NSTCG).
3. Similarly, long-term capital losses (LTCL) are offset against long-term capital gains (LTCG), resulting in either a net long-term capital gain (NLTCG) or a net long-term capital loss (NLTCL).
4. If the resulting amounts are of opposite signs (i.e., there remains a gain and a loss), those amounts are netted against each other. This produces the taxpayer's net capital gain or loss for the tax year. It is entirely long- or short-term, as dictated by the number that was larger in steps 2 and 3.

Colin reports the following capital gains (losses) from asset sales during the year.

Penguin Corporation stock (held for 7 months)	$ 1,000
Owl Corporation stock (held for 9 months)	(3,000)
Flamingo Corporation bonds (held for 14 months)	2,000
Bitcoin (held for 3 years)	4,000

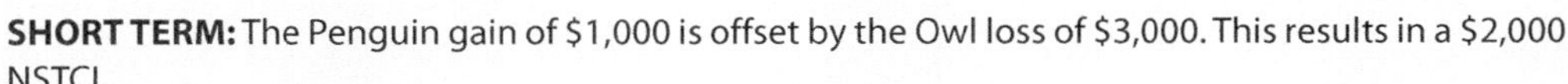

SHORT TERM: The Penguin gain of $1,000 is offset by the Owl loss of $3,000. This results in a $2,000 NSTCL.

LONG TERM: Netting the results of the sales of the bonds and the bitcoin, a $6,000 NLTCG is computed.

CONTINUE NETTING: Because there remains a gain and a loss, net these amounts against each other. A $4,000 net long-term capital gain results.

Taxing the Net Capital Gain/Loss Individuals and corporations are taxed differently on their net capital gains and losses. An individual's *net capital gain* is subject to the following *maximum* tax rates.[50] Certain upper-income taxpayers also may incur the additional Medicare tax on net investment income with respect to net capital gains. See text Section 9-5e.

	Maximum Rate[51]
Short-term gains	37%
Long-term gains	20%

[50] § 1(h). In applying the capital gain/loss netting procedure, losses are netted first against gains in the category carrying the highest tax rate.

[51] Certain assets, such as collectibles (e.g., art, antiques, stamps, etc.) and some real estate, receive a different treatment. When the 15% or 20% long-term capital gains tax rate otherwise applies, the collectibles gain is taxed at a maximum rate of 28%, and certain real estate gains are taxed at a maximum tax rate of 25%. See text Section 8-5a.

A C corporation's net capital gain does not receive any beneficial tax treatment. It is taxed as ordinary income (at a 21 percent rate).

The net capital losses of noncorporate taxpayers can be used to offset up to $3,000 of ordinary income each year. Any remaining capital loss is carried forward indefinitely.

C corporations may deduct capital losses only to the extent of capital gains. Capital losses of C corporations in excess of capital gains may not be deducted against ordinary income. Such unused capital losses are carried back three years and then carried forward five years to offset capital gains in those years.[52]

Example 28

Jones records a short-term capital loss of $5,000 during year 1 and no capital gains. If Jones is an individual, she can deduct $3,000 of this amount as an ordinary loss. The remaining $2,000 loss is carried forward to year 2 and thereafter until it is fully deducted against ordinary income or netted against other capital gains and losses.

If Jones is a C corporation, none of the capital loss is deductible in year 1. All of the $5,000 loss is carried back and offset sequentially against capital gains in the three years preceding year 1 (generating an immediate tax refund). Any remaining capital loss is carried forward and offset against capital gains in tax years 2 to 6.

Digging Deeper 6

To learn how virtual currency transactions are taxed, visit this book's companion website: www.cengage.com

LO.6

Explain the tax provision that excludes interest on state and local government obligations from gross income.

4-5b Interest on Certain State and Local Government Obligations

At the time the Sixteenth Amendment was ratified by the states, there was some question as to whether the Federal government possessed the constitutional authority to tax interest on state and local government obligations. Taxing such interest was thought to violate the doctrine of intergovernmental immunity because the tax would impair the ability of state and local governments to finance their operations.[53] Thus, interest on state and local government obligations was specifically exempted from Federal income taxation.[54] However, the Supreme Court has concluded that there is no constitutional prohibition against levying a nondiscriminatory Federal income tax on state and local government obligations.[55] Congress, however, has shown no inclination to eliminate this exclusion.

The exempt status of interest income applies solely to state and local government bonds. Thus, income received from the accrual of interest on a condemnation award or an overpayment of state tax is fully taxable.[56] Nor does the exemption apply to gains on the sale of tax-exempt securities.

Bridge Discipline — Bridge to Public Economics

The exclusion granted by the Federal government for interest paid on state and local bonds costs the U.S. Treasury approximately $40 billion per year, according to the U.S. Treasury. Such forgone revenue is referred to as a "tax expenditure." However, if the capital markets are working properly, the exclusion should produce cost savings to the state and local governments.

If the exclusion were eliminated, state and local governments would pay higher interest rates on their bonds; the investor would demand a higher interest rate to produce the same after-tax yield as that received from taxable bonds of comparable risk. Therefore, the exclusion operates as a form of revenue sharing to the benefit of the state and local governments; it can be seen as a less visible alternative to a direct grant from the Federal government to the state or local agency. It also is clear that this "expenditure" by the Federal government disproportionately is received by upper-income, high-wealth bondholders.

[52] §§ 1211 and 1212.

[53] *Pollock v. Farmer's Loan & Trust Co.*, 3 AFTR 2602, 15 S.Ct. 912 (1895).

[54] § 103(a).

[55] *South Carolina v. Baker III*, 88–1 USTC ¶9284, 61 AFTR 2d 88–995, 108 S.Ct. 1355.

[56] *Kieselbach v. Comm.*, 43–1 USTC ¶9220, 30 AFTR 370, 63 S.Ct. 303; *U.S. Trust Co. of New York v. Anderson*, 3 USTC ¶1125, 12 AFTR 836, 65 F.2d 575 (CA–2, 1933).

Macaw Corporation purchases State of Virginia bonds for $10,000 on July 1. The bonds pay $300 interest each June 30 and December 31. Macaw excludes from gross income the $300 interest received on December 31.

On March 31 of the next year, Macaw sells the bonds for $10,500 plus $150 of accrued interest. Macaw recognizes a $500 taxable gain ($10,500 – $10,000), but the $150 accrued interest still is exempt from Federal income taxation.

The interest exclusion reduces the cost of borrowing for state and local governments. A taxpayer with a 32 percent marginal Federal income tax rate requires only a 3.4 percent yield on a tax-exempt bond to obtain the same after-tax income as a taxable bond paying 5 percent interest [3.4% ÷ (1 − .32) = 5%].

Although the Internal Revenue Code excludes from Federal gross income the interest on state and local government bonds, the interest paid on U.S. government bonds is not excluded from the Federal income tax base. Congress has decided, however, that if the Federal government does not tax state and local bond interest, the state and local governments should not tax interest on U.S. government bonds.[57] However, state and local governments are free to tax each other's obligations. Thus, some states exempt the interest on the bonds they issue but tax the interest on bonds issued by other states.

The Big Picture

Return to the facts of *The Big Picture* on p. 4-1. Dr. Payne includes in gross income the $500 of interest income from the bank's money market account, but not the $500 that is earned on the Whitehall School District bonds.

4-5c Life Insurance Proceeds

Determine the extent to which life insurance proceeds are excluded from gross income.

Life insurance proceeds paid to the beneficiary because of the death of the insured are excluded from gross income.[58] Congress believed that it was good tax policy to exclude life insurance proceeds from gross income for several reasons, including the following.

- For family members, life insurance proceeds serve much the same purpose as a nontaxable inheritance.
- In a business context (as well as in a family situation), life insurance proceeds replace an economic loss suffered by the business entity (i.e., from the loss of future sales or of the decedent's professional reputation).

Sparrow Corporation purchased an insurance policy on the life of its CEO and named itself as the beneficiary. Sparrow paid $174,000 in premiums. When the company's CEO died, Sparrow collected the insurance proceeds of $600,000. The $600,000 is excluded from Sparrow's gross income.

Exceptions to Exclusion Treatment

The income tax exclusion applies only when the insurance proceeds are received because of the death of the insured. If the owner cancels the policy and receives the

[57] 31 U.S.C.A. § 742.

[58] *Estate of D. R. Daly*, 3 B.T.A. 1042 (1926).

cash surrender value, he or she must recognize gain to the extent of the excess of the amount received over the cost of the policy.[59]

Another exception to exclusion treatment applies if the policy is transferred after the insurance company issues it. If the policy is transferred for valuable consideration, the insurance proceeds are includible in the gross income of the purchaser to the extent the proceeds received exceed the amount paid for the policy plus any subsequent premiums paid.

Platinum Corporation pays premiums of $5,000 for an insurance policy with a face amount of $12,000 on the life of Beth, an officer of the corporation. Subsequently, Platinum sells the policy to Beth's spouse, Jamal, for $5,500. On Beth's death, Jamal receives the proceeds of $12,000. Jamal excludes from gross income $5,500 plus any premiums he paid subsequent to the transfer. The remainder of the proceeds constitutes gross income to Jamal, since he acquired the policy for cash consideration.

There are several major exceptions to the consideration rule.[60] These exceptions permit exclusions from gross income for transfers to the following parties. The first three exceptions facilitate the use of insurance contracts to fund **buy-sell agreements**.

1. A partner of the insured.
2. A partnership in which the insured is a partner.
3. A corporation in which the insured is an officer or a shareholder.
4. A transferee whose basis in the policy is determined by reference to the transferor's basis, such as a gift or a transfer due to a divorce.
5. The insured party under the policy.

Rick and Sita are equal partners who have a buy-sell agreement that allows either partner to purchase the interest of a deceased partner for $500,000. Neither partner has sufficient cash to buy the other partner's interest, but each holds a life insurance policy on his own life in the amount of $500,000. Rick and Sita could exchange their policies (usually at little or no taxable gain), and upon the death of either partner, the surviving partner could collect tax-free insurance proceeds. The proceeds then could be used to purchase the decedent's interest in the partnership.

Investment earnings arising from the reinvestment of life insurance proceeds generally are subject to income tax. For example, the beneficiary may elect to collect the insurance proceeds in installments that include taxable interest income. The interest portion of each installment is included in gross income.[61]

Information on accelerated death benefits can be found on this book's companion website:
www.cengage.com

Tax Planning Strategies **Life Insurance**

Framework Focus: Income and Exclusion

Strategy: Avoid Income Recognition.

Life insurance is a tax-favored investment. The annual increase in the cash surrender value of the policy is not taxable because it is subject to substantial restrictions (no income has been actually or constructively received). By borrowing on the policy's cash surrender value, the owner can receive the policy's increase in value in cash without recognizing any current gross income.

[59] *Landfield Finance Co. v. U.S.*, 69–2 USTC ¶9680, 24 AFTR 2d 69–5744, 418 F.2d 172 (CA–7).

[60] § 101(a)(2).

[61] Reg. § 1.72–7(c)(1), Reg. § 1.101–7.

4-5d Income from Discharge of Indebtedness

Describe when income must be reported from the discharge of indebtedness.

Gross income usually is generated when a creditor cancels a borrower's debt or accepts a payment for less than the amount owed. Foreclosure by a creditor is treated as a sale or exchange of the property and usually triggers gross income.[62]

Juan owed State Bank $50,000 on a note secured by some investment land. When Juan's basis in the land was $20,000 and the land's fair market value was $50,000, the bank foreclosed on the loan and took title to the land. Juan recognizes a $30,000 gain on the foreclosure, as though he had sold the land directly to State Bank.

A creditor may cancel debt to ensure the viability of the debtor. In such cases, the debtor's net worth is increased by the amount of debt forgiven. Generally, the debtor recognizes gross income equal to the amount of debt canceled.[63]

Debt Cancellation and Gross Income

Brown Corporation is unable to meet the mortgage payments on its factory building. Both the corporation and the mortgage holder are aware of the depressed market for industrial property in the area. Foreclosure would only result in the creditor obtaining unsellable property.

To improve Brown's financial position and thus improve its chances of obtaining the additional credit necessary for survival from other lenders, the creditor agrees to forgive all amounts past due and to reduce the principal amount of the mortgage. Brown's gross income is increased by the amount of the debt that was forgiven *plus* the reduction in the remaining mortgage balance.

A corporation issues bonds with a face value of $500,000. Subsequently, the corporation repurchases the bonds in the market for $150,000. It has effectively canceled its $500,000 debt with a $150,000 payment, so it recognizes $350,000 in gross income.[64]

Keri borrowed $60,000 from National Bank to purchase a warehouse. Keri agreed to make monthly principal and interest payments for 15 years. The interest rate on the note was 3%.

When the balance on the note had been reduced through monthly payments to $48,000, the bank offered to accept $45,000 in full settlement of the note. The bank made the offer because interest rates had increased to 4.5%. Keri accepted the bank's offer. As a result, she recognizes $3,000 ($48,000 – $45,000) gross income.[65]

A discharge of indebtedness generally increases the taxpayer's gross income, but the reduction in debt is excluded in each of the following situations.[66]

1. Discharges that occur when the debtor is insolvent.
2. Discharges under Federal bankruptcy law.
3. Discharge of the farm debt of a solvent taxpayer.
4. Discharge of **qualified real property business indebtedness**.
5. A seller's cancellation of a solvent buyer's indebtedness.
6. A shareholder's cancellation of a corporation's indebtedness.
7. Forgiveness of certain loans to students.
8. Discharge of acquisition indebtedness on the taxpayer's principal residence that occurs before 2026 and is due to the financial condition of the debtor.[67]

[62] *Estate of Delman v. Comm.*, 73 T.C. 15 (1979).
[63] § 61(a)(11).
[64] See *U.S. v. Kirby Lumber Co.*, 2 USTC ¶814, 10 AFTR 458, 52 S.Ct. 4 (1931).
[65] Rev.Rul. 82–202.
[66] §§ 108.
[67] §§ 108(a)(1)(E) and (h).

Insolvency and Bankruptcy

Cancellation of indebtedness income is excluded when the debtor is insolvent (i.e., the debtor's liabilities exceed the fair market value of the assets) or when the cancellation of debt results from a bankruptcy proceeding (situations 1 and 2). The insolvency exclusion is limited to the amount of insolvency. The tax law permits this exclusion to avoid imposing undue hardship on the debtor (due to a lack of wherewithal to pay) and the debtor's limited resources.

The law imposes a cost for the insolvency and bankruptcy exclusion. More specifically, the debtor must decrease certain tax benefits (capital loss carryforwards, net operating loss carryforwards, some tax credits, and suspended passive activity losses)[68] by the amount of income excluded. In addition, if the amount of excluded income exceeds these tax benefits, the debtor reduces the basis in assets.[69] Thus, excluded cancellation of indebtedness income either accelerates recognition of future income (by reducing tax benefit carryforwards) or is deferred until the debtor's assets are sold (or depreciated).

Before any debt cancellation, Maroon Corporation holds assets with a fair market value of $500,000 and related liabilities of $600,000. A creditor agrees to cancel $125,000 of liabilities. Maroon excludes $100,000 of the debt cancellation income (the amount of insolvency) and is taxed on $25,000. Maroon also reduces any tax benefits and the basis of its assets by $100,000 (the excluded income).

Qualified Real Property Indebtedness

Taxpayers (other than C corporations) can elect to exclude income from cancellation of indebtedness if the canceled debt is secured by real property used in a trade or business (situation 4). The debt must have been used to acquire or improve real property in a trade or business to qualify for the exclusion.[70]

The amount of the exclusion is limited to the *lesser of* (1) the excess of the debt over the fair market value of the real property or (2) the adjusted basis of all depreciable real property held. In addition, the basis of all depreciable real property held by the debtor is reduced by the excluded amount.

Blue, Inc. (an S corporation), owns a warehouse worth $5,000,000, with a $3,000,000 basis. The warehouse is subject to a $7,000,000 mortgage that was incurred in connection with the acquisition of the warehouse. In lieu of foreclosure, the lender decides that it will reduce the mortgage to $4,500,000. Blue may elect to exclude $2,000,000 from gross income ($7,000,000 debt − $5,000,000 value). If Blue makes the election, it reduces the aggregate basis of its depreciable realty by $2,000,000.

If the basis of the warehouse had been $1,000,000 and the warehouse was the only piece of depreciable realty that Blue owned, only $1,000,000 of the debt cancellation income would be excluded.

Seller Cancellation

When a seller of property cancels debt previously incurred by a solvent buyer in a purchase transaction, the cancellation generally does not trigger gross income to the buyer (situation 5). Instead, the reduction in debt is considered to be a reduction in the purchase price of the asset. Consequently, the basis of the asset is reduced in the hands of the buyer.[71]

[68] See Chapter 6 for a discussion of net operating loss carryforwards and suspended passive losses. Chapter 8 discusses capital loss carryforwards. Chapter 17 discusses tax credits.

[69] § 108(b).

[70] § 108(a)(1)(D).

[71] § 108(e)(5).

Snipe, Inc., purchases a truck from Sparrow Autos for $10,000 in cash and a $25,000 note payable. Two days after the purchase, Sparrow announces a sale on the same model truck, with a sales price of $28,000. Snipe contacts Sparrow and asks to be given the sales price on the truck. Sparrow complies by canceling $7,000 of the note payable. The $7,000 is excluded from Snipe's gross income, and the basis of the truck to Snipe is $28,000.

Shareholder Cancellation

If a shareholder cancels the corporation's indebtedness to him or her (situation 6) and receives nothing in return, the cancellation usually is considered a contribution of capital to the corporation by the shareholder. Thus, the corporation recognizes no gross income. Instead, its paid-in capital is increased, and its liabilities are decreased by the same amount.[72]

Student Loans

Many states make loans to students on the condition that the loan will be forgiven if students practice a profession in the state upon completing their studies. The amount of the loan that is forgiven (situation 7) is excluded from gross income. In addition, any portion of a student loan forgiven after December 31, 2020 and before January 1, 2026 is excludible from gross income. This exclusion applies to all loans made by the Federal or state government, as well as loans made by private lenders and educational institutions. However, the exclusion does not apply to debt forgiven in exchange for services rendered by the student to the lending organization.[73]

Determine the extent to which receipts can be excluded under the tax benefit rule.

4-5e Tax Benefit Rule

Generally, if a taxpayer claims a deduction for an item in one year and in a later year recovers all or a portion of the prior deduction, the recovery is included in gross income in the year received.[74]

Accrual basis MegaCorp deducted as a loss a $1,000 receivable from a customer when it appeared the amount would never be collected. The following year, the customer paid $800 on the receivable. MegaCorp reports the $800 as gross income in the year it is received.

Following this logic, the **tax benefit rule** limits income recognition when a deduction does not yield a tax benefit in the year it is taken. If MegaCorp in Example 41 reported the same Federal income tax liability in the year that the loss occurred, the $800 receipt would be excluded from gross income in the year of the recovery.

Before deducting a $1,000 loss from an uncollectible business receivable, Tulip Company reported taxable income of $200. The business bad debt deduction yields only a $200 tax benefit (assuming no loss carryback is made). That is, taxable income is reduced by only $200 (to zero) as a result of the bad debt deduction. Therefore, if the customer makes a payment on the previously deducted receivable in the following year, only the first $200 is a taxable recovery of a prior deduction. Any additional amount collected is nontaxable because only $200 of the loss yielded a reduction in taxable income (i.e., a tax benefit).

---

[72] § 108(e)(6).

[73] § 108(f)(5), as modified by the American Rescue Plan Act of 2021 (P.L. 117–2; March 11, 2021).

[74] § 111(a).

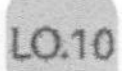

LO.10

Apply the tax provisions on loans made at below-market interest rates.

4-5f Imputed Interest on Below-Market Loans

An income tax can be reduced if gross income can be shifted to a taxpayer in a lower tax bracket. Lending income-producing property to another taxpayer without charging interest on the loan could allow such tax-shifting without requiring the taxpayer to give up ownership of the income-producing property.

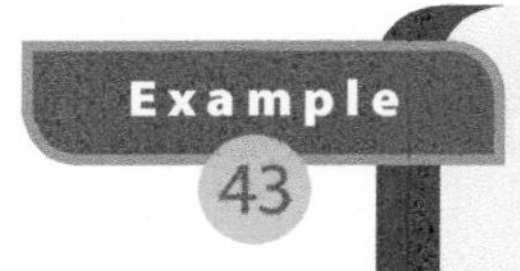

Example 43

Brown Corporation is in the 35% tax bracket and has $400,000 in a money market account earning 5% interest. Jack is the sole shareholder of Brown. He is in the 15% tax bracket and has no investment income. In view of the difference in tax rates, Jack believes that it would be better for him to receive and pay tax on the earnings from Brown's $400,000 investment. Jack does not want to receive the $400,000 from Brown as a dividend because that would trigger a tax.

Under prior law, Jack could receive the money market account from Brown in exchange for a $400,000 non-interest-bearing note, payable on Brown's demand. As a result, Jack would receive the $20,000 annual earnings on the money market account, and the combined taxes of Brown and Jack would be decreased every year by $4,000.

Decrease in Brown's tax (.05 × $400,000) × .35	($7,000)
Increase in Jack's tax (.05 × $400,000) × .15	3,000
Overall decrease in tax liability	($4,000)

The Federal income tax law does not allow this income-shifting result. Brown Corporation in this example is deemed to have received an interest payment from Jack even though no interest was actually paid.[75] This payment of **imputed interest** is taxable to Brown. Jack may be able to deduct the imaginary interest payment on his return as investment interest if he itemizes deductions. Brown then is deemed to return the interest to Jack in the form of a taxable dividend.

Imputed interest is calculated using rates that the Federal government pays on new borrowings, compounded semiannually. The Federal rates are adjusted monthly and are published by the IRS.[76] Three Federal rates exist: short-term (not over three years, including demand loans), mid-term (over three years but not over nine years), and long-term (over nine years).

If interest is charged on the loan but is less than the Federal rate, the imputed interest is the difference between the amount that would have been charged at the Federal rate and the amount actually charged.

Example 44

Assume that the Federal rate applicable to the loan in the preceding example is 3.5% through June 30 and 4% from July 1 through December 31. Brown Corporation made the loan on January 1, and the loan is still outstanding on December 31. Brown recognizes interest income of $15,140, and Jack reports interest expense of $15,140. Brown is deemed to have paid a $15,140 dividend to Jack.

Interest Calculations	
January 1 to June 30: 3.5% × $400,000 × ½ year	$ 7,000
July 1 to December 31: 4% × ($400,000 + $7,000) × ½ year	8,140
	$ 15,140

If Brown had charged 3% interest under the terms of the note, compounded annually, the deemed interest amount would have been $3,140.

Interest at the Federal rate	$ 15,140
Less interest actually charged (.03 × $400,000)	(12,000)
Imputed interest	$ 3,140

[75] § 7872(a)(1).

[76] §§ 7872(b)(2) and (f)(2).

The imputed interest rules apply to the following types of below-market loans.[77] The effects of these loans on the borrower and lender are summarized in Exhibit 4.1.

- Gift loans (loans made out of love, respect, or generosity).
- Compensation-related loans (loans made by an employer to an employee).
- Corporation-shareholder loans (loans made by a corporation to a shareholder, as in Example 43).

Exceptions and Limitations

No interest is imputed on total outstanding *compensation-related loans* or *corporation-shareholder loans* of $10,000 or less unless the purpose of the loan is tax avoidance.[78] This vague tax avoidance standard exposes practically all compensation-related and corporation-shareholder loans to possible imputed interest problems. Nevertheless, the $10,000 exception should apply when an employee's borrowing was necessitated by personal needs (e.g., to meet unexpected expenses) rather than tax considerations.

Similarly, no interest is imputed on outstanding *gift loans* of $10,000 or less between individuals, unless the loan proceeds are used to purchase income-producing property.[79] This exemption eliminates from these complex provisions immaterial amounts that do not result in sizable shifts of income.

On loans of $100,000 or less between individuals, the imputed interest cannot exceed the borrower's net investment income for the year (gross income from all investments less the related expenses).[80] Through the gift loan provision, the imputed interest rules are designed to prevent high-income individuals from shifting income to relatives in a lower marginal bracket. This shifting of investment income is considered to occur only to the extent that the borrower also recognizes net investment income. As a result, the income imputed to the lender is limited to the borrower's net investment income.

If the borrower's net investment income for the year does not exceed $1,000, no interest is imputed. However, this exemption does not apply if a principal purpose of a loan is tax avoidance. In such a case, interest is imputed, and the imputed interest is not limited to the borrower's net investment income.[81]

These exceptions to the imputed interest rules are summarized in Exhibit 4.2.

Exhibit 4.1 Effect of Certain Below-Market Loans: Imputed Interest Income and Deductions

Type of Loan		Lender	Borrower
Gift	Step 1	Interest income	Interest expense
	Step 2	Gift made*	Gift received
Compensation related	Step 1	Interest income	Interest expense
	Step 2	Compensation expense	Compensation income
Corporation to shareholder	Step 1	Interest income	Interest expense
	Step 2	Dividend paid	Dividend income

*The gift may be subject to the Federal gift tax (refer to Chapter 1).

[77] § 7872(c). Additional situations exist where these rules apply. See, for example, §§ 7872(c)(1)(D), (E).

[78] § 7872(c)(3).

[79] § 7872(c)(2).

[80] § 7872(d). The $100,000 provision applies only to gift loans.

[81] § 7872 (d)(1)(B).

Exhibit 4.2 Exceptions to the Imputed Interest Rules for Below-Market Loans

Exception	Eligible Loans	Ineligible Loans and Limitations
De minimis—aggregate loans of $10,000 or less	Gift loans	Proceeds are used to purchase income-producing assets.
	Employer-employee	Principal purpose is tax avoidance.
	Corporation-shareholder	Principal purpose is tax avoidance.
Aggregate loans of $100,000 or less	Gift loans between individuals	Principal purpose is tax avoidance. For all other loans, interest is imputed to the extent of the borrower's net investment income if it exceeds $1,000.

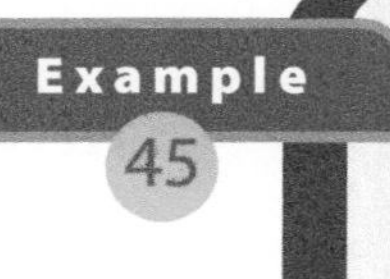

The Big Picture

Example 45

Return to the facts of *The Big Picture* on p. 4-1. Dr. Payne's loan from his parents likely is a *gift loan*, since his parents are not shareholders in the personal service corporation. Imputed interest must be computed annually with regard to this loan by both Dr. Payne and his parents, under two different tax rules: (1) the principal amount of the loan exceeds $100,000 and (2) the loan proceeds were invested in an income-producing asset.

Example 46

Vicki made interest-free gift loans as follows.

Borrower	Amount	Borrower's Net Investment Income	Purpose
Susan	$ 8,000	$–0–	Education
Dan	9,000	500	Purchase of stock
Mai	25,000	–0–	Purchase of a business
Olaf	120,000	–0–	Purchase of a residence

Assume tax avoidance is not a principal purpose of any of the loans. The loan to Susan is not subject to the imputed interest rules because the $10,000 exception applies. The $10,000 exception does not apply to the loan to Dan because the proceeds were used to purchase income-producing assets. However, under the $100,000 exception, the imputed interest is limited to Dan's investment income ($500). Because the $1,000 exception also applies to this loan, no interest is imputed.

No interest is imputed on the loan to Mai because the $100,000 exception applies. None of the exceptions apply to the loan to Olaf because the loan was for more than $100,000; he recognizes imputed interest income related to his loan.

LO.11

Use the tax rules concerning the exclusion of leasehold improvements from gross income.

4-5g Improvements on Leased Property

When a real property lease expires, the landlord regains control of both the real property and any improvements to the property (e.g., buildings and landscaping) made by the tenant during the term of the lease. Any improvements made to the leased property are excluded from the landlord's gross income unless the improvement is made to the property in lieu of rent.[82]

[82] § 109.

Mahogany Corporation leases office space to Zink and Silver, Attorneys-at-Law. When the law firm took possession of the office space, it added wall partitions, a wireless computer network, and a variety of other improvements to the space. The improvements were not made in lieu of rent payments to Mahogany. When the lease expires and Mahogany regains possession of the space, the value of the improvements is excluded from Mahogany's gross income.

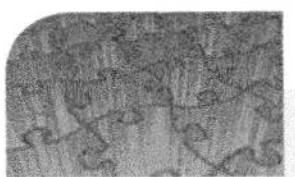

Concept Summary 4.3

Income Recognition Rules

Generally, realized income is recognized as gross income by the Federal tax law. Special rules apply for certain taxpayers and transactions.

1. Income from services and the use of property typically are taxed immediately as they are earned to the taxpayer that generated the income item.
2. Interest income is recognized as it is earned, and dividend income is taxed when the corporation makes a distribution to its shareholders from corporate E & P. Dividends can qualify for lower tax rates or offsetting deductions. Long-term capital gains also can qualify for lower tax rates.
3. Income exclusions are available for certain types of income, including life insurance proceeds received and interest income received from the debt of U.S. government agencies at the state and local levels.
4. Generally, gross income results for a borrower when a lender forgives an outstanding debt obligation. Certain taxpayers qualify for an exclusion of such income, though (e.g., in the context of a bankruptcy, a student loan, or a financially distressed residence).
5. Gross income may result when the taxpayer holds a debt investment that pays interest at a rate that is lower than what the broader market would pay.

Refocus on The Big Picture

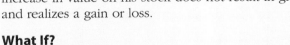

Just What Is Included in Gross Income?

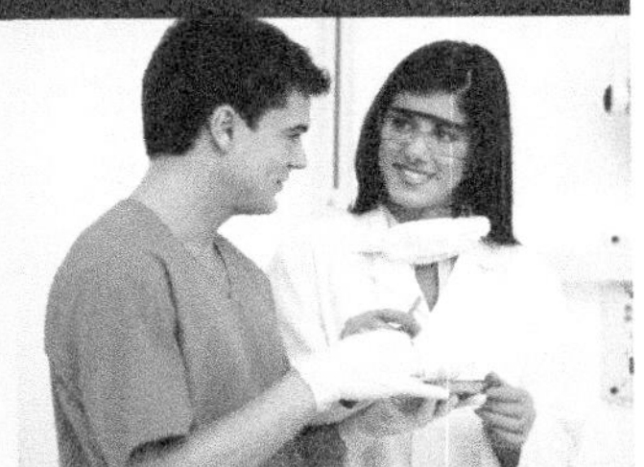

Using the accrual method of accounting, the gross income recognized by Cliff Payne's corporation is $385,500. This includes the entire $385,000 of revenue earned from providing services to patients during the year and the $500 of interest income earned on the money market account. The $500 of school district bond interest is excluded from gross income.

Dr. Payne's own gross income includes $120,000 of salary earned during the year. Even though Cliff did not cash his December paycheck until January, he is considered to have constructively received the income, because it was readily available to him. Dr. Payne may be able to reduce his taxable income with a deduction in the amount of the imputed interest expense on the below-market loan from his parents. The increase in value on his stock does not result in gross income until he sells the stock and realizes a gain or loss.

What If?

Rather than electing the accrual method, what if Dr. Payne had chosen to use the cash method of accounting for his business? Using the cash method is acceptable for certain personal service corporations and small businesses. While using the cash method would reduce the company's gross income from $385,000 to $333,000 ($385,000 amount billed less $52,000 still to be received), this is only part of the picture. Using the cash method also results in the corporation's expenses not being deducted until they are paid, which might not occur until a future year.

TYLER OLSON/SHUTTERSTOCK.COM

Suggested Readings

James Atkinson, "The Intersection of New Sec. 451 and Revenue Recognition," *The Tax Adviser*, June 2018; **tinyurl.com/451-c-TTA**.

Sinead M. Kelly, "Using Cryptocurrency as Compensation in the U.S. and Globally," *Journal of Corporate Taxation*, Mar/Apr 2020.

Patrick M. Ryle, Anthony E. Hope, Leonard Goodman, and Jay A. Soled, "The Tax Consequences Associated with E-Gaming," *Journal of Taxation*, January 2020.

Key Terms

Accounting income, 4-4
Accounting method, 4-6
Accrual method, 4-8
Assignment of income, 4-13
Buy-sell agreements, 4-22
Cash receipts method, 4-7
Claim of right doctrine, 4-9
Constructive receipt, 4-10
Economic income, 4-3
Fruit and tree metaphor, 4-13
Gross income, 4-2
Hybrid method, 4-10
Imputed interest, 4-26
Income, 4-3
Life insurance proceeds, 4-21
Original issue discount, 4-11
Qualified real property business indebtedness, 4-23
Tax benefit rule, 4-25
Taxable year, 4-6

Computational Exercises

1. **LO.3** Champ received a $10,000 distribution from NeatCo, a U.S. C corporation. NeatCo's earnings and profits for the year totaled $6,000. How much dividend income does Champ recognize?

2. **LO.5** Jesse completes the following capital asset transactions. By how much does Jesse's AGI increase/decrease as a result of these gains/losses?

Long-term gain	$10,000
Short-term gain	4,000
Short-term loss	25,000

3. **LO.8** Before any debt cancellation, the insolvent KuhnCo holds business equipment, its only asset, with a fair market value of $1,000,000 and related liabilities of $1,250,000. The lender agrees to cancel $400,000 of the liabilities. KuhnCo has no other liabilities.
   a. How much gross income does KuhnCo report as a result of the debt cancellation?
   b. How would your answer change, if at all, had the lender canceled $200,000 of the debt?

4. **LO.8** Before any debt cancellation, PeppersCo holds business land with a $2,400,000 fair market value, a $1,000,000 tax basis, and a related mortgage of $3,000,000. The lender reduces the mortgage principal by $600,000. What are the Federal income tax consequences of the debt cancellation given the following independent scenarios?
   a. Peppers is insolvent, and the land and related mortgage are the only asset and debt, respectively.
   b. The mortgage is seller financing, and Peppers is solvent.
   c. Peppers has filed for bankruptcy, and the debt is discharged by that action.

5. **LO.9** Leilei operates a sole proprietorship, using the accrual basis of tax accounting. Last year, she claimed a $10,000 bad debt deduction for a receivable from Jackie. But this year, Jackie sent her a check for $7,000, which Leilei accepted in full satisfaction of the receivable. How much gross income does Leilei record for the item this year?

6. **LO.10** Elizabeth makes the following interest-free loans during the year. The relevant Federal interest rate is 5%, and none of the loans are motivated by tax avoidance. All of the loans were outstanding for the last six months of the tax year. Identify the Federal income tax effects of these loans by computing Elizabeth's gross income from each loan.

Borrower	Amount	Borrower's Other Net Investment Income	Purpose of Loan
Richard	$ 5,000	$800	Gift
Woody	8,000	600	Stock purchase
Irene	105,000	0	Purchase principal residence

7. **LO.5** Coline has the following capital gain and loss transactions for 2022:

Short-term capital gain	$ 5,000
Short-term capital loss	(2,100)
Long-term capital gain (28%)	6,000
Long-term capital gain (15%)	2,000
Long-term capital loss (28%)	(10,500)

After the capital gain and loss netting process, what is the amount and character of Coline's gain or loss?

8. **LO.5** Elliott has the following capital gain and loss transactions for 2022:

Short-term capital gain	$ 1,500
Short-term capital loss	(3,600)
Long-term capital gain (28%)	12,000
Long-term capital gain (25%)	4,800
Long-term capital gain (15%)	6,000
Long-term capital loss (28%)	(4,500)
Long-term capital loss (15%)	(9,000)

After the capital gain and loss netting process, what is the amount and character of Elliott's gain or loss?

Problems

9. **LO.1** Howard buys wrecked cars and stores them on his property. Recently, he purchased a 1991 Ford Taurus for $400. If he can sell all of the usable parts, his total proceeds from the Taurus will be over $2,500. As of the end of the year, he has sold only the radio for $75, and he does not know how many, if any, of the remaining parts will ever be sold. What are Howard's Federal income tax issues? Critical Thinking

10. **LO.1** Determine the taxpayer's current-year (1) economic income and (2) gross income for tax purposes from the following events.

    a. Ja-ron's employment contract as chief executive of a large corporation was terminated, and he was paid $500,000 not to work for a competitor of the corporation for five years.
    b. Elliot, a 6-year-old child, was paid $5,000 for appearing in a television commercial. His parents put the funds in a savings account for the child's education.
    c. Valery found a suitcase that contained $100,000. She could not determine who the owner was.
    d. Winn purchased a lottery ticket for $5 and won $750,000 from it.
    e. Larry spent $1,000 to raise vegetables that he and his family consumed. The cost of the vegetables in a store would have been $2,400.
    f. Dawn purchased an automobile for $1,500 that was worth $3,500. The seller was in desperate need of cash.

Ethics and Equity

11. **LO.1** The roof of your corporation's office building recently suffered some damage as the result of a storm. You, the president of the corporation, are negotiating with a carpenter who has quoted two prices for the repair work: $600 if you pay in cash ("folding money") and $700 if you pay by check. The carpenter observes that the IRS can more readily discover his receipt of a check. Thus, he hints that he will report the receipt of the check (but not the cash).

    The carpenter holds another full-time job and will do the work after hours and on the weekend. He comments that he should be allowed to keep all he earns after regular working hours. Evaluate what you should do.

12. **LO.1** Megan is a college student who works as a part-time server in a restaurant. Her usual tip is 20% of the price of the meal. A customer ordered a piece of pie and said that he would appreciate prompt service. Megan fulfilled the customer's request. The customer's bill was $8, but the customer left a $100 bill on the table and did not ask for a receipt. Megan gave the cashier $8 and pocketed the $100 bill (so Megan ends up with $92).

    Megan concludes that the customer thought that he had left a $10 bill, although the customer did not return to correct the apparent mistake. The customer had commented about how much he appreciated Megan's prompt service. Megan thinks that a $2 tip would be sufficient and that the excess is like "found money." How much should Megan include in her gross income concerning this customer?

13. **LO.2** Determine Amos's gross income in each of the following cases.
    a. In the current year, Amos purchased an automobile for $25,000. As part of the transaction, Amos received a $1,500 rebate from the manufacturer.
    b. Amos sold his business. In addition to the selling price of the stock, he received $50,000 for a covenant not to compete—an agreement that he will not compete directly with his former business for five years.
    c. Amos owned some land he held as an investment. As a result of a change in the zoning rules, the property increased in value by $20,000.

Decision Making

14. **LO.2** The Bluejay Apartments, a new development, is in the process of structuring its lease agreements. The company would like to set the damage deposits high enough that tenants will keep the apartments in good condition. The company actually is more concerned about such damage than about tenants not paying their rent.
    a. Discuss the tax effects of the following alternatives.
        - $1,000 damage deposit with no rent prepayment.
        - $500 damage deposit and $500 rent for the final month of the lease.
        - $1,000 rent for the final two months of the lease and no damage deposit.
    b. Which option do you recommend? Why?

Decision Making
Planning

15. **LO.2, 11** Harper is considering three alternative investments of $10,000. Harper is in the 24% marginal tax bracket for ordinary income and 15% for qualifying capital gains in all tax years. The selected investment will be sold at the end of five years. The alternatives are:

    - A taxable corporate bond yielding 5.333% before tax and the interest reinvested at 5.333% before tax.
    - A Series EE bond that will have a maturity value of $12,200 (a 4% pretax rate of return).
    - Land that will increase in value.

    The gain on the land is classified and taxed as a long-term capital gain. The interest from the bonds is taxed as ordinary income: the interest from the corporate bond as it is earned annually, but that from the Series EE bond is recognized only upon redemption.

    How much must the land increase in value to yield a greater after-tax return than either of the bonds? For this analysis, ignore the effect of property taxes on the land. Use the future value tables in Appendix E as needed for your calculations and comparisons. Present your answer using Microsoft Excel or another spreadsheet.

16. **LO.1** Determine the taxpayer's gross income for tax purposes in each of the following situations.
   a. Deb, a cash basis taxpayer, traded a corporate bond with accrued interest of $300 for corporate stock with a fair market value of $12,000 at the time of the exchange. Deb's cost of the bond was $10,000. The value of the stock had decreased to $11,000 by the end of the year.
   b. Deb needed $10,000 to make a down payment on her house. She instructed her broker to sell some stock to raise the $10,000. Deb's cost of the stock was $3,000. Based on her broker's advice, instead of selling the stock, she borrowed the $10,000 using the stock as collateral for the debt.
   c. Deb's boss gave her two tickets to the Rabid Rabbits rock concert because Deb met her sales quota. At the time Deb received the tickets, each ticket had a face price of $200 and was selling on eBay for $300 each. On the date of the concert, the tickets were selling for $250 each. Deb and her son attended the concert.

17. **LO.2** Al is a physician who conducts his practice as a sole proprietor. During 2022, he received cash of $280,000 for medical services. Of the amount collected, $40,000 was for services provided in 2021. At the end of 2022, Al held accounts receivable of $60,000, all for services rendered in 2022. In addition, at the end of the year, Al received $12,000 as an advance payment from a health maintenance organization (HMO) for services to be rendered in 2023. Compute Al's gross income for 2022 using the:

Decision Making
Planning

   a. Cash basis of accounting.
   b. Accrual basis of accounting.
   c. Advise Al on which method of accounting he should use.

18. **LO.2** Selma operates a contractor's supply store. She maintains her books using the cash method. Selma wants to know whether the accrual basis of accounting would be preferable for her business.

   At the end of 2022, Selma's accountant computes her accrual basis income that is used on her tax return. For 2022, Selma reported cash receipts of $1,400,000, which included $200,000 collected on accounts receivable from 2021 sales. It also included the proceeds of a $100,000 bank loan. At the end of 2022, she held $250,000 in accounts receivable from customers, all from 2022 sales.
   a. Compute Selma's accrual basis gross receipts for 2022.
   b. Selma paid cash for all of the purchases. The total amount paid for merchandise in 2022 was $1,300,000. At the end of 2021, she had merchandise on hand with a cost of $150,000. At the end of 2022, the cost of merchandise on hand was $300,000. Compute Selma's gross income from merchandise sales for 2022.

19. **LO.2** Trip Garage, Inc. (459 Ellis Avenue, Harrisburg, PA 17111), is an accrual basis taxpayer that repairs automobiles. In late December 2022, the company repaired Samuel Mosley's car and charged him $1,000. Samuel did not think the problem had been fixed, so he refused to pay; as a result, Trip refused to release the automobile.

Communications

   In early January 2023, Trip made a few adjustments under the hood; Trip then convinced Samuel that the automobile was working properly. At that time, Samuel agreed to pay only $900 because he did not have the use of the car for a week. Trip said "fine," accepted the $900, and released the automobile to Samuel.

   An IRS agent thinks Trip, as an accrual basis taxpayer, should report $1,000 of income in 2022, when the work was done, and then deduct a $100 business loss in 2023. Prepare a memo to Susan Apple, the treasurer of Trip, with your recommended treatment for the disputed income.

20. **LO.1, 4** Each Saturday morning, Ted makes the rounds of the local yard sales. He has developed a keen eye for bargains, but he cannot use all of the items he thinks are "real bargains." Ted has found a way to share the benefits of his talent

Ethics and Equity

with others. If Ted spots something priced at $40 that he knows is worth $100, for example, he will buy it and list it on eBay for $70.

Ted does not include his gain in his gross income because he reasons that he is performing a valuable service for others (both the original sellers and the future buyers) and sacrificing profit he could receive. "Besides," according to Ted, "the IRS does not know about these transactions." Should Ted's ethical standards depend on his perception of his own generosity and the risk that his income-producing activities will be discovered by the IRS? Discuss.

Ethics and Equity

21. **LO.2** Accounting students understand that the accrual method of accounting is superior to the cash method for measuring the income and expenses from an ongoing business for financial reporting purposes. Often, CPAs advise their clients to use the accrual method of accounting. Yet, CPA firms generally use the cash method to prepare their own tax returns. Are the CPAs being hypocritical? Explain.

22. **LO.2** Drake Appliance Company, an accrual basis taxpayer, sells home appliances and service contracts. Determine the effects of each of the following transactions on the company's 2022 gross income assuming that the company uses any available options to defer its taxes.

    a. In December 2021, the company received a $1,200 advance payment from a customer for an appliance that Drake had special-ordered from the manufacturer. The appliance did not arrive from the manufacturer until January 2022, and Drake immediately delivered it to the customer. The sale was reported in 2022 for financial accounting purposes.

    b. In October 2022, the company sold a 6-month service contract for $240. The company also sold a 36-month service contract for $1,260 in July 2022.

    c. On December 31, 2022, the company sold an appliance for $1,200. The company received $500 cash and a note from the customer for $700 and $260 interest, to be paid at the rate of $40 a month for 24 months. Because of the customer's poor credit record, the fair market value of the note was only $600. The cost of the appliance was $750.

Ethics and Equity

23. **LO.2** Dr. Randolph, a cash basis taxpayer, knows that she will be in a lower marginal tax bracket next year. To take advantage of the expected decrease in the marginal tax rate, Randolph instructs her office manager to delay filing the medical insurance claims for services performed in November and December until January of the following year. This will ensure that the receipts will not be included in current gross income. Is Randolph abusing the cash method of accounting rules? Why or why not?

Communications
Decision Making
Planning

24. **LO.2** Your client is a new partnership, ARP Associates, which is an engineering consulting firm. Generally, ARP bills clients for services at the end of each month. Client billings are about $50,000 each month. On average, it takes 45 days to collect the receivables. ARP's expenses are primarily for salary and rent. Salaries are paid on the last day of each month, and rent is paid on the first day of each month.

    The partnership has a line of credit with a bank, which requires monthly financial statements. These must be prepared using the accrual method. ARP's managing partner, Amanda Sims, has suggested that the firm also use the accrual method for tax purposes and thus reduce accounting fees by $600.

    The partners are in the 35% (combined Federal and state) marginal tax bracket. Write a letter to your client explaining why you believe it would be worthwhile for ARP to file its tax return on the cash basis even though its financial statements are prepared on the accrual basis. ARP's address is 100 James Tower, Denver, CO 80208.

25. **LO.3** Alva received dividends on her stocks as follows.

Amur Corporation (a French corporation whose stock is traded on an established U.S. securities market)	$60,000
Blaze, Inc., a Delaware corporation	40,000
Grape, Inc., a Virginia corporation	22,000

a. Alva purchased the Grape stock three years ago, and she purchased the Amur stock two years ago. She purchased the Blaze stock 18 days before it went ex-dividend and sold it 20 days later at a $5,000 loss. Alva reported no other capital gains and losses for the year. She is in the 32% marginal tax bracket. Compute Alva's tax on her dividend income.

b. Alva's daughter, Veda, who is age 25 and who is not Alva's dependent, reported taxable income of $6,000, which included $1,000 of dividends on Grape stock. Veda purchased the stock two years ago. Compute Veda's tax liability on the dividends.

26. **LO.3** Imani and Doug were divorced on December 31, 2022, after 10 years of marriage. The couple's income received before the divorce included: Digging Deeper

Doug's salary	$41,000
Imani's salary	55,000
Rent on apartments purchased by Imani 15 years ago	8,000
Dividends on stock Doug inherited from his mother 4 years ago	1,900
Interest on a savings account in Imani's name funded with her salary	2,400

Allocate the income to Imani and Doug, applying the community property rules of:

a. California.

b. Texas.

27. **LO.4,10** Roy decides to buy a personal residence, and he goes to the bank for a $150,000 loan. The bank tells Roy that he can borrow the funds at 4% if his father will guarantee the debt. Roy's father, Hal, owns a $150,000 CD currently yielding 3.5%. The Federal rate is 3%. Hal agrees to either of the following. Decision Making

- Roy borrows from the bank with Hal's guarantee provided to the bank.
- Hal cashes in the CD (with no penalty) and lends Roy the funds at 2% interest.

Hal is in the 32% marginal tax bracket. Roy, whose only source of income is his salary, is in the 12% marginal tax bracket. The interest that Roy pays on the mortgage will be deductible by him. Which option will maximize the family's after-tax wealth?

28. **LO.6** Determine Hazel's Federal gross income from the following receipts for the year.

Gain on sale of Augusta County bonds	$800
Interest on U.S. government savings bonds	400
Interest on state income tax refund	200
Interest on Augusta County bonds	700

29. **LO.6** Katie, a resident of Virginia, is considering purchasing a North Carolina bond that yields 4.6% before tax. She is in the 35% Federal marginal tax bracket and the 5% state marginal tax bracket. Decision Making Planning

Katie is aware that State of Virginia bonds of comparable risk are yielding 4.5%. Virginia bonds are exempt from Virginia tax, but the North Carolina bond interest is taxable in Virginia.

Which of the two options will provide the greater after-tax return to Katie? Katie can deduct any state taxes paid on her Federal income tax return. In your analysis, assume that the bond amount is $100,000.

30. **LO.7** Ray and Carin are partners in an accounting firm. The partners have entered into an arm's length agreement requiring Ray to purchase Carin's partnership interest from Carin's estate if she dies before Ray. The price is set at 120% of the book value of Carin's partnership interest at the time of her death.

Ray purchased an insurance policy on Carin's life to fund this agreement. After Ray had paid $45,000 in premiums, Carin was killed in an automobile accident, and Ray collected $800,000 of life insurance proceeds. Ray used the life insurance proceeds to purchase Carin's partnership interest.

What amount should Ray include in his gross income from receiving the life insurance proceeds?

Decision Making
Digging Deeper
Planning

31. **LO.7** As a result of a cancer diagnosis in early 2022, Laura has begun chemotherapy treatments. A cancer specialist has given Laura less than one year to live. She has incurred sizable medical bills and other general living expenses and is in need of cash. Laura is considering selling stock that cost her $35,000 and has a fair market value of $50,000. This amount would be sufficient to pay her medical bills.

    However, she has read about a company (VitalBenefits.com) that would purchase her life insurance policy for $50,000. To date, Laura has paid $30,000 in premiums on the policy.

    a. Considering only the Federal income tax effects, would selling the stock or selling the life insurance policy result in more beneficial tax treatment?
    b. Assume that Laura is a dependent child and that her mother owns the stock and the life insurance policy, which is on the mother's life. Which of the alternative means of raising the cash would result in more beneficial tax treatment?

32. **LO.8** Vic, who was experiencing financial difficulties, adjusted his debts as follows. Determine the Federal income tax consequences from these events.

    a. Vic is an attorney. Vic owed his uncle $25,000. The uncle told Vic that if he serves as the executor of his estate, Vic's debt will be canceled in the uncle's will.
    b. Vic borrowed $80,000 from First Bank. The debt was secured by land that Vic purchased for $100,000. Vic was unable to pay, and the bank foreclosed when the liability was $80,000, which was also the fair market value of the property.
    c. The Land Company, which had sold land to Vic for $80,000, reduced the mortgage principal on the land by $12,000.

33. **LO.9** How does the tax benefit rule apply in the following cases?

    a. In 2020, the Orange Furniture Store, an accrual method taxpayer, sold furniture on credit for $1,000 to Sammy. Orange's cost of the furniture was $600. In 2021, Orange took a bad debt deduction for the $1,000 because Sammy would not pay his bill.

       In 2022, Sammy inherited some money and paid Orange the $1,000 he owed. Orange was in the 35% marginal tax bracket in 2020, the 12% marginal tax bracket in 2021, and the 35% marginal tax bracket in 2022.
    b. In 2021, Barb, a cash basis taxpayer, was in an accident and incurred $8,000 in medical expenses, which she claimed as an itemized deduction for medical expenses. Because of a limitation, though, the expense reduced her taxable income by only $3,000. In 2022, Barb successfully sued the person who caused the physical injury and collected $8,000 to reimburse her for the cost of her medical expenses. Barb was in the 22% marginal tax bracket in 2021 and in the 12% bracket in 2022.

34. **LO.10** Your client Aldridge is a generous individual. During the year, she made interest-free loans to various family members when the Federal interest rate was 3%. What are the Federal tax consequences of the following loans by Aldridge?

    a. On June 30, Aldridge loaned $12,000 to a cousin, Jim, to buy a used truck. Jim's only source of income was his wages on various construction jobs during the year.
    b. On August 1, Aldridge loaned $8,000 to a niece, Sonja. The loan was meant to enable Sonja to pay her college tuition. Sonja reported $1,200 interest income from CDs that her parents had given her.
    c. On September 1, Aldridge loaned $25,000 to a brother, Al, to start a business. Al reported only $220 of dividends and interest for the year.
    d. On September 30, Aldridge loaned $150,000 to her mother, Joan, so that Joan could pay the entrance fee at a retirement home. Joan's only receipts for the year were $9,000 in Social Security benefits and $500 interest income received.

35. **LO.10** Apply the imputed interest rules in the following situations.

   a. Mike loaned his sister $90,000 to buy a new home. Mike did not charge interest on the loan. The Federal rate was 4%. Mike's sister earned $900 of investment income for the year.

   b. Nico's employer maintains an emergency loan fund for its employees. During the year, Nico's spouse was very ill, and they incurred unusually large medical expenses. He borrowed $8,500 from his employer's emergency loan fund for six months. The Federal rate was 4%. Nico and his spouse earned no investment income for the year.

   c. Jody borrowed $25,000 from her controlled corporation for six months. She used the funds to pay her daughter's college tuition. The corporation charged Jody 3% interest. The Federal rate was 4%. Jody earned $3,500 of investment income for the year.

   d. Kait loaned her son, Jake, $60,000 for six months. Jake used the $60,000 to pay off college loans. The Federal rate was 4%, and Kait did not charge Jake any interest. Jake earned dividend and interest income of $2,100 for the tax year.

36. **LO.10** In the current year, Madero Corporation made a $400,000 interest-free loan to Francisco Madero, the corporation's controlling shareholder. Mr. Madero is also the corporation's chief executive officer and receives a salary of $300,000 a year. What are the tax consequences of classifying the loan as a compensation-related loan rather than as a corporation-shareholder loan?

Bridge Discipline

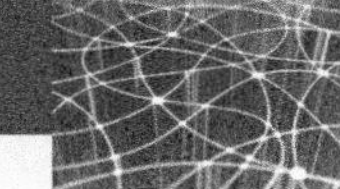

1. Find the audited financial statements of a major U.S. corporation.
   a. Summarize its most important financial accounting policies.
   b. Describe two elements of the Federal income tax law that significantly affected the corporation's earnings per share for the operating year.

2. For the same corporation, summarize three key tax accounting applications, and point out how they differ from book income principles. Summarize your findings, and present them to your classmates in no more than five PowerPoint slides. *Communications*

3. The exclusion of state and local bond interest from Federal income tax often is criticized as creating a tax haven for the wealthy. Critics, however, often fail to take into account the effect of market forces. In recent months, the long-term tax-exempt interest rate has been 2.5%, while the long-term taxable rate for bonds of comparable risk was approximately 3.75%. On the other hand, state and local governments do enjoy a savings in interest costs because of the tax-favored status of their bonds.

   To date, Congress has concluded that the benefits gained by the states and municipalities and their residents, such as the access to capital and the creation of jobs to construct and maintain critical infrastructure, outweigh any damages to our progressive income tax system. Do you agree with the proponents of the exclusion? Why or why not?

4. In a two-page paper, separately evaluate each of the following alternative proposals for taxing the income from property. *Communications*
   a. All assets would be valued at the end of the year, any increase in value that occurred during the year would be included in gross income, and any decrease in value would be deductible from gross income.
   b. No gain or loss would be recognized until the taxpayer sold or exchanged the property.

continued

c. Increases or decreases in the value of property traded on a national exchange (e.g., the New York Stock Exchange) would be reflected in gross income for the years in which the changes in value occur. For all other assets, no gain or loss would be recognized until the owner disposes of the property.

Communications

5. Various Federal stimulus provisions were designed to assist state and local governments in borrowing funds, leveraging the gross income exclusion for such bond interest so that such jurisdictions would have increased access to funds. One of the justifications for these provisions was that state and local governments cannot run budget deficits and cannot "print money," so the recent recession put them in a difficult cash-flow position.

   Audits of the use of these borrowed funds showed that some of the bond proceeds were used by the jurisdictions to participate in "public-private partnerships," where government funds were used to assist private entities in expanding in or relocating to the jurisdiction. Specifically, bond proceeds were found to have been used to provide targeted road-building and utility-construction projects to benefit large commercial entities.

   Is this an appropriate use of the gross income exclusion for state and local bond interest? Summarize your comments in an e-mail to your instructor.

Research Problems

Note: Solutions to the Research Problems can be prepared by using the Thomson Reuters Checkpoint™ online tax research database, which accompanies this textbook. Solutions can also be prepared by using research materials found in a typical tax library.

Communications

Research Problem 1. Tranquility Funeral Home, Inc., your client, is an accrual basis taxpayer that sells "pre-need" funeral contracts. Under these contracts, the customer pays in advance for goods and services to be provided at the contract beneficiary's death. These payments are refundable at the contract purchaser's request, pursuant to state law, at any time until the goods and services are furnished. Tranquility, consistent with its financial accounting reporting, includes the payments in income for the year the funeral service is provided.

An IRS agent insists that the contract payments constitute prepaid income subject to tax in the year of receipt. Your client believes the amounts involved are tax-deferred customer deposits.

Write a letter to Tranquility that contains your tax advice about how the issue should be resolved. The client's address is 400 Rock Street, Memphis, TN 38152.

Communications
Decision Making

Research Problem 2. Your client owns a life insurance policy on his own life. He has paid $6,800 in premiums, and the cash surrender value of the policy is $30,000. He borrowed $30,000 from the insurance company, using the cash surrender value as collateral. He is considering canceling the policy in payment of the loan. He would like to know the Federal income tax consequences of canceling his policy. Summarize your findings in a brief research memo.

Communications

Research Problem 3. Your client is a retailer that often issues store gift (debit) cards to customers in lieu of a cash refund. You recall that a special rule allows accrual method taxpayers to defer all or a portion of advance payments received. Determine whether this rule applies to the gift cards issued as refunds for product returns.

Research Problem 4. Your friend Jalissa is an investor in bluecoin, a virtual currency. Indicate whether and how she is subject to Federal income taxation in the following circumstances. Digging Deeper

a. Earns $1,000 in bluecoin from mining.
b. Purchases $1,000 in bluecoin from another friend.
c. Sells the purchase in part (b) in the market to a third party for $1,400.
d. Spends $1,000 of bluecoin to acquire an asset worth $1,500.
e. Spends $1,000 of bluecoin to acquire an asset worth $750.
f. Holds bluecoin that she bought in February for $1,000. On December 31, the bluecoin is worth $1,200.

Use internet tax resources to address the following questions. Look for reliable websites and blogs of the IRS and other government agencies, media outlets, businesses, tax professionals, academics, think tanks, and political outlets.

Research Problem 5. Construct a chart for your state and four of its neighboring states. Provide "Yes/No" entries for each state in the following categories. Send the chart to your classmates by e-mail. Communications

- Does the state exclude interest income from U.S. Treasury bonds?
- Does the state exclude interest income from Fannie Mae bonds?
- Does the state exclude interest income from bonds issued by governments in its own state?
- Does the state exclude interest income from bonds issued by governments in other states?

Research Problem 6. Determine the applicable Federal interest rate as of today for purposes of § 7872 below-market loans. In an e-mail to your professor, describe how the rate is determined and how you discovered the pertinent rules. Communications

Research Problem 7. From the IRS Tax Stats website (**irs.gov/statistics/soi-tax-stats-individual-income-tax-returns**), determine the number of individuals who report tax-exempt interest income on their tax return and the amount of that exempt income. Find this information for individuals at different ranges of adjusted gross income (AGI). Use the data to create pie charts (or similar visuals) of the percent of AGI represented by the tax-exempt interest income exclusion, as well as the number of individuals claiming this exclusion at different AGI levels. Analyze the IRS data, draw conclusions from it, and summarize your findings in a two- to three-paragraph e-mail sent to your instructor. Be sure your conclusions are explained and supported by the data. Communications Data Analytics

Becker CPA Review Question

1. Danny received the following interest and dividend payments this year. What amount should Danny include in his gross income? Becker

Source	Amount
City of Atlanta bond interest	$1,200
U.S. Treasury bond interest	500
State of Georgia bond interest	1,000
Ellis Company common stock dividend	400
Row Corporation bond interest	600

a. $2,500
b. $1,500
c. $3,700
d. $2,200

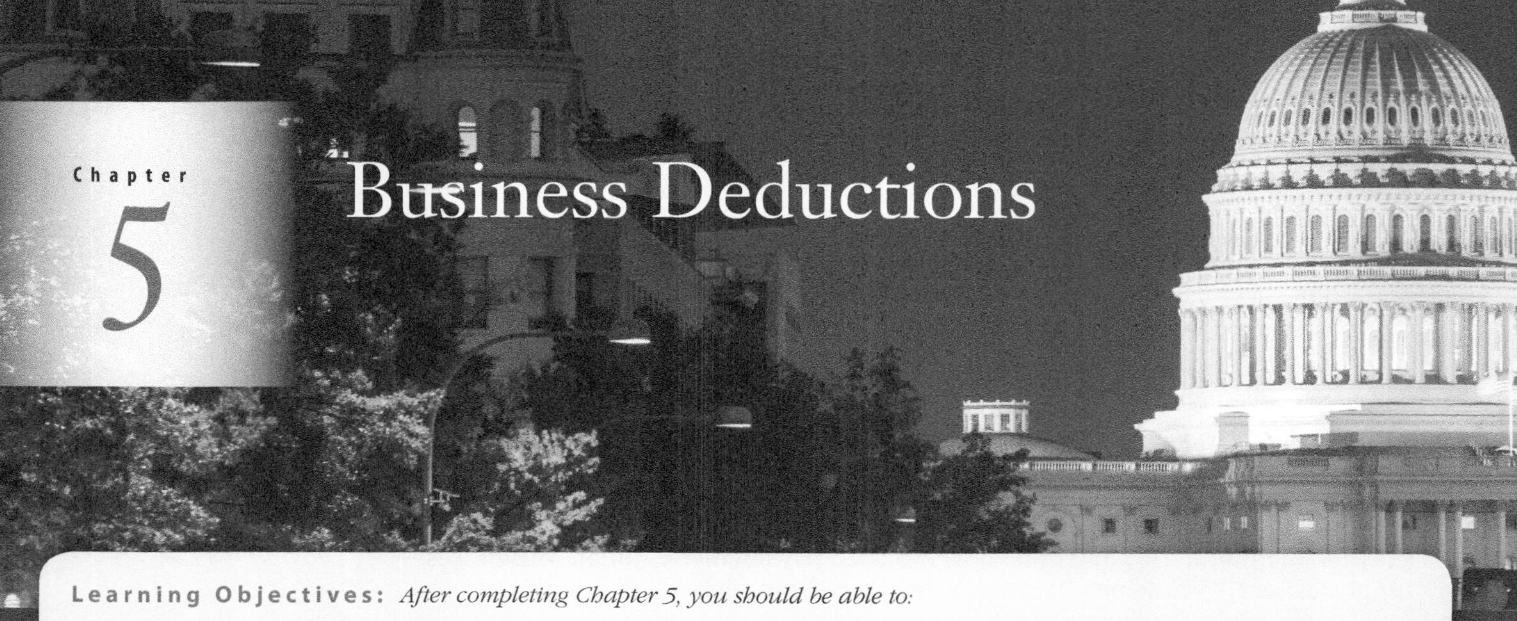

Chapter 5

Business Deductions

Learning Objectives: *After completing Chapter 5, you should be able to:*

- **LO.1** Explain the meaning and application of the ordinary, necessary, and reasonableness requirements for the deduction of business expenses.
- **LO.2** Describe and apply the cash and accrual methods of accounting for business deductions.
- **LO.3** Recognize and apply a variety of Internal Revenue Code deduction disallowance provisions.
- **LO.4** Apply the alternative tax treatments of research and experimental expenditures.
- **LO.5** Identify issues related to the deductibility of other common business expenses.
- **LO.6** Identify and measure deductible charitable contributions and determine corporate limitations on the contribution deduction.
- **LO.7** Determine the amount and timing of cost recovery available under MACRS, including additional cost recovery available in the year an asset is placed in service.
- **LO.8** Identify and apply the cost recovery limitations applicable to automobiles and property used for personal purposes, including listed property.
- **LO.9** Identify intangible assets that are eligible for amortization and calculate the amount of the amortization deduction.
- **LO.10** Determine deductible depletion expense and specify the alternative tax treatments for intangible drilling and development costs.

Chapter Outline

Tax Talk *Last year I had difficulty with my income tax. I tried to take my analyst off as a business deduction. The Government said it was entertainment. We compromised finally and made it a religious contribution.* —Woody Allen

The Big Picture

Calculating Deductible Expenses

Michael Forney, owner of a small engine service and repair business, operates his business as a C corporation with a December 31 year-end. Michael owns 80 percent of the corporation's stock, and his spouse (Kathleen) and his mother (Terry) each own 10 percent of the stock. Michael is a full-time employee at his business, and his mother helps out with the books for about two hours a week. At this time, Kathleen does not work at the business.

The following expenses, along with $435,000 of gross income, are reported in the corporation's 2023 financial statements.

Salaries and wages (including Michael's salary of $55,000 and Terry's salary of $3,000)	$150,000
Building rent	24,000
Depreciation of machinery and equipment*	13,000
Insurance (coverage for all assets of the business)	6,000
Consulting fees	6,000
Utilities	12,000
Taxes and licenses	6,000
Fine paid to city	2,500
Advertising	3,000
Interest expense	3,000
Charitable contributions	3,000
Dues paid to Small Engine Repair Institute	10,000
Political contributions	2,000

*$130,000 of new machinery and equipment were purchased this year. The depreciation for financial reporting purposes is based on straight-line depreciation over 10 years. Assume for purposes of this scenario that no depreciation may be claimed this year for assets acquired in prior years because they have been fully depreciated.

Michael would like to know the amount of his deductible expenses for tax purposes.

Michael would also like your advice on another matter. Because his business has been very profitable over the years, it has built up large cash reserves, and its cash flow continues to be strong. Even with the

continued

high levels of cash in the business, it has never paid any dividends to the shareholders. For next year, he is considering paying himself a salary of $140,000 and his mother a salary of $30,000. This would give them more cash to spend for planned vacations and home improvements.

Finally, during the year, Michael purchased another personal residence for $300,000 and converted his original residence to rental property. The original residence cost $250,000 five years ago and has a current market value of $180,000. Also during the year, he purchased a condo for $170,000, which he will rent to tenants. Michael holds these rental properties outside his small engine service and repair business. He would like to know the tax implications, if any, of these transactions.

Read the chapter and formulate your response.

As discussed in the previous chapter, the tax law takes a broad approach to measuring income: unless provided otherwise, gross income includes all income from whatever source derived. In other words, income cannot be excluded from gross income and, therefore, taxable income unless the Internal Revenue Code explicitly permits it.

The tax law takes a very different approach to deductions. A deduction is allowed only if there is a specific provision in the tax law that permits it. However, the Code goes on to allow deductions for most expenses incurred in a trade or business. This chapter discusses the general deductibility of trade or business expenses, when those expenses are deductible, certain trade or business expenses that are not deductible, and special rules surrounding the deductibility of other business expenditures. Note that dividends represent a distribution by a corporation of its profits to its shareholders and are not considered expenses. Therefore, dividends paid by a corporation are never deductible.

LO.1

Explain the meaning and application of the ordinary, necessary, and reasonableness requirements for the deduction of business expenses.

5-1 The Deductibility of Business Expenses—Overview

As just noted, an expense is not deductible under Federal tax law unless Congress creates a specific provision allowing it.[1] The Code does explicitly allow the deduction of expenses incurred in a trade or business, but only if those expenses are *ordinary, necessary,* and *reasonable* in amount.[2] Generally, an ordinary, necessary, and reasonable trade or business expense is deductible in full, without limitation or restriction.

5-1a Ordinary and Necessary Requirement

Section 162(a) permits a deduction for all **ordinary and necessary** expenses paid or incurred in carrying on a trade or business. To understand the scope of this provision, it is critical to understand the meanings of the terms *ordinary* and *necessary.* Since these terms are not defined in the Code or Regulations, the courts have dealt with these terms on numerous occasions.

An expense has been held to be *ordinary* if it is normal, usual, or customary in the type of business conducted by the taxpayer.[3] Note that an expense need not be recurring to be considered ordinary. For example, a business may incur an expense related to a rare

Example 1

Zebra Corporation was engaged in a mail-order business. The post office judged that Zebra's advertisements were false and misleading. Under a fraud order, the post office stamped "fraudulent" on all letters addressed to Zebra's business and returned them to the senders. Zebra spent $30,000 on legal fees in an unsuccessful attempt to force the post office to stop. The legal fees (although not recurring) were ordinary business expenses because they were normal, usual, or customary under the circumstances.[4]

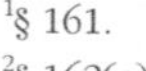

[1] § 161.

[2] § 162(a).

[3] *Deputy v. Du Pont,* 40–1 USTC ¶9161, 23 AFTR 808, 60 S.Ct. 363.

[4] *Comm. v. Heininger,* 44–1 USTC ¶9109, 31 AFTR 783, 64 S.Ct. 249 (1943).

and unusual event. However, if other businesses in a similar situation are likely to incur a similar expense, the expense can be considered ordinary, even though it is not recurring.

An expense has been held to be *necessary* if a prudent businessperson would incur the same expense and the expense is expected to be appropriate and helpful in the taxpayer's business.[5] An expense need not be indispensable or unavoidable to be considered necessary. But as Example 2 illustrates, no deduction will be allowed unless a necessary expense is also ordinary.

Pat purchased a business that had just been adjudged bankrupt. Because the business had a poor financial rating, Pat wanted to restore its financial reputation. Consequently, he paid off some of the debts owed by the former owners that had been canceled by the bankruptcy court. Because Pat had no legal obligation to make these payments, the U.S. Supreme Court decided that he was trying to generate goodwill. Although the payments were necessary (i.e., appropriate and helpful), they were *not* ordinary and their deduction *was not* allowed.[6]

5-1b Reasonableness Requirement

An expense must also be reasonable to be deductible. Although the Code applies the **reasonableness requirement** solely to salaries and other compensation for services, the courts have held that for any expense to be ordinary and necessary, it also must be reasonable in amount.[7] If an expense is unreasonable, any amount in excess of what is reasonable is not deductible.

The question of reasonableness usually arises with respect to closely held corporations where there is little or no separation of ownership and management. For example, excessive salaries, rent, and other expenses paid by a closely held corporation to its shareholders may be deemed unreasonable. What constitutes reasonableness is determined by the facts and circumstances surrounding a situation.[8] Courts will view the reasonableness of a salary paid to a shareholder of a closely held corporation in light of all relevant circumstances. For example, a court may find that an unusually large salary is reasonable despite its amount if the shareholder has unusual or unique expertise. Amounts paid to shareholders that are deemed unreasonable are generally held to be dividends.[9] Because dividends are not deductible by the corporation, the disallowance results in an increase in corporate taxable income.

The Big Picture

3

Return to the facts of *The Big Picture* on p. 5-1. The small engine service and repair business, a closely held C corporation, is owned by Michael Forney, his spouse (Kathleen), and his mother (Terry). The company has been highly profitable over the years and has never paid dividends. Michael is the key employee of the business, while his mother plays a very minor role. Assuming that their current salaries of $55,000 and $3,000 are comparable to what they could earn at similar companies for the work they do, they are likely to be considered reasonable and, therefore, deductible.

If Mr. Forney's plan to more than double his salary and increase his mother's salary by tenfold is implemented, the amounts in excess of their current salaries may be deemed unreasonable; if that is the case, the excess would be disallowed as deductible salary. Further, the disallowed amounts would likely be treated as dividends rather than salary income to Michael and Terry. Although both salaries and dividends are taxable to the shareholders, salaries are deductible by the corporation while dividends are not.

The language of § 162 is broad enough to permit the deduction of many different types of ordinary and necessary business expenses. Some of the more common deductions are listed in Exhibit 5.1.

[5] *Welch v. Helvering*, 3 USTC ¶1164, 12 AFTR 1456, 54 S.Ct. 8 (1933).

[6] *Id.*

[7] *Comm. v. Lincoln Electric Co.*, 49–2 USTC ¶9388, 38 AFTR 411, 176 F.2d 815 (CA–6), *cert. denied* 70 S.Ct. 488 (1950).

[8] *Kennedy, Jr. v. Comm.*, 82–1 USTC ¶9186, 49 AFTR 2d 82–628, 671 F.2d 167 (CA–6).

[9] See Reg. § 1.162–8.

Exhibit 5.1 Partial List of Deductible Business Expenses

Advertising	Pension and profit sharing plans
Bad debts	Rent or lease payments
Commissions and fees	Repairs and maintenance
Depletion	Salaries and wages
Depreciation	Supplies
Employee benefit programs	Taxes and licenses
Insurance	Travel and transportation
Interest	Utilities

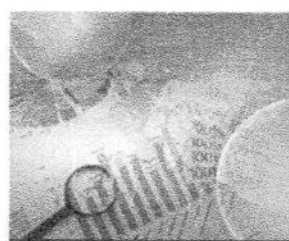

Tax Planning Strategies **Unreasonable Compensation**

Framework Focus: Tax Rate

Strategy: Changing the Nature of Distributions to Avoid Double Taxation.

The double taxation of income earned by a corporation can be avoided if distributions to shareholders are considered reasonable compensation. In substantiating the reasonableness of a shareholder-employee's compensation, an internal comparison test is sometimes useful. If it can be shown that nonshareholder-employees and shareholder-employees in comparable positions receive comparable compensation, it is indicative that compensation is not unreasonable.

Another way to substantiate the reasonableness of a shareholder-employee's compensation is to demonstrate that the shareholder-employee has been underpaid in prior years. For example, the shareholder-employee may have agreed to take a less-than-adequate salary during the unprofitable formative years of the business. He or she would expect the "postponed" compensation to be paid in later, more profitable years. To avoid problems, such an agreement should be documented, if possible, in the corporate minutes.

Keep in mind that in testing for reasonableness, the shareholder-employee's total pay package must be considered. Compensation includes all fringe benefits or perquisites, such as contributions by the corporation to a qualified pension plan, regardless of when the funds are available to the employee.

For additional discussion of the meaning of reasonable compensation, see Chapter 13.

LO.2

Describe and apply the cash and accrual methods of accounting for business deductions.

5-2 The Timing of Deduction Recognition

As discussed in Chapter 4, a taxpayer's accounting method is a major factor in determining their taxable income. The method used determines *when* an expense is deductible as well as when revenue is taxable. Usually, the method regularly used by the taxpayer in keeping the books is used for income tax purposes.[10] However, the Code and Regulations also require that the accounting method used clearly reflect income and that items be handled consistently.[11] The most common methods of accounting are the cash method and the accrual method. Most individuals and many small businesses use the cash method while larger corporations must use the accrual method. If a taxpayer owns multiple businesses and is not required to use the accrual method, it is permissible to use the cash method for some and the accrual method for others.[12]

Throughout the portions of the Code dealing with deductions, the phrase *paid or incurred* is used. A cash basis taxpayer is generally allowed a deduction in the year an expense is *paid*. An accrual basis taxpayer is allowed a deduction in the year in which the liability for the expense is *incurred*.

5-2a The Cash Method

The expenses of cash basis taxpayers are deductible only when they are actually paid, either with cash or other property. Although promising to pay or issuing a note does *not* satisfy the actually paid requirement,[13] a payment made with borrowed funds is

[10]§ 446(a).

[11]§§ 446(b) and (e); Reg. § 1.446–1(a)(2).

[12]As discussed in Chapter 4, certain taxpayers, including large C corporations, are prohibited from using the cash method.

[13]*Page v. Rhode Island Trust Co.*, 37–1 USTC ¶9138, 19 AFTR 105, 88 F.2d 192 (CA–1).

deductible. Taxpayers using the cash method are also allowed to claim a deduction at the time they charge expenses on credit cards. Effectively, they are considered to have borrowed money from the credit card issuer and simultaneously paid the expenses.[14]

Although a cash basis taxpayer must actually or constructively pay an expense for the expense to be deductible, payment does not ensure a current deduction. The Regulations require capitalization of any expenditure that creates an asset having a useful life that extends substantially beyond the end of the tax year.[15] The courts have clarified that expenditures that provide a benefit beyond the end of the tax year following the year of payment generally create an asset with a useful life that extends substantially beyond the end of the tax year and must be capitalized.[16] Thus, even cash basis taxpayers can only deduct such expenditures through amortization, depletion, or depreciation over the tax life of the asset.

Redbird, Inc., a calendar year and cash basis taxpayer, rents property from Bluejay, Inc. On July 1, 2022, Redbird pays $24,000 rent for the 24 months ending June 30, 2024.

The prepaid rent extends 18 months after the close of the tax year—substantially beyond the year of payment. Therefore, Redbird must capitalize the prepaid rent and amortize the expense on a monthly basis. Redbird's deduction for 2022 is $6,000.

Assume that Redbird is required to pay only 12 months' rent in 2022 and pays $12,000 on July 1, 2022. The entire $12,000 is deductible in 2022 when it is paid, as the benefit does not extend beyond the end of 2023.

Tax Planning Strategies **Time Value of Tax Deductions**

Framework Focus: Deductions

Strategy: Accelerate Recognition of Deductions to Achieve Tax Deferral.

Cash basis taxpayers often have the ability to make early payments for their expenses at the end of the tax year. This may allow the taxpayer to accelerate the deduction, and its related tax savings, by a full year while only accelerating the payment by a much shorter time. Given the time value of money, a tax deduction this year is worth more than the same deduction next year.

Before employing this strategy, the taxpayer must consider what next year's expected income and tax rates will be and whether a cash-flow problem may develop from early payments. Thus, a variety of considerations must be taken into account when planning the timing of tax deductions.

More on the deductibility of payments that create benefits lasting beyond the end of the tax year can be found on this book's companion website: www.cengage.com

1 Digging Deeper

5-2b The Accrual Method

An accrual basis taxpayer may not deduct an expense until both the *all events test* and the *economic performance test* are met. The all events test is met when (1) all of the events have occurred to establish the existence of a legal liability and (2) the amount of the liability can be determined with reasonable accuracy. The economic performance test is met when the party obligated to do something (i.e., to perform) to satisfy the liability does so. In situations in which a liability arises as a result of services being provided or property being transferred to the taxpayer, economic performance occurs when the service is provided or ownership of the property is transferred. If the liability is the result of the taxpayer being required to provide services or transfer property, economic performance occurs when the taxpayer provides the service or transfers the property.[17]

[14] Rev.Rul. 78–39. See also Rev.Rul. 80–335, which applies to pay-by-phone arrangements.

[15] Reg. § 1.461–1(a).

[16] *Zaninovich v. Comm.*, 80–1 USTC ¶9342, 45 AFTR 2d 80–1442, 616 F.2d 429 (CA–9). Cited by the Supreme Court in *Hillsboro National Bank v. Comm.*, 83–1 USTC ¶9229, 51 AFTR 2d 83–874, 103 S.Ct. 1134.

[17] § 461(h).

Example 5

Robin, Inc., a concert promoter, sponsored a jazz festival in a rented auditorium at City College. Robin is responsible for cleaning up after the festival, which took place on December 22, 2022, and reinstalling the auditorium seats. Because the college is closed over the Christmas holidays, the company hired by Robin to perform the work did not begin these activities until January 3, 2023. Robin cannot deduct its $1,200 labor cost until 2023 when the services are performed.

Digging Deeper 2

The recurring item exception to the economic performance test is discussed on this book's companion website: www.cengage.com

An important consequence of the economic performance test is that many expenses that are estimated for financial reporting purposes, often by employing reserves or allowance accounts, are not immediately deductible for tax purposes. These expenses typically require estimation precisely because there has been no economic performance. Instead, deductibility is deferred until economic performance has occurred.

Example 6

Oriole Airlines is required by Federal law to test its engines after 3,000 flying hours. Aircraft cannot return to flight until the tests have been conducted. An unrelated aircraft maintenance company performs the tests. Oriole estimates that the tests will cost approximately $1,500 per engine.

For financial reporting purposes, the company accrues an expense based upon $0.50 per hour of flight ($1,500 ÷ 3,000 hours) and credits an allowance account. The actual amounts paid for maintenance are offset against the allowance account.

For tax purposes, the economic performance test is not satisfied until the work has been performed. Therefore, the amount accrued for financial reporting purposes at the end of the year is not yet deductible for tax purposes.

Note that the economic performance test does not require that an expense be paid before it is deductible. In Example 6, the economic performance test is met when the engine tests are performed, even if the expense is not paid until the following year.

Digging Deeper 3

A discussion regarding the determination of book-tax differences directly from the financial statements can be found on this book's companion website: www.cengage.com

5-2c Expenses Accrued to Related Parties

Regardless of the taxpayer's general method of accounting, the Internal Revenue Code places restrictions on the deductibility of expenses accrued to *related parties*. Without these restrictions, related taxpayers who have control over both sides of a transaction would have the ability to enter into transactions that allow the immediate deduction of an expense by an accrual basis taxpayer while allowing the deferral of the related income by a cash basis taxpayer on the other side of the transaction. For example, an accrual basis, closely held corporation might borrow funds from a cash basis individual shareholder. At the end of the year, the corporation would accrue and deduct the interest expense, but the cash basis lender would not recognize interest income because no interest had yet been paid.

Section 267 specifically addresses **related-party transactions**, deferring the deduction of an expense accrued to a related party until the related party is required to recognize the item in income. Note that deferral is not required if both parties use the same general method of accounting. Likewise, deferral will not be required if the party reporting income uses the accrual method and the party taking the deduction uses the cash method.

Relationships and Constructive Ownership

For purposes of § 267, *related parties* include the following:

- Family members, including brothers and sisters (whether whole, half, or adopted), spouse, ancestors (e.g., parents and grandparents), and lineal descendants (e.g., children and grandchildren) of the taxpayer.
- Corporations and shareholders who own more than 50 percent (directly or indirectly) of the corporation's stock.[18]
- Two corporations that are members of a controlled group (discussed in Chapter 12).

[18]The provision also applies to transactions between any partner (shareholder) and a partnership (S corporation) regardless of the ownership interest held by the partner or shareholder.

Constructive ownership provisions must be considered when determining whether taxpayers are related for purposes of § 267. Under these provisions, certain taxpayers are treated as if they own the stock directly owned by others. For example, for purposes of applying the tests of § 267, taxpayers are treated as owning any stock directly owned by family members as well as their proportionate share of any stock owned by a corporation or partnership in which they have an ownership interest.

Related-Party Transactions

The stock of Sparrow Corporation is owned 20% by Ted, 30% by Ted's father, 30% by Ted's mother, and 20% by Ted's sister. Although Ted actually owns only 20% of Sparrow Corporation, he is *deemed* to own the stock owned by his father (30%), mother (30%), and sister (20%).

As a result, he directly and indirectly owns 100% of Sparrow, and Ted and Sparrow are related parties. The same outcome (100% direct and indirect ownership) results for all of the shareholders in this example.

Continue with the facts presented in Example 7. On July 1 of the current year, Ted loaned $10,000 to Sparrow Corporation at 3% annual interest, with principal and interest payable on demand. For tax purposes, Sparrow uses the accrual basis and Ted uses the cash basis. Both report on a calendar year basis.

Because Sparrow and Ted are related parties, Sparrow cannot deduct any interest accrued to Ted until Ted recognizes it as income. Because Ted is a cash basis taxpayer, the deduction is not available to Sparrow until the interest is paid.

5-2d Prepaid Expenses—The "12-Month Rule"

A special rule allows taxpayers, including accrual basis taxpayers, to deduct certain prepaid expenses. A deduction is allowed only if the benefit created by the payment doesn't extend beyond the earlier of (1) 12 months after the first date on which the taxpayer realized the benefit or (2) the end of the tax year following the tax year in which the payment was made (the "12-month rule").[19] Although this rule applies to both cash and accrual method taxpayers, it does not supersede the economic performance test discussed earlier. Therefore, it does not apply to prepayments for services, property, or the use of property for accrual basis taxpayers unless economic performance has occurred. Nor does it apply to other expenses for which special rules regarding their timing exists (e.g., interest and taxes, discussed later in this chapter). Examples of expenses eligible for the 12-month rule include insurance, dues, and licenses.[20]

"12-Month Rule"

Example 9

On November 1, 2022, Nada, a calendar year and accrual basis taxpayer, pays $6,000 for a 1-year premium on a catastrophic liability insurance policy that takes effect December 15, 2022. Nada will receive a benefit from this policy from December 15, 2022, through December 14, 2023. Her benefit does not extend beyond 12 months after the benefit begins on December 15. It also does not extend beyond the end of 2023. Therefore, this payment satisfies the requirements of the 12-month rule and Nada can deduct the $6,000 in 2022.

Assume the same facts as in Example 9, except that the benefit from the policy runs from February 1, 2023, through January 31, 2024. Nada's benefit now extends beyond the end of the tax year following the tax year in which the payment was made (December 31, 2023), so the 12-month rule requirements are not met. Nada must capitalize the $6,000 payment in 2022 and amortize it over the benefit period.

[19]Reg. § 1.263(a)-4(f).

[20]Reg. § 1.263(a)-4(f)(8) (Examples).

LO.3

Recognize and apply a variety of Internal Revenue Code deduction disallowance provisions.

5-3 Disallowance Possibilities

Although most ordinary and necessary expenses related to carrying on a trade or business are deductible, the tax law contains provisions that disallow a deduction for certain expenditures. The most frequently encountered disallowance provisions are discussed below.

5-3a Expenses Incurred in the Investigation of a Business

Recall that § 162 allows a deduction for expenses incurred in *carrying on* a trade or business. However, expenses may be incurred to investigate the creation or acquisition of a business before the business is actually conducted by the taxpayer. Such costs might include travel, engineering and architectural surveys, marketing studies, and various legal and accounting services. How such expenses are treated for tax purposes depends on the following:

- The current business, if any, of the taxpayer.
- Whether the business being investigated is actually acquired.

When the taxpayer is *not* in a business that is the same as or similar to the one being investigated, the tax result depends on whether the new business is acquired. If the taxpayer actually acquires the new business, the expenses must generally be capitalized as **startup expenditures**. However, the taxpayer may be able to immediately deduct up to $5,000 of startup expenses in the month in which business begins. (If an active business is acquired, the business is treated as beginning on the date of acquisition.) This deduction is reduced dollar-for-dollar by the amount total startup expenses exceed $50,000. As a result, the immediate deduction is totally phased out when total startup expenses reach $55,000. Therefore, the immediate deduction primarily benefits smaller businesses. Any expenses not eligible for an immediate deduction are amortized over 180 months, again beginning in the month in which business begins.[21]

Tina, a sole proprietor, owns and operates 10 restaurants located in various cities throughout the Southeast. She travels to Atlanta to discuss the acquisition of an auto dealership. She incurs legal and accounting costs associated with the potential acquisition. After incurring total investigation costs of $52,000, she acquires the auto dealership on October 1, 2022.

Tina may immediately deduct $3,000 [$5,000 − ($52,000 − $50,000)] and amortize the balance of $49,000 ($52,000 − $3,000) over a period of 180 months. For calendar year 2022, therefore, Tina can deduct $3,817 [$3,000 + ($49,000 × 3/180)].

If the taxpayer is not already in the same or similar business and the business is not acquired, the investigation expenses generally are nondeductible.[22]

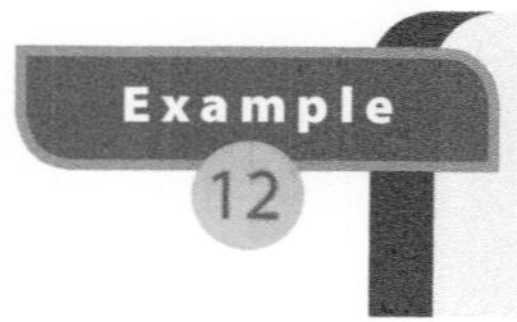

Lynn, president and sole shareholder of Marmot Corporation, incurs expenses when traveling from Rochester, New York, to California to investigate the feasibility of acquiring several auto care centers. Marmot is in the residential siding business. If no acquisition takes place, Marmot may not deduct any of the expenses.

Startup expenses include the following:

- Expenses incurred to investigate the creation or acquisition of a business by the taxpayer (e.g., market studies).
- Expenses incurred in creating or acquiring a business (e.g., incurring professional fees, identifying suppliers, and obtaining licenses).

---

[21] § 195(b).

[22] Rev.Rul. 57–418; *Morton Frank*, 20 T.C. 511 (1953).

- Expenses incurred before the day the business begins that would otherwise have been deductible under § 162 (e.g., salaries, utilities, and advertising).

If the taxpayer is already in a business that is the *same as or similar* to that being investigated (i.e., the taxpayer is investigating the expansion of an existing trade or business), all such expenses are deductible in the year paid or incurred. The tax result is the same whether or not the taxpayer decides to follow through with the expansion.[23]

The Big Picture

Example 13

Return to the facts of *The Big Picture* on p. 5-1. Michael Forney believes that his mechanical and business skills can be used to turn around other small engine businesses whose revenues have been declining. He investigates Southside Small Engine Services LLC, a nearby competitor that is for sale. Expenses paid to consultants and accountants as part of this investigation totaled $6,000. After reviewing various materials, he determined that buying Southside Small Engine Services would not be a good idea.

The $6,000 spent to investigate this potential expansion is deductible as a business expense because Mr. Forney is already in the small engine service and repair business. Investigating new business opportunities in one's current trade or business is an ordinary and necessary business expense.

An illustration of the treatment of business investigation expenses can be found on this book's companion website: www.cengage.com

4 Digging Deeper

5-3b Public Policy Limitations

The courts initially developed the general principle that a payment in violation of public policy is not deductible.[24] Although the payment may be helpful to a business and even contribute to its success, a deduction would, in effect, represent an indirect governmental subsidy for taxpayer wrongdoing.

Under legislation enacted based on this principle, deduction of the following expenses is specifically prohibited.

- Bribes and kickbacks illegal under either Federal or state law.
- Two-thirds of the treble damage payments made to claimants resulting from violation of antitrust law.[25]
- Fines and penalties paid to a government or governmental entity for violation of law.
- Amounts paid to a government or governmental entity for the investigation into the potential violation of any law.[26]

For purposes of the above rules, any entity that regulates a national securities or commodities exchange (e.g., the Securities and Exchange Commission and the Commodity Futures Trading Commission) is considered a governmental entity.

The Big Picture

Example 14

Refer to the facts of *The Big Picture* on p. 5-1. Michael Forney had not instituted proper procedures for disposing of used motor oil and other engine fluids from his business. During the current tax year, he was fined $2,500 by the city. Mr. Forney believes the fine should be deducted as an ordinary business expense. However, because the fine was assessed by and paid to a government for a law violation, the $2,500 is not deductible.

---

[23] *York v. Comm.*, 58–2 USTC ¶9952, 2 AFTR 2d 6178, 261 F.2d 421 (CA–4).

[24] *Tank Truck Rentals, Inc. v. Comm.*, 58–1 USTC ¶9366, 1 AFTR 2d 1154, 78 S.Ct. 507.

[25] §§ 162(c) and (g).

[26] § 162(f). This rule does not apply to payments that are restitution for damage caused by the taxpayer or payments for taxes.

Global Tax Issues Overseas Gun Sales Result in Large Fines

The Foreign Corrupt Practices Act (FCPA) is intended to punish taxpayers who make illegal payments to foreign officials to obtain economic advantages. Not only are such payments (usually improperly recorded as business expenses) nondeductible for income tax purposes, but serious and consistent violations can lead to the imposition of fines. Severe consequences can result from violating the bribery provisions of the FCPA, as Smith & Wesson discovered.

Smith & Wesson, a Massachusetts-based firearms manufacturer, wanted to begin selling firearms in India, Pakistan, and other foreign countries. As a new player in this international market, company officials decided to provide gifts to government officials in these countries to encourage them to do business with Smith & Wesson.

This turned out to be a costly mistake. Smith & Wesson had profits of only $100,000 from this scheme before it was uncovered, and in 2014, it agreed to pay the Securities and Exchange Commission fines of more than $2 million. Of course, the fines were not deductible because they were due to a violation of public policy [§ 162(f)].

Source: **sec.gov/News/PressRelease/Detail/PressRelease/1370542384677#.**

Interestingly, the expenses of operating an illegal business (e.g., a money laundering operation) are deductible as long as the expenses themselves are not illegal.[27] While allowing deductions related to illegal activity may seem inappropriate, recall that the law taxes net income, not gross revenue.

Example 15

Grizzly, Inc., owns and operates a restaurant. In addition, Grizzly operates an illegal gambling establishment out of the restaurant's back room. In connection with the illegal activity, Grizzly has the following expenses during the year:

Rent	$ 60,000
Payoffs to police	40,000
Depreciation on equipment	100,000
Wages	140,000
Interest	30,000
Criminal fines	50,000
Illegal kickbacks	10,000
Total	$430,000

Although the police payoffs ($40,000), fines ($50,000), and kickbacks ($10,000) are not deductible, Grizzly may nonetheless deduct the remaining $330,000 of business expenses related to the gambling operation. Of course, the revenues from the operation are included in Grizzly's gross income.

An exception applies to expenses incurred in illegal drug trafficking.[28] Drug dealers are not allowed a deduction for ordinary and necessary business expenses even if those expenses are themselves legal. Interestingly, drug dealers are nonetheless allowed to reduce their gross income by the cost of the illegal drugs.[29]

5-3c Political Contributions and Lobbying Activities

Political Contributions

No deduction is allowed for direct or indirect payments for political purposes. Historically, Congress has been reluctant to allow deductions for political expenditures even if those expenditures relate to a trade or business. It was feared that allowing such deductions might encourage abuses and enable businesses to have undue influence on the political process. Nondeductible political contributions include payments made to support a political party or to support, participate in, or influence a campaign on behalf of a candidate for public office.[30]

[27] *Comm. v. Sullivan*, 58–1 USTC ¶9368, 1 AFTR 2d 1158, 78 S.Ct. 512.

[28] § 280E.

[29] Reg. § 1.61–3(a). Gross income is defined as sales minus cost of goods sold. Thus, although § 280E prohibits any deductions for drug dealers, it does not modify the normal definition of gross income.

[30] §§ 162(e) and 276.

The Big Picture

Refer to the facts of *The Big Picture* on p. 5-1. Michael's business made political contributions to the State Senate campaigns of Tom Smith and Virginia White. The corporation made these contributions because Michael believed these candidates would be sensitive to the needs of small businesses. Therefore, he assumed that these contributions would be deductible business expenses.

However, political contributions are not deductible. Therefore, despite their connection to the corporation's business, the contributions will not reduce the corporation's taxable income.

Lobbying Expenses

Like political contributions, lobbying expenses also are not deductible. Lobbying expenses include those incurred in attempting to influence any existing or potential legislation at the Federal, state, or local level. They also include direct communications with certain high-ranking Federal government officials in an attempt to influence their official actions or positions. The disallowance extends to a pro rata portion of the membership dues of trade associations and other groups that are involved in lobbying activities.[31]

The Big Picture

Refer to the facts of *The Big Picture* on p. 5-1. Michael's business paid dues to the Small Engine Repair Institute, a trade association for similar-type businesses. The trade association estimates that 70% of its dues are used for lobbying activities. Thus, the corporation's deduction for the dues is limited to $3,000 ($10,000 × 30%).

There are two special rules related to the disallowance of lobbing expenses. First, the disallowance provision does not apply to activities devoted solely to *monitoring* legislation. Second, a *de minimis* exception allows the deduction of *in-house lobbying expenditures* incurred by the taxpayer but only if those expenditures do not exceed $2,000. In-house lobbying expenditures are those paid or incurred directly by the taxpayer rather than amounts paid to professional lobbyists or other third parties.

5-3d Expenses Related to Entertainment, Recreation, or Amusement

Taxpayers commonly incur costs to entertain potential or existing customers, clients, suppliers, or employees. These costs can be incurred either during or in association with a business meeting and may be considered ordinary and necessary trade or business expenses. However, due to the element of personal enjoyment and the related potential for abuse the deductibility of such expenses might create, Congress limits the deductibility of these expenses.

Generally, no deduction is allowed for any costs related to entertainment, amusement, or recreation activities. Nor are costs related to any facilities (e.g., airplanes, yachts, stadium boxes, hotel suites, vacation houses) used in such activities deductible. Similarly, dues related to membership in any business, social, athletic, or sporting clubs also are nondeductible.

Business meals represent an important exception to the general disallowance of entertainment expenses. Business meals, including those paid in connection with business meetings as well as those paid for employees, are generally deductible as long as they are not lavish or extravagant.[32] However, any deduction is limited to 50 percent of the cost of the meals.[33] The deduction for the cost of meals provided to employees on an employer's business premises is also subject to the 50 percent reduction.[34] There are

[31] § 162(e).

[32] § 274(k).

[33] § 274(n).

[34] These expenses will not be deductible after 2025.

several exceptions to the 50 percent cutback on the deductibility of meals. For example, the following are fully deductible:[35]

- Expenses for food or beverage provided by a restaurant (for 2021 and 2022 only);
- Expenses for meals or entertainment that must be treated by the recipient as taxable income; and
- Expenses for recreational or social activities primarily for the benefit of non-highly compensated employees.

Peach, Inc., incurs the following expenses during 2022:

Meals with potential customers at various restaurants	$ 20,000
Theater tickets and green fees for activities immediately preceding or following business meals	24,000
Rental of a luxury box at the baseball stadium for entertaining clients	30,000
Memberships in various country clubs and golf clubs	12,000
The costs of maintaining an on-site cafeteria where employees may dine for free so that they are accessible during the workday and can work during lunch	25,000
The costs of maintaining an on-site health facility so employees can work out before or after work or at lunch	27,000
The costs of an all-day summer party for employees and their families	10,000
	$148,000

Peach may deduct $42,500 of the above expenses [$20,000 for business meals provided by restaurants plus $10,000 for the employee party and $12,500 (50%×$25,000) for the on-site cafeteria]. No portion of the $24,000 spent on events preceding or following business meals, the $30,000 to rent the stadium box, the $12,000 spent on club dues, or the $27,000 maintaining the health facility are deductible.

5-3e Business Interest Expense

Interest on business debt, or *business interest*, is generally deductible. However, taxpayers may use intercompany debt as a relatively easy way of artificially shifting income between related entities. This may be particularly useful if the two entities face different tax rates or one is exempt from U.S. tax (e.g., a foreign entity). Over time, Congress has imposed various limitations on the deductibility of business interest to prevent this kind of income shifting. Currently, a limitation on the deductibility of business interest expense applies to large businesses. The deduction is limited to a taxpayer's business interest income plus 30 percent of its adjusted taxable income. Adjusted taxable income is taxable income calculated without considering (1) nonbusiness income, gain, deduction or loss; (2) any business interest income or expense; (3) the net operating loss (NOL) deduction; and (4) the deduction for qualified business income (§ 199A). In addition, for years beginning before 2022, adjusted taxable income is calculated without considering any depreciation, amortization, or depletion deduction. The limitation may impact any business that is highly leveraged, including corporations that might have used debt to finance a merger. Any disallowed interest can be carried forward indefinitely. The business interest expense limitation only applies to taxpayers with annual average gross receipts in excess of $27,000,000 (for 2022; this amount is indexed annually for inflation) over the prior three taxable years.[36]

In 2022, Robin Corporation has $50,000,000 of adjusted taxable income in addition to $1,000,000 of business interest income and $20,000,000 of business interest expense. Robin's 2022 deduction for business interest expense is limited to $16,000,000, the sum of its $1,000,000 of business interest income plus 30% of its adjusted taxable income (30% × $50,000,000 = $15,000,000). The $4,000,000 of disallowed interest expense is carried forward to future tax years.

[35] §§ 274(e) and (n).

[36] §§ 163(j) and 448(c).

5-3f Executive Compensation

The reasonableness requirement and its relevance to the deductibility of expenses paid by small businesses was discussed above. However, the reasonableness of other expenses, including those paid or incurred by larger businesses, has also gained the attention of Congress as well as the general public. Recall that allowing a deduction indirectly reduces the economic burden of an expense, allowing the taxpayer to share the cost with the larger taxpaying public. In response to concerns over the reasonableness of compensation paid to executives of large corporations, Congress enacted a limitation on the deductibility of such compensation. Specifically, the Code limits the deductibility of the compensation paid to covered employees of publicly traded corporations to $1 million per year. Covered employees are defined as the chief executive officer, the chief financial officer, and the three other most highly compensated employees of the corporation. Any individual who qualifies as a covered employee any time after 2016 will continue to be a covered employee in all future years even if he or she no longer meets one of the above descriptions. Note that the provision does not limit the amount of compensation that can be paid but only the amount that is deductible.[37] The limitation does not apply to any compensation that is excludable from the executive's gross income (discussed in Chapter 11).

On May 1, 2022, Johnette became CEO of Lowe's Depot, a publicly traded corporation that runs a chain of home supply stores. In 2022, her compensation package consists of:

Cash compensation	$1,800,000
Taxable fringe benefits	100,000
Bonus from a qualified bonus plan	5,000,000

Lowe's Depot can deduct only $1,000,000 of Johnette's compensation in 2022 and in all subsequent years that Johnette remains an employee.

5-3g Interest and Other Expenses Related to Tax-Exempt Income

In addition to expenses incurred in a trade or business, the law also allows taxpayers to deduct expenses incurred for the production of income (i.e., related to an activity engaged in for the purpose of generating income but whose activities are not extensive enough to constitute a trade or business, such as investment activities).[38] However, certain types of income (e.g., interest on municipal bonds) are tax-exempt.[39] Together, these provisions could lead to unintended consequences.

Example 21

Simone, an individual in the 35% income tax bracket, borrowed $100,000 to purchase $100,000 of municipal bonds. The bonds pay interest at a rate of 3%, but Simone must pay 4% on the loan. Before considering any potential tax consequences, the net effect of the two transactions is as follows:

Interest income earned on the bonds	$3,000
Interest expense paid on the loan	(4,000)
Net cash flow	($1,000)

However, no tax is due on the municipal interest. If the $4,000 of interest expense were deductible, the deduction would provide a tax benefit of $1,400 (35% × $4,000), turning an arrangement with a $1,000 negative pretax cash flow into a $400 profitable one due solely to the tax benefits.

[37] § 162(m). Before 2018, the $1,000,000 limit also excluded certain performance-based compensation. Contracts in place on November 2, 2017, are grandfathered into pre-2018 law as long as there are no material changes to the contract. For taxable years beginning after December 31, 2026, this provision also will apply to the next five most highly compensated employees each year, extending the limitation to a total of ten covered employees. This second group of five covered employees are determined each year and are not automatically considered covered employees in subsequent years.

[38] § 212.

[39] § 103.

To prevent the type of tax arbitrage possibilities illustrated above, the Code generally disallows the deduction of expenses paid or incurred to generate tax-exempt income.[40] The disallowance applies to interest expense that is directly related to purchasing or carrying tax-exempt bonds as well as any other expense allocable to tax-exempt income.

In January of the current year, Crane Corporation borrowed $100,000 at 4% interest. Crane used the loan proceeds to purchase 5,000 shares of stock in White Corporation. In July, Crane sold the stock for $120,000 and reinvested the proceeds in City of Denver bonds, the income from which is tax-exempt.

Assuming that the $100,000 loan remained outstanding throughout the entire year, Crane cannot deduct the interest attributable to the period when the loan was used to carry the bonds.

Digging Deeper 5

Further discussion regarding whether borrowings are directly related to tax-exempt income can be found on this book's companion website: www.cengage.com

5-3h **Other Disallowance Possibilities**

Other expenditures that are not deductible include capital expenditures and expenditures for which the taxpayer does not have adequate substantiation.

Digging Deeper 6

Further discussion of capital expenditures and other nondeductible expenses, as well as substantiation requirements, can be found on this book's companion website: www.engage.com

Apply the alternative tax treatments of research and experimental expenditures.

5-4 **Research and Experimental Expenditures**

Businesses often incur **research and experimental expenditures**, or costs to develop products or processes the viability of which is uncertain when the costs are paid or incurred. Research and experimental expenditures generally relate to research in the scientific, technological, or engineering sense. They include expenditures directly related to product or process development, such as salaries and materials, as well as the costs of obtaining a related patent. They do not include the costs of routine quality testing, consumer research, or promotions.[41] Nor do they include the costs of land or depreciable property used in the research, although the depreciation on such property may qualify.[42] In many instances, a taxpayer may incur research and experimental expenditures before actually engaging in any trade or business activity. In such instances, the expenditures are treated as described below and need not be capitalized as startup expenses.[43]

Three alternative methods were available for handling research and experimental expenditures *paid or incurred prior to 2022*.[44] The preferred method was adopted for the first taxable year in which qualified expenditures were paid or incurred. Once adopted, a taxpayer must continue to use the chosen method unless the IRS approves a request for a change.[45] Therefore, the treatment of expenditures paid or incurred prior to 2022 continues to apply to those expenditures for tax years after 2021. All research and experimental expenditures *paid or incurred after 2021* must be consistently capitalized and amortized. The proper treatment of research and experimental expenditures is discussed in detail next.

[40] § 265.
[41] Reg. § 1.174-2.
[42] § 174(c).
[43] *Snow v. Comm.*, 74–1 USTC ¶9432, 33 AFTR 2d 74–1251, 94 S.Ct. 1876.
[44] § 174.
[45] § 174(a)(2) and (b)(2).

5-4a Expense Method

Historically, Congress has sought to encourage businesses to invest in research and experimental expenditures. In tax years beginning before January 1, 2022, a taxpayer could deduct all research and experimental expenditures in the year in which they were paid or incurred, even if those expenditures created benefits that lasted beyond the end of the tax year.

5-4b Deferral and Amortization Method

Alternatively, in tax years beginning before January 1, 2022, research and experimental expenditures could be treated as deferred expenses and amortized. If this election was made, the expenditures were amortized:

1. Over a period of at least 60 months beginning in the month the taxpayer first realizes a benefit from the expenditures (i.e., when the product, process, etc., is first put to use in generating income),[46] or
2. Over a period of 10 years beginning in the year the expenditure is made.[47]

Gold Corporation, a calendar year taxpayer, decided to develop a new line of adhesives. The project began in 2020. Gold incurred the following expenses in 2020 and 2021 in connection with the project.

	2020	2021	Total
Salaries	$25,000	$18,000	$43,000
Materials	8,000	2,000	10,000
Depreciation on machinery	6,500	5,700	12,200
Total	$39,500	$25,700	$65,200

The benefits from the project will be realized starting in March 2022.

If Gold Corporation elected a 60-month deferral and amortization period, there would be no deduction prior to March 2022, the month benefits from the project begin to be realized. The deduction for 2022 is $10,867, computed as follows:

Salaries	$43,000
Materials	10,000
Depreciation	12,200
Total	$65,200
2022 deduction: $65,200 × (10 months ÷ 60 months)	$10,867
2023 deduction: $65,200 × (12 months ÷ 60 months)	$13,040

If Gold elected a 10-year deferral and amortization period, the expenses incurred in 2020 would be deducted over 10 years starting in 2020. Similarly, the expenses incurred in 2021 would be deducted over 10 years starting in 2021.

Given the time value of money, it was generally preferable to deduct research and development costs immediately. The deferral of research and experimental expenditures was preferable, however, if the taxpayer expected higher tax rates in the future.

Research and experimental expenditures incurred after 2021 must be capitalized and amortized as described above with two modifications. First, the expenditures must be amortized ratably over a 5-year period (15 years for foreign research expenses). Second, amortization will begin at the midpoint of the year the expenses are paid or incurred rather than the month in which the taxpayer first realizes benefits.[48]

[46] § 174(b)(1).
[47] § 59(e).
[48] § 174(a)(2), as amended by § 13206(a), P.L. 115-97.

Assume the same facts as Example 23, except that Gold Corporation incurs the expenses in 2022 and 2023 (rather than 2020 and 2021) and the benefits from the project will be realized starting in March 2024.

Gold's research and experimental expenses total $39,500 in 2022 and $25,700 in 2023. Gold will amortize both sets of expenses over a five-year period beginning at the mid-point of the year the expenses are incurred (in this case, July 1 of 2022 and 2023); the year benefits are realized no longer matters. Gold's research and experimental deduction in 2022 and 2023 is computed as follows:

2022 Taxable Year	
2022 expenses [$39,500 × (½ year ÷ 5 years)]	$3,950
2023 Taxable Year	
2022 expenses ($39,500 ÷ 5 years)	$ 7,900
2023 expenses [$25,700 × (½ year ÷ 5 years)]	2,570
Total research and experimental deduction	$10,470

The law also provides a credit for increasing research and experimental expenses over what the taxpayer paid or incurred in a base year or years. The amount otherwise deductible or amortizable is reduced by the available credit to prohibit the taxpayer from benefiting twice from the same expenditure.[49]

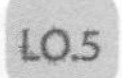

LO.5

Identify issues related to the deductibility of other common business expenses.

5-5 Issues Related to Other Common Business Deductions

In addition to the provisions discussed above, a variety of other expenses are subject to special rules and limitations. Two of the more commonly encountered expenditures are discussed below.

5-5a Interest Expense

Generally, taxpayers other than large businesses are not limited in the amount of business interest expense they may deduct. However, the deductibility of expenses (including interest) from certain other activities may be limited.[50] Further, the deductibility of interest by individuals depends on the activity to which the interest relates.[51]

Since the deductibility of interest expense associated with certain activities is limited, the IRS provides rules for allocating interest expense among activities. Under these rules, interest is allocated in the same manner as the debt with respect to which the interest is paid, and debt is allocated by tracing disbursements of the debt proceeds to specific expenditures. The interest tracing rules are complex and depend on whether loan proceeds are commingled with other cash and the length of time the loan proceeds are held before they are spent.

5-5b Taxes

As with interest expense, most state, local, and foreign taxes paid or incurred in a business or investment context are generally deductible. However, most Federal taxes are not deductible.

Although property taxes are generally deductible, the determination of a property owner's real estate taxes in the year in which property is purchased or sold may not be obvious because of how such taxes are assessed and paid. Real estate taxes for the year in which property is transferred must be apportioned between the buyer and seller of the property. The apportionment is based on the number of days the property was held by each during the real property tax year. Apportionment is required whether the tax is paid by the buyer or the seller or is prorated according to the purchase agreement. The apportionment determines who is entitled to deduct the real estate taxes in the year

[49] § 41. See Chapter 17 for a more detailed discussion of the research activities credit.

[50] See, for example, the discussion of the passive activity limits in Chapter 6.

[51] See Chapter 10 for a more detailed discussion of the deductibility of interest by individuals.

A county's real property tax year runs from January 1 to December 31. Nuthatch Corporation, the owner on January 1 of real property located in the county, sells the real property to Crane, Inc., on June 30. Crane owns the real property from June 30 through December 31. The tax for the real property tax year, January 1 through December 31, is $3,650.

Assuming that this is not a leap year, the portion of the real property tax treated as imposed upon Nuthatch, the seller, is $1,800 [(180/365) × $3,650, January 1 through June 29], and $1,850 [(185/365) × $3,650, June 30 through December 31] of the tax is treated as imposed upon Crane, the purchaser.

of sale. The required apportionment prevents the shifting of the deduction for real estate taxes from buyer to seller or vice versa. The date of sale counts as a day the property is owned by the buyer.

If the actual payment of the real estate taxes are not prorated between the buyer and seller as part of the purchase agreement, the terms of the agreement need to be adjusted to properly reflect the tax consequences. For example, if the buyer pays the entire amount of the tax, it effectively has paid the seller's portion of the real estate tax and has therefore paid more for the property than the actual price in the purchase agreement. As a result, the amount of real estate tax that is apportioned to the seller and paid by the buyer is added to the buyer's basis. The seller must increase the amount realized on the sale by the same amount.

Seth sells real estate on October 3 for a contract price of $400,000. The buyer, Winslow Company, pays the real estate taxes of $3,650 for the calendar year, which is the real estate property tax year. Assuming that this is not a leap year, $2,750 (for 275 days) is apportioned to and is deductible by the seller, Seth, and $900 (for 90 days) of the taxes is deductible by Winslow. The buyer has paid Seth's real estate taxes of $2,750 and has therefore paid $402,750 for the property. Winslow's basis is increased to $402,750, and the amount realized by Seth from the sale is increased to $402,750.

The opposite result occurs if the seller (rather than the buyer) pays the real estate taxes. In this case, the seller reduces the amount realized from the sale by the amount that has been apportioned to the buyer. The buyer is required to reduce his or her basis by a corresponding amount.

Finally, the deductibility of state, local, and foreign income taxes may raise at least two issues. The first relates to when these taxes are deductible. A tax is generally defined as a required payment to a government for which there is no direct benefit. The lack of a direct benefit suggests that the liability for income taxes can never meet the economic performance test. Therefore, taxes are generally deductible when paid regardless of a taxpayer's accounting method.[52]

The second issue relates to the state and foreign income taxes of individuals. All income taxes are considered to be the personal liability of the taxpayer. Therefore, even though a portion of an individual's income taxes may be attributable to a business (i.e., a sole proprietorship), an individual's income taxes will never be considered a business expense under § 162.[53]

5-6 Charitable Contributions

Identify and measure deductible charitable contributions and determine corporate limitations on the contribution deduction.

Although charitable contributions are neither ordinary nor necessary business expenses, Congress allows all taxpayers to deduct certain contributions. The deduction is intended to encourage taxpayers to support organizations that provide social welfare needs to communities (while reducing the costs that the government would incur to provide these services).[54] However, since most expenses deductible under § 162 are allowed without limitation or restriction, Congress expressly precludes contributions from falling under § 162 and instead addresses them separately so as to define precisely what types of contributions are encouraged and how much encouragement will be provided.

[52]Reg. § 1.461–4(g)(6).

[53]Temp.Reg. § 1.162–1T(d); *Douglas H. Tanner,* 45 T.C. 145 (1965), *aff'd per curiam* 66–2 USTC ¶9537, 18 AFTR 2d 5125, 363 F.2d 36 (CA–4); Rev. Rul. 70–40.

[54]§ 170.

5-6a Deductible Contributions

A **charitable contribution** deduction is only available for contributions made to qualified organizations.[55] Qualified organizations include:

- States or possessions of the United States or any subdivisions thereof.
- Entities created or organized in the United States and organized and operated exclusively for religious, charitable, scientific, literary, or educational purposes or for the prevention of cruelty to children or animals.

In no case is a deduction allowed for a contribution made to an individual.

A list of other types of qualified organizations can be found on this book's companion website: www.cengage.com

Contributions to qualified organizations must meet further requirements to be deductible. To qualify as a charitable contribution, a payment must be made with donative intent and with no expectation of a benefit or consideration being received from the organization. These requirements, while impacting the deductibility of a contribution, also have potential consequences for the timing of the deduction. Recall that an accrual basis taxpayer may generally only deduct an expense when both the all events and economic performance tests are met. Since no consideration results from a contribution, a contribution can never meet the economic performance test. Rather, contributions are usually only deductible when *paid* (regardless of the accounting method used by the taxpayer). However, an exception allows an *accrual basis corporation* to claim the deduction in the year preceding payment if two requirements are met. First, the contribution must be *authorized* by the board of directors by the end of that taxable year. Second, it must be *paid* on or before the due date of the corporation's tax return (i.e., the fifteenth day of the fourth month following the close of its taxable year).[56]

Example 27

On December 28, 2021, Blue Company, a calendar year, accrual basis partnership, authorizes a $5,000 donation to the Atlanta Symphony Association (a qualified charitable organization). The donation is made on April 11, 2022. Because Blue Company is a partnership, the contribution can be deducted only in 2022.[57]

However, if Blue Company is a corporation and the December 28, 2021 authorization was made by its board of directors, Blue may claim the $5,000 donation as a deduction for calendar year 2021.

5-6b Measuring Noncash Contributions

A deduction is available for contributions of property as well as cash. How a noncash contribution is measured depends on the type of property contributed. For this purpose, property must be identified as capital gain property or ordinary income property. **Capital gain property** is property that, if sold, would result in a long-term capital gain or § 1231 gain for the taxpayer. **Ordinary income property** is property that, if sold, produces income other than a long-term capital gain for the taxpayer. Examples of ordinary income property include inventory and capital assets held one year or less. Refer to Chapter 4 for a brief introduction to the distinction between capital and ordinary assets and Chapter 8 for a complete discussion of the nature of capital and § 1231 assets.

A contribution of noncash property is generally measured by the property's fair market value. This potentially allows taxpayers to include in the deduction any amount by which the property may have appreciated without also recognizing that appreciation as income. On the other hand, it prevents taxpayers from being able to recognize losses when contributing property that has depreciated. Therefore, rather than contributing depreciated property, taxpayers may want to sell the property, potentially allowing recognition of the loss, and donate the sale proceeds instead.

[55] § 170(c).

[56] § 170(a)(2).

[57] Each partner will report an allocable portion of the charitable contribution deduction as of December 31, 2022 (the end of the partnership's tax year). See Chapter 14.

Mallard Corporation is considering making a contribution to Oakland Community College. Mallard owns a parcel of land, a capital asset, which it acquired five years ago for $60,000. If Mallard were to contribute the land to Oakland, Mallard would measure the contribution at the land's fair market value on the contribution date.

If the land's fair market value on the contribution date was $100,000, Mallard would be entitled to a deduction of $100,000, even though the $40,000 of appreciation on the land has never been included in Mallard's income.

Conversely, if the land's fair market on the contribution date was $20,000, Mallard would be entitled to a deduction of only $20,000. Further, the $40,000 decline in the land's fair market value is not recognizable as a loss. In this case, Mallard may want to sell the land, recognizable the $40,000 capital loss, and donate the sales proceeds to Oakland.

In some situations, a noncash contribution must be measured at the lesser of its fair market value or its adjusted basis (i.e., it must be measured without regard to any appreciation). These situations include the following:

- Contributions of ordinary income property, and
- Contributions of capital gain property that is also tangible and personal, but only if the property is *not* used by the organization in activities related to its tax-exempt purpose.[58]

Contributions of Tangible Personal Property

White Corporation donates a painting worth $200,000 to Western States Art Museum (a qualified charity), which exhibits the painting. White had acquired the painting in 2002 for $90,000.

Because the museum put the painting to a related use, White is allowed to deduct $200,000, the fair market value of the painting.

Assume the same facts as in the previous example, except that White Corporation donates the painting to the American Cancer Society, which sells the painting and deposits the $200,000 proceeds in the organization's general fund.

White's deduction is limited to the $90,000 basis because it contributed tangible personal property that was put to an unrelated use by the charitable organization.

Black Corporation donates a painting worth $90,000 to the American Cancer Society, which sells the painting and deposits the $90,000 proceeds into the organization's general fund. Black acquired the painting several years ago for $200,000.

Because the painting is a capital asset that is tangible personal property and is put to an unrelated use by the donee organization, Black's contribution is measured by the lesser of its fair market value or adjusted basis. Since the painting's adjusted basis is greater than its fair market value, Black's contribution is $90,000. Further, Black recognizes no loss on the depreciation of the painting. Rather than contributing a depreciated asset to a qualified charity, a taxpayer should consider selling the asset, recognizing the loss, and donating the proceeds.

Special rules related to the measurement of certain noncash contributions by corporations can be found on this book's companion website: www.cengage.com

8 Digging Deeper

[58]The measurement of capital gain property contributed to certain private nonoperating foundations (defined in §§ 4942 and 509) is also limited to the basis of the property.

5-6c Limitations Imposed on Charitable Contribution Deductions

Both corporations and individuals are subject to annual limitations on the charitable contribution deduction.[59] The limitations for individual taxpayers are covered in Chapter 10.

In any tax year, a corporate taxpayer's contribution deduction is generally limited to 10 percent of taxable income (25 percent of taxable income for cash contributions for 2020 and 2021). For this purpose, taxable income is computed without regard to the charitable contribution deduction, any capital loss carryback, and the dividends received deduction. Any contributions in excess of the 10 percent limitation may be carried forward to the five succeeding tax years, subject to the same 10 percent limitation. In applying this limitation in any carryover year, the current year's contributions must be deducted first with contributions from the earliest carryover years deducted next.[60]

Annual Limitation and Carryover Rules Illustrated

Example 32

During 2022, Orange Corporation (a calendar year taxpayer) had the following income and expenses.

Income from operations	$140,000
Deductible expenses from operations	110,000
Dividends received	10,000
Charitable contributions made in May 2022	6,000

For purposes of the 10% limitation only, Orange Corporation's taxable income is $40,000 ($140,000 − $110,000 + $10,000). Consequently, the allowable charitable contribution deduction for 2022 is $4,000 (10% × $40,000). The $2,000 unused portion of the contribution can be carried forward to 2023, 2024, 2025, 2026, and 2027 (in that order) until exhausted.

Example 33

Assume the same facts as in the previous example. In 2023, Orange Corporation has taxable income (for purposes of the 10% limitation) of $50,000 and makes a charitable contribution of $4,500. The maximum deduction allowed for 2023 is $5,000 (10% × $50,000). The entire 2023 contribution of $4,500 and $500 of the 2022 charitable contribution carryforward are currently deductible. The remaining $1,500 of the 2022 contribution may be carried over until it is used (or the 5-year carryforward period ends).

LO.7

Determine the amount and timing of cost recovery available under MACRS, including additional cost recovery available in the year an asset is placed in service.

5-7 Cost Recovery Allowances

5-7a Overview

Taxpayers may deduct, or recover, the costs of most assets that are used in a trade or business or held for the production of income. *Depreciation* refers to the periodic recovery of the costs of most tangible assets, *depletion* to the recovery of the costs of natural resources, and *amortization* to the recovery of the costs of intangible assets. Depletion and amortization are discussed briefly later in this chapter. This section focuses on the role and calculation of depreciation for tax purposes.

The tax rules for recovering the cost of business assets differ from the financial accounting rules. Historically, *depreciation* for tax purposes was computed using variations of financial accounting depreciation methods. However, Congress completely revised the **depreciation** rules in 1981 by creating the **accelerated cost recovery system (ACRS)**. Generally, ACRS allowed the recovery of costs over artificially shortened recovery periods with broader availability of accelerated methods. In 1986, Congress made substantial modifications to ACRS, which resulted in the **modified accelerated cost recovery system (MACRS)**. Although the terms *depreciation* and **cost recovery** are often used

[59]The percentage limitations applicable to individuals and corporations are identified in § 170(b).

[60]The carryover rules relating to all taxpayers are in § 170(d).

interchangeably, the former normally refers to the allocation of costs over the periods they benefit for financial reporting purposes while the latter refers to the recovery of cost for tax purposes. This portion of the chapter focuses on the MACRS rules, and the chapter concludes with a discussion of the amortization of intangible property and startup expenditures and the depletion of natural resources.

Discussions of the distinction between capital expenditures and repair and maintenance costs, and the election to immediately deduct property the costs of which are immaterial, can be found on this book's companion website: www.cengage.com

9 Digging Deeper

5-7b Cost Recovery—In General

Cost recovery is available only with respect to qualifying assets used in a business or for the production of income. Cost recovery deductions are determined by the nature of the qualifying asset, when the asset is placed in service, and its basis. Thus, identifying the particular assets that qualify, their nature, when they are placed in service, and their basis is critical to determining the appropriate cost recovery deduction.

Nature of Property

MACRS provides separate cost recovery periods and methods for realty (real property) and personalty (personal property). *Realty* generally includes land and buildings permanently affixed to the land. *Personalty* is defined as any asset that is not realty. Personalty includes furniture, machinery, equipment, and any other asset that is movable. Personalty should not be confused with personal use property. Personal use property is any property (realty or personalty) that is held for personal use rather than for use in a trade or business or an income-producing activity. Cost recovery deductions are not allowed for personal use assets.

In summary, both realty and personalty can be either business use/income-producing property or personal use property. Examples include:

- A residence (realty that is personal use),
- An office building (realty that is business use),
- A dump truck (personalty that is business use), and
- Common clothing (personalty that is personal use).

Finally, assets used in a trade or business or for the production of income are eligible for cost recovery only if they are subject to wear and tear, decay or decline from

Bridge Discipline — Bridge to Finance

For many business entities, success in producing goods for sale is dependent on the efficient use of fixed assets, such as machinery and equipment. An important question for such businesses to resolve is how they should gain access to the required complement of fixed assets: that is, whether the assets should be purchased or leased. To answer this question, the taxpayer must determine which alternative is more cost-effective. Critical to this assessment is quantifying the after-tax cost (including the associated tax benefits) of each option.

Purchasing productive assets for business use often necessitates an immediate cash outflow. However, the tax savings resulting from the available depreciation expense deductions mitigate the impact of that outflow by reducing the taxpayer's taxable income and the income tax paid for the year. Consequently, the tax savings from the depreciation calculation associated with the purchase of an asset reduce the after-tax cost of employing the asset. The analysis can be refined further by evaluating the tax savings from the depreciation deductions in present value terms by quantifying the tax savings from the depreciation expense over the life of the asset. The asset's purchase also can be financed with debt.

Taxpayers who lease rather than buy an asset benefit by not giving up the use of funds that otherwise would have gone to purchase the asset. Lessees also forgo the opportunity to claim depreciation deductions; however, they reduce the cost of the leasing option by claiming the lease expense as a deduction against their tax base.

natural causes, or obsolescence. Assets that do not decline in value or that do not have a limited useful life (e.g., land, stock, and antiques) are not eligible for cost recovery.

Placed in Service Requirement

An asset becomes eligible for cost recovery when it is placed in service rather than when it is purchased. This distinction is particularly important for an asset that is purchased near the end of the tax year but not placed in service until the following tax year.

Cost Recovery Allowed or Allowable

To prevent the recovery of the same cost more than once (i.e., through periodic cost recovery during the asset's life and on the sale of the asset), the basis of property is reduced by any cost recovery deductions allowed. Furthermore, the adjusted basis of property is reduced by at least the amount of cost recovery that was allowable, or the amount that could have been taken using the appropriate cost recovery method. Therefore, even if a taxpayer fails to claim any allowable cost recovery in a given year, the basis of the property is still reduced by the amount of cost recovery that should have been claimed.

On March 15 in year 1, Heron, Inc., purchased, for $10,000, a copier to use in its business. The cost of the copier is recoverable over five years (see Exhibit 5.2), and Heron elected to use the straight-line method of cost recovery. Heron made the election because its business was new, and Heron reasoned that in the first few years of the business, a large cost recovery deduction was not needed.

Because the business was doing poorly, Heron did not deduct any cost recovery deductions in years 3 and 4. In years 5 and 6, Heron deducted the proper amount of cost recovery. The *allowed* cost recovery (cost recovery actually deducted) and the *allowable* cost recovery are computed as follows:[61]

	Cost Recovery Allowed	Cost Recovery Allowable
Year 1	$1,000	$ 1,000
Year 2	2,000	2,000
Year 3	–0–	2,000
Year 4	–0–	2,000
Year 5	2,000	2,000
Year 6	1,000	1,000
Totals	$6,000	$10,000

The adjusted basis of the copier at the end of year 6 is $0 ($10,000 cost – $10,000 *allowable* cost recovery). If Heron sells the copier for $800 in year 7, it will recognize an $800 gain ($800 amount realized – $0 adjusted basis).

Cost Recovery Basis for Personal Use Assets Converted to Business or Income-Producing Use

If a personal use asset is converted to business or income-producing use, the property's basis for cost recovery and for determining any loss on its disposition is the lower of the adjusted basis or the fair market value at the time the property was converted. This rule ensures that any loss in value that occurred when the property was a personal use asset cannot be recognized through cost recovery of the property.

[61] The cost recovery allowances are based on the half-year convention, which allows a half-year's cost recovery in the first and last years of the recovery period.

The Big Picture

Example 35

Return to the facts of *The Big Picture* on p. 5-1. Five years ago Michael Forney purchased a personal residence for $250,000. In the current year, Michael found an attractively priced larger home that he acquired for his personal residence. Because of the downturn in the housing market, however, he was not able to sell his original residence and recover his purchase price of $250,000. The residence was appraised at $180,000.

Instead of continuing to try to sell the original residence, he converted it to rental property. The basis for cost recovery of the rental property is $180,000 because the fair market value is less than the adjusted basis. The $70,000 decline in value is deemed to be personal (because it occurred while the property was held for Michael's personal use) and therefore nondeductible.

5-7c The Modified Accelerated Cost Recovery System (MACRS)

To assist taxpayers in applying the MACRS system, the IRS issues tables that provide annual cost recovery allowances based on the recovery periods, methods, and conventions specified in the Internal Revenue Code. However, those tables are based on depreciation methods and conventions that should be familiar to most accounting students. These methods and conventions are discussed below and summarized in Concept Summary 5.1.

5-7d MACRS for Personal Property

MACRS provides that the basis of eligible personalty (and certain realty) is recovered over 3, 5, 7, 10, 15, or 20 years.[62] Property included in the different cost recovery categories (class lives) is shown in Exhibit 5.2.[63] Notice that the 10-, 15-, and 20-year categories tend to apply to assets used for special purposes or in specific industries. Most general-purpose assets have recovery periods of 5 or 7 years.

Cost recovery of personalty in all but the 15- and 20-year classes is based on double-declining-balance depreciation, switching to straight-line when using straight-line over the asset's remaining recovery period yields a greater deduction. Cost recovery of property in the 15- and 20-year categories is based on the 150 percent declining-balance method.

Cost recovery of all personalty generally incorporates the **half-year convention**; that is, cost recovery in the year the asset is placed in service, as well as the year it is removed from service, is based on the simplifying assumption that the asset was used for exactly one-half of the year, allowing a half-year of cost recovery.[64] For example, the MACRS recovery period for property with a class life of 3 years begins in the middle of the year the asset is placed in service and ends 3 years later. In practical terms, this means that the cost of personalty is actually recovered over 4, 6, 8, 11, 16, or 21 tax years.

As mentioned above, the appropriate methods and conventions are built into the tables provided by the IRS. Therefore, it is generally not necessary for a taxpayer to calculate the appropriate recovery percentages. To determine the amount of the cost recovery allowance, one need only identify the asset's MACRS class life and multiply its cost by the recovery percentage from the appropriate table. The only adjustment required is the application of the part-year convention in a year in which an asset is removed from service. The MACRS percentages for personalty are shown in Exhibit 5.4 located at the end of the chapter prior to the problem materials.

Taxpayers may *elect* to instead use the straight-line method to compute cost recovery allowances for each of these classes of property. Certain property is not eligible for accelerated cost recovery and must be depreciated under an alternative depreciation system (ADS). Both the straight-line election and ADS are discussed later in the chapter.

[62] Personalty is assigned to recovery classes based on asset depreciation range (ADR) midpoint lives provided by the IRS (Rev.Proc. 87–56, 1987–2 C.B. 674). ADR lives generally represent estimates of an asset's useful economic life.

[63] § 168(e) provides the ADR ranges included in Exhibit 5.2.

[64] § 168(d)(4)(A).

Exhibit 5.2 Cost Recovery Periods/Classes: Personalty (and Certain Realty)

Class	Generally Includes Assets with the Following ADR Lives	Specific Inclusions
3-year	4 years or less	Tractor units for use over the road
		Any horse that is not a racehorse and is more than 12 years old at the time it is placed in service
		Special tools used in the manufacturing of motor vehicles, such as dies, fixtures, molds, and patterns
5-year	More than 4 years and less than 10 years	Automobiles and taxis
		Light and heavy general-purpose trucks
		Calculators and copiers
		Computers and peripheral equipment
7-year	10 years or more and less than 16 years	Office furniture, fixtures, and equipment not listed elsewhere
		Agricultural machinery and equipment
10-year	16 years or more and less than 20 years	Vessels, barges, tugs, and similar water transportation equipment
		Assets used for petroleum refining or for the manufacture of grain and grain mill products, sugar and sugar products, or vegetable oils and vegetable oil products
		Single-purpose agricultural or horticultural structures
15-year	20 years or more and less than 25 years	Land improvements
		Assets used for industrial steam and electric generation and/or distribution systems
		Assets used in the manufacture of cement
20-year	25 years or more	Farm buildings except single-purpose agricultural and horticultural structures
		Water utilities
		Railroad hydraulic and nuclear electric generating equipment

Half-Year Convention

Example 36

Robin Corporation acquires a 5-year class asset on April 10, 2022, for $30,000. Robin's cost recovery deduction for 2022 is computed as follows:

MACRS calculation based on Exhibit 5.4 ($30,000 × 0.20)	$6,000

Example 37

Assume the same facts as in the previous example. Robin sells the asset on March 5, 2024. Robin's cost recovery deduction for 2024 is $2,880 [$30,000 × 0.192 × ½ (Exhibit 5.4)].

Mid-Quarter Convention

The half-year convention is based on the simplifying presumption that assets generally will be acquired evenly throughout the tax year. However, Congress was concerned that taxpayers who placed a large portion of assets in service toward the end of the taxable year would nonetheless receive a half-year's cost recovery allowance.

To limit this unintended benefit, Congress added the **mid-quarter convention**. The mid-quarter convention applies if more than 40 percent of the cost of personality is placed in service during the last quarter of the year.[65] Under this convention, all personalty placed in service during the year is treated as if it were placed in service in the middle of the quarter in which its use actually commenced. Property placed in service during the first quarter is allowed 10.5 months (three and one-half quarters) of cost recovery in the year in which it is placed in service; the second quarter, 7.5 months (two and one-half quarters); the third quarter, 4.5 months (one and one-half quarters); and the fourth quarter, 1.5 months. The recovery percentages are shown in Exhibit 5.5.

Example 38

Silver Corporation puts into service the following new 5-year class property in 2022.

Date Placed in Service	Cost
February 15	$ 200,000
July 10	400,000
December 5	600,000
Total	$1,200,000

Because more than 40% ($600,000 ÷ $1,200,000 = 50%) of the acquisitions are in the last quarter, the mid-quarter convention applies. Silver's cost recovery allowances for the first two years are computed as follows.

2022	Mid-Quarter Convention Depreciation (Exhibit 5.5)		Total Depreciation
February 15	$200,000 × 0.35	=	$ 70,000
July 10	$400,000 × 0.15	=	60,000
December 5	$600,000 × 0.05	=	30,000
Total			$160,000

	Mid-Quarter Convention Depreciation (Exhibit 5.5)		Total Depreciation
2023			
February 15	$200,000 × 0.26	=	$ 52,000
July 10	$400,000 × 0.34	=	136,000
December 5	$600,000 × 0.38	=	228,000
Total			$416,000

Without the mid-quarter convention, Silver's 2022 cost recovery deduction would have been $240,000 [$1,200,000 × 0.20 (Exhibit 5.4)]. The mid-quarter convention reduces the taxpayer's available cost recovery deductions for assets placed in service later in the year.

[65] § 168(d)(3).

Like the half-year convention, the mid-quarter convention applies in the year an asset is removed from service as well as when it is first placed in service. When "mid-quarter" property is sold, the property is treated as though it were sold at the midpoint of the quarter in which the sale takes place. So in the quarter when sold, cost recovery is allowed for one-half of the quarter. As with the half-year convention, this is not taken into account in the cost recovery tables. Therefore, the recovery percentages in the table must be adjusted in the year in which an asset is sold.

Assume the same facts as in the previous example, except that Silver Corporation sells the $400,000 asset on October 30, 2023. The cost recovery deduction for 2023 is computed as follows (Exhibit 5.5):

February 15	$200,000 × 0.26	=	$ 52,000
July 10	$400,000 × 0.34 × (3.5/4)	=	119,000
December 5	$600,000 × 0.38	=	228,000
Total			$399,000

The adjusted basis of the $400,000 asset when sold is $221,000 [$400,000 (cost) − $60,000 (2022 cost recovery) − $119,000 (2023 cost recovery)].

Straight-Line Election

A taxpayer may *elect* to use the straight-line method for depreciable personal property.[66] If the straight-line method is elected, the basis of the property is recovered over the MACRS class life of the asset with a half-year convention or a mid-quarter convention, whichever applies. The election is available on a class-by-class and year-by-year basis. In other words, if the straight-line election is made for any property placed in service during a year, it must be applied to all property with the same class life put into service during that same year. The percentages for the straight-line election with a half-year convention appear in Exhibit 5.7.

Straight-Line Election

Terry puts into service a new 10-year class asset on August 4, 2022, for $100,000. He elects the straight-line method of cost recovery. Terry's cost recovery deduction for 2022 is $5,000 ($100,000 × 0.05). His cost recovery deduction for 2023 is $10,000 ($100,000 × 0.10). (See Exhibit 5.7 for the percentages.)

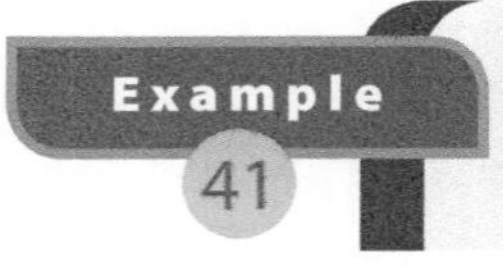

Assume the same facts as in the previous example, except that Terry sells the asset on November 21, 2023. His cost recovery deduction for 2023 is $5,000 [$100,000 × 0.10 × ½ (Exhibit 5.7)].

5-7e MACRS for Real Estate

Under MACRS, the cost of most real property is recovered using the straight-line method. The recovery period for residential rental real estate is 27.5 years. **Residential rental real estate** includes any real property if 80 percent or more of the gross rental revenues are from residential units (e.g., an apartment building). Therefore, hotels, motels, and similar establishments are not considered residential rental property. The basis of most nonresidential real estate is recovered over 39 years.[67]

The cost recovery of most MACRS real estate incorporates the **mid-month convention**.[68] Under this convention, one-half month's cost recovery is allowed for the month the

[66] §§ 168(b)(3)(D) and (5).

[67] §§ 168(b), (c), and (e). A 31.5-year life is used for such property placed in service before May 13, 1993.

[68] § 168(d)(2).

property is placed in service. If the property is sold before the end of the recovery period, one-half month's cost recovery is allowed for the month of sale.

Like personalty, the IRS provides tables to help determine cost recovery on real property. Cost recovery is computed by multiplying the property's basis by the applicable cost recovery percentage from the table. The MACRS real property rates are provided in Exhibit 5.6.

Real Estate Cost Recovery

Badger Rentals, Inc., acquired a building on April 1, 2005, for $800,000. If the building is classified as residential real estate, the cost recovery deduction for 2022 is $29,088 (0.03636 × $800,000). If the building is sold on October 7, 2022, the cost recovery deduction for 2022 is $23,028 [0.03636 × (9.5/12) × $800,000].

Assume instead that the building is acquired on March 2, 1993, for $1,000,000 and is classified as nonresidential real estate. The cost recovery deduction for 2022 is $31,740 (0.03174 × $1,000,000). If the building is sold on January 5, 2022, the cost recovery deduction for 2022 is $1,323 [0.03174 × (0.5/12) × $1,000,000]. (See the first two sections of Exhibit 5.6 for the percentages.)

Oakenwood Properties, Inc., acquired a building on November 19, 2022, for $1,200,000. If the building is classified as nonresidential real estate, the cost recovery deduction for 2022 is $3,852 (0.00321 × $1,200,000). The cost recovery deduction for 2023 is $30,768 (0.02564 × $1,200,000).

If the building is sold on May 21, 2023, the cost recovery deduction for 2023 is $11,538 [0.02564 × (4.5/12) × $1,200,000]. (See the last section of Exhibit 5.6 for the percentages.)

Special rules regarding MACRS for farm property can be found on this book's companion website: www.cengage.com

10 Digging Deeper

Qualified Improvement Property

As discussed above, the cost of nonresidential realty is recovered over 39 years. Any improvements made to this property would normally be recovered over 39 years as well. An exception to this general rule is provided for **qualified improvement property**. The cost of qualified improvement property is recovered over a 15-year period, using the half-year convention and the straight-line method.

Qualified improvement property is any improvement to an interior portion of nonresidential real property made after the property is placed in service, including leasehold improvements.[69] However, it does not include the costs of elevators or escalators or improvements that enlarge a building or modify its internal framework. The MACRS recovery percentages for qualified improvement property are included in Exhibit 5.7.

Redbud, Inc., finishes construction of an office building in July 2022. It plans to lease the third floor of the building to a tenant. In January 2023, Crimson Enterprises leases the third floor and immediately builds out the rental space to meet its needs. It spends $50,000 on cubicles, shelving, and other non-permanent additions. These improvements are qualified improvement property. Their cost will be recovered over 15 years, using the half-year convention and straight-line method.

Crimson's 2023 cost recovery deduction is $1,667 ($50,000 × 0.03333; see Exhibit 5.7 for cost recovery percentages).

[69] § 168(e)(6).

Concept Summary 5.1

MACRS: Class Lives, Methods, and Conventions

	Personalty	Realty
Class lives	3 to 20 years	Qualified Improvement Property: 15 years Residential: 27.5 years Nonresidential: 39 years
Method	200% declining balance for property with class lives less than 15 years; 150% declining balance for property with 15- or 20-year class lives	Straight-line
Convention	Half-year or mid-quarter	Half-year for qualified improvement property Mid-month for residential and other non-residential realty Mid-month

5-7f Election to Immediately Expense Certain Depreciable Assets (§ 179)

Code § 179 permits taxpayers to immediately deduct the acquisition cost of specific types of property used in a trade or business. The **§ 179 expensing election** is an annual election that applies to the acquisition cost of property placed in service each year. The aggregate cost of qualifying property that can be deducted each year is subject to a limitation that is indexed annually for inflation. The limitation for 2022 is $1,080,000 ($1,050,000 in 2021). Property to which § 179 applies includes primarily tangible personal property. However, it also includes computer software, qualified improvement property, and certain improvements made to nonresidential real property (roofs; heating, ventilation, and air conditioning units; fire protection and alarm systems; security systems).[70] The election is not available for property used for the production of income. Amounts that are expensed under § 179 reduce the asset's basis for purposes of calculating any other forms of cost recovery such as MACRS or bonus depreciation (see text Section 5-7g). As a result, any MACRS cost recovery deduction is calculated on the basis of the asset net of the § 179 expense *and* any additional first-year depreciation.

§ 179 Election and Basis

Example 45

Allison acquires and places in service business equipment (a 5-year class asset) on February 1, 2022, at a cost of $1,130,000. It is the only asset she places in service in 2022. Under § 179, Allison can elect to deduct $1,080,000 of the asset's cost in 2022. Assuming that Allison elects not to take additional first-year depreciation, she is able to use MACRS to recover the remainder of its cost ($50,000) beginning in 2022.

2022	§ 179 deduction	$1,080,000
	MACRS: ($1,130,000 − $1,080,000) × 0.20	10,000
	Total 2022 cost recovery	$1,090,000

Example 46

Assume the same facts as in Example 45. Allison sells the asset in 2024 for $50,000. Her gain on the sale is $30,800, calculated as follows:

Selling price				$50,000
Cost			$1,130,000	
Less: Cost recovery				
2022		$1,090,000		
2023	$50,000 × 0.32	16,000		
2024	$50,000 × 0.192 × ½	4,800	(1,110,800)	(19,200)
Realized gain				$30,800

[70] §§ 179(d) and (e).

Deduction Limitations

The § 179 deduction is subject to three limitations discussed and illustrated below. The limitations are applied in the order in which they are discussed.

Ceiling Amount. As discussed above, a taxpayer's § 179 deduction is subject to an annual ceiling amount, indexed for inflation ($1,080,000 in 2022; $1,050,000 in 2021). A taxpayer can choose to use *all, part, or none* of the annual § 179 amount. If a business expects its marginal tax rate to increase in the future, it may decide *not* to use the § 179 deduction. In such a situation, it may be better to defer deductions to those later years. As discussed below, the business income limitation may also lead a business owner to choose not to expense assets.

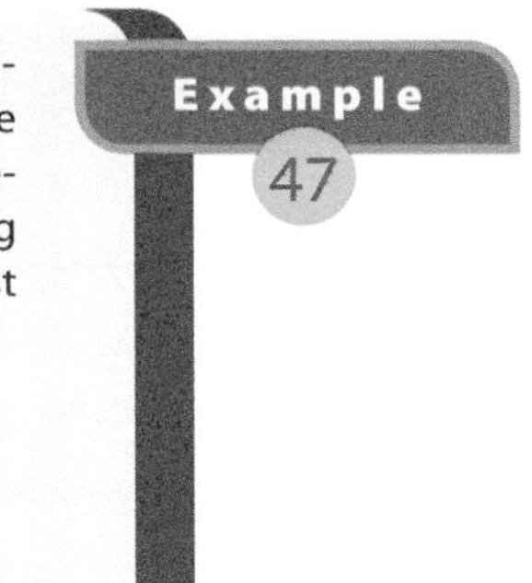

In 2022, Sonya places in service $450,000 of 7-year MACRS assets. Although she could immediately expense all of these assets, she would prefer to use § 179 on just $275,000 of the assets. She knows that combining this $275,000 immediate expense with regular MACRS depreciation effectively reduces her business income to zero, and she wants to defer the remaining deductions to future years when her marginal tax rate will be higher. As a result, Sonya's total cost recovery deduction for 2022 is:

§ 179 expense	$275,000
MACRS depreciation [($450,000 − $275,000) × 0.1429 (Exhibit 5.4)]	25,008
Total cost recovery deduction	$300,008

Property Placed in Service Maximum. The § 179 deduction is restricted to smaller businesses. This restriction is achieved by reducing the annual ceiling amount described above dollar for dollar when § 179 property placed in service during the year exceeds a specified threshold amount. Like the annual ceiling amount, the threshold amount is indexed for inflation ($2,700,000 in 2022; $2,620,000 in 2021). Thus, no § 179 deduction is allowed in 2022 if $3,780,000 ($1,080,000 + $2,700,000) or more of qualifying property is placed in service during the year.

§ 179: Property Placed in Service Maximum

During 2022, Madison places $1,245,000 of § 179 property in service for use in her business. Madison can take a $1,080,000 § 179 expense election; there is no reduction in the § 179 amount since the property placed in service maximum ($2,700,000) was not reached.

During 2022, George places $3,300,000 § 179 property in service for use in his manufacturing business (all assets are new 7-year MACRS assets). Because George placed in service more than the $2,700,000 maximum, he must reduce his § 179 deduction ($3,300,000 − $2,700,000 = $600,000). As a result, George's maximum § 179 deduction is $480,000 ($1,080,000 − $600,000). This reduction cannot be reclaimed in any way; it is permanently lost. George's total cost recovery deduction for 2022 is calculated as follows.

§ 179 expense	$480,000
MACRS depreciation [($3,300,000 − $480,000) × 0.1429 (Exhibit 5.4)]	402,978
Total cost recovery deduction	$882,978

Assume that George also places in service a $1,500,000 office building during 2022. Because the building does not qualify for § 179, it has no impact on George's § 179 allowance. Only property qualifying for § 179 is used to determine whether the § 179 ceiling amount is reduced.

Business Income Limitation. Finally, the § 179 deduction in any year is further limited to the taxpayer's business income. For this purpose, business income is calculated by deducting all business expenses except the § 179 deduction. As a result, a taxpayer's § 179 deduction cannot create (or increase) a net operating loss. For purposes of the limitation, an individual's "business income" includes income not only from a sole proprietorship but also from wages and any allocated business income from a partnership or an S corporation.

During 2022, Lance has a sole proprietorship through which he provides accounting and tax services. The business generated net income of $68,000. In addition, Lance is a 40% shareholder in a management consulting business operated as an S corporation. The S corporation pays Lance a salary of $40,000, and it recorded taxable income of $50,000. In this case, Lance's business income is $128,000 [$68,000 + $40,000 + $20,000 ($50,000 × 40%)].

Any § 179 amount in excess of business income is carried forward to future taxable years and added to other amounts eligible for expensing. The various limitations for that carryforward year (i.e., the ceiling amount, the placed in service maximum amount, and the business income limitation) are applied to the total amount of eligible property, including any amount carried over from previous years.

Jill owns a computer service and repair business and operates it as a sole proprietorship. In 2022, taxable income is $138,000 before considering any § 179 deduction. If Jill spends $2,830,000 on new equipment, her § 179 expense deduction for the year is computed as follows.

§ 179 deduction before adjustment	$1,080,000
Less: Dollar limitation reduction ($2,830,000 − $2,700,000)	(130,000)
Remaining § 179 deduction available	$ 950,000
Business income limitation	$ 138,000
§ 179 deduction allowed	$ 138,000
§ 179 deduction carryforward ($950,000 − $138,000)	$ 812,000

Effect on Basis

The basis of the property for MACRS purposes must be reduced by the § 179 amount available before applying the business income limitation.

Assume the same facts as in Example 51. Jill's adjusted basis in the equipment for cost recovery purposes is $1,880,000 ($2,830,000 cost less the $950,000 § 179 expense amount before the business income limitation). If any portion of the $812,000 carryover (due to the business income limitation) is not deducted before the equipment is sold, this amount may be added back to the basis of the equipment in determining its adjusted basis.

Section 179 and the Mid-Quarter Convention

The mid-quarter convention generally results in smaller depreciation deductions in the asset's acquisition year. However, the basis of property used to determine whether the mid-quarter convention applies is derived *after* any § 179 expense election.[71] As a result, a taxpayer may be able to avoid the mid-quarter convention by designating § 179 treatment for assets placed in service during the last quarter of the taxable year.

[71] Reg. § 1.168(d)–1(b)(4).

Financial Disclosure Insights — Tax and Book Depreciation

A common book-tax difference relates to the depreciation amounts that are reported for GAAP and Federal income tax purposes. Typically, tax depreciation deductions are accelerated; that is, they are claimed in earlier reporting periods than is the case for financial accounting purposes.

Several tax law changes since 1980 have included depreciation provisions that accelerate the related deductions relative to the expenses allowed under GAAP. Accelerated cost recovery deductions represent a means by which the taxing jurisdiction infuses the business with cash flow created by the reduction in the year's tax liabilities.

For instance, approximately one-quarter of the deferred tax liabilities recently reported by General Electric have related to depreciation. Depreciation has recently accounted for approximately one-third of the deferred tax liabilities reported by Ford and nearly all of the deferred tax liabilities reported by trucking company Ryder Systems.

5-7g Additional First-Year Depreciation (Bonus Depreciation)

Congress often uses the tax system to stimulate the economy—especially in challenging economic times. One example is **additional first-year depreciation** (also referred to as "bonus depreciation"). This provision allows taxpayers to immediately deduct a percentage of the cost of qualified property in the year it is placed in service. Since its enactment in 2002, bonus depreciation has varied between 30 and 100 percent of the cost of qualifying property. The law currently allows taxpayers to deduct 100 percent of the cost of qualifying property placed in service through 2022.[72] Qualified property generally includes most property eligible for immediate expensing under § 179 (e.g., tangible personal property, computer software, and qualified improvement property).[73]

The additional first-year depreciation is computed after any immediate expense (§ 179) deduction is claimed. Regular MACRS cost recovery is then calculated by multiplying the remaining cost recovery basis (original cost recovery basis less § 179 expensing and additional first-year depreciation) by the appropriate MACRS percentage. A taxpayer may elect *not* to claim additional first-year depreciation.

Kelly acquires equipment (a new 5-year class asset) on February 1, 2022, at a cost of $1,345,000 and elects to expense $1,080,000 under § 179. Kelly also chooses to take bonus depreciation. As a result, her total cost recovery deduction for the year is calculated as follows.

§ 179 expense	$1,080,000
Additional first-year depreciation [($1,345,000 − $1,080,000) × 100%]	265,000
Total cost recovery deduction	$1,345,000

Alternatively, Kelly could choose not to elect § 179 and still use bonus depreciation to recover the entire cost of the equipment in 2022.

Discussions of other property eligible for bonus depreciation and how to use § 179 and bonus depreciation together effectively can be found on this book's companion website: www.cengage.com

11 Digging Deeper

[72] § 168(k)(6). The additional first-year depreciation percentage decreases to 80% in 2023, 60% in 2024, 40% in 2025, and 20% in 2026. Unless Congress extends the provision, no bonus depreciation will be allowed after 2026. Different rules applied for property placed in service before September 28, 2017.

[73] § 168(k)(2). For property placed in service before September 28, 2017, bonus depreciation applied to new property only.

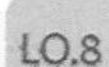

Bridge Discipline **Bridge to Economics and the Business Cycle**

Congress has passed several stimulus packages intended to stabilize and accelerate the economy. Two of these provisions, § 179 expense and bonus depreciation, allow the immediate recovery of the costs of certain assets, thus reducing their after-tax costs. However, in a weak economy, many companies are not able to take advantage of the increased deductions either because they do not have the financial resources to purchase the assets or income to allow the deduction to be taken. In such cases, the stimulus effectiveness as well as the vertical equity of the provisions are debatable.

Source: Based on Joyce Rosenberg, "Deduction Dilemma Hits Companies," *Telegraph Herald* (Dubuque, Iowa), November 9, 2008, p. B2.

LO.8

Identify and apply the cost recovery limitations applicable to automobiles and property used for personal purposes, including listed property.

5-7h Limitations Related to Automobiles and Other Property Used for Personal Purposes

Noncorporate taxpayers may use property both for business and personal purposes. For example, a sole proprietor may use an automobile to transport people and supplies from place to place for business during the week as well as for grocery shopping and running errands over the weekend. In such cases, cost recovery is generally available for the portion of the asset's cost that relates to its business use. However, limitations exist if the property is not *used predominately* for business purposes.

Property Not Used Predominantly for Business

If any property is not used predominantly (i.e., more than 50 percent) for business purposes, the § 179 deduction is not available. Failure to use **listed property** predominately for business will also preclude the use of the MACRS accelerated methods as well as bonus depreciation. Instead, the property's cost must be recovered using only the straight-line recovery method. Further, the straight-line method must continue to be used for the remainder of the asset's recovery period even if, at some later date, the property is predominantly used for business.[74]

Listed property includes:[75]

- Any passenger automobile.
- Most other property used as a means of transportation (e.g., trucks and airplanes).
- Any property of a type generally used for purposes of entertainment, recreation, or amusement.

For listed property to be considered as *predominantly used in business*, its *business use* must exceed 50 percent.[76] The use of listed property for the production of income does not qualify as business use for purposes of the more-than-50% test. However, both production-of-income and business use percentages are used to compute the cost recovery deduction.

Example 54

On September 1, 2021, Emma acquires and places in service listed 5-year recovery property. The property cost $10,000. Emma does not claim any available additional first-year cost recovery.

If Emma uses the property 40% for business and 25% for the production of income, the property is not considered as predominantly used for business. The asset cost is recovered using the straight-line method. Emma's cost recovery allowance for the year is $650 ($10,000 × 0.10 × 0.65).

If, however, Emma uses the property 60% for business and 25% for the production of income, the property is considered as used predominantly for business. Therefore, she may use the MACRS tables. Emma's cost recovery allowance for the year is $1,700 ($10,000 × 0.20 × 0.85).

[74] Reg. § 1.179-1(e)(1) and §§ 280F(b) and 168(k)(2)(F)(ii).

[75] § 280F(d)(4). Listed property also includes any computer or peripheral equipment if placed in service before December 31, 2017.

[76] § 280F(b)(3).

Change from Predominantly Business Use

If the business use percentage of listed property falls to 50 percent or less after the year the property is placed in service, the property is subject to *cost recovery recapture.* The amount required to be recaptured (i.e., included in the taxpayer's ordinary income) is the excess cost recovery. *Excess cost recovery* is the excess of the cost recovery deductions taken in prior years over the amount that would have been allowed if only the straight-line recovery method had been used since the property was placed in service.[77]

Example 55

Seth purchased a new car on January 22, 2022, at a cost of $40,000. Business use was 80% in 2022, 70% in 2023, 40% in 2024, and 60% in 2025. Seth elects not to take any available additional first-year depreciation. Seth's excess cost recovery to be recaptured as ordinary income in 2024 is computed as follows:

2022	
MACRS ($40,000 × 0.20 × 80%)	$ 6,400
Straight-line ($40,000 × 0.10 × 80%)	(3,200)
Excess	$ 3,200
2023	
MACRS ($40,000 × 0.32 × 70%)	$ 8,960
Straight-line ($40,000 × 0.20 × 70%)	(5,600)
Excess	$ 3,360
2024	
2022 excess	$ 3,200
2023 excess	3,360
Ordinary income recapture	$ 6,560

After the business usage of the listed property drops below the more-than-50% level, the straight-line method must be used for the remaining life of the property.

Example 56

Assume the same facts as in Example 55. Seth's cost recovery deduction for 2024 and 2025 is:

2024:	Straight-line ($40,000 × 0.20 × 40%)	$3,200
2025:	Straight-line ($40,000 × 0.20 × 60%)	$3,456

Limits on Cost Recovery for Automobiles

The law places further limitations on the annual cost recovery deductions for *passenger automobiles.*[78] These dollar limits were imposed because of the belief that the tax system was being used to underwrite automobiles whose cost and luxury features far exceeded what was needed for the taxpayer's business use. Any cost otherwise recoverable but limited by the annual limitation may be recovered in later years subject to the limit applicable to the subsequent year.

The following "luxury auto" depreciation limits apply based on the year the automobile was placed in service.[79]

Date Placed in Service	First Year	Second Year	Third Year	Fourth and Later Years
2021*	$10,200	$16,400	$9,800	$5,860
2019–2020	10,100	16,100	9,700	5,760
2018	10,000	16,000	9,600	5,760
2012–2017	3,160	5,100	3,050	1,875

*Because the 2022 indexed amounts were not available when we published, the 2021 amounts are used in the Examples and end-of-chapter problem materials.

[77] § 280F(b)(2).

[78] § 280F(d)(5). A passenger automobile is any four-wheeled vehicle manufactured for use on public streets, roads, and highways with an unloaded gross vehicle weight (GVW) rating of 6,000 pounds or less. This definition specifically excludes vehicles used directly in the business of transporting people or property for compensation (e.g., taxicabs, ambulances, hearses, and trucks and vans as prescribed by the Regulations).

[79] § 280F(a)(1); Rev.Proc. 2021–31.

If a new passenger automobile otherwise qualifies for additional first-year depreciation, the *luxury auto* limitation increases by $8,000 for automobiles placed in service before 2027.[80] Therefore, for acquisitions made in 2021, the initial-year cost recovery limitation increases from $10,200 to $18,200 ($10,200 + $8,000).[81]

The luxury auto limits must be reduced proportionally for any personal use of the auto. In addition, the limitation in the first year includes any amount the taxpayer elects to expense under § 179.[82] If the passenger automobile is used partly for personal use, the personal use percentage is ignored for the purpose of determining the unrecovered cost available for deduction in later years.

On July 1, 2022, Dan acquires and places in service a new automobile that cost $55,000. He does not elect § 179 expensing, and he elects not to take any available additional first-year depreciation. The car is used 80% for business and 20% for personal purposes in each tax year. Dan chooses the MACRS 200% declining-balance method of cost recovery (the auto is a 5-year asset; see Exhibit 5.4).

The depreciation computation for 2022 through 2027 is summarized in the table below. The cost recovery allowed is the lesser of the MACRS amount or the recovery limitation.

Year	MACRS Amount	Recovery Limitation	Depreciation Allowed
2022	$8,800 ($55,000 × 0.2000 × 80%)	$8,160 ($10,200 × 80%)	$ 8,160
2023	$14,080 ($55,000 × 0.3200 × 80%)	$13,120 ($16,400 × 80%)	$13,120
2024	$8,448 ($55,000 × 0.1920 × 80%)	$7,840 ($9,800 × 80%)	$ 7,840
2025	$5,069 ($55,000 × 0.1152 × 80%)	$4,688 ($5,860 × 80%)	$ 4,688
2026	$5,069 ($55,000 × 0.1152 × 80%)	$4,688 ($5,860 × 80%)	$ 4,688
2027	$2,534 ($55,000 × 0.0576 × 80%)	$4,688 ($5,860 × 80%)	$ 2,534

If Dan continues to use the car after 2027, his annual cost recovery is limited to the lesser of the unrecovered basis or the recovery limitation (i.e., $5,860 × business use percentage). For this purpose, the unrecovered basis is the adjusted basis computed as if the full recovery limitation was allowed. As a result, the unrecovered basis as of January 1, 2028 is $3,712 ($55,000 − $10,200 − $16,400 − $9,800 − $5,860 − $5,860 − $3,168*).

If Dan elects to take additional first-year depreciation in 2022, the amount of additional first-year depreciation is $44,000 ($55,000 × 80% × 100%). However, the deduction for the year would be limited to $14,560 [($8,000 + $10,200) × 80%].

*2027 MACRS amount before personal use limitation ($55,000 × 0.0576 × 100%).

Realize that the cost recovery limitations are maximum amounts. If the regular MACRS calculation produces a smaller amount of cost recovery, the smaller amount is used.

On April 2, 2022, Gail places in service a pre-owned automobile that cost $12,000. The car is used 70% for business and 30% for personal use.

The cost recovery allowance for 2022 is $1,680 ($12,000 × 0.20 × 70%), not $7,140 (the $10,200 passenger auto maximum × 70%).

[80] § 168(k)(2)(F).

[81] Different cost recovery limitations apply for trucks and vans and for electric automobiles.

[82] § 280F(d)(1).

Concept Summary 5.2 illustrates the cost recovery rules for various types of listed property.

Concept Summary 5.2

Listed Property Cost Recovery

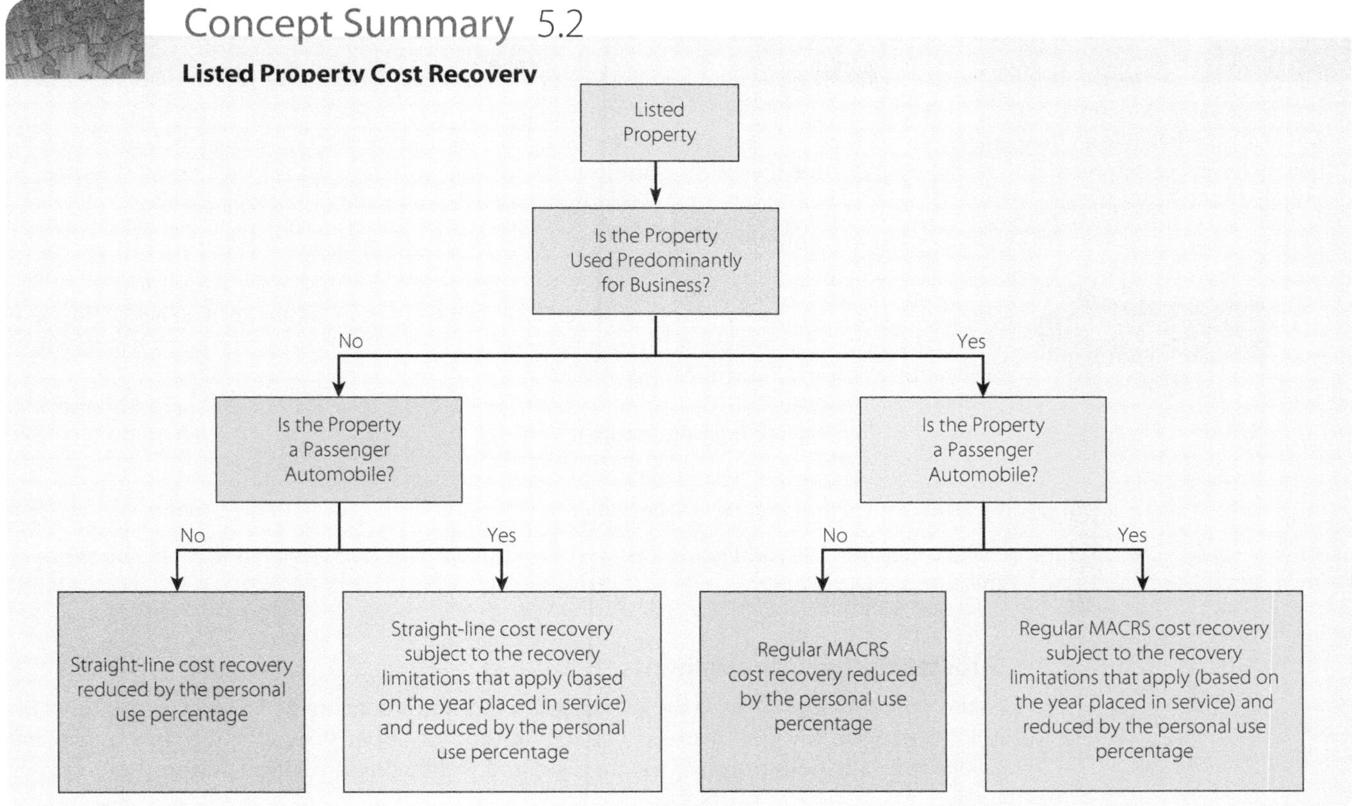

Limitation for Sport Utility Vehicles

Some sport utility vehicles (SUVs) are not considered passenger automobiles and, therefore, are not subject to the luxury automobile limitations. However, an annual limitation is placed on the § 179 deduction when the luxury auto limits do not apply to an SUV. The limitation, adjusted annually for inflation, is $27,000 in 2022. The limit is in effect for SUVs with an unloaded gross vehicle weight (GVW) rating of more than 6,000 pounds and not more than 14,000 pounds.[83]

During 2022, Jay acquires and places in service a new SUV that cost $70,700 and has a GVW of 8,000 pounds. Jay uses the vehicle 100% of the time for business purposes. The total deduction for 2022 with respect to the SUV is computed as follows:

§ 179 expense, as limited	$27,000
Standard MACRS amount [($70,700 − $27,000) × 0.20 (Exhibit 5.4)]	8,740
Total cost recovery claimed	$35,740

If Jay chooses to use bonus depreciation on the SUV, then the entire $70,700 cost will be recovered in 2022 ($27,000 § 179 and $43,700 bonus depreciation).

Leased Automobiles

Taxpayers who lease rather than purchase a passenger automobile for business purposes are not subject to the luxury auto limits. To prevent taxpayers from circumventing the luxury auto limits by deducting the lease payments associated with a luxury automobile leased for business, the Code requires these taxpayers to report an *inclusion amount* in gross income. The annual inclusion amount, based on the fair market value of the automobile, can be found in tables issued by the IRS. The annual amount is then prorated for the number of days the auto is used during the year. The prorated dollar amount then is multiplied by the business and income-producing use percentage.[84] The taxpayer deducts the lease payments multiplied by the business and income-producing usage percentage. In effect, the taxpayer's annual deduction for the lease payment is reduced by the inclusion amount.

[83] § 179(b)(5).

[84] Reg. § 1.280F–7(a).

Bridge Discipline **Bridge to Finance and Economics**

A new car, on average, loses a much larger portion of its value during the first five years through economic depreciation than it loses during later years. Depreciation accounts for about 35 percent of the ownership costs of a car during this five-year period.

Leasing a car will not eliminate the problem because the monthly lease payments are determined, in part, by the projected value of the car at the end of the lease. Because a new car loses its value faster in the earlier years, the shorter the lease, the higher the economic cost of depreciation.

Example 60

On April 1, 2022, Jim leases and places in service a passenger automobile worth $88,600. The lease is to be for a period of five years. During the taxable years 2022 and 2023, Jim uses the automobile 70% for business and 30% for personal use.

Assuming that the inclusion amounts from the IRS table for 2022 and 2023 are $12 and $27, respectively, Jim includes in gross income:

2022:	$12 × (275/365) × 70% = $6
2023:	$27 × (365/365) × 70% = $19

In each year, Jim still can deduct 70% of the lease payments made, related to his business use of the auto.

Substantiation Requirements

Listed property is subject to the substantiation requirements of § 274. A taxpayer must be able to support for any business use the amount of expense or use, the time and place of use, the business purpose for the use, and the business relationship to the taxpayer of persons using the property.

Substantiation requires adequate records or sufficient evidence corroborating the taxpayer's statement. However, these substantiation requirements do not apply to vehicles that, by reason of their nature, are not likely to be used more than a *de minimis* amount for personal purposes.[85]

5-7i Alternative Depreciation System (ADS)

The **alternative depreciation system (ADS)** must be used:[86]

- For any real property, including qualified improvement property, placed in service after 2017 by a "real property trade or business" that opts out of the interest expense limitations of § 163(j). In general, the interest expense limitation rules only apply to businesses with annual gross receipts in excess of $27 million in 2022 ($26 million in 2021).
- To calculate depreciation on listed property not used predominantly for business purposes.
- To calculate the portion of depreciation treated as an alternative minimum tax (AMT) adjustment (see Chapter 17).[87]
- To compute depreciation allowances as part of earnings and profits (see Chapter 13).

Generally, property is depreciated under the ADS using the straight-line method over a period longer than its MACRS recovery period (e.g., 5–12 years for most personal property and 30–40 years for real property). However, for AMT, depreciation of personal property is computed using the 150 percent declining-balance method with a switch to the straight-line method when appropriate. Exhibits 5.8, 5.9, and 5.10 provide cost recovery rates under the ADS method.

[85] §§ 274(d) (flush text, last sentence) and (i).

[86] § 168(g).

[87] This AMT adjustment applies for real and personal property placed in service before 1999. However, it continues to apply for personal property placed in service after 1998 if the taxpayer uses the 200% declining-balance method for regular income tax purposes.

5-8 Amortization

LO.9

Identify intangible assets that are eligible for amortization and calculate the amount of the amortization deduction.

The costs of certain intangible assets are recovered through **amortization**. Amortization, like depreciation, represents the periodic recovery of the cost of an asset. Amortization is usually determined using a straight-line recovery method. The most common amortizable intangibles assets include:

- Startup expenditures,
- Patents and copyrights, and
- Intangibles acquired as part of the acquisition of a business, including goodwill.

The amortization of startup expenditures was discussed earlier in this chapter. The costs of separately acquired patents and copyrights are amortized over their estimated useful lives beginning when the asset is placed in service.[88]

The amortization of intangibles acquired as part of the acquisition of a business is covered in § 197. Amortizable § 197 intangibles include most intangibles, including goodwill, going concern value, franchises, trademarks, copyrights, patents, and covenants not to complete. Generally, self-created intangibles are not § 197 intangibles. The cost of § 197 intangibles is amortized over 15 years beginning in the month in which the intangibles are acquired regardless of their useful lives.[89]

On June 1, Sally purchased and began operating the Falcon Café. Of the purchase price, $90,000 is allocated to goodwill.

The year's § 197 amortization deduction is $3,500 [($90,000 ÷ 15) × (7/12)].

Tax Planning Strategies — Structuring the Sale of a Business

Framework Focus: Tax Rate

Strategy: Control the Character of Income and Deductions.

On the sale of a sole proprietorship where the sales price exceeds the fair market value of the tangible assets, a planning opportunity may exist for both the seller and the buyer.

The seller's preference is for the excess amount to be allocated to *goodwill* because goodwill is a capital asset whose sale may result in favorably taxed long-term capital gain. Amounts received for a *covenant not to compete*, however, produce ordinary income, which is not subject to favorable long-term capital gain rates.

Because a covenant and goodwill both are amortized over a statutory 15-year period, the tax results of a covenant not to compete versus goodwill are the same for the *buyer*. However, the buyer should recognize that an allocation to goodwill rather than a covenant may provide a tax benefit to the seller. Therefore, the buyer, in negotiating the purchase price, should factor in the tax benefit to the seller of having the excess amount labeled goodwill rather than a covenant not to compete. Of course, if the noncompetition aspects of a covenant are important to the buyer, a portion of the excess amount can be assigned to a covenant.

5-9 Depletion

LO.10

Determine deductible depletion expense and specify the alternative tax treatments for intangible drilling and development costs.

Natural resources (e.g., oil, gas, coal, gravel, and timber) are subject to  **depletion**, a form of cost recovery that applies to natural resources. Although all natural resources, with the exception of land itself, are subject to depletion, oil and gas wells are used as an example in the following paragraphs to illustrate the related costs and issues.

[88] Reg. § 1.167(a)–14(c)(4).

[89] § 197(a).

In developing an oil or gas well, the producer typically makes four types of expenditures:

- Natural resource costs.
- Intangible drilling and development costs.
- Tangible asset costs.
- Operating costs.

Natural resources (e.g., oil under the ground) are physically limited, and the costs to acquire them are, therefore, recovered through depletion. Costs incurred in making the property ready for drilling, such as the cost of labor in clearing the property, erecting derricks, and drilling the hole, are **intangible drilling and development costs (IDCs)**. These costs generally have no salvage value and are a lost cost if the well is not productive (dry).

Costs for tangible assets such as tools, pipes, and engines are capitalized and recovered through depreciation (cost recovery). Costs incurred after the well is producing are operating costs. These costs include expenditures for items such as labor, fuel, and supplies. Operating costs are deductible as trade or business expenses. Intangible drilling and development costs and the costs of the natural resource itself receive different treatment.

5-9a Intangible Drilling and Development Costs (IDCs)

Intangible drilling and development costs can be handled in one of two ways at the option of the taxpayer. They can either be deducted immediately in the year in which they are incurred or be capitalized and recovered through depletion. The taxpayer makes the election in the first year such expenditures are incurred either by taking a deduction on the return or by adding them to the depletable basis.

Once made, the election is binding on both the taxpayer and the IRS for all such expenditures in the future. If the taxpayer fails to elect to expense IDCs (on the original timely filed return for the first year in which such expenditures are incurred), an irrevocable election to capitalize them has been made.

As a general rule, it is more advantageous to expense IDCs. The obvious benefit of an immediate write-off (as opposed to a deferred write-off through depletion) is not the only advantage. Because a taxpayer can use percentage depletion, which is calculated without reference to basis, the IDCs may be completely lost as a deduction if they are capitalized.

5-9b Depletion Methods

The cost of the natural resource itself (i.e., the oil and gas), as well as any IDCs that are capitalized, are recovered through depletion. There are two methods of calculating depletion for tax purposes: *cost depletion* and *percentage depletion*. Taxpayers may use whichever method results in the larger deduction and are free to change methods annually. These methods are described below.

Cost Depletion

Cost depletion resembles units-of-production depreciation.[90] The basis of the depletable asset is divided by the estimated recoverable units of the asset (e.g., barrels of oil or tons of ore) to arrive at the depletion per unit. This amount then is multiplied by the number of units sold (not the units produced) during the year to arrive at the cost depletion allowed.

[90] § 612.

On January 1, 2022, Pablo purchases the rights to a mineral interest for $1,000,000. At that time, the remaining recoverable units in the mineral interest are estimated to be 200,000. The depletion per unit is $5 [$1,000,000 (adjusted basis) ÷ 200,000 (estimated recoverable units)].

If 60,000 units are mined and 25,000 are sold, the cost depletion is $125,000 [$5 (depletion per unit) × 25,000 (units sold)].

If the taxpayer later discovers that the original estimate was incorrect, the depletion per unit for future calculations is redetermined using the revised estimate.[91]

Assume the same facts as in the previous example. In 2023, Pablo realizes that an incorrect estimate was made. The remaining recoverable units now are determined to be 400,000. Based on this new information, the revised depletion per unit is $2.1875 [$875,000 (adjusted basis) ÷ 400,000 (estimated recoverable units)]. The adjusted basis is the original cost ($1,000,000) reduced by the depletion claimed in 2022 ($125,000).

If 30,000 units are sold in 2023, the depletion for the year is $65,625 [$2.1875 (depletion per unit) × 30,000 (units sold)].

Percentage Depletion

Percentage depletion (also referred to as statutory depletion) is determined by multiplying the gross income from the sales of a natural resource by a specified percentage provided in the Code. The percentage varies according to the resource involved. A sample of these percentages is shown in Exhibit 5.3. The deduction for percentage depletion is limited to 50 percent of the taxable income from the property before the allowance for depletion.[92]

Example
64

CarrolCo reports gross income of $100,000 and other property-related expenses of $60,000 before depletion. Because CarrolCo is in the business of extracting and selling sulfer, it is eligible for a depletion rate of 22%. CarrollCo's depletion allowance is determined as follows:

Gross income	$100,000
Less: Other expenses	(60,000)
Taxable income before depletion	$ 40,000
Depletion allowance [the lesser of $22,000 (22% × $100,000) or $20,000 (50% × $40,000)]	(20,000)
Taxable income after depletion	$ 20,000

The adjusted basis of CarrollCo's property is reduced by $20,000, the depletion deduction allowed. If the other expenses had been only $55,000, the full $22,000 could have been deducted, and the adjusted basis would have been reduced by $22,000.

Note that percentage depletion is based on a percentage of the gross income from the property and makes no reference to cost. All other cost recovery deductions detailed in this chapter are a function of the adjusted basis (cost) of the property. Thus, when percentage depletion is used, it is possible to claim aggregate depletion deductions that exceed the original cost of the property. Nonetheless, if percentage depletion is used, the adjusted basis of the property (for computing cost depletion in a future tax year) is reduced by any depletion deducted until the basis reaches zero.

[91] § 611(a).

[92] § 613(a). Special rules apply for certain oil and gas wells (e.g., the 50% ceiling is replaced with a 100% ceiling, and the percentage depletion may not exceed 65% of the taxpayer's taxable income from all sources before the allowance for depletion). § 613A.

Exhibit 5.3 Selected Percentage Depletion Rates

22% Depletion		
Cobalt	Nickel	Sulfur
Lead	Platinum	Tin
15% Depletion		
Copper	Iron	Oil shale
Gold	Oil and gas	Silver
14% Depletion		
Borax	Limestone	Potash
Granite	Marble	Slate
10% Depletion		
Coal	Lignite and perlite	Sodium chloride
5% Depletion		
Gravel	Peat	Sand

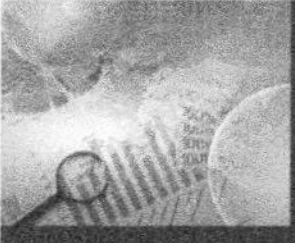

Tax Planning Strategies — Switching Depletion Methods

Framework Focus: Deductions

Strategy: Maximize Deductible Amounts.

As long as the basis of a depletable asset remains above zero, either cost depletion or percentage depletion is available. When the basis of the asset is exhausted, percentage depletion still can be taken.

Example 65

Warbler Company reports the following related to its sulfur mine:

Remaining depletable basis	$ 11,000
Gross income (10,000 units)	100,000
Expenses (other than depletion)	30,000
Percentage depletion rate	22%

Because cost depletion is limited to the remaining depletable basis of $11,000, Warbler would choose percentage depletion of $22,000 [lesser of ($100,000 × 22%) or ($70,000 × 50%)]. The basis in the mine then becomes zero.

In future years, Warbler can continue to use percentage depletion; percentage depletion is computed without reference to the remaining asset basis.

5-10 **Cost Recovery Tables**

Summary of Cost Recovery Tables

Exhibit 5.4 Regular MACRS table for personalty.
Recovery methods: 200 or 150 percent declining-balance switching to straight-line.
Recovery periods: 3, 5, 7, 10, 15, 20 years.
Convention: half-year.

Exhibit 5.5 Regular MACRS table for personalty.
Recovery methods: 200 percent declining-balance switching to straight-line.
Recovery periods: 3, 5, 7 years.
Convention: mid-quarter.

Summary of Cost Recovery Tables (continued)

Exhibit 5.6	MACRS straight-line table for realty. Recovery method: straight-line. Recovery periods: 27.5, 31.5, 39 years. Convention: mid-month.
Exhibit 5.7	MACRS straight-line table for personalty and qualified improvement property. Recovery method: straight-line. Recovery periods: 3, 5, 7, 10, 15, 20 years. Convention: half-year.
Exhibit 5.8	ADS for alternative minimum tax: 150 percent declining-balance table for personalty. Recovery method: 150 percent declining-balance switching to straight-line. Recovery periods: 3, 5, 7, 9.5, 10, 12 years. Convention: half-year.
Exhibit 5.9	ADS straight-line table for personalty. Recovery method: straight-line. Recovery periods: 5, 10, 12 years. Convention: half-year.
Exhibit 5.10	ADS straight-line table for realty. Recovery method: straight-line. Recovery period: 30, 40 years. Convention: mid-month.

Exhibit 5.4 MACRS Accelerated Depreciation for Personal Property Assuming Half-Year Convention (Percentage Rates)

For Property Placed in Service after December 31, 1986

Recovery Year	3-Year (200% DB)	5-Year (200% DB)	7-Year (200% DB)	10-Year (200% DB)	15-Year (150% DB)	20-Year (150% DB)
1	33.33	20.00	14.29	10.00	5.00	3.750
2	44.45	32.00	24.49	18.00	9.50	7.219
3	14.81*	19.20	17.49	14.40	8.55	6.677
4	7.41	11.52*	12.49	11.52	7.70	6.177
5		11.52	8.93*	9.22	6.93	5.713
6		5.76	8.92	7.37	6.23	5.285
7			8.93	6.55*	5.90*	4.888
8			4.46	6.55	5.90	4.522
9				6.56	5.91	4.462*
10				6.55	5.90	4.461
11				3.28	5.91	4.462
12					5.90	4.461
13					5.91	4.462
14					5.90	4.461
15					5.91	4.462
16					2.95	4.461
17						4.462
18						4.461
19						4.462
20						4.461
21						2.231

*Switchover to straight-line depreciation.

Exhibit 5.5 MACRS Accelerated Depreciation for Personal Property Assuming Mid-Quarter Convention (Percentage Rates)

For Property Placed in Service after December 31, 1986 (Partial Table*)

		3-Year		
Recovery Year	**First Quarter**	**Second Quarter**	**Third Quarter**	**Fourth Quarter**
1	58.33	41.67	25.00	8.33
2	27.78	38.89	50.00	61.11
		5-Year		
Recovery Year	**First Quarter**	**Second Quarter**	**Third Quarter**	**Fourth Quarter**
1	35.00	25.00	15.00	5.00
2	26.00	30.00	34.00	38.00
		7-Year		
Recovery Year	**First Quarter**	**Second Quarter**	**Third Quarter**	**Fourth Quarter**
1	25.00	17.85	10.71	3.57
2	21.43	23.47	25.51	27.55

*The figures in this table are taken from the official tables that appear in Rev.Proc. 87–57. Because of their length, the complete tables are not presented.

Exhibit 5.6 MACRS Straight-Line Depreciation for Real Property Assuming Mid-Month Convention*

For Property Placed in Service after December 31, 1986: 27.5-Year Residential Real Property

Recovery Year(s)	**The Applicable Percentage Is (Use the Column for the Month in the First Year the Property Is Placed in Service):**											
	1	**2**	**3**	**4**	**5**	**6**	**7**	**8**	**9**	**10**	**11**	**12**
1	3.485	3.182	2.879	2.576	2.273	1.970	1.667	1.364	1.061	0.758	0.455	0.152
2–18	3.636	3.636	3.636	3.636	3.636	3.636	3.636	3.636	3.636	3.636	3.636	3.636
19–27	3.637	3.637	3.637	3.637	3.637	3.637	3.637	3.637	3.637	3.637	3.637	3.637
28	1.970	2.273	2.576	2.879	3.182	3.485	3.636	3.636	3.636	3.636	3.636	3.636
29	0.000	0.000	0.000	0.000	0.000	0.000	0.152	0.455	0.758	1.061	1.364	1.667

For Property Placed in Service after December 31, 1986, and before May 13, 1993: 31.5-Year Nonresidential Real Property

Recovery Year(s)	**The Applicable Percentage Is (Use the Column for the Month in the First Year the Property Is Placed in Service):**											
	1	**2**	**3**	**4**	**5**	**6**	**7**	**8**	**9**	**10**	**11**	**12**
1	3.042	2.778	2.513	2.249	1.984	1.720	1.455	1.190	0.926	0.661	0.397	0.132
2–19	3.175	3.175	3.175	3.175	3.175	3.175	3.175	3.175	3.175	3.175	3.175	3.175
20–31	3.174	3.174	3.174	3.174	3.174	3.174	3.174	3.174	3.174	3.174	3.174	3.174
32	1.720	1.984	2.249	2.513	2.778	3.042	3.175	3.175	3.175	3.175	3.175	3.175
33	0.000	0.000	0.000	0.000	0.000	0.000	0.132	0.397	0.661	0.926	1.190	1.455

For Property Placed in Service after May 12, 1993: 39-Year Nonresidential Real Property

Recovery Year(s)	**The Applicable Percentage Is (Use the Column for the Month in the First Year the Property Is Placed in Service):**											
	1	**2**	**3**	**4**	**5**	**6**	**7**	**8**	**9**	**10**	**11**	**12**
1	2.461	2.247	2.033	1.819	1.605	1.391	1.177	0.963	0.749	0.535	0.321	0.107
2–39	2.564	2.564	2.564	2.564	2.564	2.564	2.564	2.564	2.564	2.564	2.564	2.564
40	0.107	0.321	0.535	0.749	0.963	1.177	1.391	1.605	1.819	2.033	2.247	2.461

*The official tables contain a separate row for each year. For ease of presentation, certain years are grouped in these tables. In some instances, this will produce a difference of 0.001 for the last digit when compared with the official tables.

Exhibit 5.7 MACRS Straight-Line Depreciation for Personal Property and Qualified Improvement Property Assuming Half-Year Convention*

For Property Placed in Service after December 31, 1986

MACRS Class	% First Recovery Year	Other Recovery Years: Years	Other Recovery Years: %	Last Recovery Year: Year	Last Recovery Year: %
3-year	16.67	2–3	33.33	4	16.67
5-year	10.00	2–5	20.00	6	10.00
7-year	7.14	2–7	14.29	8	7.14
10-year	5.00	2–10	10.00	11	5.00
15-year	3.33	2–15	6.67	16	3.33
20-year	2.50	2–20	5.00	21	2.50

*The official table contains a separate row for each year. For ease of presentation, certain years are grouped in this table. In some instances, this will produce a difference of 0.01 for the last digit when compared with the official table.

Note: The last two rows are used for qualified improvement property (15-year normal MACRS; 20-year ADS).

Exhibit 5.8 ADS for Alternative Minimum Tax: 150% Declining-Balance for Personal Property Assuming Half-Year Convention (Percentage Rates)

For Property Placed in Service after December 31, 1986 (Partial Table*)

Recovery Year	3-Year 150%	5-Year 150%	7-Year 150%	9.5-Year 150%	10-Year 150%	12-Year 150%
1	25.00	15.00	10.71	7.89	7.50	6.25
2	37.50	25.50	19.13	14.54	13.88	11.72
3	25.00**	17.85	15.03	12.25	11.79	10.25
4	12.50	16.66**	12.25**	10.31	10.02	8.97
5		16.66	12.25	9.17**	8.74**	7.85
6		8.33	12.25	9.17	8.74	7.33**
7			12.25	9.17	8.74	7.33
8			6.13	9.17	8.74	7.33
9				9.17	8.74	7.33
10				9.16	8.74	7.33
11					4.37	7.32
12						7.33
13						3.66

*The figures in this table are taken from the official table that appears in Rev.Proc. 87–57. Because of its length, the complete table is not presented.

**Switchover to straight-line depreciation.

Exhibit 5.9 ADS Straight-Line for Personal Property Assuming Half-Year Convention (Percentage Rates)

For Property Placed in Service after December 31, 1986 (Partial Table)*

Recovery Year	3-Year	5-Year	7-Year	10-Year	12-Year
1	16.67	10.00	7.14	5.00	4.17
2	33.33	20.00	14.29	10.00	8.33
3	33.33	20.00	14.29	10.00	8.33
4	16.67	20.00	14.29	10.00	8.33
5		20.00	14.29	10.00	8.33
6		10.00	14.29	10.00	8.33
7			14.29	10.00	8.34
8			7.14	10.00	8.33
9				10.00	8.34
10				10.00	8.33
11				5.00	8.34
12					8.33
13					4.17

*The figures in this table are taken from the official table that appears in Rev.Proc. 87–57. Because of its length, the complete table is not presented. The tables for the mid-quarter convention also appear in Rev.Proc. 87–57.

Exhibit 5.10 ADS Straight-Line for Real Property Assuming Mid-Month Convention (Percentage Rates)

For Property Placed in Service after December 31, 2017; 30-Year Residential Rental Property

Recovery Year	Month Placed in Service											
	1	2	3	4	5	6	7	8	9	10	11	12
1	3.194	2.917	2.639	2.361	2.083	1.806	1.528	1.250	0.972	0.694	0.417	0.139
2–30	3.333	3.333	3.333	3.333	3.333	3.333	3.333	3.333	3.333	3.333	3.333	3.333
31	0.139	0.417	0.694	0.972	1.250	1.528	1.806	2.083	2.361	2.639	2.917	3.194

For Property Placed in Service after December 31, 1986; 40-Year Nonresidential Real Property*

Recovery Year	Month Placed in Service											
	1	2	3	4	5	6	7	8	9	10	11	12
1	2.396	2.188	1.979	1.771	1.563	1.354	1.146	0.938	0.729	0.521	0.313	0.104
2–40	2.500	2.500	2.500	2.500	2.500	2.500	2.500	2.500	2.500	2.500	2.500	2.500
41	0.104	0.312	0.521	0.729	0.937	1.146	1.354	1.562	1.771	1.979	2.187	2.396

* Also used for residential rental property placed in service before 2018.

Refocus on The Big Picture

Calculating Deductible Expenses

MOODBOARD/GETTY IMAGES

In general, the expenses incurred in Michael's small engine service and repair business are deductible as long as they are ordinary and necessary expenses. In addition, the salaries and wages paid must be reasonable. However, his plan to increase salaries radically next year for himself and his mother probably should not be pursued, because most or all of the increase could be considered unreasonable. Charitable contributions generally are limited to 10 percent of taxable income before the charitable contribution

continued

deduction, and political contributions and the fine are not deductible. The dues paid to Small Engine Repair Institute are not fully deductible because 70 percent of the organization's efforts relate to lobbying activities. However, the amount paid to consultants to investigate a new business opportunity is fully deductible as an ordinary and necessary business expense.

Michael can elect to expense the costs of the machinery and equipment under the provisions of § 179. For the current year, the § 179 deduction is limited to $1,080,000 (2022) and cannot exceed the taxable income derived from the business (before the § 179 deduction). In this case, the entire purchase price of $130,000 is deductible.

Gross income	$ 435,500
Less: Salaries and wages	(150,000)
Building rent	(24,000)
§ 179 deduction	(130,000)
Insurance	(6,000)
Consulting fees	(6,000)
Utilities	(12,000)
Taxes and licenses	(6,000)
Advertising	(3,000)
Interest expense	(3,000)
Dues paid to Small Engine Repair Institute	(3,000)
Taxable income before the charitable contribution deduction	$ 92,500
Less: Charitable contributions	(3,000)
Taxable income	$ 89,500

As to Michael's rental properties, he will be required to report all associated rent income and expenses, including depreciation on the house he converted from personal use to rental use and on the rental condo he purchased.

What If?

Instead, assume that Michael purchased and placed in service this year $142,000 of new machinery and equipment of the type that qualifies for the § 179 deduction. In addition, Michael thinks that he can justify increasing his salary to $115,500 because of special expertise he developed recently, which will increase total salaries and wages to $210,500. Michael still can elect to expense all $142,000 of the cost of the machinery and equipment under § 179. As a result of the increased salary and § 179 deductions, however, the charitable contribution deduction now is limited to $2,000. The remainder ($1,000) is carried over to the next tax year.

Gross income	$ 435,500
Less: Salaries and wages	(210,500)
Building rent	(24,000)
§ 179 deduction	(142,000)
Insurance	(6,000)
Consulting fees	(6,000)
Utilities	(12,000)
Taxes and licenses	(6,000)
Advertising	(3,000)
Interest expense	(3,000)
Dues paid to Small Engine Repair Institute	(3,000)
Taxable income before the charitable contribution deduction	$ 20,000
Less: Charitable contributions (limited to 10% of taxable income)	(2,000)
Taxable income	$ 18,000

Suggested Readings

Bradley T. Borden and Cali A. Lieberman, "Section 179(f) Deductions and Recapture of Costs of Qualified Real Property," *Journal of Taxation*, January 2014.

Robert W. Jamison and Christopher W. Hesse, "Controlled Groups and the Sec. 179 Election for S Corporations," *The Tax Adviser*, November 2013.

John M. Malloy, Craig J. Langstraat, and James M. Plečnik, "Major Developments in Cost Segregation," *The Tax Adviser*, April 2014.

Kreig D. Mitchell, "The R&D Tax Credit for Start-Up Companies," *Practical Tax Strategies*, February 2012.

Debra T. Sinclair and Britton A. McKay, "Excess Compensation and the Independent Investor Test," *Practical Tax Strategies*, April 2013.

Christian Wood, "Implementing the New Tangible Property Regulations: The Revised 'Repair Regs' Require Thorough Assessment," *Journal of Accountancy*, January 2014.

Key Terms

Accelerated cost recovery system (ACRS), 5-20
Additional first-year depreciation, 5-31
Alternative depreciation system (ADS), 5-36
Amortization, 5-37
Capital gain property, 5-18
Charitable contribution, 5-18
Cost depletion, 5-38
Cost recovery, 5-20
Depletion, 5-37
Depreciation, 5-20
Half-year convention, 5-23
Intangible drilling and development costs (IDCs), 5-38
Listed property, 5-32
Mid-month convention, 5-26
Mid-quarter convention, 5-25
Modified accelerated cost recovery system (MACRS), 5-20
Ordinary and necessary, 5-2
Ordinary income property, 5-18
Percentage depletion, 5-39
Qualified improvement property, 5-27
Reasonableness requirement, 5-3
Related-party transactions, 5-6
Research and experimental expenditures, 5-14
Residential rental real estate, 5-26
Section 179 expensing election, 5-28
Startup expenditures, 5-8

Computational Exercises

1. **LO.2** Shanna, a calendar year and cash basis taxpayer, rents property to be used in her business from Janice. As part of the rental agreement, Shanna pays $8,400 rent on April 1, 2022, for the 12 months ending March 31, 2023.
   a. How much is Shanna's deduction for rent expense in 2022?
   b. Assume the same facts, except that the $8,400 is for 24 months' rent ending March 31, 2024. How much is Shanna's deduction for rent expense in 2022?

2. **LO.3** Vella owns and operates an illegal gambling establishment. In connection with this activity, he has the following expenses during the year:

Rent	$ 24,000
Bribes	40,000
Travel expenses	4,000
Utilities	18,000
Wages	230,000
Payroll taxes	13,800
Property insurance	1,600
Illegal kickbacks	22,000

   What are Vella's total deductible expenses for tax purposes?

3. **LO.3** Stanford owns and operates two dry cleaning businesses. He travels to Boston to discuss acquiring a restaurant. Later in the month, he travels to New York to discuss acquiring a bakery. Stanford does not acquire the restaurant but does purchase the bakery on November 1, 2022. Stanford incurred the following expenses:

Total investigation costs related to the restaurant	$28,000
Total investigation costs related to the bakery	51,000

What is the maximum amount Stanford can deduct in 2022 for investigation expenses?

4. **LO.4** Sandstorm Corporation decides to develop a new line of paints. The project begins in 2021. Sandstorm incurs the following expenses in 2021 in connection with the project:

Salaries	$85,000
Materials	30,000
Depreciation on equipment	12,500

The benefits from the project will be realized starting in July 2022. If Sandstorm Corporation chooses to defer and amortize its research and experimental expenditures over a period of 60 months, what are its related deductions in 2021 and 2022?

5. **LO.5** Tabitha sells real estate on March 2 for $260,000. The buyer, Ramona, pays the real estate taxes of $5,200 for the calendar year, which is the real estate property tax year. Assume that this is not a leap year.
   a. Determine the real estate taxes apportioned to and deductible by the seller, Tabitha, and the amount of taxes deductible by Ramona.
   b. Calculate Ramona's basis in the property and the amount realized by Tabitha from the sale.

6. **LO.7** Hamlet acquires a 7-year class asset on November 23, 2022, for $100,000 (the only asset acquired during the year). Hamlet does not elect immediate expensing under § 179. He does not claim any available additional first-year depreciation. Calculate Hamlet's cost recovery deductions for 2022 and 2023.

7. **LO.7** Lopez acquired a building on June 1, 2017, for $1,000,000. Calculate Lopez's cost recovery deduction for 2022 if the building is:
   a. Classified as residential rental real estate.
   b. Classified as nonresidential real estate.

8. **LO.7** In 2022, McKenzie purchased qualifying equipment for his business that cost $212,000. The taxable income of the business for the year is $5,600 before consideration of any § 179 deduction.
   a. Calculate McKenzie's § 179 expense deduction for 2022 and any carryover to 2023.
   b. How would your answer change if McKenzie decided to use additional first-year (bonus) depreciation on the equipment instead of using § 179 expensing?

9. **LO.8** On April 5, 2022, Kinsey places in service a new automobile that cost $60,000. He does not elect § 179 expensing, and he elects not to take any available additional first-year depreciation. The car is used 70% for business and 30% for personal use in each tax year.

   Kinsey chooses the MACRS 200% declining-balance method of cost recovery (the auto is a 5-year asset). Assume the following luxury automobile limitations: year 1: $10,200; year 2: $16,400. Compute the total depreciation allowed for 2022 and 2023.

10. **LO.10** Jebali Company reports gross income of $340,000 and other property-related expenses of $229,000 and uses a depletion rate of 14%. Calculate Jebali's depletion allowance for the current year.

Problems

11. **LO.1** Cécile owns a highly profitable restaurant run as a sole proprietorship. To protect herself from liabilities related to the business, Cécile incorporates the business, becoming the sole shareholder. However, she retains personal ownership of all of the assets (building, kitchen equipment, furniture, etc.) and rents them to the corporation, charging twice the normal rental value. What might Cécile be trying to accomplish with the rental arrangement? What is the most appropriate tax treatment?

Critical Thinking
Planning

12. **LO.2** Duck, an accrual basis corporation, sponsored a rock concert on December 29, 2022. Gross receipts were $300,000. The following expenses were incurred and paid as indicated:

Expense		Payment Date
Rental of coliseum	$ 25,000	December 21, 2022
Cost of goods sold:		
Food	30,000	December 30, 2022
Souvenirs	60,000	December 30, 2022
Performers	100,000	January 5, 2023
Cleaning of coliseum	10,000	February 1, 2023

Because the coliseum was not scheduled to be used again until January 15, the company with which Duck had contracted did not perform the cleanup until January 8–10, 2023.

a. Calculate Duck's net income from the concert for tax purposes for 2022.

b. Using the present value tables in Appendix E, what is the true cost to Duck if it had to defer the $100,000 deduction for the performers until 2023? Assume a 5% discount rate and a 21% marginal tax rate in 2022 and 2023.

13. **LO.2** Which of the following are related parties under § 267?

Father
Brother
Niece
Uncle
Cousin
Grandson
Corporation and a 45% shareholder
Corporation and a 55% shareholder

Digging Deeper

14. **LO.2** Bell, Inc., an accrual basis taxpayer, makes and sells personal computing equipment. It includes basic one-year warranty service with most of its products and, for financial reporting purposes, recognizes an estimate of the expenses related to honoring those warranties when the products are sold. Bell reports the following in its financial statements for the year.

Income Statement	
Warranty expense	$500,000
Balance Sheet	
Allowance for existing warranty contracts 1/1	30,000
Allowance for existing warranty contracts 12/31	40,000

How much warranty expense may Bell deduct for the year?

15. **LO.2, 3** Lupe, a cash basis taxpayer, owns 55% of the stock of Jasper Corporation, a calendar year accrual basis C corporation. On December 31, 2022, Jasper accrues a performance bonus of $100,000 to Lupe that it pays to him on January 15, 2023. In which year can Jasper deduct the bonus? In which year must Lupe include the bonus in gross income?

16. **LO.2, 3** Broadbill Corporation, a calendar year C corporation, has two unrelated cash method shareholders: Marcia owns 51% of the stock, and Zack owns the remaining 49%. Each shareholder is employed by the corporation at an annual salary of $240,000. During 2022, Broadbill paid each shareholder-employee $220,000 of his or her annual salary, with the remaining $20,000 paid in January 2023. How much of the 2022 salaries for Marcia and Zack is deductible by Broadbill in 2022 if the corporation is:
   a. A cash method taxpayer?
   b. An accrual method taxpayer?

17. **LO.3** Angelo, an agent for Waxwing Corporation, which is an airline manufacturer, is negotiating a sale with a representative of the U.S. government and with a representative of a developing country. Waxwing has sufficient capacity to handle only one of the orders. Both orders will have the same contract price. Angelo believes that if Waxwing authorizes a $500,000 payment to the representative of the foreign country, he can guarantee the sale. He is not sure that he can obtain the same result with the U.S. government. Identify the relevant tax issues for Waxwing.

Critical Thinking

18. **LO.3** Linda operates an illegal gambling operation and incurs the following expenses. Which of these expenses can reduce her taxable income?
   a. Bribes paid to city employees.
   b. Salaries to employees.
   c. Security cameras.
   d. Kickbacks to police.
   e. Rent on an office.
   f. Depreciation on office furniture and equipment.
   g. Tenant's casualty insurance.
   h. Utilities.

19. **LO.3** Cardinal Corporation is a trucking firm that operates in the mid-Atlantic states. One of Cardinal's major customers frequently ships goods between Charlotte and Baltimore. Occasionally, the customer sends last-minute shipments that are outbound for Europe on a freighter sailing from Baltimore. To satisfy the delivery schedule in these cases, Cardinal's drivers must substantially exceed the speed limit. Cardinal pays for any related speeding tickets. During the past year, two drivers had their licenses suspended for 30 days each for driving at such excessive speeds. Cardinal continues to pay each driver's salary during the suspension periods.

    Cardinal believes that it is necessary to conduct its business in this manner if it is to be profitable, maintain the support of the drivers, and maintain the goodwill of customers. Evaluate Cardinal's business practices.

Ethics and Equity

20. **LO.3** Quail Corporation anticipates that being positively perceived by the individual who is elected mayor will be beneficial for business. Therefore, Quail contributes to the campaigns of both the Democratic and Republican candidates. The Republican candidate is elected mayor. Can Quail deduct any of the political contributions it made? Explain.

21. **LO.3** Melissa, the owner of a sole proprietorship, does not provide health insurance for her 20 employees. She plans to spend $1,500 lobbying in opposition to legislation that would require her to provide such insurance. Discuss the tax advantages and disadvantages of paying the $1,500 to a professional lobbyist rather than spending the $1,500 on in-house lobbying expenditures.

22. **LO.3** Ella owns 60% of the stock of Peach, Inc. The stock has declined in value since she purchased it five years ago. She is going to sell 5% of the stock to a relative. Ella also is going to make a gift of 10% of the stock to another relative. Identify the relevant tax issues for Ella.

Critical Thinking
Planning

23. **LO.3** Jarret owns City of Charleston bonds with an adjusted basis of $190,000. During the year, he receives interest payments of $3,800. Jarret partially financed the purchase of the bonds by borrowing $100,000 at 5% interest. Jarret's interest payments on the loan this year are $4,900, and his principal payments are $1,100.
    a. Should Jarret report any interest income this year? Explain.
    b. Can Jarret deduct any interest expense this year? Explain.

24. **LO.3** Egret Corporation, a calendar year C corporation, was formed on March 6, 2022, and opened for business on July 1, 2022. After its formation but prior to opening for business, Egret incurred the following expenditures:

Accounting	$ 7,000
Advertising	14,500
Employee payroll	11,000
Rent	8,000
Utilities	1,000

What is the maximum amount of these expenditures that Egret can deduct in 2022?

25. **LO.3** Henrietta, the owner of a very successful hotel chain in the Southeast, is exploring the possibility of expanding the chain into a city in the Northeast. She incurs $35,000 of expenses associated with this investigation. Based on the regulatory environment for hotels in the city, she decides not to expand. During the year, she also investigates opening a restaurant that will be part of a national restaurant chain. Her expenses for this are $53,000. She proceeds with opening the restaurant, and it begins operations on September 1. Determine the amount Henrietta can deduct in the current year for investigating these two businesses.

Communications
Critical Thinking
Decision Making
Planning

26. **LO.3** Ascend, a publicly held corporation, currently pays its president an annual salary of $900,000. As a means of increasing company profitability, the board of directors increased the president's compensation effective January 1, 2017, with a performance-based compensation program. This program increased the president's compensation by $600,000 in 2017, $650,000 in 2018, $750,000 in 2019, and $800,000 in 2020 and 2021. Her compensation under this performance-based compensation program is expected to be $850,000 in 2022. Prepare a letter to Ascend's board of directors that identifies the amount of compensation that will be deductible by Ascend in 2022 and explains whether any changes should be made to the president's compensation plan in 2022. Address the letter to the board chairperson, Angela Riddle, whose address is 150 Erieview Tower, Cleveland, OH 44106.

27. **LO.3** In 2022, MSU Corporation has $500,000 of adjusted taxable income, $22,000 of business interest income, and $120,000 of business interest expense. It has average annual gross receipts of more than $27,000,000 over the prior three taxable years.
    a. What is MSU's interest expense deduction?
    b. How much interest expense can be deducted if MSU's adjusted taxable income is $300,000?

28. **LO.4** Blue Corporation, a manufacturing company, decided to develop a new line of merchandise. The project began in 2019. Blue had the following expenses in connection with the project:

	2019	2020
Salaries	$500,000	$600,000
Materials	90,000	70,000
Insurance	8,000	11,000
Utilities	6,000	8,000
Cost of inspection of materials for quality control	7,000	6,000
Promotion expenses	11,000	18,000
Advertising	-0-	20,000
Equipment depreciation	15,000	14,000
Cost of market survey	8,000	-0-

The new product will be introduced for sale beginning in April 2021. Determine the amount of the deduction for research and experimental expenditures for 2019, 2020, 2021, and 2022. If necessary, round the annual deduction to the nearest dollar.

a. Blue Corporation elects to expense the research and experimental expenditures.
b. Blue Corporation elects to amortize the research and experimental expenditures over 60 months.
c. How would your answer change if Blue Corporation incurred the expenses in 2022 and 2023 (rather than 2019 and 2020)?

29. **LO.6** In 2022, Gray Corporation, a calendar year C corporation, holds a $75,000 charitable contribution carryover from a gift made in 2017. Gray is contemplating a gift of land to a qualified charity in either 2022 or 2023. Gray purchased the land as an investment five years ago for $100,000 (current fair market value is $250,000). Before considering any charitable deduction, Gray projects taxable income of $1,000,000 for 2022 and $1,200,000 for 2023. Should Gray make the gift of the land to charity in 2022 or in 2023? Provide support for your answer. Decision Making Planning

30. **LO.6** Julieta Simms is the president and sole shareholder of Simms Corporation, 1121 Madison Street, Seattle, WA 98121. Julieta plans for the corporation to make a charitable contribution to the University of Washington, a qualified public charity. She will have the corporation donate Jaybird Corporation stock, held for five years, with a basis of $11,000 and a fair market value of $25,000. Julieta projects a $310,000 net profit for Simms Corporation in 2022 and a $100,000 net profit in 2023. Julieta calls you on December 10, 2022, and asks whether Simms should make the contribution in 2022 or 2023. Write a letter advising Julieta about the timing of the contribution. Communications Critical Thinking Decision Making Planning

31. **LO.6** On December 23, 2022, the directors of Partridge Corporation, an accrual basis calendar year taxpayer, authorized a cash contribution of $10,000 to the American Cancer Association. The payment is made on April 13, 2023. Can Partridge deduct the charitable contribution in 2022? Explain.

32. **LO.6** Aquamarine Corporation, a calendar year C corporation, makes the following donations to qualified charitable organizations during the current year: Critical Thinking

	Adjusted Basis	Fair Market Value
Painting held four years as an investment, to a church, which sold it immediately	$15,000	$25,000
Apple stock held two years as an investment, to United Way, which sold it immediately	40,000	90,000

Determine the amount of Aquamarine Corporation's charitable deduction for the current year. (Ignore the taxable income limitation.)

33. **LO.6** Joseph Thompson is president and sole shareholder of Jay Corporation. In December of the current year, Joe asks your advice regarding a charitable contribution he plans to have the corporation make to the University of Maine, a qualified public charity. Joe is considering the following alternatives as charitable contributions in December: Communications Decision Making Planning

	Fair Market Value
(1) Cash donation	$200,000
(2) Unimproved land held for six years ($110,000 basis)	200,000
(3) Maize Corporation stock held for eight months ($140,000 basis)	200,000
(4) Brown Corporation stock held for nine years ($360,000 basis)	200,000

Joe has asked you to help him decide which of these potential contributions will be most advantageous taxwise. Jay Corporation's taxable income is $3,500,000 before considering the contribution. Rank the four alternatives, and write a letter to Mr. Thompson communicating your advice. The corporation's address is 1442 Main Street, Freeport, ME 04032.

34. **LO.7** On November 4, 2020, Blue Company acquired an asset (27.5-year residential real property) for $200,000 for use in its business. In 2020 and 2021, respectively, Blue took $642 and $5,128 of cost recovery. These amounts were incorrect; Blue applied the wrong percentages (i.e., those for 39-year rather than 27.5-year property). Blue should have taken $910 and $7,272 of cost recovery in 2020 and 2021, respectively.

    On January 1, 2022, the asset was sold for $180,000. Calculate the gain or loss on the sale of the asset for that year.

35. **LO.7** Juan, a sole proprietor, acquires a new 5-year class asset on March 14, 2022, for $200,000. This is the only asset Juan acquired during the year. He does not elect immediate expensing under § 179. Juan does not claim any available additional first-year depreciation. On July 15, 2023, Juan sells the asset.
    a. Determine Juan's cost recovery for 2022.
    b. Determine Juan's cost recovery for 2023.

36. **LO.7** Debra, a sole proprietor, acquired the following new assets during 2022:

Date	Asset	Cost
April 11	Furniture	$40,000
July 28	Trucks	40,000
November 3	Computers	70,000

Determine Debra's cost recovery deductions for the current year. Debra does not elect immediate expensing under § 179. She does not claim any available additional first-year depreciation.

37. **LO.7** On May 5, 2022, Christy purchased and placed in service a hotel. The hotel cost $10,800,000, and the land cost $1,200,000 ($12,000,000 in total). Calculate Christy's cost recovery deductions for 2022 and for 2032.

38. **LO.7** Janice acquired an apartment building on June 4, 2022, for $1,600,000. The value of the land, included in the $1,600,000 purchase price, is $300,000. Janice sold the apartment building on November 29, 2028.
    a. Determine Janice's cost recovery deduction for 2022.
    b. Determine Janice's cost recovery deduction for 2028.

Critical Thinking
Decision Making
Planning

39. **LO.7** Lori, who is single, purchased 5-year class property for $200,000 and 7-year class property for $420,000 on May 20, 2022. Lori expects the taxable income derived from her business (before considering any amount expensed under § 179) to be about $550,000. Lori has determined that she should elect immediate § 179 expensing in the amount of $520,000, but she doesn't know which asset she should completely expense under § 179. She does not claim any available additional first-year depreciation.
    a. Determine Lori's total deduction if the § 179 expense is first taken with respect to the 5-year class asset.
    b. Determine Lori's total deduction if the § 179 expense is first taken with respect to the 7-year class asset.

c. What is your advice to Lori?

d. Assume that Lori is in the 24% marginal tax bracket and that she elects § 179 on the 7-year asset. Determine the present value of the tax savings from the cost recovery deductions for both assets. See Appendix E for present value factors, and assume a 6% discount rate. Round all calculations to the nearest dollar.

e. Assume the same facts as in part (d), except that Lori decides not to use § 179 on either asset. Determine the present value of the tax savings under this choice. In addition, determine which option Lori should choose.

40. **LO.7** Olga is the proprietor of a small business. In 2022, the business's income, before consideration of any cost recovery or § 179 deduction, is $250,000.

Olga spends $620,000 on new 7-year class assets and elects to take the § 179 deduction on them. She does not claim any available additional first-year depreciation. Olga's cost recovery deduction for 2022, except for the cost recovery with respect to the new 7-year assets, is $95,000. Determine Olga's total cost recovery for 2022 with respect to the 7-year class assets and the amount of any § 179 carryforward.

41. **LO.7** On June 5, 2021, Javier Sanchez purchased and placed in service a new 7-year class asset costing $560,000 for use in his landscaping business, which he operates as a single-member LLC (Sanchez Landscaping LLC). During 2021, his business generated net income of $945,780 before any § 179 immediate expense election.

a. Rather than using bonus depreciation, Javier would like to use § 179 to expense $200,000 of this asset and then use regular MACRS to recover the remaining cost. Given this information, determine the cost recovery deductions that Javier can claim with respect to this asset in 2021 and 2022.

b. Complete Javier's Form 4562 (page 1) for 2021. His Social Security number is 123-45-6789.

42. **LO.7** In 2022, Muhammad purchased a new computer for $16,000. The computer is used 100% for business. Muhammad did not make a § 179 election with respect to the computer. He does not claim any available additional first-year depreciation. If Muhammad uses the regular MACRS method, determine his cost recovery deduction for 2022 for computing taxable income and for computing his alternative minimum tax.

43. **LO.7** Jamie purchased $100,000 of new office furniture for her business in June of the current year. Jamie understands that if she elects to use ADS to compute her regular income tax, there will be no difference between the cost recovery for computing the regular income tax and the AMT. Decision Making Planning

a. Jamie wants to know the present value of the *tax cost*, after three years, of using ADS rather than MACRS. Assume that Jamie does not elect § 179 expensing, she does not claim any additional first-year depreciation, and her marginal tax rate is 32%. See Appendix E for present value factors, and assume a 6% discount rate.

b. What is the present value of the *tax savings/costs* that result over the life of the asset if Jamie uses MACRS rather than ADS?

44. **LO.8** Jabari Johnson is considering acquiring an automobile at the beginning of 2023 that he will use 100% of the time as a taxi. The purchase price of the automobile is $68,000. Johnson has heard of cost recovery limits on automobiles and wants to know the maximum amount of the $68,000 he can deduct in the first year. Communications

Write a letter to Jabari in which you present your calculations. Also prepare a memo for the tax files, summarizing your analysis. Johnson's address is 100 Morningside, Clinton, MS 39058.

45. **LO.8** On October 15, 2022, Jon purchased and placed in service a used car. The purchase price was $38,000. This was the only business use asset Jon acquired in 2022. He used the car 80% of the time for business and 20% for personal use. Jon used the regular MACRS method. Calculate the total deduction Jon may take for 2022 with respect to the car.

46. **LO.8** On June 5, 2021, Leo purchased and placed in service a new car that cost $75,000. The business use percentage for the car is always 100%. Leo does not claim any available additional first-year depreciation. Compute Leo's cost recovery deduction for 2021 and 2022.

47. **LO.8** On May 28, 2022, Mary purchased and placed in service a new $60,000 car. The car was used 60% for business, 20% for production of income, and 20% for personal use in 2022. In 2023, the usage changed to 40% for business, 30% for production of income, and 30% for personal use. Mary did not elect immediate expensing under § 179. She did not claim any available additional first-year depreciation. Compute Mary's cost recovery deduction and any cost recovery recapture in 2023.

Communications
Critical Thinking
Decision Making
Planning

48. **LO.9** Mike Saxon is negotiating the purchase of a business. The final purchase price ($2,000,000) has been agreed upon, but the allocation of the purchase price to the assets is still being discussed. Appraisals on a warehouse range from $1,200,000 to $1,500,000. If a value of $1,200,000 is used for the warehouse, the remainder of the purchase price, $800,000, will be allocated to goodwill. If $1,500,000 is allocated to the warehouse, goodwill will be $500,000.

Mike wants to know what effect each alternative will have on cost recovery and amortization during the first year. Under the agreement, Mike will take over the business on January 1 of next year. Write a letter to Mike in which you present your calculations and recommendation. Then prepare a memo for the tax files. Mike's address is 200 Rolling Hills Drive, Shavertown, PA 18708.

Ethics and Equity

49. **LO.10** Sam Jones owns a granite stone quarry. When he acquired the land, Sam allocated $800,000 of the purchase price to the quarry's recoverable mineral reserves, which were estimated at 10 million tons of granite stone. Based on these estimates, the cost depletion was $0.08 per ton. In April of the current year, Sam received a letter from the State Department of Highways notifying him that part of his property was being condemned so that the state could build a new road. At that time, the recoverable mineral reserves had an adjusted basis of $600,000 and 7.5 million tons of granite rock. Sam estimates that the land being condemned contains about 2 million tons of granite. Therefore, for the current year, Sam has computed his cost depletion at $0.11 per ton [$600,000 ÷ (7,500,000 − 2,000,000)]. Evaluate the appropriateness of what Sam is doing.

50. **LO.10** Wes acquired a mineral interest during the year for $10,000,000. A geological survey estimated that 250,000 tons of the mineral remained in the deposit. During the year, 80,000 tons were mined, and 45,000 tons were sold for $12,000,000. Other related expenses amounted to $5,000,000. Assuming that the mineral depletion rate is 22%, calculate Wes's lowest taxable income after any depletion deductions.

Bridge Discipline

1. Sparrow Corporation is considering the acquisition of an asset for use in its business over the next five years. However, Sparrow must decide whether it would be better served by leasing the asset or buying it. An appropriate asset could be purchased for $15,000, and it would qualify as a three-year asset under the MACRS classification. Assume that the election to expense assets under § 179 is not available, that any available additional first-year depreciation is not claimed, and that the asset is not expected to have a salvage value at the end of its use by Sparrow. Alternatively, Sparrow could lease the asset for a $3,625 annual cost over the five-year period. If Sparrow is in the 21% tax bracket, would you recommend that Sparrow buy or lease the asset? In your calculations, assume that 10% is an appropriate discount factor. If necessary, round annual calculations to the nearest dollar.

   Decision Making
   Planning

2. Lark Corporation is considering the acquisition of an asset for use in its business over the next five years. However, Lark must decide whether it would be better served by leasing the asset or buying it. An appropriate asset could be purchased for $15,000, and it would qualify as a three-year asset under the MACRS classification. Assume that the election to expense assets under § 179 is made but any available additional first-year depreciation is not claimed and that the asset is not expected to have a salvage value at the end of its use by Lark. Alternatively, Lark could lease the asset for a $3,625 annual cost over the five-year period. If Lark is in the 21% tax bracket, would you recommend that Lark buy or lease the asset? In your calculations, assume that 10% is an appropriate discount factor. If necessary, round annual calculations to the nearest dollar.

   Decision Making
   Planning

3. Wayside Fruit Company is a sole proprietorship owned by Neil Stephenson. The company's records reflect the following:

Sales revenue	$185,000
Operating expenses	125,000
Depreciation expense for book	13,000
Cost recovery allowance for tax	17,500
Loss on the sale of delivery truck to Neil's brother	5,000
Amount paid to fruit inspector to overlook below-standard fruit shipped to various vendors	3,000

   Compute the net income before tax for book purposes and the amount of taxable income for Wayside Fruit Company.

Research Problems

Note: Solutions to the Research Problems can be prepared by using the Thomson Reuters Checkpoint™ online tax research database, which accompanies this textbook. Solutions can also be prepared by using research materials found in a typical tax library.

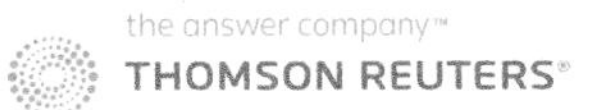

Research Problem 1. Gray Chemical Company manufactured pesticides that were toxic. Over the course of several years, the toxic waste contaminated the air and water around the company's plant. Several employees suffered toxic poisoning, and the Environmental Protection Agency cited the company for violations. In court, the judge found Gray guilty and imposed fines of $15 million. The company voluntarily set up a charitable fund for the purpose of bettering the environment and funded it with $8 million. The company incurred legal expenses in setting up the foundation and defending itself in court. The court reduced the fine from $15 million to $7 million.

Communications
Critical Thinking

Gray deducted the $8 million paid to the foundation and the legal expenses incurred. The IRS disallowed both deductions on the grounds that the payment was, in fact, a fine and in violation of public policy.

Gray's president, Ted Jones, has contacted you regarding the deductibility of the $7 million fine, the $8 million payment to the foundation, and the legal fees. Write a letter to Mr. Jones that contains your advice, and prepare a memo for the tax files. Gray's address is 200 Lincoln Center, Omaha, NE 68182.

Partial list of research aids:
§§ 162(a) and (f).
Reg. § 1.162–21(b).

Research Problem 2. In 2018, Jed James began planting a vineyard. The costs of the land preparation, labor, rootstock, and planting were capitalized. The land preparation costs do not include any nondepreciable land costs. In 2022, when the plants became viable, Jed placed the vineyard in service. Jed wants to know whether he can claim a deduction under § 179 on his 2022 income tax return for the 2018 costs for planting the vineyard.

Communications

Research Problem 3. Juan owns a business that acquires exotic automobiles that are high-tech, state-of-the-art vehicles with unique design features or equipment. The exotic automobiles are not licensed, nor are they set up to be used on the road. Rather, the cars are used exclusively for car shows or related promotional photography. With respect to the exotic automobiles, can Juan take a cost recovery deduction on his Federal income tax return? Prepare an outline for your classmates addressing this issue.

Partial list of research aids:
Bruce Selig, 70 TCM 1125, T.C.Memo. 1995–519.

Use internet tax resources to address the following questions. Look for reliable websites and blogs of the IRS and other government agencies, media outlets, businesses, tax professionals, academics, think tanks, and political outlets.

Communications
Critical Thinking
Data Analytics

Research Problem 4. Do depreciation deductions vary by entity type or by industry? Go to the IRS Tax Statistics page (**irs.gov/statistics**), and review the Excel spreadsheets containing data for corporations, partnerships, and nonfarm proprietorships by sector or industry. You can find these in the Business Tax Statistics section of the IRS site.

Evaluate the depreciation deductions by sector (19 sectors are identified in the IRS spreadsheets) and by entity using Excel. E-mail the spreadsheet to your instructor along with a brief summary of your findings.

Becker CPA Review Questions

Becker

1. Banks Corp., a calendar year corporation, reimburses employees for properly substantiated qualifying business meal expenses. The employees are present at the meals, which are neither lavish nor extravagant, and the reimbursement is not treated as wages subject to withholdings. For 2023, what percentage of the meal expense may Banks deduct?

   a. 0% c. 80%
   b. 50% d. 100%

2. Tapper Corp., an accrual basis calendar year corporation, was organized on January 2, year 1. During year 1, revenue was exclusively from sales proceeds and interest income. The following information pertains to Tapper:

Taxable income before charitable contributions for the year ended December 31, year 1	$500,000
Tapper's matching contribution to employee-designated qualified universities made during year 1	10,000
Board of Directors' authorized contribution to a qualified charity (authorized December 1, year 1, made February 1, year 2)	30,000

   What is the maximum allowable deduction that Tapper may take as a charitable contribution on its tax return for the year ended December 31, year 1?

   a. $0 c. $30,000
   b. $10,000 d. $40,000

3. Campbell Corporation, an accrual basis calendar year corporation, had income of $450,000 for financial statement purposes in year 7. This amount included book depreciation of $50,000. The related tax depreciation was $65,000. Further, the financial statements reported $100,000 of municipal bond interest income, an expense of $2,000 for life insurance premiums on the corporation's president, charitable contributions of $5,000, excess capital losses over capital gains of $3,000, income tax penalties of $10,000, state income tax of $40,000, and Federal income tax expense of $175,000. What is the amount of Campbell's taxable income for year 7?

   a. $522,000 c. $530,000
   b. $525,000 d. $565,000

4. Michael Sima, a sole proprietor craftsman, purchased an amount of equipment in the current year that exceeded the maximum allowable § 179 depreciation election limit by $20,000. Sima's total purchases of property placed in service in the current year did not exceed the § 179 phaseout threshold. All of the personal property (including the equipment) was purchased in November of the current year. Sima elected the maximum amount under § 179 and elected out of bonus depreciation. The § 179 expense election did not create or increase a loss for the current year. Which method may Sima use to depreciate the remaining equipment in the current year?

   a. Sima may not depreciate any additional equipment other than the § 179 maximum in the current year and must carry forward the excess amount to use in the following taxable year.
   b. MACRS half-year convention for personal property.
   c. MACRS mid-quarter convention for personal property.
   d. Straight-line, mid-month convention for real property.

5. Cox Construction, a company in its tenth year of business, purchased a piece of equipment on April 1, year 9, for $20,000. Cox has used it for business purposes since the initial purchase date. The company depreciated the equipment using the MACRS half-year table for 5-year assets. For tax purposes, what is the amount of accumulated depreciation for the equipment as of December 31, year 10?

a. $6,000
b. $10,400
c. $11,600
d. $12,800

6. Stem Corp. bought a machine in February of year 7 for $20,000. Then Stem bought furniture in November of year 7 for $30,000. Both assets were placed in service for business purposes immediately after purchase. No other assets were purchased during year 7. What depreciation convention must Stem use for the machine purchased in February year 7?

a. Mid-month
b. Half year
c. Mid-quarter
d. Full year

7. Data, Inc., purchased and placed in service a $5,000 computer on August 24, year 3. This is the only asset purchase during the year. Code § 179 expensing and bonus depreciation were not elected. Using the excerpt of the MACRS half-year convention table below, what is the MACRS depreciation in year 3 for the computer?

Recovery Period	5-Year	7-Year	10-Year
1	20%	14.29%	10%
2	32%	24.49%	18%
3	19.2%	17.49%	14.4%

a. $500
b. $715
c. $960
d. $1,000

8. Data, Inc., purchased and placed in service a $5,000 computer on August 24, year 3. This is the only asset purchase during the year. Code § 179 expensing and bonus depreciation were not elected. The computer was sold during year 5. Using the excerpt of the MACRS half-year convention table below, what is the MACRS depreciation in year 5 for the computer?

Recovery Period	5-Year	7-Year	10-Year
1	20%	14.29%	10%
2	32%	24.49%	18%
3	19.2%	17.49%	14.4%

a. $360
b. $437
c. $480
d. $960

9. Data, Inc., purchased and placed in service $5,000 of office furniture on August 24, year 3. This is the only asset purchase during the year. Code § 179 expensing and bonus depreciation were not elected. Using the excerpt of the MACRS half-year convention table below, what is the MACRS depreciation in year 3 for the office furniture?

Recovery Period	5-Year	7-Year	10-Year
1	20%	14.29%	10%
2	32%	24.49%	18%
3	19.2%	17.49%	14.4%

a. $500
b. $715
c. $875
d. $1,000

10. Which statement below is correct?
    a. Real property is depreciated using the half-year convention.
    b. Residential real estate is depreciated over a 39-year life.
    c. One-half month of depreciation is taken for the month that real property is disposed of.
    d. Salvage value is considered in MACRS depreciation.

11. Charlie purchased an apartment building on November 16, year 1, for $1,000,000. Determine the cost recovery for year 20.
    a. $36,360
    b. $32,100
    c. $45,500
    d. $331,850

12. Which statement below is incorrect about the § 179 deduction?
    a. The § 179 deduction is allowed even if there is a loss.
    b. The § 179 deduction may be reduced based on total purchases.
    c. Real property is generally not eligible for the § 179 deduction.
    d. Corporations may elect to take the § 179 deduction.

13. Bravo Co. acquired and placed in service $3,000,000 in machinery and equipment throughout the 2021 tax year. Bravo did not acquire any other depreciable assets during 2021. Assuming the § 179 taxable income limit does not apply, what is the maximum § 179 expense that Bravo Co. can elect and deduct in 2021?
    a. $380,000
    b. $670,000
    c. $1,050,000
    d. $2,620,000

14. Alpha Co. purchased and placed in service $100,000 of computer equipment on January 1, Year 1, and disposed of the computer equipment on March 31, Year 3. No other depreciable assets were placed in service in Year 1. Alpha uses MACRS depreciation to recover the cost of the assets. What is the amount of Alpha's MACRS depreciation in Year 1?
    a. $7,145
    b. $10,000
    c. $14,290
    d. $20,000

15. Alpha Co. purchased and placed in service $100,000 of computer equipment on January 1, Year 1, and disposed of the computer equipment on March 31, Year 3. No other depreciable assets were placed in service in Year 1. Alpha uses MACRS depreciation to recover the cost of the assets. What is the amount of Alpha's MACRS depreciation in Year 3?
    a. $8,745
    b. $9,600
    c. $17,490
    d. $19,200

16. Which of the following depreciable business-use assets are ineligible for § 179 expense or first-year bonus depreciation?
    a. Computers
    b. Office furniture
    c. Qualified improvements
    d. Office Building

Chapter

6 Losses and Loss Limitations

Learning Objectives: *After completing Chapter 6, you should be able to:*

- **LO.1** Determine the amount, classification, and timing of the bad debt deduction.
- **LO.2** State and illustrate the tax consequences of worthless securities, including § 1244 stock.
- **LO.3** Identify a casualty and determine the amount, classification, and timing of casualty and theft losses.
- **LO.4** Describe the impact of the net operating loss provisions.
- **LO.5** Explain the tax shelter problem and the reasons for at-risk and passive activity loss limitations.
- **LO.6** Explain how the at-risk limitation and the passive activity loss rules limit deductions for losses and identify taxpayers subject to these restrictions.
- **LO.7** Define an activity, material participation, and rental activity under the passive activity loss rules.
- **LO.8** Determine the relationship between the at-risk and passive activity loss limitations.
- **LO.9** Explain the special treatment available to real estate activities.
- **LO.10** Determine the consequences of the disposition of passive activities.
- **LO.11** Describe and compute the excess business loss limitation.

Chapter Outline

Tax Talk *The income tax has made more liars out of the American people than golf has. Even when you make a tax form out on the level, you don't know when it's through if you are a crook or a martyr.* —Will Rogers

The Big Picture

Receiving Tax Benefits from Losses

Robyn, an unmarried, cash basis and calendar year taxpayer, is nearing the end of a year that she would like to forget. Several years ago, she loaned $25,000 to her friend Jamil to enable him to start a business. Jamil had made scheduled payments of $7,000 (including $1,000 of interest) when he suddenly died in January. At the time of his death, he was insolvent, and Robyn's attempts to collect the debt were fruitless.

Last year Robyn invested $60,000 by purchasing stock in Owl Corporation, a closely held small business corporation started by her brother. However, the company declared bankruptcy in May of this year, and the bankruptcy trustee informed the shareholders that they should not expect to receive anything from the company.

Robyn has owned and operated a bookstore as a sole proprietorship for the past 10 years. The bookstore has been profitable, producing annual taxable income of approximately $75,000. However, due to the growth of online vendors and e-books, the business lost $180,000 this year.

In September, a tornado caused a large oak tree to blow over onto Robyn's bookstore. The cost of removing the tree and making repairs to the property was $32,000. Robyn received a check for $25,000 from her insurance company. Her adjusted basis for the bookstore building was $280,000.

Finally, Robyn invested $20,000 for a 10 percent interest in a limited partnership that owns and operates orange groves in Florida. Due to a hard freeze that damaged much of the fruit, the partnership lost $200,000 and allocated $20,000 of ordinary loss to Robyn.

Robyn has come to you for tax advice and would like to know the tax ramifications of each of the events and transactions listed above.

Read the chapter and formulate your response.

Chapter 5 introduced rules governing the deductibility of trade or business expenses. This chapter discusses deductibility of losses occurring in the course of business operations. In particular, this chapter reviews the special rules concerning the tax treatment of bad debts, casualty losses, and net operating losses. In addition, this chapter discusses tax shelters and the rules that limit a taxpayer's ability to use them to generate losses to offset other income.

In most situations, financial accounting rules treat losses as "negative gains." As this chapter and the next two chapters illustrate repeatedly, that is not necessarily true in the tax law. That is, there are frequently different rules for gains and losses under the tax law. This often takes the form of limitations on taxpayers' ability to deduct losses and to reduce tax payments. Broadly speaking, Congress has tended to limit losses in two different ways. The first way is to directly limit deductions for specific losses. Denying related party loss deductions and allowing casualty loss deductions only above a cutoff are two examples of these loss limitations. The second way that Congress limits losses is to create an overall limit on deductions. This type of limit restricts overall deductions for many different types of losses. The Net Operating Loss and the Excess Business Loss limits are examples of these.

Why would Congress choose to treat gains and losses differently? There are at least five reasons. First, Congress often seeks to prevent taxpayers from sheltering certain types of income or gains with other types of deductions or losses. For example, the passive activity loss rules effectively prevent taxpayers from using losses resulting from passive investments (e.g., the taxpayer only contributes money and does not work in that business) from offsetting salary and other types of "active" income. Second, some loss limitations deny deductions to higher-income taxpayers to make the tax system more equitable among taxpayers of varying income levels. Third, Congress attempts to prevent excessive income shifting across tax years. The net operating loss rules illustrate this motivation. Fourth, holding all else constant, denying losses increases government revenues. This gives Congress some latitude to reduce tax rates or pursue other policy goals that reduce government revenues. Fifth, the measure of taxable income for individuals generally excludes personal losses, such as loss from sale of a personal use car. This prevents possible abuse and simplifies the law. Congress made an exception for losses from certain casualties, such as a hurricane.

Taken together, these reasons for limiting losses motivate Congress to enact provisions that treat gains and losses differently—and can also make complying with the rules more difficult and costly for taxpayers. As you read the rules in this chapter, consideration of the five reasons for treating losses and gains differently can help in your understanding of these special tax loss rules.

LO.1

Determine the amount, classification, and timing of the bad debt deduction.

6-1 Bad Debts

If a taxpayer lends money or purchases a debt instrument and the debt is not repaid, the taxpayer can deduct the **bad debt**. Similarly, if an accrual basis taxpayer sells goods or provides services on credit and the account receivable subsequently becomes worthless, a bad debt deduction is permitted.[1] However, cash basis taxpayers cannot deduct bad debts arising from the sale of a product or service because these taxpayers report no income until they collect from customers. Permitting a bad debt deduction for a cash basis taxpayer would amount to a double deduction because the expenses of the product or service rendered are deducted when payments are made to suppliers and to employees or when the sale is made.

Daniela, a sole proprietor, operates a business named Executive Accounting and Tax Services. Last year Pat hired Daniela to help him with the accounting for his small business. Daniela also prepared the S corporation income tax return for the business and Pat's personal income tax return. Daniela billed

continued

[1]Reg. § 1.166–1(e). However, some financial institutions are permitted to use the reserve method for computing bad debt deductions (§ 585).

Pat $8,000 for the services she performed. Pat has never paid the bill, his business no longer exists, and his whereabouts are unknown.

If Daniela is an *accrual basis taxpayer*, she includes the $8,000 in income when the services are performed. When she determines that Pat's account will not be collected, Daniela deducts the $8,000 as a bad debt.

If Daniela is a *cash basis taxpayer*, she does not include the $8,000 in income until payment is received. When she determines that she will not collect Pat's account, she cannot deduct the $8,000 as a bad debt expense because Daniela has not yet recognized income.

The Big Picture

Example 2

Return to the facts of *The Big Picture* on p. 6-1. Because Robyn is a cash basis taxpayer, she cannot take as a bad debt deduction any unpaid accrued interest on the loan to her friend, Jamil, because Robin never recognized the receivable as income.

6-1a Specific Charge-Off Method

Most taxpayers must use the **specific charge-off method** when accounting for bad debts. A taxpayer using this method claims a deduction in the year when a specific, identifiable *business* debt becomes either partially or wholly worthless. If a taxpayer deducts a business debt as partially worthless and it becomes totally worthless in a later year, the taxpayer deducts in the later year only the remainder of the debt. A *nonbusiness* debt must be wholly worthless to claim a deduction.[2]

In the case of total worthlessness, taxpayers deduct the entire amount in the year the debt becomes worthless. The amount of the deduction depends on the taxpayer's basis in the bad debt. If the debt arose from the sale of services or products and the face amount was previously included in income, that amount is deductible. If the taxpayer purchased the debt, the deduction equals the amount the taxpayer paid for the debt instrument.

For either a business or nonbusiness debt, the taxpayer must be able to document the fact and the amount of the partial or complete worthlessness. Determining when a bad debt becomes worthless can be a difficult task. Legal proceedings need not be initiated against the debtor when the surrounding facts indicate that such action will not result in collection.

In 2020, Ross lent $1,000 to Josh, who agreed to repay the loan in two years. In 2022, Josh disappeared after the note became delinquent. If a reasonable investigation by Ross indicates that Josh cannot be found or that a suit against Josh would not result in collection, Ross can deduct the $1,000 in 2022.

Bankruptcy is generally an indication of at least partial worthlessness of a debt. Bankruptcy may create worthlessness before the settlement date. If this is the case, the deduction may be taken in the year of worthlessness.

In Example 3, assume that Josh filed for personal bankruptcy in 2021 and that the debt is a business debt. At that time, Ross learned that unsecured creditors (including Ross) were ultimately expected to receive 20 cents on the dollar.

In 2022, settlement is made, and Ross receives only $150. Ross should deduct $800 ($1,000 loan − $200 expected settlement) in 2021 and $50 in 2022 ($200 balance − $150 proceeds).

[2] § 166(a).

If a taxpayer writes off (deducts) a receivable as uncollectible and later collects it during the *same* tax year, the taxpayer must reverse the write-off entry. In contrast, the recovery of a write-off that a taxpayer deducted in an earlier tax year results in current taxable income if the loss deduction yielded a tax benefit in the prior year (under the tax benefit rule).

6-1b Business versus Nonbusiness Bad Debts

The nature of a debt depends upon whether the lender is engaged in the business of lending money or whether there is a proximate relationship between the creation of the debt and the *lender's* trade or business. Where either of these conditions is true, a bad debt receives **business bad debt** treatment. If neither condition is true, a bad debt receives **nonbusiness bad debt** treatment. The use of the borrowed funds is irrelevant when classifying the bad debt.

The Big Picture

Return to the facts of *The Big Picture* on p. 6-1. Robyn loaned her friend Jamil $25,000. Jamil used the money to start a business, which subsequently failed. When Jamil died after having made principal payments of $6,000 on the loan, he was insolvent.

Even though the proceeds of the loan were used in a business, the loan is a nonbusiness bad debt because the business was Jamil's, not Robyn's, and Robyn is not in the business of lending money.

The nonbusiness bad debt provisions are *not* applicable to a business entity (e.g., a corporation or partnership). The law assumes that any loans a business makes relate to its trade or business. Therefore, any bad debts resulting from loans made by a business receive business bad debt treatment.

Horace operates a sole proprietorship that sells premium electronic equipment. Horace uses the accrual method to account for sales of the electronic equipment. During the year, he sold $4,000 of equipment to Herbie on credit. Later that year, the account receivable becomes worthless. The loan is a business bad debt, because the debt related to Horace's business.

The distinction between a business bad debt and a nonbusiness bad debt is important. A business bad debt is deductible as an ordinary loss in the year incurred, whereas a nonbusiness bad debt is always treated as a short-term capital loss. Thus, the $3,000 capital loss limitation for individuals can limit the tax benefit from a nonbusiness bad debt, regardless of its age (refer to the discussion in text Section 4-5a and in Chapter 8).

Concept Summary 6.1 provides a summary of the tax treatment of bad debts using the specific charge-off method.

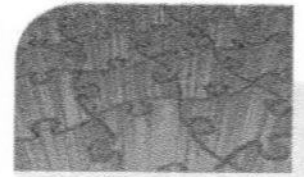

Concept Summary 6.1

The Tax Treatment of Bad Debts Using the Specific Charge-Off Method

	Business Bad Debts	Nonbusiness Bad Debts
Timing of deduction	A deduction is allowed when the debt becomes either partially or wholly worthless.	A deduction is allowed *only* when the debt becomes wholly worthless.
Recovery of amounts previously deducted	If the account recovered was written off during the current tax year, the write-off entry is reversed. If the account was written off in a previous tax year, income is created subject to the tax benefit rule.	If the account recovered was written off during the current tax year, the write-off entry is reversed. If the account was written off in a previous tax year, income is created subject to the tax benefit rule.
Character of deduction	The bad debt is deducted as an ordinary loss.	The bad debt is classified as a short-term capital loss, subject to the $3,000 capital loss limitation for individuals.

6-1c Loans between Related Parties

Loans between related parties raise the issue of whether the transaction was a *bona fide* loan or some other type of transfer, such as a gift, a disguised dividend payment, or a contribution to capital. For example, taxpayers have a tax incentive to make gifts to family members "look like" a loan because gifts are always nondeductible. The Regulations state that a bona fide debt arises from a debtor-creditor relationship based on a valid and enforceable obligation to pay a fixed or determinable sum of money. Thus, individual circumstances determine whether advances between related parties are loans. Some considerations include:

- Was a note properly executed?
- Was there a reasonable rate of interest?
- Was collateral provided?
- What collection efforts were made?
- What was the intent of the parties?

Ted, who is the sole shareholder of Penguin Corporation, lends the corporation $10,000 so that it can continue business operations. The note specifies a 2% interest rate and is payable on demand. Penguin has shown losses in each year of its five-year existence. The corporation also has liabilities greatly in excess of its assets. It is likely that Ted's transfer to the corporation would be treated as a contribution to capital rather than a liability. Consequently, no bad debt deduction would be allowed upon default by Penguin.

1 Digging Deeper

A flowchart on bad debt deduction rules can be found on this book's companion website: www.cengage.com

State and illustrate the tax consequences of worthless securities, including § 1244 stock.

6-2 Worthless Securities and Small Business Stock Losses

6-2a Worthless Securities

A loss is allowed for securities that become *completely* worthless during the year (**worthless securities**).[3] Securities include shares of stock, bonds, notes, or other evidence of indebtedness issued by a corporation or government. The losses generated are treated as capital losses (refer to text Section 4-5a) deemed to have occurred on the last day of the tax year. By treating losses as having occurred on the *last day* of the tax year, a loss that would otherwise have been classified as short term (if the date of worthlessness were used) may be classified as long term.

The Big Picture

Example 8

Return to the facts of *The Big Picture* on p. 6-1. Robyn owned stock in Owl Corporation that she acquired as an investment on October 1, 2021, at a cost of $60,000. On May 31, 2022, the stock became worthless when the company declared bankruptcy.

Because the stock is deemed to have become worthless as of December 31, 2022, Robyn has a capital loss from an asset held for more than one year (a long-term capital loss). Note that treating the worthless stock as a loss on the last day of the year results in a long-term instead of a short-term capital loss. Alternatively, if the stock qualifies as § 1244 small business stock (see the following section), Robyn has a $50,000 ordinary loss and a $10,000 long-term capital loss.

6-2b Small Business Stock (§ 1244 Stock) Losses

Congress has enacted tax rules to encourage taxpayers to form and operate small businesses. One such provision is § 1244. The general rule for losses from the sale or exchange of corporate stock is that shareholders receive capital loss treatment. However, it is

[3] § 165(g).

possible to avoid capital loss limitations if the loss arises from the sale or worthlessness of **small business stock (§ 1244 stock)**. Only *individuals*[4] who acquired the stock directly from the issuing corporation qualify for ordinary loss treatment. Section 1244 allows taxpayers to treat losses of up to $50,000 ($100,000 for married individuals filing jointly) per year as ordinary losses. Losses on § 1244 stock that exceed this limit retain their capital loss treatment.

The issuing corporation must meet certain requirements for the loss on the stock to qualify for *ordinary*—rather than a capital—loss treatment. The primary requirement is that the total capitalization of the corporation must not exceed $1 million at the time the corporation issued the stock. This limit includes all money and other property received by the corporation for stock and all capital contributions made to the corporation. Section 1244 stock can be either common or preferred.

Section 1244 applies only to losses. If § 1244 stock is sold at a gain, the provision does not apply and the gain is capital gain (which, for individuals, can result in preferential tax treatment, as discussed in text Section 4-5a).

Paulina, a single individual, was looking for an investment that would give some diversification to her stock portfolio. A friend suggested that she acquire some stock in Eagle Corporation, a new startup company. On July 1, 2020, Paulina purchased 100 shares of Eagle Corporation for $100,000. At the time Paulina acquired her stock from Eagle Corporation, the corporation had $700,000 of paid-in capital. As a result, the stock qualified as § 1244 stock. On June 20, 2022, Paulina sold all of her Eagle stock to Michael for $20,000, producing an $80,000 loss ($20,000 − $100,000). Because the Eagle stock qualifies as § 1244 stock, Paulina recognizes a $50,000 ordinary loss and a $30,000 long-term capital loss.

If Michael sells the stock later for $8,000 in a taxable transaction, the $12,000 loss ($8,000 − $20,000) would not qualify for ordinary loss treatment under § 1244 because Eagle Corporation had not issued the stock to him.

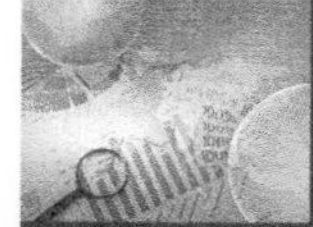

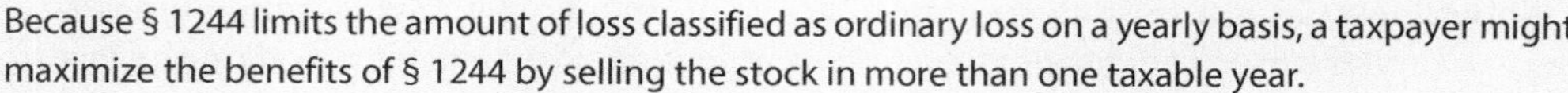

Tax Planning Strategies — Maximizing the Benefits of Small Business (§ 1244 Stock) Losses

Framework Focus: Tax Rate

Strategy: Control the Character of Income and Deductions.

Because § 1244 limits the amount of loss classified as ordinary loss on a yearly basis, a taxpayer might maximize the benefits of § 1244 by selling the stock in more than one taxable year.

Mitch, a single individual, acquired small business stock in 2020 for $150,000 (150 shares at $1,000 per share). On December 20, 2022, the stock is worth $60,000 (150 shares at $400 per share). Mitch wants to sell the stock at this time. He earns a salary of $80,000 a year, has no other capital transactions, and does not expect any in the future.

If Mitch sells all of the small business stock in 2022, his recognized loss will be $90,000 ($60,000 selling price − $150,000 cost). Code § 1244 will result in a $50,000 ordinary loss and a $40,000 long-term capital loss. In computing taxable income for 2022, Mitch could deduct the $50,000 ordinary loss but could deduct only $3,000 of the capital loss (assuming that he has no capital gains). The remainder of the capital loss could be carried over and used in future years subject to the capital loss limitations in those years.

Alternatively, if Mitch sells 82 shares in 2022, he will recognize an ordinary loss of $49,200 [82 × ($400 − $1,000)]. If Mitch then sells the remainder of the shares in 2023, he will recognize an ordinary loss of $40,800 [68 × ($400 − $1,000)], successfully avoiding the capital loss limitation. Mitch could deduct the $49,200 ordinary loss in computing 2022 taxable income and the $40,800 ordinary loss in computing 2023 taxable income and avoid any capital loss limitations.

[4] The term *individuals* for this purpose does not include a trust or an estate (but could include a partnership or an LLC).

6-3 Casualty and Theft Losses

Identify a casualty and determine the amount, classification, and timing of casualty and theft losses.

Losses on business property are deductible whether attributable to casualty, theft, or some other cause (e.g., rust, termite damage). While all *business* property losses are generally deductible, special rules govern the amount and timing of casualty and theft losses. Furthermore, individual taxpayers can deduct casualty losses on personal use (nonbusiness) property as well as on business and investment property (held in partnerships and S corporations or in an individual capacity), but a set of special limitations apply. In addition, the tax law affords special consideration to casualty gains (these usually occur when insurance proceeds exceed the basis of the property damaged).

6-3a Definition of Casualties and Thefts

The term *casualty* generally includes *fire*, *storm*, *shipwreck*, and *theft*. In addition, losses from *other casualties* are deductible. Such losses generally include any loss resulting from an event that is (1) identifiable; (2) damaging to property; and (3) sudden, unexpected, and unusual in nature. The term also includes accidental loss of property provided the loss qualifies under the same rules as any other casualty.

A *sudden event* is an event that is swift and precipitous and not gradual or progressive. An *unexpected event* is one that is ordinarily unanticipated and occurs without the intent of the taxpayer who suffers the loss. An *unusual event* is an event that is extraordinary and nonrecurring and does not commonly occur during the activity in which the taxpayer was engaged when the destruction occurred.[5] Examples include auto accidents, sonic booms, vandalism, and mine cave-ins. A taxpayer can take a deduction for a casualty loss from an automobile accident if the accident is not attributable to the taxpayer's willful act or willful negligence. Weather that causes damage (e.g., drought) must be unusual and severe for the particular region to qualify as a casualty. Furthermore, damage must be to the *taxpayer's* property to be deductible.

Events That Are Not Casualties

Not all acts of nature are treated as **casualty losses** for income tax purposes. Because a casualty must be sudden, unexpected, and unusual, progressive deterioration (such as erosion due to wind or rain) is not a casualty because it does not meet the suddenness test.

An example of an event that generally does not qualify as a casualty is insect damage. When termites caused damage over a period of several years, some courts have disallowed a casualty loss deduction.[6] On the other hand, some courts have held that termite damage over periods of up to 15 months after infestation constituted a sudden

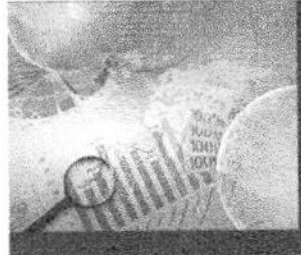

Tax Planning Strategies

Documentation of Related-Taxpayer Loans, Casualty Losses, and Theft Losses

Framework Focus: Deductions

Strategy: Maximize Deductible Amounts.

Because the validity of loans between related taxpayers might be questioned, adequate documentation is needed to substantiate a bad debt deduction if the loan subsequently becomes worthless. Documentation should include proper execution of the note (legal form) and the establishment of a bona fide purpose for the loan. In addition, it is desirable to stipulate a reasonable rate of interest and a fixed maturity date.

Because a theft loss deduction is not permitted for misplaced items, a police report and evidence of the value of the property (e.g., appraisals, pictures of the property, and purchase receipts) are necessary to document a theft.

Similar documentation of the value of property should be provided to support a casualty loss deduction because the amount of loss is measured, in part, by the decline in fair market value of the property.

Taxpayers report casualty loss deductions on Form 4684.

[5] Rev.Rul. 72–592.

[6] *Fay v. Helvering*, 41–2 USTC ¶9494, 27 AFTR 432, 120 F.2d 253 (CA–2); *U.S. v. Rogers*, 41–1 USTC ¶9442, 27 AFTR 423, 120 F.2d 244 (CA–9).

event and was, therefore, deductible as a casualty loss.[7] Despite the existence of some judicial support for the deductibility of termite damage as a casualty loss, the current position of the IRS is that termite damage is not deductible.[8]

Other examples of events that are not casualties are losses resulting from a decline in value rather than an actual loss of the property. For example, a taxpayer was allowed a loss for the actual flood damage to his property but not for the decline in market value due to the property being in a flood-prone area.[9] Similarly, a decline in value of an office building due to fire damage to nearby buildings is not deductible as a casualty.

Theft includes, but is not necessarily limited to, larceny, embezzlement, and robbery.[10] Theft does not include misplaced items.[11]

6-3b Deduction of Casualty and Theft Losses

Generally, taxpayers can deduct a casualty loss in the year the loss occurs. However, no casualty loss is permitted if a reimbursement claim with a *reasonable prospect of full recovery* exists.[12] If the taxpayer has a partial claim, only part of the loss can be claimed in the year of the casualty and the remainder is deducted in the year the claim is settled.

Fuchsia Corporation's new warehouse was completely destroyed by fire in 2022. Its cost and fair market value were $250,000. Fuchsia's only claim against the insurance company was on a $70,000 policy and was not settled by year-end. The following year, 2023, Fuchsia settled with the insurance company for $60,000. Fuchsia is entitled to a $180,000 deduction in 2022 and a $10,000 deduction in 2023.

If a taxpayer receives reimbursement for a casualty loss sustained and deducted in a previous year, an amended return is not filed for that year. Instead, the taxpayer must include the reimbursement in gross income on the return for the year in which it is received to the extent the previous deduction resulted in a tax benefit (refer to text Section 4-5e).

Golden Hawk, Inc., had a deductible casualty loss of $15,000 on its 2021 tax return. Golden Hawk's taxable income for 2021 was $60,000 after deducting the $15,000 loss. In June 2022, the corporation is reimbursed $13,000 for the prior year's casualty loss.

Golden Hawk includes the entire $13,000 in gross income for 2022 because the deduction in 2021 produced a tax benefit.

Disaster Area Losses

An exception to the general rule for the time of deduction is allowed for **disaster area losses**, which are casualties or disaster-related business losses sustained in an area designated as a disaster area by the President of the United States.[13] In such cases, the taxpayer may *elect* to treat the loss as having occurred in the taxable year immediately *preceding* the taxable year in which the disaster actually occurred. The rationale for this exception is to provide immediate tax relief to disaster victims by accelerating the tax deductions.

If the extended due date for the prior year's return has not passed, a taxpayer makes the election to claim the disaster area loss on the prior year's tax return. If a disaster area is designated after the prior year's return has been filed, it is necessary to file either an amended return or a refund claim. In any case, the taxpayers must clearly indicate their election if they make one.

[7] *Rosenberg v. Comm.*, 52–2 USTC ¶9377, 42 AFTR 303, 198 F.2d 46 (CA–8); *Shopmaker v. U.S.*, 54–1 USTC ¶9195, 45 AFTR 758, 119 F.Supp. 705 (D.Ct. Mo.).

[8] Rev.Rul. 63–232.

[9] *S. L. Solomon*, 39 TCM 1282, T.C.Memo. 1980–87.

[10] Reg. § 1.165–8(d).

[11] § 165(i). *Mary Francis Allen*, 16 T.C. 163 (1951).

[12] Reg. § 1.165–1(d)(2)(i).

[13] § 165(i).

The Big Picture

Example 13

Return to the facts of *The Big Picture* on p. 6-1. On September 28, 2022, a tornado caused an oak tree to fall on Robyn's bookstore. The amount of her uninsured casualty loss was $7,000 ($32,000 loss − $25,000 insurance recovery). Due to the extent of the damage in the area, the President of the United States designated the area a disaster area. Because Robyn's loss is a disaster area loss, she may elect to file an amended return for 2021 and take the loss in that year.

If Robyn forgoes the election, she may take the loss on her 2022 income tax return. The advantage to Robyn of claiming the deduction in 2021 is to receive the tax benefit sooner.

For information on COVID-19 losses, visit this book's companion website: www.cengage.com

2 Digging Deeper

Deduction of Theft Losses

Theft losses like other casualty losses, but the *timing* of recognition of the loss differs. A theft loss is deducted in the *year of discovery*, which may not be the same as the year of the theft. If in the year of the discovery a claim exists (e.g., against an insurance company) and there is a reasonable expectation of recovering the adjusted basis of the asset from the insurance company, no deduction is permitted.[14] In the year of settlement, the taxpayer recognizes a casualty loss if the property basis exceeds the insurance payment or a casualty gain if the payment exceeds the basis.

Sakura, Inc., owned a computer that was stolen from its offices in December 2021. The theft was discovered on June 3, 2022, and the corporation filed a claim with its insurance company that was settled on January 30, 2023.

If Sakura reasonably expected a full recovery from its insurance company, no deduction is allowed in 2022. A deduction may be available in 2023 if the actual insurance proceeds are less than the adjusted basis of the asset. (The next section discusses loss measurement rules.)

Information on the tax consequences of lost bitcoin can be found on this book's companion website: www.cengage.com

3 Digging Deeper

6-3c Loss Measurement

The rules for determining the amount of a loss depend in part on whether the loss relates to business, investment, or personal use property. Another consideration is whether the property was partially or completely destroyed.

If business property or investment property (e.g., rental property) is *completely destroyed*, the loss equals the adjusted basis[15] (typically cost less depreciation) of the property at the time of destruction.

A different measurement rule applies for *partial destruction* of business and investment property and for *partial* or *complete destruction* of personal use property held by individuals. In these situations, the loss is the lesser of:

- The adjusted basis of the property, or
- The difference between the fair market value of the property before the event and the fair market value immediately after the event.

Wynd and Rain, a law firm, owned an airplane that was used only for business purposes. The airplane was damaged in an accident. On the date of the accident, the fair market value of the plane was $52,000, and its adjusted basis was $32,000. After the accident, the plane was appraised at $24,000.

The law firm's loss deduction is $28,000 (the lesser of the adjusted basis or the decrease in fair market value). If instead the airplane had been completely destroyed in the accident, the loss deduction would have been $32,000 (the adjusted basis of the airplane). On the other hand, if the plane is for personal use, the deduction is $28,000 even if the accident totally destroys the plane. However, from 2018 through 2025, personal casualty losses are allowed only if the event relates to a Federally declared disaster (see text Section 6-3d).

[14] Reg. §§ 1.165–1(d)(2) and 1.165–8(a)(2).

[15] See text Section 7-2 for a detailed discussion of basis rules.

Any insurance recovery reduces the loss for business, investment, and personal use losses. In fact, a taxpayer may realize a gain if the insurance proceeds exceed the adjusted basis of the property. Chapter 8 discusses the treatment of net gains and losses on business property and income-producing property.

A special rule on insurance recovery applies to *personal use property*. In particular, individuals are not permitted to deduct a casualty loss for damage to insured personal use property unless the taxpayer files an insurance claim. This rule applies whether the insurance provides partial or full reimbursement for the loss.[16]

Generally, taxpayers need appraisals before and after the casualty to measure the amount of loss. However, the *cost of repairs* to the damaged property generally is acceptable as a method of establishing the loss in value.[17]

More information on loss measurement can be found on this book's companion website:
www.cengage.com

Multiple Losses

When multiple casualty losses occur during the year, the amount of each loss is computed separately. The rules for computing loss deductions where multiple losses have occurred are illustrated in Example 16.

Example 16

During the year, Swan Enterprises had the following business casualty losses:

		Fair Market Value of the Asset		
Asset	**Adjusted Basis**	**Before the Casualty**	**After the Casualty**	**Insurance Recovery**
A	$900	$600	$–0–	$400
B	300	800	250	100

The following losses are allowed:

- Asset A: $500. The complete destruction of a business asset results in a deduction of the adjusted basis of the property (reduced by any insurance recovery) regardless of the asset's fair market value.
- Asset B: $200. The partial destruction of a business asset results in a deduction equal to the lesser of the adjusted basis ($300) or the decline in value ($550), reduced by any insurance recovery ($100).

6-3d Casualty and Theft Losses of Individuals

Recall from Chapters 1 and 9 that the individual income tax formula distinguishes between deductions *for* AGI and deductions *from* AGI. Casualty and theft losses incurred by an individual in connection with a business or with rental and royalty activities are deductible *for* AGI and are limited only by the rules discussed above.[18] Losses from most other investment activities and from personal use assets generally are deducted *from* AGI. Investment casualty and theft losses (e.g., the theft of a security) are classified as other itemized deductions. Casualty and theft losses of personal use property are subject to special limitations discussed next.

Personal Use Property

In addition to the valuation rules discussed previously, individual taxpayers face three limitations on their ability to deduct personal casualty losses. First, after 2017 and before 2026, individuals can deduct a casualty loss only if it occurs in a Federally declared disaster area. Second, taxpayers must reduce each casualty loss by a $100 floor. This applies to all damaged property from a single casualty and *not* to each asset damaged or destroyed. Third, individual taxpayers can deduct only the portion of the total of *all* personal casualty losses that exceeds 10 percent of AGI.[19]

[16] § 165(h)(4)(E).

[17] Reg. § 1.165–7(a)(2)(ii).

[18] § 62(a)(1).

[19] §§ 165(c)(3) and (h).

Example 17

Rocky, who had AGI of $30,000, lost all the furniture in his apartment as a result of a flood in a Federally declared disaster area in 2022. His furniture, which he used only for personal use and had a fair market value of $12,000 and an adjusted basis of $9,000, was completely destroyed. He received $5,000 from his insurance company.

Rocky's casualty loss deduction is $900 [$9,000 basis − $5,000 insurance recovery − $100 floor − $3,000 (0.10 × $30,000 AGI)]. The $900 casualty loss is an itemized deduction (*from* AGI).

If Rocky's loss was not related to a Federally declared disaster area, his deduction would have been zero.

Learn more about Federal disaster area declarations at this book's companion website: www.cengage.com

5 Digging Deeper

Where there are both casualty and theft gains and losses from personal use property, special netting rules apply. Generally, if casualty and theft gains exceed losses during the year, the gains and losses are treated as capital gains and losses. Alternatively, if losses exceed gains, the casualty and theft gains (and losses to the extent of gains) are treated as ordinary gains and losses. Any excess losses are deductible as an itemized deduction after applying the three limitations discussed above.

For the netting of personal casualty gains and losses, there is an exception to the rule that disallows a deduction for personal casualty losses other than those in Federally declared disaster areas.[20] In this case, the taxpayer may use a personal casualty loss (or losses) *not* attributable to a Federally declared disaster to offset any personal casualty gains. After this netting process, if any loss remains, it is not deductible because it relates to a non-Federally declared disaster area casualty. If, however, a net personal casualty gain remains, it must offset any Federally declared disaster area casualty losses.

Calculating Personal Casualty Gains and Losses

Example 18

During 2022, Emmanuel has AGI of $50,000 and the following personal casualty gains and losses (after deducting the $100 floor):

Asset	Item	Gain or (Loss)
A	Personal casualty gain	$ 2,500
B	Personal casualty loss (non-Federally declared disaster area)	(2,000)
C	Personal casualty loss (Federally declared disaster area)	(9,000)

Emmanuel first offsets the non-Federally declared disaster area losses against the personal casualty gain, resulting in an excess personal casualty gain of $500, computed as follows:

Personal casualty gain	$ 2,500
Personal casualty loss (non-Federally declared disaster area)	(2,000)
Excess personal casualty gain	$ 500

Next, the excess personal casualty gain offsets the Federally declared disaster area loss. Emmanuel's overall net personal casualty loss is $8,500, computed as follows:

Personal casualty loss (Federally declared disaster area)	($ 9,000)
Less: Excess personal casualty gain	500
Overall net personal casualty loss	$ 8,500

After this second netting process, because a net personal casualty loss remains and it is from a Federally declared disaster area, Emmanuel can deduct the loss that exceeds the 10%-of-AGI floor. Emmanuel's itemized deduction for casualty losses is $3,500, computed as follows:

Net personal casualty loss	$ 8,500
Less: 10% of AGI (10% × $50,000)	(5,000)
Itemized deduction for casualty loss	$ 3,500

[20] § 165(h)(5)(B); personal casualty gains and losses are defined at § 165(h)(3).

Calculating Personal Casualty Gains and Losses

Example 19

Refer back to the facts of Example 18. How would the answer change if the casualty loss related to Asset B was $4,000 (rather than $2,500)?

Emmanuel would first offset the non-Federally declared disaster area losses against the personal casualty gain, resulting in an excess personal casualty loss of $1,500:

Personal casualty gain	$ 2,500
Personal casualty loss (non-Federally declared disaster area)	(4,000)
Excess personal casualty loss	($ 1,500)

Since this net loss relates to a non-Federally declared disaster area, the loss is *not* deductible. Emmanuel's itemized deduction for casualty losses is $4,000, computed as follows:

Personal casualty loss (Federally declared disaster area)	$ 9,000
Less: 10% of AGI (10% × $50,000)	(5,000)
Itemized deduction for casualty loss	$ 4,000

Concept Summary 6.2 summarizes the tax treatment of casualty gains and losses.

Concept Summary 6.2

Casualty Gains and Losses

	Business Use or Income-Producing Property	Personal Use Property
Event creating the loss	Any event.	Casualty from a Federally declared disaster area.
Amount	The lesser of the decline in fair market value or the adjusted basis, but always the adjusted basis if the property is totally destroyed.	The lesser of the decline in fair market value or the adjusted basis.
Insurance	Insurance proceeds received reduce the amount of the loss.	Insurance proceeds received (or for which there is an unfiled claim) reduce the amount of the loss.
$100 floor	Not applicable.	Applicable per casualty.
Gains and losses	Gains and losses are netted (see detailed discussion in Chapter 8).	Personal casualty and theft gains and losses are netted. An ordering rule requires that gains are first reduced by losses from a non-Federally declared disaster, and only then by losses from a Federally declared disaster. Only net losses from Federally declared disasters are allowed for 2018 through 2025.
Gains exceeding losses	See Chapter 8.	Treat as gains and losses from the sale of capital assets.
Losses exceeding gains	See Chapter 8.	Casualty gain is first offset by personal casualty loss not from a Federally declared disaster. If net gain results, it is then reduced by loss from Federally declared disasters. For personal use property, any loss allowed must be from a Federally declared disaster. The loss is only allowed to the extent it exceeds 10% of AGI and only if the individual itemizes deductions rather than claiming the standard deduction. The losses in excess of gains, to the extent that they exceed 10% of AGI, are itemized deductions (*from* AGI).

Digging Deeper 6

For more information on personal use property gains and losses, visit this book's companion website: www.cengage.com

6-4 Net Operating Losses

LO.4

Describe the impact of the net operating loss carryover provisions.

Taxpayers who report net operating losses, in which deductions exceed gross income, cannot compute the tax on negative income—taxable income is zero in this case. A **net operating loss (NOL)** in a particular tax year would produce no tax benefits if the Code did not provide for a carryforward of such losses to profitable years to smooth income over time.

6-4a Introduction

The requirement that every taxpayer file an annual income tax return (whether on a calendar year or a fiscal year) can lead to inequities for taxpayers who experience uneven income over a series of years. These inequities result from the application of progressive tax rates to taxable income determined annually.

To provide partial relief from this inequitable tax treatment, individuals and corporations can deduct net operating losses (NOLs) carried forward to future tax years.[21] This provision permits an NOL for any one year to offset taxable income in future years. The NOL provision provides relief only for losses from the operation of a trade or business or from casualty and theft.

Example 20

Orange Corporation realizes the following taxable income or loss over a five-year period: year 1, $50,000; year 2, ($30,000); year 3, $100,000; year 4, ($200,000); and year 5, $220,000. Blue Corporation has taxable income of $28,000 every year. Assume that there is no provision for carryback or carryover of net operating losses. Orange and Blue would have the following five-year tax liabilities (applying the corporate tax rate of 21%):

Year	Orange's Tax	Blue's Tax
1	$ 10,500	$5,880
2	–0–	5,880
3	21,000	5,880
4	–0–	5,880
5	46,200	5,880
	$ 77,700	$29,400

Note: The computation of tax is made without regard to any NOL benefit.

Even though Orange and Blue realized the same total taxable income ($140,000) over the five-year period, Orange would have to pay taxes of $77,700, while Blue would pay taxes of only $29,400.

Partnerships and S corporations cannot deduct NOLs because they pass their income through to their owners. For C corporations, the NOL equals any negative taxable income for the year, with an adjustment for the dividends received deduction (see text Section 12-4a). In addition, deductions for prior-year NOLs are not allowed when determining a current-year NOL.

6-4b General NOL Rules

The mechanism providing a tax benefit from the NOL is the provision that allows a loss deduction in profitable years of the business activity. Taxpayers can carry forward the loss to future years.

NOL Carryforwards and the 80 Percent Limit

A current-year NOL is carried forward indefinitely following the loss year. When an NOL is carried forward, the current return shows an NOL deduction for the prior year's loss. For taxable years beginning before January 1, 2021, there was no limit on an NOL deduction.[22]

[21] § 172.

[22] § 172(a)(1).

For taxable years beginning after December 31, 2020, an NOL deduction is limited to 80 percent of taxable income before any NOL deductions. If the NOL carryover is less than the 80 percent limitation amount, the taxpayer can deduct the entire carryover.[23]

Now apply the NOL rules to Example 20 for Orange Corporation. The year 2 $30,000 loss reduces Orange's year 3 income to $70,000. In addition, the $200,000 year 4 loss reduces Orange's year 5 taxable income by $176,000 (the 80% limit on NOL carryforwards applies in year 5: $220,000 × 80% = $176,000), resulting in final year 5 taxable income of $44,000 ($220,000 − $176,000).

The result of these NOL carryforwards is to reduce the income tax liability in year 3 to $14,700 and in year 5 to $9,240 ($44,000 × 21%). Thus, the NOL rules have reduced Orange Corporation's five-year income tax liabilities by $43,260 ($21,000 + $46,200 − $14,700 − $9,240). Note that Orange still pays $5,040 more total tax than Blue even with the NOL rules ($10,500 + $14,700 + $9,240 − $29,400).

Digging Deeper 7

For more information on NOLs for individuals, visit this book's companion website: www.cengage.com

LO.5

Explain the tax shelter problem and the reasons for at-risk and passive activity loss limitations.

6-5 The Tax Shelter Problem

Before Congress enacted legislation in the 1980s to reduce their effectiveness, **tax shelters** provided a popular way to avoid or defer taxes, since they could generate losses and other tax benefits to offset income from other sources. The tax avoidance potential of tax shelters attracted high-income taxpayers with high marginal tax rates. Many tax shelters merely provided an opportunity for "investors" to obtain tax deductions and credits in ventures that investors did not expect to generate before-tax profits until they sold the investment.

Although it may seem odd that a taxpayer would intentionally invest in an activity that was designed to produce losses, there is a logical explanation. The typical tax shelter took advantage of accelerated deductions related to an activity (e.g., accelerated cost recovery or depletion). These deductions generated ordinary losses in the activity's early years that could offset the investor's other sources of income (e.g., salary, interest, and dividends) and deferred the recognition of the economic profits (if any) until the activity was sold. Depending on the activity, any gain recognized on the sale might be taxed at lower capital gains rates. In addition, many tax shelters were financed with *nonrecourse debt*, which posed no risk of loss to the investor.[24] This meant that the expenditures generating the deductions were paid with borrowed funds, while the related debt produced interest deductions. Finally, many tax shelters were operated as limited partnerships, attracting multiple investors who were not required to actively participate in the activity (and who were protected from some risks related to participation). The following example illustrates what was possible *before* Congress enacted legislation to curb tax shelter abuses.

Bob, who earned a salary of $400,000 as a business executive and dividend income of $15,000, invested $20,000 for a 10% interest in a cattle-breeding tax shelter. He did not participate in running the business. Through the use of $800,000 of nonrecourse financing and available cash of $200,000, the partnership acquired a herd of an exotic breed of cattle costing $1,000,000. Depreciation, interest, and other deductions related to the activity resulted in a loss of $400,000, of which Bob's share was $40,000. Bob was allowed to deduct the $40,000 loss even though he had invested and stood to lose only $20,000 if the investment became worthless.

The net effect of the $40,000 deduction from the partnership was that a portion of Bob's salary and dividend income was "sheltered," and as a result, he was required to calculate his tax liability on only $375,000 of income [$415,000 (salary and dividends) − $40,000 (deduction)] rather than $415,000. If this deduction were available under current law and if Bob was in a combined Federal and state income tax bracket of 40%, a tax savings of $16,000 ($40,000 × 40%) would be generated in the first year alone.

[23] § 172(b)(1)(A). For losses arising in 2018, 2019, and 2020, taxpayers can carry *back* an NOL to the five prior tax years and then forward indefinitely. Code § 172(b)(1)(D).

[24] Nonrecourse debt is an obligation for which the borrower is not personally liable. An example of nonrecourse debt is a liability on real estate acquired by a partnership without the partnership or any of the partners assuming any liability for the mortgage. The acquired property generally is pledged as collateral for the loan.

Bridge Discipline **Bridge to Finance**

An important component in wealth maximization is to pay no more tax than the law requires given an investment's before-tax cash flow. Holding constant the before-tax cash flow, one way to reduce the cost of taxation in present value terms is to defer the payment of a tax into the future for as long as possible. This can be accomplished by reducing the taxpayer's tax base (i.e., taxable income) either by deferring the recognition of income or by accelerating the timing of deductions. As a result, to the extent that the tax cost associated with an investment alternative is reduced, the after-tax benefit from that investment and the investor's wealth position are enhanced.

For example, a common attribute of many tax-advantaged investments is the availability of tax losses that investors may claim on their own income tax returns. Many times these tax losses are the result of investment-level deductions, such as interest and accelerated depreciation deductions, that are bunched in the early years of the life of the investment rather than being due to economic woes of the investment itself.

Through the at-risk limitations and the passive activity loss rules, the tax law works to scale back the ability of taxpayers to claim tax losses flowing from certain investments. These limitations have a direct impact on *when* investors can claim loss deductions flowing from affected investments. The typical result of these provisions is that the loss deductions are deferred. Therefore, when evaluating competing investment alternatives, taxpayers must address the impact of these tax limitations in projecting the after-tax benefits that can be expected to follow.

A review of Example 22 shows that the taxpayer took a two-for-one write-off ($40,000 deduction, $20,000 amount invested). In the heyday of these types of tax shelters, promoters often promised tax deductions for the investor well in excess of the amount invested. Later years would often produce similar ordinary loss deductions. Then, at the end of the life of the investment, the investors would sell the assets, possibly producing long-term capital gains that enjoyed significantly lower tax rates. In response to these tax shelter results, Congress enacted rules in the 1980s to limit investors' ability to deduct the losses.

The first major law change aimed at reducing the tax benefits from tax shelters was the **at-risk limitation**. Its objective is to limit a taxpayer's deductions to the amount the taxpayer could actually lose from the investment (the amount "at risk") if it becomes worthless. Thus, in Example 22, the at-risk rule limits Bob's loss to $20,000—the amount Bob actually has risked personally by investing.

The second major attack on tax shelters came with the passage of the **passive activity loss** rules. These rules require the taxpayer to segregate all income and losses into three categories: active, portfolio, and passive. (Text Section 6-7 defines these categories.) In general, the passive activity loss limits *disallow* the deduction of passive activity losses against *active or portfolio income* even when the taxpayer is at risk to the extent of the loss. In general, passive activity losses can only offset passive activity income.

The third and most recent tax law change that limits the attractiveness of tax shelters is the "excess business loss" limit. This rule limits the dollar amount of deductible losses of noncorporate taxpayers. Text Section 6-8 covers this rule.

Thus, in Example 22, the passive activity loss rules disallow a current deduction for any of the loss. The loss from the tax shelter is a passive activity loss because Bob does not materially participate in the activity. Therefore, the $20,000 loss that is allowed under the at-risk rules ($40,000 total loss − $20,000 portion not "at risk") is disallowed under the passive activity loss rules because Bob does not report any passive activity income for the year—he reports only active and portfolio income. Consequently, Bob's current-year income must include his nonpassive activity income of $415,000. As explained later in this chapter, the disallowed $20,000 passive activity loss is suspended, but Bob can deduct it in a future year under certain conditions.

The following two sections explore the nature of the at-risk limits and the passive activity loss rules and their impact on investors. Congress intentionally structured these rules so that investors evaluating potential investments must consider mainly the pretax *economics* of the venture instead of the *tax benefits* or tax avoidance possibilities that an investment may generate.

Explain how the at-risk limitation and the passive activity loss rules limit deductions for losses and identify taxpayers subject to these restrictions.

6-6 At-Risk Limitations

The at-risk rules limit the deductibility of losses from business and income-producing activities. These rules, which apply to individuals and closely held corporations, are designed to prevent taxpayers from deducting losses that exceed their actual economic investment in an activity. The at-risk rules limit a taxpayer's deductible loss from an activity for any taxable year to the amount the taxpayer could actually lose if the activity fails.

While the amount at risk generally vacillates over time, the initial amount considered at risk includes:[25]

- The amount of cash and the adjusted basis of property contributed to the activity by the taxpayer, and
- Any amounts borrowed for use in the activity for which the taxpayer is personally liable or has pledged as security property not used in the activity.

This amount usually is increased each year by the taxpayer's share of income and is decreased by the taxpayer's share of deductible losses and withdrawals from the activity. In addition, because *general partners* are jointly and severally liable for recourse debts of the partnership, their at-risk amounts are increased when the partnership increases its debt and are decreased when the partnership reduces its debt. However, a taxpayer generally is *not* considered at risk for borrowed amounts if either of the following is true:

- The taxpayer is not personally liable for repayment of the debt (e.g., nonrecourse debt).
- The lender has an interest (other than as a creditor) in the activity.

An important exception provides that in the case of an activity involving the holding of real property, a taxpayer is considered at risk for his or her share of any *qualified nonrecourse financing* that is secured by real property used in the activity.[26]

A taxpayer may deduct a loss as long as the at-risk amount is positive. However, once the at-risk amount is exhausted, the taxpayer cannot deduct any remaining loss until the taxpayer has a positive at-risk amount.

Example 23

In 2022, Sue invests $40,000 in an oil partnership. The partnership incurs a first-year net loss, of which $60,000 is her share. Assume that Sue's interest in the partnership is subject to the at-risk limits but is not subject to the passive activity loss limits. Because Sue has only $40,000 of capital at risk, she cannot deduct more than $40,000 against her other income and must reduce her at-risk amount to zero ($40,000 at-risk amount − $40,000 loss deducted). Sue can carry over the nondeductible loss of $20,000 ($60,000 loss generated − $40,000 loss allowed) to 2023.

In 2023, Sue has taxable income of $15,000 from the oil partnership and invests an additional $10,000 in the venture. Her at-risk amount is now $25,000 ($0 beginning balance + $15,000 taxable income + $10,000 additional investment). This enables Sue to deduct the $20,000 carryover loss and requires her to reduce her at-risk amount to $5,000 ($25,000 at-risk amount − $20,000 carryover loss allowed).

Complicating the at-risk rules is that previously allowed losses must sometimes be recaptured as income to the extent the at-risk amount is reduced below zero.[27] This rule applies in situations such as those when the amount at risk is reduced below zero by distributions to the taxpayer or when the status of indebtedness changes from recourse to nonrecourse.

[25] § 465(b)(1).

[26] Section 465(b)(6) defines *qualified nonrecourse financing*. See also the related discussion in text Section 14-3e.

[27] § 465(e).

Concept Summary 6.3 summarizes the at-risk rules.

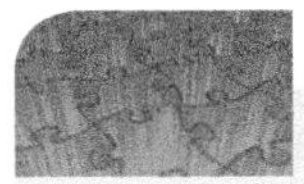

Concept Summary 6.3

Calculation of At-Risk Amount

Increases to a taxpayer's at-risk amount:

- Cash and the adjusted basis of property contributed to the activity.
- Amounts borrowed for use in the activity for which the taxpayer is personally liable or has pledged as security property that is not used in the activity.
- Taxpayer's share of amounts borrowed for use in the activity that are qualified nonrecourse financing.
- Taxpayer's share of the activity's income.

Decreases to a taxpayer's at-risk amount:

- Withdrawals from the activity.
- Taxpayer's share of the activity's deductible loss.
- Taxpayer's share of any reductions of debt for which recourse against the taxpayer exists or any reductions of qualified nonrecourse debt.

6-7 Passive Activity Loss Limits

This section identifies and explains a number of key issues in applying the passive activity loss limits.

- The limits apply only to passive activity losses incurred by certain types of taxpayers.
- These rules limit losses only if a passive activity generates them.
- Special rules exist for interests in real estate activities.
- Any suspended losses are generally allowed when a passive activity is sold.

6-7a Classification and Tax Treatment of Passive Activity Income and Loss

The passive activity loss rules in § 469 operate by requiring taxpayers to classify their income and losses into three categories: active, portfolio, or passive. Then the rules limit the extent to which losses in the passive activity category can offset income in the other categories.

Classification

Active income includes:

- Wages, salary, commissions, bonuses, and other payments for services rendered by the taxpayer.
- Profit from a trade or business in which the taxpayer is a material participant (material participation is described later in the chapter).

Portfolio income includes:

- Interest, dividends, annuities, and royalties not derived in the ordinary course of a trade or business.
- Gain or loss from the disposition of property that produces portfolio income or is held for investment purposes.

Passive activity income or loss arises from activities that are treated as passive, which include:

- Any trade or business or income-producing activity in which the taxpayer does not materially participate.
- Subject to certain exceptions (discussed later in the chapter), all rental activities, whether or not the taxpayer materially participates.

General Impact

Losses or expenses generated by passive activities can only be deducted to the extent of income from passive activities. Taxpayers cannot use excess passive losses to offset income from active or portfolio income. Instead, unused passive activity losses are suspended and carried forward to future years to offset future passive activity income. In addition, taxpayers can deduct any remaining suspended losses when they dispose of their entire interest in an activity. In that event, generally, all current and suspended passive activity losses related to the activity may offset active and portfolio income.

The Big Picture

Example 24

Return to the facts of *The Big Picture* on p. 6-1. Recall that Robyn invested $20,000 in the Florida orange grove limited partnership, which produced an allocable $20,000 loss for her this year. Assume that Robyn earns a salary of $100,000 along with $12,000 in dividends and interest from various portfolio investments. Because her at-risk basis in the partnership is $20,000, the current $20,000 loss is not limited by the at-risk rules. However, because the loss is a passive activity loss, it is not deductible against her other income. Robin must suspend and carry the loss forward to the future. If she has passive activity income from this investment or from other passive activities in the future, she can use the suspended loss to reduce or eliminate that passive activity income. If she has no passive activity income in the future, she can offset the suspended loss against other types of income only when or if she disposes of her investment in the passive activity.

Impact of Suspended Losses

The actual economic gain or loss from a passive investment (including any suspended losses) is determinable when a taxpayer disposes of his or her entire interest in the investment. This is why the passive activity loss rules described above allow an overall loss realized from the taxpayer's activity to offset passive, active, and portfolio income in the year when a fully taxable disposition occurs. However, there is a strict ordering rule for using suspended passive activity losses, as the next paragraphs describe.

A fully taxable disposition generally involves a sale of the property to a third party at arm's length and presumably for a price equal to the property's fair market value. As presented in the following example, a gain recognized on the transfer of an interest in a passive activity generally is treated as passive and is first offset by the suspended passive activity losses from that activity.

Example 25

Chloe sells an apartment building, a passive activity, with an adjusted basis of $500,000 for $580,000. In addition, she has suspended passive activity losses of $60,000 associated with the building. Her total gain, $80,000, and her taxable gain, $20,000, are calculated as follows:

Net sales price	$580,000
Less: Adjusted basis	(500,000)
Total gain	$ 80,000
Less: Suspended losses	(60,000)
Taxable gain (passive)	$ 20,000

As highlighted in Example 25, gain recognized on the sale of a passive activity generally is treated as passive and is first offset by any suspended passive activity losses from that activity. This accomplishes the purpose of determining the true economic gain or loss from the activity.

But what happens if the suspended losses exceed the gain recognized or the sale results in a loss? In this case, the excess loss can offset other income in the following order:

1. Net passive activity income or gains (if any), and
2. Nonpassive income or gains (active or portfolio).

Dean sells an apartment building, a passive activity, with an adjusted basis of $600,000 for $650,000. In addition, he has current and suspended passive activity losses of $60,000 associated with the building and has no other passive activities. His total gain of $50,000 and his deductible loss of $10,000 are calculated as follows:

Net sales price	$650,000
Less: Adjusted basis	(600,000)
Total gain	$ 50,000
Less: Suspended losses	(60,000)
Deductible loss (not passive)	($ 10,000)

Dean can deduct the $10,000 loss against his active and portfolio income. Even if the building is sold for a loss (i.e., the adjusted basis exceeds the sales price), the total loss, including the suspended losses, is deductible against portfolio and active income in the sale year.

Carryovers of Suspended Passive Activity Losses

The preceding examples assumed that the taxpayer had an interest in only one passive activity; as a result, the suspended loss related exclusively to the activity just sold. However, taxpayers sometimes own more than one passive activity, in which case any suspended losses must be allocated among those passive activities that generated losses. The allocation to an activity is made by multiplying the disallowed passive activity loss from all activities using the following fraction:

$$\frac{\textbf{Loss from one passive activity}}{\textbf{Sum of losses for taxable year from all passive activities having losses}}$$

Diego has investments in three passive activities with the following income and losses for 2021:

Activity A	($30,000)
Activity B	(20,000)
Activity C	25,000
Net passive activity loss	($25,000)
Net passive activity loss of $25,000 allocated to:	
Activity A [$25,000 × ($30,000 ÷ $50,000)]	($15,000)
Activity B [$25,000 × ($20,000 ÷ $50,000)]	(10,000)
Total suspended losses	($25,000)

Suspended losses are carried over indefinitely and are offset in the future, first against any passive activity income from the activities to which they relate and then against passive activity income from other passive activities.[28] Taxpayers subject to the passive activity loss limitation rule must maintain records to track the suspended losses and the activities to which they belong. This required tracking is important because Diego in Example 27 might, for example, sell Activity B and keep the others.

Assume that the facts are the same as in the preceding example and that in 2022, Activity A produces $10,000 of income. Diego may use $10,000 of Activity A's suspended loss of $15,000 from 2021 to offset the $10,000 income from this activity.

If Diego sells Activity A in early 2023, the remaining $5,000 suspended loss can offset any income from the activity reported by Diego in 2023 and to determine his final gain or loss.

[28] § 469(b).

Passive Activity Credits

Credits (such as the low-income housing credit and rehabilitation credit—discussed in text Section 17-2) that arise from passive activities are limited in much the same way as passive activity losses. Passive activity credits can only offset regular *tax* (not taxable income) attributable to passive activity income,[29] which equals the marginal tax from the passive activities. This computation subtracts the tax excluding the passive activities from the total tax including the passive activities.

Sam owes $50,000 of tax, disregarding net passive activity income, and $80,000 of tax, considering both net passive activity and other taxable income (disregarding the credits in both cases). The amount of tax attributable to the passive activity income is $30,000.

In the preceding example, Sam can claim a maximum of $30,000 of passive activity credits; the excess credits are carried over. He can use these passive activity credits only to reduce the *regular* tax attributable to passive activity income. A taxpayer with a net passive loss in a given tax year cannot use passive activity tax credits.

Carryovers of Passive Activity Credits

Tax credits attributable to passive activities can be carried forward indefinitely, much like suspended passive activity losses. Unlike passive activity losses, however, passive activity credits are permanently lost when the activity is disposed of in a taxable transaction where a *loss* is recognized. Credits are allowed on dispositions only when there is sufficient tax on passive activity income to absorb them. That is, taxpayers cannot ever use suspended passive activity tax credits to offset the tax on active and portfolio income.

Use of Passive Activity Credits upon Disposition of an Activity

Alicia sells a passive activity for a gain of $10,000. The activity had suspended losses of $40,000 and suspended credits of $15,000. The $10,000 gain is offset by $10,000 of the suspended losses, and the remaining $30,000 of suspended losses is deductible against Alicia's active and portfolio income. However, Alicia loses the suspended credits permanently because the sale of the activity generated no additional tax.

If Alicia in the preceding example had realized a $100,000 gain on the sale of the passive activity, the suspended credits could have been used to the extent of the regular tax attributable to the net passive activity income.

Gain on sale	$100,000
Less: Suspended losses	(40,000)
Net gain	$ 60,000

If the tax attributable to the net gain of $60,000 is $15,000 or more, the entire $15,000 of suspended credits can be used. If the tax attributable to the gain is less than $15,000, the excess suspended credits are lost.

When a taxpayer has sufficient regular tax liability from passive activities to trigger the use of suspended credits, the credits lose their character as passive activity credits. They are reclassified as regular tax credits and made subject to the same limits as other credits.

Passive Activity Changes to Active

If a former passive activity becomes active because the taxpayer increased his or her involvement in the activity, suspended losses are allowed to the extent of income from the now active business.[30] If any of the suspended loss from a prior year remains, it continues to be treated as a loss from a passive activity. The excess suspended loss can

[29] § 469(d)(2).

[30] § 469(f).

be deducted against passive activity income or carried over to the next tax year and deducted to the extent of income from the now active business in the succeeding year(s).

For several years, Rebecca has owned an interest in a passive activity that has produced losses of $80,000 during that period. Because she did not have passive activity income from other sources, she could not deduct any of the activity's passive activity losses.

In the current year, she has become a material participant in the activity and her share of the business profits totals $25,000. As a result, she may use $25,000 of the suspended passive activity loss to offset the current business profits. Rebecca's remaining suspended passive activity loss from the activity is $55,000 ($80,000 − $25,000), which is carried over to future years and used to offset income from the formerly passive activity or income from other passive activities.

6-7b Taxpayers Subject to the Passive Activity Loss Rules

The passive activity loss rules apply to individuals, estates, trusts, personal service corporations, and closely held C corporations.[31] Passive activity income or loss from investments in partnerships or S corporations (see Chapters 14 and 15) flows through to the owners, and the passive activity loss rules are applied at the owner level. Consequently, it is necessary to understand how the passive activity rules apply to both entities *and* their owners (including individual taxpayers).

Personal Service Corporations

Determination of whether a corporation is a **personal service corporation** is based on rather broad definitions. A personal service corporation is a C corporation that meets both of the following conditions:

- The principal activity is the performance of personal services.
- Owner-employees substantially perform these services.

Generally, personal service corporations include those in the fields of health, law, engineering, architecture, accounting, actuarial science, performing arts, and consulting.[32] Congress intended that applying passive activity loss limitations to personal service corporations would discourage taxpayers from sheltering service-related ordinary income by creating personal service corporations and acquiring passive activities at the corporate level.

Two tax accountants who earn an aggregate of $200,000 a year in their individual practices agree to work together in a newly formed personal service corporation. Shortly after its formation, the corporation invests in a passive activity that produces a $200,000 loss during the year. Because the passive activity loss rules apply to personal service corporations, the corporation may not deduct the $200,000 passive activity loss against the $200,000 of active income.

Additional information on personal service corporations can be found on this book's companion website: www.cengage.com

8 Digging Deeper

Closely Held C Corporations

Application of the passive activity loss rules to closely held (nonpersonal service) C corporations is also intended to prevent individuals from incorporating to avoid the passive activity loss limitations. A corporation is classified as a **closely held C corporation** if at any time during the taxable year, more than 50 percent of the value of its outstanding stock is owned, directly or indirectly, by or for five or fewer individuals. Closely held C corporations (other than personal service corporations) may use passive activity losses to offset *active* income but *not portfolio* income.

[31] § 469(a).

[32] § 448(d)(2)(A).

Example 34

Silver Corporation, a closely held (nonpersonal service) C corporation, has $475,000 of passive activity losses from a rental activity, $400,000 of active income, and $100,000 of portfolio income. The corporation may offset $400,000 of the $475,000 passive activity loss against the $400,000 of active business income but may not offset the remainder against the $100,000 of portfolio income. As a result, $75,000 of the passive activity loss is suspended ($475,000 passive activity loss − $400,000 offset against active income).

Congress intended that applying the passive activity loss limitations to closely held C corporations would discourage shareholders from transferring their portfolio investments to corporations to offset passive activity losses against portfolio income.

LO.7

Describe an activity, material participation, and rental activity under the passive activity loss rules.

6-7c Rules for Determining Passive Activities

Identifying what constitutes an activity is a necessary first step in applying the passive activity loss limitation. The rules used to delineate an activity state that in general, a taxpayer can treat one or more trade or business activities or rental activities as a single activity if those activities form an *appropriate economic unit* for measuring gain or loss. The Regulations provide guidelines for identifying appropriate economic units.[33] These guidelines are designed to prevent taxpayers from arbitrarily combining different businesses in an attempt to circumvent the passive activity loss limitation. For example, combining a profitable active business and a passive business generating losses into one activity would allow the taxpayer to offset passive activity losses against active income.

Digging Deeper 9

Additional information on defining activity can be found on this book's companion website: www.cengage.com

Taxpayers must consider all relevant facts and circumstances to determine which ventures form an appropriate economic unit. However, special rules restrict the grouping of rental and nonrental activities.[34] The following example, adapted from the Regulations, illustrates the application of the activity grouping rules.[35]

Example 35

Taj owns a men's clothing store and an internet café in Chicago. He also owns a men's clothing store and an internet café in Milwaukee. Reasonable methods of applying the facts and circumstances test may result in any of the following groupings:

- All four businesses may be grouped into a single activity because of common ownership and control.
- The clothing stores may be grouped into an activity, and the internet cafés may be grouped into an activity.
- The Chicago businesses may be grouped into an activity, and the Milwaukee businesses may be grouped into an activity.
- Each of the four businesses may be treated as a separate activity.

Once a taxpayer uses the rules above to group its activities, the taxpayer cannot change the grouping unless a material change in the facts and circumstances occurs or the original grouping was clearly inappropriate. In addition, the Regulations also grant the IRS the right to regroup activities when one of the primary purposes of the taxpayer's grouping is to avoid the passive activity loss limitation and the grouping fails to reflect an appropriate economic unit.[36]

6-7d Material Participation

As indicated previously, if a taxpayer materially participates in a nonrental trade or business activity, any loss from that activity is treated as an active loss that can offset active or portfolio income. (Participation is defined later in the chapter.) If

[33]Reg. § 1.469–4.

[34]Reg. § 1.469–4(d).

[35]Reg. § 1.469–4(c)(3).

[36]Reg. § 1.469–4(f).

a taxpayer does not materially participate, however, the loss is a passive activity loss that can only offset passive activity income. As a result, controlling whether a particular activity is active or passive is an important part of the tax strategy of a taxpayer who owns an interest in one or more businesses. It is possible for a taxpayer to influence the tax outcome by increasing or decreasing participation in different activities. Examples 36 and 37 demonstrate two of the possibilities.

Implications of Material Participation Status

Noah, a corporate executive, earns a salary of $600,000 per year. In addition, he owns a separate business in which he participates. The business produces a loss of $100,000 during the year. If Noah materially participates in the business, the $100,000 loss is an active loss that may offset his active income from his corporate employer. If he does not materially participate, the loss is passive and is suspended unless he has other passive activity income. Noah may use the suspended loss in the future only when he has passive activity income or disposes of the activity.

Junghee, an attorney, earns $350,000 a year in her law practice. In addition, she owns interests in two activities, A and B, in which she participates. Activity A, in which she does not *materially* participate, produces a loss of $50,000. Junghee has not yet met the material participation standard, described below, for Activity B, which produces income of $80,000. However, she can meet the material participation standard if she spends an additional 50 hours in Activity B during the year. Should Junghee attempt to meet the material participation standard for Activity B?

If she continues working in Activity B and becomes a material participant, the $80,000 of income from the activity is active and the $50,000 passive activity loss from Activity A must be suspended. A more favorable tax strategy is for Junghee *not to meet* the material participation standard for Activity B, thus making the income from that activity passive. This enables her to offset the $50,000 passive activity loss from Activity A against most of the passive activity income from Activity B.

To the extent possible, most taxpayers will benefit by classifying profitable activities as passive so that any passive activity losses can be used to offset that passive activity income. If the activity produces a loss, however, most taxpayers will benefit if it is classified as active to avoid the passive activity loss limitations.

Temporary Regulations[37] provide seven tests (listed in Concept Summary 6.4) that serve to determine when **material participation** is achieved.

Concept Summary 6.4

Tests to Determine Material Participation

Tests Based on Current Participation

1. The individual participates in the activity for more than 500 hours during the year.
2. The individual's participation in the activity for the taxable year constitutes substantially all of the participation in the activity of all individuals (including nonowner employees) for the year.
3. The individual participates in the activity for more than 100 hours during the year, and this participation is not less than that participation of any other individual (including nonowner employees) for the year.
4. The activity is a **significant participation activity** (where the person's participation *exceeds* 100 hours during the year), and the hours for all significant participation activities during the year are more than 500 hours.

Tests Based on Prior Participation

5. The individual materially participated in the activity for any 5 taxable years during the 10 taxable years that immediately precede the current taxable year.
6. The activity is a personal service activity, and the individual materially participated in the activity for any three preceding taxable years.

Test Based on Facts and Circumstances

7. Based on all of the facts and circumstances, the individual participates in the activity on a regular, continuous, and substantial basis during the year.

[37]Temp.Reg. § 1.469–5T(a).

Digging Deeper 10 **Learn more about the material participation tests at this book's companion website: www.cengage.com**

Participation Defined

Participation generally includes any work done by an individual in an activity that he or she owns. Participation does not include work if it is of a type not customarily done by owners *and* if one of the principal purposes for the work is to avoid the disallowance of passive activity losses or credits. Work done in an individual's capacity as an investor (e.g., reviewing financial reports in a nonmanagerial capacity) is not counted in applying the material participation tests. Participation by an owner's spouse counts as participation by the owner.[38]

Emma, a partner in a CPA firm, owns a computer store that operated at a loss during the year. To offset this loss against the income from her CPA practice, Emma would like to avoid having the computer business classified as a passive activity. During the year, she worked 480 hours in the business in management and selling activities and 30 hours doing janitorial chores. In addition, Emma's spouse participated 40 hours as a salesperson.

It is likely that Emma's 480 hours of participation in management and selling activities will count as participation in work customarily done by owners, but the 30 hours spent doing janitorial chores will not. However, the 40 hours of participation by her spouse will count. Assuming that none of the participation's principal purposes is to avoid the allowance of passive activity losses or credits, Emma will qualify as a material participant under the more-than-500-hour rule (480 + 40 = 520).

Limited Partners

A *limited* partner is a partner whose liability to third-party creditors of the partnership is limited to the amount the partner has invested in the partnership. Such a partnership must have at least one *general* partner who is fully liable in an individual capacity for the debts of the partnership to third parties. Generally, *limited partners* are not material participants unless they qualify under Test 1, 5, or 6 as shown in Concept Summary 6.4. In contrast, *general partners* can qualify as material participants by meeting any of the seven tests. If a general partner also owns a limited interest in the same limited partnership, all interests are treated as a general interest.[39]

Corporations

Personal service corporations and closely held C corporations cannot directly participate in an activity. However, a corporation is deemed to materially participate if its owners materially participate in an activity of the corporation. Together, the participating owners must own directly or indirectly more than 50 percent of the value of the outstanding stock of the corporation.[40] Alternatively, a closely held C corporation may be deemed to materially participate in an activity if, during the entire year, it has at least one full-time employee actively managing the business and at least three full-time nonowner employees working for the business. In addition, the corporation's trade or business expenses must exceed, by 15 percent, the gross income from that business for the year.[41]

6-7e Rental Activities

Subject to certain exceptions, all rental activities are treated as passive activities.[42] A **rental activity** is defined as any activity where payments are received principally for the use of tangible (real or personal) property.[43] Importantly, an activity classified as a rental activity is subject to the passive activity loss rules even if the taxpayer meets a material participation test.

[38] § 469(h)(5) and Temp.Reg. § 1.469–5T(f)(3).

[39] § 469(h)(2) and Temp.Reg. § 1.469–5T(e)(3)(ii).

[40] Temp.Reg. § 1.469–1T(g)(3)(i)(A).

[41] Temp.Reg. § 1.469–1T(g)(3)(i)(B).

[42] § 469(c)(2).

[43] § 469(j)(8).

Sarah owns a fleet of automobiles that are held for rent, and she spends an average of 60 hours a week in the activity. Assuming that her automobile business is classified as a rental activity, it is automatically subject to the passive activity rules even though Sarah spends more than 500 hours a year in its operation.

For rental activities that require significant services, the regulations include exceptions from the general rule that rental activities are passive automatically.[44] In these situations, and assuming that the activity is a trade or business, the taxpayer applies the material participation tests shown in Concept Summary 6.4 to determine whether the activity is a passive activity.

Rules defining rental activities are further explained on this book's companion website: www.cengage.com

11 Digging Deeper

Arturo owns a bicycle rental business at a nearby resort. Because the average period of customer use is seven days or less, Arturo's business is not treated as a rental activity.

This exception to the definition of a rental activity is based on the presumption that a person who rents property for seven days or less is generally required to provide significant services to the customer. Providing such services supports a conclusion that the person is engaged in a service business rather than a rental business.

If Arturo in Example 40 is a material participant, the business is treated as active. If he is not a material participant, it is treated as a passive activity. For additional discussion of the rental exceptions, see IRS Publication 925 (*Passive Activity and At-Risk Rules*).

The general rules relating to passive activity losses are reviewed in Concept Summary 6.5.

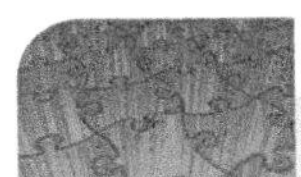

Concept Summary 6.5

Passive Activity Loss Rules: Key Issues and Answers

What is the fundamental passive activity rule?	Passive activity losses may be deducted only against passive activity income and gains. Losses not allowed are suspended and used in future years.
Who is subject to the passive activity rules?	Individuals. Estates. Trusts. Personal service corporations. Closely held C corporations.
What is a passive activity?	Trade or business or income-producing activity in which the taxpayer does not materially participate during the year or rental activities, subject to certain exceptions, regardless of the taxpayer's level of participation.
What is an activity?	One or more trades or businesses or rental activities that comprise an appropriate economic unit.
How is an appropriate economic unit determined?	Based on a reasonable application of the relevant facts and circumstances.
What is material participation?	In general, the taxpayer participates on a regular, continuous, and substantial basis. More specifically, when the taxpayer meets the conditions of one of the seven tests provided in the Regulations.
What is a rental activity?	In general, an activity where payments are received for the use of tangible property. Special rules apply to rental real estate.

[44] Temp.Reg. § 1.469–1T(e)(3).

Determine the relationship between the at-risk and passive activity loss limitations.

6-7f Interaction of At-Risk and Passive Activity Loss Limits

The determination of whether a loss is suspended under the passive activity loss rules is made *after* application of the at-risk rules, as well as other provisions relating to the measurement of taxable income. A loss that is not allowed for the year because the taxpayer is not at risk is suspended under the at-risk provisions, not under the passive activity loss rules. Further, a taxpayer's at-risk basis is reduced by the losses (but not below zero) even if the deductions are not currently usable because of the passive activity loss rules. The following examples illustrate these points.

At-Risk and Passive Activity Loss Interactions

Jack's adjusted basis in a passive activity is $10,000 at the beginning of 2020. His loss from the activity in 2020 is $4,000. Because Jack has no passive activity income, the $4,000 cannot be deducted. At year-end, Jack has an adjusted basis and an at-risk amount of $6,000 in the activity and a suspended passive activity loss of $4,000.

Jack in the preceding example has a loss of $9,000 in the activity in 2021. Because the $9,000 exceeds his at-risk amount ($6,000) by $3,000, the at-risk rules disallow the $3,000. If Jack has no passive activity income, the passive activity rules suspend the remaining $6,000 loss. At year-end, he has:

- A $3,000 loss suspended under the at-risk rules.
- $10,000 of suspended passive activity losses ($4,000 from 2020 and $6,000 from 2021).
- An adjusted basis and at-risk amount in the activity of zero.

Jack in Example 42 realizes $1,000 of passive activity income from the activity in 2022. Because the $1,000 increases his at-risk amount, $1,000 of the $3,000 unused loss from 2021 is reclassified as a passive activity loss. If he has no other passive activity income, the $1,000 income is offset by $1,000 of suspended passive activity losses. At the end of 2022, Jack has:

- No taxable passive activity income.
- $2,000 ($3,000 − $1,000) of suspended losses under the at-risk rules.
- $10,000 of (reclassified) suspended passive activity losses ($10,000 + $1,000 of reclassified suspended at-risk losses − $1,000 of passive activity losses offset against passive activity income).
- An adjusted basis and an at-risk amount in the activity of zero.

In 2023, Jack has no gain or loss from the activity in Example 43. He contributes $5,000 more to the passive activity. Because the $5,000 contribution increases his at-risk amount, the $2,000 of losses suspended under the at-risk rules is reclassified as passive. Jack gets no passive activity loss deduction in 2023. At year-end, he has:

- No suspended losses under the at-risk rules.
- $12,000 of suspended passive activity losses ($10,000 + $2,000 of reclassified suspended at-risk losses).
- An adjusted basis and an at-risk amount of $3,000 ($5,000 additional investment − $2,000 of reclassified losses).

See Concept Summary 6.6 for the interactions of the at-risk and passive activity loss limits.

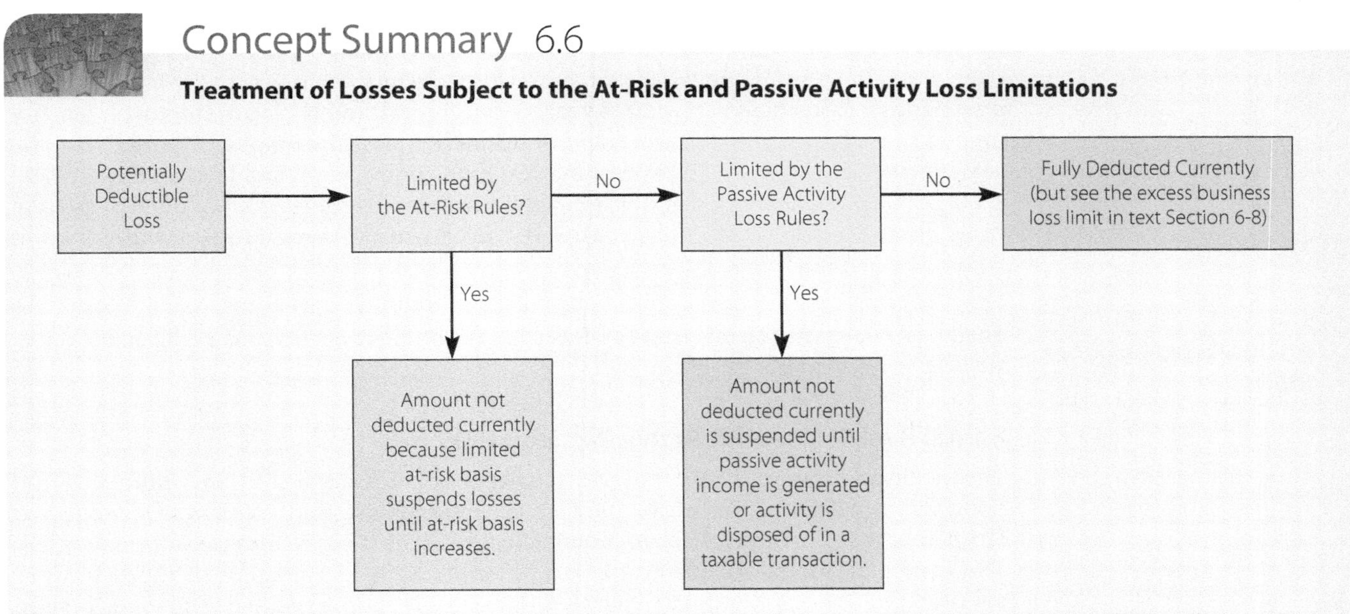

6-7g Special Passive Activity Rules for Real Estate

Explain the special treatment available to real estate activities.

The passive activity loss rules contain two exceptions related to real estate activities. These exceptions allow all or part of real estate rental losses to offset active or portfolio income even though the activity otherwise is defined as a passive activity.

Real Estate Professionals

The first exception allows certain real estate professionals to avoid passive activity treatment for rental real estate activities.[45] To potentially qualify for nonpassive treatment (of both income and losses), a taxpayer must satisfy both of the following requirements:

- More than half of the personal services that the taxpayer performs in trades or businesses are performed in real property trades or businesses in which the taxpayer materially participates.
- The taxpayer performs more than 750 hours of services in real property trades or businesses in which the taxpayer materially participates.

If these two requirements are met, taxpayers are allowed to apply the material participation tests to their rental real estate activities (i.e., the rentals are not passive activities automatically). Taxpayers who do not satisfy the above requirements (or who meet them but do not materially participate in their rental real estate activities) must continue to treat income and losses from real estate rental activities as passive activity income and losses.

During the current year, Della performs personal service activities as follows: 900 hours as a personal financial planner, 550 hours in a real estate development business, and 600 hours in a rental real estate activity. Any loss Della incurs in either real estate activity will not be subject to the passive activity loss rules if she meets one of the material participation tests. Because it is a nonrental business, the real estate development business is deemed active under the more-than-500-hour material participation test. In addition, Della meets the two requirements to qualify as a real estate professional [i.e., more than 50% of her personal services relate to real property trades or businesses (i.e., the development and rental) and these hours exceed 750]. As a result, Della can apply the material participation tests to the real estate rental activity, and she meets the more-than-500-hours test. Hence, any losses from Della's rental real estate activity can offset active and portfolio income. Likewise, any income from this activity is nonpassive (active) income.

[45] § 469(c)(7).

As discussed earlier, taxpayers generally can include a spouse's work in satisfying the material participation requirement. However, the hours worked by a spouse are *not* considered in determining whether the two tests are met for hours worked in real property trades or businesses during a year. Services performed by an employee are not treated as relating to a real estate trade or business unless the employee performing the services owns more than a 5 percent interest in the employer. In addition, a closely held C corporation may also qualify for the passive activity loss relief if more than 50 percent of its gross receipts for the year are derived from real property trades or businesses in which it materially participates.[46]

Digging Deeper 12

Additional information on real estate professionals can be found on this book's companion website: www.cengage.com

Rental Real Estate with Active Participation

The second exception to the passive activity loss limits applies to any individual and not only to real estate professionals. This exception allows individuals to deduct up to $25,000 of losses from real estate rental activities against active and portfolio income.[47] The potential annual $25,000 deduction is reduced by 50 percent of the taxpayer's adjusted gross income (AGI) in excess of $100,000. Thus, the entire deduction is phased out at $150,000 of AGI. If married individuals file separately, the $25,000 deduction is reduced to zero unless they lived apart for the entire year, in which case the loss amount is $12,500 each and the phaseout begins at $50,000 of AGI.

To qualify for the $25,000 exception, a taxpayer must meet both of the following requirements:[48]

- *Actively participate* in the real estate rental activity.
- Own 10 percent or more (in value) of all interests in the activity during the entire taxable year (or shorter period during which the taxpayer held an interest in the activity).

The difference between *active participation* and *material participation* is that the former can be satisfied without regular, continuous, and substantial involvement in operations as long as the taxpayer participates in making management decisions in a significant and bona fide sense. In this context, relevant management decisions include decisions such as approving new tenants, deciding on rental terms, and approving capital or repair expenditures.

The $25,000 allowance is available after all active participation rental losses and gains are netted and applied to other passive activity income. If a taxpayer has a real estate rental loss in excess of the amount that can be deducted under the real estate rental exception, that excess is treated as a passive activity loss, usable in future years.

Brad has $90,000 of AGI before considering rental activities. Brad also has $85,000 of losses from a real estate rental activity in which he actively participates. He also actively participates in another real estate rental activity from which he has $30,000 of income. He has other passive activity income of $36,000.

Of the net rental loss of $55,000 ($30,000 − $85,000), $36,000 is absorbed by the passive activity income, leaving $19,000 that Brad can deduct against active or portfolio income.

The $25,000 offset allowance is an aggregate of both deductions and credits in deduction equivalents. The deduction equivalent of a passive activity credit is the amount of deductions that reduces the tax liability for the taxable year by an amount equal to the credit.[49] A taxpayer with $2,200 of credits and a marginal tax rate of 22 percent would have a deduction equivalent of $10,000 ($2,200 ÷ 22%).

If total deductions and deduction equivalents exceed $25,000, the taxpayer must allocate the benefit on a pro rata basis. First, the allowance must be allocated among the losses (including real estate rental activity losses suspended in prior years) and then to credits.

[46] § 469(c)(7)(B) and Reg. § 1.469–9. In *Frank Aragona Trust*, 142 T.C. 165 (2014), the Tax Court found that a trust also could qualify for the real estate professional rule.

[47] § 469(i).

[48] § 469(i)(6).

[49] § 469(j)(5).

Deduction Equivalent Considerations

Kevin is an active participant in a real estate rental activity that produces $8,000 of income, $26,000 of deductions, and $1,500 of credits. Kevin is a single taxpayer with $98,000 of AGI (before considering this rental activity) and a 22% marginal tax rate. He can deduct the net passive activity loss of $18,000 ($8,000 − $26,000).

After deducting the loss, he has an available deduction equivalent of $7,000 ($25,000 − $18,000 passive activity loss). Because the actual credits produce a $6,818 deduction equivalent ($1,500 ÷ 25% = $6,000) and this amount is less than $7,000, Kevin may claim the entire $1,500 credit.

Example 48

Kelly is an active participant in three separate real estate rental activities. Kelly is a single taxpayer with $92,000 of AGI before considering these rental activities and is in the 22% tax bracket. The relevant tax results for each activity are as follows:

- Activity A: $20,000 of losses.
- Activity B: $10,000 of losses.
- Activity C: $1,100 of credits.

Kelly's deduction equivalent from the credits is $5,000 ($1,100 ÷ 22%). As a result, the total passive activity deductions and deduction equivalents are $35,000 ($20,000 + $10,000 + $5,000), which exceeds the maximum allowable amount of $25,000. Consequently, Kelly must allocate pro rata first from among losses and then from among credits. Deductions from losses are limited as follows:

- Activity A: $25,000 × [$20,000 ÷ ($20,000 + $10,000)] = $16,667.
- Activity B: $25,000 × [$10,000 ÷ ($20,000 + $10,000)] = $8,333.

Because the amount of passive activity deductions exceeds the $25,000 maximum, Kelly must carry forward the remaining $5,000 passive activity loss and the $1,100 passive activity credits. Kelly's suspended losses and credits by activity are as follows:

		Activity		
	Total	A	B	C
Allocated losses	$ 30,000	$ 20,000	$10,000	$ −0−
Allocated credits	1,100	−0−	−0−	1,100
Utilized losses	(25,000)	(16,667)	(8,333)	−0−
Suspended losses	5,000	3,333	1,667	−0−
Suspended credits	1,100	−0−	−0−	1,100

6-7h Disposition of Passive Activities

Determine the consequences of the disposition of passive activities.

Recall from the earlier discussion that if a taxpayer disposes of an entire interest in a passive activity, any suspended losses (and in certain cases, suspended credits) may be utilized when calculating the final taxable gain or loss on the investment. In addition, if a loss ultimately results, that loss can offset other types of income. However, the consequences may differ if the activity is disposed of in a transaction that is not fully taxable. The following sections discuss the treatment of suspended passive activity losses in two such dispositions.

Disposition of a Passive Activity at Death

When a transfer of a taxpayer's interest occurs because of the taxpayer's death, suspended losses are allowed (to the decedent) only to the extent they exceed the amount, if any, of the allowed step-up in basis.[50] Suspended losses that are equal to or less than the amount of the basis increase are, however, lost. The losses allowed generally are deducted on the final return of the deceased taxpayer.

[50] § 469(g)(2). Chapter 7 discusses this rule in depth.

Disposition of Suspended Losses at Death

Alyson dies with passive activity property having an adjusted basis of $40,000, suspended losses of $10,000, and a fair market value at the date of her death of $75,000. The increase (i.e., step-up) in basis (see text Section 7-2c) is $35,000 (fair market value at date of death in excess of adjusted basis). None of the $10,000 suspended loss is deductible on Alyson's final return or by the beneficiary. The suspended losses ($10,000) are lost because they do not exceed the step-up in basis ($35,000).

Assume the same facts as in the previous example except that the property's fair market value at the date of Alyson's death is $47,000. Because the step-up in basis is only $7,000 ($47,000 − $40,000), the suspended losses allowed are limited to $3,000 ($10,000 suspended loss at time of death − $7,000 increase in basis). The $3,000 loss available to Alyson is deducted on her final income tax return.

Disposition of a Passive Activity by Gift

In a disposition of a taxpayer's interest in a passive activity by gift, the suspended losses are added to the basis of the property.[51]

As such, the suspended losses become permanently nondeductible to both the donor and the donee. Nonetheless, a tax *benefit* may be available to the donee for another reason. The increase in the property's basis can result in greater depreciation deductions and less gain (or more loss) on a later sale of the property.

Carlton gives Maddie passive activity property having an adjusted basis of $40,000, suspended losses of $10,000, and a fair market value at the date of the gift of $100,000. Carlton cannot deduct the suspended losses in the year of the disposition. However, the suspended losses of $10,000 transfer with the property and are added to the adjusted basis of the property, resulting in a $50,000 basis in Emma's hands.

Assuming that Maddie can sell the property for $105,000 soon after she receives the gift, her taxable gain will be $55,000 ($105,000 − $50,000), which reflects the benefit from the increased basis.

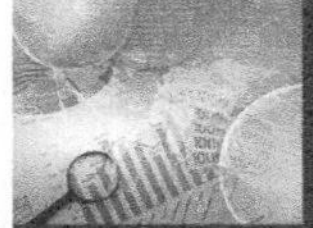

Tax Planning Strategies — Utilizing Passive Activity Losses

Framework Focus: Tax Rate

Strategy: Control the Character of Income and Deductions.

Perhaps the biggest challenge individuals face with the passive activity loss rules is to recognize the potential impact of the rules and then to structure their affairs to minimize this impact. Taxpayers who have passive activity losses (PALs) should adopt a strategy of generating passive activity income that can be sheltered by existing passive activity losses. One approach is to buy an interest in a passive activity that is generating income (referred to as a passive income generator, or PIG). Then the PAL can offset income from the PIG. From a tax perspective, it would be inefficient to buy a loss-generating passive activity unless one has passive activity income to shelter or the activity is rental real estate that can qualify for the $25,000 exception or the exception available to real estate professionals.

If a taxpayer invests in an activity that produces losses subject to the passive activity loss rules, the following strategies may help minimize the loss of current deductions:

- If money is borrowed to finance the purchase of a passive activity, the associated interest expense is generally treated as part of any passive activity loss. Consequently, by using more available (i.e., not borrowed) cash to purchase the passive investment, the investor will need less debt and will incur less interest expense. By incurring less interest expense, a possible suspended passive activity loss deduction is reduced.

continued

[51] § 469(j)(6).

- If the investor does not have sufficient cash readily available for the larger down payment, cash can be obtained by borrowing against the equity in his or her personal residence. The interest expense on such debt will be deductible under the qualified residence interest provisions (see text Section 10-4c) and will not be subject to the passive activity loss limitations. Thus, the taxpayer avoids the passive activity loss limitation and secures a currently deductible interest expense.

As explained earlier, unusable passive activity losses often accumulate and provide no current tax benefit because the taxpayer has no passive activity income. When the taxpayer disposes of the entire interest in a passive activity, however, any suspended losses from that activity reduce the taxable gain. Any remaining taxable gain can be offset by losses from other passive activities. As a result, the taxpayer should carefully select the year in which to dispose of a passive activity. It is to the taxpayer's advantage to wait until sufficient passive activity losses have accumulated to offset any gain recognized on the asset's disposition.

Bill, a calendar year taxpayer, owns interests in two passive activities: Activity A, which he plans to sell in December of this year at a gain of $100,000, and Activity B, which he plans to keep indefinitely. Current and suspended losses associated with Activity B total $60,000, and Bill expects losses from the activity to be $40,000 next year. If Bill sells Activity A this year, the $100,000 gain can be offset by the current and suspended losses of $60,000 from Activity B, producing a net taxable gain of $40,000. However, if Bill delays the sale of Activity A until January of next year, the $100,000 gain will be fully offset by the $100,000 of losses generated by Activity B ($60,000 current and prior losses + $40,000 next year's loss). Consequently, by postponing the sale by one month, he could avoid recognizing $40,000 of gain that would otherwise result.

Taxpayers with passive activity losses should consider the level of their involvement in all other trades or businesses in which they have an interest. If they show that they do not materially participate in a profitable activity, the activity becomes a passive activity. Current and suspended passive activity losses then could shelter any income generated by the profitable business. Family partnerships in which certain members do not materially participate would qualify. The silent partner in any general partnership engaged in a trade or business would also qualify.

Gail has an investment in a limited partnership that produces annual passive activity losses of approximately $25,000. She also owns a newly acquired interest in a convenience store where she works. Her share of the store's income is $35,000. If she works enough to be classified as a material participant, her $35,000 share of income is treated as active income. This results in $35,000 being subject to tax every year, while her $25,000 loss is suspended. However, if Gail reduces her involvement at the store so that she is not a material participant, the $35,000 of income receives passive treatment. Consequently, the $35,000 of income can be offset by the $25,000 passive activity loss, resulting in only $10,000 being subject to tax. Thus, by reducing her involvement, Gail ensures that the income from the profitable trade or business receives passive treatment and can then be used to absorb passive activity losses from other passive activities.

The passive activity loss rules can have a dramatic effect on a taxpayer's ability to claim passive activity losses currently. As a result, it is important to keep accurate records of all sources of income and losses, particularly any suspended passive activity losses and credits and the activities to which they relate, so that their potential tax benefit will not be lost.

The passive activity rules can also affect planning for individuals subject to the Net Investment Income Tax (text Section 9-5e).

6-8 Excess Business Losses

Describe and compute the excess business loss limitation.

Text Section 6-7 reviewed the limits Congress enacted on passive activity losses. However, taxpayers had a tax incentive to incur excessive active activity losses. In fact, that incentive would have increased after enactment of the passive activity loss limits. As part of Congress's efforts to curb excessive tax losses, the 2017 tax act limits a taxpayer's overall ability to currently deduct active business losses above a specified amount.

Specifically, a noncorporate taxpayer cannot deduct an **excess business loss**.[52] Instead, taxpayers carry the loss forward and treat it as part of the taxpayer's net operating loss (NOL) carryforward in later years (text Section 6-4 discusses NOLs).

6-8a Definition and Rules

An *excess business loss* is defined as the following items for the year attributable to the taxpayer's trades or businesses:[53]

The aggregate deductions

Less: The sum of aggregate gross income or gain

Less: A threshold amount (in 2022, $540,000 for married taxpayers filing a joint return; $270,000 for all other taxpayers). The threshold amounts are adjusted for inflation each year.

The purpose of the excess business loss limitation is to limit the amount of nonbusiness income (e.g., salaries, interest, dividends, and capital gains) that business losses can shelter with business losses. The excess business loss limitation is applied *after* the application of the § 469 passive loss rules. Given this requirement, losses from *passive* trades or businesses (e.g., a business in which the taxpayer does not materially participate) are limited first by the passive activity loss rules, and once the losses are allowed under § 469, they are subject to the excess business loss rule.

For a partnership or an S corporation, this excess business loss limitation applies at the partner or shareholder level.[54] Each partner or S corporation shareholder must consider their share of items of income, gain, deduction, or loss of the partnership or S corporation in applying the limitation each tax year.

6-8b Computing the Limit

The following examples illustrate the operation and effect of the excess business loss limitation.

Computing the Excess Business Loss Limit

In 2022, Tonya, a single taxpayer, operates a sole proprietorship in which she materially participates. Her proprietorship generates gross income of $320,000 and deductions of $600,000, resulting in a loss of $280,000. The large deductions are due to the acquisition of equipment and the use of immediate expense and additional first-year depreciation to deduct all of the acquisitions. Tonya's excess business loss is $18,000, computed as follows:

Aggregate business deductions	$ 600,000
Less: Aggregate business gross income and gains	(320,000)
Less: Threshold amount	(270,000)
Excess business loss	$ 10,000

So Tonya can deduct $270,000 of the $280,000 proprietorship loss to offset nonbusiness income. The $10,000 excess business loss becomes part of Tonya's NOL carryforward to later tax years.

Assume the same facts as in the previous example, except that Tonya is married and files a joint return. In this case, Tonya does not have an excess business loss due to the increased threshold amount.

Aggregate business deductions	$ 600,000
Less: Aggregate business gross income and gains	(320,000)
Less: Threshold amount	(540,000)
Excess business loss	$ None

As a result, Tonya's $280,000 sole proprietorship loss is fully deductible and can offset nonbusiness income (e.g., her spouse's wages or their interest and dividend income).

[52] § 461(l). This loss limitation rule applies to taxable years beginning after December 31, 2020 and before January 1, 2027.

[53] § 461(l)(3).

[54] § 461(l)(4)(A).

The excess business loss limitation applies to the aggregate gross income and deductions from all of a taxpayer's trades or businesses.[55] So a married couple filing a joint return must consolidate information from all of the couple's trades or businesses. Further, as noted in Example 55, if married taxpayers file a joint return, the losses of one spouse can offset the other spouse's nonbusiness income (up to the $540,000 limit in 2022).

The last example illustrates application of the excess business loss limitation in a flow-through entity scenario.

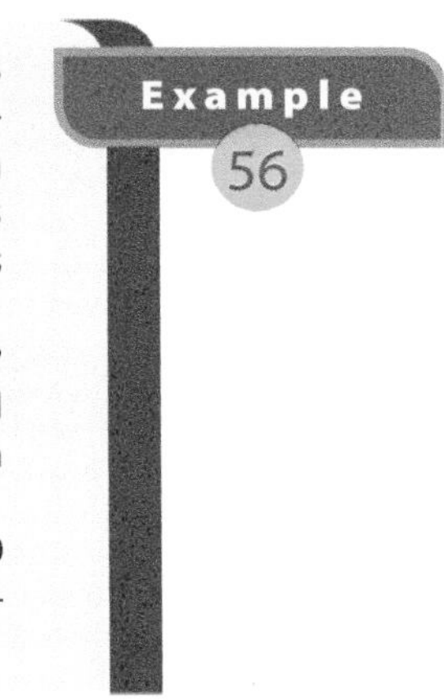

Jayson, a single taxpayer, is an S corporation shareholder and materially participates in the entity's grocery store business. During 2022, the store had a large depreciation deduction causing a substantial loss. Jayson has a flow-through loss of $345,000 from the S corporation. He also received a $78,000 salary from the corporation. At the beginning of the year, Jayson had a $520,000 basis in his S corporation shares—enough to absorb the S corporation loss. Because he materially participates in the business, it is not a passive activity.

However, Jayson's flow-through loss exceeds the $270,000 excess business loss threshold by $75,000 ($345,000 − $270,000). So Jayson can deduct $270,000 (and use it to offset his salary and other nonbusiness income). The $75,000 excess is not deductible in 2022, but carries forward as a net operating loss.

Assume that in 2023, the grocery store business generates a profit and flows through $210,000 of income to Jayson. Jayson can deduct the 2022 excess business loss of $75,000 against this flow-through income as a Net Operating Loss.

Refocus on The Big Picture

Receiving Tax Benefits from Losses

While Robyn's circumstances were unfortunate, the good news is that she will receive some tax benefits from the losses.

- *Bad debt.* Based on the facts provided, it appears that Robyn's loan to her friend, Jamil, was a bona fide nonbusiness bad debt. The amount of the loss deduction is the unpaid principal balance of $19,000 ($25,000 − $6,000). As a nonbusiness bad debt, the loss is classified as a short-term capital loss.
- *Loss from stock investment.* Likewise, the $60,000 loss on the Owl Corporation stock investment is deductible. If Robyn purchased the stock directly from the company, the stock may qualify as small business stock under § 1244. If this is the case, the first $50,000 of the loss is an ordinary loss and the remaining $10,000 loss is treated as a long-term capital loss. If the stock is not § 1244 stock, the entire $60,000 loss is treated as a long-term capital loss.
- *Loss from bookstore.* The $180,000 loss from the bookstore is reported on Schedule C of Robyn's Form 1040. It is an ordinary loss and qualifies for net operating loss (NOL) treatment if she does not have enough other taxable income this year against which the loss can be offset. Robyn can carry the loss forward to reduce taxes owed on taxable income earned in the future.
- *Casualty loss.* The loss from the damage to Robyn's bookstore is a business casualty loss. Using the cost of repairs method, the amount of the casualty loss is $7,000 ($32,000 loss − $25,000 insurance recovery). Robyn deducts this loss above the line (*for* AGI).

continued

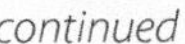

[55] § 461(l)(3)(A)(i).

- *Passive activity loss.* The $20,000 loss on the limited partnership is not deductible currently due to the passive activity loss limitation. However, the loss can be carried forward and utilized in the future to offset any passive activity income generated from the venture or other passive activities (see Example 24).

What If?

What if instead of operating orange groves, the partnership was a general partnership that owns and rents apartments to college students and Robyn actively participates in the venture? In this case, Robyn may qualify for a $20,000 ordinary loss deduction under the rental real estate with active participation exception.

Suggested Readings

Albert B. Ellentuck, "Deducting Business Bad Debts," *The Tax Adviser*, March 2016.

Hale E. Sheppard, "Special Rules for Claiming Disaster Losses: Remedies For Taxpayers Who Miss Election Deadlines," *Practical Tax Strategies*, February 2020.

Key Terms

Active income, 6-17
At-risk limitation, 6-15
Bad debt, 6-2
Business bad debt, 6-4
Casualty losses, 6-7
Closely held C corporation, 6-21
Disaster area losses, 6-8
Excess business loss, 6-32
Material participation, 6-23
Net operating loss (NOL), 6-13
Nonbusiness bad debt, 6-4
Passive activity loss, 6-15
Personal service corporation, 6-21
Portfolio income, 6-17
Rental activity, 6-24
Significant participation activity, 6-23
Small business stock (§ 1244 stock), 6-6
Specific charge-off method, 6-3
Tax shelters, 6-14
Theft losses, 6-9
Worthless securities, 6-5

Computational Exercises

1. **LO.1** Last year Aleshia identified $15,000 as a nonbusiness bad debt. In that tax year, before considering the tax implications of the nonbusiness bad debt, Aleshia had $100,000 of taxable income, of which $12,000 consisted of short-term capital gains. This year Aleshia collected $8,000 of the amount she had previously identified as a bad debt. Determine Aleshia's tax treatment of the $8,000 received in the current tax year.

2. **LO.1** Bob owns a collection agency. He purchases uncollected accounts receivable from other businesses at 60% of their face value and then attempts to collect these accounts. During the current year, Bob collected $60,000 on an account with a face value of $80,000. Determine the amount of Bob's bad debt deduction.

3. **LO.2** On May 9, 2020, Calvin acquired 250 shares of stock in Hobbes Corporation, a new startup company, for $68,750. Calvin acquired the stock directly from Hobbes, and it is classified as § 1244 stock (at the time Calvin acquired his stock, the corporation had $900,000 of paid-in capital). On January 15, 2022, Calvin sold all of his Hobbes stock for $7,000. Assuming that Calvin is single, determine his tax consequences as a result of this sale.

4. **LO.3** Determine the treatment of a loss on rental property under the following facts:

Basis	$650,000
FMV before the loss	800,000
FMV after the loss	200,000

5. **LO.6** In the current year, Ming invests $30,000 in an oil partnership. He has taxable income for the current year of $2,000 from the oil partnership and withdraws $10,000. What is Ming's at-risk amount at the end of the year?

6. **LO.6** Lucy sells her partnership interest, a passive activity, with an adjusted basis of $305,000 for $330,000. In addition, she has current and suspended losses of $28,000 associated with the partnership and has no other passive activities. Calculate the effect of these facts on Lucy's current-year adjusted gross income.

7. **LO.8** Rhonda has an adjusted basis and an at-risk amount of $7,500 in a passive activity at the beginning of the year. She also has a suspended passive activity loss of $1,500 carried over from the prior year. During the current year, she has a loss of $12,000 from the passive activity. Rhonda has no passive activity income from other sources this year. Determine the following items relating to Rhonda's passive activity as of the end of the year.
   a. Adjusted basis and at-risk amount in the passive activity.
   b. Loss suspended under the at-risk rules.
   c. Suspended passive activity loss.

8. **LO.9** Noah Yobs, who has $62,000 of AGI before considering rental activities, has $70,000 of losses from a real estate rental activity in which he actively participates. He also actively participates in another real estate rental activity from which he has $33,000 of income. He has other passive activity income of $20,000. What is Noah's adjusted gross income for the current year?

9. **LO.10** Rose dies with passive activity property having an adjusted basis of $65,000, suspended losses of $13,000, and a fair market value at the date of her death of $90,000. Of the $13,000 suspended loss existing at the time of Rose's death, how much is deductible on her final return or by the beneficiary?

Problems

10. **LO.1** Several years ago Amy Westbrook, who is in the lending business, loaned Sara Stuart $30,000 to purchase an automobile to be used for personal purposes. In August of the current year, Sara filed for bankruptcy, after paying back $1,000 of the loan to Amy. Amy was notified by the bankruptcy court that she could not expect to receive more than an additional $4,000. Amy has contacted you about the possibility of taking a bad debt deduction for the current year. Communications

    Write a letter to Amy that contains your advice as to whether she can claim a bad debt deduction for the current year. Also prepare a memo for the tax files. Amy's address is 100 Tyler Lane, Erie, PA 16563.

11. **LO.1** Monty loaned his friend Ned $20,000 three years ago. Ned signed a note and made payments on the loan. Last year, when the remaining balance was $11,000, Ned filed for bankruptcy and notified Monty that he would be unable to pay the balance on the loan. Monty treated the $11,000 as a nonbusiness bad debt. Last year before considering the tax implications of the nonbusiness bad debt, Monty had capital gains of $9,000 and taxable income of $45,000. During the current year, Ned paid Monty $10,000 in satisfaction of the debt. Determine Monty's tax treatment for the $10,000 received in the current year.

Critical Thinking

12. **LO.2** Many years ago, Jack purchased 400 shares of Canary stock. During the current year, the stock became worthless. It was determined that the company "went under" because several corporate officers embezzled a large amount of company funds. Identify the relevant tax issues for Jack.

Ethics and Equity

13. **LO.1** Jake and Mary Snow are residents of the state of New York. They are cash basis taxpayers and file a joint return for the calendar year. Jake is a licensed master plumber. Two years ago, Jake entered into a contract with New York City to perform plumbing services. During the current year, Jake was declared to be in breach of the contract, and he ceased performing plumbing services. Jake received a Form W–2 that reported $50,000 for wages paid. He also maintains that the city has not paid him $35,000 for work he performed. Jake is considering claiming a $35,000 business bad debt on his tax return. Evaluate Jake's plan.

14. **LO.1, 2** Jocelyn and Esteban file a joint return. For the current year, they had the following items:

Salaries	$120,000
Loss on sale of § 1244 stock acquired two years ago	105,000
Gain on sale of § 1244 stock acquired six months ago	20,000
Nonbusiness bad debt	19,000

Determine the impact of the above items on Jocelyn's and Esteban's income for the current year.

Decision Making
Planning

15. **LO.2** Abby, a single taxpayer, purchased 10,000 shares of § 1244 stock several years ago at a cost of $20 per share. In November of the current year, Abby receives an offer to sell the stock for $12 per share. She has the option of either selling all of the stock now or selling half of the stock now and half of the stock in January of next year. Abby's salary is $80,000 for the current year, and it will be $90,000 next year. Abby has long-term capital gains of $8,000 for the current year and will have $10,000 next year. If Abby's goal is to minimize her AGI for the two years, determine whether she should sell all of her stock this year or half of her stock this year and half next year.

Critical Thinking
Decision Making

16. **LO.3** Olaf lives in the state of Minnesota. In 2022, a tornado hit the area and damaged his home and automobile. Applicable information is as follows:

Item	Adjusted Basis	FMV Before	FMV After	Insurance Proceeds
Home	$350,000	$500,000	$100,000	$280,000
Auto	60,000	40,000	10,000	20,000

Because of the extensive damage caused by the tornado, the President designated the area a Federal disaster area.

Olaf and his wife, Anna, always file a joint return. Their 2021 tax return shows AGI of $180,000 and taxable income of $145,000. In 2022, their return shows AGI of $300,000 and taxable income (exclusive of the casualty loss deduction) of $245,000.

Determine the amount of Olaf and Anna's loss and the year in which they should take the loss.

Critical Thinking

17. **LO.3** In 2019, John opened an investment account with Randy Hansen, who held himself out to the public as an investment adviser and securities broker. John contributed $200,000 to the account in 2019. John provided Randy with a power of attorney to use the $200,000 to purchase and sell securities on John's behalf. John instructed Randy to reinvest any gains and income earned. In 2019, 2020, and 2021, John received statements of the amount of income earned by his account and included these amounts in his gross income for these years. In 2022, John discovered that Randy's purported investment advisory and brokerage activity was a fraudulent investment arrangement known as a Ponzi scheme. In reality, John's account balance

was zero, the money having been used by Randy in his scheme. Identify the relevant tax issues for John.

18. **LO.6** In 2021, Fred invested $50,000 in a general partnership. Fred's interest is not considered to be a passive activity. If his share of the partnership losses is $35,000 in 2021 and $25,000 in 2022, how much can he deduct in each year?

19. **LO.6** In the current year, Bill Parker (54 Oak Drive, St. Paul, MN 55164) is considering making an investment of $60,000 in Best Choice Partnership. If Bill makes the investment, he will participate in the business operated by Best Choice (and will meet one of the material participation tests). As as result, it will not be a passive activity. Bill's share of the entity's loss in the current year will likely be $40,000, while his share of the partnership loss next year will probably be $25,000. Write a letter to Bill in which you indicate how the losses would be treated for tax purposes in the current year and the following year. Communications

20. **LO.6** A number of years ago, Kayla acquired an interest in a partnership in which she is not a material participant. Kayla's basis in her partnership interest at the beginning of 2021 is $40,000. Kayla's share of the partnership loss is $35,000 in 2021, while her share of the partnership income is $15,000 in 2022. How much may Kayla deduct in 2021 and 2022, assuming that she owns no other passive activities?

21. **LO.6** Jorge owns two passive investments, Activity A and Activity B. He plans to dispose of Activity A in the current year or next year. Juanita has offered to buy Activity A this year for an amount that would produce a taxable passive activity gain to Jorge of $115,000. However, if the sale, for whatever reason, is not made to Juanita, Jorge believes that he could find a buyer who would pay about $7,000 less than Juanita. Passive activity losses and gains generated (and expected to be generated) by Activity B follow: Decision Making Planning

Two years ago	($35,000)
Last year	(35,000)
This year	(8,000)
Next year	(30,000)
Future years	Minimal profits

All of Activity B's losses are suspended. Should Jorge close the sale of Activity A with Juanita this year, or should he wait until next year and sell to another buyer? Jorge is in the 32% tax bracket.

22. **LO.6** Sarah has investments in four passive activity partnerships purchased several years ago. Last year the income and losses were as follows:

Activity	Income (Loss)
A	$ 30,000
B	(30,000)
C	(15,000)
D	(5,000)

In the current year, she sold her interest in Activity D for a $10,000 gain. Activity D, which had been profitable until last year, had a current loss of $1,500. How will the sale of Activity D affect Sarah's taxable income in the current year?

23. **LO.6** Leon sells his interest in a passive activity for $100,000. Determine the tax effect of the sale based on each of the following independent facts:
    a. Adjusted basis in this investment is $35,000. Losses from prior years that were not deductible due to the passive activity loss restrictions total $40,000.
    b. Adjusted basis in this investment is $75,000. Losses from prior years that were not deductible due to the passive activity loss restrictions total $40,000.

c. Adjusted basis in this investment is $75,000. Losses from prior years that were not deductible due to the passive activity loss restrictions total $40,000. In addition, suspended credits total $10,000.

24. **LO.6** In the current year, White, Inc., earns $400,000 from operations and receives $36,000 of interest income from various portfolio investments. White also pays $150,000 to acquire a 20% interest in a passive activity that produces a $200,000 loss.

a. Assuming that White is a personal service corporation, how will these transactions affect its taxable income?

b. Same as part (a), except that White is closely held but not a personal service corporation.

25. **LO.7** Jesse, an engineer, operates a separate business that he acquired eight years ago. If he participates 85 hours in the business and it incurs a loss of $34,000, under what circumstances can Jesse claim an active loss?

Critical Thinking

26. **LO.7** Rita retired from public accounting after a long and successful career of 45 years. As part of her retirement package, she continues to share in the profits and losses of the firm, albeit at a lower rate than when she was working full-time. Because Rita wants to stay busy during her retirement years, she has invested and works in a local hardware business, operated as a partnership. Unfortunately, the business has recently gone through a slump and has not been generating profits. Identify relevant tax issues for Rita.

Communications
Critical Thinking
Decision Making
Planning

27. **LO.6, 8** Kristin Graf (123 Baskerville Mill Road, Jamison, PA 18929) is trying to decide how to invest a $10,000 inheritance. One option is to make an additional investment in Rocky Road Excursions in which she has an at-risk basis of $0, suspended losses under the at-risk rules of $7,000, and suspended passive activity losses of $1,000. If Kristin makes this investment, her share of the expected profits this year will be $8,000. If her investment stays the same, her share of profits from Rocky Road Excursions will be $1,000. Another option is to invest $10,000 as a limited partner in the Ragged Mountain Winery; this investment will produce passive activity income of $9,000. Write a letter to Kristin to review the tax consequences of each alternative. Kristin is in the 24% tax bracket.

Critical Thinking
Decision Making
Planning

28. **LO.8** The end of the year is approaching, and Maxine has begun to focus on ways of minimizing her income tax liability. Several years ago, she purchased an investment in Teal Limited Partnership, which is subject to the at-risk and passive activity loss rules. (Last year Maxine sold a different investment that was subject to these rules and that produced passive activity income.) She believes that her investment in Teal has good long-term economic prospects. However, it has been generating tax losses for several years in a row. In fact, when she was discussing last year's income tax return with her tax accountant, he said that unless "things change" with respect to her investments, she would not be able to deduct losses this year.

a. What was the accountant referring to in his comment?

b. You learn that Maxine's current at-risk basis in her investment is $1,000 and that her share of the current loss is expected to be $13,000. Based on these facts, how will her loss be treated?

c. After reviewing her situation, Maxine's financial adviser suggests that she invest at least an additional $12,000 in Teal to ensure a full loss deduction in the current year. How do you react to his suggestion?

d. What would you suggest Maxine consider as she attempts to maximize her current-year deductible loss?

29. **LO.8** A number of years ago, Lee acquired a 20% interest in the BlueSky Partnership for $60,000. The partnership was profitable through 2021, and Lee's amount at risk in the partnership interest was $120,000 at the beginning of 2022. BlueSky incurred a loss of $400,000 in 2022 and reported income of $200,000 in 2023. Assuming that Lee is not a material participant, how much of his loss from BlueSky

Partnership is deductible in 2022 and 2023? Consider the at-risk and passive activity loss rules, and assume that Lee owns no other investments.

30. **LO.6** Grace acquired an activity four years ago. The loss from the activity is $50,000 in the current year (at-risk basis of $40,000 as of the beginning of the year). Without considering the loss from the activity, she has gross income of $140,000. If the activity is a convenience store and Grace is a material participant, what is the effect of the activity on her taxable income?

31. **LO.5, 6, 8** Jonathan, a physician, earns $200,000 from his practice. He also receives $18,000 in dividends and interest from various portfolio investments. During the year, he pays $45,000 to acquire a 20% interest in a partnership that operates a retail store and has no debt. The partnership produces a $300,000 loss this year. Compute Jonathan's AGI assuming that:

a. He does not participate in the operations of the partnership.

b. He is a material participant in the operations of the partnership.

32. **LO.5, 6, 8** Five years ago, Gerald invested $150,000 in a passive activity, his sole investment venture. On January 1, 2021, his amount at risk in the activity was $30,000. His shares of the income and losses were as follows:

Year	Income (Loss)
2021	($40,000)
2022	(30,000)
2023	50,000

Gerald holds no suspended at-risk or passive activity losses at the beginning of 2021. How much can Gerald deduct in 2021 and 2022? What is his taxable income from the activity in 2023? Consider the at-risk rules as well as the passive activity loss rules.

33. **LO.5, 6, 7** You have just met with Scott Myers (603 Pittsfield Drive, Champaign, IL 61821), a successful full-time real estate developer and investor. During your meeting, you discussed his tax situation because you are starting to prepare his current Federal income tax return. During your meeting, Scott mentioned that he and his wife, Susan, went to great lengths to maximize their participation in an apartment complex that they own and manage. In particular, Scott included the following activities in the 540 hours of participation for the current year:

Communications
Digging Deeper
Ethics and Equity

- Time spent thinking about the rentals.
- Time spent by Susan on weekdays visiting the apartment complex to oversee operations of the buildings (i.e., in a management role).
- Time spent by both Scott and Susan on weekends visiting the apartment complex to assess operations. Scott and Susan always visited the complex together on weekends, and both counted their hours (i.e., one hour at the complex was two hours of participation).
- Time spent on weekends driving around the community looking for other potential rental properties to purchase. Again, both Scott's hours and Susan's hours were counted, even when they drove together.

After reviewing Scott's records, you note that the apartment complex generated a significant loss this year. Prepare a letter to Scott describing your position on the deductibility of the loss.

34. **LO.11** Akiko, a single taxpayer, incurred higher than expected expenses in her active business in 2022. In addition, the economy moved into a mild recession, so her revenues were lower than in last year. Her deductible expenses totaled $2,400,000, and her taxable revenues totaled only $2,000,000. She materially participates in this business, but she also receives $320,000 in interest on a portfolio of long-term bonds. Akiko predicts that her business will break even next year and that her interest income will not change. What will be Akiko's adjusted gross income in 2022 and 2023?

35. **LO.9** During the current year, Gene, a CPA, performs services as follows: 1,800 hours in his tax practice and 50 hours in an apartment leasing operation in which he has a 15% interest. Because of his oversight duties, Gene is considered to be an active participant. He expects that his share of the loss realized from the apartment leasing operation will be $30,000 and that his tax practice will show a profit of approximately $80,000. Gene is single and has no other income. Discuss the character and treatment of the income and losses generated by these activities.

36. **LO.9** Mandy, who has AGI of $80,000 before considering rental activities, is active in three separate real estate rental activities. Mandy has a marginal tax rate of 22%. She has $12,000 of losses from Activity A, $18,000 of losses from Activity B, and income of $10,000 from Activity C. She also has $2,100 of tax credits from Activity A. Calculate the deductions and credits that she is allowed and the suspended losses and credits.

37. **LO.9** Jiu has $105,000 of losses from a real estate rental activity in which she actively participates. She has other rent income of $25,000 and other passive activity income of $32,000. Her AGI before considering these items of income and loss is $95,000. How much rental loss can Jiu deduct against active and portfolio income (ignoring the at-risk rules)? Does she have any suspended losses to carry over? Explain.

38. **LO.5, 6, 10** In the current year, Abe gives an interest in a passive activity to his daughter, Andrea. The value of the interest at the date of the gift is $25,000, and its adjusted basis to Abe is $13,000. During the time that Abe owned the investment, losses of $3,000 could not be deducted because of the passive activity loss limitations. What is the tax treatment of the suspended passive activity losses to Abe and Andrea?

Critical Thinking

39. **LO.7** Thomas believes that he has an NOL for the current year and plans to carry it forward, offsetting it against future income. In determining his NOL, Thomas offset his business income by alimony payments he made to his ex-spouse and contributions he made to his traditional Individual Retirement Account (IRA). His reason for using these items in the NOL computation is that each item is a deduction *for* AGI. Identify the relevant tax issues for Thomas.

40. **LO.11** Josie and Zach are married. Josie is a material participant in a business that specializes in monetizing intellectual property. This business suffered a $250,000 taxable loss in 2022. Zach started a business two years ago in which he materially participates. The business suffered a taxable loss of $600,000 in 2022. What is Josie's and Zach's deductible loss from these activities for the year?

Bridge Discipline

Digging Deeper

1. Marketplace, Inc., has recognized over time that a certain percentage of its customer accounts receivable will not be collected. To ensure the appropriate matching of revenues and expenditures in its financial reports, Marketplace uses the reserve method for bad debts. Records show the following pertaining to its treatment of bad debts.

Beginning allowance for bad debts	$120,000
Ending allowance for bad debts	123,000
Bad debts written off during the year	33,000

a. What was the bad debt expense for financial accounting purposes during the year?

b. What was the bad debt deduction for income tax purposes during the year?

c. Assuming that the before-tax net income for financial accounting purposes was $545,000, what is the taxable income for the year if the treatment of bad debts is the only book-tax difference?

continued

2. Heather wants to invest $40,000 in a relatively safe venture and has discovered two alternatives that would produce the following ordinary income and loss over the next three years:

Critical Thinking
Decision Making
Planning

Year	Alternative 1 Income (Loss)	Alternative 2 Income (Loss)
1	($20,000)	($48,000)
2	(28,000)	32,000
3	72,000	40,000

She is interested in the after-tax effects of these alternatives over a three-year horizon. Assume that:

- Heather's investment portfolio produces sufficient passive activity income to offset any potential passive activity loss that may arise from these alternatives.
- Heather's marginal tax rate is 24%, and her cost of capital is 6% (see Appendix E for the present value factors).
- Each investment alternative possesses equal growth potential and comparable financial risk.
- In the loss years for each alternative, there is no cash flow from or to the investment (i.e., the loss is due to depreciation), while in those years when the income is positive, cash flows to Heather equal the amount of the income.

Based on these facts, compute the present value of these two investment alternatives and determine which option Heather should choose.

3. Emily has $100,000 that she wants to invest and is considering the following two options:

Decision Making
Planning

- Option A: Investment in Redbird Mutual Fund, which is expected to produce interest income of $8,000 per year.
- Option B: Investment in Cardinal Limited Partnership (buys, sells, and operates wine vineyards). Emily's share of the partnership's ordinary income and loss over the next three years would be as follows:

Year	Income (Loss)
1	($ 8,000)
2	(2,000)
3	34,000

Emily is interested in the after-tax effects of these alternatives over a three-year horizon. Assume that Emily's investment portfolio produces ample passive activity income to offset any passive activity losses that may be generated. Her cost of capital is 8% (see Appendix E for the present value factors), and she is in the 32% tax bracket. The two investment alternatives possess equal growth potential and comparable financial risk. Based on these facts, compute the present value of these two investment alternatives and determine which option Emily should choose.

Research Problems

Note: Solutions to the Research Problems can be prepared by using the Thomson Reuters Checkpoint™ online tax research database, which accompanies this textbook. Solutions can also be prepared by using research materials found in a typical tax library.

Research Problem 1. Esther owns a large home on the Southeast Coast. Her home is surrounded by large, mature oak trees that significantly increase the value of her home. In September 2021, a hurricane damaged many of the trees surrounding her home; her region was declared a Federal disaster area as a result of the hurricane's damage. In October 2021, Esther engaged a local arborist to evaluate and treat the trees, but five of the largest trees were seriously weakened by the storm. These trees died from disease in 2022. Esther has ascertained that the amount of the casualty loss from the death of the five trees is $25,000; however, she is uncertain in which year to deduct this loss and has come to you for advice. Discuss whether the casualty loss should be deducted in the calculation of Esther's 2021 or 2022 taxable income.

Partials list of research aids:
Reg. § 1.165–1.
Oregon Mesabi Corporation, 39 B.T.A. 1033 (1939).

Research Problem 2. Five years ago, Bridget decided to purchase a limited partnership interest in a fast-food restaurant conveniently located near the campus of Southeast State University. The general partner of the restaurant venture promised her that the investment would prove to be a winner. During the process of capitalizing the business, $2,000,000 was borrowed from Northside Bank; however, each of the partners was required to pledge personal assets as collateral to satisfy the bank loan in the event that the restaurant defaulted. Bridget pledged shares of publicly traded stock (worth $200,000, basis of $75,000) to satisfy the bank's requirement.

The restaurant did a good business until just recently, when flagrant health code violations were discovered and widely publicized by the media. As a result, business has declined to a point where the restaurant's continued existence is doubtful. In addition, the $2,000,000 loan is now due for payment. Because the restaurant cannot pay, the bank has called for the collateral provided by the partners to be used to satisfy the debt. Bridget sells the pledged stock for $200,000 and forwards the proceeds to the bank. Bridget believes that her share of the restaurant's current and suspended passive activity losses can offset the $125,000 gain from the stock sale. As a result, after netting the passive activity losses against the gain, none of the gain is subject to tax.

How do you react to Bridget's position?

Research Problem 3. During 2022, your client, Kendra Adams, was the chief executive officer and a shareholder of Maze, Inc. She owned 60% of the outstanding stock of Maze. In 2019, Kendra and Maze, as co-borrowers, obtained a $100,000 loan from United National Bank. This loan was secured by Kendra's personal residence. Although Maze was listed as a co-borrower, Kendra repaid the loan in full in 2022. On Maze's Form 1120 tax returns, no loans from shareholders were reported. Discuss whether Kendra is entitled to a bad debt deduction for the amount of the payment on the loan.

Partial list of research aids:
U.S. v. Generes, 405 U.S. 93 (1972).
Dale H. Sundby, T.C.Memo. 2003–204.
Arrigoni v. Comm., 73 T.C. 792 (1980).
Estate of Herbert M. Rapoport, T.C.Memo. 1982–584.
Clifford L. Brody and Barbara J. DeClerk, T.C. Summary Opinion, 2004–149.

Use internet tax resources to address the following questions. Look for reliable websites and blogs of the IRS and other government agencies, media outlets, businesses, tax professionals, academics, think tanks, and political outlets.

Research Problem 4. Find an article that discusses tax planning for casualty losses when a Federal disaster area designation is made. Does the article convey the pertinent tax rules correctly? Then list all of the locations identified by the President as Federal disaster areas in the last two years.

Research Problem 5. Since the first bitcoin transaction in 2009, the number of circulating virtual currencies has grown to over 4,000 and some taxpayers trade the currencies multiple times each day (i.e., like a day trader). Find a reliable article on investment strategies for virtual currency and a software tool that can help the investor track the basis, fair market value, and dates of the trades. Send an email to your professor that details your findings (including an investment strategy, the name of a software tool that can help with tax recordkeeping, and whether it can produce the necessary tax reporting form for the investor).

Becker CPA Review Questions

Becker+

1. Which of the following statements regarding passive activity losses is true?
   a. A net passive activity loss may be deducted against wages.
   b. Losses on rental property are always considered passive.
   c. A passive activity is one in which the taxpayer does not materially participate.
   d. Expenses related to passive activities may be deducted from passive activity income and portfolio income.

2. Michael owns a rental house that generated a $10,000 loss this year. Michael manages the rental property but does not meet the standards for material participation. Michael is a college professor and has wages of $60,000 and $5,000 in dividend income. How is the $10,000 rental real estate loss treated on Michael's tax return?
   a. $5,000 of the loss is deductible against the passive dividend income.
   b. The rental loss is not deductible because Michael does not have any passive income.
   c. $10,000 loss is not deductible because Michael does not materially participate in the rental activity.
   d. $10,000 loss is deductible under the rental real estate exception because Michael actively participates in the rental activity.

3. What is the correct order of applying the loss limitation rules?
   a. Passive loss limits, tax basis, at-risk amount
   b. Tax basis, at-risk amount, passive loss limits
   c. At-risk amount, tax basis, passive loss limits
   d. Passive loss limits, at-risk amount, tax basis

4. Sam rents his second home. During the current year, he reported a $40,000 net loss from the rental. Assume Sam actively participates in the rental activity and no phaseout limitations apply. What is the greatest amount of the rental loss that Sam can deduct against ordinary income in the current year?
   a. $0
   b. $5,000
   c. $25,000
   d. $40,000

Part 3

Property Transactions

Chapter 7

Property Transactions: Basis, Gain and Loss, and Nontaxable Exchanges

Chapter 8

Property Transactions: Capital Gains and Losses, Section 1231, and Recapture Provisions

Part 3 presents the tax treatment of sales, exchanges, and other dispositions of property. Topics discussed include measuring basis of assets, the determination of the realized and recognized gain or loss from disposition of assets, and the characterization of the recognized gain or loss as capital or ordinary. Terminology unique to the tax law such as capital assets and § 1231 assets is explained.

Chapter 7

Property Transactions: Basis, Gain and Loss, and Nontaxable Exchanges

Learning Objectives: *After completing Chapter 7, you should be able to:*

- LO.1 Determine the gain or loss realized on property dispositions.
- LO.2 Distinguish between realized and recognized gains and losses.
- LO.3 Determine the basis of assets acquired in various ways.
- LO.4 Apply various loss disallowance provisions.
- LO.5 Apply the nonrecognition provisions and basis determination rules for like-kind exchanges.
- LO.6 Explain the nonrecognition provisions available on the involuntary conversion of property.
- LO.7 Determine the recognized gain on the sale of a principal residence.

Chapter Outline

Tax Talk *To base all of your decisions on tax consequences is not necessarily to maintain the proper balance and perspective on what you are doing.* —Barber Conable

The Big Picture

Calculating Basis and Recognized Gain for Property Transactions

Alice owns land that she received from her father 10 years ago as a gift. The land was purchased by her father in 1996 for $2,000 and was worth $10,000 at the time of the gift. Alice's father did not owe gift taxes upon making the transfer. Alice is considering selling the land, currently worth approximately $50,000, and purchasing a piece of undeveloped property in the mountains.

Alice also owns 500 shares of AppleCo stock. Three hundred shares were acquired as an inheritance when her grandfather died in 2000. Alice's grandfather paid $12,000 for the shares, and the shares were worth $30,000 at the time of his death. The other 200 shares of AppleCo were purchased by Alice two months ago for $28,000. Alice is considering selling the shares, currently worth $120 per share.

In addition, Alice owns a house that she inherited from her grandmother two years ago. Her grandmother lived in the house for over 50 years. Alice has many fond memories associated with the house because she spent many summer vacations there, and she has been reluctant to sell the house. However, a developer has recently purchased several homes in the area and has offered Alice $600,000 for the property. Based on the estate tax return, the fair market value of the house at the date of her grandmother's death was $475,000. According to her grandmother's attorney, her grandmother's basis for the house was $275,000. Alice is considering selling the house. She expects any selling expenses to be minimal because she already has identified a buyer for the property.

The building Alice used in her business was destroyed by a fire on October 5, 2022. Fortunately, the building (adjusted basis of $50,000) was insured and on November 17, 2022, she received an insurance reimbursement of $100,000 for the loss. Alice intends to invest $80,000 in a new building and use the other $20,000 of insurance proceeds to pay off credit card debt.

Alice has come to you for tax advice with respect to the property she owns. What is the recognized gain or loss for the land, stock, and house if they are sold? What tax consequences arise with respect to the involuntary conversion of her business building? Can Alice avoid paying taxes on any of the sales? Alice's objectives are to minimize the recognition of any realized gains and to maximize the recognition of any realized losses.

Read the chapter and formulate your response.

This and the following chapter explain the income tax consequences of property transactions, including the sale or other disposition of property. Specifically, Chapters 7 and 8 consider the following questions:

- Is there a realized gain or loss as a result of a property transaction?
- If so, is that gain or loss recognized for tax purposes?
- If the gain or loss is recognized, what is its tax character (i.e., ordinary or capital)?
- If the gain or loss is not recognized, what is the basis of any replacement property that is acquired?

This chapter discusses the determination of realized gains and losses, including the basis of any property involved in the transaction, and when that realized gain or loss is recognized. The next chapter covers the classification of recognized gains or losses as ordinary or capital.

For the most part, the rules discussed in Chapters 7 and 8 apply to all types of property and taxpayers. Individuals, partnerships, closely held corporations, limited liability companies, and publicly held corporations all own tangible (e.g., land, buildings, and equipment) and intangible (e.g., goodwill, patents, and stock) assets for use in business activities or as investments. Individuals are unique among taxpayers because they can also own assets that have no significant business or investment component. Because of that possibility, sometimes property transaction concepts apply differently to individual taxpayers. For example, what happens when a married couple sells their family home? Thus, the material that follows pertains to taxpayers generally, except where otherwise noted.

7-1 Determining Gain or Loss

This section addresses the determination of when a taxpayer has a gain or loss for tax purposes and how that gain or loss is measured. As discussed in Chapter 4, taxpayers do not have taxable income until there has been realization. "Realization events" generally include sales as well as certain other dispositions of assets. Once a realization event has occurred, the amount of any realized gain or loss must be determined. Many, but not all, *realized* gains and losses are also *recognized* (i.e., included in the determination of taxable income) at the time of the realization event. So while realization is an accounting concept, recognition is a tax concept that arises from various tax law provisions. Each of these ideas is discussed in further detail below and summarized in Concept Summary 7.1 at the end of this section.

LO.1

Determine the gain or loss realized on property dispositions.

7-1a Realized Gain or Loss

Realization Events

Realization events generally include transactions in which taxpayers change in a meaningful way their ownership interest in an asset, including the sale, exchange, or other disposition of the asset. The term *other disposition* is defined broadly to include virtually any disposition of property, including casualties, condemnations, thefts, and bond retirements. Usually, the key factor in determining whether a disposition has taken place is whether an identifiable event has occurred.[1] Fluctuations in the value of property are not realization events.[2] Events other than dispositions can also cause the realization of gain or loss. Examples of these other events include certain assets becoming worthless and the expiration of an option to purchase certain assets. These events can result in realized gains or losses even though there has been no disposition of an asset and the taxpayer has received nothing in return.

Heron & Associates owns Tan Corporation stock that it bought for $3,000. The stock has appreciated in value and is now worth $5,000. Heron has no realized gain because a change in value is not an identifiable event for tax purposes. Here, Heron has an *unrealized gain* of $2,000.

The same is true if the stock had declined in value to $1,000. Since there was no identifiable event, there is no realized loss. Here, Heron would have an *unrealized* loss of $2,000.

[1]Reg. § 1.1001-1(c)(1).

[2]*Lynch v. Turrish*, 1 USTC ¶18, 3 AFTR 2986, 38 S.Ct. 537 (1918).

Calculation of Realized Gain or Loss

For tax purposes, a realized gain or loss is measured as the difference between the *amount realized* from a sale or other disposition of property and the property's *adjusted basis* on the date of the realization event. If the amount realized exceeds the property's adjusted basis, the result is a **realized gain**. Conversely, if the property's adjusted basis exceeds the amount realized, the result is a **realized loss**.[3]

Lavender, Inc., sells Swan Corporation stock with a basis of $3,000 for $5,000. Lavender's realized gain is $2,000. If Lavender had sold the stock for $2,000, it would have had a realized loss of $1,000.

Amount Realized

The **amount realized** from a sale or other disposition of property is the sum of any money received (including any debt relief) plus the fair market value of any other property received.[4]

Debt relief includes any liability of the taxpayer (e.g., a mortgage on a building) that the buyer assumes as part of the sale. Debt relief also occurs if property is sold subject to the mortgage.[5] Why debt relief is included in the amount realized by a seller can be better understood by considering the economically equivalent situation in which the buyer pays additional cash to the seller who then uses the cash to pay off the debt.

Amount Realized

Juan sells a machine used in his landscaping business to Peter for $20,000 cash plus four acres of property that Peter owns in a nearby town with a fair market value of $36,000. Juan's amount realized on this sale is $56,000 ($20,000 + $36,000).

Barry owns property on which there is a mortgage of $20,000. He sells the property to Cole for $50,000 cash and Cole's agreement to assume the mortgage. Barry's amount realized from the sale is $70,000 ($50,000 cash + $20,000 debt relief).

The **fair market value** of property received in a property transaction is the price determined by a willing seller and a willing buyer when neither is compelled to sell or buy.[6] Sellers must consider all relevant factors in determining market value.[7] If the seller cannot determine the fair market value of the property received, they may use as its value the value of the property given up.[8]

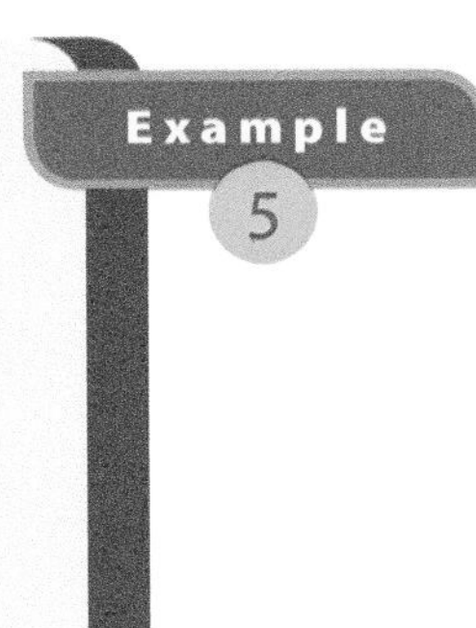

Return to the facts of Example 3. There are several ways one can determine the fair market value of the land Juan is receiving.

- Juan can hire a valuation professional to provide an appraisal.
- City or county property tax assessment information also may be helpful; the city or county assessor regularly determines the fair market value of property so that property taxes are levied appropriately.
- If the exchange is between a willing buyer and seller, determining the fair market value of Juan's landscaping machine could provide the fair market value of the land (i.e., if Juan's machine were known to be worth $56,000, Juan and Peter must agree that the land is worth $36,000 ($56,000 value of the machine – $20,000 cash paid by Peter).

---

[3] § 1001(a) and Reg. § 1.1001–1(a).

[4] § 1001(b) and Reg. § 1.1001–1(a).

[5] Reg. § 1.1001–2(a). Although a legal distinction exists between the direct assumption of a mortgage and the taking of property subject to a mortgage, the tax consequences in calculating the amount realized are the same. *Crane v. Comm.*, 47–1 USTC ¶9217, 35 AFTR 776, 67 S.Ct. 1047.

[6] *Comm. v. Marshman*, 60–2 USTC ¶9484, 5 AFTR 2d 1528, 279 F.2d 27 (CA–6).

[7] *O'Malley v. Ames*, 52–1 USTC ¶9361, 42 AFTR 19, 197 F.2d 256 (CA–8).

[8] *U.S. v. Davis*, 62–2 USTC ¶9509, 9 AFTR 2d 1625, 82 S.Ct. 1190.

Finally, the amount realized is reduced by any selling expenses (e.g., advertising, commissions, and legal fees) incurred by the seller related to the disposition. Thus, the amount realized is the net amount the taxpayer received directly or indirectly, in the form of cash or anything else of value, from the disposition of the property.

Ridge sells an office building and the associated land on October 1 of the current year. Under the terms of the sales contract, Ridge is to receive $600,000 in cash. The purchaser assumes Ridge's mortgage of $300,000 on the property. In addition, Ridge agrees to pay $15,000 of the purchaser's closing costs (a "closing cost credit"). The broker's commission on the sale is $45,000. The amount realized by Ridge is determined as follows:

Selling price:		
Cash	$600,000	
Mortgage assumed by purchaser	300,000	
		$900,000
Less:		
Broker's commission	$ 45,000	
Closing cost credit provided by Ridge	15,000	(60,000)
Amount realized		$840,000

Adjusted Basis

The **adjusted basis** of property is the property's original basis adjusted to the date of disposition.[9] Original basis is the cost or other basis of the property on the date the property is acquired. *Capital additions* increase and *capital recoveries* decrease the original basis.[10] As a result, adjusted basis equals:

Cost (or other basis) on date of acquisition
+ Capital additions
− Capital recoveries
= Adjusted basis on date of disposition

A taxpayer's original basis also includes any liability incurred to acquire the property.

Bluebird Corporation purchased manufacturing equipment for $25,000. Whether Bluebird uses $25,000 from the business's cash account to pay for this equipment or uses $5,000 from that account and borrows the remaining $20,000, the basis of this equipment will be $25,000. It does not matter whether Bluebird borrowed the $20,000 from the equipment's seller, from a local bank, or from any other lender.

Capital Additions

Capital additions include the cost of capital improvements that lengthen the property's useful life or increase its capacity or efficiency. These costs differ from repair and maintenance expenses discussed in Chapter 5. Repair and maintenance expenses do not affect the basis of an asset. Instead, taxpayers deduct these costs in the taxable year in which they are paid or incurred (if they relate to business or income-producing property).

Capital Recoveries

Capital recoveries decrease the adjusted basis of property. The more common types of capital recoveries are discussed below.

Depreciation and Cost Recovery The original basis of depreciable property is reduced by the annual depreciation charges (or cost recovery allowances) available while the

[9] § 1011(a) and Reg. § 1.1011–1.

[10] § 1016(a).

property is held by the taxpayer. The amount of depreciation that is subtracted from the original basis is the greater of the *allowed* or *allowable* cost recovery or depreciation.[11]

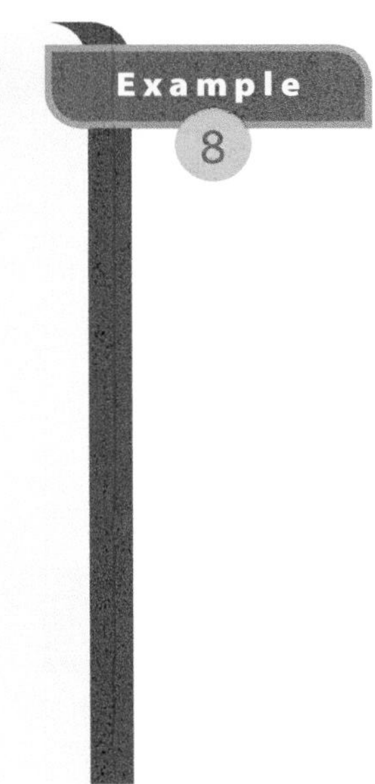

Refer back to Example 3. The machine Juan sold was acquired four years ago for $100,000. It was 7-year MACRS property. Assuming Juan did not take either an immediate expense deduction (§ 179) or bonus depreciation on the property, Juan's adjusted basis is $37,485 computed as follows:

Original cost		$100,000
Cost recovery:		
Year 1 ($100,000 × 0.1429)	$14,290	
Year 2 ($100,000 × 0.2449)	24,490	
Year 3 ($100,000 × 0.1749)	17,490	
Year 4 ($100,000 × 0.1249 × ½)	6,245	
Total cost recovery		(62,515)
Adjusted basis		$ 37,485

Since Juan's amount realized on the sale was $56,000, his realized gain is $18,515, computed as follows:

Amount realized	$ 56,000
− Adjusted basis	(37,485)
Realized gain (loss)	$ 18,515

Casualties and Thefts A casualty or theft may result in the reduction of the adjusted basis of property by the amount of any *deductible* loss resulting from the casualty or theft.[12] In addition, the adjusted basis is reduced by the amount of any insurance proceeds received. If insurance proceeds exceed the property's adjusted basis, the taxpayer may recognize a gain. In such cases, the recognized gain increases the adjusted basis of the property.[13]

Capital Recoveries: Casualties and Thefts

An insured truck owned by Falcon Corporation is destroyed in an accident. At the time of the accident, the truck's adjusted basis was $8,000 and its fair market value was $6,500. Falcon receives insurance proceeds of $6,500.

The amount of the casualty *loss* is $1,500 ($6,500 insurance insurance proceeds − $8,000 adjusted basis). The truck's adjusted basis becomes $0 ($8,000 pre-accident adjusted basis − $1,500 casualty loss − $6,500 of insurance proceeds received).

How would your answer to Example 9 change if the basis of the truck was $6,000, its fair market value was $9,000, and Falcon received a $9,000 insurance settlement?

Now Falcon has a casualty *gain* of $3,000 ($9,000 insurance proceeds − $6,000 adjusted basis). The truck's adjusted basis becomes $0 ($6,000 basis before casualty + $3,000 casualty gain − $9,000 insurance proceeds).

Certain Corporate Distributions A corporate distribution to a shareholder that is not taxable is treated as a return of capital and reduces the basis of the shareholder's stock in the corporation.[14] Corporations normally disclose this information to shareholders.

[11] § 1016(a)(2) and Reg. § 1.1016–3(a)(1)(i). Allowed depreciation is what a taxpayer has deducted on a tax return. Allowable depreciation is what a taxpayer could have legally deducted. In most cases, these amounts are the same (refer to Chapter 5).

[12] Refer to Chapter 6 for the discussion of casualties and thefts.

[13] Reg. § 1.1016–6(a).

[14] § 1016(a)(4) and Reg. § 1.1016–5(a).

Once the basis of the stock is reduced to zero, any future distributions result in a capital gain. See Chapter 13 for additional discussion.

Amortizable Bond Premium The basis in a bond purchased at a premium is reduced by the amortizable portion of the premium.[15] Investors in taxable bonds may *elect* to amortize the bond premium annually by offsetting the amortization against the bond interest income.[16] Therefore, the election enables the taxpayer to take an annual interest deduction to offset ordinary income in exchange for a larger capital gain or smaller capital loss on the disposition of the bond (due to the basis reduction).

In contrast to the treatment of taxable bonds, taxpayers *must* amortize the premium on tax-exempt bonds. Although no income offset, or deduction, is available for the amortized premium, taxpayers must nonetheless reduce the basis of tax-exempt bonds by the amortization. The law denies an amortization deduction on tax-exempt bonds because the interest income is exempt from tax. The amortization of the bond premium merely reduces the tax-exempt income earned on the bond.

Navy, Inc., purchases Eagle Corporation taxable bonds with a face value of $100,000 for $110,000, paying a premium of $10,000. The annual interest rate is 7%, and the bonds mature 10 years from the date of purchase. The annual interest income is $7,000 (7% × $100,000).

If Navy elects to amortize the bond premium, the $10,000 premium is deducted over the 10-year period. Navy's basis for the bonds is reduced each year by the amount of the amortization deduction, and Navy can deduct the amortization to offset interest income.

If the bonds were tax-exempt, amortization of the bond premium and the basis adjustment would be mandatory. However, no deduction would be allowed for the amortization.

Concept Summary 7.1

Realized Gain or Loss

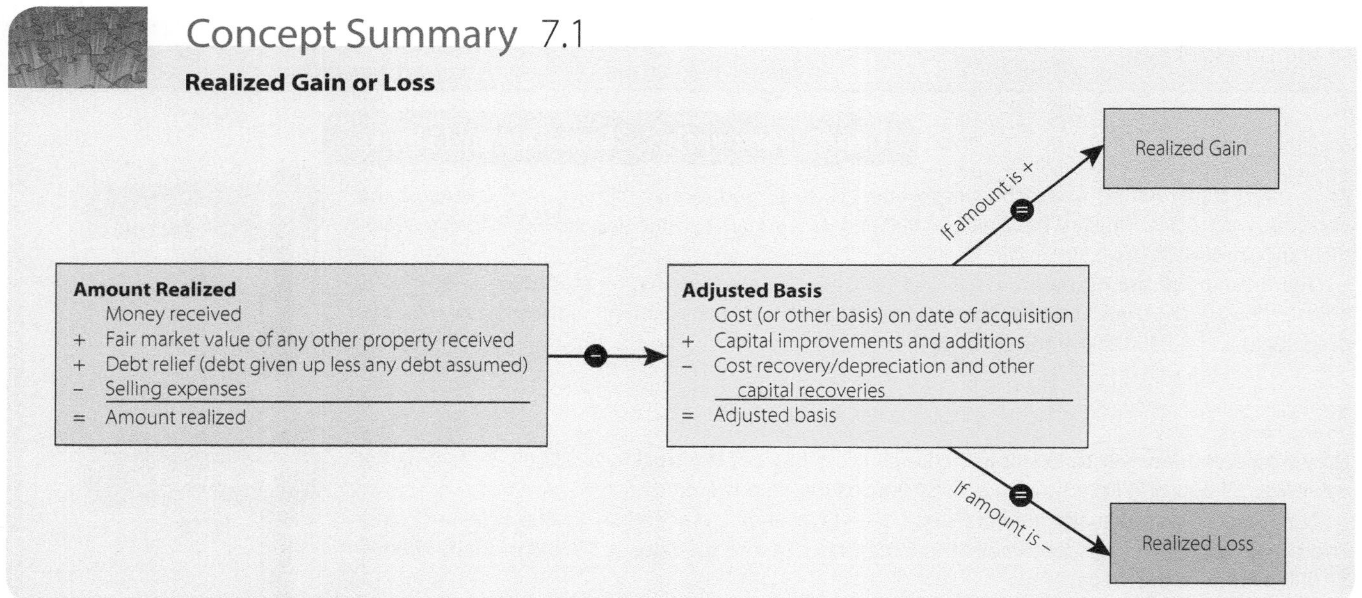

[15] § 1016(a)(5) and Reg. § 1.1016–5(b). The financial accounting treatment of bond premium amortization is the same as for tax purposes. The amortization results in a decrease in the bond investment account.

[16] § 171 and Reg. § 1.171–2. There are also rules that allow or require amortization of bond discount. The effect of discount amortization is to increase the bond's interest income and its basis. See § 454.

Bridge Discipline Bridge to Financial Accounting

As with financial accounting, when property is traded, we can use the value of the property received to assess the value of the property given up. However, certain property transactions discussed later in this chapter are treated differently for tax purposes than for financial accounting purposes. For example, the category of transactions generally referred to as "nontaxable exchanges," such as like-kind exchanges and involuntary conversions, gives taxpayers the opportunity to defer the recognition of gain on the disposition of property in qualifying transactions. The gains or losses deferred under tax law, however, are not generally deferred for financial reporting purposes. Instead, the actual gain or loss realized is reflected in the entity's financial reports.

Identifying and calculating the book-tax differences that arise from *taxable* dispositions of certain other property may not be so easy. For example, as discussed in Chapter 5, cost recovery (i.e., depreciation) rules provided by the tax law specify various ways in which an asset's cost may be recovered over time. These methods often differ from the methods used to depreciate an asset for book purposes. Consequently, the annual book-tax differences in these depreciation expense calculations are noted in the financial reports. But in addition, these cumulative differences, as reflected in the accumulated depreciation account, will also produce a book-tax difference on the asset's disposition. That is, because an asset's accumulated depreciation may differ for book and tax purposes, its adjusted basis will also differ. Consequently, when the asset is sold, the amount of gain or loss for book purposes will differ from that recognized for tax purposes.

Further discussion of the recovery of capital doctrine can be found on this book's companion website: www.cengage.com

1 Digging Deeper 

7-1b Recognized Gain or Loss

LO.2

Distinguish between realized and recognized gains and losses.

Recognized gain is the amount of the realized gain that must be included in the taxpayer's gross income.[17] A **recognized loss**, on the other hand, is the amount of a realized loss that a taxpayer can potentially deduct from its income.[18]

Unless there is an exception in the tax law, taxpayers must immediately recognize their realized gains and losses.[19] In certain cases, however, the tax law permits or requires gain or loss *deferral* to later tax years. Like-kind exchanges, which are covered later in this chapter, are one example. In addition, there are other instances when the tax law permanently *disallows* or limits deductions for certain tax losses. For example, realized losses from the sale or exchange of property between certain related parties and losses realized on the disposition of personal use assets (i.e., assets such as a residence or an automobile that are not used in either business or investment activities) are not recognized. These are discussed later in this chapter.

Concept Summary 7.2 summarizes the relation of realized and recognized gains and losses.

[17] § 61(a)(3) and Reg. § 1.61–6(a).

[18] § 165(a) and Reg. § 1.165–1(a).

[19] § 1001(c) and Reg. § 1.1002–1(a).

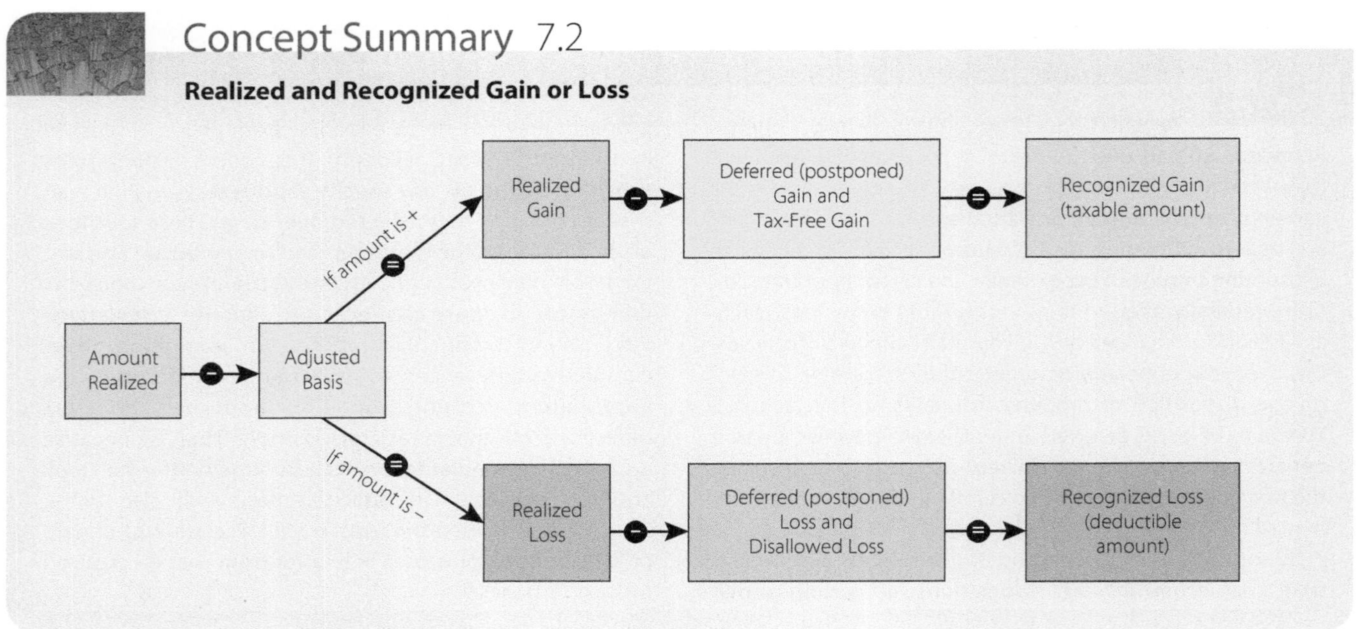

LO.3

Determine the basis of assets acquired in various ways.

7-2 Basis Considerations

A key element in calculating gain or loss from a property transaction is the asset's adjusted basis at the time of the transaction. Adjusted basis is usually an asset's unrecovered cost but can be different, especially if the taxpayer did not purchase the property.

7-2a Determination of Cost Basis

The initial basis of property generally equals the property's cost, which is the amount paid for the property in cash (including the assumption of any liabilities) or other property.[20]

A *bargain purchase* of property is an exception to the general rule for determining basis. Examples of bargain purchases include an employer transferring property to an employee for less than the property's fair market value (as compensation) and a corporation transferring property to a shareholder for less than the property's fair market value (a dividend). These transfers create gross income for the purchaser equal to the difference between fair market value and purchase price at the time the property is purchased. The basis of property acquired in a bargain purchase is the property's fair market value.[21] If the basis of the property were not increased by the bargain element, the taxpayer would be taxed on this amount again at disposition.

Wade buys land from his employer for $10,000. The fair market value of the land is $15,000.

Wade must include in his gross income the $5,000 difference between the cost and the fair market value of the land. The bargain element represents additional compensation to Wade. His basis for the land is $15,000, the land's fair market value.

[20] § 1012(a) and Reg. § 1.1012–1(a).

[21] Reg. §§ 1.61–2(d)(2)(i) and 1.301–1(j). See the discussion in Chapter 11 of the circumstances under which what appears to be a taxable bargain purchase is an excludible qualified employee discount (text Section 11-2i).

Identification Problems

Sometimes it can be difficult to determine the adjusted basis of a specific asset being sold. Identification problems generally arise when a taxpayer sells one or more assets that are indistinguishable from others that were purchased at different times for different amounts. For example, a taxpayer may purchase several shares of a company's stock at various times at different prices. If the taxpayer subsequently sells only a portion of the total shares purchased, the basis and holding period of the shares sold must be identified. If the shares being sold, and their cost, can be adequately identified, then the basis and holding period of the shares actually sold are used in determining the nature and amount of gain or loss realized (specific identification).[22] However, the taxpayer may be unable to identify the adjusted basis of the assets being sold.

In the case of stock sales, the basis of the shares sold must be determined on a first-in, first-out (FIFO) basis.[23] Thus, the holding period and cost of the stock sold are determined by referring to the purchase date and cost of the first lot of shares acquired. In times of rising stock markets, this results in using the relatively lower adjusted basis of the earlier purchased shares and a relatively higher realized gain. To avoid FIFO treatment when the sold securities are held by a broker, a taxpayer should provide specific instructions and receive written confirmation of the securities being sold. Brokers and others in similar enterprises are now required to provide investors with an annual report on the cost basis of their stocks sold during the year (to be included on Form 1099–B and reported to the IRS).

Pelican, Inc., purchased 100 shares of Olive Corporation stock two years ago for $5,000 ($50 a share) and another 100 shares of Olive stock one year ago for $6,000 ($60 a share). Pelican sells 50 shares of the stock on January 2 of the current year.

For purposes of determining the realized gain or loss, the adjusted basis of the stock sold, assuming that Pelican cannot adequately identify the shares, is $50 a share (from shares purchased two years ago, using FIFO), or $2,500. If Pelican had been able to identify the stock sold as coming from the most recently purchased lot with a cost of $60 per share, the basis deducted from proceeds would have been $3,000, thus reducing Pelican's taxable gain.

Allocation Problems

A taxpayer may acquire *several assets in a lump-sum purchase*. Because the individual assets acquired may be treated differently for tax purposes (e.g., some may not be eligible for cost recovery while the cost of others may be recoverable over different periods), the basis of each asset must be determined. To do so, the taxpayer must allocate the total cost among the individual assets. The allocation is based on the relative fair market values of the individual assets acquired.[24]

Example 14

Magenta Corporation purchases a building and land for $800,000. Because of the depressed nature of the industry in which the seller was operating, Magenta was able to negotiate a favorable purchase price. Appraisals of the individual assets indicate that the fair market value of the building is $600,000 and that of the land is $400,000.

Magenta's basis for the building is $480,000 [($600,000 ÷ $1,000,000) × $800,000], and its basis for the land is $320,000 [($400,000 ÷ $1,000,000) × $800,000].

If a business is purchased and **goodwill** is involved, a special allocation applies. Initially, the purchase price is allocated among the assets acquired, other than goodwill, based on their relative fair market values. Goodwill is then assigned the residual amount of the purchase price. The allocation is the same for both the buyer and the seller.[25]

[22] See Reg. § 1.1012–1(c)(2).

[23] Reg. § 1.1012–1(c)(1)(i) and *Kluger Associates, Inc.*, 69 T.C. 925 (1978).

[24] Reg. § 1.61–6(a).

[25] § 1060. In most cases, the seller's recognized gain associated with the goodwill is classified as capital (as discussed in Chapter 8).

Roadrunner, Inc., sells its business to Coyote Corporation. An independent appraisal indicates that the fair market values of the business assets, other than goodwill, are as follows:

Marketable securities	$ 5,000
Inventory	35,000
Building	500,000
Land	200,000

After negotiations, Roadrunner and Coyote agree on a sales price of $1,000,000. Applying the residual method, the residual purchase price is allocated to goodwill, resulting in the following basis of assets to Coyote Corporation:

Marketable securities	$ 5,000
Inventory	35,000
Building	500,000
Land	200,000
Goodwill	260,000

Note that if the purchase price was only $600,000, there would be zero goodwill and the purchase price would be allocated to the assets based on their relative fair market values to determine their adjusted bases.

An allocation issue may also arise when a corporate shareholder receives a stock dividend (i.e., the distribution of additional shares of stock by a corporation to its existing shareholders). The receipt of a stock dividend is not generally taxable to the shareholder. However, the basis of the shareholders' original stock must be allocated to the total shares owned after the dividend.[26] So although the total cost basis of the shares does not change, the per-share basis decreases because the shareholder owns more shares.

Yellow, Inc., owns 100 shares of Sparrow Corporation common stock for which it paid $1,100. Yellow receives a 10% common stock dividend, giving it a new total of 110 shares. Before the stock dividend, Yellow's basis was $11 per share ($1,100 ÷ 100 shares). The basis of each share after the stock dividend is $10 ($1,100 ÷ 110 shares).

7-2b Property Received as a Gift

When a taxpayer receives property as a gift, the donee (recipient) of the gift has paid nothing to take ownership of the asset. This would ordinarily result in a cost basis of zero. However, this would violate the statutory intent to exclude gifts from Federal income taxation. With a zero basis, the entire amount realized on a subsequent sale would be treated as realized gain. Therefore, taxpayers take a basis in property received as a gift. The basis assigned to such property depends on the following:[27]

- The date of the gift.
- The basis of the property to the donor.
- The fair market value of the property on the date of the gift.
- The amount of any Federal gift tax paid.

Gift Basis Rules, In General

If a property's fair market value on the date of the gift exceeds the donor's basis in the property (i.e., the property has appreciated in value), the donor's basis carries over to the recipient (donee).[28] This basis is referred to as a *carryover basis* and is used in determining the donee's future gain or loss.

[26] §§ 305(a) and 307(a). The holding period of the new shares includes the holding period of the old shares. § 1223(4) and Reg. § 1.1223–1(e). See Chapter 8 for a discussion of the importance of the holding period.

[27] § 1015(a).

[28] § 1015(a) and Reg. § 1.1015–1(a)(1). See Reg. § 1.1015–1(a)(3) for cases in which the facts necessary to determine the donor's adjusted basis are unknown. See Example 20 for the effect of depreciation deductions by the donee.

The Big Picture

Example 17

Return to the facts of *The Big Picture* on p. 7-1. Alice's father purchased the land in 1996 for $2,000. He gave the land to Alice 10 years ago, when the fair market value was $10,000. No gift tax was paid on the transfer. Alice is considering selling the land, which is currently worth $50,000.

If she sells the property for $50,000, Alice will have a realized gain of $48,000 ($50,000 amount realized − $2,000 basis in the land).

If the property's fair market value on the date of the gift is *lower* than the donor's basis, then special *dual basis* rules apply. Here, the donee has one basis for measuring a gain and a different basis for measuring a loss. This special rule is in place to prevent the shifting of losses (typically among family members) to the individual who would receive the greatest benefit. Under this rule, the donee's gain basis is the donor's adjusted basis and the donee's loss basis is the (lower) fair market value of the property.

The Big Picture

Example 18

Return to the facts of *The Big Picture* on p. 7-1. Instead, assume that Alice's father had purchased the land in 1996 for $12,000. He gave the land to Alice 10 years ago, when the fair market value was $10,000. No gift tax was paid on the transfer.

If Alice sells the property for $50,000, she has a realized gain of $38,000 ($50,000 amount realized − $12,000 basis in the land).

However, if the property has declined in value because of the discovery of contaminants on the property and Alice is able to sell the land for only $7,000, she will realize a loss of $3,000 ($7,000 amount realized − $10,000 basis in the land).

This loss basis rule prevents the donee from receiving a tax benefit from a decline in value that occurred while the donor held the property. Therefore, in the preceding example, Alice has a loss of only $3,000 rather than a loss of $5,000 ($7,000 − $12,000). The $2,000 difference represents the decline in value that occurred while Alice's father held the property. Ironically, however, a donee might be subject to income tax on the appreciation that occurred while the donor held the property, as illustrated in Example 17.

In any case, the operation of this dual basis rule can produce a curious anomaly: if the sales proceeds fall *between* the donor's adjusted basis and the property's fair market value at the date of gift, no gain *or* loss is recognized.

The Big Picture

Return to the facts of *The Big Picture* on p. 7-1. Instead, assume that Alice's father had purchased the land in 1996 for $12,000. He gave the land to Alice 10 years ago, when the fair market value was $10,000. No gift tax was paid on the transfer. Now Alice plans to sell the property for $11,000.

To calculate gain, she would use a basis of $12,000, her father's basis. But when a $12,000 basis is compared with the $11,000 sales proceeds, a *loss* is produced. Yet in determining loss, Alice must use the property's fair market value at the date of gift—namely, $10,000. When a $10,000 basis is compared to sales proceeds of $11,000, a *gain* is produced. Accordingly, Alice recognizes no gain or loss on this sale.

Adjustment for Federal Gift Tax Paid

If Federal gift taxes are paid by the donor on the transfer to the donee, the portion of the gift tax paid that is related to any appreciation is taken into account in determining the donee's gain basis.[29] However, basis adjustments for gift taxes are rare.

[29] § 1015(d)(6) and Reg. § 1.1015–5(c)(1). For *gifts made before 1977*, the full amount of the gift tax paid is added to the donor's basis, with basis capped at the donor's fair market value at the date of the gift. Examples illustrating these rules can be found in Reg. § 1.1015–5(c)(5) and IRS Publication 551, *Basis of Assets*.

Tax Planning Strategies — Gift Planning

Framework Focus: Tax Rate

Strategy: Shift Net Income from High-Bracket Taxpayers to Low-Bracket Taxpayers.

Framework Focus: Deductions

Strategy: Maximize Deductible Amounts.

Gifts of *appreciated property* can produce tax savings if the donee is in a lower tax bracket than the donor. The carryover basis rule effectively shifts the tax on the property's appreciation to the new owner even if all of the appreciation arose while the property was owned by the donor.

On the other hand, donors should generally avoid making gifts of property that are worth less than the donor's adjusted basis (loss property). The operation of the basis rule for losses may result in either (1) a realized loss that is not deductible by either the donor or the donee or (2) reduced tax benefits when the loss is recognized by a donee facing lower marginal tax rates. Unless the property is expected to rebound in value before it is sold, a donor would be better advised to sell the property that has declined in value, deduct the resulting loss, and then transfer the proceeds to the prospective donee.

Holding Period

The **holding period** for property acquired by gift begins on the date the donor acquired the property unless the donee's basis in the property is the property's fair market value at the date of the gift.[30] If so, the holding period starts on the date of the gift.[31] The significance of the holding period for capital assets is discussed in Chapter 8.

Basis for Depreciation

The basis for depreciation of depreciable gift property is the donee's basis for determining gain.[32] This rule is applicable even if the donee later sells the property at a loss and uses the property's fair market value at the date of gift in calculating the amount of the realized loss.

Example 20

Vito gave a machine to Tina earlier this year. At that time, the adjusted basis was $32,000 (cost of $40,000 − accumulated depreciation of $8,000), and the fair market value was $26,000. No gift tax was due. Tina's basis for determining gain is $32,000, and her loss basis is $26,000. During this year, Tina deducts depreciation (cost recovery) of $6,400 ($32,000 × 20%). (Refer to Chapter 5 for the cost recovery tables.) At the end of this year, Tina's basis determinations are calculated as follows:

	Gain Basis	Loss Basis
Donor's basis or fair market value	$32,000	$26,000
Depreciation	(6,400)	(6,400)
	$25,600	$19,600

[30] § 1223(2) and Reg. § 1.1223–1(b).

[31] Rev.Rul. 59–86.

[32] § 1011 and Reg. §§ 1.1011–1 and 1.167(g)–1.

7-2c Inherited Property

Special basis rules apply for inherited property (property acquired from a decedent). Typically, these rules are favorable to the beneficiary inheriting the property.

Basis of Inherited Property

Similar to gifts, Congress's intent is to exclude inheritances from income. Therefore, like property received as a gift, inherited property takes a basis in the hands of a recipient. Unlike property received as a gift, the basis of inherited property is generally the property's fair market value at the date of death (referred to as the *primary valuation amount*).[33] However, if the assets in an estate decline in value after the decedent's death, the administrator of the estate may elect to value the property for estate tax purposes at its fair market value six months after the date of death. This amount is referred to as the *alternate valuation amount*. If the alternate valuation amount is used for estate tax purposes, it will also become the basis of the property for the taxpayer who inherits the property.

Basis rules regarding a surviving spouse's share of community property can be found on this book's companion website: www.cengage.com

2 Digging Deeper

Basis of Inherited Property

Example 21

Linda and various other family members inherited stock in a closely held corporation from Linda's father, who died earlier this year. At the date of death, her father's basis for the stock Linda inherited was $35,000. The stock's fair market value at the date of death and the alternate valuation date was $50,000 and $52,000 respectively. The alternate valuation date was not elected. Linda's basis for income tax purposes is $50,000. This is commonly referred to as a *stepped-up basis* (i.e., the basis in the stock is stepped up from the father's $35,000 basis to the $50,000 fair market value on the date of death).

If, instead, the stock's fair market value at the date of death and the alternate valuation date was $20,000 and $21,000, respectively, Linda's basis would be $20,000. This is commonly referred to as a *stepped-down basis* (i.e., the basis in the stock is stepped down from the father's $35,000 basis to the $20,000 fair market value on the date of death).

Example 22

Returning to Example 21, assume that the stock inherited by Linda had a fair market value of $50,000 and $48,000 at the date of death and alternate valuation date, respectively. To reduce estate taxes, the administrator of the estate elected to value the estate at the alternate valuation date. Linda's basis for income tax purposes would be $48,000.

The Big Picture

Example 23

Return to the facts of *The Big Picture* on p. 7-1. Alice owns 500 shares of AppleCo stock, 300 of which were inherited from her grandfather. Her grandfather's cost basis in the stock was $12,000 (i.e., its purchase price), but the shares were worth $30,000 at the time of his death. Alice purchased the other 200 shares for $28,000.

Therefore, the basis in her 500 AppleCo shares is $58,000: the 300 shares received as an inheritance take a stepped-up basis of $30,000, and the 200 shares purchased take a cost basis of $28,000.

The alternate valuation date and amount can be elected *only if*, as a result of the election, *both* the value of the gross estate and the estate tax liability are lower than they would have been if the primary valuation date had been used.[34]

Further discussion of the alternate valuation date can be found on this book's companion website: www.cengage.com

3 Digging Deeper

[33] § 1014(a).

[34] § 2032(c). This provision prevents the alternate valuation election from being used to increase the basis of the property to the beneficiary for income tax purposes without simultaneously increasing the estate tax liability (because of estate tax deductions or credits).

Tax Planning Strategies **Inherited Property**

Framework Focus: Income

Strategy: Avoid Income Recognition.

Framework Focus: Deductions

Strategy: Maximize Deductible Amounts.

If a taxpayer *retains appreciated property* until death, the property's basis will be "stepped up" to its fair market value at that time. So no income tax will be paid on the property's appreciation by either the former owner (the decedent) or the new owner (the heir).

Alternatively, *depreciated property should be sold* prior to death. Otherwise, the property's basis in the heir's hands will be its declined fair market value, and neither the decedent nor the heir will be able to deduct the loss that occurred while the property was owned by the decedent.

Holding Period of Inherited Property

The holding period of inherited property is *deemed to be long term* regardless of when the property was acquired by the decedent and whether the property is disposed of at a gain or at a loss.[35]

Discussion and illustration of additional complexities in determining adjusted basis can be found on this book's companion website: www.cengage.com

7-3 Disallowed Losses

In certain situations, realized losses are not recognizable. Three of these situations are discussed below.

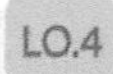

Apply various loss disallowance provisions.

7-3a Personal Use Assets

Individual taxpayers are not allowed to recognize losses on the sale, exchange, or condemnation of *personal use* assets (e.g., a residence or an automobile that is not used in any business or investment activity). An exception exists for losses resulting from certain casualties or thefts (refer to Chapter 6). In contrast, any gain realized from the disposition of personal use assets is generally recognized.

Freda sells an automobile, which she has held exclusively for personal use, for $6,000. The basis of the automobile is $5,000. Freda has a realized and recognized gain of $1,000.

If instead she sold this automobile for $4,500, she would have a realized loss of $500. However, the loss would not be recognized for tax purposes because the automobile is a personal use asset.

[35] § 1223(9).

7-3b Transactions between Related Parties

As discussed in Chapter 5, § 267 restricts the deductibility of expenses accrued to related parties. Code § 267 also disallows the immediate recognition of any losses from sales or exchanges of property directly or indirectly between those same related parties.[36] Without this restriction, taxpayers would be able to recognize losses on property sales without effectively giving up control of the property itself.

Although the loss realized in a related-party sale is not immediately recognized, it may be used to offset any future gain recognized when the property is subsequently sold to an *unrelated* party (i.e., a right of offset is created). Note that this loss offset is only available to the party who later sells the property to an unrelated party and *not* to the initial seller who realized the loss. Further, the right of offset cannot create or increase a loss. Any right of offset not used by the subsequent seller to offset some or all of the recognized gain is permanently lost.

Donald owns real estate that he originally purchased in 2017 for $1,000,000. In 2022, the property has a fair market value of $600,000. Donald believes the property will appreciate in value when a proposed shopping mall is built nearby and, therefore, does not want to lose control of it. However, he has realized a large gain on the sale of a different piece of property and would like to use the unrealized loss related to the parcel of real estate to offset the gain. So at the end of 2022, Donald sells the property to his brother, Ben, for $600,000. In 2024, after the mall is built, Ben sells the land to a developer for $850,000.

Since Ben and Donald are considered related parties under § 267, Donald cannot recognize the $400,000 loss realized on the 2022 sale to Ben. However, when Ben subsequently sells the property to the developer in 2024, his $250,000 realized gain can be reduced, but not below zero, by Donald's $400,000 unrecognized loss. As a result, Ben does not recognize a gain on the sale. The remaining $150,000 loss not recognized by Ben is permanently lost.

7-3c Wash Sales

The **wash sale** rules are designed to eliminate a taxpayer strategy to recognize a loss on the sale of stock and repurchase the stock shortly before or after the sale, leaving the taxpayer in substantially the same economic position after the sale and repurchase as before. If the wash sale rules apply, a realized loss on the sale or exchange of stock or securities is not currently recognized.

The wash sale rules apply if a taxpayer sells or exchanges stock or securities at a loss and within 30 days before *or* after the date of the sale or exchange acquires *substantially identical* stock or securities.[37] To be considered "substantially identical," stock and securities must be more than merely "similar." For example, although common stock in one corporation will be considered substantially identical to other common stock in the same corporation, common stock in one corporation will not be considered substantially identical to common stock in another corporation, even if the corporations are engaged in the same business. Buying an option to purchase substantially identical securities is

[36] § 267(a).

[37] § 1091(a) and Reg. §§ 1.1091–1(a) and (f).

treated the same as actually buying the stock. Corporate bonds and preferred stock normally are not considered substantially identical to a corporation's common stock.[38] Attempts to avoid the application of the wash sale rules by having a related taxpayer repurchase the securities have been unsuccessful.[39] The wash sale provisions do *not* apply to gains.

Although losses realized in a wash sale are not recognized, they are added to the *basis* of the stock or securities whose acquisition resulted in the nonrecognition, allowing the taxpayer to indirectly recover their basis in the old stock or securities when they dispose of the replacement stock or securities.[40] As a result, the wash sale rule operates to *defer* the recognition of the taxpayer's loss rather than to disallow it.

Oriole Manufacturing Company sold 50 shares of Green Corporation stock (basis of $10,000) for $8,000. Ten days later, Oriole purchased 50 shares of the same stock for $7,000.

Oriole's realized loss of $2,000 ($8,000 amount realized − $10,000 basis) is not recognized because it resulted from a wash sale. Oriole's basis in the newly acquired stock is $9,000 ($7,000 purchase price + $2,000 unrecognized loss from the wash sale).

Because the basis of the new stock or securities includes the unrecovered portion of the basis of the formerly held stock or securities, the *holding period* of the new stock or securities begins on the date of acquisition of the old stock or securities.[41]

If a taxpayer acquires fewer shares of substantially identical stock than the number sold, only a portion of the loss is disallowed. The portion disallowed is equal to the portion of the number of shares initially sold that are reacquired.[42] This disallowance rule does not apply to taxpayers engaged in the business of buying and selling securities.[43]

Tax Planning Strategies — Avoiding Wash Sales

Framework Focus: Deductions

Strategy: Maximize Deductible Amounts.

The wash sale rules can be avoided by replacing the sold security with a *similar* but not "substantially identical" security. For example, a taxpayer wanting to recognize an unrealized loss related to an investment in AT&T stock, but who believes the telecommunications industry will thrive in the near future, could sell the AT&T stock and immediately acquire Verizon common stock without triggering the wash sale rule even though both entities are telecommunication companies.

Nontax considerations must also come into play, however, because AT&T and Verizon are two different companies with different investment prospects. Although both securities will be affected by many of the same factors, they will also be subject to different factors that may be even more significant than the ones they share.

[38] However, if the bonds and preferred stock are convertible into common stock, they may be considered substantially identical under certain circumstances. Rev.Rul. 56–406.

[39] *McWilliams v. Comm.*, 47–1 USTC ¶9289, 35 AFTR 1184, 67 S.Ct. 1477.

[40] § 1091(d) and Reg. § 1.1091–2(a).

[41] § 1223(3) and Reg. § 1.1223–1(d).

[42] § 1091(b) and Reg. § 1.1091–1(c).

[43] § 1091(a) and Reg. § 1.1091–1(a).

7-3d Property Converted from Personal Use to Business or Income-Producing Use

As discussed previously, losses from the sale of personal use assets are not recognized for tax purposes while losses from the sale of business and income-producing assets are recognized. Can a taxpayer convert a personal use asset that has declined in value to business or income-producing use before selling the asset to recognize the loss?

The tax law prevents this practice by specifying that the *basis for determining loss* on personal use assets converted to business or income-producing use is the *lower* of the property's adjusted basis or its fair market value on the date of conversion.[44] The *gain basis* for converted property is the property's adjusted basis on the date of conversion, regardless of whether the property's use is business, income-producing, or personal in nature.

Diane's personal residence has an adjusted basis of $175,000 and a fair market value of $160,000. When she converts the personal residence to residential rental property on January 1, her basis for determining loss is $160,000 (lower of $175,000 adjusted basis and fair market value of $160,000). The $15,000 decline in value is a personal loss and can never be recognized for tax purposes. Diane's basis for determining gain is $175,000.

The basis for determining loss is also the *basis for depreciating* the converted property.[45] This is an exception to the general rule that the basis for depreciation is the basis for determining gain (e.g., property received by gift). This exception prevents the taxpayer from recovering a personal loss indirectly through depreciation of the higher original basis. Once property is converted, both its basis for loss and its basis for gain are adjusted for depreciation deductions from the date of conversion to the date of disposition.

Assume the same facts as in Example 27. The MACRS cost recovery deduction for the current year is $5,576 ($160,000 × 3.485%). Thus, at the end of the current year, Diane's adjusted basis for gain for the rental property is $169,424 ($175,000 − $5,576), and her adjusted basis for loss is $154,424 ($160,000 − $5,576).

A comprehensive example of the basis rules for personal use property converted to business or income-producing use can be found on this book's companion website: www.cengage.com

5 Digging Deeper

[44]Reg. § 1.165–9(b)(2).

[45]Reg. § 1.167(g)–1.

7-4 Nontaxable Exchanges—General Concepts

As discussed earlier, the sale or exchange of an asset results in a realized gain or loss, and most realized gains and losses are recognized immediately. However, certain exchanges may result in a change in the *form*, but not a meaningful change in the *substance*, of the assets held by a taxpayer. For example, a taxpayer may exchange a building used in a trade or business for a similar one in a different location where the business will be continued. In such a case, although the taxpayer owns a different building, the new building serves the same purpose and function as did the old. The new building may best be viewed as a continuation of the old investment.[46] In addition, these exchanges frequently do not provide the taxpayer with the *wherewithal to pay* any tax on the realized gain (i.e., the taxpayer does not have the cash that would have been received in a sale). In certain of these cases, the tax law treats these transactions as nontaxable exchanges.

A **nontaxable exchange** *postpones* (i.e., defers) recognition of realized gains or losses until the property received in the exchange is later sold in a taxable transaction. This deferral is accomplished by assigning a carryover basis to the replacement property.

Starling Management Company completes a *nontaxable exchange* of property with an adjusted basis of $10,000 and a fair market value of $12,000 for property with a fair market value of $12,000.

Starling has a realized gain of $2,000 ($12,000 amount realized − $10,000 adjusted basis). However, Starling recognizes none of its realized gain and takes a carryover basis of $10,000 in the newly acquired property.

Now assume that Starling subsequently sells the replacement property for $13,000. The recognized gain of $3,000 will include the postponed (deferred) $2,000 gain from the nontaxable transaction.

In some nontaxable exchanges, only certain property involved in the transaction may qualify for nonrecognition treatment. For example, if the taxpayer receives cash or other nonqualifying property, part or all of the realized gain from the exchange is recognized since the taxpayer has converted the exchanged asset into something substantially different and has the wherewithal to pay tax. Here, the basis of the replacement property is adjusted to reflect only the deferred gain (gain realized but not recognized).

It is important to distinguish between a nontaxable disposition (or nonrecognition transaction, as the term is used in the statute) and a tax-free transaction. As previously mentioned, the term *nontaxable* refers to postponement of recognition via some version of carryover basis. In a *tax-free* transaction, the nonrecognition is a permanent exclusion of gain (e.g., taxpayers may be able to permanently exclude a gain from the sale of a principal residence).

Either way, nontaxable and tax-free transactions are exceptions to the Code's general rule that gains and losses are recognized when they are realized. These exceptions have their own sets of requirements, limitations, and restrictions, all of which must be satisfied for a transaction to be characterized as nontaxable or tax-free. Otherwise, the general rule of recognition applies to the realized gain or loss. Like-kind exchanges and

[46]Reg. § 1.1002–1(c).

involuntary conversions are two examples of tax-deferred nonrecognition transactions. Others include certain transfers of assets by shareholders to controlled corporations (discussed in Chapter 12), certain transfers of assets by partners to partnerships (discussed in Chapter 14), and corporate reorganizations. However, the concepts discussed below related to like-kind exchanges and involuntary conversions apply to these and other nonrecognition transactions as well.

7-5 Like-Kind Exchanges—§ 1031

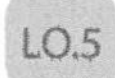

Apply the nonrecognition provisions and basis determination rules for like-kind exchanges.

Like-kind exchanges must meet the following requirements to qualify for nonrecognition:[47]

- The property given up and received by the taxpayer must be of like kind.
- The transaction is structured as an exchange.
- Both the property given up and the property received are either "used in a trade or business" *or* "held for investment."

If a transaction qualifies as a like-kind exchange, deferral of any realized gain or loss is required, and the basis and holding period of the transferred property attaches (or carries over) to the new property.

During the current year, Andy exchanged 40 acres of unimproved land in Illinois (fair market value $200,000; basis $70,000) for 10 acres of unimproved land in California (fair market value $200,000).

Although Andy has a realized gain of $130,000 on this transaction ($200,000 amount realized − $70,000 basis), none of the gain is recognized; the transaction qualifies as a like-kind exchange. Andy's basis in the new property is $70,000. This carryover basis reflects the realized gain, which is deferred ($200,000 California property fair market value − $130,000 gain deferred).

If Andy sells the California property for $200,000 cash, he will realize and recognize the deferred gain of $130,000.

One final point: the like-kind exchange rules are applied independently to each taxpayer in the exchange. For example, while one taxpayer in an exchange may qualify for like-kind treatment, the other may not.

7-5a Like-Kind Property

Like-kind property includes only *real property* held by the taxpayer for business or investment purposes.[48] However, almost all real property used in a business or for investment is considered to be of like kind. For example, an exchange of a warehouse for an office building or a manufacturing plant for a retail building would qualify as a like-kind exchange. It is irrelevant whether realty is improved or unimproved. For example, unimproved land can be exchanged for an apartment building. A taxpayer may even exchange real property used in a business for real property held for investment purposes. To qualify as like-kind property, U.S. realty must be exchanged for U.S. realty and foreign realty must be exchanged for foreign realty. In any case, real estate cannot be exchanged in a like-kind transaction for personal property.

[47] § 1031(a) and Reg. § 1.1031(a)–1(a).

[48] Before January 1, 2018, business and investment *personal property* also qualified for like-kind exchange treatment. This includes machines, equipment, furniture and fixtures, trucks, and automobiles.

Tax Planning Strategies — Like-Kind Exchanges

Framework Focus: Deductions

Strategy: Maximize Deductible Amounts.

The nonrecognition provision for like-kind exchanges is *mandatory* rather than elective. A taxpayer who wants to recognize a realized gain or loss will have to structure the transaction in a way that fails the like-kind exchange requirements. For example, a taxpayer may want to avoid like-kind treatment to recognize a realized loss.

During the current year, Stephanie exchanged her rental condo in Vail, worth $250,000 (basis of $325,000), plus $80,000 cash for a rental condo in Malibu worth $330,000. Although Stephanie has a realized loss of $75,000 on this transaction [$330,000 amount realized − $405,000 ($325,000 adjusted basis of condo transferred + $80,000 cash)], she can recognize none of the loss because the transaction qualifies as a like-kind exchange.

Stephanie could recognize the loss by instead selling her Vail condo for cash and then buying the Malibu property.

Even if a *disposition would result in a gain*, a taxpayer might want to recognize this gain in the current taxable year. If so, a like-kind exchange should be avoided. Avoiding like-kind treatment can be optimal when the taxpayer expects increasing tax rates or has:

- Unused capital loss carryovers, especially if the taxpayer is a corporation for which such carryovers are limited in duration (see Chapters 4 and 8).
- Unused net operating loss carryovers (see Chapter 6).
- Unused general business credit carryovers (see Chapter 17).
- Suspended or current passive activity losses (see Chapter 6).

Digging Deeper 6

Rules regarding multi-asset exchanges can be found on this book's companion website: www.cengage.com

7-5b Exchange Requirement

The transaction must generally involve a direct *exchange* of property to qualify as a like-kind exchange. The sale of old property and the purchase of new property, even if the old and new property are of like kind, is not an exchange. However, the Code does allow nonrecognition for certain deferred exchanges if the property to be received by the taxpayer is identified and received within a limited period following the date the taxpayer transfers the property being sold.[49]

[49] § 1031(a)(3) and Reg. § 1.1031(k)–1.

Rules regarding deferred exchanges can be found on this book's companion website: www.cengage.com

7 Digging Deeper

7-5c Boot

It is unusual to find transactions in which the value of the like-kind property given up equals the value of the like-kind property received. In most situations, at least one party must provide some other property to "even out" the exchange. Including property that is *not* like-kind property in a transaction that would otherwise qualify as a like-kind exchange will not prevent the transaction from qualifying as a like-kind exchange. However, it may trigger the recognition of some or all of a realized gain or loss. Property that is not like-kind property, including cash, is often referred to as **boot**. Although the term *boot* does not appear in the Code, tax practitioners commonly use it rather than saying "property that does not qualify as like-kind property."

The *receipt* of boot will trigger gain recognition only if there is realized gain. The recognized gain equals the *lesser* of the boot received or the realized gain. If a taxpayer recognizes gain in a like-kind exchange, the character of the gain depends on the character of the asset given up (see Chapter 8).

Implications of Boot Received

Blue, Inc., and White Corporation exchange land in a like-kind exchange. Because Blue's land (with an adjusted basis of $20,000) is worth $24,000 and White's land has a fair market value of $19,000, White also gives Blue cash of $5,000.

Blue's recognized gain is $4,000, the lesser of the realized gain of $4,000 ($24,000 amount realized − $20,000 adjusted basis) or the fair market value of the boot received of $5,000.

Assume the same facts as in the preceding example, except that White's land is worth $21,000 (not $19,000). Under these circumstances, White gives Blue cash of $3,000 to make up the difference.

Blue's recognized gain is $3,000, the lesser of the realized gain of $4,000 ($24,000 amount realized − $20,000 adjusted basis) or the fair market value of the boot received of $3,000.

The receipt of boot does not allow the recognition of a realized loss. Thus, taxpayers *never* recognize a realized loss on the exchange of like-kind property.

Implications of Boot Received

Assume the same facts as in Example 32, except that the adjusted basis of Blue's land is $30,000.

Blue's realized loss is $6,000 ($24,000 amount realized − $30,000 adjusted basis). The receipt of the boot of $5,000 does not trigger recognition of Blue's realized loss.

Giving boot does not trigger recognition if the boot consists solely of cash because the basis of cash always equals its value.

Implications of Boot Given

Example 35

Flicker, Inc., and Gadwall Corporation exchange land in a like-kind exchange. Flicker receives land with a fair market value of $75,000 and transfers land worth $63,000 (adjusted basis of $45,000) and cash of $12,000.

Flicker's realized gain is $18,000 ($75,000 amount realized − $45,000 adjusted basis of land transferred − $12,000 cash), none of which is recognized.

If, however, the boot given is noncash property with an adjusted basis that differs from its fair market value, the taxpayer giving the boot may recognize this non-like-kind gain or loss. For example, a loss realized on the transfer of stock as boot would be recognized; however, a loss realized on the transfer of personal use property as boot would not be recognized (due to disallowance of personal use losses).

Implications of Boot Given

Example 36

Assume the same facts as in the preceding example, except that Flicker transfers land worth $30,000 (adjusted basis of $36,000) and boot worth $45,000 (adjusted basis of $27,000). Flicker's net gain on this exchange is $12,000 [$75,000 amount realized − adjusted basis of $63,000 ($36,000 + $27,000)]. But Flicker is transferring two pieces of property: land (like-kind property) with a built-in realized loss of $6,000 ($30,000 fair market value − $36,000 adjusted basis) and non-like-kind property (boot) with a built-in realized gain of $18,000 ($45,000 fair market value − $27,000 adjusted basis).

In this case, the $6,000 realized loss on the like-kind property is *deferred* (not recognized) but the $18,000 realized gain on the non-like-kind property is recognized. In other words, the realized loss on the like-kind property *cannot* be used to offset the realized gain on the boot given up as part of the transaction.

7-5d Basis and Holding Period of Property Received

If an exchange qualifies as nontaxable under § 1031, the *basis of like-kind property* received in the exchange must be adjusted to reflect any gain or loss that is deferred. To arrive at the basis of the like-kind property received, its fair market value is decreased by any deferred gain or increased by any deferred loss. The *basis* of any *boot* received is the boot's fair market value because this portion of the transaction is taxable.

Basis of Like-Kind Property Received

Example 37

Vireo Property Management Company exchanges a building (used in its business) with an adjusted basis of $300,000 and a fair market value of $380,000 for land with a fair market value of $380,000. The land is to be held as an investment. The exchange qualifies as like kind (an exchange of business real property for investment real property).

Vireo's basis of its newly acquired land is $300,000 (the land's fair market value of $380,000 − $80,000 deferred gain on the building). If Vireo later sells the land for its fair market value of $380,000, Vireo recognizes the $80,000 postponed gain.

Example 38

Assume the same facts as in the preceding example, except that the building has an adjusted basis of $480,000 and a fair market value of only $380,000.

The basis in the newly acquired land is $480,000 (fair market value of $380,000 + $100,000 postponed loss on the building). If Vireo later sells the land for its fair market value of $380,000, Vireo recognizes the $100,000 postponed loss.

Bridge Discipline **Bridge to Economics**

One can assert that the "tax variable" is neutralized in nontaxable exchanges. Neutralizing potential tax consequences can have a positive result given that tax costs tend to dampen economic activity. For example, in a like-kind exchange, a taxpayer can exchange one asset for another asset of like kind without having to recognize a gain or pay a tax. The justification for the tax deferral is that the substance of the taxpayer's assets has not changed as result of the transaction. But the tax-neutral result changes when the taxpayer receives property that is not "like kind" because the substance of the taxpayer's assets has changed.

If, for example, the taxpayer receives investment land *and* cash in exchange for investment land, her ownership in the land given up has, at least in part, been converted to cash, and to that degree, not only the form but also the substance of her assets has changed. That is, the taxpayer's economic investment has changed from an ownership exclusively in land to ownership in land *and* cash. Alternatively, if the taxpayer gives up her investment in land for corporate stock in a high-tech venture, the nature of her investment also would substantively change as a result of the transaction. These differences in the substance of the taxpayer's assets after the transaction lead to the transactions being taxed.

Alternatively, the basis of property received in a like-kind exchange may be determined as follows:

Adjusted basis of like-kind property surrendered
\+ Adjusted basis of boot given
\+ Gain recognized
− Fair market value of boot received
− Loss recognized (on boot given)
= *Basis of like-kind property received*

This approach is logical in terms of the recovery of capital doctrine: the unrecovered cost or other basis is increased by additional cost (boot given) or decreased by cost recovered (boot received). Any gain recognized is included in the basis of the new property. The taxpayer has been taxed on this amount and now is entitled to recover it tax-free. Any loss recognized is deducted from the basis of the new property because the taxpayer has already received a tax benefit on that amount.

The holding period of the like-kind property surrendered in the exchange carries over and *tacks on* to the holding period of the like-kind property received.[50] This rule stems from the basic concept that the new property is a continuation of the old investment. The boot received has a new holding period (from the date of exchange) rather than a carryover holding period.

Depreciation recapture potential carries over to the property received in a like-kind exchange.[51] See Chapter 8 for a discussion of this topic.

A comprehensive example illustrating the like-kind exchange basis rules can be found on this book's companion website: www.cengage.com

8 Digging Deeper

If the taxpayer assumes a liability (or takes property subject to a liability), the law treats the liability as boot given. For the taxpayer whose liability is assumed (or whose property is taken subject to the liability), the law treats the liability relief as boot received. As discussed earlier, being relieved of a debt is equivalent to the receipt of cash (i.e., boot) followed by the repayment of the debt. The following example illustrates the effect of such a liability. In addition, the example illustrates the tax consequences for both parties involved in the like-kind exchange.

[50] § 1223(1) and Reg. § 1.1223–1(a). The tacked-on holding period applies only if the like-kind property surrendered was either a capital asset or § 1231 property.

[51] Reg. §§ 1.1245–2(c)(4) and 1.1250–2(d)(1).

Jaeger & Company and Lark Enterprises, Inc., exchange real estate investments. Jaeger gives up property with an adjusted basis of $250,000 (fair market value of $420,000) that is subject to a mortgage of $80,000 (assumed by Lark). In return for this property, Jaeger receives property with a fair market value of $340,000 (Lark's adjusted basis in the property is $200,000). Jaeger's and Lark's realized and recognized gains and their basis in the like-kind property received are computed as follows:

	Jaeger	Lark
Amount realized:		
Like-kind property received	$340,000	$420,000
Boot received:		
Mortgage assumed by Lark	80,000	
	$420,000	$420,000
Adjusted basis:		
Like-kind property given	(250,000)	(200,000)
Boot given:		
Mortgage assumed by Lark		(80,000)
Realized gain	$170,000	$140,000
Recognized gain	80,000*	-0-**
Deferred gain	$ 90,000	$140,000
Basis of property received:		
Basis of like-kind property transferred	$250,000	$200,000
Mortgage assumed		80,000
	$250,000	$280,000
Plus: Gain recognized	80,000	
Less: Boot received	(80,000)	
Basis of new property	$250,000	$280,000

*Lesser of boot received ($80,000 mortgage assumed) or realized gain ($170,000).
**No boot received. Therefore, no gain is recognized.

LO.6

Explain the nonrecognition provisions available on the involuntary conversion of property.

7-6 Involuntary Conversions—§ 1033

In most cases, taxpayers sell or exchange property when they choose to, able to take into account all of the consequences related to the transaction, including the tax consequences. There are times, however, when the taxpayer *involuntarily* (i.e., outside the taxpayer's control) disposes of property. When this happens, the taxpayer usually receives some sort of compensation (e.g., insurance proceeds or a condemnation award from a government entity). Code § 1033 provides that a taxpayer who suffers an involuntary conversion of property may postpone recognition of any *gain* realized from the conversion. The objective of this provision is to provide relief to the taxpayer who has no wherewithal to pay the tax on any gain realized from the conversion.

The deferral of gain under § 1033 generally is elective. When applicable, gain realized in an involuntary conversion is postponed when the amount realized (e.g., insurance proceeds) is reinvested in qualifying replacement property. If the amount reinvested in replacement property is *less than* the amount realized, realized gain is recognized to the extent of the deficiency.

Involuntary Conversions: General Rules

Example 40

Jason operates a charter fishing business in Panama City, Florida, taking customers out in the Gulf of Mexico on daylong fishing trips. Unfortunately, Hurricane Michael completely destroyed his boat, which had a basis of $78,000 ($120,000 cost − $42,000 of accumulated depreciation). Fortunately, Jason had insurance that paid him the full replacement cost of his boat. He filed an insurance claim the week after he lost his boat and received $175,000 in insurance proceeds three weeks later.

Jason has a realized gain of $97,000, computed as follows:

Amount realized (insurance proceeds)	$175,000
Less: Adjusted basis	(78,000)
Realized gain	$ 97,000

Jason can defer the entire realized gain provided that he uses all of the insurance proceeds to purchase a new boat.

Refer to the facts of Example 40, and assume that Jason buys a new boat for $180,000. He uses the entire insurance settlement as part of the purchase.

In this case, Jason's $97,000 realized gain is deferred, and the basis of his new boat must reflect that deferral. As a result, his new boat's basis is $83,000 ($180,000 cost − $97,000 deferred gain).

Continuing with the facts of Example 40, assume that Jason negotiates an excellent price for his new boat. In fact, he is able to replace his old boat for only $168,000 and uses the $7,000 remaining from the insurance settlement to pay for other business expenses.

Jason recognizes a $7,000 gain, which equals the difference between the $175,000 insurance settlement and the amount he paid for the new boat (the amount of the insurance proceeds he reinvested in replacement property).

The balance of the realized gain is deferred, and the basis of his new boat must reflect that deferral. As a result, his new boat's basis is $78,000 ($168,000 cost − $90,000 deferred gain).

If a *loss* is realized on an involuntary conversion, § 1033 does not apply.

Refer to the facts of Example 40, but assume that Jason had only partial coverage on his boat and his insurance settlement is only $50,000. In this case, Jason has a loss of $28,000, computed as follows:

Amount realized (insurance proceeds)	$50,000
Less: Adjusted basis	(78,000)
Realized loss	($28,000)

In this case, § 1033 will not apply to the transaction, and Jason's realized loss of $28,000 is recognized.

7-6a Involuntary Conversion Defined

An **involuntary conversion** results from the complete or partial destruction, theft, seizure, condemnation, or sale or exchange under threat of condemnation (e.g., a city seizing property under its right of eminent domain) of the taxpayer's property.[52] This description includes fires (other than arson),[53] tornadoes, hurricanes, earthquakes, floods, and other natural disasters. In these circumstances, *gain* can result from insurance proceeds received in excess of the taxpayer's adjusted basis of the property, especially if the property had replacement value insurance or if depreciation deductions have lowered the property's adjusted basis.

For condemnations, the amount realized includes the compensation paid by the public authority acquiring the taxpayer's property. Government seizures are unique events (and as a result, § 1033 includes a distinct set of rules for them). In general, for § 1033 to apply to a sale or exchange under the threat of condemnation, the taxpayer must have reasonable grounds to believe that a condemnation of the property was likely to occur.[54]

Digging Deeper 9

Rules regarding the treatment of severance damages as an involuntary conversion can be found on this book's companion website: www.cengage.com

7-6b Replacement Property

The requirements for replacement property under the involuntary conversion rules generally are more restrictive than those for like-kind exchanges. The basic requirement is that the replacement property be *similar or related in service or use* to the involuntarily converted property.[55]

Different interpretations of the phrase *similar or related in service or use* apply depending on whether the involuntarily converted property is actually used by the taxpayer (i.e., the taxpayer is an *owner-user*) or is held as an investment (i.e., the taxpayer is an *owner-investor*). Owner-users must meet the *functional use test* while owner-investors must meet the *taxpayer use test*. In most cases, the functional use test is more restrictive than the taxpayer use test. Furthermore, a special rule applies in the case of involuntary conversions that result from condemnations.

Functional Use Test

Under this test, a taxpayer's use of the replacement property and of the involuntarily converted property must be the same. For example, replacing a manufacturing plant with a wholesale grocery warehouse does not meet this test. Instead, the plant must be replaced with another manufacturing plant.

Taxpayer Use Test

The taxpayer use test for owner-investors provides much more flexibility for qualifying replacement property than the functional use test. Essentially, the properties must be used by the taxpayer (the owner-investor) in similar endeavors.[56] For example, rental property held by an owner-investor qualifies if replaced by other rental property,

[52] § 1033(a) and Reg. §§ 1.1033(a)–1(a) and −2(a).

[53] Rev.Rul. 82–74.

[54] Rev.Rul. 63–221, modified by Rev.Rul. 74–8, and *Joseph P. Balistrieri*, 38 TCM 526, T.C.Memo. 1979–115.

[55] § 1033(a) and Reg. § 1.1033(a)–1.

[56] Rev.Rul. 64–237.

regardless of the type of rental property involved. The test is met, for example, when an investor replaces a manufacturing plant (being rented) with a wholesale grocery warehouse (also being rented).[57] Replacing a rental residence with a personal residence does *not* meet the test.[58]

Special Rule for Condemnations

In addition to the functional and taxpayer use tests, the Code provides a special rule for business or investment real property that is *condemned*. This rule applies the broad like-kind classification for real estate to such circumstances. Accordingly, unimproved real property can replace improved real property.

The rules concerning the nature of replacement property are illustrated in Concept Summary 7.3.

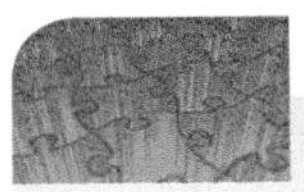

Concept Summary 7.3

Involuntary Conversions: Replacement Property Tests

Type of Property and User	Functional Use Text	Taxpayer Use Test	Special Rule for Condemnations*
Property used by the taxpayer in a trade or business or for personal purposes	X		
Property held by the taxpayer for the production of income (i.e., rental property)		X	
Any real property used by the taxpayer in a trade or business or held for the production of income that is condemned or disposed of under the threat of condemnation			X

*Applies the same test as in the case of like-kind exchanges.

7-6c Time Limitation on Replacement

In general, the taxpayer must acquire replacement property within two years after the close of the taxable year in which gain is realized.[59] Typically, gain is realized when insurance proceeds or damages are received.

[57] *Loco Realty Co. v. Comm.*, 62–2 USTC ¶9657, 10 AFTR 2d 5359, 306 F.2d 207 (CA–8).

[58] Rev.Rul. 70–466.

[59] §§ 1033(a)(2)(B) and (g)(4) and Reg. § 1.1033(a)–2(c)(3). The two-year period is extended to a four-year period if the property is located in a Federally declared disaster area. A taxpayer can apply for an extension of this time period anytime before its expiration [Reg. § 1.1033(a)–2(c)(3)]. Also, the period for filing the application for extension can be extended if a taxpayer shows reasonable cause for the delay.

Example 44

Magpie, Inc.'s building is destroyed by fire on December 16, 2021. The adjusted basis is $325,000. Magpie receives $400,000 from the insurance company on February 2, 2022. The company is a calendar year and cash method taxpayer.

The latest date for replacement is December 31, 2024 (the end of the taxable year in which realized gain occurred plus two years). The critical date is not the date the involuntary conversion occurred, but rather the date of gain realization (when the insurance proceeds are received).

In the case of a condemnation of real property used in a trade or business or held for investment, a three-year period is allowed for replacement.

Example 45

Assume the same facts as in the previous example, except that Magpie's building is condemned. On November 1, 2021, Magpie receives notification of the future condemnation, which occurs on December 16, 2021. The condemnation proceeds are received on February 2, 2022.

The latest date for replacement is December 31, 2025 (the end of the taxable year in which realized gain occurred plus three years).

The *earliest date* for replacement typically is the date the involuntary conversion occurs. However, if the property is condemned, it is possible to replace the condemned property before this date. In this case, the earliest date for replacement is the date of the threat of condemnation of the property. This rule allows the taxpayer to make an orderly replacement of the condemned property.

7-6d Nonrecognition of Gain

Nonrecognition of gain can be either mandatory or elective depending on whether the conversion is direct (into replacement property) or indirect (into money).

Direct Conversion

If the conversion is directly into replacement property rather than into money, nonrecognition of realized gain is *mandatory*. In this case, the basis of the replacement property is the same as the adjusted basis of the converted property. Direct conversion is rare in practice and usually involves condemnations.

Example 46

Oak, Inc.'s property, with an adjusted basis of $20,000, is condemned by the state. Oak receives property with a fair market value of $50,000 as compensation for the property taken.

Because the condemned property was converted directly into new property, Oak's realized gain of $30,000 is not recognized and the basis of the replacement property is $20,000 (adjusted basis of the condemned property).

Conversion into Money

More commonly, the conversion will be into money. In this case, nonrecognition is elective. If deferral is elected, the realized gain is recognized only to the extent the amount realized from the involuntary conversion exceeds the cost of the qualifying replacement property.[60] If the election is not made, the taxpayer recognizes the entire realized gain.

The basis of the replacement property is the property's cost less any postponed (deferred) gain.[61] If the taxpayer elects to postpone gain, the holding period of the replacement property includes the holding period of the converted property.

As noted earlier, § 1033 applies *only to gains* and *not to losses*. Losses from involuntary conversions are recognized if the property is held for business or income-producing purposes. Personal casualty losses are recognized (subject to the limitations discussed in Chapter 6), but condemnation losses related to personal use assets (e.g., a personal residence) are neither recognized nor postponed.

[60] § 1033(a)(2)(A) and Reg. § 1.1033(a)–2(c)(1).

[61] § 1033(b).

The Big Picture

Example 47

Return to the facts of *The Big Picture* on p. 7-1. Alice's building (used in her trade or business), with an adjusted basis of $50,000, is destroyed by a fire on October 5, 2022. Alice is a calendar year taxpayer. On November 17, 2022, she receives an insurance reimbursement of $100,000 for the loss. Assume that Alice goes ahead with her plan to invest $80,000 in a new building and to use the other $20,000 of insurance proceeds to pay off credit card debt.

- Alice has until December 31, 2024, to make the new investment and qualify for the nonrecognition election.
- Alice's realized gain is $50,000 ($100,000 insurance proceeds received − $50,000 adjusted basis of old building).
- Assuming that the replacement property qualifies as similar or related in service or use, Alice's recognized gain is $20,000. Because she reinvested $20,000 less than the insurance proceeds received ($100,000 proceeds − $80,000 reinvested), her realized gain is recognized to that extent.
- Alice's basis in the new building is $50,000. This is the building's cost of $80,000 less the postponed gain of $30,000 (realized gain of $50,000 − recognized gain of $20,000).

The Big Picture

Return to the facts of *The Big Picture* on p. 7-1. Assume the same facts as in the previous example, except that Alice receives only $45,000 of insurance proceeds. She has a realized and recognized loss of $5,000. The basis of the new building is the building's cost of $80,000.

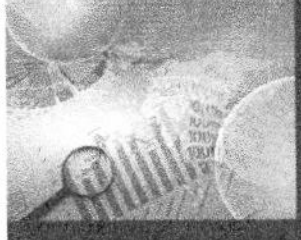

Tax Planning Strategies — Recognizing Involuntary Conversion Gains

Framework Focus: Tax Rate

Strategy: Shift Net Income from High-Bracket Years to Low-Bracket Years.

Framework Focus: Deductions

Strategy: Maximize Deductible Amounts.

Sometimes a taxpayer may prefer to *recognize a gain from an involuntary conversion* and will choose not to elect § 1033 even though replacement property is acquired. Circumstances suggesting this strategy would include:

- The taxpayer realized the gain in a low-bracket tax year (quite possibly because the events that caused the involuntary conversion, such as a flood and its aftermath, seriously disrupted the business).
- The taxpayer has a loss carryover that can offset most, if not all, of the gain from the involuntary conversion.
- The replacement property is depreciable, and the taxpayer would prefer an unreduced basis for this asset to maximize depreciation deductions in future years.

Nontax considerations might also come into play, perhaps suggesting that the property not be replaced at all. Even before the event that produced the involuntary conversion, the taxpayer might have wanted to downsize the business or terminate it outright. In any case, the taxpayer might prefer to recognize the gain, pay the tax involved, and thereby free up the remaining proceeds for other uses—business, investment, or even personal—especially if the gain is small compared to the amount of proceeds received.

LO.7

Determine the recognized gain on the sale of a principal residence.

7-7 Sale of a Principal Residence—§ 121

Recall that although losses realized on the sale or exchange of personal use assets are generally not recognizable, gains realized on the disposition of personal use assets are. However, § 121 allows individual taxpayers to exclude gain from the sale of a *principal residence*. This provision applies to the first $250,000 of realized gain, or $500,000 on certain joint returns. For this purpose, the residence must have been owned and used by the taxpayer as the primary residence for at least two of the five years preceding the date of sale. Further, the exclusion can only be used once every two years. The exclusion can be prorated, however, if a taxpayer failed to meet one or more of these time period requirements due to a change in his or her place of employment or to health issues. Moreover, a surviving spouse counts the ownership and usage periods of the decedent spouse in meeting the two-year test. This provision applies only to gains; losses on the sale or exchange of residences, like those related to other personal use assets, are not recognized for tax purposes.

Digging Deeper 10, 11, 12 **In-depth discussion of § 121 can be found on this book's companion website: www.cengage.com**

Refocus on The Big Picture

Calculating Basis and Recognized Gain for Property Transactions

DRAZEN ZIGIC/SHUTTERSTOCK.COM

Alice's basis in the land acquired as a gift is a carryover basis of $2,000. If Alice sells the land outright, she will realize and recognize a gain of $48,000. However, if she replaces the property with other real property, she should be able to qualify for favorable like-kind exchange treatment under § 1031 and defer the gain on the property disposition. If Alice receives any cash as a part of the exchange transaction, realized gain would be recognized to the extent of the cash (boot) received.

Alice's basis in the 300 shares of stock received as an inheritance is the property's $30,000 fair market value at the date of her grandfather's death. If Alice sells the 300 shares, she will realize and recognize a $6,000 gain [$36,000 sales price (300 shares × $120) − $30,000 basis].

Alice's basis in the 200 shares of stock purchased is her purchase price of $28,000. Those shares are currently worth $24,000 (200 shares × $120). Consequently, if she sells those shares, she will realize and recognize a $4,000 loss.

You advise Alice that her basis in the house is its $475,000 fair market value on the date of her grandmother's death. If Alice sells the house for $600,000, her realized and recognized gain will be $125,000.

Regarding the fire-related involuntary conversion of Alice's business building, a $50,000 realized gain occurs upon the receipt of the $100,000 of insurance proceeds. Because she intends to invest only $80,000 of the insurance proceeds in a qualifying property, Alice's recognized gain will be $20,000 ($100,000 proceeds − $80,000 reinvested). Therefore, her realized gain would be recognized to that extent (see Example 47).

continued

What If?

Alice is leaning toward selling the house. However, she knows that her grandmother would not want her to have to pay income taxes on the sale. Alice asks whether there is any way she could avoid paying taxes on the sale.

You inform Alice of the exclusion provision under § 121. Alice can qualify for this exclusion of up to $250,000 of realized gain if she owns and occupies the house as her principal residence for at least two of the five years prior to a sale.

From a tax planning perspective, what can Alice do so that none of the $50,000 of realized gain from the involuntary conversion is recognized? To have full postponement of the $50,000 realized gain, Alice would have to reinvest all of the $100,000 of insurance proceeds received in another qualified building. Under this circumstance, the basis of the replacement building would be $50,000 ($100,000 cost of replacement building − $50,000 deferred gain).

Suggested Readings

Paul Bonner, "Estate Basis Consistency and Reporting: What Practitioners Need to Know," *The Journal of Accountancy*, June 2016.

Mary B. Foster, "A Checklist for Like-Kind Real Estate Exchanges," *Journal of Real Estate Taxation*, Second Quarter 2015.

James R. Hamill, "Preserving the Residence Sale Exclusion for Mixed Use Property," *Practical Tax Strategies*, June 2013.

Christian J. Kenefick, "What Is a $10 Gold Coin Worth? Basis, FMV, and Realization Issues Abound," *Journal of Taxation*, February 2013.

Timothy M. Todd, "Whose Goodwill Is It? The Taxation of Goodwill in Owner-Entity Transactions," *Journal of Taxation*, February 2015.

Key Terms

Computational Exercises

1. **LO.1** Peyton sells an office building and the associated land on May 1 of the current year. Under the terms of the sales contract, Peyton is to receive $1,600,000 in cash. The purchaser is to assume Peyton's mortgage of $950,000 on the property. To enable the purchaser to obtain adequate financing, Peyton is to pay the $9,000 in points charged by the lender. The broker's commission on the sale is $75,000. What is Peyton's amount realized? Critical Thinking

2. **LO.3** Luciana, a nonshareholder, purchases a condominium from her employer for $85,000. The fair market value of the condominium is $120,000. What is Luciana's basis in the condominium and the amount of any income as a result of this purchase?

3. **LO.3** Sebastian purchases two pieces of equipment for $100,000. Appraisals of the equipment indicate that the fair market value of the first piece of equipment is $72,000 and that of the second piece of equipment is $108,000. What is Sebastian's basis in these two assets?

4. **LO.2, 4** Lisa sells business property with an adjusted basis of $130,000 to her son, Alfred, for its fair market value of $100,000.
   a. What is Lisa's realized and recognized gain or loss?
   b. What is Alfred's recognized gain or loss if he subsequently sells the property for $138,000? For $80,000?

5. **LO.4** Arianna's personal residence has an adjusted basis of $230,000 and a fair market value of $210,000. Arianna converts the personal residence to rental property. What is Arianna's gain basis? What is her loss basis?

6. **LO.2, 5** Logan and Johnathan exchange land, and the exchange qualifies as like kind under § 1031. Because Logan's land (adjusted basis of $85,000) is worth $100,000 and Johnathan's land has a fair market value of $80,000, Johnathan also gives Logan cash of $20,000.
   a. What is Logan's recognized gain?
   b. Assume instead that Johnathan's land is worth $90,000 and he gives Logan $10,000 cash. Now what is Logan's recognized gain?

7. **LO.2, 6** Camilo's property, with an adjusted basis of $155,000, is condemned by the state. Camilo receives property with a fair market value of $180,000 as compensation for the property taken.
   a. What is Camilo's realized and recognized gain?
   b. What is the basis of the replacement property?

Critical Thinking

8. **LO.2, 7** Constanza, who is single, sells her current personal residence (adjusted basis of $165,000) for $450,000. She has owned and lived in the house for 30 years. Her selling expenses are $22,500. What is Constanza's realized and recognized gain?

Problems

9. **LO.1** If a taxpayer sells property for cash, the amount realized consists of the net proceeds from the sale. For each of the following, indicate the effect on the amount realized if:
   a. The property is sold on credit.
   b. A mortgage on the property is assumed by the buyer.
   c. A mortgage on the property of the buyer is assumed by the seller.
   d. The buyer acquires the property subject to a mortgage of the seller.
   e. Stock that has a basis to the purchaser of $6,000 and a fair market value of $10,000 is received by the seller as part of the consideration.

10. **LO.1, 2, 4, 6** Liam owns a personal use boat that has a fair market value of $35,000 and an adjusted basis of $45,000. Liam's AGI is $100,000. Calculate the realized and recognized gain or loss if:
   a. Liam sells the boat for $35,000.
   b. Liam exchanges the boat for another boat worth $35,000.
   c. The boat is stolen and Liam receives insurance proceeds of $35,000.
   d. Would your answer in part (a) change if the fair market value and the selling price of the boat were $48,000?

11. **LO.1, 2, 4, 6** Yancy's personal residence is condemned as part of an urban renewal project. His adjusted basis for the residence is $480,000. He receives condemnation proceeds of $460,000 and invests the proceeds in stocks and bonds.
    a. Calculate Yancy's realized and recognized gain or loss.
    b. If the condemnation proceeds are $505,000, what are Yancy's realized and recognized gain or loss?
    c. What are Yancy's realized and recognized gain or loss in part (a) if the house was rental property?

12. **LO.3** Mahan purchases 1,000 shares of Bluebird Corporation stock on October 3, 2022, for $300,000. On December 12, 2022, Mahan purchases an additional 750 shares of Bluebird stock for $210,000. According to market quotations, Bluebird stock is selling for $285 per share on December 31, 2022. Mahan sells 500 shares of Bluebird stock on March 1, 2023, for $162,500.
    a. What is the adjusted basis of Mahan's Bluebird stock on December 31, 2022?
    b. What is Mahan's recognized gain or loss from the sale of Bluebird stock on March 1, 2023, assuming that the shares sold are from the shares purchased on December 12, 2022?
    c. What is Mahan's recognized gain or loss from the sale of Bluebird stock on March 1, 2023, assuming that Mahan cannot adequately identify the shares sold?

13. **LO.3** Rod Clooney purchases Kayla Mitchell's sole proprietorship for $990,000 on August 15, 2022. The assets of the business are: Communications

Asset	Kayla's Adjusted Basis	FMV
Accounts receivable	$ 70,000	$ 70,000
Inventory	90,000	100,000
Equipment	150,000	160,000
Furniture and fixtures	95,000	130,000
Building	190,000	250,000
Land	25,000	75,000
Total	$620,000	$785,000

    a. Calculate Kayla's realized and recognized gain.
    b. Determine Rod's basis for each of the assets.
    c. Write a letter to Rod informing him of the income tax consequences of the purchase. His address is 300 Riverview Drive, Delaware, OH 43015.

14. **LO.3** Roberto has received various gifts over the years. He has decided to dispose of several of these assets. What is the recognized gain or loss from each of the following transactions, assuming that no gift tax was paid when the gifts were made? All sales occurred in 2022.
    a. In 1987, he received land worth $32,000. The donor's adjusted basis was $35,000. Roberto sells the land for $95,000.
    b. In 1992, he received stock in Gold Company. The donor's adjusted basis was $19,000. The fair market value on the date of the gift was $34,000. Roberto sells the stock for $40,000.
    c. In 1998, he received land worth $15,000. The donor's adjusted basis was $20,000. Roberto sells the land for $9,000.
    d. In 2019, he received stock worth $30,000. The donor's adjusted basis was $42,000. Roberto sells the stock for $38,000.
    e. Build a spreadsheet-based solution that provides the solution to parts (a) through (d) above and uses only the donor's basis, the fair market value at the time of the gift, and the selling price as inputs. You may want to use the IF and AND functions together.

15. **LO.3** Nicky receives a car from Sam as a gift. Sam paid $48,000 for the car. He had used it for business purposes and had deducted $10,000 for depreciation up to the time he gave the car to Nicky. The fair market value of the car is $33,000.
    a. Assuming that Nicky uses the car for business purposes, what is her basis for depreciation?
    b. Assume that Nicky deducts depreciation of $6,500 and then sells the car for $32,500. What is her recognized gain or loss?
    c. Assume that Nicky deducts depreciation of $6,500 and then sells the car for $20,000. What is her recognized gain or loss?

Critical Thinking

16. **LO.3** Simon owns stock that has declined in value since acquired. He will either give the stock to his nephew, Fred, or sell it and give Fred the proceeds. If Fred receives the stock, he will sell it to obtain the proceeds. Simon is in the 12% tax bracket, and Fred's bracket is 22%. In either case, the holding period for the stock will be short-term. Identify the tax issues relevant to Simon in deciding whether to give the stock or the sale proceeds to Fred.

17. **LO.3** On September 18, 2022, Gerald received land and a building from Lei as a gift. Lei paid no gift tax on the transfer. Lei's records show the following:

Asset	Adjusted Basis	FMV
Land	$100,000	$212,000
Building	80,000	100,000

    a. Determine Gerald's adjusted basis for the land and building.
    b. Assume instead that the fair market value of the land was $87,000 and that of the building was $65,000. Determine Gerald's adjusted basis for the land and building.

18. **LO.3** Dan bought a hotel for $2,600,000 in January 2018. In May 2022, he died and left the hotel to Ed. While Dan owned the hotel, he deducted $289,000 of cost recovery. The fair market value in May 2022 was $2,800,000. The fair market value six months later was $2,850,000. Assume that an estate tax return (Form 706) is not required to be filed.
    a. What is the basis of the property to Ed?
    b. What is the basis of the property to Ed if the fair market value six months later was $2,500,000 (not $2,850,000) and the objective of the executor was to minimize the estate tax liability?

19. **LO.3, 4** Sheila sells land to Elaine, her sister, for the fair market value of $40,000. Six months later when the land is worth $45,000, Elaine gives it to Jacob, her son. (No gift tax resulted.) Shortly thereafter, Jacob sells the land for $48,000.
    a. Assuming that Sheila's adjusted basis for the land is $24,000, what are Sheila's and Jacob's recognized gain or loss on the sales?
    b. Assuming that Sheila's adjusted basis for the land is $60,000, what are Sheila's and Jacob's recognized gain or loss on the sales?

Critical Thinking
Decision Making
Planning

20. **LO.3, 4** Thania inherited 1,000 shares of Aqua, Inc. stock from Joe. Joe's basis in the stock was $35,000, and the fair market value of the stock on July 1, 2022 (the date of Joe's death), was $45,000. The shares were distributed to Thania on July 15, 2022. Thania sold the stock on July 29, 2023, for $33,000. After giving the matter more thought, she decides that Aqua is a good investment and purchases 1,000 shares for $30,000 on August 19, 2023.
    a. What is Thania's basis for the 1,000 shares purchased on August 19, 2023?
    b. Could Thania have obtained different tax consequences in part (a) if she had sold the 1,000 shares on December 27, 2022, and purchased the 1,000 shares on January 5, 2023? Explain.

21. **LO.4** Abby's home had a basis of $360,000 ($160,000 attributable to the land) and a fair market value of $340,000 ($155,000 attributable to the land) when she converted 70% of it to business use by opening a bed-and-breakfast. Four years after the conversion, Abby sells the home for $500,000 ($165,000 attributable to the land). Digging Deeper
   a. Calculate Abby's basis for gain, loss, and cost recovery for the portion of her personal residence that was converted to business use.
   b. Calculate the cost recovery deducted by Abby during the four-year period of business use assuming that the bed-and-breakfast is opened on January 1 of year 1 and the house is sold on December 31 of year 4.
   c. What is Abby's recognized gain or loss on the sale of the business use portion?

22. **LO.4** Surendra's personal residence originally cost $340,000 (ignoring the value of the land). After living in the house for five years, he converts it to rental property. At the date of conversion, the fair market value of the house is $320,000. As to the rental property, calculate Surendra's basis for: Communications Critical Thinking Decision Making
   a. Loss.
   b. Depreciation.
   c. Gain.
   d. Could Surendra have obtained better tax results if he had sold his personal residence for $320,000 and then purchased another house for $320,000 to hold as rental property? Explain.
   e. Summarize your answer to this problem in an e-mail to your instructor.

23. **LO.5** Which of the following exchanges qualify as like-kind exchanges under § 1031?
   a. Improved for unimproved real estate.
   b. Rental house for personal residence.
   c. Business land for rental house (held for investment).
   d. Warehouse for office building (both used for business).
   e. Truck for computer (both used in business).
   f. Rental house for land (both held for investment).
   g. Office furniture for office equipment (both used in business).
   h. Unimproved land in Jackson, Mississippi, for unimproved land in Toledo, Spain.
   i. General partnership interest for a general partnership interest.

24. **LO.5** In June 2022, Sue exchanges a sport-utility vehicle (adjusted basis of $16,000; fair market value of $19,500) for cash of $2,000 and a pickup truck (fair market value of $17,500). Both vehicles are for business use. Sue believes that her basis for the truck is $17,500. Is Sue correct? Why or why not? As part of your response, compute Sue's realized gain or loss (and any recognized gain or loss) on the exchange.

25. **LO.5** Daniela Fletcher owns undeveloped land (adjusted basis of $80,000 and fair market value of $92,000) on the East Coast. On January 4, 2022, she exchanges it with Lisa Martin (an unrelated party) for undeveloped land on the West Coast and $3,000 cash. Lisa has an adjusted basis of $72,000 for her land, and its fair market value is $89,000. Because the real estate market on the East Coast is thriving, on September 1, 2023, Lisa sells the land she acquired for $120,000. Communications Critical Thinking Decision Making
   a. What are Daniela's recognized gain or loss and adjusted basis for the West Coast land on January 4, 2022?
   b. What are Lisa's recognized gain or loss and adjusted basis for the East Coast land on January 4, 2022?
   c. What is Lisa's recognized gain or loss from the September 1, 2023 sale?
   d. What effect does Lisa's 2023 sale have on Daniela?
   e. Write a letter to Daniela advising her of the tax consequences of this exchange. Her address is The Corral, El Paso, TX 79968.

26. **LO.5** Katie exchanges a building and land (used in its business) for Tyler's land and building and some equipment (used in its business).

	Adjusted Basis	Fair Market Value
Katie's real property	$120,000	$300,000
Tyler's real property	60,000	220,000
Tyler's equipment	50,000	80,000

a. What are Katie's recognized gain or loss and basis for the land and building and equipment acquired from Tyler?

b. What are Tyler's recognized gain or loss and basis for the land and building acquired from Katie?

27. **LO.5** Suni owns land (adjusted basis of $90,000; fair market value of $125,000) that she uses in her business. She exchanges it for another parcel of land (worth $100,000) and stock (worth $25,000). Determine Suni's:

a. Realized and recognized gain or loss on the exchange.

b. Basis in the new land.

c. Basis in the stock Maple received.

Critical Thinking

28. **LO.5** Ross would like to dispose of some land he acquired four years ago because the land will not continue to appreciate. Its value has increased by $50,000 over the four-year period. Ross also intends to sell stock that has declined in value by $50,000 during the six months since its purchase.

Ross has four offers to acquire the stock and land. Identify the tax issues relevant to Ross in disposing of this land and stock.

Buyer 1: Exchange land.
Buyer 2: Purchase land for cash.
Buyer 3: Exchange stock.
Buyer 4: Purchase stock for cash.

29. **LO.5** What is the basis of the property received in each of the following exchanges?

a. Apartment building held for investment (adjusted basis of $145,000) for office building to be held for investment (fair market value of $225,000).

b. Land and building used as a barbershop (adjusted basis of $190,000) for land and building used as a grocery store (fair market value of $350,000).

c. Office building (adjusted basis of $45,000) for bulldozer (fair market value of $42,000), both held for business use.

d. IBM common stock (adjusted basis of $20,000) for ExxonMobil common stock (fair market value of $28,000).

e. Rental house (adjusted basis of $90,000) for mountain cabin to be held for rental use (fair market value of $225,000).

f. General partnership interest (adjusted basis of $400,000) for a limited partnership interest (fair market value of $580,000).

30. **LO.5** Steve owns real estate (adjusted basis of $12,000 and fair market value of $15,000), which he uses in his business. Steve sells the real estate for $15,000 to Aubry (a dealer) and then purchases a new parcel of land for $15,000 from Joan (also a dealer). The new parcel of land qualifies as like-kind property.

a. What are Steve's realized and recognized gain on the sale of the land he sold to Aubry?

b. What is Steve's basis for the land he purchased from Joan?

c. What factors would motivate Steve to sell his land to Aubry and purchase the land from Joan rather than exchange one parcel of land for the other?

d. Assume that the adjusted basis of Steve's original parcel of land is $15,000 and the fair market value of both parcels of land is $12,000. Respond to parts (a) through (c).

31. **LO.5** Tom Howard and Frank Pérez are good friends (and former college roommates). Each owns investment property in the other's hometown (Tom lives in Kalamazoo, MI; Frank lives in Austin, TX). To make their lives easier, they decide to exchange the investment properties. Under the terms of the exchange, Frank will transfer realty (20 acres of unimproved land; adjusted basis of $52,000; fair market value of $80,000) and Tom will exchange realty (25 acres of unimproved land; adjusted basis of $60,000; fair market value of $92,000). Tom's property is subject to a mortgage of $12,000 that will be assumed by Frank. Communications Critical Thinking Decision Making Planning

a. What are Frank's and Tom's recognized gains?

b. What are their adjusted bases?

c. As an alternative, Frank has proposed that, rather than assuming the mortgage, he will transfer cash of $12,000 to Tom. Tom would use the cash to pay off the mortgage. In an e-mail, advise Tom on whether this alternative would be beneficial to him from a tax perspective.

d. Assuming that Tom and Frank proceed with the original exchange [rather than the alternative in part (c) above], complete Form 8824 (Parts I and III) for Tom. Assume that the exchange occurs on September 16, 2021 (Tom acquired his 25-acre parcel on February 15, 2013). Tom's Social Security number is 123-45-6789.

32. **LO.5** Determine the realized, recognized, and postponed gain or loss and the new basis for each of the following like-kind exchanges: Communications Critical Thinking

	Adjusted Basis of Old Asset	Boot Given	Fair Market Value of New Asset	Boot Received
a.	$ 7,000	$ -0-	$12,000	$4,000
b.	14,000	2,000	15,000	-0-
c.	3,000	7,000	8,000	500
d.	15,000	-0-	29,000	-0-
e.	10,000	-0-	11,000	1,000
f.	17,000	-0-	14,000	-0-

g. Create a Microsoft Excel spreadsheet that—by entering the fair market value and basis of property given up and the fair market value of property received—will compute (1) realized gain or loss, (2) boot received, (3) boot given, (4) gain (loss) recognized, (5) gain (loss) deferred, and (6) the basis of like-kind property received. In separate tabs, the spreadsheet should apply the "simplified method" and the "alternative method." Ignore the implications of debt and depreciation.

Test your spreadsheet using the data in this problem (and problem 29). E-mail your spreadsheet to your instructor along with a brief summary of how you built the spreadsheet.

33. **LO.6** A warehouse owned by M&S (a partnership) and used in its business (i.e., to store inventory) is being condemned by the city to provide a right-of-way for a highway. The warehouse has appreciated by $180,000 based on an estimate of fair market value. In the negotiations, the city is offering $35,000 less than what M&S believes the property is worth. Alan, a real estate broker, has offered to purchase the property for $20,000 more than the city's offer. The partnership plans to invest the proceeds it will receive in an office building that it will lease to various tenants. Critical Thinking

a. Identify the relevant tax issues for M&S.

b. Would the answer in part (a) change if M&S's warehouse was property being held for investment rather than being used in its business? Explain.

34. **LO.6** Quentin's roadside vegetable stand (adjusted basis of $275,000) is destroyed by a tractor-trailer accident. He receives insurance proceeds of $240,000. Quentin immediately uses the proceeds plus additional cash of $45,000 to build another roadside vegetable stand at the same location. What are the Federal income tax consequences?

35. **LO.6** For each of the following involuntary conversions, indicate whether the property acquired qualifies as replacement property, any resulting recognized gain, and the basis for the property acquired.

a. Krystal owns a warehouse that is destroyed by a tornado. The space in the warehouse was rented to various tenants. The adjusted basis was $470,000. Krystal uses all of the insurance proceeds of $700,000 to build a shopping mall in a neighboring community where no property has been damaged by tornadoes. The shopping mall is rented to various tenants.

b. Javier owns a warehouse that is destroyed by fire. The adjusted basis is $300,000. Because of economic conditions in the area, Javier decides not to rebuild the warehouse. Instead, he uses all of the insurance proceeds of $400,000 to build a warehouse for use in his business in another state.

c. Bailey's personal residence is condemned as part of a local government project to widen the highway from two lanes to four lanes. The adjusted basis is $170,000. Bailey uses all of the condemnation proceeds of $200,000 to purchase another personal residence.

d. Swallow Fashions, Inc., owns a building that is destroyed by a hurricane. The adjusted basis is $250,000. Because of an economic downturn in the area caused by the closing of a military base, Swallow decides to rent space for its retail outlet rather than replace the building. It uses all of the insurance proceeds of $300,000 to buy a four-unit apartment building in another city. A realtor in that city will handle the rental of the apartments.

e. Susan and Rick's personal residence is destroyed by a tornado. They had owned it for 15 months. The adjusted basis was $170,000. Because they would like to travel, they decide not to acquire a replacement residence. Instead, they invest all of the insurance proceeds of $200,000 in a duplex, which they rent to tenants.

f. Alec and Meghann's personal residence (adjusted basis of $245,000) is destroyed in a flood. They had owned it for 18 months. Of the insurance proceeds of $350,000, they reinvest $342,000 in a replacement residence four months later.

Planning

36. **LO.6** Mitchell, a calendar year taxpayer, is the sole proprietor of a fast-food restaurant. His adjusted basis for the building and the related land is $450,000. On March 12, 2022, state authorities notify Mitchell that his property is going to be condemned so that the highway can be widened. On June 20, Mitchell's property is officially condemned, and he receives an award of $625,000. Because Mitchell's business was successful in the past, he would like to reopen the restaurant in a new location.

a. What is the earliest date Mitchell can acquire a new restaurant and qualify for gain deferral?

b. On June 30, Mitchell purchases land and a building for $610,000. Assuming that he elects the maximum postponement amount, what is his recognized gain?

c. What is Mitchell's adjusted basis for the new land and building?

d. If he does not elect § 1033, what are Mitchell's recognized gain and adjusted basis?

e. Suppose he invests the $625,000 condemnation proceeds in the stock market on June 30. What is Mitchell's recognized gain?

37. **LO.6** Emily's warehouse (adjusted basis of $450,000) is destroyed by a hurricane in October 2022. Emily, a calendar year taxpayer, receives insurance proceeds of $525,000 in January 2023. Calculate Emily's realized gain or loss, recognized gain or loss, and basis for the replacement property if she:
    a. Acquires a new warehouse for $550,000 in January 2023.
    b. Acquires a new warehouse for $500,000 in January 2023.
    c. Does not acquire replacement property.

38. **LO.7** Wesley, who is single, listed his personal residence with a real estate agent on March 3, 2022, at a price of $390,000. He rejected several offers in the $350,000 range during the summer. Finally, on August 16, 2022, he and the purchaser signed a contract to sell for $363,000. The sale (i.e., closing) took place on September 7, 2022. The closing statement showed the following disbursements:

Critical Thinking

Real estate agent's commission	$ 21,780
Appraisal fee	600
Exterminator's certificate	300
Recording fees	800
Mortgage to First Bank	305,000
Cash to seller	34,520

Wesley's adjusted basis for the house is $200,000. He owned and occupied the house for seven years. On October 1, 2022, Wesley purchases another residence for $325,000.

a. Calculate Wesley's recognized gain on the sale.
b. What is Wesley's adjusted basis for the new residence?
c. Assume instead that the selling price is $800,000. What is Wesley's recognized gain? His adjusted basis for the new residence?

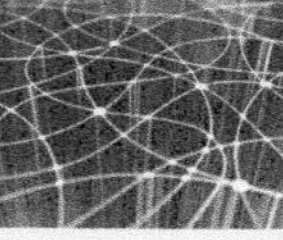

Bridge Discipline

1. In April of the current year, Blue Corporation purchased an asset to be used in its manufacturing operations for $100,000. Blue's management expects the asset to ratably provide valuable services in the production process for eight years and have a salvage value of $12,000. The asset is a five-year asset for tax purposes. Blue has adopted the half-year convention for book purposes in the year of acquisition and disposition; Blue uses MACRS for tax purposes. Neither § 179 nor bonus depreciation (additional first-year depreciation) is used for the asset.
   a. Compute the depreciation expense in the year of acquisition for book and tax purposes.
   b. Identify the book-tax difference related to the depreciation expense in the year of acquisition.
2. Refer to the facts in the preceding problem. Assume that Blue Corporation disposes of the manufacturing asset at the beginning of year 7 for $40,000. Compute the amount of gain or loss recognized for book and tax purposes. What is the book-tax difference in the year of disposition?

Research Problems

Note: Solutions to the Research Problems can be prepared by using the Thomson Reuters Checkpoint™ online tax research database, which accompanies this textbook. Solutions can also be prepared by using research materials found in a typical tax library.

Communications

Research Problem 1. Ruth Ames died on January 10, 2022. In filing the estate tax return, her executor, Melvin Sims, elects the primary valuation date and amount (fair market value on the date of death). On March 12, 2022, Melvin invests $30,000 of cash that Ruth had in her money market account in acquiring 1,000 shares of Orange, Inc. ($30 per share). On January 10, 2022, Orange was selling for $29 per share. The stock is distributed to a beneficiary, Annette Rust, on June 1, 2022, when it is selling for $33 per share.

Melvin wants you to determine the amount at which the Orange shares should appear on the estate tax return and the amount of Annette's adjusted basis for the stock. Write a letter to Melvin in which you respond to his inquiry, and prepare a memo for the tax files. His address is 100 Center Lane, Miami, FL 33124.

Research Problem 2. Terry owns real estate with an adjusted basis of $600,000 and a fair market value of $1,100,000. The amount of the nonrecourse mortgage on the property is $2,500,000. Because of substantial past and projected future losses associated with the real estate development (occupancy rate of only 37% after three years), Terry deeds the property to the creditor.

a. What are the tax consequences to Terry?
b. Assume that the data are the same, except that the fair market value of the property is $2,525,000. As a result, when Terry deeds the property to the creditor, she also receives $25,000 from the creditor. What are the tax consequences to Terry?

Critical Thinking

Research Problem 3. Randall owns an office building (adjusted basis of $250,000) that he has been renting to a group of physicians. During negotiations over a new seven-year lease, the physicians offer to purchase the building for $900,000. Randall accepts the offer with the stipulation that the sale be structured as a delayed § 1031 transaction. Consequently, the sales proceeds are paid to a qualified third-party intermediary on the closing date of September 30, 2022.

On October 2, 2022, Randall properly identifies an office building that he would like to acquire. Unfortunately, on November 10, 2022, the property Randall selected is withdrawn from the market. Working with the intermediary, on November 12, 2022, Randall identifies another office building that meets his requirements. The purchase of this property closes on December 15, 2022, and the title is transferred to Randall.

Randall treats the transaction as a like-kind exchange. Even though the original office building identified was not acquired, Randall concludes that in substance, he has satisfied the 45-day rule. He identified the acquired office building as soon as the negotiations ceased on his first choice. Should the IRS accept Randall's attempt to comply? Explain.

Use internet tax resources to address the following questions. Look for reliable websites and blogs of the IRS and other government agencies, media outlets, businesses, tax professionals, academics, think tanks, and political outlets.

Research Problem 4. Many see the "step-up in basis at death" rule as an expensive tax loophole enjoyed by the wealthy.

a. Find the latest estimates of the revenue loss to the U.S. Treasury that is attributable to this rule.

b. How does Canada's tax law determine the basis of property acquired from a decedent?

c. Send an e-mail to a member of the House Ways and Means Committee expressing a preference for retaining or eliminating the "step-up in basis" rule.

Research Problem 5. In general, the 45-day identification period and the 180-day exchange period for like-kind exchanges cannot be extended. Does this rule change if the like-kind property or the taxpayer involved in the exchange is located in a Federally declared disaster area? If so, to what extent? Use the IRS's website (**irs.gov**) to find the answer.

Becker CPA Review Questions

Becker

1. Alice gifted stock to her son, Bob, in year 5. Alice bought the stock in year 1 for $8,300. The value of the stock on the date of gift was $6,400. Bob sold the stock in year 7 for $15,800. What is Bob's recognized gain or loss on the sale in year 7?

   a. $0
   b. $7,500 gain
   c. $9,400 gain
   d. $15,800 gain

2. Jerry inherits an asset from his uncle, who purchased the asset five days before he died. Which of the following statements is correct?

   a. If Jerry sells the asset a few days after receiving it, any gain or loss on the sale will be short term.
   b. Jerry's basis in the asset is the carryover basis from his uncle.
   c. Jerry's basis is the FMV on the alternate valuation date or date it is distributed to him.
   d. Jerry's basis is the FMV on his uncle's date of death.

3. Rick purchased 100 shares of XYZ stock on April 4, year 4, for $8,600. He sold 50 shares on February 8, year 5, for $3,000. He then bought another 50 shares of XYZ on March 1, year 5, for $3,200. How much loss will Rick realize in year 5?

   a. $0
   b. $1,300
   c. $3,000
   d. $5,600

4. Agnes sold 50 shares of ABC stock to her son, Steve, in year 4 for $42,000. She bought the stock eight years ago for $50,000. Steve sold the stock to an unrelated party in year 6 for $60,000. How much gain will Steve recognize from the sale in year 6?

   a. $0
   b. $10,000
   c. $18,000
   d. $60,000

5. Chad owned an office building that was destroyed in a tornado. The adjusted basis of the building at the time was $890,000. After the deductible, Chad received an insurance check for $850,000. He used the $850,000 to purchase a new building that same year. How much is Chad's recognized loss, and what is his basis in the new building?

	Recognized Loss	New Basis
a.	$0	$850,000
b.	$0	$890,000
c.	$40,000	$850,000
d.	$40,000	$890,000

6. Chad owned an office building that was destroyed in a tornado. The adjusted basis of the building at the time was $890,000. After the deductible, Chad received an insurance check for $950,000. He used $900,000 of the insurance proceeds to purchase a new building that same year. How much is Chad's recognized gain, and what is his basis in the new building?

	Recognized Loss	New Basis
a.	$0	$890,000
b.	$0	$900,000
c.	$50,000	$890,000
d.	$60,000	$900,000

7. Marsha exchanged land used in her business in Florida with an FMV of $72,700 and an adjusted basis of $40,000 for land used in her business in Iowa with an FMV of $57,700. Marsha also assumed a $5,000 liability on the land received in the transaction and was relieved of a $20,000 liability on the land that was given up. What is Marsha's recognized gain on the transaction?

   a. $0
   b. $15,000
   c. $20,000
   d. $32,700

8. Marsha exchanged land held for investment in Florida with an FMV of $52,700 and an adjusted basis of $60,000 for land held for investment in Iowa with an FMV of $57,700. Marsha also paid $5,000 cash in the transaction. What is Marsha's basis in the land received?

   a. $55,000
   b. $57,700
   c. $60,000
   d. $65,000

9. On January 25, year 10, Mother Hall gave her daughter, Nadyne, 500 shares of common stock of XYZ, Corp. The fair market value of the stock on January 25 was $2,000. Mother Hall had paid $4,000 for the stock three years earlier. Nadyne decided a month after receiving the stock that she doesn't want to hold it and sold it for $1,000, the fair market value at the time of the sale. How much income (loss) must Nadyne include in her tax return for year 10 in regards to the sale of the stock?

   a. $0
   b. ($1,000)
   c. ($2,000)
   d. ($3,000)

10. In early year 8, Alice sold Tom, her son, 20 shares of common stock for $20,000. Alice had paid $25,000 for the stock in year 2. In late year 8, Tom sold the stock to an unrelated third party for $35,000. How much gain must Tom report in his year 8 tax return for the sale of the stock?

    a. $0
    b. $5,000
    c. $10,000
    d. $15,000

11. Marvin exchanged real property used for his printing business for new real property. The adjusted basis of the real property he gave up was $15,000. The new real property had a fair market value of $8,000, and Marvin received $8,000 in cash. What is Marvin's basis in the new real property, and how much gain must Marvin recognize on the transaction?

	Basis	**Gain**
a.	$15,000	$1,000
b.	$7,000	$0
c.	$16,000	$0
d.	$8,000	$1,000

Chapter 8

Property Transactions: Capital Gains and Losses, Section 1231, and Recapture Provisions

Learning Objectives: *After completing Chapter 8, you should be able to:*

LO.1 Explain the general scheme of taxation for capital gains and losses and distinguish capital assets from ordinary assets.

LO.2 State and explain the relevance of a sale or exchange to classification as a capital gain or loss.

LO.3 Determine the applicable holding period for a capital asset.

LO.4 Determine the tax treatment of capital gains and losses for noncorporate taxpayers.

LO.5 Determine the tax treatment of capital gains and losses for corporate taxpayers.

LO.6 Distinguish § 1231 assets from ordinary and capital assets and calculate § 1231 gain or loss.

LO.7 Determine when recapture provisions apply and derive their effects.

Chapter Outline

Tax Talk *Governments likely to confiscate wealth are unlikely to find much wealth to confiscate in the long run.* —Thomas Sowell

Capital Gains and Losses, § 1231 Gains and Losses, and Recapture

Alice owns land that she received from her father 10 years ago as a gift. The land was purchased by her father in 1996 for $2,000 and was worth $10,000 at the time of the gift. The property is currently worth about $50,000. If Alice sells the land, you previously determined in Chapter 7 that she would have a taxable gain of $48,000.

Alice also owns 500 shares of AppleCo stock, 300 of which were acquired as an inheritance when Alice's grandfather died in 2000. Alice's grandfather paid $12,000 for the AppleCo shares, and they were worth $30,000 at the time of his death. If Alice sells those shares for $120 each, you previously determined that she would have a $6,000 taxable gain. The other 200 shares were purchased by Alice two months ago for $28,000. If Alice sells those shares for $120 each, you determined that she would have a recognized loss of $4,000.

Nine months ago, Alice purchased 100 shares of Eagle Company stock for $5,000. Also on the same day, Alice invested $50,000 in a 50 percent interest in a patent that Kathy, a former college roommate who is an unemployed inventor, had obtained for a special battery she had developed to power "green" cars. To date, Kathy has been unable to market the battery to an auto manufacturer or supplier, but she has high hopes of doing so in the future.

Alice also owns a house that she inherited from her grandmother two years ago. Based on the estate tax return, the fair market value of the house at the date of her grandmother's death was $475,000, and Alice will recognize a $125,000 gain on the sale of the property.

Finally, Alice's new husband, Jeff, sold depreciable equipment used in his sole proprietorship. The business purchased the equipment for $50,000 and deducted $35,000 of depreciation before selling it for $60,000.

Now Alice would like to know more about the gains and losses and the tax liability that she and her husband can expect from these transactions.

Read the chapter and formulate your response.

Historically, for Federal income tax purposes, gains from the sale of assets classified as **capital assets** have received preferential treatment in the form of either partial exclusion or lower rates. Losses from capital assets, however, have received less desirable treatment than losses from other assets. The overall objective of these rules has been to encourage investment by reducing the tax cost of recognizing gains while at the same time limiting taxpayer use of investment losses to reduce taxes on ordinary income like wages and business profits.

During World War II, Congress extended capital asset treatment to noncapital business assets, now called "§ 1231 assets" after the Code Section that prescribes their special treatment. Later, Congress believed that this special treatment for business assets was no longer entirely warranted. Instead of repealing these rules, Congress eroded many of their benefits through *recapture provisions*. Together, these tax rules constitute one of the most complicated areas of tax law affecting both individual taxpayers and business entities.

Later, this chapter discusses more completely the lower rates currently available to capital gains, but the essential point for now is that the availability of these lower rates is confined to the excess of *net* long-term **capital gains** over *net* short-term **capital losses**. To determine the tax treatment for capital gains and losses properly, taxpayers must:

- Segregate capital from noncapital gains and losses.
- Classify the holding period as long term (i.e., more than one year) or short term (i.e., one year or less).
- Identify specific capital assets (primarily real estate and "collectibles") for which the preferential rates are not as low as they are for other capital assets.

LO.1

Explain the general scheme of taxation for capital gains and losses and distinguish capital assets from ordinary assets.

8-1 General Scheme of Property Taxation

The ultimate tax treatment of property transactions depends on whether all of the recognized gains and losses related to a given category of property produce a net gain or a net loss. For this reason, taxpayers must first properly classify recognized gains and losses. Proper classification depends on three factors (see Concept Summary 8.1):

- The *tax status* of the property.
- The manner of the property's *disposition*.
- The *holding period* of the property.

Concept Summary 8.1

Factors Impacting the Tax Treatment of Property Transactions

Characteristic	Alternatives
Tax status of property	• Capital asset • § 1231 asset • Ordinary asset
Manner of disposition	• Sale • Exchange • Casualty, theft, or condemnation
Holding period	• Short term (one year or less) • Long term (more than one year)

8-2 Capital Assets

Capital gains and losses result from the sale or exchange of capital assets. Realize that the term *capital assets* means different things to different groups. For example, economists refer to all long-term factors of production (e.g., machinery and equipment) as capital assets. Financial accountants include as assets all costs that are "capitalized." However, for income tax purposes, *capital assets* includes only a specific subset of assets. The assets most commonly identified as capital assets are investments, including corporate stocks and bonds, mutual funds, partnership interests, and government securities. However, many other assets are classified as capital assets as well.

Classification of capital versus noncapital (e.g., ordinary) can affect significantly the tax effects of a gain or loss. For example, as discussed later in this chapter, long-term capital gains generally benefit from lower rates while net capital losses frequently are not immediately recognizable. The Internal Revenue Code does not define capital assets directly. Instead, § 1221(a) defines what is *not* a capital asset. Assets excluded from classification as a capital asset include the following:

- Inventory or other property held primarily for sale to customers in the ordinary course of a business.
- Accounts and notes receivable generated from the sale of goods or services in a business.
- Real or depreciable property used in a business.
- Patents, inventions, models, or designs (whether or not patented); secret formulas or processes; certain copyrights; literary, musical, or artistic compositions; or letters, memoranda, or similar property created by or for the taxpayer.
- Supplies used in a business.

Overall, it is clear that whether or not an asset is capital depends on how it is used rather than what it is. For example, a building used by a taxpayer for personal purposes is a capital asset but one used in a trade or business is not. Generally, given the exclusions in § 1221, capital assets include most assets not associated with a trade or business. For example, capital assets include investments, whether held by an individual or a corporation. Capital assets also include many assets that people use in their daily lives, such as homes, automobiles, and furniture. Recall from text Section 7-1b, however, that losses on the sale of personal use assets are generally not deductible. As a result, the classification of personal use assets as capital assets is relevant only when their disposition produces a recognized gain. Finally, the tax law allows a few specific business-related assets to qualify as capital assets, such as goodwill purchased in a business acquisition. The discussions below examine more closely the items that § 1221 excludes from the definition of capital assets.

Further discussion on capital asset classification can be found on this book's companion website: www.cengage.com

1 Digging Deeper

Inventory

As alluded to above, inventory is not considered a capital asset. A taxpayer's business determines what is (and is not) inventory.

Inventory Determination

Example 1

Green Company buys and sells used automobiles. Its automobiles are inventory. Therefore, Green's gains from the sale of the cars are ordinary income.

Inventory Determination

Example 2

Soong sells her personal use automobile at a $500 gain. The automobile is a personal use asset and, therefore, a capital asset. Soong's gain is a capital gain.

As alluded to previously, no asset is inherently capital or ordinary. If Soong in Example 2 sells her personal use automobile to Green Company in Example 1, the automobile loses its capital asset status because it is inventory to Green Company. Similar transformations can occur if, for example, an art dealer sells a painting (inventory, *not* a capital asset) to a private collector (now a capital asset). Whether an asset is capital or ordinary, therefore, depends entirely on the relationship of that asset to the taxpayer who sold it.

Securities dealers pose a particular problem in determining whether an asset is capital. A *dealer in securities* is a merchant (e.g., a brokerage firm) that regularly engages in the purchase and resale of securities to customers. As a general rule, securities (stocks, bonds, and other financial instruments) held by a dealer are considered to be inventory and are, therefore, not subject to capital gain or loss treatment. However, a dealer might also purchase securities purely as an investment rather than for sale to clients. To prevent them from being able to exploit the different treatment of capital and ordinary gains and losses by characterizing securities as capital or not at the time of sale (i.e., characterizing securities sold at a gain as capital assets and those sold at a loss as inventory), securities dealers must clearly identify securities purchased as investments immediately upon acquisition.[1]

Digging Deeper 2

An example relating to dealers in securities can be found on this book's companion website: www.cengage.com

Accounts and Notes Receivable

Accounts and notes receivable are often created as part of a business transaction. These assets may subsequently be collected by the creditor, sold by the creditor, or become completely or partially worthless. Also, the creditor may be on the accrual or cash basis of accounting.

Collection of a receivable by an *accrual basis* taxpayer does not result in a gain or loss because it is considered a recovery of capital. If a receivable is sold, a gain or loss results if the sales price is more or less than its basis. The gain or loss is ordinary because the receivable is an ordinary asset. If the receivable is partially or wholly worthless, the creditor has a "bad debt" that may result in an ordinary deduction (see text Section 6-1).

In contrast, collection of a receivable by a *cash basis* taxpayer results in ordinary income because the asset has no basis: the taxpayer recognizes no income on the creation of the receivable. Similarly, if a cash basis taxpayer sells a receivable before collection, the result is also ordinary income. Cash basis taxpayers take no bad debt deduction because they have no basis in the receivable.

Example 3

Oriole Company, an *accrual basis taxpayer*, has accounts receivable of $100,000. Oriole recorded gross income of $100,000, resulting in a $100,000 basis for the receivable. Because Oriole needs working capital, it sells the receivables for $83,000 to a financial institution. Accordingly, it has a $17,000 ordinary loss.

If Oriole is a *cash basis taxpayer*, the sale of the receivable results in $83,000 of ordinary income because Oriole would not have recorded any income earlier and the receivable would have no tax basis.

[1]§ 1236(a).

Business Fixed Assets

Depreciable personal property and real property (both depreciable and nondepreciable) used by a business are *not* capital assets. However, § 1231 generally treats net gains from the sale of business fixed assets as capital gains, as discussed later in this chapter.

Inventions and Processes

Patents, inventions, models, or designs (whether or not patented) and secret formulas or processes, held either by the taxpayer who created them or by a taxpayer who received them from the taxpayer who created them, are not capital asssets. As a result, gains or losses from the sale or exchange of these assets do *not* receive capital gain treatment. In limited circumstances, however, the tax law treats patents as capital assets. Those special rules are discussed in text Section 8-3e.

Abigail invents a multifunctional case for a popular brand of cell phones. She has a manufacturer produce them for her and sells them via the internet. Her cost is $2.30 per case, and she sells each one for $10. To her surprise, she quickly achieves $45,000 in total sales. She has not capitalized any of the costs of developing the invention and has not patented it.

She sells all of her rights to the invention for $350,000 to a company that is in the business of producing cell phone cases. Her profit from sales of the cases is ordinary income because the cases are inventory. The $350,000 gain from selling the rights to the invention is an ordinary gain because the invention is not a capital asset.

Copyrights and Creative Works

Generally, the person whose efforts led to a copyright or creative work has an ordinary asset, not a capital asset. This rule makes the creator comparable to a taxpayer whose customary income-producing activity (e.g., salary, business profits) is taxed as ordinary income. *Creative works* include the works of authors, composers, and artists. In the case of a letter, memorandum, or other similar property, the person for whom the property was created, as well as its author, holds an ordinary asset. Finally, a person who receives a copyright or creative work from someone in whose hands the property was an ordinary asset, and who takes a carryover basis in the asset (e.g., received as a gift), also has an ordinary asset. Note, however, that a taxpayer may elect to treat the sale or exchange of a musical composition or a copyright of a musical work as the disposition of a capital asset.

Creative Works

Wanda is a part-time music composer. A music publisher purchases one of her songs for $5,000.

Wanda has a $5,000 ordinary gain from the sale of an ordinary asset unless she elects to treat the gain as a capital gain.

Ed received a letter from the President of the United States in 1995. In the current year, Ed sells the letter to a collector for $300.

Ed has a $300 ordinary gain from the sale of an ordinary asset (because the letter was created for Ed).

Isabella gives her son a song she composed. Her son sells the song to a music publisher for $5,000.

Her son has a $5,000 ordinary gain from the sale of an ordinary asset unless he elects to treat the gain as a capital gain.

If he inherits the song from Isabella, his basis for the song is its fair market value at Isabella's death. In this situation, the song is a capital asset because the son's basis is not related to Isabella's basis for the song (i.e., the song was not a *lifetime* gift).

The tax treatment of goodwill and covenants not to compete can be found on this book's companion website: www.cengage.com

3 Digging Deeper

State and explain the relevance of a sale or exchange to classification as a capital gain or loss.

8-3 Special Rules

The recognition of capital gains and losses generally requires a realization event. Recall from Chapter 7 that realization events include sales and exchanges. However, besides sales and exchanges, the tax law has identified certain other events that can lead to the recognition of capital gain or loss. In addition, Congress has identified certain situations that call for capital or ordinary treatment despite the classfication of an asset as capital or noncapital. This section details special rules for particular realization events and assets classifications.

8-3a § 1244 Stock

As discussed in text Section 6-2b, § 1244 allows losses recognized on the sale of certain stock to be classified as ordinary even though the stock is a capital asset. To qualify for § 1244 treatment, a small business corporation must have issued the stock. Further, the amount eligible for ordinary loss treatment is limited to $50,000 ($100,000 for married individuals filing jointly) per year.

8-3b Worthless Securities

Occasionally, securities such as stocks and bonds may become worthless due to the insolvency of their issuer. If the security is a capital asset, the loss is deemed to have occurred as the result of a sale or exchange on the *last day* of the tax year.[2] This last-day rule may have the effect of converting a short-term capital loss into a long-term capital loss. See text Section 6-2a for a more complete discussion of these rules.

8-3c Retirement of Corporate Obligations

Generally, amounts received on the retirement of a debt obligation (e.g., a bond or note payable) are treated as received on the sale or exchange of the obligation.[3] A debt obligation may have a tax basis to its holder different from its redemption value because it may have been acquired at a premium or discount (see Chapter 7 for a discussion of bond amortization). Consequently, the collection of the redemption value may result in a gain or loss. If the obligation is a capital asset, any gain or loss on its collection is capital because a sale or exchange has taken place.

Osprey, Inc., purchases $1,000 of Golden Eagle Corporation bonds for $1,020 in the open market. If the bonds are held to maturity and the bond premium is not amortized, the $20 difference between Osprey's collection of the $1,000 redemption value and its cost of $1,020 is treated as capital loss.

Rules regarding original issue discount and its effect on the sale or exchange of a debt obligation can be found on this book's companion website: www.cengage.com

8-3d Options

Frequently, a potential buyer of property wants to defer a final purchase decision but wants to control the sale and/or the sale price in the meantime. **Options** can achieve this kind of control. The potential purchaser (the grantee of the option) pays the property owner (the grantor of the option) for an option on the property. The grantee then becomes the option holder. An option, which usually sets the price at which a grantee can buy the property, expires after a specified period of time. Ultimately, an option may be exercised by the grantee, allowed to expire, or be sold.

Exercise of an Option by the Grantee

If an option is exercised, the amount paid for the option is added to the optioned property's selling price. This increases the gain (or reduces the loss) to the grantor resulting from the sale of the property. The grantor's gain or loss is capital or ordinary depending

[2] § 165(g)(1).

[3] § 1271(a)(1).

on the tax status of the property. The grantee adds the cost of the option to the basis of the property purchased.

Failure to Exercise an Option

If an option holder (grantee) fails to exercise the option, the lapse of the option is considered a sale or exchange of the option on the option expiration date. The resulting loss is a capital loss if the property subject to the option is (or would be) a capital asset in the hands of the grantee.

The tax treatment of an expired option for the grantor depends on the nature of the optioned property. The grantor of an option on *stocks, securities, commodities, or commodity futures* receives short-term capital gain treatment upon the expiration of the option.[4] For example, an individual investor who owns stock (a capital asset) may sell a call option, entitling the buyer of the option to acquire the stock at a specified price higher than the stock's value at the date the option is granted. The writer of the call (the grantor) receives a premium for writing the option. If the price of the stock does not increase during the option period, the option will expire unexercised. Upon the expiration of the option, the grantor must recognize a short-term capital gain equal to the premium received (whereas the grantee recognizes a loss, the character of which depends on the underlying asset). These provisions do not apply to options held for sale to customers (the inventory of a securities dealer).

Options on property *other than* stocks, securities, commodities, or commodity futures (for instance, vacant land) result in ordinary income to the grantor when the option expires regardless of whether the optioned property was a capital asset or how long the property or the option was held.

Sale of an Option

In addition to exercising an option or letting it expire, a grantee can sell or exchange it. This generally results in capital gain or loss if the option property is (or would be) a capital asset to the grantee.[5]

Robin & Associates wants to buy some vacant land for investment purposes. However, the firm cannot afford the full purchase price at the present time. Instead, Robin & Associates (the grantee) pays the landowner (the grantor) $3,000 for an option to buy the land for $100,000 anytime in the next two years. The option is a capital asset to Robin because if it actually purchased the land (the option property), the land would be a capital asset.

Three months after purchasing the option, Robin sells it to a third party for $7,000. The firm has a $4,000 ($7,000 − $3,000) capital gain on this sale.

If Robin instead allows the option to expire without purchasing the land, the firm will recognize a capital loss of $3,000. Conversely, the grantor of the option would recognize $3,000 of ordinary income.

The Big Picture

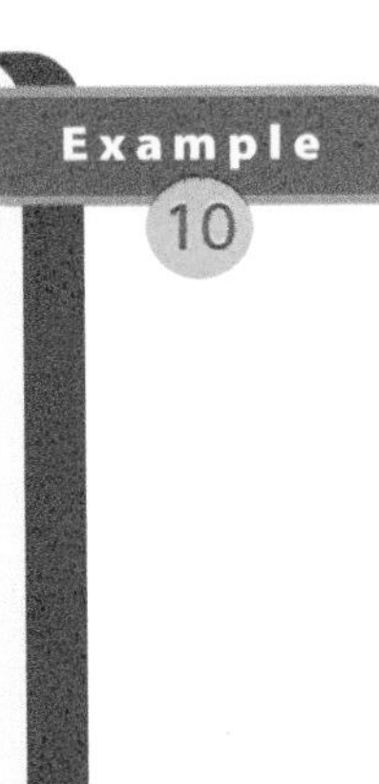

Return to the facts of *The Big Picture* on p. 8-1. On February 1 of the current year, Alice purchases 100 shares of Eagle Company stock for $5,000. On April 1 of the current year, she writes a call option on the stock, giving the grantee the right to buy the stock for $6,000 during the following six-month period. Alice (the grantor) receives a call premium of $500 for writing the call.

- If the call is exercised by the grantee on August 1 of the current year, Alice has $1,500 ($6,000 + $500 − $5,000) short-term capital gain from the sale of the stock. The grantee has a $6,500 basis for the stock ($500 option premium + $6,000 purchase price).
- Investors sometimes get nervous and want to "lock in" gains or losses.
  - Assume that prior to the grantee's exercise of the call, Alice decides to sell her stock for $6,000 and enters into a closing transaction by purchasing a call on 100 shares of Eagle Company stock for $5,000.

continued

[4] § 1234(b).

[5] § 1234(a)(1) and Reg. § 1.1234–1(a)(1).

- Because the Eagle stock is selling for $6,000, Alice must pay a call premium of $1,000.
- She recognizes a $500 short-term capital loss [$500 (call premium received) − $1,000 (call premium paid)] on the closing transaction.
- On the actual sale of the Eagle stock, Alice has a short-term capital gain of $1,000 [$6,000 (selling price) − $5,000 (cost)].
- The original grantee is not affected by Alice's closing transaction. The original option is still in existence, and the grantee's tax consequences depend on what action the grantee takes—exercising the option, letting the option expire, or selling the option.

• Assume that the original option expired unexercised. Alice has a $500 short-term capital gain equal to the call premium received for writing the option. This gain is not recognized until the option expires. The grantee has a loss from expiration of the option. The nature of the loss will depend upon whether the option was a capital asset or an ordinary asset.

Concept Summary 8.2 identifies the consequences of various transactions involving options to both the grantor and grantee.

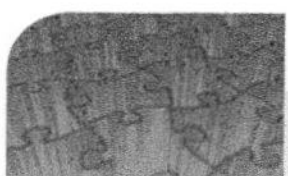

Concept Summary 8.2

Options: Consequences to the Grantor and Grantee

	Effect on	
Event	**Grantor (Option Writer)**	**Grantee (Option Holder)**
Option is granted.	Receives value for the option and has a contract obligation (a liability).	Pays for the option and has a contract right (an asset).
Option is exercised.	Amount received for option increases proceeds from sale of the option property.	Amount paid for option becomes part of the basis of the option property purchased.
Option expires.	Recognizes a short-term capital gain if the option property is stocks, securities, commodities, or commodity futures. Otherwise, gain is ordinary income.	Recognizes a capital or ordinary loss depending on the nature of the property to the grantee if it had been acquired.
Option is sold or exchanged by grantee.	No immediate impact on grantor.	Recognizes a capital or ordinary loss depending on the nature of the property to the grantee if it had been acquired.

8-3e Patents

As discussed earlier, § 1221 excludes **patents** from the definition of capital asset. Despite this, § 1235 gives long-term capital gain or loss treatment to a *patent holder* that transfers *all substantial rights* to the patent. If the transfer meets this requirement, any gain or loss is *automatically a long-term* capital gain or loss.

Substantial Rights

To receive capital gain or loss treatment, *all substantial rights* to the patent must be transferred. All substantial rights have not been transferred if, for example, the transferee's right to the use of the patent is limited geographically or is for a period less than the remaining legal life of the patent. All the facts and circumstances of the transaction, not just the language of the transfer document, must be considered in determining whether all substantial rights have been transferred.[6]

Example 11 illustrates the special treatment for patents.

[6]Reg. § 1.1235–2(b)(1).

The Big Picture

Example 11

Return to the facts of *The Big Picture* on p. 8-1. Kathy transfers her remaining 50% share of the rights in the battery patent to the Green Battery Company in exchange for a lump-sum payment of $1,000,000 plus $0.50 for each battery sold.

Assuming that Kathy has transferred all substantial rights, the question of whether the transfer is a sale or exchange of a capital asset is not relevant. Kathy automatically has a long-term capital gain from both the lump-sum payment received and the per-battery royalty to the extent that those proceeds exceed her basis for the patent.

Kathy also had an automatic long-term capital gain when she sold the other 50% of her rights in the patent to Alice, because Kathy transferred an undivided interest (i.e., where all owners have a claim to the entire patent and the income it produces) that included all substantial rights in the patent.

Whether Alice gets long-term capital gain treatment on a transfer to Green Battery will depend on whether she is a holder (see the following discussion and Example 12).

Holder Defined

The *holder* of a patent must be an *individual* (usually the invention's creator or an individual who purchases the patent rights from the creator before the invention is actually produced for sale). However, the creator's employer is not eligible for long-term capital gain treatment. Normally, the employer will have an ordinary asset because the patent was developed as part of its business.

The Big Picture

Example 12

Continuing with the facts of Example 11, Kathy is the holder of the patent because she is the inventor and was not an employee when she invented the battery. When Alice purchased a 50% interest in the patent nine months ago, she became a holder if the patent had not yet been "reduced to practice." Because batteries were apparently not being manufactured at the time of the purchase, the patent had not been reduced to practice.

Consequently, Alice is also a holder, and she has an automatic long-term capital gain or loss when she transfers all substantial rights in her interest in the patent to Green Battery Company. Alice's basis for her share of the patent is $50,000, and the proceeds from the transfer of her share of the patent are $1,000,000 plus $0.50 for each battery sold. Thus, Alice will have a long-term capital gain even though she has not held her interest in the patent for more than one year.

Compare the results here to those in Example 4. There, Abigail sold all substantial rights, but she had no patent and the invention had been "reduced to practice" because it was being manufactured and sold.

Rules regarding the treatment of franchises, trademarks, and trade names can be found on this book's companion website: www.cengage.com

5 Digging Deeper

8-3f Lease Cancellation Payments

The tax treatment of payments received for canceling a lease depends on whether the recipient of the payments is the **lessor** or the **lessee** and whether the lease is a capital asset.

Lessee Treatment

Lease cancellation payments received by a lessee are treated as an exchange.[7] The treatment of these payments depends on the underlying use of the property and how long the lease has existed.[8]

- If the property was used personally (e.g., an apartment used as a residence), the payment results in a capital gain (and long term if the lease existed for more than one year).
- If the property was used for business and the lease existed for one year or less, the payment results in ordinary income.
- If the property was used for business and the lease existed for more than one year, the payment results in a § 1231 gain.

Merganser, Inc., owns an apartment building that it is going to convert into an office building. Vicki is one of the apartment tenants who receives $1,000 from Merganser to cancel the lease.

Vicki has a capital gain of $1,000 (which is long term or short term depending upon how long she has held the lease). Merganser has an ordinary deduction of $1,000.

Lessor Treatment

Payments received by a lessor (the landlord) for a lease cancellation are always ordinary income because they are considered to be in lieu of rental payments.[9]

Finch & Company owns an apartment building near a university campus. Hui-Fen is one of the tenants. Hui-Fen is graduating early and offers Finch $800 to cancel the apartment lease. Finch accepts the offer.

Finch has ordinary income of $800. Hui-Fen has a nondeductible payment because the apartment was personal use property.

Digging Deeper 6

Special rules for the sale of real property subdivided for sale by investors can be found on this book's companion website: www.cengage.com

LO.3

Determine the applicable holding period for a capital asset.

8-4 Holding Period

8-4a General Rules

Property must be held more than one year to qualify for long-term capital gain or loss treatment.[10] The sale or exchange of property held for one year or less results in short-term capital gain or loss. The **holding period** is generally deemed to start on the day *after* the property was acquired and includes the day of disposition.

The Big Picture

Return to the facts of *The Big Picture* on p. 8-1. Assume that Alice purchased the 200 shares of AppleCo stock on January 15, 2022. If she sells them on January 16, 2023, Alice's holding period is more than one year and the gain or loss is long term.

If instead Alice sells the stock on January 15, 2023, the holding period is exactly one year and the gain or loss is short term.

[7] § 1241 and Reg. § 1.1241–1(a).

[8] Reg. § 1.1221–1(b) and PLR 200045019. If the lease was held for more than one year before cancellation, it is a § 1231 asset.

[9] Reg. § 1.61–8(b).

[10] § 1222(3).

An asset's holding period is based on calendar months and fractions of calendar months and not on the number of days. To be held for more than one year, a capital asset acquired on the last day of any month must not be sold until on or after the first day of the thirteenth succeeding month.[11]

Purple, Inc., purchases a capital asset on March 31, 2022. If Purple sells the asset on March 31, 2023, the holding period is one year and Purple will have a short-term capital gain or loss.

If Purple sells the asset on April 1, 2023, the holding period is more than one year and it will have a long-term capital gain or loss.

8-4b Special Holding Period Rules

There are several special holding period rules.[12] The application of these rules varies depending upon the type of asset involved and how it was acquired.

Nontaxable Exchanges

If property is acquired in a nontaxable transaction and takes a basis, in whole or in part, equal to the basis of the property surrendered (e.g., in a like-kind exchange, involuntary conversion, or as part of a wash sale) and the property surrendered is a capital asset or a § 1231 asset, the holding period of the newly acquired property is deemed to include the taxpayer's holding period of the surrendered property. In other words, if the basis of an asset carries over from one asset to another, so does its holding period. In such cases, the holding period of the surrendered property is said to be *tacked on* to the holding period of the newly acquired asset.

Holding Period Rules

Red Manufacturing Corporation exchanges some vacant real estate it owns (a capital asset) for land closer to its factory.

The transaction is a like-kind exchange, and Red's basis in the new land is equal to its basis in the land it surrendered. Therefore, its holding period of the new land includes the holding period of the old land.

A lightning strike destroyed Vireo Company's generator (a § 1231 asset) in March. Vireo uses all of the insurance proceeds it received to acquire a comparable generator.

The destruction of the old generator and acquisition of the new generator qualifies as a nontaxable involuntary conversion, and the basis of the new generator is equal to that of the old. Therefore, the holding period of the new generator is deemed to include the holding period of the old generator.

Similarly, if a taxpayer holds property that has a basis determined by the basis of the same property in the hands of the previous owner, the taxpayer's holding period is deemed to include the holding period of the previous owner. See the discussion of these items in text Section 7-2b.

[11] Rev.Rul. 66–7.

[12] § 1223.

Carryover Basis

Example 19

Kareem acquired 100 shares of Robin Corporation stock for $1,000 on December 31, 2018. He transferred the shares by gift to Megan on December 31, 2021, when the stock was worth $2,000. Kareem's basis of $1,000 becomes the basis for determining gain or loss on a subsequent sale by Megan. Megan's holding period begins with the date the stock was acquired by Kareem.

Example 20

Assume the same facts as in the preceding example, except that the fair market value of the shares was only $800 on the date of the gift. If Megan sells the stock for a loss, her basis in the stock will be its value on the date of the gift. Accordingly, the tacked-on holding period rule does not apply, and Megan's holding period begins with the date of the gift.

So if she sells the shares for $500 on April 1, 2022, Megan has a $300 recognized capital loss, the holding period is from December 31, 2021, to April 1, 2022, and the loss is short term.

Inherited Property

The holding period for inherited property is treated as long term regardless of how long the property is actually held by the heir. The holding period of the decedent or the decedent's estate is not relevant to the heir's holding period.

Example 21

Shonda inherits Blue Company stock from her father, who died in March 2022. She receives the stock on April 1, 2022, and sells it on November 1, 2022. Even though Shonda held the stock for less than one year, she receives long-term capital gain or loss treatment on the sale.

8-4c Short Sales

A **short sale** occurs when a taxpayer sells borrowed property and repays the lender with substantially identical property either held on the date of the sale or purchased after the sale. The repayment of the lender "closes" the short sale. Short sales typically involve corporate stock. The seller's objective is to make a profit in anticipation of a decline in the stock's price. If the price declines, the seller in a short sale recognizes a net profit equal to the difference between the (higher) sales price of the borrowed stock and the (lower) price paid for its replacement.

Under § 1233, a short sale gain or loss is a capital gain or loss to the extent the short sale property constitutes a capital asset of the taxpayer. This gain or loss is not recognized until the short sale is closed. Generally, the holding period of the short sale property is determined by how long the property used to close the short sale was held.

Short Sales

Example 22

On January 4, Green & Associates sold short 100 shares of Osprey Corporation for $1,500. Green closed the transaction on July 28 of the same year by purchasing 100 shares of Osprey for $1,000 and delivering them to the broker from whom the securities were borrowed. Because this stock was held less than one year (actually, less than a day), Green's $500 gain ($1,500 sale price − $1,000 basis) is short term.

Assume the same facts as in the preceding example, except that the January 4 short sale was not closed until January 28 of the *following* year. The result is the same, because the stock was acquired and used to close the transaction on the same day; that is, it was not held more than a year.

If a taxpayer owns securities that are "substantially identical" to those sold short, § 1259 subjects the short sale to potential *constructive sale treatment*, and the taxpayer recognizes gain (but not loss) as of that date even though the short sale was not yet closed. Similarly, if the taxpayer has not closed the short sale by delivering the short sale securities to the broker from whom the securities were borrowed before January 31 of the year following the short sale, the short sale is deemed to have closed on the short sale date. The holding period in such circumstances is determined by how long the securities in question were held.

Assume the same facts as in Example 22, except that Green & Associates owned 100 shares of Osprey Corporation when it sold short 100 shares on January 4. Green does not close the short sale before January 31 of the following year. Green must recognize any gain on its 100 shares of Osprey as of January 4 of the current year. If Green owned those shares more than one year as of that date, the gain is long term.

Tax Planning Strategies — Timing Capital Gains

Framework Focus: Income and Exclusions

Strategy: Postpone Recognition of Income to Achieve Tax Deferral.

Framework Focus: Deductions

Strategy: Maximize Deductible Amounts.

Taxpayers have considerable control over the timing of their capital gains through the mechanism of realization. Accordingly, a taxpayer might want to defer recognizing a large capital gain in a year with *substantial itemized deductions*, such as large personal casualty losses or medical expenditures. In so doing, the taxpayer minimizes the loss of such deductions due to AGI limitations. See additional discussion in Chapter 10.

Nontax considerations, of course, often dictate when assets are sold. If a particular stock is peaking in popularity, selling it might be a wise investment strategy, even if the taxpayer's current tax situation is not optimal.

Similarly, if a taxpayer needs cash to start a business, purchase a home, or pay for a child's education or medical costs, the capital asset might need to be sold at a time when investment *and* tax considerations counsel otherwise. In these circumstances, however, a taxpayer might choose to *borrow* the money required and use the capital asset as collateral for the loan rather than sell the asset. A loan does not trigger tax consequences, and the taxpayer can continue to hold the asset until a more opportune time—albeit at the cost of paying interest, which may be nondeductible.

In-depth coverage of short sales can be found on this book's companion website: www.cengage.com **7 Digging Deeper**

LO.4

Determine the tax treatment of capital gains and losses for noncorporate taxpayers.

8-5 Tax Treatment of Capital Gains and Losses of Noncorporate Taxpayers

This section discusses how capital gains and losses are taxed to noncorporate taxpayers (individuals, trusts, and estates). The next section of this chapter considers the rules for corporations.

8-5a Net Capital Gains

Net gains from the sale or exchange of capital assets are taxed at various rates depending upon the holding period of the assets generating the net gain, the taxpayer's regular tax rate, and the type of asset involved. Therefore, taxpayers must first net their capital gains and losses to determine how they are taxed. This netting process is discussed below.

Net Short-Term Gains

Net gains attributable to capital assets held one year or less are taxed at the same rates as *ordinary income*. Accordingly, the applicable tax rates vary from 10 percent to 37 percent. Although short-term capital gains receive no preferential tax treatment compared to ordinary income, they do have one advantage: they can absorb capital losses without limit. As discussed later in this section, *capital losses* are deducted first against capital gains (without limit). Any capital losses in excess of capital gains can be deducted against ordinary income, but only up to $3,000 per year.[13] Thus, someone with a large capital loss will find short-term capital gains attractive even though such gains do not qualify for lower tax rates.

Example 25

Kay generated a $50,000 long-term capital loss on the sale of her employer's stock (not a small business stock) that she had acquired over the previous 10 years. Kay holds other, appreciated, stock purchased within the last year that she is thinking about selling (since she thinks the prices are going to decline). If Kay decides to sell this stock and realizes a short-term capital gain, she will be able to use her capital loss to reduce the net gain she must recognize.

If Kay's short-term capital gains total $60,000, her capital loss will offset $50,000 of these gains, leaving only a $10,000 net short-term gain to be taxed at Kay's ordinary tax rate.

On the other hand, if Kay's short-term capital gains total $45,000, her capital loss will offset the entire short-term gain. In this case, none of her short-term gains are taxed. However, only $3,000 of the remaining $5,000 net long-term capital loss is immediately deductible against Kay's ordinary income.

Net Long-Term Gains

Net gains attributable to capital assets held more than one year are classified as *long-term* gains and are eligible for special (lower) tax rates. A taxpayer qualifies for a 0 percent rate on these gains if the taxpayer is in the 10 percent or the majority of the 12 percent regular tax bracket after taxing other taxable income.

A taxpayer qualifies for a 15 percent rate on these gains if the taxpayer is in the 22 percent, 24 percent, and 32 percent brackets or a portion of the 35 percent regular rate bracket after considering other taxable income. In 2022, the 15 percent tax rate applies until taxable income exceeds $517,200 for married taxpayers filing jointly, $488,500 for heads of household, $459,750 for single taxpayers, and $258,600 for married taxpayers filing separately.

A taxpayer qualifies for a 20 percent rate on these gains if taxable income exceeds the maximum taxable income thresholds for the 15 percent alternative tax rate. Thus, the benefit of these long-term capital gain tax rates can be significant. The threshold amounts above, as well as the thresholds that apply to the regular marginal tax rates, are indexed annually for inflation.

[13] § 1211(b).

The 0%/15%/20% rates apply to most net long-term capital gains and any qualified dividend income based on the taxpayer's filing status and taxable income. Relatively few taxpayers in the 10 or 12 percent tax brackets realize capital gains. In addition, there are few taxpayers who are in the highest income tax bracket and subject to the 20 percent rate. Thus, the tax rate that generally applies to most net long-term capital gains for most taxpayers is 15 percent. Concept Summary 8.3 reviews these rates and their taxable income cutoffs.

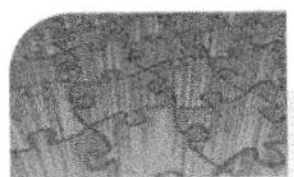

Concept Summary 8.3

Alternative Tax Rates on Net Capital Gains (NCG)
(Based on Filing Status and Taxable Income)

2022: FILING STATUS

Single		Married, Filing Jointly		Married, Filing Separately		Head of Household		NCG Tax Rate
Taxable Income		Taxable Income		Taxable Income		Taxable Income		
Greater Than	No More Than	Greater Than	No More Than	Greater Than	No More Than	Greater Than	No More Than	
$ –0–	$ 41,675	$ –0–	$ 83,350	$ –0–	$ 41,675	$ –0–	$ 55,800	0%
41,675	459,750	83,350	517,200	41,675	258,600	55,800	488,500	15%
459,750		517,200		258,600		488,500		20%

Example 26

Wang, a single taxpayer, realized an $80,000 net long-term capital gain in 2022. If Wang's taxable income, excluding the capital gain, was $220,000, his total taxable income would be $300,000. However, the tax rate applicable to his long-term capital gain is only 15% and the related tax would be $12,000 ($80,000 × 15%). The tax on his other taxable income would be calculated using his ordinary rates up to and including 35%.

Tax Planning Strategies — Gifts of Appreciated Securities

Framework Focus: Tax Rate

Strategy: Shift Net Income from High-Bracket Taxpayers to Low-Bracket Taxpayers.

Persons with appreciated securities that have been held over one year may reduce the tax due on their sale by giving the securities to someone (often a child) who is in the *lowest tax bracket*. The donor's holding period carries over, along with their basis, and the donee's lower tax rate applies when the securities are sold. As a result, the gain could be taxed at the donee's 0 percent rather than the donor's 15 or 20 percent. The donee should be at least age 19 (or 24 in the case of a full-time student) by year-end, however, or the *kiddie tax* may nullify most of the tax advantage being sought. The kiddie tax subjects the gain to the parents' tax rate. See Chapter 9.

Such gifts usually bear no gift tax due to the $16,000 annual exclusion. But once the property is transferred by the donor, it belongs to the donee. It is not available to the donor, nor may it be used to pay a parent's essential support obligations. Moreover, these assets may affect a child's eligibility for need-based financial aid when applying to college.

There are two major exceptions, however, to the general capital gains rates. The first exception relates to so-called *28% property*, which consists of the following items.

- **Collectibles** (e.g., works of art, rugs, antiques, gems, coins, stamps, and alcoholic beverages) held more than one year.[14]
- The taxable portion of the gain on sales of *qualified small business stock* (see the end of this section).

[14] §§ 1(h)(5) and 408(m) and Prop. Reg. § 1.408–10(b).

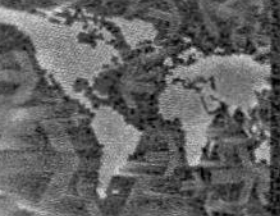

Global Tax Issues — Capital Gain Treatment in the United States and Other Countries

Not all countries apply an alternative tax rate or other incentive to long-term capital gains. In many countries, those gains are taxed in the same manner as other income. Although the U.S. system of identifying and taxing capital assets is complex, it provides a potential benefit to all U.S. taxpayers regardless of the level of their income or their tax bracket.

These assets are labeled *28% property* because the net long-term gains they produce are taxed at a *maximum* rate of 28 percent. Taxpayers in a lower tax bracket would pay tax on long-term gains from 28% property at that lower rate. As a result, the benefit of the applicable tax rates for gains on *28% property* is as follows.

Ordinary Income Tax Rates	Applicable Tax Rates	Differential (Percentage Points)
10%	10%	None
12%	12%	None
22%	22%	None
24%	24%	None
32%	28%	4%
35%	28%	7%
37%	28%	9%

Note that gains on *28% property* receive preferential tax treatment only when realized by taxpayers in the top three ordinary income tax brackets.

Taxation of Collectibles Gains

Example 27

Kelsey is in the 12% tax bracket due to her income. She generates $2,000 of gains on the sale of a coin collection she has had since she was a child. Although collectibles are 28% property, her gains will be taxed at only 12%, consistent with her lower ordinary income tax bracket.

Example 28

Ashley is in the top ordinary tax bracket (37%). She sells a stamp collection she has owned for several years for a $3,000 gain. The stamps are 28% property and will be taxed at the preferential 28% tax rate since Ashley's ordinary tax rate exceeds 28%.

The second major exception involves depreciable real estate that has been held more than one year. Some—but not all—of the gain attributable to depreciation deductions on real estate such as apartments, office buildings, shopping centers, and warehouses is taxable at 25 percent rather than 0, 15, or 20 percent. The amount that is taxed in this manner is limited to the gain attributable to depreciation that is *not* already "recaptured" as ordinary income under § 1250, as explained later in this chapter. Accordingly, these gains are called *unrecaptured § 1250 gain*. The 25 percent rate is a *maximum* rate, so the benefit of this tax rate for gains from the sale of depreciable real estate really only impacts taxpayers in the 32 percent to 37 percent tax brackets and saves them from 7 percentage points to a maximum of 12 percentage points.

Concept Summary 8.4 reviews the tax treatment given to capital gains recognized by noncorporate taxpayers.

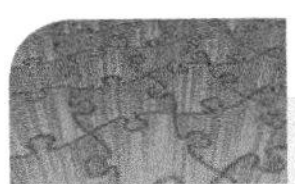

Concept Summary 8.4

Capital Gains of Noncorporate Taxpayers

Type of Asset	Applicable Rate
Held not more than one year (short term).	10%–37%, same as ordinary income.
Collectibles held more than one year (*28% property*).	Lower of taxpayer's marginal rate on ordinary income or 28%.
Taxable portion (50%, 25%, or 0%) of gain on qualified small business stock held more than five years (*28% property*; see text Section 8-5d for a detailed explanation of the special treatment given to "qualified small business stock").	Lower of taxpayer's marginal rate on ordinary income or 28%.
Unrecaptured § 1250 gain on depreciable real estate held more than one year.	Lower of taxpayer's marginal rate on ordinary income or 25%.
Other capital assets held more than one year (regular long term).	0%, 15%, or 20% depending on specific taxable income thresholds.

8-5b Net Capital Losses

As explained previously, capital gains can be classified into four general categories.

- Short term—taxed as ordinary income.
- *28% property*—taxed at no more than 28 percent.
- *Unrecaptured § 1250 gain*—taxed at no more than 25 percent.
- Regular long term—taxed at 0 percent, 15 percent, or 20 percent.

A taxpayer can also have losses from capital assets in *three* of these four categories. The *unrecaptured § 1250 gain* category applies only to gain. Noncorporate taxpayers may immediately recognize no more than $3,000 of net capital losses. Any excess capital loss may be carried forward indefinitely, subject to the same $3,000 limit each year.

Annemarie has taxable income of $100,000 before considering a net capital loss of $30,000. She recognizes $3,000 of the net capital loss currently, reducing her taxable income to $97,000. She carries forward the remaining $27,000 net capital loss. Assuming Annemarie recognizes no additional capital gains or losses, she will recognize $3,000 of her capital loss carryforward each year for the next nine years.

8-5c Capital Gain and Loss Netting Process

When both gains and losses occur in the year, their treatment depends on the taxpayer's *net* capital gain or loss. To determine the source of the net gain or loss, individual gains and losses must be netted against each other in the following order.

Step 1. Group all gains and losses into four groups: short-term, *28% property*, *unrecaptured § 1250 gain*, and regular long-term categories.

Step 2. Net the gains and losses within each category to obtain net short-term, net *28% property*, net *unrecaptured § 1250 gain*, and net regular long-term gain or loss.

Step 3. Offset the net *28% property gain or loss and unrecaptured § 1250 gain* amounts if they are of opposite sign. Add them if they have the same sign. Then offset the resulting amount against the regular net long-term amount if they are of opposite sign, or add the amounts if they have the same sign.

Step 4. Offset the result of step 3 with the net short-term gain or loss from step 2 if they are of opposite sign.

These netting rules result in short-term losses offsetting the *highest-taxed gain first.* Consequently, if there is a net short-term capital loss, it first offsets any net *28% property gain*, any remaining loss offsets *unrecaptured § 1250 gain*, and then any remaining loss offsets regular long-term gain.

If the result of step 4 is *only* a short-term capital gain, the taxpayer is not eligible for a reduced tax rate. If the result of step 4 is a loss, a **net capital loss (NCL)** exists and the taxpayer may be eligible for a *capital loss deduction*. If there was no offsetting in step 4 because the short-term and step 3 results were both gains *or* if the result of the offsetting is a *28% property*, an *unrecaptured § 1250 property*, and/or a regular long-term gain, a **net capital gain (NCG)** exists and the taxpayer may be eligible for a reduced tax rate. The net capital gain may consist of regular long-term gain, *unrecaptured § 1250 gain*, and/or *28% property gain*. Each of these gains may be taxed at a different rate.

Special Tax Rates and Capital Gain and Loss Netting Process

Example 30

Joe is in the 35% Federal income tax bracket, with taxable income that does not exceed the cutoff for the 20% capital gain rate. He is taxed as follows.

Ordinary income	35%
Unrecaptured § 1250 gain	25%
28% gain	28%
Short-term capital gain	35%
Other long-term capital gain	15%

Example 31

This example shows how a *net long-term capital loss* is applied. In 2022, Joe sold assets resulting in a $3,000 short-term capital gain, a $1,000 collectibles capital gain, a $3,000 long-term capital gain, and an $8,000 long-term capital loss.

Step	Short-Term	28% Gain	Unrecaptured § 1250 Gain	Regular Long-Term	Comment
1	$ 3,000	$ 1,000		$ 3,000	
				(8,000)	
2	$ 3,000	$ 1,000		($ 5,000)	Net each category of gains and losses.
3		(1,000)	→	1,000	Netted because of opposite sign.
		$ -0-		($ 4,000)	
4	(3,000)	→	→	3,000	The net short-term gain is netted against the net regular long-term loss, and the remaining loss is eligible for the capital loss deduction.
	$ -0-			($ 1,000)	

Special Tax Rates and Capital Gain and Loss Netting Process

Example 32

This example shows how *net short-term* and *regular long-term capital losses* are applied. In 2022, Joe sold assets resulting in a $3,000 short-term capital gain, a $5,000 short-term capital loss, a $15,000 collectibles capital gain, a $7,000 collectibles loss, a $4,000 unrecaptured § 1250 gain, a $3,000 long-term capital gain, and an $8,000 long-term capital loss.

Step	Short-Term	28% Gain	Unrecaptured § 1250 Gain	Regular Long-Term	Comment
1	$ 3,000	$15,000	$4,000	$ 3,000	
	(5,000)	(7,000)		(8,000)	
2	($ 2,000)	$ 8,000	$4,000	($ 5,000)	Net each category of gains and losses.
3		(5,000)	←	5,000	Net regular long-term loss is netted against *28% gain first.* There is no remaining long-term loss to offset against the unrecaptured § 1250 gain.
		$ 3,000		$ -0-	
4	2,000 →	(2,000)			Short-term loss is netted against *28% gain* next.
	$ -0-	$ 1,000	$4,000		
		Net *28% gain*	Net *25% gain*		

If a net loss remains after applying these rules for offsetting losses, a noncorporate taxpayer deducts up to $3,000 of that loss against ordinary income.[15] Noncorporate taxpayers must carry over losses that exceed $3,000 to future years and apply them first against capital gains and then deduct up to $3,000 per year. Capital loss carryovers expire, however, when the taxpayer dies.

Use of Capital Loss Carryovers

Example 33

James incurred a $10,000 loss on his only capital asset transaction in 2022. If he has no other capital asset transactions from that point on, James will deduct his $10,000 loss as follows.

Year	Deduction
2022	$3,000
2023	3,000
2024	3,000
2025	1,000

Example 34

Assume the same facts as in the preceding example, except that James realizes a capital gain of $4,500 in 2024. At that time, his remaining capital loss carryover is $4,000 ($10,000 − $6,000 deducted previously). Because his capital gain in 2024 (i.e., $4,500) exceeds this loss carryforward, James can deduct the entire $4,000 against that year's capital gain.

Example 35

Assume the same facts as in Example 34, except that James dies in late 2023. His remaining capital loss carryforward of $4,000 ($10,000 − $6,000 deducted in 2022 and 2023) expires unused.

[15] § 1211(b)(1). Married persons filing separate returns are limited to a $1,500 deduction per tax year.

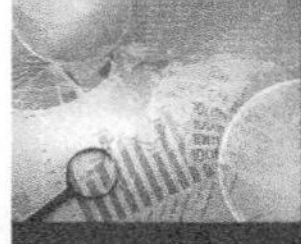

Tax Planning Strategies — Matching Gains with Losses

Framework Focus: Income and Exclusions

Strategy: Avoid Income Recognition.

A taxpayer who has already realized a large capital gain may want to consider disposing of an asset that has declined in value. Doing so will shelter the capital gain from taxation and will also allow the immediate recognition of the capital loss. Without the capital gain, a capital loss may be deductible only in $3,000 annual increments.

Similarly, a taxpayer with a large realized capital loss might use the occasion to sell some appreciated assets. Doing so would enable the taxpayer to use the capital loss immediately and at the same time realize the benefit of the asset appreciation at little or no tax cost.

On the other hand, matching capital losses and long-term capital gains means that the taxpayer utilizes the capital loss against income that would otherwise qualify for a preferential tax rate. If the taxpayer's ordinary income is taxed at a higher rate, he or she might prefer to deduct the loss against that higher taxed income, even on a schedule of $3,000 per year. In such an analysis, the *time value of money* must be considered; a current-year deduction offsetting income taxable at 0, 15, or 20 percent might be worth more than a series of annual deductions that will offset income taxed at higher rates spread over several years.

Nontax considerations, such as investment prospects for the assets in question, are also important. Future investment prospects are often unknowable or at least highly speculative, while tax effects can be determined with relative certainty—which explains some of the late December selling activity in publicly traded securities and mutual funds.

When a taxpayer's net capital loss exceeds $3,000 and derives from more than one category, the losses are used in the following order: first, short-term; then, *28% property*; and finally, regular long-term. Taxpayers carry forward unused short-term and long-term losses separately and do not net them together.

During the current year, Nancy incurs a short-term capital loss of $2,500 and a long-term capital loss of $8,500. Nancy will recognize a $3,000 loss against her ordinary income consisting of the $2,500 short-term loss and $500 of the long-term loss. The remaining $8,000 ($11,000 realized loss − $3,000 recognized) carries forward as a long-term capital loss.

Digging Deeper 8

Further discussion of qualified dividend income can be found on this book's companion website: www.cengage.com

8-5d **Small Business Stock**

To encourage the formation of new, small businesses, a special *exclusion* is available to noncorporate taxpayers who derive capital gains from the sale or exchange of **qualified small business stock**.[16] Any amount not excluded from income is taxed at a maximum rate of 28 percent (as noted earlier). The exclusion amount varies depending on when the qualified small business stock was acquired:

- 100 percent of the gain is excluded for qualified stock acquired after September 27, 2010.
- 75 percent of the gain is excluded for qualified stock acquired after February 17, 2009, and before September 28, 2010.
- 50 percent of the gain is excluded for qualified stock acquired before February 18, 2009.

As a result, the maximum effective tax rate on gains from the sale of qualified small business stock is 0 percent (28% × 0%), 7 percent (28% × 25%), or 14 percent (28% × 50%).

[16]§ 1202(a).

Example 37

Yolanda realized a $100,000 gain on the sale of qualified small business stock that she acquired in 2008. Yolanda's marginal tax rate is 32% without considering this gain. Because she acquired the stock before February 18, 2009, Yolanda excludes $50,000 of this gain (50%) from her gross income. The other $50,000 is taxed at the maximum rate of 28%. As a result, Yolanda owes Federal income tax of $14,000 on the stock sale ($50,000 × 28%), for an effective tax rate of 14% on the entire $100,000 gain.

If, instead, Yolanda acquired the stock any time after September 27, 2010, she would exclude 100% of the gain.

The exclusion is only available on the sale of qualified small business stock held by the taxpayer more than five years. Stock is qualified small business stock if all of the following requirements are met:

- The stock must have been newly issued after August 10, 1993, by a regular corporation, not a Subchapter S corporation.
- The issuing corporation must use at least 80 percent of its assets, determined by their value, in the *active conduct* of a trade or business.
- When the stock was issued, the issuing corporation's assets must not have exceeded $50 million, at adjusted basis, including the proceeds of the stock issuance.
- The corporation does not engage in banking, financing, insurance, investing, leasing, farming, mineral extraction, hotel or motel operations, restaurant operations, or any business whose principal asset is the *reputation or skill* of its employees (such as accounting, architecture, health, law, engineering, or financial services).

In addition to meeting these conditions, the amount of gain eligible for the exclusion is limited to the *greater* of 10 times the taxpayer's basis in the stock or $10 million per taxpayer per company, computed on an aggregate basis.[17]

Rachel purchased $100,000 of qualified small business stock when it was first issued in October 2005. In 2023, she sold the stock for $4,000,000. Her gain is 3,900,000 ($4,000,000 − $100,000). Although this amount exceeds 10 times her basis ($100,000 × 10 = $1,000,000), it is *less* than $10,000,000. As a result, the entire $3,900,000 gain is eligible for a 50% exclusion.

Transactions that fail to satisfy *any* of the conditions are taxed as capital gains (and losses) realized by noncorporate taxpayers generally.

Gains on the sale of qualified small business stock are also eligible for deferral if the stock was held more than six months and the sale proceeds are invested in other qualified small business stock within 60 days.[18] Any gain postponed reduces the basis of the stock purchased. Gain must be recognized to the extent the sale proceeds exceed the cost of new qualified business stock. However, that gain will be eligible for the exclusion discussed above if the stock sold was held for more than five years.

Assume the same facts as in the preceding example, except that Rachel sold her stock in January 2023 and used $3,500,000 of the sale proceeds to purchase other qualified small business stock one month later. Rachel recognizes gain to the extent that she does not reinvest the sale proceeds—namely, $500,000 ($4,000,000 sale proceeds − $3,500,000 reinvested). A 50% exclusion will apply, however, to the $500,000.

Rachel's basis for the stock purchased in February 2023 is $100,000 ($3,500,000 purchase price − $3,400,000 postponed gain; the postponed gain is the $3,900,000 original gain less the $500,000 gain recognized in 2023).

[17] § 1202(b). For married persons filing separately, the limitation is $5 million.

[18] § 1045(a).

Tax Fact Capital Gains for the Wealthy?

Almost all individual taxpayers, regardless of income level, receive preferential treatment for capital gains and qualified dividends in the form of a lower tax rate. Many argue, however, that the lower rates nonetheless add a level of regressivity to the tax, or at least reduce its progressivity, because capital gains and qualified dividends are realized disproportionately by higher-income taxpayers. The most recently available data regarding the proportion of AGI comprised of preferentially taxed income, by AGI level, is illustrated below.

Source: *Statistics of Income-2019; Individual Income Tax Returns (Publication 1304), Figure F.*, Internal Revenue Service. Washington D.C.

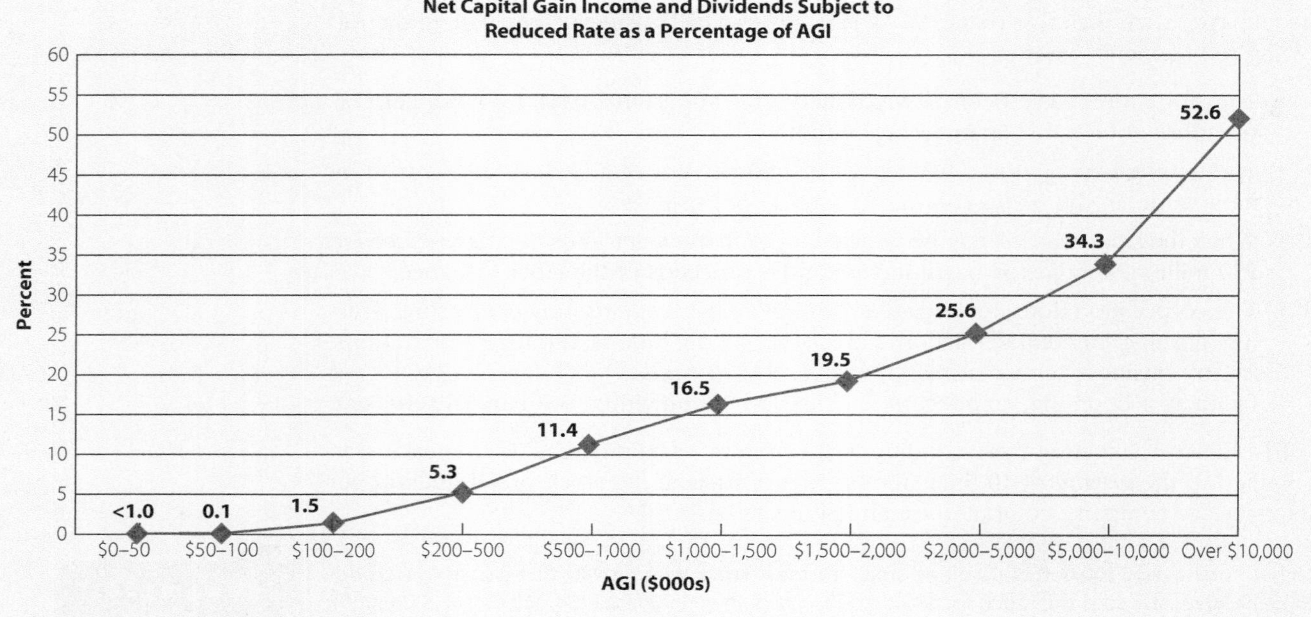

LO.5

Determine the tax treatment of capital gains and losses for corporate taxpayers.

8-6 Tax Treatment of Capital Gains and Losses of Corporate Taxpayers

The treatment of a corporation's net capital gain or loss differs dramatically from the rules for noncorporate taxpayers discussed in the preceding section. Briefly, the differences are as follows.

- Net capital gains are taxed at the ordinary income tax rates.
- Capital losses offset only capital gains. Corporations cannot deduct net capital losses against other taxable income.
- There is a three-year carryback and a five-year carryforward period for net capital losses.[19] Capital loss carrybacks and carryforwards are always treated as short term, regardless of their original nature.

Note that with the treatment given to corporate capital gains and losses, no substantive advantage results to the taxpayer as a result of generating net capital gains. However, the classification of gains as capital or ordinary remains important because capital losses can only offset capital gains. Corporations that realize capital losses have an incentive to realize capital gains during the five-year carryover window to ensure the capital loss may be recognized.

[19] § 1212(a)(1).

Sparrow Corporation has a $15,000 long-term capital loss for the current year and $57,000 of other taxable income. Sparrow may not deduct the $15,000 long-term capital loss against its other income.

The $15,000 long-term capital loss becomes a $15,000 short-term capital loss for carryback and carryforward purposes. This amount may offset capital gains in the three-year carryback period or, if not absorbed there, offset capital gains in the five-year carryforward period. Any amount remaining after this carryforward period expires is permanently lost.

8-7 Section 1231 Gains and Losses

Distinguish § 1231 assets from ordinary and capital assets and calculate § 1231 gain or loss.

Businesses own many assets that are used in the business rather than held for resale. In financial accounting, such assets are known as "fixed assets." For example, a foundry's 15-ton stamping machine is a fixed asset. It is also a depreciable asset. The building housing the foundry is another fixed asset. Chapter 5 discussed how to depreciate such assets. Chapter 7 discussed how to determine the adjusted basis and the amount of gain or loss from their disposition. The remainder of this chapter largely deals with how to *classify* the gains and losses from the disposition of fixed assets. This classification determines the *character* of the gain or loss. Gain or loss character, along with the process of netting the gains and losses, determine their taxation.

8-7a Relationship to Capital Gains and Losses

At first glance, the *classification of fixed assets* would seem straightforward. Code § 1221(a)(2) specifically excludes from capital assets any depreciable or real property "used in a trade or business." Accordingly, the foundry's stamping machine and the building housing the foundry described earlier are not capital assets. Therefore, one would expect gains to be taxed as ordinary income and losses to be deductible as ordinary losses. However, net gains realized on the disposition of these assets sometimes receive more favorable treatment.

The disposition of assets used in a trade or business and held for more than one year is covered by § 1231. This provision requires taxpayers to aggregate gains and losses from the disposition of **§ 1231 property** at the end of the taxable year. Net gains generally are treated as long-term capital gains, eligible for the lower capital gain tax rates available to noncorporate taxpayers and allowing the recognition of the taxpayers' capital losses. However, net losses are treated as ordinary, avoiding the limitations on the ability to recognize capital losses.[20] As a result, taxpayers cannot determine a particular disposition's character as capital or ordinary until the taxable year has ended and the taxpayer's **§ 1231 gains and losses** are tabulated. However, § 1231 potentially provides taxpayers with "the best of both worlds," the treatment of net gains as capital and net losses as ordinary.

Section 1231 Treatment

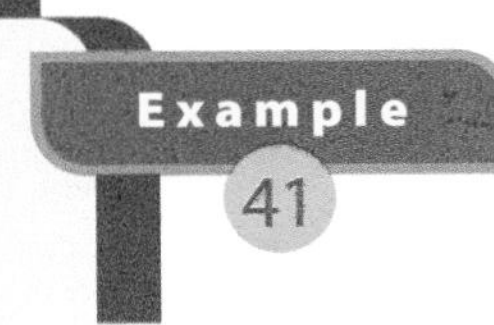

Brown & Co. sells a building at a $5,000 gain and equipment at a $3,000 loss. Both properties were § 1231 assets because they were used in Brown's trade or business and held for the long-term holding period (more than one year). Brown has a net § 1231 gain of $2,000, and that net gain *may* (depending on various recapture rules discussed later in this chapter) be treated as a long-term capital gain.

Chickadee, Inc., sells equipment at a $10,000 loss and business land at a $2,000 gain. Both properties were held for more than one year and, therefore, are § 1231 assets. Chickadee has a net § 1231 loss of $8,000 that is treated as an ordinary loss.

[20] In text Sections 8-8 and 8-9, the recapture of some of the beneficial capital gain treatment through the imposition of § 1245 and § 1250 is discussed.

Digging Deeper 9 A historical perspective of § 1231 can be found on this book's companion website: www.cengage.com

8-7b Definition of Section 1231 Assets

Generally

Generally, § 1231 property includes property used in a trade or business, More specifically, § 1231 property includes the following.

- Depreciable personal property and all real property used in a business (e.g., machinery and equipment, buildings and land).
- Certain *purchased* intangible assets (such as patents and goodwill) that are eligible for amortization.
- Certain natural resources (e.g., timber), livestock, and unharvested crops.

Digging Deeper 10 Rules regarding § 1231 treatment for natural resources and livestock can be found on this book's companion website: www.cengage.com

Section 1231 property generally does *not* include the following.

- Property not held more than one year.
- Inventory and property held primarily for sale to customers.
- A patent, invention, model, or design (whether or not patented); a secret formula or process; certain copyrights; literary, musical, or artistic compositions; and certain U.S. government publications.
- Accounts receivable and notes receivable arising in the ordinary course of the trade or business.

Casualty or Theft of Nonpersonal Use Capital Assets

Generally, § 1231 covers gains and losses related to assets that are used in a trade or business. However, as explained further below, the benefits of § 1231 are extended to certain capital assets as well if the taxpayer recognizes those gains and losses as the result of a casualty or theft. However, the only capital assets to which § 1231 may apply are those held *in connection with* a trade or business (whether or not they are "used" in the trade or business; e.g., artwork owned by a corporation that is not an art dealer) or for the production of income (e.g., a building owned and leased by an individual who is not a real estate professional).[21] Together, these are referred to as "nonpersonal use capital assets." Code § 1231 will never apply to gains or losses related to capital assets that are not used by the taxpayer in some capacity or that are used by individuals for personal purposes even if those gains or losses are the result of a casualty or theft.

Recall from Chapter 6 that casualties, thefts, and condemnations are *involuntary conversions* and gains from such conversions need not be recognized if the proceeds are timely reinvested in similar property. Because § 1231 serves only to characterize recognized gains or losses, it has no impact on realized gains or losses that are deferred.

Note further that this special rule does not apply to *condemnation* gains and losses. As a result, if a § 1231 asset is disposed of by condemnation, any resulting gain or loss will automatically receive § 1231 treatment.

[21] § 1231(a)(3).

8-7c General Procedure for § 1231 Computation

Like the tax treatment of capital gains and losses, the ultimate treatment of § 1231 gains and losses depends on the taxpayer's *net* gain or loss on the disposition of § 1231 property. Consequently, the ultimate tax treatment of individual § 1231 gains and losses depends on the results of a netting procedure. The steps in that procedure are discussed below and summarized in Concept Summary 8.5.

Step 1: Net Gains and Losses from Casualties

Net all recognized long-term gains and losses resulting from casualties of both § 1231 and nonpersonal use capital assets.

a. If the casualty gains exceed the casualty losses, treat the net gain as a § 1231 gain.
b. If the casualty losses exceed the casualty gains, treat all casualty losses and gains as ordinary.

This preliminary netting process is beneficial because it maintains ordinary loss treatment for net losses from casualties even if the taxpayer might have net gains from other dispositions of § 1231 assets.

Step 2: Net All § 1231 Gains and Losses

Net all § 1231 gains and losses including any net casualty gain from step 1(a) above.

a. If the gains exceed the losses, the net § 1231 gain is treated as a long-term capital gain (after applying the "lookback" provisions discussed below in step 3) and netted with the taxpayers other capital gains and losses.
b. If the losses exceed the gains, the net § 1231 loss is treated as an ordinary loss and deducted against ordinary income.

Section 1231 Computations

Example 43

Falcon Management, Inc., recognized the following gains and losses this year.

Gains and Losses from the Sale of Capital Asssets	
Long-term capital gain	$3,000
Long-term capital loss	(400)
Short-term capital gain	1,000
Short-term capital loss	(200)
Casualties	
Gain from insurance recovery on fire loss to building, owned five years	$ 1,200
Loss from theft of computer (uninsured), owned two years	(1,000)
§ 1231 Gains and Losses from Sale of Depreciable Business Assets Held Long Term	
Asset A	$ 300
Asset B	1,100
Asset C	(500)
Gains and Losses from Sale of Depreciable Business Assets Held Short Term	
Asset D	$ 200
Asset E	(300)

continued

Falcon had no net § 1231 losses in prior tax years.

Falcon's gains and losses receive the following tax treatment. [The gains on the business building and Assets A and B are *after* any depreciation recapture (discussed later in the chapter).]

- **Step 1:** The netting of the § 1231 and nonpersonal use capital asset casualties includes two items—the $1,200 gain from the business building and the $1,000 loss from the computer—resulting in a net $200 gain. Because they net to a gain, that gain is treated as a § 1231 gain and added to the other § 1231 gains.
- **Step 2:** The gains from § 1231 transactions (Assets A and B and the § 1231 casualty gain) exceed the losses (Asset C) by $1,100 ($1,600 − $500). Because these § 1231 gains and losses net to a gain, the net § 1231 gain is a long-term capital gain and is added to Falcon's other long-term capital gains.

Falcon's net long-term capital gain is $3,700 ($3,000 + $1,100 from § 1231 transactions − $400 long-term capital loss). Its net short-term capital gain is $800 ($1,000 − $200). The result is a net capital gain of $4,500. Because Falcon is a corporation, this gain will be taxed at ordinary rates. If Falcon were an individual rather than a corporation, the $3,700 net long-term capital gain portion would be eligible for preferential capital gain treatment and the $800 net short-term capital gain would be taxed as ordinary income.

Falcon treats the gain and loss from Assets D and E as ordinary gain and loss because § 1231 does not apply unless the assets have been held more than one year.[22]

Impact of the Gains and Losses on Falcon's Taxable Income	
Ordinary Gains and Losses	
Gain from sale of Asset D	$ 200
Loss from sale of Asset E	(300)
Net ordinary loss	(100)
Capital Gains and Losses	
Net long-term capital gain	$ 3,700
Net short-term capital gain	800
Net capital gain	$ 4,500

Example 44

Assume the same facts as in the preceding example, except that the loss from Asset C was $1,700 instead of $500.

- **Step 1:** The treatment of the casualty gains and losses is the same.
- **Step 2:** The losses from § 1231 transactions now exceed the gains by $100 ($1,700 − $1,600). As a result, the net § 1231 loss is deducted in full as an ordinary loss.

Capital gain income is $3,400 ($2,600 long-term + $800 short-term).

Impact of the Gains and Losses on Falcon's Taxable Income	
Ordinary Gains and Losses	
Gain from sale of Asset D	$ 200
Loss from sale of Asset E	(300)
Net § 1231 loss	(100)
Net ordinary loss	(200)
Capital Gains and Losses	
Net long-term capital gain	$ 2,600
Net short-term capital gain	800
Net capital gain	$ 3,400

[22] § 1231(b)(1).

Step 3: § 1231 Lookback Provision

Because the treatment of any one § 1231 gain or loss in a year depends on the net § 1231 gain or loss for the year, taxpayers may exploit the provision by grouping losses in one year (and receiving ordinary loss treatment for the entire amount) and gains in another (receiving capital gain treatment for the entire amount). The **§ 1231 lookback** requirement reduces taxpayer's ability to artificially exploit the benefits of § 1231 by requiring taxpayers to recognize current year net § 1231 gains as ordinary to the extent they recognized net § 1231 losses as ordinary losses in prior years (i.e., to "recapture" prior net § 1231 losses). Specifically, the net § 1231 gain from step 2(a) is offset by the "nonrecaptured net § 1231 losses" for the five preceding taxable years.[23] For transactions in 2022, the lookback years are 2017, 2018, 2019, 2020, and 2021.

a. To the extent of the nonrecaptured net § 1231 loss, the current-year net § 1231 gain is ordinary income. The *nonrecaptured net § 1231 losses* are losses that have not already been used to offset net § 1231 gains in a later tax year.
b. The remaining net § 1231 gain exceeding the lookback recapture is given long-term capital gain treatment.

Section 1231 Lookback Provision

Komodo Manufacturing Corporation sold used equipment and some business real estate during 2022 for a net § 1231 gain of $25,000. During 2021, Komodo had no § 1231 transactions, but in 2020, it had a net § 1231 loss of $17,000. This loss causes $17,000 of the 2022 gain to be reclassified as ordinary income. The remaining 2022 gain of $8,000 ($25,000 of § 1231 gain − $17,000 previously nonrecaptured loss) is treated as a long-term capital gain.

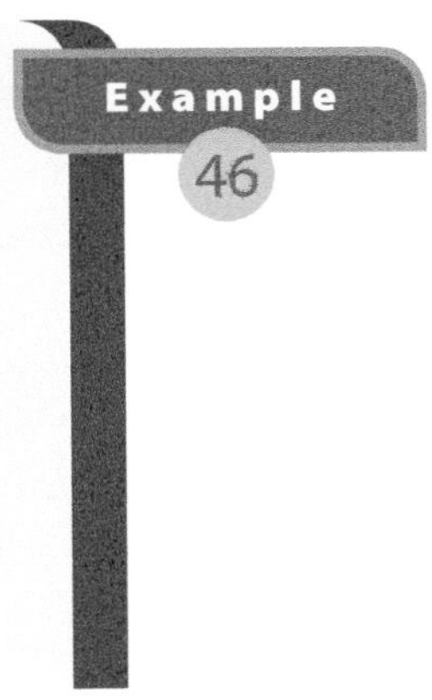

Assume the same facts as in the preceding example, except that Komodo had a net § 1231 loss of $37,000 in 2020 and a net § 1231 gain of $10,000 in 2021.

- The 2020 net § 1231 loss of $37,000 would cause the net § 1231 gain of $10,000 in 2021 to be classified as ordinary income, and $27,000 ($37,000 loss − $10,000 recaptured) would carry over to 2022.
- The remaining nonrecaptured § 1231 loss of $27,000 from 2020 results in a complete reclassification of the § 1231 gain of $25,000 from 2022, making that entire gain ordinary income.
- The remaining nonrecaptured § 1231 loss from 2020 is $2,000 ($27,000 nonrecaptured § 1231 loss carried to 2022 − $25,000 recaptured in 2022). This recapture potential carries over to 2023.

[23] § 1231(c).

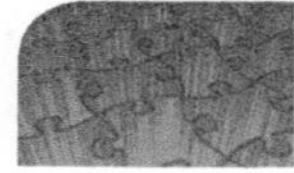

Concept Summary 8.5

Section 1231 Netting Procedure

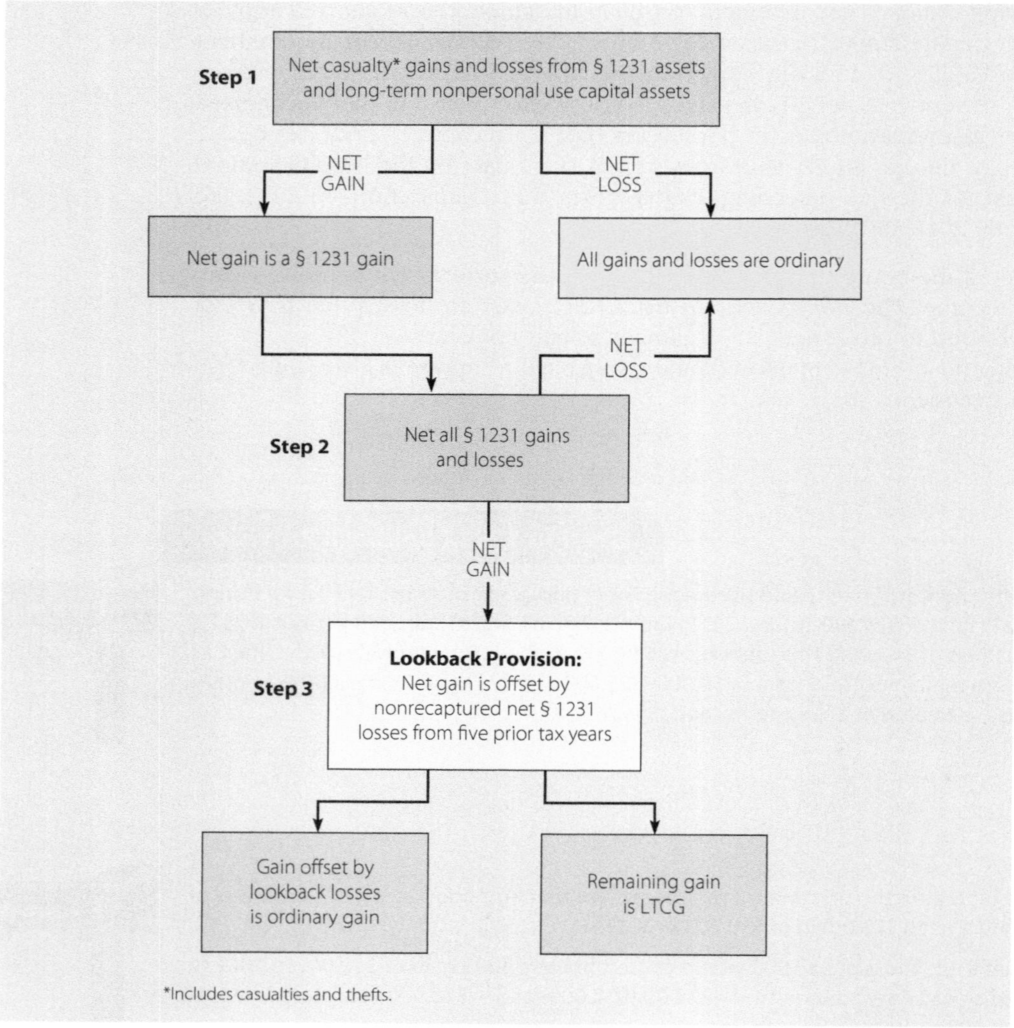

*Includes casualties and thefts.

LO.7

Determine when recapture provisions apply and derive their effects.

8-8 Section 1245 Recapture

As explained earlier, when Congress concluded that § 1231 was unduly generous, it chose to require the *recapture* of some of § 1231's benefits rather than repeal that section altogether. The lookback rule just discussed recaptures some or all of the *net* § 1231 gain as ordinary income. In contrast, the depreciation recapture rules discussed below reclassify § 1231 gains from selling an *individual asset* as ordinary income.

These recapture rules apply exclusively to § 1231 gains; they do not affect losses. In essence, depreciation recapture takes part—often all—of the gain from the sale or exchange of a § 1231 asset and classifies it as *ordinary income* before the netting process of § 1231 begins. Accordingly, recaptured gain is computed *first*, without considering other § 1231 transactions that occurred during the taxable year. This section discusses the § 1245 recapture rules, and text Section 8-9 discusses the § 1250 recapture rules.

Under § 1245, taxpayers must treat all gain recognized on the sale or exchange of § 1245 property as ordinary gain up to the amount of cost recovery, including § 179 expense and bonus depreciation, previously taken on the disposed property. Practically, therefore, § 1231 gain results only if the taxpayer disposes of § 1245 property for more than its original cost. That is, when § 1245 applies, only the excess of the sales price over the original cost, or the gain due to an asset's appreciation, is eligible for § 1231 treatment. As described more completely in the next section, § 1245 applies primarily to personal property like machinery and equipment.

The Big Picture

Example 47

Return to the facts of *The Big Picture* on p. 8-1. Recall that Alice's husband, Jeff, had purchased, for $50,000, depreciable equipment for use in his business and had deducted $35,000 of depreciation. As a result, the equipment's adjusted basis is $15,000.

If Jeff sold the equipment for $45,000, his gain would be $30,000 ($45,000 amount realized − $15,000 adjusted basis). If it were not for § 1245, the $30,000 gain would be § 1231 gain. However, because § 1245 treats as ordinary income (not as § 1231 gain) any gain to the extent of depreciation taken, the entire $30,000 gain would be ordinary income.

The Big Picture

Example 48

Continue with the facts of Example 47, except that Jeff sold the equipment for $60,000 instead of $45,000. Jeff would have a gain of $45,000 ($60,000 amount realized − $15,000 adjusted basis). The § 1245 gain would be $35,000 (equal to the depreciation taken), and the remaining gain of $10,000 (equal to the excess of the sales price over the original cost) would be § 1231 gain.

The Big Picture

Example 49

Continue with the facts of Example 47, except that Jeff sold the equipment for $8,000 instead of $45,000. Jeff would have a loss of $7,000 ($8,000 amount realized − $15,000 adjusted basis). Because there is a loss, there is no depreciation recapture. All of the loss is § 1231 loss.

Section 1245 recapture applies to the portion of *recognized* gain from the sale or other disposition of § 1245 property that is caused by prior depreciation.[24] Code § 1245 merely *reclassifies* gain as ordinary income; it does not change the *amount* of recognized gain. Thus, in Example 48, Jeff recaptures as ordinary income only the $30,000 of actual gain, not the entire $35,000 of depreciation taken. In other words, § 1245 recaptures the *lesser* of the accumulated depreciation taken on the asset sold or the gain recognized.

The method of depreciation (e.g., accelerated or straight-line) does not matter. Because all depreciation taken is potentially subject to recapture, § 1245 recapture often is referred to as *full recapture*. Any remaining gain after subtracting the amount recaptured as ordinary income usually will be § 1231 gain. The remaining gain is casualty gain, however, if the asset is disposed of in a casualty event. For example, if the equipment in Example 48 had been disposed of by casualty and the $60,000 received had been an insurance recovery, Jeff still would have a gain of $45,000, and $35,000 of that gain still would be recaptured by § 1245 as ordinary gain. The other $10,000 of gain, however, would enter the netting process as a casualty gain.

[24]The term *depreciation* includes § 167 depreciation, § 168 cost recovery, § 179 immediate expensing, § 168(k) additional first-year depreciation, and § 197 amortization.

Bridge Discipline **Bridge to Financial Accounting**

Much of the tax law is intended to influence taxpayer behavior to accomplish some economic, social, or political goal rather than measure taxpayers' ability to pay. Because of this, the Code differentiates certain kinds of income and expenses from others, providing preferential treatment to some (e.g., municipal bond interest is tax-favored relative to interest on corporate bonds) and limiting the tax benefits of others (e.g., fines and penalties are not deductible).

Conversely, the purpose of financial accounting is not to change the behavior of the reporting entity, but to provide information to the users of the financial statements. Therefore, financial accounting makes far fewer distinctions when classifying the reporting entity's revenues and expenses.

The treatment of capital gains and losses is one of the most long-lived of these tax-related distinctions. The "best of both worlds" treatment afforded by § 1231 is over 70 years old. Whereas the tax deductibility of a capital loss may be limited, its characterization as capital for tax purposes does not affects its inclusion in a company's financial income.

Differences in classification of income and deductions created solely by the tax code must be reported in the Schedule M–1 or M–3 of the C corporation, S corporation, partnership, and limited liability entity. Many of these items must also be reported as permanent or temporary differences in the financial statements pursuant to ASC 740.

8-8a **Section 1245 Property**

Generally, **§ 1245 property** includes all depreciable personal property (e.g., machinery and equipment) that is § 1231 property. Buildings and their structural components usually are not § 1245 property. The following property is *also* subject to § 1245 treatment.

- Amortizable personal property such as goodwill, patents, copyrights, and leaseholds of § 1245 property.
- Professional baseball and football player contracts.
- Certain depreciable tangible real property (other than buildings and their structural components) employed as an integral part of certain activities such as manufacturing and production. For example, a natural gas storage tank where the gas is used in the manufacturing process is § 1245 property.
- Certain "qualified" real property, including qualified improvement property, to the extent that § 179 expense was taken (refer to text section 5-7f).[25]
- Single-purpose agricultural and horticultural structures and petroleum storage facilities (e.g., a greenhouse or silo).

8-8b **Observations on § 1245**

- In most instances, the total depreciation taken will exceed the recognized gain on § 1245 property. It is uncommon for machinery, equipment, or furniture to sell for more than its original cost. Therefore, the disposition of § 1245 property usually results in ordinary income rather than § 1231 gain (refer to Example 48).
- Recapture is required regardless of the depreciation method used.
- Recapture applies regardless of the holding period of the property. Of course, the entire recognized gain would be ordinary income if the property was not held more than one year, because then § 1231 would not apply.

[25] § 1245(a)(3)(C).

- Code § 1245 does not apply to losses, which receive § 1231 treatment.
- Gains from the disposition of § 1245 assets also may be treated as passive activity gains (refer to Chapter 6).

8-9 Section 1250 Recapture

Whereas § 1245 recapture applies to depreciable personal property, § 1250 recapture applies to *depreciable real property* (principally buildings and their structural components), such as apartments, office buildings, factories, stores, and warehouses. Intangible real property, such as leaseholds of **§ 1250 property**, also is included.

Section 1250 recapture is limited to a property's *excess depreciation*, which is the depreciation actually deducted minus straight-line depreciation. Since real property placed in service after 1986 can only be recovered using straight-line depreciation, there is *no § 1250 recapture* upon the disposition of most real property held longer than one year.

Because qualified improvement property is eligible for bonus depreciation, the disposition of such property can give rise to excess depreciation and § 1250 recapture. Section 1250 also remains relevant in determining the tax rate on certain capital gains of individual taxpayers (see text Section 8-9a) and the depreciation recapture for corporations (see text Section 8-9b).

Concept Summary 8.6 compares and contrasts the § 1245 and § 1250 depreciation recapture rules.

Concept Summary 8.6

Comparison of § 1245 and § 1250 Depreciation Recapture

	§ 1245	§ 1250
Property affected	All depreciable personal property and § 197 intangibles such as goodwill, patents, and copyrights. Qualified improvement property on which § 179 was taken.	Nonresidential real property acquired after 1969 and before 1981 on which accelerated depreciation was taken. Qualified improvement property on which bonus depreciation was taken. Residential rental real property acquired after 1975 and before 1987 on which accelerated depreciation was taken.
Depreciation recaptured	Any gain due to depreciation, including § 179 expense, bonus (additional first-year) depreciation, and amortization. Limited for qualified improvement property to gain due to § 179 expense.	Any gain due to the excess of accelerated depreciation, including bonus depreciation available on qualified improvement property, over straight-line depreciation. Because straight-line depreciation has been required of most real property since 1986, § 1250 depreciation recapture is unusual.
Treatment of gain exceeding recapture gain	Usually § 1231 gain.	Usually § 1231 gain.
Treatment of loss	No depreciation recapture; loss is usually § 1231 loss.	No depreciation recapture; loss is usually § 1231 loss.

8-9a Unrecaptured § 1250 Gain (Real Estate 25% Gain)

As noted previously in the chapter, *noncorporate taxpayers* pay tax at a maximum rate of 25 percent on their **unrecaptured § 1250 gain**. This gain represents that part of the gain on § 1250 property that is attributable to depreciation that was not recaptured by § 1250. Recall that for property placed in service after 1986, § 1250 generally does not apply, because such property is depreciated using the straight-line method under MACRS. As a result, *all* of the gain attributable to depreciation on such assets is *unrecaptured § 1250 gain*.

Example 50

Linda, a noncorporate taxpayer, placed two apartment buildings in service at an original cost of $100,000 each. On each building, she claimed depreciation deductions of $78,000. Thus, her adjusted basis for each building is $22,000 ($100,000 cost − $78,000 depreciation deducted). She now sells these buildings for $96,000 and $110,000, respectively. She computes the amount and character of her gains as follows. Because the buildings were depreciated using the straight-line method, there is no § 1250 recapture.

	Building A	Building B
Amount realized	$ 96,000	$110,000
Adjusted basis	(22,000)	(22,000)
Recognized gain	$ 74,000	$ 88,000
Depreciation recaptured as ordinary income by § 1250	(–0–)	(–0–)
§ 1231 gain	$ 74,000	$ 88,000
Unrecaptured § 1250 gain potentially taxed at 25%	74,000	78,000
Remaining § 1231 gain potentially taxed at 0/15/20%	None	$ 10,000

8-9b Additional § 1250 Recapture for Corporations

Although depreciation recapture is generally the same for all taxpayers, *corporate taxpayers* that sell depreciable real estate face an additional amount of § 1250 depreciation recapture. Code § 291 requires recapture of 20 percent of the excess of the amount that would be recaptured under § 1245 (had § 1245 applied) over the amount actually recaptured under § 1250. For depreciable real property acquired after 1986, this simplifies to 20 percent of the § 1245 recapture amount.

Example 51

Red Corporation purchases nonresidential real property on May 1, 2007, for $800,000. Straight-line depreciation is taken in the amount of $316,239 before the property is sold on October 8, 2022, for $1,200,000.

First, determine the recognized gain:

Sales price		$1,200,000
Less: Adjusted basis—		
Cost of property	$ 800,000	
Less: Cost recovery	(316,239)	(483,761)
Recognized gain		$ 716,239

continued

Because the property is § 1250 property sold by a corporation, the recognized gain is characterized as follows:

Ordinary income		
Recapture generally required by § 1250		$ 0
§ 291 recapture		
§ 1245 recapture if § 1245 had applied	316,239	
Recapture generally required by § 1250	0	
	316,239	
	× 20%	63,248
Total ordinary income (§ 1250 recapture with § 291)		$ 63,248
§ 1231 gain		652,991
Total recognized gain		$ 716,239

Special rules regarding recapture on sales between related parties can be found on this book's companion website: www.cengage.com

11 Digging Deeper

8-10 Depreciation Recapture and Nontaxable and Tax-Free Transactions

Because §§ 1245 and 1250 only reclassify recognized gains, they are not immediately relevant in nontaxable or tax-free transactions. However, the recapture potential related to an asset involved in these transactions often remains after the transaction.

8-10a Gifts

Gifting property does not trigger depreciation recapture; however, the recapture potential carries over to the donee.[26]

Wade gives his daughter, Helen, § 1245 property with an adjusted basis of $1,000. The amount of recapture potential is $700. Helen uses the property in her business and claims further depreciation of $100 before selling it for $1,900.

Helen's recognized gain is $1,000 [$1,900 amount realized − $900 adjusted basis ($1,000 carryover basis − $100 depreciation taken by Helen)], of which $800 is recaptured as ordinary income ($100 depreciation taken by Helen + $700 recapture potential carried over from Wade). The remaining gain of $200 is § 1231 gain. Even if Helen had used the property for personal purposes, the $700 recapture potential would have carried over.

8-10b Death

Although not an attractive tax planning technique, death eliminates all recapture potential.[27] Depreciation recapture potential is eliminated when property passes from a decedent to an estate or an heir.

Assume the same facts as in the preceding example, except that Helen receives the property as a result of Wade's death and the property has a fair market value of $1,700 when Wade dies. The $700 recapture potential from Wade is extinguished at his death. Helen has a basis in the property equal to its fair market value at Wade's death ($1,700).

Helen will have a $300 gain when the property is sold because the selling price ($1,900) exceeds the property's adjusted basis of $1,600 ($1,700 basis to Helen − $100 depreciation taken by Helen) by $300. Because of § 1245, Helen has ordinary income of $100. The remaining gain of $200 is § 1231 gain.

[26] §§ 1245(b)(1) and 1250(d)(1) and Reg. §§ 1.1245–4(a)(1) and 1.1250–3(a)(1).

[27] §§ 1245(b)(2) and 1250(d)(2).

8-10c Certain Nontaxable Transactions

In certain transactions, the transferor's adjusted basis for the property carries over to the transferee. If this is the case, any depreciation recapture potential also carries over to the transferee.[28] Included in this category are the following transfers of property:

- Nontaxable incorporations under § 351 (see Chapter 12).
- Certain subsidiary liquidations under § 332 (see Chapter 13).
- Nontaxable contributions to a partnership under § 721 (see Chapter 14).
- Nontaxable corporate reorganizations.

Gain may be recognized in these transactions if boot is received. If gain is recognized, it is treated as ordinary income to the extent of the recapture potential or the recognized gain, whichever is lower.[29]

8-10d Like-Kind Exchanges and Involuntary Conversions

As explained in Chapter 7, realized gain is recognized to the extent of boot received in a like-kind exchange. Realized gain is also recognized to the extent the proceeds from an involuntary conversion are not reinvested in similar property. Any recognized gain is subject to recapture as ordinary income under §§ 1245 and 1250. However, since only real property can be the subject of a like-kind exchange, § 1245 recapture is not likely because it generally only applies to tangible personal property. Code § 1250 recapture also is not likely because it infrequently applies to dispositions of real property. On the other hand, unrecaptured § 1250 gain (25% gain) is likely to be present if depreciable real property was the subject of the exchange. Any remaining recapture potential carries over to the property received in the exchange.

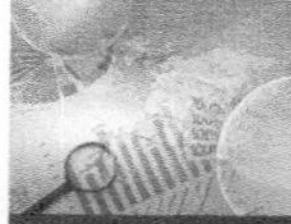

A discussion of the relation of recapture to installment sales and property dividends can be found on this book's companion website: www.cengage.com

Tax Planning Strategies — Timing of Recapture

Framework Focus: Tax Rate

Strategy: Shift Net Income from High-Bracket Years to Low-Bracket Years.
Shift Net Income from High-Bracket Taxpayers to Low-Bracket Taxpayers.

Because recapture is usually not triggered until the property is sold or disposed of, it may be possible to plan for recapture in low-bracket or loss years. If a taxpayer has net operating loss carryovers, the recognition of ordinary income from recapture may be advisable to absorb the loss carryovers.

Angel Corporation has a $15,000 net operating loss carryover. It owns a machine that it plans to sell in the early part of next year. The expected gain of $17,000 from the sale of the machine will be recaptured as ordinary income under § 1245. Angel sells the machine before the end of this year and offsets $15,000 of the ordinary income by the net operating loss carryover.

It is also possible to postpone recapture or to shift the burden of recapture to others. For example, recapture is avoided upon the disposition of a § 1231 asset if the taxpayer replaces the property by entering into a like-kind exchange. In this instance, recapture potential is merely carried over to the newly acquired property.

Recapture can be shifted to others through the gratuitous transfer of § 1245 or § 1250 property to family members. A subsequent sale of such property by the donee will trigger recapture to the donee rather than the donor (refer to Example 52). This technique is advisable when the donee is in a lower income tax bracket than the donor.

[28] §§ 1245(b)(3) and 1250(d)(3); Reg. §§ 1.1245–2(a)(4) and (c)(2), 1.1245–4(c) and 1.1250–2(d)(1) and (3).

[29] §§ 1245(b)(3) and 1250(d)(3); Reg. §§ 1.1245–4(c) and 1.1250–3(c).

Refocus on The Big Picture

Capital Gains and Losses, § 1231 Gains and Losses, and Recapture

The land, stock, and home owned by Alice are all capital assets and will produce capital gain or loss when sold. Accordingly, Alice will have a long-term capital gain of $48,000 from the sale of the land, a long-term capital gain of $6,000 from the sale of 300 shares of inherited AppleCo stock, a short-term capital loss of $4,000 from the sale of the other 200 shares of AppleCo stock, and a $125,000 long-term capital gain from the sale of the house. The treatment given to the Eagle stock will depend on the nature of its disposition (see Example 10).

For the patent, because Alice is a "holder" of the patent, it will qualify for the beneficial capital gain rate regardless of the holding period if the patent should produce income in excess of her $50,000 investment. However, if Alice loses money on the investment, she will be able to deduct only $3,000 of the loss per year against her ordinary income (assuming that there are no offsetting capital gains in the year of a sale).

The depreciable property owned by Alice's husband is § 1231 property. The $45,000 gain from the sale of the property ($60,000 amount realized − $15,000 adjusted basis) is subject to depreciation recapture under § 1245. Accordingly, the first $35,000 of the gain (up to the amount of depreciation taken on the property) is taxed as ordinary income. The remaining $10,000 is § 1231 gain and is given long-term capital gain treatment.

As a result of these transactions where the amount of gain or loss is determined, Alice and her husband have a net long-term capital gain of $189,000 ($48,000 + $6,000 + $125,000 + $10,000) and a net short-term capital loss of $4,000. The long-term capital gain and short-term capital loss are netted, so the final result is a net capital gain of $185,000, which is taxed at the 15 or 20 percent tax rate. Alice and her husband also report $35,000 of ordinary income on their joint income tax return because of the depreciation recapture provisions. Note that the total gain reported is $221,000 ($186,000 + $35,000). This equals the sum of the individual gains and losses realized ($48,000 + $6,000 − $4,000 + $1,000 + $125,000 + $45,000).

What If?

What if the depreciable business property was worth only $10,000 when it was sold? In this case, there is no depreciation recapture, and the $5,000 loss is deductible as an ordinary loss under § 1231.

DRAZEN ZIGIC/SHUTTERSTOCK.COM

Suggested Readings

Paul L. Caron and Jay A. Soled, "New Prominence of Basis in Estate Planning," *Tax Notes Today*, March 28, 2016.

Geoff Colvin, "Was Bob Dylan's Sale of His Massive Music Catalogue a Tax Maneuver?," *Fortune*, December 8, 2020.

Melanie James, "Factors Influencing Reduction in Value for Potential Capital Gains Tax," *Practical Tax Strategies*, April 2014.

John Przybylski, "Managing Capital Gain to Minimize the Pain," *Practical Tax Strategies*, July 2015.

Richard L. Schmalbeck and Jay A. Soled, "Reforming Real Estate Depreciation Recapture," *Tax Notes Today*, Feburary 17, 2015.

Key Terms

Capital assets, 8-2
Capital gains, 8-2
Capital losses, 8-2
Collectibles, 8-15
Holding period, 8-10
Lessee, 8-9
Lessor, 8-9
Net capital gain (NCG), 8-18
Net capital loss (NCL), 8-18
Options, 8-6
Patents, 8-8
Qualified small business stock, 8-20
Section 1231 gains and losses, 8-23
Section 1231 lookback, 8-27
Section 1231 property, 8-23
Section 1245 property, 8-30
Section 1245 recapture, 8-29
Section 1250 property, 8-31
Section 1250 recapture, 8-31
Short sale, 8-12
Unrecaptured § 1250 gain, 8-32

Computational Exercises

1. **LO.1** Dexter owns a large tract of land and subdivides it for sale. Assume that Dexter meets all of the requirements of § 1237 and during the tax year sells the first eight lots to eight different buyers for $22,000 each. Dexter's basis in each lot sold is $15,000, and he incurs total selling expenses of $900 on each sale. What is the amount of Dexter's capital gain and ordinary income?

Digging Deeper

2. **LO.2** Shelia purchases $50,000 of newly issued Gingo Corporation bonds for $45,000. The bonds have original issue discount (OID) of $5,000. After Sheila amortized $2,300 of OID and held the bonds for four years, she sold the bonds for $48,000. What is the amount and character of her gain or loss?

3. **LO.2** Olivia wants to buy some vacant land for investment purposes. She currently cannot afford the full purchase price. Instead, Olivia pays the landowner $8,000 to obtain an option to buy the land for $175,000 anytime in the next four years. Fourteen months after purchasing the option, Olivia sells the option for $10,000. What is the amount and character of Olivia's gain or loss?

4. **LO.4** Coline has the following capital gain and loss transactions for 2022.

Short-term capital gain	$ 5,000
Short-term capital loss	(2,100)
Long-term capital gain (28%)	6,000
Long-term capital gain (15%)	2,000
Long-term capital loss (28%)	(10,500)

After the capital gain and loss netting process, what is the amount and character of Coline's net capital gain or loss?

5. **LO.4** Elliott has the following capital gain and loss transactions for 2022.

Short-term capital gain	$ 1,500
Short-term capital loss	(3,600)
Long-term capital gain (28%)	12,000
Long-term capital gain (25%)	4,800
Long-term capital gain (15%)	6,000
Long-term capital loss (28%)	(4,500)
Long-term capital loss (15%)	(9,000)

After the capital gain and loss netting process, what is the amount and character of Elliott's net capital gain or loss?

6. **LO.6, 7** Renata Corporation purchased equipment in 2020 for $180,000 and has taken $83,000 of regular MACRS depreciation. Renata Corporation sells the equipment in 2022 for $110,000. What is the amount and character of Renata's gain or loss?

7. **LO.6, 7** Jacob purchased business equipment for $56,000 in 2019 and has taken $35,000 of regular MACRS depreciation. Jacob sells the equipment in 2022 for $26,000. What is the amount and character of Jacob's gain or loss?

8. **LO.6, 7** Shannon owns two items of business equipment. Both were purchased in 2018 for $100,000, both have a 7-year MACRS recovery period, and both have an adjusted basis of $37,490. Shannon is considering selling these assets in 2022. One of them is worth $60,000, and the other is worth $23,000. Because both items were used in her business, Shannon simply assumes that the loss on one will offset the gain from the other and that the net gain or loss will increase or reduce her business income. What is the amount and character of Shannon's gain or loss? Planning

9. **LO.7** An apartment building was acquired in 2013 by an individual taxpayer. The depreciation taken on the building was $123,000, and the building was sold for a $34,000 gain. What is the amount of unrecaptured § 1250 gain?

10. **LO.7** In a § 1031 like-kind exchange, Rafael exchanges a business building that originally cost $200,000. On the date of the exchange, the building given up has an adjusted basis of $85,000 and a fair market value of $110,000. Rafael pays $15,000 and receives a building with a fair market value of $125,000. What is the amount and character of Rafael's gain or loss?

11. **LO.7** Gaston Corporation distributes § 1245 property as a dividend to its shareholders. The property's fair market value is $580,000, and the adjusted basis is $560,000. In addition, the amount of the recapture potential is $55,000. What is the amount and character of Gaston's gain or loss? Digging Deeper

Problems

12. **LO.1** An individual taxpayer sells some used assets at a garage sale. Why are none of the proceeds taxable in most situations? Critical Thinking

13. **LO.1** Alison owns a painting that she received as a gift from her aunt 10 years ago. The aunt created the painting. Alison has displayed the painting in her home and has never attempted to sell it. Recently, a visitor noticed the painting and offered Alison $5,000 for it. If Alison decides to sell the painting, what tax issues does she face? Critical Thinking

14. **LO.1** During the year, Eugene had the four property transactions summarized below. Eugene is a collector of antique glassware and occasionally sells a piece to get funds to buy another. What are the amount and nature of the gain or loss from each of these transactions?

Property	Date Acquired	Date Sold	Adjusted Basis	Sales Price
Antique vase	06/18/11	05/23/22	$37,000	$42,000
Blue Growth Fund (100 shares)	12/23/13	11/22/22	22,000	38,000
Orange bonds	02/12/14	04/11/22	34,000	42,000*
Green stock (100 shares)	02/14/22	11/23/22	11,000	13,000

*The sales price included $750 of accrued interest income.

Critical Thinking
Decision Making
Planning

15. **LO.1** Rennie owns a video game arcade. He buys vintage video games from estates, often at much less than the retail value of the property. He usually installs the vintage video games in a special section of his video game arcade that appeals to players of "classic" video games. Recently, Rennie sold a classic video game that a customer "just had to have." Rennie paid $11,250 for it, owned it for 14 months, and sold it for $18,000. Rennie had suspected that this particular classic video game would be of interest to collectors; so he had it refurbished, put it on display in his video arcade, and listed it for sale on the internet. No customers in the arcade had played it other than those testing it before considering it for purchase. Rennie would like the gain on the sale of the classic video game to be a long-term capital gain. Did he achieve that objective? Why or why not?

16. **LO.1** George is the owner of numerous classic automobiles. His intention is to hold the automobiles until they increase in value and then sell them. He rents the automobiles for use in various events (e.g., antique automobile shows) while he is holding them. In 2022, he sold a classic automobile for $1,500,000. He had held the automobile for five years, and it had a tax basis of $750,000.

    a. Was the automobile a capital asset? Why or why not?
    b. Assuming a rate of return of 7%, how much would he have had to invest five years ago (instead of putting $750,000 into the car) to have had $1,500,000 this year? See Appendix E for the present value factors.

Communications
Planning

17. **LO.1** Faith Godwin is a dealer in securities. She has spotted a fast-rising company and would like to buy and hold its stock for investment. The stock is currently selling for $2 per share, and Faith thinks it will climb to $40 a share within two years. Faith's coworkers have told her that there is "no way" she can get long-term capital gain treatment when she purchases stock because she is a securities dealer. Faith has asked you to calculate her potential gain and tell her whether her coworkers are right. Draft a letter to Faith, responding to her request. Her address is 200 Catamon Drive, Great Falls, MT 59406.

Digging Deeper

18. **LO.1** Eagle Partners meets all of the requirements of § 1237 (subdivided realty). In 2022, Eagle Partners begins selling lots and sells four separate lots to four different purchasers. Eagle Partners also sells two contiguous lots to another purchaser. The sales price of each lot is $30,000. The partnership's basis for each lot is $15,000. Selling expenses are $500 per lot.

    a. What are the realized and recognized gain?
    b. Explain the nature of the gain (i.e., ordinary income or capital gain).
    c. Would your answers change if, instead, the lots sold to the fifth purchaser were not contiguous? If so, how?

Digging Deeper

19. **LO.1, 2** Benny purchased $400,000 of Peach Corporation face value bonds for $320,000 on November 13, 2021. The bonds had been issued with $80,000 of original issue discount because Peach was in financial difficulty in 2021. On December 3, 2022, Benny sold the bonds for $283,000 after amortizing $1,000 of the original issue discount. What are the nature and amount of Benny's gain or loss?

20. **LO.2** Carla was the owner of vacant land that she was holding for investment. She paid $2,000,000 for the land in 2019. Raymond was an investor in vacant land. He thought Carla's land might be the site of an exit ramp from a new freeway. Raymond gave Carla $836,000 for an option on her land in 2020. The option was good for two years and gave Raymond the ability to purchase Carla's land for $4,765,000.

The freeway was not approved by the government, and Raymond's option expired in 2022. Does Carla have $836,000 of long-term capital gain upon the expiration of the option? Explain.

21. **LO.2, 3, 4** Mac, an inventor, obtained a patent on a chemical process to clean old aluminum siding so that it can be easily repainted. Mac has a $50,000 tax basis in the patent. Mac does not have the capital to begin manufacturing and selling this product, so he has done nothing with the patent since obtaining it two years ago.

Communications
Critical Thinking
Decision Making
Planning

Now a group of individuals has approached him and offered two alternatives. Under one alternative, they will pay Mac $600,000 (payable evenly over the next 15 years) for the exclusive right to manufacture and sell the product. Under the other, they will form a business and contribute capital to it to begin manufacturing and selling the product; Mac will receive 20% of the company's shares of stock in exchange for all of his patent rights. Discuss which alternative is better for Mac. Share your analysis and conclusions in an e-mail to your instructor.

22. **LO.2** Blue Corporation and Fuchsia Corporation are engaged in a contract negotiation over the use of Blue's trademarked name, DateSiteForSeniors. For a one-time payment of $45,000, Blue licensed Fuchsia to use the name DateSiteFor Seniors, and the nonexclusive license requires that Fuchsia pay Blue a royalty every time a new customer signs up on Fuchsia's website. Blue is a developer of "website ideas" that it then licenses to other companies such as Fuchsia. Did Fuchsia purchase a franchise right from Blue, or did Fuchsia purchase the name DateSiteForSeniors from Blue?

Digging Deeper

23. **LO.2** Freys, Inc., sells a 12-year franchise to Reynaldo. The franchise contains many restrictions on how Reynaldo may operate its store. For instance, Reynaldo cannot use less than Grade 10 Idaho potatoes; must fry the potatoes at a constant 410 degrees; must dress store personnel in Freys-approved uniforms; and must have a Freys sign that meets detailed specifications on size, color, and construction. When the franchise contract is signed, Reynaldo makes a noncontingent $160,000 payment to Freys. During the same year, Reynaldo pays Freys $300,000—14% of Reynaldo's sales. How does Freys treat each of these payments? How does Reynaldo treat each of the payments?

Digging Deeper

24. **LO.3** Aliya held vacant land that qualified as an investment asset. She purchased the vacant land on April 10, 2018. She exchanged the vacant land for a rental house in a qualifying like-kind exchange on January 22, 2022. Aliya was going to hold the house for several years and then sell it. However, she got an "offer she could not refuse" and sold it on November 22, 2022, for a substantial gain. What was Aliya's holding period for the house?

25. **LO.3** Dennis sells short 100 shares of ARC stock at $20 per share on January 15, 2022. He buys 200 shares of ARC stock on April 1, 2022, at $25 per share. On May 2, 2022, Dennis closes the short sale by delivering 100 of the shares purchased on April 1.

Digging Deeper

a. What are the amount and nature of Dennis's loss upon closing the short sale?
b. When does the holding period for the remaining 100 shares begin?
c. If Dennis sells (at $27 per share) the remaining 100 shares on January 20, 2023, what will be the nature of his gain or loss?

Communications

26. **LO.1, 3, 4** Liana Amiri (single with no dependents) has the following transactions in 2022:

AGI (exclusive of capital gains and losses)	$240,000
Long-term capital gain	22,000
Long-term capital loss	(8,000)
Short-term capital gain	19,000
Short-term capital loss	(23,000)

What is Liana's net capital gain or loss? Draft a letter to Liana describing how the net capital gain or loss will be treated on her tax return. Assume that Liana's income from other sources puts her in the 37% bracket. Liana's address is 300 Ireland Avenue, Shepherdstown, WV 25443.

Decision Making
Planning

27. **LO.4** Sally is single and has taxable income of $170,000 as of November 30 of this year. She wants to sell a Rodin sculpture that has appreciated $90,000 since she purchased it six years ago, but she does not want to pay more than $15,000 of additional tax on the transaction. Sally also owns various stocks, some of which are currently worth less than their basis. How can she achieve her desired result?

28. **LO.5** Platinum, Inc., has determined its taxable income as $215,000 before considering the results of its capital gain or loss transactions. Platinum has a short-term capital loss of $24,000, a long-term capital loss of $38,000, and a short-term capital gain of $39,000. What is Platinum's taxable income? What (if any) are the amount and nature of its capital loss carryover?

Ethics and Equity

29. **LO.1, 4** A taxpayer is an antiques collector and is going to sell an antique purchased many years ago for a large gain. The facts and circumstances indicate that the taxpayer might be classified as a dealer rather than an investor in antiques. The taxpayer will save $40,000 in taxes if the gain is treated as long-term capital gain rather than as ordinary income. The taxpayer is considering the following options as ways to ensure the $40,000 tax savings.

- Give the antique to his daughter, who is an investment banker, to sell.
- Merely assume that he has held the antique as an investment.
- Exchange the antique in a like-kind exchange for another antique he wants.

One of the tax preparers the taxpayer has contacted has said that he would be willing to prepare the return under the second option. Would you? Why or why not? Evaluate the other options.

Communications

30. **LO.1, 4** In 2022, Beth Jarow had a $28,000 loss from the sale of a personal residence. She also purchased from an individual inventor for $7,000 (and resold in two months for $18,000) a patent on a rubber bonding process. The patent had not yet been reduced to practice. Beth purchased the patent as an investment. In addition, she had the following capital gains and losses from stock transactions:

Long-term capital loss	($ 6,000)
Long-term capital loss carryover from 2021	(12,000)
Short-term capital gain	21,000
Short-term capital loss	(7,000)

What is Beth's net capital gain or loss? Draft a letter to Beth, explaining the tax treatment of the sale of her personal residence. Assume that Beth's income from other sources puts her in the 24% bracket. Beth's address is 1120 West Street, Ashland, OR 97520.

Critical Thinking
Planning

31. **LO.1, 3, 4** Bridgette is known as the "doll lady." She started collecting dolls as a child, always received one or more dolls as gifts on her birthday, never sold any dolls, and eventually owned 600 dolls. She is retiring and moving to a small apartment and has decided to sell her collection. She lists the dolls on an internet auction site and, to her great surprise, receives an offer from another doll collector of $45,000

for the entire collection. Bridgette sells the entire collection, except for five dolls she purchased during the last year. She had owned all of the dolls sold for more than a year. What tax factors should Bridgette consider in deciding how to report the sale?

32. **LO.1, 2, 4** Harriet, who is single, is the owner of a sole proprietorship. Two years ago Harriet developed a process for preserving doughnuts that gives the doughnut a much longer shelf life. The process is not patented or copyrighted, and only Harriet knows how it works. Harriet has been approached by a company that would like to buy the process. Harriet insists that she receive a long-term employment contract with the acquiring company as well as be paid for the rights to the process. The acquiring company offers Harriet a choice of two options: (1) $650,000 in cash for the process and a 10-year covenant not to compete at $65,000 per year or (2) $650,000 in cash for a 10-year covenant not to compete and $65,000 per year for 10 years in payment for the process. Which option should Harriet accept? What is the tax effect on the acquiring company of each approach?

Critical Thinking
Decision Making
Digging Deeper

33. **LO.4** Julio sold his corporation to a competitor, Exeter LLC, for $100,000,000. Julio incorporated his business seven years ago by investing $500,000 plus his proprietary know-how. There have been no other corporate shareholders. Compute Julio's after-tax cash flow from the sale, assuming he is in the 37% tax bracket and has no other property sales during the year.

34. **LO.6** A sculpture that Korliss Kane held for investment was destroyed in a flood. The sculpture was insured, and Korliss had a $60,000 gain from this casualty. He also had a $17,000 loss from an uninsured antique vase that was destroyed by the flood. The vase also was held for investment. Korliss had no other property transactions during the year and has no nonrecaptured § 1231 losses from prior years. Both the sculpture and the vase had been held more than one year when the flood occurred (i.e., both are long-term nonpersonal use capital assets). Compute Korliss's net gain or loss, and identify how it would be treated. Also write a letter to Korliss, explaining the nature of the gain or loss. Korliss's address is 2367 Meridian Road, Hannibal, MO 63401.

Communications

35. **LO.6** Geranium, Inc., has the following net § 1231 results for each of the years shown. What is the nature of the net gain in 2021 and 2022?

Tax Year	Net § 1231 Loss	Net § 1231 Gain
2017	$18,000	
2018	33,000	
2019	42,000	
2020		$41,000
2021		30,000
2022		41,000

36. **LO.6** Jinjie owns two parcels of land (§ 1231 assets). One parcel can be sold at a loss of $60,000, and the other parcel can be sold at a gain of $70,000. Jinjie has no nonrecaptured § 1231 losses from prior years. The parcels could be sold at any time because potential purchasers are abundant. Jinjie has a $35,000 short-term capital loss carryover from a prior tax year and no capital assets that could be sold to generate long-term capital gains. Both land parcels have been held more than one year. What should Jinjie do based upon these facts? (Assume that tax rates are constant, and ignore the present value of future cash flows.)

Critical Thinking
Decision Making
Planning

37. **LO.6, 7** Siena Industries (a sole proprietorship) sold three § 1231 assets on October 10, 2022. Data on these property dispositions are as follows.

Asset	Cost	Acquired	Depreciation	Sold for
Rack	$100,000	10/10/18	$62,000	$86,000
Forklift	35,000	10/16/19	23,000	4,000
Bin	87,000	03/12/21	34,000	60,000

a. Determine the amount and the character of the recognized gain or loss from the disposition of each asset.

b. Assuming that Siena has no nonrecaptured net § 1231 losses from prior years, analyze these transactions and determine the amount (if any) that will be treated as a long-term capital gain.

Communications

38. **LO.6, 7** On December 1, 2020, Lavender Manufacturing Company (a corporation) purchased another company's assets, including a patent. The patent was used in Lavender's manufacturing operations; $49,500 was allocated to the patent, and it was amortized at the rate of $275 per month. On July 30, 2022, Lavender sold the patent for $95,000. Twenty months of amortization had been taken on the patent. What are the amount and nature of the gain Lavender recognizes on the disposition of the patent? Write a letter to Lavender, discussing the treatment of the gain. Lavender's address is 6734 Grover Street, Boothbay Harbor, ME 04538. The letter should be addressed to Bill Cubit, Controller.

39. **LO.6, 7** Javier is the sole proprietor of a sporting goods business. During 2022, the following transactions occurred.

- Unimproved land adjacent to Javier's store was condemned by the city on February 1. The condemnation proceeds were $15,000. The land, acquired in 1989, had a basis of $40,000. Javier has additional parking across the street and plans to use the condemnation proceeds to build his inventory.
- A delivery truck used in Javier's business was sold on January 2 for $3,500. The truck was purchased on January 2, 2018, for $6,000. On the date of sale, the adjusted basis was zero.
- Javier sold a rowing machine at an auction. Net proceeds were $4,900. The rowing machine was purchased as used equipment 17 years ago for $5,200 and is fully depreciated.
- Javier sold an apartment building for $300,000 on September 1. The property was purchased on September 1, 2019, for $150,000 and was being depreciated over a 27.5-year MACRS life using the straight-line method. At the date of sale, the adjusted basis was $124,783. Javier actively managed the property as a trade or business.
- Javier's personal yacht was stolen on September 5. The yacht had been purchased in August at a cost of $25,000. The fair market value immediately preceding the theft was $19,600. Javier was insured for 50% of the original cost, and he received $12,500 on December 1.
- Javier sold a Buick on May 1 for $9,600. The vehicle had been used exclusively for personal purposes. It was purchased on September 1, 2018, for $20,800.
- A trampoline stretching machine (owned two years and used in Javier's business) was stolen on May 5, but the business's insurance company will not pay any of the machine's value because Javier failed to pay the insurance premium. The machine had a fair market value of $8,000 and an adjusted basis of $6,000 at the time of theft.
- Javier had AGI of $102,000 from sources other than those described above.
- Javier has no nonrecaptured § 1231 lookback losses.

a. For each transaction, what are the amount and nature of recognized gain or loss?

b. What is Javier's 2022 AGI?

40. **LO.7** Nicholas owns business equipment with a $155,000 adjusted basis; he paid $200,000 for the equipment, and it is currently worth $173,000. Nicholas dies suddenly, and his son Alvin inherits the property. What is Alvin's basis for the property? What happens to the § 1245 depreciation recapture potential?

41. **LO.7** Heron Company purchases commercial realty on November 13, 2004, for $650,000. Straight-line depreciation of $287,492 is claimed before the property is sold on February 22, 2022, for $850,000. What are the tax consequences of the sale of realty if Heron is:
   a. A C corporation?
   b. A sole proprietorship?

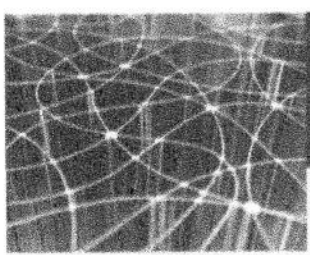

Bridge Discipline

1. Using an online research service, find the audited financial statements of a major U.S. corporation.
   a. List some of the items the corporation reports as having different treatment for tax and financial accounting purposes. These items often are mentioned in the footnotes to the statements.
   b. List two or more such items that seem to increase the taxpayer's after-tax income and two or more that seem to decrease it.

Research Problems

Note: Solutions to the Research Problems can be prepared by using the Thomson Reuters Checkpoint™ online tax research database, which accompanies this textbook. Solutions can also be prepared by using research materials found in a typical tax library.

Research Problem 1. Your long-term client Clyde has a major "classification" problem he needs help with. Clyde had worked for many years as the chief executive of Red Industries, Inc., and had been a major shareholder. Clyde and the company had a falling out, and Clyde was terminated. Clyde and Red executed a document under which Clyde's stock in Red would be redeemed and Clyde would agree not to compete against Red in its geographic service area. After extensive negotiations between the parties, Clyde agreed to surrender his Red stock in exchange for $600,000. Clyde's basis in his shares was $143,000, and he had held the shares for 17 years. The agreement made no explicit allocation of any of the $600,000 to Clyde's agreement not to compete against Red. How should Clyde treat the $600,000 payment on his 2022 tax return?

Research Problem 2. Your client Ali has a "basis" issue he needs help with. Ali owns 100 shares of Brown Corporation stock. He purchased the stock at five different times and at five different prices per share as indicated. Decision Making

Share Block	Number of Shares	Per-Share Price	Purchase Date
A	10	$60	10/10/2002
B	20	20	08/11/2003
C	15	15	10/24/2004
D	35	30	04/23/2005
E	20	25	07/28/2005

On April 28, 2022, Ali will sell 40 shares of Brown stock for $40 per share. All of Ali's shares are held by his stockbroker. The broker's records track when the shares were purchased. May Ali designate the shares he sells? If so, which shares should he sell? Assume that Ali wants to maximize his gain because he has a capital loss carryforward.

Research Problem 3. Siva, a new client of yours, owns various plots of land in Fulton County, Georgia. He acquired the land at various times during the last 20 years. About every fourth year, Siva subdivides into lots one of the properties he owns. He then has water, sewer, natural gas, and electricity hookups put in each lot and paves new streets. Siva has always treated his sales of such lots as sales of capital assets. His previous tax returns were prepared by an accountant whose practice you recently purchased. Has the proper tax treatment been used on the prior tax returns? Explain.

Partial list of research aids:
§§ 1221 and 1237.
Jesse W. and Betty J. English, 65 TCM 2160, T.C.Memo. 1993–111.

Use internet tax resources to address the following questions. Look for reliable websites and blogs of the IRS and other government agencies, media outlets, businesses, tax professionals, academics, think tanks, and political outlets.

Research Problem 4. Find a website, other than the IRS website, that discusses the taxation of short sales of securities.

Research Problem 5. Perform a Google search to find information about capital gains tax rates worldwide (and across U.S. states). Try searching for "capital gains rate by country (state)." What jurisdiction has the highest capital gains tax rate? What U.S. states have high capital gains tax rates?

Becker CPA Review Questions

Becker

1. A gain on the sale of which of the following assets will not result in a capital gain?
   a. Stock in a public company
   b. A home used as a personal residence
   c. Goodwill of a corporation
   d. Inventory of a corporation

2. Conner purchased 300 shares of Zinco stock for $30,000 in year 1. On May 23, year 6, Conner sold all the stock to his daughter Alice for $20,000, its then fair market value. Conner realized no other gain or loss during year 6. On July 26, year 6, Alice sold the 300 shares of Zinco for $25,000. What was Alice's recognized gain or loss on her sale?
   a. $0
   b. $5,000 long-term gain
   c. $5,000 short-term loss
   d. $5,000 long-term loss

3. Brad and Angie are married and file a joint return. For year 14, they had income from wages in the amount of $100,000 and had the following capital transactions to report on their income tax return:

Carryover of capital losses from year 13	$200,000
Loss on sale of stock purchased in March year 14, sold on October 10, year 14, and repurchased on November 2, year 14	20,000
Gain on the sale of stock purchased 5 years ago and sold on March 14, year 14	15,000
Gain on the sale of their personal residence (all qualifications have been met for the maximum allowable gain exclusion)	675,000
Loss on the sale of their personal automobile	10,000
Gain on the sale of their personal furniture	5,000
Loss on the sale of investment property (land only)	150,000

   What is the amount of capital loss carryover to year 15?
   a. ($155,000)
   b. ($152,000)
   c. ($132,000)
   d. ($125,000)

4. A piece of depreciable machinery is sold. It has been held for three years and qualifies as § 1231 property. The selling price is greater than the adjusted basis but less than the original purchase price. Which statement below is correct?
   a. All of the gain will be subject to § 1245 recapture.
   b. Only a portion of the gain will be subject to § 1245 recapture.
   c. None of the gain will be subject to § 1245 recapture.
   d. Code § 1245 recapture will not apply because there is a loss on the sale.

5. Wally, Inc., sold the following three personal property assets in year 6:

Asset	Purchase Date	Cost	Accumulated Depreciation	Selling Price
A	5/1/year 3	$5,000	$3,000	$2,300
B	8/13/year 4	1,200	500	2,000
C	2/18/year 4	3,800	1,800	1,500

   What is Wally's net § 1231 gain or loss in year 6?
   a. $500 loss
   b. $300 gain
   c. $800 gain
   d. $1,600 gain

6. Wally, Inc., sold the following three personal property assets in year 6:

Asset	Purchase Date	Cost	Accumulated Depreciation	Selling Price
A	5/1/year 3	$5,000	$3,000	$1,300
B	8/13/year 4	1,200	500	1,100
C	2/18/year 4	3,800	1,800	1,500

   What is Wally's net § 1231 gain or loss in year 6?
   a. $500 loss
   b. $700 loss
   c. $1,200 loss
   d. $1,200 gain

7. Wally, Inc., sold the following three personal property assets in year 6:

Asset	Purchase Date	Cost	Accumulated Depreciation	Selling Price
A	5/1/year 3	$5,000	$3,000	$2,300
B	8/13/year 4	1,200	500	2,000
C	2/18/year 6	3,800	1,800	1,500

   What is Wally's net § 1231 gain or loss in year 6?
   a. $500 loss
   b. $300 gain
   c. $800 gain
   d. $1,600 gain

8. Wally, Inc., sold the following three personal property assets in year 6:

Asset	Purchase Date	Cost	Accumulated Depreciation	Selling Price
A	5/1/year 3	$5,000	$3,000	$2,300
B	8/13/year 4	1,200	500	2,000
C	2/18/year 6	3,800	1,800	1,500

   What is Wally's § 1245 recapture in year 6?
   a. $500 loss
   b. $300 gain
   c. $800 gain
   d. $1,600 gain

9. Net § 1231 losses are:
   a. Deducted as a capital loss against other capital gains and nothing against ordinary income.
   b. Deducted as a capital loss against other capital gains and up to $3,000 against ordinary income.
   c. Not allowed as a deduction.
   d. Deducted as an ordinary loss.
10. Code § 1245 recapture applies to which of the following?
   a. Code § 1231 real property sold at a gain with accumulated depreciation in excess of straight line.
   b. Code § 1231 personal property sold at a gain with accumulated depreciation.
   c. Code § 1231 real property sold at a gain with accumulated depreciation equal to straight-line depreciation.
   d. Code § 1231 personal property sold at a loss.
11. Code § 1250 recapture applies to which of the following?
   a. Code § 1231 real property sold at a gain with accumulated depreciation in excess of straight line.
   b. Code § 1231 personal property sold at a gain with accumulated depreciation.
   c. Code § 1231 real property sold at a gain with accumulated depreciation equal to straight-line depreciation.
   d. Code § 1231 personal property sold at a loss.

Taxation of Individuals

Part 4 focuses on key tax concepts and rules for individuals. The topics are unique to individual taxpayers, including filing status, itemized deductions, sole proprietorship provisions, and the kiddie tax. Special business deductions including for qualified business income and self-employed retirement plans are covered. In addition, education credits, the earned income credit, estimated tax payments, and filing procedures are explained.

Chapter 9

Individuals as Taxpayers

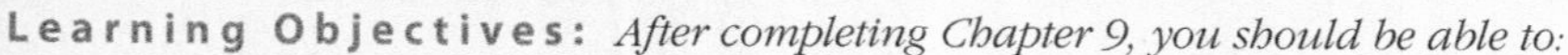

Learning Objectives: *After completing Chapter 9, you should be able to:*

- **LO.1** Describe and apply the components of the Federal income tax formula for individuals.
- **LO.2** Explain the standard deduction and when it should be used in determining taxable income.
- **LO.3** Explain the rules for determining dependency status.
- **LO.4** Identify the proper filing status of an individual and the related filing requirements.
- **LO.5** Identify and apply the methods available for determining the tax liability of individuals.
- **LO.6** Identify individuals subject to the kiddie tax and calculate the tax.

Chapter Outline

Tax Talk *I'm proud of paying taxes in the United States. The only thing is—I could be just as proud for half the money.* —Arthur Godfrey

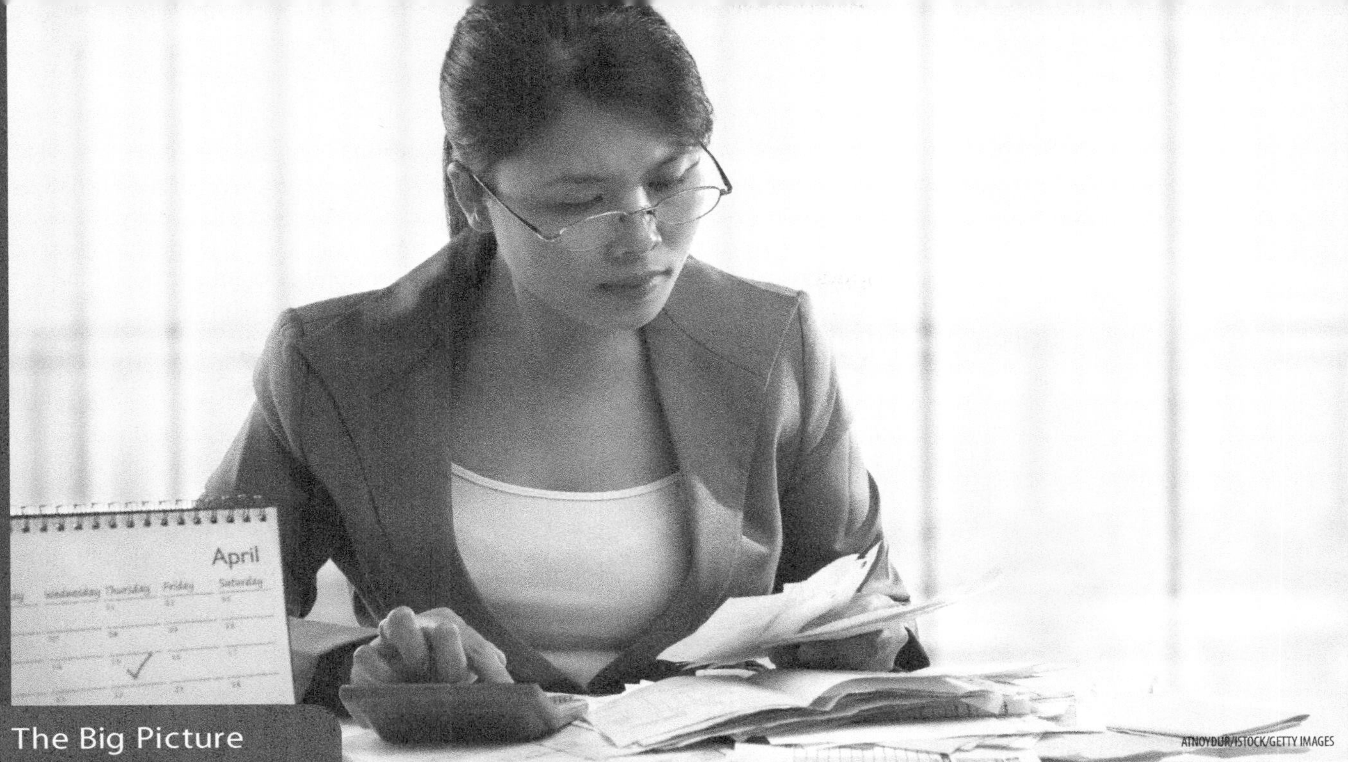

ATNOYDUR/ISTOCK/GETTY IMAGES

The Big Picture

A Divided Household

Polly maintains a household in which she lives with her unemployed husband, Nick, and stepdaughter, Paige. A family friend, Maude, also lived with Polly until February when Maude was fatally injured in an automobile accident. Polly provides more than half of the support of Paige and, before the accident, Maude. Polly also paid for Maude's hospitalization and funeral expenses. Paige, an accomplished gymnast, graduated from high school last year. Paige has a part-time job but spends most of her time training and looking for an athletic scholarship to the "right" college. In March, Nick left for parts unknown and has not been seen or heard from since. Polly was more surprised than distressed over Nick's unexpected departure.

Based on these facts, what are Polly's income tax concerns for the current year?

Read the chapter and formulate your response.

Part 4 of this text focuses on individuals as taxpayers. Although determining the taxable income of most individuals is relatively simple, the manner in which the tax law is applied to individuals has tremendous significance. Individual taxpayers pay nearly 85 percent of all Federal income taxes collected, making the tax laws that apply to them of great economic and social consequence. Further, the sheer number of individuals impacted by the tax law, most of them eligible voters, often makes the taxation of individuals a heated personal and political issue as well. As you will see, Congress uses the provisions related to individual taxpayers to attempt to address a host of economic and social matters.

Most of the ideas already covered in this text apply to individuals as well as to other types of taxpayers and tax reporting entities. For example, § 61 requires individuals to include all types of income in their gross income, unless a specific exclusion applies. Code § 161 severely limits the deductibility of individuals' expenses, although § 162 provides an exception for most ordinary and necessary expenses incurred in carrying on a trade or business. In addition to providing Congress the opportunity to significantly influence behavior and, therefore, policy through the tax system, individual taxpayers, in their capacities as wage earners, business owners, investors, consumers, and social beings, raise interesting and unique issues not relevant to other taxpayers and tax reporting entities. It is those issues that are unique to individuals, or that apply to individuals in unique ways, that are the focus of this and the next two chapters.

LO.1

Describe and apply the components of the Federal income tax formula for individuals.

9-1 The Individual Tax Formula

This chapter examines the general framework for determining the taxable income of an individual as well as how the tax on that income is determined. To compute taxable income, it is necessary to understand the tax formula illustrated in Concept Summary 9.1.

Concept Summary 9.1

Individual Income Tax Formula

Income (broadly defined)	$xx,xxx
Less: Exclusions	(x,xxx)
Gross income	$xx,xxx
Less: Deductions *for* adjusted gross income	(x,xxx)
Adjusted gross income (AGI)	$xx,xxx
Less: The greater of—	
Total itemized deductions *or* standard deduction	(x,xxx)
Less: Personal and dependency exemptions*	(x,xxx)
Less: Deduction for qualified business income**	(x,xxx)
Taxable income	$xx,xxx
Tax on taxable income (see Tax Tables or Tax Rate Schedules)	$ x,xxx
Less: Tax credits (including income taxes withheld and prepaid)	(xxx)
Tax due (or refund)	$ xxx

* Exemption deductions are not allowed from 2018 through 2025.

** Only applies from 2018 through 2025 (see text Section 11-4d).

Note: For 2021, individuals who do not itemize deductions may subtract from adjusted gross income cash charitable contributions of up to $600 if married filing jointly or $300 if unmarried.

The tax rate structure applicable to individuals is progressive, with rates ranging from 10 percent to 37 percent.[1] For comparison, the lowest rate structure, which was in effect from 1913 to 1915, ranged from 1 to 7 percent, and the highest, in effect during 1944 to 1945, ranged from 23 to 94 percent. The tax rates that apply to any particular individual are determined not only by their taxable income but also by their filing status (explained later).

[1]The current Tax Rate Schedules that apply to individuals can be found in Appendix A and in the inside front cover of the hardbound text.

Once the individual's tax has been computed, prepayments and credits are subtracted to determine whether the taxpayer owes additional tax or is entitled to a refund.

9-1a Components of the Tax Formula

The components of the tax formula are examined in detail throughout Part 4 of this text. A brief introduction of each is offered below to provide an overview of the general framework applicable to individuals.

Income (Broadly Defined)

As discussed in Chapter 4, "income" is broadly defined to include all sources of income, both taxable and nontaxable. In general, the courts have further defined "income" as any realized increase in wealth.[2] Income does not include recoveries of capital or amounts for which the taxpayer has an obligation to repay. Income is not recognizable for tax purposes until it is realized.

When Dan's apartment lease ends, he decides to buy a house. Consequently, the owner of the apartment building returns to Dan the $600 damage deposit he previously made. To make a down payment on the house, Dan sells stock for $50,000 (original cost of $28,000) and borrows $200,000 from a bank.

Only the $22,000 gain from the sale of the stock is income to Dan. The $600 damage deposit and the $28,000 cost of the stock are a return of capital. The $200,000 bank loan is not income as Dan has an obligation to repay that amount (the loan does not increase his wealth).

Exclusions

For various reasons, Congress has chosen to exclude certain types of income from the income tax base. The principal income exclusions are listed in Exhibit 9.1. The exclusions most commonly encountered by individual taxpayers (primarily employee fringe benefits) are discussed in detail in Chapter 11.

Exhibit 9.1 Partial List of Exclusions from Gross Income

Accident and health insurance proceeds
Alimony received (for divorces executed after 2018)
Annuity payments (to the extent proceeds represent a recovery of the taxpayer's investment)
Child support payments
Damages for personal injury or sickness
Fringe benefits of employees:
- Educational assistance payments provided by employer
- Employer-provided accident and health insurance
- Group term life insurance (for coverage up to $50,000)
- Meals and lodging (if furnished for convenience of employer)
- Tuition reductions for employees of educational institutions
- Miscellaneous benefits

Gains from sale of principal residence (subject to statutory ceiling)
Gifts and inheritances received
Interest from state and local bonds
Life insurance paid at death of insured
Scholarship grants (to a limited extent)
Social Security benefits (to a limited extent)
Workers' compensation benefits

[2] *Comm. v. Glenshaw Glass Co.*, 55–1 USTC ¶9308, 47 AFTR 162, 348 U.S. 426.

Gross Income

The Internal Revenue Code defines gross income broadly as "except as otherwise provided ..., all income from whatever source derived."[3] The "except as otherwise provided" phrase refers to exclusions. Therefore, gross income includes all sources of income that are not specifically excluded from the tax base. Since several items are determined with respect to gross income, it is important to be able to distinguish it from income, more broadly defined, and from adjusted gross income discussed below. Gross income includes, but is not limited to, the items in Exhibit 9.2.

Exhibit 9.2 Partial List of Gross Income Items

Alimony received (related to divorces before 2019)	Interest
Bargain purchase from employer	Jury duty fees
Bonuses	Partnership income
Breach of contract damages	Pensions
Business income	Prizes (with some exceptions)
Commissions	Professional fees
Compensation for services	Punitive damages
Debts forgiven (with some exceptions)	Rents
Dividends	Rewards
Embezzled funds	Royalties
Farm income	Salaries
Fees	Severance pay
Gains from illegal activities	Strike and lockout benefits
Gains from sale of property	Tips and gratuities
Gambling winnings	Treasure trove (found property)
Hobby receipts	Wages

Example 2

Beth received the following during the year:

Salary	$30,000
Interest on savings account	900
Gift from her aunt	10,000
Prize won in state lottery	1,000
Alimony from former spouse (divorced in 2015)	12,000
Child support from former spouse	6,000
Damages for injury in auto accident	25,000
Ten $50 bills in an unmarked envelope found in an airport lounge (airport authorities could not locate anyone who claimed ownership)	500
Federal income tax refund for last year's tax overpayment	120

In addition, her stock investments increased in value by $5,000.

Beth must include $44,400 in computing taxable income.

Salary	$30,000
Interest	900
Lottery prize	1,000
Alimony	12,000
Money found at airport	500
Gross Income	$44,400

The $120 Federal tax refund and $25,000 of damages are recoveries of capital and, therefore, not considered income for tax purposes. The $5,000 increase in the value of her investments is not considered income because it is unrealized. The $10,000 gift and $6,000 child support are both excludible income (covered in Chapter 10).

[3] § 61(a).

Deductions *for* Adjusted Gross Income

Deductions available to individuals fall into two broad categories, each taken into account at different places in the tax formula. As you will see, where in the formula expenses are deductible can be just as important as whether they are deductible.

The first category of deductions are those available *for* adjusted gross income (i.e., deductions that are subtracted from gross income to arrive at adjusted gross income). Deductions for adjusted gross income (AGI) include the following:[4]

- Ordinary and necessary expenses incurred in a trade or business.
- Part of the self-employment tax paid.
- Alimony payments related to divorces executed prior to 2019.
- Contributions to certain retirement plans, including Individual Retirement Accounts.
- Contributions to Health Savings Accounts.
- The capital loss deduction (limited to $3,000).

Expenses deductible *for* AGI generally reduce a taxpayer's taxable income unconditionally, without taxpayer-specific limitations. The effect of deductions *for* AGI is illustrated below.

Mason, age 45, earned a salary of $78,000 in the current year. He contributed $4,000 to his traditional Individual Retirement Account (IRA), sold stock held as an investment for a short-term capital loss of $2,000, and paid $4,600 in alimony to his former spouse (the couple divorced in 2017). His AGI is determined as follows:

Gross income		
Salary		$ 78,000
Less: Deductions *for* AGI		
IRA contribution	$4,000	
Capital loss	2,000	
Alimony paid	4,600	(10,600)
AGI		$ 67,400

Deductions *from* Adjusted Gross Income

Expenses deductible *from* AGI (commonly referred to as **itemized deductions**) are generally personal expenses. As a general rule, personal expenses are not deductible; however, as discussed in Chapter 1, Congress allows the deduction of certain personal expenses for various reasons, such as to influence taxpayers' behavior to facilitate various social and economic objectives. Itemized deductions are discussed in Chapter 10. A partial list of itemized deductions is included in Exhibit 9.3.

[4] See § 62 for a comprehensive list of items that are deductible *for* AGI. Deductions *for* AGI are sometimes known as *above-the-line* deductions because on the tax return, they are taken before the "line" designating AGI.

Exhibit 9.3 Partial List of Itemized Deductions

Medical expenses in excess of 7.5% of AGI
State and local income or sales taxes*
Real estate taxes*
Personal property taxes*
Interest on home mortgage (subject to certain limitations)
Investment interest (up to the amount of net investment income)
Charitable contributions (within specified percentage limitations)
Casualty and theft losses in excess of 10% of AGI

*Only $10,000 of combined state and local taxes is deductible.

Distinguishing deductions *for* AGI and itemized deductions (*from* AGI) is important for at least two reasons. First, AGI is used in computing limitations on certain itemized deductions such as medical expenses, charitable contributions, and certain casualty losses. For example, medical expenses are deductible only to the extent they exceed 7.5 percent of AGI, and charitable contribution deductions generally may not exceed 50 percent of AGI (60 percent for certain cash donations). These limitations might be described as a percentage *floor* under the medical expense deduction and a percentage *ceiling* on the charitable contribution deduction. Thus, whether a deduction is available for AGI or from AGI affects the amount of other deductions.

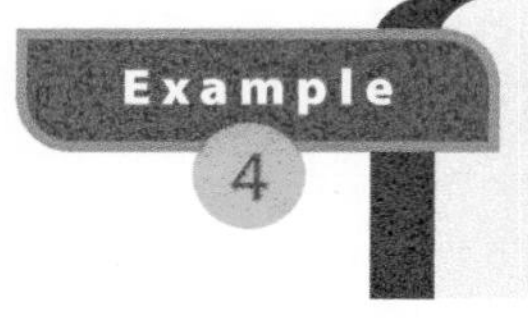

Assume the same facts as in Example 3, except that Mason also had unreimbursed medical expenses of $8,000. Medical expenses may be included in his itemized deductions to the extent they exceed 7.5% of AGI. In computing his itemized deductions, Mason may include medical expenses of $2,945 [$8,000 medical expenses − $5,055 (7.5% × $67,400 AGI)]

Second, as discussed further below, taxpayers may choose to deduct the greater of their total itemized deductions or the standard deduction. Therefore, even though a taxpayer may incur an expense that qualifies as an itemized deduction, it may not reduce taxable income if total itemized deductions do not exceed the standard deduction. Expenses that qualify as deductions *for* AGI, however, are available to reduce taxable income whether the taxpayer uses the standard deduction or not.

The Standard Deduction

In lieu of claiming itemized deductions, taxpayers can claim the **standard deduction**. As discussed later in the chapter, the standard deduction amount varies depending on filing status, age, and blindness. The standard deduction amount is adjusted each year for the effects of inflation.

Personal and Dependency Exemptions

Prior to 2018, exemption deductions were allowed for the taxpayer, the taxpayer's spouse, and each dependent of the taxpayer. Exemption deductions are suspended for 2018 through 2025. However, as discussed in this and subsequent chapters, whether someone qualifies as a taxpayer's dependent remains important for several reasons.

Qualified Business Income Deduction

From 2018 through 2025, a deduction for a portion of a taxpayer's qualified business income (QBI) is allowed. In general, this deduction relates to business income generated by noncorporate businesses (e.g., sole proprietorships, S corporations, partnerships, and LLCs) and included in the taxpayer's individual taxable income. Generally, the deduction is the *lesser* of (1) 20 percent of qualified business income or (2) 20 percent of modified taxable income. The QBI deduction is unique in that although it is deductible *from* AGI, it is not an itemized deduction. Rather, it is deductible in addition to itemized deductions, available whether or not the taxpayer chooses to use the standard deduction. This deduction is discussed further in Chapter 11.

Taxable Income

The determination of taxable income is illustrated in Example 5.

Example 5

Grace, age 25, is not married and has her disabled and dependent mother living with her. This qualifies Grace for head-of-household filing status and a standard deduction of $19,400 in 2022. In 2022, Grace earned a $44,000 salary as a high school teacher. Her other income consisted of $1,100 interest on a certificate of deposit (CD) and $500 of nontaxable interest on municipal bonds she had received as a graduation gift in 2014. During 2022, she sold stock that resulted in a deductible capital loss of $1,000. Her itemized deductions are $11,000. Grace's taxable income for the year is computed as follows:

Income (broadly defined)		
Salary		$44,000
Interest on a CD		1,100
Interest on municipal bonds		500
Total income		$45,600
Less: Exclusion—		
Interest on municipal bonds		(500)
Gross income		$45,100
Less: Deduction *for* adjusted gross income—capital loss		(1,000)
Adjusted gross income (AGI)		$44,100
Less: The *greater* of—		
Total itemized deductions	$11,000	
or the standard deduction for head of household	19,400	(19,400)
Less: Deduction for qualified business income		(-0-)
Taxable income		$24,700

The exclusion of $500 (i.e., interest from municipal bonds) is subtracted in determining gross income, while the capital loss of $1,000 is classified as a deduction *for* AGI. Grace chose to itemize her deductions *from* AGI as they exceed the standard deduction (see Exhibit 9.3). Grace's income tax is determined later in this chapter in Example 37.

9-2 Standard Deduction

LO.2

Explain the standard deduction and when it should be used in determining taxable income.

One purpose of the standard deduction is to exempt part of a taxpayer's income from Federal income taxes, making that income available to pay for basic living expenses before any income tax is imposed. Practically, the allowance of a standard deduction also reduces the number of taxpayers who itemize, reducing compliance complexity for taxpayers as well as the audit effort required of the IRS.

9-2a Basic and Additional Standard Deduction

The standard deduction is the sum of two components: the *basic* standard deduction and the *additional* standard deduction.[5] Exhibit 9.4 lists the basic standard deduction allowed for taxpayers in each filing status (discussed further below). Most taxpayers are allowed to use the full standard deduction. However, certain taxpayers are not allowed to claim *any* standard deduction, and the standard deduction is *limited* for others. These provisions are discussed later in the chapter.

A taxpayer who is age 65 or over *or* blind qualifies for an *additional standard deduction* with the amount again depending on the taxpayer's filing status (see amounts in Exhibit 9.5). Two additional standard deductions are allowed for a taxpayer who is age 65 or over *and* blind. The additional standard deduction provisions also apply for a qualifying spouse who is age 65 or over or blind, but a taxpayer may not claim an additional standard deduction for a dependent. Both the basic and additional standard deduction amounts are adjusted annually for inflation.

Taxpayers are allowed to deduct the *greater* of their itemized deductions or the *total* standard deduction (the sum of the basic standard deduction and any additional standard deduction amounts). The choice is elective and may be changed each year. For example, a taxpayer who buys a home may change from using the standard deduction to itemizing deductions (because of mortgage interest and property tax deductions). The taxpayer's age can also impact the choice. Prior to 2018, approximately 30 percent of taxpayers itemized their deductions. As a result of the increased standard deduction and elimination of some itemized deductions by the TCJA of 2017, the number of itemizers dropped to 11 percent in 2018. In 2019, the most recent year for which data is available, 12 percent of all individual taxpayers itemized their deductions.

Standard versus Itemized Deduction

Juan and Lisa Fernandez have been renting an apartment while saving money for a down payment on a house. Early in 2022, they purchased a house. Interest paid on their home mortgage in 2022 amounted $9,800, and they paid property taxes of $5,500. In addition, they had charitable contributions of $8,000 and paid state income taxes of $4,000. In total, their itemized deductions amount to $27,300. They should compute their taxable income using this amount rather than the $25,900 standard deduction.

Prior to 2022, Sara, who is single, had always chosen to itemize. In 2022, however, she reaches age 65. Her itemized deductions for 2022 are 13,800, but her total standard deduction is $14,700 [$12,950 (basic standard deduction) + $1,750 (additional standard deduction)].

Sara should compute her taxable income for 2022 using the standard deduction ($14,700) because it exceeds her itemized deductions ($13,800).

Exhibit 9.4 Basic Standard Deduction Amounts

Filing Status	2021	2022
Single	$12,550	$12,950
Married, filing jointly	25,100	25,900
Surviving spouse	25,100	25,900
Head of household	18,800	19,400
Married, filing separately	12,550	12,950

Digging Deeper 1

Some individuals may not claim the standard deduction. Find out who at this book's companion website: www.cengage.com

[5] § 63(c)(1).

Exhibit 9.5 **Amount of Each Additional Standard Deduction**

Filing Status	2021	2022
Single	$1,700	$1,750
Married, filing jointly	1,350	1,400
Surviving spouse	1,350	1,400
Head of household	1,700	1,750
Married, filing separately	1,350	1,400

9-2b Limitations on the Standard Deduction for Dependents

To prevent taxpayers from shifting income to a dependent and using the dependent's standard deduction to shield the income from tax, the standard deduction available to individuals who qualify as a dependent of another taxpayer is limited. When filing their own tax return, a *dependent's* basic standard deduction in 2022 is limited to the greater of $1,150 or the sum of the individual's earned income for the year plus $400.[6] This limitation applies only to the basic standard deduction. A dependent who is 65 or over or blind or both also is allowed the additional standard deduction amount on his or her own return (refer to Exhibit 9.5).

Dependent Standard Deduction

Gabrielle, who is 17 years old and single, qualifies as a dependent of her parents. During 2022, she received $1,200 of interest (unearned income) on a savings account. She also earned $450 from a part-time job. When Gabrielle files her own tax return, her standard deduction is $1,150 (the greater of $1,150 or the sum of earned income of $450 plus $400).

Assume the same facts as in Example 8, except that Gabrielle is 67 years old and qualifies as her son's dependent. In this case, when Gabrielle files her own tax return, her standard deduction is $2,900 [$1,150 (see Example 8) + $1,750 (the additional standard deduction allowed because Gabrielle is age 65 or over)].

Aleshia, who is 16 years old and single, earned $800 from a summer job and had no unearned income during 2022. She qualifies as a dependent of her parents. Her standard deduction is $1,200 (the greater of $1,150 or the sum of earned income of $800 plus $400).

Javier, who is 20 years old, single, and a full-time college student, qualifies as a dependent of his parents. He worked as a musician during the summer of 2022, earning $12,750. Javier's standard deduction is $12,950 (the greater of $1,150 or the sum of earned income of $12,750 plus $400, but limited to the $12,950 standard deduction for a single taxpayer).

[6] § 63(c)(5). Both the $1,150 amount and the $400 amount are subject to adjustment for inflation each year. In 2021, the amounts were $1,100 and $350.

Explain the rules for determining dependency status.

9-3 Dependents

As discussed above, the standard deduction ensures taxpayers a given level of income to meet basic living expenses before the income tax is imposed. Historically, taxpayers have also been allowed exemptions to adjust the level of untaxed income allowed for the number of individuals supported by the taxpayer. Exemption deductions have been allowed for the taxpayer (**personal exemptions**) as well as for eligible dependents (**dependency exemptions**). However, Congress suspended the deduction for exemptions from 2018 through 2025 and increased the standard deduction amount.

Even though the exemption deduction has been suspended, understanding when someone qualifies as a "dependent" remains important. For example, the definition of a dependent is used for a variety of purposes including determining eligibility for the child credit and the dependent credit and the deductibility of medical expenses (all discussed in Chapter 10) as well as the limitation on the standard deduction discussed above. The exemption amount, still used in determining the dependency status of certain dependents, is $4,400 in 2022 ($4,300 in 2021). A person may qualify as another's dependent by meeting the definition of either a qualifying child or a qualifying relative.[7]

9-3a Qualifying Child

In addition to a dependency exemption, having a qualifying child may make the taxpayer eligible for the following:

- Head-of-household filing status (discussed below).
- Earned income tax credit (discussed in Chapter 10).
- Child tax credit (discussed in Chapter 10).
- Credit for child and dependent care expenses (discussed in Chapter 10).

A **qualifying child** must meet the relationship, residence, age, and support tests.[8]

Relationship Test

To be considered a qualifying child of a taxpayer, someone must be the taxpayer's child (including adopted, step, and foster children), sibling (including step and half siblings), or a *descendant* of any of these parties (e.g., grandchild, nephew, and niece). An adopted child includes a child placed with the taxpayer even though the adoption is not final. An eligible foster child is a child who is placed with the taxpayer by an authorized placement agency or by a judgment decree or other order of any court of competent jurisdiction.

Residence Test

A qualifying child must live with the taxpayer for more than half of the year. Temporary absences (e.g., school, vacation, medical care, military service, detention in a juvenile facility) are disregarded.[9]

Age Test

At the end of the tax year, a qualifying child must be (1) under age 19 or (2) under age 24 *and* a full-time student. A student who was in school during any part of five months of the year is considered full-time.[10] Also, an individual cannot be older than the

[7] § 152.
[8] § 152(c).
[9] § 152.
[10] §§ 152(c)(3)(A) and 152(f)(2).

taxpayer claiming him or her as a qualifying child (e.g., a brother cannot claim his older sister as a qualifying child). Anyone disabled during any part of the year is considered to meet the age test.[11]

The Big Picture

Return to the facts of *The Big Picture* on p. 9-1. Is Paige a qualifying child of Polly? Paige satisfies the relationship and residence tests, but the answer to the age test remains unclear. Because she is not a full-time student or disabled, she must be under 19 to meet the age test.

Support Test

To be a qualifying child, an individual must not be self-supporting (i.e., provide more than one-half of his or her own support). Support includes amounts provided for food, shelter, clothing, medical and dental care, education, recreation, and similar items. In the case of an individual who is a child of the taxpayer and a full-time student, scholarships are not taken into account for purposes of the support test.[12]

Shawn, age 23, is a full-time student and lives with his parents and an older cousin. During 2022, Shawn receives his support from the following sources: 30% from a part-time job, 30% from a scholarship, 20% from his parents, and 20% from the cousin.

Based on the information provided, Shawn is a qualifying child of his parents. He passes the relationship and residence tests. Further, he is considered to provide only 43% [30% self/(30% self + 20% from parents + 20% from cousin)] of his own support. (Note: Shawn cannot be his cousin's qualifying child due to the relationship test.)

Tiebreaker Rules

In some situations, a child may be a qualifying child of more than one person. In this event, the tax law specifies the person for whom the child will qualify.[13] Called "tiebreaker rules," these rules are summarized in Concept Summary 9.2.

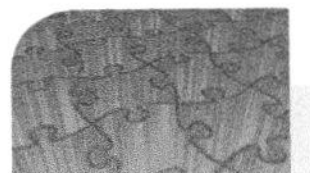

Concept Summary 9.2

Tiebreaker Rules for Determining Dependency Status

Persons Eligible to Treat Qualified Child as Dependent	Person Prevailing
Only one of the persons is the parent.	Parent
Both persons are the parents, and the child lives longer with one parent.	Parent with the longer period of residence
Both persons are the parents, and the child lives with each the same period of time.	Parent with the higher adjusted gross income (AGI)
None of the persons are the parent.	Person with highest AGI

Examples of the tiebreaker rules can be found on this book's companion website: www.cengage.com **2 Digging Deeper**

[11] Within the meaning of § 22(e)(3) for purposes of the credit for the elderly or disabled.

[12] § 152(f)(5).

[13] § 152(c)(4).

9-3b Qualifying Relative

Someone may also be considered a dependent of a taxpayer by being designated as a **qualifying relative**. A qualifying relative must meet the following relationship, gross income, and support tests.[14]

Relationship Test

The relationship test for a qualifying relative is more expansive than that for a qualifying child. In addition to the relatives included in the qualified child test, the following will meet the test for a qualified relative:

- Lineal ascendants (e.g., parents and grandparents).
- Collateral ascendants (e.g., uncles and aunts).
- Certain in-laws (e.g., son-, daughter-, father-, mother-, brother-, and sister-in-law).[15]

Children who do not satisfy the qualifying child definition (e.g., a 25-year-old daughter) might meet the qualifying relative criteria.

Inez provides more than half of the support of her son, James. James is age 20, is not disabled or a full-time student, and generates income of $2,400 from a part-time job. James is not a qualifying child due to the age test, but is a qualifying relative.

Qualifying relatives also include individuals who are "members of the household" (i.e., live with the taxpayer for the entire year) whether or not they are otherwise related to the taxpayer. For example, cousins are not "qualifying relatives" (cousins are not on the list above), but a cousin can meet the relationship test if a "member of the household." Member-of-the-household status is not available for anyone whose relationship with the taxpayer violates local law or anyone who was a spouse during any part of the year.[16] However, an ex-spouse can qualify as a member of the household in a year following the divorce.

As the relationship test indicates, the category designation of "qualifying relative" is somewhat misleading since persons other than relatives can qualify. Furthermore, not all relatives will qualify (although relatives who are not listed could be a "member of the household").

The Big Picture

Return to the facts of *The Big Picture* on p. 9-1. Although Maude is unrelated to Polly, she qualifies as Polly's dependent by being a member of the household. If Maude meets the other criteria to be considered a dependent, Polly also can deduct the medical expenses she paid on Maude's behalf.

Gross Income Test

An individual's gross income must be *less* than the exemption amount—$4,400 in 2022 ($4,300 in 2021)—to be a qualifying relative. As described in the tax formula, gross

[14] § 152(d).

[15] Once established by marriage, in-law status continues to exist and survives divorce.

[16] §§ 152(d)(2)(H) and (f)(3).

income includes any income that is taxable. In the case of scholarships, for example, any amount that is taxable (e.g., received for room and board) is included in gross income and any amount that is excludable (e.g., used for books and tuition) is not. See the discussion of scholarships in Chapter 10.

Gross Income Test

Haylie provides more than half of the support of her son, Tom, who does not live with her. Tom, age 26, is a full-time student in medical school, earns $3,000 from a part-time job, and receives a $12,000 scholarship covering his tuition.

Based on the information available, Tom is Haylie's dependent. He is a qualifying relative since his gross income, $3,000, is less than the exemption amount, meeting the gross income test. (Note: Tom is not a qualifying child; he fails both the residence and the age tests.)

Aaron provides more than half of the support of his widowed aunt, Myrtle, who does not live with him. Myrtle's income for the year is as follows: dividend income of $1,100, earnings from pet sitting of $1,200, nontaxable Social Security benefits of $6,000, and nontaxable interest from City of Milwaukee bonds of $8,000.

Because Myrtle's gross income is only $2,300 ($1,100 + $1,200), she meets the gross income test and may qualify as Aaron's dependent.

The Big Picture

Return to the facts of *The Big Picture* on p. 9-1. Assuming that Paige is not a qualifying child (see Example 12), can she be a qualifying relative? She meets the relationship and support tests, but what about the gross income test?

If her income from her part-time job is less than $4,400 (the 2022 exemption amount), she does qualify and would be Polly's dependent.

Support Test

For an individual to be considered the taxpayer's qualifying relative, the taxpayer must furnish over half of the individual's support. As with a qualifying child, support includes food, shelter, clothing, medical and dental care, education, recreation, and similar items. As also described earlier, in the case of an individual who is a child of the taxpayer and a full-time student, scholarships are not taken into account for purposes of the support test.

Waleed contributed $3,400 (consisting of food, clothing, and medical care) toward the support of his nephew, Aroosa, who lives with him. Aroosa earned $1,300 from a part-time job and received $2,000 from a student loan to attend a local university. Assuming that the other dependency tests are met, Waleed can claim Aroosa as a dependent because he contributed more than half of Aroosa's support.

If an individual does not spend funds that have been received from any source, the unspent amounts are not counted for purposes of the support test.

Emily contributed $3,000 to her father's support during the year. In addition, her father received $2,400 in Social Security benefits, $200 of interest, and wages of $600. Her father deposited the Social Security benefits, interest, and wages in his own savings account and did not use any of the funds for his support. Thus, the Social Security benefits, interest, and wages are not considered to be part of his support. Emily's father is her dependent if the other tests are met.

An individual's own funds, however, must be taken into account if applied toward support. The initial source of the funds is not relevant.

Dominic contributes $8,000 toward his parents' total support of $20,000. The parents, who do not live with Dominic, obtain the other $12,000 from savings and a home equity loan on their residence. Although the parents have no income, their use of savings and borrowed funds are counted as part of their support. Because Dominic does not satisfy the support test, he cannot treat his parents as dependents.

Capital expenditures for items such as furniture, appliances, and automobiles are included for purposes of the support test if the item does, in fact, constitute support.

Tebin purchased a television costing $950 and gave it to his mother, who lives with him. The television was placed in the mother's bedroom and was used exclusively by her. Tebin should include the cost of the television in determining the support of his mother.

Multiple Support Agreements An exception to the support test is available when an individual receives support from multiple taxpayers. A **multiple support agreement** allows a group of taxpayers—none of whom provide more than 50 percent of the support of a potential qualifying relative—to designate one member of the group to be treated as passing the support test.[17] To use a multiple support agreement to meet the support test, the group must collectively provide more than 50 percent of the individual's support and the designated member must provide over 10 percent. This provision is often used by the children of aged dependent parents when none of the children individually meet the support test.

The person designated to meet the support test under a multiple support agreement must also meet all other requirements to treat the individual as a qualifying relative. For example, a person who does not meet the relationship or member-of-the-household requirement cannot claim the individual as a dependent under a multiple support agreement.

Wanda, who resides with her son, Adam, received a total of $12,000 from the the following individuals during the year. This constituted all of her support for the year.

	Amount	Percentage of Total
Adam, a son	$ 5,760	48%
Bob, a son	1,200	10
Carol, a daughter	3,600	30
Diane, a friend	1,440	12
	$12,000	100%

If Adam and Carol file a multiple support agreement, either may treat Wanda as a dependent. Wanda cannot be considered a dependent of Bob because Bob did not contribute *more than 10%* of her support. Bob's consent is not required for Adam and Carol to file a multiple support agreement. Diane does not meet the relationship or member-of-the-household test and cannot be a party to the agreement. The decision as to who claims Wanda rests with Adam and Carol. It is possible for Carol to claim Wanda even though Adam furnished more of Wanda's support.

[17] § 152(d)(3).

The filing requirements for those who are party to a multiple support agreement can be found on this book's companion website: www.cengage.com

3 Digging Deeper

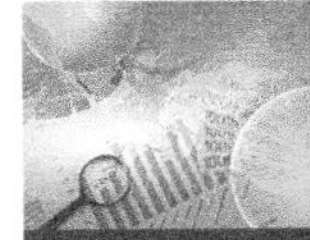

Tax Planning Strategies — Multiple Support Agreements and the Medical Expense Deduction

Framework Focus: Deductions

Strategy: Maximize Deductible Amounts.

Generally, medical expenses are deductible only if they are paid on behalf of the taxpayer, his or her spouse, and their dependents.[18] Because deductibility may rest on dependency status, planning is important in arranging multiple support agreements.

During the year, Suzanne will be supported by her two sons (Gary and Alan) and her daughter (Maria). Each will furnish approximately one-third of the required support. If the parties decide that Maria should treat Suzanne as her dependent under a multiple support agreement, only Suzanne's medical expenses that are paid by Maria will be deductible.

In planning a multiple support agreement, the parties should consider who is most likely to have total medical expenses that exceed the 7.5%-of-AGI limitation. In Example 24, for instance, Maria might be a poor choice if she and her family do not expect to incur many medical expenses of their own.

Children of Divorced or Separated Parents Another exception to the support test applies when parents with children are divorced or separated. Unmarried parents living apart for the last six months of the year also are covered by these rules. As illustrated in Concept Summary 9.2, a child of such parents will be considered the qualifying child of the parent having custody of the child for the greater part of the year (i.e., the custodial parent). If both parents have custody for an equal period of time, the child will be the qualifying child of the parent with the higher adjusted gross income.

However, a child may be considered the qualifying child of the noncustodial parent if the custodial parent signs a waiver declaring he or she will not treat the child as a dependent and the parents together meet the following conditions:[19]

- They would have been entitled to claim the child as a dependent had they been married and filed a joint return.
- They have custody (either jointly or singly) of the child for more than half of the year.

More on the dependency status of children of divorced or separated parents can be found on this book's companion website: www.cengage.com

4 Digging Deeper

9-3c Other Rules for Determining Dependents

In addition to being either a qualifying child or qualifying relative, a dependent must meet the joint return and the citizenship tests.

[18] See the discussion of medical expenses in Chapter 10.

[19] § 152(e)(2) and Reg. § 1.152-4.

Joint Return Test

An individual who is married and files a joint return with his or her spouse generally cannot be considered a dependent of another taxpayer.[20] The joint return rule does not apply, however, if the following conditions are met:[21]

- The reason for filing is to claim a refund for tax withheld.
- No tax liability would exist for either spouse on separate returns.
- Neither spouse is required to file a return.

Paul provides over half of the support of his son, Quinn. He also provides over half of the support of Vera, who is Quinn's wife. During the year, both Quinn and Vera had part-time jobs. To recover the taxes withheld, they file a joint return. If Quinn and Vera have income low enough that they are not *required* to file a return, both will be considered Paul's dependents.

Tax Planning Strategies **Problems with a Joint Return**

Framework Focus: Deductions

Strategy: Maximize Deductible Amounts.

A married person who files a joint return generally will not be considered a dependent of another taxpayer. If a joint return has been filed, dependency status may still be established if separate returns are substituted on a timely basis (on or before the due date of the return).

While preparing a client's 2021 income tax return on April 2, 2022, a tax practitioner discovered that the client's daughter had filed a joint return with her husband in late January 2022. Presuming that the daughter otherwise qualifies as the client's dependent, dependency status is not lost if she and her husband file separate returns on or before April 15, 2022.

Citizenship Test

To qualify as a dependent, an individual must be a U.S. citizen, a U.S. resident, or a resident of Canada or Mexico for some part of the calendar year in which the taxpayer's tax year begins. However, from 2018 through 2025, a taxpayer may not claim a dependent tax credit (see text Section 10-5b) unless the individual is a U.S. citizen or a U.S. resident.[22]

9-3d Comparison of Dependent Categories

Concept Summary 9.3 provides a comparison of the tests that must be met for the two categories of dependents. The following summarizes the differences:

- The relationship test required for qualifying relative status is much broader than the similarly named test required for qualifying child status. Several more relations, as well as non-related members of the same household, qualify as relatives under the former test.
- The support test for the qualifying child classification focuses on the support provided by the child. Conversely, the support test for the qualifying relative classification focuses on the support provided by the relative providing the support.
- The qualifying child category has no gross income limitation, whereas the qualifying relative category has no age restriction.

[20] § 152(b)(2).

[21] Prop Reg § 1.152–1(a)(2).

[22] §§ 152(b)(3) and 24(h)(4)(B).

Concept Summary 9.3

Tests for Dependency Status

Test	Qualifying Child	Qualifying Relative
Relationship:		
• Children (natural, step, or adopted) and their *descendants*, and siblings and stepsiblings and their *descendants*.	X	
• Children (natural, step, or adopted) and their *descendants*, siblings and their children, parents and their *ascendants*, uncles and aunts, stepparents and stepsiblings, and certain in-laws.		X
• Member of the household (live with taxpayer for *entire* year; relative or non-relative).		X
Residence	X	
Age	X	
Support:		
• Not self-supporting ("child" furnishes one-half or less of his or her support).	X	
• Taxpayer furnishes over one-half of the support of potential dependent.		X
Gross income *less* than the exemption amount		X
Joint return (potential dependent cannot file joint return)	X	X
Citizenship or residency (potential dependent must meet test)	X	X

9-4 Filing Status and Filing Requirements

LO.4

Identify the proper filing status of an individual and the related filing requirements.

Once taxable income has been calculated, a two-step process is used in determining income tax due (or refund available). First, the taxpayer's filing status and then whether a tax return must be filed must be determined. Second, the tax has to be computed and adjusted for available tax credits—see Concept Summary 9.1 and the tax formula. This section deals with the filing status and filing requirements.

9-4a Filing Status

Every year taxpayers must determine their **filing status**. Filing status is used, in part, to capture differences in taxpayers' relative abilities to pay that are not captured by their incomes. The taxpayer's filing status is used to determine:

- The taxpayer's standard deduction;
- The amount of other exclusions, deductions, and credits available to the taxpayer; and
- The tax rates used to calculate the taxpayer's tax liability.

The five available filing statuses are:

- Single.
- Married, filing jointly.
- Married, filing separately.
- Surviving spouse (also referred to as a qualifying widow or widower).
- Head of household.

The amount of tax imposed on a given level of income varies considerably depending on the taxpayer's filing status. This is illustrated in the following example.

The following amounts of tax are computed using the 2022 Tax Rate Schedules for a taxpayer (or taxpayers in the case of a joint return) with $60,000 of taxable income (see Appendix A).

Filing Status	Amount of Tax
Single	$8,817
Married, filing jointly	6,789
Married, filing separately	8,817
Head of household	7,317

Besides the effect from the tax rates that will apply, filing status also has an impact on the amount of the standard deduction that is allowed—see Exhibits 9.4 and 9.5 earlier in the chapter.

Single Taxpayers

A taxpayer who is unmarried (including a taxpayer who is legally separated or divorced) and does not qualify for head-of-household status (discussed below) will file as a single taxpayer.

Married Taxpayers

A married couple may choose to file separately or jointly. If married individuals choose to file separate returns, each reports only his or her own income, deductions, and credits and determines tax using the married filing separately Tax Rate Schedule. If the couple reside in a community property state, generally, they must split the income and report it as such.[23] If the couple files jointly, they report their combined income, deductions, and credits and determine their combined tax using the married filing jointly Tax Rate Schedule.

The joint return Tax Rate Schedule is constructed by doubling the amount of income subject to tax at each rate for a married individual filing separately. Therefore, if married individuals have the same amount of income, the married separate and married joint Tax Rate Schedules will produce the same amount of total tax. However, if their incomes are sufficiently different, filing separately can result in higher taxes as the higher-earning spouse is forced into a higher marginal tax bracket. Filing separately may also reduce the exclusions and deductions available (e.g., the standard deduction is not available to a married individual filing separately if the spouse itemizes, and certain credits may not be allowed). Therefore, most married couples should choose to file a joint return. However, special circumstances (e.g., significant medical expenses incurred by one spouse subject to the 7.5%-of-AGI limitation) may warrant the decision to file separately. It may be necessary to compute the tax under both assumptions to determine the most advantageous filing status. It should be noted that filing a joint return carries the potential disadvantage of joint and several liability. This means that the IRS can pursue the collection of the tax due for that year against either spouse.

Digging Deeper 5

More on the history of the joint filing status can be found on this book's companion website: www.cengage.com

[23]Form 8958 (Allocation of Tax Amounts Between Certain Individuals in Community Property States) is used for this purpose.

A legally married same-sex couple is recognized as married for Federal tax purposes. According to the IRS, registered domestic partners or partners in civil unions, though, are not "spouses" under Federal law. Therefore, they cannot file Federal tax returns using married filing jointly or married filing separately status.[24] However, some states (e.g., California) do recognize registered domestic partners as married for tax purposes and thus taxpayers may have a different filing status for Federal and state tax purposes.

A discussion of the marriage tax can be found on this book's companion website: www.cengage.com 6 Digging Deeper

The joint return rates also apply for two years following the death of one spouse if the surviving spouse maintains a household for a dependent child. The child must be a son, stepson, daughter, or stepdaughter who qualifies as a dependent of the taxpayer (the gross income and joint return tests are waived for this purpose). This is referred to as **surviving spouse** status.[25]

Head of Household

Unmarried individuals who maintain a household for a dependent (or dependents) can file as a **head of household** rather than as single. The tax rates applicable to a head of household are lower than those applicable to a single person but not as low as those applicable to a married couple filing jointly.[26] Head-of-household status is reserved for taxpayers who meet three requirements:

1. the taxpayer is considered unmarried at the end of the year,
2. the taxpayer pays more than half the cost of maintaining a home, and
3. a qualifying person lived with the taxpayer in the home for over half of the year.

A qualifying person includes a qualifying child and a qualifying relative (other than someone who qualifies as a relative under the member-of-the-household classification). An important exception to the qualifying person rules permits the parent of a taxpayer to meet the definition of a qualifying person even when that parent does not live in the home for more than half of the year.[27]

Bridge Discipline — Bridge to Equity or Fairness

Much has been made in the press and in political circles over the years concerning the so-called **marriage penalty**. This marriage penalty refers to the additional income tax that married couples might pay over and above the aggregate amount two single individuals would pay with equal amounts of income. The marriage penalty arose because of the nature of the income tax rate structure that applies to individual taxpayers.

Relevant practical, policy, and ethical issues related to this dilemma include the following:

- Do two unmarried individuals living apart have the same ability to pay as a married couple with the same combined income?
- Should two unmarried individuals who live together pay the same amount of combined tax as a married couple with the same combined income?

Long aware of the marriage penalty, Congress reduced its effect by increasing the standard deduction available to married filers to 200 percent of that applicable to single persons and doubling the amount of income subject to tax at each rate below the 35 percent bracket for joint filers relative to single filers. However, it remains possible for two single individuals each in the 35 percent marginal tax bracket to face a higher total combined tax liability by marrying (compare the Tax Tables for these filing statuses).

In addition, some tax rules apply less favorably for married couples than for single individuals. For example, the net investment income tax (see text Section 9-5e) can apply to a married couple filing jointly with over $250,000 of income while the threshold for a single person is $200,000 (rather than $125,000).

[24] Reg. § 301.7701–18 and *U.S. v. Windsor*, 2013–2 USTC ¶50,400, 111 AFTR 2d 2013–2385, 133 S.Ct. 2675.

[25] § 2(a)(1). The IRS label for surviving spouse status is "qualifying widow(er) with dependent child."

[26] § 2(b).

[27] § 2(b)(1)(B).

Head-of-Household Status

Tam's 18-year-old unmarried son lived with her all year. He did not provide more than half of his own support and does not meet the tests to be a qualifying child of anyone else. Because he is a qualifying child and is single, he is a qualifying person for head-of-household filing status.

Haukea's boyfriend and her boyfriend's 10-year-old daughter live with Haukea all year in her home. Even though her boyfriend may be a qualifying relative if the gross income and support tests are met, he is not a qualifying person for head-of-household purposes because he is not related to Haukea. The boyfriend's 10-year-old daughter is not a qualifying child, and because she is the boyfriend's qualifying child, she is not Haukea's qualifying relative. As a result, she is not Haukea's qualifying person for head-of-household purposes.

Rick, an unmarried individual, lives in New York City and maintains a household in Detroit for his dependent parents. Rick may use the head-of-household rates even though his parents do not reside in his New York home.

The Big Picture

Return to the facts of The Big Picture on p. 9-1. Assuming that Polly can be treated as single (i.e., not married), can Maude qualify Polly for head-of-household filing status? The answer is no. Even though Maude can be claimed as Polly's dependent (see Example 15), she does not meet the relationship test.

Digging Deeper 7

Information on a paid preparer's responsibilities when preparing a return for a taxpayer filing as Head of Household can be found on this book's companion website: www.cengage.com

Abandoned Spouse Rules

Recall that filing separately may cause a married taxpayer to lose the benefit of certain exclusions and deductions. Congress has enacted provisions that allow married taxpayers, commonly referred to as abandoned spouses, to file as a head of household if the following conditions are satisfied:

- The taxpayer does not file a joint return.
- The taxpayer paid more than half the cost of maintaining his or her home for the tax year.
- The taxpayer's spouse did not live in the home during the last six months of the tax year.
- The home was the principal residence of the taxpayer's son, daughter, stepson, stepdaughter, foster child, or adopted child for more than half the year, and the child can be claimed as a dependent.[28]

The resulting tax burden using the relatively favorable head-of-household status is lower than when using the married filing separately rate schedule.

The Big Picture

Example 32

Return to the facts of The Big Picture on p. 9-1. Can Polly qualify as an abandoned spouse? Yes, if she can claim Paige as a dependent—either as a qualifying child (see Example 12) or as a qualifying relative (see Example 18). If so, Polly can use the head-of-household filing status. If not, her filing status is married filing separately.

[28] § 7703(b).

Global Tax Issues Filing a Joint Return

John is a U.S. citizen and resident, but he spends much of his time in London, where his employer sends him on frequent assignments. John is married to Victoria, a citizen and resident of the United Kingdom.

Can John and Victoria file a joint return for U.S. Federal income tax purposes? Although § 6013(a)(1) specifically precludes the filing of a joint return if one spouse is a nonresident alien, another Code provision permits an exception. Under § 6013(g), the parties can elect to treat the nonqualifying spouse as a "resident" of the United States. This election would allow John and Victoria to file jointly.

But should John and Victoria make this election? If Victoria has considerable income of her own (from non-U.S. sources), the election could be ill-advised. As a nonresident alien, Victoria's non-U.S. source income ordinarily *would not* be subject to the U.S. income tax. If she is treated as a U.S. resident, however, her non-U.S. source income *will be subject to U.S. tax*. Under the U.S. worldwide approach to taxation, all income (regardless of where earned) of anyone who is a *resident* or *citizen* of the United States is subject to tax.

9-4b Filing Requirements

General Rules

In general, an individual must file a tax return if gross income equals or exceeds the applicable standard deduction.[29] For example, a single taxpayer under age 65 must file a tax return in 2022 if gross income equals or exceeds $12,950. Because the standard deduction amount is subject to an annual inflation adjustment, the gross income thresholds for determining whether a tax return must be filed normally change every year.

The additional standard deduction for those age 65 or older is considered in determining the gross income filing requirements. For example, the 2022 filing requirement for a single taxpayer age 65 or older is $14,700 ($12,950 basic standard deduction + $1,750 additional standard deduction).

A self-employed individual with net earnings of $400 or more from a business or profession must file a tax return regardless of the amount of gross income.

Even though an individual has gross income below the filing level amounts and therefore does not owe any tax, he or she must file a return to obtain a tax refund of any tax that might have been withheld from their income by a payer. A return is also necessary to obtain the benefits of the earned income credit (see Chapter 10). In addition, an individual who needs to reconcile the amount of premium tax credit received in advance during the year or owed to them (to help pay for health insurance obtained through the Marketplace) must file a return (see Chapter 10).

Filing Requirements for Dependents

Computation of the gross income filing requirement for an individual who is a dependent of another taxpayer is subject to more complex rules. For example, such an individual must file a return if he or she has either earned income in excess of the standard deduction amount or unearned income in excess of the greater of $1,150 or the sum of unearned income plus $400.

More information on the filing requirements for dependents can be found on this book's companion website: www.cengage.com

8 Digging Deeper

[29] § 6012(a)(1).

Identify and apply the methods available for determining the tax liability of individuals.

9-5 Tax Determination

The computation of income tax due (or refund) involves applying the proper set of tax rates to taxable income to determine the tentative tax liability for the year and then adjusting the liability for available credits. The tax liability will usually be computed using either the Tax Tables or the Tax Rate Schedules. In certain cases, however, the application of the kiddie tax or the recognition of long-term capital gains will cause a modification of the means by which the tax is determined.

9-5a Tax Rate Schedule Method

The **Tax Rate Schedules** reflect the tax rate brackets as laid out in the Internal Revenue Code.[30] The 2022 rate schedule for single taxpayers is reproduced in Exhibit 9.6. This schedule is used to illustrate the tax computation in Examples 33 and 34.

Pat is single and had $5,810 of taxable income in 2022. His tax is $581 ($5,810 × 10%).

Chris is single and had taxable income of $102,000 in 2022. His tax is $18,316 [$15,213.50 + 24% ($102,000 − $89,075)]. His marginal tax rate is 24%, and his average tax rate is 17.96% ($18,316 ÷ $102,000) (see text Section 1-2a).

Exhibit 9.6 2022 Tax Rate Schedule for Single Taxpayers

If Taxable Income Is			
Over	**But Not Over**	**The Tax Is:**	**Of the Amount Over**
$ -0-	$ 10,275	10%	$ -0-
10,275	41,775	$ 1,027.50 + 12%	10,275
41,775	89,075	4,807.50 + 22%	41,775
89,075	170,050	15,213.50 + 24%	89,075
170,050	215,950	34,647.50 + 32%	170,050
215,950	539,900	49,335.50 + 35%	215,950
539,900		162,718.00 + 37%	539,900

[30] § 1.

9-5b Tax Table Method

A taxpayer with taxable income less than $100,000 is required to compute his or her tax liability using the **Tax Table**. Although the Tax Table is derived from the Tax Rate Schedules, the tax calculated using the two methods may vary slightly. This variation occurs because the tax for a particular income range in the Tax Table is based on the midpoint of the range from the Schedules.

Liang is single and has taxable income of $30,000 for calendar year 2021. To determine Liang's tax using the Tax Table (see Appendix A), find the $30,000 to $30,050 income line. The tax of $3,404 is actually the tax that the 2021 Tax Rate Schedule (see Appendix A) would yield on taxable income of $30,025 (i.e., the midpoint amount between $30,000 and $30,050).

Restrictions on the availability of the tax table method can be found on this book's companion website: www.cengage.com

9 Digging Deeper

9-5c Computation of Net Taxes Payable or Refund Due

The *pay-as-you-go* feature of the Federal income tax system requires payment of all or part of the taxpayer's income tax liability during the year. These payments are made through Federal income tax withholding by employers, estimated tax paid by the taxpayer, or both.[31] The payments are applied against the tax liability to determine whether the taxpayer will get a refund or must pay additional tax.

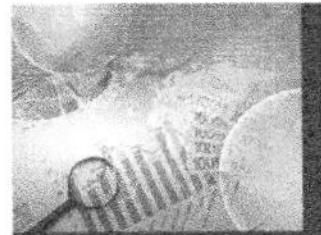

Tax Planning Strategies — Shifting Income and Deductions across Time

Framework Focus: Tax Rate

Strategy: Shift Net Income from High-Bracket Years to Low-Bracket Years.

Given the time value of money, good tax planning generally involves deferring the recognition of income and accelerating the recognition of deductions. However, the progressive tax rates faced by individuals will sometimes call for just the opposite. For example, a cash basis taxpayer who is in the 12 percent bracket this year but expects to be in the 24 percent bracket next year should, if possible, defer payment of deductible expenses until next year to maximize the tax benefit of the deduction.

A note of caution is in order with respect to shifting income and expenses between years. Congress has recognized the tax planning possibilities of such shifting and has enacted many provisions to limit a taxpayer's ability to do so. Some of these limitations on the shifting of income and deductions are discussed in Chapters 4 through 6.

[31] See § 3402 for withholding and § 6654 for estimated payments.

Employers are required to withhold income tax on compensation paid to their employees and to pay this tax to the government on the employee's behalf. The employer must provide each employee a Form W–2 (Wage and Tax Statement), which documents wages and taxes withheld (including income, Social Security, and Medicare taxes). The employee should receive this form by January 31 after the year in which the income tax is withheld.

If taxpayers receive income that is not subject to withholding or income from which not enough tax is withheld, they may have to pay estimated tax. Form 1040–ES (Estimated Tax for Individuals) is used for these payments, with estimates due quarterly.

The income tax liability also is reduced by any available tax credits. Unlike tax deductions, which reduce taxable income on which the tax liability is based, tax credits (including tax withheld) reduce the tax liability dollar for dollar.

Gail is a taxpayer in the 24% tax bracket. As a result of incurring $1,000 in adoption expenses, she is entitled to a $1,000 adoption expense credit. She also contributed $1,000 to the American Cancer Society and included this amount in her itemized deductions.

The credit for adoption expenses results in a $1,000 reduction of Gail's tax liability for the year. The contribution to the American Cancer Society reduces taxable income by $1,000 and results in a $240 reduction in Gail's tax liability ($1,000 reduction in taxable income × 24% tax rate).

Selected tax credits for individuals are discussed in Chapter 10. Following are some of the more common credits available to individuals:

- Child tax credit.
- Dependent credit.
- Credit for child and dependent care expenses.
- Education tax credits.
- Earned income credit.
- Premium tax credit.

The computation of net taxes payable or refund due can be illustrated by returning to the facts of Example 5.

Grace is not married and has her disabled and dependent mother living with her. Recall that Example 5 established that Grace has taxable income of $24,700. Further assume that she has the following income tax withheld, $2,000; estimated tax payments, $600; and a dependent tax credit, $500. Grace's net taxes payable (refund due) is computed as follows:

Income tax (from 2022 Tax Rate Schedule for head of household)		2,671
Less: Tax credits and prepayments—		
Dependent tax credit	$ 500	
Income tax withheld	2,000	
Estimated tax payments	600	(3,100)
Net taxes payable (refund due, if negative)		($ 429)

9-5d Kiddie Tax—Unearned Income of Dependent Children

LO.6

Identify individuals subject to the kiddie tax and calculate the tax.

Historically, some taxpayers have reduced their taxes by transferring ownership of income-producing assets to their children. Transferring the assets shifted the unearned income produced by these assets to the children who were in a lower tax bracket. Current tax law reduces the benefits of such income shifting by taxing the net unearned income of children using the marginal tax rate of their parents. **Unearned income** includes taxable interest, dividends, capital gains, rents, royalties, the taxable portion of scholarships, pension and annuity income, and income (other than earned income) received as the beneficiary of a trust.

This provision, commonly referred to as the **kiddie tax**, generally applies to any child who is under age 19 (or under age 24 if a full-time student) and has unearned income of more than $2,300 in 2022 ($2,200 in 2021).[32] The kiddie tax does not apply if the child has earned income that exceeds half of his or her support, if the child is married and files a joint return, or if both parents are deceased.

Net Unearned Income

In 2022, the net unearned income of a dependent child, the base on which the kiddie tax is applied, is computed as follows:

Unearned income

Less: $1,150

Less: The *greater* of:

 $1,150 of the standard deduction, *or*

 The amount of allowable itemized deductions directly connected with the production of the unearned income

Equals: Net unearned income

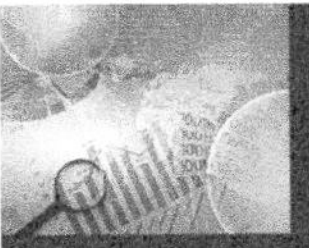

Tax Planning Strategies **Income of Certain Children**

Framework Focus: Tax Rate

Strategy: Shift Net Income from High-Bracket Taxpayers to Low-Bracket Taxpayers

Taxpayers can use several strategies to avoid or minimize the effect of the kiddie tax. With the cutoff age being 19 (under 24 for full-time students), many children are vulnerable to the application of the kiddie tax. Parents should consider giving a younger child assets that defer the inclusion in gross income until the child reaches a nonvulnerable age. For example, U.S. government Series EE savings bonds can be used to defer income until the bonds are cashed in.

Growth stocks typically pay little in the way of dividends. However, the unrealized appreciation on an astute investment may more than offset the lack of dividends. The child can hold the growth stock until he or she reaches a safe age. If the stock is sold then at a profit, the profit is taxed at the child's low rates.

Taxpayers in a position to do so can employ their children in their business and pay them a reasonable wage for the work they actually perform (e.g., light office help such as filing). The child's earned income is sheltered by the standard deduction, and the parents' business is allowed a deduction for the wages. The kiddie tax rules have no effect on earned income, even if it is earned from the parents' business.

[32] § 1(g)(2).

If the amount of net unearned income (regardless of source) is positive, an amount of taxable income up to the net unearned income is taxed at the parents' marginal tax rate. The child's remaining taxable income is taxed at the child's rate. If net unearned income is not a positive amount, the child's tax is computed using the appropriate tax rate schedule (likely single). All amounts above are adjusted yearly for inflation.

Election to Report Certain Unearned Income on Parents' Return

If a child who is subject to the kiddie tax is required to file a tax return and meets all of the following requirements, the parents may elect instead to report on their own tax return the child's unearned income that exceeds $2,300.

- Gross income is from interest and dividends only.
- Gross income is more than $1,150 but less than $11,500 ($1,100 and $11,000 in 2021, respectively).
- No estimated tax has been paid in the name and Social Security number of the child, and the child is not subject to backup withholding.

The parent(s) must also pay an additional tax to cover the tax on the child's income that is not taxed at the parents' rate, equal to the smaller of $110 or 10 percent of the child's gross income over $1,150. Again, these amounts are all for 2022 and adjusted annually for inflation.

If the parental election is made, the child is treated as having no gross income and is not required to file a tax return. In this case, Form 8814 (Parents' Election to Report Child's Interest and Dividends) must be filed as part of the parents' tax return.

Parents who have substantial itemized deductions based on AGI may find that making the parental election increases total taxes for the family unit. Taxes should be calculated both with and without the parental election to determine the appropriate choice.

Digging Deeper 10

An example of the calculation of the kiddie tax can be found on this book's companion website: www.cengage.com

9-5e Additional Taxes for Certain Individuals

An individual may owe income-based taxes in addition to the income tax. These other taxes include the following:

- Alternative minimum tax (see discussion in Chapter 17)
- Self-employment tax (see discussion in Chapter 11)
- Additional Medicare Tax and Net Investment Income Tax

The purpose of the Additional Medicare Tax and Net Investment Income Tax is to increase the preexisting Medicare tax and extend it to the unearned investment income of higher-income taxpayers. The Additional Medicare Tax is computed at a rate of 0.9 percent on wages and self-employment income in excess of threshold amounts. The threshold amount is $250,000 for married taxpayers ($125,000 if married filing separately) and $200,000 for all other taxpayers.[33] An employer must withhold the 0.9% tax on wages paid to any employee that exceed $200,000 for the year (regardless of

[33] § 3101(b)(2). The base amounts are not indexed for inflation.

the employee's filing status). Unlike the base Medicare tax, the Additional Medicare Tax is imposed only on the employee, not also the employer. The net result of the Additional Medicare Tax is to increase the marginal rate of the Medicare tax on the earned income of higher-income taxpayers to 3.8 percent (2.9 percent basic tax + 0.9 percent additional tax).

The Net Investment Income Tax (NIIT) extends the Medicare tax to the unearned investment income of higher-income taxpayers. The tax is imposed at a rate of 3.8 percent of the lesser of:

- Net investment income, or
- The excess of modified adjusted gross income (MAGI) over $250,000 for married taxpayers filing a joint return ($125,000 if married filing separately) and $200,000 for all other taxpayers.[34]

In general, "net investment income" includes interest, dividends, annuities, royalties, rents, income from passive activities, and net gains from the sale of investment property, reduced by deductions allowed in generating such income. For purposes of computing the NIIT, MAGI is defined as AGI increased by any foreign earned income exclusion (adjusted for related deductions). See Chapter 11 for discussion of the foreign earned income exclusion.

Rajiv is single and has the following income for 2022: wages of $220,000, interest income of $6,000, and capital gain of $28,000. Rajiv owes Additional Medicare Tax of $180 [0.9% × ($220,000 − $200,000)]. In addition, he owes NIIT of $1,292 computed as follows:

3.8% × the lesser of:

- Net investment income of $34,000 ($6,000 + $28,000), or
- Modified adjusted gross income of $254,000 ($220,000 + $6,000 + $28,000) over $200,000, or $54,000

Unlike many threshold amounts, the ones for the NIIT and the Additional Medicare Tax are not adjusted annually for inflation. These additional taxes must be paid during the year through income tax withholdings or estimated tax payments.

9-6 Tax Return Filing Procedures

9-6a Selecting the Proper Form

Because the 2022 tax forms had not been released when this text was published, the following comments apply to the 2021 forms.

Most taxpayers use the basic Form 1040 to report their taxable income and tax liability. Then depending on their various activities (e.g., business, investment, personal), supplemental schedules may be required.

[34] § 1411(b). The base amounts are not indexed for inflation.

If the taxpayer:	**File:**
Has additional income to report (e.g., unemployment compensation, prize or award money, or gambling winnings). *OR* Has any deductions *for* AGI to claim (e.g., student loan interest, self-employment tax, individual retirement account contributions, or educator expenses).	Schedule 1 (Form 1040)
Owes the alternative minimum tax or needs to make an excess advance premium tax credit repayment. *OR* Owes other taxes (e.g., the self-employment tax, household employment taxes, or additional taxes on IRAs or other qualified retirement plans and tax-favored accounts).	Schedule 2 (Form 1040)
Can claim a nonrefundable credit other than the child tax credit or the dependent credit (e.g., the foreign tax credit, education credits, or general business credit). *OR* Can claim a refundable credit other than the earned income credit, American Opportunity credit, or additional child tax credit (e.g., the net premium tax credit or health coverage credit). *OR* Has other payments to report (e.g., an amount paid with an extension to file or excess Social Security tax withheld).	Schedule 3 (Form 1040)

Other forms and schedules may be needed to supplement Form 1040 and Schedules 1 through 3. For example, a self-employed taxpayer will need to complete Schedule C (Form 1040) as a supplement to Schedule 1, while also computing their self-employment tax liability by completing Schedule SE (Form 1040), as a supplement to Schedule 2.

Taxpayers who are over the age of 65 by the end of the tax year may file Form 1040–SR rather than Form 1040, although the forms are mostly identical.

9-6b **The E-File Approach**

The **e-file** program is used by the vast majority of individual taxpayers (and is mandatory for most tax return preparers). The required tax information is transmitted to the IRS electronically either directly from the taxpayer (i.e., an "e-file online return") or indirectly through an "Authorized *e-file* Provider." These providers are tax professionals who have been accepted into the electronic filing program by the IRS. Providers often are the preparers of the return as well.

Taxpayers also can use IRS Free File (with online fillable forms) or use commercial software to file a tax return at no cost. A number of software providers offer free e-filing services. These services are generally available only to taxpayers who have AGI of $73,000 or less. Eligibility requirements and a list of the software providers are available on the IRS website: **irs.gov/filing/e-file-options**.

All taxpayers and tax return preparers must attest to the returns they file. For most taxpayers, this is done through an electronic return signature using a personal identification number (a Self-Select PIN). Or the taxpayer can authorize a tax preparer to

Tax Fact What Mode of Tax Filing Is Right for You?

Based on recent statistics, e-filing has become the primary mode of filing tax returns. Of the approximately 151 million individual tax returns filed during the 2021 filing season, 90 percent were filed electronically.

Source: **efile.com/efile-tax-return-direct-deposit-statistics/**

generate a PIN by signing Form 8879 (IRS *e-file* Signature Authorization). If certain paper documents must be submitted, a one-page form must be completed and filed when the return is e-filed. Form 8453 (U.S. Individual Income Tax Transmittal for an IRS e-file Return) is used to submit required attachments for both self- and practitioner-prepared electronic returns.

The e-file approach has two major advantages over paper filing. First, it eliminates many reporting errors. Second, it reduces the time required for processing a refund.

9-6c When and Where to File

Tax returns of individuals are due on or before the fifteenth day of the fourth month following the close of the tax year. For the calendar year taxpayer, the usual filing date is on or before April 15 of the following year.[35] When the due date falls on a Saturday, Sunday, or legal holiday, the filing deadline is the next business day.

If a taxpayer is unable to file the return by the specified due date, a six-month extension of time can be obtained by filing Form 4868 (Application for Automatic Extension of Time to File U.S. Individual Income Tax Return).[36]

Although obtaining an extension excuses a taxpayer from a penalty for failure to file, it does not insulate against the penalty for failure to pay. If more tax is owed, the filing of Form 4868 should be accompanied by an additional payment to cover the balance due. The return should be sent or delivered to the IRS Regional Service Center listed in the instructions for each type of return or contained in software applications.[37]

9-6d Modes of Payment

Payments of taxes due can be made by check, money order, IRS Direct Pay (electronic funds withdrawal from a bank account), the Electronic Federal Tax Payment System (EFTPS), and a number of major credit cards. The use of a credit or debit card results in a charge to the taxpayer.

[35] § 6072(a).

[36] Reg. § 1.6081–4. See also IRS Publication 17 (*Your Federal Income Tax*).

[37] The appropriate Regional Service Center address can be found at **irs.gov/filing/where-to-file-paper-tax-returns-with-or-without-a-payment**.

Refocus on The Big Picture

A Divided Household

ATNOYDUR/ISTOCK/GETTY IMAGES

Of major concern to Polly is her filing status. If she qualifies as an abandoned spouse, she is entitled to file as head of household. If not, she is considered to be a married person filing separately. Moreover, to be an abandoned spouse, Polly must be able to consider Paige as a dependent. To be a dependent, Paige must meet the requirements of a qualifying child or a qualifying relative.

For qualifying child purposes, Paige must meet the age test (i.e., either under 19 or under 24 and a full-time student). (A disabled child exception seems highly unlikely.) Because Paige currently is not a full-time student, is she under age 19? If so, she is a qualifying child (see Example 12). If Paige is not a qualifying child, is she a qualifying relative? Here, the answer depends on meeting the gross income test (see Example 18). How much did Paige earn from her part-time job? If her earnings are under $4,400, she satisfies the gross income test. Thus, if Paige can be claimed as a dependent under either the qualifying child or the qualifying relative category, Polly is an abandoned spouse entitled to head-of-household filing status (see Example 32). If not, she is a married person filing separately.

Maude will be considered to be Polly's dependent because she is a member of the household. It does not matter that she died in February. Because Maude is her dependent, Polly can claim the medical expenses she paid on Maude's behalf. The funeral expenses, however, are not deductible (see Example 15).

Does Maude qualify Polly for head-of-household filing status? No—although she is a dependent, Maude does not meet the relationship test (see Example 31).

What If?

Assume that Nick left for parts unknown in August (not March). Now Polly cannot qualify as an abandoned spouse. Her spouse lived in the home during part of the last six months of the year. Consequently, Polly is treated as married and cannot qualify for head-of-household filing status. She must file as a married person filing separately.

Suggested Readings

David R. Baldwin, Robert Caplan, Mary Kay Foss, Shannon Hudson, David H. Kirk, Frank Lin, Dana McCartney, and Darren Neuschwander, "Developments in Individual Taxation," *The Tax Adviser*, March 2021.

Andrew Lafond and Bruce A. Leauby, "Help Wanted: Hire Your Kids for Tax Savings," *Practical Tax Strategies*, October 2013.

Michaele L. Morrow, Mitchell Franklin, and Timothy A. Gagnon "Tax Considerations for Marriage: I do…or do not," 149 Tax Notes 1059 (2015).

Key Terms

Dependency exemptions, 9-10
E-file, 9-28
Filing status, 9-17
Head of household, 9-19
Itemized deductions, 9-5
Kiddie tax, 9-25
Marriage penalty, 9-19
Multiple support agreement, 9-14
Personal exemptions, 9-10
Qualifying child, 9-10
Qualifying relative, 9-12
Standard deduction, 9-6
Surviving spouse, 9-19
Tax Rate Schedules, 9-22
Tax Table, 9-23
Unearned income, 9-25

Computational Exercises

1. **LO.2** Brett and Abby are dependents of their parents, and each has income of $2,100 for the year. Brett's standard deduction for the year is $1,150, while Abby's is $2,500. Because their income is the same, what causes the difference in the amount of the standard deduction? Issue ID

2. **LO.2** Compute the 2022 standard deduction for the following taxpayers.
   a. Ellie is 15 and claimed as a dependent by her parents. She has $800 in dividend income and $1,400 in wages from a part-time job.
   b. Ruby and Woody are married and file a joint tax return. Ruby is age 66, and Woody is 69. Their taxable retirement income is $10,000.
   c. Shonda is age 68 and single. She is claimed by her daughter as a dependent. Her earned income is $500, and her interest income is $125.
   d. Frazier, age 55, is married but is filing a separate return. His wife itemizes her deductions.

3. **LO.4** Paul and Sonja, who are married, had itemized deductions of $13,200 and $400, respectively, during 2022. Paul suggests that they file separately—he will itemize his deductions *from* AGI, and she will claim the standard deduction. Issue ID
   a. Evaluate Paul's suggestion.
   b. What should they do?

4. **LO.5** Compute the 2022 tax liability and the marginal and average tax rates for the following taxpayers (use the 2022 Tax Rate Schedules in Appendix A for this purpose).
   a. Chandler, who files as a single taxpayer, has taxable income of $94,800.
   b. Lazare, who files as a head of household, has taxable income of $57,050.

5. **LO.5** George and Aimee are married. George has wage income of $190,000, and Aimee has a sole proprietorship that generated net income of $85,000. They also have interest and dividend income of $21,000. Compute any NIIT and Additional Medicare Tax they owe for the current year.

6. **LO.6** In 2022, Jack, age 12, has interest income of $4,900 from funds he inherited from his aunt and no earned income. He has no investment expenses. Christian and Danielle (his parents) have taxable income of $82,250 and file a joint return. Assume that no parental election is made. Determine Jack's net unearned income and total tax liability. Digging Deeper

Problems

7. **LO.1** Which of the following items are *inclusions* in gross income?
   a. During the year, stock that the taxpayer purchased as an investment doubled in value.
   b. Amount an off-duty motorcycle police officer received for escorting a funeral procession.
   c. While his mother was in the hospital, the taxpayer sold her jewelry to help pay for the hospital bills.
   d. Child support payments received.
   e. A damage deposit the taxpayer recovered when he vacated the apartment he had rented.
   f. Interest received by the taxpayer on an investment in general purpose bonds issued by IBM.

g. Amounts received by the taxpayer, a baseball "Hall of Famer," for autographing sports equipment (e.g., balls and gloves).

h. Tips received by a bartender from patrons. (Taxpayer is paid a regular salary by the cocktail lounge that employs him.)

i. Taxpayer sells his Super Bowl tickets for three times what he paid for them.

j. Taxpayer receives a new BMW from his grandmother when he passes the CPA exam.

8. **LO.1** Which of the following items are *exclusions* from gross income?

a. Alimony payments received from a 2016 divorce settlement.

b. Damages award received by the taxpayer for personal physical injury—none were for punitive damages.

c. A new golf cart won in a church raffle.

d. Amount collected on a loan previously made to a college friend.

e. Insurance proceeds paid to the taxpayer on the death of her uncle—she was the designated beneficiary under the policy.

f. Interest income on City of Chicago bonds.

g. Jury duty fees.

h. Stolen funds the taxpayer had collected for a local food bank drive.

i. Reward paid by the IRS for information provided that led to the conviction of the taxpayer's former employer for tax evasion.

j. An envelope containing $8,000 found (and unclaimed) by the taxpayer in a bus station.

9. **LO.1, 2, 3, 4** Compute the taxable income for 2022 in each of the following independent situations.

a. Drew and Meg, ages 40 and 41, respectively, are married and file a joint return. In addition to four dependent children, they have AGI of $125,000 and itemized deductions of $27,000.

b. Sybil, age 40, is single and supports her dependent parents, who live with her, as well as her grandfather, who is in a nursing home. She has AGI of $80,000 and itemized deductions of $8,000.

c. Scott, age 49, is a surviving spouse. His household includes two unmarried stepsons who qualify as his dependents. He has AGI of $75,000 and itemized deductions of $10,100.

d. Amelia, age 33, is an abandoned spouse who maintains a household for her three dependent children. She has AGI of $58,000 and itemized deductions of $10,650.

e. Chang, age 42, is divorced but maintains the home in which he and his daughter, Jill, live. Jill is single and qualifies as Chang's dependent. Chang has AGI of $64,000 and itemized deductions of $9,900.

10. **LO.1, 2, 3** Compute the taxable income for 2022 for Emily on the basis of the following information. Her filing status is single.

Salary	$85,000
Interest income from bonds issued by Xerox	1,100
Alimony payments received (divorce occurred in 2014)	6,000
Contribution to traditional IRA	6,000
Gift from parents	25,000
Short-term capital gain from stock investment	2,500
Amount lost in football office pool	500
Age	40

11. **LO.1, 2, 3** Compute the taxable income for 2022 for Aiden on the basis of the following information. Aiden is married but has not seen or heard from his spouse since 2020.

Salary	$80,000
Interest on bonds issued by the City of Boston	3,000
Interest on CD issued by Wells Fargo Bank	2,000
Cash dividend received on Chevron common stock	2,200
Life insurance proceeds paid on death of aunt (Aiden was the designated beneficiary of the policy)	200,000
Inheritance received on death of aunt	100,000
Jackson (a cousin) repaid a loan Aiden made to him in 2016 (no interest was provided for)	5,000
Itemized deductions (state income tax, property taxes on residence, interest on home mortgage, and charitable contributions)	9,700
Number of dependents (children, ages 17 and 18, and mother-in-law, age 70)	3
Age	43

12. **LO.2** In choosing between the standard deduction and itemizing deductions *from* AGI, what effect, if any, does each of the following have? Issue ID
    a. The age of the taxpayer(s).
    b. The health (i.e., physical condition) of the taxpayer.
    c. Whether taxpayers rent or own their residence.
    d. Taxpayer's filing status (e.g., single, married, filing jointly).
    e. Whether married taxpayers decide to file separate returns.
    f. The taxpayer's uninsured personal residence was recently destroyed by a wildfire (the region was declared a disaster area by the Federal government).
    g. The number of dependents supported by the taxpayer.

13. **LO.2, 3, 4** In 2022, David is age 78, is a widower, and is a dependent of his son. How does this situation affect the following?
    a. David's own individual filing requirement.
    b. The standard deduction allowed to David.
    c. The availability of any additional standard deduction.

14. **LO.2** Determine the amount of the standard deduction allowed for 2022 in the following independent situations. In each case, assume that the taxpayer is the dependent of another taxpayer.
    a. Curtis, age 18, has income as follows: $700 interest from a certificate of deposit and $12,800 from repairing cars.
    b. Mattie, age 18, has income as follows: $600 cash dividends from investing in stock and $4,700 from lifeguarding at a local pool.
    c. Jason, age 16, has income as follows: $675 interest on a bank savings account and $800 for painting a neighbor's fence.
    d. Ayla, age 15, has income as follows: $400 cash dividends from a stock investment and $500 from grooming pets.
    e. Sarah, age 67 and a widow, has income as follows: $500 from a bank savings account and $3,200 from babysitting.

15. **LO.3** Analyze each of the characteristics in considering the indicated test for dependency as a qualifying child or qualifying relative. In the last two columns, after each listed test (e.g., gross income), state whether the particular test is Met, Not Met, or Not Applicable (NA).

Characteristic	Qualifying Child Test	Qualifying Relative Test
a. Taxpayer's son has gross income of $7,000	Gross income	Gross income
b. Taxpayer's niece has gross income of $3,000	Gross income	Gross income
c. Taxpayer's uncle lives with him	Relationship	Relationship
d. Taxpayer's daughter is 25 and disabled	Age	Age
e. Taxpayer's daughter is age 18, has gross income of $8,000, and does not live with him	Residence, Gross income	Gross income
f. Taxpayer's cousin does not live with her	Relationship, Residence	Relationship
g. Taxpayer's brother does not live with her	Residence	Relationship
h. Taxpayer's sister has dropped out of school, is age 17, and lives with him	Relationship, Residence, Age	Relationship
i. Taxpayer's older nephew is age 23 and a full-time student	Relationship, Age	Relationship
j. Taxpayer's grandson lives with her and has gross income of $7,000	Relationship, Residence	Relationship, Gross income

16. **LO.3** Caden and Lily are divorced on March 3, 2021. For financial reasons, however, Lily continues to live in Caden's apartment and receives her support from him. Caden does not claim Lily as a dependent on his 2021 Federal income tax return but does so on his 2022 return. Explain.

17. **LO.3** For tax year 2022, determine the number of dependents in each of the following independent situations.

    a. Ben and Molly (ages 48 and 46, respectively) are married and furnish more than 50% of the support of their two children, Libby (age 18) and Sam (age 24). During the year, Libby earns $4,500 providing transportation for elderly persons with disabilities, and Sam receives a $5,000 scholarship that is used entirely for tuition at the law school he attends.

    b. Audry (age 45) was divorced this year. She maintains a household in which she, her ex-husband (Clint), and his mother (Olive) live and furnishes more than 50% of their support. Olive is age 91 and blind.

18. **LO.3** Wesley and Camilla (ages 90 and 88, respectively) live in an assisted care facility and for 2021 and 2022 received their support from the following sources:

	Percentage of Support
Social Security benefits	16%
Son	20
Niece	29
Cousin	12
Brother	11
Family friend (not related)	12

    a. Which persons are eligible to treat Wesley and Camilla as dependents under a multiple support agreement?

    b. Must Wesley and Camilla be claimed by the same person(s) for both 2021 and 2022? Explain.

    c. Who, if anyone, can claim their medical expenses?

19. **LO.2, 3, 4, 5** Taylor, age 18, is a dependent of her parents. For 2022, she has the following income: $6,250 of wages from a summer job, $800 of interest from a money market account, and $300 of interest from City of Chicago bonds. Digging Deeper

a. What is Taylor's taxable income for 2022?

b. What is Taylor's tax for 2022? [Her parents file a joint return and have taxable income of $135,000 (no dividends or capital gains).]

20. **LO.1, 3, 5** Charlotte (age 40) is a surviving spouse and provides all of the support of her four minor children who live with her (all are under age 16). She also maintains the household in which her parents live and furnished 60% of their support. Besides interest on City of Miami bonds in the amount of $5,500, Charlotte's father received $2,400 from a part-time job. Charlotte has a salary of $80,000, a short-term capital loss of $2,000, a cash prize of $4,000 from a church raffle, and itemized deductions of $10,500. Using the Tax Rate Schedules, compute Charlotte's 2022 tax liability. Ignore any credits for which she may qualify.

21. **LO.1, 2, 3, 4, 5** Morgan (age 45) is single and provides more than 50% of the support of Tammy (a family friend), Jen (a niece, age 18), and Jerold (a nephew, age 18). Both Tammy and Jen live with Morgan, but Jerold (a French citizen) lives in Canada. Morgan earns a salary of $95,000, contributes $5,000 to a traditional IRA, and receives sales proceeds of $15,000 for an RV that cost $60,000 and was used for vacations. She has $8,200 in itemized deductions. Using the Tax Rate Schedules, compute Morgan's 2022 tax liability. Ignore any credits for which she may qualify.

22. **LO.4** Bob and Carol have been in and out of marital counseling for the past few years. Early in 2022, they decide to separate. However, because they are barely able to get by on their current incomes, they cannot afford separate housing or the legal costs of a divorce. So Bob moves out of their house in March and takes up residence in their detached garage (which has an enclosed workshop and bathroom). Carol stays in the house with their two children and pays more than half of the costs of maintaining their residence. Bob does not enter the house for the remainder of the year. Can Carol qualify as an abandoned spouse? Explain. Ethics and Equity

23. **LO.4** Which of the following individuals are required to file a tax return for 2022? Should any of these individuals file a return even if filing is not required? Why or why not?

a. Patricia, age 19, is a self-employed single individual with gross income of $5,200 from an unincorporated business. Business expenses amounted to $4,900.

b. Mike is single and is 67 years old. His gross income from wages was $12,750.

c. Ronald is a dependent child under age 19 who received $6,800 in wages from a part-time job.

d. Sam is married and files a joint return with his spouse, Lana. Both Sam and Lana are 67 years old. Their combined gross income was $24,250.

e. Quinn, age 20, is a full-time college student who is claimed as a dependent by his parents. For 2022, Quinn has taxable interest and dividends of $2,500.

24. **LO.4, 5** Sarah and Brandi are engaged and plan to get married. During 2022, Sarah is a full-time student and earns $9,000 from a part-time job. With this income, student loans, savings, and nontaxable scholarships, she is self-supporting. For the year, Brandi is employed and has wages of $61,000. How much income tax, if any, can Brandi save if she and Sarah marry in 2022 and file a joint return? Decision Making

25. **LO.5** Jayden calculates his 2022 income tax by using both the Tax Tables and the Tax Rate Schedules. Because the Tax Rate Schedules yield a slightly lower tax liability, he plans to pay this amount.

a. Why is there a difference?

b. Is Jayden's approach permissible? Why or why not?

Digging Deeper

26. **LO.1, 6** Paige, age 17, is a dependent of her parents in 2022. During 2022, Paige earned $3,900 pet sitting and $4,300 in interest on a savings account. Her parents report taxable income of $120,000 on their joint return (no qualified dividends or capital gains). What are Paige's taxable income and tax liability for 2022?

Digging Deeper

27. **LO.1, 6** Terri, age 16, is a dependent of her parents in 2022. During the year, Terri earned $5,000 in interest income and $3,000 from part-time jobs.
    a. What is Terri's taxable income?
    b. How much of Terri's income is taxed at her rate? At her parent's rate?
    c. Can the parental election be made? Why or why not?

Tax Return Problems

Tax Forms Problem

ProConnect™ Tax

1. Lance H. and Wanda B. Dean are married and live at 431 Yucca Drive, Santa Fe, NM 87501. Lance works for the convention bureau of the local Chamber of Commerce, while Wanda is employed part-time as a paralegal for a law firm.

   During 2021, the Deans had the following receipts:

Salaries ($60,000 for Lance, $42,000 for Wanda)		$102,000
Interest income—		
City of Albuquerque general purpose bonds	$1,000	
Ford Motor Company bonds	1,100	
Ally Bank certificate of deposit	400	2,500
Child support payments from John Allen		7,200
Annual gifts from parents		26,000
Settlement from Roadrunner Touring Company		90,000
Lottery winnings		600
Federal income tax refund (for tax year 2020)		400

   Wanda was previously married to John Allen. When they divorced several years ago, Wanda was awarded custody of their two children, Penny and Kyle. (Note: Wanda has never issued a Form 8332 waiver.) Under the divorce decree, John was obligated to pay alimony and child support—the alimony payments were to terminate if Wanda remarried.

   In July, while going to lunch in downtown Santa Fe, Wanda was injured by a tour bus. As the driver was clearly at fault, the owner of the bus, Roadrunner Touring Company, paid her medical expenses (including a one-week stay in a hospital). To avoid a lawsuit, Roadrunner also transferred $90,000 to her in settlement of the personal injuries she sustained.

   The Deans had the following expenditures for 2021:

Medical expenses (not covered by insurance)		$7,200
Taxes—		
Property taxes on personal residence	$3,600	
State of New Mexico income tax (includes amount withheld from wages during 2021)	4,200	7,800
Interest on home mortgage (First National Bank)		6,000
Charitable contributions (cash)		3,600
Life insurance premiums (policy on Lance's life)		1,200
Contribution to traditional IRA (on Wanda's behalf)		6,000
Traffic fines		300
Contribution to the reelection campaign fund of the mayor of Santa Fe		500
Funeral expenses for Wayne Boyle		6,300

The life insurance policy was taken out by Lance several years ago and designates Wanda as the beneficiary. As a part-time employee, Wanda is excluded from coverage under her employer's pension plan. Consequently, she provides for her own retirement with a traditional IRA obtained at a local trust company. Because the mayor is a member of the local Chamber of Commerce, Lance felt compelled to make the political contribution.

The Deans' household includes the following, for whom they provide more than half of the support:

	Social Security Number*	Birth Date
Lance Dean (age 42)	123-45-6786	12/16/1979
Wanda Dean (age 40)	123-45-6787	08/08/1981
Penny Allen (age 19)	123-45-6788	10/09/2002
Kyle Allen (age 16)	123-45-6789	05/03/2005
Wayne Boyle (age 75)	123-45-6785	06/15/1946

*In the interest of privacy and to protect against taxpayer identification misuse, Social Security numbers used throughout the textbook have been replaced with fictitious numbers.

Penny graduated from high school on May 9, 2021, and is undecided about college. During 2021, she earned $8,500 (placed in a savings account) playing a harp in the lobby of a local hotel. Wayne is Wanda's widower father, who died on January 20, 2021. For the past few years, Wayne qualified as a dependent of the Deans.

Federal income tax withheld is $3,900 (Lance) and $1,800 (Wanda). The proper amount of Social Security and Medicare tax was withheld. The Deans received the appropriate coronavirus recovery rebates (economic impact payments); related questions in ProConnect Tax should be ignored.

Determine the Federal income tax for 2021 for the Deans on a joint return by completing the appropriate forms. They do not own and did not use any virtual currency during the year, and they do not want to contribute to the Presidential Election Campaign Fund. If an overpayment results, it is to be refunded to them. Suggested software: ProConnect Tax. Note: For 2021, non-itemizers may deduct up to $300 of cash charitable contributions (see text Section 10-4d).

Communications
Decision Making
Planning
Tax Forms Problem

ProConnect™ Tax

2. Logan B. Taylor is a widower whose wife, Sara, died on June 6, 2019. He lives at 4680 Dogwood Lane, Springfield, MO 65801. He is employed as a paralegal by a local law firm. During 2021, he had the following receipts:

Salary		$ 80,000
Interest income—		
Money market account at Omni Bank	$ 300	
Savings account at Boone State Bank	1,100	
City of Springfield general purpose bonds	3,000	4,400
Inheritance from Daniel		60,000
Life insurance proceeds		200,000
Amount from sale of St. Louis lot		80,000
Proceeds from estate sale		9,000
Federal income tax refund (for 2020 tax overpayment)		700

Logan inherited securities worth $60,000 from his uncle, Daniel, who died in 2021. Logan also was the designated beneficiary of an insurance policy on Daniel's life with a maturity value of $200,000. The lot in St. Louis was purchased on May 2, 2016, for $85,000 and held as an investment. As the neighborhood has deteriorated, Logan decided to cut his losses and sold the lot on January 5, 2021, for $80,000. The estate sale consisted largely of items belonging to Sara and Daniel (e.g., camper, boat, furniture, and fishing and hunting equipment). Logan estimates that the property sold originally cost at least twice the $9,000 he received and has declined or stayed the same in value since Sara and Daniel died.

Logan's expenditures for 2021 include the following:

Medical expenses (including $10,500 for dental)		$13,500
Taxes—		
State of Missouri income tax (includes withholdings during 2021)	$4,200	
Property taxes on personal residence	4,500	8,700
Interest on home mortgage		5,600
Contribution to church (paid pledges for 2021 and 2022)		4,800

Although Logan and his dependents are covered by his employer's health insurance policy, he is subject to a deductible and dental care is not included. The $10,500 dental charge was for Helen's implants. Helen is Logan's widowed mother, who lives with him (see below). Logan normally pledges $2,400 ($200 per month) each year to his church. On December 5, 2021, on the advice of his pastor, he prepaid his pledge for 2022.

Logan's household, all of whom he supports, includes the following:

	Social Security Number	**Birth Date**
Logan Taylor (age 48)	123-45-6787	08/30/1973
Helen Taylor (age 70)	123-45-6780	01/13/1951
Asher Taylor (age 23)	123-45-6783	02/18/1998
Mia Taylor (age 22)	123-45-6784	07/16/1999

Helen receives a modest Social Security benefit. Asher, a son, is a full-time student in dental school and earns $4,500 as a part-time dental assistant. Mia, a daughter, does not work and is engaged to be married.

Part 1—Tax Computation

Using the appropriate forms and schedules, compute Logan's income tax for 2021. Federal income tax of $4,200 was withheld from his wages. If Logan has any overpayment on his income tax, he wants the refund sent to him. Assume that the proper amounts of Social Security and Medicare taxes were withheld. Logan received the appropriate coronavirus recovery rebates (economic impact payments); related questions in ProConnect Tax should be ignored. Logan does not own and did not use any virtual currency during the year, and he does not want to contribute to the Presidential Election Campaign Fund. Suggested software: ProConnect Tax.

Part 2—Follow-Up Advice

In early 2022, the following take place:

- Helen decides that she wants to live with one of her daughters and moves to Arizona.
- Asher graduates from dental school and joins an existing practice in St. Louis.
- Mia marries, and she and her spouse move in with his parents.
- Using the insurance proceeds he received on Daniel's death, Logan pays off the mortgage on his personal residence.

Logan believes that these events may have an effect on his tax position for 2022. Therefore, he requests your advice.

Write a letter to Logan explaining in general terms the changes that will occur for tax purposes. Assume that Logan's salary and other factors not mentioned (e.g., property and state income taxes) will remain the same.

Research Problems

Note: Solutions to the Research Problems can be prepared by using the Thomson Reuters Checkpoint™ online tax research database, which accompanies this textbook. Solutions can also be prepared by using research materials found in a typical tax library.

Communications

Research Problem 1. Kathy and Brett Ouray married in 2004. They began to experience marital difficulties in 2018 and, in the current year, although they are not legally separated, consider themselves completely estranged. They have contemplated getting a divorce. However, because of financial concerns and because they both want to remain involved in the lives of their three sons, they have not yet filed for divorce. In addition, their financial difficulties have meant that Kathy and Brett cannot afford to live in separate residences. So although they consider themselves emotionally estranged, they and their three sons all reside in a single-family home in Chicago, Illinois.

Although Brett earns significantly more than Kathy, both contribute financially to maintaining their home and supporting their teenage sons. In one of their few and brief conversations this year, they determined that Brett had contributed far more than Kathy to the maintenance of their home and the support of their sons. Thus, Brett has decided that for the current tax year, they will file separate Federal income tax returns and that he will use the head-of-household filing status. While they live under the same roof, Brett believes that he and Kathy should maintain separate households. Given this fact and the fact that he provides significantly more for the support of his and Kathy's sons, he believes that he is eligible for head-of-household filing status. Advise Brett on which filing status is most appropriate for him in the current year. His address is 16 Lahinch, Chicago, IL 60608.

Use internet tax resources to address the following questions. Look for reliable websites and blogs of the IRS and other government agencies, media outlets, businesses, tax professionals, academics, think tanks, and political outlets.

Research Problem 2. Locate IRS Form 2120 (at **irs.gov**), and answer the following questions.

a. Who must sign the form?
b. Who must file the form?
c. Can it be used for someone who is not related to the taxpayer? Explain.

Research Problem 3. What purpose is served by Form 8857? Read the directions to the form, and see IRS Publication 971 for additional information.

Research Problem 4. A nonresident alien earns money in the United States that is subject to Federal income tax. What guidance does the IRS provide about what tax form needs to be used and when it should be filed? In terms of the proper filing date, does it matter whether the earnings were subject to income tax withholding? Explain.

Communications
Data Analytics

Research Problem 5. How do U.S. individuals generate their income? Does it vary by size of income (AGI)? Go to the IRS tax statistics website (**irs.gov/statistics**), and look for recent information on "sources of income" using the Individual Statistical Tables by Size of Adjusted Gross Income. Compare the following types of income by size of AGI: (1) wages, (2) capital gain distributions, (3) sales of capital assets, and (4) sales of property other than capital assets. Cluster the data into no more than six AGI categories. Present your findings in a visual (e.g., bar chart), and summarize your findings in a one-page memo to your instructor.

Becker CPA Review Questions

Becker

1. Bob provides more than half of his mother's support. His mother earns $6,000 per year as a hairdresser. She lives in an apartment across town. Bob is unmarried and has no children. What is Bob's most advantageous filing status?
   a. Single
   b. Head of household
   c. Qualifying single
   d. Supporting single

2. Jane is 20 years old and is a sophomore at Lake University. She is a full-time student and does not have any gross income. Jane spends the holidays and summers at home with her parents. Her total support for the current tax year is $30,000, including a scholarship for $5,000 to cover her tuition. Jane used $12,000 of her savings, and her grandparents provided $13,000. Which of the following statements regarding the dependency rules for Jane is true?
   a. If Jane's parents (rather than her grandparents) provided the $13,000, then they would not be able to claim Jane as a dependent because Jane provided more than half of her own support.
   b. Jane's grandparents can claim her as a dependent because Jane did not provide more than half of her own support.
   c. Jane's grandparents cannot claim her as a dependent because Jane provided more than half of her own support.
   d. Jane does not qualify as a dependent for either her parents or grandparents.

3. In the current tax year, Blake Smith provided more than half of the support for his cousin, niece, and a close family friend. Blake lives alone and sends a monthly support check to each person. None of the individuals whom Blake supports has any income or files a tax return. All three individuals are U.S. citizens. Which of the three people Blake supports can he claim as a dependent on his tax return?
   a. Cousin
   b. Niece
   c. Family friend
   d. None

4. Jeff and Rhonda are married and have two children, Max and Jen. Max is 20, attends college in the Los Angeles area full-time, and works as a stunt double for a television show while he is in school. Max earns $15,000 per year as a stunt double and lives at home when school is not in session. Jeff and Rhonda pay for Max's tuition and all of his living expenses. Jen, who lives at home, is 18 years old and makes $18,000 per year working full-time as an office administrator. Jeff and Rhonda pay for 65 percent of Jen's living expenses. In addition, Rhonda's mother, Joanne (a widow), resides with the family, earns $3,000 per year in taxable interest and dividends from her investments, and receives $9,000 per year in nontaxable Social Security benefits. Jeff and Rhonda receive no rent from Joanne and provide all the support she needs for the year. Everyone mentioned is a U.S. citizen. How many people qualify as dependents for Jeff and Rhonda's income tax return?
   a. Two
   b. Three
   c. Four
   d. Five

5. Katherine and Bill Grant have two children. Kelly is 22 years old and is a full-time student. She lives on campus at an out-of-state university but will return home for the summer. Kelly earns $5,000 a year working part-time. Her parents provide her with $15,000 of support, and her grandparents provide her with $15,000 of support. Jake is 15 years old and lives at home. He is fully supported by his parents. Jake's friend Luke also lives with the Grants. Luke is 15 years old and moved into the Grant home in April. The Grants pay all of Luke's support. How many total dependents may Katherine and Bill Grant claim for the current year?
   a. One
   b. Three
   c. Two
   d. Zero

6. Bill and Anne Chambers are married and file a joint return. They have no children. Their college friend, Ryan, lived with them for the entire current tax year. Ryan is 40 years old and earned $2,000 at a part-time job and received $25,000 in municipal bond interest. Ryan is a citizen of the United States and is unmarried. Which of the following statements is true regarding claiming Ryan as a dependent on the Chambers' tax return?
   a. If Ryan earns $15,000 in self-employment income in addition to the part-time job and municipal bond interest, he will qualify as a dependent on the Chambers' tax return.
   b. Ryan qualifies as a dependent for the Chambers under the qualifying child rules.
   c. As long as Ryan does not provide more than half of his own support, he qualifies as a dependent for the Chambers under the qualifying relative rules because he lived with them for the entire year.
   d. As long as the Chambers provide more than half of Ryan's support, he qualifies as a dependent for the Chambers under the qualifying relative rules.

7. Susie, John, Luke, and Will provide support for their 80-year-old mother, Joyce. Joyce lives by herself in an apartment in Miami, Florida. Joyce earned $5,000 this year working at her church. Joyce provides 5% of her own support. Susie provides 30% of Joyce's support, John provides 10% of Joyce's support, Luke provides 15% of Joyce's support, and Will provides 40% of Joyce's support. Under a multiple support agreement, who may claim Joyce as a dependent?
   a. Susie, Luke, John, and Will
   b. Susie, Luke, and Will
   c. Susie and Will
   d. Will

8. Heather is single and has one son, Rhett, who is 19 years old. Rhett lived at home for four months of the current tax year before moving away to take a full-time job in another city. Heather provided more than half of Rhett's support for the taxable year. Rhett earned $20,000 in gross income and is unmarried. Which of the following statements regarding the dependency rules for Rhett is true?
   a. Heather may claim Rhett as a dependent because he is a qualifying child.
   b. Heather may claim Rhett as a dependent because he is a qualifying relative.
   c. Rhett fails the age limit test for a qualifying child.
   d. Rhett must live with Heather for the entire year to meet the qualifying relative test.

9. Jonathan Jones is a 19-year-old full-time college student at the local community college. He lives in an apartment near campus during the school year and returns home for the summer break and holidays. Jonathan earned $5,000 this year working at the campus bookstore. His parents gave him $20,000 and his grandparents gave him $10,000 this year in support. Which of the following statements is true?
   a. Jonathan does not qualify as a dependent for his parents because his gross income is too high.
   b. Jonathan does not meet the residency test for qualifying child.
   c. Jonathan's grandparents can claim him as a dependent.
   d. Jonathan's parents can claim him as a dependent.

Chapter

10 Individuals: Income, Deductions, and Credits

Learning Objectives: *After completing Chapter 10, you should be able to:*

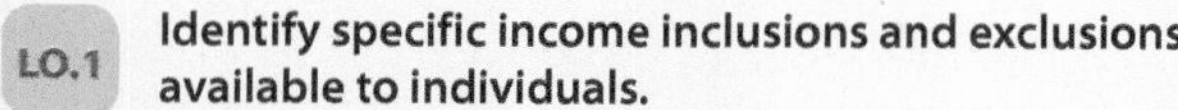

LO.1 Identify specific income inclusions and exclusions available to individuals.

LO.2 Determine an individual's allowable itemized deductions.

LO.3 Explain and illustrate the adoption expenses credit, child tax credit, education tax credits, credit for child and dependent care expenses, earned income credit, and premium tax credit.

Chapter Outline

Tax Talk *A tax loophole is something that benefits the other guy. If it benefits you, it is tax reform.* —Russell B. Long

The Big Picture

The Tax Implications of Life!

Danae and David Steele, ages 35 and 37, respectively, recently married and have come to you for tax advice. They have several questions about their tax situation. Both are employed, and they expect to have combined wages from all sources of $70,000 for the current year.

In the current year, Danae enrolled in the masters of accounting program at State University. She would like to become a CPA but will need to complete additional accounting coursework to achieve this goal. As a result of her previous accounting work experience and undergraduate business degree, Danae was appointed as a teaching assistant for an introductory accounting course. In addition to a $450 monthly salary, the position also provides for a waiver of $4,500 of her tuition for the semester. She also paid $250 of interest during the year on student loans still outstanding from her undergraduate education.

Danae and David received a wedding gift of $10,000 from her grandmother, and the couple earned $250 of interest on a savings account they opened with the money. David sold stock for $1,000 that was purchased two years ago for $5,000.

Early in the year, David was crossing a street in the pedestrian crosswalk when a delivery van struck him. David suffered a severe injury to his right arm that required him to miss work for a month. Shortly after the accident, given their medical expenses and the fact that David couldn't work for a month, a friend set up a GoFundMe page to raise money for the family. The initial request was for $8,000. Through the generosity of friends, family and strangers, their campaign raised $12,500. David and Danae used the money to pay medical expenses, their rent, and the remaining balance of Danae's tuition.

continued

As a result of the accident, David and Danae also initiated a lawsuit against the delivery company. After many meetings and much negotiation, the delivery company's insurance company settled the case in December. They paid the couple the following.

Compensatory damages:	
Medical expenses	$ 30,000
Injury to David's right arm	100,000
Pain and suffering	50,000
Loss of income	15,000
Legal fees	25,000
Punitive damages	160,000
	$380,000

This is David's second marriage, and he pays alimony to his ex-wife (they divorced in 2016). He has custody of his 15-year-old son, Stephen, who lives with him and Danae for nine months each year. The Steeles rent their home, paid $3,500 of state income taxes, paid a $412 motor vehicle registration tax on their personal car, incurred additional medical expenses of $20,000, and made $2,500 of charitable contributions.

Without calculating Danae and David's tax liability, what are the tax implications of the transactions noted above? Are there other tax deductions or credits for which they may qualify or other tax issues of which they should be made aware?

Read the chapter and formulate your response.

This chapter focuses on the computation of taxable income for individual taxpayers. Recall that taxable income is the base on which the tax liability is calculated. In the simplest of terms, taxable income is determined by calculating *gross income* and then reducing that amount by allowable *tax deductions*. Prior chapters discussed these terms in a general sense. This chapter explains rules that apply specifically to individual taxpayers with respect to both income and deduction amounts. In addition, the chapter discusses individual tax credits that may further reduce an individual's tax liability.

LO.1

Identify specific income inclusions and exclusions available to individuals.

10-1 Overview of Income Provisions Applicable to Individuals

The definition of gross income is broad enough to include almost all receipts of money, property, or services. However, the tax law provides for the exclusion of certain types of income.[1] The following income *inclusions* and *exclusions*, which apply to all taxpayers (including individuals), were discussed in Chapter 4:

- Interest from state and local bonds (exclusion).
- Life insurance paid on death of the insured (exclusion).
- Imputed interest on below-market loans (inclusion).
- Income from discharge of indebtedness (inclusion unless a specific exclusion applies).
- Income included per the tax benefit rule (inclusion).

Many *exclusions* available only to individuals are for *fringe benefits* received by *employees* (refer to Exhibit 9.1 in Chapter 9). Fringe benefits are discussed in Chapter 11. Additional inclusions and exclusions for individuals are discussed next.

[1]See §§ 101–140.

Bridge Discipline **Bridge to Economics and Finance**

As is the case for business entities, a primary financial goal for individual taxpayers is maximizing the *after-tax value* of their assets over time. This approach requires not only selecting the best investment alternatives but also choosing those investments with the most favorable tax attributes. Fundamental to this notion is recognizing the key role the government plays in all economic activity through its taxing authority. As a result, investors should consider economically sound strategies that minimize the extent to which the government can stake a claim to their success. For example, taxpayers can reduce the government's share of their wealth accumulations by deferring the payment of taxes until future years and by taking advantage of investment strategies for which tax incentives are available. Taxpayers should choose the investment alternatives that provide the best after-tax return over time and not necessarily those that lead to the least amount of taxation.

These points can be illustrated by examining two classic strategies. One of the best ways for individuals to maximize their personal wealth is to invest to the extent possible in qualified retirement savings programs [e.g., Individual Retirement Accounts, § 401(k) plans]. Contributions to such accounts provide a current tax deduction. In addition, earnings in the account are not subject to taxation until they are withdrawn, which, in most cases, is in retirement. Postponing the tax in these two ways reduces the present value of the tax cost, which increases the after-tax value of the investment. Another strategy involves investing in tax-free municipal bonds, which produce interest income that is free of Federal income tax. However, the return on a municipal bond should be compared with the after-tax returns on comparable taxable bonds. In other words, the taxpayer should evaluate how the implicit tax (in the form of a lower return) associated with a municipal bond compares with the explicit tax (in the form of taxable interest) associated with a taxable bond.

10-2 Specific Inclusions Applicable to Individuals

The general principles governing the determination of gross income have occasionally yielded results that Congress found unacceptable. Thus, Congress has provided more specific rules for determining the amount of gross income from certain sources. The following provisions applicable to individuals are discussed in this chapter:

- Alimony and separate maintenance payments.
- Prizes and awards.
- Unemployment compensation.
- Social Security benefits.

10-2a Alimony and Separate Maintenance Payments

When a married couple divorce or legally separate, state law generally requires a division of the property accumulated during the marriage. In addition, one spouse may have a legal obligation to support the other spouse. The Code distinguishes between the support payments (alimony or separate maintenance) and the property division in terms of the tax consequences of each. Further, if payments are made that are intended to provide for the support of a child, the tax law provides that these payments are distinguishable from both alimony and property settlements.

Alimony and separate maintenance payments made under a divorce agreement executed after 2018 are *neither* taxable to the recipient *nor* deductible by the payor.[2] However, payments made under an agreement entered into on or before December 31, 2018, are *includible* in the gross income of the party receiving the payments and *deductible* by the party making the payments. As a result, the Schedule 1 (Form 1040) requires a taxpayer to enter the date of the divorce where alimony payments are reported on the schedule.

[2] §§ 71 and 215.

Pete and Tina were divorced in 2018. Tina is required to pay Pete $15,000 of alimony each year. As a result per the tax law in effect at the time of their divorce, Pete must include the $15,000 in his gross income; Tina is allowed to deduct $15,000 from her gross income.

If their divorce had been finalized in 2019 (or later), Pete would not be required to include the alimony in his income and Tina would not be allowed a deduction for the alimony paid.

Property Settlements

A transfer of property other than cash to a former spouse under a divorce decree or agreement is not a taxable event. The transferor is not entitled to a deduction and does not recognize gain or loss on the transfer. The transferee does not recognize income and has a basis equal to the transferor's basis.[3]

Paul transfers stock to Rosa as part of a divorce settlement. The cost of the stock to Paul was $12,000, and the stock's fair market value at the time of the transfer is $15,000. Rosa later sells the stock for $16,000. Neither Paul nor Rosa recognizes any gain or income from the transfer of the stock to Rosa. Rosa has a realized and recognized gain of $4,000 ($16,000 − $12,000) when she sells the stock.

Requirements for Alimony

Because a payor may face a higher marginal tax rate than a recipient of alimony, couples divorcing before 2019 may have had an incentive to have payments treated as alimony rather than as part of a property settlement. To clarify the appropriate treatment of payments between former spouses subsequent to a divorce, Congress developed the following rules. Payments made under pre-2019 agreements are *classified as alimony* only if the following conditions are satisfied:

- The payments are in cash. (This distinguishes alimony from a property division.)
- The agreement or decree does not specify that the payments are not alimony. (This allows the parties to determine by agreement whether the payments will be alimony.)
- The payor and alimony recipient are not members of the same household at the time the payments are made. (This ensures the payments are for maintaining two households.)
- There is no liability to make the payments for any period after the death of the alimony recipient. (Payments due after death would be a property interest that could be transferred to heirs.)[4]

More information on payments related to divorce can be found on this book's companion website: www.cengage.com

Child Support

Taxpayers do *not* realize income from the receipt of child support payments made by their former spouse. This result occurs because the money is received subject to the duty to use the money for the child's benefit. The payor is not allowed to deduct the child support payments because the payments are made to satisfy the payor's legal obligation to support the child.

In many cases, it may be difficult to determine whether payments subject to pre-2019 agreements are intended to be alimony or child support. This issue is often resolved by applying the following rule: If the amount of the payments would be reduced upon the occurrence of a contingency related to a child (e.g., the child attains age 21 or dies), the amount of the future reduction in the payment is deemed child support. In addition,

[3] § 1041.

[4] See *Divorced or Separated Individuals* (IRS Publication 504) for additional information about the tax consequences of divorce.

to the extent a taxpayer's alimony and child support obligations are not met in full in a year, any payments received are categorized first as child support and then any excess is categorized as alimony. These rules are applied even though the divorce agreement specifies other amounts for the support of the child.[5]

Under a divorce agreement entered into in 2017, Grace is required to make monthly alimony payments of $500 to Matt. However, when Matt and Grace's child reaches age 21, marries, or dies (whichever occurs first), the payments will be reduced to $300 per month. Matt has custody of their child. Because the required payments will be reduced by $200 per month due to the relevant contingencies, $200 of the monthly payments will be considered child support for Federal tax purposes regardless of how they are labeled. Only $300 of the monthly payment will be considered alimony.

If Grace makes payments of only $350 per month, the first $200 is treated as child support with the remaining $150 considered alimony.

10-2b **Prizes and Awards**

The fair market value of prizes and awards (other than scholarships) must be included in gross income.[6] Therefore, lottery winnings, door prizes, and performance awards from an employer to an employee are fully taxable to the recipient.

One exception permits a prize or an award to be excluded from gross income if *all* of the following requirements are satisfied:

- The prize or award is received in recognition of religious, charitable, scientific, educational, artistic, literary, or civic achievement (e.g., Nobel Prize, Pulitzer Prize, or faculty teaching award).
- The recipient was selected without taking any action to enter the contest or proceeding.
- The recipient is not required to render substantial future services as a condition for receiving the prize or award.
- The recipient transfers the prize or award to a qualified governmental unit or nonprofit organization.[7]

Another exception allows the exclusion of certain employee achievement awards in the form of tangible personal property (e.g., a smart watch) but not cash or cash equivalents (e.g., gift certificates, meals, lodging, or tickets to theatre or sporting events). To qualify for the exclusion, the awards must be made in recognition of length of service or safety achievement. Generally, the ceiling on the excludible amount for an employee is $400 per taxable year. However, if the award is made as a part of a tax-qualified plan, the ceiling on the exclusion is $1,600 per taxable year.[8]

Olympic and Paralympic Game athletes are allowed to exclude the value of any medal and cash award received if the medal winner's income is $1 million or less. The rationale offered for this exclusion is that the athletes "perform a valuable patriotic service."[9]

A taxpayer can also avoid including prizes and awards in gross income by refusing to accept the prize or award.[10]

More about the taxation of prizes can be found on this book's companion website: www.cengage.com

2 Digging Deeper

10-2c **Unemployment Compensation**

The unemployment compensation program is sponsored and operated by the Federal and state governments to provide a source of income for people who have been employed and are temporarily out of work. Prior to 1986, the IRS exempted unemployment

[5]§§ 71(c)(2) and (c)(3) and *Allen H. Johnson*, 107 TCM 1358, T.C.Memo. 2014–67.

[6]§ 74.

[7]§ 74(b).

[8]§ 74(c). Qualified plan awards are defined in § 274(j) and explained in *Business Expenses*, Chapter 2 (IRS Publication 535).

[9]P.L. 114–239 (10/7/16), adding § 74(d) effective for awards received after 2015. Also see H.R. Rep. No. 114–762 (9/20/16).

[10]See Rev.Rul. 57–374 and Rev.Proc. 87–54.

benefits from tax. These payments were considered social benefit programs for the promotion of the general welfare. In 1986, in order to reduce the unemployment compensation recipient's potential disincentive to work, Congress amended the Code to make these benefits taxable.[11]

10-2d Social Security Benefits

The amount of Social Security benefits included in a taxpayer's gross income is based on two factors: (1) the taxpayer's ability to pay and (2) the amount of benefits considered to be a recovery of the taxpayer's contributions, or a recovery of capital. If a taxpayer's income exceeds a specified base amount, as much as 85 percent of Social Security retirement benefits must be included in gross income. The taxable amount of benefits is determined through the application of one of two formulas described in § 86.

Digging Deeper 3

Additional information about the tax treatment of Social Security benefits can be found on this book's companion website: www.cengage.com

Digging Deeper 4

Learn more about the tax treatment of Social Security benefits received while living abroad on this book's companion website: www.cengage.com

10-3 Specific Exclusions Applicable to Individuals

Given the all-inclusive definition of gross income, an amount can be excluded from gross income only if the taxpayer can locate specific authority for such an exclusion. The discussion that follows focuses on common exclusion items available to individual taxpayers.

10-3a Gifts and Inheritances

From the implementation of the Federal income tax in 1913, Congress has allowed the recipient of a gift to exclude its value from gross income. The exclusion applies to gifts made during the life of the donor (*inter vivos* gifts) and transfers that take effect upon the death of the donor (bequests and inheritances).[12] However, the recipient of a gift of income-producing property is subject to tax on the income subsequently earned from the property.

"Gifts" are often made in a business setting. For example, a salesperson gives a purchasing agent free samples, an employee receives cash from an employer upon retirement, or a corporation makes payments to employees who were victims of a natural disaster. In these and similar instances, it is frequently unclear whether the payment was a gift or represents compensation for past, present, or future services.

The courts have defined a gift as "a voluntary transfer of property by one to another without adequate (valuable) consideration or compensation therefrom."[13] If the payment is intended to be for services rendered, it is not a gift, even though the payment is made without legal or moral obligation and the payor receives no economic benefit from the transfer. To qualify as a gift, the payment must be made "out of affection, respect, admiration, charity or like impulses."[14] Thus, the cases about this issue have been decided on the basis of the donor's intent.[15]

In the case of cash or other property received by employees from their employer, Congress has eliminated any ambiguity. Transfers from an employer to an employee cannot be categorized as a gift.[16]

Amounts received as a result of a crowdfunding campaign may meet the definition of a gift. Crowdfunding involves raising funds, often a small amount from a large group of people, for artistic or technology projects, as well as for personal or charitable undertakings. Under the broad definition of gross income provided in the tax law, crowdfunded

[11]§ 85. The American Rescue Plan Act of 2021 (P.L. 117–2) provides that for 2020, up to $10,200 of unemployment compensation can be excluded from income.

[12]§ 102.

[13]*Estate of D. R. Daly*, 3 B.T.A. 1042 (1926).

[14]*Robertson v. U.S.*, 52–1 USTC ¶9343, 41 AFTR 1053, 72 S.Ct. 994.

[15]See, for example, *Comm. v. Duberstein*, 60–2 USTC ¶9515, 5 AFTR 2d 1626, 80 S.Ct. 1190.

[16]§ 102(c). But see § 139 for qualified disaster situations.

amounts received are included in the recipient's income. However, if such funds are given without an expectation of receiving anything in return (e.g., as payment for someone's medical expenses rather than as payment for a future music album), then such amounts may meet the criterion to be considered a gift and, as such, would be excluded from income.

The Big Picture

Example 4

Return to the facts of *The Big Picture* on p. 10-1. The $12,500 received by David and Danae as a result of their GoFundMe campaign should be categorized as a gift and, as such, excluded from their income. The contributors to the campaign do not seem to have been motivated by the expectation of receiving anything in return; the contributions resulted from the generosity of their friends and family as well as strangers. As a result, the payments meet the tax law definition of a gift.

However, any amounts contributed to the campaign by David's employer would likely not meet the definition of a gift because David provides services to his employer.

What is considered a "gift"? Learn more on this book's companion website: www.cengage.com 5 Digging Deeper

10-3b Scholarships

General Information

Payments or benefits received by a student at an educational institution may be categorized as (1) scholarships, (2) compensation for services, or (3) a gift.

The **scholarship** rules are intended to provide exclusion treatment for education-related benefits that cannot qualify as gifts but are not compensation for services. To be excluded from income, the scholarship must be used for qualified tuition and related expenses such as books and supplies (not housing or food).[17] The recipient must also be a candidate for a degree at an educational institution.[18]

If the payments or benefits are received as compensation for services (past or present), the fact that the recipient is a student generally does not mean the amounts can be excluded from gross income.[19] Thus, teaching and research assistants are usually considered employees, and their stipend is taxable compensation. However, an exception allows nonprofit educational institutions to provide qualified tuition reduction plans for their employees where tuition reduction amount can be excluded from the employee's gross income. The exclusion also applies to tuition reductions granted to the employee's spouse and dependent children.[20]

Amounts received to be used for educational purposes (other than amounts received from family members) cannot be excluded as gifts because conditions attached to the receipt of the funds mean that the payments were not made out of "detached generosity."

The Big Picture

Return to the facts of *The Big Picture* on p. 10-1. State University waives a portion of tuition for all graduate teaching assistants. Per § 117(d), a qualified tuition reduction is not included in the gross income of the recipient if (either for undergraduate or graduate students) it is provided for engaging in teaching or research activities. Thus, while the $450 Danae receives each month is considered compensation for services and is included in her gross income, the $4,500 tuition waiver is excluded from her gross income if it is provided as a part of her teaching appointment.

[17] § 117(b). See also irs.gov/newsroom/tax-benefits-for-education-information-center.

[18] § 117(a).

[19] Reg. § 1.117–2(a). See *C. P. Bhalla*, 35 T.C. 13 (1960), for a discussion of the distinction between a scholarship and compensation. See also *Bingler v. Johnson*, 69–1 USTC ¶9348, 23 AFTR 2d 1212, 89 S.Ct. 1439. For potential exclusion treatment, see the discussion of qualified tuition reduction plans in text Section 11-2e.

[20] § 117(d).

Aliyah enters a contest sponsored by a local newspaper. Each contestant is required to submit an essay on local environmental issues. The prize is one year's tuition at State University. Aliyah wins the contest. The newspaper has a legal obligation to her, as the contest winner. Thus, the benefit is not a gift. However, because the tuition payment aids Aliyah in pursuing her studies and is not compensation for services, the payment is categorized as a scholarship.

Athletic scholarships are generally excluded from income because they are granted to assist students in paying for their education and are not considered a payment for services. The NCAA also allows athletic scholarships to include a "cost of attendance" amount. In addition to tuition, fees, books, and room and board, an athletic scholarship can include expenses like academic-related supplies, transportation, and other similar items. The value of these benefits may differ from campus to campus. However, only the amounts received for tuition, books, and supplies can be excluded from gross income.[21]

A scholarship recipient may exclude from gross income the amount used for tuition and related expenses (fees, books, supplies, and equipment required for courses) provided the conditions of the grant do not require that the funds be used for other purposes.[22]

Kelly received an athletic scholarship from State University. The scholarship pays her tuition, $9,000, and books and supplies, $2,400. She also received $4,500 a year for costs of attendance, which she uses to pay for housing, food, laundry, and transportation.

The tuition and the cost of books and supplies are excluded from gross income as a scholarship. The $4,500 received to pay for the costs of attendance does not qualify for the scholarship exclusion. As a result, Kelly must include that amount in her gross income.

Timing Issues

Frequently, the scholarship recipient is a cash basis taxpayer who receives the money in one tax year but pays the educational expenses in a subsequent year. The amount eligible for exclusion may not be known at the time the money is received. In that case, the transaction is held open until the educational expenses are paid.[23]

In August 2022, Sanjay received $10,000 as a scholarship for the 2022–2023 academic year. Sanjay's expenditures for tuition, books, and supplies were as follows:

August–December 2022	$3,000
January–May 2023	4,500
	$7,500

Sanjay's gross income for 2023 includes $2,500 ($10,000 − $7,500) that is not excludible as a scholarship. None of the scholarship is included in his gross income in 2022.

10-3c Damages

A person who suffers harm caused by another is often entitled to **compensatory damages**. The tax consequences of the receipt of damages depend on the type of harm the taxpayer has experienced. The taxpayer may seek recovery for (1) a loss of income, (2) expenses incurred, (3) property destroyed, or (4) personal injury.

[21]Rev.Rul. 77–263.

[22]§ 117(b). See also **irs.gov/newsroom/tax-benefits-for-education-information-center**.

[23]Prop.Reg. § 1.117–6(b)(2).

Generally, reimbursement for a loss of income is taxed in the same manner as the income replaced (see the exception under Personal Injury discussed next). The recovery of an expense is not income unless the expense was deducted; if the expense was deducted, the damages generally are taxable under the tax benefit rule (refer to text Section 4-5e).

A payment for damaged or destroyed property is treated as an amount received in a sale or exchange of the property. Thus, the taxpayer has a realized gain if the damages received exceed the property's basis. Damages for personal injuries receive special treatment under the Code.

Personal Injury

The legal theory of personal injury damages is that the amount received is intended "to make the plaintiff (the injured party) whole as before the injury."[24] It follows that if the damages received were subject to tax, the after-tax amount received would be less than the actual damages incurred and the injured party would not be "whole as before the injury." With respect to personal injury damages, a distinction is made between compensatory damages and **punitive damages**.

Compensatory damages are intended to compensate the taxpayer for the damages incurred. Only those compensatory damages received for *physical personal injury or physical sickness* can be excluded from gross income.[25] Such exclusion treatment applies to amounts received for loss of income associated with the physical personal injury or physical sickness. Compensatory damages awarded on account of emotional distress cannot be excluded from gross income (except to the extent of any amount received for medical care). Likewise, any amounts received for age discrimination or injury to one's reputation cannot be excluded.

Punitive damages are amounts the party that caused the harm must pay to the victim as punishment for outrageous conduct. Punitive damages are not intended to compensate the victim, but rather to punish the party who caused the harm. It follows that amounts received as punitive damages may actually place the victim in a better economic position than before the harm was experienced. Thus, punitive damages are included in gross income.

These rules are summarized in Concept Summary 10.1.

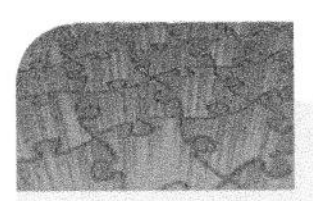

Concept Summary 10.1

Taxation of Damages

Type of Claim	Taxation of Award or Settlement
Breach of contract (generally loss of income)	Taxable.
Property damages	Gain to the extent damages received exceed basis. A loss is deductible for business property and investment property to the extent of basis over the amount realized. A loss may be deductible for personal use property (see discussion of casualty losses in text Section 6-3).
Personal injury	
Physical	All compensatory amounts are excluded unless previously deducted (e.g., medical expenses). Amounts received as punitive damages are included in gross income.
Nonphysical	Compensatory damages and punitive damages are included in gross income.

[24] *C. A. Hawkins*, 6 B.T.A. 1023 (1928).

[25] § 104(a)(2).

The Big Picture

Return to the facts of *The Big Picture* on p. 10-1. The damages David received were awarded as a result of a physical personal injury. Therefore, all of the compensatory damages can be excluded, even the compensation for the loss of income of $15,000. The punitive damages David received, however, must be included in his gross income.

10-3d Workers' Compensation

State workers' compensation laws require the employer to pay fixed amounts for specific job-related injuries. These state laws were enacted to allow the employee to recover the damages without suing the employer. Although the payments are intended, in part, to compensate for a loss of future income, Congress has specifically excluded workers' compensation benefits from gross income.[26]

10-3e Accident and Health Insurance Benefits

The income tax treatment of **accident and health insurance benefits** depends on whether the policy providing the benefits was purchased by the taxpayer or the taxpayer's employer. Benefits collected under an accident and health insurance policy purchased by the taxpayer are excludible even though the payments are a substitute for income.[27]

Quynh purchases a medical and disability insurance policy. The insurance company pays Quynh $1,000 per week to replace wages she loses while in the hospital. Although the payments serve as a substitute for income, the amounts received are tax-exempt benefits collected under Quynh's insurance policy.

A different set of rules applies if the accident and health insurance protection was purchased by the individual's employer, as discussed in text Section 11-2a.

10-3f Educational Savings Bonds

Because of the rising cost of attending college, Congress has attempted to assist low- to middle-income parents in saving for their children's college education with specific tax benefits for such saving. One such benefit is an interest income exclusion on **educational savings bonds**.[28] The interest on Series EE U.S. government savings bonds may be excluded from gross income if the bond proceeds are used to pay qualified higher education expenses. The bonds must be issued to a taxpayer age 24 or older.

Qualified higher education expenses consist of tuition and fees paid to an eligible educational institution for the taxpayer, spouse, or dependent. If the redemption proceeds (both principal and interest) exceed the qualified higher education expenses, only a pro rata portion of the interest will qualify for exclusion.

Tracy's redemption proceeds from qualified savings bonds during the taxable year are $6,000 (principal of $4,000 and interest of $2,000). Tracy's qualified higher education expenses are $5,000. Because the redemption proceeds exceed the qualified higher education expenses, only $1,667 [($5,000 ÷ $6,000) × $2,000] of the interest is excludible.

Once a taxpayer's modified adjusted gross income exceeds a threshold amount, the exclusion is phased out. *Modified adjusted gross income (MAGI)* is adjusted gross income prior to the foreign earned income exclusion and the educational savings bond exclusion. The threshold amounts are adjusted for inflation each year. For 2022, the phaseout

[26] § 104(a)(1).

[27] § 104(a)(3).

[28] § 135.

begins at $85,800. The phaseout is completed when MAGI exceeds the threshold amount by more than $15,000. The otherwise excludible interest is reduced by the amount calculated as follows:

MAGI – $85,800 / $15,000		Excludible interest before phaseout	=	Reduction in excludible interest

On a joint return, $128,650 is substituted for $85,800 (in 2022), and $30,000 is substituted for $15,000.[29]

Example 12

Assume the same facts as in Example 11, except that Tracy's MAGI for 2022 is $87,000. Tracy is single. The phaseout results in Tracy's interest exclusion being reduced by $133 {[($87,000 − $85,800) ÷ $15,000] × $1,667}. Therefore, Tracy's exclusion is $1,534 ($1,667 − $133).

10-3g Wrongful Incarceration

Code § 139F exempts amounts received as damages for being wrongfully incarcerated. The exclusion applies to an individual convicted of a Federal or state crime who is later exonerated.

10-4 Itemized Deductions

LO.2

Determine an individual's allowable itemized deductions.

Taxpayers are allowed to deduct *from* AGI specified expenditures as itemized deductions. Itemized deductions can be classified as follows:

- Expenses that are *personal* in nature.
- Expenses related to (1) the *production or collection of income* and (2) the *management of property* held for the production of income.[30]

Expenses in the latter category are sometimes referred to as *nonbusiness expenses*. While trade or business expenses (discussed previously) must be incurred in connection with business activity, nonbusiness expenses are expenses incurred in connection with an income-producing activity that does not qualify as a trade or business. If the nonbusiness expense is incurred in connection with rental or royalty property, it is classified as a deduction *for* AGI (similar to trade or business expenses). Otherwise, it is classified as a deduction *from* AGI. Itemized deductions include, but are not limited to, the expenses listed in Exhibit 10.1.

Exhibit 10.1 Partial List of Itemized Deductions

Personal Expenditures

Medical expenses in excess of 7.5% of AGI

State and local income taxes or sales taxes

Real estate taxes

Personal property taxes

Home mortgage interest expense

Charitable contributions (limited to a maximum of 60% or 50% of AGI)

Casualty losses incurred in a Federally declared disaster area (in excess of 10% of AGI)

Expenditures Related to Income-Producing Activities

Investment interest (to the extent of net investment income)

[29]The indexed amounts for 2021 were $83,200 and $124,800.

[30]§ 212.

The election to itemize is appropriate when total itemized deductions exceed the standard deduction associated with the taxpayer's filing status (see text Section 9-2). Itemized deductions are reported on Schedule A (Form 1040) and filed with an individual's Federal income tax return (Form 1040). Commonly encountered itemized deductions are discussed next.

10-4a Medical Expenses

Medical expenses paid for the care of the taxpayer, spouse, and dependents are allowed as an itemized deduction to the extent the expenses are not reimbursed. The medical expense deduction is limited to the amount by which such expenses exceed 7.5 percent of the taxpayer's AGI.[31]

The threshold percentage, sometimes referred to as a "floor," is used to restrict deductions, because expenses below the floor are not deductible. Here, the floor is significant. Only medical expenses in excess of the "7.5%-of-AGI floor" are deductible. As a result, a medical expense deduction is rare (especially for high-income taxpayers).

The Big Picture

Example 13

Return to the facts of *The Big Picture* on p. 10-1. In addition to the medical expenses incurred associated with David's accident that were later reimbursed by the delivery company's insurance company, the Steeles had other qualifying medical expenses. Assuming that their AGI for the year is \$200,000, they will need to itemize their deductions and have more than \$15,000 (\$200,000 × 7.5%) in unreimbursed medical expenses to receive a tax benefit from those expenses. Thus, their itemized deduction for medical expenses would equal whatever qualifying medical expenses were incurred that exceeded the \$15,000 threshold.

Medical Expenses Defined

The term *medical care* includes expenditures incurred for the "diagnosis, cure, mitigation, treatment, or prevention of disease, or for the purpose of affecting any structure or function of the body."[32] Medical expense also includes premiums paid for health care insurance, prescription medicine and insulin, and lodging while away from home for the purpose of obtaining medical care. Examples of deductible and nondeductible medical expenses appear in Exhibit 10.2.

Cosmetic Surgery

Amounts paid for cosmetic surgery are not deductible medical expenses unless the surgery is medically necessary. Cosmetic surgery is necessary when it ameliorates the effects of (1) a deformity arising from a congenital abnormality, (2) a personal injury, or (3) a disfiguring disease.[33]

Nursing Home Care

The cost of care in a nursing home or home for the aged, including meals and lodging, can be included in deductible medical expenses if the primary reason for being in the home is to get medical care. If the primary reason for being there is personal, any costs for medical or nursing care are deductible medical expenses, but the cost of meals and lodging are not considered medical expenses.

Capital Expenditures

When capital expenditures are incurred for medical purposes, they must be deemed medically necessary by a physician, used primarily by the patient, and the expense must be reasonable in order to be deductible. Examples of such expenditures include dust

[31] § 213(a). The Consolidated Appropriations Act (2021) made the 7.5% threshold permanent.

[32] § 213(d)(1)(A).

[33] § 213(d)(9)(A)

Exhibit 10.2 Examples of Deductible and Nondeductible Medical Expenses Paid by Taxpayer

Deductible	Nondeductible
Medical (including dental, mental, and hospital) care	Funeral, burial, or cremation expenses
Prescription drugs and insulin	Nonprescription drugs (except insulin)
Special equipment:	Bottled water
Wheelchairs	Toiletries, cosmetics
Crutches	Diaper service, maternity clothes
Artificial limbs	Programs for the general improvement of health:
Eyeglasses (including contact lenses)	Weight reduction
Hearing aids	Health spas
Transportation for medical care	Social activities (e.g., dancing and swimming lessons)
Medical and hospital insurance premiums	Elective cosmetic surgery
Long-term care insurance premiums (subject to limitations)	
Cost of alcohol and drug rehabilitation	
Certain costs to stop smoking	
Weight reduction programs related to obesity	
Personal protective equipment to prevent the spread of COVID-19 ; COVID-19 home testing kits	

elimination systems,[34] elevators,[35] and vans specially designed for wheelchair-bound taxpayers. Other expenditures that may qualify are swimming pools (if the taxpayer does not have access to a neighborhood pool) and air conditioners if they do not become permanent improvements (e.g., window units).[36]

Both a capital expenditure for a permanent improvement and related operating and maintenance costs may qualify as medical expenses. The allowable costs are deductible in the year incurred but are limited to the amount by which the cost exceeds the increase in value of the related property. Also note that although depreciation is required for most other capital expenditures, it is not required for those qualifying for medical purposes (in other words, the entire cost of a qualifying capital expenditure is immediately deductible).

Medical Expenses for Spouse and Dependents

In computing the medical expense deduction, a taxpayer may include medical expenses for a spouse and for a person who was a dependent at the time the expenses were paid or incurred. Of the requirements that normally apply in determining dependency status, neither the gross income nor the joint return test applies in determining dependency status for medical expense deduction purposes.

Transportation, Meals, and Lodging

Payments for transportation to and from a point of treatment for medical care are also considered deductible medical expenses (subject to the AGI floor). These costs include bus, taxi, train, or plane fare; charges for ambulance service; and out-of-pocket expenses for the use of an automobile. A mileage allowance of 18 cents per mile (for 2022) may be used instead of actual out-of-pocket automobile expenses.[37] Whether the taxpayer chooses to claim out-of-pocket automobile expenses or the 18 cents per mile automatic mileage option, related parking fees and tolls can also be deducted. Also included are transportation expenditures for someone such as a family member or nurse who must accompany the patient. The cost of meals while en route to obtain medical care is not considered a deductible or a medical expense.

[34] Ltr.Rul. 7948029.

[35] *Riach v. Frank*, 62–1 USTC ¶9419, 9 AFTR 2d 1263, 302 F.2d 374 (CA–9, 1962).

[36] Reg. § 1.213–1(e)(1)(iii).

[37] Notice 2022–3. In 2021, the allowance was 16 cents per mile.

Digging Deeper 6

Additional information about medical expenses can be found on this book's companion website: www.cengage.com

Health Savings Accounts

Qualifying individuals may make deductible contributions to a **Health Savings Account (HSA)**. An HSA is a qualified trust or custodial account administered by a qualified HSA trustee, which can be a bank, an insurance company, or another IRS-approved trustee.[38] A taxpayer can use an HSA in conjunction with a high-deductible medical insurance policy to help reduce the overall cost of medical coverage. The high-deductible policy provides coverage for extraordinary medical expenses (in excess of the deductible), and expenses not covered by the policy can be paid with funds withdrawn tax-free from the HSA.

Example 14

Antonio, who is married and has three dependent children, carries a high-deductible medical insurance policy with a deductible of $4,400. He establishes an HSA and contributes the maximum allowable amount to the HSA in 2022.

During 2022, Antonio's family incurs medical expenses of $7,000. The high-deductible policy covers $2,600 of the expenses ($7,000 expenses − $4,400 deductible). Antonio can withdraw $4,400 from the HSA to pay the medical expenses not covered by the high-deductible policy.

High-Deductible Plans High-deductible policies are less expensive than low-deductible policies, so taxpayers with low medical costs can benefit from the lower premiums and use funds from the HSA to pay costs not covered by the high-deductible policy. A plan must meet two requirements to qualify as a high-deductible plan in 2022.[39]

1. The annual deductible is not less than $1,400 for self-only coverage ($2,800 for family coverage).
2. The annual limit on total out-of-pocket costs (excluding the premiums) under the plan does not exceed $7,050 for self-only coverage ($14,100 for family coverage).

Tax Treatment of HSA Contributions and Distributions To establish an HSA, a taxpayer contributes funds to a custodial account.[40] As illustrated in the preceding example, funds can be withdrawn from an HSA to pay medical expenses that are not covered by the high-deductible policy. The following general tax rules apply to HSAs:

1. Contributions made by the taxpayer to an HSA are deductible *from* gross income to arrive at AGI (deduction *for* AGI). Thus, the taxpayer does not need to itemize to take the deduction.
2. Earnings on HSAs are not subject to taxation unless distributed, in which case taxability depends on how the funds are used.[41]
   - Distributions from HSAs are excluded from gross income if they are used to pay for medical expenses not covered by the high-deductible policy.
   - Distributions that are not used to pay for medical expenses are included in gross income and are subject to an additional 20 percent penalty if made before age 65, death, or disability. Any distributions made by reason of death or disability or distributions made after the HSA beneficiary becomes eligible for Medicare are taxed but not subject to the penalty.

HSAs have at least two other attractive features. First, an HSA is portable. Taxpayers who switch jobs can take their HSAs with them. Second, anyone under age 65 who has a high-deductible plan and is not covered by another policy that is not a high-deductible plan can establish an HSA.

[38] § 223(a).

[39] § 223(c)(2). In 2021, the annual deductible limits were $1,400 (self-only coverage) and $2,800 (family coverage), and the annual out-of-pocket cost limits were $7,000 (self-only coverage) and $14,000 (family coverage).

[40] § 223(d).

[41] § 223(f).

Deductible Amount The annual deduction for contributions to an HSA is limited to an amount that depends on whether the taxpayer has self-only coverage or family coverage. The annual limit for an individual who has self-only coverage in 2022 is \$3,650, while the annual limit for an individual who has family coverage in 2022 is \$7,300. These amounts are subject to annual cost-of-living adjustments.[42] An eligible taxpayer who has attained the age of 55 by the end of the tax year may make an additional annual (catch-up) contribution of up to \$1,000. A deduction is not allowed after the individual becomes eligible for Medicare coverage.

Determining the Maximum HSA Contribution Deduction

Liu (age 45), who is married and self-employed, carries a high-deductible medical insurance policy with family coverage and an annual deductible of \$4,000. In addition, he has established an HSA. In 2022, Liu's maximum annual contribution to the HSA is \$7,300.

During 2022, Adam, who is self-employed, made 12 monthly payments of \$1,200 for an HSA contract that provides medical insurance coverage with a \$3,600 deductible. The plan covers Adam, his wife, and their two children. Of the \$1,200 monthly fee, \$675 was for the high-deductible policy, and \$525 was deposited into an HSA.

Because Adam is *self-employed*, he can deduct \$8,100 of the amount paid for the high-deductible policy (\$675 per month × 12 months) as a deduction *for* AGI (refer to text Section 11-4b). In addition, the \$6,300 (\$525 × 12) contributed to the HSA is a deduction *for* AGI. Note that the \$6,300 HSA deduction does not exceed the \$7,300 annual ceiling.

10-4b Taxes

A deduction is allowed for certain state and local taxes paid or accrued by a taxpayer.[43] However, it is important to understand the difference between a tax and a fee, because fees are not deductible unless incurred as a business expense or as an expense in the production of income. The IRS defines a tax as follows:

> The word *taxes* has been defined as an enforced contribution, exacted pursuant to legislative authority in the exercise of taxing power, and imposed and collected for the purpose of raising revenue to be used for public or governmental purposes and not as payment for a privilege granted or service rendered.[44]

As a result, fees for dog licenses, automobile inspections, automobile titles and registration, hunting and fishing licenses, bridge and highway tolls, driver's licenses, parking meter deposits, and postage are not taxes.

Not all taxes are deductible. For example, Federal income taxes are not deductible. Other taxes are not deductible if they relate to personal, rather than business, activities. An example is the excise tax included in the cost of purchasing gasoline. Deductible and nondeductible taxes are summarized in Exhibit 10.3.

From 2018 through 2025, the maximum itemized deduction for the nonbusiness state and local taxes discussed next (personal and real property taxes, income or sales taxes) is limited to \$10,000. This maximum is the same for taxpayers filing individually and jointly. A \$5,000 maximum applies for married taxpayers filing separately. This limit applies to the taxes deductible from AGI that are not directly imposed on business and investment activity or property.

[42] § 223(b)(2). See Rev.Proc. 2021–25. The annual limits were \$3,600 and \$7,200 in 2021.

[43] Most deductible taxes are listed in § 164, while nondeductible items are included in § 275.

[44] Rev.Rul. 81–191.

Exhibit 10.3 Deductible and Nondeductible Taxes

Deductible*	Nondeductible
State, local, and foreign real property taxes	Federal income taxes
State and local personal property taxes	FICA taxes imposed on employees
State and local income taxes *or* sales/use taxes	Employer FICA taxes paid on domestic household workers
Foreign income taxes	Estate, inheritance, and gift taxes
	Federal, state, and local excise taxes (e.g., gasoline, tobacco, and spirits)
	Foreign income taxes if the taxpayer chooses the foreign tax credit option
	Taxes on real property to the extent such taxes are to be apportioned and treated as imposed on another taxpayer
	Special assessments for streets, sidewalks, curbing, and other similar improvements

*Per § 164(b)(6), from 2018 through 2025, the aggregate itemized deduction for these four taxes cannot exceed $10,000.

Personal Property Taxes

Deductible personal property taxes must be *ad valorem* (assessed in relation to the value of the property). A motor vehicle tax based on weight, model, year, or horsepower is not an ad valorem tax. In contrast, a motor vehicle tax based on the value of the car is an ad valorem tax and, as such, is a deductible tax.

The Big Picture

Return to the facts of *The Big Picture* on p. 10-1. Assume that their state imposes a motor vehicle registration tax equal to 2% of the value of the vehicle plus 40 cents per hundredweight. The Steeles own a car having a value of $20,000 and weighing 3,000 pounds. They pay an annual registration tax of $412. Of this amount, $400 (2% × $20,000 of value) is deductible as a personal property tax (subject to the $10,000 annual aggregate deduction limit) if they itemize their deductions. The remaining $12, the portion based on the weight of the car, is not deductible. Any other amount included in the annual fee (e.g., processing charges) is not considered a tax.

Real Estate Taxes

Real estate taxes of individuals are generally deductible. Taxes on personal use property and investment property are deductible as itemized deductions. Taxes on business property are deductible as business expenses. Real property taxes on property that is sold during the year must be allocated between the buyer and the seller (refer to text Section 5-5b).

State and Local Income Taxes and Sales Taxes

State and local *income* taxes paid by an individual are deductible only as itemized deductions, even if the taxpayer's sole source of income is from a business, rents, or royalties.

Cash basis taxpayers are entitled to deduct state income taxes in the year in which the payment is made. This includes taxes withheld by the employer, amounts paid with the state income tax return when filed, and estimated state income tax payments.[45] If the taxpayer overpays state income taxes, the refund received is included in gross income in the year received to the extent the deduction reduced the taxable income in the prior year.

[45]Rev.Rul. 71–190. See also Rev.Rul. 82–208, where a deduction is not allowed when the taxpayer cannot, in good faith, reasonably determine that there is additional state income tax liability.

Tax Planning Strategies **Timing the Payment of Deductible Taxes**

Framework Focus: Deductions

Strategy: Accelerate Recognition of Deductions to Achieve Tax Deferral.

It is sometimes possible to defer or accelerate the payment of certain deductible taxes, such as state income tax, real property tax, and personal property tax. For example, the final installment of estimated state income tax is generally due after the end of a given tax year. However, accelerating the payment of the final installment could result in larger itemized deductions for the current year as long as consideration is given to the $10,000 itemized deduction maximum.

Leona, a cash basis, unmarried taxpayer, had $800 of state income tax withheld from her paychecks during 2022. Also in 2022, Leona paid $100 that was due when she filed her 2021 state income tax return and made estimated payments of $300 toward her 2022 state income tax liability. When Leona files her 2022 Federal income tax return in April 2023, she elects to itemize deductions, which amount to $15,500, including the $1,200 of state income tax payments and withholdings, all of which reduce her taxable income.

As a result of overpaying her 2022 state income tax, Leona receives a refund of $200 early in 2023. She will include this amount in her 2023 gross income in computing her Federal income tax. Whether Leona receives a check from the state for $200 or applies the $200 toward her 2023 state income tax does not change this outcome.

Individuals can elect to deduct either their state and local income taxes *or* their sales/use taxes paid as an itemized deduction. This election is intended to provide equity to taxpayers living in states that do not have a state income tax (but do have sales taxes). Taxpayers making this election can either deduct actual sales/use tax payments *or* the amount specified in an IRS table (available on the IRS website). The amount in the table can be increased by sales tax paid on the purchase of motor vehicles, boats, and other specified items.

See this book's companion website to learn about the distinction between taxes deductible for AGI versus from AGI: www.cengage.com 7 Digging Deeper

10-4c Interest

For Federal income tax purposes, whether interest expense is tax deductible is dictated by the context in which the interest expense is incurred. Business interest is fully deductible as an ordinary and necessary expense. Most personal (consumer) interest such as interest paid on credit cards and car loans is not deductible. However, interest on qualified student loans, investment interest, and qualified residence (home mortgage) interest is deductible, subject to the limits discussed next.

Interest on Qualified Student Loans

Taxpayers who pay interest on a qualified student loan may be able to deduct the interest as a deduction *for* AGI. The deduction is allowable only to the extent the proceeds of the loan are used to pay qualified education expenses to qualified educational institutions. The maximum annual deduction is $2,500. However, in 2022, the deduction is phased out for taxpayers with modified AGI (MAGI) between $70,000 and $85,000 ($145,000 and $175,000 on joint returns). The deduction is not available for taxpayers who are claimed as dependents or for married taxpayers filing separately.[46]

[46] §§ 221(c) and (e)(2). See § 221(b)(2)(C) for the definition of MAGI. The 2021 MAGI threshold amounts were $70,000 and $85,000 ($140,000 and $170,000 on joint returns).

In 2022, Curt and Rita, who are married and file a joint return, paid $3,000 of interest on a qualified student loan. Their MAGI was $152,500. Their maximum potential deduction for qualified student loan interest is $2,500, but it must be reduced by $625 as a result of the phaseout rules.

$$\$2{,}500 \text{ interest} \times \frac{\$152{,}500 \text{ (MAGI)} - \$145{,}000 \text{ (AGI phaseout floor)}}{\$30{,}000 \text{ (phaseout range)}} = \$625 \text{ reduction}$$

Curt and Rita are allowed a student loan interest deduction of $1,875 ($2,500 maximum deduction − $625 reduction) for AGI.

Investment Interest

Years ago wealthy taxpayers used the interest deduction in the tax law to create wealth. They would borrow to purchase investments that would appreciate over time and then deduct the interest on the debt as an ordinary deduction when paid. Later, when the asset was sold at a gain, only a capital gains tax was due on the appreciation. Thus, today's interest deduction could lead to tomorrow's capital gain.

In response, Congress limited the deductibility of **investment interest**, which is interest paid on debt borrowed for the purpose of purchasing or continuing to hold investment property. The deduction for investment interest allowed during the tax year is limited to the lesser of the investment interest paid or net investment income.[47]

Net investment income, which serves as the ceiling on the deductibility of investment interest, is the excess of investment income over investment expenses. Investment income includes gross income from interest, annuities, and royalties not derived in the ordinary course of a trade or business. However, investment income does not include any income taken into account when calculating income or loss from a passive activity.

Investment expenses are those deductible expenses directly connected with the production of investment income, such as property taxes on investment holdings. Investment expenses do not include interest expense and, from 2018 through 2025, any expenses that are miscellaneous itemized deductions (e.g., brokerage charges and investment counsel fees).

After net investment income is determined, the allowable deductible investment interest expense is calculated.

Ethan's financial records for the year reflect the following:

Interest income from bank savings account	$10,000
Taxable annuity receipts	5,500
Local ad valorem property tax on investments	200
Investment interest expense	17,000

Ethan's investment income amounts to $15,500 ($10,000 + $5,500), and deductible investment expenses total $200. Therefore, his net investment income is $15,300 ($15,500 − $200). Consequently, the investment interest deduction is limited to $15,300, the lesser of investment interest expense ($17,000) or net investment income.

The amount of investment interest disallowed is carried over to future years. In Example 20, the amount that is carried over to the following year is $1,700 ($17,000 investment interest expense − $15,300 deduction allowed). No limit is placed on the length of the carryover period.

Tax planning tips for investment interest expense can be found on this book's companion website: www.cengage.com

[47] § 163(d)(1).

Qualified Residence Interest

Qualified residence interest is interest paid or accrued during the taxable year on indebtedness (subject to limitations) secured by any property that is a qualified residence of the taxpayer. Qualified residence interest falls into two categories: (1) interest on **acquisition indebtedness** and (2) interest on **home equity loans**. Before each of these categories is discussed, however, the term *qualified residence* must be defined.

A qualified residence includes the taxpayer's principal residence and one other residence of the taxpayer or spouse. The principal residence meets the requirement for nonrecognition of gain upon sale under § 121 (see text Section 7-7). The one other residence, or second residence, is used as a residence if not rented or, if rented, meets the requirements for a personal residence under the rental of vacation home rules of § 280A. A taxpayer who has more than one second residence can choose the qualified second residence each year (i.e., the taxpayer can select a different second residence each year). A residence includes a house, a cooperative apartment, and a condominium, as well as a mobile home or boat that has living quarters (sleeping, bathroom, and cooking facilities).

Although in most cases interest paid on a home mortgage is fully deductible, there are limitations.[48] A deduction is allowed for interest paid or accrued during the tax year on aggregate acquisition indebtedness. *Acquisition indebtedness* refers to amounts incurred in acquiring, constructing, or substantially improving the taxpayer's qualified residence that serves as security for that indebtedness. The amount of acquisition indebtedness is limited based on when the debt was incurred. If the debt is incurred after December 15, 2017, and before January 1, 2026, acquisition indebtedness is limited to $750,000 ($375,000 for married taxpayers filing separate returns). Debt incurred on or before December 15, 2017, is limited to $1 million ($500,000 for married taxpayers filing separate returns). The higher limits will apply to all homeowners after 2025 irrespective of the date of borrowing.

Prior to 2018, qualified residence interest also included interest on home equity loans. Such loans utilize the personal residence of the taxpayer as security for the loan, typically in the form of a second mortgage. Because home equity loan proceeds can be used for personal purposes (e.g., auto purchases and medical expenses), what would otherwise have been nondeductible personal interest was converted to deductible qualified residence interest.

From 2018 through 2025, qualified residence interest includes only interest on acquisition indebtedness.[49] Thus, interest paid on a home equity loan is not deductible unless the funds are used to build or substantially improve the taxpayer's primary residence.[50] For example, assume that a taxpayer with acquisition indebtedness takes out a home equity loan secured by his primary residence to improve that residence. All of the interest paid on both loans is fully deductible as long as the total of these debts does not exceed $750,000. However, if the taxpayer took out the home equity loan to pay for a vacation and pay down credit card balances, the home equity loan interest would not be deductible. If proceeds of a home equity loan were used to pay for business expenses, the interest would be deductible business interest.[51]

Larry owns a personal residence with a fair market value of $600,000 and an outstanding first mortgage of $420,000. Therefore, his equity in his home is $180,000 ($600,000 − $420,000). Larry borrows $75,000 that is secured by a second mortgage on his home to put an addition on his home.

All of Larry's interest is deductible; both loans are secured by his residence, and the total of the loans ($420,000 + $75,000) does not exceed $750,000 or the value of his residence. If Larry had used the home equity loan proceeds to buy a new car and boat, the home equity loan interest would not be deductible.

[48] § 163(h)(3).

[49] § 163(h)(3)(F)(i)(I).

[50] IR-2018-32 (February 21, 2018).

[51] From 2018 through 2025, the treatment of interest expense on an equity debt that was not used to improve the home is determined using the interest tracing rules of Reg. § 1.163–8T and Reg. § 1.163–15.

Prior to 2022, mortgage insurance premiums paid by the taxpayer on a qualified residence are deductible, subject to a phaseout based on AGI, as qualified residence interest.[52]

Interest Paid for Services Mortgage loan companies commonly charge a fee, often called a loan origination fee, for finding, placing, or processing a mortgage loan. Loan origination fees are typically nondeductible amounts included in the basis of the acquired property. Other fees, sometimes called **points** and expressed as a percentage of the loan amount, are paid to reduce the interest rate charged over the term of the loan. Essentially, the payment of points is a prepayment of interest and is considered compensation to a lender solely for the use of money. To be deductible, points must be in the nature of interest and cannot be a form of service charge or payment for specific services.[53]

In general, points are capitalized and then amortized and deductible ratably over the life of the loan. However, the purchaser of a principal residence may deduct qualifying points in the year of payment. This exception also covers points paid to obtain funds for improvements to a personal residence.[54]

Points paid to refinance acquisition indebtedness (i.e., an existing home mortgage) cannot be immediately deducted but must be capitalized and amortized as an interest deduction over the life of the new loan.[55]

Sandra purchased her residence many years ago, obtaining a 30-year mortgage at an annual interest rate of 6%. In the current year, Sandra refinances the mortgage to reduce the interest rate to 4%. To obtain the refinancing, she has to pay points of $2,600. The $2,600, which is considered prepayment of interest, must be capitalized and amortized over the remaining life of the mortgage.

Prepayment Penalty

When a mortgage or loan is paid off in full in a lump sum before its term (i.e., paid off early), the lending institution may require an additional payment from the borrower (normally, a specific percentage of the loan balance). This is known as a prepayment penalty and is considered to be interest (e.g., personal, investment, or qualified residence) in the year paid. The general rules for deductibility of interest also apply to prepayment penalties.

Tax-Exempt Securities

The tax law provides that no deduction is allowed for interest on debt incurred to purchase or carry tax-exempt securities.[56] The meaning of the phrase *to purchase or carry* has been examined in many court cases.

Prepaid Interest

Accrual method reporting is imposed on cash basis taxpayers for interest prepayments that extend beyond the end of the taxable year.[57] Such payments must be allocated to the tax years to which the interest payments relate. These provisions are intended to prevent cash basis taxpayers from accelerating tax deductions by prepaying interest.

Classification of Interest Expense

Whether interest is deductible *for* AGI or as an itemized deduction (*from* AGI) depends on whether the indebtedness has a business, investment, or personal purpose. If the debt proceeds are used for a business expense (other than performing services as an employee) or for an expense related to the production of rent or royalty income, the interest is

[52] §§ 163(h)(3)(E).
[53] Rev.Rul. 69–188.
[54] § 461(g)(2).
[55] Rev.Rul. 87–22.
[56] § 265(a)(2).
[57] § 461(g)(1).

Concept Summary 10.2

Deductibility of Personal, Student Loan, Investment, and Mortgage Interest

Type	Deductible	Comments
Personal (consumer) interest	No	Includes any interest that is not qualified residence interest, qualified student loan interest, investment interest, or business interest. Examples include interest on car loans and credit card debt.
Qualified student loan interest	Yes	Deduction *for* AGI; subject to limitations.
Investment interest (*not* related to rental or royalty property)	Yes	Itemized deduction; limited to net investment income for the year; disallowed interest can be carried over to future years.
Investment interest (related to rental or royalty property)	Yes	Deduction *for* AGI; limited to net investment income for the year; disallowed interest can be carried over to future years.
Qualified residence interest (acquisition indebtedness)	Yes	Itemized deduction; limited to indebtedness of $750,000 (up to $1 million if incurred on or before December 15, 2017).
Qualified residence interest (home equity indebtedness)	Potentially	From 2018 to 2025, generally not deductible. However, such interest expense could be deductible depending on the use of the proceeds of the loan (e.g., acquisition indebtedness or business expenses).

Generally, the classification rules for interest expense are provided in Reg. § 1.163–8T and Reg. § 1.163–15.

deductible *for* AGI. Business expenses appear on Schedule C of Form 1040, and expenses related to rents or royalties are reported on Schedule E. If the indebtedness is incurred for personal use, such as qualified residence interest, any deduction allowed is taken *from* AGI and is reported on Schedule A of Form 1040 (thus, the taxpayer must itemize deductions to receive the benefit of this deduction). Note, however, that allowable student loan interest is deductible *for* AGI. If the taxpayer is an employee who incurs debt in relation to his or her employment, the interest is considered to be personal interest and is not deductible. Concept Summary 10.2 reviews the tax treatment of the various types of interest expense incurred by individual taxpayers.

10-4d Charitable Contributions

As discussed in text Section 5-6, § 170 allows individuals to deduct contributions made to qualified domestic organizations. Such contributions serve certain social welfare needs and thus relieve the government of the cost of providing these services to the community.

Criteria for a Gift

A **charitable contribution** is defined as a gift of property made to a qualified organization.[58] The major elements needed to qualify a contribution as a gift are a donative intent, the absence of consideration, and acceptance by the donee. Consequently, the taxpayer has the burden of establishing that the transfer was made from motives of disinterested generosity as established by the courts.[59] This test can be subjective and has led to problems of interpretation.

Benefit Received Rule

When a donor derives a tangible benefit from a contribution, the value of the benefit is not deductible.

---

[58] § 170(c).

[59] *Comm. v. Duberstein*, 60–2 USTC ¶9515, 5 AFTR 2d 1626, 80 S.Ct. 1190.

Jacob purchases a ticket at $100 for a special performance of the local symphony (a qualified charity). If the price of a ticket to a symphony concert is normally $35, Jacob is allowed only $65 as a charitable contribution. Even if Jacob does not attend the concert, his deduction is limited to $65.

If, however, Jacob does *not* accept the ticket from the symphony (or returns it prior to the event), he can deduct the full $100.

Contributions in Exchange for State and Local Tax Credits

Several states provide a state or local tax credit to taxpayers who donate to specified state or local funds or public charities. Primarily due to concerns that state and local governments might expand the availability of these programs to help taxpayers "work around" the $10,000 state and local tax deduction limit, the IRS issued proposed rules limiting the Federal tax benefits of such contributions. Under these rules, if taxpayers receive a state or local tax credit greater than 15 percent of the contributions made, the taxpayers must reduce their charitable contribution deduction by the amount of the credit.[60]

In 2022, Prisha, a resident of State G, donated $5,000 to State G's Scholar Program. This donation provides Prisha with a 60% state income tax credit [$3,000 ($5,000 × 60%)] that can be used to reduce her overall state income tax liability. In making this contribution, Prisha is attempting to convert a state income tax payment (with an overall deduction limit of $10,000 per year) into a charitable contribution (with a potentially more favorable AGI limit).

On Prisha's 2022 Federal income tax return, she must reduce this charitable contribution by $3,000 because the credit she received was more than 15% of the contribution made. As a result, Prisha's charitable contribution deduction for this $5,000 donation is reduced to $2,000 ($5,000 donation − $3,000 state tax credit).

Contribution of Services

No deduction is allowed for the value of one's services contributed to a qualified charitable organization. However, unreimbursed expenses related to the services rendered may be deductible. For example, the cost of a uniform (without general utility) that is required to be worn while performing services may be deductible, as are certain out-of-pocket transportation costs incurred for the benefit of the charity. In lieu of the out-of-pocket costs for an automobile, a standard mileage rate of 14 cents per mile is allowed.[61] Deductions are also permitted for transportation, reasonable expenses for lodging, and the cost of meals while away from home that are incurred in performing the donated services. Such travel expenses are not deductible if the travel involves a significant element of personal pleasure, recreation, or vacation.[62]

Nondeductible Items

In addition to the benefit received rule and the restrictions placed on the contribution of services, the following items may not be deducted as charitable contributions:

- Dues, fees, or bills paid to country clubs, lodges, fraternal orders, or similar groups.
- Cost of raffle, bingo, or lottery tickets.
- Cost of tuition.
- Payment for the right to purchase tickets for seating at an athletic event in a university stadium.[63]

[60] Reg. § 1.170A–1(h)(3). Reg. § 1.164–3(j) allows an individual with state and local taxes below the $10,000 cap to treat the disallowed charitable contribution amount as a state tax deduction (not to exceed the $10,000 cap).

[61] § 170(i).

[62] § 170(j).

[63] § 170(l).

- Value of blood given to a blood bank.
- Payments to homeowners associations.
- Gifts to individuals.
- Rental value of property used by a qualified charity.

Sarah's neighbor, Dylan, is very ill and has been in the hospital for several weeks. Dylan's insurance will not cover all of his medical bills. As a result, a neighborhood friend set up a crowdfunding website, allowing people to contribute money that will be used to help Dylan pay his medical bills. Sarah transferred $700 to the crowdfunding campaign.

Sarah may not deduct the $700 as a charitable contribution because the payment was made for the benefit of an individual rather than to a (qualified) charitable organization (see text Section 10-4d).

Time of Deduction

A charitable contribution generally is deducted in the year the payment is made. This rule applies to both cash and accrual basis individuals. A contribution is ordinarily deemed to have been made on the date of delivery of the property to the donee. For example, if a gift of common stock is made to a qualified charitable organization, the gift is considered complete on the day of delivery or mailing. However, if the donor delivers the stock certificate to her bank, her broker, or the issuing corporation, the gift is considered complete on the date the stock is transferred on the books of the corporation.

A contribution made by check is considered delivered on the date of mailing. Thus, a contribution made by a check mailed on December 31, 2022, is deductible on the taxpayer's 2022 tax return. If the contribution is charged on a credit card, the date the charge is made determines the year of deduction.

Record-Keeping Requirements

In order to claim a charitable contribution deduction, the taxpayer must have appropriate documentation. The specific type of documentation required depends on the amount of the contribution and whether the contribution is made in cash or noncash property.[64] For example, for a single contribution of $250 or more, no charitable deduction is allowed unless the taxpayer receives written acknowledgment of the donation from the charity that notes the donation and states whether the donor received anything in return from the donee. In addition, special rules may apply to gifts of certain types of property (e.g., used cars, boats, and airplanes) where Congress has found taxpayer abuse of the rules in the past. Further, for certain gifts of noncash property, Form 8283 (Noncash Charitable Contributions) must be attached to the taxpayer's return.

The taxpayer must have the required documentation before the tax return with the claimed contribution is filed (and no later than the due date, including extensions, of that tax return). Failure to comply with the reporting rules typically results in disallowance of the charitable contribution deduction. In addition, substantial penalties may apply if the taxpayer significantly overvalues any contributed property.

Valuation Requirements

Property donated to a charity is generally valued at fair market value at the time the gift is made. Little guidance is provided about the measurement of the fair market value. IRS guidance states that "The fair market value is the price at which the property would change hands between a willing buyer and a willing seller, neither being under any compulsion to buy or sell and both having reasonable knowledge of relevant facts."[65]

Generally, charitable organizations do not attest to the fair market value of the donated property. Nevertheless, the taxpayer must maintain reliable, written evidence of the value of the donation. For certain donations, a qualified appraisal is required.

---

[64] Documentation thresholds and requirements are provided in § 170(f).

[65] Reg. § 1.170A–1(c)(2).

Global Tax Issues — Choose the Charity Wisely

Maiya, a U.S. citizen of Nepali descent, was distressed by the damage caused by a major earthquake in Nepal. She donated $100,000 to the Earthquake Victims' Relief Fund, a Nepali charitable organization that was set up to help victims of the earthquake. Raju, also a U.S. citizen of Nepali descent, donated $100,000 to help with the relief effort. However, Raju's contribution went to his church, which sent the proceeds of a fund drive to the Earthquake Victims' Relief Fund in Nepal. Maiya's contribution is not deductible, but Raju's is. Why? Contributions to charitable organizations are not deductible unless the organization is a U.S. charity.

Digging Deeper 9

More information about the requirements for charitable contribution deductions can be found on this book's companion website: www.cengage.com

Limitations on Charitable Contribution Deduction

The potential charitable contribution deduction is the total of all donations, both money and property, that qualify for the deduction. However, the charitable contribution deduction is subject to a number of limitations (based on the taxpayer's AGI, the type of property contributed, and the charity receiving the property). In general:

- If the qualifying contributions for the year total 20 percent or less of AGI, they are fully deductible.
- If the qualifying contributions are more than 20 percent of AGI, the deductible amount may be limited to 20 percent, 30 percent, 50 percent, or 60 percent of AGI depending on the type of property given and the type of organization to which the donation is made.
- In any case, the maximum charitable contribution deduction may not exceed 60 percent of AGI for the tax year.

To correctly calculate the amount of a charitable contribution deduction, it is also necessary to understand the distinction between **capital gain property** and **ordinary income property**. These rules, which were discussed in text Section 5-6, are summarized in Concept Summary 10.3.

The following sections explain when the various percentage limitations apply.

Fifty Percent Ceiling

Contributions made to public charities may not exceed 50 percent of an individual's AGI for the year. The 50 percent ceiling on contributions applies to public charities such as churches; schools; hospitals; and Federal, state, or local governmental units. The 50 percent ceiling also applies to contributions to private operating foundations and certain private nonoperating foundations.

In the remaining discussion of charitable contributions, public charities and private foundations (both operating and nonoperating) that qualify for the 50 percent ceiling will be referred to as 50 percent organizations.

Temporary Sixty Percent Ceiling

From 2018 through 2025, the deduction limit for *cash donations* made to 50 percent organizations is 60 percent of AGI. The increase in the charitable contribution deduction percentage is intended to offset the potential decrease in charitable donations that could result from fewer individuals itemizing their deductions. Most policy organizations believe that the increased ceiling will have little, if any, effect on the expected decline in individual donations to charities.

Concept Summary 10.3

Determining the Deduction for Contributions of Appreciated Property by Individuals

If the Type of Property Contributed Is:	And the Property Is Contributed to:	The Contribution Is Measured by:	But the Deduction Is Limited to:
Capital gain property	A 50% organization	Fair market value of the property	30% of AGI
Ordinary income property	A 50% organization	The basis of the property*	50% of AGI
Capital gain property (and the property is tangible personal property put to an unrelated use by the donee)	A 50% organization	The basis of the property*	50% of AGI
Capital gain property	A private nonoperating foundation that is not a 50% organization	The basis of the property*	The lesser of: 20% of AGI or 50% of AGI minus other contributions to 50% organizations
Cash	A 50% organization	The amount of cash	60% of AGI (100% for 2020 and 2021)

*If the fair market value of the property is less than the adjusted basis (i.e., the property has declined in value instead of appreciating), the fair market value is used.

Thirty Percent Ceiling

A 30 percent ceiling applies to contributions of cash and ordinary income property to private nonoperating foundations that are not 50 percent organizations. The 30 percent ceiling also applies to contributions of appreciated capital gain property to 50 percent organizations.[66]

In the event the contributions for any one tax year involve a combination of 60, 50, and 30 percent property, the allowable deduction comes first from the 60 percent property, next from the 50 percent property, and then from the 30 percent property.[67]

During the year, Lisa makes the following donations to her church: cash of $2,000 and unimproved land worth $30,000. Lisa purchased the land four years ago for $22,000 and held it as an investment. Therefore, it is capital gain property. Lisa's AGI for the year is $60,000. Disregarding percentage limitations, Lisa's potential charitable contribution deduction is $32,000 [$2,000 (cash) + $30,000 (fair market value of land)].

In applying the percentage limitations, however, the *current* deduction for the land is limited to $18,000 [30% (limitation applicable to capital gain property) × $60,000 (AGI)]. Thus, the total current deduction is $20,000 [$2,000 (cash) + $18,000 (land)]. Note that the total deduction does not exceed $30,000, which is 50% of Lisa's AGI.

Twenty Percent Ceiling

A 20 percent ceiling applies to contributions of appreciated capital gain property to private nonoperating foundations that are not 50 percent organizations. In addition, only the basis of the contributed property is allowed as a deduction.

[66]Under a special election, a taxpayer may choose to permanently forgo a deduction of the appreciation on capital gain property. Referred to as the reduced deduction election, this enables the taxpayer to move from the 30% limitation to the 50% limitation. See § 170(b)(1)(C)(iii).

[67]§ 170(b)(1)(G)(iii)(II).

Tax planning tips for non-cash donations can be found on this book's companion website: www.cengage.com

Additional Provisions for 2020 and 2021

As a result of COVID-19 related legislation, charitable contributions made in the 2020 and 2021 tax years enjoy additional tax benefits. First, in both 2020 and 2021, the deduction limit for cash contributions is increased to 100 percent of AGI (from 60 percent of AGI).[68] Second, in 2020, individuals who did not itemize deductions were allowed to claim a deduction *for* AGI of up to $300 for charitable contributions made in cash.[69] Third, in 2021, individuals who do not itemize are allowed to claim a *from* AGI deduction of up to $300 for charitable contributions made in cash ($600 for married couples filing jointly); this deduction is in addition to the taxpayer's standard deduction.[70]

Contribution Carryovers

Contributions that exceed the percentage limitations for the current year can be carried over for five years.[71] In the carryover process, such contributions do not lose their identity for limitation purposes. Thus, if the contribution originally involved 30 percent property, the carryover will continue to be classified as 30 percent property in the carryover year.

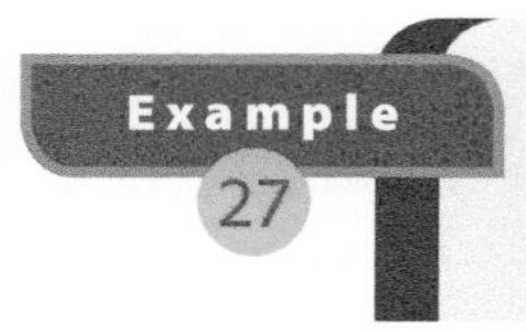

Assume the same facts as in Example 26. Because only $18,000 of the $30,000 value of the land (the deductible amount) is deducted in the current year, the balance of $12,000 may be carried over to the following year. The carryover will still be treated as a donation of capital gain property and will be subject to the 30%-of-AGI limitation in the carryover year.

In applying the percentage limitations, current charitable contributions must be claimed first before any carryovers can be considered. If carryovers involve more than one year, they are utilized in a first-in, first-out order.

10-4e Other Itemized Deductions

In general, no deduction is allowed for personal, living, or family expenses.[72] However, a number of expenses and losses are deductible on Schedule A (Form 1040).

- Gambling losses and gambling expenses up to the amount of gambling winnings.
- Impairment-related work expenses of a handicapped person.
- Federal estate tax on income earned or received by a person after his or her death (e.g., a bonus, interest income).[73]

[68]CARES Act § 2205(a) (P.L. 116–136); Consolidated Appropriations Act, 2021 §213 (P.L. 116–260).

[69]§§ 62(a)(22) and (f).

[70]§ 170(p).

[71]§ 170(d); Reg. § 1.170A–10.

[72]§ 262.

[73]These deductions are addressed in § 165 (gambling losses), § 67 (impairment-related work expenses), and § 691 (estate tax deduction).

Example 28

Jean is single and had the following transactions in 2022:

Medicines that required a prescription	$ 830
Doctor and dentist bills paid and not reimbursed	3,120
Medical insurance premium payments	9,200
Contact lenses	370
Transportation for medical purposes on March 1, 2022 (324 miles × 18 cents per mile + $10 parking)	68
State income tax withheld (exceeds the sales tax from the sales tax table)	7,900
Real estate taxes paid	6,580
Interest paid on qualified residence mortgage (acquisition indebtedness)	4,340
Qualifying charitable contributions (paid by check); proper documentation exists	2,160
Transportation in performing charitable services throughout 2022 (800 miles × 14 cents per mile + $7 parking and tolls)	119
Unreimbursed employee business expenses	1,870
Tax return preparation fee	450
Safe deposit box (used for keeping investment documents and tax records)	170

Jean's AGI is $120,000. The total of her itemized deductions is $21,207, as calculated below. This amount is greater than her 2022 standard deduction of $12,950.

Itemized Deductions

Medical and Dental Expenses		
Total	$13,588	
Less: 7.5% of AGI	(9,000)	
Deductible amount		$ 4,588
Taxes Paid		
State and local income taxes	$ 7,900	
Real estate taxes	6,580	
Total	$14,480	
Deduction limited to $10,000		10,000
Interest Paid		
Home mortgage interest		4,340
Gifts to Charity		
Gifts by cash or check	$ 2,160	
Other than by cash or check	119	
Total deduction		2,279
Total Itemized Deductions		$21,207

Prior to 2018, certain other personal expenses were deductible to the extent, in total, they exceeded 2 percent of the taxpayer's AGI (and only if the taxpayer itemized deductions instead of claiming the standard deduction). These miscellaneous itemized deductions included unreimbursed employee business expenses, certain investment expenses, tax return preparation fees (other than for portions of the return related to business), and expenses related to hobbies. From 2018 through 2025, these expenses are not deductible. This explains why, in Example 28, Jean's unreimbursed employee expenses, tax return preparation fee, and safe deposit box rental cost are not tax deductible.

Explain and illustrate the adoption expenses credit, child tax credit, education tax credits, credit for child and dependent care expenses, earned income credit, and premium tax credit.

10-5 Individual Tax Credits

A tax credit and an income tax deduction are not the same thing: income tax deductions reduce a taxpayer's tax base while tax credits reduce a taxpayer's tax liability. Thus, a credit is a dollar-for-dollar reduction in a taxpayer's tax liability. Several commonly encountered tax credits available to individuals are discussed in this section.

Tax Planning Strategies **Effective Utilization of Itemized Deductions**

Framework Focus: Deductions

Strategy: Maximize Deductible Amounts.

An individual may use the standard deduction in one year and itemize deductions in another year. Therefore, it is possible to obtain tax benefits by shifting itemized deductions from one year to another. For example, if a taxpayer's itemized deductions and the standard deduction are approximately the same for each year of a two-year period, the taxpayer should use the standard deduction in one year and shift itemized deductions (to the extent permitted by law) to the other year. The individual could, for example, prepay a charitable pledge for a particular year or avoid paying end-of-the-year medical expenses to shift the deduction to the following year.

10-5a Adoption Expenses Credit

The **adoption expenses credit** assists taxpayers who incur nonrecurring costs directly associated with the adoption process, such as adoption fees, attorney fees, court costs, social service review costs, and transportation costs.[74]

In 2022, up to $14,890 of costs incurred to adopt an eligible child qualify for the credit. An eligible child is either:

- Under 18 years of age at the time of the adoption, or
- Physically or mentally incapable of taking care of himself or herself.

In general, taxpayers claim the credit in the year the adoption is completed. If the adoption is not completed, the credit can be claimed in the following year. A married couple must file a joint return to claim the credit.

The amount of the credit that is otherwise available is phased out ratably over a $40,000 range once AGI exceeds $223,410. Although the credit is nonrefundable, any unused adoption expenses credit may be carried forward for up to five years, utilized on a first-in, first-out basis.

10-5b Child and Dependent Tax Credits

The **child tax credit** and the **dependent tax credit** allow individual taxpayers to claim a tax credit based solely on the *number* of their qualifying children and dependents. These credits are two of several "family-friendly" provisions in the Federal income tax law. To be eligible for the child tax credit, the child must be under age 17 (under age 18 for 2021), must be a U.S. citizen, and must be a dependent of the taxpayer. The dependent tax credit is available for each dependent of the taxpayer (other than a qualifying child).

The child tax credit is $2,000 per qualifying child; the dependent tax credit is $500 for non-qualifying-child dependents.[75] The child tax credit phases out as AGI exceeds $400,000 (for married taxpayers filing jointly) or $200,000 (for all other taxpayers).

Due to the COVID-19 pandemic, Congress temporarily increased the child tax credit. For 2021, the credit was increased to $3,000 ($3,600 for a qualifying child under age 6 at the end of the year).

The portion of the child tax credit in excess of $2,000 for 2021 ($1,600 per child under age 6 and $1,000 per child age 6 and older) was subject to its own phaseout rule. For 2021, the additional child tax credit phased out as AGI exceeded $150,000 (married, filing jointly), $112,500 (head of household), or $75,000 (other taxpayers). The additional credit was reduced by $50 for each $1,000 (or fraction thereof) of AGI over the applicable threshold amount. This phaseout did not reduce the $2,000 child tax credit amount (which has its own phaseout rule, noted above).

[74] § 23.

[75] § 24.

In 2021, the child tax credit was fully refundable. In 2022, the child tax credit is partially refundable (up to $1,500 per child, but no more than 15 percent of earned income in excess of $2,500). The dependent tax credit is also subject to a phaseout; it is not refundable.

10-5c Credit for Child and Dependent Care Expenses

The **credit for child and dependent care expenses** mitigates the inequity experienced by working taxpayers who must pay for child care services to work outside the home.[76] This credit is a specified percentage of expenses incurred to enable the taxpayer to work or to seek employment. The credit percentage varies based on the taxpayer's AGI, and expenses are capped at a maximum of $6,000 in 2022 ($16,000 in 2021).

Eligibility

To be eligible for the credit, an individual must have either:

- A dependent under age 13, or
- A dependent or spouse who is physically or mentally incapacitated and who lives with the taxpayer for more than one-half of the year.

Generally, married taxpayers must file a joint return to obtain the credit.

Eligible Employment-Related Expenses

Eligible expenses include amounts paid for household services and care of a qualifying individual that are incurred to enable the taxpayer to be employed. The care can be provided in the home (e.g., by a nanny) or outside the home (e.g., at a day-care center).

Out-of-the-home expenses incurred for an older dependent or spouse who is physically or mentally incapacitated qualify for the credit if that person regularly spends at least eight hours each day in the taxpayer's household. This makes the credit available to taxpayers who care for handicapped older children and relatives who are 65 and older in the home. Child care payments to a relative are eligible for the credit unless the relative is a child (under age 19) of the taxpayer.

Earned Income Ceiling

Qualifying employment-related expenses are limited to an individual's earned income. For married taxpayers, this limitation applies to the spouse with the lesser amount of earned income. Special rules are provided for taxpayers with nonworking spouses who are disabled or are full-time students. If a nonworking spouse is physically or mentally disabled or is a full-time student, they are deemed to have earned income for purposes of this limitation. The deemed amount is $250 per month if there is one qualifying individual in the household (e.g., a dependent child under age 13) or $500 per month if there are two or more qualifying individuals in the household. In the case of a student-spouse, the student's income is treated as earned only for the months the student is enrolled on a full-time basis.[77]

Calculation of the Credit

Many taxpayers incurred additional expenses for child and dependent care during the COVID-19 pandemic. Thus, Congress increased the amount of expenses qualifying for the credit, increased the credit rate, and changed the income eligibility rules for 2021 (allowing more taxpayers to claim the credit at its highest rate). In 2022, these items returned to their previous levels.

In general, the credit is equal to a percentage of *unreimbursed* employment-related expenses up to $3,000 for one qualifying individual ($8,000 in 2021) and $6,000 for two or more individuals ($16,000 in 2021). In 2022, the credit rate starts at 35 percent and decreases to 20 percent as AGI increases (50 percent to 0 percent in 2021); see Exhibits 10.4 and 10.5.

---

[76] § 21.

[77] § 21(d).

Example 29

During 2022, Nancy worked full-time while her spouse, Ron, attended college for 10 months during the year. The couple has two children under 13. Nancy earned $82,000 and incurred $6,200 of child care expenses. Ron is deemed to have earned $500 for each of the 10 months (or a total of $5,000).

Because Nancy and Ron report AGI of $82,000, their credit rate is 20%. Nancy and Ron are limited to $5,000 in qualified child care expenses ($6,200 of child care expenses, limited to Ron's deemed earned income of $5,000). As a result, they are entitled to a child care credit of $1,000 (20% × Ron's deemed income of $5,000; see Exhibit 10.5) for the year.

Exhibit 10.4 2021 Child and Dependent Care Credit Computations

Adjusted Gross Income		Credit	Adjusted Gross Income		Credit
Over	But Not Over	Rate	Over	But Not Over	Rate
$ 0	$125,000	50%	$155,000	$157,000	34%
125,000	127,000	49%	157,000	159,000	33%
127,000	129,000	48%	159,000	161,000	32%
129,000	131,000	47%	161,000	163,000	31%
131,000	133,000	46%	163,000	165,000	30%
133,000	135,000	45%	165,000	167,000	29%
135,000	137,000	44%	167,000	169,000	28%
137,000	139,000	43%	169,000	171,000	27%
139,000	141,000	42%	171,000	173,000	26%
141,000	143,000	41%	173,000	175,000	25%
143,000	145,000	40%	175,000	177,000	24%
145,000	147,000	39%	177,000	179,000	23%
147,000	149,000	38%	179,000	181,000	22%
149,000	151,000	37%	181,000	183,000	21%
151,000	153,000	36%	183,000	400,000	20%
153,000	155,000	35%	400,000	*	*

*The 20% rate phases out for taxpayers with AGI over $400,000. Specifically, a 1% reduction occurs for each additional $2,000 of AGI in excess of $400,000. As a result, the credit percentage is zero once AGI exceeds $498,000.

Exhibit 10.5 2022 Child and Dependent Care Credit Rates

Adjusted Gross Income		
Over	But Not Over	Applicable Rate of Credit
$ 0	$15,000	35%
15,000	17,000	34%
17,000	19,000	33%
19,000	21,000	32%
21,000	23,000	31%
23,000	25,000	30%
25,000	27,000	29%
27,000	29,000	28%
29,000	31,000	27%
31,000	33,000	26%
33,000	35,000	25%
35,000	37,000	24%
37,000	39,000	23%
39,000	41,000	22%
41,000	43,000	21%
43,000	No limit	20%

10-5d Education Tax Credits

The **American Opportunity credit** and the **lifetime learning credit** [78] are available to help qualifying low- and middle-income individuals defray the cost of higher education. The credits are available for qualifying tuition and related expenses incurred by students pursuing undergraduate or graduate degrees or vocational training. Books and other course materials are eligible for the American Opportunity credit (but not the lifetime learning credit).[79] Room and board are ineligible for both credits.

Maximum Credit

The American Opportunity credit permits a maximum credit of $2,500 per year (100 percent of the first $2,000 of tuition expenses plus 25 percent of the next $2,000 of tuition expenses) for the *first four years* of postsecondary education. The lifetime learning credit permits a credit of 20 percent of qualifying expenses (up to $10,000 per year) incurred in a year in which the American Opportunity credit is not claimed. Generally, the lifetime learning credit is used for individuals who are beyond the first four years of postsecondary education.

Eligible Individuals

Both education credits are available for qualified expenses incurred by a taxpayer, taxpayer's spouse, or taxpayer's dependent. The American Opportunity credit is available per eligible student, while the lifetime learning credit is calculated per taxpayer. To be eligible for the American Opportunity credit, a student must take at least one-half of the full-time course load for at least one academic term at a qualifying educational institution. No comparable requirement exists for the lifetime learning credit. Therefore, taxpayers who are seeking new job skills or maintaining existing skills through graduate training or continuing education are eligible for the lifetime learning credit. Taxpayers who are married must file a joint return to claim either education credit.

Income Limitations and Refundability

Both education credits are subject to income limitations, which differ by credit. Forty percent of the American Opportunity credit is refundable, and the credit can be used to offset a taxpayer's alternative minimum tax (AMT) liability (the lifetime learning credit is neither refundable nor an AMT liability offset).[80]

Both credits are phased out beginning when the taxpayer's AGI (modified for this purpose) reaches $80,000 ($160,000 for married taxpayers filing jointly).[81] Each credit is phased out proportionally over a $10,000 ($20,000 for married taxpayers filing jointly) phaseout range. As a result, each credit is eliminated when modified AGI reaches $90,000 ($180,000 for married taxpayers filing jointly).

American Opportunity Credit: Calculation and Limitation

Tom and Jennifer are married and file a joint tax return. Their modified AGI is $158,000, and they have two children, Lora and Sam. Tom and Jennifer paid $7,500 of tuition and $8,500 for room and board for Lora (a freshman) and $8,100 of tuition plus $7,200 for room and board for Sam (a junior). Both Lora and Sam are full-time students and are their parents' dependents.

Lora's tuition and Sam's tuition are qualified expenses for the American Opportunity credit. For 2022, Tom and Jennifer may claim a $2,500 American Opportunity credit for both Lora's and Sam's expenses [(100% × $2,000) + (25% × $2,000)]; in total, they qualify for a $5,000 American Opportunity credit.

[78] § 25A.

[79] § 25A(i)(3).

[80] If the credit is claimed for a taxpayer subject to § 1(g) (the "kiddie tax"), the credit is not refundable.

[81] These amounts are not adjusted for inflation. Prior to 2021, the lifetime learning credit was subject to a similar phaseout.

American Opportunity Credit: Calculation and Limitation

Example 31

Assume the same facts as in Example 30, except that Tom and Jennifer's modified AGI for 2022 is $172,000 instead of $158,000. In this case, Tom and Jennifer can claim a $2,000 American Opportunity credit rather than a $5,000 credit.

The potential $5,000 American Opportunity credit is reduced because their modified AGI exceeds the $160,000 limit for married taxpayers. The reduction is computed as the amount by which modified AGI exceeds the limit, expressed as a percentage of the phaseout range, or [($172,000 − $160,000) ÷ $20,000], resulting in a 60% reduction. Therefore, the maximum available credit for 2021 is $2,000 ($5,000 × 40% allowable portion).

Taxpayers are prohibited from receiving a double tax benefit associated with qualifying educational expenses. Therefore, taxpayers who claim an education credit may not deduct the expenses, nor may they claim the credit for amounts that are otherwise excluded from gross income (e.g., scholarships and employer-paid educational assistance).

Digging Deeper 11

Information reporting for education credits is explained on this book's companion website:
www.cengage.com

10-5e Earned Income Credit

The **earned income credit** provides income tax equity to the working poor. In addition, the credit helps to offset the cost of other Federal taxes, such as the gasoline tax, that impose a relatively larger burden on low-income taxpayers. Further, the credit encourages and rewards work. As discussed below, a taxpayer's EITC increases as earnings increase (until reaching the maximum). This creates an incentive for people to seek employment or to increase their work hours.[82]

Eligibility Requirements

Eligibility for the credit depends not only on whether the taxpayer meets the earned income and AGI thresholds but also on whether they have a *qualifying child.* The term *qualifying child* generally has the same meaning here as it does for purposes of determining who qualifies as a dependent.

In addition to being available for taxpayers with qualifying children, the earned income credit is also available to certain workers without children. In general, this provision is available only to such taxpayers ages 25 through 64 who cannot be claimed as a dependent on another taxpayer's return. (In 2021, the minimum age to claim the credit was reduced to 19 (except for certain full-time students) and the maximum age was eliminated.)

Amount of the Credit

The earned income credit is determined by multiplying a maximum amount of earned income by the appropriate credit percentage. Generally, earned income includes employee compensation and net earnings from self-employment; it excludes items such as interest, dividends, pension benefits, nontaxable employee compensation, and alimony. If a taxpayer has children, the credit percentage used in the calculation depends on the number of qualifying children.

[82]§ 32. Due to the COVID-19 pandemic, taxpayers could use either 2019 or 2021 earned income in calculating their 2021 earned income credit (a similar provision applied in 2020). The earned income credit is not available if the taxpayer's unearned income (e.g., interest and dividends) exceeds $10,300 in 2022 ($10,000 in 2021). See § 32(i).

In 2022, the maximum earned income credit is $3,733 ($10,980 × 34%) for a taxpayer with one qualifying child, $6,164 ($15,410 × 40%) for a taxpayer with two qualifying children, and $6,935 ($15,410 × 45%) for a taxpayer with three or more qualifying children. However, the maximum earned income credit is phased out completely if the taxpayer's earned income or AGI exceeds certain thresholds. To the extent the greater of earned income or AGI exceeds $26,260 in 2022 for married taxpayers filing a joint return ($20,130 for other taxpayers), the difference, multiplied by the appropriate phaseout percentage, is subtracted from the maximum earned income credit.

Information about the Premium Tax Credit can be found in the online ACA appendix and on this book's companion website: www.cengage.com

12 Digging Deeper

Refocus on The Big Picture

The Tax Implications of Life!

ESB PROFESSIONAL/SHUTTERSTOCK.COM

While Danae and David's employment earnings of $70,000 are taxable, they should be aware that their employers may have provided them with a number of tax-free fringe benefits. In addition, if Danae and David paid monthly premiums for accident and health care plans or contributed to a flexible spending account, those amounts may reduce their taxable income (these items are discussed in text Section 11-2h). The $10,000 gift received from Danae's grandmother can be excluded from gross income. However, the $250 of interest earned on the money is included in income.

While Danae's tuition waiver of $4,500 can be excluded from gross income, the $450 monthly payment is compensation and, as such, is included in the couple's gross income. With respect to the damages awarded, all of the compensatory damages of $220,000 can be excluded from gross income because they relate to personal physical injury or sickness. However, the punitive damages of $160,000 must be included in gross income. The amounts received from the crowdfunding campaign can be excluded from gross income since these amounts were given to the couple with no expectation of receiving anything in return from them.

Danae and David have several deductions *for* adjusted gross income. In addition to the alimony paid by David, $3,000 of the capital loss from the stock sale is deductible *for* AGI and interest on the qualified student loan is deductible *for* AGI (subject to a phaseout).

While medical expenses, state income taxes, personal property taxes, and charitable contributions are deductible *from* AGI, Danae and David should claim the standard deduction for a married couple since it appears to exceed their itemized deductions.

Danae and David will determine their tax liability using the tax rate schedule for married couples filing a joint return.

They may be eligible for one or more tax credits, including the child tax credit and an education tax credit related to Danae's tuition. If Stephen has unearned income in excess of certain thresholds, they should also be made aware of the potential application of the "kiddie" tax.

What If?

What if Danae and David purchase a house in the current year? What are the likely tax implications of owning a new home? If they purchase a new home, mortgage interest and property taxes paid on the home are treated as additional itemized deductions. Depending on the amount of these deductions, Danae and David's itemized deductions might then exceed the standard deduction amount, giving them a larger tax deduction and further reducing their tax liability.

Suggested Readings

Elisa Anchan and Ryan Oberly, "Donor Naming Considerations," *Taxation of Exempts*, Jul/Aug 2020.

Luke Bailey, "Individual Coverage Health Reimbursement Arrangements—A New Alternative for Employer-Provided Health Coverage," *Corporate Taxation*, Jan/Feb 2021.

Sheldon Banoff and Richard Lipton, "Turbo-Charging Your Tax Deductions: Do They Really Ad(d) Up?" *Journal of Taxation*, March 2021.

Paul C. Lau, Ron Marcuson, and Elizabeth Hoffman, "Tackling Taxes—Taxation of Settlement and Litigation Judgement: Part I," *Taxes-The Tax Magazine*, March 11, 2020.

Brian T. Whitlock, "Untaxingly Yours—New Rules Expand Health Reimbursement Accounts," *Taxes—The Tax Magazine*, January 10, 2020.

Key Terms

Accident and health insurance benefits, 10-10
Acquisition indebtedness, 10-19
Adoption expenses credit, 10-28
Alimony and separate maintenance payments, 10-3
American Opportunity credit, 10-31
Capital gain property, 10-24
Charitable contribution, 10-21
Child tax credit, 10-28
Compensatory damages, 10-8
Credit for child and dependent care expenses, 10-29
Dependent tax credit, 10-28
Earned income credit, 10-32
Educational savings bonds, 10-10
Health Savings Account (HSA), 10-14
Home equity loans, 10-19
Investment interest, 10-18
Lifetime learning credit, 10-31
Medical expenses, 10-12
Net investment income, 10-18
Ordinary income property, 10-24
Points, 10-20
Punitive damages, 10-9
Qualified residence interest, 10-19
Scholarship, 10-7

Computational Exercises

1. **LO.1** Casper and Cecile divorced in 2018. As part of the divorce settlement, Casper transferred stock to Cecile. Casper purchased the stock for $25,000, and it had a market value of $43,000 on the date of the transfer. Cecile sold the stock for $40,000 a month after receiving it. In addition, Casper is required to pay Cecile $1,500 a month in alimony. He made five payments to her during the year. What are the tax consequences for Casper and Cecile regarding these transactions?

2. **LO.1** Sally was an all-state soccer player during her junior and senior years in high school. She accepted an athletic scholarship from State University. The scholarship provided the following:

Tuition and fees	$15,000
Housing and meals	6,000
Books and supplies	1,500
Transportation	1,200

Determine the effect of the scholarship on Sally's gross income.

3. **LO.1** Jarrod receives a scholarship of $18,500 from East State University to be used to pursue a bachelor's degree. He spends $12,000 on tuition, $1,500 on books and supplies, $4,000 for room and board, and $1,000 for personal expenses. How much may Jarrod exclude from his gross income?

4. **LO.2** Pierre, a cash basis, unmarried taxpayer, had $1,400 of state income tax withheld during 2022. Also in 2022, Pierre paid $455 that was due when he filed his 2021 state income tax return and made estimated payments of $975 toward his 2022 state income tax liability. When Pierre files his 2022 Federal income tax return in April 2023, he elects to itemize deductions, which amount to $15,650, including the state income tax payments and withholdings, all of which reduce his taxable income.
   a. What is Pierre's 2022 state income tax deduction?
   b. As a result of overpaying his 2022 state income tax, Pierre receives a refund of $630 early in 2023. The standard deduction for single taxpayers for 2022 was $12,950. How much of the $630 will Pierre include in his 2023 gross income?

5. **LO.2** Troy's financial records for the year reflect the following:

Interest income from bank savings account	$ 900
Taxable annuity receipts	1,800
City ad valorem property tax on investments	125
Investment interest expense	3,200

   Calculate Troy's net investment income and his current investment interest deduction. How is a deduction for any potential excess investment interest treated?

6. **LO.2** Miller owns a personal residence with a fair market value of $195,000 and an outstanding first mortgage of $157,500, which was entirely used to acquire the residence. This year Miller gets a home equity loan of $10,000 to purchase a new fishing boat for personal use. How much of this mortgage debt is treated as qualified residence indebtedness?

7. **LO.2** Donna donates stock in Chipper Corporation to the American Red Cross on September 10, 2022. She purchased the stock for $18,100 on December 28, 2021, and it had a fair market value of $27,000 when she made the donation.
   a. What is Donna's charitable contribution deduction?
   b. Assume instead that the stock had a fair market value of $15,000 (rather than $27,000) when it was donated to the American Red Cross. What is Donna's charitable contribution deduction?
   c. What documentation should you request from Donna to confirm the amount of her charitable contribution deduction?

8. **LO.2** Barbara incurred the following expenses during 2022:

Membership dues at a health club she joined at the suggestion of her physician to improve her general physical condition	$ 840
Multiple vitamins and antioxidant vitamins	240
Smoking cessation program	3,500
Nonprescription nicotine gum	250
Insulin	2,600
Funeral expenses for her mother, who passed away in June	7,200

   Barbara's AGI for 2022 is $54,000. What is Barbara's medical expense deduction for 2022?

9. **LO.2** Thomas purchased a personal residence from Monique. To sell the residence, Monique agreed to pay $5,500 in points related to Thomas's mortgage. Discuss the deductibility of the points.

10. LO.3 Paola and Isidora are married; file a joint tax return; report modified AGI of $148,000; and have one dependent child, Dante. The couple paid $12,000 of tuition and $10,000 for room and board for Dante (a freshman). Dante is a full-time student. Determine the amount of the American Opportunity credit for 2022.

11. LO.3 In 2022, Santiago and Amy are married and file a joint tax return claiming their three children, ages 12, 14, and 19, as dependents. All parties are U.S. citizens. The couple's AGI is $140,000. Determine any available child tax credit and dependent tax credit.

12. LO.3 In 2022, Ivanna, who has three children under age 13, worked full-time while her spouse, Sergio, attended college for nine months during the year. Ivanna earned $47,000, and the couple incurred $6,400 of child care expenses. Determine Ivanna and Sergio's child and dependent care credit.

Problems

Critical Thinking

13. LO.1 William and Abigail, who live in San Francisco, have been experiencing problems in their marriage. They have a 3-year-old daughter, April, who stays with William's parents during the day because both William and Abigail are employed. Abigail worked to support William while he attended medical school, and now she has been accepted by a medical school in Mexico. Abigail has decided to divorce William and attend medical school. April will stay in San Francisco because of her strong attachment to her grandparents and because they can provide her with excellent day care. Abigail knows that William will expect her to contribute to the cost of raising April. Abigail also believes that to finance her education, she must receive cash for her share of the property they accumulated during their marriage. In addition, she believes that she should receive some reimbursement for her contribution to William's support while he was in medical school. She expects the divorce proceedings to take several months. Identify the relevant tax issues for Abigail.

Decision Making

14. LO.1 Patrick and Eva are planning to divorce in 2022. Patrick has offered to pay Eva $12,000 each year until their 11-year-old daughter reaches age 21. Alternatively, Patrick will transfer to Eva common stock that he owns with a fair market value of $100,000. What factors should Eva and Patrick consider in deciding between these two options?

15. LO.1 For each of the following, determine the amount that should be included in gross income:

    a. Peyton was selected the most valuable player in the Super Bowl. In recognition of this, he was awarded an automobile with a value of $60,000. Peyton did not need the automobile, so he asked that the title be put in his parents' names.
    b. Jacob was awarded the Nobel Peace Prize. When he was presented the check for $1,400,000, Jacob said, "I do not need the money. Give it to the United Nations to use toward the goal of world peace."
    c. Linda appeared on a television game show during the year, winning $6,000 of cash and $4,000 of furniture and appliances.

16. LO.1 Herbert was employed for the first six months of 2022 and earned $90,000 in salary. During the next six months, he collected $8,800 of unemployment compensation, borrowed $12,000 (using his personal residence as collateral), and withdrew $2,000 from his savings account (including $60 of interest earned this year). He received dividends of $550. In December, he won $1,500 in the lottery on a $5 ticket. Calculate Herbert's gross income.

17. **LO.1** Adrian was awarded an academic scholarship to State University for the 2022–2023 academic year. He received $6,500 in August and $7,200 in December 2022. Adrian had enough personal savings to pay all expenses as they came due. Adrian's expenditures for the relevant period were as follows:

Tuition, August 2022	$3,700
Tuition, January 2023	3,750
Room and board	
August–December 2022	2,800
January–May 2023	2,500
Books and educational supplies	
August–December 2022	1,000
January–May 2023	1,200

Determine the effect on Adrian's gross income for 2022 and 2023.

18. **LO.1** Determine the effect on gross income in each of the following cases:
   a. Eloise received $150,000 in settlement of a sex discrimination case against her former employer.
   b. Nell received $10,000 for damages to her personal reputation. She also received $40,000 in punitive damages.
   c. Beth received $10,000 in compensatory damages and $30,000 in punitive damages in a lawsuit she filed against a tanning parlor for severe burns she received from using its tanning equipment.
   d. Joanne received compensatory damages of $75,000 and punitive damages of $300,000 from a cosmetic surgeon who botched her nose job.

19. **LO.2** Emma Doyle is employed as a corporate attorney. For calendar year 2022, she had AGI of $75,000 and paid the following medical expenses: Communications

Medical insurance premiums	$3,700
Doctor and dentist bills for Bob and April (Emma's parents)	6,800
Doctor and dentist bills for Emma	5,200
Prescription medicines for Emma	400
Nonprescription insulin for Emma	350

Bob and April would qualify as Emma's dependents, except that they file a joint return. Emma's medical insurance policy does not cover them. Emma filed a claim for reimbursement of $2,800 of her own expenses with her insurance company in December 2022 and received the reimbursement in January 2023. What is Emma's maximum allowable medical expense deduction for 2022? Prepare a memo for your firm's tax files in which you document your conclusions.

20. **LO.2** Reba is a single taxpayer. Lawrence, Reba's 84-year-old dependent grandfather, lived with Reba until this year, when he moved to Lakeside Nursing Home because he needs specialized medical and nursing care. During the year, Reba made the following payments on behalf of Lawrence:

Room at Lakeside	$11,000
Meals for Lawrence at Lakeside	2,200
Doctor and nurse fees at Lakeside	1,700
Cable TV service for Lawrence's room at Lakeside	380
Total	$15,280

Lakeside has medical staff in residence. Disregarding the AGI floor, how much, if any, of these expenses qualify for a medical expense deduction by Reba?

21. **LO.2** Paul suffers from emphysema and severe allergies and, upon the recommendation of his physician, has a dust elimination system installed in his personal residence. In connection with the system, Paul incurs and pays the following amounts during 2022.

Doctor and hospital bills	$ 4,500
Dust elimination system	10,000
Increase in utility bills due to the system	450
Cost of certified appraisal	300

In addition, Paul pays $750 for prescribed medicines.

The system has an estimated useful life of 20 years. The appraisal was to determine the value of Paul's residence with and without the system. The appraisal states that his residence was worth $350,000 before the system was installed and $356,000 after the installation. Paul's AGI for the year was $50,000. How much is Paul's medical expense deduction in 2022?

22. **LO.2** Nichole, who is single and uses the cash method of accounting, lives in a state that imposes an income tax. In April 2022, she files her state income tax return for 2021 and pays an additional $1,000 in state income taxes. During 2022, her withholdings for state income tax purposes amount to $7,400, and she pays estimated state income tax of $700. In April 2023, she files her state income tax return for 2022, claiming a refund of $1,800. Nichole receives the refund in August 2023. Nichole has no other state or local tax expenses.

a. Assuming that Nichole itemized deductions in 2022, how much may she claim as a deduction for state income taxes on her Federal return for calendar year 2022 (filed in April 2023)?

b. Assuming that Nichole itemized deductions in 2022 (which totaled $20,000), how will the refund of $1,800 that she received in 2023 be treated for Federal income tax purposes?

c. Assume that Nichole itemized deductions in 2022 (which totaled $20,000) and that she elects to have the $1,800 refund applied toward her 2023 state income tax liability. How will the $1,800 be treated for Federal income tax purposes?

d. Assuming that Nichole did not itemize deductions in 2022, how will the refund of $1,800 received in 2023 be treated for Federal income tax purposes?

Communications
Decision Making

23. **LO.2** In 2022, Kathleen Tweardy incurs $30,000 of interest expense related to her investments. Her investment income includes $7,500 of interest, $6,000 of qualified dividends, and a $12,000 net capital gain on the sale of securities. Kathleen asks you to compute the amount of her deduction for investment interest, taking into consideration any options she might have. In addition, she would like your suggestions about any tax planning alternatives that are available. Write a letter to her that contains your advice. Kathleen lives at 11934 Briarpatch Drive, Midlothian, VA 23113.

24. **LO.2** Helen Derby borrowed $150,000 to acquire a parcel of land to be held for investment purposes. During the current year, she reported AGI of $90,000 and paid interest of $12,000 on the loan. Other items related to Helen's investments include the following:

Interest and annuity income	$11,000
Long-term capital gain on sale of stock	3,500
Real estate tax on the investment land	800

a. Determine Helen's investment interest deduction for the current year.

b. Discuss the treatment of the portion of Helen's investment interest that is disallowed for the current year.

c. Complete Helen's Form 4952 for the current year. For this purpose, assume that she chooses not to include the long-term capital gain as investment income. Her Social Security number is 123-45-6789.

25. **LO.2** The Wilmoths plan to purchase a house and would like to determine the after-tax cost of financing its purchase. Given their projected taxable income, the Wilmoths are in the 24% Federal income tax bracket and the 8% state income tax bracket (i.e., an aggregate marginal tax bracket of 32%). Assume that the Wilmoths will benefit from itemizing their deductions for both Federal and state tax purposes. The total cash outlay during the first year of ownership will be $23,400 ($1,200 principal payments, $22,200 qualified residence interest payments). Determine the initial year after-tax cost of financing the purchase of the home.

26. **LO.2** In December of each year, Eleanor Young contributes 10% of her gross income to the United Way (a 50% organization). Eleanor, who is in the 24% marginal tax bracket, is considering the following alternatives for satisfying the contribution. Communications Decision Making Digging Deeper

	Fair Market Value
(1) Cash donation	$23,000
(2) Unimproved land held for six years ($3,000 basis)	23,000
(3) Blue Corporation stock held for eight months ($3,000 basis)	23,000
(4) Gold Corporation stock held for two years ($28,000 basis)	23,000

Eleanor has asked you to help her decide which of the potential contributions listed above will be most tax advantageous. Evaluate the four alternatives, and write a letter to Eleanor to communicate your advice. Her address is 2622 Bayshore Drive, Berkeley, CA 94709.

27. **LO.2** Ramon had AGI of $180,000 in 2022. He is considering making a charitable contribution this year to the American Heart Association, a qualified charitable organization. Determine the current allowable charitable contribution deduction in each of the following independent situations, and indicate the treatment for any amount that is not deductible currently. Identify any planning ideas to minimize Ramon's tax liability. Decision Making Digging Deeper Planning

a. A cash gift of $95,000.
b. A gift of OakCo stock worth $95,000 on the contribution date. Ramon acquired the stock as an investment two years ago at a cost of $84,000.
c. A gift of a painting worth $95,000 that Ramon purchased three years ago for $60,000. The charity has indicated that it would sell the painting to generate cash to fund medical research.
d. Ramon has decided to donate cash to the American Heart Association of $113,000. However, he is considering delaying his donation until next year, when his AGI will increase to $300,000 and he will be in the 32% income tax bracket, an increase from his current-year income tax bracket of 24%. Ramon asks you to determine the tax savings from the tax deduction in present value terms if he were to make the donation this year rather than delaying the donation until next year. See Appendix E for the present value factors, and assume a 6% discount rate.

28. **LO.2** Linda, who files as a single taxpayer, had AGI of $280,000 for 2022. She incurred the following expenses and losses during the year:

Medical expenses (before the 7.5%-of-AGI limitation)	$33,000
State and local income taxes	4,800
State sales tax	1,300
Real estate taxes	6,000
Home mortgage interest	5,000
Automobile loan interest	750
Credit card interest	1,000
Charitable contributions	7,000
Casualty loss (before 10% limitation but after $100 floor; not in a Federally declared disaster area)	34,000
Unreimbursed employee business expenses	7,600

Calculate Linda's allowable itemized deductions for the year.

29. **LO.3** Jason, a single parent, lives in an apartment with his three minor children, whom he supports. Jason earned $27,400 during 2022 and uses the standard deduction. Calculate the amount, if any, of Jason's earned income credit.

30. **LO.3** Paul and Karen Kent are married, and both are employed (Paul earns $44,000 and Karen earns $9,000 during 2022). Paul and Karen have two dependent children, both under the age of 13 (Samuel and Joy). So they can work outside the home, Paul and Karen pay $3,800 ($1,900 for each child) to Sunnyside Day Care Center (422 Sycamore Road, Fort Worth, TX 76028; Employer Identification Number: 11-2345678) to care for their children while they are working. Assuming that Paul and Karen file a joint return, what, if any, is their tax credit for child and dependent care expenses?

31. **LO.3** Jim and Mary Jean are married and have two dependent children under the age of 13. Both parents are employed outside the home and, during 2022, earn salaries as follows: $130,000 (Jim) and $5,200 (Mary Jean). To care for their children while they work, they pay Eleanor (Jim's mother) $5,600. Eleanor does not qualify as a dependent of Jim and Mary Jean. Assuming that Jim and Mary Jean file a joint tax return, what, if any, is their credit for child and dependent care expenses?

Communications
Digging Deeper

32. **LO.3** Jenna, a longtime client of yours, is an architect and the president of the local Rotary chapter. To keep up to date with the latest developments in her profession, she attends continuing education seminars offered by the architecture school at State University. During 2022, Jenna spends $2,000 on course tuition to attend such seminars. She also spends another $400 on architecture books during the year.

    Jenna's daughter, Caitlin, is a senior majoring in engineering at the University of the Midwest. During the 2022 calendar year, Caitlin incurs the following expenses: $8,200 for tuition ($4,100 per semester) and $750 for books and course materials. Caitlin, who Jenna claims as a dependent, lives at home while attending school full-time. Jenna is married, files a joint return, and reports a combined AGI with her husband of $121,000.

    a. Calculate Jenna's education tax credits for 2022.
    b. Calculate Jenna's education tax credits if their combined AGI was $162,000.
    c. In her capacity as president of the local Rotary chapter, Jenna has asked you to prepare a 30- to 45-minute speech outlining the different ways the tax law helps defray (1) the cost of higher education and (2) the cost of continuing education once someone is in the workforce. Prepare an outline of possible topics for presentation. A tentative title for your presentation is "How Can the Tax Law Help Pay for College and Continuing Professional Education?"

Critical Thinking

33. **LO.3** Mark and Lisa are approaching an exciting time in their lives as their oldest son, Austin, graduates from high school and moves on to college. What are some of the tax issues Mark and Lisa should consider as they think about paying for Austin's college education?

Critical Thinking
Decision Making
Planning

34. **LO.3** Joyce, a single parent, lives in an apartment with her two minor children (ages 8 and 10), whom she supports. Joyce earns $33,000 during 2022. She uses the standard deduction and files as head of household.

    a. Calculate the amount, if any, of Joyce's earned income credit.
    b. During the year, Joyce is offered a new job that has greater future potential than her current job. If she accepts the job offer, her earnings for the year will be $39,000; however, she is afraid she will not qualify for the earned income credit. Using after-tax cash-flow calculations, determine whether Joyce should accept the new job offer. Since the child tax credit will be the same under either scenario, you can ignore it for purposes of this analysis.

Tax Return Problems

Decision Making

Planning

Tax Forms Problem

ProConnect™ Tax

1. Alice J. and Bruce M. Byrd are married taxpayers who file a joint return. Their Social Security numbers are 123-45-6784 and 111-11-1113, respectively. Alice's birthday is September 21, 1974, and Bruce's is June 27, 1973. They live at 473 Revere Avenue, Lowell, MA 01850. Alice is the office manager for Lowell Dental Clinic, 433 Broad Street, Lowell, MA 01850 (Employer Identification Number 98-7654321). Bruce is the manager of a Super Burgers fast-food outlet owned and operated by Plymouth Corporation, 1247 Central Avenue, Hauppauge, NY 11788 (Employer Identification Number 11-1111111).

   The following information is shown on their Wage and Tax Statements (Form W–2) for 2021.

Line	Description	Alice	Bruce
1	Wages, tips, other compensation	$58,000	$62,100
2	Federal income tax withheld	4,500	5,300
3	Social Security wages	58,000	62,100
4	Social Security tax withheld	3,596	3,850
5	Medicare wages and tips	58,000	62,100
6	Medicare tax withheld	841	900
15	State	Massachusetts	Massachusetts
16	State wages, tips, etc.	58,000	62,100
17	State income tax withheld	2,950	3,100

   The Byrds provide over half of the support of their two children, Cynthia (born January 25, 1997, Social Security number 123-45-6788) and John (born February 7, 2001, Social Security number 123-45-6780). Both children are full-time students and live with the Byrds except when they are away at college. Cynthia earned $6,200 from a summer internship in 2021, and John earned $3,800 from a part-time job. Both children received scholarships covering tuition and materials.

   During 2021, the Byrds provided 60% of the total support of Bruce's widower father, Sam Byrd (born March 6, 1945, Social Security number 123-45-6787). Sam lived alone and covered the rest of his support with his Social Security benefits. Sam died in November, and Bruce, the beneficiary of a policy on Sam's life, received life insurance proceeds of $1,600,000 on December 28.

   The Byrds had the following expenses relating to their personal residence during 2021:

Property taxes	$5,000
Qualified interest on home mortgage (acquisition indebtedness)	8,700
Repairs to roof	5,750
Utilities	4,100
Fire and theft insurance	1,900

   The Byrds had the following medical expenses for 2021:

Medical insurance premiums	$4,500
Doctor bill for Sam incurred in 2020 and not paid until 2021	7,600
Operation for Sam	8,500
Prescription medicines for Sam	900
Hospital expenses for Sam	3,500
Reimbursement from insurance company, received in 2021	3,600

The medical expenses for Sam represent most of the 60% that Bruce contributed toward his father's support.

Other relevant information follows:

- When they filed their 2020 state return in 2021, the Byrds paid additional state income tax of $900.
- During 2021, Alice and Bruce attended a dinner dance sponsored by the Lowell Police Disability Association (a qualified charitable organization). The Byrds paid $300 for the tickets. The cost of comparable entertainment would normally be $50.
- The Byrds contributed $5,000 to Lowell Presbyterian Church and gave used clothing (cost of $1,200 and fair market value of $350) to the Salvation Army. All donations are supported by receipts, and the clothing is in very good condition.
- Via a crowdfunding site (**gofundme.com**), Alice and Bruce made a gift to a needy family who lost their home in a fire ($400). In addition, they made several cash gifts to homeless individuals downtown (estimated to be $65).
- In 2021, the Byrds received interest income of $2,750, which was reported on a Form 1099–INT from Second National Bank, 125 Oak Street, Lowell, MA 01850 (Employer Identification Number 98-7654322).
- The home mortgage interest was reported on Form 1098 by Lowell Commercial Bank, PO Box 1000, Lowell, MA 01850 (Employer Identification Number 98-7654323). The mortgage (outstanding balance of $425,000 as of January 1, 2021) was taken out by the Byrds on May 1, 2017.
- Alice's employer requires that all employees wear uniforms to work. During 2021, Alice spent $850 on new uniforms and $566 on laundry charges.
- Bruce paid $400 for an annual subscription to the *Journal of Franchise Management* and $741 for annual membership dues to his professional association.
- Neither Alice's nor Bruce's employer reimburses for employee expenses.
- The Byrds do not keep the receipts for the sales taxes they paid and had no major purchases subject to sales tax.
- This year the Byrds gave each of their children $2,000, which was then deposited into their Roth IRAs.
- Alice and Bruce paid no estimated Federal income tax, and they did not engage in any virtual currency transactions during the year. Neither Alice nor Bruce wants to designate $3 to the Presidential Election Campaign Fund. The Byrds received the appropriate coronavirus recovery rebates (economic impact payments); related questions in ProConnect Tax should be ignored.

Part 1—Tax Computation

Compute net tax payable or refund due for Alice and Bruce Byrd for 2021, and complete their 2021 Federal tax return using appropriate forms and schedules. If they have overpaid, they want the amount to be refunded to them. Suggested software: ProConnect Tax.

Part 2—Tax Planning

Alice and Bruce are planning some significant changes for 2022. They have provided you with the following information and asked you to project their taxable income and tax liability for 2022.

The Byrds will invest the $1,600,000 of life insurance proceeds in short-term certificates of deposit (CDs) and use the interest for living expenses during 2022. They expect to earn total interest of $32,000 on the CDs.

Bruce has been promoted to regional manager, and his salary for 2022 will be $88,000. He estimates that state income tax withheld will increase by $4,000 and the Social Security tax withheld will be $5,456.

Alice, who has been diagnosed with a serious illness, will take a leave of absence from work during 2022, so she will not receive a salary or incur any work-related expenses during the year. The estimated cost for her medical treatment is $15,400, of which $6,400 will be reimbursed by their insurance company. Their medical insurance premium will increase to $9,769. Property taxes on their residence are expected to increase to $5,100. The Byrds' home mortgage interest expense and charitable contributions are expected to be unchanged from the prior year.

John will graduate from college in December 2021 and will take a job in New York City in January 2022. His starting salary will be $46,000.

Assume that all of the information reported in 2021 will be the same in 2022 unless other information has been presented above.

2. Paul and Donna Decker are married taxpayers, ages 44 and 42, respectively, who file a joint return for 2022. The Deckers live at 1121 College Avenue, Carmel, IN 46032. Paul is an assistant manager at Carmel Motor Inn, and Donna is a teacher at Carmel Elementary School. They present you with W–2 forms that reflect the following information: Tax Computation Problem

	Paul	Donna
Salary	$68,000	$56,000
Federal tax withheld	6,770	6,630
State income tax withheld	1,400	1,100
FICA (Social Security and Medicare) withheld	5,202	4,284
Social Security numbers	111-11-1112	123-45-6789

Donna is the custodial parent of two children from a previous marriage who reside with the Deckers through the school year. The children, Larry and Jane Parker, reside with their father, Bob, during the summer. Relevant information for the children follows:

	Larry	Jane
Age	17	18
Social Security numbers	123-45-6788	123-45-6787
Months spent with Deckers	9	9

Under the divorce decree, Bob pays child support of $150 per month per child during the nine months the children live with the Deckers. Bob says that he spends $200 per month per child during the three summer months they reside with him. Donna and Paul can document that they provide $2,000 of support per child per year. The divorce decree is silent as to which parent can claim the exemptions for the children.

In August, Paul and Donna added a suite to their home to provide more comfortable accommodations for Hannah Snyder (Social Security number 123-45-6786), Donna's mother, who had moved in with them in February 2021 after the death of Donna's father. Not wanting to borrow money for this addition, Paul sold 300 shares of Acme Corporation stock for $50 per share on May 3, 2022, and used the proceeds of $15,000 to cover construction costs. The Deckers had purchased the stock on April 29, 2017, for $25 per share. They received dividends of $750 on the jointly owned stock a month before the sale.

Hannah, who is 66 years old, received $7,500 in Social Security benefits during the year, of which she gave the Deckers $2,000 to use toward household expenses and deposited the remainder in her personal savings account. The Deckers determine that they have spent $2,500 of their own money for food, clothing, medical expenses, and other items for Hannah. They do not know what the rental value of Hannah's suite would be, but they estimate it would be at least $300 per month.

Interest paid during the year included the following:

Home mortgage interest (paid to Carmel Federal Savings and Loan)	$7,890
Interest on an automobile loan (paid to Carmel National Bank)	1,660
Interest on Citibank Visa card	620

In July, Paul hit a submerged rock while boating. Fortunately, he was uninjured after being thrown from the boat and landing in deep water. However, the boat, which was uninsured, was destroyed. Paul had paid $25,000 for the boat in June 2021, and its value was appraised at $18,000 on the date of the accident.

The Deckers paid doctor and hospital bills of $12,700 and were reimbursed $2,000 by their insurance company. They spent $640 for prescription drugs and medicines and $5,904 for premiums on their health insurance policy. They have filed additional claims of $1,200 with their insurance company and have been told they will receive payment for that amount in January 2023. Included in the amounts paid for doctor and hospital bills were payments of $380 for Hannah and $850 for the children.

Additional information of potential tax consequence follows:

Real estate taxes paid	$6,850
Sales taxes paid (per table)	1,379
Contributions to their church	4,600
Appraised value of books donated to public library	740
Refund of state income tax for 2021 (the Deckers itemized on their 2021 Federal tax return, and their total state and local taxes were less than $10,000, and their total itemized deductions exceeded their standard deduction by $5,400)	1,520

Compute net tax payable or refund due for the Deckers for 2022.

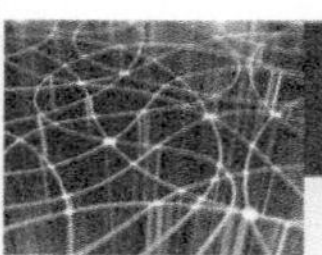

Bridge Discipline

1. George comes to you asking for your advice. He wants to invest $10,000 either in a debt security or in an equity investment. His choices are shown below.

   - Redbreast Corporation bond, annual coupon rate of 7.5%.
   - City of Philadelphia general obligation bond, annual coupon rate of 6.0%.
   - Blue Corporation 7.5% preferred stock (produces qualified dividend income).

   These alternatives are believed to carry comparable risk. Assuming that George is in the 35% marginal tax bracket (and that dividends are taxed at a 15% rate), which investment alternative could be expected to produce the superior annual after-tax rate of return?

2. Assume the same facts as in Problem 1, except that George is a C corporation rather than an individual and is in the 25% marginal tax bracket (combined Federal and state rate). Which investment strategy would maximize George, Inc.'s annual return?

Research Problems

Note: Solutions to the Research Problems can be prepared by using the Thomson Reuters Checkpoint™ online tax research database, which accompanies this textbook. Solutions can also be prepared by using research materials found in a typical tax library.

Research Problem 1. Jane suffers from a degenerative spinal disorder. Her physician said that swimming could help prevent the onset of permanent paralysis and recommended the installation of a swimming pool at her residence for her use. Jane's residence had a market value of approximately $500,000 before the swimming pool was installed. The swimming pool was built, and an appraiser estimated that the value of Jane's home increased by $98,000 because of the addition.

The pool cost $194,000, and Jane claimed a medical expense deduction of $96,000 ($194,000 − $98,000) on her tax return. Upon audit of the return, the IRS determined that an adequate pool should have cost $70,000 and would increase the value of her home by only $31,000. Thus, the IRS claims that Jane is entitled to a deduction of only $39,000 ($70,000 − $31,000).

a. Is there any ceiling limitation on the amount deductible as a medical expense? Explain.
b. Can capital expenditures be deductible as medical expenses? Explain.
c. What is the significance of a "minimum adequate facility"? Should aesthetic or architectural qualities be considered in the determination? Why or why not?

Research Problem 2. Ken and Mary Jane Blough, your neighbors, have asked you for advice after receiving correspondence in the mail from the IRS. You learn that the IRS is asking for documentation in support of the itemized deductions the Bloughs claimed on a recent tax return. The Bloughs tell you that their income in the year of question was $75,000. Because their record-keeping habits are poor, they felt justified in claiming itemized deductions equal to the amounts that represent the average claimed by other taxpayers in their income bracket. These averages are calculated and reported by the IRS annually based on actual returns filed in an earlier year. Accordingly, they claimed medical expenses of $7,102, taxes of $6,050, interest of $10,659, and charitable contributions of $2,693. What advice do you give the Bloughs?

Partial list of research aids:
Cheryl L. de Werff, T.C. Summary Opinion, 2011–29.

Research Problem 3. Ashby and Curtis, married professionals, have a 2-year-old son, Jason. Curtis works full-time as an electrical engineer, but Ashby has not worked outside the home since Jason was born. Since Jason is getting older, Ashby thinks that Jason would benefit from attending nursery school several times a week, which would give her an opportunity to reinvigorate her love of painting at a nearby art studio. Ashby thinks that if she is lucky, the proceeds from the sale of her paintings will pay for the nursery school tuition. Ashby plans to claim the credit for child and dependent care expenses because the care provided Jason at the nursery school is required for her to pursue her art career. Can Ashby and Curtis claim the credit for child and dependent care expenses for the nursery school expenditure? Why or why not?

Use internet tax resources to address the following questions. Look for reliable websites and blogs of the IRS and other government agencies, media outlets, businesses, tax professionals, academics, think tanks, and political outlets.

Research Problem 4. The Federal government incurs a cost for every item that is deductible in the computation of taxable income. These costs, which take the form of forgone tax revenue, are often referred to as "tax expenditures." The Joint Committee on Taxation regularly estimates the current and projected tax expenditures associated with a long list of provisions in the tax law. Locate the Joint Committee on Taxation's most recent analysis, and identify the current tax expenditure associated with the deductions for medical expenses, interest on student loans, mortgage interest, and charitable contributions. How are these costs expected to change over the next five years? How is the concept of tax expenditures helpful to tax policy analysts?

Research Problem 5. One income exclusion that some states allow that the Federal government does not is for lottery winnings. Does your state have an exclusion for lottery winnings? If so, how does it work? Why do you think a state might allow winnings from its own state lottery to be excluded from state income taxes?

Research Problem 6. Taxpayers who purchase health insurance coverage through the Health Insurance Marketplace may be eligible for the premium tax credit under § 36B. Use the IRS website to determine which taxpayers are eligible for the credit. Send a one-page summary of your findings to your instructor.

Becker CPA Review Questions

Becker

1. Stephen is a graduate student at West University. He works part-time at the campus coffee shop earning $5,000 this year. Stephen also receives a $25,000 scholarship that pays for his tuition, fees, and books. What amount does Stephen include in his gross income?

   a. $25,000
   b. $5,000
   c. $30,000
   d. $0

2. Kim was seriously injured at her job. As a result of her injury, she received the following payments.

   - $5,000 reimbursement from employer-provided health insurance for medical expenses paid by Kim. The premiums this year paid by Kim's employer totaled $6,000.
   - $15,000 disability pay. Kim has disability insurance provided by her employer as a nontaxable fringe benefit. Kim's employer paid $6,000 in disability premiums this year on behalf of Kim.
   - $10,000 received for damages for personal physical injury.
   - $200,000 in punitive damages.

   What amount is taxable to Kim?

   a. $215,000
   b. $225,000
   c. $236,000
   d. $0

3. In the current year, Wells paid the following expenses:

Premiums on an insurance policy against loss of earnings due to sickness or accident	$3,000
Physical therapy after spinal surgery	2,000
Premium on an insurance policy that covers reimbursement for the cost of prescription drugs	500

   In the current year, Wells recovered $1,500 of the $2,000 that she paid for physical therapy through insurance reimbursement from a group medical policy paid for by her employer. Disregarding the adjusted gross income percentage threshold, what amount could be claimed on Wells's current-year income tax return for medical expenses?

   a. $4,000
   b. $3,500
   c. $1,000
   d. $500

4. Which of the following credits is considered "refundable"?
   a. Child and dependent care credit
   b. Retirement plan contribution credit
   c. Child tax credit
   d. Credit for elderly

5. Jim spent four years earning his undergraduate degree at a local university. He began his first year of law school in January of the current year. Assuming he is under the phaseout limitation, what education tax credit is Jim eligible for in the current year?
   a. American Opportunity credit
   b. Earned income credit
   c. Lifetime learning credit
   d. Professional education and training credit

6. Which of the following statements is true regarding the taxation of Social Security benefits?
   a. 85% is the maximum amount of taxable Social Security benefits.
   b. 50% is the maximum amount of taxable Social Security benefits.
   c. If a taxpayer's only source of income is $10,000 of Social Security benefits, then 50% of the benefits are taxable.
   d. If a taxpayer's only source of income is $10,000 of Social Security benefits, then 85% of the benefits are taxable.

7. Bill and Jane Jones were divorced on January 1, 2018. They have no children. In accordance with the divorce decree, Bill transferred the title of their house over to Jane. The home had a fair market value of $250,000 and was subject to a $100,000 mortgage. Under the divorce agreement, Bill is to make $1,000 monthly mortgage payments on the home for the remainder of the mortgage. In the current year, Bill made 12 mortgage payments. What amount is taxable to Jane in the current year?
   a. $12,000
   b. $250,000
   c. $100,000
   d. $0

8. Jake pays the following amounts to his former spouse during the current year:

Regular alimony payments	$ 12,000
Child support	10,000
Residence as part of a property settlement	115,000

   What amount can Jake deduct as alimony for the current year? Assume the divorce occurred before 2019.
   a. $0
   b. $12,000
   c. $22,000
   d. $137,000

Chapter 11

Individuals as Employees and Proprietors

Learning Objectives: *After completing Chapter 11, you should be able to:*

LO.1 **Distinguish between employee and independent contractor status.**

LO.2 **Explain the exclusions from income available to employees who receive fringe benefits.**

LO.3 **Apply the rules for computing deductible expenses of work, including transportation, travel, moving, education, and entertainment expenses.**

LO.4 **Explain the difference between accountable and nonaccountable employee plans.**

LO.5 **Understand the opportunities available to build wealth through Individual Retirement Accounts.**

LO.6 **Explain the tax provisions applicable to proprietors.**

LO.7 **Distinguish between business and hobby activities and apply the rules limiting the deduction of hobby losses.**

Chapter Outline

Tax Talk *The taxpayer—that's someone who works for the Federal government but doesn't have to take a civil service examination.*—Ronald Reagan

The Big Picture

Self-Employed versus Employee—What's the Difference?

Marcus and Mary Herman come to you for tax advice. Marcus is a self-employed consultant. Last year his business generated revenues of $165,000 and incurred expenses of $18,000 for rent and utilities for an office. Marcus also spent $8,000 purchasing depreciable equipment used in the business and paid a part-time assistant $12,000 for work performed during the year. He also hired Ellen to help him in his consulting practice. Marcus paid Ellen $40,000 for her work during the year.

Marcus paid $3,000 for his own health insurance and $500 for term life insurance; he did not contribute to any retirement plans. Mary is employed as a consultant by a large firm. Her salary last year was $85,000. Her employer paid $3,000 of premiums for her health insurance and provided $50,000 of group term life insurance to each of its employees. Mary is not covered by a qualified retirement plan at work, but she contributed $6,000 to a traditional IRA.

Mary routinely travels for her job and was reimbursed by her employer for all travel expenses. In addition, she spent $500 on other employee business expenses that were not reimbursed by her employer.

What are the tax consequences of these items? Can Marcus and Mary deduct the expenses they incurred? Are there other tax planning opportunities the couple may be missing or tax issues of which they should be aware?

Read the chapter and formulate your response.

Generally, individuals earn business income as employees or through self-employment. Self-employed individuals are commonly referred to as independent contractors but are also described as freelancers, external consultants, micro-business owners, entrepreneurs, proprietors, or individuals who work in the "gig economy."

In many cases, properly categorizing an individual as an employee or as self-employed for tax purposes is a complex determination. This chapter begins with a discussion of the factors that must be considered in determining whether an individual is an employee or is self-employed. This is followed by a discussion of tax provisions applicable to employees and then by a discussion of tax provisions related to self-employed individuals.

LO.1

Distinguish between employee and independent contractor status.

11-1 Employee versus Independent Contractor

When one person performs services for another person or for an entity, the person performing the services either is an employee or is self-employed (i.e., an **independent contractor**). Globalization, advances in technology, and economic factors have led to increases in self-employment. Some individuals view self-employment as a way to be their own boss, have a flexible work schedule, and do work they truly love. Employers often see hiring self-employed individuals (rather than employees) as a means to achieve greater workforce flexibility and control costs. In any circumstance, the proper determination of employment status is important and is often scrutinized.

From an employer's perspective, misclassification of an individual as self-employed rather than as an employee is not uncommon. This misclassification can be unintentional, resulting from the difficulty in applying a complex set of rules related to employee versus independent contractor status. However, classifying someone as a contractor instead of as an employee may be an intentional (although improper) strategy to avoid certain costs. Unlike employees, self-employed individuals need not be included in various fringe benefit programs (e.g., group term life insurance and retirement plans). Further, employers are not required to pay FICA and unemployment taxes (see text Section 11-4e) on compensation paid to independent contractors.

From the worker's perspective, categorization as an employee may avoid certain risks associated with self-employment that employees generally do not assume. For example, a self-employed individual assumes responsibility for employment-related tax obligations and assumes the legal responsibilities associated with performing the job. Allowable business expenses of self-employed taxpayers are generally classified as deductions *for* AGI and are reported on Schedule C (Profit or Loss from Business) of Form 1040.[1] With the exception of reimbursement under an **accountable plan** (see text Section 11-3f), expenses of employees are deductions *from* AGI. From 2018 through 2025, the deduction for these expenses (i.e., miscellaneous itemized deductions) is suspended. As a result, such deductions provide no tax benefit to the employee during this period.[2]

Failure to categorize an individual's work status correctly can have serious tax consequences; tax deficiencies as well as interest and penalties may result for the employer and the employee. The next section discusses the factors that are considered in the proper classification of an individual as an employee or as an independent contractor.

11-1a Factors Considered in Classification

The most important consideration in classifying an individual as an independent contractor or an employee is determining whether an employer-employee relationship exists. The common law definition of an employee originated in the courts and is summarized in various IRS pronouncements; one such pronouncement specifies 20 factors that are regularly used to determine whether a worker is a common law employee or an independent contractor (and, thus, self-employed).[3]

[1]§§ 62(a)(1) and 162(a). A Schedule SE (Self-Employment Tax) also is filed.

[2]§ 67(g), added by the Tax Cuts and Jobs Act (TCJA) of 2017.

[3]Rev.Rul. 87–41. Also see IRS Publication 1779 (*Independent Contractor or Employee*).

Bridge Discipline **Bridge to Equity or Fairness and Business Law**

Max performs services for Calico, Inc. Amy performs services for Amber, Inc. Max and Amy's work products are very similar. Yet, Max is classified as an employee, and Amy is classified as an independent contractor. Does such a legal classification produce equitable results in terms of the effects it has on Max and Amy?

In distinguishing between an employee and an independent contractor, the overriding theme of the existing legal guidance is that an employee is subject to the will and control of the employer as to what is to be done and how it is to be done. In other words, an employer has the right to control and direct the individual who performs the services, not only as to the result to be accomplished by the work but also as to the details and means by which the result is accomplished. Among the factors generally considered in determining whether this right exists are the following.

- Degree of control exercised over the details of the work.
- Provision of facilities used in the work.
- Opportunity for profit or loss.
- Right to terminate employment.
- Whether work is part of regular business.
- Permanency of the relationship.
- Relationship that the parties believe they are creating.
- Manner of payment (e.g., by the job or by the hour).
- Skill required.
- Offering of the services to the general public rather than to one individual or entity.
- Distinct occupation or recognized trade or calling involved.
- Custom in the trade.

An employee-employer relationship exists when the employer has the right to specify the end result and the ways and means by which that result is to be attained.[4] In general, this means that a worker is classified as an employee if the employer identifies what should be done and how it should be done. If the individual is told what to do but is allowed to determine independently how to do it, an employee-employer relationship likely does not exist.

If the business provides the following items to a worker, an employee-employer relationship likely exists.

- Furnishing tools or equipment and a place to work.
- Providing support services, including the hiring of assistants to help do the work.
- Training the worker to obtain needed job skills.
- Allowing participation in various workplace fringe benefits (e.g., accident and health plans, group life insurance, and retirement plans).
- Paying for services based on time rather than the task performed.

Alternatively, independent contractors are more likely to have unreimbursed business expenses, a significant investment in tools and work facilities, and less permanency in their business relationships. Independent contractors, moreover, anticipate a profit from their work, make their services available in a marketplace, and are likely to be paid a flat fee on a per-job basis.

In resolving employment status, each case is tested on its own merits; the right to control the means and methods of accomplishment is most often the definitive test.

Code § 6041(a) requires businesses that pay $600 or more in a calendar year to a contractor to issue Form 1099–NEC (Nonemployee Compensation) to the IRS and the contractor by January 31 of the following year. While this helps the contractor determine their income tax obligations, it is crucial that this business owner (contractor) maintain proper records of all receipts and expenses to be able to satisfy their income and other tax obligations.

Additional information about worker classification can be found on this book's companion website: www.cengage.com

1 Digging Deeper

[4]Reg. § 31.3401(c)–1(b).

The Big Picture

Example 1

Return to the facts of *The Big Picture* on p. 11-1. Marcus is a consultant whose major client accounts for 60% of his billings. He does the routine consulting work at the client's request. He is paid a monthly retainer in addition to amounts charged for extra work. Marcus is a self-employed individual. Even though most of his income comes from one client, he still has the right to determine *how* the end result of his work is attained.

The Big Picture

Example 2

Return to the facts of *The Big Picture* on p. 11-1. Ellen is a recent MBA graduate hired by Marcus to assist him in the performance of services for the client mentioned in Example 1. Ellen is under his supervision; he reviews her work and pays her an hourly fee. Ellen is considered Marcus's employee.

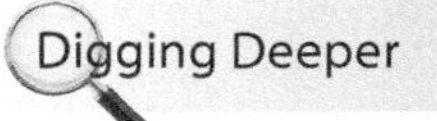

Digging Deeper 2

Information about statutory employees can be found on this book's companion website: www.cengage.com

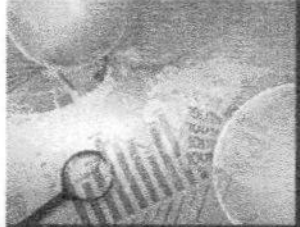

Tax Planning Strategies — Self-Employed Individuals

Framework Focus: Deductions

Strategy: Maximize Deductible Amounts.

Some taxpayers, such as personal trainers and consultants, might be classified as either employees or independent contractors depending on their relationship with the service recipient or payor. These taxpayers should consider all factors and not automatically assume that one status is preferable to the other.

It is advantageous to deduct one's business expenses *for* AGI. However, an independent contractor may incur additional expenses such as local gross receipts taxes, license fees, franchise fees, personal property taxes, and occupation taxes. Record-keeping and filing requirements can also be quite burdensome.

One of the most expensive considerations is the **self-employment tax** imposed on independent contractors and other self-employed individuals. Such individuals are required to pay double the amount of Social Security and Medicare taxes that are imposed on an employee with the same amount of earned income (wages). Even though a deduction *for* AGI is allowed for one-half of the self-employment tax paid, an employee and an independent contractor are not in the same tax position where equal amounts are earned. This discussion continues in text Section 11-4e.

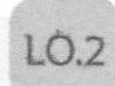

LO.2

Explain the exclusions from income available to employees who receive fringe benefits.

11-2 Exclusions Available to Employees

Several gross income exclusions that are available to *all taxpayers* were discussed in Chapter 4; these include interest income on obligations of state and local governments, life insurance proceeds, and income from discharge of indebtedness. Other exclusions, available only to *individuals*, were discussed in Chapter 10; these include gifts and inheritances, scholarships, and compensation for injuries and sickness.

Another class of exclusions available only to *employees* is referred to as qualified fringe benefits. The popularity of fringe benefits is attributable to the fact that the cost of such benefits is deductible by employers and excludible from income by employees. The next sections discuss several of the most popular fringe benefits available to employees.

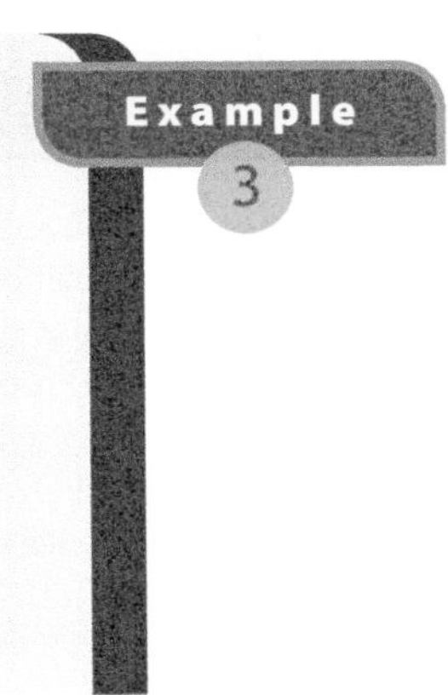

Cardinal Corporation, which has a marginal tax rate of 21%, provides health insurance coverage to employees at a cost of $1,000 per employee. Because Cardinal can deduct the health insurance premiums paid to provide this coverage, the net cost to the corporation is $790 per employee ($1,000 cost − $210 tax savings). The employee excludes the value of this fringe benefit from gross income, so the employee has no tax cost related to the health insurance.

The average employee of Cardinal Corporation is in the 12% income tax bracket. If Cardinal did not provide the health insurance coverage and the employee paid a $1,000 premium, the employee would use after-tax dollars to acquire the coverage. The employee would then need to earn $1,136 to pay for $1,000 of coverage [$1,136 wages − ($1,136 × 12% tax)]. The after-tax cost to the corporation of $1,136 in wages is $897 ($1,136 wages − $239 corporate tax savings). Thus, the cost of health insurance coverage is $107 less per employee ($897 − $790) if it is provided as a qualified fringe benefit, because the insurance is both deductible by the corporation and excludible by the employee.

11-2a Employer-Sponsored Accident and Health Plans

Congress encourages employers to provide employees, retired former employees, and their dependents with accident and health benefits, disability insurance, and long-term care plans. The *premiums* are deductible by the employer and are excluded from the employee's gross income.[5] Although § 105(a) provides the general rule that employees have includible income when they collect insurance *benefits*, two exceptions are provided.

Code § 105(b) generally excludes payments received for medical care of the employee, spouse, and dependents. However, if the payments are for expenses that do not meet the Code's definition of medical care,[6] the amount received is included in gross income. In addition, taxpayers include in gross income any amounts received for medical expenses that were deducted on a prior tax return.

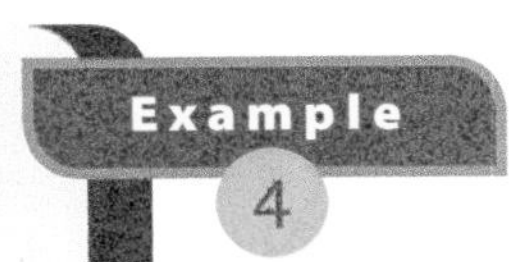

In 2022, Tab's employer-sponsored health insurance plan paid $4,000 for hair transplants that did not meet the Code's definition of medical care. As a result, Tab includes $4,000 in his gross income in 2022.

Code § 105(c) excludes payments for the permanent loss or the loss of the use of a member or function of the body or the permanent disfigurement of the employee, the spouse, or a dependent. However, payments that are a substitute for salary (e.g., related to the period of time absent from work) are included in income.

Jill loses an eye in an automobile accident unrelated to her work. As a result of the accident, Jill incurs $2,000 of tax-deductible medical expenses. She collects $100,000 from an accident insurance policy carried by her employer. The benefits are paid according to a schedule of amounts that vary with the part of the body injured (e.g., $100,000 for loss of an eye and $150,000 for loss of a hand).

Because the payment is for loss of a *member or function of the body*, the $100,000 is excluded from Jill's gross income. Jill was absent from work for a week as a result of the accident. Her employer also provides her with insurance for the loss of income due to illness or injury. Jill collects $7,500, which is included in her gross income.

[5] § 106, Reg. § 1.106–1, and Rev.Rul. 82–196.

[6] See text Section 10-4a for an additional discussion of medical expenses.

Bridge Discipline **Bridge to Economic and Societal Needs**

The media frequently report on challenges facing senior citizens. Organizations such as the AARP effectively lobby for the rights of senior citizens through direct lobbying in Washington, D.C., and through grassroots efforts throughout the country. With the "graying of America," these concerns and lobbying efforts are likely to be magnified.

The Internal Revenue Code contains a number of provisions that are "senior citizen friendly." Among these are the following.

- Exclusion from gross income, except for taxpayers above certain income levels, of Social Security benefits (§ 86).
- Exclusion from gross income of certain life insurance proceeds paid on account of death (§ 101).
- Exclusion from gross income of medical insurance premiums and benefits (§§ 105 and 106).
- Limited exclusion from gross income of gain on the sale of a principal residence (§ 121).
- Limited exclusion from gross income of long-term care insurance premiums and benefits (§ 7702B).
- Tax-deferred treatment of retirement plans (§§ 401–436).

11-2b Medical Reimbursement Plans

As discussed previously, amounts received through insurance coverage (benefits) are excluded from income under § 105 or § 106. Instead of providing the employee with insurance coverage for hospital and medical expenses, the employer may agree to reimburse the employee for these expenses (a self-insured arrangement). Generally, the benefits received under a self-insured plan can be excluded from the employee's gross income if the plan does not discriminate in favor of highly compensated employees.[7]

There is an alternative means of accomplishing a medical reimbursement plan. The employer can purchase a medical insurance plan with a high deductible (e.g., the employee is responsible for the first $2,800 of the family's medical expenses) and then make contributions to the employee's **Health Savings Account (HSA)**.[8] The employer can make contributions each month up to the maximum contribution of 100 percent of the deductible amount. Under a high-deductible plan, the monthly deductible amount is limited to one-twelfth of $3,650 for self-only coverage; for an individual with family coverage, the monthly deductible amount is limited to one-twelfth of $7,300.

Withdrawals from the HSA must be used to reimburse the employee for the medical expenses paid by the employee that are not covered under the high-deductible plan. The employee is not taxed on the employer's contributions to the HSA, the earnings on the funds in the account, or the withdrawals made for medical expenses.[9]

Digging Deeper 3 **Long-term care insurance is discussed on this book's companion website:** www.cengage.com

[7] § 105(h). Also see § 106 and Rev.Rul. 61–146. Employers should make sure that such reimbursement plans fall within the requirements of the Affordable Care Act to avoid an excise tax. See § 4980D, Notice 2013–54 and Notice 2015–17. Also see rules on Qualified Small Employer Health Reimbursement Arrangements (QSEHRA) at § 9831(d) and Notice 2017–67.

[8] §§ 106(d) and 223. See additional coverage in text Section 10-4a.

[9] §§ 106(d), 223(b), and 223(d). The 2022 inflation-adjusted amounts are published in Rev.Proc. 2021–25. The amounts for 2021 were $3,600 and $7,200.

11-2c Meals and Lodging Furnished for the Convenience of the Employer

Under the following conditions, the value of meals and lodging provided to the employee and the employee's spouse and dependents is excluded from gross income.[10]

- The meals and/or lodging are *furnished by the employer* on the employer's *business premises* for the *convenience of the employer*. For 2021 and 2022, employers can deduct 100 percent of meals provided by a restaurant; from 2023 to 2025, the employer may only deduct 50 percent of the cost of the meals provided. After 2025, employers may not claim a deduction for these meals. However, if the employer continues to provide such meals, their value remains as an exclusion for the employees.
- In the case of lodging, the *employee is required* to accept the lodging as a condition of employment.

The courts have interpreted these requirements strictly, as discussed next.

Furnished by the Employer

The following two questions have been raised with regard to the *furnished by the employer* requirement.

- Who is considered an *employee*?
- What is meant by *furnished*?

The IRS and some courts have reasoned that because a partner is not an employee, the exclusion does not apply to a partner. However, the Tax Court and the Fifth Circuit Court of Appeals have ruled in favor of the taxpayer on this issue.[11]

The Supreme Court held that a *cash meal allowance* was ineligible for the exclusion because the employer did not actually furnish the meals.[12] Similarly, one court denied the exclusion where the employer paid for the food and supplied the cooking facilities but the employee prepared the meal.[13]

On the Employer's Business Premises

The *on the employer's business premises* requirement, applicable to both meals and lodging, has resulted in much litigation. The Regulations define business premises as simply "the place of employment of the employee."[14] The Sixth Circuit Court of Appeals held that a residence, owned by the employer and occupied by an employee, located two blocks from the motel that the employee managed was *not* part of the business premises.[15] However, the Tax Court considered an employer-owned house located

[10] § 119(a). The value of meals and lodging also is excluded from FICA and FUTA tax. *Rowan Companies, Inc. v. U.S.*, 81–1 USTC ¶9479, 48 AFTR 2d 81–5115, 101 S.Ct. 2288.

[11] Rev.Rul. 80; *Comm. v. Doak*, 56–2 USTC ¶9708, 49 AFTR 1491, 234 F.2d 704 (CA–4); but see *G. A. Papineau*, 16 T.C. 130 (1951); *Armstrong v. Phinney*, 68–1 USTC ¶9355, 21 AFTR 2d 1260, 394 F.2d 661 (CA–5).

[12] *Comm. v. Kowalski*, 77–2 USTC ¶9748, 40 AFTR 2d 77–6128, 98 S.Ct. 315.

[13] *Tougher v. Comm.*, 71–1 USTC ¶9398, 27 AFTR 2d 71–1301, 441 F.2d 1148 (CA–9).

[14] Reg. § 1.119–1(c)(1).

[15] *Comm. v. Anderson*, 67–1 USTC ¶9136, 19 AFTR 2d 318, 371 F.2d 59 (CA–6).

across the street from the hotel that was managed by the taxpayer to be on the business premises of the employer.[16]

Perhaps these two cases can be reconciled by comparing the distance from the lodging facilities to the place where the employer's business was conducted. Seemingly, the closer the lodging is to the business operations, the more likely the convenience of the employer is served.

For the Convenience of the Employer

The *convenience of the employer* test is intended to focus on the employer's motivation for furnishing the meals and lodging rather than on the benefits received by the employee. If the employer furnishes the meals and lodging primarily to enable employees to perform their duties properly, the "convenience" test is met.

The Regulations provide the following examples to illustrate where the "convenience" test is met:[17]

- A restaurant requires its service staff to eat their meals on the premises during the busy lunch and breakfast hours.
- A bank furnishes meals on the premises for its tellers, to limit the time the employees are away from their booths during busy times.
- A worker is employed at a construction site in a remote part of Alaska. The employer must furnish meals and lodging due to the inaccessibility of other facilities.

Required as a Condition of Employment

The *required as a condition of employment* test applies only to lodging. If the employee's use of the housing would serve the convenience of the employer but the employee is not required to use the housing, the exclusion is not available. In addition, if the employee has the option of accepting a benefit of cash or lodging, the condition-of-employment test is not satisfied.

Khalid is the manager of a large apartment complex. The employer requires Khalid to live on the premises but does not charge him rent. The rental value of his apartment is $9,600 a year. Although Khalid considers the rent-free housing a significant benefit, he is not required to include the value of the housing in his gross income.

Other housing exclusions are available for certain employees of educational institutions, ministers of the gospel, and military personnel.

11-2d Group Term Life Insurance

An employee can claim a limited exclusion for group term life insurance benefits that are provided by the employer. The premiums on the first $50,000 of group term life insurance protection are excludible from the employee's and former employee's gross income.

[16] *J. B. Lindeman*, 60 T.C. 609 (1973).

[17] Reg. § 1.119–1(f).

The benefits of this exclusion are available only to employees. Proprietors and partners are not considered employees. Moreover, only a broad-scale coverage of employees satisfies the group requirement (e.g., shareholder-employees would not constitute a qualified group). The exclusion applies only to term insurance (protection for a period of time but with no cash surrender value) and not to ordinary life insurance (lifetime protection plus a cash surrender value that can be drawn upon before death).

As mentioned previously, the exclusion applies to the first $50,000 of group term life insurance protection. For each $1,000 of coverage in excess of $50,000, the employee must include the amounts indicated in Exhibit 11.1 in gross income.[18]

More on group term life insurance can be found on this book's companion website:
www.cengage.com

4 Digging Deeper

Finch Corporation provides its employees with a group term life insurance policy with coverage equal to the employee's annual salary. Keith, age 52, is president of the corporation and receives an annual salary of $350,000. Keith must include $828 in gross income related to the insurance protection for the year.

$$\frac{\$350{,}000 - \$50{,}000}{\$1{,}000} \times \$0.23 \times 12\text{ months} = \$828$$

If the plan discriminates in favor of certain key employees (e.g., officers), the key employees are not eligible for the exclusion.[19] In such a case, the key employees include in gross income the *greater* of actual premiums paid by the employer or the amount calculated from the Uniform Premiums table in Exhibit 11.1. The other (i.e., non-key) employees still are eligible for the $50,000 exclusion and use the Uniform Premiums table to compute the income from excess insurance protection.

11-2e Qualified Tuition Reduction Plans

Employees (including retired and disabled former employees) of nonprofit educational institutions can exclude from gross income a tuition waiver that is provided pursuant to a qualified tuition reduction plan. The exclusion applies to tuition reductions granted to the employee, the employee's spouse, and the employee's dependent children.[20]

[18] Reg. § 1.79–3(d)(2).

[19] § 79(d).

[20] § 117(d).

Exhibit 11.1 Uniform Premiums for $1,000 of Group Term Life Insurance Protection

Attained Age on Last Day of Employee's Tax Year	Cost of $1,000 of Protection for a One-Month Period*
Under 25	$ 0.05
25–29	0.06
30–34	0.08
35–39	0.09
40–44	0.10
45–49	0.15
50–54	0.23
55–59	0.43
60–64	0.66
65–69	1.27
70 and above	2.06

*Reg. § 1.79–3, effective for coverage after June 30, 1999.

11-2f Other Employee Fringe Benefits

Certain other fringe benefits available to employees also are excluded from gross income.

- The employee does not include in gross income the value of child and dependent care services paid for by the employer and incurred to enable the employee to work. In 2022, the exclusion cannot exceed $5,000 per year ($2,500 if married and filing separately). For a married couple, the annual exclusion cannot exceed the earned income of the spouse who has the lesser amount of gross income. For an unmarried taxpayer, the exclusion cannot exceed the taxpayer's earned income.[21]
- The value of the use of a gym or other athletic facilities by employees, their spouses, and their dependent children may be excluded from an employee's gross income. The facilities must be on the employer's premises, and substantially all of the use of the facilities must be by employees and their family members.[22]
- When an employee's personal account is credited with frequent flyer miles after taking a trip that the employer paid for, no gross income is recognized.[23]
- Qualified employer-provided educational assistance (tuition, fees, books, and supplies) at the undergraduate and graduate levels is excludible from gross income. The exclusion does not cover meals, lodging, transportation costs, or educational payments for courses involving sports, games, or hobbies. The exclusion is subject to an annual statutory ceiling of $5,250 per employee.[24]
- If an employer has a qualified adoption assistance program, an employee can exclude up to $14,890 of adoption expenses that are paid or reimbursed by the employer.[25] If the child has special needs (is not physically or mentally capable of caring for himself or herself), the $14,890 exclusion from gross income applies even if the actual adoption expenses are less than that amount. For 2021, the exclusion is phased out as adjusted gross income increases from $223,410 to $263,410.

[21] § 129. In 2021, these amounts were $10,500 and $5,250, respectively. The exclusion applies to the same types of expenses that, if paid by the employee (and not reimbursed by the employer), would be eligible for the credit for child and dependent care expenses; see text Section 10-5c.

[22] § 132(j)(4).

[23] Ann. 2002–18.

[24] § 127. To provide assistance to some employees, the CARES Act (P.L. 116–136) modified this rule to allow educational assistance to include principal and interest on a student loan. This treatment was extended through 2025 by the Consolidated Appropriations Act 2021 (P.L. 116–260).

[25] § 137. A credit relating to the expenditures of the parents also is available under § 23, as discussed in text Section 10-5a.

11-2g **Cafeteria Plans**

Generally, if an employee is offered a choice between cash and some other form of compensation, the employee is deemed to have received the cash even when the noncash option is elected. As a result, the employee recognizes gross income regardless of the option chosen.

An exception to this constructive receipt treatment is provided under the cafeteria plan rules. Under such a plan, the employee can choose between cash and nontaxable benefits (e.g., group term life insurance, health and accident protection, child care). If the employee chooses the otherwise nontaxable benefits, the cafeteria plan rules allow the benefits to be excluded from the employee's gross income.[26]

Cafeteria plans provide flexibility in tailoring the employee pay package to fit individual needs. Some employees (often younger employees) prefer cash, while others (often older employees) will opt for the fringe benefit program. However, long-term care insurance cannot be part of a cafeteria plan. Thus, an employer that wants to provide long-term care benefits must provide such benefits separately from the cafeteria plan.[27]

Hawk Corporation offers its employees (on a nondiscriminatory basis) a choice of any one or all of the following benefits.

Benefit	Cost
Group term life insurance	$ 200
Hospitalization insurance for family members	2,400
Child care payments	1,800
	$4,400

If a benefit is not selected, the employee receives cash equal to the cost of the benefit. Kay, an employee, has a spouse who works for another employer that provides hospitalization insurance but no child care payments. Kay elects to receive the group term life insurance, the child care payments, and $2,400 of cash. Only the $2,400 is included in Kay's gross income.

11-2h **Flexible Spending Plans**

Flexible spending plans (often referred to as flexible benefit plans) operate much like cafeteria plans. Under these plans, the employee accepts lower cash compensation (up to $2,850 in 2022) in return for the employer's agreement to pay certain costs without the employee recognizing gross income. For example, assume that the employer's health insurance policy does not cover dental expenses. Under a flexible spending plan, an employee estimates his or her dental expenses for the upcoming year and agrees to a salary reduction equal to the estimated dental expenses. The employer then pays or reimburses the employee for the actual dental expenses incurred, up to the amount of the salary reduction. If the employee's actual dental expenses are less than the reduction in cash compensation, the employee cannot recover the difference. Hence, these plans often are referred to as *use or lose* plans. To avoid the loss of unpaid amounts, the IRS allows a payment until two-and-a-half months (March 15 for calendar year plans) after the end of the plan year to count toward the prior year's plan. As is the case for cafeteria plans, flexible spending plans cannot be used to pay long-term care insurance premiums.

[26]§ 125.

[27]§ 125(f).

Concept Summary 11.1 reviews the exclusions discussed to this point in the chapter.

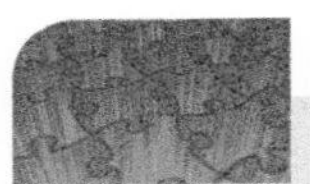

Concept Summary 11.1

Employee Fringe Benefits

Type of Benefit	Exclusion
Accident, health, and long-term care insurance and medical reimbursement (§§ 105 and 106)	Insurance premiums paid by the employer and benefits collected by the employee
High-deductible health insurance and contributions to employee's Health Savings Account (§§ 106 and 223)	Employer premiums on high-deductible medical insurance plus contributions to Health Savings Account (statutory limits, indexed for inflation)
Meals and lodging furnished for the convenience of the employer (§ 119)	Value of meals and lodging on the employer's premises
Group term life insurance (§ 79)	Premiums on up to $50,000 of protection
Qualified tuition reduction [§ 117(d)]	Value of tuition waiver
Child care provided by the employer or reimbursement for employee's cost (§ 129)	Services provided or reimbursement of expenses up to $5,000 a year
Athletic facilities on the employer's premises (§ 132)	Value of services
Educational assistance for tuition, fees, books, and supplies* (§ 127)	Limited to $5,250 annually
Adoption assistance (§ 137)	Expenses up to $14,890 annually, subject to AGI phaseout
Flexible spending plans (§ 125)	Limited to $2,850 annually

* Through 2025 also includes principal and interest on certain student loans.

11-2i General Classes of Excluded Benefits

An employer can provide many forms and types of economic benefits to its employees. Under the all-inclusive concept of income, the benefits are taxable unless one of the provisions previously discussed specifically excludes the item from gross income. The amount of the resulting gross income is the fair market value of the benefit. This reasoning can lead to results that are unsatistfactory, as illustrated in the following example.

Ryan is employed in New York as a ticket clerk for Trans National Airlines. He has a sick mother in Miami, Florida, but Ryan has no money for plane tickets. Trans National has daily flights from New York to Miami that often leave with empty seats. The cost of a round-trip ticket is $400. If Trans National allows Ryan to fly without charge to Miami, under general gross income rules, Ryan recognizes income equal to the value of a ticket. However, as discussed next, this is one of several classes of excluded benefits provided for in the Code.

Because Congress believed that taxing fringe benefits often yielded harsh results (as demonstrated in the example), it established broad classes of nontaxable employee benefits that include:

- No-additional-cost services.
- Qualified employee discounts.
- Working condition fringes.
- *De minimis* fringes.
- Qualified transportation fringes.
- Qualified moving expense reimbursements.
- Qualified retirement planning services.

The value of these employer-provided benefits is excluded from the employee's gross income[28] under circumstances that are discussed next.

No-Additional-Cost Services

The circumstances of Example 9 illustrate the rationale for the **no-additional-cost service** fringe benefit. The value of the services received is excluded from an employee's gross income if all of the following conditions are satisfied.

- The employee receives services, as opposed to property.
- The employer does not incur substantial additional costs, including forgone revenue, in providing the services to the employee.
- The services are offered to customers in the ordinary course of the business in which the employee works.[29]

In Example 9, although the airplane may burn slightly more fuel because Ryan is on board and Ryan may receive the same snacks as paying customers, the additional costs to the airline are not substantial. As a result, the flight qualifies as a no-additional-cost service and the value of the flight is excluded from Ryan's gross income.

On the other hand, assume that Ryan is given a reserved seat on a flight that is frequently full. The employer would be forgoing revenue to allow Ryan to fly. This forgone revenue would be a substantial additional cost, and the value of the benefit would be included in Ryan's gross income.

Further details about no-additional-cost benefits can be found on this book's companion website: www.cengage.com 5 Digging Deeper

The no-additional-cost exclusion extends to the employee's spouse and dependent children and to retired and disabled former employees.[30] However, the exclusion is not extended to highly compensated employees unless the benefit is available on a nondiscriminatory basis to all employees.

Qualified Employee Discounts

When the employer sells goods or services (other than no-additional-cost benefits just discussed) to the employee for a price that is less than the price charged to regular customers, the employee recognizes gross income equal to the discount. However, a **qualified employee discount** can be excluded from the gross income of the employee subject to the following conditions and limitations.

- The exclusion is not available for discounted sales of real property (e.g., a house) or for personal property of the type commonly held for investment (e.g., common stock).
- The property or services must be from the same line of business in which the employee works.
- In the case of *property*, the exclusion is limited to the *gross profit component* of the price to customers.
- In the case of *services*, the exclusion is limited to 20 percent of the customer price.

[28] See, generally, § 132.

[29] § 132(b) and Reg. § 1.132–2.

[30] § 132 and Reg. § 1.132–1(b).

Silver Corporation, which operates a department store, sells a television to its employee Kylie for $300. The regular customer price is $500, and the gross profit rate is 25%. Silver also sells Kylie a service contract for $120. The regular customer price for the contract is $150. Kylie must include $75 in gross income as follows.

Customer price for property	$ 500	
Less: Gross profit (25%)	(125)	
Employee price	(300)	
Excess discount		$ 75
Customer price for service contract	$ 150	
Less: 20% maximum exclusion	(30)	
Employee price	(120)	
Excess discount		-0-
Total gross income recognized by Kylie		$ 75

As in the case of no-additional-cost benefits, the exclusion applies to employees, an employee's spouse and dependent children, and retired and disabled former employees.

Working Condition Fringes

Generally, an employee may exclude from gross income the cost of property or services provided by the employer if the employee could deduct the cost of those items if they had actually paid for them. These benefits are called **working condition fringes**.

Jayden is a CPA employed by an accounting firm. The employer pays Jayden's annual dues to professional organizations. Jayden is not required to include the payment of the dues in gross income; if he had paid the dues, he would have deducted the amount as an employee business expense (as discussed later in this chapter).

In many cases, this exclusion merely avoids reporting income and an offsetting deduction. Unlike the other fringe benefits discussed previously, working condition fringes can be made available on a discriminatory basis and still qualify for the exclusion.

De Minimis Fringes

As the term suggests, ***de minimis* fringe benefits** are so small in amount that accounting for them is impractical and, as such, their value is excluded from the employee's gross income. Examples of *de minimis* fringes include the following.

- Occasional personal use of a company copying machine, occasional company cocktail parties or picnics for employees, occasional money for meals or ride-sharing services for employees because of overtime work, and certain holiday gifts of property with a low fair market value.
- The value of meals consumed in a subsidized eating facility (e.g., an employees' cafeteria) operated by the employer if the facility is located on or near the employer's business premises, if revenue equals or exceeds direct operating costs, and if nondiscrimination requirements are met. This exclusion applies irrespective of whether the employer can deduct any of the facility's costs.

When taxpayers venture beyond established norms, there is obviously room for disagreement as to what is *de minimis*. According to the IRS, cash or gift cards never are considered *de minimis*.[31]

[31]TAM 200437030 and IRS Publication 15B, *Employer's Tax Guide to Fringe Benefits*.

Generally, the value of personal use of an employer-provided cell phone is excluded as a *de minimis* fringe benefit if the phone is provided primarily for business reasons, such as to enable the employee to be in contact with clients when the employee is away from the office.

Qualified Transportation Fringes

The intent of the exclusion for **qualified transportation fringes** is to encourage employees to use mass transit for commuting to and from work. Qualified transportation fringes include the following benefits provided by the employer to the employee.

1. Transportation in a commuter highway vehicle, like a dedicated bus or van, between the employee's residence and the place of employment.
2. A transit pass.
3. Qualified parking.

These exclusions have annual limits. For 2022, the exclusion is $280 per month ($270 in 2021).

Qualified parking includes the following.

- Parking provided to an employee on or near the employer's business premises.
- Parking provided to an employee on or near a location from which the employee commutes to work via mass transit, in a commuter highway vehicle, or in a carpool.

Qualified transportation fringes may be provided directly by the employer or may be in the form of cash reimbursements.

Gray Corporation's offices are located in the center of a large city. The company pays for parking spaces to be used by the company officers. Emma, a vice president, receives $300 of such benefits each month during 2022. The parking space rental qualifies as a qualified transportation fringe. Of the $300 benefit received each month, $280 is excludible from gross income. The balance of $20 is included in Emma's gross income. The same result would occur if Emma paid for the parking and was reimbursed by her employer.

Employers cannot deduct qualified transportation fringe benefits provided to employees [§ 274(a)(4)]. However, if the employer provides the benefit, the employee may exclude the amount from gross income within the limits stated above.

Qualified Moving Expense Reimbursements

A qualified moving expense is defined as an expense that would be deductible under § 217. For 2018 through 2025, the moving expense exclusion only applies to members of the Armed Forces on active duty.

Qualified Retirement Planning Services

Qualified retirement planning services include any retirement planning advice or information that an employer who maintains a qualified retirement plan provides to an employee or the employee's spouse. This exclusion is intended to motivate more employers to provide retirement planning services to their employees.

Nondiscrimination Provisions

For no-additional-cost services, qualified employee discounts, and qualified retirement planning services that are discriminatory in favor of *highly compensated employees*, exclusion treatment is denied. However, non-highly compensated employees can exclude the value of these benefits from gross income.[32]

[32] §§ 132(j)(1) and (m)(2).

Dove Company's officers are allowed to purchase goods from the company at a 25% discount. All other employees are allowed only a 15% discount. The company's gross profit margin on these goods is 30%. Because the officers receive more favorable discounts, the plan is discriminatory in favor of the officers. With regard to all other employees, the discount is "qualified" because it is available to all employees (other than the officers who receive a more favorable discount) and the discount is less than the company's gross profit.

Peggy, an officer in the company, purchased goods from the company for $750 when the price charged to customers was $1,000. Peggy reports $250 in gross income because the plan is discriminatory.

Mason, an employee of the company who is not an officer, purchased goods for $850 when the customer price was $1,000. Mason is not required to recognize gross income because he received a qualified employee discount.

De minimis fringe benefits (except for subsidized eating facilities) and working condition fringe benefits can be provided on a discriminatory basis.

A review of employee fringe benefits is provided in Concept Summary 11.2.

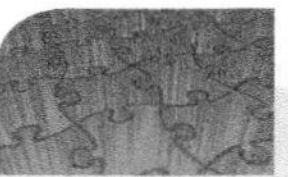

Additional information on *de minimis* fringe benefits can be found on this book's companion website: www.cengage.com

Concept Summary 11.2

General Classes of Fringe Benefits

Benefit	Description and Examples	Coverage Allowed	Effect of Discrimination
1. No-additional-cost services	The employee takes advantage of the employer's excess capacity (e.g., free flights for airline employees).	Current, retired, and disabled employees; their spouses and dependent children. Partners are treated as employees.	No exclusion for highly compensated employees.
2. Qualified discounts on goods	The employee is allowed a discount no greater than the gross profit margin on goods sold to customers.	Same as (1).	Same as (1).
3. Qualified discounts on services	The employee is allowed a discount (maximum of 20%) on services the employer offers to customers.	Same as (1).	Same as (1).
4. Working condition fringes	Expenses paid by the employer that would be deductible if paid by the employee (e.g., a mechanic's tools). Includes auto salesperson's use of a car held for sale.	Current employees, partners, directors, and independent contractors.	No effect.
5. *De minimis* items	Expenses so immaterial that accounting for them is not warranted (e.g., occasional meal money).	Any recipient of a fringe benefit.	No effect.
6. Qualified transportation fringes	Transportation benefits provided by the employer to employees, including a transit pass and qualified parking.	Current employees.	No effect.
7. Qualified moving expense reimbursements	Qualified moving expenses paid or reimbursed by the employer.	From 2018–2025, members of the Armed Forces on active duty only.	No effect.
8. Qualified retirement planning services	Qualified retirement planning services provided by the employer.	Current employees and spouses.	Same as (1).

11-2j Foreign Earned Income

Individual taxpayers are generally subject to U.S. income tax on all income earned regardless of the income's geographic origin. As a result, a U.S. citizen who earns income in another country could experience double taxation: the same income would be taxed in the United States and in the other country.

Out of a sense of fairness, and so as not to discourage U.S. citizens from working abroad, Congress has provided alternative forms of relief from taxes on foreign earned income. Taxpayers can elect *either* (1) to include the foreign income in their taxable income and then claim a credit for foreign taxes paid or (2) to exclude up to $112,000 of the foreign earnings from their U.S. gross income (the **foreign earned income exclusion**).[33] The foreign tax credit option is discussed in text Section 17-3; the following discussion explains why most taxpayers choose the exclusion.

Foreign earned income consists of the earnings from the individual's personal services rendered in a foreign country (other than as an employee of the U.S. government). To qualify for the exclusion, the taxpayer must be either of the following.

- A bona fide resident of the foreign country (or countries).
- Present in a foreign country (or countries) for at least 330 days during any 12 consecutive months.

The following rules apply in calculating the exclusion and tax owed.

- The exclusion must be computed on a daily basis when the exclusion period straddles two years.
- The tax on the income in excess of the excluded amount is calculated at the marginal rate that would apply without the exclusion (i.e., as though the excluded income were included in taxable income).

Sandra's trips to and from a foreign country in connection with her work encompassed the following dates.

Arrived in Foreign Country	Returned to the United States
March 11, 2021	February 16, 2022

During the 12 consecutive months ending on March 11, 2022, Sandra was present in the foreign country for at least 330 days (365 days less 12 days in February and 11 days in March 2022 equals 342 days). Therefore, all income earned in the foreign country through March 11, 2022, is eligible for the exclusion.

The exclusion is limited to an indexed amount of $112,000 for 2022 ($108,700 in 2021). For married persons, both of whom have foreign earned income, the exclusion is computed separately for each person. If all of the days in the tax year are not qualifying days (i.e., days present in the other country), the taxpayer must compute the maximum exclusion on a daily basis ($112,000 divided by the number of days in the entire year and multiplied by the number of qualifying days).

Calculating the Exclusion and Tax

Keith qualifies for the foreign earned income exclusion. He was present in France for all of 2022. Keith's salary for 2022 is $120,000. Because all of the days in 2022 are qualifying days, Keith can exclude $112,000 of his $120,000 salary.

Assume instead that only 342 days were qualifying days. Then Keith's exclusion is limited to $104,942, computed as follows.

$$\$112{,}000 \text{ maximum exclusion} \times \frac{342 \text{ days outside the U.S.}}{365 \text{ days in the year}} = \$104{,}942 \text{ exclusion allowed}$$

[33] § 911(d).

Calculating the Exclusion and Tax

In 2022, Carol, who is not married, had taxable income of $30,000 after excluding $112,000 of foreign earned income. Without the benefit of the exclusion, Carol's taxable income would have been $142,000 ($30,000 + $112,000). The tax on the taxable income of $30,000 is calculated using the marginal rate applicable to income between $112,000 and $142,000, which is 24%. As a result, Carol's tax liability is $7,200 ($30,000 × 24%).

LO.3

Apply the rules for computing deductible expenses of work, including transportation, travel, moving, education, and entertainment expenses.

11-3 Expenses Relating to Time at Work

In general, as discussed in Chapter 5, business expenses that are ordinary and necessary are deductible in the calculation of taxable income. However, this general rule does not mean that all work-related expenses will be deductible by all taxpayers without limit.

First, an individual's classification as an employee or an independent contractor affects how business expenses are deducted in the calculation of taxable income. Unreimbursed business expenses incurred by an employee are categorized as miscellaneous itemized deductions. Such expenses are deductible only to the extent they exceed a 2%-of-AGI floor. *However*, from 2018 through 2025, the deduction for such miscellaneous itemized deductions is suspended. As a result, the only employee business expenses that are currently deductible are those that are reimbursed by an employer (and these expenses, once reimbursed, have no effect on an employee's taxable income). In contrast, business expenses incurred by an independent contractor are deductible *for* AGI. Thus, such expenses are not limited by an AGI floor.

Second, irrespective of whether business expenses are incurred by an employee or independent contractor, certain business expenses are limited by tax law provisions beyond the "ordinary and necessary" requirement.

The calculation of the deduction for a variety of business expenses is discussed next.

11-3a Transportation Expenses

Deductible, unreimbursed employment-related **transportation expenses** include only the cost of transporting the taxpayer from one place to another in the course of employment when the taxpayer is not away from home in travel status. Such costs include taxi or ride-share fares, automobile expenses, tolls, and parking.

Commuting Expenses

Commuting between home and one's place of employment is a personal, nondeductible expense. The fact that one person drives 30 miles to work and another person walks six blocks is of no significance.[34] However, the expenses of getting from one job to another job or from one workstation to another workstation are deductible transportation expenses rather than nondeductible commuting expenses.

Digging Deeper 7

Commuting expenses are discussed in more detail on this book's companion website: www.cengage.com

[34] *U.S. v. Tauferner*, 69–1 USTC ¶9241, 23 AFTR 2d 69–1025, 407 F.2d 243 (CA–10).

Cynthia holds two jobs: a full-time job with Blue Corporation and a part-time job with Wren Corporation. She customarily leaves home at 7:30 A.M. and drives 30 miles to the Blue plant, where she works until 5:00 P.M. After dinner at a nearby café, Cynthia drives 20 miles to Wren and works from 7:00 to 11:00 P.M. Cynthia is eligible to deduct commuting expenses based on 20 miles (the distance between jobs).

Instead, assume that Cynthia has an office in the home that qualifies as a principal place of business. In this circumstance, the transportation between her home and various work locations is not a deductible commuting expense.

Computation of Automobile Expenses

A taxpayer has two choices in computing deductible automobile expenses. The first alternative is to use the actual operating cost, which includes depreciation (see text Section 5-7), fuel, oil, repairs, licenses, and insurance costs. Records must be kept that document the automobile's use for personal and business purposes. Only the percentage allocable to business transportation and travel is allowed as a deduction. The percentage of business use is usually arrived at by comparing the business mileage with total mileage—both business and personal.

The second alternative is the **automatic mileage method**, also called the standard mileage method. This method simplifies record keeping, as the taxpayer only has to multiply the automatic mileage rate by the business miles driven to compute the deduction. For 2022, the deduction is based on 58.5 cents per mile for business miles (56 cents for 2021).[35] Parking fees and tolls are allowed in addition to expenses computed using the automatic mileage method.

Generally, a taxpayer may elect either method for any particular year. However, a taxpayer may not use the standard mileage method for a vehicle after claiming depreciation deductions for that vehicle. In addition, the standard mileage rate cannot be used if five or more vehicles are in use (for business purposes) at the *same* time.[36]

Additional information on the standard mileage rate, including the effect on the automobile's basis, can be found on this book's companion website: www.cengage.com — 8 Digging Deeper

11-3b Travel Expenses

A deduction is allowed for **travel expenses** related to a taxpayer's work. Travel expenses are more broadly defined in the Code than are transportation expenses. Travel expenses include transportation expenses and meals and lodging while working away from home. Deductible travel expenses also include reasonable laundry and incidental expenses. However, a deduction for meals and lodging is available only if a taxpayer is away from their home, as discussed next.

Additional information about travel expenses can be found on this book's companion website: www.cengage.com — 9 Digging Deeper

Away-from-Home Requirement

The crucial test for the deductibility of travel expenses is whether the taxpayer is away from home overnight. "Overnight" need not be a 24-hour period, but it must be a period substantially longer than an ordinary day's work and must require rest, sleep, or a relief-from-work period.[37] Thus, a one-day business trip is not considered travel for tax purposes, and meals and lodging for such a trip are not deductible.

[35] Notice 2022–3.

[36] These and other requirements are detailed in Rev.Proc. 2019–46.

[37] *U.S. v. Correll*, 68–1 USTC ¶9101, 20 AFTR 2d 5845, 88 S.Ct. 445; Rev.Rul. 75–168.

Temporary Assignments

Taxpayers must be away from home for a temporary period. If the taxpayer is reassigned to a new location for an indefinite period of time, that new location becomes the tax home. "Temporary" indicates that the assignment's termination is expected within a reasonably short period of time. The position of the IRS is that the tax home is the business location of the taxpayer. Thus, travel expenses are not deductible if a taxpayer is reassigned for an indefinite period and does not move their place of residence to the new location.

Temporary Becomes Permanent

Malcolm maintains a consulting practice in Los Angeles. Due to new client responsibilities, Malcolm decided to open an office in San Diego. Malcolm worked out of the new office for three months to train a new manager and to assist in setting up the new office. He tried commuting from his home in Los Angeles for a week and decided that he could not continue driving several hours a day. He rented an apartment in San Diego, where he lived during the week. He spent weekends with his wife and children at their home in Los Angeles.

Malcolm's rent, meals, laundry, incidentals, and automobile expenses in San Diego are deductible. To the extent that Malcolm's transportation expense related to his weekend trips home exceeds what his cost of meals and lodging would have been, the excess is personal and nondeductible.

Assume that in the previous example, Malcom decided that he was the best person to manage the new office in San Diego and so decided to move there permanently. His wife and children continued to live in Los Angeles until the end of the school year. Malcolm is no longer "away from home" because the assignment is not temporary. His travel expenses are not deductible.

To curtail controversy in this area, the Code specifies that a taxpayer "*shall not* be treated as *temporarily* away from home during any period of employment if such period exceeds 1 year."[38]

Digging Deeper 10

For more information on the away-from-home rule, visit this book's companion website: www.cengage.com

Determining the Tax Home

Under ordinary circumstances, determining the location of a taxpayer's tax home does not present a problem. The tax home is the area in which the taxpayer works. When the taxpayer has more than one place of employment, the tax home is determined by considering the time spent, the level of activity involved, and the income earned at each job.

It is possible for a taxpayer never to be considered away from their tax home. In other words, the tax home follows the taxpayer. Under such circumstances, all meals and lodging remain personal and are not deductible.

Jim is single and works full-time as a long-haul truck driver. He lists his mother's home as his address and stays there during holidays. However, he contributes nothing toward its maintenance.

Because Jim has no regular place of duty or place where he regularly lives, his tax home is where he works (i.e., on the road). As an itinerant (transient), he is never away from home, and all of his meals and lodging while on the road are personal and not deductible.

The result reached in Example 21 is justified on the grounds that there is no duplication of living expenses in the case of itinerant taxpayers.[39]

[38] § 162(a).

[39] Rev.Rul. 73–539 and *James O. Henderson*, 70 TCM 1407, T.C.Memo. 1995–559, *aff'd* by 98–1 USTC ¶50,375, 81 AFTR 2d 98–1748, 143 F.3d 497 (CA–9).

Combined Business and Pleasure Travel

Deductible travel expenses need not be incurred in the performance of specific work functions. Travel expenses incurred to attend a professional convention are deductible if attendance is connected with the taxpayer's trade or business. For example, a lawyer could deduct travel expenses incurred to attend a meeting of the American Bar Association.

To limit the possibility of a taxpayer claiming a tax deduction for what is essentially a personal vacation, several provisions have been enacted to restrict deductions associated with combined business and pleasure trips. If the business/pleasure trip is from one point in the United States to another point in the United States (*domestic travel*), the transportation expenses are deductible only if the trip is primarily for business.[40] Meals, lodging, and other expenses are allocated between business and personal days. If the trip is primarily for pleasure, transportation expenses are not deductible.

In the current year, Hana travels from Seattle to New York primarily for business. She spends five days conducting business and three days sightseeing and attending shows. Her plane and taxi fare amounts to $1,160. Her meals amount to $200 per day, and lodging and incidental expenses are $350 per day.

Hana can deduct the transportation expenses of $1,160 because the trip is primarily for business (five days of business versus three days of sightseeing). Deductible meals are limited to five days and are not subject to a 50% reduction since they were consumed in a local restaurant (see text Section 11-2c) for a total of $500 [5 days × ($200 × 50%)]. Lodging and incidental expenses are limited to $1,750 (5 days × $350).

If instead Hana's trip to New York is primarily a vacation, apart from a few hours spent meeting with people in her company's New York office, her transportation expenses are not deductible.

When the trip is outside the United States (*foreign travel*), different rules apply.[41] Transportation expenses must be allocated between business and personal days *unless* (1) the taxpayer is away from home for seven days or less (ignoring the day travel begins but counting the day travel ends) or (2) less than 25 percent of the time was for personal purposes. No allocation is required if the taxpayer has no substantial control over arrangements for the trip or the desire for a vacation is not a major factor in taking the trip. If the trip is primarily for pleasure, no transportation charges are deductible. Days devoted to travel are considered business days. Weekends, legal holidays, and intervening days are considered business days provided that both the preceding and succeeding days were business days. Compare Examples 22 and 23.

To learn more about special rules for conventions held outside of North America, visit this book's companion website: www.cengage.com

11 Digging Deeper

In the current year, Robert takes a trip from New York to Japan primarily for business purposes. He is away from home from June 10 through June 19. He spends three days vacationing and seven days (including two travel days) conducting business. His airfare is $4,000, his meals amount to $200 per day (all at local restaurants), and lodging and incidental expenses are $300 per day.

Because Robert is away from home for more than seven days and more than 25% of his time is devoted to personal travel, only 70% (7 days business/10 days total) of the transportation is deductible. His potential deductions are computed as follows.

continued

[40] Reg. § 1.162–2(b)(1).

[41] § 274(c) and Reg. § 1.274–4. For purposes of the seven-days-or-less exception, the departure travel day is not counted.

Transportation (70% × $4,000)	$2,800
Lodging ($300 × 7)	2,100
Meals ($200 × 7)	1,400
Total deductions	$6,300

If Robert was gone the same period of time but spent only two (rather than three) days vacationing, no allocation of transportation would be required. Because the pleasure portion of the trip would then be less than 25% of the total, all of the airfare would qualify for the travel deduction.

The foreign travel rules do not operate to bar a deduction to an employer if the expense is *compensatory* in nature. For example, the value of a trip to Rome won by a top salesperson is included in the gross income of the employee and is fully deductible by the employer.

Tax Planning Strategies **Transportation and Travel Expenses**

Framework Focus: Deductions

Strategy: Maximize Deductible Amounts.

Detailed records of all transportation and travel expenses should be kept. Because the automatic (standard) mileage allowance often is modest in amount, a new, expensive automobile used primarily for business may generate a larger deductible expense based on actual cost. The election to expense some or all of the cost of the automobile via cost recovery (the immediate expensing provisions, § 179, or MACRS depreciation), insurance, repairs and maintenance, and other related costs may result in automobile expenses greater than the automatic mileage allowance.

Additionally, if a taxpayer wants to sightsee or vacation on a business trip, it may be beneficial to schedule business on both a Friday and a Monday to turn the weekend into business days for allocation purposes. It is especially crucial to schedule appropriate business days when foreign travel is involved.

11-3c Education Expenses

In general, a self-employed taxpayer can deduct **education expenses**, provided the expenses are:

- To meet the specific legal requirements to keep a job, or
- To maintain or improve existing skills required in the present job.

Education expenses are *not* deductible if the education is for either of the following purposes.

- To meet the minimum educational standards for qualification in the taxpayer's existing job, or
- To qualify the taxpayer for a new trade or business.[42]

From 2018 through 2025, employees incurring education expenses that are not reimbursed by the employer may not deduct these expenses (they are employee business expenses and, as such, miscellaneous itemized deductions). However, employees

[42]Reg. §§ 1.162–5(b)(2) and (3).

should determine if any other education deduction or credit may apply, such as the lifetime learning credit (text Section 10-5d) or the educator expense deduction for AGI (text Section 11-3e).

A deduction is generally allowed for education related to new duties of a self-employed taxpayer if the new duties involve the same general work. For example, the IRS has ruled that a practicing dentist's education expenses incurred to become an orthodontist are deductible.[43] Fees incurred for professional qualification exams (the bar exam, for example) and fees for review courses (such as a CPA review course) generally are not deductible.[44]

Employer or Legal Requirements to Keep a Job

Taxpayers can deduct education expenses if additional courses are required by the employer or are imposed by law. For example, some states require a minimum of a bachelor's degree plus additional courses to retain a teaching job, while others require teachers to make satisfactory progress toward a master's degree to keep their positions. If the required education is the minimum degree required for the job, no deduction is allowed.

Expenses incurred for education required by law for various professions (e.g., medicine, law, and accounting) also qualify for a deduction.

Maintaining or Improving Existing Skills

The "maintaining or improving existing skills" requirement in the Code has been difficult for both taxpayers and the courts to interpret. For example, a business consultant may be permitted to deduct the costs of obtaining an advanced degree on the grounds the advanced management education is undertaken to maintain and improve existing management skills. The consultant can also deduct the costs of specialized, nondegree management courses that are taken to maintain or improve existing skills. However, expenses incurred by a self-employed accountant to obtain a law degree are not deductible, because the education constitutes training for a new trade or business.[45]

Allowable Expenses

Education expenses include books and supplies, tuition, transportation (e.g., from the office to night school), and travel (e.g., meals and lodging while away from home at an executive education training program).

Another deduction item relating to education is the limited deduction of interest on student loans; see text Section 10-4c.[46]

11-3d Entertainment and Meal Expenses

Many businesses incur entertainment and meal expenses. While such expenses can help build business activity, a personal element also is involved in these activities. As a result, Congress decided to limit these deductions. No deduction is allowed with respect to:

1. An activity generally considered to be entertainment, amusement, or recreation;
2. Membership dues with respect to any club organized for business, pleasure, recreation, or other social purposes; or
3. A facility or portion thereof used in connection with any of the above items.

---

[43] Rev.Rul. 74–78.

[44] Reg. § 1.212–1(f) and Rev.Rul. 69–292.

[45] Reg. § 1.162–5(b)(3)(ii), Example (1).

[46] § 221.

Taxpayers still may generally deduct 50 percent of the food and beverage expenses associated with operating their trade or business (e.g., a business meal with a current or potential client or meals consumed by employees during work travel). However, due to the impact of the COVID-19 pandemic on restaurants, Congress provided a temporary *100 percent* deduction for meals and beverages provided by a restaurant that are paid or incurred in 2021 and 2022.[47]

Additional information on meal expenses can be found on this book's companion website: www.cengage.com

The 50 percent rule has a number of additional exceptions.[48] One exception covers the situation where the full value of the meals is included in the compensation of the employee (or independent contractor). Expenses directly related to business meetings of employees also are not subject to the 50 percent rule (and are fully deductible). A similar exception applies to employer-paid recreational or social activities for employees (e.g., the annual holiday party or spring picnic). In addition, businesses that have retreats and/or other off-site training events are generally allowed to deduct 100 percent of the meals provided to participants at those sites.[49]

Example 24

Myrtle wins an all-expense-paid trip to Europe for selling the most insurance for her company during the year. Her employer treats this trip as additional compensation to Myrtle. The 50 percent rule does not apply to the employer's deduction for the expenses of the trip.

Business Meals

A meal is deductible by a business only if all of the following conditions are met.[50]

- The expense is reasonable (i.e., not lavish or extravagant).
- The taxpayer (or an employee) is present at the meal.
- The food and beverages are provided to a current or potential business customer or client.
- If combined with entertainment, the meal and beverages cost is separately itemized on the bill or receipt.

Business Meals

During 2022, Lance Smith submits a proposed consulting contract to a local business. He invites the two business owners to dinner at a local restaurant to discuss the contract and pays for the meal. During the meal, Lance answers questions about the proposed contract. Lance can deduct 100% of this qualified business meal.

Assume the same facts as Example 25, except that Lance buys dinner for the two business owners but does not attend the dinner. Since Lance was not present at the meal, no deduction is allowed.

[47] § 274(n)(2)(D). The expenses must be paid or incurred after December 31, 2020, and before January 1, 2023. While the statutory language does not provide a definition of the term *restaurant*, the IRS provided that in Notice 2021-25.

[48] §§ 274(e) and (n).

[49] *Jacobs*, 148 T.C. 490 (2017); acq. in result only (Action on Decision 2019-01).

[50] § 274(k); Regs. § 1.274-11 and § 1.274-12.

If the taxpayer is in travel status, the expense of the meal can be deducted, subject to the 50 percent rule (100 percent in 2021 and 2022 for meals provided by a restaurant).

Business Gifts

Although not subject to the 50 percent limit on meals, business gifts are deductible only to the extent of $25 per donee per year.[51] Gifts costing $4 or less (e.g., pens with the employee's or company's name on them) or promotional materials are not subject to the $25 limit. In addition, incidental costs such as engraving of jewelry and nominal charges for gift-wrapping, mailing, and delivery are not included in the cost of the gift in applying the limitation. Records must be maintained to substantiate business gifts.

11-3e Other Expenses of Work

In addition to those expenses discussed previously, the Code provides for the deduction of a number of other work-related expenses. The home office deduction and educator expenses are discussed in this section.

Office in the Home

Self-employed individuals are only allowed a deduction for **office in the home expenses** if a portion of the residence is used *exclusively and on a regular basis* as either:

- The principal place of business for any trade or business of the taxpayer, or
- A place of business used by clients, patients, or customers.

From 2018 through 2025, employees are not allowed to deduct expenses related to an office in the home because these expenses are considered miscellaneous itemized deductions.

The precise meaning of "principal place of business" has been the subject of considerable debate between taxpayers and the IRS.[52] The term *principal place of business* includes a place of business that satisfies both of the following requirements.[53]

- The office is used by the taxpayer to conduct administrative or management activities of a trade or business.
- There is no other fixed location of the trade or business where the taxpayer conducts these activities.

Dr. Sunder is a self-employed anesthesiologist. During the year, she spends 30 to 35 hours per week administering anesthesia and postoperative care to patients in three hospitals, none of which provides her with an office. She also spends two or three hours per day in a room in her home that she uses exclusively as an office. Dr. Sunder does not meet patients there, but she performs a variety of tasks related to her medical practice (e.g., contacting surgeons, bookkeeping, and reading medical journals).

A deduction for this office in the home is allowed because Dr. Sunder conducts administrative or management activities there, and she has no other fixed location where these activities can be carried out.

[51] 274(b)(1). Multiple gifts to members of the same customer's family are consolidated (so there will be only one $25 deduction allowed).

[52] See the restrictive interpretation arrived at in *Comm. v. Soliman*, 93–1 USTC¶ 50,014, 71 AFTR 2d 93–463, 113 S.Ct. 701.

[53] § 280A(c)(1).

The exclusive use requirement means that a specific part of the home must be used solely for business purposes. A deduction, if permitted, requires an allocation of total expenses of operating the home between business and personal use based on floor space or number of rooms.

Additional information on the home office deduction can be found on this book's companion website: www.cengage.com

Even if the taxpayer meets the above requirements, the allowable home office expenses cannot exceed the gross income from the business less all other business expenses attributable to the activity. That is, the home office deduction cannot create a loss. Furthermore, the home office expenses that are allowed as itemized deductions otherwise (e.g., mortgage interest and real estate taxes) must be deducted first.

The home office expenses of a self-employed individual are deductible *for* AGI. Any disallowed home office expenses are carried forward and used in future years subject to the same limitations.

Example 28

Patrick is a certified public accountant employed by a regional CPA firm as a tax manager. He also has a business refinishing furniture that he operates out of his home. For this business, he uses two rooms in the basement of his home exclusively and regularly. The floor space of the two rooms is 240 square feet, which constitutes 10% of the total floor space of his 2,400-square-foot residence. Gross income from the business totals $8,000. Expenses of the business (other than home office expenses) are $6,500. Patrick incurs the following home office expenses.

Real property taxes on residence	$ 4,000
Interest expense on residence	7,500
Operating expenses of residence (including homeowners insurance)	2,000
MACRS depreciation on residence (based on 10% business use)	350

Patrick's deductions are determined as follows.

Business income		$ 8,000
Less: Other business expenses		(6,500)
Net income from the business (before the office in the home deduction)		$ 1,500
Less: Allocable taxes ($4,000 × 10%)	$400	
Allocable interest ($7,500 × 10%)	750	(1,150)
Subtotal		$ 350
Less: Allocable operating expenses of the residence ($2,000 × 10%)		(200)
Subtotal		$ 150
Less: Allocable MACRS depreciation ($350, limited to remaining income)		(150)
Remaining home office expenses		$ -0-

Patrick has a carryover deduction of $200 (the unused excess MACRS depreciation). Because he is self-employed, the allocable taxes and interest ($1,150), the other deductible office expenses ($200 + $150), and $6,500 of other business expenses are deductible *for* AGI.

Educator Expenses

Many teachers pay for professional development courses or purchase school supplies for classroom use for which they are not reimbursed by their employer. Such expenses could be considered miscellaneous itemized deductions. However, the deduction for such amounts is currently suspended.

An additional provision applies to elementary and secondary school teachers that provides modest relief. Eligible educators must work at least 900 hours during a school year as a teacher, an instructor, a counselor, a principal, or an aide. If they meet these requirements, teachers may deduct the costs they incur for books, supplies, professional development courses, computer equipment and related software and services, other equipment, and supplementary materials they use in the classroom. The annual ceiling on this *for* AGI deduction is $300 ($250 for 2021).[54] Personal protective equipment, disinfectant, and other supplies used for the prevention of the spread of COVID-19 also qualify.[55]

11-3f **Classification of Employee Expenses**

LO.4

Explain the difference between accountable and nonaccountable employee plans.

The classification of employee expenses depends on whether they are reimbursed by the employer under an accountable plan. If such expenses are reimbursed, then neither the reimbursement nor the expense is reported by the employee. In effect, this result is equivalent to reporting the reimbursement as income and treating the expenses as deductions *for* AGI.[56] Alternatively, if the expenses are reimbursed under a nonaccountable plan or are not reimbursed at all, they are classified as deductions *from* AGI and are currently nondeductible miscellaneous itemized deductions.

Accountable Plans

An accountable plan requires the employee to satisfy these two requirements.

- Substantiate the expenses. An employee provides an adequate accounting by submitting a record (e.g., completing an employer-provided travel expense reimbursement form), with receipts and other substantiation, to the employer.[57]
- Return any excess reimbursement or allowance. An "excess reimbursement or allowance" is any amount the employee does not adequately account for as an ordinary and necessary business expense.

The law provides that no deduction is allowed for any travel, entertainment, business gift, or listed property (e.g., automobiles and computers) expenses unless properly substantiated by adequate records. The records should contain the following information:[58]

- The amount of the expense.
- The time and place of travel or entertainment (or date of gift).
- The business purpose of the expense.
- The business relationship of the taxpayer to the person entertained (or receiving the gift).

As a result, the taxpayer must keep records (e.g., in a calendar or by other means) to document these expenses. Documentary evidence (e.g., itemized receipt) is required to support any expenditure for lodging while traveling away from home and for any other expenditure of $75 or more. If a taxpayer fails to keep adequate records, a written or oral statement of the exact details of the expense will be required, along with other corroborating evidence.[59]

For further information on the substantiation of expenses, visit this book's companion website: www.cengage.com

14 Digging Deeper

[54] § 62(a)(2)(D).

[55] Consolidated Appropriations Act, 2021 § 275 (P.L. 116–260). Applies to items purchased after March 12, 2020.

[56] § 62(a)(2).

[57] Reg. § 1.162–17(b)(4).

[58] § 274(d).

[59] Reg. § 1.274–5T(c)(3).

Nonaccountable Plans

A **nonaccountable plan** is a plan in which an adequate accounting or return of excess amounts, or both, is not required. All expense reimbursements are reported in full as wages on the employee's Form W–2. Any allowable expenses, to the extent they are deductible, are deductible in the same manner as unreimbursed expenses.

If an employer offers an accountable plan and requires employees to return excess reimbursements or allowances but an employee fails to follow the rules of the plan, the expenses and reimbursements are subject to nonaccountable plan treatment.

Unreimbursed Employee Expenses

Unreimbursed employee business expenses (including 50 percent of any meals) are treated as miscellaneous itemized deductions. Such expenses are not deductible from 2018 through 2025.

Digging Deeper 15

How are frequent flyer miles earned by an employee taxed? Find out on this book's companion website: www.cengage.com

LO.5

Understand the opportunities available to build wealth through Individual Retirement Accounts.

11-3g Contributions to Individual Retirement Accounts

Traditional and Roth Individual Retirement Accounts, or IRAs, are commonly used to provide individual savings for retirement. The tax rules that govern deductible contributions, taxable distributions, age requirements, and possible penalties for early withdrawals or excess contributions are discussed in the following section.

Traditional IRAs

An individual can contribute to a traditional **Individual Retirement Account (IRA)** assuming that the person (or spouse) has earned income. These contributions may be deductible depending on income level and access to another work-related retirement plan. For 2022, the contribution ceiling is the lesser of $6,000 (or $12,000 for spousal IRAs) or 100 percent of compensation.[60] An individual who attains the age of 50 by the end of the tax year can make an additional "catch-up" IRA contribution of up to $1,000 annually.

If the taxpayer is an active participant in another qualified retirement savings plan, the traditional IRA deduction limitation is phased out *proportionately* between certain AGI ranges, as shown in Exhibit 11.2.[61] If AGI is above the phaseout range, no IRA deduction is allowed.

AGI is calculated taking into account any passive activity losses and taxable Social Security benefits and ignoring any foreign income exclusion, savings bonds interest exclusion, and the IRA deduction itself. As long as the deduction is not completely phased out, the allowable IRA deduction cannot be less than $200.

Exhibit 11.2 Phaseout of Traditional IRA Deduction of an Active Participant in 2022

AGI, Filing Status	Phaseout Begins*	Phaseout Ends*
Single and head of household	$ 68,000	$ 78,000
Married, filing joint return	109,000	129,000
Married, filing separate return	–0–	10,000

*These amounts are indexed annually for inflation. For the 2022 amounts, see Notice 2021–61.

[60] §§ 219(b)(1) and (c)(2). The limit may be adjusted annually for inflation in $500 increments.

[61] § 219(g).

IRA Deduction Calculation

Dan, who is single, earns compensation income of $74,000 in 2022. He is an active participant in his employer's qualified retirement plan. Dan contributes $6,000 to a traditional IRA. The deductible amount is reduced from $6,000 by $3,600 because of the phaseout (see Exhibit 11.2).

$$\frac{\$6{,}000 \text{ (amount into phaseout range)}}{\$10{,}000 \text{ (phaseout range)}} \times \$6{,}000 \text{ contribution} = \$3{,}600$$

As a result, only $2,400 ($6,000 − $3,600) of Dan's $6,000 contribution is tax deductible.

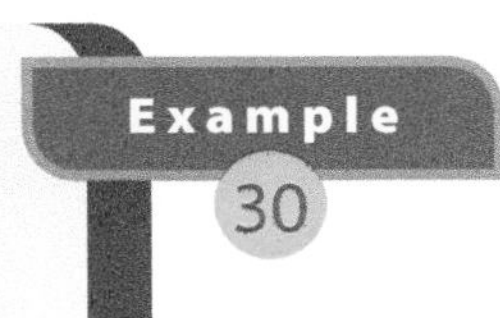

Bonnie, an unmarried individual who is 45, is an active participant in her employer's qualified retirement plan in 2022. With an AGI of $77,800, Bonnie's IRA deduction limit would be $120 {$6,000 − [($77,800 − $68,000)/$10,000 × $6,000]} per the phaseout calculation. However, because of the floor amount, she is allowed a $200 IRA deduction.

An individual is not considered an active participant in a qualified plan merely because the individual's spouse is an active participant in such a plan for any part of a plan year. Thus, even when filing jointly, the nonparticipating individual may take a full $6,000 deduction regardless of the participation status of their spouse unless the couple has AGI above $204,000. A deduction phaseout begins at AGI of $204,000 and ends at $214,000 (phaseout over the $10,000 range) rather than beginning and ending at the phaseout amounts in Exhibit 11.2.[62]

Nell is covered by a qualified employer retirement plan at work. Her husband, Nick, is not an active participant in a qualified plan. If Nell and Nick's combined AGI is $135,000, Nell cannot make a deductible IRA contribution because she exceeds the income threshold for an active participant. However, because Nick is not an active participant and their combined AGI does not exceed $204,000, he can make a fully deductible contribution of $6,000 to an IRA.

To the extent an individual is ineligible to make a deductible contribution to an IRA, *nondeductible contributions* can be made to the account. The nondeductible contributions are subject to the same dollar limits as deductible contributions ($6,000 of earned income, $12,000 for a spousal IRA). Income in the account accumulates tax-free until distributed. Where nondeductible contributions are made, only the account earnings are taxed upon distribution; the individual's account basis equals the contributions made.

Roth IRAs

A Roth IRA is a *nondeductible* alternative to the traditional deductible IRA. Earnings inside a Roth IRA are not taxable, and all qualified distributions from a Roth IRA are tax-free.[63]

The maximum allowable annual contribution to a Roth IRA for 2022 is the lesser of $6,000 ($12,000 for spousal IRAs) or 100 percent of the individual's compensation for the year. Contributions to a Roth IRA must be made by the due date (excluding extensions) of the taxpayer's tax return.

A taxpayer can make tax-free withdrawals from a Roth IRA after an initial five-year holding period if any of the following requirements are satisfied.

- The distribution is made on or after the date on which the participant attains age 59½.

[62] § 219(g)(7). However, a special rule in § 219(g)(4) allows a married person filing a separate return to avoid the phaseout rules even though the spouse is an active participant. The individual must live apart from the spouse at all times during the taxable year and must not be an active participant in another qualified plan.

[63] § 408A.

- The distribution is made to a beneficiary (or the participant's estate) on or after the participant's death.
- The participant becomes disabled.
- The distribution is used for qualified first-time homebuyer's expenses (maximum $10,000).

Amy establishes a Roth IRA at age 42 and contributes $5,000 per year for 20 years. The account is now worth $149,400, consisting of $100,000 of nondeductible contributions and $49,400 in accumulated earnings that have not been taxed. Amy may withdraw the $149,400 tax-free from the Roth IRA because she is over age 59½ and has met the five-year holding period requirement.

If the taxpayer receives a distribution from a Roth IRA and does not satisfy the aforementioned requirements, some of the distribution may constitute gross income. If the distribution represents a return of capital, it is not taxable. Conversely, if the distribution represents a payout of earnings, it is taxable. Under the ordering rules for Roth IRAs, distributions are treated as first made from contributions (return of capital).

Assume the same facts as in the previous example, except that Amy is only age 50 and receives a distribution of $55,000. Because her basis for the Roth IRA is $100,000 (contributions made), the distribution is tax-free, and her basis in the account is reduced to $45,000 ($100,000 − $55,000).

Contributions to Roth IRAs are subject to income limits. In 2022, the maximum annual contribution of $6,000 is phased out beginning at AGI of $129,000 for single taxpayers and $204,000 for married taxpayers who file a joint return. The phaseout range is $10,000 for married taxpayers filing jointly and $15,000 for single taxpayers. For a married taxpayer filing separately, the phaseout begins with AGI of $0 and is phased out over a $10,000 range.

Bev, who is single and an independent contractor, would like to contribute $6,000 to her Roth IRA in 2022. Her AGI is $139,000. As a result, her contribution is limited to $2,000 ($6,000 − $4,000), calculated as follows.

$$\frac{\$10{,}000 \text{ (amount into phaseout range)}}{\$15{,}000 \text{ (phaseout range)}} \times \$6{,}000 \text{ contribution} = \$4{,}000 \text{ reduction}$$

Unlike a traditional IRA, which requires withdrawals at age 72, there are no required withdrawals from a Roth IRA.[64] Such savings can be accumulated over the taxpayer's lifetime and then passed to heirs without incurring Federal income or estate taxes.[65]

Rollovers and Conversions

Often when employees change jobs, they do not want to leave their retirement savings with their former employer. As a result, retirement savings in a qualified plan may be directly transferred from that plan to an IRA or may be "rolled over" into an IRA. Amounts that are directly transferred to another plan are not included in the owner's gross income. Rollover distributions will not be included in gross income as long as the funds received are transferred to an IRA within 60 days of receipt.[66]

In addition, a traditional IRA may be rolled over or converted to a Roth IRA. The tax consequences depend on whether the contributions made to the traditional IRA were deductible or nondeductible. If deductible contributions were made, the basis for the IRA is zero. Thus, the entire amount of the rollover or conversion is included in gross income. If nondeductible contributions were made, the basis for the IRA is equal to the sum of the contributions. Thus, only the IRA earnings included in the rollover or conversion are included in gross income.

See Concept Summary 11.3 for an overview of some of the primary differences between traditional and Roth IRAs.

[64] 408A(c)(4).

[65] Additional details on traditional and Roth IRAs can be found in IRS Publication 590, *Individual Retirement Accounts (IRAs)*.

[66] § 402(c)(3).

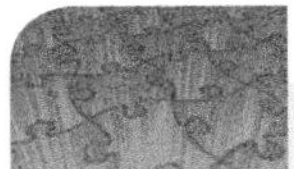

Concept Summary 11.3

Comparison of IRAs

	Traditional		
	Deductible IRA	**Nondeductible IRA**	**Roth IRA**
Maximum contribution (per year)	$6,000*	$6,000*	$6,000*
Tax-deductible contribution	Yes	No	No
Tax-free growth of income	Yes	Yes	Yes
Beginning of AGI phaseout for active participant (2022)	$68,000 single, $109,000 joint	N/A	$129,000 single, $204,000 joint
Income tax on distributions	Yes, for entire distribution	Yes, for the earnings portion	No, if satisfy 5-year holding period**
50% excise tax: age 72 insufficient distributions	Yes	Yes	No
10% early withdrawal penalty (before age 59½)	Yes, with exceptions†	Yes, with exceptions†	Yes, with exceptions†

*The total of deductible, nondeductible, and Roth IRA contributions may not exceed $6,000 per year.

**In addition, the distribution must satisfy one of the following: made after age 59½, used for qualified first-time homebuyer expenses, made to participant who is disabled, or made to a beneficiary on or after the participant's death.

†Qualified education and first-time homebuyer costs (up to $10,000) avoid the 10% penalty.

11-4 Individuals as Proprietors

LO.6

Explain the tax provisions applicable to proprietors.

A sole proprietorship is *not* a taxable entity separate from the individual who owns the proprietorship. The owner reports the results of business operations of the proprietorship on Schedule C of Form 1040. The net profit or loss reported on the Schedule C is included in the taxable income of the individual proprietor. The proprietor reports all of the net profit from the business irrespective of the amount actually withdrawn from the proprietorship during the year.

Income and expenses of the proprietorship retain their character when reported by the proprietor. For example, ordinary income of the proprietorship is treated as ordinary income when reported by the proprietor, and capital gain of the proprietorship is treated as capital gain when reported by the proprietor. In addition, a deduction for qualified business income (§ 199A, discussed later in this section) is available for sole proprietors. In general, this deduction is 20 percent of proprietorship net income and is claimed on the proprietor's Form 1040 in determining taxable income.

George is the sole proprietor of George's Bicycle Shop. Gross income of the business is $200,000, and operating expenses are $110,000. George also sells a capital asset held by the business for a $10,000 long-term capital gain. During the year, he withdraws $60,000 cash from the business for living expenses.

George reports the operating income and expenses of the business on Schedule C, resulting in net profit (ordinary income) of $90,000 ($200,000 − $110,000). George reports all of the $90,000 net profit from the business on Form1040, irrespective of his cash withdrawal. He also reports a $10,000 long-term capital gain on his personal tax return (Schedule D of Form1040).

11-4a Accounting Periods and Methods

A taxpayer's accounting method determines when an item is includible in gross income and when an item is deductible in calculating taxable income. Proprietors may choose among various accounting methods, just as other business entities do (refer to Chapters

4 and 5). The cash method is commonly used by proprietorships that provide services, while the accrual or hybrid method generally is required if inventory is a material income-producing factor of the business and the taxpayer is not a *small business*.

Because a proprietorship is not an entity separate from the proprietor, the proprietorship must use the same tax year-end as the proprietor. This does not preclude the use of a fiscal year for a proprietorship, but most proprietorships use the calendar year.

11-4b **Income and Deductions of a Proprietorship**

The broad definition of gross income in § 61(a) applies equally to individuals and business entities, including proprietorships, corporations, and partnerships. Thus, asset inflows into a proprietorship are to be treated as income unless a Code section provides for an exclusion from income (e.g., interest on state and local bonds, appreciation on investments). Refer to Chapter 4 for a detailed discussion of gross income.

Generally, the provisions that govern business deductions are not entity-specific. The § 162 requirement that trade or business expenses be *ordinary and necessary* (refer to text Section 5-1) applies to proprietorships as well as corporations, partnerships, and other business entities. However, certain deductions are available only to self-employed taxpayers. These deductions are addressed next.

Medical Insurance Premiums

A self-employed taxpayer may deduct *for* AGI any insurance premiums paid for medical coverage.[67] The deduction is allowed for premiums paid on behalf of the taxpayer, the taxpayer's spouse, and dependents of the taxpayer. The deduction is not allowed if the taxpayer (or taxpayer's spouse) is eligible to participate in an employer-provided health plan.

This deduction is reported on Schedule 1 of the Form 1040 rather than on Schedule C. Premiums paid for medical coverage of the *employees* of a self-employed taxpayer are deductible as business expenses on Schedule C, however.

Ellen, a sole practitioner of an unincorporated accounting practice, has two dependent children. This year she paid health insurance premiums of $12,000 for her own coverage and $8,000 for coverage of her two children. Ellen can claim health insurance premiums of $20,000 as a deduction *for* AGI in computing her taxable income.

Self-Employment Tax

The tax on self-employment income is levied to provide Social Security and Medicare benefits (old age, survivors, and disability insurance and hospital insurance) for self-employed individuals. Individuals with net earnings of $400 or more from self-employment are subject to the self-employment tax.[68] For 2022, the self-employment tax is 15.3 percent of self-employment income up to $147,000 and 2.9 percent of self-employment income in excess of that amount. This wage base is anually indexed for inflation.

Net earnings from self-employment include gross income from a trade or business less allowable trade or business deductions, plus the taxpayer's distributive share of any business-related partnership income or loss, and any net income from rendering personal services as an independent contractor.[69]

In computing the tax, net SE earnings are reduced by 7.65 percent (to 92.35 percent of the total) to reflect a deduction for the "employer's half" of the total 15.3 percent tax. Self-employed taxpayers are allowed a deduction *for* AGI equal to one-half of the self-employment tax liability.[70]

[67] § 162(l).
[68] § 6017.
[69] § 1402(a)(12).
[70] § 164(f).

If an individual who is self-employed also receives wages subject to the FICA tax from working as an employee of another organization, the amount of the Social Security portion on which the self-employment tax is computed is reduced. However, a combination of FICA wages and self-employment earnings will not reduce the Medicare component of the self-employment tax, because there is no ceiling on this component of the tax.

Computing Self-Employment Taxes

In 2022, Kelly recorded $86,000 of net earnings from a data imaging services business that she owns. During the year, she also received wages of $71,700 as an employee of a small accounting firm. The amount of Kelly's self-employment income subject to the Social Security tax (12.4%) is $75,300 ($147,000 − $71,700), producing a tax of $9,337 ($75,300 × 12.4%); note that $75,300 is less than Kelly's net SE income ($86,000 × 0.9235 = $79,421), so the smaller amount is used.

All of Kelly's net self-employment income ($79,421) is subject to the 2.9% Medicare portion of the self-employment tax. Thus, Kelly's Medicare tax on this income is $2,303 ($79,421 × 2.9%). In total, Kelly's self-employment tax liability is $11,640 [$9,337 (Social Security) + $2,303 (Medicare)].

Continue with the facts in the previous example. If Kelly's wages from working at the accounting firm were only $50,000, then her ceiling for Social Security taxation would be $97,000 ($147,000 − $50,000). Because her net self-employment income ($79,421) is less than this amount, Kelly would compute her self-employment tax on $79,421 of net SE income.

11-4c Retirement Plans for Self-Employed Individuals

Individual Retirement Accounts (discussed earlier in this chapter) are available to both employees and self-employed individuals. Other options for self-employed individuals include, but are not limited to, **Simplified Employee Pension (SEP) plans** and SIMPLE plans, both of which are discussed next.

SEP Plans

Self-employed individuals (e.g., partners and sole proprietors) can establish and receive qualified retirement benefits under SEP plans. Such a plan allows a self-employed individual to make contributions toward their own retirement (as well as employees' retirement) while avoiding the complexity that arises in other qualified retirement plans.[71] Contributions are made directly to a traditional individual retirement account (SEP IRA). Fundamentally, a SEP IRA can be thought of as a traditional IRA (with higher contribution limits) that is funded by employer contributions.

A self-employed individual may annually contribute the lesser of $61,000 (in 2022) or 25 percent of compensation to a SEP IRA. In applying the 25 percent ceiling, the annual compensation amount considered can be no more than $305,000.[72] For purposes of the contribution limits, a self-employed individual's compensation is defined as net earnings from self-employment.[73] However, net earnings from self-employment are reduced by the deductible portion of self-employment tax as well as the deduction for contributions made on the individual's behalf to the SEP IRA.[74]

[71] § 401(k)(8).

[72] § 408(k)(2) and Notice 2021-61.

[73] § 1402(c).

[74] SEP Plan FAQs, **www.irs.gov/retirement-plans**.

An individual can maintain a SEP for their self-employed business even if they participate in an employer's retirement plan at a second job. However, because a SEP is considered a defined contribution plan, contributions to a SEP must be added to contributions to other defined contribution plans in calculating contribution limits.

Finally, contributions to SEP IRAs are not required to be made annually. However, in years that a contribution is made, such contributions must be made to the SEP IRAs of all participants who are 21 or older, worked for the employer during three of the five prior years, and received at least $650 in compensation for the year. This includes part-time employees, seasonal employees, and employees who die or terminate their employment during the year.[75]

Pat, a sole proprietor, reports earned income of $150,000 in 2022 (after the deduction for one-half of self-employment tax but before any SEP IRA contribution). The maximum contribution Pat may make to a her SEP IRA is $61,000, the lesser of $150,000 or $61,000.

SIMPLE Plans

Employers with 100 or fewer employees who do not maintain another qualified retirement plan may establish a *savings incentive match plan for employees* (SIMPLE plan).[76] The plan can be in the form of a § 401(k) plan or an IRA. A SIMPLE § 401(k) plan is not subject to the nondiscrimination rules that apply to § 401(k) plans.

All employees who received at least $5,000 in compensation from the employer during any two preceding years and who reasonably expect to receive at least $5,000 in compensation during the current year must be eligible to participate in the plan. The decision to participate is up to the employee. A *self-employed individual* also may establish a SIMPLE plan.

The contributions made by the employee (a salary reduction is made) must be expressed as a percentage of compensation rather than as a fixed dollar amount. The SIMPLE plan must not permit the elective employee contribution for the year to exceed $14,000 in 2022 ($13,500 in 2021).[77] The SIMPLE elective deferral limit is increased under a "catch-up" provision for employees age 50 and over. The amount is $3,000 in 2022 and is indexed for inflation in $500 increments.

Generally, the employer must either match elective employee contributions up to 3 percent of the employee's compensation or provide nonmatching contributions of 2 percent of compensation for each eligible employee.

No other contributions may be made to the plan other than the employee elective contribution and the required employer matching contribution (or nonmatching contribution under the 2 percent rule). All contributions are fully vested on behalf of the employee. An employer is required to make the required matching or nonmatching contributions to a SIMPLE § 401(k) plan once it is established, whereas an employer's contributions to a traditional § 401(k) plan or a SEP IRA may be discretionary.

[75] § 408(k)(2)

[76] § 408(p).

[77] § 408(p)(2)(E)(i). The $14,000 statutory amount is indexed for inflation in $500 increments. As a result, the maximum amount that may be contributed to the plan for an employee under age 50 for 2022 is $23,150 [$14,000 employee contributions + $9,150 ($305,000 compensation ceiling × 3%) employer match].

Tax Planning Strategies

Factors Affecting Retirement Plan Choices

Framework Focus: Deductions

Strategy: Maximize Deductible Amounts.

An IRA might not be the best retirement plan option for many self-employed taxpayers. The maximum amount that can be deducted is $6,000 per year ($12,000 for a spousal plan), which may be too low to fund an adequate level of retirement income for the employee. Other options (i.e., SEP IRA, Keogh plan, SIMPLE plan) allow larger contributions and larger deductions.

However, a self-employed individual who establishes any one of these types of plans is required to cover most employees of the business under such plans. This can result in substantial expenditures not only for the required contributions but also for expenses of administering the plan. An advantage of an IRA is that coverage of employees is not required.

11-4d Deduction for Qualified Business Income

The deduction for **qualified business income** (QBI) became a part of the Internal Revenue Code as a result of the TCJA of 2017.[78] The rationale for the deduction relates to the TCJA's reduction of the corporate tax rate to 21 percent. The following discussion, in which the single level of tax paid by businesses operating in noncorporate form is compared to the double taxation experienced by businesses operating in corporate form, illustrates the rationale for the deduction for QBI.

Assume that a corporation has $10v0 of taxable income in 2022. If that corporation distributed all of its after-tax profit as a dividend to individual shareholders, the maximum combined (corporate and individual) tax rate on that $100 would be approximately 37 percent. That is, after paying Federal income taxes of $21, the corporation would distribute the remaining $79 to shareholders as a dividend. For an individual shareholder in the highest tax bracket, such a dividend would be taxed at a maximum rate of 20 percent. Thus, the shareholder would pay $16 in Federal income tax as a result of the receipt of the distribution. The remaining after-tax income equals $63. This means that a combined 37 percent in Federal income taxes was paid on the corporation's business income.[79]

If that same $100 was earned in 2022 by the sole proprietorship of a taxpayer in the highest income tax bracket, the income would also be taxed at a maximum rate of 37 percent.[80] Thus, without the deduction for QBI, the (historic) tax benefit of operating in noncorporate form would have been eliminated by the TCJA of 2017.

Generally, the deduction for QBI is equal to 20 percent of a noncorporate entity's qualified business income. By allowing a 20 percent deduction, the maximum tax rate on

[78] § 199A, Tax Cuts and Jobs Act (TCJA) 2017, Pub. L. 115–97, § 11012.

[79] 37% = [($21 corporate tax + $16 tax on dividends)/$100 corporate taxable income]. For ease of explanation, the presence of shareholders other than individuals is ignored in the example.

[80] For ease of explanation, taxes other than the individual income tax (e.g., the 3.8% Medicare tax) are ignored in the example.

noncorporate business income is approximately 30, rather than 37, percent, all else equal. Using the numbers in the previously described scenario, if the sole proprietor's $100 taxable income represented the business's QBI, then taxable income would be reduced by a $20 QBI deduction. The sole proprietor would pay tax on the remaining $80 of taxable income at a 37 percent maximum individual tax rate, resulting in Federal income tax of $30. All else equal, the TCJA retains the tax advantage to operating in noncorporate form.

This section begins by discussing the general rules for and key terms in the calculation of the deduction for QBI. The limitations that apply with respect to high-income taxpayers and service businesses are discussed after the general provisions.

General Rule

Generally, § 199A permits an individual to deduct 20 percent of the qualified business income generated by a sole proprietorship.[81] More precisely, the deduction is the *lesser of*:

1. 20 percent of QBI, or
2. 20 percent of modified taxable income.[82]

The general rule includes a number of terms that require definition and clarification.

Qualified business income (QBI), referenced in (1.) above, is defined as the ordinary income less the ordinary deductions a taxpayer reports from a "qualified trade or business." An individual taxpayer's QBI also includes the distributive share of QBI from each partnership or S corporation interest held by the taxpayer.

Qualified business income does not include certain types of investment income, such as:

- Capital gains or capital losses (including any net § 1231 gain included in capital gain and loss computations);
- Dividends;
- Interest income (unless "properly allocable" to a trade or business, such as lending); or
- Certain other investment items.

Additionally, qualified business income does not include:

- "Reasonable compensation" paid to the taxpayer by a qualified trade or business; or
- Guaranteed payments made to a partner for services rendered.[83]

As noted in the definition of QBI, in order to qualify for the deduction, the taxpayer's QBI must be earned in a "qualified trade or business" (QTB). (The term *qualified* appears in a variety of contexts in § 199A.) At the most basic level, such a business is conducted by the taxpayer in the United States.[84] For taxpayers who fall below the taxable income thresholds specified in § 199A (in 2022, $340,100 for married taxpayers filing jointly; $170,050 for single and head-of-household taxpayers), a QTB is defined broadly. Such a business includes any trade or business other than providing services as an employee.[85]

Irrespective of the amount calculated in (1.), part (2.) of the deduction calculation provides that the § 199A deduction cannot exceed 20 percent of the taxpayer's modified taxable income. Modified taxable income is taxable income *before* the deduction for qualified business income reduced by any net capital gain. In computing modified

[81] § 199A(a) and (b). Note that the deduction is also available for QBI generated by a partnership or an S corporation.

[82] If the taxpayer has more than one qualified trade or business, the QBI deduction is determined for each business independently [§ 199A(b)(1)(A)]. These amounts are then combined [into the "combined qualified business income amount" of § 199A(a)(1)(A)] and compared to the modified taxable income limitation in part (2) of the general rule.

[83] § 199A(c)(4).

[84] § 199A(c)(3)(A). As a result, foreign trade or business income does not qualify for the deduction. Certain Puerto Rico activities qualify for the deduction.

[85] § 199A(d)(1).

taxable income, the term *net capital gain* includes both a net capital gain plus any qualified dividend income.[86]

Finally, the QBI deduction is a deduction *from* AGI. The deduction is the last deduction taken in determining an individual's taxable income.[87] The deduction is available whether a taxpayer uses the standard deduction or itemizes deductions. Examples 40, 41, and 42 illustrate the basic calculation of the QBI deduction.

A taxpayer's deduction for QBI must be determined separately for each qualified trade or business. These independent calculations are combined into the "qualified business income amount" which is then compared to the taxpayer's overall modified taxable income limit.

Basic QBI Deduction Computation

Sanjay, a married taxpayer, operates a candy store as a sole proprietor. The business has no employees; Sanjay provides all services to customers. In 2022, Sanjay's qualified business income is $210,000 [his Schedule C (Form 1040) net income reduced by his self-employment tax deduction]. Sanjay's AGI is $275,900, which includes wages earned by his spouse but no other income. He and his spouse take the standard deduction ($25,900). Sanjay's modified taxable income is $250,000 ($275,900 − $25,900).

Sanjay's QBI deduction is $42,000, the lesser of:

1. 20% of qualified business income ($42,000; $210,000 × 20%), or
2. 20% of modified taxable income ($50,000; $250,000 × 20%).

As a result, Sanjay's taxable income is $208,000 {$250,000 of taxable income before the QBI deduction less the $42,000 QBI deduction [the lesser of the amounts calculated in (1) and (2)]}.

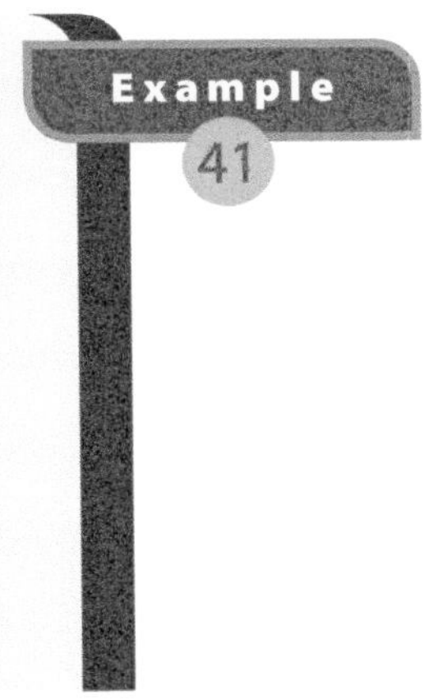

Assume that Abby is a single taxpayer who does not itemize deductions and operates a sole proprietorship. In 2022, her business generates $140,000 of business income, $40,000 of deductible business expenses (including her self-employment tax deduction), and $2,950 of interest income from her business deposits. She has no other sources of income. Abby's AGI is $102,950.

Abby has $100,000 of qualified business income ($140,000 − $40,000); the interest income does not qualify as QBI. Her modified taxable income is $90,000 ($102,950 AGI − $12,950 standard deduction).

Abby's QBI deduction is $18,000, the lesser of:

1. 20% of qualified business income ($20,000; $100,000 × 20%), or
2. 20% of modified taxable income ($18,000; $90,000 × 20%).

As a result, Abby's taxable income is $72,000 {$90,000 of taxable income before the QBI deduction less the $18,000 QBI deduction [the lesser of the amounts calculated in (1) and (2)]}.

Assume the same facts as in the previous example, except that Abby has $2,950 of qualified dividend income rather than interest income. Abby's AGI remains $102,950, and her taxable income before the QBI deduction remains $90,000 ($102,950 AGI − $12,950 standard deduction).

Abby's modified taxable income is now $87,050 [$90,000 taxable income before the QBI deduction less $2,950 of "net capital gain" (the qualified dividend income)].

Abby's QBI deduction is $17,410, the lesser of:

1. 20% of qualified business income ($20,000; $100,000 × 20%), or
2. 20% of modified taxable income ($17,410; $87,050 × 20%).

As a result, Abby's taxable income is $72,590 {$90,000 of taxable income before the QBI deduction less the $17,410 QBI deduction [the lesser of the amounts calculated in (1) and (2)]}.

[86] Reg. § 1.199A–3(b)(2)(ii).

[87] § 63(b)(3).

Limitations on the QBI Deduction

There are *three limitations* on the QBI deduction. An overall limitation based on modified taxable income [part (2.) of the deduction calculation, discussed previously] applies to all taxpayers. A second limitation is in place for high-income taxpayers, and a third limitation applies to certain types of service businesses of high-income taxpayers.

As noted previously, the second and third limitations only apply when taxable income before the QBI deduction exceeds $340,100 (married taxpayers filing a joint return) or $170,050 (single and head-of-household taxpayers). Once these thresholds are reached, the following two *independent* limitations are applied.

1. *Limitation based on wages and capital investment.* The QBI deduction is capped based on the percentage of the W–2 wages paid by the business (i.e., wages paid to its employees) *or* based on a smaller percentage of W–2 wages paid and a percentage of the cost of its depreciable property used to produce QBI.[88]
2. *Limitation for "specified services" businesses.* The QBI deduction generally is not available for income earned from "specified service" businesses.[89] "Specified service" businesses include physicians, dentists, attorneys, accountants, consultants, investment advisers, entertainers, and athletes (among others), but not engineers and architects.

These limitations, discussed in more detail below, are fully phased in once taxable income (before the QBI deduction) exceeds $440,100 for married taxpayers filing jointly and $220,050 for single and head-of-household taxpayers. Note that these limitations, where applicable, are compared with the overall limitation (based on modified taxable income) to determine the taxpayer's deduction for QBI.

Limitation Based on Wages and Capital Investment

The **W–2 Wages/Capital Investment Limit**, which applies once a taxpayer's income exceeds the thresholds mentioned previously, limits the 20 percent QBI deduction to the *greater of*:

1. 50 percent of the "W–2 wages" paid by the QTB, or
2. 25 percent of the "W–2 wages" paid by the QTB plus 2.5 percent of the taxpayer's share of the unadjusted basis immediately after acquisition of all tangible depreciable property (including real estate) used in the QTB as long as such property has not been fully depreciated prior to the close of the taxable year.

"W–2 wages" include the total amount of wages subject to income tax withholding, compensation paid into qualified retirement accounts, and certain other forms of deferred compensation paid to the employees of the business.[90] For labor-intensive businesses, 50 percent of the W–2 wages paid by the business will likely be the relevant limit on the QBI deduction.

W–2 Wages Limit

Example 43

Simone, a married taxpayer, operates a business as a sole proprietor. In 2022, the business has one employee, who is paid $80,000. Assume that the business has no significant assets. During 2022, Simone's qualified business income is $230,000 and her modified taxable income is $250,000 (this is also her taxable income before the QBI deduction).

Since Simone's taxable income before the QBI deduction is below the income threshold for married taxpayers filing a joint return ($340,100), the W–2/Capital Investment Limitation does not apply. As a result, Simone's QBI deduction is $46,000, the lesser of:

1. 20% of qualified business income ($46,000; $230,000 × 20%), or
2. 20% of modified taxable income ($50,000; $250,000 × 20%).

continued

[88] § 199A(b)(2)(B).

[89] § 199A(d)(2).

[90] §§ 199A(b)(4).

Assume the same facts as in the previous example, except that Simone's qualified business income is $500,000 and her modified taxable income is $600,000 (this is also her taxable income before the QBI deduction).

Because Simone's taxable income before the QBI deduction exceeds $440,100, the W–2/Capital Investment Limitation fully applies. As a result, her QBI deduction is $40,000, the lesser of:

1. 20% of qualified business income ($100,000; $500,000 × 20%), or
2. 50% of W–2 wages ($40,000; $80,000 × 50%)

And *no more than*:

3. 20% of modified taxable income ($120,000; $600,000 × 20%).

For capital-intensive businesses (e.g., real estate), an alternate limit exists. It begins with 25 percent of W–2 wages paid by the QTB and adds to this amount 2.5 percent of the unadjusted basis (immediately after acquisition) of "qualified property."

Qualified property includes depreciable tangible property—real or personal—that is used by the QTB during the year and whose "depreciable period" has not ended before the end of the taxable year. Land and intangible assets are *not* qualified property. The "depreciable period" for "qualified property" under § 199A is a minimum of 10 years.[91]

Example
45

Tom and Eileen are married and file a joint return. In 2022, their taxable income before the QBI deduction is $500,000 (this is also their modified taxable income). Tom has $400,000 in QBI from a restaurant he operates as a sole proprietorship. Tom employed four individuals (cook, bartender, and wait staff) during the year and paid $150,000 in W–2 wages in total. Tom owns the building in which the restaurant is located. He bought the building (and its furniture and fixtures) four years ago for $600,000, and the land then was worth $100,000; thus, the unadjusted acquisition basis (purchase price less the value of the land) of the building, furniture, and fixtures was $500,000.

Because their taxable income before the QBI deduction exceeds the $440,100 threshold, the W–2 Wages/Capital Investment Limit is applicable. Their QBI deduction is $75,000, computed as follows.

1. 20% of qualified business income ($400,000 × 20%)		$ 80,000
2. But no more than the *greater of*:		
• 50% of W–2 wages ($150,000 × 50%), or		$ 75,000
• 25% of W–2 wages ($150,000 × 25%) plus	$37,500	
2.5% of the unadjusted basis of qualified property ($500,000 × 2.5%)	12,500	$ 50,000
And *no more than*:		
3. 20% of modified taxable income ($500,000 × 20%)		$100,000

Many owners of pass-through businesses, especially landlords, have no employees. As a result, the 25 percent of W–2 wages plus 2.5 percent of the unadjusted basis of qualified property limit is most likely to affect them.

[91]§ 199A(b)(6)(B).

Jiaxiu, a single taxpayer, owns a five-unit apartment building that he purchased five years ago. His unadjusted basis in the building (purchase price less the value of the land) is $500,000. His taxable income before the QBI deduction is $250,000 in 2022 (this is also his modified taxable income). He has no employees in his business, and his QBI is $220,000.

Because his taxable income before the QBI deduction exceeds the $220,050 threshold, the W–2 Wages/ Capital Investment Limit is applicable. His QBI deduction is $12,500, computed as follows.

1. 20% of qualified business income ($220,000 × 20%)		$44,000
2. But no more than the *greater of*:		
• 50% of W–2 wages ($0 × 50%), or		$ -0-
• 25% of W–2 wages ($0 × 25%) plus	$ -0-	
2.5% of the unadjusted basis of qualified property ($500,000 × 2.5%)	12,500	$12,500
And *no more than*:		
3. 20% of modified taxable income ($250,000 × 20%)		$50,000

In Examples 45 and 46, the taxpayers are either below the taxable income threshold or at least $100,000 over the taxable income threshold. Between these ranges, the W–2 Wages/Capital Investment Limit is phased in. More precisely, this limit does not apply to taxpayers with taxable income (before the QBI deduction) less than the threshold amount ($340,100 for married taxpayers filing jointly; $170,050 for single and head-of-household taxpayers). The limit does apply to taxpayers whose taxable income (before the QBI deduction) exceeds the threshold amount by more than $100,000 (married filing jointly) or $50,000 (all other taxpayers). If, however, the taxpayer's taxable income before the QBI deduction is between these two amounts *and the W–2 Wages/Capital Investment portion of the QBI limits the taxpayer's QBI deduction*, the W–2 Wages/ Capital Investment limit is phased in. The calculation of the phase-in is not discussed in this chapter, though it is included in Concept Summary 11.4.

Limitation for "Specified Services" Businesses

For high-income taxpayers (in 2022, $440,100 for married couples; $220,050 for all other taxpayers), § 199A excludes any "specified service trade or business" from the definition of a qualified trade or business.[92] A specified service trade or business includes those involving:

- The performance of services in certain fields including health, law, accounting, actuarial science, performing arts, consulting, athletics, financial services, and brokerage services;
- Services consisting of investing and investment management, trading or dealing in securities, partnership interests, or commodities; and
- Any trades or business where the business's principal asset is the reputation of one or more of its employees or owners.

Architects and engineers are specifically excluded from this definition.[93]

[92] §§ 199A(d)(1)(A) and (d)(2).

[93] § 199A(d)(2)(A).

Concept Summary 11.4

An Overview of the 2022 Qualified Business Income Deduction

How to Use the Concept Summary: ***First,*** identify all qualified trades or businesses (QTB) of the taxpayer and the related qualified business income (QBI). ***Then*** for each QTB, move through the flowchart to determine the QBI amount for each QTB. Once this process is complete, combine all of the QBI amounts (this is the "combined qualified business income amount"). ***Finally,*** apply the *overall limitation* (based on modified taxable income). The QBI deduction is the *lesser of:*

1. The combined "qualified business income (QBI) amount," or
2. 20% of modified taxable income.*

* Modified taxable income is taxable income *before* the QBI deduction less any "net capital gain" (including any qualified dividend income).

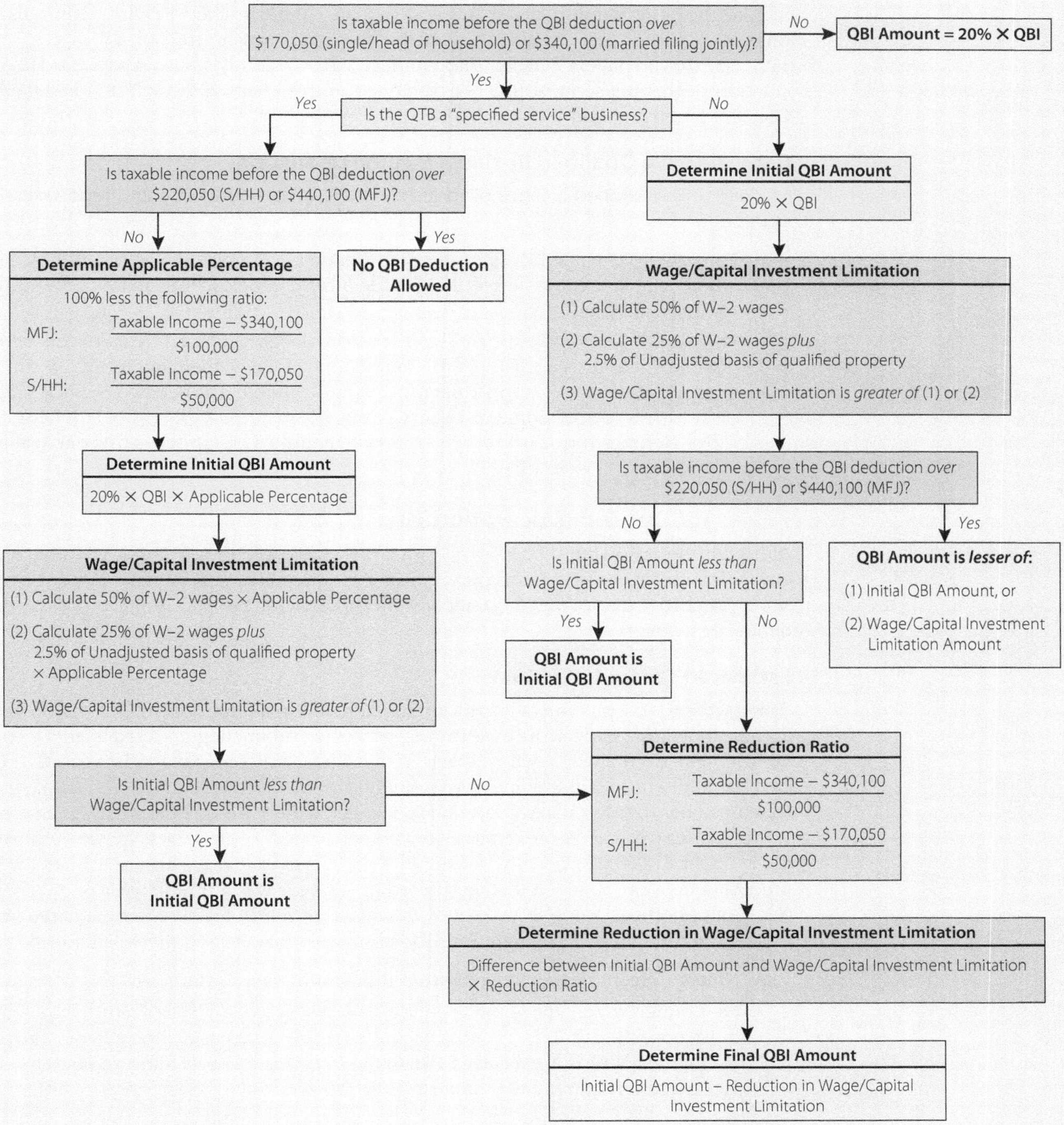

Is taxable income before the QBI deduction *over* \$170,050 (single/head of household) or \$340,100 (married filing jointly)?

- *No* → **QBI Amount = 20% × QBI**
- *Yes* → Is the QTB a "specified service" business?

Specified service business — *Yes*:

Is taxable income before the QBI deduction *over* \$220,050 (S/HH) or \$440,100 (MFJ)?

- *Yes* → **No QBI Deduction Allowed**
- *No* ↓

Determine Applicable Percentage

100% less the following ratio:

MFJ: $\dfrac{\text{Taxable Income} - \$340{,}100}{\$100{,}000}$

S/HH: $\dfrac{\text{Taxable Income} - \$170{,}050}{\$50{,}000}$

Determine Initial QBI Amount

20% × QBI × Applicable Percentage

Wage/Capital Investment Limitation

(1) Calculate 50% of W-2 wages × Applicable Percentage

(2) Calculate 25% of W-2 wages *plus* 2.5% of Unadjusted basis of qualified property × Applicable Percentage

(3) Wage/Capital Investment Limitation is *greater of* (1) or (2)

Is Initial QBI Amount *less than* Wage/Capital Investment Limitation?

- *Yes* → **QBI Amount is Initial QBI Amount**
- *No* → Determine Reduction Ratio (below)

Specified service business — *No*:

Determine Initial QBI Amount

20% × QBI

Wage/Capital Investment Limitation

(1) Calculate 50% of W-2 wages

(2) Calculate 25% of W-2 wages *plus* 2.5% of Unadjusted basis of qualified property

(3) Wage/Capital Investment Limitation is *greater of* (1) or (2)

Is taxable income before the QBI deduction *over* \$220,050 (S/HH) or \$440,100 (MFJ)?

- *Yes* → **QBI Amount is *lesser of*:** (1) Initial QBI Amount, or (2) Wage/Capital Investment Limitation Amount
- *No* → Is Initial QBI Amount *less than* Wage/Capital Investment Limitation?
  - *Yes* → **QBI Amount is Initial QBI Amount**
  - *No* → Determine Reduction Ratio

Determine Reduction Ratio

MFJ: $\dfrac{\text{Taxable Income} - \$340{,}100}{\$100{,}000}$

S/HH: $\dfrac{\text{Taxable Income} - \$170{,}050}{\$50{,}000}$

Determine Reduction in Wage/Capital Investment Limitation

Difference between Initial QBI Amount and Wage/Capital Investment Limitation × Reduction Ratio

Determine Final QBI Amount

Initial QBI Amount – Reduction in Wage/Capital Investment Limitation

In Example 40, Sanjay operated a sole proprietorship that generated QBI of $210,000 and he was able to claim a QBI deduction of $42,000.

However, if Sanjay's spouse had a salary of $300,000 (instead of $64,000), he would not be able to claim a QBI deduction since their taxable income before the QBI deduction exceeds $440,100 [$210,000 (QBI) + $300,000 (spouse's wages) − $25,900 (standard deduction) = $484,100]. The *income of Sanjay's spouse* triggered the limitation.

Example 47 illustrates an important consideration in the calculation of the deduction. The QBI deduction phaseout for a specified services business is based on *taxable income* before the QBI deduction (*not* on QBI). *Any* income that contributes to taxable income can cause the specified services QBI deduction to be reduced.

Like the W–2 Wages/Capital Investment Limit, the Specified Services Limit also is phased in where the taxpayer is over the specified income threshhold by less than $100,000 (for taxpayers married filing jointly, $50,000 for all other taxpayers). The calculation of this phase-in is also not discussed in this chapter, though it is included in Concept Summary 11.4.

Reporting the Qualified Business Income Deduction

The IRS has developed a series of forms and schedules to calculate and report the QBI deduction.

- Form 8995 (Qualified Business Income Deduction Simplified Computation) is used when taxable income before the QBI deduction is below the limitation thresholds for the year.
- Form 8995–A (Qualified Business Income Deduction) is used by taxpayers whose taxable income before the QBI deduction exceeds the limitation thresholds. A series of schedules supplement the form: Schedule A (Specified Service Trades or Businesses), Schedule B (Aggregation of Business Operations), Schedule C (Loss Netting and Carryforward), and Schedule D (Patrons of Agricultural or Horticultural Cooperatives).

11-4e Estimated Tax Payments

Although the following discussion is primarily applicable to self-employed taxpayers, employed taxpayers may be required to pay estimated tax if they have income that is not subject to withholding (e.g., income from consulting work, rental property, dividends, or interest).

Estimated Tax for Individuals

Estimated tax is the amount of tax (including alternative minimum tax and self-employment tax) an individual expects to owe for the year after subtracting tax credits and income tax withheld. An individual who expects to owe Federal income tax for the year of $1,000 or more and whose withholding does not equal or exceed the required annual payment (discussed below) must make quarterly payments.[94] Otherwise, a penalty may be assessed.

No quarterly payments are required and no penalty will apply if the taxpayer's estimated tax is under $1,000. No penalty will apply if the taxpayer had a zero tax liability for the preceding tax year provided that the preceding tax year was a taxable year of 12 months (i.e., not a short year) *and* the taxpayer was a U.S. citizen or resident for that entire year.

The required annual payment must be computed first. This is the smaller of:

- Ninety percent of the tax shown on the current year's return; or
- One hundred percent of the tax shown on the preceding year's return (the return must cover the full 12 months of the preceding year). If the AGI on the preceding year's return exceeds $150,000 ($75,000 if married filing separately), the 100 percent requirement is increased to 110 percent.

[94] §§ 6654(c)(1) and 6654(e)(1).

In general, one-fourth of this required annual payment is due on April 15, June 15, and September 15 of the tax year and January 15 of the following year. An equal part of withholding is deemed paid on each due date. For example, if $10,000 has been withheld during the year, $2,500 is applied to each quarter. If the quarterly estimates are determined to be $3,000, then $500 ($3,000 – $2,500) must be paid each quarter. Payments are submitted with the payment voucher for the appropriate quarter from Form 1040–ES.

Penalty on Underpayments

A nondeductible penalty is imposed on the amount of underpaid estimated tax. The rate for this penalty is adjusted quarterly to reflect changes in the average prime rate. An underpayment occurs when any installment (the sum of estimated tax paid and income tax withheld) is less than 25 percent of the required annual payment. The penalty is applied to the amount of the underpayment for the period of the underpayment.[95]

Example 48

Marta made the following payments of estimated tax for 2022 and had no income tax withheld.

April 15, 2022	$1,400
June 15, 2022	2,300
September 15, 2022	1,500
January 17, 2023	1,800

Marta's actual tax for 2022 is $8,000, and her tax in 2021 was $10,000. Therefore, each installment should have been at least $1,800 [($8,000 × 90%) × 25%]. Of the payment on June 15, $400 will be credited to the unpaid balance of the first quarterly installment due on April 15,[96] thereby effectively stopping the underpayment penalty for the first quarter. Of the remaining $1,900 payment on June 15, $100 is credited to the September 15 payment, resulting in this third quarterly payment being $200 short. Then $200 of the January 17 payment is credited to the September 15 shortfall, ending the underpayment period for that amount. The January 17, 2023 installment is now underpaid by $200, and a penalty will apply from January 17, 2023, to April 17, 2023 (unless some tax is paid sooner).

In summary, Marta's underpayments for each quarter are as follows.

1st installment due	$400 from April 15 to June 15, 2022
2nd installment due	Paid in full
3rd installment due	$200 from September 15, 2022, to January 17, 2023
4th installment due	$200 from January 17 to April 17, 2023

If a possible underpayment of estimated tax is indicated, Form 2210 is filed to compute the penalty due or to justify that no penalty applies.

11-5 Hobby Losses

LO.7

Distinguish between business and hobby activities and apply the rules limiting the deduction of hobby losses.

Expenses incurred by a self-employed taxpayer are deductible only if the taxpayer can show that the activity was entered into for the purpose of making a profit.[97]

Certain activities can have attributes that make it difficult to determine if the primary motivation for the activity is to make a profit or is for personal pleasure. Examples include raising horses and operating a farm that is also used as a weekend residence. While personal losses are not deductible, losses attributable to profit-seeking activities may be deducted and used to offset a taxpayer's other income. Activities that have both personal and profit-seeking motives are classified as hobbies, and the tax law limits the deductibility of **hobby losses**.

The income and deductions from a hobby are reported separately on the tax return. Hobby income always is reported as *other income* on line 8 of Schedule 1 (Form 1040). The deductions (and how they are limited and reported) are discussed in more detail next.

[95] § 6654(b)(2).

[96] Payments are credited to unpaid installments in the order in which the installments are required to be paid. § 6654(b)(3).

[97] Reg. § 1.183–1(a).

11-5a General Rules

If an individual can show that an activity has been conducted with the intent to earn a profit, losses from the activity are fully deductible (and reported, along with any income, on Schedule C). The hobby loss rules apply only if the activity is not engaged in for profit. Hobby expenses are deductible only to the extent of hobby income.[98]

The Regulations stipulate that the following nine factors should be considered in determining whether an activity is profit-seeking or a hobby.[99]

- Whether the activity is conducted in a businesslike manner.
- The expertise of the taxpayers or their advisers.
- The time and effort expended.
- The expectation that the assets of the activity will appreciate in value.
- The taxpayer's previous success in conducting similar activities.
- The history of income or losses from the activity.
- The relationship of profits earned to losses incurred.
- The financial status of the taxpayer (e.g., if the taxpayer does not have substantial amounts of other income, this may indicate that the activity is engaged in for profit).
- Elements of personal pleasure or recreation in the activity.

The presence or absence of one or more factors is not by itself determinative of whether the activity is profit-seeking or is a hobby. Rather, the decision is a subjective one that is based on an analysis of all of the facts and circumstances.

11-5b Presumptive Rule of Profit-Seeking

The Code provides a rebuttable presumption that an activity is profit-seeking if the activity shows a profit in at least three of the previous five tax years.[100] If the activity involves horses, a profit in at least two of the previous seven tax years meets the presumptive rule. If these profitability tests are met, the activity is presumed to be a trade or business rather than a hobby. In this situation, the IRS bears the burden of proving that the activity is a hobby rather than trade- or business-related. On the other hand, if the three-year test (two for horses) is not met, then the activity is presumed to be a hobby and the taxpayer has the burden to prove that the activity is profit-seeking. The history of profits and losses would be one of the factors used to determine whether the activity was a hobby or business.

Camille and Walter are married taxpayers who enjoy a busy lifestyle. Camille, who is an executive for a large corporation, is paid a salary of $800,000. Walter is a collector of antiques. Several years ago he opened an antique shop in a local shopping center, and he spends most of his time buying and selling antiques. He occasionally earns a small profit from this activity but more frequently incurs substantial losses.

If Walter's losses are business-related, they are fully deductible against Camille's salary income on a joint return. In resolving this issue, consider the following.

- Initially determine whether Walter's antique activity has met the three-out-of-five years profit test.
- If that presumptive rule is not met, the activity may nevertheless qualify as a business if Walter can show that the intent is to engage in a profit-seeking activity. It is not necessary to show actual profits.
- Determine if the operation is for profit, using the nine factors identified in the Regulation (text Section 11-5a).

[98] § 183(b)(2).

[99] Reg. §§ 1.183–2(b)(1) through (9).

[100] § 183(d).

11-5c Determining the Taxable Amount

If an activity is a hobby, the gross income generated is taxable. Gross income means revenue less cost of goods sold. Other expenses are deductible only to the extent of the gross income from the hobby. These expenses are deducted in the following order.

1. Amounts deductible under other Code sections without regard to the nature of the activity, such as property taxes and home mortgage interest.
2. Amounts deductible under other Code sections as if the activity had been engaged in for profit but only if those amounts do not affect adjusted basis. Examples include maintenance, utilities, and selling expenses.
3. Amounts for depreciation, amortization, and depletion.[101]

If a taxpayer itemizes deductions, property taxes and mortgage interest are deductible irrespective of hobby income. From 2018 through 2025, any other hobby expenses are not deductible because they are considered miscellaneous itemized deductions. However, all of the gross income from the hobby is included in taxable income.

Jane, the vice president of an oil company, reports AGI of $80,000. She paints in her spare time. She uses a home studio, comprising 10% of her home's square footage. During the current year, Jane incurs the following expenses.

Frames	$ 2,800
Art supplies	900
Home studio expenses	
Total home property taxes	2,000
Total home mortgage interest	10,000
Total home maintenance and utilities	4,600
Calculated depreciation on 10% of home	500

During the year, Jane sold paintings for a total of $5,660. Jane's cost of goods sold is comprised of frame and art supply costs related to paintings sold this year. If the activity is a hobby, Jane determines her potential deductions under the hobby loss rules as follows.

Gross income [$5,660 less ($2,800 + $900)]	$ 1,960
Deduct: Property taxes and mortgage interest (10% of $12,000)	(1,200)
Net income	$ 760

Jane includes the $1,960 of hobby income in AGI, increasing her AGI to $81,960. The taxes and interest are itemized deductions, deductible in full (assuming Jane itemizes deductions rather than claiming the standard deduction). The remaining painting-related expenses are miscellaneous itemized deductions, which are currently not deductible. Because the property taxes and home mortgage interest are otherwise deductible, Jane is taxed on the $1,960 of gross income from her hobby.

[101] Reg. § 1.183–1(b)(1).

Refocus on The Big Picture

Self-Employed versus Employee—What's the Difference?

ISTOCK.COM/NEUSTOCKIMAGES

Marcus may deduct the ordinary and necessary business expenses incurred by his proprietorship. This includes the $18,000 for rent and utilities, the $12,000 paid to his part-time assistant, and the $40,000 paid to Ellen for consulting work. The $8,000 paid for equipment can be depreciated or may be immediately deducted under the first-year expensing provisions. As a self-employed taxpayer, Marcus may deduct the $3,000 of health insurance premiums paid, but only if he is not eligible to participate in the health plan maintained by Mary's employer. Marcus cannot deduct the premiums of $500 paid for his life insurance policy.

Marcus may want to consider contributing to his own IRA or establishing a SEP IRA or SIMPLE plan to allow for greater retirement contributions. Marcus should be aware that in addition to paying income tax on the net income earned by his business, he also owes self-employment tax at a combined rate of 15.3 percent, but he can claim an income tax deduction for half of the self-employment tax paid.

While Mary will owe income tax on her $85,000 salary, the health insurance premiums of $3,000 and group term life insurance premiums paid by her employer qualify as tax-free fringe benefits. In addition, as long as Mary is required to substantiate her travel expenses as part of an accountable plan, none of the travel-related reimbursements need to be included in her gross income. Because Mary is not covered by a qualified retirement plan at work, she can deduct the entire contribution made to her traditional IRA.

While the $500 of employee business expenses is technically deductible, the deduction for these expenses is currently suspended. While Mary is not subject to self-employment tax, she did incur a 7.65 percent payroll tax related to Social Security and Medicare. Her employer paid the additional 7.65 percent of those taxes.

What If?

Marcus is considering moving his office into a vacant room in their home. Can he deduct expenses associated with his home office?

As a self-employed individual, Marcus can deduct the costs of a home office as long as the office is used exclusively and on a regular basis as either the principal place of business or a place of business used by his clients and customers. Deductible expenses would include a portion of mortgage interest and property taxes paid on the home; a portion of utilities, repairs and maintenance, and other household expenses; and depreciation on the business portion of the home.

Suggested Readings

Vorris J. Blankenship, "Sec. 403(b) Retirement Plans: A Comparison with 401(k) Plans," *The Tax Adviser*, January 1, 2021.

Cathalene Bowler and Dennis Schmidt, "Estimated Tax Rules and Strategies for Individuals," *Journal of Taxation*, October 2018.

Kimberly S. Krieg and Sarah C. Lyon, "COVID-19 and Household Employees," *Practical Tax Strategies*, December 2020.

Percy Lee. "An Unregulated Asset in a Regulated World: Whether and How Employers Should Pay Employees in Cryptocurrency," *Journal of Taxation*, October 2021.

Annette Nellen, Caroline Bruckner, and Jennifer Brown, "Taxes and the Growing Gig Workforce: What to Know," *Journal of Taxation*, June 2018.

Michael T. Odom, QBI Deduction: Interaction with Various Code Provisions." *The Tax Adviser*, December 1, 2020.

Key Terms

Accountable plan, 11-2
Automatic mileage method, 11-19
Cafeteria plans, 11-11
De minimis fringe benefits, 11-14
Education expenses, 11-22
Estimated tax, 11-42
Flexible spending plans, 11-11
Foreign earned income exclusion, 11-17
Health Savings Account (HSA), 11-6
Hobby losses, 11-43
Independent contractor, 11-2
Individual Retirement Account (IRA), 11-28
No-additional-cost service, 11-13
Nonaccountable plan, 11-28
Office in the home expenses, 11-25
Qualified business income, 11-35
Qualified employee discount, 11-13
Qualified transportation fringes, 11-15
Self-employment tax, 11-4
Simplified employee pension (SEP) plans, 11-33
Transportation expenses, 11-18
Travel expenses, 11-19
W–2 Wages/Capital Investment Limit, 11-38
Working condition fringes, 11-14

Computational Exercises

1. **LO.2** Valentino is a patient in a nursing home for 45 days in 2022. While in the nursing home, he incurs total costs of $13,500. Medicare pays $8,000 of the costs. Valentino receives $15,000 from his long-term care insurance policy, which pays while he is in the facility. Assume that the Federal daily excludible amount for Valentino is $390. Of the $15,000, what amount may Valentino exclude from his gross income?

   Digging Deeper

2. **LO.2** Mio was transferred from New York to Germany. He lived and worked in Germany for 340 days in 2022. Mio's salary for 2022 is $190,000. What is Mio's foreign earned income exclusion? (In your computation, round any division to four decimal places before converting to a percentage. For example, 0.473938 would be rounded to 47.39%.)

3. **LO.6** In 2021, Henry Jones (Social Security number 123-45-6789) works as a freelance driver, finding customers using various platforms like Uber and Grubhub. He is single and has no other sources of income. His qualified business income from driving is $61,200.
   a. Compute Henry's QBI deduction and his tax liability for 2021.
   b. Complete Henry's 2021 Form 8995 (Qualified Business Income Deduction Simplified Computation).

4. **LO.3** Tyler, a self-employed taxpayer, travels from Denver to Miami primarily on business. He spends five days conducting business and two days sightseeing. His expenses are $400 (airfare), $150 per day (meals at local restaurants), and $300 per night (lodging). What are Tyler's deductible expenses if this travel took place in 2022? In 2023?

5. **LO.3** In November 2022, Kortney (who is a self-employed management consultant) travels from Chicago to Barcelona (Spain) on business. She is gone for 10 days (including 2 days of travel), during which time she spends 5 days conducting business and 3 days sightseeing. Her expenses are $1,500 (airfare), $200 per day (meals at local restaurants), and $400 per night (lodging). Because Kortney stayed with relatives while sightseeing, she paid for only 5 nights of lodging.
   What is Kortney's deduction for:
   a. Airfare?
   b. Meals?
   c. Lodging?

6. **LO.3** Samantha recently was employed by an accounting firm. During the year, she spends $2,500 for a CPA exam review course and begins working on a law

degree in night school. Her law school expenses were $4,200 for tuition and $450 for books (which are not a requirement for enrollment in the course). Assuming no reimbursement, how much of these expenses can Samantha deduct?

7. **LO.3** In 2022, Robert takes four key clients and their spouses to dinner at a local restaurant. Business discussions occurred over dinner. Expenses were $700 (drinks and dinner) and $140 (tips to servers). If Robert is self-employed, how much can he deduct for this event?

8. **LO.3** Andrew sends Godiva chocolates to 10 of his key clients at Christmas. The chocolates cost $50 a box not including $4 for gift wrapping and shipping. How much can Andrew deduct?

9. **LO.6** In 2022, Miranda records net earnings from self-employment of $168,500. She has no other gross income. Determine the amount of Miranda's self-employment tax and her *for* AGI income tax deduction.

10. **LO.5** Myers, who is single, reports compensation income of $75,000 in 2022. He is an active participant in his employer's qualified retirement plan. Myers contributes $6,000 to a traditional IRA. Of the $6,000 contribution, how much can Myers deduct?

11. **LO.5** Meredith, who is single, would like to contribute $6,000 to her Roth IRA. Her AGI is $130,000.
    a. What is the maximum amount that Meredith can contribute? Show your calculations in Microsoft Excel.
    b. Assume that Meredith's AGI is $100,000 and she plans to put $6,000 each year into her Roth IRA, hoping to earn 6% annually. What amount will accumulate in her Roth at the end of 20 years? *Hint*: Use the time value of money tables found in text Appendix E.
    c. In part (b), instead assume that Meredith puts the $6,000 into the Roth IRA for 15 years at 6%. How much will accumulate at the end of this period?

Problems

12. **LO.1** Mason performs services for Isabella. In determining whether Mason is an employee or an independent contractor, comment on the relevance of each of the factors listed below.
    a. Mason performs services only for Isabella and does not work for anyone else.
    b. Mason sets his own work schedule.
    c. Mason reports his job-related expenses on a Schedule C.
    d. Mason obtained his job skills from Isabella's training program.
    e. Mason performs the services at Isabella's business location.
    f. Mason is paid based on time worked rather than on task performed.

13. **LO.2** Rex, age 55, is an officer of Blue Company, which provides him with the following nondiscriminatory fringe benefits in 2022.
    - Hospitalization insurance premiums for Rex and his dependents. The cost of the coverage for Rex is $2,900 per year, and the additional cost for his dependents is $3,800 per year. The plan has a $3,000 deductible, but his employer contributed $1,500 to Rex's Health Savings Account (HSA). Rex withdrew only $800 from the HSA, and the account earned $50 of interest during the year.

- Insurance premiums of $840 for salary continuation payments. Under the plan, Rex will receive his regular salary in the event he is unable to work due to illness. Rex collected $4,500 on the policy to replace lost wages while he was ill during the year.
- Rex is a part-time student working on his bachelor's degree in engineering. His employer reimbursed his $5,200 tuition under a plan available to all full-time employees.

Determine the amounts that Rex must include in gross income.

14. **LO.2** Casey is in the 12% marginal tax bracket, and Mei is in the 35% marginal tax bracket. Their employer is experiencing financial difficulties and cannot continue to pay for the company's health insurance plan. The annual premiums are approximately $8,000 per employee. Decision Making

    The employer has proposed to either (1) require the employee to pay the premiums or (2) reduce each employee's pay by $10,000 per year with the employer paying the premium. Which option is less objectionable to Casey, and which is less objectionable to Mei?

15. **LO.2** Belinda spent the last 60 days of 2022 in a nursing home. The cost of the services provided to her was $18,000 ($300 per day). Medicare paid $8,500 toward the cost of her stay. Belinda also received $7,500 of benefits under a long-term care insurance policy she purchased. Assume that the Federal daily excludible amount is $390. What is the effect of each of these items on Belinda's gross income? Digging Deeper

16. **LO.2** Does the taxpayer recognize gross income in the following situations?

    a. Ava is a filing clerk at a large insurance company. She is permitted to leave the premises for her lunch, but she usually eats in the company's cafeteria because it is quick and she is on a tight schedule. On average, she pays $2 for a lunch that would cost $12 at a restaurant; it cost her employer $10 to prepare. However, if the prices in the cafeteria were not so low and the food was not so delicious, she would probably bring her own lunch at a cost of $3 per day.

    b. Scott is an executive for an international corporation located in New York City. Often he works late, taking calls from the company's European branch. Scott often stays in a company-owned condominium when he has a late-night work session. The condominium is across the street from the company office and has the technology needed to communicate with employees and customers throughout the world.

    c. Ira recently moved to take a new job. For the first month on the new job, Ira was searching for a home to purchase or rent. During this time, his employer permitted Ira to live in an apartment that the company maintains for customers during the buying season. The month that Ira occupied the apartment was not during the buying season, however, and the apartment would not otherwise have been occupied.

17. **LO.2** Tim is the vice president of western operations for Maroon Oil Company and is stationed in San Francisco. He is required to live in an employer-owned home, which is three blocks from his company office. The company-provided home is equipped with high-speed internet access and several telephone lines. Tim receives telephone calls and e-mails that require immediate attention any time of day or night because the company's business is spread all over the world. A full-time administrative assistant resides in the house to assist Tim with the urgent business matters.

    Tim often uses the home for entertaining customers, suppliers, and employees. The fair market value of comparable housing is $9,000 per month. Tim also is provided with free parking at his company's office. The value of the parking is $370 per month. Calculate the amount associated with the company-provided housing and free parking that Tim must include in his gross income for 2022.

Communications

18. **LO.1, 2, 4** Finch Construction Company provides the carpenters it employs with all required tools. However, the company believes that this practice has led to some employees not taking care of the tools and to the mysterious disappearance of some of the tools.

The company is considering requiring all of its employees to provide their own tools. Each employee's salary would be increased by $1,500 to compensate for the additional cost. Write a letter to Finch's management, explaining the tax consequences of this plan to the carpenters. Finch's address is 300 Harbor Drive, Vermillion, SD 57069.

Decision Making

19. **LO.2** Rosa's employer has instituted a flexible benefits program. Rosa will use the plan to pay for her daughter's dental expenses and other medical expenses that are not covered by health insurance. Rosa is in the 24% marginal tax bracket and estimates that the medical and dental expenses not covered by health insurance will be within the range of $2,000 to $3,000. Her employer's plan permits her to set aside as much as $2,850 in the flexible benefits account. Rosa does not itemize her deductions.

    a. Rosa puts $1,850 into her flexible benefits account, and her actual expenses are $2,850. What is her cost of underestimating the expenses?
    b. Rosa puts $2,850 into her flexible benefits account, and her actual expenses are $1,850. What is her cost of overestimating her expenses?
    c. What is Rosa's cost of underfunding as compared with the cost of overfunding the flexible benefits account?
    d. Does your answer in part (c) suggest that Rosa should fund the account closer to the low end or to the high end of her estimates?

20. **LO.2** Sparrow Corporation would like you to review its employee fringe benefits program with regard to the tax consequences of the plan for the company's president (Polly), who is also the majority shareholder.

    a. The company has a qualified retirement plan. The company pays the cost of employees attending a retirement planning seminar. The employee must be within 10 years of retirement, and the cost of the seminar is $1,500 per attendee.
    b. The company owns a parking garage that is used by customers, employees, and the general public. Only the general public is required to pay for parking. The charge to the general public for Polly's parking for the year would have been $3,600 (a $300 monthly rate).
    c. The company owns a condominium at the beach, which it uses to entertain customers. Employees are allowed to use the facility without charge when the company has no scheduled events. Polly used the facility 10 days during the year. The dates of Polly's personal use had a rental value of $1,000.
    d. The company is in the household moving business. Employees are allowed to ship goods without charge whenever there is excess space on a truck. Polly purchased a dining room suite for her daughter. Company trucks delivered the furniture to the daughter. Regular freight charges would have been $750.
    e. The company has a storage facility for household goods. Officers are allowed a 20% discount on charges for storing their goods. All other employees are allowed a 10% discount. Polly's discounts for the year totaled $900.

21. **LO.2** Ted works for Azure Motors, an automobile dealership. All employees can buy a car at the company's cost plus 2%. The company does not charge employees the $300 dealer preparation fee that nonemployees must pay. Ted purchased an automobile for $29,580 ($29,000 + $580). The company's cost was $29,000. The price for a nonemployee would have been $33,900 ($33,600 + $300 preparation fee). What is Ted's gross income from the purchase of the automobile?

22. **LO.2** Several of Egret Company's employees have asked the company to create a hiking trail that employees could use during their lunch hours. The company owns vacant land that is being held for future expansion but would have to spend approximately $50,000 if it were to make a trail. Nonemployees would be allowed to use the facility as part of the company's effort to build strong community support. What are the relevant tax issues for the employees? Critical Thinking

23. **LO.2** Bluebird, Inc., does not provide its employees with any tax-exempt fringe benefits. The company is considering adopting a hospital and medical benefits insurance plan that will cost approximately $9,000 per employee. To adopt this plan, the company may have to reduce salaries and/or lower future salary increases. Bluebird is in the 25% (combined Federal and state rates) bracket. Planning

    Bluebird also is responsible for matching the Social Security and Medicare taxes withheld on employees' salaries (at the full 7.65% rate). The hospital and medical benefits insurance plan will not be subject to the Social Security and Medicare taxes, and the company is not eligible for the small business credit for health insurance. The employees generally fall into two marginal tax rate groups, specifically:

Income Tax	Social Security and Medicare Tax	Total
12%	7.65%	19.65%
24%	1.45%	25.45%

The company has asked you to assist in its financial planning for the hospital and medical benefits insurance plan by computing the following.

a. How much taxable compensation is the equivalent of $9,000 of exempt compensation for each of the two classes of employees?
b. What is the company's after-tax cost of the taxable compensation computed in part (a)?
c. What is the company's after-tax cost of the exempt compensation?
d. Briefly explain your conclusions from the preceding analysis.

24. **LO.2** George is a U.S. citizen who is employed by Hawk Enterprises, a global company. Beginning on June 1, 2022, George began working in London. He worked there until January 31, 2023, when he transferred to Paris. He worked in Paris the remainder of 2023. His salary for the first five months of 2022 was $100,000, and it was earned in the United States. His salary for the remainder of 2022 was $175,000, and it was earned in London.

    George's 2023 salary from Hawk was $300,000, with part being earned in London and part being earned in Paris. What is George's gross income in 2022 and 2023? (Assume that the foreign earned income exclusion is the same in both 2022 and 2023.)

25. **LO.3** During 2022, José, a self-employed technology consultant, made gifts in the following amounts.

To Haley (José's personal assistant) at Christmas	$36
To Darryl (a key client)—$3 was for gift wrapping	53
To Darryl's wife (not a client of the bank) on her birthday	20
To Veronica (José's office manager) at Christmas	30

In addition, on professional assistants' day, José takes Haley to lunch at a local restaurant at a cost of $82. Presuming that José has adequate substantiation, how much can he deduct?

26. **LO.3** Kristen, an independent management consultant, is based in Atlanta. During March and April of 2022, she is contracted by a national hardware chain to help implement revised human resource policies in Jackson (Mississippi) temporarily. During this period, Kristen flies to Jackson on Sunday night, spends the week at the district office, and returns home to Atlanta on Friday afternoon. The cost of returning home is $550, while the cost of spending the weekend in Jackson would have been $490.

a. Presuming no reimbursement for these expenses, how much, if any, of these weekend expenses may Kristen deduct?

b. Would your answer in part (a) change if the amounts involved were reversed (i.e., the trip home would have cost $490; staying in Jackson would have cost $550)? Explain.

27. **LO.3** In June of 2022, Enrique and Denisse Espinosa traveled to Denver to attend a three-day conference sponsored by the American Society of Implant Dentistry. Denisse, a self-employed practicing oral surgeon, participated in scheduled technical sessions dealing with the latest developments in surgical procedures. On two days, Enrique attended group meetings where various aspects of family tax planning were discussed. On the other day, he went sightseeing. Enrique does not work for his wife, but he prepares their tax returns and manages the family investments. Expenses incurred in connection with the conference are summarized as follows.

Airfare (two tickets)	$2,000
Lodging (single and double occupancy are the same rate—$250 each day)	750
Meals at local restaurants ($200 × 3 days)*	600
Conference registration fee (includes $120 for Family Tax Planning sessions)	620
Car rental	300

*Split equally between Enrique and Denisse Espinosa.

How much, if any, of these expenses can the Espinosas deduct?

28. **LO.3** On Thursday, Justin flies from Baltimore (where his sole proprietorship office is located) to Cadiz (Spain). He conducts business on Friday and Tuesday; vacations on Saturday, Sunday, and Monday (a legal holiday in Spain); and returns to Baltimore on Thursday. Justin was scheduled to return home on Wednesday, but all flights were canceled due to bad weather. As a result, he spent Wednesday watching floor shows at a local casino.

a. For tax purposes, what portion of Justin's trip is regarded as being for business?

b. Suppose Monday had not been a legal holiday. Would this change your answer to part (a)? Explain.

c. Under either part (a) or (b), how much of Justin's airfare qualifies as a deductible business expense?

Ethics and Equity

29. **LO.3** Veronica is a key employee of Perdiz Corporation, an aerospace engineering concern located in Seattle. Perdiz would like to establish an office on the east coast of Florida and wants Veronica to be in charge of the branch. Veronica is hesitant about making the move because she fears she will have to sell her residence in Seattle at a loss. Perdiz buys the house from Veronica for $420,000, its cost to her. She has owned and occupied the house as her principal residence for eight years. One year later Perdiz resells the property for $370,000.

Nothing regarding the sale of the residence is ever reflected on Veronica's income tax returns. Perdiz absorbs all of Veronica's moving expenses. As an ethical tax professional, do you have any qualms as to the way these matters have been handled for income tax purposes? Explain.

30. **LO.3, 4** Christine is a full-time fourth-grade teacher at Vireo Academy. During 2022, she spends $1,400 for classroom supplies. On the submission of adequate substantiation, Vireo reimburses her for $500 of these expenses—the maximum reimbursement allowed for supplies under school policy. [The reimbursement is not shown as income (Box 1) of Form W–2 given to Christine by Vireo.] What are the income tax consequences of the $1,400 if Christine:

a. Itemizes her deductions *from* AGI?

b. Chooses the standard deduction?

31. **LO.3** Ava recently graduated from college and is interviewing for a position in marketing. Gull Corporation has offered her a job as a sales representative that will require extensive travel and entertainment but provide valuable experience. Under the offer, she has two options: she receives a salary of $53,000, and she absorbs all expenses; she receives a salary of $39,000, and Gull reimburses for all expenses. Gull assures Ava that the $14,000 difference in the two options will be adequate to cover the expenses incurred. What issues should have an impact on Ava's choice? Critical Thinking Decision making Planning

32. **LO.6** Ashley (a single taxpayer) is the owner of ABC LLC. The LLC (a sole proprietorship) generates QBI of $900,000 and is not a "specified services" business. ABC paid total W–2 wages of $300,000, and the total unadjusted basis of property held by ABC is $30,000. Ashley's taxable income before the QBI deduction is $740,000 (this is also her modified taxable income). What is Ashley's QBI deduction for 2022? Decision Making

33. **LO.5** Jong, age 29, is single and an active participant in a qualified retirement plan. Her modified AGI is $70,000 in 2022.
    a. Calculate the amount Jong can contribute to a traditional IRA and the amount she can deduct.
    b. Assume instead that Jong is a participant in a SIMPLE IRA and that she elects to contribute 4% of her compensation to the account, while her employer contributes 3%. What amount will be contributed for 2022? What amount will be vested?

34. **LO.5** Carri and Dane, ages 34 and 32, respectively, have been married for 11 years, and both are active participants in employer-qualified retirement plans. Their total AGI in 2022 is $207,000, and they earn salaries of $89,000 and $95,000, respectively. What amount may Carri and Dane:
    a. Contribute to regular IRAs?
    b. Deduct for their contributions in part (a)?
    c. Contribute to Roth IRAs?
    d. Deduct for their contributions in part (c)?

35. **LO.6** Govind, age 31, earns a salary of $26,000 and is not an active participant in any other qualified plan. His wife, Olga, reports $600 of compensation income. What is the maximum total deductible contribution to their IRAs?

36. **LO.6** Answer the following independent questions with respect to traditional IRA contributions for 2022.
    a. Juan, age 41, earns a salary of $28,000 and is not an active participant in any other qualified plan. His wife, Agnes, generates no earned income. What is the maximum total deductible contribution to their IRAs?
    b. Abby, age 29, reports earned income of $25,000, and her husband, Sam, records earned income of $2,600. They are not active participants in any other qualified plan. What is the maximum contribution to their IRAs?
    c. Leo's employer makes a contribution of $3,500 to Leo's simplified employee pension plan. If Leo is single, he reports earned income of $32,000, and his AGI is $29,000, what amount, if any, can he contribute to an IRA?

37. **LO.7** Alex, who is single, conducts an activity in the current year that is appropriately classified as a hobby. The activity produces the following revenues and expenses.

Revenue	$18,000
Property taxes	3,000
Materials and supplies	4,500
Utilities	2,000
Advertising	5,000
Insurance	750
Depreciation	4,000

Without regard to this hobby, Alex's AGI is $62,000. Determine the amount of gross income that Alex must report and the amount of expenses he is permitted to deduct.

Tax Return Problems

Critical Thinking

Planning

ProConnect™ Tax

1. Beth R. Jordan lives at 2322 Skyview Road, Mesa, AZ 85201. She is a tax accountant with Mesa Manufacturing Company, 1203 Western Avenue, Mesa, AZ 85201 (employer identification number 11-1111111). She also writes computer software programs for tax practitioners and has a part-time tax practice. Beth is single and has no dependents. Beth's birthday is July 4, 1975, and her Social Security number is 123-45-6785. She did not engage in any virtual currency transactions during the year, and she wants to contribute $3 to the Presidential Election Campaign Fund. Beth received the appropriate coronavirus recovery rebates (economic impact payments); related questions in ProConnect Tax should be ignored.

   The following information is shown on Beth's Wage and Tax Statement (Form W–2) for 2021.

Line	Description	Amount
1	Wages, tips, other compensation	$65,000.00
2	Federal income tax withheld	9,500.00
3	Social Security wages	65,000.00
4	Social Security tax withheld	4,030.00
5	Medicare wages and tips	65,000.00
6	Medicare tax withheld	942.50
15	State	Arizona
16	State wages, tips, etc.	65,000.00
17	State income tax withheld	1,954.00

   During the year, Beth received interest of $1,300 from Arizona Federal Savings and Loan and $400 from Arizona State Bank. Each financial institution reported the interest income on a Form 1099–INT. She received qualified dividends of $800 from Blue Corporation, $750 from Green Corporation, and $650 from Orange Corporation. Each corporation reported Beth's dividend payments on a Form 1099–DIV.

   Beth received a $1,100 income tax refund from the state of Arizona on April 29, 2021. On her 2020 Federal income tax return, she used the standard deduction.

   Fees earned from her part-time tax practice in 2021 totaled $3,800. She paid $600 to have the tax returns processed by a computerized tax return service.

   On February 8, 2021, Beth bought 500 shares of Gray Corporation common stock for $17.60 a share. On September 12, 2021, she sold the stock for $14 a share.

   On January 2, 2021, Beth acquired 100 shares of Blue Corporation common stock for $30 a share. She sold the stock on December 19, 2021, for $55 a share. Both stock transactions were reported to Beth on Form 1099–B; basis was not reported to the IRS.

   Beth bought a used sports utility vehicle for $6,000 on June 5, 2021. She purchased the vehicle from her brother-in-law, who was unemployed and was in need of cash. On November 2, 2021, she sold the vehicle to a friend for $6,500.

   During the year, Beth records revenues of $16,000 from the sale of a software program she developed. She incurred the following expenditures in connection with her software development business.

Cost of personal computer	$7,000
Cost of printer	2,000
Furniture	3,000
Supplies	650
Fee paid to computer consultant	3,500

Beth elected to expense the maximum portion of the cost of the computer, printer, and furniture allowed under the provisions of § 179. These items were placed in service on January 15, 2021, and used 100% in her business.

Although her employer suggested that Beth attend an in-person conference on current developments in corporate taxation, Beth was not reimbursed for the travel expenses of $1,420 she incurred in attending. The $1,420 included $200 for the cost of meals.

During the year, Beth paid $300 for prescription medicines and $2,875 for medical bills. Medical insurance premiums were paid for her by her employer.

Beth paid real property taxes of $1,766 on her home. Interest on her home mortgage (Valley National Bank) was $3,845, and credit card interest was $320. Beth contributed $2,080 in cash to various qualifying charities during the year. Professional dues and subscriptions totaled $350. Beth paid estimated Federal income taxes of $1,000.

Part 1—Tax Computation

Compute Beth Jordan's 2021 Federal income tax payable (or refund due), and complete her 2021 tax return using appropriate forms and schedules. Suggested software: ProConnect Tax.

Part 2—Tax Planning

Beth is anticipating significant changes in her life in 2022, and she has asked you to estimate her taxable income and tax liability for 2022. She just received word that she has been qualified to adopt a 2-year-old daughter. Beth expects that the adoption will be finalized in 2022 and that she will incur approximately $2,000 of adoption expenses. In addition, she expects to incur approximately $3,500 of child and dependent care expenses relating to the care of her new daughter, which will enable her to keep her job at Mesa Manufacturing Company.

However, with the additional demands on her time, she has decided to discontinue her two part-time jobs (i.e., the part-time tax practice and her software business), and she will cease making estimated income tax payments. In your computations, assume that all other 2022 income and expenses will be the same as 2021 amounts.

Communications
Critical Thinking
ProConnect™ Tax

2. David R. and Ella M. Cole (ages 39 and 38, respectively) are husband and wife who live at 1820 Elk Avenue, Denver, CO 80202. David is a self-employed consultant specializing in retail management, and Ella is a dental hygienist for a chain of dental clinics.

   David earned consulting fees of $145,000 in 2021. He maintains his own office and pays for all business expenses. The Coles are adequately covered by the medical plan provided by Ella's employer but have chosen not to participate in its § 401(k) retirement plan.

   David's employment-related expenses for 2021 are summarized below.

Airfare	$8,800
Lodging	4,835
Meals from restaurants (during travel status)	2,400
Entertainment	3,600
Ground transportation (e.g., limos, rental cars, and taxis)	800
Business gifts	900
Office supplies (includes postage, overnight delivery, and copying)	1,500

   The entertainment involved taking clients to sporting and musical events. The business gifts consisted of $50 gift certificates to a national restaurant. These were sent by David during the holidays to 18 of his major clients.

In addition, David drove his 2019 Ford Expedition 11,000 miles for business and 3,000 for personal use during 2021. He purchased the Expedition on August 15, 2018; David always has used the automatic (standard) mileage method for tax purposes. Parking and tolls relating to business use total $340 in 2021.

When the Coles purchased their present residence in April 2018, they devoted 450 of the 3,000 square feet of living space to an office for David. The property cost $440,000 ($40,000 of which is attributable to the land) and has since appreciated in value. Expenses relating to the residence (except for mortgage interest and property taxes; see below) are reported as follows.

Insurance	$2,600
Repairs and maintenance	900
Utilities	4,700
Painting office area; area rugs and plants (in the office)	1,800

In terms of depreciation, the Coles use the MACRS percentage tables applicable to 39-year nonresidential real property. As to depreciable property (e.g., office furniture), David tries to avoid capitalization and uses whatever method provides the fastest write-off for tax purposes.

Ella works at a variety of offices as a substitute when a hygienist is ill or on vacation or when one of the clinics is particularly busy (e.g., prior to the beginning of the school year). Besides her transportation, she must provide and maintain her own uniforms. Her expenses for the year are summarized below.

Uniforms	$690
State and city occupational licenses	380
Professional journals and membership dues in the American Dental Hygiene Association	340
Correspondence study course (taken online) dealing with teeth whitening procedures	420

Ella's salary for the year is $42,000, and her Form W–2 for the year shows income tax withholdings of $4,000 (Federal) and $1,000 (state) and the proper amount of Social Security and Medicare taxes.

In addition to those items already mentioned, the Coles had the following receipts during 2021.

Interest income—		
State of Colorado general purpose bonds	$2,500	
IBM bonds	800	
Wells Fargo Bank	1,200	$ 4,500
Federal income tax refund for year 2020		510
Life insurance proceeds paid by Eagle Assurance Corporation		200,000
Inheritance of savings account from Sarah Cole		50,000
Sales proceeds from two ATVs		9,000

For several years, the Coles household has included David's divorced mother, Sarah, who has been claimed as their dependent. Late last year Sarah unexpectedly died. Unknown to Ella and David, Sarah had a life insurance policy and a savings account (with David as the designated beneficiary of each).

In 2020, the Coles purchased two ATVs for $14,000. After several near mishaps, they decided that the sport was too dangerous. In 2021, they sold the ATVs to their neighbor.

Additional expenditures for the year include the following.

Funeral expenses for Sarah		$ 4,500
Taxes—		
Real property taxes on personal residence	$6,400	
Colorado state income tax due (paid in April 2021 for tax year 2020)	310	6,710
Mortgage interest on personal residence (Rocky Mountain Bank)		6,600
Contributions to traditional IRAs for Ella and David ($6,000 + $6,000)		12,000

In 2021, the Coles made quarterly estimated tax payments of $6,000 (Federal) and $500 (state) for a total of $24,000 (Federal) and $2,000 (state).

Using the appropriate forms and schedules, compute David and Ella's joint Federal income tax for 2021. Disregard the alternative minimum tax (AMT) and various education credits. Relevant Social Security numbers are:

David Cole	123-45-6788
Ella Cole	123-45-6787

The Coles have never owned or used any virtual currency. The Coles received the appropriate coronavirus recovery rebates (economic impact payments; related questions in ProConnect Tax should be ignored). They do not want to contribute to the Presidential Election Campaign Fund. Also, the Coles want any overpayment of tax refunded to them and not applied toward next year's tax liability. David will have a self-employment tax liability. Suggested software: ProConnect Tax.

Bridge Discipline

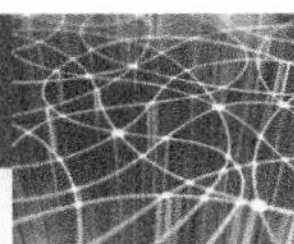

1. Justin performs services for Partridge, Inc., and receives compensation of $85,000 for the year. Determine the tax consequences of Social Security and Medicare on Justin's take-home pay if:
   a. Justin is classified as an employee of Partridge.
   b. Justin is classified as an independent contractor.

2. The Code contains provisions that are "friendly" to specific groups of taxpayers. Among these are the following.
   - Senior citizens.
   - Married taxpayers.
   - Employed taxpayers.
   - Taxpayers with children.
   - Self-employed taxpayers.

   Provide justification for the special treatment for each of the above groups, and give an example of such special treatment for each group.

Research Problems

Note: Solutions to the Research Problems can be prepared by using the Thomson Reuters Checkpoint™ online tax research database, which accompanies this textbook. Solutions can also be prepared by using research materials found in a typical tax library.

Communications

Research Problem 1. The employees of the city of Greenville must make mandatory contributions to the city's postretirement health benefit plan. The employees' contributions are placed in a trust and are used exclusively for the employees' benefits. The employees believe that because they are required to make the contributions from their base salaries, the result should be the same as if the employer made the contribution and had reduced their salaries by the amount of the contributions. As a result, the employees believe they should be permitted to exclude the payments from gross income. The employees have asked you to research the issue.

Communications
Critical Thinking

Research Problem 2. Rick Beam has been an independent sales representative for various textile manufacturers for many years. His products consist of soft goods such as tablecloths, curtains, and drapes. Rick's customers are clothing store chains, department stores, and smaller specialty stores. The employees of these companies who are responsible for purchasing merchandise are known as buyers. These companies generally prohibit their buyers from accepting gifts from manufacturers' sales representatives.

Each year Rick gives cash gifts (never more than $25) to most of the buyers who are his customers. Generally, he cashes a large check in November and gives the money personally to the buyers around Christmas. Rick says, "This is one of the ways that I maintain my relationship with my buyers." He maintains adequate substantiation of all of the gifts.

Rick's deductions for these gifts have been disallowed by the IRS based on § 162(c)(2). Rick is confused and comes to you, a CPA, for advice.

a. Write a letter to Rick concerning his tax position on this issue. Rick's address is 948 Octavia Street, Baton Rouge, LA 70821.

b. Prepare a memo for your files supporting the advice you have given.

Critical Thinking

Research Problem 3. Aaron, a resident of Minnesota, has been a driver for Green Delivery Service for the past six years. For this purpose, he leases a truck from Green, and his compensation is based on a percentage of the income resulting from his pickup and delivery services. Green allows its drivers to choose their 10-hour shifts and does not exercise any control on how these services are carried out (e.g., the route to be taken or the order in which parcels are delivered or picked up). Under Green's operating agreement with its drivers, Green can terminate the arrangement after 30 days' notice. In practice, however, Green allows its truckers to quit immediately without giving advance notice. The agreement also identifies the drivers as independent contractors.

Green maintains no health or retirement plans for its drivers, and each year it reports their income by issuing Forms 1099–NEC (and not Forms W–2). Green requires its drivers to maintain a commercial driver's license and be in good standing with the state highway law enforcement division.

Citing the employment tax Regulations in §§ 31.3121(d)–1(c)(2) and 31.3306(i)–1(b), an IRS agent contends that Aaron is an independent contractor and, therefore, is subject to the self-employment tax. Based on *Peno Trucking, Inc.* (93 TCM 1027, T.C.Memo. 2007–66), Aaron disagrees and contends that he is an employee (i.e., not self-employed). Who is correct? Why?

Use internet tax resources to address the following questions. Look for reliable websites and blogs of the IRS and other government agencies, media outlets, businesses, tax professionals, academics, think tanks, and political outlets.

Research Problem 4. Prepare no more than five Powerpoint slides on the topic "Should a Millennial Establish a Roth IRA and Contribute to It?" for a talk with your school's Investment Club. For a hypothetical taxpayer, graph the difference in account balances for Roth versus traditional IRAs given a starting date of age 25 and retirement dates of ages 65 and 70.

Research Problem 5. Isabelle was contemplating making a contribution to her traditional IRA in 2021. She determined she would contribute $6,000 in December 2021 but forgot about making the contribution until she was preparing her 2021 tax return in February 2022. Use the website of any well-known IRA provider (e.g., Fidelity, Vanguard, T. Rowe Price) to determine if Sarah can make a deductible 2021 contribution to her IRA after the tax year has ended.

Becker CPA Review Questions

Becker

1. Linda is an employee of JRH Corporation. Which of the following would be included in Linda's gross income?
   a. Premiums paid by JRH Corporation for a group term life insurance policy for $50,000 of coverage for Linda.
   b. $1,000 of tuition paid by JRH Corporation to State University for Linda's master's degree program.
   c. A $2,000 trip given to Linda by JRH Corporation for meeting sales goals.
   d. $1,200 paid by JRH Corporation for an annual parking pass for Linda.

2. Bob and Nancy are married and file a joint return in 2022. They are both under age 50 and employed, with wages of $50,000 each. Their total AGI is $117,000. Neither of them is an active participant in a qualified plan. What is the maximum traditional IRA deduction they can take for the current year?
   a. $0
   b. $6,000
   c. $9,600
   d. $12,000

3. Where is the deduction for qualified business income (QBI) applied in the individual tax formula?
   a. As an adjustment to arrive at adjusted gross income
   b. As an itemized deduction
   c. As an alternative to the standard deduction
   d. As a deduction from adjusted gross income separate from the standard deduction and itemized deductions

4. Which of the following is considered a specified service trade or business (SSTB) for purposes of the qualified business income deduction?
   a. Accounting firm
   b. Manufacturing company
   c. Engineering firm
   d. Architectural services

5. Bob is a farmer and is required to use the accrual method. At the beginning of the year, Bob has inventory, including livestock held for resale, amounting to $10,000. During the year, Bob purchased livestock totaling $3,000. Bob's ending inventory was $4,000. Bob's net sales for the year totaled $17,000. What is Bob's gross profit for the current year?

   a. $9,000
   b. $17,000
   c. $8,000
   d. $13,000

6. What is the basic deduction calculation for the qualified business income deduction?

   a. 30% × Qualified business income (QBI)
   b. 20% × W–2 wages
   c. 20% × Qualified business income (QBI)
   d. 30% × W–2 wages

7. Which of the following is the overall limitation to the qualified business income (QBI) deduction?

   a. Lesser of: 50% of combined QBI or 20% of the taxpayer's taxable income in excess of net capital gain
   b. Lesser of: combined QBI or 20% of the taxpayer's taxable income in excess of net capital gain
   c. Lesser of: 50% of W–2 wages or 25% of W–2 wages plus 2.5% of the unadjusted basis of qualified property
   d. Taxable income limitations based on filing status

8. Calculate the taxpayer's 2022 qualified business income deduction for a qualified trade or business:

Filing status:	Single
Taxable income:	$100,000
Net capital gains:	$0
Qualified business income (QBI):	$30,000
W–2 wages:	$10,000

   a. $5,000
   b. $70,000
   c. $20,000
   d. $6,000

9. Calculate the taxpayer's 2022 qualified business income deduction for a qualified trade or business:

Filing status:	Single
Taxable income:	$180,000
Net capital gains:	$0
Qualified business income (QBI):	$80,000
W–2 wages:	$20,000

   a. $16,000
   b. $10,000
   c. $2,700
   d. $14,806

Part 5 Business Entities

Chapter 12
Corporations: Organization, Capital Structure, and Operating Rules

Chapter 13
Corporations: Earnings & Profits and Distributions

Chapter 14
Partnerships and Limited Liability Entities

Chapter 15
S Corporations

Part 5 focuses on the tax rules for common types of legal entities with which to conduct business. The discussion includes an analysis of the tax rules relevant in the life cycle of a business (from formation to termination of the entity) and taxation of business activities. The specific business entities covered are the C corporation, the S corporation, the partnership, and the LLC. Rules also are reviewed as to the Federal income tax treatment of distributions from a C corporation, and special provisions for noncorporate businesses.

Chapter 12

Corporations: Organization, Capital Structure, and Operating Rules

Learning Objectives: *After completing Chapter 12, you should be able to:*

- **LO.1** Identify major tax and nontax considerations associated with the corporate form of business.
- **LO.2** Explain the tax consequences of incorporating and transferring assets to controlled corporations.
- **LO.3** Compute the adjusted basis of shareholder stock and corporate contributed assets.
- **LO.4** Describe the special rules that apply when a corporation assumes shareholder liabilities.
- **LO.5** Explain the tax aspects of the capital structure of a corporation.
- **LO.6** Characterize the tax differences between debt and equity investments.
- **LO.7** List and apply the tax rules unique to computing corporate taxable income.
- **LO.8** Compute the corporate income tax.
- **LO.9** Describe the reporting process for corporations.

Chapter Outline

Tax Talk *Taxes owing to the Government … are the price that business has to pay for protection and security.* —Benjamin N. Cardozo

Growing into the Corporate Form

Amber has operated her business as a sole proprietorship since it was formed 10 years ago. Now, however, she has decided to incorporate the business as Garden, Inc., because the corporate form offers several important nontax advantages, including limited liability. Also, the incorporation would enable her husband, Jimmy, to become a part owner in the business.

Amber is also anxious to take advantage of the reduced corporate tax rate in the 2017 tax act. Amber expects to transfer her business assets in exchange for Garden stock, while Jimmy will provide accounting and legal services for an equity interest. Amber's sole proprietorship assets available for transfer to the new corporation are as follows:

	Adjusted Basis	Fair Market Value
Accounts receivable	$ -0-	$ 50,000
Building	100,000	400,000
Other assets	300,000	550,000
	$400,000	$1,000,000

Aware of the problem of double taxation associated with operating as a regular corporation, Amber is considering receiving some corporate debt at the time of the incorporation. The interest expense on the debt will then provide a deduction for Garden, Inc. Amber's main concern is whether the incorporation will be a taxable transaction. Can the transaction be structured to avoid tax?

Read the chapter and formulate your response.

Taxpayers can choose to operate a business using several different organizational forms. Taxation is one of many factors that taxpayers consider when choosing an organizational form. This chapter deals with the unique tax consequences of organizing and operating an entity as a regular corporation, including:

- Classification of the entity as a corporation.
- The tax consequences to the shareholders and the corporation when forming a corporation.
- The capital structure of the corporation.
- Calculating the corporate income tax liability.
- Corporate tax filing requirements.

LO.1

Identify major tax and nontax considerations associated with the corporate form of business.

12-1 An Introduction to Corporate Income Taxation

Internal Revenue Code Subchapter C and Subchapter S govern the taxation of corporate taxpayers. Corporations governed by Subchapter C are referred to as **C corporations** or **regular corporations**. Corporations governed by Subchapter S are referred to as **S corporations**.

S corporations generally do not pay Federal income tax because their ordinary business income or loss flows through to the shareholders. In addition, certain items flow through the S corporation to the shareholders and retain their separate character. Shareholders report their share of ordinary income and other separately stated items on their individual income tax returns according to their stock ownership interests.

12-1a Double Taxation of Corporate Income

Unlike proprietorships, partnerships, and S corporations, C corporations are subject to an entity-level Federal income tax. The corporation computes tax on its taxable income using a flat 21 percent rate.[1] When a corporation distributes its income, the corporation's shareholders report dividend income on their own tax returns. This results in *double taxation*: income that has already been taxed at the corporate level is taxed again at the shareholder level, either when the corporation pays dividends or as capital gains when shareholders sell their stock.

Digging Deeper 1

Additional information on the corporate income tax rate for the past century can be found on this book's companion website: www.cengage.com

Global Tax Issues **U.S. Corporate Taxes and International Business Competitiveness**

In a 2021 study, the Tax Foundation examined the impact of national tax systems on international business competitiveness. In its report, the Tax Foundation ranked the international tax competitiveness of the 37 members of the Organization for Economic Co-operation and Development (OECD) by examining each country's tax policies. The rankings were based on many tax policy factors, including corporate and individual tax rates, consumption taxes, payroll and property taxes, and international tax rules.

The United States ranked 21st out of the 37 OECD countries in overall international tax competitiveness, largely due to its comparative rankings on corporate taxes (19th) and individual tax rules (23rd). Estonia claimed the top ranking in the report, followed by Latvia, New Zealand, and Switzerland.

One of the primary goals underlying the enactment of the TCJA of 2017 was to increase the international competitiveness of U.S. businesses. The reduction in the corporate tax rate to 21 percent was the centerpiece of that legislation. The Tax Foundation's 2017 study ranked the United States 30th out of 35 countries.

Source: **files.taxfoundation.org/20211014170634/International-Tax-Competitiveness-Index-2021.pdf**

[1]Before 2018, corporate taxpayers computed their tax liability using a progressive rate structure, with marginal rates ranging from 15% to 39%.

Taxation of Dividends

Double taxation stems, in part, from the nondeductibility of a C corporation's dividend distributions. This gives shareholders of a closely held corporation an incentive to try to convert dividend distributions into tax deductible expenses. A common way to do this is to increase compensation to shareholder-employees. However, the IRS scrutinizes compensation and other economic transactions (e.g., loans, leases, and sales) between shareholders and closely held corporations to ensure that payments are reasonable in amount and not just attempts to deduct payments to shareholders by labeling them as something other than dividends.[2]

To reduce the severity of double taxation, Congress reduced the tax rate applicable to the dividend income of individuals. Qualified dividend income is taxed at the same preferential rate as long-term capital gains—20 percent, 15 percent, or 0 percent. Most commonly, the 15 percent rate applies. However, the 20 percent rate applies to high-income taxpayers and the 0 percent rate applies to lower-income taxpayers. In addition, a 3.8 percent additional tax applies to net investment income in excess of modified adjusted gross income of $200,000 ($250,000 if married filing jointly), thus increasing the double taxation of dividend income for high-income taxpayers.[3] Examples 1 and 2 illustrate the effects of corporate double taxation and how that compares to a business entity not subject to double taxation.

Susanna, an individual taxpayer in the 35% marginal tax rate bracket, can generate $100,000 of additional taxable income in the current year. If the income is taxed to Susanna, the associated tax is $35,000 ($100,000 × 35%).

If, however, Susanna can shift the income to a newly created corporation, the corporate tax is $21,000. The lower corporate marginal tax rates result in a tax *savings* of $14,000 ($35,000 − $21,000).

Any attempt to take advantage of the difference between the corporate and individual marginal tax rates also must consider the effect of double taxation. When the preferential rate for dividend income is considered, however, tax savings opportunities may still exist.

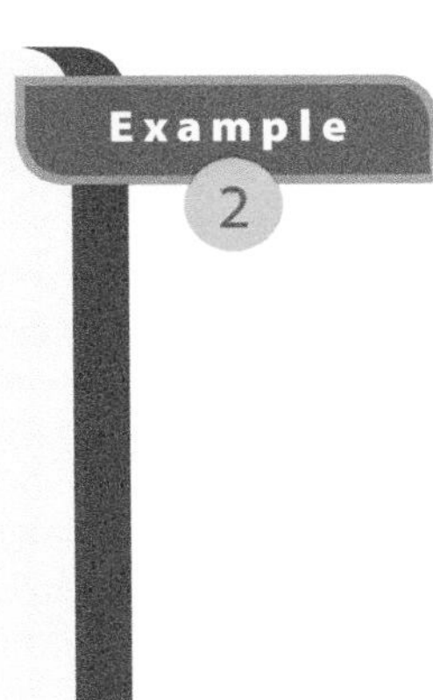

Assume in Example 1 that the corporation distributes all of its after-tax earnings to Susanna as a dividend and that a 15% capital gain rate applies to her. The dividend results in income tax of $11,850 [($100,000 − $21,000) × 15%] to Susanna.

As a result, even after double taxation, the combined tax burden of $32,850 ($21,000 paid by the corporation + $11,850 paid by the shareholder) represents an income tax *savings* of $2,150 when compared to the $35,000 of tax that results from taxing the $100,000 of income at Susanna's 35% marginal rate. The present value of these tax savings increases if the corporation distributes only part of its earnings as dividends.

In contrast, the opposite result occurs if Susanna is in a lower tax bracket or if the $100,000 of business income generates a qualified business income deduction for her (covered in text Section 11-4d). That is, the income tax Susanna pays on business income earned directly would be less than the corporate income tax after considering the double taxation effect (see Example 3).

12-1b Comparison of Corporations and Other Forms of Doing Business

When comparing C corporations to other business forms, there are a number of factors to consider, including:

- Tax rates;
- § 199A deduction (see text Section 11-4d for details);
- Character of business income;
- Business losses;

[2]See Chapter 13 for a discussion of constructive dividends.

[3]See text Section 8-5 for a discussion of the taxation of net capital gains and text Section 9-5e on the 3.8% net investment income tax.

- Employment taxes; and
- State taxes.

The paragraphs below discuss each of these factors.[4]

Tax Rates As noted earlier, a flat rate of 21 percent applies to corporate taxable income for taxable years beginning after 2017. Before 2018, the marginal tax rates for corporations ranged from 15 percent to 39 percent.

In contrast to the flat corporate rate, individuals face marginal tax rates that range from 10 percent to 37 percent, depending on income level. In some cases, taxes will be greater in the corporate form. However, the corporate form of doing business presents tax savings opportunities when the applicable corporate marginal rate is *lower* than the applicable individual marginal rate. The post-2017 flat 21 percent corporate rate significantly increases the likelihood of these tax savings opportunities, especially for corporations that pay little or no dividends (as in Example 1).

§ 199A Deduction Recall from Chapter 11 that most proprietorship and partnership income qualifies for the 20 percent qualified business income deduction (§ 199A). Example 3 illustrates a one-year tax comparison of a business operated as a corporation, a sole proprietorship that qualifies for the § 199A deduction, and a proprietorship that does not qualify for that deduction.

Example 3

Albert owns 100% of A Corporation, Betty is the sole proprietor of B Company, and Cai is the sole proprietor of C Company. Each business generated $500,000 of taxable income and before-tax cash flow. A Corporation and B Company produce a product, but C Company provides accounting services. A Corporation will distribute $200,000 of its after-tax income to Albert. All three owners face a 37% marginal tax rate on ordinary income. What is the after-tax cash flow and effective tax rate for each business?

B Company qualifies for the § 199A deduction, but C Company does not because it provides accounting services and its taxable income exceeds the threshold for that deduction. The table below compares the tax and cash flow consequences for each business.

	A Corporation	B Company	C Company
Taxable income and before-tax cash flow	$ 500,000	$500,000	$500,000
Corporate tax @ 21%	(105,000)	–0–	–0–
Cash available to owners	$ 395,000	$500,000	$500,000
§ 199A deduction @ 20%	–0–	(100,000)	–0–
Taxable income to owners	$ 395,000	$400,000	$500,000
Shareholder tax on $200,000 of dividend income @ 23.8%	($ 47,600)	$ –0–	$ –0–
Individual tax on ordinary income @ 37%	$ –0–	($148,000)	($185,000)
Before-tax cash flow	$ 500,000	$500,000	$500,000
Corporate tax	(105,000)	–0–	–0–
Shareholder tax on dividend income	(47,600)	–0–	–0–
Individual tax on ordinary income	–0–	(148,000)	(185,000)
After-tax cash flow	$ 347,400	$352,000	$315,000
Effective tax rate	30.5%	29.6%	37.0%

As Example 3 illustrates, the § 199A deduction results in rough parity between qualifying flow-through entities and corporations for reasonable corporate payout ratios. However, the greater the dividend distributions, the lower the after-tax cash flow and the higher the effective tax rate. The "tax-optimal" strategy is to eliminate dividend payments, but this

[4]Chapter 18 presents a detailed comparison of sole proprietorships, partnerships, S corporations, and C corporations as forms of doing business.

Tax Fact Corporations' Reporting Responsibilities

Like individuals, corporations are required to report their taxable income and other financial information to the IRS on an annual basis. The forms used depend on the type and size of the corporation. The IRS reports that taxpayers filed about 6,840,000 corporate tax returns. Of these, only 23.3 percent were filed by C corporations. Over 92 percent of C and S corporations submit their returns electronically.

Type of Corporation	Form	Percentage
C corporation	1120	23.3%
C corporation	Others	3.0
S corporation	1120S	73.7
		100.0%

Based on projections, the IRS expects to receive approximately 6.35 million corporate income tax returns during the 2020 filing season.

Source: Fiscal Year Return Projections for the United States: 2021–2028, IRS, Publication 6292, Fall 2021, Table 1.

may be inconsistent with the cash needs and investment expectations of the shareholders. Thus, it is important to perform the type of analysis in Example 3 when deciding whether to incorporate. Note that Examples 1 through 3 ignore other tax issues that taxpayers must consider in selecting the proper form of doing business, but they illustrate potential tax savings that taxpayers can achieve by taking advantage of tax rate differentials.

Character of Business Income Unlike other forms of business, the tax attributes of income and expense items of a C corporation do not pass through the corporate entity to the shareholders. As a result, if the business will tend to generate tax-favored income (e.g., tax-exempt income or long-term capital gains), it may be better to organize the business as a flow-through entity so that the owners can take advantage of tax-favored income.

Business Losses C corporation losses are treated differently than losses of other business forms. Proprietorships, partnerships, and S corporations allow their owners to deduct losses from these entities, subject to limits. In contrast, a C corporation retains its losses for use against its own future income. Therefore, owners that expect losses (e.g., in the early years of the business) should consider avoiding forming a corporation until the business becomes profitable.

Franco plans to start a business this year. He expects that the business will incur operating losses for the first three years and then become highly profitable. Franco decides to operate as an S corporation while incurring losses because they will flow through and result in deductions on his personal return. When the business becomes profitable, Franco intends to switch to C corporation status because his personal tax rate exceeds the 21% corporate rate.

Employment Taxes The net income of a proprietorship is subject to the self-employment tax (15.3 percent), as are some partnership allocations of income to partners. Alternatively, wages paid to a shareholder-employee of a corporation (C or S) are subject to payroll taxes. Owners must compare the combined corporation-employee payroll tax burden with the self-employment tax in the proprietorship and partnership business forms. This analysis should include the benefit of the deduction available to a corporation for payroll taxes paid, as well as the deduction available to an individual for one-half of the self-employment taxes paid.

State Taxes At the entity level, state corporate income taxes and/or franchise taxes apply to corporations. Some states impose a corporate income tax or franchise tax on all business forms (including partnerships and S corporations). If a business will operate in multiple states, state taxes become more important (Chapter 16 discusses the taxation of multistate corporations). Most states tax owners on their share of the income of sole proprietorships, S corporations, and partnerships (along with dividend distributions).

Bridge Discipline Bridge to Finance

Investment brokers and promoters often try to entice individuals to invest their disposable income in ventures designed to produce handsome returns. In most situations, the type of business entity in which the funds are invested takes the form of a "flow-through" entity, such as a limited partnership. Such investment ventures rarely operate as regular corporations.

A limited partnership is the favored investment vehicle for several reasons. One of the most significant reasons is that the investors who become limited partners are protected from exposure to unlimited liability. In addition, any operating losses of the entity (which owners may expect in the venture's early years) flow through to the partners and, as a result, potentially provide an immediate tax benefit on the partners' returns. Another potential advantage of the partnership form is avoidance of the previously discussed double taxation of corporate earnings.

The tax attributes of the various forms of business entities are compared in Concept Summary 12.1.

12-1c Nontax Considerations

Nontax considerations may outweigh tax considerations and lead owners to conclude that they should operate a business as a corporation. Here are some of the more important *nontax considerations*:

- Sole proprietors and general partners in partnerships face the danger of *unlimited liability*. That is, business creditors can file claims against the assets of the business *and* the *personal* assets of proprietors or general partners. State corporate law protects the personal assets of shareholders.

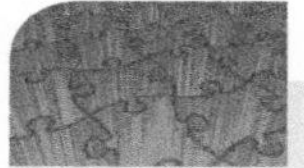

Concept Summary 12.1

Tax Treatment of Business Forms Compared

	Sole Proprietorships	Partnerships	S Corporations	Regular (C) Corporations
Entity tax return	None	Form 1065	Form 1120S	Form 1120
Taxation of entity income	No separate entity-level income tax. Proprietorship's income and expenses are reported on owner's Form 1040 (Schedule C). Character of entity income and expenses retained at owner level.	No separate entity-level income tax. Partnership's income and expenses are allocated and reported (on Schedule K–1) to partners who report these items on their returns (e.g., Form 1040 for individual partners). Character of entity income and expenses retained at partner level.	Generally, no separate entity-level income tax. S corporation's income and expenses are allocated and reported (Schedule K–1) to shareholders who report these items on their returns (e.g., Form 1040 for individual shareholders). Character of entity income and expenses retained at shareholder level.	Corporate income tax applies at a flat 21% rate.
Taxation of withdrawals/ distributions from entity	Withdrawals by owner are not subject to separate tax.	Distributions to partners are generally not subject to separate tax.	Distributions to shareholders are generally not subject to separate tax.	Character of entity income and expenses not retained at shareholder level. Instead, distributions to shareholders are generally taxed as dividend income. Preferential tax rates (0%/15%/20%) apply to qualified dividends.
Employment taxes	Schedule C income subject to self-employment tax.	Some partnership income allocations subject to self-employment tax.	Compensation paid to shareholder/employees subject to payroll taxes. Shareholder's allocated portion of entity income not subject to self-employment tax.	Compensation paid to shareholder/employees subject to payroll taxes.

- The corporate form of business provides a vehicle for *raising capital* through widespread stock ownership. Most major businesses in the United States operate as corporations.
- Shares of stock in a corporation are *freely transferable*; a partner's sale of his or her partnership interest must be approved by the other partners.
- A corporation continues to exist if shareholders die or sell their stock. In contrast, death or withdrawal of a partner may terminate the existing partnership and cause financial difficulties that result in dissolution of the entity. Thus, *continuity of life* is a distinct advantage of the corporate form.
- Corporations have *centralized management*. All management responsibility is assigned to a board of directors, which appoints officers to carry out the corporation's business. Partnerships often have decentralized management, in which every partner has a right to participate in the organization's business decisions. **Limited partnerships**, though, can also centralize their management.

12-1d Limited Liability Companies

The **limited liability company (LLC)** is a business form that blends some corporate form advantages into a flow-through entity. All 50 states and the District of Columbia have passed laws that allow LLCs, and thousands of companies have chosen LLC status. As with a corporation, operating as an LLC allows its owners (called "members") to avoid unlimited liability, which is a primary *nontax* consideration in choosing a business form. The tax advantage of LLCs is that qualifying businesses can elect treatment as a proprietorship or partnership for tax purposes, thereby avoiding the problem of double taxation associated with regular corporations.[5]

12-1e Entity Classification

There is a long history of taxpayers and the IRS disagreeing about taxing a business as a corporation or as a partnership. To ease this problem, the Treasury Department issued **Check-the-box Regulations**.[6] The Regulations enable taxpayers to choose the tax status of a business entity without regard to its corporate (or noncorporate) characteristics. These rules simplified tax administration considerably and eliminated much of the litigation that arose under prior law.

Under the Check-the-box Regulations, an unincorporated entity with *more than one* owner is, by default, classified as a partnership. An unincorporated entity with *only one* owner is, by default, classified as a **disregarded entity**, which the Regulations treat as a sole proprietorship for an individual owner or as a branch or a division of a corporate owner. If the entity wants to use its default status, it simply files the appropriate tax return. If a taxpayer wants to use a different status or change its status, it does so by "checking a box" on Form 8832. Thus, an LLC (single or multi-member) can choose to be taxed as a C corporation and, if it otherwise qualifies, even elect S corporation status.[7] Although an LLC does not typically pay Federal income taxes, LLCs must report and pay employment and excise taxes.

Additional information on entity classification can be found on this book's companion website: www.cengage.com

2 Digging Deeper

[5]Regarding the nontax characteristics of LLCs, some states allow an LLC to have centralized management, but not continuity of life or free transferability of interests. Other states allow LLCs to adopt any or all of the corporate characteristics of centralized management, continuity of life, and free transferability of interests. The comparison of business entities in Chapter 18 includes a discussion of LLCs.

[6]Reg. §§ 301.7701–1 through −4, and −7.

[7]The status election is not available to entities that are incorporated under state law or to entities that are required to be taxed as corporations under Federal law (e.g., certain publicly traded partnerships). State law does not treat LLCs as corporations, so they default to either partnership or proprietorship status.

LO.2

Explain the tax consequences of incorporating and transferring assets to controlled corporations.

12-2 Organization of and Transfers to Controlled Corporations

Property transactions producing realized gain or loss normally produce tax consequences. As a result, unless special provisions in the Code apply, a transfer of property to a corporation in exchange for stock is a taxable transaction. The gain or loss equals the difference between the fair market value of the stock and other assets the shareholder received and the shareholder's tax basis in the property transferred to the corporation.

12-2a Section 351 Rationale and General Rules

In contrast to the typical result of full gain or loss recognition, the Code permits nonrecognition of gain or loss in limited circumstances. For example, both § 1031 (like-kind exchanges—see Chapter 7) and § 351 (transfers of property to controlled corporations) postpone gain or loss recognition until a substantive change in the taxpayer's investment occurs (e.g., a sale of property or ownership shares to outsiders). When taxpayers exchange some of their property for other property of a like kind, § 1031 provides that gain (or loss) realized on the exchange is not recognized because a substantive change in the taxpayer's investment has not occurred. The rules accomplish this deferral by reducing the taxpayer's basis in the assets received by the deferred gain or by increasing the basis by the deferred loss. This substituted basis results in taxpayers recognizing the gain or loss when they sell the new property for cash or non-like-kind property.

Similarly, Exhibit 12.1 illustrates that § 351 defers gain or loss when shareholders transfer property to a controlled corporation (defined later in the chapter) in exchange for the corporation's own stock. There are at least three reasons why Congress granted this tax deferral treatment. First, contributing property to a corporation leaves an owner's economic status unchanged when incorporating business assets; only the form of the investment has changed. The investment in the business assets carries over to an investment in corporate stock. Second, when a shareholder receives only stock in the corporation, the shareholder receives no cash to pay a tax on any realized gain. As a result, the wherewithal to pay concept discussed in Chapter 1 provides justification for tax deferral. As noted later, however, when a shareholder receives property other than stock (i.e., cash or other "boot") from the corporation, the shareholder recognizes some or all of the realized gain. A third justification for the nonrecognition of gain or loss provisions under § 351 is that Congress believes tax rules should not impede a taxpayer's judgment about the best choice of entity form for conducting business.

Exhibit 12.1 Transfers to Controlled Corporations Under § 351

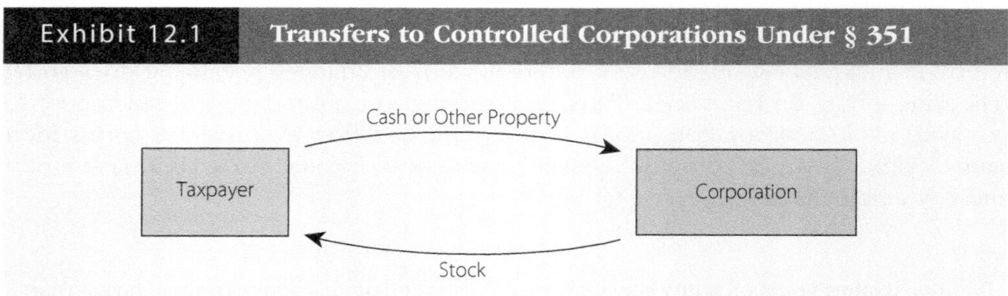

Ron is considering incorporating his sole proprietorship. He worries about his personal liability for the obligations of the business. Ron realizes that if he incorporates, depending on state law, he will be liable only for the debts of the business that he personally guarantees. If Ron incorporates his business, he will transfer the following assets to the corporation:

continued

	Tax Basis	Fair Market Value
Cash	$ 10,000	$ 10,000
Furniture and fixtures	20,000	60,000
Land and building	240,000	300,000
	$270,000	$370,000

Ron will receive stock in the newly formed corporation worth $370,000. Without the nonrecognition provisions of § 351, Ron would recognize a taxable gain of $100,000 ($370,000 − $270,000) on the transfer.

Under § 351, however, Ron recognizes no gain because his economic status has not changed. Ron's investment in the assets of his sole proprietorship ($270,000) carries over to his investment in the incorporated business, which is now in the form of his ownership of stock in the corporation. This reduction to his stock basis below its fair market value results in a $100,000 gain *deferral* and not gain *exclusion*. As a result, § 351 provides for tax neutrality on the initial incorporation of Ron's sole proprietorship.

If Ron's basis in the assets was $450,000 instead of $270,000, then § 351 would result in Ron deferring the $80,000 loss ($370,000 – $450,000) by not recognizing the loss and taking a $450,000 basis in the stock he received.

In a manner similar to a like-kind exchange, gain and loss deferral is not absolute. If a taxpayer transfers property to a corporation and receives "boot" (money or property other than stock), § 351(b) requires gain recognition to the extent of the lesser of the gain realized or the boot received (the amount of money and the fair market value of other property received). The tax character of the gain (e.g., ordinary, capital) depends on the type of asset transferred.[8] Loss on a § 351 transaction is never recognized. As discussed in more detail later, a substituted basis for the shareholder's stock accomplishes gain or loss deferral by reducing the stock basis by the deferred gain or increasing it by the deferred loss.[9] The major shareholder consequences of a taxable property transaction versus one that is tax deferred are identified in Concept Summary 12.2.

Concept Summary 12.2

Shareholder Consequences: Taxable Corporate Formation versus Tax-Deferred § 351 Transaction

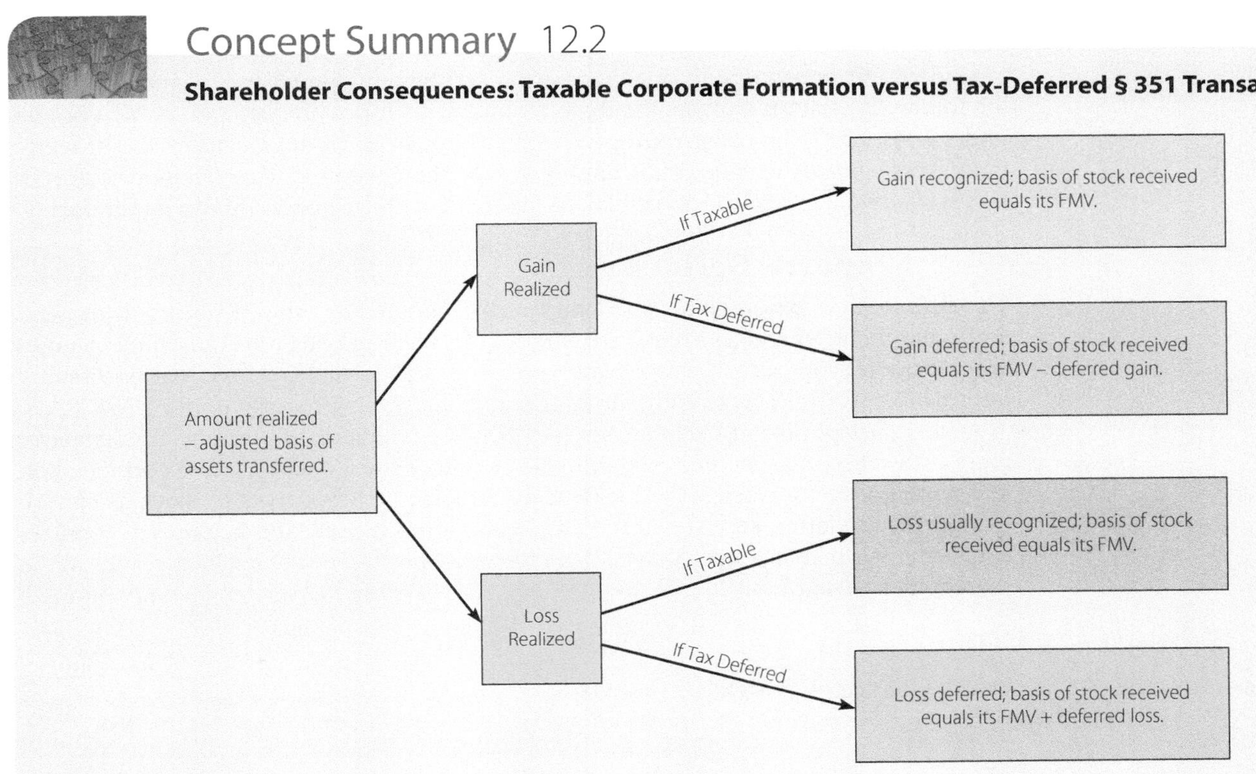

[8] Rev.Rul. 68–55, 1968–1 C.B. 140.

[9] § 358(a). See the discussion preceding Example 26.

Amanda and Calvin form Quail Corporation. Amanda transfers equipment with an adjusted basis of $30,000 and a fair market value of $60,000 for 50% of Quail's stock. Calvin transfers equipment with an adjusted basis of $70,000 and a fair market value of $60,000 for the remaining 50% of the stock. The transfers qualify under § 351.

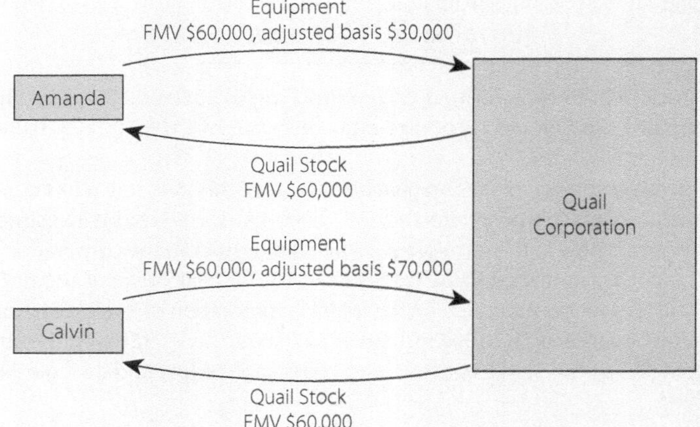

Amanda has a deferred gain of $30,000, and Calvin has a deferred loss of $10,000. Both have a substituted basis in the stock of Quail Corporation. Amanda has a basis of $30,000 in her stock, and Calvin has a basis of $70,000 in his stock. Therefore, if either Amanda or Calvin later disposes of the Quail stock in a taxable transaction (e.g., a sale), this deferred gain/loss will then be fully recognized—a $30,000 gain to Amanda and a $10,000 loss to Calvin.

Alternatively, suppose that Amanda and Calvin each received Quail stock worth $50,000 and cash of $10,000. In this case, Amanda would recognize $10,000 of the $30,000 realized gain because she received boot of $10,000. In contrast, Calvin's receipt of boot would not trigger the loss recognition because receiving boot can only trigger gain. This rule means that a shareholder can never recognize a loss if § 351 applies to a transaction. Additional discussion of gain/loss recognition and the basis of stock received appears later in the chapter.

Code § 351 is *mandatory* if a transaction satisfies this provision's requirements. As the following sections explain, the three requirements for nonrecognition of gain or loss under § 351 are (1) *property is transferred*, (2) in exchange for *stock*, and (3) the property transferors *control* the corporation after the exchange. Therefore, if recognition of gain or loss is *desired*, the taxpayer must plan to fail to meet at least one of these requirements.

12-2b Property Defined

The definition of **property** for § 351 purposes is broad. For example, along with plant and equipment, unrealized receivables of a cash basis taxpayer and installment notes are considered property.[10] Proprietary processes and formulas as well as proprietary information such as a patentable invention also qualify as property under § 351.[11]

Code § 351 specifically excludes services from the definition of property. So a taxpayer must always report as income the fair market value of stock and any other consideration as compensation for services.[12] Consequently, when a taxpayer receives stock as consideration for rendering services to the corporation, the income the taxpayer recognizes equals the fair market value of the stock received. This immediate taxation results in the shareholder having basis in this stock equal to the value of the service income reported.

[10] *Hempt Brothers, Inc. v. U.S.*, 74–1 USTC ¶9188, 33 AFTR 2d 74–570, 490 F.2d 1172 (CA–3), and Reg. § 1.453–9(c)(2).

[11] Rev.Rul. 64–56; Rev.Rul. 71–564.

[12] §§ 61 and 83 generally tax service income when the service provider receives unrestricted compensation for providing the services.

Ann and Sanjit form Olive Corporation and transfer the following consideration:

	Consideration Transferred		
	Basis to Transferor	Fair Market Value	Number of Shares Issued
From Ann:			
Personal services rendered to Olive Corporation	$ -0-	$20,000	200
From Sanjit:			
Installment note receivable	5,000	40,000	
Inventory	10,000	30,000	800
Proprietary process	-0-	10,000	

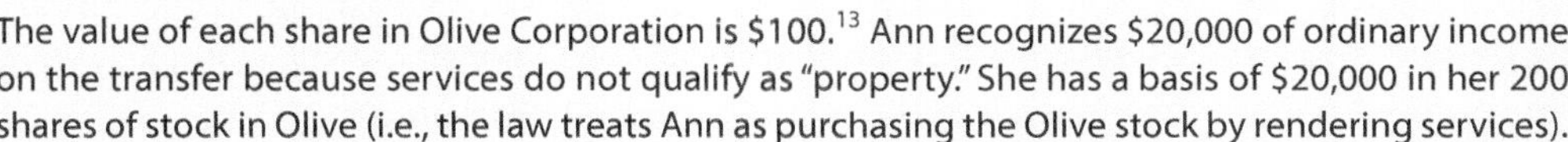

The value of each share in Olive Corporation is $100.[13] Ann recognizes $20,000 of ordinary income on the transfer because services do not qualify as "property." She has a basis of $20,000 in her 200 shares of stock in Olive (i.e., the law treats Ann as purchasing the Olive stock by rendering services).

In contrast, Sanjit recognizes no gain on the transfer because all of the consideration he transferred to Olive qualifies as "property" and he has "control" of Olive after the transfer. (See the discussion concerning control on the next page.) Sanjit has a substituted basis of $15,000 in the Olive stock.

Issues involving intangible assets and § 351 can be found on this book's companion website: www.cengage.com

3 Digging Deeper

12-2c Stock Transferred

Shareholder nonrecognition of gain occurs only when the shareholder receives stock. Stock includes common and most preferred shares. However, the Regulations state that the term *stock* does not include stock rights and stock warrants.[14] In addition, it does not include "nonqualified preferred stock," which possesses many of the attributes of debt.[15]

As a result, any corporate debt or **securities** (i.e., long-term debt such as bonds) are boot because they do not qualify as stock. Therefore, shareholder receipt of the corporation's debt in exchange for the transfer of appreciated property to a controlled corporation can cause gain recognition, but only if the shareholder realizes a gain on the contribution.

The Big Picture

Return to the facts of *The Big Picture* on p. 12-1. Assume that the proposed transaction qualifies under § 351, but Amber decides to receive some corporate debt along with the stock.

If Amber receives Garden stock worth $900,000 and Garden debt of $100,000 in exchange for the property transferred, Amber realizes a gain of $600,000 [$1,000,000 (value of consideration received) − $400,000 (basis in the transferred property)]. However, because the transaction qualifies under § 351, Amber recognizes only $100,000 of gain because the $100,000 of Garden debt is boot. Amber defers the remaining $500,000 realized gain.

Information on nonqualified preferred stock can be found on this book's companion website: www.cengage.com

4 Digging Deeper

[13]The value of closely held stock normally is presumed to equal the value of the property transferred.

[14]Reg. § 1.351–1(a)(1)(ii).

[15]§ 351(g). Examples of nonqualified preferred stock include preferred stock that is redeemable within 20 years of issuance and whose dividend rate is based on factors other than corporate performance. See also Reg. § 1.351–1(a)(1)(ii).

12-2d Control of the Corporation

For a transaction to qualify as nontaxable under § 351, the transferor(s) of the property must **control** the corporation immediately after the exchange. The property transferors must own stock possessing at least 80 percent of the total combined voting power of all classes of stock entitled to vote *and* at least 80 percent of the total *number of shares* of all other classes of stock.[16]

Control Immediately after the Transfer

Control after the exchange can apply to a single person or to several taxpayers if they are all parties in an integrated transaction. To satisfy the timing requirement, the Regulations provide that when more than one person is involved, the exchange does not necessarily require simultaneous exchanges by two or more persons. The Regulations do, however, require that the rights of the parties (i.e., those transferring property to the corporation) be previously set out and determined. Also, shareholders should execute the agreement to transfer property "with an expedition consistent with orderly procedure," and the transfers should occur close together in time.[17]

The Point at Which Control Is Determined

Jack exchanges property with a basis of $60,000 and a fair market value of $100,000 for 70% of the stock of Gray Corporation. The other 30% is owned by Jane, who acquired it several years ago. The fair market value of Jack's stock is $100,000.

Jack recognizes a taxable gain of $40,000 on the transfer because he does not have control immediately after the exchange and his transaction cannot be integrated with Jane's for purposes of the control requirement.

Lana, Leo, and Lori incorporate their respective businesses by forming Green Corporation. Lana exchanges her property for 300 shares in Green on January 7, 2022. Leo exchanges his property for 400 shares in Green on January 14, 2022, and Lori exchanges her property for 300 shares in Green on March 5, 2022.

The three exchanges are part of a prearranged plan, so the control requirement is met. The nonrecognition provisions of § 351 apply to all of the exchanges.

Once control has been achieved, it is not necessarily lost if, shortly after the transaction, stock received by shareholders in a § 351 exchange is sold or given to persons who are not parties to the exchange.[18]

Naomi and Eric form Eagle Corporation. They transfer appreciated property to the corporation with each receiving 50 shares of Eagle stock. Shortly after the formation, Naomi gives 25 shares to her son.

Because Naomi was not committed to making the gift, she met the control test "immediately after the exchange." Therefore, Naomi and Eric meet the requirements of § 351 and neither recognizes gain on the exchange.

A different result might occur if a plan for the ultimate disposition of the stock existed *before* the exchange.

[16] § 368(c). Nonqualified preferred stock is treated as stock, not boot, for purposes of this control test.

[17] Reg. § 1.351–1(a)(1).

[18] *Wilgard Realty Co. v. Comm.*, 42–1 USTC ¶9452, 29 AFTR 325, 127 F.2d 514 (CA–2).

Assume the same facts as in Example 11, except that Naomi was obligated to immediately give 25 shares to a business associate pursuant to a plan to satisfy an outstanding obligation.

In this case, the formation of Eagle would be taxable to Naomi and Eric because of their lack of control (i.e., Naomi and Eric, the property transferors, would have owned only 75% of the stock).

Tax Planning Strategies **Utilizing § 351**

Framework Focus: Income and Exclusions

Strategy: Avoid Income Recognition.

When using § 351, ensure that all parties transferring property (including cash) collectively receive control of the corporation. Simultaneous transfers are not necessary, but a long period of time between transfers makes the transaction vulnerable to taxation if the transfers are not properly documented as part of a single plan. To do this, the parties should document and preserve evidence of their intentions. Also, it is helpful to have some reasonable explanation for any delay in the transfers.

To meet the requirements of § 351, mere momentary control on the part of the transferor may not suffice if loss of control is compelled by a prearranged agreement.[19]

For many years, Paula operated a business as a sole proprietor employing Brooke as manager. To dissuade Brooke from quitting and going out on her own, Paula promised her a 30% interest in the business. To fulfill this promise, Paula transferred the business to newly formed Green Corporation in return for all of its stock. Immediately thereafter, Paula transfers 30% of the stock to Brooke. As a consequence, she fails to meet the 80% control requirement.

Code § 351 probably does not apply to Paula's transfer to Green Corporation. It appears that she was under an obligation to relinquish control. If this preexisting obligation exists, § 351 will not be available to Paula because, as the sole property transferor, she does not have 80% control of Green Corporation. If there is no obligation and the loss of control was voluntary on Paula's part, momentary control would suffice.[20]

Later transfers of property to an existing corporation must satisfy the 80 percent control requirement to avoid gain recognition. For these later transfers, a transferor's interest does not count toward control if the value of stock received is relatively small compared with the value of stock already owned. Further, the primary purpose of the transfer may not be to qualify other transferors for § 351 treatment.[21] (For a complete discussion of this issue, see "Transfers to Existing Corporations" on p. 12-15.)

Transfers for Property and Services

Taxpayers can lose § 351 treatment if persons who do not transfer property own "too much" stock. Example 14 shows how a service contributor can also cause a property contributor to fail the control test and thus have to recognize gain (or loss) on his or her contribution to the corporation.

The Big Picture

Return to the facts of *The Big Picture* on p. 12-1. Assume that Amber transfers her $1,000,000 of property to Garden, Inc., and receives 50% of its stock. Jimmy receives the other 50% of the stock for services rendered (worth $1,000,000).

Both Amber and Jimmy report income from the transfers. Jimmy has ordinary income of $1,000,000 because he provides services for stock. Amber recognizes a taxable gain of $600,000 [$1,000,000 (fair market value of the stock in Garden) − $400,000 (basis in the transferred property)]. As the sole transferor of property, she receives only 50% of Garden's stock and so she fails the control test.

[19] Rev.Rul. 54–96, 1954–1 C.B. 111.

[20] Compare *Fahs v. Florida Machine and Foundry Co.*, 48–2 USTC ¶9329, 36 AFTR 1161, 168 F.2d 957 (CA–5), with *John C. O'Connor*, 16 TCM 213, T.C.Memo. 1957–50, *aff'd* in 58–2 USTC ¶9913, 2 AFTR 2d 6011, 260 F.2d 358 (CA–6).

[21] Reg. § 1.351–1(a)(1)(ii).

As noted earlier, a person receiving stock in exchange for services and for property transferred is taxed on the stock value related to those services but not on the stock issued for property if § 351 applies. In addition, all stock received by the person transferring both property and services counts in determining whether the transferors acquired control of the corporation.[22]

The Big Picture

Example 15

Assume the same facts as in Example 14, except that Jimmy transfers property worth $800,000 (basis of $260,000) in addition to services rendered to Garden, Inc. (valued at $200,000).

Now Jimmy becomes a part of the control group. Amber and Jimmy, as property transferors, together receive 100% of the corporation's stock. Consequently, § 351 applies to the exchanges. Amber recognizes no gain. Jimmy recognizes no gain on the transfer of the property, but he must recognize ordinary income equal to the value of the shares issued for services rendered. Thus, Jimmy recognizes $200,000 of ordinary income currently.

Transfers for Services and Nominal Property

Note that to be part of the group meeting the 80 percent control test, the person contributing services must transfer property having more than a "relatively small value" compared with the value of services performed. Code § 351 will not apply when a small amount of property is transferred and the primary purpose of the transfer is to qualify the transaction under § 351 for other transferors.[23] The regulations do not define a "relatively small" property contribution. However, the IRS generally considers a service contributor also to be a property contributor if the value of the property transferred equals or exceeds 10 percent of the value of the services provided. The IRS therefore considers property contributions that are less than 10 percent of the value of the services to be relatively small.

Determining Control Group Membership When Services Are Rendered

Ava and Rick form Grouse Corporation. Ava transfers land worth $100,000 with a basis of $20,000. Rick transfers equipment worth $50,000 with an adjusted basis of $10,000 and provides services worth $50,000. Ava and Rick each receive 50% of the Grouse stock.

Because the value of the property Rick transfers is not small relative to the value of the services he renders, his stock in Grouse Corporation is counted in determining control under § 351; thus, Ava and Rick jointly own 100% of the stock in Grouse. In addition, all of Rick's stock, not just the shares received for the equipment, counts in determining control.

As a result, Ava does not recognize gain on the transfer of the land. Rick similarly does not recognize the gain on his equipment; however, he must recognize income of $50,000 on the transfer of services. Even though the transfer of the equipment qualifies Rick as a property contributor under § 351, his transfer of services for stock is still taxable compensation income.

Assume the same facts as in Example 16, except that the value of Rick's property is $2,000 and the value of his services is $98,000.

In this situation, the value of the property is small relative to the value of the services (and well below the 10% IRS threshold); therefore, Rick does not qualify as a property transferor. Consequently, the transaction is fully taxable to both Ava and Rick. In this situation, Ava, the sole property transferor, lacks at least 80% control of Grouse Corporation following the transfer.

As a result, she will fully recognize her realized gain. Further, because the control test ignores Rick's shares, the § 351 deferral is not available to him. He will recognize income of $98,000 relating to the services provided along with any realized gain or loss on the transfer of the additional $2,000 of property.

[22]Reg. § 1.351–1(a)(2), Ex. 3.

[23]Reg. § 1.351–1(a)(1)(ii).

Transfers to Existing Corporations

Once a corporation is operational, § 351 also applies to any later transfers of property for stock by either new or existing shareholders. That is, § 351 does not apply solely at the time of corporate formation.

Tyrone and Pooja formed Blue Corporation three years ago. Both Tyrone and Pooja transferred appreciated property to Blue in exchange for 50 shares each in the corporation. The original transfers qualified under § 351, and neither Tyrone nor Pooja recognized gain or loss on the exchange. In the current year, Tyrone transfers property worth $90,000 with an adjusted basis of $5,000 for 50 additional Blue shares.

Tyrone has a taxable gain of $85,000 on the transfer. The exchange does not qualify under § 351 because Tyrone does not have 80% control of Blue Corporation immediately after the transfer—he now owns 100 shares of the 150 shares outstanding, or a 66⅔% interest.

If current shareholders transfer property with a small value relative to the value of stock already owned, a special rule applies (similar to the nominal property rule noted for service contributors). In particular, if the purpose of the transfer is to qualify a transaction under § 351, the ownership of the current shareholders does not count toward control even if they contribute property with new shareholders. Thus, in the preceding example, if Pooja had contributed $200 for one share of stock at the time of Tyrone's contribution, Pooja's ownership would not count toward the 80 percent control requirement and Tyrone would still have had a taxable exchange.

12-2e Basis Determination and Other Issues

LO.3 **Compute the adjusted basis of shareholder stock and corporate contributed assets.**

Recall that § 351(a) postpones gain or loss recognition until the taxpayer's investment changes substantively. It is the basis rules described below that result in gain or loss postponement until the shareholder disposes of the stock.

Basis of Stock to Shareholder

A shareholder that transfers property to a corporation in a § 351 transaction takes a *substituted basis* in the corporate stock instead of a fair market value basis. The stock basis equals the basis the taxpayer had in the property transferred plus any gain recognized on the exchange of property minus the value of boot received. For computing stock basis, boot received includes liabilities transferred by the shareholder to the corporation. In contrast, because boot triggers realized gain recognition, a shareholder takes a fair market value basis in boot received.[24] Exhibit 12.2 summarizes this substituted basis computation.

Exhibit 12.2 Shareholder's Basis of Stock Received in Exchange for Property

Adjusted basis of property transferred	$xx,xxx
Plus: Gain recognized	xxx
Minus: Boot received (including any liabilities transferred)	(xxx)
Minus: Adjustment for loss property (if elected)	(xxx)
Equals: Basis of stock received	$xx,xxx

Note that a service contributor also includes in its stock basis the value of services contributed because these are always taxable to the contributing shareholder.

Basis of Property to Corporation

Just as a shareholder's stock embeds deferred gain or loss into the stock basis, a similar *carryover* basis rule exists for computing the basis of the corporation's property. This rule provides that the property's basis to the corporation equals the basis in the hands of the transferor plus any gain recognized on the transfer by the transferor-shareholder.[25]

[24] § 362(a). Recall from earlier discussions that the basis of stock received for services equals its fair market value.

[25] § 362(a).

Exhibit 12.3 summarizes the basis calculation for property received by a corporation. Examples 19 and 20 illustrate these basis rules.

Exhibit 12.3 Corporation's Basis in Property Received

Adjusted basis of property transferred	$xx,xxx
Plus: Gain recognized by transferor-shareholder	xxx
Minus: Adjustment for loss property (if required)	(xxx)
Equals: Basis of property to corporation	$xx,xxx

Basis Determination

Example 19

Kesha and Ned form Brown Corporation. Kesha transfers land (basis of $30,000 and fair market value of $70,000); Ned invests cash ($60,000). They each receive 50 shares in Brown Corporation, worth $1,200 per share, but Kesha also receives $10,000 of cash from Brown. The transfers of property, the realized and recognized gain on the transfers, and the basis of the stock in Brown Corporation to Kesha and Ned are as follows:

	A	B	C	D	E	F
	Basis of Property Transferred	**FMV of Stock Received**	**Boot Received**	**Realized Gain (B + C − A)**	**Recognized Gain (Lesser of C or D)**	**Basis of Stock in Brown (A − C + E)**
From Kesha:						
Land	$30,000	$60,000	$10,000	$40,000	$10,000	$30,000
From Ned:						
Cash	60,000	60,000	-0-	-0-	-0-	60,000

Brown Corporation has a basis of $40,000 in the land (Kesha's basis of $30,000 plus her recognized gain of $10,000).

Assume the same facts as in Example 19, except that Kesha's basis in the land is $68,000 (instead of $30,000). Because recognized gain cannot exceed realized gain, the transfer generates only $2,000 of gain to Kesha. The realized and recognized gain and the basis of the stock in Brown Corporation to Kesha are as follows:

	A	B	C	D	E	F
	Basis of Property Transferred	**FMV of Stock Received**	**Boot Received**	**Realized Gain (B + C − A)**	**Recognized Gain (Lesser of C or D)**	**Basis of Stock in Brown (A − C + E)**
Land	$68,000	$60,000	$10,000	$2,000	$2,000	$60,000

Brown's basis in the land is $70,000 ($68,000 basis to Kesha + $2,000 gain recognized by Kesha).

Concept Summary 12.3 shows the shareholder and corporate consequences of a transfer of property to a corporation for stock, with and without the application of § 351. The facts applicable to shareholder Kesha's transfer in Example 19 are used to illustrate the differences between the transaction being tax-deferred and taxable.

Basis Adjustment for Loss Property

Concept Summary 12.3 shows that when Kesha contributes property in a § 351 transaction, Kesha and the corporation reduce the basis of Kesha's stock and the basis of the contributed assets. This *duplicates* the gain potential for the two entities. Despite this, the tax law does not allow taxpayers to duplicate losses in a similar manner. Accordingly, when a taxpayer contributes **built-in loss property** to a corporation, the aggregate basis of the assets transferred by a shareholder can exceed their fair market value. When this built-in loss situation exists, an anti-loss duplication rule requires the corporation

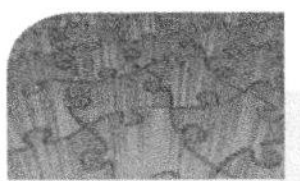

Concept Summary 12.3

Tax Consequences to the Shareholders and Corporation: With and Without the Application of § 351 (Based on the Facts of Example 26)

	With § 351			Without § 351		
Shareholder	**Gain/Loss Recognized**	**Stock Basis**	**Other Property Basis**	**Gain/Loss Recognized**	**Stock Basis**	**Other Property Basis**
Kesha	Realized gain recognized to extent of boot received; loss not recognized.	Substituted (see Exhibit 12.2).	FMV	All realized gain or loss recognized.	FMV	FMV
	$10,000	$30,000	$10,000	$40,000	$60,000	$10,000

	With § 351		Without § 351	
Corporation	**Gain/Loss Recognized**	**Property Basis**	**Gain/Loss Recognized**	**Property Basis**
Brown	No gain or loss recognized on the transfer of corporate stock for property.	Carryover (see Exhibit 12.3).	No gain or loss recognized on the transfer of corporate stock for property.	FMV
	$0	$40,000	$0	$70,000

Note that the benefit to Kesha of deferring $30,000 of gain under § 351 comes with a cost: her stock basis is $30,000 (rather than $60,000), and the corporation's basis in the property received is $40,000 (rather than $70,000). In this sense, the deferred gain reduces the basis of the stock for Kesha ($30,000 stock basis = $60,000 FMV − $30,000 deferred gain) and the basis of the land for Brown Corporation ($40,000 land basis = $70,000 FMV − $30,000 deferred gain) below their fair market values.

to reduce the basis in the separate loss properties by allocating the net built-in loss proportionately among the contributed loss assets that resulted in the net overall built-in loss.[26] This rule prevents a high shareholder stock basis *and* a high corporate asset basis. The next two examples illustrate this rule.

Example 21

In a transaction qualifying under § 351, Charles transfers the following assets to Gold Corporation in exchange for all of its stock:

	Tax Basis	Fair Market Value	Built-In Gain/(Loss)
Equipment	$100,000	$ 90,000	($10,000)
Land	200,000	230,000	30,000
Building	150,000	100,000	(50,000)
	$450,000	$420,000	($30,000)

Charles's stock basis is $450,000 [$450,000 (basis of the property transferred) + $0 (gain recognized) − $0 (boot received)]. However, Gold must reduce its basis in the loss assets transferred by the net built-in loss ($30,000) in proportion to each asset's share of the loss.

	Unadjusted Tax Basis	Adjustment	Adjusted Tax Basis
Equipment	$100,000	($ 5,000)*	$ 95,000
Land	200,000		200,000
Building	150,000	(25,000)**	125,000
	$450,000	($ 30,000)	$420,000

$$* \frac{\$10{,}000 \text{ (loss attributable to equipment)}}{\$60{,}000 \text{ (total built-in loss)}} \times \$30{,}000 \text{ (net built-in loss)} = \$5{,}000 \text{ (adjustment to basis in equipment).}$$

$$** \frac{\$50{,}000 \text{ (loss attributable to building)}}{\$60{,}000 \text{ (total built-in loss)}} \times \$30{,}000 \text{ (net built-in loss)} = \$25{,}000 \text{ (adjustment to basis in building).}$$

[26] § 362(e)(2). This adjustment is determined separately for each property transferor. This adjustment also is required in the case of a contribution to capital by a shareholder.

Note the end result for Example 21:

- Charles still has a built-in loss in his stock basis. As a result, if he sells the Gold Corporation stock, he will recognize a loss of $30,000 [$420,000 (presumed selling price of the stock) − $450,000 (basis in the stock)].
- Gold Corporation can no longer recognize a loss on the sale of *all* of its assets [$420,000 (selling price based on value of assets) − $420,000 (adjusted basis in assets) = $0 (gain or loss)].

If a corporation is subject to the built-in loss adjustment, an alternative approach is available. If the shareholder and the corporation *both* elect, the shareholder reduces the basis in the corporate stock rather than the corporation's property. Given capital gain rates that generally are lower than the corporate tax rate, it is frequently desirable for the corporation and individual shareholders to elect this treatment.

Assume the same facts as in the previous example. If Charles and Gold elect, Charles can reduce his stock basis to $420,000 ($450,000 − $30,000). As a result, Gold's aggregate basis in the assets is $450,000. If Charles has no intention of selling his stock, this election could be desirable since it benefits Gold by giving the corporation a higher depreciable basis in the equipment and building.

Note the end result of Example 22:

- Charles has no built-in loss. As a result, if he sells the Gold Corporation stock, he will recognize no gain or loss [$420,000 (presumed value of the stock) − $420,000 (basis in the stock)].
- Gold Corporation has a built-in loss. As a result, if it sells *all* of its assets [$420,000 (presumed value of assets) − $450,000 (basis in assets)], Gold recognizes a loss of $30,000.

Consequently, as shown in the two previous examples, the built-in loss adjustment places the loss with *either* the shareholder or the corporation but not both.

Corporate Treatment When Stock Is Issued for Services

A corporation's transfer of its stock for property is not a taxable exchange.[27] A transfer of shares for services is also not a taxable transaction to a corporation.[28] But another issue arises: can a corporation deduct as a business expense the fair market value of the stock it issues in consideration of services? Yes, unless the services are a capital expenditure.[29]

The Big Picture

Example 23

Return to the facts of *The Big Picture* on p. 12-1. Amber transfers her $1,000,000 of property to Garden, Inc., and receives 50% of the stock. In addition, assume that Jimmy transfers property worth $800,000 (basis of $260,000) and agrees to serve as manager of the corporation for one year (services worth $200,000) for 50% of the stock.

Amber's and Jimmy's transfers qualify under § 351. Neither Amber nor Jimmy is taxed on the transfer of his or her property. However, Jimmy has ordinary income of $200,000, the value of the services he will render to Garden, Inc. Garden has a basis of $260,000 in the property it acquired from Jimmy, and it may claim a compensation expense deduction under § 162 for $200,000. Jimmy's stock basis is $460,000 [$260,000 (basis of property transferred) + $200,000 (income recognized for services rendered)].

The Big Picture

Example 24

Assume in the preceding example that Jimmy receives the Garden stock as consideration for the appreciated property and for providing legal services in organizing the corporation. The value of Jimmy's legal services is $200,000.

Jimmy has no gain on the transfer of the property but has income of $200,000 for the value of the services rendered. Garden, Inc., has a basis of $260,000 in the property it acquired from Jimmy but must now capitalize the $200,000 as an organizational expenditure. Jimmy's stock basis is $460,000 [$260,000 (basis of property transferred) + $200,000 (income recognized for services rendered)].

[27] § 1032.

[28] Reg. § 1.1032–1(a).

[29] Rev.Rul. 62–217, 1962–2 C.B. 59.

Holding Period for Shareholder and Transferee Corporation

The shareholder's holding period for stock received for a capital asset or for § 1231 property includes the holding period of the property transferred to the corporation. The holding period of the property is *tacked on* to the holding period of the stock. The holding period for stock received for any other property (e.g., cash or inventory) begins on the day after the exchange.

The corporation's holding period for property acquired in a § 351 transfer is the holding period of the transferor-shareholder regardless of the character of the property to the transferor. For instance, whether the property transferred is an ordinary asset (e.g., inventory), a § 1231 asset, or a capital asset, the corporation's holding period is the same as the transferor's.[30]

12-2f Assumption of Liabilities—§ 357

LO.4

Describe the special rules that apply when a corporation assumes shareholder liabilities.

It is not uncommon to form a corporation by transferring assets *and* liabilities of an unincorporated business. Liabilities assumed by the other party are equivalent to cash received and are treated as boot. Without a provision to the contrary, the transfer of mortgaged property to a controlled corporation could require recognition of gain by the transferor if the corporation took over the mortgage. Paying tax on this "gain" could discourage corporate formations.

For this reason, § 357(a) provides that when a corporation assumes a liability in a § 351 transaction, the liability is not treated as boot received for gain recognition purposes. (However, liabilities assumed by the corporation are treated as boot in determining the basis of the stock received.) As a result, the liabilities the corporation assumes reduce the basis of the stock the shareholder receives.

The Big Picture

Example 25

Return to the facts of *The Big Picture* on p. 12-1. Suppose that you learn that Amber's husband, Jimmy, becomes disinterested in becoming a stockholder in Garden, Inc., and that Amber's building is subject to a liability of $70,000 that Garden assumes. Consequently, Amber receives 100% of the Garden stock, is relieved of the $70,000 liability, and contributes property with an adjusted basis of $400,000 and fair market value of $1,000,000.

The exchange is tax-free under § 351 because § 357(a) precludes treating the debt relief as boot for determining recognized gain. However, the basis to Amber of the Garden stock is $330,000 [$400,000 (basis of property transferred) − $70,000 (amount of the liability assumed by Garden)].

While treating contributed debt as something other than boot seems like it should be an easy rule to apply, it creates two potential problems. The first is that shareholders might contribute debt that they only recently incurred and "pocket the cash." The shareholder might have done this innocently, or deliberately, to get some cash without

Global Tax Issues **Does § 351 Cover the Incorporation of a Foreign Business?**

When a taxpayer wants to incorporate a business overseas by moving assets across U.S. borders, the deferral mechanism of § 351 applies in certain situations, but not in others. In general, § 351 is available to defer gain recognition when starting up a new corporation outside the United States unless so-called tainted assets are involved. Under § 367, tainted assets, which include assets such as inventory and accounts receivable, are treated as having been sold by the taxpayer prior to the corporate formation; therefore, their transfer results in the current recognition of gain. The presence of tainted assets triggers gain because Congress does not want taxpayers to be able to shift the gain outside U.S. jurisdiction. The gain recognized is ordinary or capital depending on the nature of the asset involved.

[30] §§ 1223(1) and (2).

recognizing gain. The second problem arises from the stock basis calculation discussed previously: reducing the stock basis by the debt relief can result in a stock basis that is less than zero, which makes little sense. The paragraphs below discuss each of these problems and the tax law's solutions in detail.

Exception (1): Tax Avoidance or No Bona Fide Business Purpose

Code § 357(b) provides that if the principal purpose of the assumption of the liabilities is to avoid tax *or* if there is no bona fide business purpose behind the exchange, the liabilities are treated as boot. Satisfying the bona fide business purpose under § 357(b) is not difficult if the shareholder incurs the liabilities in the transferor's normal course of conducting a trade or business. But what if the shareholder borrows money shortly before transferring the property and uses the proceeds for personal purposes?[31] This type of situation is economically equivalent to the corporation transferring both stock and cash to the shareholder, resulting in boot treatment for the liabilities assumed.

Dan transfers real estate (basis of $140,000 and fair market value of $190,000) to a controlled corporation in return for stock in the corporation. Shortly before the transfer, Dan mortgages the real estate and uses the $20,000 of proceeds to meet personal obligations. Thus, along with the real estate, the mortgage is transferred to the corporation.

In this case, the assumption of the mortgage lacks a bona fide business purpose. Consequently, § 357(b) treats the debt relief as boot received, and Dan has a taxable gain on the transfer of $20,000:[32]

Stock	$ 170,000
Release of liability—treated as boot	20,000
Total amount realized	$ 190,000
Less: Basis of real estate	(140,000)
Realized gain	$ 50,000
Recognized gain	$ 20,000

The effect of the application of § 357(b) is to taint *all* liabilities transferred, even if *some* have a bona fide business purpose.

Tim, an accrual basis taxpayer, incorporates his sole proprietorship. Among the liabilities transferred to the new corporation are trade accounts payable of $100,000 and a credit card bill of $5,000. Tim had used the credit card to purchase an anniversary gift for his spouse.

Under these circumstances, § 357(b) treats *all* of the $105,000 of liabilities as boot and triggers gain recognition up to the amount of realized gain.

Exception (2): Liabilities in Excess of Basis

The second exception in § 357(c) states that if the corporation assumes shareholder liabilities that exceed the shareholder's adjusted basis of contributed property, the difference is taxable gain. Without this provision, if liabilities exceed the basis in the property exchanged, a taxpayer will have a negative basis in the stock received in the controlled corporation.[33] Section 357(c) precludes the negative basis possibility by treating the excess over basis as gain to the transferor.

[31]See, for example, *Campbell, Jr. v. Wheeler*, 65–1 USTC ¶9294, 15 AFTR 2d 578, 342 F.2d 837 (CA–5).

[32]§ 351(b).

[33]*Jack L. Easson*, 33 T.C. 963 (1960), *rev'd* in 61–2 USTC ¶9654, 8 AFTR 2d 5448, 294 F.2d 653 (CA–9).

Example 28

Andre transfers land and equipment with adjusted bases of $350,000 and $50,000, respectively, to a newly formed corporation in exchange for 100% of the stock. The corporation assumes $500,000 of liabilities on the transferred land.

Without § 357(c), Andre's basis in the stock of the new corporation would be negative $100,000 [$400,000 (bases of properties transferred) + $0 (gain recognized) − $0 (boot received) − $500,000 (liabilities assumed)].

Code § 357(c), however, causes Andre to recognize gain of $100,000 ($500,000 liabilities assumed − $400,000 bases of assets transferred). As a result, the stock has a zero basis in Andre's hands, determined as follows:

Bases in the properties transferred ($350,000 + $50,000)	$ 400,000
Plus: Gain recognized	100,000
Less: Boot received	(−0−)
Less: Liabilities assumed	(500,000)
Basis in the stock received	$ −0−

As a result, Andre recognizes $100,000 of gain and avoids a negative stock basis. Note that this result does not depend on the value of the contributed land and equipment. Andre would recognize $100,000 of gain under § 357(c) even if he realized a loss on the exchange.

The definition of liabilities under § 357(c) *excludes* obligations that would have been deductible to the transferor had those obligations been paid before the transfer. Therefore, accounts payable of a cash basis taxpayer are ignored when applying § 357(c) and in computing the shareholder's stock basis.

Tina, a cash basis taxpayer, incorporates her sole proprietorship. In return for all of the stock of the new corporation, she transfers the following items:

	Adjusted Basis	Fair Market Value
Cash	$10,000	$10,000
Unrealized accounts receivable (amounts due to Tina but not yet received by her)	−0−	40,000
Trade accounts payable	−0−	30,000
Note payable	5,000	5,000

Because uncollected accounts receivable and unpaid trade accounts payable have a zero basis for cash basis taxpayers, those taxpayers recognize no income until they collect the receivables and no deduction until they pay the accounts payable. In contrast, the note payable has a basis because it was issued for cash or other consideration.

In this situation, Tina disregards the accounts payable for determining her recognized gain and for determining her stock basis. Thus, because the balance of the note payable does not exceed the basis of the assets transferred, Tina does not have a problem of liabilities in excess of basis (i.e., the note payable of $5,000 does not exceed the aggregate basis in the cash and accounts receivable of $10,000).

If §§ 357(b) and (c) both apply to the same transfer, § 357(b) applies.[34] This could be significant because § 357(b) does not automatically create gain on the transfer, as does § 357(c). Instead, it merely converts the liability to boot. That is, § 357(b) will result in recognized gain only if there is a realized gain, while § 357(c) will always result in gain even if the overall transaction results in a realized loss. So depending on the facts, either provision could result in more or less gain than the other, as Example 30 illustrates.

[34] § 357(c)(2)(A).

Seo-Yeon owns land with a basis of $100,000 and a fair market value of $1,000,000. The land is subject to a mortgage of $300,000. One month prior to transferring the land to Robin Corporation, Seo-Yeon borrows an additional $200,000 for personal purposes and gives the lender a second mortgage on the land. Therefore, upon the incorporation, Robin Corporation issues stock worth $500,000 to Seo-Yeon and assumes the mortgages on the land.

Both § 357(b) and § 357(c) apply to the transfer. The mortgages on the property exceed the basis of the property. Thus, Seo-Yeon has a gain of $400,000 under § 357(c). Seo-Yeon borrowed $200,000 just prior to the transfer and used the loan proceeds for personal purposes. Under § 357(b), Seo-Yeon has boot of $500,000 in the amount of the liabilities, which triggers $500,000 of recognized gain. Note that *all* of the liabilities are treated as boot, not just the "tainted" $200,000 liability.

	§ 357(b) Result	§ 357(c) Result
Amount realized:		
Robin Corporation stock	$ 500,000	$ 500,000
Release of mortgage on land	300,000	300,000
Release of second mortgage—personal purposes	200,000	200,000
Total amount realized	$1,000,000	$1,000,000
Basis of land	(100,000)	(100,000)
Realized gain	$ 900,000	$ 900,000
Gain recognized under § 357(b) ($300,000 + $200,000)	$ 500,000	
Gain recognized under § 357(c) [($300,000 + $200,000) − $100,000]		$ 400,000

Unfortunately for Seo-Yeon, the relatively more onerous rule of § 357(b) dominates over § 357(c), requiring her to recognize a $500,000 gain.

Concept Summary 12.4 summarizes the tax rules that apply when liabilities are transferred in property transactions, including the special rules that apply in § 351 transactions.

Concept Summary 12.4

Tax Consequences of Liability Assumption

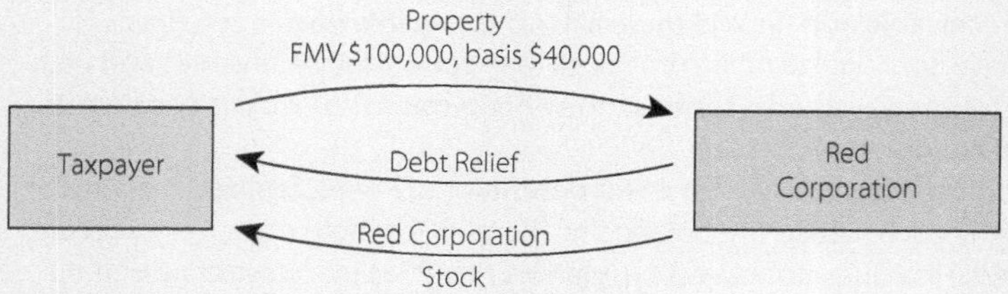

General rule: § 1001	If Red Corporation takes property subject to Taxpayer's liability or assumes Taxpayer's liability, Taxpayer is treated as having received cash due to the debt relief. Therefore, if the liability is $20,000, Taxpayer is treated as receiving Red stock of $80,000 and cash of $20,000 in a fully taxable transaction. Gain realized and recognized is $60,000.
Special rule in a § 351 transaction: § 357(a)	Assume the same facts as above, except that the transfer is a § 351 transaction. Taxpayer is not treated as receiving cash of $20,000 for gain recognition purposes (the debt relief is *not* treated as boot). Therefore, gain recognition is avoided. The debt relief will, however, reduce the Taxpayer's basis in Red Corporation stock.
Exception to § 351 transaction rule: Tax avoidance or no bona fide business purpose: § 357(b)	Assume the same facts as above, except that the transfer is a § 351 transaction and the liability does *not* have a business purpose. Taxpayer is treated as receiving cash of $20,000 for gain recognition purposes (the debt relief *is* treated as boot). Therefore, $20,000 of the realized gain is recognized.
Exception to § 351 transaction rule: Liabilities in excess of basis: § 357(c)	Assume the same facts as above, except that the transfer is a § 351 transaction, the liability is $45,000, the Red stock is worth $55,000, and § 357(b) does not apply. Taxpayer recognizes a $5,000 gain (excess of $45,000 liability over $40,000 property basis).

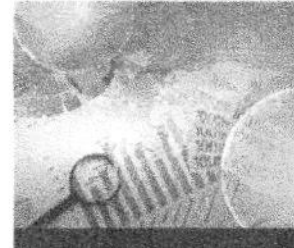

Tax Planning Strategies — Avoiding § 351

Framework Focus: Tax Rate

Strategy: Shift Net Income from High-Bracket Years to Low-Bracket Years. Control the Character of Income and Deductions.

Code § 351(a) provides for the nonrecognition of gain on transfers to controlled corporations. As such, it is often regarded as a relief provision favoring taxpayers. In some situations, however, avoiding § 351(a) may produce a more advantageous tax result. The transferors might prefer to recognize gain on the transfer of property if the tax cost is low. For example, they may be in low tax brackets or expect their tax rate to rise in the future, or the gain may be a capital gain that available capital losses could offset at no current tax cost. Recognizing gain will also lead to a stepped-up basis in the transferred property in the corporation. This higher basis can result in lower future gains and additional depreciation and amortization deductions.

Another reason a particular transferor might want to avoid § 351 concerns possible loss recognition. Recall that § 351 refers to the nonrecognition of both gains and losses. Code § 351(b)(2) specifically states: "No loss to such recipient shall be recognized." A transferor who wants to avoid gain or loss deferral has several alternatives:

- Purposely structure the contribution to fail the control test. A shareholder group that controls less than 80 percent of the corporate stock avoids § 351.
- Sell the property to the corporation for its stock. The IRS could attempt to collapse the "sale," however, by taking the approach that the transfer really falls under an earlier § 351(a) contribution.[35]
- Sell the property to the corporation for other property or boot. Because the transferor receives no stock, § 351 is inapplicable.
- Transfer the property to the corporation in return for its debt or for nonqualified preferred stock. Recall that § 351 does not apply to a transferor who receives corporate debt or nonqualified preferred stock. In both this and the previous alternatives, watch for the possible disallowance of the loss under the related-party rules.

The deferral provisions in § 351 effectively transfer gains and some losses from shareholders to the corporation. This can increase or decrease future corporate tax liabilities. That is, transferring a gain asset creates a deferred tax liability for the corporation, but transferring a loss asset creates a deferred tax asset. Shareholders could justifiably consider this in determining the number of shares granted, even if the properties transferred have the same fair market value.

Iris and Ivan form Wren Corporation with the following investments: property by Iris (basis of $40,000 and fair market value of $50,000) and property by Ivan (basis of $60,000 and fair market value of $50,000). Each receives 50% of the Wren stock. Has Ivan acted wisely in settling for only 50% of the stock?

At first, it would appear so because Iris and Ivan each invested property of the same value ($50,000). But what about tax considerations? By applying the general carryover basis rules, the corporation now has a basis of $40,000 in Iris's property and $60,000 in Ivan's property. In essence, Iris has shifted a possible $10,000 gain to the corporation, while Ivan has transferred a $10,000 potential loss. Thus, an equitable allocation of the Wren stock would call for Ivan to receive a greater percentage interest than Iris would receive.

This issue is further complicated by the special basis adjustment required when a shareholder such as Ivan contributes property with a built-in loss to a corporation. (See the discussion of this basis adjustment for loss property in the next section.) In this situation, if Wren is to take a carryover basis in Ivan's property, Ivan must reduce his stock basis by the $10,000 built-in loss. This reduced stock basis, of course, could lead to a greater tax burden on Ivan when he sells the Wren stock. This may suggest additional support for Ivan having a greater percentage interest than Iris has.

[35] *U.S. v. Hertwig*, 68–2 USTC ¶9495, 22 AFTR 2d 5249, 398 F.2d 452 (CA–5).

12-2g Recapture Considerations

The depreciation recapture rules do not apply to a § 351 transfer to a controlled corporation (unless the shareholder receives boot).[36] Instead, any recapture potential of the property carries over to the corporation as it steps into the shoes of the transferor-shareholder for purposes of basis determination. However, to the extent gain is recognized, the recapture rules apply. These rules prevent taxpayers from converting ordinary income into § 1231 gain by transferring the property to a controlled corporation.

Paul transfers equipment (adjusted basis of $30,000, original cost of $120,000, and fair market value of $100,000) to a controlled corporation in return for stock. If Paul had sold the equipment, it would have yielded a gain of $70,000, all of which would have been treated as ordinary income under the § 1245 depreciation recapture rules.

If the transfer qualifies for § 351 treatment, Paul has no recognized gain and no depreciation to recapture. If the corporation later disposes of the equipment in a taxable transaction, it must take into account the § 1245 recapture potential originating with Paul. So, for example, if the corporation were to sell the asset shortly after incorporation for $100,000, all of the $70,000 gain recognized would be given ordinary treatment because of the depreciation recapture rules.

Alternatively, if Paul had received boot of $60,000 on the transfer, all of the recognized gain would have been recaptured as ordinary income. The remaining $30,000 ($90,000 − $60,000) of recapture potential would have carried over to the corporation.

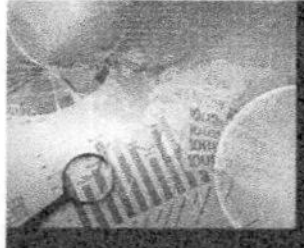

Tax Planning Strategies

Other Considerations When Incorporating a Business

Framework Focus: Tax Rate

Strategy: Control the Character of Income and Deductions.
Shift Net Income from High-Bracket Taxpayers to Low-Bracket Taxpayers.

Framework Focus: Deductions

Strategy: Maximize Deductible Amounts.

Framework Focus: Income and Exclusions

Strategy: Avoid Income Recognition.

When a business is incorporated, the organizers must determine which assets and liabilities should be transferred to the corporation. A transfer of assets that produces passive income (rents, royalties, dividends, and interest) can cause the corporation to be a personal holding company in a tax year when operating income is low. Thus, the corporation could be subject to the personal holding company penalty tax (see the discussion in Chapter 13).

A transfer of the accounts payable of a cash basis taxpayer may prevent the organizer from taking a tax deduction if the accounts are paid by the corporation. Therefore, the parties should decide who will receive the greatest benefit from the deduction and then plan accordingly.

Leasing property to the corporation may be a more attractive alternative than transferring ownership. Leasing provides the taxpayer with the opportunity of withdrawing money from the corporation in a deductible form without the payment being characterized as a nondeductible dividend. If the property is donated to a family member in a lower tax bracket, the lease income can be shifted as well. If the depreciation and other deductions available in connection with the property are larger than the lease income, a high-tax-rate taxpayer could retain the property until the income exceeds the deductions.

continued

[36] §§ 1245(b)(3) and 1250(d)(3).

The Big Picture

Example 33

Return to the facts of *The Big Picture* on p. 12-1. If Amber decides to retain the $50,000 of cash basis accounts receivable rather than transfer them to the newly formed Garden, Inc., she will recognize $50,000 of ordinary income upon their collection.

Alternatively, if the receivables are transferred to Garden as the facts suggest, the corporation will recognize the ordinary income as the receivables are collected. However, a subsequent corporate distribution to Amber of the cash collected could be subject to double taxation as a dividend (see Chapter 13 for further discussion). Given the alternatives available, Amber needs to evaluate which approach is better for the parties involved.

Another way to shift income to other taxpayers is by using corporate debt. Shareholder debt in a corporation can be given to family members with low marginal tax rates. This technique also shifts income without a loss of control of the corporation.

12-3 Capital Structure of a Corporation

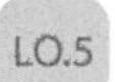

LO.5

Explain the tax aspects of the capital structure of a corporation.

Shareholders can form or expand a corporation using equity financing, debt financing, or a combination of the two. Evaluating the relative tax and nontax advantages and disadvantages of these two basic elements in the capital structure of a corporation can help the corporation decide how to finance its activities.

12-3a Capital Contributions

Corporations recognize no gain or loss when they issue shares of stock (including treasury stock) for money or property.[37] This is also true for voluntary or required shareholder contributions of money or property when the corporation issues no shares in return. The **capital contributions** represent an additional price paid for the shares held by the shareholders and are treated as additions to the capital of the corporation.[38]

In addition, corporations sometimes receive assets from *nonshareholders*. If a civic or government entity contributes property to a corporation to induce the corporation to locate in a particular community, the contributions are not tax-free capital contributions. Instead, the corporation includes these contributions in the corporation's gross income and takes a fair market value basis in the assets.[39] However, a governmental tax abatement granted to a corporation for locating in the jurisdiction is not taxable. The abatement just reduces future payments and related deductions for state and local taxes and is therefore ignored when granted.

Example 34

A city donates land worth $400,000 to Teal Corporation as an inducement for Teal to locate in the city. The city also agrees to reduce the standard real estate tax rate for Teal by 50% on newly constructed property in the city.

The receipt of the land produces $400,000 of gross income to Teal, and the land's basis to the corporation is $400,000. However, the real estate tax abatement is not taxable to Teal.

A corporation recognizes income if a nonshareholder (a customer or potential customer) contributes assets to a corporation, regardless of how the corporation labels these contributions. Further, a corporation must recognize income if a nonshareholder transfers property to a corporation in exchange for goods or services.

[37] § 1032.

[38] § 118 and Reg. § 1.118–1.

[39] Reg. § 1.118–1. See also *Teleservice Co. of Wyoming Valley*, 27 T.C. 722 (1957), *aff'd* in 58–1 USTC ¶9383, 1 AFTR 2d 1249, 254 F.2d 105 (CA–3), *cert. den.* 78 S.Ct. 1360 (1958).

A cable television company charges its customers an initial fee to hook up to a new cable system installed in the area. These payments are used to finance the total cost of constructing the cable company's infrastructure. The customers will make monthly payments for the cable service.

The initial payments are used for capital expenditures, but they represent payments for services to be rendered by the cable company. As such, they are taxable income and are not contributions to capital.

Characterize the tax differences between debt and equity investments.

12-3b Debt in the Capital Structure

Various tax and nontax characteristics of debt and equity are relevant when developing the capital structure of a corporation. The relative amounts of debt and equity are a strategic variable for the corporation.

Advantages of Debt

The advantages of issuing long-term debt are numerous. Interest on debt is deductible by the corporation, but dividend payments are not.[40] Further, the shareholders are not taxed on debt repayments unless the repayments exceed basis. In contrast, property distributions from a corporation to its shareholders are not tax-free if the corporation has earnings and profits (see text Section 4-4b and Chapter 13). The tax law taxes these distributions as dividends to the extent of the corporation's earnings and profits.

Another distinction between debt and equity relates to the taxation of dividend and interest income. Individual shareholders enjoy taxation of dividend income at long-term capital gain tax rates. However, shareholders pay tax on interest income at the shareholder's ordinary income tax rates.

Wade transfers cash of $100,000 to a newly formed corporation for 100% of its stock. In its initial year, the corporation has net income and "earnings and profits" of $40,000. If the corporation distributes $7,500 to Wade, the distribution is a taxable dividend to Wade with no corresponding deduction to the corporation.

Assume, instead, that Wade transfers to the corporation cash of $50,000 for stock. In addition, he lends the corporation $50,000. The note is payable in equal annual installments of $5,000 and bears interest at the rate of 5%. At the end of the year, the corporation pays Wade interest of $2,500 ($50,000 × 5%) and a note repayment of $5,000. The interest payment is taxable to Wade and a deductible expense to the corporation. The $5,000 principal repayment on the loan is neither taxed to Wade nor deductible by the corporation.

Based on current tax rates, the table below computes the after-tax impact on Wade and the corporation under each alternative. For both Wade and the corporation, the better outcome occurs when the distribution is comprised of a note repayment and interest. That is, the after-tax income to Wade is higher, and the after-tax cost to the corporation is lower, under the debt scenario.

	If the Distribution Is	
	$7,500 Dividend	**$5,000 Note Repayment and $2,500 Interest**
*After-tax benefit to Wade**		
[$7,500 × (1 − 15%)]	$6,375	
{$5,000 + [$2,500 × (1 − 35%)]}		$6,625
After-tax cost to corporation		
No deduction to corporation	$7,500	
{$5,000 + [$2,500 × (1 − 21%)]}		$6,975

*Assumes that Wade's dividend income is taxed at the 15% capital gains rate and that his interest income is taxed at the 35% ordinary income rate.

[40] However, § 163(j) limits business interest deductions to business interest income plus 30% of taxable income (see discussion that follows).

Reclassification of Debt as Equity (Thin Capitalization Problem)

The tax and nontax advantages of debt create incentives for taxpayers to classify equity as debt. It is unlikely that a bank would loan money to a corporation that has little or no shareholder investment. However, shareholders could make it look like they are "loaning" money to the corporation instead of contributing additional equity just to obtain the tax advantages of debt. This is called a **"thin capitalization"** problem in which a corporation appears to have artificially low equity and high debt.

When the IRS concludes that a corporation is thinly capitalized, the IRS reclassifies some or all debt as equity and denies the corporation the tax advantages of debt financing. That is, the government can treat the debt as stock for tax purposes if the debt has too many equity-like features. This will result in treating principal and deductible interest payments as nondeductible dividends. However, now that individual rates are higher (up to 37 percent) than corporate rates (21 percent), the IRS may be less inclined to raise this issue because the conversion of interest income to dividend income could produce a tax benefit to individual investors that outweighs the tax cost of nondeductible dividends.

Code § 385 lists several factors that the IRS uses to determine whether a debtor-creditor relationship or a shareholder-corporation relationship exists. Until recently, taxpayers have had to rely solely on numerous judicial decisions to determine whether a true debtor-creditor relationship exists. In late 2016, the Treasury Department released regulations under § 385 that seek to curb thin capitalization of closely held corporations.[41] However, some tax professionals assert that these rules have not answered important questions. As a result, the long line of judicial decisions establishing key guidelines and principles are likely to have continuing relevance. Together, Congress, the Treasury Department, and the courts identify the following factors as important characteristics in distinguishing between debt and equity:

- Whether the debt instrument is in proper form. An open account advance is more easily characterized as a contribution to capital than a loan evidenced by a properly written note executed by the shareholder.[42]
- Whether the debt instrument bears a reasonable rate of interest and has a definite maturity date. When a shareholder advance does not provide for interest, the return expected is that inherent in an equity interest (e.g., a share of the profits or an increase in the value of the shares).[43] Likewise, a lender unrelated to the corporation will usually be unwilling to commit funds to the corporation for an indefinite period of time (i.e., no definite due date).
- Whether the debt is paid on a timely basis. A lender's failure to insist upon timely repayment (or satisfactory renegotiation) indicates that the return sought does not depend upon interest income and the repayment of principal.
- Whether payment is contingent on earnings. A lender ordinarily will not advance funds that are likely to be repaid only if the venture is successful.
- Whether the debt is subordinated to other liabilities. Subordination tends to reduce a significant characteristic of the creditor-debtor relationship. Creditors should have the right to share with other general creditors in the event of the corporation's dissolution or liquidation. Subordination also destroys another basic attribute of creditor status—the power to demand payment at a fixed maturity date.[44]
- Whether holdings of debt and stock are proportionate (e.g., each shareholder owns the same percentages of debt and stock). When debt and equity obligations are held in the same proportion, shareholders are, apart from tax considerations, indifferent as to whether corporate distributions are in the form of interest or dividends.

[41]See final and temporary Reg. §§ 1.385–1 to –4T (T.D. 9790).

[42]*Estate of Mixon, Jr. v. U.S.*, 72–2 USTC ¶9537, 30 AFTR 2d 72–5094, 464 F.2d 394 (CA–5).

[43]*Slappey Drive Industrial Park v. U.S.*, 77–2 USTC ¶9696, 40 AFTR 2d 77–5940, 561 F.2d 572 (CA–5).

[44]*Fin Hay Realty Co. v. U.S.*, 68–2 USTC ¶9438, 22 AFTR 2d 5004, 398 F.2d 694 (CA–3).

- Whether funds loaned to the corporation are used to finance initial operations or capital asset acquisitions. Funds used to finance initial operations or to acquire capital assets the corporation needs to operate are generally obtained through equity investments.
- Whether the corporation has a high ratio of shareholder debt to shareholder equity. Thin capitalization indicates that the corporation lacks reserves to pay interest and principal on debt when corporate income is insufficient to meet current needs.[45] In determining a corporation's debt-equity ratio, courts look at the relation of the debt both to the book value of the corporation's assets and to their fair market value.[46]

Code § 385 gives the IRS the authority to classify an instrument either as *wholly* debt or equity or as *part* debt and *part* equity. This flexible approach is important because it is sometimes difficult to classify some instruments either wholly as stock or wholly as debt. Because the principles above are relevant mainly for closely held corporations, a partial debt, partial equity approach also provides the IRS with a better avenue to address these issues in publicly traded corporations.

LO.7

List and apply the tax rules unique to computing corporate taxable income.

12-4 Taxing Corporate Operations

The rules related to gross income, deductions, and losses discussed in previous chapters of this text generally apply to corporations. However, corporations face unique limitations on certain deductions. Conversely, corporations can deduct certain items not generally available to other entities. This section discusses these special rules regarding the determination of the corporate income tax liability.

12-4a Deductions Available Only to Corporations

Certain deductions are specific to corporate taxpayers. These provisions include the dividends received deduction and the organizational expenditures deduction.

Dividends Received Deduction

The purpose of the **dividends received deduction** is to mitigate multiple taxation of corporate income. Without the deduction, dividends paid between corporations could be subject to several levels of tax. For example, suppose that Corporation A is owned by Corporation B and that individuals own Corporation B. If Corporation A pays Corporation B a dividend and B passes the dividend on to its shareholders, the dividend is taxable to Corporation B and Corporation B's shareholders. In addition, Corporation A had already paid tax on the business income that resulted in the dividend paid to Corporation B. Thus, three levels of tax resulted in this example. The dividends received deduction alleviates this inequity by reducing or eliminating the dividend income taxable to corporations that receive dividends from other corporations.

As Exhibit 12.4 illustrates, the amount of the dividends received deduction depends on the percentage of ownership (voting power and value) the recipient corporate shareholder holds in a *domestic corporation* making the dividend distribution. So if one corporation owns 30 percent of the stock of another corporation, the dividends received deduction percentage is 65 percent, resulting in taxation of the other 35 percent of the dividend.[47]

The dividends received deduction cannot exceed a taxable income limitation that equals the corporation's taxable income multiplied by the dividends received deduction percentage. Thus, if a corporate shareholder owns less than 20 percent of the stock in the distributing corporation, the dividends received deduction is limited to 50 percent of taxable income if that amount is less than 50 percent of the dividends received. For this purpose, taxable income is computed without regard to the net operating loss

[45] A court held that a debt-equity ratio of approximately 14.6:1 was not excessive. See *Tomlinson v. 1661 Corp.*, 67–1 USTC ¶9438, 19 AFTR 2d 1413, 377 F.2d 291 (CA–5). A 26:1 ratio was found acceptable in *Delta Plastics, Inc.*, 85 TCM 940, T.C.Memo. 2003–54.

[46] In *Bauer v. Comm.*, 84–2 USTC ¶9996, 55 AFTR 2d 85–433, 748 F.2d 1365 (CA–9), a debt-equity ratio of 92:1 resulted when book value was used. But the ratio ranged from 2:1 to 8:1 when equity included both paid-in capital and accumulated earnings.

[47] § 243(a). Dividends from foreign corporations generally do not qualify for a dividends received deduction. But see §§ 245 and 245A.

Exhibit 12.4 Dividends Received Deduction

Percentage of Ownership by Corporate Shareholder	Deduction Percentage
Less than 20%	50%
20% or more (but less than 80%)	65%
80% or more*	100%

*The payor corporation must be a member of an affiliated group with the recipient corporation.

(NOL) deduction, the dividends received deduction, and any capital loss carryback. In a somewhat counterintuitive exception, however, the taxable income limitation *does not apply* if the corporation has an NOL for the current taxable year.[48]

The following steps are useful in the computation of the deduction:

1. Multiply the dividends received by the deduction percentage (See Exhibit 12.4.).
2. Multiply the taxable income by the same deduction percentage.
3. The deduction is limited to the lesser of Step 1 or Step 2, unless deducting the amount derived in Step 1 results in an NOL. If it does, the amount derived in Step 1 is used. This is referred to as the *NOL exception*.

Example 37

Red, White, and Blue Corporations, three unrelated calendar year corporations, report the following information for the year:

	Red Corporation	White Corporation	Blue Corporation
Gross income from operations	$ 400,000	$ 320,000	$ 230,000
Expenses from operations	(340,000)	(340,000)	(340,000)
Dividends received from domestic corporations (less than 20% ownership)	200,000	200,000	200,000
Taxable income before the dividends received deduction	$ 260,000	$ 180,000	$ 90,000

In determining the dividends received deduction, use the three-step procedure described above.

	Red	White	Blue
Step 1 (50% × $200,000)	$100,000	$100,000	$100,000
Step 2			
50% × $260,000 (taxable income)	$130,000		
50% × $180,000 (taxable income)		$ 90,000	
50% × $90,000 (taxable income)			$ 45,000
Step 3			
Lesser of Step 1 or Step 2	$100,000	$ 90,000	
Step 1 amount results in an NOL			$100,000

Only White Corporation is subject to the 50% of taxable income limitation (Step 2). The NOL exception does not apply because subtracting $100,000 (Step 1) from $180,000 (taxable income before the dividends received deduction) does not yield a negative figure. Blue Corporation qualifies under the NOL exception because subtracting $100,000 (Step 1) from $90,000 (taxable income before the dividends received deduction) yields a negative figure. Thus, Blue Corporation can deduct the entire dividends received deduction while White Corporation cannot.

In summary, each corporation has a dividends received deduction for the year as follows: $100,000 for Red Corporation, $90,000 for White Corporation, and $100,000 for Blue Corporation.

[48]Further, the limitation does not apply in the case of the 100% deduction available to members of an affiliated group. § 246(b)(2).

Corporations can take a dividends received deduction only if the corporation has held the stock for more than 45 days.[49] Congress enacted this restriction to close a tax loophole involving dividends on stock that is held only briefly. When stock is purchased shortly before a dividend record date and soon thereafter sold ex-dividend, a capital loss corresponding to the amount of the dividend often results (ignoring other market valuation changes). If the dividends received deduction was allowed in such cases, the capital loss resulting from the stock sale would exceed the taxable portion of the related dividend income and produce a net tax *benefit* from the dividend.

On October 1, 2022, Pink Corporation declares a $1 per share dividend for shareholders of record as of November 1, 2022, and payable on December 1, 2022. Black Corporation purchases 10,000 shares of Pink stock on October 28, 2022, for $25,000 and sells those 10,000 shares ex-dividend on November 4, 2022, for $15,000. (This example assumes no fluctuation in the market price of the Pink stock other than from paying the dividend.) The sale results in a short-term capital loss of $10,000 ($15,000 amount realized − $25,000 basis). On December 1, Black receives a $10,000 dividend from Pink.

Without the holding period restriction, Black Corporation would recognize a $10,000 deduction (subject to the capital loss limitation) but only $5,000 of income [$10,000 dividend − $5,000 dividends received deduction ($10,000 × 50%)], or a $5,000 net loss. However, because Black did not hold the Pink stock for more than 45 days, Black cannot claim a dividends received deduction.

Additional information on the DRD can be found on this book's companion website: www.cengage.com

Organizational Expenditures Deduction

Expenses incurred in connection with the organization of a corporation normally are capitalized because they benefit the corporation during its life. But over what period should corporations amortize their organizational expenses? Taxpayers ordinarily cannot deduct amortization expenses if they cannot estimate a useful life for the organizational costs, and corporations have an indefinite life. Congress enacted § 248 to solve this problem for corporations.

Under § 248, a corporation may *elect* to deduct the first $5,000 of **organizational expenditures** and amortize any remaining expenditures over the 180-month period beginning with the month in which the corporation begins business.[50] Section 248 also requires corporations to reduce the immediate deduction dollar for dollar when total organizational expenditures exceed $50,000. Organizational expenditures include:

- Legal and accounting services related to organizing the corporation (e.g., drafts of the corporate charter and bylaws, minutes of organizational meetings, and terms of original stock certificates).
- Expenses of temporary directors and of organizational meetings of directors or shareholders.
- Fees paid to the state of incorporation.

Expenditures that *do not qualify* as organizational expenditures include those connected with issuing or selling shares of stock or other securities (e.g., commissions, professional fees, and printing costs) or with expenditures to transfer assets to a corporation. These expenditures reduce the amount of capital raised and are not deductible.

[49]The stock must be held more than 45 days during the 91-day period beginning on the date that is 45 days before the ex-dividend date (or in the case of preferred stock, more than 90 days during the 181-day period beginning on the date that is 90 days before the ex-dividend date). § 246(c).

[50]The month in which a corporation begins business may not be obvious. Ordinarily, a corporation begins business when it starts the business operations for which it was organized. Reg. § 1.248–1(d). For a similar problem in the Subchapter S area, see Chapter 15.

Example 39

Stork Corporation (a calendar year C corporation) began business on July 1 of the current year and incurred $52,000 of organizational expenditures. Stork wants to expense as much of these expenditures as possible, electing to amortize any amount it cannot expense. Stork's current-year deduction is $4,633, determined as follows:

Immediate expense [$5,000 − ($52,000 − $50,000)]	$3,000
Amortization [($52,000 − $3,000) ÷ 180] × 6 months in tax year	1,633
Total	$4,633

To qualify for the election, the expenditure must be *incurred* before the end of the tax year in which the corporation begins business. In this regard, the corporation's method of accounting is of no consequence. Thus, an expense incurred by a cash basis corporation in its first tax year qualifies even though the expense is not paid until a subsequent year.

A corporation is assumed to have elected to deduct and amortize organizational expenditures for the taxable year in which it begins business. A corporation can forgo the election by capitalizing its organizational expenditures on a timely filed return for its first taxable year. In that case, the corporation deducts the capitalized organizational costs when it ceases to do business and liquidates.

Example 40

Black Corporation, an accrual basis, calendar year taxpayer, was formed and began operations on April 1, 2022. The following expenses were incurred during its first year of operations (April 1–December 31, 2022):

Expenses of temporary directors and of organizational meetings	$15,500
Fee paid to the state of incorporation	2,000
Accounting services incident to organization	18,000
Legal services for drafting the corporate charter and bylaws	32,000
Expenses incident to the printing and sale of stock certificates	48,000

Black Corporation elects to amortize the $67,500 of organizational costs under § 248. Because of the dollar cap (i.e., dollar-for-dollar reduction for amounts in excess of $50,000), none of the $5,000 expensing allowance is available. The monthly amortization is $375 [($15,500 + $2,000 + $18,000 + $32,000) ÷ 180 months], and $3,375 ($375 × 9 months) is deductible for tax year 2022.

Note that the $48,000 of expenses incident to the printing and sale of stock certificates does not qualify for the election. Black Corporation must capitalize these expenses as a reduction of paid-in capital.

Organizational expenditures differ from *startup expenditures*.[51] Startup expenditures include various investigation expenses involved in entering a new business (e.g., travel, market surveys, financial audits, and legal fees) and operating expenses such as rent and payroll that are incurred by a corporation before it actually begins to produce any gross income. Taxpayers can elect to deduct startup expenditures in the same manner as organizational expenditures. So corporations can deduct up to $5,000 (subject to the phaseout for startup expenditures that exceed $50,000) and any remaining amounts amortized over a period of 180 months. The deduction occurs and the amortization deductions begin in the month and year in which the corporation begins business. The same rules that apply to organizational expenditures also apply to startup expenditures. This means that taxpayers can deduct up to $5,000 of organizational expenditures (and amortize the rest) and do the same for startup expenditures.

12-4b Business Interest Expense Limitation

A limitation on the deduction for business interest applies to certain taxpayers.[52] Business interest is interest paid or accrued on trade or business debt. Although the limitation applies to any business, the rules are most likely to affect large corporations and flow-through entities due to a small business exception.

[51] § 195. The deduction for startup expenditures is also available to noncorporate taxpayers.

[52] § 163(j).

Tax Planning Strategies **Organizational Expenditures**

Framework Focus: Deductions

Strategy: Maximize Deductible Amounts.

To qualify for the 180-month amortization procedure of § 248, only organizational expenditures incurred in the first taxable year of the corporation can be considered. This rule could prove to be an unfortunate trap for corporations formed late in the year.

Thrush Corporation is formed in December 2021. Qualified organizational expenditures are incurred as follows: $62,000 in December 2021 and $30,000 in January 2022. If Thrush uses the calendar year for tax purposes, only $62,000 of the organizational expenditures qualify for amortization.

One solution to the problem posed by this example may be for Thrush Corporation to adopt a fiscal year that ends on or beyond January 31. All organizational expenditures will then have been incurred before the close of the first tax year. Alternatively, the corporation could wait until January 2022 to be formed.

Under § 163(j), the deduction for business interest for any year is limited to the sum of:

1. The taxpayer's *business interest income* for the year and
2. 30 percent of the taxpayer's *adjusted taxable income* for the year.

Any business interest deduction disallowed by reason of the limitation is treated as business interest paid or accrued in the succeeding tax year. The carryforward period is unlimited.

The business interest deduction limitation does not apply to certain small businesses. In general, the small business exception applies to taxpayers with average gross receipts for the prior three-year period of $26 million or less.

Business Interest Income

"Business interest income" is the amount of interest income includible in gross income for the year that relates to a trade or business. Congress believes that a corporation typically will have neither investment interest income nor investment interest expense; instead, Congress assumes that all corporate interest income and interest expense relates to the corporation's trade or business.[53]

Adjusted Taxable Income

"Adjusted taxable income"[54] is taxable income computed without regard to:

1. Any nonbusiness income, gain, deduction, or loss;
2. Any business interest or business interest income;
3. Any net operating loss (NOL) deduction;
4. Any deduction for qualified business income (§ 199A); and
5. Any deduction allowable for depreciation, amortization, or depletion.[55]

[53]TCJA of 2017 Joint Explanatory Statement, p. 288. The Joint Explanatory Statement relies on the rationale that since § 163(d)—the investment interest expense limitation—does not apply to corporations, any interest income and interest expense should relate to the corporation's trade or business activities (not investment activities).

[54]§ 163(j)(8)(A).

[55]The depreciation, amortization, and depletion adjustment only applies to taxable years beginning before January 1, 2022; § 163(j)(8)(A)(v).

The Treasury Department and the IRS are authorized to provide other adjustments to the computation of adjusted taxable income.[56] The 30 percent of adjusted taxable income amount cannot be less than zero.[57]

Business Interest Expense Limitation

In 2021, Tangerine Corporation, a calendar year C corporation, has $5,000,000 of adjusted taxable income, $75,000 of business interest income, and $600,000 of business interest expense.

Tangerine's business interest deduction limitation is $1,575,000 [$75,000 (business interest income) + $1,500,000 (30% × $5,000,000 adjusted taxable income)]. As a result, Tangerine can deduct all $600,000 of its business interest expense.

Assume the same facts as in Example 42, except that Tangerine has $2,000,000 of business interest expense. Here, the deduction for business interest is limited to $1,575,000, and the disallowed amount of $425,000 ($2,000,000 − $1,575,000) is carried forward to next year and treated as business interest in that year.

If Tangerine satisfies the small business exception (i.e., had average gross receipts for the prior three-year period of $26,000,000 or less, which is the small business threshold for 2021), the limitation on business interest does not apply and the entire $2,000,000 of business interest is deductible in the current year.

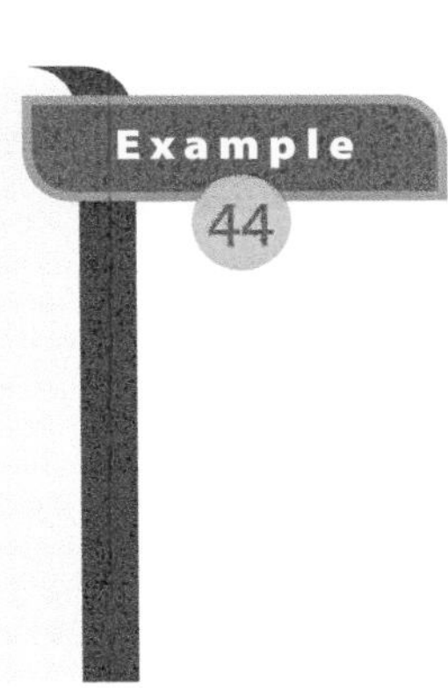

In 2022, Eagle Corporation, a calendar year C corporation, has ($1,000,000) of adjusted taxable income, $40,000 of business interest income, and $100,000 of business interest expense.

Eagle's business interest deduction limitation is $40,000 [$40,000 (business interest income) + $0 (30% × adjusted taxable income amount, but not less than zero)]. As a result, Eagle's current-year deduction for business interest is limited to $40,000, and the disallowed amount of $60,000 ($100,000 − $40,000) is carried forward to next year and treated as business interest in that year.

If Eagle satisfies the small business exception (i.e., had average gross receipts for the prior three-year period of $27,000,000 or less, which is the small business threshold for 2022), the limitation on business interest does not apply and the entire $100,000 of business interest is deductible in the current year.

Other Rules

Flow-Through Entities In the case of a partnership or S corporation, the business interest deduction limitation applies at the entity level. The general carryforward rule for disallowed business interest does not apply to partnerships (or S corporations); rather, a partner or S corporation shareholder can deduct the disallowed interest under a special carryforward rule. A partner's (or S corporation shareholder's) adjusted taxable income is determined without regard to the partner's (or shareholder's) distributive share of the partnership's (or S corporation's) items of income, gain, deduction, or loss.[58]

[56] § 163(j)(8)(B).
[57] § 163(j)(1), flush language.
[58] § 163(j)(4).

Trade or Business The term *trade or business* does not include performing services as an employee.[59] As a result, an individual cannot include W–2 wages in adjusted taxable income for purposes of computing the interest deduction limitation. The term also does not include certain real property trades or businesses and certain farming businesses.

LO.8

Compute the corporate income tax.

12-4c Determining the Corporate Income Tax Liability

Corporate income tax rates have fluctuated over the years. The current top statutory corporate income tax rate was reduced from 46 percent to 35 percent over 30 years ago. The U.S. corporate income tax rate is a flat 21 percent for tax years beginning after 2017 (including for PSCs).

The Big Picture

Example 45

Return to the facts of *The Big Picture* on p. 12-1. Assume that Amber incorporates her business as a calendar year C corporation and that it has taxable income of $51,500. The corporation's income tax liability is $10,815 ($51,500 × 21%).

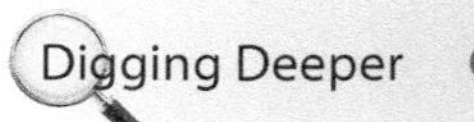

Digging Deeper 6

Important information on controlled groups can be found on this book's companion website: www.cengage.com

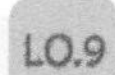

LO.9

Describe the reporting process for corporations.

12-5 Procedural Matters

This section covers various aspects of the corporate income tax return, including filing requirements, estimated tax payments, and special disclosure schedules on the return.

12-5a Filing Requirements for Corporations

A corporation must file a Federal income tax return (Form 1120) whether or not it has taxable income. A corporation that did not exist during an entire annual accounting period must file a return for the portion of the year it existed. In addition, a corporation must file a return even though it has ceased to do business if it has valuable claims for which it will bring suit. A corporation is relieved of filing income tax returns only when it ceases to do business and retains no assets.[60]

The due date for Form 1120 is on or before the fifteenth day of the fourth month following the close of a corporation's tax year.[61] Corporations with assets of $10 million or more generally must file electronically. A C corporation, other than a personal service corporation, can use either a calendar year or a fiscal year to report its taxable income. The tax year of the shareholders has no effect on the corporation's tax year.

[59] § 163(j)(7).

[60] § 6012(a)(2) and Reg. § 1.6012–2(a).

[61] § 6072(a). A corporation with a June 30 year-end must file a Form 1120 by the fifteenth day of the *third* month following the close of its fiscal year through 2025 [P.L. 114–41, § 2006(a)(3)(B)]. If the due date falls on a Saturday, Sunday, or legal holiday, the due date is the next business day.

12-5b **Estimated Tax Payments**

A corporation must make payments of estimated tax unless it reasonably expects its tax liability will be less than $500. The required annual payment is the *lesser* of:

- 100 percent of the corporation's tax for the current year, or
- 100 percent of the tax for the preceding year (if that was a 12-month tax year, the return filed showed a tax liability, and the corporation's taxable income was less than $1 million in each of the last three tax years).

Corporations make estimated payments in four installments due on or before the fifteenth day of the fourth month, the sixth month, the ninth month, and the twelfth month of the corporate taxable year.[62] The full amount of the unpaid tax is due on the due date of the return without regard to extensions. A corporation failing to pay its required estimated tax payments will be subjected to a nondeductible penalty on the amount by which the installments are less than the tax due.

12-5c **Schedule M–1—Reconciliation of Income (Loss) per Books with Income per Return**

Schedule M–1 of Form 1120 is a schedule that *reconciles* financial accounting net income or loss with taxable income reported on the corporation's income tax return by listing the corporation's book-tax differences. The purpose of this schedule is to list the differences between financial accounting net income and Federal taxable income. Schedule M–1 is used by corporations with less than $10 million of total assets.

The starting point on Schedule M–1 is net income (loss) per books. Corporations enter additions and subtractions for items that affect financial accounting net income and taxable income differently. The following items are entered as *additions* to financial accounting income (see lines 2 through 5 of Schedule M–1):

- Federal income tax expense per books (subtracted in computing net income per books but not deductible in computing taxable income).
- The excess of capital losses over capital gains (subtracted for financial accounting purposes but not deductible by corporations for income tax purposes).
- Income that is reported in the current year for tax purposes but is not reported in computing net income per books (e.g., prepaid income).
- Various other expenses that reduce net income per books but are not deducted in computing taxable income (e.g., charitable contributions in excess of the 10 percent ceiling applicable to corporations).

The following *subtractions* are entered on lines 7 and 8 of Schedule M–1.

- Income reported for financial accounting purposes but excluded from taxable income (e.g., tax-exempt interest).
- Deductions taken on the tax return but not expensed in computing net income per books (e.g., tax depreciation in excess of financial accounting depreciation).

The result of combining net income with these additions and subtractions is taxable income (before the NOL deduction and the dividends received deduction). Concept Summary 12.5 provides a conceptual diagram of Schedule M–1.

[62] § 6655. If the due date falls on a Saturday, Sunday, or legal holiday, the due date is the next business day. See § 6655(g)(2) for the definition of a *large corporation*.

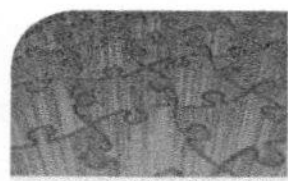

Concept Summary 12.5

Conceptual Diagram of Schedule M–1 (Form 1120)

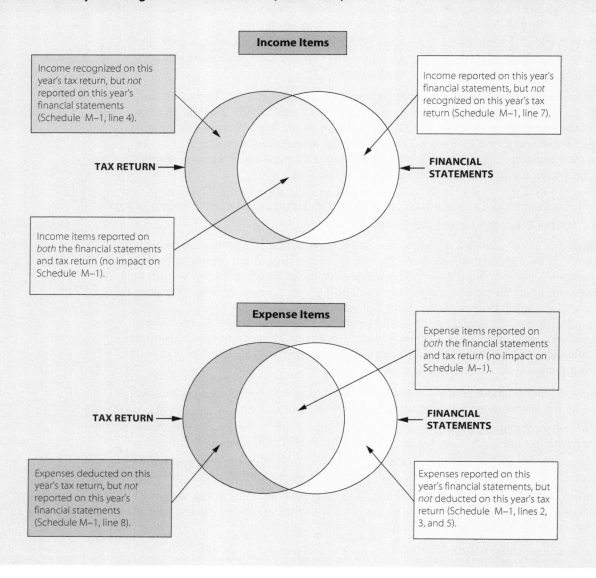

Example 46

During the current year, Tern Corporation had the following transactions:

Net income per books (after tax)	$89,400
Taxable income	50,000
Federal income tax expense per books	10,500
Interest income from tax-exempt bonds	5,000
Interest paid on loan, the proceeds of which were used to purchase the tax-exempt bonds	500
Life insurance proceeds received as a result of the death of a key employee	50,000
Premiums paid on key employee life insurance policy	2,600
Excess of capital losses over capital gains	2,000

continued

For book and tax purposes, Tern Corporation determines depreciation under the straight-line method. Tern's Schedule M–1 for the current year is constructed as follows:

Schedule M-1 Reconciliation of Income (Loss) per Books With Income per Return
Note: The corporation may be required to file Schedule M-3. See instructions.

1	Net income (loss) per books	89,400	7	Income recorded on books this year not included on this return (itemize): Tax-exempt interest $ 5,000 *Life insurance proceeds on key employee* $50,000	55,000
2	Federal income tax per books	10,500	8	Deductions on this return not charged against book income this year (itemize):	
3	Excess of capital losses over capital gains	2,000	a	Depreciation $	
4	Income subject to tax not recorded on books this year (itemize):		b	Charitable contributions $	
5	Expenses recorded on books this year not deducted on this return (itemize):				
a	Depreciation $				
b	Charitable contributions $				
c	Travel and entertainment $				
	Prem.–life ins. $2,600; Int.–tax-exempt bonds $500	3,100	9	Add lines 7 and 8	55,000
6	Add lines 1 through 5	105,000	10	Income (page 1, line 28)—line 6 less line 9	50,000

12-5d Schedule M–2—Analysis of Unappropriated Retained Earnings per Books

Schedule M–2 reconciles unappropriated retained earnings at the beginning of the year with unappropriated retained earnings at year-end. Corporations reconcile these *financial statement* amounts by adding net income per books to the beginning balance of retained earnings and then subtracting distributions to shareholders made during the year. Other sources of increases or decreases in retained earnings are also listed on Schedule M–2.

Assume the same facts as in the preceding example. Tern Corporation's beginning balance in unappropriated retained earnings is $125,000. During the year, Tern distributed a cash dividend of $30,000 to its shareholders. Based on this additional information, Tern's Schedule M–2 for the current year is constructed as follows:

Schedule M-2 Analysis of Unappropriated Retained Earnings per Books (Schedule L, Line 25)

1	Balance at beginning of year	125,000	5	Distributions: a Cash	30,000
2	Net income (loss) per books	89,400		b Stock	
3	Other increases (itemize):			c Property	
			6	Other decreases (itemize):	
			7	Add lines 5 and 6	30,000
4	Add lines 1, 2, and 3	214,400	8	Balance at end of year (line 4 less line 7)	184,400

Corporations with less than $250,000 of gross receipts and less than $250,000 in assets do not have to complete Schedule L (balance sheet) and Schedules M–1 and M–2 of Form 1120. These rules are intended to ease the compliance burden on small business.

Information about small businesses can be found on this book's companion website: www.cengage.com

7 Digging Deeper

12-5e Schedule M–3—Net Income (Loss) Reconciliation for Corporations with Total Assets of $10 Million or More

Corporate taxpayers with total assets of $10 million or more are required to report much greater detail about differences between income (loss) reported for financial accounting purposes and income (loss) reported for tax purposes. This expanded reconciliation of book and taxable income (loss) is reported on **Schedule M–3**.[63]

[63]Corporations that are not required to file Schedule M–3 may do so voluntarily. Any corporation that files Schedule M–3 is not allowed to file Schedule M–1. Corporations (and partnerships) with $10 million to $50 million of total assets may elect to file Schedule M–1 in lieu of Schedule M–3, Parts II and III. Electing entities must still file Schedule M–3, Part I (lines 1–12). Entities with less than $10 million of assets that voluntarily file Schedule M–3 also may elect the reduced Schedule M–3 filing requirements.

Bridge Discipline **Bridge to Financial Accounting**

Measures of corporate income for financial reporting and income tax purposes differ because the objectives of these measures differ. Income measures for financial reporting purposes are intended to help various stakeholders have a clear view of the corporation's financial position and operational results. Income measures for Federal income tax purposes, on the other hand, must comply with the relevant provisions of the Internal Revenue Code. The tax law is intended not only to raise revenues to fund government operations but also to reflect the objectives of government fiscal policy.

As a consequence of these differing objectives, revenue and expense measurements used to determine taxable income may differ from those used in financial reporting. In most cases, differences between book and tax measurements are temporary in nature. Two such temporary differences relate to the different methods of calculating depreciation expense and the limits placed on the deductibility of net capital losses for tax purposes. Permanent differences between book and tax income, such as the dividends received deduction and the domestic production activities deduction, also may exist.

Accounting standards for reporting income tax expenses and liabilities require that the tax impact of *temporary* differences be recognized currently in the financial statements. Because many temporary differences allow a firm to postpone its tax payments to later years, the financial statements must show the amount of the expense that is paid currently and that portion that is to be paid in a later period. The portion of the taxes to be paid in a later period is shown as a liability for such future income taxes. The liability for future income taxes is referred to as a deferred income tax liability.

See Chapter 3 for a complete discussion of this topic.

Schedule M–3 is a response, at least in part, to a variety of financial reporting scandals. One objective of Schedule M–3 is to create greater transparency between corporate financial statements and tax returns. Another objective is to identify corporations that engage in aggressive tax practices by requiring that corporations disclose transactions that create book-tax differences on their tax returns.

Total assets for purposes of the $10 million test and the income and expense amounts required by Schedule M–3 are determined from the taxpayer's financial reports. If the taxpayer files Form 10–K with the Securities and Exchange Commission (SEC), that statement is used. If no 10–K is filed, information from another financial source is used, in the following order: certified (audited) financial statements, prepared financial statements, or the taxpayer's books and records.

Digging Deeper 8 **Information on Schedule M–3 can be found on this book's companion website:** www.cengage.com

12-5f **Effect of Taxes on Financial Statements**

Given the differences between taxable income and net income per books, what effect do these differences have on an entity's financial statements? How are income tax accruals arrived at and reported for accounting purposes? What other types of disclosures regarding present and potential tax liabilities are required to satisfy the accounting standards? Recall that Chapter 3 discussed answers to these and other questions at length.

A corporation with total assets of $10 million or more must file Schedule UTP (Uncertain Tax Position Statement) with its Form 1120. In general, a corporation must report tax positions taken on a current or prior year's Federal income tax return and for which the corporation recorded a reserve for Federal income tax in its audited financial statements (or for which the corporation recorded no reserve because of an expectation to litigate). Financial reporting of tax positions is discussed in Chapter 3.

Digging Deeper 9 **Learn about consolidated returns at this book's companion website:** www.cengage.com

Refocus on The Big Picture

Growing into the Corporate Form

KURHAN/SHUTTERSTOCK.COM

Amber, the sole property transferor, must acquire at least 80 percent of the stock issued by Garden, Inc., for the transaction to qualify for tax-deferred treatment under § 351. Otherwise, she will recognize $600,000 of taxable gain as a result of the transfer. As a corollary, Jimmy must not receive more than 20 percent of Garden's stock in exchange for services (see Example 14). Even if the requirements of § 351 are met, any debt issued by the corporation will be treated as boot and will result in at least some gain recognition to Amber (see Example 8). Therefore, Amber must evaluate the cost of recognizing gain now versus the benefit of Garden obtaining an interest deduction later.

What If?

Can the § 351 transaction be modified to further reduce personal and business tax costs, both at the time of formation and in the future? Several strategies may be worth considering:

- Have Jimmy transfer some property along with the services rendered to Garden, Inc. As long as Jimmy transfers property with more than a relatively small value compared to the value of services performed, Jimmy will be considered part of the control group. This would allow Amber to own less than 80 percent of the new corporation and still have the transaction qualify under § 351.
- Instead of having Garden issue debt on formation, Amber might withhold certain assets. For example, if the building is not transferred, it can be leased to the corporation. The resulting rent payment would mitigate the double taxation problem by reducing Garden's taxable income via a rent deduction (but would increase Amber's taxable income).

Suggested Readings

David B. Friedel and Yaw O. Awuah, "Sec. 351 Control Requirement: Opportunities and Pitfalls," *The Tax Adviser*, July 2014.

Jeffrey L. Rubinger and Nadia E. Kruler, "Service Applies Substance Over Form Doctrine to Disallow Dividends-Received Deduction," *Journal of Taxation*, July 2013.

Key Terms

Built-in loss property, 12-16
C corporations, 12-2
Capital contribution, 12-25
Check-the-box Regulations, 12-7
Control, 12-12
Disregarded entity, 12-7
Dividends received deduction, 12-28
Limited liability company (LLC), 12-7
Limited partnerships, 12-7
Organizational expenditures, 12-30
Property, 12-10
Regular corporations, 12-2
S corporations, 12-2
Schedule M–1, 12-35
Schedule M–3, 12-37
Securities, 12-11
Thin capitalization, 12-27

Computational Exercises

1. **LO.2** Marie and Ramesh form Roundtree Corporation with the transfer of the following. Marie performs personal services for the corporation with a fair market value of $80,000 in exchange for 400 shares of stock. Ramesh contributes an installment note receivable (basis $25,000; fair market value $30,000), land (basis $50,000; fair market value $170,000), and inventory (basis $100,000; fair market value $120,000) in exchange for 1,600 shares. Determine Marie and Ramesh's current income, gain, or loss; calculate the basis that each takes in the Roundtree stock.

2. **LO.2** Grady exchanges property with a basis of $12,000 and fair market value of $18,000 for 60% of the stock of Eadie Corporation. Pedro acquired the other 40% of the stock five years ago. Calculate Grady's current income, gain, or loss and the basis he takes in his shares of Eadie stock as a result of this transaction.

3. **LO.3, 4** Jocelyn contributes land with a basis of $60,000 and fair market value of $90,000 and inventory with a basis of $5,000 and fair market value of $8,000 in exchange for 100% of Zion Corporation stock. The land is subject to a $15,000 mortgage. Determine Jocelyn's recognized gain or loss and the basis in the Zion stock received.

4. **LO.3, 4** Diego transfers real estate with an adjusted basis of $260,000 and fair market value of $350,000 to a newly formed corporation in exchange for 100% of the stock. The corporation assumes the liability on the transferred real estate in the amount of $300,000. Determine Diego's recognized gain on the transfer and the basis for his stock.

5. **LO.2, 3** Yvonne and Simon form Ion Corporation. Yvonne transfers equipment with a basis of $110,000 and fair market value of $165,000. Simon invests $130,000 of cash. They each receive 100 shares in Ion Corporation worth $130,000, but Yvonne also receives $35,000 of cash from Ion. Calculate Ion Corporation's basis in the equipment. In addition, determine Yvonne and Simon's basis in the Ion stock.

6. **LO.6** Chaz transfers cash of $60,000 to a newly formed corporation for 100% of the stock. In its initial year, the corporation has net income of $15,000. The income is credited to the earnings and profits account of the corporation. The corporation distributes $5,000 to Chaz.
   a. How do Chaz and the corporation treat the $5,000 distribution?
   b. Assume, instead, that Chaz transfers to the corporation cash of $30,000 for stock and cash of $30,000 for a note of the same amount. The note is payable in equal annual installments of $3,000 each (beginning at the end of the corporation's initial year of operations) and bears interest at the rate of 6%. At the end of the year, the corporation pays an amount to meet this obligation (i.e., the annual $3,000 principal payment plus the interest due). Determine the total amount of the payment and its tax treatment to Chaz and the corporation.

7. **LO.7** Crane and Loon Corporations, two unrelated C corporations, have the following transactions for the current year:

	Crane	Loon
Gross income from operations	$180,000	$300,000
Expenses from operations	255,000	310,000
Dividends received from domestic corporations (15% ownership)	100,000	230,000

   a. Compute the dividends received deduction for Crane Corporation.
   b. Compute the dividends received deduction for Loon Corporation.

8. **LO.7** Cherry Corporation, a calendar year C corporation, is formed and begins business on April 1 of the current year. In connection with its formation, Cherry incurs organizational expenditures of $54,000. Determine Cherry Corporation's deduction for organizational expenditures for the current year.

9. **LO.8** Compute the income tax liability for each of the following unrelated calendar year C corporations.
   a. Darter Corporation has taxable income of $68,000.
   b. Owl Corporation has taxable income of $10,800,000.
   c. Toucan Corporation, a personal service corporation, has taxable income of $170,000.

Problems

10. **LO.1** Janice is the sole owner of Catbird Company. In the current year, Catbird had operating income of $100,000, a long-term capital gain of $15,000, and a charitable contribution of $5,000. Janice withdrew $70,000 of profit from Catbird. How should Janice report this information on her individual tax return if Catbird Company is:
    a. An LLC?
    b. An S corporation?
    c. A C corporation?

11. **LO.1** Can a sole proprietor form as a single-member limited liability company (LLC)? If so, how would such an LLC be taxed?

12. **LO.1** In the current year, Riflebird Company had operating income of $220,000, operating expenses of $175,000, and a long-term capital loss of $10,000. How do Riflebird Company and Roger, the sole owner of Riflebird, report this information on their respective Federal income tax returns for the current year under the following assumptions?
    a. Riflebird Company is a proprietorship (Roger did not make any withdrawals from the business).
    b. Riflebird Company is a C corporation (no dividends were paid during the year).

13. **LO.1** Ellie and Linda are equal owners in Otter Enterprises, a calendar year business. During the current year, Otter Enterprises has $320,000 of gross income and $210,000 of operating expenses. In addition, Otter has a long-term capital gain of $15,000 and makes distributions to Ellie and Linda of $25,000 each. Discuss the impact of this information on the taxable income of Otter, Ellie, and Linda if Otter is:
    a. A partnership.
    b. An S corporation.
    c. A C corporation.

14. **LO.1** In the current year, Azure Company has $350,000 of net operating income before deducting any compensation or other payments to its sole owner, Sasha. In addition, Azure has interest on municipal bonds of $25,000. Sasha has significant income from other sources and is in the 37% marginal tax bracket. Based on this information, determine the income tax consequences to Azure Company and to Sasha during the year for each of the following independent situations. (Ignore the deduction for qualified business income and the 3.8% Medicare surtax on net investment income.)
    a. Azure is a C corporation and pays no dividends or salary to Sasha.
    b. Azure is a C corporation and distributes $75,000 of dividends to Sasha.

c. Azure is a C corporation and pays $75,000 of salary to Sasha.
d. Azure is a sole proprietorship, and Sasha withdraws $0.
e. Azure is a sole proprietorship, and Sasha withdraws $75,000.

Critical Thinking

15. **LO.2** Sarah incorporates her small business but does not transfer the machinery and equipment used by the business to the corporation. Sarah instead leases the machinery and equipment to the corporation for an annual rent. What tax reasons might Sarah have for not transferring the machinery and equipment to the corporation when the business was incorporated?

16. **LO.2, 3** Seth, Pete, Cara, and Jen form Kingfisher Corporation with the following consideration:

	Consideration Transferred		
	Basis to Transferor	**Fair Market Value**	**Number of Shares Issued**
From Seth—			
Inventory	$30,000	$96,000	30*
From Pete—			
Equipment ($30,000 of depreciation taken by Pete in prior years)	45,000	99,000	30**
From Cara—			
Proprietary process	15,000	90,000	30
From Jen—			
Cash	30,000	30,000	10

*Seth receives $6,000 in cash in addition to the 30 shares.
**Pete receives $9,000 in cash in addition to the 30 shares.

Assume that the value of each share of Kingfisher stock is $3,000. As to these transactions, provide the following information:

a. Seth's recognized gain or loss. Identify the nature of any such gain or loss.
b. Seth's basis in the Kingfisher Corporation stock.
c. Kingfisher Corporation's basis in the inventory.
d. Pete's recognized gain or loss. Identify the nature of any such gain or loss.
e. Pete's basis in the Kingfisher Corporation stock.
f. Kingfisher Corporation's basis in the equipment.
g. Cara's recognized gain or loss.
h. Cara's basis in the Kingfisher Corporation stock.
i. Kingfisher Corporation's basis in the proprietary process.
j. Jen's recognized gain or loss.
k. Jen's basis in the Kingfisher stock.
l. During discussions relating to the formation of Kingfisher, Seth mentions that he may be interested in either (1) just selling all of his inventory in the current year for its fair market value of $96,000 or (2) proceeding with his involvement in Kingfisher's formation as shown above but followed by a sale of his stock five years later for $90,000. What would be the tax cost of these alternative plans, stated in present value terms? Referring to Appendix E, assume a discount rate of 6%. Further, assume that Seth's marginal income tax rate is 35% and his capital gains rate is 15%.
m. Prepare your solution to part (l) using spreadsheet software such as Microsoft Excel.

17. **LO.2, 3** Tom and Gail form Owl Corporation with the following consideration: Planning

	Consideration Transferred		
	Basis to Transferor	Fair Market Value	Number of Shares Issued
From Tom—			
Cash	$ 50,000	$ 50,000	
Installment note	240,000	350,000	40
From Gail—			
Inventory	$ 60,000	$ 50,000	
Equipment	125,000	250,000	
Patentable invention	15,000	300,000	60

Tom purchased the $350,000 face value installment note last year for $240,000. As to these transactions, provide the following information:

a. Tom's recognized gain or loss.
b. Tom's basis in the Owl Corporation stock.
c. Owl Corporation's basis in the installment note.
d. Gail's recognized gain or loss.
e. Gail's basis in the Owl Corporation stock.
f. Owl Corporation's basis in the inventory, equipment, and patentable invention.
g. How would your answers to the preceding questions change if Tom received common stock and Gail received preferred stock?
h. How would your answers change if Gail was a partnership?
i. Gail is considering an alternative to the plan as presented above. She is considering selling the inventory to an unrelated third party for $50,000 in the current year instead of contributing it to Owl. After the sale, she will transfer the $50,000 sales proceeds along with the equipment and patentable invention to Owl for 60 shares of Owl stock. Whether or not she pursues the alternative, she plans to sell her Owl stock in six years for an anticipated sales price of $700,000. In present value terms and assuming she later sells her Owl stock, determine the tax cost of (1) contributing the property as originally planned or (2) pursuing the alternative she has identified. Referring to Appendix E, assume a discount rate of 6%. Further, assume Gail's marginal income tax rate is 32% and her capital gains rate is 15%.

18. **LO.2** Luciana, Jon, and Clyde incorporate their respective businesses and form Starling Corporation. On March 1 of the current year, Luciana exchanges her property (basis of $50,000 and value of $150,000) for 150 shares in Starling Corporation. On April 15, Jon exchanges his property (basis of $70,000 and value of $500,000) for 500 shares in Starling. On May 10, Clyde transfers his property (basis of $90,000 and value of $350,000) for 350 shares in Starling. Decision Making

a. If the three exchanges are part of a prearranged plan, what gain will each of the parties recognize on the exchanges?
b. Assume that Luciana and Jon exchanged their property for stock four years ago, while Clyde transfers his property for 350 shares in the current year. Clyde's transfer is not part of a prearranged plan with Luciana and Jon to incorporate their businesses. What gain will Clyde recognize on the transfer?
c. Returning to the original facts, if the property that Clyde contributes has a basis of $490,000 (instead of $90,000), how might the parties otherwise structure the transaction?

Critical Thinking

19. **LO.2** Dan Knight and Patricia Chen form Crane Corporation. Dan transfers land (worth $200,000, basis of $60,000) for 50% of the stock in Crane. Patricia transfers machinery (worth $150,000, adjusted basis of $30,000) and provides services worth $50,000 for 50% of the stock.
    a. Will the transfers qualify under § 351? Explain.
    b. What are the tax consequences to Dan and Patricia?
    c. What is Crane Corporation's basis in the land and the machinery?

20. **LO.2** John organized Toucan Corporation 10 years ago. He contributed property worth $1,000,000 (basis of $200,000) for 2,000 shares of stock in Toucan (representing 100% ownership). John later gave each of his children, Julie and Rachel, 500 shares of the stock. In the current year, John transfers property worth $350,000 (basis of $170,000) to Toucan for 1,000 more of its shares. What gain, if any, will John recognize on the transfer?

Communications
Decision Making

21. **LO.2** Rhonda owns 50% of the stock of Peach Corporation. She and the other 50% shareholder, Rachel, have decided that additional contributions of capital are needed if Peach is to remain successful in its competitive industry. The two shareholders have agreed that Rhonda will contribute assets having a value of $200,000 (adjusted basis of $15,000) in exchange for additional shares of stock. After the transaction, Rhonda will hold 75% of Peach Corporation and Rachel's interest will fall to 25%.
    a. What gain is realized on the transaction? How much of the gain will be recognized?
    b. Rhonda is not satisfied with the transaction as proposed. How will the consequences change if Rachel agrees to transfer $1,000 of cash in exchange for additional stock? In this case, Rhonda would own slightly less than 75% of Peach, and Rachel's interest would be slightly more than 25%.
    c. If Rhonda still is not satisfied with the result, what should be done to avoid any gain recognition?
    d. Summarize your solution in an e-mail, and send it to your instructor.

22. **LO.2, 3, 4** Adam transfers property with an adjusted basis of $50,000 with a fair market value of $400,000 to Swift Corporation for 90% of the stock. The property is subject to a liability of $60,000, which Swift assumes.
    a. What is the basis of the Swift stock to Adam?
    b. What is the basis of the property to Swift Corporation?

23. **LO.2, 3, 4** Allie forms Broadbill Corporation by transferring land (basis of $125,000, fair market value of $775,000), which is subject to a mortgage of $375,000. One month prior to incorporating Broadbill, Allie borrows $100,000 for personal reasons and gives the lender a second mortgage on the land. Broadbill Corporation issues stock worth $300,000 to Allie and assumes the mortgages on the land.
    a. What are the tax consequences to Allie and to Broadbill Corporation?
    b. How would the tax consequences to Allie differ if she had not borrowed the $100,000?

Decision Making
Planning

24. **LO.2, 3** Rafael transfers the following assets to Crane Corporation in exchange for all of its stock. (Assume that neither Rafael nor Crane plans to make any special tax elections at the time of incorporation.)

Assets	Rafael's Adjusted Basis	Fair Market Value
Inventory	$ 60,000	$100,000
Equipment	150,000	105,000
Shelving	80,000	65,000

    a. What is Rafael's recognized gain or loss?
    b. What is Rafael's basis in the stock?

c. What is Crane's basis in the inventory, equipment, and shelving?

d. If Rafael has no intentions of selling his Crane stock for at least 15 years, what action would you recommend that Rafael and Crane Corporation consider? How does this change the previous answers?

25. **LO.2, 3, 4** Kesha, a sole proprietor, is engaged in a cash basis service business. In the current year, she incorporates the business to form Kiwi Corporation. She transfers assets with a basis of $500,000 and a fair market value of $1,200,000, a bank loan of $450,000 that Kiwi assumes, and $80,000 in trade payables in return for all of Kiwi's stock. What are the tax consequences of the incorporation of the business?

26. **LO.2** Nancy and her daughter, Kathleen, have been working together in a cattery called "The Perfect Cat." Nancy formed the business several years ago as a sole proprietorship, and it has been very successful. Assets currently have a fair market value of $450,000 and a basis of $180,000. On the advice of their tax accountant, Nancy decides to incorporate "The Perfect Cat." Because of Kathleen's participation, Nancy would like her to receive shares in the corporation. What are the relevant tax issues? Critical Thinking

27. **LO.2** Early in the year, Charles, Lane, and Tami form the Harrier Corporation for the express purpose of developing a shopping center. All parties are experienced contractors, and they transfer various business assets (e.g., building materials, land) to Harrier in exchange for all of its stock. Three months after it is formed, Harrier purchases two cranes from Lane for their fair market value of $400,000 by issuing four annual installment notes of $100,000 each. Because the adjusted basis of the cranes is $550,000, Lane plans to recognize a § 1231 loss of $150,000 in the year of the sale. Does Lane have any potential income tax problem with this plan? Explain. Ethics and Equity

28. **LO.2, 3** Rasa and Jane form Osprey Corporation. Rasa transfers property with a basis of $25,000 and fair market value of $200,000 for 50 shares in Osprey Corporation. Jane transfers property with a basis of $50,000 and fair market value of $165,000 and agrees to serve as manager of Osprey for one year; in return, Jane receives 50 shares in Osprey. The value of Jane's services to Osprey is $35,000.

a. What gain or income will Rasa and Jane recognize on the exchange?

b. What basis will Osprey Corporation have in the property transferred by Rasa and Jane? How should Osprey treat the value of the services that Jane renders?

29. **LO.2, 3** Assume in Problem 28 that Jane receives the 50 shares of Osprey Corporation stock in consideration for the appreciated property and for the provision of accounting services in organizing the corporation. The value of Jane's services is $35,000.

a. What gain or income does Jane recognize?

b. What is Osprey Corporation's basis in the property transferred by Jane? How should Osprey treat the value of the services that Jane renders?

30. **LO.2, 3** In January of the current year, Wanda transferred machinery worth $200,000 (adjusted basis of $30,000) to a controlled corporation, Oriole, Inc. The transfer qualified under § 351. Wanda had deducted $165,000 of depreciation on the machinery while it was used in her proprietorship. Later during the year, Oriole sells the machinery for $190,000. What are the tax consequences to Wanda and to Oriole on the sale of the machinery?

31. **LO.5** Red Corporation wants to set up a manufacturing facility in a midwestern state. After considerable negotiations with a small town in Ohio, Red accepts the following offer of land worth $3,000,000 and cash of $1,000,000.
    a. How much gain or income, if any, must Red Corporation recognize?
    b. What basis will Red Corporation have in the land?
    c. Assume that in addition to the facts given, the small town offers to reduce the established property tax rate by 40% on new assets acquired by Red during the two-year period after locating in the town. What are the Federal income tax consequences of the property tax abatement?

Communications
Critical Thinking

32. **LO.6** Emily Patrick (36 Paradise Road, Northampton, MA 01060) formed Teal Corporation a number of years ago with an investment of $200,000 of cash, for which she received $20,000 in stock and $180,000 in bonds bearing interest of 8% and maturing in nine years. Several years later, Emily lent the corporation an additional $50,000 on open account. In the current year, Teal Corporation becomes insolvent and is declared bankrupt. During the corporation's existence, Emily was paid an annual salary of $60,000. Write a letter to Emily in which you explain how she should treat her losses for tax purposes.

33. **LO.7** In each of the following independent situations, determine the dividends received deduction for the calendar year C corporation. The corporate shareholders own less than 20% of the stock in the corporations paying the dividends.

	Almond Corporation	Banana Corporation	Cherry Corporation
Income from operations	$ 700,000	$ 800,000	$ 900,000
Expenses from operations	(600,000)	(860,000)	(910,000)
Qualifying dividends	100,000	100,000	100,000

34. **LO.7** Gull Corporation, a cash method, calendar year C corporation, was formed and began business on November 1, 2022. Gull incurred the following expenses during its first year of operations (November 1, 2022–December 31, 2022):

Expenses of temporary directors and organizational meetings	$21,000
Fee paid to state of incorporation	3,000
Expenses for printing and sale of stock certificates	11,000
Legal services for drafting the corporate charter and bylaws (not paid until January 2023)	19,000

    a. Assuming that Gull Corporation elects under § 248 to expense and amortize organizational expenditures, what amount may be deducted in 2022?
    b. Assume the same facts as above, except that the amount paid for the legal services was $28,000 (instead of $19,000). What amount may be deducted as organizational expenditures in 2022?

35. **LO.7** Egret Corporation, a calendar year C corporation, was formed on March 6, 2022, and opened for business on July 1, 2022. After its formation but prior to opening for business, Egret incurred the following expenditures:

Accounting	$ 7,000
Advertising	14,500
Employee payroll	11,000
Rent	8,000
Utilities	1,000

What is the maximum amount of these expenditures that Egret can deduct in 2022?

36. **LO.8** In each of the following *independent* situations, determine the corporation's income tax liability. Assume that all corporations use a calendar year for tax purposes and that the tax year involved is 2022.

	Taxable Income
Purple Corporation	$ 65,000
Azul Corporation	290,000
Pink Corporation	12,350,000
Turquoise Corporation	19,000,000
Teal Corporation (a personal service corporation)	130,000

37. **LO.9** Emerald Corporation, a calendar year and accrual method taxpayer, provides the following information and asks you to prepare Schedule M–1 for 2022:

Net income per books (after-tax)	$268,200
Federal income tax per books	31,500
Tax-exempt interest income	15,000
Life insurance proceeds received as a result of death of corporate president	150,000
Interest on loan to purchase tax-exempt bonds	1,500
Excess of capital losses over capital gains	6,000
Premiums paid on life insurance policy on life of Emerald's president	7,800

38. **LO.9** The following information for 2022 relates to Sparrow Corporation, a calendar year, accrual method taxpayer.

Net income per books (after-tax)	$205,050
Federal income tax per books	55,650
Tax-exempt interest income	4,500
MACRS depreciation in excess of straight-line depreciation used for financial accounting purposes	7,200
Excess of capital loss over capital gains	9,400
Nondeductible meals and entertainment	5,500
Interest on loan to purchase tax-exempt bonds	1,100

Based on the above information, use Schedule M–1 of Form 1120, which is available on the IRS website, to determine Sparrow's taxable income for 2022.

39. **LO.9** In the current year, Woodpecker, Inc., a C corporation with $8,500,000 in assets, deducted amortization of $40,000 on its financial statements and $55,000 on its Federal tax return. Is Woodpecker required to file Schedule M–3? If a Schedule M–3 is filed by Woodpecker, how is the difference in amortization amounts treated on that schedule? Digging Deeper

40. **LO.9** Dove Corporation, a calendar year C corporation, had the following information for 2022: Critical Thinking

Net income per books (after-tax)	$386,250
Taxable income	120,000
Federal income tax per books	25,200
Cash dividend distributions	150,000
Unappropriated retained earnings as of January 1, 2022	796,010

Based on the above information, use Schedule M–2 of Form 1120 (see Example 47 in the text) to determine Dove's unappropriated retained earnings balance as of December 31, 2022.

Digging Deeper

41. **LO.9** In the current year, Pelican, Inc., incurs $50,000 of nondeductible fines and penalties. Its depreciation expense is $245,000 for financial statement purposes and $310,000 for tax purposes. How is this information reported on Schedule M–3?

Digging Deeper

42. **LO.9** In January 2022, Pelican, Inc., established an allowance for uncollectible accounts (bad debt reserve) of $70,000 on its books and increased the allowance by $120,000 during the year. As a result of a client's bankruptcy, Pelican, Inc., decreased the allowance by $60,000 in November 2022. Pelican, Inc., deducted the $190,000 of increases to the allowance on its 2022 income statement, but was not allowed to deduct that amount on its tax return. On its 2022 tax return, the corporation was allowed to deduct the $60,000 actual loss sustained because of its client's bankruptcy. On its financial statements, Pelican, Inc., treated the $190,000 increase in the bad debt reserve as an expense that gave rise to a temporary difference. On its 2022 tax return, Pelican, Inc., took a $60,000 deduction for bad debt expense. How is this information reported on Schedule M–3?

Tax Return Problem

Tax Forms Problem

ProConnect™ Tax

1. On November 1, 2010, Janet Morton and Kim Wong formed Pet Kingdom, Inc., to sell pets and pet supplies. Pertinent information regarding Pet Kingdom is summarized as follows.
   - Pet Kingdom's business address is 1010 Northwest Parkway, Dallas, TX 75225; its telephone number is (214) 555-2211; and its e-mail address is petkingdom@pki.com.
   - The employer identification number is 11-1111112, and the principal business activity code is 453910.
   - Janet and Kim each own 50% of the common stock; Janet is president and Kim is vice president of the company. No other class of stock is authorized.
   - Both Janet and Kim are full-time employees of Pet Kingdom. Janet's Social Security number is 123-45-6788, and Kim's Social Security number is 123-45-6787.
   - Pet Kingdom is an accrual method, calendar year taxpayer. Inventories are determined using FIFO and the lower of cost or market method. Pet Kingdom uses the straight-line method of depreciation for book purposes and accelerated depreciation (MACRS) for tax purposes.
   - During 2021, the corporation distributed cash dividends of $250,000.

Pet Kingdom's financial statements for 2021 are shown below.

Income Statement

Income		
Gross sales		$ 5,750,000
Sales returns and allowances		(200,000)
Net sales		$ 5,550,000
Cost of goods sold		(2,300,000)
Gross profit		$ 3,250,000
Dividends received from stock investments in less-than-20%-owned U.S. corporations		43,750
Interest income:		
State bonds	$ 15,000	
Certificates of deposit	20,000	35,000
Total income		$ 3,328,750

continued

Expenses			
Salaries—officers:			
Janet Morton	$262,500		
Kim Wong	262,500	$525,000	
Salaries—clerical and sales		725,000	
Taxes (state, local, and payroll)		238,000	
Repairs and maintenance		140,000	
Interest expense:			
Loan to purchase state bonds	$ 9,000		
Other business loans	207,000	216,000	
Advertising		58,000	
Rental expense		109,000	
Depreciation*		106,000	
Charitable contributions		38,000	
Employee benefit programs		60,000	
Premiums on term life insurance policies on lives of Janet Morton and Kim Wong; Pet Kingdom is the designated beneficiary		40,000	
Total expenses			(2,255,000)
Net income before taxes			$ 1,073,750
Federal income tax			(221,734)
Net income per books			$ 852,016

*Depreciation for tax purposes is $136,000. You are not provided enough detailed data to complete a Form 4562 (depreciation). If you solve this problem using Intuit ProConnect, enter the amount of depreciation on line 20 of Form 1120.

Balance Sheet

Assets	January 1, 2021	December 31, 2021
Cash	$ 1,200,000	$ 1,039,461
Trade notes and accounts receivable	2,062,500	2,147,000
Inventories	2,750,000	3,030,000
Stock investment	1,125,000	1,125,000
State bonds	375,000	375,000
Certificates of deposit	400,000	400,000
Prepaid Federal tax	-0-	2,266
Buildings and other depreciable assets	5,455,000	5,455,000
Accumulated depreciation	(606,000)	(712,000)
Land	812,500	812,500
Other assets	140,000	128,500
Total assets	$13,714,000	$13,802,727

Liabilities and Equity	January 1, 2021	December 31, 2021
Accounts payable	$ 2,284,000	$ 1,840,711
Other current liabilities	175,000	155,000
Mortgages	4,625,000	4,575,000
Capital stock	2,500,000	2,500,000
Retained earnings	4,130,000	4,732,016
Total liabilities and equity	$13,714,000	$13,802,727

During 2021, Pet Kingdom made estimated tax payments of $56,000 each quarter to the IRS. Prepare a Form 1120 for Pet Kingdom for tax year 2021. Suggested software: ProConnect Tax Online.

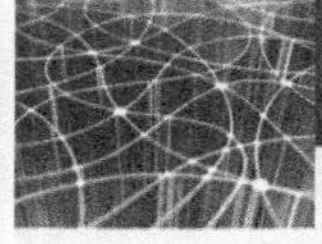

Bridge Discipline

1. Charles is planning to invest $10,000 in a venture whose management is undecided about whether to structure it as a regular corporation or as a partnership. Charles will hold a 10% interest in the entity. Determine the treatment to Charles if the entity is a corporation and if it is a partnership. Charles is in the 37% marginal tax bracket. Also, assume that the passive activity rules do not apply to Charles.
   a. If the entity incurs an $80,000 operating loss in year 1, what is Charles's cash outflow if the entity is a corporation? A partnership? Do not consider the 3.8% additional tax on net investment income in the analysis.
   b. In year 2, the entity earns operating income of $200,000 and makes no distributions to any of the owners. What is the Federal income tax burden on Charles if the investment is a corporation? A partnership?
   c. In year 3, the entity earns operating income of $200,000 and distributes all of that year's after-tax proceeds to the owners. What amount of cash is available to Charles if the entity operates as a corporation (assume that any distribution is a qualified dividend)? A partnership?

2. On your review of the books and records of Ridge Corporation, you note the following information pertaining to its tax provision:

Net income per books	$615,100
Book income tax expense	144,900
Dividends received deduction	70,000
Capital gains	50,000
Capital losses	(60,000)
MACRS depreciation	80,000
Book depreciation	65,000

   a. Calculate Ridge's taxable income and Federal income tax liability for the year.
   b. Calculate Ridge's deferred income tax liability.

3. Bengal Corporation's reported book income was $30,000,000. Bengal's net income included straight-line depreciation of $3,500,000, $25,000 of City of Denver bond interest, $4,000,000 of dividend income from a 30%-owned U.S. corporation, and $6,800,000 of Federal income tax expense. Bengal Corporation paid $8,000,000 to the U.S. government toward its current-year tax liability. Bengal's MACRS deduction for the year totaled $2,000,000. How much Federal income tax will Bengal owe (or receive as a refund)?

Research Problems

Note: Solutions to the Research Problems can be prepared by using the Thomson Reuters Checkpoint™ online tax research database, which accompanies this textbook. Solutions can also be prepared by using research materials found in a typical tax library.

Research Problem 1. Mateo is a real estate broker who specializes in commercial real estate. Although he usually buys and sells on behalf of others, he also maintains a portfolio of property of his own. He holds this property, mainly unimproved land, either as an investment or for sale to others.

In early 2017, Irene and Al contact Mateo regarding a tract of land located just outside the city limits. Mateo bought the property, which is known as the Moore farm, several years ago for $600,000. At that time, no one knew that it was located on a geological fault line. Irene, a well-known architect, and Al, a building contractor, want Mateo to join them in developing the property for residential use. They are aware of the fault line but believe that they can circumvent the problem by using newly developed design and construction technology. Because of the geological flaw, however, they regard the Moore farm as being worth only $450,000. Their intent is to organize a corporation to build the housing project, and each party will receive stock commensurate to the property or services contributed.

After consulting his tax adviser, Mateo agrees to join the venture if certain modifications to the proposed arrangement are made. The transfer of the land would be structured as a sale to the corporation. Instead of receiving stock, Mateo would receive a note from the corporation. The note would be interest-bearing and be due in five years. The maturity value of the note would be $450,000—the amount that even Mateo concedes is the fair market value of the Moore farm.

Your tax senior has asked you to determine the income tax consequences that will result from Mateo's suggested approach. You should compare this result with what would happen if Mateo merely transferred the Moore farm in return for stock in the new corporation.

Research Problem 2. A new client, John Dobson, recently formed John's Premium Steakhouse, Inc., to operate a new restaurant. The restaurant will be a first-time business venture for John, who recently retired after 30 years of military service. John transferred cash to the corporation in exchange for 100% of its stock, and the corporation has leased a building and restaurant equipment. John has asked you for guidance on the tax treatment of various expenses (e.g., licensing, training, advertising) he expects the corporation to incur during the restaurant's pre-opening period. Research the tax treatment of startup expenditures, including the point at which a business begins for purposes of determining what expenses are included. Prepare a memo for the client files, describing the results of your research.

Communications

Partial list of research aids:
§ 195.
Reg. § 1.195–1.

Research Problem 3. Lynn Jones, along with Shawn, Walt, and Donna, are trying to decide whether they should organize a corporation and transfer their shares of stock in several corporations to this new corporation. All of their shares are listed on the New York Stock Exchange and are readily marketable. Lynn would transfer shares in Brown Corporation, Shawn would transfer stock in Rust Corporation, Walt would transfer stock in White Corporation, and Donna would transfer stock in several corporations. The stock would be held by the newly formed corporation for investment purposes. Lynn asks you, her tax adviser, whether she would have gain on the transfer of her substantially appreciated shares in Brown Corporation if she transferred the shares to a newly formed corporation. Your input will be critical as they make their decision. Prepare a letter to your client, Lynn Jones, and a memo for the firm's files. Lynn's address is 1540 Maxwell Avenue, Highland, KY 41099.

Communications
Decision Making

Use internet tax resources to address the following question. Look for reliable websites and blogs of the IRS and other government agencies, media outlets, businesses, tax professionals, academics, think tanks, and political outlets.

Research Problem 4. Limited liability company (LLC) status has become a popular form of operating a business in the United States. Investigate how the growth of LLC status has affected the relative number of new businesses that have chosen to operate as corporations.

Becker CPA Review Questions

Becker

1. Gearty and Olinto organized The Worthington Corp., which issued voting common stock with a fair market value of $240,000. They each transferred property in exchange for stock as follows:

	Property	Adjusted Basis	Fair Market Value	Percentage of The Worthington Corp. Stock Acquired
Gearty	Building	$80,000	$164,000	60%
Olinto	Land	10,000	96,000	40%

The building was subject to a $20,000 mortgage that was assumed by The Worthington Corp. What was The Worthington Corp.'s basis in the building?

a. $60,000
b. $80,000
c. $144,000
d. $104,000

2. Gearty and Olinto organized The Worthington Corp., which issued voting common stock with a fair market value of $240,000. They each transferred property in exchange for stock as follows:

	Property	Adjusted Basis	Fair Market Value	Percentage of The Worthington Corp. Stock Acquired
Gearty	Building	$80,000	$164,000	60%
Olinto	Land	10,000	96,000	40%

The building was subject to a $20,000 mortgage that was assumed by The Worthington Corp. What amount of gain did Gearty recognize on the exchange?

a. $0
b. $20,000
c. $84,000
d. $104,000

3. Ron, David, and Mary formed Widget, Inc. Ron and David each received 40% of the stock, and Mary received the remaining 20%. Ron contributed land with an FMV of $70,000 and an adjusted basis of $20,000. The corporation also assumed a $30,000 liability on the property. David contributed land with an FMV of $30,000 and an adjusted basis of $15,000. David also contributed $10,000 in cash. Mary received her stock for services rendered. She normally would bill $20,000 for these services. What is Mary's basis in the corporate stock received?

a. $0
b. $10,000
c. $15,000
d. $20,000

4. In the current year, Acorn, Inc., had the following items of income and expense:

Sales	$500,000
Cost of sales	250,000
Dividends received	25,000

The dividends were received from a corporation of which Acorn owns 30%. In Acorn's current-year corporate income tax return, what amount should be reported as income before special deductions?

a. $525,000
b. $505,000
c. $275,000
d. $250,000

5. Hirsch, Incorporated, is a calendar year corporation that has had revenues of less than $500,000 since inception. In year 12, Hirsch had a net operating loss of $50,000 that was able to be used in full in year 13. For year 13, Hirsch expects to have taxable income prior to NOL deduction of $100,000. How will Hirsch avoid a penalty for underpayment of estimated Federal taxes in year 13?
   a. Hirsch must pay 100% of the tax shown on its year 13 return via estimated taxes to avoid an underpayment penalty.
   b. Hirsch must pay the amount of taxes owed on its year 12 return via estimated taxes to avoid an underpayment penalty.
   c. Hirsch must pay 90% of the tax shown on its year 13 return via estimated taxes to avoid an underpayment penalty.
   d. Hirsch may pay the lower of the amount of taxes owed in year 12 or 100% of the tax shown on the return for year 13 via estimated taxes to avoid an underpayment penalty.

Chapter 13

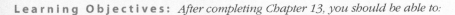

Corporations: Earnings & Profits and Distributions

Learning Objectives: *After completing Chapter 13, you should be able to:*

LO.1 **Explain the role that earnings and profits play in determining the tax treatment of distributions.**

LO.2 **Compute a corporation's earnings and profits (E & P).**

LO.3 **Apply the rules for assigning earnings and profits to distributions.**

LO.4 **Evaluate the tax effects of noncash dividends on the recipient shareholder and the corporation making the distribution.**

LO.5 **Identify the nature and treatment of constructive dividends.**

LO.6 **Distinguish between taxable and nontaxable stock dividends.**

LO.7 **Discuss the tax treatment of stock redemptions and corporate liquidations.**

Chapter Outline

Tax Talk *The relative stability of profits after taxes is evidence that the corporation profits tax is, in effect, almost entirely shifted; the government simply uses the corporation as a tax collector.* —K. E. Boulding

The Big Picture

Taxing Corporate Distributions

Plainwell Ice Cream Corporation, a premium ice cream manufacturer, has had a very profitable year. To share its profits with its two shareholders, Waffle Cone Corporation and Luis, it distributes cash of $200,000 to Cone and real estate worth $300,000 (adjusted basis of $20,000) to Luis, a married individual filing a joint return. The real estate is subject to a mortgage of $100,000, which Luis assumes. The distribution is made on December 31, Plainwell's year-end.

Plainwell experienced both good and bad years in the past. More often than not, however, it has lost money. Despite this year's banner profits, Plainwell's GAAP-based balance sheet indicates a year-end deficit in retained earnings. Consequently, for financial reporting purposes, the distribution of cash and land is treated as a liquidating distribution, resulting in a reduction of Plainwell's paid-in capital account.

The tax consequences of the distributions to Plainwell and its shareholders depend on a variety of factors that are not directly related to the financial reporting treatment. Identify these factors, and explain the tax effects of the distributions to both the entity and its two shareholders.

Read the chapter and formulate your response.

Generally, a corporation cannot deduct distributions made to its shareholders. In contrast, shareholders may be required to treat distributions as fully subject to tax, a nontaxable recovery of capital, or capital gain.

Because distributions provide no deduction to the paying corporation and often require income recognition by the shareholders, corporate income seemingly is subject to a double income tax (i.e., at both the corporate and shareholder levels). Because of the possibility of a double income tax when dealing with corporations, the tax treatment of distributions often raises issues such as the following.

- The availability of earnings to be distributed.
- The basis of the shareholder's stock.
- The character of the property being distributed.
- Whether the shareholder gives up ownership in return for the distribution.
- Whether the distribution is liquidating or nonliquidating.

13-1 Corporate Distributions—Overview

Explain the role that earnings and profits play in determining the tax treatment of distributions.

To the extent that a distribution is made from corporate earnings and profits (E & P), the shareholder receives a **dividend**, usually taxed in a preferential manner.[1] Generally, corporate distributions are presumed to be paid out of E & P (discussed in text Section 13-2a) and are treated as dividend income, *unless* the parties to the transaction can show otherwise.

The portion of a corporate distribution that is not taxed as a dividend (because of insufficient E & P) is nontaxable to the extent of the shareholder's basis in the stock. The stock basis is reduced accordingly. If the distribution exceeds the shareholder's basis, the excess is treated as a gain from the sale or exchange of the stock.[2]

At the beginning of the year, Amber Corporation (a calendar year taxpayer) holds accumulated E & P of $30,000. The corporation reports no current E & P. During the year, the corporation distributes $40,000 to its *equal* shareholders, Bob and Bonnie (i.e., each receives $20,000). Only $30,000 of the $40,000 distribution is a taxable dividend.

Suppose Bob's basis in his stock is $8,000, while Bonnie's basis is $4,000. Under these conditions, Bob recognizes a taxable dividend of $15,000 and reduces the basis of his stock from $8,000 to $3,000. The $20,000 Bonnie receives from Amber Corporation is accounted for as follows.

- Taxable dividend of $15,000.
- Reduction in stock basis from $4,000 to zero.
- Taxable gain of $1,000.

13-2 Earnings and Profits (E & P)

The notion of **earnings and profits** is similar in many respects to the financial accounting concept of retained earnings. Both are measures of the firm's accumulated capital. However, these two concepts differ in a fundamental way. The computation of retained earnings is based on financial accounting rules, while E & P is determined using rules specified in the tax law.

Congress has not provided a specific definition of *earnings and profits* in the Internal Revenue Code. Rather, it has provided adjustments that are made to a corporation's taxable income to arrive at E & P. The Treasury (through regulations), the IRS (through rulings), and the courts (through case law) have provided additional guidance. All of these rules must be taken into account when calculating E & P.

[1]§§ 301(c)(1) and 316(a). Corporate shareholders can claim a dividends received deduction. See text Section 12-4a. Others typically pay a tax on dividends at a maximum 15% or 20% rate.

[2]§ 301(c).

Tax Fact Who Pays Dividends?

The vast majority of dividends paid by C corporations come from the very largest enterprises (measured by size of total assets) as reported on Forms 1120 for the latest tax year for which data are available.

Cash and stock dividends for the year totaled about $836 billion. Only about 11 percent of all dividend payments during a tax year are made by C corporations with less than $500 million in total assets.

Percentage of Dividends Paid, by Size of Corporate Assets

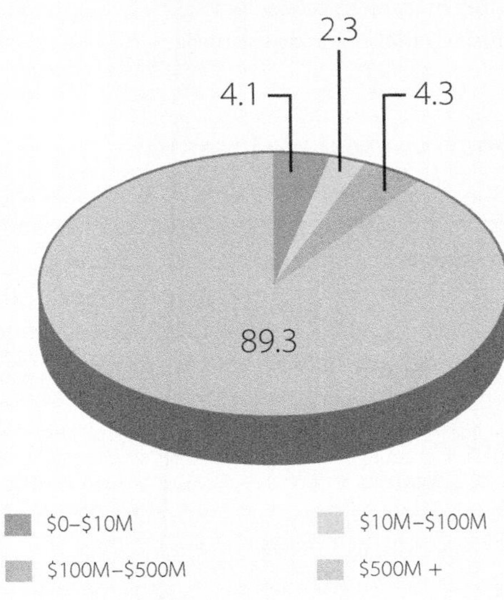

E & P is a measure of the dividend-paying capacity of a corporation (i.e., a measure of *economic income*). As a result, when a corporation makes a distribution to a shareholder, E & P represents the maximum amount of dividend income shareholders must recognize as a result of a distribution by the corporation. As a result, the effect of a specific transaction on the E & P account often can be determined by considering whether the transaction increases or decreases the corporation's ability to pay a dividend.

13-2a Computation of E & P

LO.2

Compute a corporation's earnings and profits (E & P).

Earnings and profits is computed by applying a series of adjustments to a C corporation's taxable income, providing a measure of the corporation's dividend-paying capacity (or economic income).[3] In general, E & P determinations are applied in the same manner for cash and accrual basis taxpayers.

Accumulated E & P is fixed as of the beginning of the tax year; it is the sum of the undistributed earnings of the entity since the later of its incorporation date or February 28, 1913. **Current E & P** is that portion of E & P attributable to the current tax year's operations. It is computed by using the corporation's Federal taxable income and then applying a series of adjustments to more closely approximate the cash flow of the entity.[4]

Additions to Taxable Income

To determine current E & P, one must add certain previously excluded income items back to taxable income. Included among these positive adjustments are interest income on municipal bonds, excluded life insurance proceeds (in excess of cash surrender value), and Federal income tax refunds from taxes paid in prior years.

[3]Reg. § 1.312–6(a).

[4]Section 312 describes many of the adjustments to taxable income necessary to determine E & P. Reg. § 1.312–6 addresses the effect of accounting methods on E & P.

The dividends received deduction is added back to taxable income to determine E & P; this item does not decrease the corporation's assets. This treatment occurs because the deduction does not impair the corporation's ability to pay dividends: this is a deduction that does not reduce E & P.

Eagle Corporation paid $120,000 of Federal income taxes this year. Eagle also received $6,000 of tax-exempt interest income from State X bonds.

The Federal income taxes are subtracted from taxable income to compute Eagle's E & P because this amount is not available for distribution to shareholders. In contrast, the tax-exempt interest is added to taxable income to compute Eagle's E & P; the interest is not part of taxable income, but it represents funds available for distribution.

Subtractions from Taxable Income

Some of the corporation's nondeductible expenditures are subtracted from taxable income to arrive at current E & P. These negative adjustments include the nondeductible portion of business meals and entertainment expenses; related-party losses; expenses incurred to produce tax-exempt income; Federal income taxes paid; nondeductible key employee life insurance premiums (net of increases in cash surrender value); and nondeductible fines, penalties, and lobbying costs.

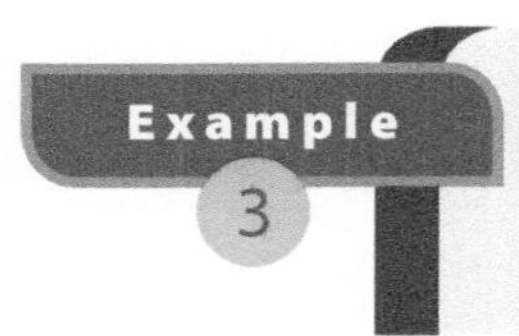

Crane Corporation sells property (basis of $10,000) to its sole shareholder for $8,000. Because of the related-party loss disallowance rules, Crane cannot deduct the $2,000 loss in computing its taxable income. However, because the overall economic effect of the transaction is a decrease in its assets by $2,000, the loss reduces Crane's current E & P for the year of the sale.

Timing Adjustments

Some E & P adjustments shift the effect of a transaction from the year of its inclusion in or deduction from taxable income to the year in which it has an economic effect on the corporation. Charitable contribution carryovers, net operating loss carryovers, and capital loss carryovers all give rise to this kind of adjustment.

During 2022, Raven Corporation makes charitable contributions, $12,000 of which cannot be deducted in arriving at its taxable income for the year because of the 10% of taxable income limitation. Consequently, the $12,000 is carried forward to 2023 and available for deduction in that year.

The excess charitable contribution reduces Raven's 2022 current E & P by $12,000 and increases its current E & P for 2023, when the deduction is allowed, by a like amount. Raven paid cash to the charity in 2022, thereby reducing its dividend-paying capacity. For 2023, the charitable contribution carryover reduces Raven's taxable income for that year (the starting point for computing E & P), but no cash outlay was made in that year; the payment is reversed since it already has been taken into account in determining Raven's 2022 current E & P.

Gains and losses from property transactions generally affect the determination of E & P only to the extent they are recognized for tax purposes. As a result, gains and losses deferred under the like-kind exchange provision and gains deferred under the involuntary conversion gains do not affect E & P until recognized, and no timing adjustment is required for these items.

Accounting Method Adjustments

Some E & P adjustments arise because the accounting methods used for determining E & P generally are more conservative than those allowed for calculating taxable income. For example, the installment method is not permitted for E & P purposes even though, in some cases, it is allowed when computing taxable income. Accordingly, an adjustment is required for the deferred gain attributable to sales of property made during the year under the installment method. Specifically, all principal payments are treated as having been received in the year of sale.[5]

In 2022, Cardinal Corporation, a calendar year taxpayer, sells unimproved real estate (basis of $20,000) for $100,000. Under the terms of the sale, a 4% interest rate applies, and payments of principal are scheduled to be $60,000 in 2023 and $40,000 in 2024. Cardinal does not elect out of the installment method.

Because Cardinal's 2022 taxable income will not reflect any of the gain from the sale, the corporation must make an $80,000 positive adjustment for that year (the deferred gain from the sale) in computing current E & P. Then negative E & P adjustments are required in 2023 and 2024 (i.e., when the deferred gain is recognized under the installment method).

Treatment of the gain for regular tax and E & P purposes by Cardinal is summarized as follows.

Tax Year	Regular Tax	E & P Treatment	E & P Adjustment
2022	$ -0-	$80,000	+$80,000
2023	48,000*	-0-	−48,000
2024	32,000	-0-	−32,000

*$80,000 gain × $60,000 principal received this year ÷ $100,000 total principal to be received.

A similar analysis can be used for most of the timing and accounting method adjustments.

The alternative depreciation system (ADS) is used in computing E & P.[6] This method requires straight-line depreciation with a half-year convention, over a recovery period equal to the Asset Depreciation Range (ADR) midpoint life.[7] If MACRS cost recovery is used for income tax purposes, a positive or negative adjustment equal to the difference between MACRS and ADS must be made each year. Finally, no additional first-year (bonus) depreciation is allowed under the ADS.[8]

Likewise, when assets are sold, an additional adjustment to taxable income is required to account for the difference in gain or loss resulting from the difference in income tax basis and E & P basis.[9] The adjustments arising from depreciation are illustrated in the following example.

Example
6

On January 2, 2020, White Corporation purchased equipment with an ADR midpoint life of 10 years for $30,000. The equipment was then depreciated over its 7-year MACRS class life. No § 179 or additional first-year depreciation was claimed. The asset was sold on July 2, 2022, for $27,000. For purposes of determining taxable income and E & P, cost recovery claimed on the equipment is summarized below.

Year	Cost Recovery Computation	MACRS	ADS	E & P Adjustment
2020	$30,000 × 14.29%	$ 4,287		
	$30,000 ÷ 10-year ADR recovery period × ½ (half-year for first year of service)		$1,500	$2,787
2021	$30,000 × 24.49%	7,347		
	$30,000 ÷ 10-year ADR recovery period		3,000	4,347
2022	$30,000 × 17.49% × ½ (half-year for year of disposal)	2,624		
	$30,000 ÷ 10-year ADR recovery period × ½ (half-year for year of disposal)		1,500	1,124
	Total cost recovery	$14,258	$6,000	$8,258

continued

[5]§ 312(n)(5).

[6]§ 312(k)(3)(A).

[7]See § 168(g)(2). The ADR midpoint life for most assets is set out in Rev.Proc. 87–56. The recovery period is 5 years for automobiles and light-duty trucks and 40 years for real property. For assets with no class life, the recovery period is 12 years.

[8]§ 168(k)(2)(D). In general, additional first-year depreciation (also called "bonus depreciation") is allowed for qualified property placed in service after 2011 and before 2027. No bonus depreciation is scheduled for tax years after 2026. Different rules applied between 2008 and 2011 and prior to 2005. See text Section 5-7g.

[9]§ 312(f)(1).

Each year, White Corporation increases its taxable income by the adjustment amount indicated above to determine E & P. In addition, when computing 2022 E & P, White reduces taxable income by $8,258 to account for the excess gain recognized for income tax purposes.

	Income Tax	E & P
Amount realized	$ 27,000	$ 27,000
Adjusted basis for income tax ($30,000 cost − $14,258 MACRS)	(15,742)	
Adjusted basis for E & P ($30,000 cost − $6,000 ADS)		(24,000)
Gain on sale	$ 11,258	$ 3,000
Adjustment amount ($3,000 − $11,258)	($ 8,258)	

In addition to more conservative depreciation methods, the E & P rules impose limitations on the deductibility of § 179 expense.[10] Specifically, this expense is deducted over a period of five years for E & P purposes (20 percent per year). Therefore, in any year that § 179 is elected, 80 percent of the resulting expense is added back to taxable income to determine current E & P. In each of the following four years, a subtraction from taxable income equal to 20 percent of the § 179 expense is made.

On January 2, 2021, LarsonCo placed in service a five-year depreciable asset. The acquisition price of the asset was $50,000, and LarsonCo claimed a § 179 deduction for the full amount. Treatment of the § 179 amounts for regular tax and E & P purposes is summarized as follows.

Tax Year	Regular Tax	E & P Treatment	E & P Adjustment
2021	$50,000	$10,000	+$40,000
2022	-0-	10,000	−10,000
2023	-0-	10,000	−10,000
2024	-0-	10,000	−10,000
2025	-0-	10,000	−10,000

The E & P rules also require specific accounting methods in various situations, making adjustments necessary when certain methods are used for income tax purposes. Examples include the following.

- E & P requires cost depletion rather than percentage depletion.
- When accounting for long-term contracts, E & P rules require the percentage of completion method rather than the completed contract method.
- E & P does not allow for the amortization of organizational expenses; any such expense deducted when computing taxable income must be added back.
- The E & P computation requires an adjustment for changes in the LIFO recapture amount (the excess of FIFO over LIFO inventory value) during the year. Increases in the LIFO recapture amount are added to taxable income and decreases are subtracted, to the extent of prior-year increases.
- E & P rules also specify that intangible drilling costs and mine exploration and development costs be amortized over a period of 60 months and 120 months, respectively.[11]

[10] § 312(k)(3)(B).

[11] § 312(n).

13-2b Summary of E & P Adjustments

E & P serves as a measure of the earnings of the corporation that are available for distribution as taxable dividends to the shareholders. Current E & P is determined by making a series of adjustments to the corporation's taxable income. These adjustments are reviewed in Concept Summary 13.1.

Crimson Corporation (a calendar year, accrual basis taxpayer) reports taxable income of $429,000 in 2022. In addition, it provides the following information.

Federal income tax liability paid	$ 90,090
Tax-exempt interest income	6,250
Business meal expenses provided by a restaurant (total)	10,000
Entertainment expenses	3,000
Premiums paid on key employee life insurance*	8,500
Life insurance proceeds from key employee life insurance policy*	250,000
Excess of capital losses over capital gains	22,000
MACRS cost recovery deduction	82,000
E & P depreciation (straight-line depreciation using ADS)	64,000
Section 179 expense elected and deducted during 2019 for regular tax purposes	120,000
Dividends received from domestic corporations (less than 20% owned)	35,000

*Term policy; no cash surrender value.

Crimson sold property using the installment method during 2020. The property was sold for $120,000 and had an $84,000 adjusted basis when sold. During 2022, Crimson received a $30,000 payment on the installment note.

Crimson did not claim any § 179 expense for 2022. Compute Crimson's current E & P.

Taxable income	$ 429,000
Federal income tax liability paid	(90,090)
Tax-exempt interest income	6,250
Disallowed portion of business meal expenses	0**
Entertainment expenses	(3,000)
Life insurance premiums paid	(8,500)
Proceeds from life insurance policy	250,000
Excess capital losses	(22,000)
Excess of MACRS cost recovery over E & P (ADS) depreciation	18,000***
Allowable portion of 2019 § 179 expenses (20% × $120,000)	(24,000)
Dividends received deduction (50% × $35,000)	17,500
Installment sale gain	(9,000)****
Current E & P	$ 564,160

**For 2021 and 2022, business meals provided by a restaurant are not subject to the 50% disallowance rule.

***$82,000 MACRS − $64,000 ADS

****[($120,000 sales price − $84,000 adjusted basis) ÷ $120,000 sales price] × $30,000 payment received

13-2c Allocating E & P to Distributions

LO.3 **Apply the rules for assigning earnings and profits to distributions.**

When a positive balance exists in both the current and accumulated E & P accounts, corporate distributions are deemed to be made first from current E & P and then from accumulated E & P.

When more than one distribution is made during the year and total distributions exceed the amount of current E & P, it becomes necessary to allocate current and accumulated E & P to each distribution made during the year. First, dollars of current E & P are applied using the following formula.

Then accumulated E & P is applied in chronological order, beginning with the earliest distribution. This allocation is important if any shareholder sells stock during the year.

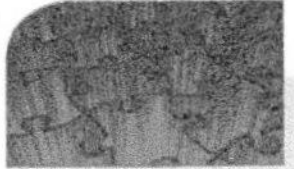

Concept Summary 13.1

Computing E & P

Transaction	Adjustment to Taxable Income to Determine Current E & P	
	Addition	Subtraction
Tax-exempt income	X	
Dividends received deduction	X	
Collection of proceeds from insurance policy on life of corporate employee (in excess of cash surrender value)	X	
Deferred gain on installment sale (all of the gain is added to E & P in year of sale)	X	
Future recognition of installment sale gross profit		X
Excess capital loss		X
Excess charitable contribution (over 10% limitation) in year incurred		X
Deduction of charitable contribution, NOL, or capital loss carryovers in succeeding taxable years (increase E & P because deduction reduces taxable income while E & P was reduced in a prior year)	X	
Federal income taxes paid		X
Federal income tax refund	X	
Loss on sale between related parties		X
Nondeductible fines, penalties, lobbying costs, meals, and entertainment		X
Payment of premiums on insurance policy on life of corporate employee (in excess of increase in cash surrender value of policy)		X
Realized gain (not recognized) on an involuntary conversion	No effect	
Realized gain or loss (not recognized) on a like-kind exchange	No effect	
Excess percentage depletion (only cost depletion can reduce E & P)	X	
Accelerated depreciation (E & P is reduced only by straight-line, units-of-production, or machine hours depreciation)	X	X
Additional first-year (bonus) depreciation	X	
§ 179 expense in year elected (80%)	X	
§ 179 expense in four years following election (20% each year)		X
Increase (decrease) in LIFO recapture amount	X	X
Intangible drilling costs deducted currently (reduce E & P in future years by amortizing costs over 60 months)	X	
Mine exploration and development costs (reduce E & P in future years by amortizing costs over 120 months)	X	

Example 9

On January 1 of the current year, Black Corporation holds accumulated E & P of $10,000. Current E & P for the year amounts to $30,000, earned evenly throughout the year. Megan and Matt are the sole *equal* shareholders of Black from January 1 to July 31.

On August 1, Megan sells all of her stock to Helen. Black makes two distributions to shareholders during the year: $40,000 to Megan and Matt ($20,000 to each) on July 1 and $40,000 to Matt and Helen ($20,000 to each) on December 1. Current and accumulated E & P are applied to the two distributions as follows.

continued

	Source of Distribution		
	Current E & P	Accumulated E & P	Return of Capital
July 1 distribution ($40,000)	$15,000	$10,000	$15,000
December 1 distribution ($40,000)	15,000	-0-	25,000

Because 50% of the total distributions are made on July 1 and December 1, respectively, one-half of current E & P is assigned to each of the two distributions. Accumulated E & P is applied in chronological order, so the entire amount attaches to the July 1 distribution. The tax consequences to the shareholders follow.

	Shareholder		
	Megan	Matt	Helen
July distribution ($40,000)			
Dividend income—			
From current E & P ($15,000)	$ 7,500	$ 7,500	$ -0-
From accumulated E & P ($10,000)	5,000	5,000	-0-
Return of capital ($15,000)	7,500	7,500	-0-
December distribution ($40,000)			
Dividend income—			
From current E & P ($15,000)	-0-	7,500	7,500
From accumulated E & P ($0)	-0-	-0-	-0-
Return of capital ($25,000)	-0-	12,500	12,500
Total distribution	$20,000	$40,000	$20,000
Total dividend income	$12,500	$20,000	$ 7,500
Nontaxable return of capital (assuming sufficient basis in the stock investment)	$ 7,500	$20,000	$12,500

Because the balance in the accumulated E & P account is exhausted when it is applied to the July 1 distribution, Megan has more dividend income than Helen does, even though both receive equal distributions during the year. In addition, each shareholder's basis is reduced by the nontaxable return of capital; any excess over basis results in taxable gain.

When the tax years of the corporation and its shareholders are not the same, it may be impossible to determine the amount of current E & P so that a timely return can be filed. For example, if shareholders use a calendar year and the corporation uses a fiscal year, current E & P may not be known until after the shareholders' tax returns have been filed. To address this timing issue, one presumes that current E & P is sufficient to cover every distribution made during the year until the parties can show otherwise.

Example 10

Griffen Corporation uses a June 30 fiscal year for tax purposes. Kayla, Griffen's only shareholder, uses a calendar year. On July 1, 2022, Griffen has a zero balance in its accumulated E & P account. For fiscal year 2022–2023, the corporation incurs a $5,000 deficit in current E & P. On August 1, 2022, Griffen distributed $10,000 to Kayla. The distribution is dividend income to Kayla and is reported when she files her income tax return for the 2022 calendar year, on or before April 15, 2023.

Because Kayla cannot prove until June 30, 2023, at the earliest, that the corporation has generated a deficit in current E & P for the fiscal year, she must assume that the $10,000 distribution is fully drawn from a positive current E & P. Thus, she includes the $10,000 as dividend income on her 2022 Form 1040.

When Kayla learns of the deficit, she can file an amended return for 2022 showing the $10,000 as a nontaxable return of capital. Alternatively, Kayla can file for an extension for her 2022 return while she awaits Griffen Corporation's fiscal year-end.

Additional difficulties arise when either the current or the accumulated E & P account is less than zero. In particular, when current E & P is positive and accumulated E & P has a deficit balance, accumulated E & P is *not* netted against current E & P. Instead, the distribution is treated as a taxable dividend to the extent of the positive current E & P balance.

The Big Picture

Example 11

Return to the facts of *The Big Picture* on p. 13-1. Recall that Plainwell Ice Cream Corporation recorded a deficit in GAAP-based retained earnings at the start of the year and record profits during the year. Assume that these financial results translate into an $800,000 deficit in accumulated E & P at the start of the year and current E & P of $600,000. In addition, for purposes of this example, assume that there is no mortgage on the real estate.

In this case, current E & P would exceed the total cash and property distributed to the shareholders. The distributions are treated as taxable dividends; they are deemed to be paid from current E & P even though Plainwell's accumulated E & P still is negative at the end of the year.

In contrast to the previous rule, when a deficit exists in current E & P and a positive balance exists in accumulated E & P, the accounts are netted at the date of distribution. If the resulting balance is zero or negative, the distribution is a nontaxable return of capital to the extent of basis; any excess over basis results in a taxable gain. If a positive balance results, the distribution is a dividend to the extent of the balance. Any loss in current E & P is deemed to accrue ratably throughout the year unless the parties can show otherwise. Various E & P rules are indicated in Concept Summary 13.2.

Example 12

At the beginning of the current year, Gray Corporation (a calendar year taxpayer) holds accumulated E & P of $10,000. During the year, the corporation incurs a $15,000 deficit in current E & P that accrues ratably. On July 1, Gray distributes $6,000 in cash to Jennifer, its sole shareholder.

To determine how much of the $6,000 cash distribution represents dividend income to Jennifer, the balances of both accumulated and current E & P as of July 1 are determined and netted. This occurs because of the deficit in current E & P.

	Source of Distribution	
	Current E & P	**Accumulated E & P**
January 1		$10,000
July 1 (½ of $15,000 deficit in current E & P)	($7,500)	2,500

The balance in E & P just before the July 1 distribution is $2,500. Thus, of the $6,000 distribution, $2,500 is taxed as a dividend, and $3,500 represents a nontaxable return of capital. After the distribution, Jennifer's stock basis is $4,000 ($7,500 – $3,500).

Assume instead that Gray's current E & P deficit amounts to $30,000 and that Jennifer's stock basis is $5,000.

	Source of Distribution	
	Current E & P	**Accumulated E & P**
January 1		$10,000
July 1 (½ of $30,000 current E & P deficit)	($15,000)	(5,000)

The balance in E & P just before the July 1 distribution is ($5,000). As a result, there is zero dividend income. The distribution first is treated as a return of capital (to the extent of Jennifer's stock basis) and then as a taxable gain. Now Jennifer's basis is reduced to zero, and she reports a taxable capital gain of $1,000.

Bridge Discipline **Bridge to Finance**

Investors often have tried to read the dividend policies of a corporation as indicators of the strength of the entity: constant dividend payments indicated a stable financial structure for the corporation, while dividend increases were a predictor of good times and triggered stock price increases. Reductions in historic dividend payment patterns foreshadowed financial difficulties and often caused a quick and sizable drop in share price.

Nobel Prize winners Merton Miller, University of Chicago, and Franco Modigliani, MIT, saw things differently. They viewed dividends as a remnant of various financing sources available to the corporation: if it was cheaper to finance future growth by retaining profits and decreasing or eliminating dividend payments, so be it. The entity must reduce its cost of capital wherever possible, and under this interpretation, a dividend decrease might indicate the internal financial strength of the corporation. Conversely, the payment of a dividend reduces the capital available to the entity, thereby forcing the entity to finance its operations and growth from some third-party source and risking future weakness if the cost of that capital increases.

Miller and Modigliani found that stock price and dividend policy were unrelated and that changes in dividend patterns should not affect the capitalized value of the business. Even with lower tax rates on dividends, few shareholders complain that the typical growth stock rarely pays dividends. Nevertheless, shares of companies that pay dividends on average outperform those that don't pay dividends.

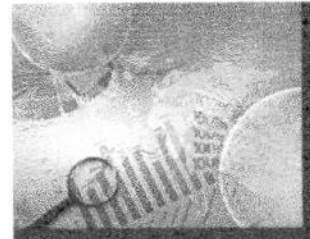

Tax Planning Strategies **Corporate Distributions**

Framework Focus: Income and Exclusions

Strategy: Avoid Income Recognition.

Concerning the discussion of corporate distributions, the following points are pertinent.

- Because E & P is used to determine a shareholder's dividend income, its periodic determination is essential to corporate planning. Thus, an E & P account should be established and maintained, particularly if the possibility exists that a corporate distribution might be a return of capital.
- Accumulated E & P is the sum of all past years' current E & P. Because there is no statute of limitations on the computation of E & P, the IRS can redetermine a corporation's current E & P for a tax year long ago. Such a change affects accumulated E & P and has a direct effect on the taxability of current distributions to shareholders.
- Distributions can be planned to avoid or minimize dividend exposure.

Example 13

Flicker Corporation holds accumulated E & P of $100,000 as of January 1 of the current year. During the year, it expects to generate earnings from operations of $80,000 and to sell an asset for a loss of $100,000. Thus, it anticipates a current E & P deficit of $20,000. Flicker also expects to make a cash distribution of $60,000 during the year.

A tax-effective approach by Flicker would be to recognize the loss as soon as possible and immediately thereafter make the cash distribution to the shareholders. Suppose these two steps

continued

take place on January 1. Because the current E & P now shows a deficit, the accumulated E & P account must be brought up to date (refer to Example 12). Thus, at the time of the distribution, the combined E & P balance is zero [$100,000 (beginning balance in accumulated E & P) − $100,000 (existing deficit in current E & P)], and the $60,000 distribution to the shareholders constitutes a return of capital. Current deficits are deemed to accrue pro rata throughout the year unless the parties can prove otherwise; here, they can.

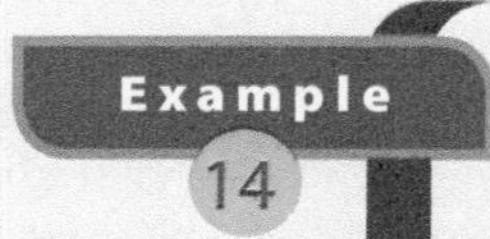

Example 14

After several unprofitable years, Darter Corporation has a deficit in accumulated E & P of $100,000 as of January 1, 2022. Starting in 2022, Darter expects to generate annual E & P of $50,000 for the next four years and would like to distribute this amount to its shareholders. The corporation's cash position (for dividend purposes) will correspond to the current E & P generated. Compare the following possibilities; Darter shareholders are indifferent between the two alternatives.

1. On December 31 of 2022, 2023, 2024, and 2025, Darter Corporation distributes cash of $50,000.
2. On December 31 of 2023 and 2025, Darter Corporation distributes cash of $100,000.

The two alternatives are illustrated as follows.

Year	Accumulated E & P (First of Year)	Current E & P	Distribution	Amount of Dividend
		Alternative 1		
2022	($100,000)	$50,000	$ 50,000	$50,000
2023	(100,000)	50,000	50,000	50,000
2024	(100,000)	50,000	50,000	50,000
2025	(100,000)	50,000	50,000	50,000
		Alternative 2		
2022	($100,000)	$50,000	$ –0–	$ –0–
2023	(50,000)	50,000	100,000	50,000
2024	(50,000)	50,000	–0–	–0–
2025	–0–	50,000	100,000	50,000

Alternative 1 produces $200,000 of dividend income because each $50,000 distribution is fully paid from current E & P. Alternative 2, however, produces only $100,000 of dividend income to the shareholders. The remaining $100,000 is a return of capital. Why?

When Darter made its first distribution of $100,000 on December 31, 2023, it had a deficit of $50,000 in accumulated E & P (the original deficit of $100,000 is reduced by the $50,000 of current E & P from 2022). Consequently, the $100,000 distribution yields a $50,000 dividend (the current E & P for 2023), and $50,000 is treated as a return of capital. As of January 1, 2024, Darter's accumulated E & P now has a deficit balance of $50,000, because a distribution cannot increase a deficit in E & P. After adding the remaining $50,000 of current E & P from 2024, the balance as of January 1, 2025, is zero. Thus, the second distribution of $100,000 made on December 31, 2025, also yields $50,000 of dividends (the current E & P for 2025) and a $50,000 return of capital.

By adjusting the distribution schedule only slightly, Darter shareholders cut in half their gross income from the payments.

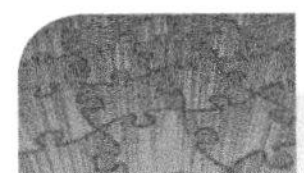

Concept Summary 13.2

Allocating E & P to Distributions

Current E & P at Time of Distribution	Accumulated E & P at Time of Distribution	Outcome	Illustration
Positive	**Positive**	Current E & P is applied first to distributions on a pro rata basis; then accumulated E & P is applied (as necessary) in chronological order beginning with the earliest distribution.	Example 9
		Unless the parties can show otherwise, it is presumed that current E & P covers all distributions.	Example 10
Positive	**Deficit**	Current and accumulated E & P are *not* netted. Distributions are dividends to the extent of current E & P. If the distribution exceeds the current E & P, the excess first reduces the stock basis to zero, and then it generates a taxable gain.	Example 11
Deficit	**Positive**	Current and accumulated E & P are netted. Any loss in current E & P is deemed to accrue ratably throughout the year, unless the corporation can show otherwise.	
		(1) If *positive:* Distribution is a dividend to the extent of the balance. If the distribution exceeds the net E & P, the excess first reduces the stock basis to zero and then generates a taxable gain.	Example 12
		(2) If *negative:* Distribution is treated as a return of capital, first reducing the stock basis to zero, then generating taxable gain.	Example 12
Deficit	**Deficit**	Entire distribution is treated as a return of capital, first reducing the basis of the stock to zero, then generating taxable gain.	

13-3 Noncash Dividends

Evaluate the tax effects of noncash dividends on the recipient shareholder and the corporation making the distribution.

The previous discussion assumed that all distributions by a corporation to its shareholders are in the form of cash. Although most corporate distributions are paid in cash, a corporation may distribute a noncash or **property dividend** for various reasons. For example, the shareholders may want a particular asset that is held by the corporation. Alternatively, a corporation that is strapped for cash still may want to distribute some profits to its shareholders and must use a noncash asset.

Bridge Discipline **Bridge to Investments**

Most investors look to the stocks of utilities, real estate investment trusts, and consumer products companies as the source of steady dividend payments. Alternatively, an investor could put together an effective portfolio using only stocks and mutual funds that regularly produce higher dividend yields.

Dividends can be important to the investor because:

- They may be attractive in a tax-sheltered account, like a § 401(k) plan, such that the tax inefficiency ("double taxation") of the dividends is not recognized immediately by the investor.
- Generally, a dividend-paying company is a profitable company, and corporate profits can be hard to come by.
- Earning and reinvesting dividends is an easy way to put into place an investment policy of dollar-cost averaging, a technique that forces the investor to buy more shares when prices are low and fewer shares when prices are high. Dollar-cost averaging often implements a contrarian investment strategy.

Distributions of noncash assets are treated for tax purposes in the same way as distributions of cash, except for effects attributable to any difference between the basis and the fair market value of the distributed property. Distributions of property with a basis that differs from fair market value raise several tax questions.

- *For the shareholder:*
  - What is the amount of the distribution?
  - What is the basis of the property in the shareholder's hands?
- *For the corporation:*
  - Is a gain or loss recognized as a result of the distribution?
  - What is the effect of the distribution on E & P?

13-3a Noncash Dividends—Effect on the Shareholder

When a corporation distributes property rather than cash to a shareholder, the amount distributed is measured by the fair market value of the property on the date of distribution.[12] As with a cash distribution, the portion of a property distribution covered by existing E & P is a dividend, and any excess is treated as a return of capital. If the fair market value of the property distributed exceeds the corporation's E & P and the shareholder's stock basis, a capital gain usually results.

The amount distributed is reduced (but not below zero) by any liabilities to which the distributed property is subject immediately before and after the distribution and by any liabilities of the corporation assumed by the shareholder. The basis in the distributed property to the shareholder is the fair market value of the property on the date of the distribution.

The Big Picture

Return to the facts of *The Big Picture* on p. 13-1. Plainwell Ice Cream Corporation distributed property with a $300,000 fair market value and $20,000 adjusted basis to Luis, one of its shareholders. The property was subject to a $100,000 mortgage, which Luis assumed.

As a result, Luis reports a distribution of $200,000 [$300,000 (fair market value) − $100,000 (liability)], which is taxed as a dividend. The basis of the property to Luis is $300,000, its fair market value.

Example 16

Red Corporation owns 10% of Tan Corporation. Tan holds ample E & P to cover any distributions made during the year. One distribution made to Red consists of a vacant lot with a basis of $50,000 and a fair market value of $30,000. Red recognizes dividend income of $30,000 (before the dividends received deduction), and its basis in the lot becomes $30,000.

Distributing property that has depreciated in value as a property dividend may reflect poor income tax planning. Note what happens in Example 16. Basis of $20,000 disappears due to the loss (Tan's basis $50,000, fair market value $30,000). As an alternative, if Tan Corporation sells the lot, it can use the $20,000 loss to reduce its taxable income for the year. Then Tan can distribute the $30,000 cash proceeds to its shareholders.

13-3b Noncash Dividends—Effect on the Corporation

Recognition of Gain or Loss

All distributions of appreciated property trigger a recognized gain to the distributing corporation.[13] In effect, a corporation that distributes appreciated property is treated as if it had sold the property to the shareholder for its fair market value. However, the distributing corporation does *not* recognize any realized loss on the distributed property.

[12] § 301.

[13] § 311.

The Big Picture

Return to the facts of *The Big Picture* on p. 13-1. Plainwell Ice Cream Corporation distributed property with a fair market value of $300,000 and an adjusted basis of $20,000 to Luis, one of its shareholders. As a result, Plainwell recognizes a $280,000 gain on the distribution.

Siesta Corporation distributes land with a basis of $30,000 and a fair market value of $10,000. Siesta does not recognize a loss on the distribution.

If the distributed property is subject to a liability in excess of basis or the shareholder assumes the liability, a special rule applies. For purposes of determining gain on the distribution, the fair market value of the property is treated as being at least the amount of the liability.[14]

Assume that the land in Example 18 is subject to a liability of $35,000, which is assumed by the shareholder who receives the land. The corporation recognizes gain of $5,000 on the distribution ($35,000 liability − $30,000 basis in the land).

Effect of Distributions on E & P

Distributions reduce E & P by the amount of money distributed and by the greater of the fair market value or the adjusted basis of property distributed, less the amount of any liability on the property.[15] E & P is increased by gain recognized when appreciated property is distributed as a property dividend.

Effects of Noncash Distributions

Crimson Corporation distributes property (basis $10,000 and fair market value $20,000) to Lei, its shareholder. Crimson recognizes a $10,000 gain, which is added to its E & P. E & P then is reduced by $20,000, the fair market value of the distributed property. Lei reports dividend income of $20,000 (presuming sufficient E & P from other events).

Assume the same facts as in Example 20, except that the property's adjusted basis to Crimson is $25,000. Crimson's E & P is reduced by $25,000, the property's adjusted basis, which is greater than the property's fair market value. Lei reports dividend income of $20,000 (the fair market value of the property received).

Assume the same facts as in Example 21, except that the property is subject to a liability of $6,000, which Lei assumes. E & P now is reduced by $19,000 [$25,000 (adjusted basis) − $6,000 (liability)]. Lei records a dividend of $14,000 [$20,000 (amount of the distribution) − $6,000 (liability)], and her basis in the property is $20,000, its fair market value.

Under no circumstances can a distribution, whether cash or noncash, either generate a deficit in E & P or add to a deficit in E & P. Deficits arise only through recognized corporate losses.

[14] § 311(b)(2).

[15] §§ 312(a), (b), and (c).

Bridge Discipline **Bridge to Finance**

The double taxation of corporate income always has been controversial. Arguably, taxing dividends twice creates several undesirable economic distortions, including:

- An incentive to invest in noncorporate rather than corporate entities.
- An incentive for corporations to finance operations with debt rather than with equity because interest payments are deductible. Notably, this behavior increases the vulnerability of corporations in economic downturns.
- An incentive for corporations to retain earnings and structure distributions of profits to avoid the double tax.

Collectively, these distortions may raise the cost of capital for corporate investments. In addition, elimination of the double tax would make the United States more competitive globally, since the taxing systems of a majority of U.S. trading partners assess only one tax on corporate income.

While many support a reduced or zero tax rate on dividends, others contend that the double tax should remain in place to rein in the concentration of economic power held by publicly traded corporations. Those favoring retention of the double tax also note that the benefits of reduced tax rates on dividends flow disproportionately to the wealthy.

Teal Corporation holds accumulated E & P of $10,000 at the beginning of the current tax year. During the year, it records current E & P of $15,000. At the end of the year, it distributes cash of $30,000 to its sole shareholder, Walter. Walter's basis in his Teal shares is $18,000.

Teal's E & P at the end of the year is reduced to zero by the dividend distribution. The remaining $5,000 of the distribution to Walter cannot generate a deficit in E & P; it is a nontaxable return of capital and reduces the basis in Walter's shares. Walter's stock basis now is $13,000 ($18,000 − $5,000).

Source of Distribution	Effects
Current E & P	($15,000)
Accumulated E & P	(10,000)
Return of capital	5,000

Identify the nature and treatment of constructive dividends.

13-4 Constructive Dividends

Any measurable economic benefit conveyed by a corporation to its shareholders can be treated as a dividend for Federal income tax purposes even though it is not declared or designated as a dividend by the entity's board of directors. A so-called **constructive dividend** typically is not issued pro rata to all shareholders.[16] Nor must the distribution satisfy the requirements of a dividend as set forth by applicable state law. Instead, a constructive dividend is strictly a creation of the Federal income tax law.

Constructive dividends usually arise in the context of closely held corporations. Here the dealings between the parties are less structured, and frequently, documentation of the transactions is not rigorous.

The constructive dividend might be seen as a substitute for actual distributions. Usually, it is intended to accomplish some tax objective not available through the direct payment of dividends. The shareholders may be attempting to distribute corporate profits in a form, such as compensation, that is deductible to the corporation. Alternatively, the shareholders may be seeking benefits for themselves while avoiding their own recognition of gross income.

[16]See *Lengsfield v. Comm.*, 57–1 USTC ¶9437, 50 AFTR 1683, 241 F.2d 508 (CA–5).

Not all constructive dividends are deliberate attempts to avoid formal dividends; many are entered into inadvertently. An awareness of the various constructive dividend situations is essential to protect the parties from unanticipated, undesirable tax consequences.

13-4a Types of Constructive Dividends

The most frequently encountered types of constructive dividends include the following.

Shareholder Use of Corporate-Owned Property

A constructive dividend can occur when a shareholder uses the corporation's property for personal purposes at no cost. Personal use of corporate-owned automobiles, airplanes, yachts, waterfront property, and entertainment facilities is commonplace in some closely held corporations. The shareholder recognizes dividend income to the extent of the fair rental value of the property for the period of its personal use.[17]

Bargain Sale of Corporate Property to a Shareholder

Shareholders often purchase property from a corporation at a cost below the fair market value of the property. These bargain sales produce dividend income to the extent that the property's fair market value on the date of sale differs from the amount the shareholder paid for the property.[18]

Bargain Rental of Corporate Property

A bargain rental of corporate property by a shareholder also produces dividend income. Here the measure of the constructive dividend is the excess of the property's fair rental value over the rent actually paid.

Payments for the Benefit of a Shareholder

If a corporation pays a shareholder's personal expenses, the payment is treated as a constructive dividend. The obligation involved need not be legally binding on the shareholder; it may, in fact, be motivated by a moral or charitable purpose.[19] Forgiveness of shareholder debt by the corporation also constitutes a constructive dividend.[20] Excessive rentals paid by a corporation for the use of shareholder property create a constructive dividend equal to the amount paid in excess of the fair rental value.

Unreasonable Compensation

A salary payment to a shareholder-employee that is determined to be **unreasonable compensation** frequently is treated as a constructive dividend. As a consequence, it is not deductible by the corporation. In determining the reasonableness of salary payments, the following factors have been considered by the courts and the IRS.

- The employee's qualifications.
- A comparison of salaries with dividend distributions.
- The prevailing rates of compensation for comparable positions in comparable business concerns.
- The nature and scope of the employee's work.
- The size and complexity of the business.
- A comparison of salaries paid with both gross and net income.

[17] *Daniel L.Reeves*, 94 TCM 287, T.C.Memo. 2007–273.

[18] Reg. § 1.301–1(j).

[19] *Montgomery Engineering Co. v. U.S.*, 64–2 USTC ¶9618, 13 AFTR 2d 1747, 230 F.Supp. 838 (D.Ct. N.J.), *aff'd* in 65–1 USTC ¶9368, 15 AFTR 2d 746, 344 F.2d 996 (CA–3).

[20] Reg. § 1.301–1(m).

Global Tax Issues A Worldwide View of Dividends

From an international perspective, U.S. double taxation of dividends is unusual. Most developed countries have adopted a policy of *corporate integration*, which imposes a single tax on corporate profits.

Corporate integration takes several forms. One popular approach is to impose a tax at the corporate level but allow shareholders to claim a credit for corporate-level taxes paid when dividends are received. A second alternative is to allow a corporate-level deduction for dividends paid to shareholders. A third approach is to allow shareholders to exclude corporate dividends from income.

Facing tradeoffs between equity and the economic distortions introduced by double taxation and the prevalence of corporate integration throughout the world, U.S. tax law continues to struggle with the issue of how corporate distributions should be taxed.

- The taxpayer's salary policy toward all employees.
- For small corporations with a limited number of officers, the amount of compensation paid to the employee in question in previous years.
- For large corporations, whether a "reasonable investor," acting in the best interests of the entity, would have agreed to the level of compensation paid.[21]

Loans to Shareholders

Advances to shareholders that are not bona fide loans usually are reclassified as constructive dividends. Whether an advance qualifies as a bona fide loan is a question of fact to be determined in light of the particular circumstances. Factors considered in determining whether the advance is a bona fide loan include the following.[22]

- Whether the advance is on open account or is evidenced by a written instrument.
- Whether the shareholder furnished collateral or other security for the advance.
- How long the advance has been outstanding.
- Whether any repayments have been made.
- The shareholder's ability to repay the advance.
- The shareholder's use of the funds (e.g., payment of routine bills versus nonrecurring, extraordinary expenses).
- The regularity of the advances.
- The dividend-paying history of the corporation.

13-4b Shareholder Treatment of Constructive Dividends

For tax purposes, constructive distributions are treated like cash distributions.[23] As a result, a corporate shareholder is entitled to the dividends received deduction (refer to text Section 12-4a). The constructive distribution constitutes dividend income only to the extent of the corporation's current and accumulated E & P.[24]

Digging Deeper 1

Information on the disappearing dividend tax can be found on this book's companion website: www.cengage.com

[21]*Mayson Manufacturing Co. v. Comm.*, 49–2 USTC ¶9467, 38 AFTR 1028, 178 F.2d 115 (CA–6) and *Alpha Medical v. Comm.*, 99–1 USTC ¶50,461, 83 AFTR 2d 99–1922, 172 F.3d 942 (CA–6).

[22]*Fin Hay Realty Co. v. U.S.*, 68–2 USTC ¶9438, 22 AFTR 2d 5004, 398 F.2d 694 (CA–3).

[23]*Simon v. Comm.*, 57–2 USTC ¶9989, 52 AFTR 698, 248 F.2d 869 (CA–8).

[24]*DiZenzo v. Comm.*, 65–2 USTC ¶9518, 16 AFTR 2d 5107, 348 F.2d 122 (CA–2).

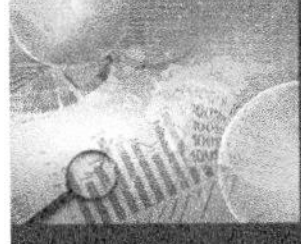

Tax Planning Strategies **Constructive Dividends**

Framework Focus: Income and Exclusions

Strategy: Avoid Income Recognition.

Tax planning can be particularly effective in avoiding constructive dividend situations. Shareholders should try to structure their dealings with the corporation on an arm's length basis. For example, reasonable rent should be paid for the use of corporate property, and a fair price should be paid for its purchase. The parties should make every effort to support the amount involved with appraisal data or market information obtained from reliable sources at or near the time of the transaction.

Dealings between shareholders and a closely held corporation should be as formal as possible. In the case of loans to shareholders, for example, the parties should provide for an adequate rate of interest and written evidence of the debt. Shareholders also should establish and follow a realistic repayment schedule.

If shareholders want to distribute corporate profits in a form deductible to the corporation, a balanced mix of the possible alternatives lessens the risk of constructive dividend treatment. Rent for the use of shareholder property, interest on amounts borrowed from shareholders, or salaries for services rendered by shareholders are all feasible substitutes for dividend distributions.

Much can be done to protect against the disallowance of unreasonable compensation. Example 24 is an illustration, all too common in a family corporation, of what *not* to do.

Bob Cole wholly owns Eagle Corporation. Corporate employees and their annual salaries include Rebecca, Bob's wife ($120,000); Sam, Bob's son ($80,000); Bob ($640,000); and Wong, an unrelated longtime friend ($320,000). The operation of Eagle is shared about equally between Bob and Wong. Rebecca performed significant services for Eagle during its formative years but now merely attends the annual meeting of the board of directors. Sam is a full-time student and occasionally signs papers for the corporation in his capacity as treasurer.

Eagle has not made a cash distribution for 10 years, although it holds substantial accumulated E & P. Rebecca, Sam, and Bob run the risk of a finding of unreasonable compensation, based on the following factors.

- Rebecca's salary is vulnerable unless proof is available that some or all of her $120,000 annual salary is payment for services rendered to the corporation in prior years and that she was underpaid for those years.[25]
- Sam's salary also is vulnerable; he does not appear to earn the $80,000 paid to him by the corporation. Although neither Sam nor Rebecca is a shareholder, each one's relationship to Bob is enough of a tie-in to raise the unreasonable compensation issue.
- Bob's salary could be challenged by the IRS. Why is Bob receiving $320,000 more than Wong when it appears that they share equally in the operation of the corporation?
- The fact that Eagle has not distributed any cash over the past 10 years, even though it is capable of doing so, also may increase the likelihood of constructive dividend treatment.

What could have been done to improve the tax position of the parties in Example 24? Rebecca and Sam are not entitled to a significant salary, as neither seems to be performing any services for the corporation. Bob probably should reduce his compensation to correspond to that paid to Wong. He then can attempt to distribute corporate earnings to himself in some other form.

continued

[25]See, for example, *R. J. Nicoll Co.*, 59 T.C. 37 (1972).

Paying some dividends to Bob also might help to alleviate the problems raised in Example 24. The IRS has been successful in denying a deduction for salary paid to a shareholder-employee, even when the payment was reasonable, in a situation where the corporation had not distributed any dividends.[26] Most courts, however, have not denied deductions for compensation solely because a dividend was not paid. A better approach is to compare an employee's compensation with the level of compensation prevalent in the particular industry.

The corporation can substitute *indirect* compensation for Bob by paying expenses that benefit him personally but are nevertheless deductible to the corporation. For example, premiums paid by the corporation for sickness, accident, and hospitalization insurance for Bob are deductible to the corporation and generally nontaxable to him.[27] Any payments under the policy are not taxable to Bob unless they exceed his medical expenses.[28]

The corporation also can pay for travel and entertainment expenses incurred by Bob on behalf of the corporation. If these expenditures are primarily for the benefit of the corporation, Bob recognizes no gross income, and the corporation claims a deduction.[29] The tax treatment of these benefits is discussed in text Section 11-3.

When testing for reasonableness, the IRS looks at the total compensation package, including indirect compensation payments to a shareholder-employee.

What Is the Employee's Compensation?

Cora, the president and sole shareholder of Willet Corporation, is paid an annual salary of $400,000 by the corporation. She would like to draw funds from the corporation but is concerned that additional salary payments might cause the IRS to contend that her salary is unreasonable.

Cora does not want Willet to pay any dividends. She also wants to donate $50,000 to her alma mater to establish scholarships for needy students. Willet Corporation could make the contribution on its president's behalf. The payment clearly benefits Cora, but the amount of the contribution is not taxed to her.[30] Willet claims a charitable contribution deduction for the payment.

Example 26

Assume in Example 25 that Cora has made an individual pledge to the university to provide $50,000 for scholarships for needy students. Willet Corporation satisfies Cora's pledge by paying the $50,000 to the university. The $50,000 will be taxed to Cora. In this context, the $50,000 payment to the university may be treated as *indirect* compensation to Cora.[31]

In determining whether Cora's salary is unreasonable, both the *direct* payment of her $400,000 salary and the *indirect* $50,000 payment are considered. Cora's total compensation package is $450,000. Cora may be eligible for a charitable contribution deduction (see text Section 10-4d).

Certain activities can combine both business and personal dimensions (e.g., a business trip to Hawaii). A country club membership can generate both business and personal use. Such items can be attractive as forms of indirect compensation, but disentangling the business and personal use of business assets can be a challenge.

[26] *Charles McCandless Tile Service v. U.S.*, 70–1 USTC ¶9284, 25 AFTR 2d 70–870, 422 F.2d 1336 (Ct.Cls.). The court in *McCandless* concluded that a return on equity of 15% of net profits was reasonable.

[27] Reg. § 1.162–10.

[28] The medical reimbursement plan must meet certain nondiscrimination requirements. § 105(h)(2).

[29] Reg. § 1.62–2(c)(4).

[30] *Henry J. Knott*, 67 T.C. 681 (1977), *acq.* 1979–2 C.B. 2

[31] *Schalk Chemical Co. v. Comm.*, 62–1 USTC ¶9496, 9 AFTR 2d 1579, 304 F.2d 48 (CA–9).

Ultimately, whether a constructive dividend exists when indirect compensation is used often depends on the employer's policies and related documentation substantiating some business justification for the usage. Many companies have policies that allow for the "limited personal use" of certain corporate assets (such as computers, telephones, mobile devices, copy machines, conference rooms, and vehicles). This "limited personal use" exception typically is allowed as long as the employee's use is occasional, is not for outside employment, does not result in excessive costs, and does not interfere with work responsibilities.

13-5 Stock Dividends

LO.6

Distinguish between taxable and nontaxable stock dividends.

On occasion, a C corporation issues a dividend in the form of its own stock (i.e., instead of using cash or other property). This may occur because the entity is short of cash or because it wants to dispose of some treasury stock that it holds. A **stock dividend** is triggered by a board directive. Stock dividends are rare events; about 2 percent of all C corporation distributions during a typical tax year involve the corporation's own shares.

As a general rule, stock dividends are excluded from income if they are pro rata distributions of stock or stock rights paid on common stock.[32] However, there are exceptions to this general rule.

Additional information on stock rights can be found on this book's companion website: www.cengage.com

If a stock dividend is not taxable, the corporation's E & P is not reduced.[33] If a stock dividend is taxable, the distributing corporation treats the distribution in the same manner as any other taxable distribution.

If a stock dividend is taxable, the shareholder's basis of the newly received shares is fair market value and the holding period starts on the date of receipt. If a stock dividend is not taxable, the basis of the stock on which the dividend is distributed is reallocated.[34]

If the dividend shares are identical to these formerly held shares, basis in the old stock is reallocated by dividing the taxpayer's cost in the old stock by the total number of shares. If the dividend stock is not identical to the underlying shares (e.g., a stock dividend of preferred on common), basis is determined by allocating the basis of the formerly held shares between the old and new stock according to the fair market value of each. The holding period includes the holding period of the previously held stock.[35]

Stock Dividends

Example 27

Gail bought 1,000 shares of common stock two years ago for $10,000. In the current tax year, Gail receives 10 shares of common stock as a nontaxable stock dividend. To determine Gail's basis in the new shares, the existing basis of $10,000 is divided by 1,010 (the number of shares outstanding after the distribution). Consequently, each share of stock now has a basis of $9.90 instead of the pre-dividend $10 basis.

Example 28

Assume instead that Gail received a nontaxable preferred stock dividend of 100 shares. The preferred stock has a fair market value of $1,000, and the common stock, on which the preferred is distributed, has a fair market value of $19,000. After the receipt of the stock dividend, the basis of the common stock is $9,500, and the basis of the preferred is $500, computed as follows.

continued

[32]Companies often issue stock dividends or authorize stock splits to keep the stock price in an affordable range. Stock splits do not change the total value of an investment. For example, 100 shares at $100 will become 200 shares at $50 after the split. However, some studies show that a stock split often leads to an upward price trend over the year following the split.

[33]§ 312(d)(1).

[34]§ 307(a).

[35]§ 1223(5).

Fair market value of common	$19,000
Fair market value of preferred	1,000
	$20,000
Basis of common: $\frac{19}{20}$ × $10,000	$ 9,500
Basis of preferred: $\frac{1}{20}$ × $10,000	$ 500

Digging Deeper 3

Additional information on stock dividends can be found on this book's companion website: www.cengage.com

LO.7

Discuss the tax treatment of stock redemptions and corporate liquidations.

13-6 Stock Redemptions

Many investors are tempted to use a "no dividends" strategy in working with a healthy corporation whose accumulated profits and market value continue to rise over time.

Example 29

Sally invests $100,000 in the new Cream Corporation. Cream is successful in generating operating profits, and it reinvests its accumulated profits in the business rather than paying dividends. Fifteen years later, Sally's shares are worth $300,000, and her share of Cream's E & P exceeds $1,000,000. Sally sells the shares for a $200,000 long-term capital gain, taxed at a rate of only 20%. By selling her stock to a third party, Sally can reduce the sales proceeds by her stock basis, resulting in a significant tax savings to her, at no detriment to Cream.

A similar strategy would seem to work where several shareholders can act in concert. Using a **stock redemption** to carry out this strategy, the corporation buys back shares from its shareholders in a market transaction. Stock redemptions occur for numerous reasons, including the following.

- To acquire the holdings of a retiring or deceased shareholder.
- To carry out a property settlement related to a divorce.
- To increase the per-share price of the stock as it trades in a market.
- To implement a business succession plan (e.g., using a buy-sell agreement to transfer shares from one generation of shareholders to a younger one).

Bridge Discipline **Bridge to Finance**

Stock buybacks are popular among U.S. corporations as a means to manipulate share prices. If a buyback is executed properly, all shareholders retain their respective levels of control over the entity, but because fewer shares now are available on the market, an artificial increase in share price occurs. Often, the market temporarily "overcorrects" for the buyback, probably because of the publicity the transaction attracts in the press, and the corporation's total capitalized value actually increases.

Most stock buybacks result in dividend income to the shareholders. Stock redemptions of this type generally do not qualify for capital gain/loss treatment under the tax law. Thus, parties must measure the costs associated with an effective distribution of retained earnings in this way. If dividend income is subject to a favorable tax rate or if the corporate owner of the redeemed shares qualifies for the dividends received deduction, there are few impediments to the plans for the buyback.

Some analysts see an increase in stock buyback activity as a sign of an increasingly healthy economy. A combination of large corporate cash balances and low market interest rates, and significant cuts in effective income tax rates, also can accelerate the buyback market.

Global Tax Issues — Non-U.S. Shareholders Prefer Capital Gain Treatment in Stock Redemptions

As a general rule, non-U.S. shareholders of U.S. corporations are subject to U.S. income tax on dividend income but not on capital gains. In some situations, a nonresident alien or business entity is taxed on a capital gain from the disposition of stock in a U.S. corporation, but only if the stock was effectively connected with the conduct of a U.S. trade or business of the individual. See text Section 16-2.

Whether a stock redemption qualifies for capital gain treatment therefore takes on added significance for non-U.S. shareholders. If one of the qualifying stock redemption rules can be satisfied, the non-U.S. shareholder typically will avoid U.S. income tax on the transaction. If, instead, dividend income is the result, a 30 percent withholding tax typically applies.

Stock redemptions generally result in dividend income for the shareholder whose stock is redeemed, rather than a capital gain or loss, unless the shareholder surrenders significant control in the entity as a result of the redemption. Capital gain/loss treatment largely is restricted to stock buybacks where either:

- All of the shareholder's stock is redeemed.[36]
- After the redemption, the investor is a minority shareholder and owns less than 80 percent of the interest owned in the corporation before the redemption.[37]

Information on disproportionate and other redemptions can be found on this book's companion website: www.cengage.com

4 Digging Deeper

In measuring the investor's stock holdings before and after the redemption, shares owned by related taxpayers also are counted.[38]

Stock attribution rules can be found on this book's companion website: www.cengage.com

5 Digging Deeper

Mike and Cheryl are husband and wife, and each owns 100 shares in Mauve Corporation, the total of all of Mauve's outstanding stock. Mauve's operations have produced a sizable aggregated operating profit over the years, such that its E & P exceeds $5,000,000. Mike and Cheryl have realized appreciation of $600,000 on their original investment of $100,000 each, and they would like to enjoy some of the cash that Mauve has accumulated during their holding period.

At Mike's request, instead of paying a dividend, Mauve buys back one-half of Mike's shares for $350,000. This seems to produce a $300,000 long-term capital gain [$350,000 (sales proceeds) − $50,000 (basis in 50 shares of Mauve stock)], but it results in a $350,000 dividend for Mike, since the redemption did not reduce the control of Mauve that Mike and Cheryl can exercise.

When the transaction is treated as a dividend, the investor's basis in the redeemed shares *does not disappear*; rather, it attaches to any remaining shares that he or she owns. Corporate E & P is reduced by the amount of any recognized dividend.

Stock redemptions also can result in capital gain/loss treatment when the shareholder dies or when the corporation downsizes.[39] Other tax consequences for the redeeming corporation are summarized as follows.

- If noncash property is used to acquire the redeemed shares, the corporation recognizes any realized gain (but not loss) on the distributed assets.[40]
- When the shareholder is taxed as having received a capital gain, E & P of the redeeming corporation *disappears* to the extent of the percentage of shares redeemed relative to the shares outstanding before the buyback.[41]

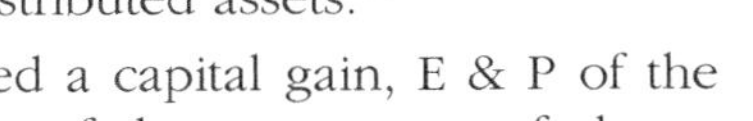

[36] § 302(b)(3).

[37] § 302(b)(2).

[38] Code § 318 is used for this purpose.

[39] For example, see §§ 302(b)(4) and 303.

[40] § 311.

[41] The E & P reduction cannot exceed the amount of the redemption proceeds. § 312(n)(7).

Tax Planning Strategies — Stock Redemptions

Framework Focus: Tax Rates

Strategy: Control the Character of Income and Deductions.

Stock redemptions offer several possibilities for tax planning.

- Usually, a stock redemption triggers dividend treatment. A preferential tax rate on dividend income reduces some of the adverse consequences of a nonqualified stock redemption for noncorporate shareholders.
- Dividend treatment for a stock redemption may be preferable to a redemption that produces a capital gain if the distributing corporation has little or no E & P or where the distributee-shareholder is another C corporation. In the latter situation, dividend treatment may be preferred due to the availability of the dividends received deduction.
- Stock redemptions are well suited for purchasing the interest of a retiring or deceased shareholder. Rather than the remaining shareholders buying the stock of the exiting shareholder, corporate funds are used to redeem the stock from the retiring shareholder or from the decedent shareholder's estate. The ability to use the corporation's funds to buy out a shareholder's interest also can be advantageous in property settlements between divorcing taxpayers.
- A qualifying stock redemption financed by installment notes can provide tax benefits to both the corporation and the shareholder. For the corporation, the related interest expense is deductible (subject to the business interest expense limitation; see text Section 12-4b). The shareholder can use the installment method to defer the gain recognition attributable to the notes, as noted in text Section 4-3b.

13-7 Corporate Liquidations

When a corporation makes a nonliquidating distribution (e.g., a cash dividend or a stock redemption), the entity continues as a going concern. With a complete liquidation, however, corporate existence terminates, as does the shareholder's ownership interest. A complete liquidation, like a qualifying stock redemption, produces capital gain/loss treatment to the *shareholder*. However, the tax effects of a liquidation to the *corporation* vary somewhat from those of a redemption. Gain/loss treatment is the general rule for the liquidating corporation, although some losses are disallowed.

13-7a The Liquidation Process

Shareholders may decide to liquidate a corporation for one or more reasons, including the following.

- The corporate business has been unsuccessful.
- The shareholders want to acquire the corporation's assets.
- Another person or entity wants to purchase the corporation's assets. The purchaser may buy the shareholders' stock and then liquidate the corporation to acquire the assets. Alternatively, the purchaser may buy the assets directly from the corporation. After the assets are sold, the corporation distributes the sales proceeds to its shareholders and liquidates.

A **corporate liquidation** exists when a corporation ceases to be a going concern. The corporation continues solely to wind up its affairs, pay debts, and distribute any remaining assets to its shareholders. Legal dissolution under state law is not required for a liquidation to be complete for tax purposes. A liquidation can exist even if the corporation retains a nominal amount of assets to pay remaining debts and preserve legal status.[42]

13-7b Liquidating and Nonliquidating Distributions Compared

As noted previously, a *nonliquidating* property distribution, whether in the form of a dividend or a stock redemption, triggers gain (but not loss) to the distributing corporation. For the shareholder, the receipt of cash or property produces dividend income to

[42]Reg. § 1.332–2(c).

the extent of the corporation's E & P or, in the case of a qualifying stock redemption, results in a capital gain or loss.

However, a complete liquidation produces different tax consequences to the liquidating corporation.[43] With certain exceptions, a liquidating corporation recognizes gain *and* loss upon the distribution of its assets. Thus, a liquidation usually results in income tax for both the corporation and the shareholders; this can be seen as a form of double taxation.

Goose Corporation, with an E & P balance of $40,000, makes a cash distribution of $50,000 to one of its shareholders. The shareholder's basis in the Goose stock is $24,000. If the distribution is not a qualifying stock redemption or in complete liquidation, the shareholder recognizes dividend income of $40,000 (the amount of Goose's E & P) and treats the remaining $10,000 of the distribution as a return of capital (i.e., stock basis is reduced to $14,000).

If the distribution is a qualifying stock redemption or is pursuant to a complete liquidation, the shareholder recognizes a capital gain of $26,000 ($50,000 distribution − $24,000 stock basis).

Information on parent-subsidiary liquidations can be found on this book's companion website: www.cengage.com

6 Digging Deeper

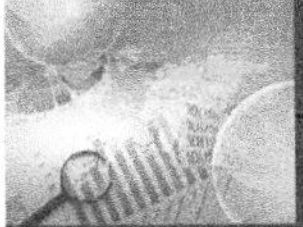

Tax Planning Strategies **Corporate Liquidations**

Framework Focus: Tax Rates

Strategy: Avoid Double Taxation.

Usually, distributions in liquidation are taxed at both the corporate level and the shareholder level. When a corporation liquidates, it can, as a general rule, deduct losses on assets that have depreciated in value. These assets should not be distributed in the form of a property dividend or stock redemption, because losses are not recognized on nonliquidating distributions.

Shareholders faced with large prospective gains in a liquidation may consider shifting part or all of that gain to other taxpayers. One approach is to donate the liquidating corporation's stock to charity, producing a deduction equal to the stock's fair market value.

Alternatively, the stock may be transferred by gift to family members. Some or all of the later capital gain on liquidation could be taxed at the reduced tax rate on long-term capital gains. However, possible gift tax issues on the stock transfer must be considered (see text Section 1-3d). Effective planning for stock transfers in the context of a liquidation therefore is crucial in arriving at the desired tax result.

13-8 Restrictions on Corporate Accumulations

Two provisions of the Code are designed to prevent corporations and their shareholders from avoiding the double tax on dividend distributions. Both provisions impose a penalty tax on undistributed income retained by the corporation. The rules underlying these provisions are complex and beyond the scope of this text. However, a brief description is provided as an introduction.

The *accumulated earnings tax*[44] imposes a 20 percent tax on the current year's corporate earnings that have been accumulated without a reasonable business need. The burden of proving what constitutes a reasonable need is borne by the taxpayer. In determining the excessive accumulated income, most businesses are allowed a $250,000 minimum exemption. Thus, most corporations can accumulate $250,000 in earnings over a series of years without fear of an accumulated earnings tax. Beyond the exemption amount, a C corporation's earnings can be accumulated, without incurring the penalty tax, for:

[43] § 331.

[44] §§ 531–537.

- Working capital needs (e.g., to purchase inventory or pay salaries and taxes),
- Retirement of debt incurred in connection with the business,
- Investment or loans to suppliers or customers (if necessary to maintain the corporation's business), or
- Realistic business contingencies, including lawsuits or self-insurance.

The *personal holding company (PHC) tax*[45] acts to discourage the sheltering of gross income in corporations owned by individuals who are subject to high marginal income tax rates. The PHC tax is applied at a 20 percent rate; in any tax year, the IRS cannot impose both the PHC tax and the accumulated earnings tax on the same corporation. Generally, an entity is considered a PHC and may be subject to the tax if:

- More than 50 percent of the value of the outstanding stock was owned by five or fewer individuals at any time during the last half of the year, and
- A substantial portion (60 percent or more) of the corporation's income is comprised of dividends, interest, rents, royalties, or certain personal service income.

Refocus on The Big Picture

Taxing Corporate Distributions

A number of factors affect the tax treatment of Plainwell Ice Cream Corporation's distributions. The amount of current and accumulated E & P (which differs from the financial reporting concept of retained earnings) partially determines the tax effect on the shareholders. Given that Plainwell had a highly profitable year, it is possible that current E & P equals or exceeds the amount of the distributions. If so, they are dividends to the shareholders rather than a return of capital.

Waffle Cone Corporation receives $200,000 of dividend income that is mostly offset by the dividends received deduction. The amount of the offsetting deduction depends on the ownership percentage that Waffle Cone holds in Plainwell. In this situation, Waffle Cone likely would qualify for a dividends received deduction of $130,000 ($200,000 × 65%). Luis reports $200,000 of dividend income (i.e., $300,000 value of the real estate less the $100,000 mortgage). Assuming that Plainwell is a U.S. corporation and that Luis has held his stock for the entire year, the distribution is a qualified dividend. As a result, the dividend is subject to reduced income tax rates. Luis's basis in the real estate is its fair market value at distribution, or $300,000.

From Plainwell's perspective, the distribution of the appreciated property triggers a recognized gain, equal to $280,000 ($300,000 fair market value less $20,000 adjusted basis). While the gain increases Plainwell's E & P, the distributions to the shareholders reduce it by $200,000 for the cash and $200,000 for the real estate ($300,000 fair market value reduced by the $100,000 mortgage).

What If?

What if the balance of current E & P is less than the combined value of the cash and real estate distributed to the shareholders? Current E & P is applied pro rata to the cash and the real estate. Because the amounts received by the two shareholders are equal ($200,000 each), the current E & P applied is taxed as a dividend and is treated as described above.

To the extent the distributions are not paid from current E & P, accumulated E & P is applied in a pro rata fashion (both distributions were made on December 31). However, if Plainwell reports a deficit in accumulated E & P, the remaining amounts distributed to the two shareholders are first a tax-free recovery of stock basis, and any excess is taxed as a sale of the stock (probably classified as capital gain).

[45] §§ 541–547.

Suggested Readings

Matt Egan, "Are Stock Buybacks Deepening America's Inequality?", **money.cnn.com/2018/03/05/investing/stock-buybacks-inequality-tax-law/index.html**, March 5, 2018.

Matthew DiLallo, "Dividend Reinvestment," **tinyurl.com/fool-drips**, October 12, 2020.

Key Terms

Accumulated E & P, 13-3
Constructive dividend, 13-16
Corporate liquidation, 13-24
Current E & P, 13-3
Dividend, 13-2
Earnings and profits, 13-2
Property dividend, 13-13
Stock dividend, 13-21
Stock redemption, 13-22
Unreasonable compensation, 13-17

Computational Exercises

1. **LO.1** At the beginning of the year, Myrna Corporation (a calendar year taxpayer) holds E & P of $32,000. The corporation generates no additional E & P during the year. On December 31, the corporation distributes $50,000 to its sole shareholder, Abby, whose stock basis is $10,000. How does the Federal income tax law treat this distribution?

2. **LO.3** On January 1 of the current year, Rhondell Corporation holds accumulated E & P of $13,000. Current E & P for the year is $84,000, earned evenly throughout the year. Elizabeth and Jonathan are the sole equal shareholders of Rhondell from January 1 to April 30. On May 1, Elizabeth sells all of her stock to Marshall.

   Rhondell makes two distributions to shareholders during the year, as indicated below. Analyze the distributions by completing the table that follows. Assume that the shareholders have sufficient basis in their stock for any amount that is treated as return of capital.

Total Distribution	From Current E & P	From Accumulated E & P	Return of Capital
April 30, $42,000 cash	________	________	________
December 31, $58,000 cash	________	________	________

3. **LO.5** Global Corporation distributed property with an $850,000 fair market value and a $415,000 adjusted basis to Kang, one of its shareholders. The property was subject to a $230,000 mortgage, which Kang assumed. Global's accumulated E & P totals $3,000,000.

   What is the amount of Kang's dividend income on the distribution? What is Kang's basis in the property received?

4. **LO.5** Fargo Corporation holds $5,000,000 in accumulated E & P. It distributes to Leilei, one of its shareholders, land worth $310,000; basis of the land to Fargo is $260,000. Determine the Federal income tax consequences of the distribution to Fargo.

5. LO.7 During the current year, Gnatcatcher, Inc. (E & P of $1,000,000), distributed $200,000 each to Brandi and Yuen in redemption of some of their Gnatcatcher stock. The two shareholders are not related; they acquired their shares five years ago. Brandi and Yuen are in the 32% income tax bracket, and each had a $45,000 basis in her redeemed stock.
   a. Assume that the distribution to Brandi is a qualifying stock redemption. Determine Brandi's tax liability on the distribution.
   b. Assume that the distribution to Yuen is a nonqualified stock redemption. Determine Yuen's tax liability on the distribution.

6. LO.7 Rosalie owns 50% of the outstanding stock of Salmon Corporation. In a qualifying stock redemption, Salmon distributes $80,000 to Rosalie in exchange for one-half of her shares, which have a basis of $100,000. Compute Rosalie's recognized loss, if any, on the redemption.

Digging Deeper

7. LO.7 Derk owns 250 shares of stock in Rose Corporation. The remaining 750 shares of Rose are owned as follows: 150 by Derk's daughter Rosalie, 200 by Derk's aunt Penelope, and 400 by a partnership in which Derk holds an 80% interest. Determine the number of shares that Derk owns (directly and indirectly) in Rose Corporation.

8. LO.7 Caramel Corporation has 5,000 shares of stock outstanding. In a qualifying stock redemption, Caramel distributes $145,000 in exchange for 1,000 of its shares. At the time of the redemption, Caramel has recorded paid-in capital of $800,000 and E & P of $300,000. Calculate the reduction to Caramel's E & P as a result of the distribution.

Problems

9. LO.1, 3 At the start of the current year, Blue Corporation (a calendar year taxpayer) holds accumulated E & P of $100,000. Blue's current E & P is $60,000. At the end of the year, it distributes $200,000 ($100,000 each) to its equal shareholders, Pooja and Jon. Their basis in the stock is $11,000 for Pooja and $26,000 for Jon. How is the distribution treated for tax purposes?

10. LO.2 Cardinal Corporation, a calendar year taxpayer, receives dividend income of $250,000 from a corporation in which it holds a 10% interest. Cardinal also receives interest income of $35,000 from municipal bonds. (The municipality used the proceeds from the bond issue to construct a public library.) Cardinal borrowed funds to purchase the municipal bonds and pays $20,000 of interest on the loan. Excluding these three items, Cardinal's taxable income is $500,000, on which it paid Federal income tax of $131,250 during the year.
    a. What is Cardinal's taxable income after these items are taken into account?
    b. What is Cardinal's accumulated E & P at the end of the tax year if its beginning E & P balance was $150,000?

11. LO.2 Compute current E & P for Sparrow Corporation (a calendar year, accrual basis taxpayer). Sparrow reported the following transactions during 2022, its second year of operation.

Taxable income	$330,000
Federal income tax liability paid	69,300
Tax-exempt interest income	5,000
Meals expense provided by a restaurant (total)	3,000
Premiums paid on key employee life insurance	3,500
Increase in cash surrender value attributable to life insurance premiums	700
Proceeds from key employee life insurance policy	130,000
Cash surrender value of life insurance policy at distribution	20,000

Excess of capital losses over capital gains	$ 13,000
MACRS deduction	26,000
Straight-line depreciation using ADS lives	16,000
Section 179 expense elected during 2021	25,000
Dividends received from domestic corporations (less than 20% owned)	35,000

- Sparrow uses the LIFO inventory method, and its LIFO recapture amount increased by $10,000 during 2022.
- Sparrow sold some property on installments during 2021. The property was sold for $40,000 and had an adjusted basis then of $32,000. During 2022, Sparrow received a $15,000 payment on the installment sale.

12. **LO.1, 2, 3** On September 30, Silver Corporation, a calendar year taxpayer, sold a parcel of land (basis of $400,000) for a $1,000,000 note. The note is payable in five installments, with the first payment due next year. Because Silver did not elect out of the installment method, none of the $600,000 gain is taxed this year.

    Silver Corporation had a $300,000 deficit in accumulated E & P at the beginning of the year. Before considering the effect of the land sale, Silver had a deficit in current E & P of $50,000.

    Javiera, the sole shareholder of Silver, has a basis of $200,000 in her stock. If Silver distributes $900,000 to Javiera on December 31, how much gross income must she report for Federal income tax purposes?

13. **LO.2** In determining Blue Corporation's current E & P for the current tax year, how should taxable income be adjusted as a result of the following transactions?
    a. A capital loss carryover from one year ago, fully used this year.
    b. Nondeductible business meal expenses.
    c. Interest income on municipal bonds.
    d. Nondeductible lobbying expenses.
    e. Loss on a sale between related parties.
    f. Federal income tax refund from last year's return, received this year.

14. **LO.1, 3** Sparrow Corporation is a calendar year taxpayer. At the beginning of the current year, Sparrow holds accumulated E & P of $33,000. The corporation incurs a deficit in current E & P of $46,000 that accrues ratably throughout the year. On June 30, Sparrow distributes $20,000 to its sole shareholder, Libby. If Libby's stock has a basis of $4,000, how is she taxed on the distribution? Critical Thinking

15. **LO.1, 3** Complete the following schedule for each case. Unless otherwise indicated, assume that the shareholders have ample basis in the stock investment. All taxpayers use a calendar tax year.

	Accumulated E & P Beginning of Year	Current E & P	Cash Distributions (All on Last Day of Year)	Dividend Income	Return of Capital
a.	($200,000)	$ 70,000	$130,000	______	______
b.	150,000	(120,000)	210,000	______	______
c.	90,000	70,000	150,000	______	______
d.	120,000	(60,000)	130,000	______	______
e.	Same as part (d), except that the distribution of $130,000 is made on June 30 and the corporation uses the calendar year for tax purposes.			______	______

16. **LO.1, 3** YiLing, the sole shareholder of Brown Corporation, sold her stock to Calvin on July 30 for $270,000. YiLing's basis in the stock was $200,000 at the beginning of the year. Brown had accumulated E & P of $120,000 on January 1

and current E & P of $240,000. During the year, Brown made the following distributions: $450,000 cash to YiLing on July 1 and $150,000 cash to Calvin on December 30. How will YiLing and Calvin be taxed on the distributions? How much gain will YiLing recognize on the sale of her stock to Calvin?

Critical Thinking

17. **LO.1, 2** In each of the following independent situations, indicate the effect on taxable income and E & P, stating the amount of any increase (or decrease) in each as a result of the transaction. Assume that E & P has already been increased by taxable income.

	Transaction	Taxable Income Increase (Decrease)	E & P Increase (Decrease)
a.	Realized gain of $80,000 on involuntary conversion of building ($10,000 of gain is recognized).	________	________
b.	Mining exploration costs incurred on May 1 of current year; $24,000 is deductible from current-year taxable income.	________	________
c.	Sale of equipment to unrelated third party for $240,000; basis is $120,000 (no election out of installment method; no payments are received in current year).	________	________
d.	Dividends of $20,000 received from 5% owned corporation, together with dividends received deduction (assume that the taxable income limit does not apply).	________	________
e.	Additional first-year (bonus) depreciation of $45,000 claimed in current year.	________	________
f.	Section 179 expense deduction of $25,000 in current year.	________	________
g.	Continue with the facts of (f) for the next tax year.	________	________
h.	MACRS depreciation of $80,000. ADS depreciation would have been $90,000.	________	________
i.	Federal income taxes of $80,000 paid in current year.	________	________

18. **LO.2** Penguin Corporation (a cash basis, calendar year taxpayer) recorded the following income and expenses in the current year.

Income from services	$400,000
Salaries paid to employees	70,000
Tax-exempt interest income	24,000
Dividends from a corporation in which Penguin holds a 12% interest	40,000
Short-term capital loss on the sale of stock	17,000
Estimated Federal income taxes paid	110,000

Penguin purchased 7-year MACRS property in the current year for $80,000; it did not claim any § 179 or additional first-year depreciation. The property has a 10-year ADR midpoint life. Determine Penguin's taxable income and current E & P.

19. **LO.1, 3** At the beginning of the year, Teal Corporation held accumulated E & P of $210,000. On March 30, Teal sold an asset at a loss of $200,000. For the calendar year, Teal incurred a deficit in current E & P of $305,000, which includes the loss on the sale of the asset. If Teal made a distribution of $50,000 to its sole shareholder on April 1, how is the shareholder taxed? Her basis in the stock was $72,000.

20. **LO.1, 3** Green Corporation (a calendar year taxpayer) had a deficit in accumulated E & P of $250,000 at the beginning of the current year. Its net profit for the

period January 1 through July 30 was $300,000, but its E & P for the entire taxable year was only $40,000. If Green made a distribution of $60,000 to its sole shareholder on August 1, how will the shareholder be taxed?

21. **LO.1, 3** Black Corporation and Tom each own 50% of Tan Corporation's common stock. On January 1, Tan holds a deficit in accumulated E & P of $200,000. Its current E & P is $90,000. During the year, Tan makes cash distributions of $40,000 each to Black and Tom.
    a. How are the two shareholders taxed on the distribution?
    b. What is Tan's accumulated E & P at the end of the year?

22. **LO.1, 4** Heather, an individual, owns all of the outstanding stock in Silver Corporation. Heather purchased her stock in Silver nine years ago, and her basis is $56,000. At the beginning of this year, the corporation has $76,000 of accumulated E & P and no current E & P (before considering the effect of the distributions as noted below). What are the tax consequences to Heather (amount and type of income and basis in property received) and Silver Corporation (gain or loss and effect on E & P) in each of the following situations? Critical Thinking
    a. Silver distributes land to Heather. The land was held as an investment and has a fair market value of $54,000 and an adjusted basis of $42,000.
    b. Assume that Silver has no current or accumulated E & P prior to the distribution. How would your answer to part (a) change?
    c. Assume that the land distributed in part (a) is subject to a $46,000 mortgage (which Heather assumes). How would your answer change?
    d. Assume that the land has a fair market value of $54,000 and an adjusted basis of $62,000 on the date of the distribution. How would your answer to part (a) change?

23. **LO.1, 4** Lime Corporation, with E & P of $500,000, distributes land (worth $300,000, adjusted basis of $350,000) to Harry, its sole shareholder. The land is subject to a liability of $120,000, which Harry assumes. What are the tax consequences to Lime and to Harry?

24. **LO.4** Raven Corporation owns three machines that it uses in its business. It no longer needs two of these machines and is considering distributing them to its two shareholders as a property dividend. The machines have a fair market value of $20,000 each. The basis of each machine is as follows: A, $27,000; B, $20,000; and C, $12,000. Raven has asked you for advice. What do you recommend? Decision Making Planning

25. **LO.1, 2, 3, 4** Cerulean Corporation has two equal shareholders, Marco and Avery. Marco acquired his Cerulean stock three years ago by transferring property worth $700,000, basis of $300,000, for 70 shares of the stock. Avery acquired 70 shares in Cerulean Corporation two years ago by transferring property worth $660,000, basis of $110,000. Cerulean's accumulated E & P as of January 1 of the current year is $350,000. Critical Thinking

    On March 1 of the current year, the corporation distributed to Marco property worth $120,000, basis to Cerulean of $50,000. It distributed cash of $220,000 to Avery. On July 1 of the current year, Avery sold her stock to Harpreet for $820,000. On December 1 of the current year, Cerulean distributed cash of $90,000 each to Harpreet and Marco. What are the tax issues?

26. **LO.1, 2, 4** Petrel Corporation has accumulated E & P of $85,000 at the beginning of the year. Its current-year taxable income is $320,000. On December 31, Petrel distributed business property (land, fair market value $140,000, adjusted basis $290,000) to Juan, its sole shareholder. Juan assumes a $70,000 liability on the property. Critical Thinking Decision Making Planning

    Included in the determination of Petrel's current taxable income is $16,000 of income recognized from an installment sale in a previous year. In addition, the corporation incurred a Federal income tax liability of $67,200, paid life insurance premiums of $4,500, and received term life insurance proceeds of $150,000 on the death of an officer.

a. What is Juan's gross income from the distribution?

b. What is Petrel's E & P after the property distribution?

c. What is Juan's tax basis in the property received?

d. How would your answers to parts (a) and (b) change if Petrel had sold the property at its fair market value, used $70,000 of the proceeds to pay off the liability, and distributed the remaining cash and any tax savings to Juan?

Critical Thinking

27. **LO.5** Parrot Corporation is a closely held company with accumulated E & P of $300,000 and current E & P of $350,000. Tom and Jerry are brothers; each owns a 50% share in Parrot, and they share management responsibilities equally. What are the tax consequences of each of the following independent transactions involving Parrot, Tom, and Jerry? How does each transaction affect Parrot's E & P?

a. Parrot sells an office building (adjusted basis of $350,000; fair market value of $300,000) to Tom for $275,000.

b. Parrot lends Jerry $250,000 on March 31 of this year. The loan is evidenced by a note that is payable on demand. No interest is charged on the loan (the current applicable Federal interest rate is 3%).

c. Parrot owns an airplane that it leases to others for a specified rental rate. Tom and Jerry also use the airplane for personal use and pay no rent. During the year, Tom used the airplane for 120 hours, and Jerry used it for 160 hours. The rental value of the airplane is $350 per hour, and its maintenance costs average $80 per hour.

d. Tom leases equipment to Parrot for $20,000 per year. The same equipment can be leased from another company for $9,000 per year.

Decision Making
Planning

28. **LO.5** Rover Corporation would like to transfer excess cash to its sole shareholder, Aleshia, who is also an employee. Aleshia is in the 24% tax bracket, and Rover is in the 21% bracket.

Because Aleshia's contribution to Rover's profit is substantial, Rover believes that a $25,000 bonus in the current year is reasonable compensation and should be deductible in full. However, Rover is considering paying Aleshia a $25,000 dividend because Aleshia's tax rate on dividends is lower than the corporate tax rate on compensation. Is Rover correct in believing that a dividend is the better choice? Why or why not?

Communications
Digging Deeper

29. **LO.6** Your client, Raptor Corporation, declares a dividend permitting its common shareholders to elect to receive 9 shares of cumulative preferred stock or 3 additional shares of Raptor common stock for every 10 shares of common stock held. Raptor has only common stock outstanding (fair market value of $45 per share). One shareholder elects to receive preferred stock, while the remaining shareholders choose the common stock.

Raptor asks you whether the shareholders recognize any gross income on the receipt of the stock. Prepare a letter to Raptor's president, Sarah Isaacs, or a memo for the tax research file regarding this matter. Raptor's address is 1812 S. Camino Seco, Tucson, AZ 85710.

Digging Deeper

30. **LO.6** Kendra purchased 10,000 shares of Gold Corporation common stock six years ago for $160,000. In the current year, Kendra received 800 shares of preferred stock as a dividend on her common stock, while the other holders of common stock received a common stock dividend. The preferred stock that Kendra received is worth $80,000, and her common stock has a fair market value of $240,000.

Gold holds ample E & P to cover any distributions made during the year. What is Kendra's basis in the preferred and common stock after the dividend is received? When does her holding period commence for the preferred stock?

31. **LO.6** Denim Corporation declares a nontaxable dividend payable in rights to subscribe to common stock. One right and $60 entitle the holder to subscribe to one share of stock. One right is issued for every two shares of stock owned. At the date of distribution of the rights, the market value of the stock is $110 per share, and the market value of the rights is $55 each. Lauren owns 300 shares of stock that she purchased two years ago for $9,000. Lauren receives 150 rights, of which she exercises 105 to purchase 105 additional shares. She sells the remaining 45 rights for $2,475. What are the tax consequences of this transaction to Lauren? Digging Deeper

32. **LO.6** Your client, Jacob Corcoran, bought 10,000 shares of Grebe Corporation stock two years ago for $24,000. Last year, Jacob received a nontaxable stock dividend of 2,000 shares in Grebe. In the current tax year, Jacob sold all of the stock received as a dividend for $18,000. Prepare a letter to Jacob or a memo for the tax research file describing the tax consequences of the stock sale. Jacob's address is 925 Arapahoe Street, Boulder, CO 80304. Communications Digging Deeper

33. **LO.7** Joseph and Erica, husband and wife, jointly own all of the stock in Velvet Corporation. The two are currently involved in divorce proceedings, and pursuant to those negotiations, they have agreed that only one of them will remain a shareholder in Velvet after the divorce. Because Erica has been more involved in Velvet's management and operations over the years, the parties have agreed that Joseph's ownership should be acquired by either Erica or Velvet. What issues should be considered in determining whether Erica or Velvet should acquire Joseph's shares in the corporation? Critical Thinking Planning

34. **LO.1, 7** Julio is in the 32% tax bracket. He acquired 2,000 shares of stock in Gray Corporation seven years ago at a cost of $50 per share. In the current year, Julio received a payment of $150,000 from Gray Corporation in exchange for 1,000 of his shares in Gray. Gray has E & P of $1,000,000. What tax liability would Julio incur on the payment in each of the following situations? Assume that Julio has no capital losses.
    a. The stock redemption qualifies for sale or exchange treatment.
    b. The stock redemption does not qualify for sale or exchange treatment.

35. **LO.1, 7** How would your answer to Problem 34 differ if Julio were a corporate shareholder rather than an individual shareholder and the stock ownership in Gray Corporation represented a 25% interest?

36. **LO.1, 7** Assume in Problem 34 that Julio takes a capital loss carryover of $50,000 into the current tax year. Julio records no other capital gain transactions during the year. What amount of the capital loss may Julio deduct in the current year in the following situations? Decision Making Planning
    a. The payment from Gray Corporation is a qualifying stock redemption for tax purposes.
    b. The payment from Gray is a nonqualified stock redemption for tax purposes.
    c. If Julio had the flexibility to structure the transaction as described in either part (a) or (b), which form would he choose?

37. **LO.1, 7** How would your answer to parts (a) and (b) of Problem 36 differ if Julio were a corporate shareholder (in the 21% tax bracket) rather than an individual shareholder and the stock ownership in Gray Corporation represented a 25% interest?

38. **LO.7** Silver Corporation has 2,000 shares of common stock outstanding. Howard owns 600 shares, Howard's grandfather owns 300 shares, Howard's mother owns 300 shares, and Howard's son owns 100 shares. In addition, Maroon Corporation owns 500 shares. Howard owns 70% of the stock of Maroon. Digging Deeper
    a. Applying the stock attribution rules, how many shares does Howard own in Silver?
    b. Assume that Howard owns only 40% of the stock in Maroon. How many shares does Howard own, directly and indirectly, in Silver?

c. Assume the same facts as in part (a) above, but in addition, Howard owns a 25% interest in the Yellow Partnership. Yellow owns 200 shares in Silver. How many shares does Howard own, directly and indirectly, in Silver?

Digging Deeper 39. **LO.7** Shonda owns 1,000 of the 1,500 shares outstanding in Rook Corporation (E & P of $1,000,000). Shonda paid $50 per share for the stock seven years ago. The remaining stock in Rook is owned by unrelated individuals. What are the tax consequences to Shonda in the following independent situations?

a. Rook redeems 450 shares of Shonda's stock for $225,000.

b. Rook redeems 600 shares of Shonda's stock for $300,000.

Digging Deeper 40. **LO.7** Broadbill Corporation (E & P of $650,000) has 1,000 shares of common stock outstanding. The shares are owned by the following individuals: Tammy, 300 shares; Yvette, 400 shares; and Jeremy, 300 shares. Each of the shareholders paid $50 per share for the Broadbill stock four years ago.

In the current year, Broadbill distributes $75,000 to Tammy in redemption of 150 of her shares. Determine the tax consequences of the redemption to Tammy and to Broadbill under the following independent circumstances.

a. Tammy and Jeremy are grandmother and grandson.

b. The three shareholders are siblings.

Digging Deeper 41. **LO.7** For the last 11 years, Lime Corporation has owned and operated four different trades or businesses. Lime also owns stock in several corporations that it purchased for investment purposes.

The stock of Lime is held equally by Sultan, an individual, and by Turquoise Corporation. Sultan and Turquoise each own 1,000 shares in Lime, purchased 9 years ago at a cost of $200 per share.

Determine whether either of the following independent transactions qualifies as partial liquidations under § 302(b)(4). In each transaction, determine the tax consequences to Lime, to Turquoise, and to Sultan. Lime holds E & P of $2,100,000 on the date of the distribution. Lime redeems 250 shares from each shareholder.

a. Lime sells one of its business lines (basis $500,000, fair market value $700,000) and distributes the proceeds equally to Sultan and Turquoise.

b. Lime equally distributes stock investments (basis $425,000, fair market value $700,000) that it holds in other corporations to Sultan and Turquoise.

Digging Deeper 42. **LO.7** Dove Corporation (E & P of $800,000) has 1,000 shares of stock outstanding. The shares are owned as follows: Julia, 600 shares; Maxine (Julia's sister), 300 shares; and Janine (Julia's daughter), 100 shares. Dove owns land (basis $300,000, fair market value $260,000) that it purchased as an investment seven years ago.

Dove distributes the land to Julia in exchange for all of her shares in the corporation. Julia had a basis of $275,000 in the shares. What are the tax consequences for both Dove and Julia if the distribution is:

a. A qualifying stock redemption?

b. A liquidating distribution?

Critical Thinking 43. **LO.5** Pink Corporation has several employees. Their names and salaries are listed below.

Judy	$470,000
Holly (Judy's daughter)	100,000
Terry (Judy's son)	100,000
John (an unrelated third party)	320,000

Holly and Terry are the only shareholders of Pink. Judy and John share equally in the management of the company's operations. Holly and Terry are both full-time college students at a university 200 miles away. Pink has substantial E & P and never has distributed a dividend. Discuss any income tax issues related to Pink's salary arrangement.

Bridge Discipline

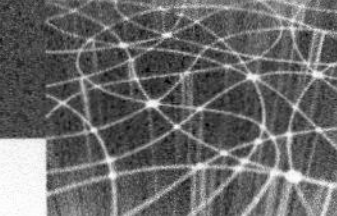

1. Find the audited financial statements of four major U.S. corporations, each in a different operating industry (e.g., manufacturing, energy, financial services, health care).
   a. Compute the total return on each corporation's stock for the past two years.
   b. Compute the dividend yield of the stock for the past two years.

2. Find a report involving the buyback of common stock by a publicly traded U.S. corporation. In no more than four PowerPoint slides, summarize the transaction, and discuss the tax and finance motivations for the redemption presented in the article. Communications

3. A dividend is declared by the corporation's board of directors, and it is paid to each shareholder in an equal fashion. Evaluate this statement from an accounting and Federal income tax standpoint. Summarize your position in no more than four PowerPoint slides in preparation for a presentation to your classmates in Business Law I. Communications

Research Problems

Note: Solutions to the Research Problems can be prepared by using the Thomson Reuters Checkpoint™ online tax research database, which accompanies this textbook. Solutions can also be prepared by using research materials found in a typical tax library.

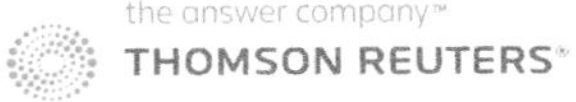

Research Problem 1. Kenny Merinoff and his daughter, Mia, own all of the outstanding stock of Flamingo Corporation. Mia and Kenny are officers in the corporation and, together with Kenny's uncle, Ira, comprise the entire board of directors. Flamingo uses the cash method of accounting and adopted a calendar year-end. Communications

In late 2014, the board of directors adopted the following legally enforceable resolution (agreed to in writing by each of the officers).

> Salary payments made to an officer of the corporation that are disallowed in whole or in part as a deductible expense for Federal income tax purposes shall be reimbursed by such officer to the corporation to the full extent of the disallowance. It shall be the duty of the board of directors to enforce the collection of each such amount.

In 2020, Flamingo paid Kenny \$800,000 in compensation. Mia received \$650,000. As part of an audit in late 2021, the IRS found the compensation of both officers to be excessive. It disallowed deductions for \$400,000 of the payment to Kenny and \$350,000 of the payment to Mia. The IRS recharacterized the disallowed payments as constructive dividends. Complying with the resolution by the board of directors, both Kenny and Mia repaid the disallowed compensation to Flamingo Corporation in 2022.

Mia and Kenny have asked you to determine how their repayments are treated for Federal income tax purposes. Mia still is working as a highly compensated executive for Flamingo, while Kenny is retired and living off of his savings. Prepare a memo for your firm's tax research files describing the results of your review.

Partial list of research aids:
§ 1341.
Vincent E. Oswald, 49 T.C. 645 (1968).

Communications **Research Problem 2.** Emerald Corporation must change its method of accounting for Federal income tax purposes. The change will require that an adjustment to income be made over three tax periods. Jonas, the sole shareholder of Emerald, wants to better understand the implications of this adjustment for E & P purposes, as he anticipates a distribution from Emerald in the current year. Prepare a memo for your firm's files describing the results of your research.

Partial list of research aids:
§ 481(a).
Rev.Proc. 97–27.

Use internet tax resources to address the following questions. Look for reliable websites and blogs of the IRS and other government agencies, media outlets, businesses, tax professionals, academics, think tanks, and political outlets.

Communications
Data Analytics

Research Problem 3. Just how common are dividend distributions? Are dividends concentrated in the companies traded on the New York Stock Exchange, or do closely held corporations pay dividends in a similar manner? Did dividends decrease during the Great Recession of 2008 and 2009? Search for answers to these questions on the internet and/or in academic journal articles.

In addition, using data from the IRS Tax Statistics website (**irs.gov/statistics**), find and analyze corporate balance sheet data (overall and by size of total assets) to provide answers to the questions above. Summarize the data you find in a Microsoft Excel spreadsheet and e-mail it, along with a three-paragraph summary of your findings, to your instructor.

Communications **Research Problem 4.** Publicly traded corporations reacquire their own shares for various reasons. Through the use of a tender offer, a corporation can purchase a substantial percentage of the company's stock. Prepare an outline discussing (1) why publicly traded corporations reacquire their own shares and (2) how the tender offer process works for both corporations and shareholders. E-mail your outline to your professor.

Becker CPA Review Questions

Becker

1. On January 1, year 5, Olinto Corp., an accrual basis, calendar year C corporation, had $35,000 in accumulated earnings and profits. For year 5, Olinto had current earnings and profits of $15,000 and made two $40,000 cash distributions to its shareholders, one in April and one in September of year 5. What amount of the year 5 distributions is classified as dividend income to Olinto's shareholders?

   a. $15,000
   b. $35,000
   c. $50,000
   d. $80,000

2. Fox Corp. owned 2,000 shares of Duffy Corp. stock that it bought in year 0 for $9 per share. In year 8, when the fair market value of the Duffy stock was $20 per share, Fox distributed this stock to a noncorporate shareholder. Fox's recognized gain on this distribution was:

   a. $40,000
   b. $22,000
   c. $18,000
   d. $0

3. Ridge Corp., a calendar year C corporation, made a nonliquidating cash distribution to its shareholders of $1,000,000 with respect to its stock. At that time, Ridge's current and accumulated earnings and profits totaled $750,000 and its total paid-in capital for tax purposes was $10,000,000. Ridge had no corporate shareholders. Ridge's cash distribution:

   I. Was taxable as $750,000 in dividend income to its shareholders.

   II. Reduced its shareholders' adjusted bases in Ridge stock by $250,000.

   a. I only
   b. II only
   c. Both I and II
   d. Neither I nor II

4. Jane is the sole shareholder of Buttons, Inc. Buttons has a deficit of $60,000 in accumulated earnings and profits (E & P) at the beginning of the current year. Current E & P is $35,000. If Buttons pays out a cash distribution to Jane during the current year of $50,000, how much is a taxable dividend to Jane?

   a. $0
   b. $35,000
   c. $50,000
   d. $85,000

5. Jane is the sole shareholder of Buttons, Inc. Buttons has accumulated earnings and profits (E & P) of $65,000 at the beginning of the current year. The current E & P is $35,000. Buttons pays out a property distribution to Jane during the current year with an FMV of $150,000 and an adjusted basis of $130,000. How much is a taxable dividend to Jane?

   a. $35,000
   b. $100,000
   c. $120,000
   d. $150,000

6. ABC Corp. paid two cash distributions during year 5. The first was $42,000, and the second was $33,000. Accumulated earnings and profits (E & P) at the end of year 4 were $80,000. Current E & P for year 5 is $30,000. How will the second distribution be allocated between current E & P and accumulated E & P?

	Current E & P	**Accumulated E & P**
a.	$13,200	$19,800
b.	$16,500	$16,500
c.	$19,800	$13,200
d.	$30,000	$30,000

7. ABC Corp. paid two cash distributions during year 5. The first was $42,000, and the second was $33,000. Accumulated earnings and profits (E & P) at the end of year 4 were $10,000. Current E & P for year 5 is $30,000. How will the first distribution be allocated between current E & P and accumulated E & P?

	Current E & P	**Accumulated E & P**
a.	$16,800	$25,200
b.	$16,800	$10,000
c.	$25,200	$16,800
d.	$30,000	$10,000

8. Generally, in a direct distribution of assets to the shareholders that results in a complete corporate liquidation:

   a. There is no taxable event.

   b. The corporation recognizes no gain or loss because it transfers the assets to the shareholders at the corporation's basis immediately before the distribution.

   c. The shareholders recognize dividend income in the amount of the fair market value of property received.

   d. The shareholders recognize gain or loss to the extent the fair market value of the distributed assets differs from the adjusted basis of the stock.

Chapter 14

Partnerships and Limited Liability Entities

Learning Objectives: *After completing Chapter 14, you should be able to:*

LO.1 Identify governing principles and theories of partnership taxation.

LO.2 Apply the tax rules regarding the formation of a partnership with cash and property contributions.

LO.3 Determine the tax treatment of expenditures of a newly formed partnership and identify elections available to the partnership.

LO.4 Calculate partnership taxable income and describe how partnership items affect a partner's income tax liability.

LO.5 Determine a partner's basis in the partnership interest.

LO.6 Apply the tax law's limitations on deducting partnership losses.

LO.7 Apply the tax laws regarding transactions between a partner and the partnership.

LO.8 Explain how LLPs and LLCs differ and list the tax advantages and disadvantages of using an LLC.

Chapter Outline

Tax Talk *If you are truly serious about preparing your child for the future, don't teach him to subtract—teach him to deduct.* —Fran Lebowitz

RODERICK PAUL WALKER/ALAMY STOCK PHOTO

The Tax Consequences of Partnership Formation and Operations

For 15 years, Maria has owned and operated a seaside bakery and café called The Beachsider. Each morning, customers line up on the boardwalk in front of the building and enjoy fresh coffee and croissants while waiting for a table. "The building is too small," Maria commented to her landlord, Kyle. "Is there any way we can expand?" The Beachsider is one of several older buildings on 3 acres of a 10-acre parcel that Kyle inherited 30 years ago. The remaining 7 acres are undeveloped.

Kyle and Maria talked to Josh, a real estate developer, and he proposed an expansion to The Beachsider and upgrades to the other buildings. The improvements would preserve the character of the original retail center, and the remaining acreage would be available for future expansion. Kyle and Maria were impressed with Josh's vision and excited about the plans to upgrade the property and expand Maria's business.

The parties agreed to form a partnership to own and operate The Beachsider and to improve and lease the other buildings. Josh summarized the plan as follows: "Kyle and Maria will each contribute one-half of the capital we need. Kyle's real estate is valued at about $2,000,000. Maria's bakery equipment and the café furnishings are valued at about $500,000. The improvements will cost about $1,500,000 of cash, which Maria has agreed to contribute to the partnership."

Josh continued, "You have agreed that I do not need to contribute any capital to the partnership. I will oversee the construction, and when it is complete, I will vest in a 5 percent interest in the partnership's capital. On an ongoing basis, I will oversee the partnership's operations in exchange for a fixed salary and 20 percent of the partnership's ongoing profits. The construction is estimated to be completed in June of this year, and my capital interest is estimated to be valued at $200,000 at that time."

What are the tax consequences if the trio forms Beachside Properties as a limited liability company (LLC) to own and operate the retail center? What issues might arise later in the life of the entity?

Read the chapter and formulate your response.

Much of the new business in today's world of commerce is conducted through what the Internal Revenue Code would classify as *partnerships.* As evidence of their popularity, approximately 3.6 million partnership tax returns are filed with the IRS annually.

Whether termed a *joint venture* or some other designation, a partnership is formed when individuals or separate business entities get together for the specific purpose of earning profits by jointly operating a trade or business. For example, a group can limit its goals to a specific list of agreed-to projects or to a given time period, or businesses can work together without altering any of their underlying capital structures. In many service professions, such as law, medicine, and accounting, state laws prohibit the owners from using a corporation to limit their liability to clients or patients; there, the partnership form prevails.

LO.1

Identify governing principles and theories of partnership taxation.

14-1 Overview of Partnership Taxation

There are several types of partnership entities, each suited for different situations. Partnerships are used in almost every imaginable industry, and their popularity among business owners continues to rise.

The tax law addressing the transactions of partners and partnerships is found in Subchapter K of the Internal Revenue Code. These provisions comprise only a few short pages in the Code, however. Most of the details of partnership tax law have evolved through extensive Regulations and a healthy number of court cases.

14-1a Forms of Doing Business—Federal Tax Consequences

This chapter and the next chapter analyze business forms that offer certain advantages over C corporations. These entities are partnerships and Subchapter S corporations ("S corporations"), which are called *flow-through* or *pass-through* entities because the owners of the trade or business elect to avoid treating the enterprise as a separate taxable entity. Instead, the owners are taxed on a proportionate share of the firm's taxable income, which "flows through" to them at the end of each of its taxable years regardless of the amount of cash or property distributions the owners receive during the year. The entity serves as an information provider to the IRS and its owners with respect to the proportionate allocation of income, and the tax liability falls directly on the owners for their share of the partnership's income.

A partnership may be especially advantageous in many cases. A partnership's income is subject to only a single level of taxation, whereas C corporation income can be subject to *double taxation.* Corporate income is taxed at the entity level at rates up to 21 percent. Any after-tax corporate income that is distributed to the entity's owners may be taxed again as a dividend at the owner level.

In addition, the entity offers certain planning opportunities not available to other business structures. Both C and S corporations are subject to rigorous allocation and distribution requirements (generally, each allocation or distribution is proportionate to the ownership interest of the shareholder). A partnership, though, may adjust its allocations of income and cash flow among the partners each year according to their needs as long as certain standards are met. Any previously unrealized income (such as appreciation of corporate assets) of a C corporation is recognized at the entity level when the corporation liquidates, but a partnership generally may liquidate tax-free. Finally, many states impose reporting and licensing requirements on corporate entities, including S corporations. These include franchise or capital stock tax returns that may require annual assessments and costly professional preparation assistance. Partnerships, on the other hand, often have no reporting requirements beyond Federal and state informational tax returns.

Although partnerships may avoid many of the income tax and reporting burdens faced by other entities, they are subject to all other taxes in the same manner as any other business. Thus, the partnership files returns and pays the outstanding amount of pertinent sales taxes, property taxes, and payroll taxes.

Tax Fact **Partnership Power**

Partnerships and limited liability entities represent a sizable number of business enterprises, and they generate a significant part of the net income of the economy, especially in the investment sectors.

Partnerships are used in almost every type of industry—from agriculture to health care to waste management. Almost half of all partnerships are engaged in some sort of real estate business. Certain elements of the tax law make partnerships especially appealing for activities such as research and development and oil and gas exploration and extraction.

All kinds of service activities are operated through some sort of partnership (especially limited liability partnerships): partnerships are common in the accounting, law, education, and transportation services industries.

Here are some statistics about the activities of these entities from the 2019 tax year.

Number of partnerships, LLCs, etc.	3,624,145
Number of partners/members	22,405,728
Reported partnership net income—total	$491 billion
Number of limited partnerships	411,439
Number of limited liability entities	2,731,022

Source: *IRS Tax Stats.*

In summary, partnerships offer advantages to both large and small businesses. For smaller business operations, a partnership allows owners to combine their resources at low cost. For larger business operations, a partnership offers a unique ability to raise capital with low filing and reporting costs (compared to corporate bond issuances, for example). Additional discussion as to the choice of legal form in which to conduct a business is included in Chapter 18.

14-1b **Definition of a Partnership**

A partnership is an association of two or more persons formed to carry on a trade or business, with each contributing money, property, labor, or skill, and with all expecting to share in profits and losses. A "person" can be an individual, a corporation, or another partnership. For Federal income tax purposes, a partnership includes a syndicate, a group, a pool, a joint venture, or another unincorporated organization through which any business, financial operation, or venture is carried on. The entity must not otherwise be classified as a corporation, trust, or estate.[1]

An eligible noncorporate entity can "check the box" on the partnership tax return, indicating that the entity wants to be taxed as a partnership.[2] A partnership must have at least two owners, so a sole proprietor or one-owner limited liability entity cannot "check the box" and be taxed as a partnership.[3]

Businesses operating in several forms are taxed as partnerships. Provisions controlling these legal forms of doing business typically are dictated by the laws of the states in which the businesses operate.

- In a **general partnership (GP)**, the partners share profits and losses in some specified manner as dictated by the partnership agreement. All partners may participate in management of the partnership, since there are no limited partners. Creditors can reach the assets of the business and the personal assets of the general partners to satisfy any outstanding debts. A general partner can be bankrupted by a judgment against the entity, even though the partner did not cause the violation triggering the damages. General partnerships often are used for operating activities and corporate joint ventures.
- In a **limited partnership (LP)**, profits and losses are shared as the partners agree, but ownership interests are either general (creditors can reach the personal assets of the partner) or limited (a partner's exposure to entity liabilities is limited to the partner's own capital investment). Usually, the general partners conduct most of the partnership business, and they have a greater say in making decisions that affect

[1] § 7701(a)(2).

[2] Reg. §§ 301.7701–1 to –3, as discussed in text Section 12-1e.

[3] § 761(a).

Bridge Discipline Bridge to Finance

As movies have become more expensive to produce, many production studios have turned to limited partnerships or LLCs as a lucrative source of investment capital. For example, several well-known studios have sold limited partnership or LLC interests in entities formed to produce specific movies.

The sponsoring studio usually injects capital for a small (1–5 percent) general partnership interest, and the limited partners contribute the remaining capital—millions of dollars in most cases.

These film-financing partnerships are not necessarily private operations. A layperson with a well-connected tax or investment adviser can become a partner in the next Channing Tatum project, perhaps financed by Silver Screen Partners. Partnership shares sell for multiples of $100,000 or more, and in return, the investor can become part-owner in an entity that is certain to throw off operating losses for many years to come.

Especially interested in movie financing of this type can be non-U.S. investors. The use of partnerships and limited liability entities is a common way to attract cross-border investment, since many developed countries treat such joint ventures favorably under their tax laws, allowing deferral of income recognition and lower tax withholding on the income of these entities.

U.S. investors are attracted to joint venture financing of film projects in several countries, including Germany and Canada, and U.S. states, including Illinois and Louisiana, that offer generous tax credits for projects that are filmed and processed chiefly within their borders. The partnership tax regime can offer an immediate flow-through of these tax benefits.

The next time you go to a movie, watch the credits and think about the large number of people who invested cash in the movie, all benefiting from the partnership tax laws!

the entity operations. Limited partnerships often are used to raise capital for real estate development, oil and gas exploration, and various financial product investment vehicles.

- The **limited liability partnership (LLP)** is used chiefly in the service professions, such as accounting, medicine, law, and consulting. The primary difference between an LLP and a general partnership is that an LLP partner is not personally liable for acts of negligence, fraud, or malpractice committed by other partners.
- The **limited liability company (LLC)** is discussed in more detail later in this chapter. This entity is taxed as a partnership, but its capital structure resembles that of a corporation, with shares for sale and an owner's liability limited almost strictly to the extent of his or her equity investment. Most states allow LLCs to be owned solely by one person. In that case, the entity is treated for Federal income tax purposes as an individual or C corporation, following the tax filing status of the single LLC member.

14-1c Partnership Taxation and Reporting

A partnership is not itself a taxable entity.[4] Typically, a partnership combines income and expenses related to the entity's trade or business activities into a single income or loss amount that flows through to the partners at the end of the entity's tax year.[5] Partners report their **distributive share** of the partnership's income or loss for the year on their tax returns. As a result, the partnership itself pays no Federal income tax on its income; instead, the partners' individual tax liabilities are affected by the activities of the entity.

Partnership Flow-Throughs

Adam is a 40% partner in the ABC Partnership. Both Adam's and the partnership's tax years end on December 31. This year the partnership generates $200,000 of ordinary taxable income. However, because the partnership needs capital for expansion and debt reduction, Adam makes no cash withdrawals during the year. He meets his living expenses by reducing his investment portfolio. Adam is taxed on his $80,000 distributive share of the partnership's income ($200,000 × 40%), even though he received no distributions from the entity during the year. This allocated income is included in Adam's gross income.

[4] § 701.

[5] § 702.

Partnership Flow-Throughs

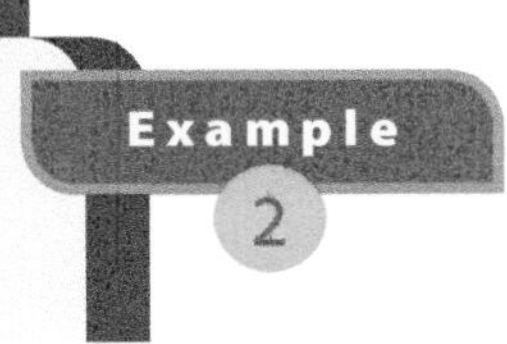

Assume the same facts as in Example 1, except that the partnership realizes a taxable loss of $100,000. Adam's $40,000 proportionate share of the loss flows through to him from the partnership, and he can deduct the loss. (Note: Loss limitation rules discussed later in the chapter may result in some or all of this loss being deducted by Adam in a later year.)

Separately Stated Items

Many items of partnership income, expense, gain, or loss retain their tax identity as they flow through to the partners. These **separately stated items** include those items that may affect any two partners' tax liability computations differently.[6] For example, the § 179 expense of a partnership is separately stated because one partner might be able to deduct his or her share of the expense completely and another's deduction might be limited.

Separately stated items include recognized gains and losses from property transactions, dividend income, immediately expensed tangible personal property (§ 179), and expenditures that individual partners would treat as itemized deductions (e.g., charitable contributions).

Items that are not separately stated, because all partners treat them the same on their income tax returns, are aggregated and form the *ordinary income* of the partnership. Thus, profits from product sales, advertising expenses, and depreciation recapture amounts are combined to form the entity's ordinary income. This amount then is allocated among the partners and flows through to their tax returns. The ordinary income that flows through to a general partner, as well as any salary-like guaranteed payments (discussed in text Section 14-4a) received, usually is subject to self-employment tax as well as Federal income tax.[7]

Beth is a 25% partner in the BR Partnership, a manufacturer of solar energy panels. The cash basis entity collected sales income of $60,000 and incurred $15,000 in business expenses. In addition, it sold a corporate bond for a $9,000 long-term capital gain. Finally, the partnership made a $1,000 contribution to the local Performing Arts Fund. The fund is a qualifying charity. BR and all of its partners use a calendar tax year.

Beth is allocated ordinary taxable income of $11,250 [($60,000 − $15,000) × 25%] from the partnership. She also reports her allocated share of the entity's long-term capital gain ($2,250) and charitable contributions ($250).

The partnership ordinary income increases Beth's gross income and is subject to both income and self-employment taxes. Beth's share of BR's capital gain and charitable contribution is combined with her other similar activities for the year as though she had incurred them herself. These items could be treated differently on the tax returns of the various partners (e.g., because a partner may be subject to a percentage limitation on charitable contribution deductions), so they are not included in the computation of ordinary partnership income. Instead, the items flow through to the partners separately.

Tax Reporting Rules

Even though it is not a taxpaying entity, the partnership files an information tax return, Form 1065. This return is due by the fifteenth day of the third month following the end of the tax year. For a calendar year partnership, this deadline is March 15. An automatic six-month extension is available (to September 15 for a calendar year partnership) for filing the Form 1065.

As part of the Form 1065, the partnership prepares a Schedule K–1 for each partner showing that partner's share of partnership items. Each partner receives a copy of Schedule K–1 for use in preparing the respective partner's tax return.

[6] § 703(a)(1).

[7] § 1402(a).

The partnership incurs a penalty if it fails to file a timely (by the extended due date) Form 1065. For partnership returns required to be filed in 2023, the penalty is $220 per month times the numbers of partners, up to a maximum of 12 months.

Look at Form 1065 at **irs.gov**, and refer to it during the following discussion. The ordinary income and expense items generated by the partnership's trade or business activities are netted to produce a single income or loss amount. The partnership reports this ordinary income or loss from its trade or business activities on Form 1065, page 1. Schedule K (page 4 of Form 1065) accumulates all items that must be separately reported to the partners, including net trade or business income or loss (from page 1). The amounts on Schedule K are allocated among and reported by the partners on each owner's Schedule K–1.

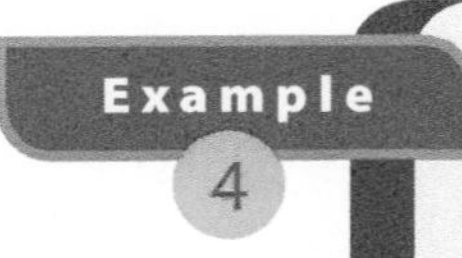

The BR Partnership in Example 3 reports its $60,000 of sales income on Form 1065, page 1, line 1. The $15,000 of business expenses are reported in the appropriate amounts on page 1, line 2 or lines 9–20. Partnership ordinary income of $45,000 is shown on page 1, line 22, and on Schedule K, line 1. The $9,000 capital gain and the $1,000 charitable contribution are reported only on Schedule K, on lines 9a and 13a, respectively.

Beth receives a Schedule K–1 from the partnership that shows her shares of partnership ordinary income of $11,250, long-term capital gain of $2,250, and charitable contributions of $250 on lines 1, 9a, and 13 (code A), respectively.

She combines these amounts with similar items from other sources on her personal tax return. For example, if she has a $5,000 long-term capital loss from a stock transaction during the year, her overall net capital loss is $2,750. She then evaluates this net amount to determine the amount she may deduct on her Form 1040.

The partnership reconciles book income with its tax return data on Schedule M–1 or Schedule M–3. This reconciliation is similar to the book-tax reconciliation prepared by a C corporation, as discussed in text Sections 3-1a and 12-5.

Schedule M–3 generally is required in lieu of Schedule M–1 if the partnership owns $10 million or more in assets at the end of the year or it reports gross receipts of at least $35 million. The net taxable income calculated on the Analysis of Net Income (Loss) schedule should agree with the reconciled taxable income on Schedule M–1 or Schedule M–3. Schedule L shows an accounting-basis balance sheet, and Schedule M–2 reconciles partners' beginning and ending capital accounts.

14-1d Partner's Ownership Interest in a Partnership

Each partner typically owns both a **capital interest** and a **profits (loss) interest** in the partnership. A capital interest is measured by a partner's **capital sharing ratio**, which is the partner's percentage ownership of the capital of the partnership. A partner's capital interest can be determined in several ways. The most widely accepted method measures the capital interest as the percentage of net asset value (asset value remaining after payment of all partnership liabilities) a partner would receive upon immediate liquidation of the partnership.

A profits (loss) interest relates to the partner's share of current partnership operating results. **Profit and loss sharing ratios** usually are specified in the partnership agreement. They are used to determine each partner's allocation of partnership ordinary taxable income (loss) and separately stated items.[8] The partnership can change its profit and loss allocations at any time by amending the partnership agreement.

[8] § 704(a).

Bridge Discipline Bridge to Business Law

Although a written **partnership agreement** is not required by most U.S. states, many rules governing the tax consequences to partners and their partnerships refer to such an agreement. Remember that a partner's distributive share of income, gain, loss, deduction, or credit is determined in accordance with the partnership agreement. Consequently, if taxpayers operating a business in partnership form want a measure of certainty as to the tax consequences of their activities, a carefully drafted partnership agreement is crucial.

An agreement that sets forth the obligations, rights, and powers of the partners should prove invaluable in settling controversies among them and provide some degree of certainty as to the tax consequences of the partners' actions.

The partnership agreement may provide for a **special allocation** of certain items to specified partners, or it may allocate items in a different proportion from the general profit and loss sharing ratios. These items are reported separately to the partner receiving the allocation. For a special allocation to be recognized for tax purposes, it also must produce nontax economic consequences to the partners receiving the allocation.[9]

Partnership Special Allocations

When the George-Helen Partnership was formed, George contributed cash and Helen contributed some City of Boise bonds that she had held for investment purposes. The partnership agreement allocates all of the tax-exempt interest income from the bonds ($15,000 this year) to Helen as an inducement for her to remain a partner.

This is an acceptable special allocation for income tax purposes; it reflects the differing economic circumstances that underlie the partners' contributions to the capital of the entity. Because Helen would have received the tax-exempt income if she had not joined the partnership, she can retain the tax-favored treatment via the special allocation.

Assume the same facts as in Example 5. Three years after it was formed, the George-Helen Partnership purchased some City of Butte bonds. The municipal bond interest income of $15,000 flows through to the partners as a separately stated item, so it retains its tax-exempt status.

The partnership agreement allocates all of this income to George because he is subject to a higher marginal income tax rate than is Helen. The partnership then allocates $15,000 more of the partnership's ordinary income to Helen than to George. These allocations are not effective for income tax purposes because they have no purpose other than reducing the partners' combined income tax liability.

A partner has a **basis in the partnership interest**, just as he or she would have a tax basis in any asset owned. When income flows through to a partner from the partnership, the partner's basis in the partnership interest increases accordingly. When a loss flows through to a partner, the basis in the partnership interest is reduced.[10] A partner's basis is important when determining the treatment of distributions from the partnership to the partner, establishing the deductibility of partnership losses, and calculating gain or loss on the disposition of the partnership interest.

[9] § 704(b).

[10] §§ 705, 722, and 723.

Example 7

The Philly Clinic (Philly) contributes $20,000 of cash to acquire a 30% capital and profits interest in the Red Robin LLC. In its first year of operations, the LLC earns ordinary income of $40,000 and makes no distributions to its members. Philly's initial basis is the $20,000 it paid for the interest. Philly recognizes ordinary income of $12,000 (30% interest × $40,000 ordinary income) and increases its basis in Red Robin by the same amount, to $32,000.

The Code provides for increases and decreases in a partner's basis so that the income or loss from partnership operations is taxed only once. In Example 7, if Philly sold its interest at the end of the first year for $32,000, it would recognize no gain or loss. If the Code did not provide for an adjustment to the owner's basis for flow-through amounts, Philly's basis still would be $20,000. In that case, Philly would recognize a gain of $12,000 in addition to being taxed on its $12,000 share of the flow-through income from Red Robin.

Digging Deeper 1

Discussion of the aggregate and entity concepts can be found on this book's companion website: www.cengage.com

LO.2

Apply the tax rules regarding the formation of a partnership with cash and property contributions.

14-2 Formation of a Partnership: Tax Effects

14-2a Gain or Loss on Contributions to the Partnership

When a taxpayer transfers property to an entity in exchange for valuable consideration, a taxable exchange usually results. Typically, both the taxpayer and the entity realize and recognize gain or loss on the exchange. The gain or loss recognized by the transferor is the difference between the fair market value of the consideration received and the adjusted basis of the property transferred.[11]

As a general rule, however, neither the partner nor the partnership recognizes the gain or loss that is realized when a partner contributes property to a partnership in exchange for a partnership interest. Instead, recognition of any realized gain or loss is deferred under § 721.[12] This treatment is similar to the treatment of assets transferred to a controlled corporation.[13] However, these rules apply whenever an owner makes a contribution to the capital of the partnership or LLC, not just when the entity is formed.

Creating a Partnership

Example 8

In exchange for a 60% profits and loss interest worth $60,000, Alicia transfers two assets to the Wren LLC on the day the entity is created. She contributes cash of $40,000 and retail display equipment (basis to her as a sole proprietor, $8,000; fair market value, $20,000). Because an exchange has occurred between two parties, Alicia *realizes* a $12,000 gain on this transaction. The gain realized is the fair market value of the LLC interest of $60,000 less the basis of the assets that Alicia surrendered to the entity [$40,000 (cash) + $8,000 (equipment)].

Under § 721, Alicia *does not recognize* the $12,000 realized gain in the year of contribution. Alicia might not have had sufficient cash if she had been required to pay tax on the $12,000 gain. All that she received from the entity was an illiquid LLC interest; she received no cash with which to pay any resulting tax liability.

[11] §§ 1001(a) and (c).

[12] § 721.

[13] § 351.

Creating a Partnership

Assume the same facts as in Example 8, except that the equipment Alicia contributes to the LLC has an adjusted basis of $25,000. She has a $5,000 *realized* loss [$60,000 – ($40,000 + $25,000)], but she cannot deduct the loss. Realized losses as well as realized gains are deferred by § 721.

Unless it was essential that the entity receive Alicia's display equipment rather than similar equipment purchased from an outside supplier, Alicia should have considered selling the equipment to a third party. This would have allowed her to recognize a $5,000 loss in the year of the sale. Alicia then could have contributed $60,000 of cash (including the proceeds from the sale) for her interest in the entity, and Wren would have had funds to purchase similar equipment.

Five years after Wren (Examples 8 and 9) was created, Alicia contributes another piece of equipment to the entity. This property has a basis of $35,000 and a fair market value of $50,000. Alicia will be able to defer recognition of the $15,000 realized gain. Section 721 is effective *whenever* an owner makes a contribution to the capital of the partnership or LLC, not just when the entity is formed.

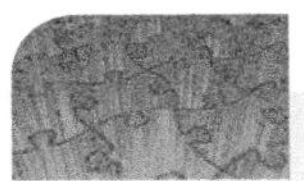

Concept Summary 14.1

Partnership/LLC Taxation: Tax Reporting

1. Compared with a C corporation, a partnership may offer some advantages, including a single level of taxation, the availability of certain planning opportunities, and simplified administration and reporting.
2. Entities treated as a partnership for tax purposes include general partnerships, limited partnerships, limited liability companies (LLCs), and limited liability partnerships (LLPs).
3. Partnership income and losses flow through to the partners and are reported on the partners' tax returns. The partnership reports ordinary income or loss as well as *separately stated items* to the partners. Under certain conditions, items may be *specially allocated* to specified partners.
4. The partnership files Form 1065 as an information return and prepares a Schedule K-1 to report each partner's share of income and deductions.

14-2b Exceptions to Nonrecognition

Contributions to the capital of a partnership or limited liability entity sometimes trigger recognized gain or loss. Realized gain or loss may be recognized when:

- Appreciated stocks are contributed to an investment partnership,
- The transaction is essentially a disguised sale or exchange of properties,
- The partnership interest is received in exchange for services rendered to the partnership by the partner.

Investment Partnership

If the transfer consists of appreciated stocks and securities and the partnership is an investment partnership, it is possible that the contributing partner will recognize the inherent realized gain at the time of the contribution.[14] This rule prevents investors from using the partnership form to diversify their investment portfolios on a tax-free basis.

Disguised Exchange

If a transaction is essentially a taxable exchange of properties, tax on the gain is not deferred under the nonrecognition provisions of § 721.[15]

[14] § 721(b).

[15] Reg. § 1.731–1(c)(3).

Sara owns land, and Bob owns stock. Sara would like to have Bob's stock, and Bob wants Sara's land. If Sara and Bob both contribute their property to newly formed SB Partnership in exchange for interests in the partnership, the tax on the transaction appears to be deferred under § 721. The tax on a subsequent distribution by the partnership of the land to Bob and the stock to Sara also appears to be deferred under partnership distribution rules.

Not so! Tax law disregards the passage of the properties through the partnership and holds, instead, that Sara and Bob exchanged the land and stock directly. Thus, the transaction is treated as any other taxable exchange.

Disguised Sale

Immediate gain recognition also occurs in the context of a **disguised sale** of property or of a partnership interest. A disguised sale occurs when a partner contributes property to a partnership and soon thereafter receives a distribution from the partnership. This distribution could be viewed as a payment by the partnership for purchase of the property.[16]

Kim transfers property to the existing KLM Partnership. The property has an adjusted basis of $10,000 and a fair market value of $30,000. Two weeks later, the partnership distributes $30,000 of cash to Kim. Lacking an exception under the distribution rules, the $30,000 of cash received would not be taxable to Kim if the basis for her partnership interest prior to the distribution was greater than the amount distributed.

However, the transaction appears to be a disguised purchase-sale transaction rather than an asset contribution and distribution. Therefore, Kim recognizes gain of $20,000 on transfer of the property, and the partnership is deemed to have purchased the property for $30,000.

If the distribution occurs more than two years after the property contribution or if it is deemed "reasonable" in relation to the partner's invested capital, the distribution is *not* presumed to be a disguised sale.

Services

Another exception to the nonrecognition provision of § 721 occurs when a partner receives a capital interest in the partnership as compensation for services rendered to the partnership. This is not a tax-deferred transaction because services are not treated as "property" that can be transferred to a partnership on a tax-free basis. Instead, the partner performing the services recognizes ordinary compensation income equal to the fair market value of the partnership interest received.[17]

The partnership may deduct the amount included in the *service partner's* income if the services are of a deductible nature. If the services are not deductible by the partnership, they are capitalized. For example, architectural plans created by a partner are capitalized into the basis of a structure built with those plans. Alternatively, day-to-day management services performed by a partner for the partnership usually are deductible by the partnership.

Bill, Carol, and Dave form the BCD Partnership, with each receiving a one-third capital and profits interest in the entity. Dave receives his one-third interest as compensation for the accounting and tax planning services he rendered to the partnership. The value of a one-third capital interest in the partnership (for each of the parties) is $20,000.

The partnership deducts $20,000 for Dave's services in computing ordinary income. Dave recognizes $20,000 of compensation income, and he takes a $20,000 basis in his partnership interest. The same result would occur if the partnership had paid Dave $20,000 for his services and he immediately contributed that amount to the entity for a one-third ownership interest.

[16] § 707(a)(2)(B).

[17] § 83(a).

Tax treatment of services for an interest in a partnership's future profits can be found on this book's companion website: www.cengage.com

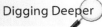

2 Digging Deeper

14-2c Tax Issues Related to Contributed Property

When a partner makes a tax-deferred contribution of an asset to the capital of a partnership, the entity assigns a *carryover basis* to the property.[18] The partnership's basis in the asset (the asset's "inside basis") is equal to the basis the partner held in the property prior to its transfer to the partnership. The partner's basis in the new partnership interest (the owner's "outside basis") equals the prior basis in the contributed asset.[19] The tax term for this basis concept is *substituted basis*. Thus, two assets are created out of one when a partnership is formed—namely, the property in the hands of the new entity and the new asset (the partnership interest) in the hands of the partner. Both assets are assigned a basis that is derived from the partner's basis in the contributed property.

The holding period of a partner's ownership interest includes that of the contributed property when the property was a § 1231 asset or capital asset in the partner's hands. When other assets, including cash, are contributed, the holding period starts on the day the interest is acquired.

Example 14

On June 1, José transfers property to the JKL LLC in exchange for a one-third interest in the entity. The property has an adjusted basis to José of $10,000 and a fair market value of $30,000. José incurs a $20,000 realized gain on the exchange ($30,000 − $10,000), but he does not recognize any of the gain. Jose's basis for his interest in JKL is the amount necessary to recognize the $20,000 deferred gain if his interest later is sold for its $30,000 fair market value. This amount, $10,000, is the substituted basis.

The basis of the property contributed to JKL is the amount necessary to allow for the recognition of the $20,000 deferred gain if the property later is sold for its $30,000 fair market value. This amount, also $10,000, is the carryover basis.

The holding period for the contributed asset also carries over to the entity. Thus, JKL's holding period for the asset includes the period during which José owned the asset individually.

Depreciation Method and Period

If depreciable property is contributed to the partnership, the partnership usually is required to use the same cost recovery method and life as had been used by the partner. The partnership merely "steps into the shoes" of the partner and continues the same cost recovery calculations.

Intangible Assets

If a partner contributes an existing intangible asset to the partnership, the partnership generally will "step into the shoes" of the partner in determining future amortization deductions. Code § 197 intangible assets are amortized over 15 years and include purchased goodwill, going-concern value, information systems, customer- or supplier-related intangible assets, patents, licenses obtained from a governmental unit, franchises, trademarks, covenants not to compete, and other items.

[18] § 723.

[19] § 722.

Receivables, Inventory, and Built-In Losses

To prevent ordinary income from being converted into capital gain, gain or loss is treated as ordinary when the partnership disposes of either of the following.[20]

- Contributed receivables that were unrealized in the contributing partner's hands at the contribution date. Such receivables include the right to receive payment for goods or services.
- Contributed property that was inventory in the contributor's hands on the contribution date if the partnership disposes of the property within *five years of the contribution*. For this purpose, inventory includes all tangible property except capital and real or depreciable business assets.

A similar rule is designed to prevent a capital loss from being converted into an ordinary loss. Under the rule, if contributed property is disposed of at a loss and the property had a "built-in" capital loss on the contribution date, the loss is treated as a capital loss if the partnership disposes of the property *within five years of the contribution*. The capital loss is limited to the "built-in" loss on the date of contribution.[21]

The Big Picture

Example 15

Return to the facts of *The Big Picture* on p. 14-1. Recall that Kyle, Maria, and Josh decide to structure their venture as an LLC. Assume that Kyle has a basis of $600,000 in the $2,000,000 of real estate he contributed and that Maria has a $0 basis in the bakery equipment and the café furnishings.

When Beachside Properties LLC is formed, no tax arises for the LLC or for Kyle or Maria. Kyle does not recognize his $1,400,000 realized gain, nor does Maria recognize her $500,000 realized gain.

Kyle takes a substituted basis of $600,000 for his interest, and Maria takes a substituted basis of $1,500,000 ($1,500,000 of contributed cash + $0 for contributed property). Beachside Properties assumes a carryover basis of $600,000 for the real estate contributed by Kyle and $0 for the property contributed by Maria. To the extent that the buildings and other land improvements are depreciable, the LLC "steps into Kyle's shoes" in calculating depreciation deductions.

When Josh vests in his 5% capital interest in the LLC, the $200,000 value of the interest is taxable to him, because it is a capital interest received in exchange for services. Beachside Properties probably will capitalize this amount because it relates to construction activities. Josh's 20% share of the future profits of the LLC are taxed to him as they flow through from the LLC.

14-2d Inside and Outside Bases

Reference has been made previously to the partnership's inside basis and the partners' outside basis. **Inside basis** refers to the adjusted basis of each partnership asset, as determined from the partnership's tax accounts. **Outside basis** represents each partner's basis in his or her partnership interest. Each partner "owns" a share of the partnership's inside basis for all of its assets, and all partners should maintain a record of their respective outside bases.

LO.3

Determine the tax treatment of expenditures of a newly formed partnership and identify elections available to the partnership.

14-2e Tax Accounting Elections

Numerous tax accounting elections must be made when a new partnership is formed. These elections are formal decisions on how a particular transaction or tax attribute should be handled. Most of these elections must be made by the partnership rather than

[20] § 724. For this purpose, § 724(d)(2) waives the holding period requirement in defining § 1231 property.

[21] § 724(c).

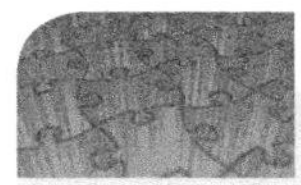

Concept Summary 14.2

Partnership Formation and Basis Computation

1. Generally, partners or partnerships do not recognize gain or loss when property is contributed in exchange for capital interests.
2. Partners take a substituted basis in the partnership interest (*outside basis*) equal to the basis of the property contributed to the partnership.
3. The partnership takes a carryover basis in assets received (*inside basis*) equal to the partner's basis in those assets.
4. The partnership's holding period for contributed property may include the contributing partner's holding period.
5. Income or gain is recognized by a contributing partner when services are contributed or when the capital contribution is a disguised sale or exchange.
6. Special rules may apply when the partnership disposes of contributed receivables, inventory, or loss assets.

by the partners individually.[22] For example, the *partnership* makes the elections involving the following tax accounting items.

- Inventory methods.
- Tax year and accounting method (cash, accrual, or hybrid).
- Cost recovery methods and assumptions.
- Immediate cost recovery deductions for certain tangible personal property.
- Amounts and treatment (i.e., deduction or credit) of research and experimentation costs.
- Amortization of organizational expenditures and amortization period.

Each partner is bound by the decisions made by the partnership relative to these items. If the partnership fails to make an election, a partner cannot make the election individually.

Although most elections are made by the partnership, each *partner* separately makes a specific election for the following relatively narrow tax accounting issues.

- Whether to take a deduction or a credit for taxes paid to foreign countries.
- Whether to claim the cost or percentage depletion method for oil and gas wells.

14-2f **Initial Costs of a Partnership**

In its initial stages, a partnership incurs expenses relating to some or all of the following: forming the partnership (organizational expenditures), admitting partners to the partnership, marketing and selling partnership units to prospective partners (**syndication costs**), acquiring assets, starting business operations (startup costs), negotiating contracts, and dealing with other items.

Many of these expenditures are not currently deductible. However, the Code permits a deduction or ratable (straight-line) amortization of "organizational" and "startup" costs. Costs incurred to acquire tangible assets are included in the initial basis of the acquired assets, leading to depreciation deductions. "Syndication costs" may be neither amortized nor deducted.[23]

[22] § 703(b).

[23] § 709(a).

Organizational Expenditures

Organizational expenditures are incurred incident to the creation of the partnership and are capital in nature. Such costs include accounting and legal fees associated with the partnership formation. Costs incurred for the following purposes are *not* organizational expenditures.

- Acquiring assets for the partnership.
- Transferring assets to the partnership.
- Admitting partners, other than at formation.
- Removing partners, other than at formation.
- Negotiating operating contracts.

For Federal income tax purposes, a partnership may deduct up to $5,000 of organizational expenditures in the year in which it begins business. This amount is reduced, however, by organizational expenditures that exceed $50,000. Any organizational expenditures that cannot be deducted under this provision are amortizable over 180 months beginning with the month in which the partnership begins business.[24]

The election to deduct organizational expenditures is made by entering the proper amounts on the first partnership return. Lacking such a computation, no deduction or amortization of the organizational expenditures is allowed until the entity is liquidated.

The Bluejay LLC, which was formed on March 1, incurs $52,000 in organizational expenditures. Bluejay uses a calendar tax year. On its first tax return for the period March–December, Bluejay can deduct $5,722 for these items. This deduction is the sum of:

- **$5,000 reduced by the $2,000 ($52,000 − $50,000) amount by which the organizational expenditures exceed $50,000 = $3,000.**
- **$2,722 ($49,000 × 10/180) amortization of the remaining $49,000 ($52,000 − $3,000) of organizational expenditures for 10 months.**

If Bluejay had failed to make a proper election to deduct or amortize the organizational expenditures, none of these costs would have been deductible until the entity liquidated.

Startup Costs

Operating costs that are incurred after the entity is formed but before it begins business are known as startup costs. Like organizational expenditures, startup costs are capitalized and may be immediately expensed and/or amortized.[25] Such costs include marketing surveys prior to conducting business, pre-operating advertising expenses, costs of establishing an accounting system, and salaries paid to executives and employees before the start of business.

For Federal income tax purposes, startup costs follow the same rules as organization expenditures. A partnership may deduct up to $5,000 of startup costs in the year in which it begins business. This amount is reduced, however, by the startup costs that exceed $50,000.

Costs that are not deductible under this provision are amortizable over 180 months beginning with the month in which the partnership begins business. If the deduction for startup costs is not claimed, no deduction or amortization of the startup costs is allowed until the entity is liquidated.

Digging Deeper 3

In-depth coverage of asset acquisition costs, accounting methods, and required tax year can be found on this book's companion website: www.cengage.com

[24] § 709(b).

[25] § 195.

14-3 Operations of the Partnership

LO.4

Calculate partnership taxable income and describe how partnership items affect a partner's income tax liability.

A key consideration in the taxation of partnerships is that a variety of entities can be partners and each may be affected differently by the partnership's operations. In particular, any combination of individuals, corporations, trusts, estates, or other partnerships may be partners. Furthermore, at the end of each year, every partner receives a share of the partnership's income, deductions, credits, and alternative minimum tax (AMT) preferences and adjustments.[26]

These flow-through items ultimately may be reported and taxed on a wide variety of income tax returns [e.g., Forms 1040 (Individuals), 1041 (Fiduciaries), 1120 (C corporations), and 1120S (S corporations)], each facing different limitations and rules. Thus, the ultimate tax treatment of partnership operations is directly affected by how the partnership reports its operating results.

14-3a Schedules K and K–1

A partnership measures and reports two kinds of income: ordinary business income and separately stated items. A separately stated item is any item with tax attributes that could affect partners differently. Separately stated items are segregated and reported separately on the partnership's Schedule K and each partner's Schedule K–1. All other (nonseparately stated) income and expenses are reported as income from operations on page 1 of the partnership's Form 1065; the net amount then is also reported on Schedules K and K–1. Items passed through separately include the following.[27]

- Net short-term and net long-term capital gains or losses.
- Section 1231 gains and losses.
- Charitable contributions.
- Portfolio income items (qualified and ordinary dividends, interest, and royalties).
- Expenses related to portfolio income.
- Immediately expensed tangible personal property (§ 179).
- Disallowed business interest expense.[28]
- AMT preference and adjustment items.
- Self-employment income.[29]
- Passive activity items (e.g., rental real estate income or loss).
- Intangible drilling and development costs.[30]
- General business tax credits.[31]
- Qualified business income deduction information.

A partnership is not allowed to claim the following deductions.

- Net operating loss (NOL).
- Dividends received deduction.
- Items that are allowed only to individuals, such as the standard deduction.

[26] § 702(a).

[27] § 702(a). For tax years beginning in 2021 (or later), a partnership also prepares Schedules K–2 (partnership foreign activities) and K–3 (partner's share of Schedule K–2 items).

[28] See § 163(j).

[29] See § 1402(a).

[30] See text Section 5-9a.

[31] See § 38.

The Big Picture

Example 17

Return to the facts of *The Big Picture* on p. 14-1. In its second year of operations, Beachside Properties LLC reports income and expenses from operating the café as well as rent income and expenses from leasing the other buildings. Beachside's activities are summarized as follows.

Sales revenue	$2,000,000
Cost of sales	800,000
W–2 wages paid to employees	500,000
Cost recovery deductions	91,984
Utilities, supplies, and other expenses	128,016
Taxes and licenses (including payroll taxes)	60,000
Contribution to charity	6,000
Short-term capital gain	12,000
Net income from rental real estate	300,000
Qualified dividends received	4,000
Tax-exempt income (bond interest)	2,100
Alternative minimum tax (AMT) adjustment (cost recovery)	18,224
Payment of medical expenses on behalf of Kyle	4,000
Net operating loss (NOL) from last year's operations	250,000
Cash distribution to Maria	20,000

Refer to Form 1065 at **irs.gov**. Beachside's ordinary income is determined and reported on the partnership return as follows.

Nonseparately Stated Items (Ordinary Income)	
Sales revenue	$2,000,000
Cost of sales	(800,000)
W–2 wages paid to employees	(500,000)
Cost recovery deductions	(91,984)
Utilities, supplies, and other expenses	(128,016)
Taxes and licenses (including payroll taxes)	(60,000)
Ordinary income [Form 1065, page 1, line 22, and Form 1065, page 4 (Schedule K), line 1]	$ 420,000

Beachside's separately stated income and deduction items are:

Separately Stated Income and Deductions (Schedule K)	
Net income from rental real estate (line 2)	$ 300,000
Qualified dividends received (line 6b)	4,000
Short-term capital gain (line 8)	12,000
Contribution to charity (line 13a)	(6,000)

Beachside is not allowed a deduction for payment of Kyle's medical expenses. This payment probably is handled as a distribution to Kyle, who may report it as a medical expense on his Form 1040, Schedule A in determining itemized deductions.

Maria's distribution is not deducted by Beachside. That amount instead reduces Maria's basis in her LLC interest.

The AMT adjustment is not a separate component of Beachside's ordinary income. It is reported to Beachside's members so that they can properly calculate any AMT liability of their own.

Beachside reports the following additional information the members may utilize in preparing their own income tax returns.

continued

Beachside reported an operating loss last year. The LLC could not deduct that loss; instead, the loss was passed through to the LLC members last year. Partnerships and LLCs do not incur net operating loss carryforwards.

Additional Information (Schedule K)	
AMT adjustment—cost recovery (line 17a)	$18,224
Tax-exempt income—bond interest (line 18a)	2,100
Distributions (line 19a)	24,000
Investment income (line 20a)	4,000

The LLC members' pass-through income represents net earnings (loss) from self-employment and is reported on line 14a.

The Big Picture

Continue with the facts in Example 17, but now consider the entity's book-tax reconciliation. Beachside Properties LLC must prepare the Analysis of Net Income (Loss) and Schedule M–1 on Form 1065, page 5. In preparing these schedules, the LLC combines the ordinary income of $420,000 and the four separately stated income and deduction amounts in Example 17 to arrive at "net income" of $730,000. This amount is shown on line 1 of the Analysis of Net Income (Loss) and is the amount to which book income is reconciled on Schedule M–1, line 9.

The Big Picture

Example 19

Assume the same facts as in Example 17, but now consider the effect of the LLC's operations on one of its members. Maria, a 40% owner, will receive a Schedule K–1 from Beachside Properties, on which she is allocated a 40% share of ordinary income and separately stated items. Thus, on her Form 1040, Maria includes $168,000 of ordinary income, a $2,400 charitable contribution, a $4,800 short-term capital gain, $120,000 of passive activity rent income, and $1,600 of qualified dividend income. Maria's Schedule K–1 also reports the $20,000 cash distribution received.

Maria discloses her $840 share of tax-exempt interest on the first page of Form 1040. In determining her AMT liability (if any), Maria will take into account a $7,290 positive adjustment ($18,224 × 40%).

Discussion of the failure to file a partnership return penalty can be found on this book's companion website: www.cengage.com

4 Digging Deeper

Distributions, Withdrawals

Asset distributions and withdrawals by partners during the year do not affect the partnership's income determination. These items usually are treated as made on the last day of the partnership's tax year. Such distributions reduce the partner's outside basis in the entity by the amount of the cash received, or by the inside basis of the asset to the entity, but not below zero. The entity's inside basis in assets is similarly reduced. The partner usually assigns to the received property a basis equal to the entity's inside basis in the distributed asset.[32]

[32]§§ 732 and 733.

Example 20

Bueno Company is a partner in the BB Partnership. The basis in Bueno's partnership interest is $10,000. The partnership distributes $3,000 cash to Bueno at the end of the year. Bueno does not recognize any gain on the distribution. It reduces its basis in BB by $3,000 (the amount of the distribution) to $7,000. Bueno's basis in the cash received is $3,000.

BB also distributes to Bueno a plot of land worth $5,000, with a $2,000 basis to BB. Neither BB nor Bueno recognizes a gain from this distribution. Bueno assigns the land a $2,000 basis, and it reduces its basis in BB by the same amount.

The result in Example 20 arises whether or not a similar distribution is made to other partners. In a partnership, all partners need not receive a pro rata distribution at the same time as long as capital account balances are maintained appropriately.

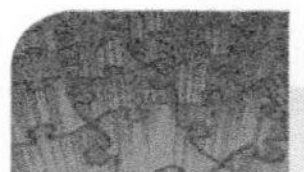

Digging Deeper 5

Rules on the treatment of partnership distributions can be found on this book's companion website: www.cengage.com

14-3b Partnership Allocations

After ordinary income, separately stated items, and other related information are determined at the partnership level, those amounts are allocated among the partners and reported on their tax returns. Allocations are made as required by the partnership agreement, using the profit and loss sharing ratios agreed to by the owners.

Concept Summary 14.3

Tax Reporting of Partnership Activities

Item	Partnership Level (Form 1065)	Partner Level (Schedule K–1)
1. Compute partnership ordinary income.	Page 1, line 22. Schedule K, line 1.	Line 1. Each partner's share is passed through for separate reporting. Each partner's basis is increased.
2. Compute partnership ordinary loss.	Page 1, line 22. Schedule K, line 1.	Line 1. Each partner's share is passed through for separate reporting. Each partner's basis is decreased. The amount of a partner's loss deduction may be limited. Losses that may not be deducted are carried forward for use in future years.
3. Separately reported income and deduction items such as portfolio income, capital gain and loss, AMT and foreign tax items, and § 179 deductions.	Schedule K, various lines.	Various lines. Each partner's share of each item is passed through for separate reporting.
4. Net earnings from self-employment.	Schedule K, line 14a, code A.	Line 14, code A.

Alternatively, two key special allocation rules also can affect a partner's Schedule K–1 results.[33]

Economic Effect

The partnership agreement can provide that any partner may share capital, profits, and losses in ratios that are tailored to their needs.[34] For example, a partner could have a 25 percent capital sharing ratio yet be allocated 30 percent of the profits and 20 percent of the losses of the partnership, or, as in Examples 5 and 6, a partner could be allocated a specific amount or items of income, deduction, gain, or loss. Such special allocations are permissible if they meet the **economic effect test**.[35] The economic effect rules prevent partners from shifting income and loss items merely to reduce current income taxes. The rules also ensure that a partner bears the economic burden of a loss or deduction allocation and receives the economic benefit of an income or gain allocation.[36]

Further discussion of the economic effect test can be found on this book's companion website: www.cengage.com

6 Digging Deeper

Precontribution Gain or Loss

Certain income, gain, loss, and deductions relative to contributed property may not be allocated under the economic effect rules. Instead, **precontribution gain or loss** is allocated among the partners to take into account the variation between the basis of the property and its fair market value on the date of contribution. For nondepreciable property, this means that *built-in* gain or loss on the date of contribution is allocated to the contributing partner when the property eventually is disposed of by the partnership in a taxable transaction.[37]

The Big Picture

Example 21

Return to the facts of *The Big Picture* on p. 14-1. When Beachside Properties LLC was formed, among other items, Kyle contributed land (value of $800,000 and basis of $600,000) and buildings (value of $1,200,000 and basis of $0). Maria contributed equipment and furnishings (value of $500,000 and basis of $0).

For book purposes, Beachside records the land and other properties at their fair market values. For tax purposes, the LLC takes carryover bases in the properties. The LLC must keep track of the differences between the basis in each property and the value at the contribution date. If any of this property is sold, the gain is allocated to the contributing partner to the extent of any previously unrecognized built-in gain.

For example, if Beachside sells the land contributed by Kyle for $1,100,000, the gain is calculated and allocated as follows.

	Book	Tax
Amount realized	$1,100,000	$1,100,000
Less: Adjusted basis	(800,000)	(600,000)
Gain realized	$ 300,000	$ 500,000
Built-in gain allocated solely to Kyle	(–0–)	(200,000)
Remaining gain (allocated among members)	$ 300,000	$ 300,000

For Federal income tax purposes, Kyle recognizes $320,000 of the gain [($300,000 × 40%) + $200,000], Maria recognizes $120,000 ($300,000 × 40%), and Josh recognizes $60,000 ($300,000 × 20%).

[33] The Code requires or allows certain other allocations not discussed here.
[34] § 704(a).
[35] § 704(b)(2).
[36] See Reg. § 1.704–1(b)(2).
[37] § 704(c)(1).

Qualified Business Income Deduction

Noncorporate owners of flow-through entities including partners can claim a deduction from income equal to 20 percent of the income that is allocated to them from the entity.[38] If the owner's taxable income (before the **QBI deduction**) is less than certain thresholds ($340,100 for taxpayers filing joint returns and $170,050 for single and head-of-household taxpayers), the deduction is calculated as 20 percent of qualified business income (QBI). QBI includes the ordinary net income from the pass-through entity, including rental income. However, QBI does not include other separately stated items of income, gain, or loss.

Hugh is a single taxpayer. He owns a 25% interest in HG Partnership. The partnership records ordinary net income of $600,000. Hugh's share of partnership ordinary net income is $150,000. His share of W–2 wages paid by HG Partnership is $50,000, and his share of the unadjusted basis of qualified property is $400,000. The partnership is his sole source of income. Hugh's tentative § 199A deduction is $30,000 ($150,000 × 20%).

If the owner's taxable income exceeds the appropriate threshold, the allowable deduction may be reduced. In this case, the § 199A deduction is the lesser of the 20 percent QBI deduction or the greater of 50 percent of W–2 wages paid by the business or 25 percent of the W–2 wages plus 2.5 percent of unadjusted basis of tangible depreciable property. The limitation phases in over $100,000 of taxable income for taxpayers filing joint returns and $50,000 for all other returns. For instance, for a single taxpayer, the limitation is fully phased in when taxable income exceeds $220,050 ($170,050 threshold + $50,000). An additional limitation applies if the income is from specified service businesses. In this instance, if the taxpayer's income exceeds the appropriate threshold, the taxpayer gets no deduction. The deduction is calculated at the partner level. Therefore, the entity must report on Schedules K–1 any information the partners need to complete their tax returns.

Continue with the facts of Example 22. Now assume that Hugh's taxable income from all sources is $250,000. In this case, taxable income (before QBI deduction) exceeds $220,050, so the W–2/tangible property limitation is fully phased in. Hugh's QBI deduction would be $25,000: the lesser of (1) 20% of QBI or (2) the greater of 50% of allocated W–2 wages or 25% of allocated W–2 wages plus 2.5% of unadjusted basis of tangible depreciable property.

1. 20% of QBI ($150,000 × 20%)		$30,000
2. Greater of		
a. 50% of W–2 wages ($50,000 × 50%)	$25,000	
b. 25% of W–2 wages plus 2.5% of unadjusted basis of depreciable property [($50,000 × 25%) + ($400,000 × 2.5%)]	$22,500	
		$25,000

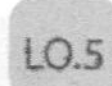

Determine a partner's basis in the partnership interest.

14-3c Basis of a Partnership Interest

A partner's basis in the partnership interest is important for determining the treatment of distributions from the partnership to the partner, establishing the deductibility of partnership losses, and calculating gain or loss on the partner's disposition of the partnership interest.

A partner's basis is not reflected anywhere on the Schedule K–1. Instead, each partner maintains a personal record of the basis in his or her partnership interest.

Initial Basis in the Partnership Interest

A partner's basis in a newly formed partnership usually equals (1) the adjusted basis in any cash or other property contributed to the partnership plus (2) the fair market value of any services the partner performed for the partnership (i.e., the amount of ordinary income reported by the partner for services rendered to the partnership).

[38] § 199A.

Bridge Discipline Bridge to Financial Accounting

The equivalent in financial accounting to the partner's income tax basis in his or her partnership interest is the **capital account**. A partner's ending balance in the capital account is not required to be the same as his or her basis in the partnership interest. Just as the tax and accounting bases of a specific asset may differ, a partner's capital account and basis in the partnership interest usually are not equal.

Whereas asset contributions and most distributions from the partnership do not create financial accounting income, the capital account is "written up or down" to aggregate fair market value when the entity is formed. For most partnerships with simple financial transactions, *changes* to the capital account parallel closely the annual changes to the partner's basis in the partnership. Basis in one's partnership interest cannot be a negative number, but the capital account can become negative.

Oddly, the Schedules K–1 for the partners require an accounting for their capital accounts, but there is no required reconciliation for the partner's tax basis on the Schedule K–1. As a result, the tax adviser may find that a new partnership client has poor records with respect to the basis amounts of the partners, and a reconstruction must take place so that future computations will be correct.[39]

A partnership interest also can be acquired after the partnership has been formed. The method of acquisition controls how the partner's initial basis is computed. If the partnership interest is purchased from another partner, the purchasing partner's basis is the amount paid (cost basis) for the partnership interest. The basis of a partnership interest acquired by gift is the donor's basis for the interest plus, in certain cases, some or all of the transfer (gift) tax paid by the donor. The basis of a partnership interest acquired through inheritance generally is the fair market value of the interest on the date the partner dies.

Basis Adjustments Due to Entity Operations

After the partnership begins its activities, or after a new partner is admitted to the partnership, the partner's basis is adjusted for numerous items. The following items *increase* a partner's basis.

- The partner's proportionate share of partnership income (including capital gains and tax-exempt income).
- The partner's proportionate share of any increase in partnership liabilities.

The following items *decrease* the partner's basis in the partnership.

- The partner's proportionate share of partnership deductions and losses (including capital losses).
- The partner's proportionate share of nondeductible expenses.
- The partner's proportionate share of any reduction in partnership liabilities.[40]

Under no circumstances can a partner's basis in the partnership's interest be reduced below zero.

Increasing the basis for the partner's share of partnership taxable income is logical, because the partner already has been taxed on the income. By increasing the partner's basis, the partner is not taxed again on the income when the interest is sold or the partner receives a distribution from the partnership.

It also is logical that tax-exempt income should increase the partner's basis. If the income is tax-exempt in the current period, it should not contribute to the recognition of gain when the partner either sells the interest or receives a distribution from the partnership. Decreasing the basis for the partner's share of deductible losses, deductions, and noncapitalizable, nondeductible expenditures is done for the same reasons.

[39]Sometimes, lacking adequate information with which to make this computation, the capital account is used for this purpose, because it is "close enough" and forms a good surrogate for the partner's basis in the partnership.

[40]§§ 705 and 752.

Tax Fact What Do Partnerships Do?

Partnerships report over $36 trillion in assets on their 2019 Form 1065 balance sheets. The partnership form seems to be especially popular for businesses operating in the financial services and real estate industries. Manufacturing assets tend not to be found as frequently in these entities.

Assets of Partnerships, by Industry

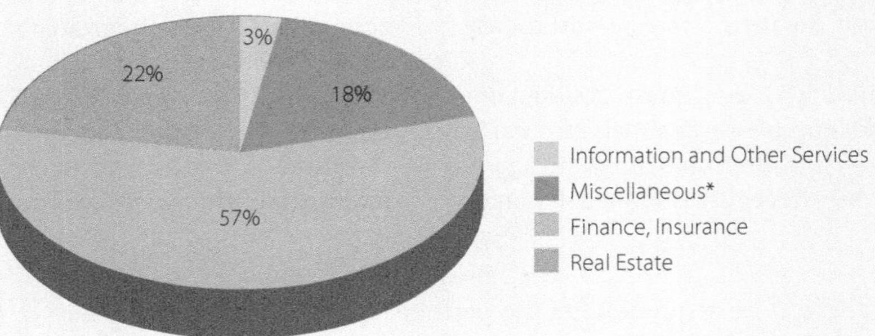

*Includes aggregated amounts from the agriculture, health care, construction, manufacturing, wholesale and retail trade, education, and arts and entertainment sectors.

Source: *IRS Tax Stats.*

Example 24

Yuri is a one-third member in the XYZ LLC. His proportionate share of operations during the current year consists of $20,000 of ordinary business income and $10,000 of tax-exempt income. None of the income is distributed to Yuri.

The basis of Yuri's LLC interest before adjusting for his share of income is $35,000, and the fair market value of the interest before considering the income items is $50,000.

The unrealized gain inherent in Yuri's investment in XYZ is $15,000 ($50,000 − $35,000). Yuri's proportionate share of the income items should increase the fair market value of the interest to $80,000 ($50,000 + $20,000 + $10,000). When the basis of Yuri's interest is increased to $65,000 ($35,000 + $20,000 + $10,000), the unrealized gain inherent in Yuri's investment remains at $15,000.

Thus, $20,000 of ordinary business income is taxed to Yuri this year and should not be taxed again when Yuri either sells his interest or receives a distribution. Similarly, the tax-exempt income is exempt this year and should not increase Yuri's gain when he either sells his interest or receives a distribution from XYZ.

Partnership Liabilities

A partner's basis includes the partner's share of partnership debt.[41] Partnership debt includes most debt that is considered a liability under financial accounting rules. However, partnership debt for this purpose does *not* include the accounts payable of a cash basis partnership and certain contingent liabilities.

Partnership debt is classified as either recourse or nonrecourse.[42] For **recourse debt**, the partnership or at least one of the partners is personally liable. This liability can exist, for example, through the operation of state law or through personal guarantees that a partner makes to the creditor. If the entity defaults on the loan, the lender can pursue the other assets of the borrower, including personal use property.

For **nonrecourse debt**, no partner is personally liable. Lenders of nonrecourse debt generally require that collateral be pledged against the loan. Upon default, the lender can claim only the collateral, not the partners' personal assets.

[41] § 752.

[42] Reg. § 1.752–1(a). All of the debts of an LLC generally are treated as nonrecourse debt for its members, because it is the entity, and not the members, that is ultimately liable for repayment.

Liabilities and Partnership Interest Basis

The Bay Partnership financed its asset acquisitions with debt. If the partnership defaults on the debt, the lender can place a lien on the partners' salaries and personal assets. This constitutes recourse debt.

The Tray LLC financed its asset acquisitions with debt. If the entity defaults on the debt, the lender can repossess the equipment purchased with the loan proceeds. This constitutes non-recourse debt.

A partner's share of entity-level debt usually increases as a result of increases in outstanding partnership debt. This increase is treated as a cash contribution and creates additional basis in the partnership for the partner, against which flow-through losses can be deducted.

Example 27

Ji-hun and Becky contribute property to form the JB Partnership. Ji-hun contributes cash of $30,000. Becky contributes land with a basis and fair market value of $45,000, subject to a liability of $15,000. The partnership borrows $50,000 to finance construction of a building on the contributed land. At the end of the first year, the accrual basis partnership owes $3,500 in trade accounts payable to various vendors. No other operating activities occurred. If Ji-hun and Becky share equally in liabilities, the partners' bases in their partnership interests are determined as follows.

Ji-hun's Basis		Becky's Basis	
Contributed cash	$30,000	Basis in contributed land	$45,000
		Less: Debt assumed by partnership	(15,000)
Share of debt on land (assumed by partnership)	7,500	Share of debt on land (assumed by partnership)	7,500
Share of construction loan	25,000	Share of construction loan	25,000
Share of trade accounts payable	1,750	Share of trade accounts payable	1,750
Basis, end of year 1	$64,250	Basis, end of year 1	$64,250

A decrease in a partner's share of partnership debt is treated as a cash distribution and decreases the partner's basis. Because distributions are taken into consideration before any current-year losses from the partnership, this ordering procedure limits the partner's ability to deduct current-year flow-through losses.

In-depth coverage of the partnership debt allocation rules can be found on this book's companion website: www.cengage.com

7 Digging Deeper

14-3d Partner's Basis, Gain, and Loss

The partner's basis in an ownership interest also is affected by (1) postacquisition contributions of cash or property to the partnership and (2) postacquisition distributions of cash or property from the partnership.

Ed is a one-third member in ERM LLC. On January 1, Ed's basis in his interest was $50,000. The calendar year, accrual basis entity generated ordinary taxable income of $210,000. It also received $60,000 of tax-exempt interest income from City of Buffalo bonds. It paid $3,000 in nondeductible fines and penalties.

continued

On July 1, Ed contributed $20,000 cash and a computer (zero basis to him) to ERM. Ed's monthly cash draw from the LLC is $3,000; this is not a guaranteed payment. The only entity liabilities are trade accounts payable. On January 1, the trade accounts payable totaled $45,000; this account balance was $21,000 on December 31. Ed's shares of the entity's liabilities is one-third for basis purposes.

Ed's basis in the LLC on December 31 is $115,000, computed as follows.

Beginning basis in the LLC interest	$ 50,000
Share of ordinary income	70,000
Share of tax-exempt income	20,000
Share of nondeductible fines and penalties	(1,000)
Ed's basis in noncash capital contribution (computer)	-0-
Additional cash contributions	20,000
Capital withdrawal ($3,000 per month)	(36,000)
Share of net decrease in ERM liabilities [1/3 × ($45,000 − $21,000)]	(8,000)
Ending basis in the LLC interest	$115,000

If Ed withdraws cash of $115,000 from ERM the next year, the withdrawal is tax-free to him and reduces his basis to zero. The distribution is tax-free because Ed has recognized his share of net income throughout his association with the entity via the annual flow-through of his share of the ERM income and expense items to his personal tax return.

If Ed receives a $20,000 cash withdrawal of his share of the municipal bond interest income, that amount retains its nontaxable character; his basis was increased when ERM received the interest income.

Noncash Distributions

When a distribution involves something other than cash, the recipient partner (1) reduces the basis in the partnership interest and (2) assigns a basis to the asset received, both by the amount of the inside basis of the distributed asset. When cash and another asset are distributed at the same time, the partner first accounts for the cash received.

Loss never is recognized when a partnership makes a distribution other than possibly in its own liquidation. A partner recognizes gain only when receiving *cash* in an amount in excess of the basis in the partnership interest.

Distributions of Noncash Assets

Example 29

Pert Corporation has a $100,000 basis in the PQR Partnership. Pert receives a distribution from PQR in the form of a plot of land (basis to PQR of $40,000, fair market value of $50,000). Pert does not recognize gain from the distribution. Pert's basis in the land is $40,000 (i.e., a carryover basis), and its basis in PQR now is $60,000 ($100,000 − $40,000).

Pert Corporation has a $100,000 basis in the PQR Partnership. Pert receives a distribution from PQR in the form of a plot of land (basis to PQR of $40,000, fair market value of $50,000) and $75,000 of cash.

Pert does not recognize any gain from the distribution because the cash received ($75,000) does not exceed Pert's partnership basis ($100,000). Pert's basis in the land is $25,000, the basis in PQR remaining after accounting for the cash ($100,000 partnership basis − $75,000 cash = $25,000 basis assigned to land). Pert's basis in the partnership now is zero ($25,000 basis after accounting for the cash − $25,000 assigned to the land).

Distributions of Noncash Assets

Pert Corporation has a $100,000 basis in the PQR Partnership. Pert receives a distribution from PQR in the form of a plot of land (basis to PQR of $40,000, fair market value of $50,000) and $125,000 of cash. Pert recognizes $25,000 of gain from the distribution ($125,000 cash received − $100,000 basis in PQR). Pert's basis in the land is $0, since there is no basis in PQR remaining after accounting for the cash. Pert's basis in the partnership also is zero.

Capital Changes

When a partnership interest is sold, exchanged, or retired, the partner must compute the basis as of the date the transaction occurs. The partner recognizes gain or loss on the disposition of the partnership interest, and this usually is a capital gain or loss. Income "bunching" may occur if the partner recognizes the pass-through of operating income in the same tax year during which the sale of the interest occurs. To the extent the partner is allocated a share of ordinary income items (i.e., "hot assets") that have yet to be recognized by the partnership, some of the capital gain is converted to ordinary income.[43]

Hot Assets

When its basis in the TUV Partnership is $100,000, taking into account all earnings to date and the sale-date liabilities of the partnership, Kurt Corporation sells its interest in the entity to Gloria for $120,000. At the time of the sale, Kurt's share of the built-in gain in TUV's hot assets is $8,000. Kurt recognizes $8,000 of ordinary income and $12,000 of capital gain (i.e., the total gain of $20,000 is comprised of $8,000 of ordinary income and $12,000 of capital gain).

When its basis in the TUV Partnership is $100,000, taking into account all earnings to date and the sale-date liabilities of the partnership, Kurt Corporation sells its interest in the entity to Gloria for $120,000. At the time of the sale, Kurt's share of the built-in gain in TUV's hot assets is $28,000. Kurt recognizes $28,000 of ordinary income and $8,000 of capital loss (i.e., the total gain of $20,000 is comprised of $28,000 of ordinary income and $8,000 of capital loss).

14-3e Loss Limitations

LO.6

Apply the tax law's limitations on deducting partnership losses.

Partnership losses flow through to the partners for use on their tax returns. However, the amount and nature of the partner's deductible losses may be limited. When limitations apply, all or some of the losses are suspended and carried forward until the rules allow them to be used. Only then can the losses decrease the partner's tax liability.

Several different limitations may apply to partnership losses that are passed through to a partner. The first allows the deduction of *losses* only to the extent the partner has a positive basis in the partnership interest. The partnership interest basis cannot be reduced below zero.

Losses that are deductible under this basis limitation may then be subject to the *at-risk* limitations. Losses are deductible under this provision only to the extent the partner is at risk for the partnership interest. Any losses that survive this second limitation may be subject to a third limitation, the *passive activity loss* rules. If a loss passes the three limitations, a noncorporate partner must consider whether the excess business loss limitation applies. Only losses that make it through all of these applicable limitations are eligible to be deducted on the partner's tax return.

[43]Partnership items that hold unrecognized ordinary income are known as *hot assets*. Hot assets include the unrealized receivables of a cash basis partnership and a broadly defined concept of inventory. §§ 751(a) and (d).

Example 34

Meg is a 50% member in MQ Telecomm Services LLC. On January 1, Meg's basis in her LLC interest is $50,000, and her at-risk amount is $35,000. Her share of losses from MQ for the year is $60,000, all of which is a passive activity loss. Meg owns another investment that generated $25,000 of passive activity income during the year. She has no other passive or active losses. Meg can deduct $25,000 of the MQ losses on her Form 1040.

Applicable Provision	Deductible Loss	Suspended Loss
Basis limitation	$50,000	$10,000
At-risk limitation	35,000	15,000
Passive activity loss limitation	25,000	10,000
Excess business loss limitation	25,000	-0-

Meg can deduct only $50,000 under the basis limitation rule. Of this $50,000, only $35,000 is deductible under the at-risk limitation. Under the passive activity loss limitation, passive activity losses can only be deducted against passive activity income. The net passive income/loss is $0, so the excess business loss limitation does not apply. Thus, Meg can deduct only $25,000 on her return. The remaining $35,000 of losses is suspended under the various loss limitation provisions.

Basis Limitation

A partner may deduct losses and deductions from the partnership only to the extent of the partner's basis in the partnership.[44] Items that cannot be deducted because of this rule are suspended and carried forward indefinitely for use against future increases in the partner's basis. Such increases might result from additional capital contributions, from sharing in additional partnership debts, or from future partnership income.

Example 35

Carol and Dan do business as the CD Partnership, sharing profits and losses equally. All parties use the calendar year. At the start of the current year, the basis of Carol's partnership interest is $25,000. The partnership sustains an operating loss of $80,000 in the current year. Only $25,000 of Carol's $40,000 distributive share of the partnership loss can be deducted under the basis limitation. As a result, the basis of Carol's partnership interest is zero as of January 1 of the following year, and Carol must carry forward the remaining $15,000 of partnership losses.

Now assume that CD earns a profit of $70,000 for the next calendar year. Carol reports net partnership income of $20,000 ($35,000 share of income − $15,000 carryforward loss). At the end of that year, Carol's partnership interest basis is $20,000 ($0 beginning basis + $35,000 income − $15,000 loss).

Concept Summary 14.4 later in the chapter shows that contributions to capital, partnership income items, and distributions from the partnership are taken into account before loss items. This *losses last* rule can produce some unusual results in taxation of partnership distributions and deductibility of losses.

Tax Planning Strategies **Make Your Own Tax Shelter**

Framework Focus: Deductions

Strategy: Maximize Deductible Amounts.

In Example 35, Carol's entire $40,000 share of the current-year partnership loss could have been deducted under the basis limitation in the current year if she had contributed an additional $15,000 or more to the entity's capital by December 31 of the first tax year. Alternatively, if the partnership had incurred additional debt by the end of the first tax year, Carol's basis might have been increased to permit some or all of the loss to be deducted in that year.

Thus, if partnership losses are projected for a given year, careful tax planning can ensure their deductibility under the basis limitation. Note, however, that the effects of the at-risk and passive activity limitations as discussed on the next page also must be considered.

[44] § 704(d).

The Basis Limitation on Losses

The Ellen-Glenn Partnership is owned equally by two partners: Ellen and the Glenn Hospital. At the beginning of the year, Ellen's basis in her partnership interest is $0. Her share of partnership income is $12,000 for the year, and she receives a $10,000 distribution from the partnership.

Under the basis adjustment ordering rules of Concept Summary 14.4, as shown on the next page, Ellen's basis first is increased by the $12,000 of partnership income; then it is decreased by her $10,000 distribution. She reports her $12,000 share of partnership taxable income on her personal tax return. Her basis in the partnership at the end of the year is $2,000 ($0 beginning basis + $12,000 income − $10,000 distribution).

Example 37

Assume the same facts as in Example 36, except that Ellen's share of partnership operating results is a $12,000 loss instead of $12,000 of income. She again receives a $10,000 distribution.

A distribution of cash in excess of basis in the partnership interest results in a gain to the distributee partner to the extent of the excess. Ellen's distribution is considered before the deductibility of the loss is evaluated under the basis limitation.

Therefore, Ellen recognizes gain on the $10,000 distribution because she has a $0 basis in her partnership interest. Unfortunately for Ellen, the operating loss cannot be deducted under the basis limitation rule because Ellen still holds a $0 basis in her partnership interest. The loss is suspended, and Ellen carries it forward to a future tax year.

At-Risk Limitation

Under the at-risk rules (see text Section 6-6), a partner's deductions for certain pass-through losses are limited to amounts that are economically invested in the partnership. Invested amounts include the cash and the adjusted basis of property contributed by the partner and the partner's share of partnership earnings that have not been distributed.[45]

Losses that are not deductible under the at-risk rules are suspended and carried forward indefinitely. When a positive at-risk amount arises in a future tax year, the suspended loss is allowed.

When some or all of the partners are personally liable for partnership recourse debt, that debt is included in the basis of the partnership for those partners. Usually, those partners also include the debt in their amount at risk.

No partner, however, carries any financial risk on nonrecourse debt. Therefore, as a general rule, partners cannot include nonrecourse debt in their amount at risk even though that debt is included in the basis of their partnership interest. This rule has an important exception, however. Real estate nonrecourse financing provided by a bank, retirement plan, or similar party or by a Federal, state, or local government generally is deemed to be at risk.[46] Such debt is termed **qualified nonrecourse financing**.

Losses and At-Risk Amounts

Kelly invests $5,000 in the Kelly Green Limited Partnership as a 5% general partner. Shortly thereafter, the partnership acquires the master recording of a well-known vocalist for $250,000 ($50,000 from the partnership and $200,000 secured from a local bank via *recourse* debt). Kelly's share of the recourse debt is $10,000, and her basis in the interest is $15,000 ($5,000 cash investment + $10,000 debt share).

Because the debt is recourse, Kelly's at-risk amount also is $15,000. Kelly's share of partnership losses in the first year of operations is $11,000. Kelly can deduct the full $11,000 of partnership losses under both the basis and the at-risk limitations because this amount is less than both her outside basis and at-risk amount.

[45] § 465.

[46] § 465(b)(6).

Losses and At-Risk Amounts

Example 39

Assume the same facts as in Example 38, except that the bank loan is nonrecourse. Kelly's basis in the partnership interest still is $15,000, but she can deduct only $5,000 of the flow-through loss. The amount she has at risk in the partnership does not include the nonrecourse debt. (The debt does not relate to real estate, so it cannot be qualified nonrecourse debt.)

The $6,000 suspended loss ($11,000 loss pass-through − $5,000 deduction) is deducted in a future tax year when a positive at-risk amount exists. This might occur because the entity has generated an undistributed net profit or because of a capital contribution by Kelly.

Passive Activity Rules

Partnership losses also may be disallowed under the passive activity rules. Recall from text Section 6-7 that an activity is considered passive if the taxpayer (in this case, a partner) does not materially participate in the activity or if the activity is considered a rental activity.

Losses from passive partnership activities are aggregated by each partner with his or her other passive activity income and losses. Passive activity losses generally are deducted only to the extent they offset passive activity income. Any excess passive activity loss is suspended and carried forward to future years. The passive activity limitation applies after the partnership interest basis and at-risk limitations.

Limitation on the Deduction of Excess Business Losses

Another provision limits the total amount of net business losses that can be deducted by an active owner. The rule limits the maximum loss in 2022 to $540,000 for married filing joint tax returns and $270,000 for all other tax returns. Any loss in excess of these amounts can be carried forward indefinitely.[47]

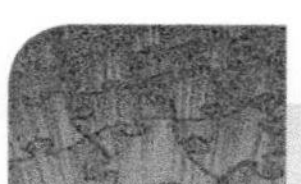

Concept Summary 14.4

Partner's Basis in Partnership Interest

Basis generally is adjusted in the following order.

Initial basis: Amount paid for partnership interest or gift or inherited basis (including share of partnership debt).

+ Partner's subsequent asset contributions and allocable debt increases.
+ Partner's share of the partnership's:
  - Income items.
  - Tax-exempt income items.
  - Excess of depletion deductions over adjusted basis of property subject to depletion.

− Partner's distributions and withdrawals and allocable debt decreases.

− Partner's share of the partnership's:
  - Separately stated deductions.
  - Nondeductible items not chargeable to a capital account.
  - Special depletion deduction for oil and gas wells.
  - Loss items.

The basis of a partner's interest never can be negative.

Entity-level liabilities, and thus a partner's basis in the partnership, may change from day to day, but the partner's basis generally needs to be computed only once or twice a year.

LO.7

Apply the tax laws regarding transactions between a partner and the partnership.

14-4 Transactions between Partner and Partnership

Many types of transactions occur between a partnership and its partners. A partner may contribute property to the partnership, perform services for the partnership, or receive distributions from the partnership. A partner may borrow money from or lend money to the partnership. Property may be bought and sold between a partner and

[47] § 461(l).

the partnership. Several of these transactions were discussed earlier in the chapter. The remaining types of partner-partnership transactions are the focus of this section.

14-4a Guaranteed Payments

A **guaranteed payment** is a payment for services performed by the partner or for the use of the partner's capital. The payment is not determined by reference to partnership income. Guaranteed payments usually are expressed as a fixed-dollar amount or as a percentage of capital the partner has invested in the partnership. Whether the partnership deducts or capitalizes the guaranteed payment depends on the nature of the payment.

Donna, Deepak, and Diane formed the accrual basis DDD Partnership. DDD and each of the partners are calendar year taxpayers. According to the partnership agreement, Donna is to manage the partnership and receive a $21,000 distribution from the entity every year, payable in 12 monthly installments. Deepak is to receive an amount that is equal to 8% of his capital account, as it is computed by the firm's accountant at the beginning of the year, payable in 12 monthly installments. Diane is DDD's advertising specialist. She withdraws 4% of the partnership's net income for personal use. Donna and Deepak receive guaranteed payments from the partnership, but Diane does not.

Guaranteed payments resemble the salary or interest payments of other businesses and receive somewhat similar income tax treatment. In contrast to the provision that usually applies to withdrawals of assets by partners from their partnerships, guaranteed payments are deductible (or capitalized) by the entity. Deductible guaranteed payments, like any other deductible expense of a partnership, can create an ordinary loss for the entity.

The partner's guaranteed payment is reported as a separately stated item on Schedules K and K–1. The partner uses this information (in lieu of a Form W–2 or 1099) to report the income on the partner's tax return. Partners receiving a guaranteed payment report ordinary income and treat it as paid on the last day of the entity's tax year.

Guaranteed Payments: Income and Deductions

Example 41

Continue with the situation introduced in Example 40. For calendar year 2022, Donna receives the $21,000 as provided by the partnership agreement, Deepak's guaranteed payment is $17,000, and Diane withdraws $20,000 under the personal expenditures clause. Before considering these amounts, the partnership's ordinary income for the year is $650,000.

DDD can deduct its payments to Donna and Deepak, so the final amount of its ordinary income is $612,000 ($650,000 − $21,000 − $17,000). Thus, each of the equal partners is allocated $204,000 of ordinary partnership income ($612,000 ÷ 3). In addition, Donna reports the $21,000 guaranteed payment as gross income, and Deepak includes the $17,000 guaranteed payment in his gross income.

Diane's partnership draw is a distribution from her interest basis and is not taxed separately to her.

Assume the same facts as in Example 41, except that the partnership uses a "natural business" tax year that ends on March 31, 2023. Thus, even though Donna received 9 of her 12 payments for fiscal 2023 in the 2022 calendar year, all of Donna's guaranteed payments are taxable to her in 2023. Similarly, all of Deepak's guaranteed payments are taxable to him in 2023 rather than when they are received.

The deduction for, and the gross income from, guaranteed payments is allowed on the same date that all of the other income and expense items relative to the partnership are allocated to the partners (i.e., on the last day of the entity's tax year).

14-4b Other Transactions between a Partner and a Partnership

Many common transactions between a partner and the partnership are treated as if the partner were an outsider, dealing with the partnership at arm's length. Loan transactions, rental payments, and sales of property between the partner and the partnership generally are treated in this manner.

The Eastside Co-op, a one-third partner in the ABC Partnership, owns a tract of land the partnership wants to purchase. The land has a fair market value of $30,000 and a basis to Eastside of $17,000. If Eastside sells the land to ABC, Eastside recognizes a $13,000 gain on the sale, and ABC takes a $30,000 cost basis in the land. If the land has a fair market value of $10,000 on the sale date, Eastside recognizes a $7,000 loss.

Digging Deeper 8

Rules regarding the timing of partnership deductions for payments to partners can be found on this book's companion website: www.cengage.com

Sales of Property

No loss is recognized on a sale of property between a person and a partnership when the person owns, directly or indirectly, more than 50 percent of partnership capital or profits.[48] The disallowed loss may not vanish entirely, however. If the person later sells the property at a gain, the disallowed loss reduces the gain that would otherwise be recognized.

Barry sells land (basis, $30,000; fair market value, $20,000) to the BCD LLC, of which he owns a 60% capital interest. BCD pays him $20,000 for the land. Barry cannot deduct his $10,000 realized loss. Barry and the LLC are related parties, and the loss is disallowed.

When BCD sells the land to an outsider at a later date, it receives a sales price of $34,000. The entity can offset the recognition of its $14,000 realized gain on the subsequent sale ($34,000 sales proceeds − $20,000 basis) by the $10,000 prior disallowed loss ($20,000 − $30,000). Thus, BCD recognizes only a $4,000 gain on its sale of the land.

Using a similar rationale, any gain that is realized on a sale or exchange between a partner and a partnership in which the partner owns a capital or profits interest of more than 50 percent is recognized as ordinary income unless the asset is a capital asset to both the seller and the purchaser.[49]

The Kent School purchases some land (basis, $30,000; fair market value, $45,000) for $45,000 from the JJ Realty LLC, in which Kent owns a 90% profits interest. The land was a capital asset to JJ. If Kent holds the land as a capital asset, JJ recognizes a $15,000 capital gain. However, if Kent is a real estate developer and the land is not a capital asset to it, JJ recognizes $15,000 of ordinary income from the sale, even though it held the land as a capital asset.

14-4c Partners as Employees

A partner does not qualify as an employee under Federal tax law, specifically for purposes of payroll taxes (e.g., FICA or FUTA). Moreover, because a partner is not an employee, the partnership cannot deduct its payments for the partner's fringe benefits, and the partner reports as gross income the value of the fringe benefits received. Nonetheless, a general partner's share of ordinary partnership income and guaranteed payments for services generally are classified as Federal self-employment (SE) income.[50]

[48] § 707(b)(1).
[49] § 707(b)(2).
[50] § 1402(a) and Prop.Reg. § 1.1402(a)–2.

The partner pays an SE tax in addition to the Federal income tax on pass-through items, and the additional Medicare taxes also may apply. The combination of these tax obligations can become expensive. Tax liabilities on SE income of a partner include:

- A 12.4 percent tax on the first $147,000 for 2022 ($142,800 for 2021) of SE income for the individual's account in the FICA retirement system.
- A 2.9 percent tax on all SE income to support the Medicare system.

Tax Planning Strategies

Transactions between Partners and Partnerships

Framework Focus: Deductions

Strategy: Maximize Deductible Amounts.

To ensure that no negative tax results occur, partners should be careful when engaging in transactions with the partnership. A partner who owns a majority of the partnership generally should not sell property at a loss to the partnership because the loss is disallowed. Similarly, a majority partner should not sell a capital asset to the partnership at a gain if the asset is to be used by the partnership as other than a capital asset. The gain on this transaction is taxed as ordinary income to the selling partner rather than as capital gain.

As an alternative to selling property to a partnership, a partner may lease it to the partnership. The partner recognizes rent income, and the partnership has a rent deduction. A partner who needs more cash immediately can sell the property to an outside third party; then the third party can lease the property to the partnership for a fair rental.

A partner who is an individual may be subject to additional taxes that support the Federal Medicare system, on flow-through items from the entity. Certain upper-income taxpayers must pay:

- A 0.9 percent tax on SE income,[51] and
- A 3.8 percent tax on flow-through net investment income (NII), including interest and dividend income, passive/portfolio income, and capital gains. NII does not include tax-exempt interest income, but it does include the share of pass-through operating income for a passive or limited partner.[52]

Further discussion of the net investment income tax can be found on this book's companion website: www.cengage.com

9 Digging Deeper

Concept Summary 14.5

Partner-Partnership Transactions

1. Partners can transact business with their partnerships in a non-partner capacity. These transactions include the sale and exchange of property, rentals, and loans of funds.
2. A payment to a partner may be classified as a guaranteed payment if it is for services or use of the partner's capital and is not based on partnership income. A guaranteed payment usually is deductible by the partnership and is included in the partner's income on the last day of the partnership's tax year.
3. Losses are disallowed between a partner and a partnership when the partner owns (directly or indirectly) more than a 50% interest in the partnership's capital or profits.
4. Income from a related-party sale is treated as ordinary income if the property is not a capital asset to both the transferor and the transferee.
5. Partners are not employees of their partnership, so the entity cannot deduct payments for partner fringe benefits, nor need it withhold or pay any payroll tax for payments to partners.
6. A partner may be subject to self-employment and the additional Medicare taxes on guaranteed payments received and on a distributive share of flow-through income.

[51] § 1401(b)(2)(A). Form 8959 is used to compute this tax.

[52] § 1411. Form 8960 is used to compute this tax.

Explain how LLPs and LLCs differ and list the tax advantages and disadvantages of using an LLC.

14-5 Limited Liability Companies

The *limited liability company (LLC)* combines partnership taxation with limited personal liability for all owners of the entity. All states and the District of Columbia have passed legislation permitting the establishment of LLCs. The following sections explain the taxation, advantages, and disadvantages of using LLCs.

14-5a Taxation of LLCs

A properly structured LLC can elect to be treated as a partnership for income tax purposes. Because LLC members are not personally liable for the debts of the entity, the LLC effectively is treated as a limited partnership with no general partners. This treatment may result in an unusual application of partnership taxation rules.

The IRS has not specifically ruled on most aspects of LLC taxation, but the following comments explain how an LLC member would be taxed, assuming that the LLC has elected to be treated as a partnership.

- Formation of a new LLC is treated in the same manner as formation of a partnership. Generally, no gain or loss is recognized by the LLC member or the LLC, the member takes a substituted basis in the LLC interest, and the LLC takes a carryover basis in the assets it receives.
- An LLC's income and losses are allocated proportionately. Special allocations are permitted as long as they are supported by a nontax economic effect.
- An LLC member contributing property with built-in gains can be subject to tax on certain distributions within seven years of the contribution.
- A loss must meet the partnership interest basis, at-risk, and passive activity loss requirements to be currently deductible. Because debt of an LLC is considered nonrecourse to each of the members, it is not included in the at-risk limitation unless it is "qualified nonrecourse financing."
- The initial accounting period and accounting method elections are available to an LLC.
- Property takes a carryover or substituted basis when distributed from an LLC.

14-5b Advantages of an LLC

An LLC offers certain advantages over a limited partnership.

- Generally, none of the members of an LLC is personally liable for the entity's debts. In contrast, general partners in a limited partnership have personal liability for partnership recourse debts.
- Limited partners cannot participate in the management of a partnership. All owners of an LLC have the legal right to participate in the entity's management.

An LLC also offers certain advantages over an S corporation (see Chapter 15), including the following.

- An LLC can have an unlimited number of owners, but an S corporation is limited to 100 shareholders.
- Any taxpayers, including corporations, nonresident aliens, other partnerships, and trusts, can be owners of an LLC. S corporation shares can be held only by specified parties.
- The transfer of property to an LLC in exchange for an ownership interest in the entity is governed by partnership tax provisions rather than corporate tax provisions. Thus, the transfers need not satisfy the 80 percent control requirement needed for tax-free treatment under the corporate tax statutes (see text Section 12-2d).

- The S corporation taxes on built-in gains and investment income do not apply to LLCs.
- An owner's basis in an LLC includes the owner's share of almost all LLC liabilities under the law. Only certain entity liabilities are included in the S corporation shareholder's basis.
- An LLC may make special allocations, whereas S corporations must allocate income, loss, etc., only on a per-share/per-day basis.

14-5c Disadvantages of an LLC

Only a limited body of case law interprets the various state statutes, so the application of specific provisions in a specific state may be uncertain. An additional uncertainty for LLCs that operate in more than one jurisdiction pertains to which state's law will prevail and how it will be applied.

Among other factors, statutes differ from state to state as to the type of business an LLC can conduct—primarily the extent to which a service-providing firm can operate as an LLC. Special rules also may apply where the LLC has only one member.

Despite these uncertainties and limitations, LLCs are being formed at increasing rates, and the ranks of multistate LLCs also are rising quickly.

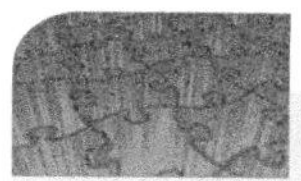

Concept Summary 14.6

Advantages and Disadvantages of the Partnership Form

The partnership form may be attractive when one or more of the following factors is present.

- The entity is generating net taxable losses and/or valuable tax credits, which will be of use to the owners.
- The owners want to avoid complex corporate administrative and filing requirements.
- The owners want to make special allocations of certain income or deduction items that are not possible under the C or S corporation forms.
- Other means of reducing the effects of the double taxation of corporate business income (e.g., compensation to owners, interest, and rental payments) have been exhausted.
- The entity does not generate material amounts of tax preference and adjustment items, which increase the AMT liabilities of its owners.
- The entity is generating passive activity income, which its owners can use to claim immediate deductions for passive activity losses they have generated from other sources.
- The owners hold adequate bases in their ownership interests to facilitate the deduction of flow-through losses and the assignment of an adequate basis to assets distributed in kind to the owners.

The partnership form may be less attractive when one or more of the following factors is present.

- The tax rate paid by the owners on the entity's income is greater than that payable by the entity as a C corporation, and the income is not expected to be distributed soon. (If earnings are distributed by a C corporation, double taxation would likely occur.)
- The entity is generating net taxable income without distributing any cash to the owners. The owners may not have sufficient cash with which to pay the tax on the entity's earnings.
- The type of income the entity is generating (e.g., business and portfolio income) is not as attractive to its owners as passive activity income would be, because the owners could offset passive activity income by the passive activity losses they have generated on their own.
- The entity is in a high-exposure business, and the owners want protection from personal liability. An LLC or LLP structure may be available, however, to limit personal liability.
- The owners want to reduce exposure to Federal self-employment and additional Medicare taxes.

14-6 **Summary**

Partnerships and LLCs are popular among business owners; there are more than twice as many partnerships and limited liability entities as there are C corporations subject to Federal income tax law. This may be partly because formation of the entity is relatively simple and tax-free. The Code places very few restrictions on who can be a partner. Partnerships are especially attractive when operating losses are anticipated or when marginal rates that would apply to partnership income are less than those that would be paid by a C corporation. Partnerships do not offer the limited liability of a corporate entity, but the use of limited partnerships, LLCs, and LLPs can offer some liability protection to the owners.

Partnerships are tax-reporting, not taxpaying, entities. Distributive shares of ordinary income and separately stated items are taxed to the partners on the last day of the tax year. Special allocations and guaranteed payments are allowed and offer partners the ability to tailor the cash-flow and taxable amounts that are distributed by the entity to its owners. Deductions for flow-through losses may be limited by the related-party, passive activity, excess business loss, and at-risk rules, as well as by the partner's basis in the partnership. The flexibility of the partnership rules makes this form continually attractive to new businesses, especially in a global setting.

Refocus on The Big Picture

The Tax Consequences of Partnership Formation and Operations

RODERICK PAUL WALKER/ALAMY STOCK PHOTO

After considering the various types of partnerships, Kyle, Maria, and Josh decided to form Beachside Properties as an LLC. Upon formation of the entity, there was no gain or loss recognized by the LLC or any of its members (see Example 15). Beachside Properties computes its income as shown in Example 17 and allocates the income as illustrated in Example 19. The LLC's income affects the members' bases and capital accounts. An important consideration for the LLC members is whether their distributive shares and guaranteed payments will be treated as self-employment income.

What If?

What happens in the future when the LLC members decide to expand or renovate Beachside's facilities? At that time, the existing members can contribute additional funds, the entity can receive capital from new members, or the entity can borrow money. A partnership or limited liability entity is not subject to the 80 percent control requirement applicable to the formation of a corporation and subsequent transfers to it. Therefore, new investors can contribute cash or other property in exchange for interests in the entity—and the transaction will qualify for tax-deferred treatment.

Suggested Readings

Susan L. Megaard and Michael M. Megaard, "Reducing Self-Employment Taxes on Owners of LLPs and LLCs," *Business Entities*, March/April 2012.

Darla Mercado, "One Way to Play the New Tax Law: Start an LLC," ***cnbc.com***, January 25, 2018.

Eric J. Toder, "Tax Reform and Small Business," ***taxpolicycenter.org***, April 15, 2015.

Key Terms

Basis in the partnership interest, 14-7
Capital account, 14-21
Capital interest, 14-6
Capital sharing ratio, 14-6
Disguised sale, 14-10
Distributive share, 14-4
Economic effect test, 14-19
General partnership (GP), 14-3
Guaranteed payment, 14-29
Inside basis, 14-12
Limited liability company (LLC), 14-4
Limited liability partnership (LLP), 14-4
Limited partnership (LP), 14-3
Nonrecourse debt, 14-22
Organizational expenditures, 14-14
Outside basis, 14-12
Partnership agreement, 14-7
Precontribution gain or loss, 14-19
Profit and loss sharing ratios, 14-6
Profits (loss) interest, 14-6
QBI deduction, 14-20
Qualified nonrecourse financing, 14-27
Recourse debt, 14-22
Separately stated items, 14-5
Special allocation, 14-7
Syndication costs, 14-13

Computational Exercises

1. **LO.4** Enerico contributes $100,000 cash in exchange for a 40% interest in the calendar year ABC LLC. This year ABC generates $80,000 of ordinary taxable income and has no separately stated items. Enerico withdraws $10,000 cash from the partnership at the end of the tax year.
   a. Compute Enerico's gross income from ABC's ordinary income for the tax year.
   b. Compute Enerico's gross income from the LLC's cash distribution.

2. **LO.2** Henrietta transfers cash of $75,000 and equipment with a fair market value of $25,000 (basis to her as a sole proprietor, $10,000) in exchange for a 40% profit and loss interest worth $100,000 in the XYZ Partnership.
   a. Compute Henrietta's realized and recognized gains from the asset transfers.
   b. Compute Henrietta's basis in her interest in XYZ.
   c. What is XYZ's basis in the equipment that it now holds?

3. **LO.2** Wozniacki and Wilcox form Jewel LLC, with each investor receiving a one-half interest in the capital and profits of the LLC. Wozniacki receives the one-half interest as compensation for tax planning services rendered prior to the formation of the LLC. Wilcox contributes $50,000 cash. The value of a one-half capital interest in the LLC (for each of the parties) is $50,000.
   a. Compute Wozniacki's realized and recognized gain from joining Jewel.
   b. Compute Wozniacki's basis in his interest in Jewel.
   c. How does Jewel treat the services that Wozniacki has rendered?

4. **LO.5** At the beginning of the tax year, Barnaby's basis in the BBB Partnership was $50,000, including his $5,000 share of partnership debt. At the end of the tax year, his share of the entity's debt was $8,000.

   Barnaby's share of BBB's ordinary income for the year was $20,000, and he received cash distributions totaling $12,000. In addition, his share of the partnership's tax-exempt income was $1,000. Determine Barnaby's basis at the end of the tax year.

5. **LO.3** Candlewood LLC began its business on September 1; it uses a calendar tax and an accounting year. Candlewood incurred $6,500 in legal fees for drafting the LLC's operating agreement and $3,000 in accounting fees for tax advice of an organizational nature, for a total of $9,500 of organizational costs.

   Candlewood also incurred $30,000 of preopening advertising expenses and $24,500 of salaries and training costs for new employees before opening for business, for a total of $54,500 of startup costs. The LLC desires to take the largest deduction available for these costs. Compute Candlewood's deductions for the first year of its operations for:
   a. Organizational expenditures.
   b. Startup expenses.

6. LO.4, 5 Franco owns a 60% interest in the Dulera LLC. On December 31 of the current tax year, his basis in the LLC interest is $128,000. The fair market value of the interest is $140,000. Dulera then distributes to Franco $30,000 cash and equipment with an adjusted basis of $5,000 and a fair market value of $8,000.
   a. Compute Franco's basis in Dulera after the distribution.
   b. Compute Franco's basis in the equipment he received from Dulera.

Digging Deeper

7. LO.4, 5 When Bruno's basis in his interest in the MNO LLC is $150,000, he receives cash of $55,000, a proportionate share of inventory, and land in a distribution that liquidates MNO and his interest in the LLC. The inventory has a basis to the entity of $45,000 and a fair market value of $48,000. The land's basis is $70,000, and its fair market value is $60,000. Compute Bruno's recognized gain or loss from the liquidating distribution and his tax basis in the inventory and land.

Problems

Critical Thinking

8. LO.2 Janda and Kelsey contributed $1,000,000 each to the JKL LLC in exchange for 45% capital and profits interests in the entity. Lilli will contribute no cash but has agreed to manage the LLC's business operations in exchange for an $80,000 annual salary and a 10% interest in the LLC's capital and profits (valued at $200,000). What are the consequences of the entity formation and Lilli's compensation arrangement to the LLC members? To the LLC itself?

9. LO.2 Emma and Laine form the equal EL Partnership. Emma contributes cash of $100,000. Laine contributes property with an adjusted basis of $40,000 and a fair market value of $100,000.
   a. How much gain, if any, must Emma recognize on the transfer? Must Laine recognize any gain? If so, how much?
   b. What is Emma's tax basis in her partnership interest? Her § 704(b) book basis?
   c. What is Laine's tax basis in her partnership interest? Her § 704(b) book basis?
   d. What tax basis does the partnership take in the property transferred by Laine?
   e. How will the partnership account for the difference between the basis and value of the property transferred by Laine?

Decision Making
Planning

10. LO.2 Kenisha and Shawna form the equal KS LLC with a cash contribution of $360,000 from Kenisha and a property contribution (adjusted basis of $380,000, fair market value of $360,000) from Shawna.
   a. How much gain or loss, if any, does Shawna realize on the transfer? Does Shawna recognize any gain or loss? If so, how much?
   b. What is Kenisha's tax basis in her LLC interest?
   c. What is Shawna's tax basis in her LLC interest?
   d. What tax basis does the LLC take in the property transferred by Shawna?
   e. Are there more effective ways to structure the formation? Explain.

11. LO.2 Liz and John formed the equal LJ Partnership on January 1 of the current year. Liz contributed $80,000 of cash and land with a fair market value of $90,000 and an adjusted basis of $75,000. John contributed equipment with a fair market value of $170,000 and an adjusted basis of $20,000. John previously used the equipment in his sole proprietorship.
   a. How much gain or loss will Liz, John, and LJ realize?
   b. How much gain or loss will Liz, John, and LJ recognize?
   c. What bases will Liz and John take in their partnership interests?
   d. What bases will LJ take in the assets it receives?
   e. How will LJ depreciate any assets it receives from the partners?

12. **LO.2, 5** Sam and Drew are equal members of the SD LLC, formed on June 1 of the current year. Sam contributed land that he inherited from his uncle Garza in 2009. Garza had purchased the land in 1984 for $30,000. The land was worth $100,000 when Garza died. The fair market value of the land was $200,000 at the date it was contributed to SD.

    Drew has significant experience developing real estate. After SD is formed, he will prepare a plan for developing the property and secure zoning approvals for the LLC. Drew usually would bill a third party $50,000 for these efforts. Drew also will contribute $150,000 of cash in exchange for his 50% interest in SD. The value of Drew's 50% interest is $200,000.

    a. How much gain or income does Sam recognize on his contribution of the land to SD? What is the character of any gain or income recognized?
    b. What basis does Sam take in his LLC interest?
    c. How much gain or income will Drew recognize on the formation of SD? What is the character of any gain or income recognized?
    d. What basis will Drew take in his LLC interest?

13. **LO.2, 5** Continue with the facts presented in Problem 12. At the end of the first year, SD distributes $100,000 cash to Sam. No distribution is made to Drew.

    a. How does Sam treat the payment?
    b. How much income or gain would Sam recognize as a result of the distribution?
    c. Under general tax rules, what basis would SD take in the land Sam contributed?

14. **LO.3** On July 1 of the current year, the R&R Partnership was formed as a limited partnership to operate a bed-and-breakfast. The partnership paid $3,000 in legal fees for drafting the partnership agreement and $5,000 for accounting fees related to organizing the entity. It also paid $10,000 in syndication costs to locate and secure investments from limited partners.

    In addition, before opening the inn for business, the entity paid $15,500 for advertising and $36,000 in costs related to an open house just before the grand opening of the property. The partnership opened the inn for business on October 1.

    a. How are these expenses classified?
    b. How much may the partnership deduct in its initial year of operations?
    c. How are costs treated that are not deducted currently?

15. **LO.2, 4** Phoebe and Parker are equal members of Phoenix Investors LLC. They are real estate investors who formed the entity several years ago with equal cash contributions. Phoenix then purchased a parcel of land.

    On January 1 of the current year, to acquire a one-third interest in the entity, Reece contributed to Phoenix some land she had held for investment. Reece purchased the land five years ago for $75,000; its fair market value at the contribution date was $90,000. No special allocation agreements were in effect before or after Reece was admitted to the LLC. Phoenix holds all land for investment.

    Immediately before Reece's property contribution, the Phoenix balance sheet was as follows.

	Basis	FMV		Basis	FMV
Land	$30,000	$180,000	Phoebe, capital	$15,000	$ 90,000
			Parker, capital	15,000	90,000
	$30,000	$180,000		$30,000	$180,000

    a. At the contribution date, what is Reece's basis in her interest in Phoenix?
    b. When does the LLC's holding period begin for the contributed land?

c. On June 30 of the current year, the LLC sold the land contributed by Reece for $90,000. What is the LLC's recognized gain or loss? How is it allocated among the LLC members?

d. Prepare a balance sheet reflecting basis and fair market value for the entity immediately after the land sale. No other transactions occurred during the year.

16. **LO.4, 5, 7** Amy and Mitchell share equally in the profits, losses, and capital of the accrual basis AM Products LLC. Amy is a managing member of the LLC (treated as a general partner) and is a U.S. person.

At the beginning of the current tax year, Amy's *tax basis capital account* has a balance of $300,000, and the LLC has debts of $200,000 payable to unrelated parties. All debts are recourse to the LLC, but neither of the LLC members has personally guaranteed them. The following information about AM's operations for the current year is obtained from the LLC's records.

Sales revenue	$1,400,000
Other "ordinary and necessary" operating expenses (e.g., utilities, repairs, and rent)	500,000
W–2 wages to employees	200,000
Depreciation expense	300,000
Interest income	4,000
Long-term capital gain	6,000
Charitable contribution (cash)	4,000
Cash distribution to Amy	20,000
Unadjusted basis of partnership property immediately after acquisition	1,600,000

Year-end LLC debt payable to unrelated parties is $140,000. All transactions are reflected in Amy's beginning capital account and tax basis in the same manner. All AM Products' activities are eligible for the qualified business income deduction.

a. Calculate Amy's tax basis in her LLC interest at the beginning and end of the tax year. Use her capital account as a starting point.

b. What income, gains, losses, and deductions does Amy report on her income tax return?

c. What other calculations is Amy required to make?

d. Prepare Amy's tax basis capital account roll forward from the beginning to the end of the tax year. How does her ending capital account differ from her ending tax basis in the LLC interest as calculated in part (a)?

e. Using the information from parts (a) to (d), prepare Amy's Schedule K–1 as if you were the preparer of AM Products LLC's tax return. Provide all information that Amy needs to the extent you can. For Parts I and II (items A to F), omit any missing information (e.g., last names, addresses, EINs).

f. Using the Schedule K–1, how much would you estimate as Amy's ending tax basis in the partnership agreement? How did you arrive at this amount?

17. **LO.7** This year the Tastee Partnership reported income before guaranteed payments of $92,000. Stella owns a 90% profits interest and works 1,600 hours per year in the business. Euclid owns a 10% profits interest (with a basis of $30,000 at the beginning of the tax year) and performs no services for the partnership during the year. For services performed during the year, Stella receives a "salary" of $6,000 per month. Euclid withdrew $10,000 from the partnership during the year as a normal distribution of cash from Tastee (i.e., not for services).

a. What is the amount of guaranteed payments made by the partnership this year?

b. How much is the partnership's ordinary income after any permitted deduction for guaranteed payments?

c. How much income will Stella report?

d. How much income will Euclid report?

18. **LO.6** Tobias is a 50% partner in Solomon LLC, which does not invest in real estate. On January 1, Tobias's adjusted basis for his LLC interest is $130,000, and his at-risk amount is $105,000. His share of losses from Solomon for the current year is $150,000, all of which is passive. Tobias owns another investment that produced $90,000 of passive activity income during the year. (Assume that Tobias is a single taxpayer, there were no distributions or changes in liabilities during the year, and the Solomon loss is Tobias's only loss for the year from any activity.)

    How much of Solomon's losses may Tobias deduct on his Form 1040? How much of the loss is suspended, and what Code provisions cause the suspensions?

19. **LO.3** Cerulean, Inc., Coral, Inc., and Crimson, Inc., form the Three Cs Partnership on January 1 of the current year. Cerulean is a 50% partner, and Crimson and Coral are 25% partners. For reporting purposes, Crimson uses a fiscal year with an October 31 year-end, Coral uses the calendar year, and Cerulean uses a fiscal year with a February 28/29 year-end. What is the required tax year for Three Cs under the least aggregate deferral method? Digging Deeper

20. **LO.2, 4, 5** The JM Partnership was formed to acquire land and subdivide it as residential housing lots. On March 1, 2019, Jessica contributed land valued at $600,000 to the partnership in exchange for a 50% interest. She had purchased the land in 2011 for $420,000 and held it for investment purposes (capital asset). The partnership holds the land as inventory.

    On the same date, Matt contributed land valued at $600,000 that he had purchased in 2009 for $720,000. He became a 50% owner. Matt is a real estate developer, but he held this land personally for investment purposes. The partnership holds this land as inventory.

    In 2020, the partnership sells the land contributed by Jessica for $620,000. In 2021, the partnership sells the real estate contributed by Matt for $580,000.

    a. What is each partner's initial basis in his or her partnership interest?
    b. What is the amount of gain or loss recognized on the sale of the land contributed by Jessica? What is the character of this gain or loss?
    c. What is the amount of gain or loss recognized on the sale of the land contributed by Matt? What is the character of this gain or loss?
    d. How would your answer in part (c) change if the property was sold in 2026?

21. **LO.2, 5** Lee, Brad, and Rick form the LBR Partnership on January 1 of the current year. In return for a 25% interest, Lee transfers property (basis of $15,000, fair market value of $17,500) subject to a nonrecourse liability of $10,000. The liability is assumed by the partnership. Brad transfers property (basis of $16,000, fair market value of $7,500) for a 25% interest, and Rick transfers cash of $15,000 for the remaining 50% interest.

    a. How much gain must Lee recognize on the transfer?
    b. What is Lee's basis in his interest in the partnership?
    c. How much loss may Brad recognize on the transfer?
    d. What is Brad's basis in his interest in the partnership?
    e. What is Rick's basis in his interest in the partnership?
    f. What basis does the LBR Partnership take in the property transferred by Lee?
    g. What is the partnership's basis in the property transferred by Brad?

22. **LO.2, 5** Assume the same facts as in Problem 21, except that the property contributed by Lee has a fair market value of $27,500 and is subject to a nonrecourse mortgage of $20,000. Digging Deeper

    a. What is Lee's basis in his partnership interest?
    b. How much gain must Lee recognize on the transfer?
    c. What is Brad's basis in his partnership interest?
    d. What is Rick's basis in his partnership interest?
    e. What basis does the LBR Partnership take in the property transferred by Lee?

Critical Thinking
Decision Making
Planning

23. **LO.5, 6** The BCD Partnership plans to distribute cash of $20,000 to partner Brad at the end of the tax year. The partnership reported a loss for the year, and Brad's share of the loss is $10,000. Brad holds a basis of $15,000 in the partnership interest, including his share of partnership liabilities. The partnership expects to report substantial income in future years.
    a. How does Brad calculate the ending basis in the BCD Partnership interest?
    b. How much gain or loss must Brad report for the tax year due to the distribution?
    c. Will the deduction for any of the $10,000 loss be suspended? Why or why not?
    d. Could any planning opportunities be used to minimize the tax ramifications of the distribution? Explain.

Critical Thinking

24. **LO.2, 3** The Parakeet Partnership was formed on August 1 of the current year and admitted Morlan and Merriman as equal partners on that date. The partners both contributed $300,000 of cash to establish a children's clothing store in the local mall. The partners spent August and September buying inventory, equipment, supplies, and advertising for their "Grand Opening" on October 1. The partnership will use the accrual method of accounting. The following are some of the costs incurred during the partnership's first year of operations. Parakeet uses a calendar tax year.

Legal fees to form partnership	$ 8,000
Advertising for "Grand Opening"	18,000
Advertising after opening	30,000
Consulting fees for establishing accounting system	20,000
Rent, at $2,000 per month	10,000
Utilities, at $1,000 per month	5,000
Salaries to salesclerks (beginning in October)	50,000
Payments to Morlan and Merriman for services ($6,000 per month each for three months)	36,000
Tax return preparation expense	12,000

In addition, on October 1, the partnership purchased all of the assets of Granny Newcombs, Inc. Of the total purchase price for these assets, $252,000 was allocated to the Granny Newcombs trade name and logo.

Determine how each of the listed costs is treated by the partnership, and identify the period over which the costs can be deducted, if any.

25. **LO.4** Bill and Mary filed a joint Federal income tax return this year. Mary owns a 30% interest in MAJIC Partnership, a women's dress boutique. Mary's share of the partnership's net income is $280,000. Her shares of the partnership's W–2 wages and unadjusted basis of depreciable property are $100,000 and $300,000, respectively.
    a. What is Bill and Mary's maximum QBI deduction if their total taxable income is $300,000?
    b. What is the maximum QBI deduction if Bill and Mary's total taxable income is $450,000?
    c. What is the maximum QBI deduction if MAJIC's income was from qualified services and Bill and Mary's total taxable income was $450,000?

26. **LO.7** Four GRRLs Partnership is owned by four unrelated friends. Lacy holds a 40% interest; each of the others owns 20%. Lacy sells investment property to the partnership for its fair market value of $200,000. Her tax basis in the property was $250,000.
    a. How much loss, if any, may Lacy recognize?
    b. If Four GRRLs later sells the property for $260,000, how much gain must it recognize?
    c. How would your answers in parts (a) and (b) change if Lacy owned a 60% interest in the partnership?
    d. If Lacy's basis in the investment property was $120,000 (instead of $250,000) and she was a 60% partner, how much, if any, gain would she recognize on the sale of the property to Four GRRLs? How is it characterized?

27. **LO.7** Burgundy, Inc., and Violet Gomez are equal partners in the calendar year BV LLC. Burgundy uses a fiscal year ending April 30, and Violet uses a calendar year. Burgundy receives an annual guaranteed payment of $100,000 for use of capital contributed by Burgundy. BV's taxable income (after deducting the payment to Burgundy) is $80,000 for 2022 and $90,000 for 2023.
   a. How much income from BV must Burgundy report for its tax year ending April 30, 2023?
   b. How much income from BV must Violet report for her tax year ending December 31, 2023?

28. **LO.4, 7** Ming and Denise, mother and daughter, operate a local restaurant as an LLC. The MD LLC earned a profit of $200,000 in the current year. Denise's equal LLC interest was acquired by gift from Ming. Assume that capital is a material income-producing factor and that Ming manages the day-to-day operations of the restaurant without any help from Denise. Reasonable compensation for Ming's services is $50,000. Digging Deeper
   a. How much of the MD income is allocated to Ming?
   b. What is the maximum amount of LLC income that can be allocated to Denise?
   c. Assuming that Denise is 15 years old, has no other income, and is claimed as a dependent by Ming, how is Denise's income from the restaurant taxed?

29. **LO.5** In each of the following independent cases in which the partnership owns no hot assets, indicate the following. All of the partners received proportionate distributions. Digging Deeper
   - Whether the partner recognizes gain or loss.
   - Whether the partnership recognizes gain or loss.
   - The partner's adjusted basis for the property distributed.
   - The partner's outside basis in the partnership after the distribution.

   a. Kim receives $20,000 of cash in partial liquidation of her interest in the partnership. Kim's outside basis for her partnership interest immediately before the distribution is $3,000.
   b. Kourtni receives $40,000 of cash and land with a $30,000 inside basis to the partnership (value $50,000) in partial liquidation of her interest. Kourtni's outside basis for her partnership interest immediately before the distribution is $80,000.
   c. Assume the same facts as in part (b), except that Kourtni's outside basis for her partnership interest immediately before the distribution is $60,000.
   d. Klois receives $50,000 of cash and inventory with a basis of $30,000 and a fair market value of $50,000 in partial liquidation of her partnership interest. Her basis was $90,000 before the distribution.

30. **LO.4, 5, 7** At the beginning of the tax year, Melodie's basis in the MIP LLC was $60,000, including Melodie's $40,000 share of the LLC's liabilities. At the end of the year, MIP distributed to Melodie cash of $10,000 and inventory (basis of $6,000, fair market value of $10,000). MIP repaid all of its liabilities by the end of the year. Digging Deeper
   a. If this is a proportionate current distribution, what is the tax effect of the distribution to Melodie and MIP? After the distribution, what is Melodie's basis in the inventory and in her MIP interest?
   b. Would your answers to part (a) change if this had been a proportionate liquidating distribution? Explain.

31. **LO.2, 4, 5** Suzy contributed assets valued at $360,000 (basis of $200,000) in exchange for her 40% interest in Suz-Anna GP (a general partnership in which both partners are active owners). Anna contributed land and a building valued at $640,000 (basis of $380,000) in exchange for the remaining 60% interest. Anna's property was encumbered by qualified nonrecourse financing of $100,000, which was assumed by the partnership. Digging Deeper

The partnership reports the following income and expenses for the current tax year.

Sales	$560,000
Utilities, salaries, depreciation, other operating expenses	360,000
Short-term capital gain	10,000
Tax-exempt interest income	4,000
Charitable contributions (cash)	8,000
Distribution to Suzy	10,000
Distribution to Anna	20,000

At the end of the year, Suz-Anna held recourse debt of $100,000 for partnership accounts payable and qualified nonrecourse financing of $200,000.

a. What is Suzy's basis in Suz-Anna after formation of the partnership? Anna's basis?

b. What income and separately stated items does Suz-Anna report on Suzy's Schedule K–1? What income deductions and taxes does Suzy report on her tax return?

c. All partnership debts are shared proportionately. At the end of the tax year, what are Suzy's basis and amount at risk in her partnership interest?

Critical Thinking
Digging Deeper

32. **LO.2, 4, 5, 8** Continue with the facts presented in Problem 31, except that Suz-Anna was formed as an LLC instead of a general partnership.

a. How would Suz-Anna's ending liabilities be treated?

b. How would Suzy's basis and amount at risk be different? Explain.

Communications
Ethics and Equity

33. **LO.4** The Sparrow Partnership plans to distribute $200,000 cash to its partners at the end of the year. Marjorie is a 40% partner and would receive $80,000. Her basis in the partnership is only $10,000, however, so she would recognize a $70,000 gain if she receives the proposed cash distribution.

Marjorie has asked Sparrow instead to purchase a parcel of land that she has found on which she will build her retirement residence. The partnership then will distribute that land to her. Under the partnership distribution rules, Marjorie would take a $10,000 basis in the land worth $80,000. Her basis in the partnership would be reduced to $0, but recognition of the $70,000 gain is deferred.

Do you think this is an appropriate transaction? Explain your conclusion in an e-mail to your instructor.

Tax Return Problem

Tax Forms Problem

ProConnect™ Tax

1. Ryan Ross (111-11-1112), Oscar Omega (222-22-2223), Clark Carey (333-33-3334), and Kim Kardigan (444-44-4445) are equal active members in ROCK the Ages LLC. ROCK serves as agent and manager for prominent musicians in the Los Angeles area. The LLC's Federal ID number is 55-5555556. It uses the cash basis and the calendar year and began operations on January 1, 2009. Its current address is 6102 Wilshire Boulevard, Suite 2100, Los Angeles, CA 90036. ROCK was the force behind such music icons as Adrianna Venti, Drake Malone, Elena Gomez, Tyler Quick, Queen Bey, and Bruno Mercury and has had a very profitable year. The following information was taken from the LLC's income statement for the current year.

Revenues	
Fees and commissions	$4,800,000
Taxable interest income from bank deposits	1,600
Tax-exempt interest	3,200
Net gain on stock sales	4,000
Total revenues	$4,808,800

Expenses	
Advertising and public relations	$ 380,000
Charitable contributions	28,000
Section 179 expense	20,000
Employee W–2 wages	1,000,000
Guaranteed payment (services), Ryan Ross, office manager	800,000
Guaranteed payment (services), other members	600,000
Business meals subject to 50% disallowance	200,000
Business restaurant meals and travel (100% deductible)	320,000
Legal and accounting fees	132,000
Office rentals paid	80,000
Interest expense on operating line of credit	10,000
Insurance premiums	52,000
Office expense	200,000
Payroll taxes	92,000
Utilities	54,800
Total expenses	$3,968,800

Recently, ROCK has taken advantage of bonus depreciation and § 179 deductions and fully remodeled the premises and upgraded its leasehold improvements. This year ROCK wrapped up its remodel with the purchase of $20,000 of office furniture for which it will claim a § 179 deduction. (For simplicity, assume that ROCK uses the same cost recovery methods for both tax and financial purposes.) There is no depreciation adjustment for alternative minimum tax purposes.

ROCK invests much of its excess cash in non-dividend-paying growth stocks and tax-exempt securities. During the year, the LLC sold two securities. On June 15, ROCK purchased 1,000 shares of Tech, Inc. stock for $100,000; it sold those shares on December 15 for $80,000. On March 15 of last year, ROCK purchased 2,000 shares of BioLabs, Inc. stock for $136,000; it sold those shares for $160,000 on December 15 of the current year. These transactions were reported to the IRS on Forms 1099–B; ROCK's basis in these shares *was* reported.

Net income per books is $840,000. On January 1, the members' tax basis capital accounts equaled $200,000 each. No additional capital contributions were made this year. In addition to their guaranteed payments, each member withdrew $250,000 cash during the year. All contributions and distributions have been in cash, so the LLC has no net unrecognized § 704(c) gain or loss. The LLC's balance sheet as of December 31 of this year is as follows.

	Beginning	**Ending**
Cash	$ 444,000	$??
Tax-exempt securities	120,000	120,000
Marketable securities	436,000	300,000
Leasehold improvements, furniture, and equipment	960,000	980,000
Accumulated depreciation	(960,000)	(980,000)
Total assets	$1,000,000	$??

	Beginning	**Ending**
Operating line of credit	$ 200,000	$ 160,000
Capital, Ross	200,000	??
Capital, Omega	200,000	??
Capital, Carey	200,000	??
Capital, Kardigan	200,000	??
Total liabilities and capital	$1,000,000	$??

All debt is shared equally by the members. Each member has personally guaranteed the debt of the LLC. All members are active in LLC operations.

For our purposes, assume the LLC is not considered an SSTB, and ROCK's operations constitute one active trade or business for purposes of the passive activity and at-risk limitations. (Note that the § 179 deduction is a business-related expense.) The LLC's UBIA (unadjusted basis immediately after acquisition) equals the total original cost of all leasehold improvements, or $980,000.

The appropriate business code for the entity is 711410. For the Form 1065, page 5, Analysis of Net Income, put all partners' allocations in cell 2(b)(ii), per IRS instructions for an LLC.

a. Complete the 2021 Form 1065 for ROCK the Ages LLC with appropriate forms and schedules. Suggested software: ProConnect Tax. Use tax-basis information for Schedules L and M–2. Provide any special information the LLC members might need, including net income from self-employment and information for the § 199A calculation. Attach additional statements if needed, and leave information blank if not available.

b. Continue by preparing Schedules K–1 for ROCK's members. Pay attention to any special allocation required for Ryan Ross. Ross's address is 15520 W. Earlson Street, Pacific Palisades, CA 90272. (Leave other addresses blank.)

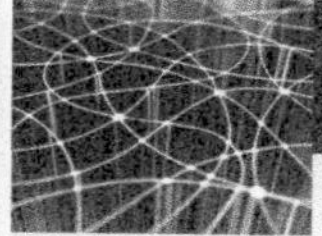

Bridge Discipline

1. What is the function of a partner's capital account under the rules of generally accepted accounting principles (GAAP)? What is the partner's initial balance in the capital account? How and when does the capital account increase and decrease? What is the GAAP treatment of distributions to a partner?

2. Jim Dunn, Amy Lauersen, and Tony Packard have agreed to form a partnership. In return for a 30% capital interest, Dunn transferred machinery (basis $268,000, fair market value $400,000) subject to a liability of $100,000. The liability was assumed by the partnership. Lauersen transferred land (basis $450,000, fair market value $300,000) for a 30% capital interest. Packard transferred cash of $400,000 for the remaining 40% interest. Compute the initial values of Dunn's:
   a. Basis in his partnership interest for tax purposes.
   b. Capital account for financial reporting purposes.

3. To what extent are the personal assets of a general partner, limited partner, or member of an LLC subject to (a) contractual liability claims, such as trade accounts payable, and (b) malpractice claims against the entity? Answer the question for partners or members in a general partnership, an LLP, a nonprofessional LLC, and a limited partnership.

Research Problems

Note: Solutions to the Research Problems can be prepared by using the Thomson Reuters Checkpoint™ online tax research database, which accompanies this textbook. Solutions can also be prepared by using research materials found in a typical tax library.

Communications
Critical Thinking
Planning

Research Problem 1. Your clients, Grayson Investments, Inc. (Ana Marks, President), and Blake Caldwell, each contributed $200,000 of cash to form the Realty Management Partnership, a limited partnership. Grayson is the general partner, and Blake is the limited partner. The partnership used the $400,000 cash to make a down payment on a building. The rest of the building's $4,000,000 purchase price was financed with an interest-only nonrecourse loan of $3,600,000, which was obtained from an independent third-party bank.

The partnership allocates all partnership items equally between the partners except for the MACRS deductions and building maintenance, which are allocated 70% to Blake and 30% to Grayson. The partnership wants to satisfy the "economic effect" requirements of Reg. §§ 1.704–1 and 1.704–2 and will reallocate MACRS, if necessary, to satisfy the requirements of the Regulations.

Under the partnership agreement, liquidation distributions will be paid in proportion to the partners' positive capital account balances. Capital accounts are maintained as required in the Regulations. Grayson Investments has an unlimited obligation to restore its capital account, and Blake is subject to a qualified income offset provision under Reg. § 1.704–1(b)(2)(ii)(d).

Assume that all partnership items, except for MACRS, will net to zero throughout the first three years of the partnership operations. Also assume that each year's MACRS deduction will be $200,000 (to simplify the calculations).

Draft a letter to the partnership evaluating the allocation of MACRS in each of the three years under Reg. §§ 1.704–1 and –2. The partnership's address is 53 East Marsh Ave., Smyrna, GA 30082. Do not address the "substantial" test.

Research Problem 2. Barney Chang and Aldrin, Inc., a domestic C corporation, have decided to form BA LLC. The new entity will produce a product that Barney recently developed and patented. Barney and Aldrin each will own a 50% capital and profits interest in the LLC. Barney is a calendar year taxpayer, and Aldrin is taxed using a June 30 fiscal year-end. BA does not have a "natural business year" and elects to be taxed as a partnership. Digging Deeper

a. Determine the taxable year of the LLC under the Code and Regulations.

b. Two years after formation of BA, Barney sells half of his interest (25%) to Aldrin. Can BA retain the taxable year determined in part (a)? Why or why not?

Use internet tax resources to address the following questions. Look for reliable websites and blogs of the IRS and other government agencies, media outlets, businesses, tax professionals, academics, think tanks, and political outlets.

Research Problem 3. Find an article posted by a law firm that comments on pitfalls to avoid in drafting partnership agreements. Ideally, use the home page of a firm that has offices in your state. Summarize the posting in no more than four PowerPoint slides, and send your file to your instructor. Communications

Research Problem 4. Find a blog that concentrates on the taxation of partners and partnerships. Post a message defining the terms *inside basis* and *outside basis* and illustrating why the distinction between them is important. Respond to any replies you receive. Print your message and one or two of the replies. Communications

Research Problem 5. Determine the statutory tax treatment in your state of a one-member LLC. Write an e-mail to your professor comparing this rule with Federal tax law. Communications

Research Problem 6. Construct a graph that shows the increases in the numbers of LLCs and LLPs filing Federal tax returns for five-year periods beginning with 1970. Explain any trends in the data that you identify. Send your report as an e-mail to your instructor. Communications

Becker CPA Review Questions

Becker

1. Gray is a 50% partner in Fabco Partnership. Gray's tax basis in Fabco on January 1, year 4, was $5,000. Fabco made no distributions to the partners during year 4 and recorded the following.

Ordinary income	$20,000
Tax-exempt income	8,000
Portfolio income	4,000

What is Gray's tax basis in Fabco on December 31, year 4?

a. $21,000
b. $16,000
c. $12,000
d. $10,000

2. Nick, Chris, Stacey, and Mike are each 25% partners in Liberty Partnership, a general partnership. During the current year, the partnership had revenues of $300,000 and nonseparately stated business expenses of $100,000, including a guaranteed payment of $30,000 to Nick for services provided to the partnership. Liberty also recorded interest income of $10,000 and charitable contributions of $16,000. With regard to activity in the partnership, what should Stacey report on her income tax return for the current year?

	Ordinary Income	Interest Income	Charitable Contributions
a.	$200,000	$10,000	$16,000
b.	80,000	2,500	4,000
c.	57,500	2,500	4,000
d.	50,000	2,500	4,000

3. Duffy Associates is a partnership engaged in real estate development. Olinto, a civil engineer, billed Duffy $40,000 in the current year for consulting services rendered. In full settlement of this invoice, Olinto accepted a $15,000 cash payment plus the following:

	Fair Market Value	Carrying Amount on Duffy's Books
10% partnership interest in Duffy	$10,000	N/A
Automobile	7,000	$3,000

What amount should Olinto, a cash basis taxpayer, report in his current-year return as income for the services rendered to Duffy?

a. $15,000
b. $28,000
c. $32,000
d. $40,000

4. On January 2 of the current year, Black acquired a 50% interest in New Partnership by contributing property with an adjusted basis of $7,000 and a fair market value of $9,000, subject to a mortgage of $3,000. What was Black's basis in New at January 2 of the current year?

a. $3,500
b. $4,000
c. $5,500
d. $7,500

5. At partnership inception, Black acquires a 50% interest in Decorators Partnership by contributing property with an adjusted basis of $250,000. Black recognizes a gain if:

I. The fair market value of the contributed property exceeds its adjusted basis.
II. The property is encumbered by a mortgage with a balance of $100,000.

a. I only
b. II only
c. Both I and II
d. Neither I nor II

6. When a partner's share of partnership liabilities increases, that partner's basis in the partnership interest:
   a. Increases by the partner's share of the liabilities.
   b. Decreases by the partner's share of the liabilities.
   c. Decreases, but not to less than zero.
   d. Is not affected.

7. Peter, a 25% partner in Gold & Stein Partnership, received a $20,000 guaranteed payment in the current year for deductible services rendered to the partnership. Guaranteed payments were not made to any other partner. Gold & Stein's current-year partnership income consisted of:

Net business income before guaranteed payments	$80,000
Net long-term capital gains	10,000

   What amount of income should Peter report from Gold & Stein Partnership on his current-year tax return? (Disregard the character of the income and just calculate the total increase to Peter's income.)

   a. $37,500
   b. $27,500
   c. $22,500
   d. $20,000

8. Hart's adjusted basis of his interest in a partnership was $30,000. He received a nonliquidating distribution of $24,000 cash plus a parcel of land with a fair market value and partnership basis of $9,000. Hart's basis for the land is:

   a. $9,000
   b. $6,000
   c. $3,000
   d. $0

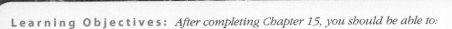

Chapter

15 S Corporations

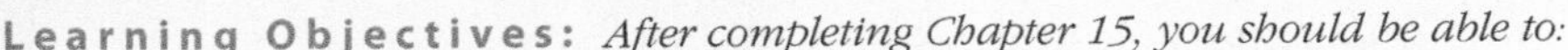

Learning Objectives: *After completing Chapter 15, you should be able to:*

LO.1 Explain the tax effects associated with S corporation status.

LO.2 Identify corporations that qualify for the S election.

LO.3 Explain how to make and terminate an S election.

LO.4 Compute nonseparately stated income and allocate income, deductions, and credits to shareholders.

LO.5 Determine how distributions to S corporation shareholders are taxed.

LO.6 Calculate a shareholder's basis in S corporation stock.

LO.7 Explain the tax effects of losses on S shareholders.

LO.8 Compute the entity-level taxes on S corporations.

Chapter Outline

Tax Talk *In levying taxes and in shearing sheep it is well to stop when you get down to the skin.* —Austin O'Malley

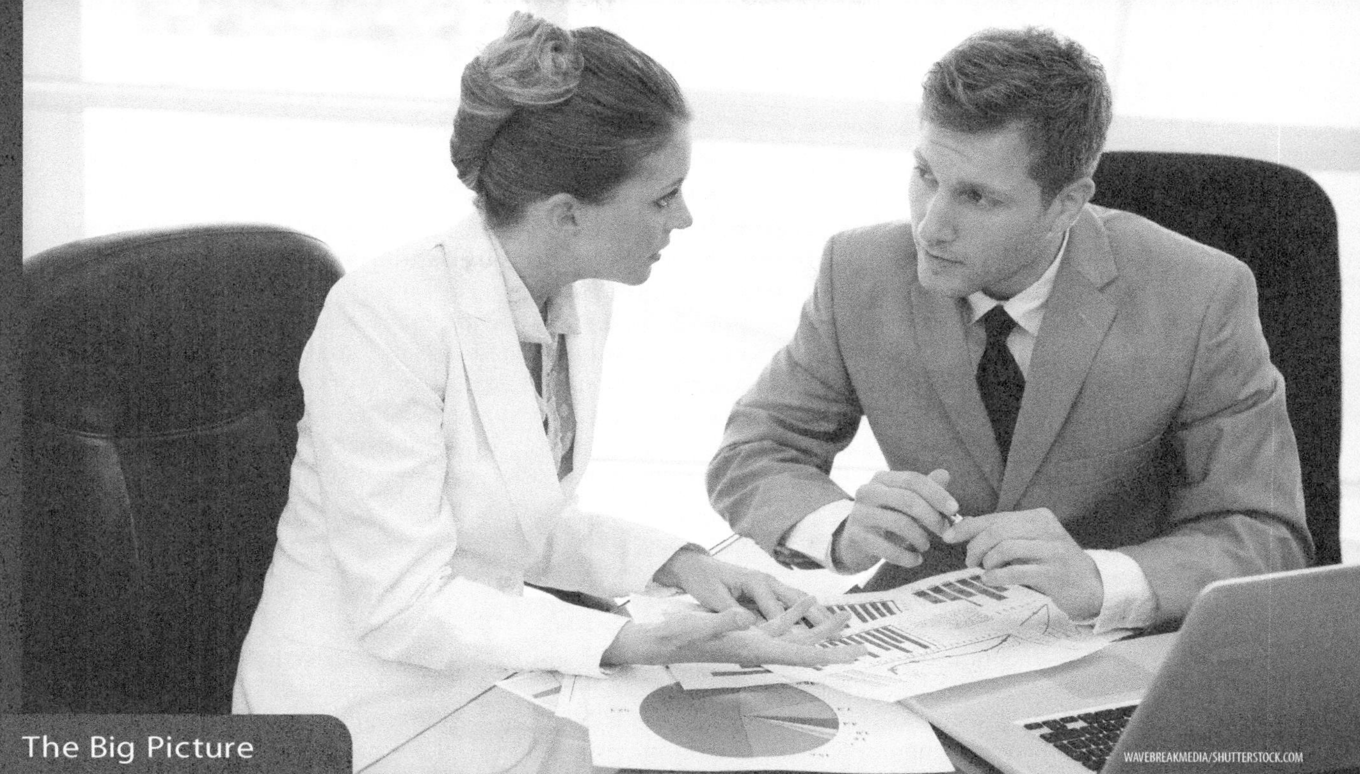

The Big Picture

Converting a C Corporation to an S Corporation

Fowle, Inc., has been operating as a C corporation for a number of years, consistently earning taxable income of less than $100,000 per year. The company has accumulated its earnings for a variety of business needs and has not paid dividends to date. Thus, the corporation has been able to take advantage of lower C corporation tax rates and has avoided double taxation problems so far.

Fowle receives some tax-exempt income, generates a small amount of passive income, and holds about $200,000 of C corporation earnings and profits. The company's sole owner, David, currently draws a salary of $92,000. Fowle has issued two classes of stock, voting common and nonvoting preferred.

The company now is facing increased competition as a result of cheaper imports from China. David expects very large operating losses for the next few years. David would like to know if there is a way that he can deduct the anticipated losses.

Read the chapter and formulate your response.

Explain the tax effects associated with S corporation status.

An individual establishing a business has a number of choices as to the form of business entity under which to operate. Chapters 12 and 13 outline many of the rules, advantages, and disadvantages of operating as a regular C corporation. Chapter 14 discusses the partnership entity as well as the limited liability company (LLC) and limited liability partnership (LLP) forms.

Another alternative, the **S corporation**, provides many of the benefits of partnership taxation and provides the owners limited liability protection from creditors. The S corporation rules, which are contained in **Subchapter S** of the Internal Revenue Code (§§ 1361–1379), were enacted to allow flexibility in the entity choice that businesspeople face. As a result, S status combines the legal environment of C corporations with taxation similar to that applying to partnerships. S corporation status is obtained through an election by a *qualifying* corporation with the consent of its shareholders.

15-1 An Overview of S Corporations

S corporations (like C corporations) are organized under state law. Other than for income tax purposes, they are recognized as separate legal entities and generally provide shareholders with the same liability protection available to C corporations. As a rule, where the S corporation provisions are silent, C corporation rules apply.

The S corporation rules should be seen as supplementary to the Federal income tax rules for all C corporations (see Chapters 12 and 13) and to those for partnerships and limited liability entities (contained in Code Subchapter K; see Chapter 14). Some provisions apply only to electing S corporations (addressed throughout this chapter), but S corporations also must apply certain tax rules of Subchapters C and K.

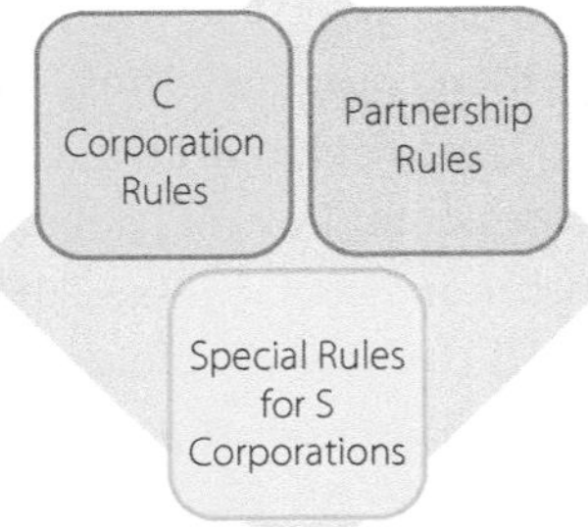

Today the choice of a flow-through entity for a closely held business often is between an S corporation (a Federal tax entity) and an LLC (a state tax entity). Both are flow-through entities for Federal income tax purposes and provide limited liability for the owners under nontax state law. In the typical year, over 4.8 million S corporations file Federal income tax returns, and filings are received from over 2 million LLCs and 4 million partnership returns.

As the following examples illustrate, S corporations can be advantageous even when the individual tax rate exceeds the corporate tax rate.

S Corporation Advantages

An S corporation earns $300,000, and all after-tax income is distributed currently. The marginal individual tax rate applicable to the entity's shareholders is 37% for ordinary income and 20% for dividend income (ignoring the 3.8% investment income tax). Assume that the corporate tax rate is 21%, and the S corporation shareholders receive the full 20% qualified business income deduction (see text Section 15-3b). The entity's available after-tax earnings, compared with those of a similar C corporation, are computed below.

continued

	C Corporation	S Corporation
Earnings	$300,000	$300,000
Less: Corporate income tax	(63,000)	(-0-)
Amount available for distribution	$237,000	$300,000
Less: Income tax at owner level	(47,400)*	(88,800)**
Available after-tax earnings	$189,600	$211,200

*$237,000 × 20% dividend income tax rate.
**($300,000 − $60,000 qualified business income deduction) × 37%.

The S corporation generates an extra $21,600 of after-tax earnings ($211,200 − $189,600) when compared with a similar C corporation (and even when using the highest individual marginal tax rate). The C corporation might be able to reduce this disadvantage by paying out its earnings as deductible compensation, rents, or interest to its owners. In addition, tax at the owner level is deferred or avoided by not distributing after-tax earnings.

A new corporation elects S status and incurs a net operating loss (NOL) of $300,000. The shareholders may use their proportionate shares of the NOL to offset other taxable income in the current year, providing an immediate tax savings. In contrast, a newly formed C corporation is required to carry the NOL forward and receives no tax benefit in the current year. Hence, an S corporation can accelerate the use of NOL deductions and thereby provide a greater present value for the tax savings generated by the loss.

15-2 Qualifying for S Corporation Status

LO.2 **Identify corporations that qualify for the S election.**

There are certain conditions that a corporation must meet before S corporation status is available.

15-2a Definition of a Small Business Corporation

To achieve S corporation status, a corporation *first* must qualify as a **small business corporation**. A small business corporation:

- Is a *domestic* corporation (incorporated and organized in the United States).
- Is eligible to elect S corporation status.
- Issues only one class of stock.
- Is limited to a maximum of 100 shareholders.

Bridge Discipline **Bridge to Business Law**

An S corporation is a corporation for all purposes other than its Federal and state income tax law treatment. The entity registers as a corporation with the secretary of state of the state of its incorporation. It issues shares and may hold some treasury stock. Dealings in its own stock are not taxable to the S corporation.

The corporation itself is attractive as a form of business ownership because it offers limited liability to all shareholders from the claims of customers, employees, and others. This is not the case for any type of partnership, where there always is at least one general partner bearing the ultimate personal liability for the operations of the entity. Forming an entity as an S corporation facilitates the raising of capital for the business, since an infinite number of shares can be divided in any way imaginable, so as to pass income and deductions, gains, losses, and credits through to the owners, assuming that the fairly generous "type of shareholder" requirements continue to be met.

An S corporation must comply with all licensing and registration requirements of its home state under the rules applicable to corporate entities. Some states levy privilege taxes on the right to do business in the corporate form, and the S corporation typically is not exempted from this tax.

Because an S corporation is a separate legal entity from its owners, shareholders can be treated as employees and receive qualified retirement and fringe benefits under the Code as well as unemployment and worker's compensation protection through the corporation. Some limitations apply to the deductibility of the shareholders' fringe benefits though.

The tax fiction of the S corporation is attractive to investors as demonstrated by the fact that about two-thirds of all U.S. corporations have an S election in effect.

- Has only individuals, estates, and certain trusts and exempt organizations as shareholders.
- Has no nonresident alien shareholders.[1]

In addition to non-U.S. corporations, S status is also not permitted for certain banks or insurance companies. S corporations are permitted to have wholly owned C and S corporation subsidiaries.[2] No maximum or minimum dollar sales or capitalization restrictions apply to S corporations.

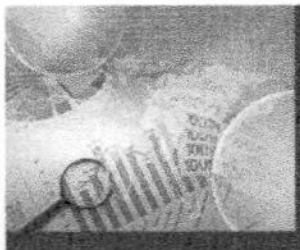

Tax Planning Strategies **When to Elect S Corporation Status**

Framework Focus: Deductions

Strategy: Maximize Deductible Amounts.

Framework Focus: Tax Rate

Strategy: Shift Net Income from High-Bracket Taxpayers to Low-Bracket Taxpayers.
Shift Net Income from High-Tax Jurisdictions to Low-Tax Jurisdictions.

A number of considerations will affect a decision to make an S election.

- If shareholders have high marginal income tax rates relative to C corporation rates, avoid an S election.
- If current and future corporate losses are anticipated, S corporation status is advisable.
- If a C corporation holds an NOL carryover from prior years, the losses cannot be used in an S corporation year (except with respect to built-in gains).
- There may be tax advantages to the S shareholder who receives a flow-through of passive activity income.
- Some states treat S corporations as C corporations and apply a corporate income tax to them.
- Tax-exempt income at the S level does not lose its special tax treatment for shareholders.
- An S corporation avoids the corporate personal holding company tax and accumulated earnings tax.

One Class of Stock

A small business corporation may have only one class of stock issued and outstanding.[3] This restriction permits differences in voting rights but not differences in distribution or liquidation rights.[4] Thus, two classes of common stock that are identical, except that one class is voting and the other is nonvoting, are treated as a single class of stock for S corporation purposes.

In contrast, voting common stock and voting preferred stock (with a preference on dividends) are treated as two classes of stock. Authorized and unissued stock or treasury stock of another class does not disqualify the corporation. Likewise, unexercised stock options, phantom stock, stock appreciation rights, warrants, and convertible debentures usually do not constitute a second class of stock.[5]

Although the one-class-of-stock requirement seems straightforward, it is possible for debt to be reclassified as stock, resulting in an unexpected loss of S corporation status.[6] To mitigate concern over possible reclassification of debt as a second class of stock, the law provides a set of *safe harbor* provisions. Neither straight debt[7] nor short-term advances[8] constitute a second class of stock.

[1] Federal tax law uses the term *alien* to describe a person who is not a U.S. citizen [see § 7701(b)].

[2] Other eligibility rules exist. § 1361(b).

[3] § 1361(b)(1)(D) and (c)(4).

[4] § 1361(c)(4).

[5] Reg. § 1.1361–1(l)(1).

[6] Refer to the discussion of debt-versus-equity classification in Chapter 12.

[7] § 1361(c)(5)(A).

[8] Reg. § 1.1361–1(l)(1).

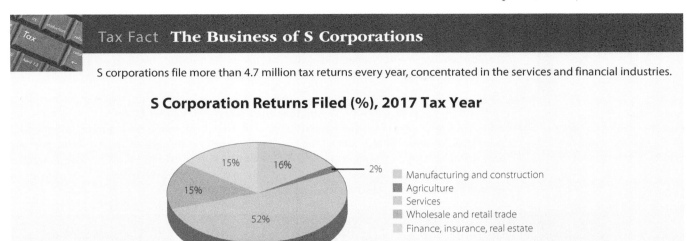

Tax Fact The Business of S Corporations

S corporations file more than 4.7 million tax returns every year, concentrated in the services and financial industries.

S Corporation Returns Filed (%), 2017 Tax Year

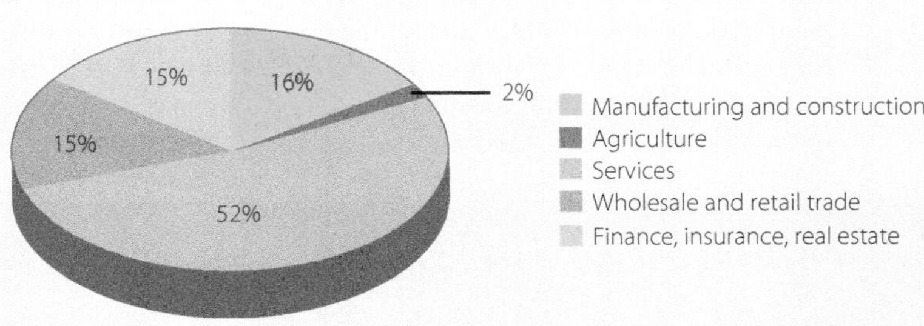

The Big Picture

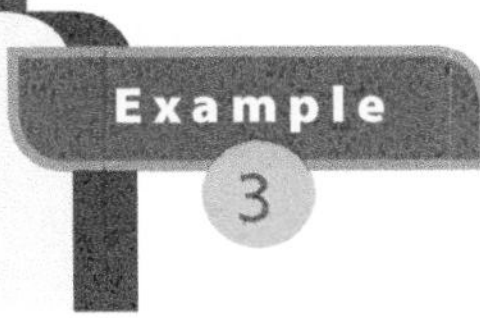

Return to the facts of *The Big Picture* on p. 15-1. Fowle, Inc., could elect to be an S corporation, except that one class of stock is voting common and the other class is nonvoting preferred. If S status is desired, a recapitalization of the Fowle stock is required, perhaps issuing nonvoting common in place of the preferred stock, which would satisfy the one-class-of-stock requirement.

Additional information on the one-class-of-stock requirement can be found on this book's companion website: www.cengage.com

1 Digging Deeper

Shareholder Limitations

An S corporation is limited to 100 shareholders. However, several exceptions allow the number of shareholders to exceed 100. For instance, if shares of stock are owned jointly by two individuals, they generally are treated as separate shareholders. However, a group of family members (e.g., ancestors, descendants, spouses, and former spouses) may be counted as one shareholder for purposes of determining the number of shareholders.[9]

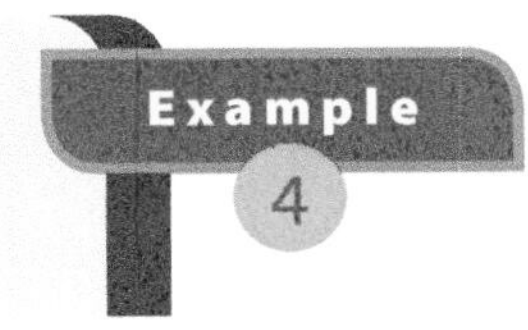

Fred and Wilma (husband and wife) jointly own 10 shares in Oriole, Inc., an S corporation, with the remaining 90 shares outstanding owned by 99 other shareholders. Fred and Wilma are divorced. Both before and after the divorce, the 100-shareholder limit is met, and Oriole can qualify as a small business corporation.

S corporation shareholders may be individuals, estates, or certain trusts and exempt organizations.[10] This limitation prevents partnerships, corporations, most LLCs, LLPs, and most IRAs from owning S corporation stock. Without this rule, partnerships and corporate shareholders could easily circumvent the 100-shareholder limitation.

[9] §§ 1361(c)(1)(A)(ii) and (B)(i). Reg. § 1.1361–1(e) provides a definition of who is a family member.

[10] § 1361(b)(1)(B). A one-member LLC typically is an eligible S shareholder.

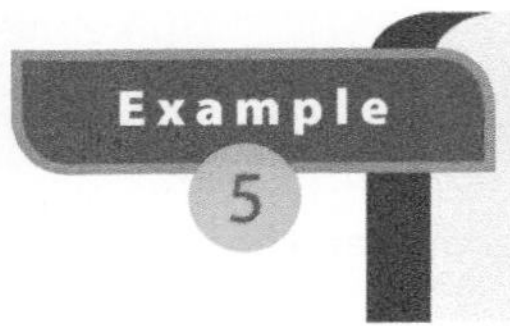

Paul and 200 other individuals want to form an S corporation. Paul reasons that if the group forms a partnership, the partnership can then form an S corporation and act as a single shareholder, thereby avoiding the 100-shareholder rule. Paul's plan will not work, because partnerships cannot own stock in an S corporation.

Individuals who are not U.S. citizens *must live in the United States* to own S corporation stock.[11] Someone who is neither a U.S. citizen nor a U.S. resident is termed a nonresident alien (NRA). Shareholders who live in community property states and are married to a NRA[12] cannot own S corporation stock, because the NRA spouse is treated as owning half of the stock.[13] Similarly, if a resident alien shareholder permanently moves outside the United States, the S election is terminated.

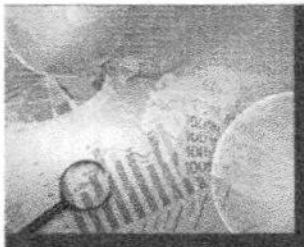

Tax Planning Strategies **Beating the 100-Shareholder Limit**

Framework Focus: Tax Rate

Strategy: Avoid Double Taxation.

Although partnerships and corporations cannot own small business corporation stock, S corporations themselves can be partners in a partnership or shareholders in a corporation. In this way, the 100-shareholder requirement can be bypassed in a limited sense. For example, if two S corporations, both with 80 shareholders, form a partnership, the shareholders of both corporations can enjoy the limited liability conferred by S corporation status and a single level of tax on the resulting profits even though there are 160 shareholders involved.

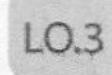
LO.3

Explain how to make and terminate an S election.

15-2b **Making the Election**

To become an S corporation, the entity must file a valid election with the IRS. The election is made on Form 2553. For the election to be valid, all shareholders must consent. For S corporation status to apply in the current tax year, the election must be filed either in the previous year or on or before the fifteenth day of the third month of the current year.[14]

The Big Picture

Return to the facts of *The Big Picture* on p. 15-1. Suppose that in 2022, David decides to elect that Fowle, Inc., become an S corporation beginning January 1, 2023. Fowle's S election can be made at any time in 2022 or by March 15, 2023. An election after March 15, 2023, will not be effective until the 2024 calendar tax year.

Even if the 2½-month deadline is met, an S election is not valid unless the corporation qualifies as a small business corporation for the *entire* tax year. Otherwise, the election is effective for the following tax year.

A corporation that does not yet exist cannot make an S corporation election.[15] A new corporation's 2½-month election period begins at the earliest of any of the following events.

- When the corporation has shareholders.
- When it acquires assets.
- When it begins doing business.[16]

[11]§ 1362(b)(1)(C).

[12]Assets acquired by a married couple are generally considered community property in these states: Alaska (by election), Arizona, California, Idaho, Louisiana, Nevada, New Mexico, Texas, Washington, and Wisconsin.

[13]See *Ward v. U.S.*, 81–2 USTC ¶9674, 48 AFTR 2d 81–5942, 661 F.2d 226 (Ct.Cls.), where the court found that the stock was owned as community property. Because the taxpayer-shareholder (a U.S. citizen) was married to a citizen and resident of Mexico, the nonresident alien prohibition was violated. If the taxpayer-shareholder had held the stock as separate property, the S election would have been valid.

[14]§ 1362(b). Extensions of time to file Form 2553 may be possible in certain situations; see Rev.Proc. 2007–62.

[15]See, for example, *T.H. Campbell & Bros., Inc.*, 34 TCM 695, T.C.Memo. 1975–149; Ltr.Rul. 8807070.

[16]Reg. § 1362-6(a)(2)(ii)(C). Also see, for example, *Nick A. Artukovich*, 61 T.C. 100 (1973).

15-2c Shareholder Consent

A qualifying election requires the consent of all of the corporation's shareholders.[17] Consent must be in writing, and it generally must be filed by the election deadline. Both spouses must consent if they own their stock jointly (as joint tenants, tenants in common, tenants by the entirety, or community property).[18] In certain circumstances (e.g., a shareholder is out of the country when the consent form is due), one may receive an extension of time to file a consent. For current-year S elections, any person who was a shareholder during any part of the year must sign the consent.

Tax Planning Strategies **Making a Proper Election**

Framework Focus: Tax Rate

Strategy: Avoid Double Taxation.

- Because S corporation status is *elected*, strict compliance with the requirements is demanded by both the IRS and the courts. Any failure to meet a condition in the law may lead to loss of the S election and raise the specter of double tax.
- Make sure that all shareholders timely file a proper consent. If any doubt exists concerning the shareholder status of an individual, it would be wise to request that he or she sign a consent anyway.[19] Missing consents are fatal to the election, whereas there is no problem with submitting too many consents.
- Make sure the election is timely and properly filed. Either deliver the election to an IRS office in person or send it by certified or registered mail or via a major overnight delivery service. The date used to determine timeliness is the postmark date, not the date the IRS receives the election.

Additional information on shareholder consent can be found on this book's companion website: www.cengage.com

2 Digging Deeper

15-2d Loss of the Election

An S election remains in force until it is revoked or lost. Election or consent forms are not required for future years. However, an S election can terminate if any of the following occurs.[20]

- Shareholders owning a majority of shares (voting and nonvoting) voluntarily revoke the election.
- A new shareholder owning more than one-half of the stock affirmatively refuses to consent to the election.
- The corporation no longer qualifies as a small business corporation.
- The corporation does not meet the passive investment income limitation.

Voluntary Revocation

A **voluntary revocation** of the S election requires the consent of shareholders owning a majority of shares on the day the revocation is to be made.[21] A revocation filed up to and including the fifteenth day of the third month of the tax year is effective for the entire tax year unless a later date is specified. Similarly, unless an effective date is specified, a revocation made after the first 2½ months of the current tax year is effective for the following tax year.

---

[17] § 1362(a)(2).

[18] Rev.Rul. 60–183; *William Pestcoe*, 40 T.C. 195 (1963); Reg. § 1.1362–6(b)(3)(iii). This rule likely also applies to all family members who are being treated as one shareholder.

[19] See *William B. Wilson*, 34 TCM 463, T.C.Memo. 1975–92.

[20] § 1362(d).

[21] § 1362(d)(1)(B).

The shareholders of Petunia Corporation, a calendar year S corporation, voluntarily revoke the S election on January 5 of the current year (not a leap year). They do not specify a future effective date in the revocation. If the revocation is properly executed and timely filed, Petunia will be a C corporation for the entire current tax year. If the revocation is not made until June, Petunia remains an S corporation this year and becomes a C corporation at the beginning of the next year.

A corporation can revoke its S status *prospectively* by specifying a future date when the revocation is to be effective. A revocation that designates a future effective date splits the corporation's tax year into a short S corporation year and a short C corporation year. The day on which the revocation occurs is treated as the first day of the C corporation year. The corporation allocates income or loss for the entire year on a pro rata basis using the number of days in each short year.

Assume the same facts as in the preceding example, except that Petunia designates July 1 as the revocation date. Accordingly, June 30 is the last day of the S corporation's tax year. The C corporation's tax year runs from July 1 to December 31 of the current year. Income or loss for the 12-month period is allocated between the two short years (i.e., 184/365 to the C corporation year).

Rather than allocating on a pro rata basis, the corporation can elect to compute the actual income or loss attributable to the two short years. This election requires the consent of everyone who was a shareholder at any time during the S corporation's short year and everyone who owns stock on the first day of the C corporation's year.[22]

Assume the same facts as in the preceding example, except that all of Petunia's shareholders consent to allocate the income or loss to the two short years based on its actual realization. Assume further that Petunia experiences a total loss of $102,000, of which $72,000 is incurred in the first half of the year, and only $30,000 is allocated to the C corporation year.

Loss of S Corporation Status

If an S corporation fails to qualify as a small business corporation at any time after the election has become effective, its status as an S corporation ends. The termination occurs on the day the corporation ceases to be a small business corporation.[23] Thus, if the corporation ever has more than 100 shareholders, has a second class of stock, or has a nonqualifying shareholder or it otherwise fails to meet the definition of a small business corporation, the S election terminates immediately.

Peony Corporation has been a calendar year S corporation for three years. On August 13, one of its 100 shareholders sells *some* of her stock to an outsider. Peony now has 101 shareholders, and it ceases to be a small business corporation. Peony is an S corporation through August 12 and a C corporation from August 13 to December 31.

Passive Investment Income Limitation

The Code provides a **passive investment income (PII)** limitation for S corporations that previously were C corporations or for S corporations that have merged with C corporations. If an S corporation holds C corporation earnings and profits (E & P) and it generates passive investment income in excess of 25 percent of its gross receipts for three consecutive tax years, the S election is terminated as of the beginning of the fourth year.[24]

[22] § 1362(e)(3).

[23] § 1362(d)(2)(B).

[24] § 1362(d)(3)(A)(ii).

For 2020, 2021, and 2022, Chrysanthemum Corporation, a calendar year S corporation, derived passive investment income in excess of 25% of its gross receipts. If Chrysanthemum holds accumulated E & P from years in which it was a C corporation, its S election is terminated as of January 1, 2023.

PII includes dividends, interest, rents, gains and losses from sales of capital assets, and royalties net of investment deductions. Rents are not considered PII if the corporation renders significant personal services to the occupant.

Violet Corporation owns and operates an apartment building. The corporation provides utilities for the building, maintains the lobby, and furnishes trash collection for tenants. These activities are not considered significant personal services, so any rent income earned by the corporation will be considered PII.

Alternatively, if Violet also provides maid services to its tenants (personal services beyond what normally would be expected from a landlord in an apartment building), the rent income would no longer be PII.

Reelection after Termination

After an S election has been terminated, the corporation must wait five years before reelecting S corporation status. The five-year waiting period is waived if:

- There is a more-than-50% change in ownership of the corporation after the first year for which the termination is applicable, or
- The event causing the termination was not reasonably within the control of the S corporation or its majority shareholders.[25]

Conditions that a corporation must meet before S corporation status is available are illustrated in Exhibit 15.1.

Tax Planning Strategies **Preserving the S Election**

Framework Focus: Tax Rate

Strategy: Avoid Double Taxation.

Unexpected loss of S corporation status can be costly to a corporation and its shareholders. Given the complexity of the rules facing these entities, constant attention is necessary to preserve the S election.

- As a starting point, the corporation's management and shareholders should be made aware of the various transactions that can lead to the loss of an election.
- Because most violations of the S corporation requirements result from transfers of stock, the corporation and its shareholders should consider adopting a set of stock transfer restrictions.

A carefully designed set of restrictions could prevent sale of stock to nonqualifying entities or violation of the 100-shareholder rule. Similarly, stock could be repurchased by the corporation under a buy-sell agreement upon the death of a shareholder, thereby preventing nonqualifying trusts from becoming shareholders.[26]

---

[25] § 1362(g) and Reg. § 1.1362–5(a).

[26] Most such agreements do not create a second class of stock. Rev.Rul. 85–161; *Portage Plastics Co. v. U.S.*, 72–2 USTC ¶9567, 30 AFTR 2d 72–5229, 470 F.2d 308 (CA–7).

Exhibit 15.1 **Conditions Required to Elect S Corporation Status**

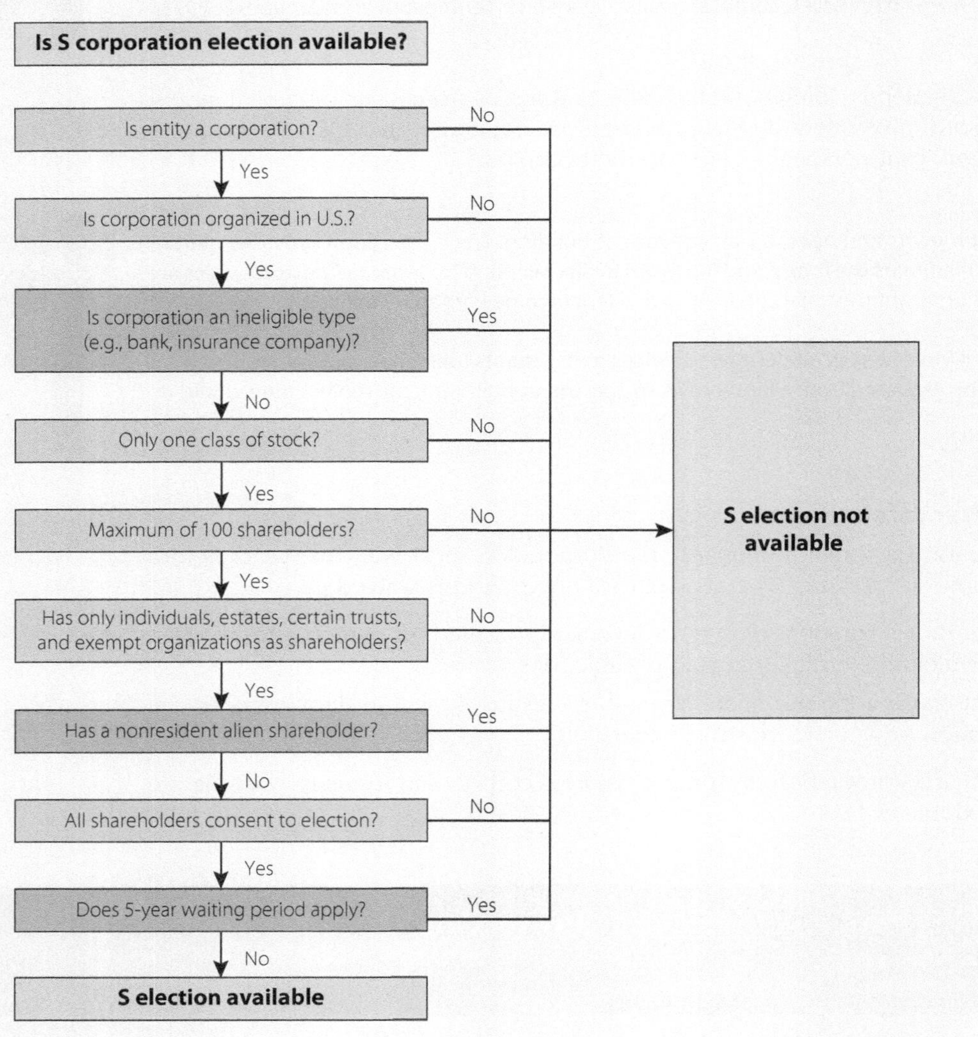

Compute nonseparately stated income and allocate income, deductions, and credits to shareholders.

15-3 Operational Rules

S corporations are treated much like partnerships for tax purposes. Each year the S corporation determines nonseparately stated income or loss and separately stated income, deductions, and credits. These items are taxed only once, as they pass through to shareholders without incurring a corporate-level income tax. All items are allocated to each shareholder based on average ownership of stock throughout the year.[27] The *flow-through* of each item of income, deduction, and credit from the corporation to the shareholder is illustrated in Exhibit 15.2.

15-3a Computation of Taxable Income

An S corporation's taxable income or loss is determined in a manner similar to the tax rules that apply to partnerships, except that S corporations recognize gains (but not losses) on distributions of appreciated property to shareholders.[28] With a few exceptions,

[27] §§ 1366(a), (b), and (c).

[28] § 1363(b).

Exhibit 15.2 Flow-Through of Items of Income and Loss to S Corporation Shareholders

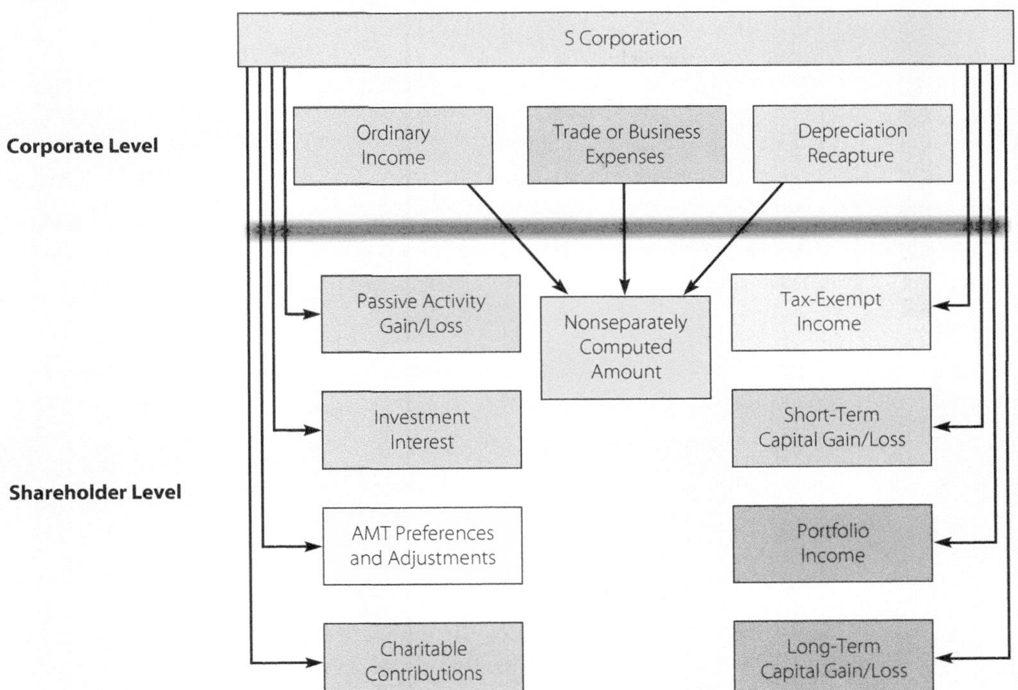

S corporations generally make tax accounting and other elections at the corporate level.[29] Other special provisions affecting only the computation of C corporation income, such as the dividends received deduction, do not extend to S corporations.[30]

In general, S corporation items are divided into (1) nonseparately stated income or loss and (2) separately stated income, losses, deductions, and credits that could uniquely affect the tax liability of any shareholder in a different manner depending on other factors in the shareholder's tax situation. In essence, nonseparately stated items are aggregated into an undifferentiated amount that constitutes S corporation ordinary income or loss.

Example 13

The following is the income statement for Larkspur, Inc., an S corporation.

Sales		$ 40,000
Less: Cost of goods sold		(23,000)
Gross profit on sales		$ 17,000
Less: Interest expense	$1,200	
Charitable contributions	400	
Advertising expenses	1,500	
Other operating expenses	2,000	(5,100)
Book income from operations		$ 11,900
Add: Tax-exempt interest income	$ 300	
Dividend income	200	
Long-term capital gain	500	1,000
Less: Short-term capital loss		(150)
Net income per books		$ 12,750

Larkspur's ordinary income (i.e., S corporation nonseparately stated income) is calculated as follows, using net income for book purposes as the starting point.

continued

[29]Certain elections are made at the shareholder level (e.g., the choice between a foreign tax deduction or credit; see Chapter 16).

[30]§ 703(a)(2).

Net income per books		$12,750
Separately stated items		
Remove: Tax-exempt interest income	$300	
Dividend income	200	
Long-term capital gain	500	(1,000)
Add: Charitable contributions	$400	
Short-term capital loss	150	550
Ordinary income (nonseparately stated income)		$12,300

Larkspur's $12,300 nonseparately stated income, as well as each of the five separately stated items, is divided among the shareholders based upon their stock ownership.

An S corporation reports details as to the differences between book income and pass-through items on its Form 1120S, Schedule M–1 or M–3.

Digging Deeper 3

For more information on Schedule M–3, visit this book's companion website: www.cengage.com

15-3b Qualified Business Income Deduction

To bring the taxation of flow-through entities such as S corporations closer to the C corporation 21 percent rate, shareholders of certain S corporations (and other qualified flow-through entities) may deduct up to 20 percent of certain qualified business income (QBI). With the full 20 percent deduction, the pass-through top rate is 29.6 percent (80% × 37%), ignoring payroll and other taxes. Income earned by a C corporation that is distributed after tax as a dividend to the shareholders may be subject to a maximum Federal income tax rate of 39.8 percent [21% + (79% × 23.8%)], which includes the 3.8 percent investment income tax rate.

The **qualified business income deduction (QBID)** is based on the following formula:

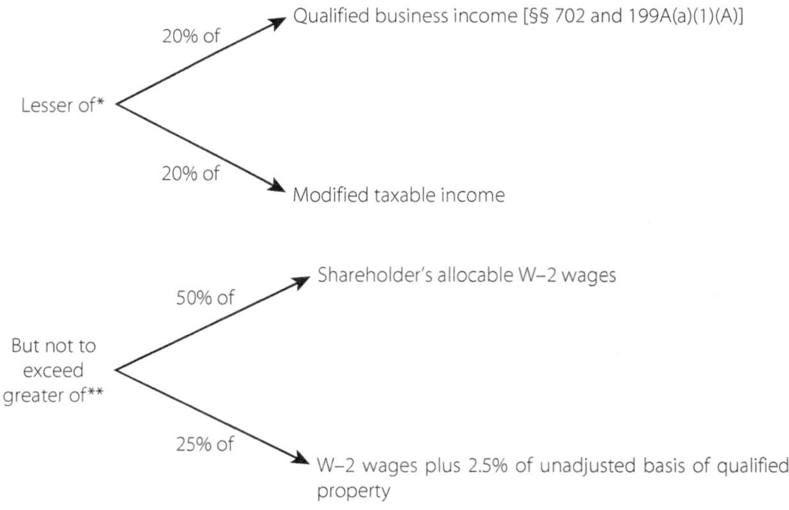

*Deduction limited for certain specified service-type S corporations where taxable income exceeds $170,050 (single; phased out at $220,050) and $340,100 (joint; phased out at $440,100). The phaseout percentage is the ratio of the excess over the threshold amount to $50,000 for individual taxpayers or $100,000 if married filing jointly.

**Does not apply if taxable income is equal to or less than $170,050 (single; phased out at $220,050) or $340,100 (joint; phased out at $440,100).

There are some important limitations on the QBID. The deduction is the smaller of 20 percent of qualified business income or modified taxable income reduced by net capital gains.[31] Taxable income for this purpose is computed without considering the

[31] § 199A(a).

QBID. QBI does not include any service-related income paid by the S corporation, including reasonable compensation paid to the S corporation shareholder.[32]

QBI is the net amount of domestic qualified items of income, gains, deductions, and losses in the determination of taxable income with respect to the S shareholders qualified businesses. In case of a qualified business loss in one year, the loss is carried over to the next year to reduce QBI (but not below zero). Further, QBI does not include certain investment-type gains, deductions, or losses.

The W–2 wages limitation is the greater of (1) 50 percent of wages paid by the S corporation or (2) the sum of 25 percent of the W–2 wages plus 2.5 percent of the unadjusted basis (determined immediately after purchase) of all depreciable property.[33] An S corporation's W–2 wages are the sum of wages paid subject to withholding, elective deferrals, and deferred compensation (including wages paid to S corporation owners).

QBI Deduction

Example 14

Fran is a single taxpayer. She owns a 25% interest in Flower Inc., which is an S corporation. Flower has ordinary net income of $600,000. Fran's share of S corporation ordinary net income is $150,000. Her share of W–2 wages paid by Flower is $50,000, and her share of the unadjusted basis of qualified property is $400,000. Income from the partnership is her sole source of income. Fran's tentative § 199A deduction would be $30,000 ($150,000 × 20%).

From Example 14, assume that Fran's taxable income from all sources is $300,000. In this case, her taxable income from all sources exceeds the $220,050 threshold. As a result, Fran must determine her QBI deduction, including the W–2 wages/capital investment limitation.

Fran's QBI deduction is $25,000, computed as follows:

1. 20% of QBI ($150,000 × 20%)		$30,000
2. Greater of:		
a. 50% of W–2 wages ($50,000 × 50%), or	$25,000	
b. 25% of W–2 wages plus 2.5% of unadjusted basis of depreciable property ($50,000 × 25% + $400,000 × 2.5%)	$22,500	$25,000

15-3c Allocation of Income and Loss

Each shareholder is allocated a pro rata portion of nonseparately stated income or loss and all separately stated items. The pro rata allocation method assigns an equal amount of each of the S items to each day of the year.[34] If a shareholder's stock holding changes during the year, this allocation assigns the shareholder a pro rata share of each item for each day the stock is owned. On the date of transfer, the transferor is considered to own the stock.[35]

S corporation item × **Percentage of shares owned** × **Percentage of year shares were owned** = **Amount of item to be reported**

Pat, a shareholder, owned 10% of Larkspur's stock (from Example 13) for 100 days and 12% for the remaining 265 days. Using the required per-day allocation method, Pat's share of the S corporation ordinary income is $1,409, the total of $12,300 × [10% × (100/365)] plus $12,300 × [12% × (265/365)]. All of Pat's Schedule K–1 totals flow through to the appropriate lines on his individual income tax return (Form 1040).

[32] § 199A(e)(5)(A).

[33] § 199A(b)(2)(B)(ii). For more detail, see D. L. Crumbley and J. R. Hasselback, "Attractiveness of S Corporations After 2017," *Tax Notes*, February 26, 2018.

[34] §§ 1366(a)(1) and 1377(a)(1).

[35] Reg. § 1.1377–1(a)(2)(ii).

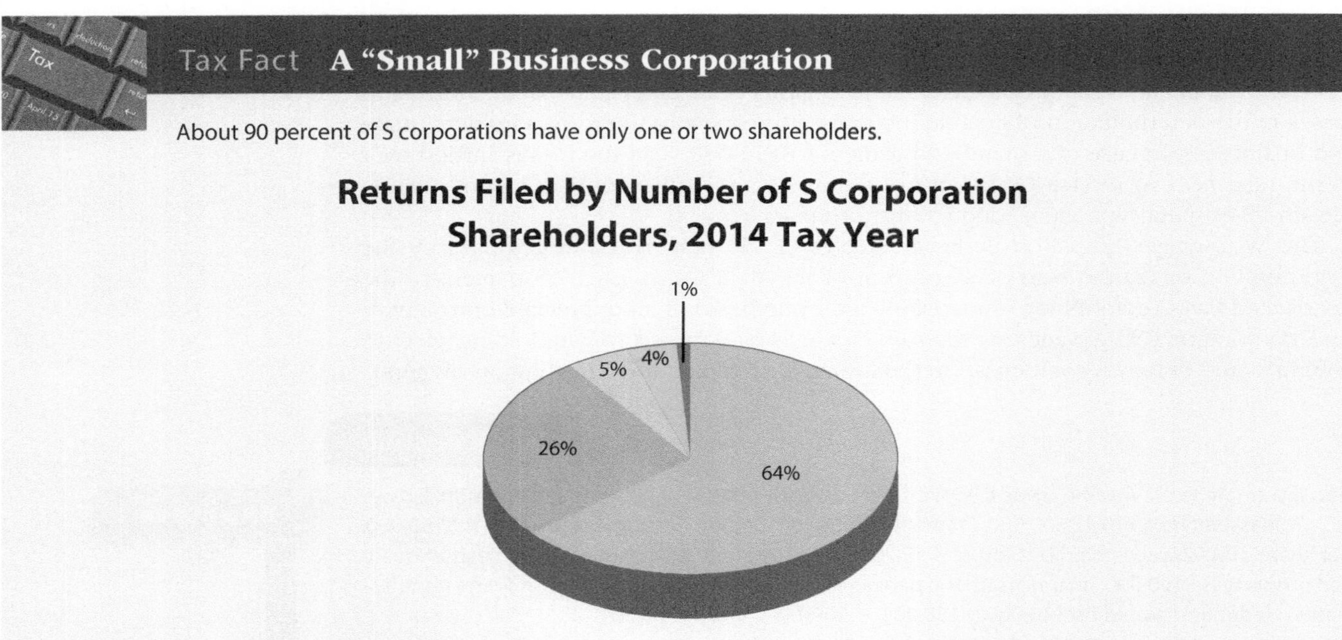

The Short-Year Election

If a shareholder's interest is completely terminated during the tax year by a sale or by a disposition following death, all shareholders owning stock during the year and the corporation may elect to treat the S taxable year as two taxable years. The first year ends on the date of the termination. Under this election, there is an interim closing of the books, and the shareholders report their shares of the S corporation items as they occurred during the short tax year.[36]

The short-year election provides an opportunity to shift income, losses, and credits among shareholders (e.g., items that have a clearly identifiable date of occurrence). The election is desirable in circumstances where more loss can be allocated to taxpayers with higher marginal tax rates.

Alicia, the owner of all of the shares of an S corporation, transfers her stock to Cindy halfway through the tax year. There is a $100,000 NOL for the entire tax year, but $30,000 of the loss occurs during the first half of the year. Without a short-year election, $50,000 of the loss is allocated to Alicia and $50,000 is allocated to Cindy.

If the corporation makes the short-year election, Cindy is allocated $70,000 of the loss. In this case, the sales price of the stock probably would be increased to recognize the tax benefits being transferred from Alicia to Cindy.

Determine how distributions to S corporation shareholders are taxed.

15-3d Tax Treatment of Distributions to Shareholders

S corporations do not generate E & P while the S election is in effect. Indeed, all profits are taxed in the year earned, as though they were distributed on a pro rata basis to the shareholders. Thus, distributions from S corporations do not constitute dividends in the traditional sense—there is no corporate E & P to distribute.

[36] § 1377(a)(2).

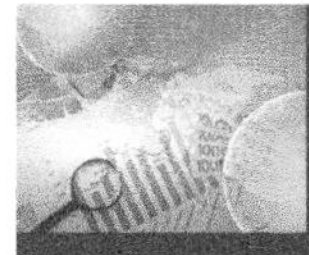

Tax Planning Strategies **Salary Structure**

Framework Focus: Tax Rate

Strategy: Shift Net Income from High-Bracket Taxpayers to Low-Bracket Taxpayers. Avoid Double Taxation.

The amount of any salary paid to a shareholder-employee of an S corporation can have varying tax consequences and should be considered carefully. Larger amounts might be advantageous if the maximum contribution allowed under the employee's retirement plan has not been reached. Smaller amounts may be beneficial if the parties are trying to shift taxable income to lower-bracket shareholders, reduce payroll taxes, curtail a reduction of Social Security benefits, or restrict losses that do not pass through because of the basis limitation.

A strategy of decreasing compensation and correspondingly increasing distributions to shareholder-employees often results in substantial savings in employment taxes. However, a shareholder of an S corporation cannot always perform substantial services and arrange to receive distributions rather than compensation so that the corporation may avoid paying employment taxes. The shareholder may be deemed an employee, and any distributions will be recharacterized as wages subject to FICA and FUTA taxes.[37] For planning purposes, some level of compensation should be paid to all shareholder-employees to avoid any recharacterization of distributions as deductible salaries—especially in personal service corporations.[38]

The qualified business income (QBI) deduction rules (§ 199A) complicate the issue of salary versus distribution as wages paid to an S corporation shareholder are included in W–2 wages when computing the QBI limitation. However, the 20 percent QBI deduction is only allowed for business income allocated to the shareholder and does not include the shareholder's wages from the S corporation.

It is possible, however, for S corporations to have an accumulated E & P (AEP) account. This can occur when:

- The S corporation was previously a C corporation, or
- A C corporation with its own AEP merged into the S corporation.

Distributions from S corporations are measured as the cash received plus the fair market value of any other distributed property. The tax treatment of distributions differs depending upon whether the S corporation holds AEP. Concept Summary 15.1 outlines the taxation of distributions.

S Corporation with No AEP

If the S corporation holds no AEP, the distribution is a tax-free recovery of capital to the extent it does not exceed the basis of the shareholder's stock. When the amount of the distribution exceeds the stock basis, the excess is treated as a gain from the sale or exchange of property (capital gain in most cases). The vast majority of S corporations fall into this favorable category.

Hyacinth, Inc., a calendar year S corporation, holds no AEP. During the year, Juan, an individual shareholder of the corporation, receives a cash distribution of $12,200 from Hyacinth. Juan's basis in his stock is $9,700. Juan recognizes a capital gain of $2,500, the excess of the distribution over the stock basis ($12,200 − $9,700). The remaining $9,700 is tax-free, but it reduces Juan's basis in his stock to zero.

[37] Rev.Rul. 74–44; *Spicer Accounting, Inc. v. U.S.*, 91–1 USTC ¶50,103, 66 AFTR 2d 90–5806, 918 F.2d 90 (CA–9); *Radtke v. U.S.*, 90–1 USTC ¶50,113, 65 AFTR 2d 90–1155, 895 F.2d 1196 (CA–7); *Joseph M. Grey Public Accountant, P.C.*, 119 T.C. 121 (2002); *David E. Watson, P.C. v. U.S.*, 2012–2 USTC ¶50,203, 109 AFTR 2d 2012–1059, 668 F.3d 1008 (CA–8). The IRS uses salary surveys and other statistical methods to determine the appropriate compensation level. *McAlary Ltd.*, T.C. Summary Opinion 2013–62.

[38] FS-2008-25, Wage Compensation for S Corporation Officers, August 2008.

Concept Summary 15.1

Distributions from an S Corporation

Where Earnings and Profits Exist	Where No Earnings and Profits Exist
1. Distributions are tax-free to the extent of the accumulated adjustments account (AAA).*	
2. Distributions from accumulated E & P (AEP) constitute dividend income.†	
3. Distributions are tax-free to the extent of the other adjustments account (OAA).*	
4. Any residual distribution is nontaxable to the extent of the shareholder's basis in stock.*	1. Distributions are nontaxable to the extent of shareholder's basis in stock.*
5. Excess is treated as gain from a sale or exchange of stock (capital gain in virtually all cases).	2. Excess is treated as gain from a sale or exchange of stock (capital gain in virtually all cases).

*The distribution reduces the shareholder's stock basis. A shareholder's stock basis serves as the upper limit on the amount that may be received tax-free.
†The AAA bypass election is available to pay out AEP before reducing the AAA [§ 1368 (e)(3)].

S Corporation with AEP

A more complex set of rules applies to S corporations that hold AEP. These rules treat distributions of pre-election (C corporation) and post-election (S corporation) earnings differently. Distributions of AEP are taxed as dividends and do not reduce stock basis, while distributions of previously taxed S corporation earnings are tax-free to the extent of the shareholder's basis in the stock.

Distributions are deemed to be first from previously taxed, undistributed earnings of the S corporation. These distributions are tax-free and are determined by reference to a special account, the **accumulated adjustments account (AAA)**.[39] Next, AEP is distributed as taxable dividends (i.e., as payments from AEP). After AEP is depleted, tax-free distributions are made from the **other adjustments account (OAA)**, as discussed below. Remaining amounts of the distribution are received tax-free until the shareholder's stock basis reaches zero,[40] with any excess being treated typically as capital gain.

Ordering Rules for Distributions

Example 19

Short, a calendar year S corporation, distributes $1,300 of cash to its only shareholder, Otis, on December 31. Otis's basis in his stock is $1,400, AAA is $500, and Short has $750 of AEP before the distribution.

The first $500 of the distribution is a tax-free recovery of basis from the AAA. The next $750 is a taxable dividend distribution from AEP. The remaining $50 of cash is a tax-free recovery of basis. Immediately after the distribution, Short records a zero balance in AAA and AEP. Otis's stock basis now is $850.

	Corporate AAA	Corporate AEP	Otis's Stock Basis
Beginning balance	$ 500	$ 750	$1,400
Distribution from AAA	(500)		(500)
Distribution from AEP		(750)	
Distribution from stock basis			(50)
Ending balance	$-0-	$-0-	$ 850

[39] For S corporations in existence prior to 1983, an account similar to the AAA was used. This account, called *previously taxed income* (PTI), can be distributed in cash tax-free to shareholders after AAA has been distributed. See §§ 1368(c)(1) and (e)(1).

[40] § 1368(c).

Ordering Rules for Distributions

Assume the same facts as in the preceding example. The next year Short's income totals zero. It distributes $1,000 to Otis. Of the distribution, $850 is a tax-free recovery of the stock basis, and $150 is taxed to Otis as a capital gain.

With the consent of all of its shareholders, an S corporation can elect to have a distribution treated as if it first were made from AEP rather than from the AAA. This mechanism is known as an **AAA bypass election**. This election may be desirable when making distributions to move the entity to the no-AEP system of accounting for distributions, at a maximum tax cost of 20 percent of the AEP (i.e., the maximum income tax rate applied to dividends for most shareholders).

Rotor, an S corporation, has $1,000 of AEP and a balance of $10,000 in the AAA. An AAA bypass election for Rotor's next shareholder distribution would eliminate the need to track the AAA and would greatly simplify the accounting for future distributions. The cost for this simplification is the tax on $1,000 of dividend income.

Accumulated Adjustments Account (AAA)

The AAA is the cumulative total of undistributed nonseparately and separately stated income and deduction items for the S corporation. The AAA provides a mechanism to ensure that earnings of an S corporation are taxed only once. Changes to the AAA are reported annually in Schedule M–2 on page 4 of the Form 1120S.

The initial AAA balance is zero when an S election is made. AAA then is computed at the end of each tax year rather than at the time of a distribution. The ending balance in the AAA account is calculated first by adding to the beginning balance any current nonseparately computed income and positive separately stated items (except tax-exempt income). The next step is to reduce the balance by any distributions from AAA. The last step is to reduce the balance by any other negative items.

AAA is applied to the distributions made during the year on a pro rata basis (in a fashion similar to the application of current E & P, discussed in Chapter 13). The determination of AAA is summarized in Exhibit 15.3.

Although adjustments to AAA and stock basis adjustments are similar, there are some important differences between the two amounts. In particular,

- The AAA is not affected by tax-exempt income and related expenses.
- The AAA can have a negative balance. All losses decrease the AAA balance, even those in excess of the shareholder's basis. However, distributions may not make the AAA negative or increase a negative balance in the account.
- Every shareholder has a proportionate interest in the AAA, regardless of the amount of his or her stock basis.[41] In fact, AAA is a corporate account, so there is no connection between the amount and any specific shareholder.[42] Thus, the benefits of AAA can be shifted from one shareholder to another. For example, when an S corporation shareholder sells stock to another party, any AAA balance on the purchase date can be distributed tax-free to the purchaser.

Other Adjustments Account

The OAA tracks the entity's net items that affect basis but not the AAA, such as tax-exempt income and any related nondeductible expenses. Distributions from this account are tax-free.

---

[41] § 1368(c).

[42] § 1368(e)(1)(A).

Exhibit 15.3 Adjustments to the Corporate AAA

Increase by:

1. Schedule K income items other than tax-exempt income.
2. Nonseparately computed income.

Decrease by:

3. Distribution(s) from AAA (but not below zero).
4. Negative Schedule K items other than distributions (e.g., losses, deductions).

Schedule M–2

Page 4 of the Form 1120S includes Schedule M–2, a reconciliation of beginning and ending balances in the AAA and OAA accounts. Most tax professionals recommend that the Schedule M–2 be kept current even if the entity has retained no AEP so that if future events require the use of these amounts, they need not be reconstructed after the fact.

Poinsettia, an S corporation, records the following items.

AAA, beginning of year	$ 8,500
OAA, beginning of year	-0-
Ordinary income	25,000
Tax-exempt interest income	4,000
Key employee life insurance proceeds received	5,000
Payroll penalty expense	2,000
Charitable contributions	3,000
Unreasonable compensation	5,000
Premiums on key employee life insurance	2,100
Distributions to shareholders	16,000

Poinsettia's Schedule M–2 appears as follows.

Schedule M-2 **Analysis of Accumulated Adjustments Account, Shareholders' Undistributed Taxable Income Previously Taxed, Accumulated Earnings and Profits, and Other Adjustments Account** (see instructions)

		(a) Accumulated adjustments account	(b) Shareholders' undistributed taxable income previously taxed	(c) Accumulated earnings and profits	(d) Other adjustments account
1	Balance at beginning of tax year	8,500			0
2	Ordinary income from page 1, line 21	25,000			
3	Other additions				9,000**
4	Loss from page 1, line 21	( )			
5	Other reductions	(10,000*)			(2,100)
6	Combine lines 1 through 5	23,500			6,900
7	Distributions	16,000			
8	Balance at end of tax year. Subtract line 7 from line 6	7,500			6,900

**$2,000 (payroll penalty) + $3,000 (charitable contributions) + $5,000 (unreasonable compensation).*
***$4,000 (tax-exempt interest income) + $5,000 (life insurance proceeds).*

Effect of Terminating the S Election

Normally, distributions to shareholders from a C corporation are taxed as dividends to the extent of E & P. However, any distribution of *cash* by a C corporation to shareholders during a one-year period[43] following an S election termination receives a different treatment. Such a distribution is treated as a tax-free recovery of stock basis to the extent that it does not exceed the AAA.[44] Because *only* cash distributions reduce the AAA during this *post-election termination period*, a corporation should not make property distributions during this time. Instead, the entity should sell property and distribute the proceeds to shareholders.

[43] § 1377(b).

[44] § 1371(e).

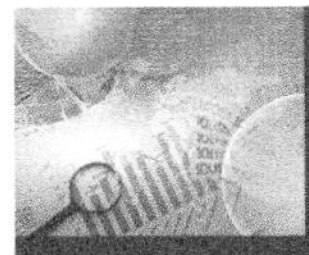

Tax Planning Strategies The Accumulated Adjustments Account

Framework Focus: Tax Rate

Strategy: Avoid Double Taxation.

The AAA is needed to determine the tax treatment of distributions from S corporations with AEP *and* distributions made during the post-termination election period. Therefore, it is important for all S corporations (even those with no AEP) to maintain a current AAA (and OAA) balance. Without an accurate AAA balance, distributions could needlessly be classified as taxable dividends. Alternatively, it will be costly to reconstruct the AAA after the S election terminates.

Distributions should be made when AAA is positive. If future years bring operating losses, AAA is reduced and shareholder exposure to AEP and taxable dividends increases.

The Big Picture

Example 23

Return to the facts of *The Big Picture* on p. 15-1. Assume that Fowle has operated as an S corporation for many years and that the entity turned profitable once it mastered the pricing methods of its import markets. Then David decides to terminate the S election as of the end of the year. On December 31 of that year, Fowle's AAA balance totals $1,300,000.

David can receive a nontaxable distribution of cash during the next year to the full extent of the entity's AAA balance. Any cash distributions received during the next year reduce the basis of David's Fowle stock but not below zero.

15-3e Tax Treatment of Noncash Distributions by the Corporation

An S corporation recognizes a gain on any distribution of appreciated property as if the asset were sold to the shareholder at its fair market value.[45] The corporate gain is passed through to the shareholders, and the asset's basis to the receiving shareholder is stepped up to fair market value. The character of the gain—capital gain or ordinary income—depends upon the type of asset being distributed.

The S corporation does not recognize a loss when distributing assets that are worth less than their basis. As with gain property, the shareholder's basis is equal to the asset's fair market value. Thus, the potential loss is postponed until the shareholder sells the stock of the S corporation. Because loss property receives a step-down in basis without any loss recognition by the S corporation, distributions of loss property should be avoided. See Concept Summary 15.2.

Noncash Distributions by an S Corporation

Yarrow, Inc., an S corporation for 12 years, distributes to Xiang, one of its shareholders, a tract of land held as an investment. The land was purchased for $22,000 many years ago and currently is worth $82,000. Yarrow recognizes a capital gain of $60,000, which increases the AAA by $60,000. The gain flows through proportionately to all of Yarrow's shareholders and is taxed to them.

This tax-free noncash distribution reduces AAA and Xiang's S stock basis by $82,000 (fair market value). The tax consequences are the same for appreciated property whether (a) it is distributed to shareholders and they dispose of it or (b) the corporation sells the property and distributes the proceeds to its shareholders.

[45] § 311(b).

Concept Summary 15.2

Consequences of Noncash Distributions

	Appreciated Property	Depreciated Property
S corporation	Realized gain is recognized by the corporation, which passes it through to the shareholders. This gain increases a shareholder's stock basis, generating a basis in the property equal to FMV. On the distribution, the shareholder's stock basis is reduced by the FMV of the property (but not below zero).	Realized loss is not recognized. The shareholder takes an FMV basis in the property, and stock basis is reduced by the same amount. AAA is reduced by the amount of the unrecognized loss.
C corporation	Realized gain is recognized under § 311(b) and increases E & P (net of tax). The shareholder reports a taxable dividend to the extent of corporate E & P equal to the property's FMV (reduced by any liabilities assumed). The shareholder takes a basis in the asset equal to its FMV.	Realized loss is not recognized. The shareholder takes an FMV basis in the property.
Partnership	No gain is recognized by the partnership or partner. The partner takes a carryover basis in the asset, but the asset basis is limited to the partner's basis in the partnership.	Realized loss is not recognized. The partner takes a carryover basis in the asset, but the asset basis is limited to the partner's basis in the partnership.

Noncash Distributions by an S Corporation

Example 25

Continue with the facts of Example 24. If the land had been purchased for $82,000 and was currently worth $22,000, Xiang would take a $22,000 basis in the land. The $60,000 realized loss is not recognized at the corporate level. The loss does reduce Yarrow's AAA, though not an attractive result for Yarrow shareholders. However, if the S corporation sells the asset to an unrelated party, it does recognize the loss and reduces AAA.

Example 26

Assume the same facts as in Examples 24 and 25, except that Yarrow is a C corporation (E & P balance of $1,000,000) or a partnership. Assume that Xiang's basis before the distribution in her corporate stock or partnership interest is $100,000, and ignore any corporate-level taxes. Compare the results.

	Appreciated Property		
	S Corporation	C Corporation	Partnership
Entity gain/loss	$60,000	$60,000	$ –0–
Owner's gain/loss/dividend	60,000	82,000	–0–
Owner's basis in land	82,000	82,000	22,000

	Property That Has Declined in Value		
	S Corporation	C Corporation	Partnership
Entity gain/loss	$ –0–	$ –0–	$ –0–
Owner's gain/loss/dividend	–0–	22,000	–0–
Owner's basis in land	22,000	22,000	82,000

15-3f Shareholder's Basis in S Stock

Calculate a shareholder's basis in S corporation stock.

The calculation of the initial tax basis of stock in an S corporation is similar to that for the basis of stock in a C corporation and depends upon the manner in which the shares are acquired (e.g., gift, inheritance, purchase, exchange under § 351). Once the initial tax basis is determined, various transactions during the life of the corporation affect the shareholder's basis in the stock. Although each shareholder is required to compute his or her own basis in the S shares, neither Form 1120S nor Schedule K–1 provides a place for tracking this amount.

A shareholder's basis is increased by stock purchases and capital contributions. Operations during the year cause the following additional upward adjustments to basis.[46]

- Nonseparately computed income.
- Separately stated income items (e.g., tax-exempt income).

Basis then is reduced by distributions not reported as income by the shareholder (e.g., an AAA distribution). Next, the following items reduce basis (but not below zero).

- Nondeductible expenses of the corporation (e.g., fines, penalties, and illegal kickbacks).
- Nonseparately computed loss.
- Separately stated loss and deduction items.

As under the partnership rules, basis first is increased by income items; then it is decreased by distributions and finally by losses.[47] In most cases, this *losses last* rule is advantageous to the S shareholder.

In its first year of operation, Iris, Inc., a calendar year S corporation, earns income of $2,000. Before accounting for the entity's operating results, assume that the stock basis of Iris's sole shareholder, Marty, is zero. Therefore, Marty's stock basis is increased to $2,000. On February 2 in its second year of operation, Iris distributes $2,000 to Marty. During the remainder of the second year, the corporation incurs a $2,000 loss.

Under the S corporation ordering rules, the $2,000 distribution is tax-free AAA to Marty. The distribution is accounted for before the loss. The $2,000 loss is suspended until Marty generates additional stock basis (e.g., from capital contributions or future entity profits).

A shareholder's basis in S corporation stock never is reduced below zero. Once stock basis reaches zero, any additional basis reductions (losses or deductions but *not* distributions) decrease the shareholder's basis in loans made to the S corporation (but not below zero). Any excess of losses or deductions over both stock and loan bases is not deductible in the current year. Thus, until additional basis is created due to capital contributions or flow-through income, the loss deductions are suspended.

When there is a capital contribution or an item of flow-through income after both stock and loan bases have been reduced to zero, basis first is restored to the shareholder loans up to the original principal amount.[48] Then basis in the stock is restored. A distribution in excess of stock basis does not reduce any debt basis. If a loss and a distribution occur in the same year, the loss reduces the stock basis *after* the distribution.

[46] § 1367(a).
[47] Reg. § 1.1367–1(f).
[48] § 1367(b)(2); Reg. § 1.1367–2(e).

Sofia, a sole shareholder, holds a $7,000 stock basis and a $2,000 basis in a loan she made to Romulus, a calendar year S corporation with zero AEP. At the beginning of the year, the corporation's AAA and OAA balances are zero. Ordinary income for the year is $8,200. During the year, the corporation also received $2,000 of tax-exempt interest income.

Cash of $17,300 is distributed to Sofia on November 15. As a result, Sofia recognizes $100 capital gain from the distribution.

	Corporate AAA	Corporate OAA	Sofia's Stock Basis	Sofia's Loan Basis
Beginning balance	$ –0–	$ –0–	$ 7,000	$2,000
Ordinary income	8,200		8,200	
Tax-exempt income		2,000	2,000	
Subtotal	$ 8,200	$ 2,000	$17,200	$2,000
Distribution ($17,300)				
From AAA	(8,200)		(8,200)	
From OAA		(2,000)	(2,000)	
From stock basis			(7,000)	
Ending balance	$ –0–	$ –0–	$ –0–	$2,000
Distribution in excess of stock basis (capital gain)			$ 100	

Pass-through losses can reduce loan basis, but distributions do not. Stock basis cannot be reduced below zero, so the $100 excess distribution does not reduce Sofia's loan basis.

The basis rules for S corporation stock are similar to the rules for determining a partner's basis in a partnership interest. However, a partner's basis in the partnership interest includes the partner's direct investment plus a *ratable share* of partnership liabilities.[49] If a partnership borrows from a partner, the partner receives a basis increase as if the partnership had borrowed from an unrelated third party.[50]

In contrast, corporate borrowing has no effect on the stock basis of an S corporation shareholder. The fact that a shareholder has guaranteed a loan made to the corporation by a third party has no effect on the shareholder's loan basis unless payments actually have been made as a result of that guarantee. Direct loans from a shareholder to the S corporation have a tax basis only for the shareholder making the loan.

If a loan's basis has been reduced and is not restored, income is recognized when the corporation repays the loan. If the corporation issued a note as evidence of the debt, repayment constitutes an amount received in exchange for a capital asset and the amount that exceeds the shareholder's basis is capital gain.[51] However, if the loan is made on open account, the repayment constitutes ordinary income to the extent it exceeds the shareholder's basis in the loan. Thus, a written note should be provided to avoid the ordinary income implications of an open account.

The Big Picture

Return to the facts of *The Big Picture* on p. 15-1. Assume that Fowle has made an S election. At the beginning of 2022, David's basis in his Fowle stock was $90,000. During the year, he made a $40,000 loan to the corporation, using a written debt instrument and market interest rates.

Fowle generated a $93,000 taxable loss for 2022. Thus, at the beginning of 2023, David's stock basis was zero, and the basis in his loan to Fowle was $37,000.

Fowle repaid the loan in full on March 1, 2023. David recognizes a $3,000 capital gain as a result of the repayment.

[49] § 752(a).

[50] Reg. § 1.752–1(e).

[51] *Joe M. Smith*, 48 T.C. 872 (1967), *aff'd* and *rev'd* in 70–1 USTC ¶9327, 25 AFTR 2d 70–936, 424 F.2d 219 (CA–9); Rev.Rul. 64–162. An open account loan is treated as evidenced by a note if the shareholder's net payable at the end of the tax year exceeds $25,000. Reg. § 1.1367–2.

More information on S stock basis can be found on this book's companion website: www.cengage.com 4 Digging Deeper

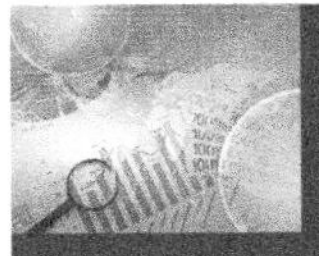

Tax Planning Strategies Working with Suspended Losses

Framework Focus: Income and Exclusion

Strategy: Avoid Income Recognition.

Distributions made to shareholders with suspended losses usually create capital gain income because there is no stock basis to offset. Typically, distributions should be deferred until the shareholder creates stock basis in some form. In this way, no gross income is recognized until the suspended losses are fully used.

The Big Picture

Example 30

Continue with the facts of Example 29, except that Fowle's loss cannot be deducted by David because he has a zero basis in both the stock and debt of the entity. David purchases $5,000 of additional stock in Fowle. David gets an immediate deduction for his investment due to his $93,000 in suspended losses. Alternatively, if Fowle shows a $5,000 profit for the year, David pays no tax on the flow-through income since it is offset by the suspended losses.

However, if Fowle distributes $5,000 to David in 2022 without earning any profit for the year and prior to any capital contribution by him, David recognizes a $5,000 capital gain, because the distribution exceeds the zero stock basis.

15-3g Treatment of Losses

LO.7

Explain the tax effects of losses on S shareholders.

Net Operating Loss

One major advantage of an S election is the ability to pass through net operating losses (NOLs) of the corporation directly to the shareholders. A shareholder can deduct its share of the entity's operating loss on its own tax return for the year in which the S corporation's tax year ends. The corporation does not deduct the NOL. A shareholder's basis in the stock is reduced by any NOL pass-through, but not below zero. The entity's AAA is reduced by the same deductible amount.[52]

Deductions for an S corporation's pass-throughs (e.g., NOL, capital loss, and charitable contributions) cannot exceed a shareholder's stock basis *plus* the basis of any loans made by the shareholder to the corporation.[53] A shareholder can carry forward a loss pass-through to the extent the loss for the year exceeds basis. Any loss carried forward may be deducted *only* by the *same* shareholder if and when the basis in the stock of or loans to the corporation is restored.[54]

[52]§§ 1368(a)(1)(A) and (e)(1)(A).

[53]See *Donald J. Sauvigne*, 30 TCM 123, T.C.Memo. 1971–30.

[54]§ 1366(d).

Example 31

Ginny owns 10% of the stock of Pilot, a calendar year S corporation. Her basis in the shares is $10,000 at the beginning of year 1. The indicated events are accounted for under the S corporation rules as follows.

Tax Year	Event	Tax Consequences
1	Ginny's share of Pilot's operating loss is $15,000.	Ginny deducts $10,000. Her stock basis is reduced to zero. She has a $5,000 suspended loss.
2	Ginny's share of Pilot's operating loss is $4,000.	No current deduction is allowed for the loss, since Ginny has no stock basis to offset. Her suspended loss is now $9,000.
3	Ginny's share of Pilot's operating loss is $7,000. She purchases an additional $10,000 of stock from Pilot.	The purchase creates $10,000 of stock basis. Ginny deducts $10,000—the current $7,000 loss and $3,000 of the suspended loss. Stock basis again is zero, and the new suspended loss is $6,000.
4	Ginny sells all of her Pilot shares to Christina on January 1.	The $6,000 suspended loss disappears—it cannot be transferred to Christina.

Concept Summary 15.3 provides a summary of the treatment of S corporation losses.

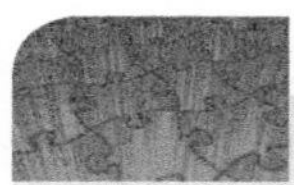

Concept Summary 15.3

Treatment of S Corporation Losses

Step 1. Allocate total loss to the shareholder on a daily basis based upon stock ownership.

Step 2. If the shareholder's loss exceeds his or her stock basis, apply any excess to the basis of corporate indebtedness to the shareholder. Loss allocations do not reduce stock or loan basis below zero.

Step 3. Where a flow-through loss exceeds the stock and loan basis, any excess is suspended and carried over to succeeding tax years.

Step 4. In succeeding tax years, any net increase in basis restores the debt basis first up to its original amount.

Step 5. Once debt basis is restored, any remaining net increase restores stock basis.

If the S election terminates, any suspended loss carryover may be deducted during the post-termination period to the extent of the stock basis at the end of this period. Any loss remaining at the end of this period is lost forever.

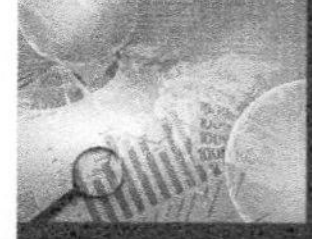

Tax Planning Strategies **Loss Considerations**

Framework Focus: Deductions

Strategy: Maximize Deductible Amounts.

A net loss in excess of tax basis may be carried forward and deducted only by the same shareholder in succeeding years. Thus, before disposing of the stock, a shareholder should increase stock/loan basis to flow through the loss. The next shareholder cannot acquire the loss carryover.

The NOL provisions create a need for sound tax planning during the last election year and the post-termination transition period. If it appears that the S corporation is going to sustain an NOL or use up any loss carryover, each shareholder's basis should be analyzed to determine whether it can absorb the owner's share of the loss. If basis is insufficient to absorb the loss, further investments should be considered before the end of the post-termination period. Such investments can be accomplished through additional stock purchases from the corporation or from other shareholders to increase basis.

continued

A calendar year C corporation records a $20,000 NOL during the previous year. The corporation makes a valid S election for the current year and incurs another $20,000 NOL. At all times during the current year, the stock of the corporation was owned by the same 10 shareholders, each of whom owned 10% of the stock.

Tim, one of the shareholders, holds a stock basis of $1,800 at the beginning of the current year. None of the C corporation NOL may be carried forward into the S year. Although Tim's share of the S corporation NOL is $2,000, his deduction for the loss is limited to $1,800 with a $200 carryover to the next year.

At-Risk Rules

As discussed in Chapters 6 and 14, S corporation shareholders, like partners, are limited in the amount of loss they may deduct by their "at-risk" amounts.

An at-risk amount is determined separately for each shareholder. A shareholder usually is considered at risk with respect to an activity to the extent of cash and the adjusted basis of other property contributed to the electing corporation, any amount borrowed for use in the activity for which the taxpayer has personal liability for payment from personal assets, and the net fair market value of personal assets that secure nonrecourse borrowing.

Any losses that are suspended under the at-risk rules are carried forward to future tax years. The S stock basis limitations and at-risk limitations are applied before the passive activity limitations (see below).

Carl has a basis of $35,000 in his S corporation stock. He takes a $15,000 nonrecourse loan from a local bank and lends the proceeds to the S corporation. Carl now has a stock basis of $35,000 and a loan basis of $15,000.

Carl's share of this year's S corporation loss is $40,000. Due to the at-risk rules, he can deduct only $35,000 of S corporation losses, reducing his S corporation stock basis to zero.

Passive Activity Losses and Credits

S corporations are not directly subject to the passive activity limits, but corporate rental activities are inherently passive, and other activities of an S corporation may be passive unless the shareholder(s) materially participate(s) in operating the business.

If the corporate activity involves rentals or the shareholders do not materially participate, the shareholders can apply these losses or credits only against income from other passive activities.

Passive activity gains and income flow through to the shareholder as investment income, and this income is subject to the additional Medicare tax (see Chapter 9).

15-3h Limitation on the Deduction of Excess Business Losses

A fourth limitation applies to the deduction of business losses of pass-through entities. Section 461(l) limits the total amount of net business losses that can be deducted from an active owner's tax return. This rule limits the maximum deductible loss in 2022 to $540,000 for married filing joint tax returns and $270,000 for all other tax returns. Any loss in excess of these amounts can be carried forward indefinitely. This limitation applies after the rules for stock basis, at-risk, and passive activity losses are applied.

15-3i Other Operational Rules

Several other points may be made about the possible effects of various Code provisions on S corporations.

- An S corporation must make estimated tax payments with respect to any tax on a net recognized built-in gain and excess passive investment income tax (discussed next).
- Any family member who renders services or furnishes capital to an S corporation must be paid reasonable compensation. Otherwise, the IRS can make adjustments to reflect the value of the services or capital. This rule may make it more difficult for related parties to shift S corporation taxable income to children or other family members.
- The flow-through of S items to a shareholder is not self-employment income and is not subject to the self-employment tax.[55] Compensation for services rendered to an S corporation is, however, subject to FICA taxes for the employee-shareholder, but it is not considered wages for purposes of the 20 percent QBI deduction. This treatment of earned income of S corporations is attractive compared to the treatment of a proprietorship or a partnership, whose income is taxed as self-employment income to the owners.
- A number of qualified fringe benefits, which typically are received by employees on a tax-free basis, are subject to Federal income tax when received by a more-than-2% shareholder-employee of an S corporation. These benefits include the value of group term life insurance, medical insurance, and meals and lodging furnished for the convenience of the employer. These items are treated as wages and are subject to most payroll taxes. The employee can deduct medical insurance premiums on his or her Form 1040.
- An S corporation is liable for a penalty if it does not file its Form 1120S on a timely basis. The penalty for returns filed in 2023 is $220 per month times the number of S shareholders, for up to 12 months.[56]
- An accrual basis S corporation uses the cash method of accounting for purposes of deducting business expenses and interest owed to a cash basis related party.[57] Thus, the timing of the shareholder's income and the corporate deduction must match.
- The S election is not recognized by the District of Columbia and a few states, including New Hampshire and Tennessee. Thus, some or all of the entity's income may be subject to a state-level income tax.
- An S corporation may issue § 1244 stock to its shareholders to obtain ordinary loss treatment (see Chapter 8).
- Loss deductions may be disallowed due to a lack of a profit motive. If the activities at the corporate level are not profit-motivated, the losses may be disallowed under the hobby loss rules (see Chapter 11).[58]

Bridge Discipline **Bridge to Public Finance**

Proceeds from the Federal self-employment tax are used by the Federal government to fund retirement and health care entitlements. Any shortfalls in these funds mean that the following may occur.

- Citizens needing retirement annuities and/or health care services will receive less than is needed. This may not be a desirable result in a moral or ethical sense, since life will be more difficult than it otherwise might be for those of modest means.
- Retirement income and health care services must be funded from general revenues, meaning almost exclusively funds from the Federal income tax. This represents a mismatch of payor and payee, an income redistribution result that would not be attractive to some. In a zero-sum sense, benefits of this sort reduce funding for other budgetary needs of the Federal government (e.g., for defense, transportation, or research).

---

[55] Rev.Rul. 59–221.

[56] § 6699. The penalty is waived if the entity can show reasonable cause for the failure to file.

[57] § 267(b).

[58] § 183; *Michael J. Houston*, 69 TCM 2360, T.C.Memo. 1995–159; *Mario G. De Mendoza, III*, 68 TCM 42, T.C.Memo. 1994–314.

15-4 Entity-Level Taxes

LO.8

Compute the entity-level taxes on S corporations.

In almost all cases, an S corporation does *not* pay any Federal income tax, because all items flow through to the shareholders. But an S corporation that previously was a C corporation may be required to pay a built-in gains tax, a LIFO recapture tax, a general business credit recapture, or a passive investment income tax.

15-4a Tax on Pre-Election Built-In Gain

Without the **built-in gains tax**, it would be possible to avoid the corporate double tax on a disposition of appreciated property by electing S corporation status.

Zinnia, Inc., a C corporation, owns a single asset with a basis of $100,000 and a fair market value of $500,000. If Zinnia sells this asset and distributes the cash to its shareholders, there are two levels of tax, one at the corporate level and one at the shareholder level. Alternatively, if Zinnia distributes the asset to its shareholders as a dividend, a double tax still results.

In an attempt to avoid the double tax, Zinnia elects S corporation status. It then sells the asset and distributes the proceeds to shareholders. Without the built-in gains tax, the gain would be taxed only once, at the shareholder level. The distribution of the sales proceeds would be a tax-free reduction of the stock basis and the AAA. However, the built-in gains tax ensures that Zinnia would not avoid the double tax. (See Example 35.)

The built-in gains tax generally applies to C corporations that convert to S status. It is a *corporate-level* tax on any built-in gain recognized when the S corporation disposes of an asset in a taxable disposition within five calendar years after the date on which the S election took effect.[59]

General Rules

The base for the built-in gains tax includes any unrealized gain on appreciated assets (e.g., real estate, cash basis receivables, goodwill) held by a corporation on the day it elects S status. The highest corporate tax rate (21 percent) is applied to the unrealized gain when any of the assets are sold. Any gain from the sale (net of the built-in gains tax)[60] also passes through as a taxable gain to shareholders.

Assume the same facts as in the preceding example. A corporate-level built-in gains tax must be paid by Zinnia if it sells the asset after electing S status. Upon sale of the asset, Zinnia owes a tax of $84,000 ($400,000 × 21%). In addition, Zinnia's shareholders report a $316,000 taxable flow-through gain ($400,000 − $84,000). The built-in gains tax effectively imposes a double tax on Zinnia and its shareholders, as would have been the case had Zinnia remained a C corporation.

For more information on built-in gains, visit this book's companion website: www.cengage.com — 5 Digging Deeper

The amount of built-in gain recognized in any year is limited to an *as if* taxable income for the year, computed as if the corporation were a C corporation. Any built-in gain that escapes taxation due to the taxable income limitation is carried forward and recognized in future tax years. Thus, a corporation can defer a built-in gain tax liability if it has a low or negative taxable income.

[59] § 1374(d)(7)(B).

[60] § 1366(f)(2).

Vinca, an S corporation, recognizes $400,000 of built-in gains during the year. Had Vinca been a C corporation, its taxable income would have been $300,000. Thus, the amount of built-in gain subject to tax is $300,000. The excess built-in gain of $100,000 is carried forward and taxed in the next year (assuming adequate C corporation taxable income in that year).

There is no statutory limit on the carryforward period, but the gain would effectively expire at the end of the built-in gain recognition period.[61]

An S corporation can offset built-in gains with NOLs or unexpired capital losses from C corporation years.

Yowler, an S corporation, reports a built-in gain of $100,000 and taxable income of $90,000. Yowler holds a $12,000 NOL carryforward and an $8,000 capital loss carryforward from C corporation years prior to its S election. Yowler also has a business credit carryforward of $4,000. Yowler's built-in gains tax liability is calculated as follows.

Lesser of taxable income or built-in gain	$ 90,000
Less: NOL carryforward from C year	(12,000)
Capital loss carryforward from C year	(8,000)
Tax base	$ 70,000
Highest corporate income tax rate	× 0.21
Tentative tax	$ 14,700
Less: Business credit carryforward from C year	(4,000)
Built-in gains tax liability	$ 10,700

The $10,000 realized (but not taxed) built-in gain in excess of taxable income is carried forward to the next year as long as the next year is within the built-in gain recognition period.

Tax Planning Strategies Managing the Built-In Gains Tax

Framework Focus: Income and Exclusion

Strategy: Avoid Income Recognition.
Postpone Recognition of Income to Achieve Tax Deferral.

Although limitations exist on contributions of loss property to the corporation before S status is elected, it still is possible for a corporation to minimize built-in gains and maximize built-in losses prior to the S election. A cash basis S corporation can accomplish this by reducing receivables, accelerating payables, and accruing compensation costs.

To further reduce or defer the tax, the corporation may take advantage of the taxable income limitation by shifting income and deductions to minimize taxable income in years when built-in gain is recognized. Although the postponed built-in gain is carried forward to future years, the time value of money makes the postponement beneficial. For example, paying compensation to shareholder-employees in place of a distribution creates a deduction that reduces taxable income and postpones the built-in gains tax.

Built-in *loss* property may be sold in the same year built-in gain property is sold to reduce or eliminate the built-in gains tax. Generally, the taxpayer should sell built-in loss property in a year when an equivalent amount of built-in gain property is sold. Otherwise, the built-in loss could be wasted.

Tulip, Inc., an S corporation, holds a built-in gain of $110,000 and reports current taxable income of $120,000 before payment of salaries to its shareholders. If Tulip pays at least $120,000 in salaries to the shareholders (rather than making a distribution), its taxable income drops to zero and the built-in gains tax is postponed. Thus, Tulip may want to keep its salaries higher to postpone the built-in gains tax in future years and reap a benefit from the time value of money. Of course, paying the salaries may increase the associated payroll tax liabilities.

[61] § 1374(d)(7); Notice 90–27.

LIFO Recapture Tax

When a C corporation uses the FIFO method for its last year before making the S election, any built-in gain is recognized and taxed as the inventory is sold. A LIFO-basis corporation would not recognize this gain unless the corporation invaded the LIFO layer during the built-in gains tax period. To preclude a deferral of gain recognition by a C corporation that elects S status, any LIFO recapture amount at the time of the S election is subject to a corporate-level tax.

The taxable LIFO recapture amount equals the excess of the inventory's value under FIFO over the LIFO value. The resulting tax, determined by including the LIFO recapture amount in the last C corporation tax return, is payable in four equal installments, with the first payment due on or before the due date for the corporate return for the last C corporation year (without regard to any extensions). The remaining three installments are paid on or before the due dates of the succeeding corporate returns. No interest is due if payments are made by the due dates, and no estimated taxes are due on the four tax installments. No refund is allowed if the LIFO value is higher than the FIFO value.

Daffodil Corporation converts from a C corporation to an S corporation at the beginning of the year. Daffodil used the LIFO inventory method and held an ending LIFO inventory of $110,000 (FIFO value of $190,000) before the S election. Daffodil's marginal tax rate on its final C corporation tax return is 21%.

Daffodil adds the $80,000 LIFO recapture amount to its C corporation taxable income, resulting in an increased tax liability of $16,800 ($80,000 × 21%). Daffodil pays one-fourth of the tax ($4,200) with its final C corporation tax return. The three succeeding installments of $4,200 each are paid with Daffodil's first three S corporation tax returns.

15-4b Passive Investment Income Penalty Tax

A tax is imposed on the excess passive income of S corporations that possess C corporation AEP. The tax rate is the highest corporate income tax rate for the year (21 percent). The rate is applied to excess net passive income (ENPI), which is determined using the following formula.

Passive investment income (PII) includes gross receipts derived from royalties, rents, dividends, interest, and annuities. Only the net gain from the disposition of capital assets is taken into account in computing PII gross receipts.[62] Net passive income is PII reduced by any deductions directly connected with the production of that income. Any PII tax reduces the gross income that flows through to the shareholders.

Tax Fact The S Corporation Economy

Total assets controlled by S corporations make up a significant part of the economy. The 5.3 million S corporations that file Federal tax returns, representing over 7 million shareholders, employ $3.6 trillion in assets in their investments and operations.

Here are some more data about the S corporation sector.

- Trade or business income accounts for over 85 percent of all S corporation net income.
- About 70 percent of all S corporations report a positive amount of gross income.
- About 60 percent of all S corporations report business gross receipts of $250,000 or less.

[62] §§ 1362(d)(3)(B) and (C).

The excess net passive income (ENPI) cannot exceed a hypothetical C corporate taxable income for the year before considering special C corporation deductions (e.g., the dividends received deduction) or an NOL carryover.[63]

Example 40

Lilac Corporation, an S corporation, records gross receipts totaling $264,000 (of which $110,000 is PII). Expenditures directly connected to the production of the PII total $30,000. Therefore, Lilac reports net PII of $80,000 ($110,000 − $30,000), and its PII exceeds 25% of its gross receipts by $44,000 [$110,000 PII − (25% × $264,000)]. Excess net passive income (ENPI) is $32,000, calculated as follows.

$$\text{ENPI} = \frac{\$44{,}000}{\$110{,}000} \times \$80{,}000 = \$32{,}000$$

Lilac's PII tax is $6,720 ($32,000 × 21%).

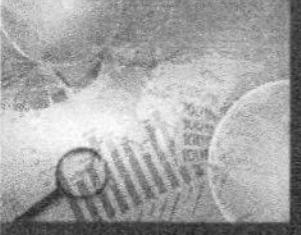

Tax Planning Strategies **Avoid PII Pitfalls**

Framework Focus: Tax Rate

Strategy: Avoid Double Taxation.

Watch for a possible violation of the PII limitation. Avoid a consecutive third year with excess passive income when the corporation has accumulated E & P from C corporation years. In this connection, assets that produce passive income (e.g., stocks and bonds, certain rental assets) might be retained by the shareholders in their individual capacities and kept out of the corporation.

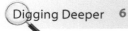

Digging Deeper 6

Further details on the passive investment income penalty can be found on this book's companion website: www.cengage.com

15-5 **Summary**

The S corporation rules are elective and can be used to benefit a number of owners of small businesses.

- When the business is profitable, the S corporation election removes the threat of double taxation on corporate profits.
- When the business is generating losses, deductions for allocable losses are immediately available to the shareholders.

About 70 percent of all U.S. corporations operate under the S rules. Flow-through income is taxed to the shareholders, who increase basis in their corporate stock accordingly. In this manner, subsequent distributions to shareholders can be made tax-free. Flow-through losses reduce stock and debt basis, but loss deductions are suspended when basis reaches zero. Flow-through items that could be treated differently by various shareholders are separately stated on Schedule K–1 of the Form 1120S.

The S rules are designed for the closely held business with a simple capital structure. Eligibility rules are not oppressive, and they do not include any limitations on the corporation's capitalization value, sales, number or distribution of employees, or other operating measures. Accounting for an S corporation's shareholder distributions can be complex though, and maintenance of S status must be monitored on an ongoing basis.

[63] §§ 1374(d)(4) and 1375(a) and (b).

Corporate-level taxes seldom are assessed on S corporations, but they guard against abuses of the S rules, such as shifting appreciated assets from higher C corporation rates to lower individual rates (the built-in gains tax) or doing the same with investment assets (the tax on excessive PII).

Refocus on The Big Picture

Converting a C Corporation to an S Corporation

WAVEBREAKMEDIA/SHUTTERSTOCK.COM

As long as Fowle, Inc., is a C corporation, David cannot deduct on his individual tax return the losses the business incurs. However, the corporation can carry any net operating losses (NOLs) forward to reduce taxes paid if the company becomes profitable again.

If David wants to deduct the losses on his individual return, the corporation should make an S election or possibly become an LLC. Assuming that Fowle meets the one class of stock requirement, an S election may be appropriate. The election should be made before any losses are incurred because any regular corporate NOLs do not flow through to an S shareholder.

Fowle should make a timely election on Form 2553, and David must consent to the election in writing. For the S election to be effective this year, it should be made on or before the fifteenth day of the third month of the current year.

The S corporation's tax-exempt interest income flows through to David. The entity may want to reconsider its salary and fringe benefits levels for David, so as to minimize the creation of a payroll tax burden, and to manage the restrictions on deductions for fringe benefits provided to an S shareholder. Fowle's tax-exempt interest can be distributed to David tax-free only after all of the entity's AEP has been accounted for.

What If?

What if David expects the loss years to be followed by increased profitability as the company shifts some of its manufacturing to other countries with cheaper labor and material costs? In this case, David expects that the corporation will make significant distributions to him. How might this affect David's decision about whether the corporation should make an S election?

David should be aware of several rules that may result in income tax being paid by the S corporation or by him as the shareholder. First, distributions from an S corporation may be treated as taxable dividends to a shareholder to the extent the S corporation has earnings and profits dating to its years as a C corporation. While distributions are deemed to be made first from accumulated net S corporation earnings (i.e., the balance in AAA), distributions in excess of that amount may be treated as a taxable dividend, being paid from AEP (accumulated E & P).

In addition, David should be aware that an S corporation that has been a C corporation in the past may be required to pay a built-in gains tax or LIFO recapture tax. The base for the built-in gains tax includes any unrealized gain on appreciated assets held by Fowle, Inc., on the day the company becomes an S corporation. The Federal corporate income tax rate is applied to the unrealized gains when any of the assets are sold within a specified number of years. If Fowle uses the LIFO inventory method, any LIFO recapture amount at the time of the S election also is subject to a corporate-level tax.

Suggested Readings

John J. Buttita and Debra M. Doyle, "A Practical Approach to Choice of Family Business Entity Under the New Tax Act," *Journal of Taxation*, December 2018.

Kristin Hill, Robert W. Jamison Jr., Robert S. Keller, Kenneth N. Orbach, Alexander Scott, Kevin J. Walsh, and Sheryll Wilson, "Current Developments in S Corporations," *The Tax Adviser*, June 2021.

Tony Nitti, "S Corporation Shareholder Compensation: How Much Is Enough?" *The Tax Adviser*, August 2011.

Key Terms

AAA bypass election, 15-17
Accumulated adjustments account (AAA), 15-16
Built-in gains tax, 15-27
Other adjustments account (OAA), 15-16
Passive investment income (PII), 15-8
Qualified business income deduction (QBID), 15-12
S corporation, 15-2
Small business corporation, 15-3
Subchapter S, 15-2
Voluntary revocation, 15-7

Computational Exercises

1. **LO.4** Dion, an S shareholder, owned 20% of MeadowBrook's stock for 292 days and 25% for the remaining 73 days in the year. Using the per-day allocation method, compute Dion's share of the following S corporation items.

	Schedule K Totals	Dion's Schedule K–1 Totals
Ordinary income	$60,000	________
Tax-exempt interest	1,000	________
Charitable contributions	3,400	________

2. **LO.4, 6** Greiner, Inc., a calendar year S corporation, holds no AEP. During the year, Chad, an individual shareholder, receives a $30,000 cash distribution from Greiner. Prior to the distribution, Chad's basis in his Greiner stock is $25,000.
   a. Determine Chad's ordinary income and capital gain, if any, from the distribution.
   b. What is the basis of Chad's Greiner stock after accounting for the distribution?

3. **LO.5, 6** Holbrook, a calendar year S corporation, distributes $15,000 cash to its only shareholder, Cody, on December 31. Cody's basis in his stock is $20,000, Holbrook's AAA balance is $8,000, and Holbrook holds $2,500 AEP before the distribution. Complete the chart below using spreadsheet software such as Microsoft Excel.

	Basis in Stock	Distribution from Account	Effect on Stock Basis
From AAA account	________	________	________
From AEP account	________	________	________
From Cody's stock basis	________	________	________

4. **LO.5** Vogel, Inc., an S corporation for five years, distributes a tract of land held as an investment to Jamari, its majority shareholder. The land was purchased for $45,000 ten years ago and is currently worth $120,000.
   a. As a result of the distribution, what is Vogel's recognized capital gain? How much is reported as a distribution to shareholders?
   b. What is the net effect of the distribution on Vogel's AAA?
   c. Assume instead that the land had been purchased for $120,000 and was currently worth $45,000. How much would Vogel recognize as a loss? What would be the net effect on Vogel's AAA? What would be Jamari's basis in the land?

5. **LO.7** Kaiwan, Inc., a calendar year S corporation, is partly owned by Sharrod, whose beginning stock basis is $32,000. During the year, Sharrod's share of a Kaiwan long-term capital gain (LTCG) is $5,000, and his share of an ordinary loss is $18,000. Sharrod then receives a $20,000 cash distribution. Compute the following.
   a. Sharrod's deductible loss.
   b. Sharrod's suspended loss.
   c. Sharrod's new basis in the Kaiwan stock.

Problems

6. **LO.2** Which of the following can be a shareholder of an S corporation?
   a. Partnership.
   b. Limited liability partnership.
   c. Corporation.
   d. One-member limited liability company.

7. **LO.2** Isaac and 121 of his close friends want to form an S corporation. Isaac reasons that if he and his friends form a partnership, the partnership then can establish an S corporation and act as a single shareholder, thereby avoiding the 100 shareholder rule. Will Isaac's plan work? Why or why not?

8. **LO.2** Joey lives in North Carolina, a common law state. He is a shareholder in an S corporation. If he marries a nonresident alien, will the S election terminate? Would your answer change if he lived in Louisiana? Explain.

9. **LO.3** On March 5, 2022, the two 50% shareholders of a calendar year corporation decide to elect S status. One of the shareholders, Mila, purchased her stock from a previous shareholder (a nonresident alien) on January 18, 2022. Identify any potential problems for Mila or the corporation. Critical Thinking

10. **LO.5, 6** Scott Tierney owns 21% of an S corporation. He is confused with respect to the amounts of the corporate AAA and his stock basis. Write a memo to the tax research file, identifying the key differences between AAA and an S shareholder's stock basis. Communications

11. **LO.6** For each of the following independent statements, indicate whether the transaction will increase (+), decrease (−), or have no effect (*NE*) on the basis of a shareholder's stock in an S corporation.
   a. Expenses related to tax-exempt income.
   b. Short-term capital gain.
   c. Nonseparately computed loss.
   d. Section 1231 gain.
   e. Depletion *not* in excess of basis.
   f. Separately computed income.
   g. Nontaxable return-of-capital distribution by the corporation.
   h. Advertising expenses.
   i. Business gifts in excess of $25.
   j. Depreciation recapture income.
   k. Dividends received by the S corporation.
   l. LIFO recapture tax paid.
   m. Collection of a bad debt previously deducted.
   n. Long-term capital loss.
   o. Cash distribution to shareholder out of AAA (with positive stock basis).

Critical Thinking

12. **LO.6, 7** Junie's share of her S corporation's net operating loss is $50,000, but her stock basis is only $30,000. Point out the Federal income tax consequences that Junie must face.

13. **LO.5, 6** Mary is a shareholder in CarrollCo, a calendar year S corporation. At the beginning of the year, her stock basis is $10,000, her share of the AAA is $2,000, and her share of corporate AEP is $6,000. At the end of the year, Mary receives a $6,000 cash distribution from CarrollCo.

    Mary's share of S corporation items includes a $2,000 long-term capital gain and a $10,000 ordinary loss. Determine the effects of these events on Mary's share of CarrollCo's AAA, on CarrollCo's AEP, and on Mary's stock basis using spreadsheet software such as Microsoft Excel.

14. **LO.4** The profit and loss statement of Kitsch Ltd., an S corporation, shows $100,000 book income. Kitsch is owned equally by four shareholders. From supplemental data, you obtain the following information about items that are included in book income.

Selling expenses	($21,200)
Tax-exempt interest income	3,000
Dividends received	9,000
§ 1231 gain	7,000
Depreciation recapture income	11,000
Net income from passive real estate rentals	5,000
Long-term capital loss	(6,000)
Salary paid to owners (each)	(12,000)
Cost of goods sold	(91,000)

    a. Compute Kitsch's nonseparately stated income or loss for the tax year.
    b. What would be the share of this year's nonseparately stated income or loss items for James Billings, one of the Kitsch shareholders?
    c. What is James Billings's share of tax-exempt interest income, if any? Is the income taxable to him this year?

15. **LO.4** Maul, Inc., a calendar year S corporation, incurred the following items.

Tax-exempt interest income	$ 7,000
Sales	140,000
Depreciation recapture income	12,000
Long-term capital gain	20,000
§ 1231 gain	7,000
Cost of goods sold	(42,000)
Administrative expenses	(15,000)
Depreciation expense (MACRS)	(17,000)
Charitable contributions	(7,000)

    a. Calculate Maul's nonseparately computed income or loss.
    b. If Carl is a 40% shareholder of Maul, what is Carl's share of Maul's long-term capital gain?

16. **LO.4** Zebra, Inc., a calendar year S corporation, incurred the following items this year. Sammy is a 40% Zebra shareholder throughout the year.

Sales	$100,000
Cost of goods sold	(40,000)
Depreciation expense (MACRS)	(10,000)
Administrative expenses	(5,000)
§ 1231 gain	21,000
Depreciation recapture income	25,000

Short-term capital loss from stock sale	($ 6,000)
Long-term capital loss from stock sale	(4,000)
Long-term capital gain from stock sale	15,000
Charitable contributions	(4,500)

a. Calculate Sammy's share of Zebra's nonseparately computed income or loss.
b. Calculate Sammy's share of Zebra long-term capital gain, if any.
c. Calculate Sammy's share of charitable contributions, if any.

17. **LO.4** On January 1, Bobby and Alicia own equally all of the stock of an electing S corporation called Prairie Dirt Delight. The company has a $60,000 loss for the year (not a leap year). On the 219th day of the year, Bobby sells his half of the stock to his son, Bubba. How much of the $60,000 loss, if any, is allocated to Bubba?

18. **LO.4, 5** McLin, Inc., is a calendar year S corporation. Its AAA balance is zero. Decision Making
   a. McLin holds $90,000 of AEP. Tobias, the sole shareholder, has an adjusted basis of $80,000 in his stock. Determine the tax aspects if a $90,000 salary is paid to Tobias. Ignore the 20% QBI deduction.
   b. Same as part (a), except that McLin pays Tobias a $90,000 cash distribution from AEP.

19. **LO.4, 5** Tiger, Inc., a calendar year S corporation, is owned equally by four shareholders: Ann, Becky, Chris, and David. Tiger owns investment land that was purchased for $160,000 four years ago. On September 14, when the land is worth $240,000, it is distributed to David. Assuming that David's basis in his S corporation stock is $270,000 on the distribution date, discuss any Federal income tax ramifications. Ignore the QBI deduction.

20. **LO.4, 5, 6** Spence, Inc., a calendar year S corporation, generates an ordinary loss of $110,000 and makes a distribution of $140,000 to its sole shareholder, Storm Nelson. Nelson's stock basis and AAA at the beginning of the year both total $200,000. Write a memo to your senior manager, Ahmad McMullin, discussing the tax treatment of Spence's activities. Communications

21. **LO.5** Polly has been the sole shareholder of a calendar year S corporation since its inception. Polly's stock basis is $15,500, and she receives a distribution of $19,000. Corporate-level accounts indicate a $6,000 balance in AAA and a $500 balance in AEP. How is Polly taxed on the distribution? What is her stock basis after the distribution?

22. **LO.4, 7** Sweetie, a calendar year S corporation, reports an ordinary loss of $80,000 and a capital loss of $20,000. Mei Freiberg owns 30% of the corporate stock and holds a $24,000 basis in the stock. Determine the amounts of the ordinary loss and capital loss, if any, that flow through to Freiberg. Prepare a memo for the tax research files explaining your computations. Communications

23. **LO.4, 5, 6** Valence Corporation's Form 1120S shows ordinary income of $88,000 for the year. Daniel owns 40% of the Valence stock throughout the year. The following information is obtained from the corporate records.

Salary paid to Daniel	($40,000)
Tax-exempt interest income	5,000
Charitable contributions	(6,000)
Dividends received from a non-U.S. corporation	5,000
Long-term capital loss	(6,000)
Depreciation recapture income	11,000
Refund of prior-year state income taxes	5,000
Cost of goods sold	(80,000)

Short-term capital loss	($ 7,000)
Administrative expenses	(18,000)
Short-term capital gain	14,000
Selling expenses	(11,000)
Daniel's beginning stock basis	32,000
Daniel's additional stock purchases	9,000
Beginning AAA	45,000
Daniel's loan to corporation	20,000

a. Compute Valence's book income or loss.
b. Compute Daniel's ending stock basis.
c. Calculate ending corporate AAA.

24. **LO.5** If the beginning balance in Swan, Inc.'s OAA is $6,700 and the following transactions occur, what is Swan's ending OAA balance?

Depreciation recapture income	$ 21,600
Payroll tax penalty	(4,200)
Tax-exempt interest income	4,012
Nontaxable life insurance proceeds	100,000
Life insurance premiums paid (nondeductible)	(3,007)

25. **LO.5, 6** Cougar, Inc., is a calendar year S corporation. Cougar's Form 1120S shows nonseparately stated ordinary income of $80,000 for the year. Johnny owns 40% of the Cougar stock throughout the year. The following information is obtained from Cougar's corporate records.

Tax-exempt interest income	$ 3,000
Salary paid to Johnny	(52,000)
Charitable contributions	(6,000)
Dividends received from a non-U.S. corporation	5,000
Short-term capital loss	(6,000)
Depreciation recapture income	11,000
Interest income from certificate of deposit	5,000
Cost of goods sold	(72,000)
Long-term capital loss	(7,000)
Administrative expenses	(18,000)
Long-term capital gain	14,000
Selling expenses	(11,000)
Johnny's beginning stock basis	32,000
Johnny's additional stock purchases	9,000
Beginning AAA	31,000
Johnny's loan to corporation	20,000

a. Compute Cougar's book income or loss.
b. Compute Johnny's ending stock basis.
c. Calculate Cougar's ending AAA balance.

Critical Thinking

26. **LO.6, 7** Orange, Inc., a calendar year corporation in Clemson, South Carolina, elects S corporation status for 2022. The company generated a $74,000 NOL in 2021 and another NOL of $43,000 in 2022.

Orange stock always is owned by the same four shareholders, each owning 25% of the stock. Pete, one of the shareholders, holds a $6,020 basis in this Orange stock at the beginning of 2022. Identify the Federal income tax issues that Pete faces.

Critical Thinking

27. **LO.7** Samuel sold 1,000 shares of his stock in Maroon, Inc., an S corporation. He sold the stock for $15,700 after he had owned it for six years. Samuel had paid $141,250 for the stock, which was issued under § 1244. Samuel is married and separately owns the 1,000 shares. Determine the appropriate Federal income tax treatment of any gain or loss on the stock sale.

28. **LO.7** Blue is the owner of all of the shares of an S corporation. Blue is considering receiving a salary of $110,000 from the business. She will pay the 7.65% FICA taxes on the salary, and the S corporation will pay the same amount of FICA tax. If Blue reduces her salary to $50,000 and takes an additional $60,000 as a cash distribution from AAA, how will her Federal income tax liabilities change?

Critical Thinking
Decision Making
Planning

29. **LO.1** One of your clients, Texas, Inc., is considering electing S status. Both of Texas's equal shareholders paid $30,000 for their stock. As of the beginning of 2022, Texas's Subchapter C NOL carryforward is $110,000. Its taxable income projections for the next few years are as follows. Will you counsel Texas to make the S election in 2022? Explain.

Critical Thinking
Decision Making
Planning

2022	$40,000
2023	25,000
2024	25,000
2025	25,000

30. **LO.6, 7** C&C Properties is an S corporation that owns two rental real estate undertakings: Carrot Plaza and Cantaloupe Place. Each property produces an annual $10,000 operating loss. C&C's Schedule K aggregates the results of the two locations into one number.

Dan and Marta, C&C's two equal shareholders, each hold a $7,000 stock basis in C&C as of the beginning of the year. Marta actively participates in the Cantaloupe location, but not at Carrot. Dan actively participates at neither location. Determine the amount of the available loss pass-throughs for both shareholders.

Critical Thinking

Tax Return Problem

1. John Parsons (123-45-6781) and George Smith (123-45-6782) are 70% and 30% owners, respectively, of Premium, Inc. (11-1111120), a candy company located at 1005 16th Street, Cut and Shoot, TX 77303. Premium's S election was made on January 15, 2012, its date of incorporation. The following information was taken from the company's 2021 income statement.

Tax Forms Problem

ProConnect™ Tax

Interest income	$ 100,000
Gross sales receipts	2,410,000
Beginning inventory	9,607
Direct labor	(203,102)
Direct materials purchased	(278,143)
Direct other costs	(249,356)
Ending inventory	3,467
Salaries and wages	(442,103)
Officers' salaries ($75,000 each to Parsons and Smith)	(150,000)
Repairs	(206,106)
Depreciation expense, tax and book	(15,254)
Interest expense	(35,222)
Rent expense (operating)	(40,000)
Taxes	(65,101)
Charitable contributions (cash)	(20,000)
Advertising expenses	(20,000)
Payroll penalties	(15,000)
Other deductions	(59,899)
Book income	704,574

A comparative balance sheet appears below.

	January 1, 2021	December 31, 2021
Cash	$ 47,840	$?
Accounts receivable	93,100	123,104
Inventories	9,607	3,467
Prepaid expenses	8,333	17,582
Building and equipment	138,203	185,348
Accumulated depreciation	(84,235)	(?)
Land	2,000	2,000
Total assets	$214,848	$844,422
Accounts payable	$ 42,500	$ 72,300
Notes payable (less than 1 year)	4,500	2,100
Notes payable (more than 1 year)	26,700	24,300
Capital stock (100 shares outstanding)	30,000	30,000
Retained earnings	111,148	?
Total liabilities and capital	$214,848	$844,422

Premium's accounting firm provides the following additional information.

Distributions to shareholders	$100,000
Beginning balance, Accumulated adjustments account	111,148
Ordinary business income for QBI	639,574
W–2 wages for QBI	795,205
UBIA of qualified property	125,000

Prepare Premium's Form 1120S and Schedule K–1s for John Parsons and George Smith, 5607 20th Street, Cut and Shoot, TX 77303. Suggested software: ProConnect Tax.

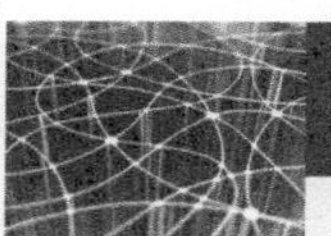

Bridge Discipline

1. Using an online research service, determine whether your state:
   a. Allows flow-through treatment for Federal S corporations.
   b. Requires any state-specific form to elect or elect out of S treatment at the state level.
   c. Places any additional withholding tax burdens on out-of-state U.S. shareholders or on non-U.S. shareholders of an S corporation.
   d. Requires any additional information disclosures or compliance deadlines for S corporations operating in the state *other than* to the revenue department (e.g., a report that must be filed with the secretary of state).
   e. Accepts "composite" or "block" income tax returns.
   f. Imposes a tax directly on the S corporation.

Communications

2. Using no more than five slides, at least two of which include a chart or graphic to illustrate your observations, prepare a presentation for your fellow students at the annual Pay It Forward conference at the university student union. In your talk, discuss the societal implications of the rule that excludes from the self-employment tax any flow-through income (other than salary and wages) that is assigned to a shareholder in an S corporation while taxing that of the owners of a partnership or an LLC.

Research Problems

Note: Solutions to the Research Problems can be prepared by using the Thomson Reuters Checkpoint™ online tax research database, which accompanies this textbook. Solutions can also be prepared by using research materials found in a typical tax library.

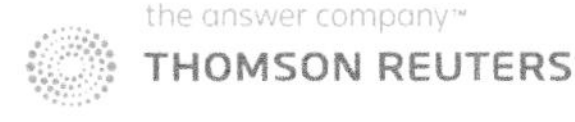

Critical Thinking
Digging Deeper

Research Problem 1. Glow and Bro organized an S corporation and intended to have only one class of stock. They agreed that all distributions should be proportional to their stock ownership. During 2020, Bro withdrew large sums of money from the S corporation without Glow's knowledge. Glow's share of pass-through income was $500,000 on the Schedule K–1, but he only received $30,000 of cash distributions. The S corporation became bankrupt. The IRS determined that the two owners did not receive distributions that were proportionate to their ownership, but it taxed Glow (who is in the 37% tax bracket) on the $500,000.

Glow argued that a second class of stock was created: these substantially disproportionate distributions appear to create a preference in distribution, creating a second class of stock. Thus, the election was terminated, the entity was a C corporation, and Glow should be taxed only on the $30,000 distribution, taxed as a dividend because the entity was a C corporation. Glow also argued that the S corporation should take a theft loss deduction for Bro's withdrawals.

You are the U.S. Tax Court judge hearing the dispute. What are the proper Federal income tax results? Elaborate.

Research Problem 2. Sean Moon is president, secretary, treasurer, sole director, and sole shareholder of Streetz, an S corporation real estate company. He manages all aspects of the company's operations, and he is the only person working at the company that holds a real estate broker's license. Sean works 12-hour days and takes few days off. Corporate records indicate the following.

Year	Gross Receipts	Net Income
1	$376,453	$122,605
2	405,244	161,660
3	518,189	231,454

Sean and his wife, Kim, filed joint Federal income tax returns, but they did not report any wages or salaries on their returns. During year 3, Sean transferred $240,000 from Streetz to his personal account.

You are an expert witness for the IRS. Identify the items that you would present to the U.S. Tax Court with respect to the amount of Sean's compensation that is subject to employment taxes and any other taxes due for year 3 (especially the additional Medicare net investment income tax). *Hint*: This is a reasonable compensation issue.

Communications

Research Problem 3. A client forwards Field Service Advice 200230030 to you and inquires how the government can force an S corporation shareholder to have a negative basis in their stock. Using the Thomson Reuters Checkpoint™ online tax research database, search FSA 200230030 and prepare an outline summarizing the Field Service Advice. E-mail your outline to your instructor.

Use internet tax resources to address the following questions. Look for reliable websites and blogs of the IRS and other government agencies, media outlets, businesses, tax professionals, academics, think tanks, and political outlets.

Communications
Data Analytics

Research Problem 4. Prepare a graph of the growth in the number of S elections since 1980, using increments of no more than five years. On the same graph, show the maximum Federal income tax rates for those years as they applied to individuals and to C corporations. Send your graph and other observations in an e-mail to your instructor with some explanatory comments as to what you found. You might use the IRS Data Book and other items at **irs.gov/taxstats**.

Communications
Data Analytics

Research Problem 5. Based on the most recent data from **irs.gov/taxstats** or the *IRS Data Book*, use Microsoft Excel to prepare a pie chart showing the total number of business tax returns filed, including sole proprietorships (nonfarm), partnerships, C corporations, S corporations, and Forms 1120–RIC and 1120–REIT.

Becker CPA Review Questions

Becker

1. Village Corp., a calendar year corporation, began business in year 1. Village made a valid S corporation election on December 5, year 4, with the unanimous consent of its shareholders. The eligibility requirements for S status continued to be met throughout year 5. On what date did Village's S status become effective?

   a. January 1, year 4
   b. January 1, year 5
   c. December 5, year 4
   d. December 5, year 5

2. Fox Corp., an S corporation, had an ordinary loss of $36,500 for the year ended December 31, year 2. At January 1, year 2, Duffy owned 50% of Fox's stock. Duffy held the stock for 40 days in year 2 before selling the entire 50% interest to an unrelated third party. Duffy's basis for the stock was $10,000. Duffy was a full-time employee of Fox until the stock was sold. Duffy's share of Fox's loss was:

   a. $0
   b. $2,000
   c. $10,000
   d. $18,250

3. An S corporation has 30,000 shares of voting common stock and 20,000 shares of nonvoting common stock issued and outstanding. The S election can be revoked voluntarily with the consent of the shareholders holding, on the day of the revocation, the following number of outstanding shares.

	Shares of Voting Stock	Shares of Nonvoting Stock
a.	0	20,000
b.	7,500	5,000
c.	10,000	16,000
d.	20,000	0

4. The Haas Corp., a calendar year S corporation, has two equal shareholders. For the year ended December 31, year 6, Haas had net income of $60,000, which included $50,000 from operations and $10,000 from investment interest income. There were no other transactions that year. Each shareholder's basis in the stock of Haas will increase by:

   a. $50,000
   b. $30,000
   c. $25,000
   d. $0

5. Zinco Corp. was a calendar year S corporation. Zinco's S status terminated on April 1, year 6, when Case Corp. became a shareholder. During year 6 (365-day calendar year), Zinco had nonseparately computed income of $310,250. If no election was made by Zinco, what amount of the income, if any, was allocated to the S short year for year 6?

   a. $233,750
   b. $155,125
   c. $76,500
   d. $0

6. The Matthew Corporation, an S corporation, is equally owned by three shareholders—Emily, Alejandra, and Kristina. The corporation is on the calendar year basis for tax and financial purposes. On April 1 of the current year, Emily sold her one-third interest in the Matthew Corporation equally to the other two shareholders. For the current year, the corporation had nonseparately stated ordinary income of $900,000. For the current year, how much ordinary income should be allocated to Kristina on her Schedule K–1?

   a. $25,000
   b. $75,000
   c. $337,500
   d. $412,500

7. After a corporation's status as an S corporation is revoked or terminated, how many years is the corporation required to wait before making a new S election, in the absence of IRS consent to an earlier election?

   a. 1
   b. 3
   c. 5
   d. 10

8. An S corporation may deduct:

   a. Charitable contributions within the percentage of income limitation applicable to corporations.
   b. Net operating loss carryovers.
   c. Foreign income taxes.
   d. Compensation of officers.

9. XYZ Inc., was a C corporation through the end of year 6. Starting at the beginning of year 7, XYZ elected S corporation status. At the end of year 6, XYZ had accumulated earnings and profits (E & P) of $53,700. At the end of year 7, XYZ had a balance of $32,000 in its accumulated adjustments account (AAA). During year 8, XYZ had ordinary income of $15,300 and made distributions of $100,000. What amount of the distribution will be a nontaxable distribution out of S corporation earnings to the shareholders of XYZ at the end of year 8?

   a. $1,000
   b. $47,300
   c. $52,700
   d. $53,700

10. On March 4, Year 1, Miqdadi Corporation, a calendar year corporation, elected S status, and all of its shareholders consented to the election. All of the eligibility requirements had been met by the corporation for S status during the portion of the year that was pre-election. On which date is the earliest that Miqdadi Corporation can be recognized as an S corporation?

    a. January 1, Year 1.
    b. March 4, Year 1.
    c. January 1, Year 2.
    d. March 4, Year 2.

11. As of January 1, Year 6, Kane owned all the 100 issued shares of Manning Corp., a calendar year S corporation. On the 41st day of Year 6, Kane sold 25 of the Manning shares to Rodgers. For the year ended December 31, Year 6 (a 365-day calendar year), Manning had $73,000 in nonseparately stated income and made no distributions to its shareholders. What amount of nonseparately stated income from Manning should be reported on Kane's Year 6 tax return?

    a. $56,750
    b. $54,750
    c. $16,250
    d. $0

Part 6

Special Business Topics

Part 6 covers several topics that are relevant to all types of taxpayers. Business entities operate in both the international and state arenas. Therefore, multijurisdictional taxation is addressed for both multinational and multistate operations. A review then follows of tax credits allowed to reduce the Federal income tax liability on business income and the application of the AMT to individual taxpayers. Part 6 concludes with a comparative analysis of the different types of business entities discussed throughout the text.

Chapter

16 Multijurisdictional Taxation

Learning Objectives: *After completing Chapter 16, you should be able to:*

LO.1 Discuss the computational and compliance issues that arise when a taxpayer operates in more than one taxing jurisdiction.

LO.2 Identify the sources of tax law applicable to a taxpayer operating in more than one country.

LO.3 Outline the U.S. tax effects related to the offshore operations of a U.S. taxpayer.

LO.4 Describe the tax effects related to the U.S. operations of a non-U.S. taxpayer.

LO.5 Identify the sources of tax law applicable to a taxpayer operating in more than one U.S. state.

LO.6 Apply principles designed to compute state taxable income for a taxpayer operating in more than one U.S. state.

LO.7 Synthesize key aspects of international and multistate tax systems to identify common rules and issues taxpayers face in both systems.

Chapter Outline

Tax Talk *Don't tax you, don't tax me; tax the fellow behind the tree.* —U.S. Sen. Russell B. Long

Don't tax you, don't tax me; tax the companies across the sea. —U.S. Rep. Dan Rostenkowski

MONKEY BUSINESS IMAGES/SHUTTERSTOCK.COM

The Big Picture

Going International

VoiceCo, a domestic corporation, designs, manufactures, and sells specialty microphones for use in theaters. All of its activities take place in Florida, although it ships products to customers all over the United States. When it received inquiries about its products from foreign customers, VoiceCo decided to test the foreign market and placed ads in foreign trade journals. Soon it was taking orders from non-U.S. customers.

VoiceCo is concerned about its potential foreign income tax exposure. Although it has no assets or employees in the foreign jurisdictions, it now is involved in international commerce. Is VoiceCo subject to income taxes in foreign countries? Must it pay U.S. income taxes on the profits from its foreign sales? What if VoiceCo pays taxes to other countries? Does it receive any benefit from these payments on its U.S. tax return?

Later VoiceCo established a manufacturing plant in Ireland to meet the European demand for its products. VoiceCo incorporated the Irish operation as a controlled foreign corporation (CFC) named VoiceCo-Ireland. How does U.S. corporate income tax law affect these events?

Read the chapter and formulate your response.

One of the tax planning principles that has been discussed throughout this text relates to the use of favorable tax jurisdictions—moving income into lower-taxed districts and deductions into higher-taxed ones. Many individuals dream of moving all of their income and wealth to a tax-friendly state or a proverbial island in the tropics, never to be taxed again. This chapter examines the temptations that attract taxpayers to this idea and various ways in which this goal can and cannot be accomplished.

LO.1

Discuss the computational and compliance issues that arise when a taxpayer operates in more than one taxing jurisdiction.

16-1 The Multijurisdictional Taxpayer

Companies large and small must deal with the consequences of earning income through activities in different jurisdictions. A small business may have its center of operations in a single city but have customers in many states and countries. Consider the typical U.S. multinational corporation. Its assets, employees, customers, suppliers, lenders, and owners are located in numerous locations, crossing city, county, state, national, and "virtual" borders.

RobotCo, a corporation created and organized in Delaware, produces and sells robotic manufacturing equipment for the auto industry. It holds its valuable patents and intangible property in Delaware and Bermuda. The company has manufacturing operations in Ireland, Singapore, Germany, Texas, and New Jersey. It operates distribution centers in Canada, the United Kingdom, Germany, Hong Kong, Texas, New Jersey, Georgia, California, Illinois, and Arizona. RobotCo's sales force spends time in Europe, Asia, Mexico, Canada, and almost every state in the union. RobotCo's engineers likewise provide technical service to customers wherever they may be located. RobotCo also maintains a substantial web presence.

RobotCo must determine its potential exposure to tax in each of these jurisdictions. Such exposure usually is based on RobotCo's nexus (or economic connection) to the various locations. Unfortunately for all concerned, each of these taxing jurisdictions uses a different taxing system and methods, imposes taxes under differing structures, and even defines the tax base differently. How does RobotCo divide its income among the various jurisdictions that want a piece of its tax dollars, determine its tax costs, mitigate any potential double taxation, and file the appropriate returns with this diverse set of taxing authorities? Such questions and more must be addressed by modern-day businesses.

Thousands of state and local jurisdictions are involved in the taxation of interstate transactions through income, property, sales, or other taxes. State and local taxes make up over one-third of all taxes collected in the United States. Global trade also represents a major portion of the U.S. economy. In 2020, U.S. exports of goods and services amounted to $2.1 trillion, with imports reaching $2.8 trillion. Hundreds of countries and many more political subdivisions participated in the taxation of these transactions. These interstate and international trade flows, along with cross-state and cross-country investments, create significant Federal, state, and local tax consequences for both U.S. and foreign entities.

16-2 U.S. Taxation of Multinational Transactions

Cross-border transactions create the need for special tax considerations for both the United States and its trading partners. From a U.S. perspective, international tax laws should promote the global competitiveness of U.S. enterprises and at the same time protect the tax revenue base of the United States. These two objectives sometimes conflict, however. The need to deal with both objectives contributes to the complexity of the rules governing the U.S. taxation of cross-border transactions.

Bridge Discipline **Bridge to International Law**

Many provisions of the U.S. tax law relating to international transactions are thinly disguised extensions of a principle of international law—the ability of sovereign countries to protect the safety and privacy of their citizens abroad.

For instance, U.S. tax auditors often have difficulty obtaining or reviewing the documentation supporting deductions claimed by U.S. taxpayers operating overseas. Banking, credit card, and other records that are available (in the course of business or forcibly by summons) for strictly U.S. transactions are not always available once those same transactions cross national borders.

How could the U.S. tax base include rental and royalty income of a U.S. investor operating through a corporation in another country when property ownership and taxation records are not available for substantiation or audit outside the country of the investment? Perhaps this explains why the U.S. tax base typically excludes such items.

Conversely, when the taxing agencies of multiple countries are allowed by law to trade among themselves information about business operations and taxpayers, the fairness and completeness of the taxing process may improve. But such lengthening of the reach of the taxing authorities results from diplomatic negotiations among the countries, not from the passage of legislation.

U.S. persons engage in activities outside the United States for many different reasons. Consider two U.S. corporations that have established sales subsidiaries in foreign countries. Dedalus, Inc., operates in Germany, a high-tax country, because customers demand local attention from sales agents. Mulligan, Inc., operates in the Cayman Islands, a tax haven country, simply to shift income outside the United States. U.S. tax law must fairly address both situations with the same law.

U.S. multinational taxpayers—and tax professionals—must understand the Federal tax rules related to international business so that these rules can be incorporated into their overall tax plans. Generally, this involves reducing the exposure to double taxation of business profits, locating cash and other assets where they will be the most productive, and decreasing the present value of tax liabilities (for example, by accelerating losses and deductions, deferring taxable income recognition, and taking advantage of favorable tax rules where possible).

U.S. international tax provisions are concerned primarily with two types of potential taxpayers: U.S. persons earning income from outside the United States, and non-U.S. persons earning income from inside the United States.[1] U.S. persons earning income only from within the country do not create any international tax issues and are taxed under the purely domestic provisions of the Internal Revenue Code. Non-U.S. persons earning income from outside the United States are not within the taxing jurisdiction of the United States (unless this income is somehow directly connected to U.S. operations).

The U.S. taxation of international transactions can be organized in terms of "outbound" and "inbound" taxation. **Outbound taxation** refers to the U.S. taxation of foreign-source income earned by U.S. taxpayers. **Inbound taxation** refers to the U.S. taxation of U.S.-source income earned by foreign taxpayers. Exhibit 16.1 illustrates these concepts.

U.S. taxpayers often "internationalize" gradually over time. A U.S. business may operate on a strictly domestic basis for several years, then explore offshore markets by exporting its products abroad, and later license its products to a foreign manufacturer or enter into a joint venture with a foreign partner. If its forays into non-U.S. markets are successful, the U.S. business may create a foreign subsidiary and move a portion of its operations abroad by establishing a sales or manufacturing facility.

[1]The term *person* includes an individual, corporation, partnership, trust, estate, or association. § 7701(a)(1). The terms *domestic* and *foreign* are defined in §§ 7701(a)(4) and (5).

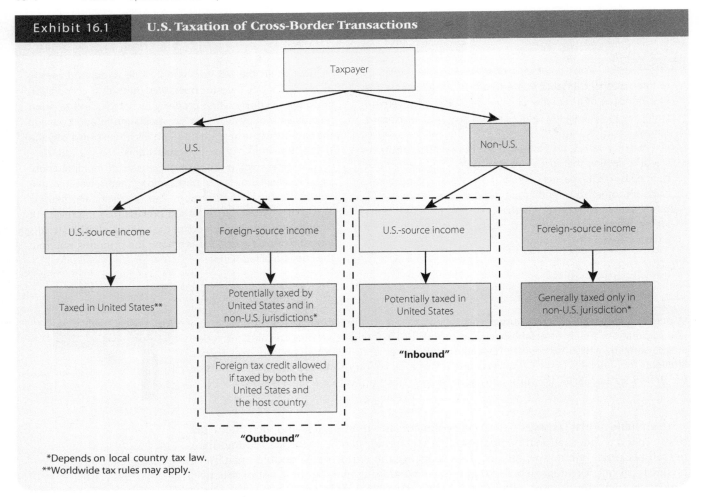

Exhibit 16.1 **U.S. Taxation of Cross-Border Transactions**

Taxpayer

U.S.

Non-U.S.

U.S.-source income

Taxed in United States**

Foreign-source income

Potentially taxed by United States and in non-U.S. jurisdictions*

Foreign tax credit allowed if taxed by both the United States and the host country

"Outbound"

U.S.-source income

Potentially taxed in United States

"Inbound"

Foreign-source income

Generally taxed only in non-U.S. jurisdiction*

*Depends on local country tax law.
**Worldwide tax rules may apply.

Both U.S. and offshore entities generally move into international markets in this manner. In this timeline, each step generates increasingly significant international income tax consequences. Exhibit 16.2 shows a typical timeline for a business "going global."

Information on filing deadlines when outside of the country can be found on this book's companion website: www.cengage.com

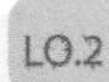

Identify the sources of tax law applicable to a taxpayer operating in more than one country.

16-2a **Sources of Law**

U.S. individuals and companies operating across national borders are subject to the laws of every jurisdiction in which they operate or invest. Accordingly, the source of law depends on the nature of a taxpayer's connection with a particular country.

For U.S. persons, the Internal Revenue Code addresses the tax consequences of earning income anywhere in the world. However, U.S. persons also must comply with the local tax law of the other nations in which they operate.

Exhibit 16.2 **Global Activities Timeline**

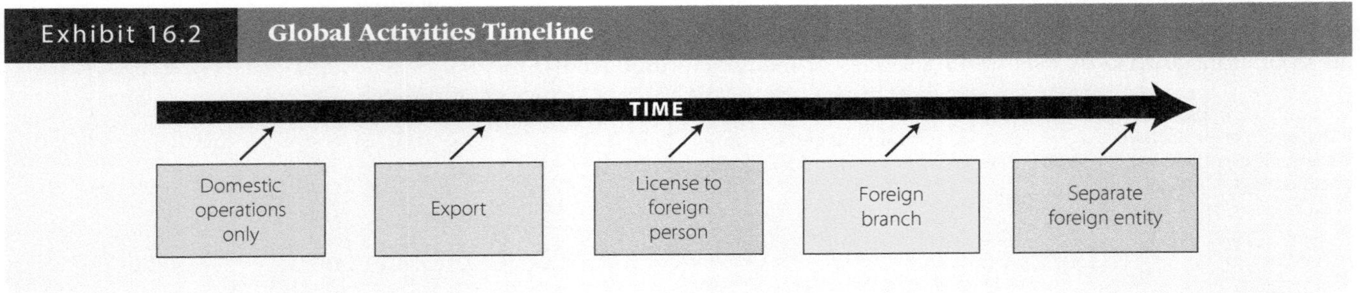

For non-U.S. persons, U.S. statutory law is relevant to income they earn that is connected to U.S. income-producing activities, whether those activities involve a passive investment or an active trade or business. Whether non-U.S. persons also are subject to potential tax in their home countries on their U.S. income depends on their own local tax law.

It is difficult for the United States (or any country) to craft local tax laws that equitably address all of the potential issues that arise when two countries attempt to tax the same income. Furthermore, any uncertainty as to tax consequences can be an impediment to global business investment. Consequently, countries might enter into **income tax treaties** with each other to provide more certainty to taxpayers.

Tax treaties are the result of specific negotiations with a treaty partner, so each treaty is unique. Nevertheless, all tax treaties are organized in the same way and address similar issues. For example, all treaties include provisions regarding the taxation of investment income, business profits from a **permanent establishment (PE)**, personal service income, and exceptions for certain persons (e.g., athletes, entertainers, students, and teachers).

Permanent establishment (PE) is an important concept that is defined in all income tax treaties. A person has a PE within a country when its activities within that country rise beyond a minimal level. Tax treaties outline the activities that create a PE, including an office, plant, or other fixed place of business. Treaties also specify certain activities that do not create a PE (e.g., a temporary construction project). Once a person has a PE within a country, the business profits associated with the PE become subject to tax in that country.

Amelia, Inc., a U.S. corporation, sells boating supplies to customers in the United States and Canada. Amelia has no assets in Canada. All Canadian sales transactions are conducted via the internet or telephone from Amelia's Florida office. Because Amelia does not have any assets in Canada or conduct any activities within Canada, it does not have a Canadian PE. Consequently, Canada does not impose an income tax on the profit associated with Amelia's Canadian sales. However, if Amelia opens a sales office in Canada, a PE will exist, and Canada will tax the profits associated with the PE.

Although the United States has entered into almost 70 income tax treaties, many jurisdictions where U.S. taxpayers operate are not covered by a treaty. Where there is no tax treaty, the more subjective test of whether a person is "engaged in a trade or business" within a country replaces the PE determination. Both the PE concept and the engaged in a trade or business concept are closely related to the determination of whether a person has *nexus* within a jurisdiction for state and local tax purposes (discussed later in this chapter).

16-2b Tax Issues

Outline the U.S. tax effects related to the offshore operations of a U.S. taxpayer.

Authority to Tax

The United States taxes the *worldwide* income of U.S. taxpayers.[2] The United States claims the right to tax all of a U.S. person's income because of the protection of U.S. law provided to a person connected to the United States through citizenship, residency, or place of organization. Because non-U.S. governments also may tax some of the U.S. person's income when it is earned within the other country's borders, U.S. taxpayers may be subjected to double taxation.

There are two broad methods of taxing cross-border income. Under the *territorial* approach, a country simply exempts from tax the income derived from sources outside

[2]Gross income for a U.S. person includes all income from whatever source derived. "Source" in this context means not only type of income (e.g., wages or interest) but also geographic source (e.g., the United States or Belgium). § 61.

Tax Fact U.S. Income Tax Treaties in Force

The United States has entered into income tax treaties with the following nations.

Armenia	France	Lithuania	South Africa
Australia	Georgia	Luxembourg	Spain
Austria	Germany	Malta	Sri Lanka
Azerbaijan	Greece	Mexico	Sweden
Bangladesh	Hungary	Moldova	Switzerland
Barbados	Iceland	Morocco	Tajikistan
Belarus	India	Netherlands	Thailand
Belgium	Indonesia	New Zealand	Trinidad
Bulgaria	Ireland	Norway	Tunisia
Canada	Israel	Pakistan	Turkey
China	Italy	Philippines	Turkmenistan
Cyprus	Jamaica	Poland	Ukraine
Czech Republic	Japan	Portugal	United Kingdom
Denmark	Kazakhstan	Romania	Uzbekistan
Egypt	Korea	Russia	Venezuela
Estonia	Kyrgyzstan	Slovak Republic	
Finland	Latvia	Slovenia	

its borders. Most European and Asian countries have adopted this approach.[3] The second approach is to tax the *worldwide* income of all domestic persons and then provide a **foreign tax credit (FTC)** against home country taxes for taxes paid to other countries on the same income. When the foreign tax credit is available, the United States allows its taxpayers to reduce their U.S. tax liability by some or all of the foreign income taxes paid on income earned outside the United States.

Gator Enterprises, Inc., a U.S. corporation, operates a manufacturing branch in Italy because of customer demand there, local availability of raw materials, and the high cost of shipping finished goods. This branch income is taxed in the United States as part of Gator's worldwide income, but it also is taxed in Italy. Without the availability of a foreign tax credit to mitigate this double taxation, Gator Enterprises would suffer an excessive tax burden and could not compete with local Italian companies.

The United States uses the territorial approach in taxing non-U.S. persons. Such inbound taxpayers generally are subject to tax only on income earned within U.S. borders.

Purdie, Ltd., a corporation based in the United Kingdom, operates in the United States. Although it is not a U.S. person, Purdie is taxed in the United States on its U.S.-source business income. If Purdie, Ltd., could operate free of U.S. tax, its U.S.-based competitors would face a serious disadvantage.

[3] In some cases, countries allow the territorial exemption from home country taxation only if the income has been subject to tax in another country. Other countries, however, exempt such income even if no source country tax is imposed.

The United States offers a form of territorial taxation to U.S. corporations as a political response designed to increase the competitiveness of U.S. businesses in the global marketplace. A 100% dividends received deduction is available when a non-U.S. subsidiary remits profits earned overseas to its U.S. parent as a dividend. Structurally, the worldwide taxation approach remains as the chief means by which U.S. persons are taxed on multinational income, but this deduction allows the U.S. corporation some movement toward a territorial system, and it encourages the repatriation of current earnings to the United States by many corporations.

Although the worldwide taxing system still undergirds the income taxation of U.S. persons' cross-border transactions, recent tax law changes overlay these rules, especially for large entities. These changes:

- Provide incentives for U.S. businesses to locate jobs in the United States and repatriate overseas profits to the United States, and
- Prevent U.S. entities from shifting taxable income outside the United States into low-tax-rate countries.

Income Sourcing

Determining the source of net income is a critical component in calculating the U.S. tax consequences to both U.S. and foreign persons. The sourcing rules are used in computing the foreign tax credit (discussed later in the chapter) and in determining the Federal income tax base for non-U.S. persons.

A number of specific provisions contained in §§ 861 through 865 address the income-sourcing rules for all types of income, including interest, dividends, rents, royalties, services, and sales of assets. Generally, the sourcing rules assign income to a geographic source based on the location where the economic activity producing the income took place. In some cases, this relationship is clear, and in others, the connection is more obscure.

Sourcing Rules

Wickless, Inc., a U.S. corporation, provides scuba diving lessons to customers in Florida and in the Bahamas. These services are sourced based on the place where the activity is performed. The services performed in Florida are U.S.-source income, and those performed in the Bahamas are foreign-source income.

Example 7

Brown, Inc., a U.S. corporation, receives dividend income from Takeda Corporation, a Japanese corporation, based on its ownership of Takeda common stock. Brown purchased the stock in the United States and receives all payments in the United States. At first glance, it appears that all of the activities related to earning the dividend income take place in the United States. Nevertheless, the dividend income is treated as foreign source because it is paid by a non-U.S. corporation.[4]

In addition to sourcing income, the U.S. rules require taxpayers to assign deductions to U.S.- or foreign-source categories. Deductions that are directly related to an activity or property first are allocated to classes of income to which they directly relate (e.g., sales, services, rentals). Then the deductions are apportioned between the U.S. and foreign groupings using a reasonable basis (e.g., revenue, gross profit, assets, units sold, time spent). If a deduction is not definitely related to any class of gross income, the deduction is first assigned to all classes of gross income and then apportioned between U.S.- and foreign-source income.

Many deductions may be allocated and apportioned based on any reasonable method the taxpayer chooses.[5] However, the U.S. tax rules impose a specific method for certain types of deductions, including interest and research and experimentation expenses. Interest expense is allocated and apportioned based on the theory that borrowed money can be raised and spent in any country, without being earmarked to any specific

[4]Code § 861(a)(2) establishes that only dividends from domestic corporations are U.S.-source income.

[5]Reg. § 1.861–8.

Tax Fact Where Do We Stand?

Drastic reductions in marginal business income tax rates have rippled through the world. Even perpetually high-tax countries such as Sweden and the United Kingdom have cut back marginal tax rate structures to remain competitive, and often they have changed the tax base to match similar revisions of the U.S. tax law.

As a result of this dramatic evolution in international tax rates, the average marginal business income tax rate in developed countries now lies between 25 and 30 percent, down from perhaps 50 percent in the 1960s. These numbers do not take into account, though, the dependence of many U.S. trading partners on transaction taxes, such as the value added tax and wealth-based taxes, which make difficult an apples-to-apples comparison of rates alone.

After 2017, when the top Federal statutory tax rate was dropped to 21% from 35%, the United States is near the global average in corporate tax rates.

Top Statutory Corporate Income Tax Rates for Selected Countries	
Canada	26.20%
France	28.40%
Germany	29.90%
Ireland	12.50%
Japan	29.70%
Mexico	30.00%
Sweden	20.60%
United Kingdom	19.00%
United States	25.80%

Note: Tax rates include additional taxes on corporate taxable income levied by states, cities, provinces, cantons, and other smaller jurisdictions. Deductions, exemptions, and credits can reduce an entity's effective tax rate below the top statutory rate.

***Source:* OECD 2021 Statutory Corporate Income Tax Rates (stats.oecd.org/Index.aspx?DataSetCode=CTS_CIT).**

location or use (i.e., it is *fungible*). For example, if a taxpayer borrows to support its manufacturing activity, this frees up other funds for use to support its investment activities, regardless of where the borrowing and spending actually occurred. Accordingly, interest expense is allocated and apportioned to all activities and property of the taxpayer. Taxpayers must allocate and apportion interest expense on the basis of asset location, using the tax book value of the assets.

The Big Picture

Example 8

Return to the facts of *The Big Picture* on p. 16-1. Assume that VoiceCo makes an overseas investment and generates $2,000,000 of gross income and $50,000 of expenses, all related to its microphone manufacturing and sales. The expenses can be allocated and then apportioned on the basis of gross income.

	Gross Income			Apportionment	
	Foreign	**U.S.**	**Allocation**	**Foreign**	**U.S.**
Sales	$1,000,000	$500,000	$37,500*	$25,000	$12,500**
Manufacturing	400,000	100,000	12,500	10,000	2,500***
Totals			$50,000	$35,000	$15,000

* $50,000 × ($1,500,000/$2,000,000) = $37,500.
** $37,500 × ($500,000/$1,500,000) = $12,500.
*** $12,500 × ($100,000/$500,000) = $2,500.

If VoiceCo could show that $45,000 of the expenses were directly related to its sales income, the $45,000 would be allocated directly to that class of gross income, with the remainder allocated and apportioned between U.S. and foreign sources ratably.

		Apportionment	
	Allocation	**Foreign**	**U.S.**
Sales	$45,000	$30,000	$15,000
Manufacturing	5,000	4,000	1,000
Totals	$50,000	$34,000	$16,000

Tax Planning Strategies Sourcing Income from Sales of Inventory

Framework Focus: Tax Rate

Strategy: Control the Character of Income and Deductions.

Generally, income from the sale of personal property is sourced according to the residence of the seller. Several important exceptions exist for inventory. Income from the sale of purchased inventory is sourced in the country in which the sale takes place under the "title passage" rule. This approach provides the taxpayer with flexibility regarding the sourcing of income and deductions, and it allows for the creation of zero-taxed foreign-source income.

USCo, a domestic corporation, purchases inventory for resale from unrelated parties and sells the inventory to customers in the United States and Brazil. If title on the Brazilian sales passes in the United States (i.e., risks of loss shift to the Brazilian customers at the shipping point), the inventory income is U.S.-source. If title passes outside the United States (e.g., at the customer's warehouse in Brazil), the inventory income is foreign-source.

Although the Code identifies the income item as foreign source, this income likely is not subject to any Brazilian income tax because USCo has no employees, assets, or activities in Brazil. Although the income is subject to U.S. tax in either case (because it represents taxable income to a U.S. person), in the latter case, USCo has generated foreign-source income with no corresponding foreign income tax. This will prove useful in managing USCo's ability to use foreign tax credits, as discussed next.

When a taxpayer both produces and sells inventory, the income is sourced to the country of production.

The Big Picture

Example 9

Return to the facts of *The Big Picture* on p. 16-1. Assume that VoiceCo makes an overseas investment and generates both U.S.-source and foreign-source gross income for the current year. VoiceCo's assets (measured at tax book value) are as follows.

Assets generating U.S.-source income	\$18,000,000
Assets generating foreign-source income	5,000,000
Total VoiceCo assets	\$23,000,000

VoiceCo incurs interest expense of \$800,000 for the current year. Interest expense is apportioned to foreign-source income as follows.

$$\frac{\$5{,}000{,}000\text{ (foreign assets)}}{\$23{,}000{,}000\text{ (total assets)}} \times \$800{,}000\text{ (interest expense)} = \$173{,}913$$

Foreign Tax Credit

The United States can tax its citizens and residents on their worldwide taxable income. To reduce the possibility of double taxation, a foreign tax credit (FTC) is in place.

A qualified taxpayer is allowed a tax credit for foreign income taxes paid or accrued. All of the taxes paid by the taxpayer to various countries on its operations are combined to compute the FTC. The credit is a dollar-for-dollar reduction of U.S. income tax liability.

Example 10

Caulkin Tools, Inc., a U.S. corporation, operates a branch operation in Largo from which it earns taxable income of \$750,000 for the current year. Caulkin pays income tax of \$100,000 on these earnings to the Largo tax authorities. Caulkin also includes the \$750,000 in gross income for U.S. tax purposes.

Before considering the FTC, Caulkin owes \$157,500 in U.S. income taxes on this foreign-source income. Thus, total taxes on the \$750,000 could equal \$257,500 (\$100,000 + \$157,500), a 34% effective rate.

But Caulkin takes an FTC of \$100,000 against its U.S. tax liability on the foreign-source income. Caulkin's total taxes on the \$750,000 now are \$157,500 (\$100,000 + \$57,500), a 21% effective rate.

The FTC is elective for the tax year. Lacking an election to take the FTC, a deduction is claimed for foreign taxes paid or incurred. One cannot take a credit and a deduction for the same foreign income taxes, and in most situations, the FTC is more valuable to the taxpayer.

FTC Limits The United States does not grant an FTC for all foreign taxes paid, and there are limits on the amount of foreign taxes that can be taken as a credit. First, only foreign *income* taxes are potentially creditable. Second, the FTC allowed in any tax year is limited to the U.S. tax imposed on the foreign-source income included on the U.S. tax return.[6] Thus, taxpayers are allowed a credit for the lesser of the foreign income taxes paid or accrued or the following limitation.

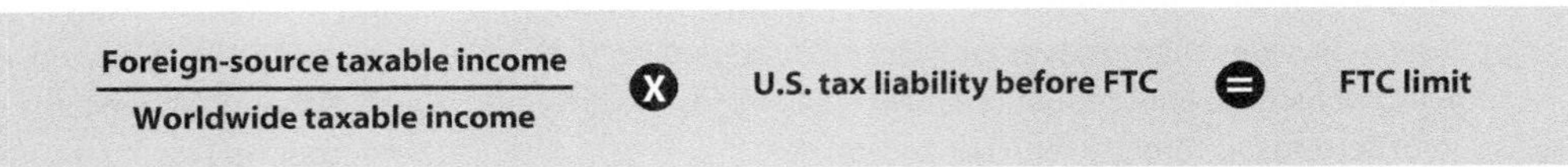

Worldwide taxable income is the total taxable income reported on the taxpayer's U.S. tax return. Any potential FTCs disallowed because of the FTC limitation may be carried back 1 year or forward 10 years, subject to the FTC limits in those tax years.

Lassaline, Inc., a domestic corporation, invests in the bonds of non-U.S. corporations. Lassaline's worldwide taxable income for the tax year is $1,200,000, consisting of $1,000,000 of profits from U.S. sales and $200,000 of interest income from foreign sources. Foreign taxes of $90,000 were withheld on these interest payments.

Lassaline's U.S. tax before the FTC is $252,000. Its FTC is limited to $42,000 [($200,000/ $1,200,000) × $252,000]. Thus, Lassaline's net U.S. tax liability is $210,000 after allowing the $42,000 FTC. The remaining $48,000 of FTCs ($90,000 − $42,000) may be carried back or forward.

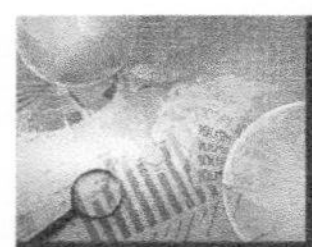

Tax Planning Strategies **Utilizing the Foreign Tax Credit**

Framework Focus: Tax Credits

Strategy: Maximize Tax Credits.

The FTC limitation can prevent the total amount of foreign taxes paid in high-tax jurisdictions from being credited against U.S. income tax liabilities. Taxpayers can overcome this problem by using the sourcing rules to:

- Generate ***income*** items that are ***foreign-source***, so as to maximize net foreign-source income, the numerator of the FTC fraction.
- Realize ***deduction*** items as ***U.S.-source***, so as to minimize any reduction in net foreign-source income, the numerator of the FTC fraction.

A U.S. taxpayer's ability to use FTCs directly relates to its level of foreign-source income relative to its total taxable income. To the extent a U.S. taxpayer can keep the average tax rate on its foreign-source income at or below the U.S. tax rate on such income, the foreign taxes will be fully creditable. Consequently, combining high- and low-tax foreign-source income is an important income tax planning objective.

[6] §§ 901 and 903 provide definitions of creditable foreign taxes. § 904 contains the FTC limitation rules.

Example 12

Compare the following scenarios where Genius, a U.S. corporation, incurs FTC situations that differ depending on its ability to mix high- and low-taxed income. In the first scenario, Genius earns only $500,000 of highly taxed foreign-source income. In the second scenario, it also generates $100,000 of low-taxed foreign-source income.

	Only Highly Taxed Income	With Low-Taxed Income
Foreign-source income	$500,000	$600,000
Foreign taxes	275,000	280,000
U.S.-source income	700,000	700,000
U.S. taxes (21%)	252,000	273,000
FTC limitation	105,000*	126,000**

* ($500,000/$1,200,000) × $252,000 = $105,000.
** ($600,000/$1,300,000) × $273,000 = $126,000.

When the low-taxed income is added, Genius's actual foreign taxes increase by only $5,000 ($280,000 versus $275,000), but its FTC limitation increases by $21,000 (from $105,000 to $126,000). The ability to "cross-credit" high- and low-taxed foreign income is available, though, only when all of the foreign-source income is classified in the same income basket, as discussed next.

To limit the ability of U.S. taxpayers to cross-credit foreign taxes, the FTC rules provide for several **separate foreign tax credit income categories** (or baskets), including those for passive (investment) and general operating income. In any tax year, taxpayers are allowed to credit the lesser of foreign income taxes paid or accrued or the FTC limit only *within each separate basket*. The taxpayer's FTC for the year is the sum of the separately computed amounts; FTCs are not combined among the baskets.

The separate FTC limitation categories for different types of income each use this same basic FTC limitation formula. The baskets affect the amount of FTC that can be taken, generally by segregating income subject to a high level of foreign tax from lower-taxed foreign income.

Example 13

BenCo, Inc., a U.S. corporation, operates a foreign branch in Adagio that earns taxable income of $1,500,000 from manufacturing operations and $600,000 from passive activities. BenCo pays Adagio income taxes of $600,000 (40%) and $100,000 (16⅔%), respectively, on this foreign-source income.

The corporation earns $4,000,000 of U.S.-source taxable income, resulting in worldwide taxable income of $6,100,000. BenCo's U.S. taxes before the FTC are $1,281,000 (at 21%). The following table illustrates the effect of the separate limitation baskets on cross-crediting.

Separate Foreign Income Category	Net Taxable Amount	Foreign Taxes	U.S. Tax before FTC at 21%	FTC Allowed with Separate Limits
General	$1,500,000	$600,000	$315,000	$315,000
Passive	600,000	100,000	126,000	100,000
Total	$2,100,000	$700,000	$441,000	$415,000

Without the separate limitation provisions, the FTC would be the lesser of (1) $700,000 foreign taxes or (2) $441,000 share of U.S. tax [($2,100,000/$6,100,000) × $1,281,000]. Here, the "basket" provisions decrease the FTC by $26,000 ($441,000 – $415,000). The foreign-source income taxed at the foreign tax rate of 40% cannot be aggregated with foreign-source income taxed at only 16⅔%.

Information on the international economy and its relevance to tax rules can be found on this book's companion website: www.cengage.com

2 Digging Deeper

Financial Disclosure Insights Overseas Operations and Book-Tax Differences

Non-U.S. operations account for a large portion of the permanent book-tax differences of U.S. business entities. These differences may relate to different tax bases, different tax rate structures, or special provisions concerning tax-based financing with the other country. For instance, lower tax rates applied by Ireland, Bermuda, and the Netherlands recently reduced Apple's current-year tax rate by about 25%.

Tax planning strategies using non-U.S. operations also are found in the deferred tax asset and liability accounts. For example, IBM recently reported a deferred tax asset relating to delays in using its FTCs amounting to about $900 million. For the operating arm of General Electric, that amount was about $1.5 billion.

Controlled Foreign Corporations

To minimize current U.S. tax liability, taxpayers often attempt to shift the income-generating activity to a foreign entity, often in a low-tax-rate country. For example, a U.S. person can create a foreign holding company to own the stock of foreign operating affiliates or intangible assets, such as patents and trademarks. A non-U.S. corporation also can be used to accumulate income from sales or service activities by acting as an intermediary between the U.S. corporation and an offshore customer. The subsidiary would be used to purchase goods from the U.S. parent or domestic affiliates and then resell the goods to overseas customers or provide services on behalf of the U.S. parent or affiliates.

In some cases, the use of intermediate overseas subsidiaries is based on a substantive business purpose. In other cases, they are employed only to reduce the present value of income tax costs. Because of this potential for abuse, Congress has enacted various provisions to limit the use of income-shifting techniques.

The most important of these provisions are those affecting **controlled foreign corporations (CFCs)**. Subpart F of the Code provides that certain types of "tainted" income generated by CFCs are included in current-year gross income by the U.S. shareholders, without regard to actual distributions. U.S. shareholders must include in gross income their pro rata share of **Subpart F income**. This rule applies to U.S. shareholders who own stock in the corporation on the last day of the tax year or on the last day the foreign corporation is a CFC. Subpart F and CFC rules thus create an immediate "flow-through" of taxable income from the foreign subsidiary to its U.S. shareholders.

Jordan, Ltd., a calendar year foreign corporation, is a CFC for the entire tax year. Taylor, Inc., a U.S. corporation, owns 60% of Jordan's one class of stock for the entire year. Jordan earned $100,000 of Subpart F income for the year and makes no actual distributions during the year. Taylor, a calendar year taxpayer, includes $60,000 in gross income as a constructive dividend for the tax year.

To the extent Jordan has paid any foreign income taxes, Taylor may claim an indirect foreign tax credit for the portion of the foreign taxes related to the $60,000 constructive dividend.

What Is a CFC? A CFC is any non-U.S. corporation in which U.S. shareholders own on any day during the foreign corporation's taxable year more than 50 percent of the total combined voting power of all classes of voting stock, or the total value of the stock of the corporation. The offshore subsidiaries of most multinational U.S. parent corporations are CFCs. About 100,000 CFCs exist, largely in the United Kingdom, Canada, China, Mexico, Germany, and the Netherlands.

For the purposes of determining whether a foreign corporation is a CFC, a **U.S. shareholder** is a U.S. person who owns, or is considered to own, 10 percent or more of the total combined voting power of all classes of voting stock of the foreign corporation. Stock owned directly, indirectly, and constructively is counted. Indirect ownership involves stock held through a foreign entity, such as a foreign corporation, foreign partnership, or foreign trust. This stock is considered to be actually owned proportionately by the shareholders, partners, or beneficiaries.

Subpart F Income Only certain income earned by the CFC triggers immediate U.S. taxation as a constructive dividend. This tainted income, often referred to as *Subpart F income*, can be characterized as income that is easily shifted or has little or no economic connection with the CFC's country of incorporation. Examples include:

- Passive/portfolio income such as interest, dividends, rents, and royalties.
- Sales income where neither the manufacturing activity nor the customer base is in the CFC's country and either the property supplier or the customer is related to the CFC.
- Service income where the CFC is providing services on behalf of its U.S. owners outside the CFC's country.

Concept Summary 16.1 illustrates the events involved in creating Subpart F income.

Concept Summary 16.1

Subpart F Income and a CFC

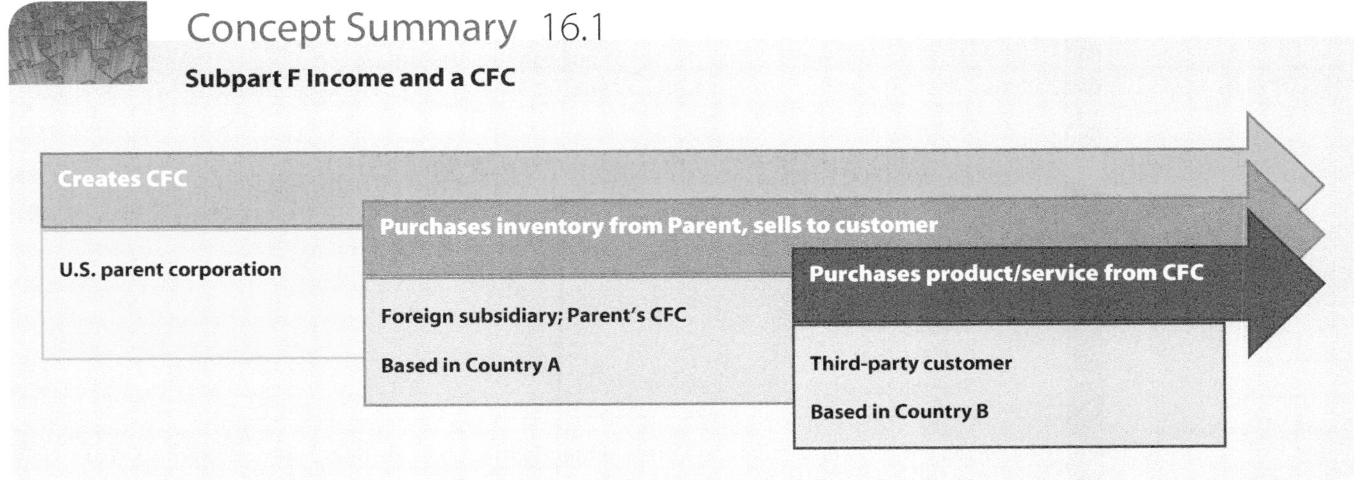

Subpart F Income

Example 15

Collins, Inc., a domestic corporation, sells $1,000,000 of its products to customers in Europe. All manufacturing and sales activities take place in the United States. Collins has no employees, assets, or operations in Europe and thus is not subject to income tax in any European jurisdiction.

Collins, Inc. (U.S. Corporation)
$1,000,000 Sale of Inventory
Non-U.S. Customers

Collins reported the following tax consequences from these inventory sales.

Sales revenue	$1,000,000
Cost of goods sold	(600,000)
Net income	$ 400,000
U.S. tax at 21%	$ 84,000

Assume that Collins instead creates a wholly owned foreign subsidiary in the Cayman Islands, where no income taxes are imposed on corporate income. Collins then sells the inventory to the subsidiary at an intercompany transfer price of $700,000, and the subsidiary sells the inventory to the ultimate European customers for $1,000,000. The subsidiary does not further process the inventory and is only minimally involved in the sales function; Collins's employees arrange the transactions with the ultimate customers. In essence, the sale to the subsidiary can be seen as a "paper" transaction.

continued

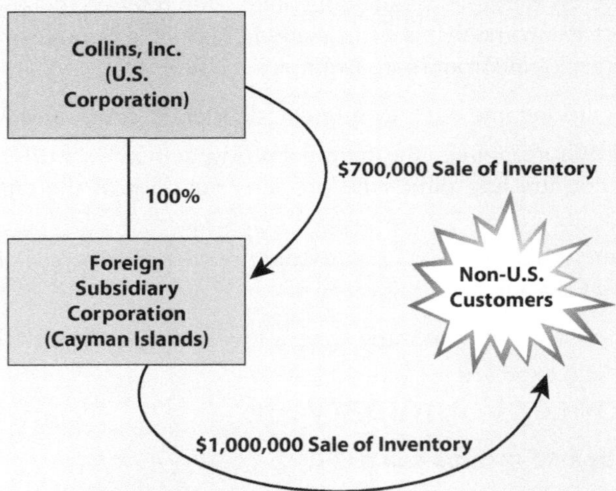

If there were no tax law restrictions, this structure would create the following tax consequences.

	Collins, Inc.	Foreign Subsidiary
Sales revenue	$ 700,000	$1,000,000
Cost of goods sold	(600,000)	(700,000)
Net income	$ 100,000	$ 300,000
U.S. tax at 21%	$ 21,000	
Foreign tax at 0%		$ -0-

Because the Cayman subsidiary is not engaged in a U.S. trade or business, it is not subject to any U.S. tax on its income. Thus, at first glance, it appears that using the foreign subsidiary significantly reduces Collins's current tax cost from $84,000 to $21,000.

However, Collins will find this strategy attacked by the U.S. taxing authorities on two fronts, either of which results in the loss of all or most of the tax savings.

First, the IRS may use the transfer pricing rules of § 482 to claim that the $700,000 intercompany transfer price between Collins and its subsidiary is not a correct **arm's length price**. The IRS may claim that the transfer price should be $1,000,000 because the subsidiary does not add any value to the inventory through further processing or sales activities and all of the risks of the transaction are borne by Collins. With this transfer pricing adjustment, Collins will record a $400,000 profit from the sales and the same $84,000 tax cost as if it had not used the foreign subsidiary as an intermediary.

Second, under the Subpart F rules, the subsidiary's $300,000 income creates a constructive dividend for Collins, thus producing a $63,000 tax cost ($300,000 × 21%). Combined with its original $21,000 tax, Collins's total tax cost for the sales is $84,000 ($21,000 + $63,000), and the use of the foreign subsidiary does not achieve any tax savings.

Example 16

Assume that in Example 15, Collins's foreign subsidiary instead was incorporated in Ireland, where the tax rate on such sales income is 12.5%. The subsidiary purchases raw materials from Collins and performs substantial manufacturing activity in Ireland before selling the inventory to customers in Hong Kong.

In this case, the sales income is not Subpart F income. Because of the substantial activity provided by the Ireland subsidiary, there is economic substance to the non-U.S. entity that generates the income.

The fact that the Irish subsidiary pays a substantially lower tax rate than the U.S. parent does not by itself trigger a constructive dividend. However, Collins must still document the appropriateness of its intercompany transfer price on raw material sales to its Irish subsidiary.

Additional coverage of transfer pricing can be found on this book's companion website: www.cengage.com

3 Digging Deeper

Subpart F Income—Summary The Subpart F and CFC rules create an immediate flow-through of Federal taxable income, regardless of whether distributions are made to the U.S. shareholder. This is similar to the income treatment of partnerships, S corporations, and similar entities. See Chapters 14 and 15.

Any time a CFC earns income that has little economic connection to its local country, the income potentially can create a constructive dividend to the CFC's U.S. shareholders. Alternatively, if the CFC is actively generating the income, it likely escapes the definition of Subpart F income.

Murphy, Inc., a U.S. corporation owns all of GreenCo, Ltd., an Irish manufacturing corporation, and SwissCo, a Swiss distribution corporation. Both GreenCo and SwissCo are CFCs. GreenCo sells its inventory production to SwissCo. SwissCo sells the inventory to unrelated customers located in Switzerland, Italy, and Germany.

Because SwissCo does not manufacture the inventory and acquires it from a related supplier, any sales to customers outside Switzerland will produce Subpart F income and a constructive dividend to Murphy, Inc. This is true even though SwissCo is engaged in an active business and is not merely a "paper" corporation. To avoid Subpart F treatment, Murphy, Inc., could create a distribution company within each country where it operates to sell to customers only within that country.

Additional Tax for Base Erosion The Code provides another sanction for large C corporations that appear to shift "too much" taxable income to other countries where a lower income tax rate may be available. The *base erosion anti-abuse* provision applies to U.S. and non-U.S. corporations with average annual gross receipts of at least $500 million for the prior three tax years.

An alternative tax computation applies to the entity when "excessive" deductible interest, rents, royalties, management fees, and similar payments are made to a related (25 percent ownership) non-U.S. person; such payments often are used to shift taxable income to the country where the payment is received. If these base erosion items total at least 3 percent of total deductible expenses for the year, the entity pays a Federal corporate income tax equal to the *greater of* the corporation's regular tax liability, or:

10% ⊗ **Taxable income (after adding back the base erosion items)**

The base erosion tax is similar in nature to provisions adopted in the last decade by other developed countries that want to keep the income tax base indicative of where multinational profits are earned. The provisions effectively act as a minimum tax to keep a taxpayer from unduly reducing its U.S. taxable income to zero (or close to it) by using income-shifting deductions and other devices with a related party.

The tax sometimes is called the "BEAT," or the base erosion anti-abuse tax. Base erosion items do not include those related to cost of goods sold or those where a withholding tax already applies. The 10 percent tax rate increases to 12.5 percent after 2025.

Special Tax Rate for Intangible Income

The U.S. tax law provides an extra incentive for domestic C corporations to generate taxable income overseas in the form of intangible income, with most personnel and activities still in the United States. A lower tax rate (effectively 13.125 percent) applies to income from intangible assets that the U.S. entity employs overseas. The discounted tax rate is meant to encourage U.S. C corporations to conduct international business that leverages U.S. expertise (especially in technological fields) in profitable operations around the world. The lower tax rate is meant to affect how domestic C corporations position their assets and personnel in various countries.

Tax Fact The Inbound Sector

Inbound corporate operations produce a small but significant portion of U.S. income tax collections.

With a lower income tax rate applying after 2017 to inbound transactions, perhaps the amount of taxable income attracted from these sources will increase over time.

Number of Forms 1120-F filed	20,000
Taxable income reported	$9.1 billion
Net tax liability	$3.4 billion

The special tax rate does not apply to income that otherwise is taxed under Subpart F. The base for the lower tax rate, sometimes known as foreign-derived intangible income (FDII), is limited to the entity's foreign-source taxable income for the year.

LO.4

Describe the tax effects related to the U.S. operations of a non-U.S. taxpayer.

Inbound Issues

Generally, only the U.S.-source income of nonresident alien individuals and foreign corporations is subject to U.S. taxation. This reflects the reach of the U.S. tax jurisdiction. This constraint, however, does not prevent the United States from also taxing the foreign-source income of nonresident alien individuals and foreign corporations when that income is effectively connected with the conduct of a U.S. trade or business.

A **nonresident alien (NRA)** is an individual who is not a citizen or resident of the United States. *Citizenship* is determined under the immigration and naturalization laws of the United States. A person is treated as a *resident* of the United States for income tax purposes if he or she meets either the green card test or the substantial presence test. If either of these tests is met for the calendar year, the individual is deemed a U.S. resident for the year.

Two important definitions determine the U.S. tax consequences to non-U.S. persons with U.S.-source income: "the conduct of a U.S. trade or business" and "**effectively connected income**." Specifically, for a foreign person's noninvestment income to be subject to U.S. taxation, the non-U.S. person must be considered engaged in a U.S. trade or business and must earn income effectively connected with that business.

General criteria for determining whether a U.S. trade or business exists include the location of production activities, management, distribution activities, and other business functions. The Code does not explicitly define a U.S. trade or business, but case law has described the concept as activities carried on in the United States that are regular, substantial, and continuous.

Once a non-U.S. person is considered engaged in a U.S. trade or business, all U.S.-source income other than investment and capital gain income is considered effectively connected to that trade or business and is therefore subject to U.S. taxation. Effectively connected income is taxed at the same rates that apply to U.S. persons, and deductions for expenses attributable to that income are allowed.

Certain U.S.-source income that is *not* effectively connected with the conduct of a U.S. trade or business is subject to a flat 30 percent tax. This income includes dividends, certain interest, rents, royalties, certain compensation, premiums, annuities, and other income of this type. This tax generally is levied by a withholding mechanism that requires the payors of the income to withhold 30 percent of gross amounts (or a lower rate as established by a treaty). This method improves the collectability of Federal taxes from nonresidents and non-U.S. corporations.

Robert, a citizen and resident of New Zealand, produces wine for export. During the current year, Robert earns $500,000 from exporting wine to unrelated wholesalers in the United States. The title to the wine passes to the U.S. wholesalers in New York. Robert has no offices or employees in the United States. The income from the wine sales is U.S.-source income, but because Robert is not engaged in a U.S. trade or business, the income is not subject to taxation in the United States.

Robert begins operating a hot dog cart in New York City. This activity constitutes a U.S. trade or business. Consequently, all U.S.-source income other than investment income is taxed in the United States as income effectively connected with a U.S. trade or business. Thus, both the hot dog cart profits and the $500,000 in wine income are taxed in the United States.

Several exceptions exempt non-U.S. persons from U.S. taxation on their U.S. investment income that is not connected with a U.S. business. For example, certain U.S.-sourced portfolio debt investments and capital gains (other than gains on U.S. real property investments) are exempt from U.S. tax for most non-U.S. investors. Gains from investments in U.S. real property usually are subject to U.S. income taxation. Concept Summary 16.2 summarizes the U.S. income taxation of non-U.S. persons.

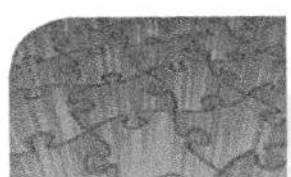

Concept Summary 16.2

U.S. Income Tax Treatment of a Non-U.S. Person's Income*

Type of Income	Tax Rate
U.S.-source investment income	Generally 30% withholding on gross amount (or lower treaty rate) with certain limited exceptions.
U.S.-source income effectively connected with a U.S. trade or business	Regular individual or corporate rates applied against net income (after deductions).
Gain on U.S. real property (direct or indirect ownership)	Taxed as if effectively connected to a U.S. trade or business.
Capital gains (other than on U.S. real property) not effectively connected to a U.S. trade or business	Foreign corporation: Not subject to U.S. tax. Individual: Generally not taxed but may be subject to a 30% U.S. tax if taxpayer is physically present in the United States for 183 days or more in a taxable year.
Foreign-source business income	Generally not subject to U.S. taxation unless attributable to a U.S. office or fixed place of business.

*Subject to change under treaty provisions.

16-3 Crossing State Lines: State and Local Income Taxation in the United States

Few taxpayers sell goods and services solely in the U.S. state where they are based. Sales in other states are attractive for a variety of business reasons, including ease of selling via the internet, the expansion of market share, and the achievement of economies of scale. By extending its operations into other states, a firm may be able to lower its labor and distribution costs, obtain additional sources of long-term debt and equity, and perhaps find a more favorable tax climate.

Many of the same issues discussed earlier in the chapter concerning international operations are encountered when a multistate operation is in place. Both international and multistate operations raise basic questions such as where the transaction is subject to tax and how that jurisdiction's tax rules apply.

However, as state and local income taxation has evolved in the United States, differences in terminology, definitions, and scope of the tax have arisen. In addition, the sheer number of income taxing districts at the state and local levels makes an encounter with the state and local income tax laws of the United States a challenging experience.

16-3a Sources of Law

LO.5

Identify the sources of tax law applicable to a taxpayer operating in more than one U.S. state.

Think of how complicated a tax professional's work would be if there were several hundred different Internal Revenue Codes, each with its own Regulations, rulings, and court decisions. That description is hardly an exaggeration of the state and local income tax law faced by a taxpayer operating in more than one jurisdiction. Unless a

Financial Disclosure Insights Tax Rates in Non-U.S. Jurisdictions

When Congress changes the U.S. tax law, it seldom applies tax rate changes retroactively or prospectively—the rate changes usually are applicable on the date the tax bill is effective. Other countries do not always enact tax law changes in this way. Sometimes a country will adopt a schedule of tax rate increases or decreases to go into effect over a period of years.

Tax legislation of this sort can have an important effect on the U.S. taxpayer's effective tax rate as computed in the footnotes to the financial statements. When another country adopts prospective tax rate changes, an increase or a decrease in the effective tax rate is reported with respect to the deferred tax accounts for GAAP purposes. Specifically, the effective tax rate decreases when a tax rate cut is scheduled in a country that does business with the U.S. party, and the rate increases when a tax rate increase is adopted for future tax years. In the last three decades, most developed countries have been cutting business income tax rates.

firm's salable goods or services are designed, made, and sold strictly within one taxing jurisdiction, the multistate regime comes into effect.

Almost every U.S. state taxes the recognized income of proprietors, corporations, and other entities that have a presence in the state.[7] All of those states have constitutional provisions allowing an income tax and aggregated legislation defining the tax base, specifying when the tax is due and from whom, and otherwise administering the tax. A separate revenue department interprets the law and administers the annual taxing process.

Every one of these systems is distinct and different in multiple ways—the name and location of the chief tax official, the definitions of what is taxable and deductible and what is not, the due dates and filing requirements applicable to the tax, and the taxpayer-friendliness of the audit and appeals system.

Tax Fact State Tax Revenue Sources

The corporate income tax accounts for only a small portion of total tax revenues of the states. Each year, over $2 trillion in taxes are collected by the states (i.e., more than $6,000 per U.S. individual). Property taxes typically are collected by cities, counties, and other local-level jurisdictions.

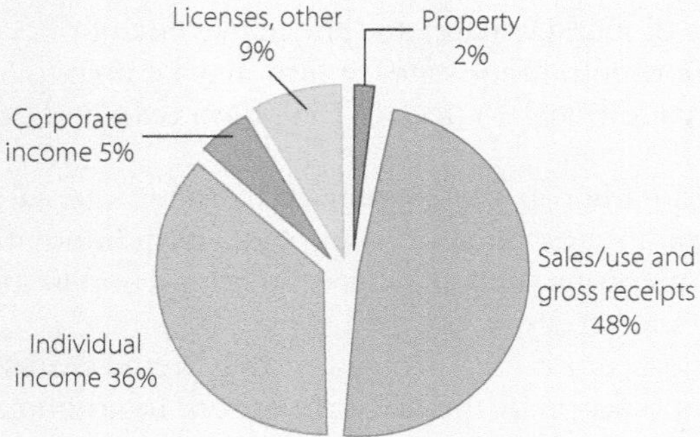

Source: U.S. Census Bureau, 2020 State Government Tax Tables; **https://www.census.gov/data/tables/2020/econ/stc/2020-annual.html**.

[7]Some states tax the investment income of individuals, but those taxes are not addressed in this chapter. Nevada, South Dakota, Washington, and Wyoming do not have a corporate income tax. Washington uses a business and occupation tax; a few states impose a tax on the gross receipts (not on the net income) of a business.

Income taxes are levied by states, cities, counties, villages, commuter districts, school districts, stadium boards, and numerous other bodies that have been granted such taxing authority by their states. By one estimate, a business taxpayer might possibly be exposed to over 1,000 different income taxing jurisdictions in the United States at the state and local levels. Politicians often think they can gain economic development advantages over neighboring states by granting special tax breaks—"Locate your assembly plant here, and we'll reduce your property taxes for five years." Economic development goals, as well as fluctuating needs to either increase or decrease tax revenues, mean that state and local tax laws are constantly changing.

The Federal government has mostly stayed out of the fray and not attempted to force states and localities to use a single common tax formula and administrative organization. Only in **Public Law 86–272** (P.L. 86–272) has Congress attempted to bring consistency to the multistate income tax process. This 1959 law prohibits a state from imposing income taxes on a business if the only contact in the state is **solicitation of orders** for sales of tangible personal property by employees that are approved and shipped from outside the state.

Still, the states have taken some steps to coordinate their activities. Several groups of states exchange information as to the seller and purchase price for cross-border sales so that income and sales/use tax obligations can be computed and collected properly. A few states have reciprocity arrangements with their neighbors to straighten out the complications that can arise when an employee lives in one jurisdiction but works in another.

Harry works at the Illinois plant of Big Corporation, but he lives in Iowa. His wages are subject to Iowa tax. If Illinois and Iowa had a reciprocity agreement in place, either (1) Big would collect income tax at Iowa's rates and remit the tax to the Iowa revenue department or (2) Big would collect Illinois tax, and that state would keep the withholdings paid, in full satisfaction of Harry's Iowa tax obligations for the year.

About half of the states are members of the **Multistate Tax Commission (MTC)**, a body that proposes legislation to the states and localities and issues its own regulations and informational materials. A majority of the non-MTC members also follow the agency's rules virtually without exception. The Uniform Division of Income for Tax Purposes Act (UDITPA) is made available to states and localities interested in a coherent set of income assignment rules, and it forms the basis for the income tax statutes in most of the MTC member states.

The MTC, which provides very specific formulas and definitions to be used in computing state taxable income, is as close as the states have come so far to a multilateral tax treaty process. If all states and localities followed all of the MTC rules, taxpayers would be unable to gain any "border advantages" or disadvantages. But political concerns likely will keep this coordinated result from ever happening.

16-3b Tax Issues

The key issues facing a state or locality in drafting and implementing an income tax model are the same as those facing the international tax community. The results of the deliberative process, though, have produced somewhat different sets of rules and terminology.

Authority to Tax

A business is taxable in the state in which it is resident, organized, or incorporated. Tax liabilities also arise in other jurisdictions where **nexus** exists; that is, a sufficient presence in the other state has been established on an ongoing basis. Such presence might come about because the corporation was organized there, the proprietor lives there, an in-state customer made a purchase, or the business employed people or equipment within the borders of the state. The precise activities that create nexus vary from jurisdiction to jurisdiction, although states must follow P.L. 86–272 and the regulations of the MTC (although some MTC states may have modified model provisions of UDITPA).[8]

When a taxpayer operates in more than one state, total taxable income for the year is split among the jurisdictions in which the operations take place. Portions of the total income amount are assigned to each of the business locations, so several tax returns and payments will be due. For a taxpayer considering an expansion of operations, the tax adviser can make an important contribution in helping to decide with which state(s) nexus will be created.

The nexus rules of state/local taxation serve much the same function as do the permanent establishment provisions of international taxation. The PE standards are based in the language of the applicable tax treaty and interpretive court decisions. They look for real estate holdings and manufacturing equipment. Permanent establishment is found when an office in the host country participates significantly in the making of a sales or service contract.

Digging Deeper 4

For insights on state tax and modernizing tax laws, visit this book's companion website: www.cengage.com

LO.6

Apply principles designed to compute state taxable income for a taxpayer operating in more than one U.S. state.

Income Measurement

The multistate business, like its international counterpart, must divide the taxable income generated for the year among the states in which it operates. Then tax liability is computed for the states in which nexus has been established. The computational template illustrated in Exhibit 16.3 indicates how most states derive their shares of the entity's aggregate taxable income. Usually, the starting point for this computation is Federal taxable income.

State modification items come about because each state creates its own tax base in the legislative process, and some of the rules adopted may differ from those used in the Internal Revenue Code. The modification items reflect such differences in the tax base. For example, modifications might be created to reflect the following differences between state and Federal taxable income.

- The state might allow a different cost recovery or depreciation schedule.
- The state might tax interest income from its own bonds or from those of other states.
- The state might allow a deduction for Federal income taxes paid.

Exhibit 16.3 **Computing State Corporate Income Tax Liability**

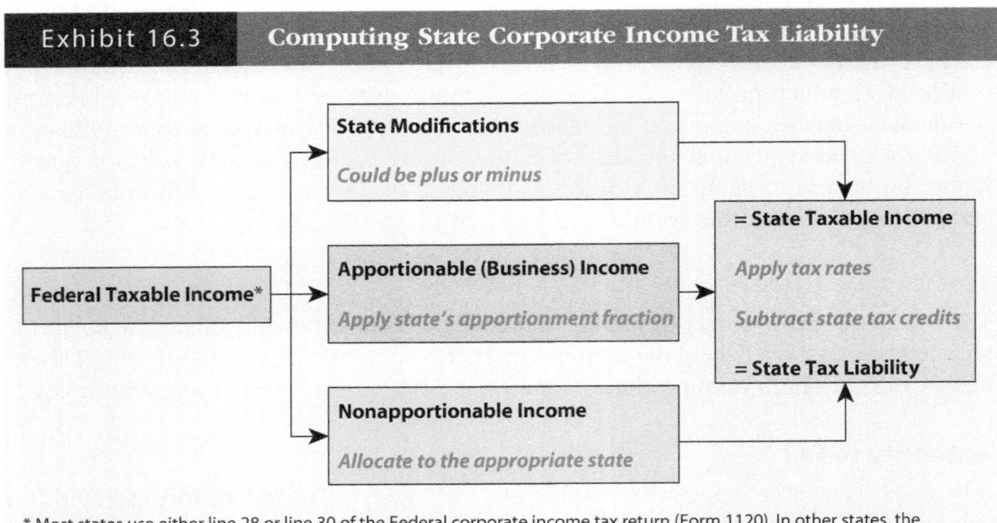

* Most states use either line 28 or line 30 of the Federal corporate income tax return (Form 1120). In other states, the corporation is required to identify and report each element of income and deduction on the state return.

[8]Income and sales/use tax regimes use different nexus standards in most states. This chapter concentrates on income tax nexus provisions.

Tax Planning Strategies **Nexus: To Have or Have Not**

Framework Focus: Tax Rate

Strategy: Shift Net Income from High-Tax Jurisdictions to Low-Tax Jurisdictions.

Most taxpayers try to avoid establishing nexus in a new state, for example, by giving a sales representative a cash auto allowance rather than a company car, by restricting the location of inventory to only a few states, or by limiting a salesperson's activities to those that are protected by the solicitation standard of P.L. 86–272. This effort to avoid nexus stems in part from the additional compliance burden that falls on the taxpayer when a new set of income tax returns, information forms, and deadlines must be dealt with in the new state.

Another concern is that the marginal tax rate that applies to the net taxable income generated by the taxpayer may increase. Such a tax increase occurs, of course, only when the applicable tax rate in the new state is higher than the rate that would apply in the home state. If a business already is based in a low-tax state, its aggregate tax liability is sure to increase.

Still, nexus is not necessarily a bad thing. Consider what happens if a business based in California, Massachusetts, Illinois, or another high-tax jurisdiction purposely creates nexus in a low- or no-tax state. If the new state applies a lower marginal rate than is available in the home state or offers special exemptions or exclusions that match the taxpayer's operations, the aggregate tax bill can decrease. Then the planning efforts include determining which activities will *create* nexus in the new jurisdiction and meeting or maintaining that standard.

For instance, an entertainer based in Manhattan is subject to the high income taxes of New York City and New York State. By establishing a permanent office in Tennessee, nexus will be created, and some portion of the taxpayer's income will be subject to taxation there instead of in New York. These are permanent savings, accruing immediately to after-tax income and the share price of the stock of the taxpayer.

- The state might allow a net operating loss (NOL) deduction only for losses generated in the state.
- The state's NOL deduction might reflect different carryover periods than Federal law allows.

State tax modifications are made even if the taxpayer operates only in its home state.

Allocation and Apportionment The next step in computing state taxable income is to **allocate** items of nonbusiness income and loss to the states in which such items are derived. For instance, a Kansas entity might recognize some net income from the rental of a Missouri office building to a tenant. The net rental amount is in Federal taxable income, but it must appear only and fully in Missouri taxable income. So by means of the modification process, the rents are removed from the taxable income for both states and then added back into Missouri taxable income. The allocation process is very much like the income-sourcing procedures employed in international taxation.

HammerCo reports $400,000 in taxable income for the year from its sales operations based exclusively in State A and State B. HammerCo recognized net rent income of $60,000 from a building it owns in State A. It earned $20,000 in interest income from State B bonds. This amount is excluded from Federal taxable income, and it is taxed under State A law but not by State B. HammerCo also claimed a Federal NOL carryforward of $75,000 from a prior period. State A follows Federal law for NOLs, but State B does not allow such carryovers. Thus, Federal taxable income totals $385,000 ($400,000 + $60,000 − $75,000).

continued

HammerCo's modifications to determine the state tax base, after starting with Federal taxable income, are as follows.

State A		State B	
Amount	**Modification**	**Amount**	**Modification**
− $60,000	Total nonbusiness income	− $60,000	Total nonbusiness income
+ $20,000	Municipal bond interest income	+ $75,000	Remove Federal NOL deduction
+ $60,000	Net rent income from State A rentals		

The business income of the taxpayer is **apportioned** among the states in which it operates. The apportionment percentage for the state is multiplied times the apportionable income of the taxpayer to measure the extent of the taxpayer's exposure to the state's income tax. The application of the apportionment percentage is illustrated in Exhibit 16.3.

Most states apply an apportionment procedure involving three factors, each meant to estimate the taxpayer's relative activities in the state.

- The **sales factor** = In-state sales/total sales.
- The **payroll factor** = In-state payroll/total payroll.
- The **property factor** = In-state property/total property.

The state's apportionment percentage is the average of these three factors. This three-factor apportionment can be traced to the earliest days of state income taxation. Today most states require the taxpayer to add additional weight to the sales factor, believing it to be the most accurate and measurable reflection of the taxpayer's in-state activities. It is common to "double-weight" the sales factor, and many states use a sales-factor-only apportionment procedure.

Example 21

LinkCo, Inc., operates in two states. It reports the following results for the year. LinkCo's apportionment percentages for both states are computed as shown. Amounts are stated in millions of dollars.

	State A	State B	Totals
Sales	$30	$20	$50
Payroll	40	20	60
Property	45	5	50
Sales factor	$30/$50 = 0.6	$20/$50 = 0.4	
Payroll factor	$40/$60 = 0.67	$20/$60 = 0.33	
Property factor	$45/$50 = 0.9	$5/$50 = 0.1	
Apportionment percentage	(0.6 + 0.67 + 0.9) ÷ 3 = 0.72	(0.4 + 0.33 + 0.1) ÷ 3 = 0.28	

Note that 100% of LinkCo's income is apportioned between the two states: 72% to State A and 28% to State B.

Now assume that State A double-weights the sales factor. LinkCo's apportionment percentages are computed as follows.

	State A	State B	Totals
Sales	$30	$20	$50
Payroll	40	20	60
Property	45	5	50
Sales factor	$30/$50 = 0.6	$20/$50 = 0.4	
Payroll factor	$40/$60 = 0.67	$20/$60 = 0.33	
Property factor	$45/$50 = 0.9	$5/$50 = 0.1	
Apportionment percentage	(0.6 + 0.6 + 0.67 + 0.9) ÷ 4 = 0.69	(0.4 + 0.33 + 0.1) ÷ 3 = 0.28	

continued

State B's apportionment computations are not affected by A's double-weighting of the sales factor. The percentages now do not total 100%. The effect of the special weighting is to reduce LinkCo's tax liability in A. This is likely LinkCo's "home state" given the location of its personnel and plant and equipment.

Finally, assume that State B uses a "sales-factor-only" weighting. The A apportionment percentage is 0.69, and the B percentage is 0.4. Now the apportionment percentages *exceed* 100%.

Many states follow the regulations of the MTC and the outline of the UDITPA in defining and applying the apportionment factors. But because the states do not follow identical rules in the makeup of the factors, the apportionment percentages seldom total precisely to 100 percent of Federal taxable income. Some other aspects of the three-factor approach include the following.

- Sales are assigned using the tax accounting methods of the taxpayer. Sales are assigned using the "ultimate destination" concept; that is, a sale is usually assigned to the state of the purchaser.
- If a sale is made into a state with no income tax or a state with which the taxpayer has not established nexus, tax is likely escaped. But over a third of the states apply a **throwback rule** that causes the sale to be sourced to the state of the seller (i.e., by overriding the "ultimate destination" rule).
- Payroll is assigned to the state in which the employee's services primarily are performed. Payroll includes wages, bonuses, commissions, and taxable fringe benefits. Some states exclude officer compensation because it can distort the computations. Some states exclude contributions to a § 401(k) plan.
- The property factor uses an average historical cost basis, net of accumulated depreciation. Idle property is ignored, but construction in progress is included. Property in transit is assigned to the state of its presumed destination.
- Property leased but not owned by the taxpayer is included in the property factor at eight times the annual rentals paid.

Many states use specialized apportionment percentages for industries whose sales and asset profile is not properly reflected in the traditional three-factor formula. For instance, the airline industry might divide its income based on passenger-miles beginning and ending in the state. Truckers might be able to divide taxable income among the states based on in-state vehicle-trips or tons-per-day. Communications companies might use the in-state miles of cable or number of wireless devices to make up an apportionment formula.

The Unitary Theory About 30 states use or allow a **unitary approach** in computing the apportionment factors. Conglomerates are required, or can elect, to base their computations on the data for all of their affiliated corporations, not just the legal entities that do business with the state. Affiliates included under the unitary theory share a majority ownership with a parent or group of shareholders. They also often share data processing, sales force, and marketing resources.

The *combined return* that the unitary business files includes much more data than might be expected on a separate-entity basis, but the taxing jurisdictions often believe that the unitary figures offer a more accurate reflection of the taxpayer's activity within the state and that, therefore, a more accurate tax liability can be derived.

Financial Disclosure Insights State/Local Taxes and the Tax Expense

In applying GAAP principles for a business entity, state and local tax expenses are found in several places in the taxpayer's financial reports. In the tax footnote, the state/local tax costs often are reported in dollar and/or percentage terms in both current and deferred components. The following are examples of state/local tax expenses that were reported for 2020.

	Current State/Local Tax Expense ($ million)	Deferred State/Local Tax Expense ($ million)
Eli Lilly	($47.3)	($20.5)
eBay	87.0	(8.0)
Netflix	65.8	164.7
Ford Motor	(6.0)	12.0

Example 22

Kipp Industries is a holding company for three subsidiaries: GrapeCo operating in California, PotatoCo operating in Idaho, and BratCo operating in Germany. Only GrapeCo has nexus with California. But because California is a unitary state, the California apportionment percentage is computed also using PotatoCo and BratCo data.

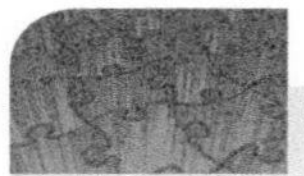

Concept Summary 16.3

Corporate Multistate Income Taxation

1. A taxpayer is subject to income tax in the state in which it resides or is organized.
2. A taxpayer is subject to income tax in states where it has a business presence and enjoys the resources of the host state in conducting its operations.
3. A multistate taxpayer must divide its aggregate taxable income for the year among the states in which it conducts business.
4. Nonbusiness income is allocated to the state in which it is generated.
5. Business income is apportioned among the states in which the taxpayer has nexus.
6. Apportionment usually is conducted using a formula based on the relative sales, employment, and asset holdings in the various states.
7. Most states weight the sales factor higher than the other apportionment factors.
8. Some states apply a special apportionment formula for certain industries when the traditional three-factor formula could distort the income division procedure in some way.
9. About 30 states employ the unitary theory in deriving the apportionment factors, using the data from a group of corporations to compute the apportionment formula. Other states allow or require a consolidated return from a conglomerate.

Digging Deeper 5

Information on unclaimed property as a revenue source can be found on this book's companion website: www.cengage.com

Tax Planning Strategies Where Should My Income Go?

Framework Focus: Tax Rate

Strategy: Shift Net Income from High-Tax Jurisdictions to Low-Tax Jurisdictions.

Every state defines its apportionment factors in a slightly different manner. The multistate taxpayer needs to keep track of these differences and place activities in the state that will serve them best.

Planning with the sales factor includes a detailed analysis of the destination point of the product shipments for the year, especially when the firm has customers in low- and no-tax states. The property factor should include only assets that are used in the taxpayer's trade or business, not the investment, leasing, or research functions. Permanently idle property is excluded from the property factor as well. The payroll factor can be manipulated by hiring independent contractors to carry out certain sales and distribution work or by relocating highly paid managers to low-tax states.

By setting up an investment holding company in a no- or low-tax state such as Delaware or Nevada and transferring income-producing securities and intangible assets to that entity, significant tax reductions can be obtained. When the net investment income is paid back to the parent corporation, the dividends received deduction eliminates the tax liability there.

Use of the unitary system does not always result in a tax increase, although the additional record-keeping burden of operating in a unitary state cannot be understated. If the affiliates make available less profitable operations or a presence in low- or no-tax states or countries, the current tax liability may be reduced. The record-keeping burden can be reduced if the taxpayer makes a **waters'-edge election**, which allows it to include only affiliate data from within the boundaries of the United States.

Return to the facts of Example 22. If Kipp Industries files a waters'-edge election, the unitary group that files a California income tax return can be limited to GrapeCo and PotatoCo since BratCo operates outside the United States.

16-4 Common Challenges

Synthesize key aspects of international and multistate tax systems to identify common rules and issues taxpayers face in both systems.

Practical and policy issues facing the U.S. states, developed countries, and the taxpayers operating in all of them show a great degree of similarity between the multistate and international tax regimes. Terminology may differ, and the evolution of tax solutions may take radically different paths, but the key issues that face the multijurisdictional community are at once challenging and rewarding.

16-4a Authority to Tax

The old-economy orientation of the nexus and permanent establishment rules presents great difficulty in today's economy, as jurisdictions attempt to describe the income and sales/use tax base fairly. An electronic presence also uses the resources of the host country and should trigger a tax in the visited jurisdiction. Mathematically, the apportionment and sourcing rules should result in some tax liability in the host jurisdiction. It is improper to maintain that no presence exists and no tax should be paid when a business has customers in a state.

The notion of *physical presence* as the only factor giving a state the authority to tax is becoming less important over time. For example, just-in-time manufacturing and purchasing strategies reduce the need for warehousing by some taxpayers. Human capital can be dispersed through telecommuting, video conferencing,

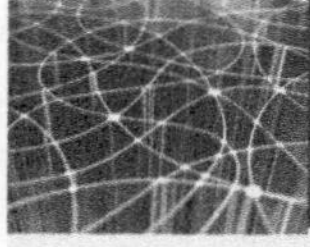

Bridge Discipline **Bridge to Cost Accounting and Executive Compensation**

Multijurisdictional companies operate across state and country borders. The transfer price used by a company can have a significant effect on the amount of profits subject to taxation within a particular taxing jurisdiction. Companies face other concerns when establishing transfer pricing policies. For example, the internal determination of how a division of the company is performing may be based on transfer pricing between related entities within the global group. Furthermore, the compensation of the managers within those divisions may be tied directly to divisional performance.

If an intercompany price is set in a manner that optimizes the global tax position, a separate cost accounting policy may be required to determine an entity's profitability for purposes of compensating employees. Tax advisers often face resistance from operations managers when suggesting improved transfer pricing methods, because such improvements often change the traditional division of profits among different parts of the business.

and project rotation using work-group software that provides acceptable levels of data security. As business activities become almost exclusively wireless, the standard of presence will likely continue to diminish, since the buyer and the seller are both "everywhere."

Digging Deeper 6 **An overview to modernization of nexus rules can be found on this book's companion website: www.cengage.com**

16-4b **Division of Income**

The multistate apportionment procedure could use an overhaul. The fact that a majority of states change the weighting of the sales factor indicates that some other income division method might better serve taxpayers and governments. Three-factor apportionment was designed for an age of traveling sales representatives and sales of built, grown, and manufactured goods. Sales reps were assigned territories they could drive through on short notice, so they usually lived close to their customer base. In that case, the sales and payroll factors could be highly redundant.

Today, with communication and distribution systems more highly developed, the sales factor appears incrementally to be the preferred income-sourcing device; this resembles a customer-based sourcing rule. Sales of goods and services should be assigned based on a destination test so that the transaction is assigned to the state of the purchaser.

The three-factor formula further breaks down for income derived from specialized industries, as evidenced by the special computational methods allowed by many states. Perhaps the economy is so specialized today that income simply cannot be assigned by the use of one simple formula. Nonetheless, more uniformity among the states as to definitions and computational rules for the factors would be welcome.

The U.S. Treasury has held hearings in the last decade concerning the adoption of an apportionment approach to the sourcing of international taxable income. Although formulary apportionment would represent a more reliable and predictable method of dividing multinational income and deduction amounts, the data collection burden that such a system would create may be too much to expect from most of the trading partners in the short term.

16-4c **Transfer Pricing**

The transfer pricing system used in international trade requires the taxpayer to keep a database of comparable prices and transactions, even though often no such comparability exists. Especially when dealing with proprietary goods and design, it may be impossible to find comparable goods and, therefore, an acceptable transfer price for them. One solution to this situation would be to allow additional definitions of comparable

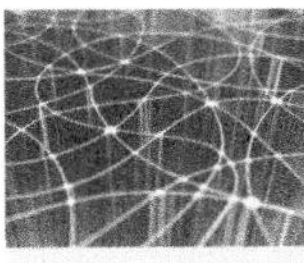

Bridge Discipline **Bridge to Economic Development and Political Science**

The tax professional occasionally is in a position to negotiate with a state or city taxing jurisdiction to garner tax relief for a client as an incentive to locate a plant or distribution center in that geographic area. In times when construction budgets are high and interstate competition is fierce to attract or retain businesses that are making location decisions, such tax concessions can be significant.

For instance, to encourage a business to build a large distribution center in the area, community leaders might be agreeable to:

- Paying for roads, sewer, water, and other improvements through taxpayer bonds;
- Reducing property taxes by 50 percent for the first 10 years of the center's operations; and
- Permanently excluding any distribution-related vehicles and equipment from the personal property tax.

An incentive-granting community provides the concessions even though the influx of new workers will place a great strain on public school facilities and likely necessitate improvements in traffic patterns and other infrastructure.

Consider the position of a large employer that has been located in the area for more than 50 years. By how much should it be willing to absorb the tax increases that result when economic development concessions are used to attract new, perhaps temporary, businesses to the area? Should the employer challenge the constitutionality of the grant of such sizable tax breaks to some, but not all, business taxpayers in the jurisdiction? Should higher "impact fees" be assessed on new developments?

Does your analysis change if the new business competes with the longtime resident for sales? For employees? For political power?

goods, or of ranges of acceptable transfer prices, perhaps subjected to audit on a rotating five-year basis. The use of advance pricing agreements further allows a greater degree of control by the governments in data collection and analysis, ideally prior to the undertaking of the sales or manufacturing transactions. The anti-base-erosion tax might restrict these arrangements.

Examples of transfer pricing strategies can be found on this book's companion website: www.cengage.com

7 Digging Deeper

16-4d Tax Havens

When taxpayers perceive effective tax rates as too high, planning usually includes seeking out a **tax haven**. If income-producing securities or profitable service operations can be moved to another jurisdiction, ideally one with significantly lower marginal tax rates on that type of income, permanent tax savings can be achieved. A tax haven usually has adopted rules that allow taxpayers to establish residency with a minimal presence, and the jurisdiction provides little or no cooperation in international exchanges of tax and financial information. The Bahamas, the Netherlands, and the Cayman Islands, among other countries, often are seen as tax havens.

When a government witnesses a loss of its tax base due to the transfer of assets and income out of the jurisdiction, anti-tax-haven legislation is discussed, but it seldom is effective. The U.S. international tax regime shows several distinct attempts to find and tax income moved offshore, but those taxes collect only nominal revenues in the typical tax year. Income-shifting devices currently used by multistate taxpayers have been attacked by the states in various ways, but legislators hesitate to be too aggressive, probably out of fear of the state being branded "anti-business."

Perhaps a separate set of nexus rules could be created to address the most portable types of income, such as that from interest and dividends. But this difficult problem likely needs a multilateral solution, which is unlikely to be found in the short term among states and countries, each with unique revenue shortfalls and political profiles.

16-4e Interjurisdictional Agreements

Treaties are documents that address many issues other than the taxable income computation. They involve several players within the governmental structure, and they take several years to draft and adopt. Tax treaties involving the United States are only bilateral, meaning that it is difficult to anticipate and coordinate the interaction of several treaties as they apply to a single taxpayer.

At the multistate level, the Federal government has been slow to take up issues involving a synchronization of the income tax systems used by the states. Although this reluctance may be partly for strictly constitutional reasons, it exists largely because of the difficulties presented by the lack of uniformity among the states' tax laws and enforcement efforts.

But the future must hold a greater degree of cooperation among various taxing jurisdictions, at least in the trading of information and the coordination of enforcement efforts. The United States must create additional treaties or information-sharing agreements with countries in South America and Africa. Sharing data, while still respecting the confidentiality needs of the taxpayer and requirements of the governments, represents a technologically sound method of collecting taxes in today's multijurisdictional economy.

Refocus on The Big Picture

Going International

MONKEY BUSINESS IMAGES/SHUTTERSTOCK.COM

Income earned from non-U.S. sales is taxed currently to VoiceCo in the United States under the worldwide approach to cross-border income taxation. If VoiceCo receives Subpart F income from its Irish subsidiary, current income taxation results, but VoiceCo can claim foreign tax credits, which help alleviate the double taxation that would otherwise result. Or if the subsidiary pays a dividend to the parent, a 100 percent dividends received deduction may be available, thereby exempting the dividend from current U.S. income taxation.

What If?

VoiceCo is considering building a new manufacturing facility in another state in the United States. How will VoiceCo's expansion decision be affected by state tax considerations? In making the decision to expand, VoiceCo should consider a variety of state tax issues, including whether the state imposes a corporate income tax at all and, if so, whether the state requires unitary reporting. Other relevant issues affecting the tax calculation in the state include what apportionment formula is used by the state, whether the state has a throwback rule, and whether the state will offer tax incentives for the relocation.

Suggested Readings

"Base Erosion and Profit Shifting," **oecd.org/tax/beps/**, 2018.

Daniel and Elke Asen, "International Tax Competitiveness Index," *Tax Foundation*, October 2019.

"State Business Incentives Database," **stateincentives.org**.

Key Terms

Allocate, 16-21
Apportioned, 16-22
Arm's length price, 16-14
Controlled foreign corporations (CFCs), 16-12
Effectively connected income, 16-16
Foreign tax credit (FTC), 16-6
Inbound taxation, 16-3
Income tax treaties, 16-5
Multistate Tax Commission (MTC), 16-19
Nexus, 16-19
Nonresident alien (NRA), 16-16
Outbound taxation, 16-3
Payroll factor, 16-22
Permanent establishment (PE), 16-5
Property factor, 16-22
Public Law 86–272, 16-19
Sales factor, 16-22
Separate foreign tax credit income categories, 16-11
Solicitation of orders, 16-19
Subpart F income, 16-12
Tax haven, 16-27
Throwback rule, 16-23
Unitary approach, 16-23
U.S. shareholder, 16-12
Waters'-edge election, 16-25

Computational Exercises

1. **LO.3** Cordeio, Inc., is a calendar year taxpayer and a CFC for the entire tax year. Yancy Company, a U.S. corporation, owns 75% of Cordeio's one class of stock for the entire year. Cordeio's Subpart F income for the year is $450,000, and no distributions were made to the parent. Determine Yancy's gross income from the Subpart F constructive dividend from Cordeio.

2. **LO.3** Enders, Inc., a domestic corporation, reports $290,000 total taxable income for the year, consisting of $208,800 in U.S.-source business profits and $81,200 of income from foreign investment securities. Overseas tax authorities withheld $24,000 in income taxes on the investment income. Enders's U.S. tax before the FTC is $60,900.
   a. Compute Enders's foreign tax credit for the year.
   b. Express your answer as a Microsoft Excel formula.

3. **LO.6** Castle Corporation conducts business and has nexus in States 1, 2, and 3. All of the states use a three-equal-factors apportionment formula, with the factors evenly weighted. Castle generates $555,000 apportionable income and $75,000 allocable income related to State 3 activities. Castle's sales, payroll, and property are divided evenly among the three states. Compute taxable income for:
   a. State 1.
   b. State 2.
   c. State 3.
   d. Express your computation as a Microsoft Excel formula that will provide the correct solution for all three states.

4. LO.6 Fillon operates manufacturing facilities in States A and B. Fillon has nexus with both states; apportionment factors are 0.70 for A and 0.30 for B. Taxable income for the year totaled $150,000, with a $200,000 A profit and a $50,000 B loss. Calculate taxable income for the year for:
   a. State A.
   b. State B.

5. LO.6 Beckett Corporation has nexus with States A and B. Apportionable income for the year totals $800,000. Beckett's apportionment factors for the year use the following data. Compute Beckett's B taxable income for the year; B uses a three-factor apportionment formula with a double-weighted sales factor.

	State A	State B	Totals
Sales	$960,000	$640,000	$1,600,000
Property	180,000	–0–	180,000
Payroll	220,000	–0–	220,000

6. LO.6 Vogel Corporation owns two subsidiaries. Song, located in State A, generated $500,000 taxable income this year. Bird, located in State B, generated a $100,000 loss for the period.
   a. Determine Song's taxable income in States A and B, assuming that the subsidiaries constitute independent corporations under the tax law.
   b. How does your answer change if the companies constitute a unitary business?

Problems

7. LO.3 BlueCo, a domestic corporation, incorporates GreenCo, a new wholly owned entity in Germany. Under both German and U.S. legal principles, this entity is a corporation. BlueCo faces a 21% U.S. tax rate.

   GreenCo earns $1,500,000 in net profits from its German manufacturing activities, and GreenCo makes no dividend distributions to BlueCo. How much Federal income tax will BlueCo pay for the current year as a result of GreenCo's earnings, assuming that it incurs no deemed dividend under Subpart F?

8. LO.3 Evaluate this statement: It is unfair that the United States taxes some of its citizens and residents on their worldwide income.

9. LO.3 Describe the different approaches used by countries to tax the earnings of their citizens and residents generated outside the borders of the country.

10. LO.3 Chock, a U.S. corporation, purchases inventory for resale from distributors within the United States and resells this inventory at a $1,000,000 profit to customers outside the United States. Title to the goods passes outside the United States. What is the source of Chock's inventory sales income?

11. LO.3 Willa, a U.S. corporation, owns the rights to a patent related to a medical device. Willa licenses the rights to use the patent to IrishCo, which uses the patent in its manufacturing facility located in Ireland. What is the source of the $1,000,000 royalty income Willa received from IrishCo for the use of the patent?

12. LO.3 USCo incurred $100,000 in interest expense for the current year. The tax book value of USCo's assets generating foreign-source income is $5,000,000. The tax book value of USCo's assets generating U.S.-source income is $45,000,000. How much of the interest expense is allocated and apportioned to foreign-source income?

13. **LO.3** QuinnCo could not claim all of the income taxes it paid to Japan as a foreign tax credit (FTC) this year. What computational limit probably kept QuinnCo from taking its full FTC? Explain.

14. **LO.3** FoldIt, a U.S. business, paid income taxes to Mexico relative to profitable sales of shipping boxes it made in that country. Can it claim a deduction for these taxes in computing U.S. taxable income? A tax credit? Both? Explain.

15. **LO.3** ABC, Inc., a domestic corporation, reports $50,000,000 of taxable income, including $15,000,000 of foreign-source taxable income from services rendered, on which ABC paid $2,500,000 in foreign income taxes. The U.S. tax rate is 21%. What is ABC's foreign tax credit?

16. **LO.3** Fleming, Inc., a domestic corporation, operates in both Canada and the United States. This year the business generated taxable income of $400,000 from foreign sources and $300,000 from U.S. sources. All of Fleming's foreign-source income is in the general operating income basket. Fleming's total worldwide taxable income is $700,000. Fleming pays Canadian taxes of $152,000. What is Fleming's allowed FTC for the tax year? Fleming's U.S. tax rate is 21%.

17. **LO.3** Drake, Inc., a U.S. corporation, operates a branch sales office in Turkey. During the current year, Drake earned $500,000 in taxable income from U.S. sources and $100,000 in taxable income from sources in Turkey. Drake paid $40,000 in income taxes to Turkey. All of the income is characterized as general operating income. Compute Drake's U.S. income tax liability after consideration of any foreign tax credit. Drake's U.S. tax rate is 21%.

18. **LO.3** Crank, Inc., a U.S. corporation, operates a branch sales office in Ghana. During the current year, Crank earned $200,000 in taxable income from U.S. sources and $50,000 in taxable income from sources in Ghana. Crank paid $5,000 in income taxes to Ghana. All of the income is characterized as general operating income. Compute Crank's U.S. income tax liability after consideration of any foreign tax credit. Crank's U.S. tax rate is 21%.

19. **LO.3** Night, Inc., a domestic corporation, earned $300,000 from foreign manufacturing activities on which it paid $36,000 of foreign income taxes. Night's foreign sales income is taxed at a 50% foreign tax rate. Both sales and manufacturing income are assigned to the general limitation basket. What amount of foreign sales income can Night earn without generating any excess FTCs for the current year? Assume a 21% U.S. rate. Critical Thinking

20. **LO.3** Orion, Inc., a U.S. corporation, reports foreign-source income and pays foreign taxes for the tax year as follows.

	Income	Taxes
Passive basket	$150,000	$ 13,000
General basket	300,000	150,000

Orion's worldwide taxable income is $600,000, and U.S. taxes before the FTC are $126,000 (assume a 21% rate). What is Orion's U.S. tax liability after the FTC?

21. **LO.3** Discuss the policy reasons for the existence of the Subpart F rules. Give two examples of Subpart F income. Critical Thinking

22. **LO.3** USCo owns 65% of the voting stock of LandCo, a Country X corporation. Terra, an unrelated Country Y corporation, owns the other 35% of LandCo. LandCo owns 100% of the voting stock of OceanCo, a Country Z corporation. Assuming that USCo is a U.S. shareholder, do LandCo and OceanCo meet the definition of a CFC? Explain.

23. **LO.3** Is a foreign corporation owned equally by 100 unrelated U.S. citizens considered to be a controlled foreign corporation (CFC)? Explain.

24. **LO.3** Hart Enterprises, a domestic corporation, owns 100% of OK, Ltd., an Irish corporation. OK's gross income for the year is $10,000,000. Determine whether any of the following transactions produce Subpart F gross income for the current year.
    a. OK earned $600,000 from sales of products purchased from Hart and sold to customers outside Ireland.
    b. OK earned $1,000,000 from sales of products purchased from Hart and sold to customers in Ireland.
    c. OK earned $400,000 from sales of products purchased from unrelated suppliers and sold to customers in Germany.
    d. OK purchased raw materials from Hart, used these materials to manufacture finished goods, and sold these goods to customers in Italy. OK earned $300,000 from these sales.
    e. OK earned $50,000 in dividend income from Canada and Mexico passive investments.

25. **LO.3** HiramCo, a U.S. entity, operates a manufacturing business in both Mexico and Costa Rica, and it holds its investment portfolio in Sweden. How many foreign tax credit computations must HiramCo make? Be specific, and use the term *basket* in your answer.

26. **LO.4** Give a simple answer to Andre's question: "If I move to the United States, how will the Federal government tax my widget sales and capital gains?" Andre will be living in New York City, where state and local taxes are very high. Ignore the effects of tax treaties in your answer.

27. **LO.4** Evaluate the following statement: Non-U.S. persons never are subject to U.S. taxation on U.S.-source investment income so long as they are not engaged in a U.S. trade or business.

Communications

28. **LO.3, 4** Write a memo for the tax research file on the difference between "inbound" and "outbound" activities in the context of U.S. taxation of international income.

29. **LO.4** Velocity, Inc., a non-U.S. corporation, earned $500,000 U.S.-source income from royalties that it collected and $400,000 interest from its investment in U.S. Treasury bonds. Compute Velocity's U.S. income tax on these amounts.

30. **LO.5** Evaluate this statement: A state can tax only its resident individuals and the corporations and partnerships that are organized in-state.

Communications
Critical Thinking
Planning

31. **LO.5** You are working with the top management of one of your clients in selecting the U.S. location for a new manufacturing operation. Craft a plan for the CEO to use in discussions with the economic development representatives of each of the top candidate states. In no more than three PowerPoint slides, list some of the tax incentives the CEO should request from a particular state during the bilateral negotiations between the parties. Your list should be both creative and aggressive in its requests.

Decision Making

32. **LO.5** Considering only the aggregate state income tax liability, how should Norris, who sells widgets from its domicile State A, deploy its sales force? The states that entail the taxpayer's entire customer base use the following flat income tax rates.

State A	5%
State B	3
State C	6
State D	0

33. **LO.5** Continue to consider the case of the taxpayer in Problem 32. Is it acceptable to you if Norris purposely shifts its sales force among the states to reduce its tax liabilities? In your response, first explain the tax-related motivations of the taxpayer in this regard. Ethics and Equity

34. **LO.6** Compute state taxable income for HippCo, Inc. Its Federal taxable income for the year is $1,000,000. Its operations are confined to Oregon and Montana. HippCo generates only business and interest income for the year.

   - Federal cost recovery deductions totaled $200,000. Montana used this amount, but Oregon allowed only $120,000.
   - Interest income of $25,000 from Oregon bonds was excluded from Federal taxable income. Oregon taxes all municipal bond income, while Montana taxes all such interest except that from its own bonds.
   - Interest income from Treasury bonds that was recognized on the Federal return came to $11,000. Neither state taxes such income.

35. **LO.6** Continue with the facts of Problem 34. Using the format of Exhibit 16.3, compute state taxable income for HippCo, assuming also that the taxpayer recognized $225,000 of net rent income during the year from a warehouse building in Montana. Federal taxable income still is $1,000,000.

36. **LO.6** PinkCo, Inc., operates in two states, both of which equally weight the three apportionment factors. PinkCo reports the following results for the year. Compute the apportionment percentage for both states. Amounts are stated in millions of dollars.

	State A	State B	Totals
Sales	$25	$ 75	$100
Payroll	20	30	50
Property	0	100	100

37. **LO.6** Repeat the computations of Problem 36, but now assume that State B uses a double-weighted sales factor in its apportionment formula.

38. **LO.6** Repeat the computations of Problem 36, but now assume that State A is a sales-factor-only state and that State B uses the following weights: sales 0.70, payroll 0.15, and property 0.15.

39. **LO.6** State A enjoys a prosperous economy with high real estate values and compensation levels. State B's economy has seen better days—property values are depressed, and unemployment is higher than in other states. Most consumer goods are priced at about 10% less in B as compared with prices in A. Both A and B apply unitary income taxation on businesses that operate in-state. Does unitary taxation distort the assignment of taxable income between A and B? Explain. Critical Thinking

40. **LO.6** Hernandez, which has been an S corporation since inception, is subject to tax in States Y and Z. On Schedule K of its Federal Form 1120S, Hernandez reported ordinary income of $500,000 from its business, taxable interest income of $10,000, capital loss of $30,000, and $40,000 of dividend income from a corporation in which it owns 30%. Communications

    Both states apportion income by use of a three-factor formula that equally weights sales, payroll, and the average cost of property; both states treat interest and dividends as business income. In addition, both Y and Z follow Federal provisions with respect to the determination of corporate taxable income. Y recognizes S status, but Z does not.

    Based on the following information, write a memo to the shareholders of Hernandez, detailing the amount of taxable income on which Hernandez will pay tax in Y and Z. Hernandez corporate offices are located at 5678 Alabaster Circle, Bowling Green, KY 42103.

	State Y	State Z
Sales	$1,000,000	$800,000
Property (average cost)	500,000	100,000
Payroll	800,000	200,000

Communications
Critical Thinking
Planning

41. **LO.6** Prepare a PowerPoint presentation (maximum of six slides) entitled "Planning Principles for Our Multistate Clients." The slides will be used to lead a 20-minute discussion with colleagues in the corporate tax department. Keep the outline general, but assume that your colleagues already work with clients operating in at least 15 states. Address only income tax issues.

Communications
Critical Thinking

42. **LO.3, 7** Miha Ohua is the CFO of a U.S. company that has operations in Europe and Asia. The company has several manufacturing subsidiaries in low-tax foreign countries where the tax rate averages 6%. These subsidiaries purchase raw materials used in the production process from related subsidiaries located in countries where the tax rate averages 33%.

    Miha is considering establishing a transfer price for the raw materials so that the higher-tax subsidiaries charge a low price for the raw materials. In this way, little of the profit is left in these subsidiaries, and most of the profits end up in the low-tax subsidiaries. This approach might reduce the U.S. company's overall global tax rate. Write a memo to Miha, outlining the issues with this plan.

Bridge Discipline

1. What type of information-sharing agreements does the IRS have with the revenue agency of the Bahamas? Canada? Germany? Israel? Argentina? Discuss.

Communications

2. Submit a paper to your instructor of no more than two pages discussing the treatment of state and local taxes that is found in the text of U.S. income tax treaties with two other countries that you choose.

Communications

3. Several U.S. states finance their operations without the benefit of a corporate income tax. Prepare five to seven PowerPoint slides, and make a presentation to your school's Accounting Club. In your presentation, discuss the public economic and policy effects of using nontraditional revenue sources to fund state operating and infrastructure projects. Compare the taxing and expenditure process used in your state with at least two of these jurisdictions: Alaska; Hawaii; Michigan; Texas; Washington, D.C.; and Washington State.

Critical Thinking

4. The trend in state income taxation is to adopt an apportionment formula that places extra weight on the sales factor. Several states now use sales-factor-only apportionment. Explain why this development is attractive to the taxing states.

Research Problems

Note: Solutions to the Research Problems can be prepared by using the Thomson Reuters Checkpoint™ online tax research database, which accompanies this textbook. Solutions can also be prepared by using research materials found in a typical tax library.

Research Problem 1. Jerry Jeff Keen, the CFO of Boots Unlimited, a Texas corporation, has come to you regarding a potential restructuring of business operations. Boots long has manufactured its western boots in plants in Texas and Oklahoma.

Communications
Critical Thinking

Recently, Boots has explored the possibility of setting up a manufacturing subsidiary in Ireland, where manufacturing profits are taxed at 12.5%. Jerry Jeff sees this as a great idea, given that the alternative is to continue all manufacturing in the United States, where profits are taxed at 21%. Boots plans to continue all of the cutting, sizing, and hand tooling of leather in its U.S. plants. This material will be shipped to Ireland for final assembly, with the finished product shipped to retail outlets all over Europe and Asia. Your initial concern is whether the income generated by the Irish subsidiary is Subpart F income. Address this issue in a research memo, along with any planning suggestions.

Partial list of research aids:
§ 954(d).
Reg. § 1.954–3(a).
Bausch & Lomb, 71 TCM 2031, T.C.Memo. 1996–57.

Research Problem 2. Polly Ling is a successful professional golfer. She is a resident of a country that does not have a tax treaty with the United States. Ling plays matches around the world, about one-half of which are in the United States. Ling's reputation is without blemish; in fact, she is known as being exceedingly honest and upright, and many articles discuss how she is a role model for young golfers due to her tenacious and successful playing style and her favorable character traits. Every year she reports the most penalty strokes on herself among the participants in women's matches, and this is seen as reinforcing her image as an honest and respectful competitor.

This combination of quality play and laudable reputation has brought many riches to Ling. She comes to you with several Federal income tax questions. She knows that as a non-U.S. resident, any of her winnings from tournament play that occurs in the United States are subject to U.S. income taxation. But what about each of the following items? How does U.S. tax law affect Ling? Apply the sourcing rules in this regard, and determine whether the graduated U.S. Federal income tax rate schedules apply.

- Endorsement income from YourGolf for wearing clothing during matches with its logo prominently displayed. Ling must play in at least 10 tournaments per year that are televised around the world. She also must participate in photo sessions and in blogs and tweets associated with the tournaments. Payment to Ling is structured as a flat fee, with bonuses paid if she finishes in the top five competitors for each match. This is known as an *on-court endorsement*.
- Endorsement income from GolfZone for letting the company use her likeness in a video game that simulates golf tournaments among known golfers and other players that the (usually middle-aged men and women) gamers identify. In this way, the gamer seems to be playing against Ling on famous golf courses. Two-thirds of all dollar sales of the game licenses are to U.S. customers.
- Endorsement income from Eliteness for appearing in print and internet ads that feature Ling wearing the company's high-end watches. One-fifth of all dollar sales of the watches are to U.S. customers. The latter two items are known as *off-court endorsements*.

Partial list of research aids:
Goosen, 136 T.C. (2011).

Use internet tax resources to address the following questions. Look for reliable websites and blogs of the IRS and other government agencies, media outlets, businesses, tax professionals, academics, think tanks, and political outlets.

Communications

Research Problem 3. Find the text of various tax treaties currently in force in the United States. In an e-mail to your instructor, address the following items.

a. How does the U.S. income tax treaty with Germany define "business profits" for multinational businesses?
b. How does the U.S. income tax treaty with Japan treat the FIRPTA provisions?
c. List five countries with which the United States has entered into an estate tax treaty.
d. What is the effective date of the latest income tax treaty with the United Kingdom?
e. List three countries with which the United States does not have in force a bilateral income tax treaty.

Research Problem 4. Make a list of five countries with which the United States does *not* have in force a bilateral income tax treaty.

Communications

Research Problem 5. Choose 10 countries, one of which is the United States. Create a table showing whether each country applies a worldwide or territorial approach to international income taxation. Then list the country's top income tax rate on business profits. Send a copy of this table to your instructor.

Communications
Data Analytics

Research Problem 6. Locate data on the size of the international economy, including data on international trade, foreign direct investment of U.S. firms, and investments in the United States by foreign firms. Useful websites include **census.gov** and **bea.gov**. Prepare an analysis of these data for a three-year period, using spreadsheet and graphing software, and e-mail your findings to your instructor.

Communications

Research Problem 7. Read the "tax footnote" of five publicly traded U.S. corporations. Find the effective state/local income tax rates of each. Create a PowerPoint presentation (maximum of five slides) for your instructor, summarizing the search and reporting your findings.

Data Analytics

Research Problem 8. Identify three states considered to be in the same economic region as your own.

a. For each of the three states and your own state, answer the following questions, creating a table with your answers. Answers to most can be found at the website **taxadmin.org**.
   i. What is the overall tax burden per capita, and where does it rank among all states?
   ii. What is the overall tax burden as a percentage of personal income, and where does it rank among all states?
   iii. From what source(s) does it raise most of its revenues (e.g., sales/use tax, highway tolls)?
   iv. What is the highest marginal tax rate on corporate income?
   v. What is its apportionment formula, including factors and weights?
b. What advice or insight might you provide to your state legislature regarding your state's tax system, based on your findings for part (a)?

Becker CPA Review Questions

1. Olinto, Inc., reports taxable income (before special deductions and net operating loss deduction) of $92,000. Included in that amount is $12,000 interest and dividends income. Forty percent of Olinto's property, payroll, and sales are in its home state. What amount of this taxable income will be taxed by Olinto, Inc.'s home state?

   a. $12,000
   b. $36,800
   c. $44,000
   d. $90,000

2. In which of the following cases will Federal law prohibit a state from imposing a tax on net income?

   a. The business has a retail outlet store in the state.
   b. The business has its corporate headquarters in the state and generates sales from there.
   c. Orders are taken within the state, accepted at corporate headquarters outside of the state, and shipped from a location outside of the state.
   d. Orders are taken within the state, accepted at corporate headquarters outside of the state, and shipped from a location inside the state.

3. Which of the following statements best describes a multistate corporation's approach to the apportionment and allocation of its income?

   I. The corporation will allocate its nonbusiness income.
   II. The corporation will apportion its business income.

   a. I only.
   b. II only.
   c. Both I and II.
   d. Neither I nor II.

4. Reiki, Inc., operates stores in Massachusetts and Vermont. Reiki's payroll, property, and sales by state are as follows.

State	Payroll	Property (Ending)	Property (Average)	Sales
Massachusetts	$200,000	$175,000	$195,000	$ 750,000
Vermont	350,000	225,000	200,000	900,000
Total	550,000	400,000	395,000	1,650,000

   What is Reiki's apportionment factor for Massachusetts (round to two decimal places)?

   a. 41.86%
   b. 44.12%
   c. 45.45%
   d. 43.73%

Chapter 17

Business Tax Credits and the Alternative Minimum Tax

Learning Objectives: *After completing Chapter 17, you should be able to:*

- **LO.1** Explain the difference in the use of credits and deductions to achieve social and economic objectives.
- **LO.2** Identify and calculate various business-related tax credits.
- **LO.3** Explain the rationale for the alternative minimum tax (AMT).
- **LO.4** Present and explain the formula for computing the AMT for individuals.
- **LO.5** Identify the adjustments made in calculating AMTI.
- **LO.6** Identify the preferences that are included in calculating AMTI.
- **LO.7** Compute the AMT.
- **LO.8** Apply the AMT credit in the alternative minimum tax structure.

Chapter Outline

Tax Talk *A government which robs Peter to pay Paul can always count on the support of Paul.* —George Bernard Shaw

ISTOCK.COM/MONKEY BUSINESS IMAGES

The Big Picture

Dealing with Tax Credits and the AMT

Mike, the CEO of Progress Corporation, is committed to helping revitalize the crumbling downtown area in his hometown. The area has experienced high unemployment as companies have left for the suburbs, and Mike is considering expanding his business and purchasing an old office building in a historic section of downtown. The building, a certified historic structure, will require substantial renovations, and Mike has heard that there are tax credits that might help reduce his costs. He would also like to hire inner-city workers and help working families by providing on-site child care. He is interested in learning whether his company might take advantage of any other tax credits offered by the Federal government that might reduce his costs.

Read the chapter and formulate your response.

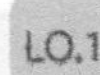

Explain the difference in the use of credits and deductions to achieve social and economic objectives.

Federal tax law often serves other purposes besides merely raising revenue for the government. Evidence of equity, social, and economic considerations is found throughout the tax law. Congress has generally used **tax credits** to promote social or economic objectives or to work toward greater tax equity among different types of taxpayers. For example, the disabled access credit was enacted to accomplish a social objective: to encourage taxpayers to renovate older buildings so that they would be accessible to the disabled and be in compliance with the Americans with Disabilities Act. The foreign tax credit has as its chief purpose the economic and equity objectives of mitigating the burden of multiple taxation on a single stream of income that may be subject to tax in more than one country.

A tax credit is much different than an income tax deduction. Income tax deductions reduce a taxpayer's tax base so that the tax benefit of a deduction depends on a taxpayer's tax rate. Tax credits, on the other hand, reduce a taxpayer's tax liability directly. Therefore, the benefit of a credit, and the incentive it provides, is the same across taxpayers regardless of their tax rate.

Assume that Congress wants to encourage a certain activity. One way to accomplish this objective is to allow a tax credit of 25% for any expenditures paid or incurred related to the activity. Another way is to allow an itemized deduction for the expenditures. Abby, Bill, and Carmen are considering making expenditures related to the activity. Assume that Abby's tax rate is 12% and Bill's tax rate is 35% and that they both itemize their deductions. Carmen does not incur enough expenses to itemize deductions. The following tax benefits are available to each taxpayer for a $1,000 expenditure.

	Abby	Bill	Carmen
Tax benefit if a 25% credit is allowed	$250	$250	$250
Tax benefit if an itemized deduction is allowed	120	350	-0-

As these results indicate, tax credits provide benefits on a more equitable basis than do tax deductions—all three taxpayers reduce their tax liabilities by the same amount. Equally apparent is that the deduction approach in this case benefits only taxpayers who itemize deductions, while the credit approach benefits all taxpayers who make the specified expenditure.

Given the availability of numerous deductions and credits, some taxpayers with significant economic income may nonetheless be able to pay little or no Federal income tax. The alternative minimum tax (AMT) is designed to limit the aggregate benefit of certain deductions and credits otherwise available to taxpayers to ensure that those with economic income cannot reduce their tax liability below a minimum amount based on their ability to pay.

This chapter examines the most commonly-used tax credits available to business taxpayers as well as the AMT. Note that corporations have not been subject to the AMT since 2017. However, the AMT targets several types of income and deductions related to individual taxpayers, including many associated with business activities.

LO.2

Apply various business-related tax credits.

17-1 General Business Tax Credit Overview

As alluded to above, Congress has generally used tax credits to achieve social or economic objectives or to promote equity among different types of taxpayers. Though many credits enacted by Congress are unrelated to businesses or business activities, this chapter focuses on business-related credits. Most business-related credits are combined into the general business tax credit. This section of the chapter introduces the operation of the general business credit.

17-1a General Business Credit

The **general business credit** is comprised of a number of specific credits, each of which is computed separately under its own set of rules. The general business credit combines these credits into one amount for the purpose of imposing an overall limit on the annual credits that can be used to offset a taxpayer's income tax liability.

Tax Fact Business Tax Credits

The amount of business tax credits claimed by corporations fluctuates significantly based on the type of credit. The amount of each credit for 2018 varies from a low of $227,000 to over $100,000,000,000.

Credit Type	Amount of Credits (reported in thousands of dollars)
Foreign tax credit	$103,455,878
Research activities credit	23,335,464
Low-income housing credit	7,596,112
Renewable electricity production credit	5,536,382
Work-opportunity credit	1,403,678
Rehabilitation credit	780,486
Employer-Provided family and medical leave	67,524
Credit for employer provided childcare facilities and services	16,453
Biodiesel and renewable diesel fuels credit	6,917
Small employer health insurance premiums credit	2,368
Disabled access credit	294
Credit for contributions for small employer pension plan startup costs	227

Source: IRS Tax Statistics.

The general business credit is limited to the taxpayer's net income tax reduced by the greater of:[1]

- The *tentative minimum tax* [see the discussion of the alternative minimum tax (AMT) later in this chapter], or
- 25 percent of the *net regular tax liability* that exceeds $25,000.[2]

Net regular tax liability is the regular tax liability reduced by certain nonrefundable credits (e.g., credit for child and dependent care expenses and foreign tax credit).

Example 2

Tanager Corporation's general business credit for the current year is $130,000. Tanager's net regular tax liability is $150,000. Tanager has no other tax credits. The general business credit allowed for the tax year is computed as follows.

Net regular tax liability		$150,000
Reduced by: Net regular tax liability	$150,000	
	(25,000)	
	$125,000	
	× 25%	
		(31,250)
General business credit allowed for tax year		$118,750

Tanager then has $11,250 ($130,000 − $118,750) of unused general business credits that may be carried back or forward.

17-1b Treatment of Unused General Business Credits

Unused general business credits are initially carried back one year and reduce the tax liability of the year to which it is carried back. As a result, the taxpayer may receive a tax refund as a result of the carryback. Any remaining unused credits are then carried forward 20 years.[3]

[1] § 38(c). This rule works to keep the general business credit from completely eliminating the tax liability for many taxpayers.

[2] § 38(c)(3)(B). The $25,000 amount is apportioned among the members of a controlled group.

[3] § 39(a)(1).

A FIFO method is applied to the carryback, carryovers, and utilization of credits earned during a particular year. The FIFO method minimizes the potential for loss of a general business credit benefit due to the expiration of credit carryovers and generally works to the taxpayer's benefit.

Titan Company generated a general business credit of $40,000 in 2022. It has also generated general business credit carryovers, none of which could be used in prior years, as follows:

2019	$ 4,000
2020	6,000
2021	2,000
Total carryovers	$ 12,000

Assume that Titan may take a general business credit of $50,000 in 2022 based on its 2022 tax liability. Titan will use its available credits in 2022 as follows:

Carryovers used	
2019	$ 4,000
2020	6,000
2021	2,000
Credit generated in 2022	38,000
	$ 50,000
Remaining 2022 credit carried forward to 2023	$ 2,000

Each component of the general business credit is determined separately under its own set of rules. Some of the more important credits that make up the general business credit are explained here in the order listed in Exhibit 17.1.

17-2 Specific Credits in General Business Credit

There are over 30 business credits included in the general business credit. The following sections discuss the credits that are most commonly used by businesses.

17-2a Tax Credit for Rehabilitation Expenditures

The **rehabilitation expenditures credit** is intended to discourage businesses from moving from economically distressed areas and to encourage the preservation of historic structures. The credit is 20 percent of qualified rehabilitation expenditures related to a *certified historic structure* (either residential or nonresidential). The 20 percent credit is taken ratably over a five-year period starting with the year the rehabilitated building is placed in service. Taxpayers who claim the rehabilitation credit must reduce the basis of the rehabilitated building by the credit allowed.[4]

Exhibit 17.1 Principal Components of the General Business Credit

The general business credit combines (but is not limited to) the following.

- Tax credit for rehabilitation expenditures
- Work opportunity tax credit
- Research activities credit
- Various energy credits
- Low-income housing credit
- Disabled access credit
- Credit for small employer pension plan startup costs
- Credit for employer-provided child care
- Small employer health insurance credit
- Employer-provided family and medical leave credit

[4] § 50(c).

Bridge Discipline **Bridge to Finance**

Any evaluation of the cash-flow benefit of tax deductions and credits should take into account the net present value of that benefit. The general business credit and the related carryback and carryover provisions can be used to illustrate the cash-flow impact. Assume that Blonde, Inc., is considering in 2022 making $400,000 of expenditures that qualify for the general business credit and that the $400,000 of tax savings is an important factor in making the expenditure. However, further examination suggests that the amount that may be used to reduce the current year tax liability is only $150,000. Further, none can be used in 2021 (the carryback year), so the remaining $250,000 will be carried forward. The $250,000 of unused general business credit is expected to offset Blonde's future tax liability as follows.

2023	$50,000
2024	75,000
2025	125,000

Assuming a 4 percent discount rate, the present value of the tax savings is only $378,545. Failure to consider the timing and net present value of the tax benefits may lead to the wrong business decision.

2022	$150,000 × 1.0000	=	$150,000
2023	50,000 × 0.9615	=	48,075
2024	75,000 × 0.9246	=	69,345
2025	125,000 × 0.8890	=	111,125
			$378,545

The carryforward period for the general business credit is 20 years. However, using a 4 percent discount rate, one dollar in 20 years is worth about 46 cents ($1 × 0.4564) today. The annual limitation on the general business credit and the resulting carryover could make the net present value of the credit significantly lower than the amount of the credit itself.

The Big Picture

Return to the facts of *The Big Picture* on p. 17-1. Assume that Progress spends $60,000 to rehabilitate the office building (adjusted basis of $40,000).

Progress is allowed a credit of $12,000 (20% × $60,000) for rehabilitation expenditures. The credit is spread over five years ($2,400 per year). However, the corporation may only increase the basis of the building by $48,000 [$60,000 (rehabilitation expenditures) − $12,000 (credit allowed)].

To qualify for the credit, buildings must be substantially rehabilitated. A building has been *substantially rehabilitated* if qualified rehabilitation expenditures exceed the *greater of*:

- The adjusted basis of the property before the rehabilitation expenditures, or
- $5,000.

Qualified rehabilitation expenditures do not include the cost of acquiring a building, the cost of facilities related to a building (such as a parking lot), and the cost of enlarging an existing building. Stringent rules also require the retention of the building's original internal and external walls.

17-2b Work Opportunity Tax Credit

The **work opportunity tax credit**[5] was enacted to encourage employers to hire individuals from a variety of targeted and economically disadvantaged groups. Examples include long-term unemployed individuals (those unemployed for at least 27 weeks), qualified ex-felons, high-risk youths, participants in the Federal Supplemental Nutrition Assistance Program (SNAP), veterans, summer youth employees, and long-term family assistance recipients.

Computation of the Work Opportunity Tax Credit: General

The credit generally is equal to 40 percent of the first $6,000 of wages (per eligible employee) for the first 12 months of employment. The credit is not available for wages paid to an employee after the *first year* of employment. If the employee's first year

[5] § 51. The credit is available for qualifying employees who start work before 2026.

overlaps two of the employer's tax years, however, the employer may take the credit over two tax years. If the credit is claimed, the employer's tax deduction for wages is reduced by the amount of the credit.

To qualify an employer for the 40 percent credit, the employee must (1) be certified by a designated local agency as being a member of one of the targeted groups and (2) have completed at least 400 hours of service to the employer. If an employee meets the first condition but not the second, the credit is reduced to 25 percent, provided the employee has completed a minimum of 120 hours of service to the employer.

Digging Deeper 1

More on the applicability of the work opportunity tax credit to qualified summer youth employees can be found on this book's companion website: www.cengage.com

On June 1, 2022, Maria, a calendar year taxpayer, hires Joe, a member of a certified group, and obtains the required certification to qualify Maria for the work opportunity credit. During his seven months of work in 2022, Joe is paid $3,500 for 500 hours of work. Maria is allowed a credit of $1,400 ($3,500 × 40%) for 2022.

Joe continues to work for Maria in 2023 and is paid $7,000 through May 31, 2023. Because up to $6,000 of first-year wages are eligible for the credit, Maria is also allowed a 40% credit on $2,500 [$6,000 − $3,500 (wages paid in 2022)] of 2023 wages paid. The credit is $1,000 ($2,500 × 40%). None of Joe's wages paid after May 31, 2023, the end of the first year of Joe's employment, are eligible for the credit.

The Big Picture

Return to the facts of *The Big Picture* on p. 17-1. In January 2022, Progress Corporation hires four individuals who are certified to be members of a qualifying targeted group. Each employee works 1,000 hours and is paid wages of $8,000 during the year.

Progress's work opportunity credit is $9,600 [($6,000 × 40%) × 4 employees]. If the tax credit is taken, Progress reduces its deduction for wages paid by $9,600. No credit is available for wages paid to these employees after their first year of employment.

17-2c Research Activities Credit

To encourage business-related research and development (R & D), a credit is allowed for certain qualifying expenditures paid or incurred by a taxpayer. The **research activities credit** is the *sum* of three components: (1) an incremental research activities credit, (2) a basic research credit, and (3) an energy research credit.[6]

Incremental Research Activities Credit

The incremental research activities credit equals 20 percent of the *excess* of qualified research expenses for the taxable year (the credit year) over a base amount. Determining the *base amount* involves a complex series of computations meant to approximate recent historical levels of research activity by the taxpayer. Thus, the credit is allowed only for increases in research expenses.[7]

In general, *research expenditures* qualify if the research relates to discovering technological information that is intended for use in the development of a new or improved business component of the taxpayer. If the research is performed in-house (by the taxpayer or its employees), all of the expenses qualify. If the research is contracted to others outside the taxpayer's business, only 65 percent of the amount paid qualifies for the credit.[8]

[6] § 41. A qualified startup company (less than $5 million in gross receipts) can offset the credit against its payroll tax liability.

[7] An alternative simplified credit procedure is also available. See §§ 41(c)(4) and (5).

[8] § 41(b)(3)(A). In the case of payments to a qualified research consortium, § 41(b)(3)(A) provides that 75% of the amount paid qualifies for the credit. In contrast, for amounts paid to an energy research consortium, § 41(b)(3)(D) allows the full amount to qualify for the credit.

Bobwhite Company incurs the following research expenditures.

In-house wages, supplies, computer time	$135,000
Payment to Cutting Edge Scientific (a contractor)	100,000

Bobwhite's qualified research expenditures are $200,000 [$135,000 + ($100,000 × 65%)]. If the base amount is $100,000, the incremental research activities credit is $20,000 [($200,000 − $100,000) × 20%].

The research incremental credit is *not* allowed for:[9]

- Research conducted once commercial production begins.
- Surveys and studies such as market research, testing, or routine data collection.
- Research conducted *outside* the United States (other than research undertaken in Puerto Rico or U.S. possessions).
- Research in the social sciences, arts, or humanities.

In addition to qualifying for the research credit, research expenditures also can be capitalized and amortized or, in years beginning before 2022, immediately deducted in the year incurred. However, to prevent a double benefit for the same expenditure, any deduction must be reduced by the amount of the credit.[10,11]

An example of the relationship between the research activities credit and the related deduction can be found on this book's companion website: www.cengage.com 2 Digging Deeper

Basic Research Credit

Corporations (other than S corporations or personal service corporations) are allowed an additional 20 percent credit for basic research expenditures incurred in *excess* of a base period amount.[12] *Basic research* is defined generally as any original investigation for the advancement of scientific knowledge not having a specific commercial objective. Basic research conducted outside the United States and in the social sciences, arts, or humanities does not qualify. The base period amount is a complex calculation generally representing the average basic research expenses incurred over the previous three years.

Energy Research Credit

This component of the research credit encourages taxpayers to support an energy research consortium, an exempt organization conducting energy research. The credit is equal to 20 percent of payments made to these organizations.

17-2d Low-Income Housing Credit

To encourage building owners and real estate developers to make affordable housing available for low-income individuals, Congress offers a credit to owners of qualified low-income housing projects.[13] As is the case with many other business credits, the low-income housing credit is motivated more by social than business concerns. To qualify for the credit, property must be certified by the appropriate state or local agency authorized to provide low-income housing credits. These credits are issued based on a nationwide allocation, dictated chiefly by budgetary and housing policy concerns.

[9] § 41(d).

[10] §§ 174 and 280C(c). Recall the discussion of rules for deducting research and experimental expenditures in Chapter 5. Although the immediate deduction for research and experimental expenditures expired at the end of 2021, Congress was considering at the time of this text's publication an extension of the deduction.

[11] A taxpayer may instead choose to retain the full deduction and reduce the credit by the maximum corporate tax rate (i.e., 21%). Though reducing the credit and reducing the deduction will generally yield the same tax benefit for a corporation, reducing the credit may be preferable if the corporation's general business credit is limited.

[12] § 41(e).

[13] § 42.

The credit is available over a ten-year period as long as the property continues to meet the eligibility requirements. The credit each year is equal to the property's qualified basis multiplied by the credit rate. A property's qualified basis generally is its adjusted basis at the end of the year in which it is placed in service multiplied by a fraction that represents the portion of the property rented to low-income tenants. Tenants are low-income tenants if their income does not exceed a specified percentage of the area median gross income. The credit rate is computed by the Treasury as the amount necessary to produce total credits over the 10-year period with a present value of up to 70 percent of the qualified basis of the property. Generally, first-year credits are prorated based on the date the project is placed in service.

A partnership spends $1,000,000 to build a qualified low-income housing project. The complex is completed on January 1 of the current year. The entire project is rented to low-income families. Assume the credit rate for property placed in service during January of the current year is 7.25%.[14]

The partners are allocated a credit of $72,500 ($1,000,000 × 7.25%) in the current year and in each of the following nine years. If only 75% of the project was used by low-income tenants, the credit would be reduced to $54,375 ($1,000,000 × 75% × 7.25%).

Recapture of a portion of the credit may be required if the number of units set aside for low-income tenants falls below a minimum threshold, or if the taxpayer disposes of the property or their interest in it.

17-2e Energy Credits

The Internal Revenue Code contains a variety of **energy credits** for businesses and individuals to encourage the conservation of natural resources and the development of energy sources other than oil and gas. The primary goals of the tax provisions are to improve energy-related infrastructure and encourage higher levels of energy conservation. Credit amounts and expiration dates differ for the various provisions.

Some of the more widely applicable provisions include credits for:

- Businesses that buy fuel cell and microturbine power plants.
- Taxpayers who purchase alternative power motor vehicles and refueling property.

17-2f Disabled Access Credit

The **disabled access credit** is designed to encourage eligible small businesses to make their facilities more accessible to disabled individuals. The credit, created as part of the Americans with Disabilities Act of 1990, is calculated at the rate of 50 percent of the eligible expenditures that exceed $250 but do not exceed $10,250. As a result, the maximum credit is $5,000 ($10,000 × 50%).[15]

An *eligible small business* is a business that during the previous year either had gross receipts of $1 million or less or had no more than 30 full-time employees. A sole proprietorship, a partnership, a regular corporation, or an S corporation can qualify as such an entity.

Eligible expenditures include any reasonable and necessary amounts that are paid or incurred to make older buildings accessible (only buildings first placed in service before November 6, 1990, qualify). Qualifying projects include installing ramps, widening doorways, and adding raised markings on elevator control buttons. Costs to assist hearing- or visually-impaired employees or customers who interact with the business also qualify. These costs can include both personnel (e.g., an interpreter) or equipment (e.g, audio or visual equipment or modifications to existing equipment).

The property's tax basis is reduced by the amount of the credit.

[14]The credit rate applicable to new projects is adjusted monthly.

[15]§ 44.

This year Red, Inc., an eligible small business, makes $11,000 of capital improvements to a building that had been placed in service in June 1990. The improvements make Red's business more accessible to the disabled and are eligible expenditures for purposes of the disabled access credit.

The amount of the credit is $5,000 [($10,250 maximum − $250 floor) × 50%]. Although $11,000 of eligible expenditures are incurred, only $10,000 qualifies for the credit. The capital improvements have a depreciable basis of $6,000 [$11,000 (cost) − $5,000 (amount of the credit)].

17-2g Credit for Small Employer Pension Plan Startup Costs

Small businesses are entitled to a nonrefundable credit for administrative costs associated with establishing and maintaining certain qualified retirement plans.[16] While these costs (e.g., payroll system changes, retirement-related education programs, and consulting fees) are deductible as ordinary and necessary business expenses, the credit lowers the after-tax cost of establishing a qualified retirement program and encourages eligible employers to offer retirement plans for their employees.

The **credit for small employer pension plan startup costs** is available only to businesses with 100 or fewer employees who each earns at least $5,000 of compensation. The credit is generally equal to 50 percent of qualified startup costs.

The maximum credit is limited to the greater of

- $500 or
- the lesser of
  - $250 times the number of employees eligible for the plan or
  - $5,000.

The credit can be claimed for qualifying costs incurred in each of the three years beginning with the tax year in which the retirement plan becomes effective, resulting in a maximum total credit of $15,000. Any deduction for the startup costs must be reduced by the amount of the credit taken.

Maple Company, with 65 full-time employees, decides to establish a qualified retirement plan. In the process, it pays consulting fees of $21,200 to a firm that will provide educational seminars to Maple's employees and will assist the payroll department in making necessary changes to the payroll system.

Maple claims a credit for the pension plan startup costs of $ 5,000, 50% of $21,200, limited to the greater of

- $500 or
- the lesser of
  - $16,250 ($250 × 65 employees) or
  - $5,000.

If Maple had only 10 employees, its credit would be limited to $2,500 ($250 × 10 employees).

17-2h Credit for Employer-Provided Child Care

An employer's expenses to provide for the care of employee's children is a deductible business expense. Alternatively, employers may claim a credit for providing child care facilities to their employees during normal working hours.[17]

The **credit for employer-provided child care**, limited annually to $150,000, is composed of the aggregate of two components: 25 percent of qualified child care expenses and 10 percent of qualified child care resource and referral services. *Qualified child care expenses*

[16] § 45E.

[17] § 45F.

include the costs of acquiring, constructing, rehabilitating, expanding, and operating a child care facility. *Child care resource and referral services* include amounts paid or incurred under a contract to provide child care resource and referral services to an employee.

Any qualifying expenses otherwise deductible by the taxpayer are reduced by the amount of the credit. In addition, the taxpayer's basis for any property acquired or constructed and used for qualifying purposes is reduced by the amount of the credit. If within 10 years of being placed in service a child care facility ceases to be used for a qualified use, the taxpayer must recapture a portion of the credit previously claimed.[18]

The Big Picture

Return to the facts of *The Big Picture* on p. 17-1. During the year, Progress Corporation constructs a child care facility for $400,000 to be used by its employees who have preschool-aged children in need of child care services while their parents are at work. In addition, Progress incurs salary costs of $100,000 for child care workers and other administrative costs associated with the facility.

As a result, Progress's credit for employer-provided child care is $125,000 [($400,000 + $100,000) × 25%]. Correspondingly, the basis of the facility is reduced to $300,000 ($400,000 − $100,000), and the deduction for salaries and administrative costs is reduced to $75,000 ($100,000 − $25,000).

17-2i Small Employer Health Insurance Credit

Under the Affordable Care Act (ACA), a tax credit is available to a qualified small employer for nonelective contributions to purchase health insurance for its employees.[19] The insurance must be purchased through a Small Business Health Options Program (SHOP) Marketplace established as part of the ACA. The credit is available only for two consecutive tax years.

To qualify for the credit in 2022, the employer must have no more than 25 full-time equivalent employees whose annual full-time wages average no more than $57,400 ($55,600 in 2021). The employer must pay at least half the cost of the health insurance premiums.[20] The credit is 50 percent of the health insurance premiums paid. It is subject to a phaseout if the employer has more than 10 full-time equivalent employees and/or has annual full-time wages that average more than $28,700 ($27,800 in 2021).[21]

Global Tax Issues — Sourcing Income in Cyberspace—Getting It Right When Calculating the Foreign Tax Credit

The overall limitation on the foreign tax credit plays a critical role in restricting the amount of the credit available to a taxpayer. In the overall limitation formula, the taxpayer must characterize the year's taxable income as either earned (or sourced) inside or outside the United States. As a general rule, a relatively greater percentage of foreign-source income in the formula leads to a larger foreign tax credit. But classifying income as either foreign or U.S. source is not always a simple matter.

The existing income-sourcing rules were developed long before the existence of the internet, and taxing authorities are finding it challenging to apply these rules to internet transactions. Where does a sale take place when the web server is in Scotland, the seller is in India, and the customer is in Illinois? Where is a service performed when all activities take place over the internet? These questions and more must be answered by the United States and its trading partners as the internet economy grows in size and importance.

[18] § 45F(d).

[19] § 45R.

[20] §§ 45R(d)(1) and (4). The wage amount is indexed for inflation each year.

[21] § 45R(c). The credit percentage for tax-exempt employers is 35%.

17-2j Credit for Employer-Provided Family and Medical Leave

Employers can claim a general business credit equal to 12.5 percent of the wages paid to qualifying employees while they are on family and medical leave.[22] To claim the **credit for employer-provided family and medical leave**, employers must pay during the leave a minimum of 50 percent of the wages normally paid to an employee. If the wages paid during the leave *exceed* 50 percent of normal wages, the credit is increased by 0.25 percentage point for each percentage point above 50 percent.

The credit is capped at 25 percent of wages paid (this would be allowed if the employer paid 100 percent of the employee's wages during the leave). The credit is limited to 12 weeks of leave per employee during any taxable year.

An employer must have a written policy in place that allows all qualifying full-time employees no less than two weeks of annual paid family and medical leave (non-full-time employees must be offered leave on a pro rata basis). Wages paid as vacation leave, personal leave, or other medical or sick leave are not considered to be family and medical leave when determining how many weeks the employer has provided family and medical leave. The credit applies to wages paid in taxable years beginning after 2017 and before 2026.

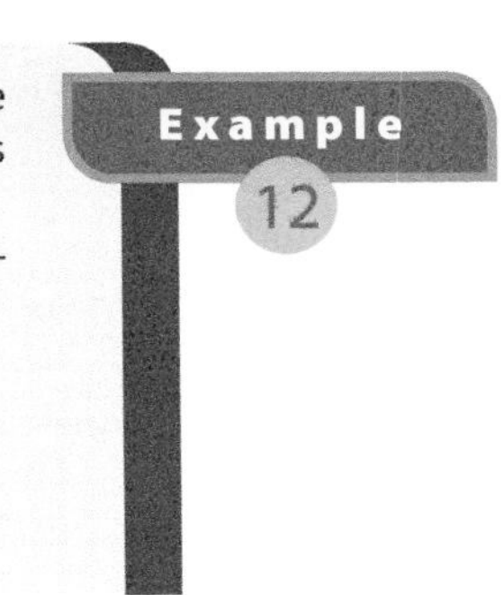

Rocket Corporation has a qualifying paid family and medical leave policy in place with 1,200 eligible employees. Twenty-five percent of the employees take family and medical leave for six weeks this year. The employees are paid 60% of their normal annual wages of $52,000 during the six weeks.

Sixty percent exceeds the required minimum 50% payment rate by 10 percentage points. Therefore, the credit percentage is 15 percent [12.5% + (0.25 × 10)]. Rocket's credit is:

15% × ($52,000/52 weeks x 6 weeks) × (1,200 employees × 25%) =
15% × $6,000 wages × 300 employees = $270,000

Rocket's family and medical leave credit is $270,000.

Concept Summary 17.1 provides an overview of the tax credits discussed in this chapter.

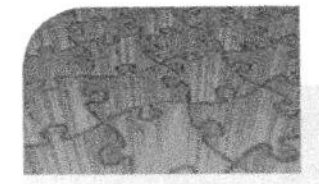

Concept Summary 17.1

Tax Credits included in the General Business Credit

Credit	Computation	Comments
General business (§ 38)	May not exceed net income tax minus the greater of tentative minimum tax or 25% of net regular tax liability that exceeds $25,000.	Components include tax credit for rehabilitation expenditures, work opportunity tax credit, research activities credit, low-income housing credit, disabled access credit, credit for small employer pension plan startup costs, and credit for employer-provided child care. Unused credit may be carried back 1 year and forward 20 years. FIFO method applies to carrybacks, carryovers, and credits earned during current year.

continued

[22] § 45S, added by the TCJA of 2017. "Family and medical leave" is as defined by the Family and Medical Leave Act of 1993.

Tax Credits—(Continued)

Credit	Computation	Comments
Rehabilitation expenditures (§ 47)	Qualifying investment times rehabilitation percentage; rate for certified historic structures is 20%.	Part of general business credit and therefore subject to same carryback, carryover, and FIFO rules. Purpose is to discourage businesses from moving from economically distressed areas to new locations.
Work opportunity (§ 51)	Credit is limited to 40% of the first $6,000 of wages paid to each eligible employee.	Part of the general business credit and therefore subject to the same carryback, carryover, and FIFO rules. Purpose is to encourage employment of members of economically disadvantaged groups.
Research activities (§ 41)	Incremental credit is 20% of excess of computation-year expenditures over a base amount. Basic research credit is allowed to certain corporations for 20% of cash payments to qualified organizations that exceed a specially calculated base amount. An energy research credit is allowed for 20% of qualifying payments made to an energy research consortium.	Part of general business credit and therefore subject to same carryback, carryover, and FIFO rules. Purpose is to encourage high-tech and energy research in the United States.
Low-income housing (§ 42)	Appropriate rate times eligible basis (portion of project attributable to low-income units).	Part of general business credit and therefore subject to same carryback, carryover, and FIFO rules. Recapture may apply. Purpose is to encourage construction of housing for low-income individuals. Credit is available each year for 10 years.
Energy credits	Various items to encourage individuals and businesses to "go green."	Part of general business credit and therefore subject to same carryback, carryover, and FIFO rules.
Disabled access (§ 44)	Credit is 50% of eligible access expenditures that exceed $250 but do not exceed $10,250. Maximum credit is $5,000.	Part of general business credit and therefore subject to same carryback, carryover, and FIFO rules. Purpose is to encourage small businesses to become more accessible to disabled individuals. Available only to eligible small businesses.
Credit for small employer pension plan startup costs (§ 45E)	The credit equals 50% of qualified startup costs incurred by eligible employers. Maximum annual credit is the *lesser* of (1) $5,000 or (2) $250 times the number of non-highly compensated employees. Deduction for related expenses is reduced by the amount of the credit.	Part of general business credit and therefore subject to same carryback, carryover, and FIFO rules. Purpose is to encourage small employers to establish qualified retirement plans for their employees.
Credit for employer-provided child care (§ 45F)	Credit is equal to 25% of qualified child care expenses plus 10% of qualified expenses for child care resource and referral services. Maximum credit is $150,000. Deduction for related expenses or basis must be reduced by the amount of the credit.	Part of general business credit and therefore subject to same carryback, carryover, and FIFO rules. Purpose is to encourage employers to provide child care for their employees' children during normal working hours.
Small Employer Health Insurance Credit (§ 45R)	The credit is 50% of the health insurance premiums paid (subject to a phaseout).	To qualify for the credit, the employer must have no more than 25 full-time equivalent employees whose annual full-time wages average no more than $57,400 (2022).
Credit for employer-provided family and medical leave (§ 45S)	Credit is equal to 12.5% of wages paid to qualifying employees while they are on family and medical leave (limited to 12 weeks per employee per year). Employers must pay a minimum of 50% of the wages normally paid; if wages paid during the leave *exceed* 50% of normal wages, the credit is increased by 0.25% for each percentage point above 50% to a maximum credit of 25%.	Nonrefundable credit. Part of general business credit and therefore subject to same carryback, carryover, and FIFO rules. Purpose is to encourage employers to provide leave to their employees for family and medical purposes (e.g,, birth of a child; care for a sick child, spouse, or parent).

17-3 Foreign Tax Credit

Businesses can also benefit from other tax credits that are not part of the general business credit. Perhaps the most commonly used of these is the **foreign tax credit (FTC)**. Foreign-sourced income earned by a U.S. person is subject to the U.S. income tax under the worldwide system of business taxation. If the non-U.S country in which the income is earned also imposes an income tax, the possibility of double taxation arises. Double taxation is most often addressed through applicable tax treaties that assign taxable income to only one of the countries involved or through the allowance of tax credits and exemptions in the taxpayer's home country. The foreign tax credit allows U.S. taxpayers a credit for the income taxes paid in a non-treaty country.[23]

The credit is limited, however, to the U.S. tax attributable to the foreign income. The limitation is calculated as follows.[24]

In any year in which the FTC is limited, the disallowed amount is allowed in another tax year as a carryover. Unused FTCs are carried back 1 year and forward 10 years. FTC carryovers tend to occur when the effective tax rate that applies to the dual-taxed income is lower in the United States than it is in the other country.

The FTC is an annual taxpayer election. If the FTC is not elected, a deduction is allowed for the foreign taxes paid.

BlueCo, a U.S. corporation, manufactures and sells most of its products in the United States. It also conducts business in the European Union through various branches. During the current year, BlueCo reports taxable income of $700,000, of which $500,000 is U.S.-source and $200,000 is foreign-source. Foreign income taxes paid amounted to $45,000. BlueCo's U.S. income tax liability before the foreign tax credit is $147,000. Its allowable FTC and FTC carryforward are determined as follows:

(1) Foreign taxes paid	$45,000
(2) U.S. tax associated with dual-taxed income	
$\frac{\$200,000 \text{ (Foreign-source TI)}}{\$700,000 \text{ (Total TI)}} \times \$147,000 \text{ (U.S. tax)}$	$42,000
(3) FTC allowed [lesser of (1) or (2)]	$42,000
(4) FTC carryforward [(1) − (2), but not below $0]	$ 3,000

17-4 Alternative Minimum Tax (AMT)

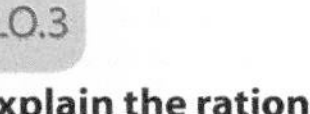

Explain the rationale for the alternative minimum tax (AMT).

The tax law has always included incentives intended to influence the economic and social behavior of taxpayers. As a result, some taxpayers are able to take advantage of these incentives to significantly minimize or entirely avoid any Federal income tax liability in a particular year. In such circumstances, although taxpayers are legally minimizing their tax liabilities, concerns arise about the potential inequity that results when taxpayers with substantial economic incomes use these incentives to avoid paying income tax.[25] To alleviate this concern, the **alternative minimum tax (AMT)** was enacted. The goal of

[23]The credit is allowed via § 27, but the qualifications and calculation procedure for the FTC are contained in §§ 901–908. Although taxpayers can claim a deduction rather than a credit for the foreign taxes paid, in most instances, the credit is advantageous since it is a direct offset against the tax liability.

[24]§ 904.

[25]Joint Committee on Taxation, *General Explanation of the Tax Reform Act of 1986 ("Blue Book")*, (JCS-10-87) May 4, 1987, pp. 432–433.

the AMT is to ensure that all taxpayers with more than modest economic incomes pay some minimum amount of tax. This is accomplished by requiring the taxpayer to pay the greater of the regular tax liability or the liability determined under the AMT formula. In 2017, approximately 5 million individual taxpayers paid a total of $37.7 billion in additional taxes due to the AMT. However, changes made by the TCJA significantly reduced the number of taxpayers paying AMT. For instance, IRS data show that only $2.6 billion in revenue was collected from the individual AMT for the 2019 tax year.[26]

Currently, the AMT applies to individuals, trusts, and estates. The focus of this section of the chapter is on the AMT as it applies to individual taxpayers.[27] In theory all individual taxpayers subject to the Federal income tax are subject to the AMT. Whether a taxpayer has an AMT liability depends on a number of factors, including the taxpayer's income, geographic location, and family situation as well as the exclusions, deductions, and credits utilized in the calculation of their regular Federal income tax liability as discussed in detail below.

LO.4

Present and explain the formula for computing the AMT for individuals.

17-4a Calculating the AMT: The AMT Formula

Alternative Minimum Taxable Income

The starting point for determining the AMT is **alternative minimum taxable income (AMTI)**. AMTI is intended to better capture a taxpayer's economic income, or ability to pay tax, by reducing the benefits of certain tax incentives available in the calculation of regular taxable income. Because most gross income and deductions are similarly included in both AMTI and regular taxable income, the law does not take a direct approach to calculating AMTI.[28] Rather, it begins with regular taxable income and requires a set of modifications as illustrated in Exhibit 17.2. In other words, the law requires taxpayers to take an indirect approach to calculating AMTI by reconciling AMTI to regular taxable income.

As shown in Exhibit 17.2, differences between regular taxable income and AMTI are categorized as either adjustments or preferences. Most adjustments relate to timing differences that arise because of different methods used to calculate regular taxable income and AMTI. Adjustments that are caused by timing differences will eventually reverse; positive adjustments will be offset by negative adjustments in the future and vice versa.[29]

Depreciation provides a good example of a timing difference. In general, AMT depreciation methods are slower than regular tax depreciation methods. Initially then, there will be less depreciation for AMT purposes than for regular tax purposes. This difference will result in positive timing differences until AMT depreciation is larger than regular tax depreciation, when the timing difference will become negative. However, over time, the same amount of depreciation will be deducted for regular tax and AMT purposes because the asset's basis for regular tax and AMT depreciation is the same.

In contrast to adjustments, preferences represent permanent differences between the regular tax treatment and the AMT treatment of certain items.[30] Certain deductions and exclusions allowed to taxpayers for regular income tax purposes provide significant tax savings. Adding these deductions and exclusions back to regular taxable income as preferences when determining AMTI reduces the benefit derived from them. Examples of preferences include percentage depletion in excess of the property's adjusted basis and excess intangible drilling costs. Both adjustments and preferences are discussed in more detail later in the chapter.

Calculating AMTI is the first step in the determination of whether a taxpayer will have an alternative minimum tax liability. To complete the AMT calculation, as shown in Exhibit 17.2, the exemption, rates, credit, and regular tax liability must all be considered.

[26] **irs.gov/statistics/soi-tax-stats-individual-income-tax-returns#prelim.**

[27] Between 1986 and 2017, C corporations were required to calculate and pay AMT in a manner similar to individuals. The TCJA of 2017 eliminated the corporate AMT for tax years beginning after 2017.

[28] A "direct approach" means that in calculating regular taxable income, gross income is reduced by deductions to arrive at taxable income.

[29] § 56.

[30] § 57.

Exhibit 17.2 Alternative Minimum Tax Formula for Individuals

Taxable income
Plus or minus: Adjustments
Plus: Preferences
Equals: Alternative minimum taxable income (AMTI)
Minus: Exemption
Equals: Alternative minimum tax (AMT) base
Multiplied by: 26% or 28% rate
Equals: Tentative minimum tax before foreign tax credit
Minus: AMT foreign tax credit
Equals: Tentative minimum tax (TMT)
Minus: Regular tax liability (less any foreign tax credit)
Equals: AMT (if TMT > regular tax liability)

Exemption Amount

After calculating AMTI, the taxpayer determines the AMT **exemption amount**. The purpose of the AMT exemption is to ensure that taxpayers with minimal positive adjustments or preferences are not subject to an AMT liability. Note that the exemption amounts for AMT are significantly higher than those for regular tax purposes.

The initial exemption amounts for 2022 are listed below.[31] These exemption amounts are phased out at a rate of 25 percent of the amount by which AMTI exceeds certain thresholds (see Example 14). The exemption amount and the phaseout thresholds are both tied to the taxpayer's filing status.

		Phaseout	
Status	**Exemption**	**Begins at**	**Ends at**
Married, joint	$118,100	$1,079,800	$1,552,200
Single or head of household	75,900	539,900	843,500
Married, separate	59,050	539,900	776,100

Once AMTI equals the end of the phaseout range, a taxpayer's exemption amount will equal zero. Example 14 illustrates the calculation of the phaseout of the AMT exemption.

Harry, who is single, records AMTI of $680,000 for the year. His $75,900 initial exemption amount is reduced by $35,025 [($680,000 − $539,900) × 25% phaseout rate]. Harry's AMT exemption is $40,875 ($75,900 exemption − $35,025 reduction).

AMT Liability

As shown in Exhibit 17.2, AMTI less the exemption amount equals the AMT base. This base amount is multiplied by the tax rate and reduced by any credits that are allowed, resulting in the tentative minimum tax (TMT).

[31] The exemption amounts are indexed annually for inflation. § 55(d)(4).

The relationship between the regular tax liability and the TMT is key to the AMT calculation. If the regular tax liability exceeds the TMT, the taxpayer's AMT liability is zero. However, if the TMT exceeds the regular tax liability, the excess is the taxpayer's AMT liability. Technically, the AMT is a surtax; both tax law and the Form 6251 categorize any excess of TMT over the taxpayer's regular tax liability as the AMT amount.[32] For practical purposes, the taxpayer pays whichever tax liability is greater—that calculated using the regular income tax rules or that calculated using the AMT rules.

A graduated, two-tier AMT rate schedule applies in calculating the TMT. In 2022, a 26 percent rate applies on an AMT base up to $206,100 ($103,050 for married, filing separately); a 28 percent rate applies to any remaining AMT base above that amount.[33] Any net capital gain or qualified dividend income included in the AMT base is taxed at the favorable tax rates for such amounts rather than at the AMT rates.

Anna, an unmarried individual, reports regular taxable income of $650,000. Anna itemizes deductions; she has positive adjustments of $70,000 and preferences of $65,000. Anna's regular tax liability for 2022 is $203,455. Her AMT in 2022 is calculated as follows.

Taxable income	$650,000
Plus: Adjustments	70,000
Plus: Preferences	65,000
Equals: AMTI	$785,000
Minus: AMT exemption [$75,900 − 25%($785,000 − $539,900)]	14,625
Equals: AMT base	$770,375
TMT [($206,100 × 26%) + ($770,375 − $206,100) × 28%]	$211,583
Minus: Regular tax liability	203,455
Equals: AMT	$ 8,128

Anna will pay the IRS a total of $211,583, consisting of her regular tax liability of $203,455 plus her AMT of $8,128.

Credits against regular tax liability are allowed to some taxpayers depending on their economic circumstances or the type of business activity in which they engage. Personal nonrefundable credits (e.g., Adoption Credit, Lifetime Learning Credit, and Saver's Credit) can offset any AMT liability as well as any regular tax liability.[34]

Michael has total personal nonrefundable credits of $11,000, regular tax liability of $133,000, and tentative minimum tax of $126,000. The entire $11,000 credit is available to offset Michael's $133,000 tax liability.

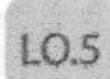

Identify the adjustments made in calculating AMTI.

17-4b AMT Adjustments

As discussed previously, most **adjustments** relate to timing differences that arise because of differences in how an item is treated for regular tax and AMT purposes. As a result, it is necessary to determine the difference between amounts determined under the methods used in calculating regular taxable income and the amounts determined using the methods allowed for AMT purposes.

The remainder of this section discusses specific AMT adjustments.

Depreciation

Although an AMT adjustment for depreciation is sometimes required, the relevance of the adjustment has declined over time. For example, the alternate depreciation system (ADS) must be used to compute AMT depreciation on real property placed in service

[32] § 55(a).

[33] §§ 55(b)(1)(A) and (d)(4)(B).

[34] § 26(a)(2).

before 1999.[35] As discussed in text Section 5-7i, although both ADS and MACRS use the straight-line depreciation method for realty, ADS uses a 40-year recover period rather than the 27.5- or 39-year recovery periods required by MACRS.[36] However, no AMT adjustment is required for realty placed in service after 1998.

ADS is also required for personal property when computing AMT depreciation. The ADS system generally requires the cost of personal property to be recovered using 150 percent declining-balance depreciation rather than the 200 percent declining-balance method on which MACRS is based (See Exhibit 5.8 in Chapter 5). Further, the use of § 179 expense or bonus depreciation is not generally allowed for AMT purposes. However, a special exception applies for personal property placed in service between 2011 and 2027. The cost of personal property placed in service in those years that is eligible for bonus depreciation is recovered for AMT purposes in the same manner as it is for regular tax purposes, including the use of § 179 expense, bonus depreciation, and MACRS.[37] Recall that a taxpayer may elect not to use bonus depreciation to recover the cost of an asset for regular tax purposes. Nonetheless, if the asset was *eligible* for such expensing, no AMT depreciation adjustment is required either in the year placed in service or in any succeeding year.[38] As discussed in text Section 5-7g, property eligible for bonus depreciation includes most tangible property with a recovery period of 20 years or less, as well as software and certain other intangibles. Beginning in 2018, bonus depreciation was expanded to cover used property.[39] Therefore, no AMT adjustment is necessary for most personal property placed in service between 2011 and 2027.

Bonus Depreciation and AMT Depreciation

Elison owns and operates a small after-school tutoring business. In early 2022, he purchased and placed in service furniture costing $18,000. Rather than use MACRS for the furniture, Emerson immediately deducted 100% of the cost of the furniture using bonus depreciation. No AMT depreciation adjustment is required in 2022 because bonus depreciation applies for both regular tax and AMT purposes.[40]

Assume the same facts as in Example 17, except that Elison elects not to use bonus depreciation on the furniture for regular tax purposes. He believes that his business will be more profitable in the future and would like to ensure that he has tax deductions available to offset this future income.

In 2022, Elison's regular tax depreciation deduction for the furniture is $2,572 ($18,000 × 0.1429). Even though bonus depreciation is not being used for regular tax purposes, no AMT depreciation adjustment is needed because the property was *eligible* for bonus depreciation.

Where AMT depreciation adjustments are required (e.g., for public utility property and certain property owned by car dealerships ineligible for bonus depreciation), the amount and direction of the adjustment is driven by a difference in the accelerated-depreciation percentage for regular tax and AMT purposes. For personal property, the MACRS recovery period and convention (see text Section 5-7d) are used to calculate regular tax depreciation as well as AMT depreciation. However, where the depreciation deduction for regular tax purposes is calculated using the 200 percent declining-balance method, AMT depreciation is calculated using the 150 percent declining-balance method.[41] (See Exhibit 5.8 in Chapter 5.) Example 19 illustrates the adjustment calculation.

[35] § 56(a)(1)(A).

[36] The 39-year life generally applies to nonresidential real property placed in service on or after May 13, 1993.

[37] § 168(k)(2)(G).

[38] § Rev.Proc. 2017–33, 2017–19 I.R.B. 1236, § 4.04.

[39] § 168(k).

[40] Assume instead that the furniture is placed in service in 2023, when the bonus depreciation percentage is 80%. If Elison claims bonus depreciation equal to 80% of the cost of the furniture ($14,400) and then uses MACRS to recover the remaining 20% ($3,600), his total depreciation deduction for regular tax purposes will be $14,914 [$14,400 + $514 ($3,600 × 0.1429)]. Since the depreciation of property eligible for bonus depreciation is the same for both regular tax and AMT purposes, no adjustment will be required in 2023.

[41] § 56(a)(1)(A)(ii).

Sawyer placed an $8,000 asset ineligible for bonus depreciation in service in year 1. The MACRS recovery period for such an asset is three years. Annual regular tax (using 200% declining balance) and AMT depreciation (using 150% declining balance) amounts are as follows.

Tax Year	Regular Income Tax Deduction	AMT Deduction	AMT Adjustment
1	$2,666	$2,000	$ 666
2	3,556	3,000	556
3	1,185	2,000	(815)
4	593	1,000	(407)

As is shown in Example 19, the same conventions are used for regular tax and AMT depreciation. Thus, the asset is fully depreciated over four years for both regular tax and AMT purposes, because the same recovery period and the half-year convention are applied in both calculations. The AMT depreciation deduction is initially smaller because of the lesser declining balance percentage used for AMT purposes. As a result, the adjustments in year 1 and year 2 are positive; regular taxable income is increased by these amounts to arrive at the AMTI. In the last two years of the asset's life, the AMT adjustments are negative. Regular income will be decreased by these amounts to arrive at AMTI. In total, the same amount of depreciation is taken for both regular tax and AMT purposes.

All personal property is taken into consideration in computing one net AMT depreciation adjustment regardless of the date placed in service. Using this netting process, the AMT adjustment for a tax year is the difference between the total regular tax depreciation for all personal property and the total depreciation computed for that property for AMT purposes. In other words, the same principles that apply in Example 19 apply in aggregate.

Adjusted Gain or Loss

When property is sold or disposed of during the year, the gain or loss reported for regular income tax purposes may differ from the gain or loss determined for AMT purposes. Such a difference will be caused by the use of different depreciation methods for regular tax and AMT purposes, resulting in a different adjusted basis. An AMT adjustment must be made to regular taxable income to capture any such differences.[42]

Return to the facts in Example 19. Sawyer sells the asset he placed in service in year 1 on September 1 of year 3 for $12,500. In the year of sale, two AMT adjustments result: the depreciation adjustment for year 3 and any gain (or loss) adjustment resulting from the sale.

The regular income tax depreciation for year 3 is $593 [$8,000 cost × 14.81% (Chapter 5, Exhibit 5.4) × 0.5]. AMT depreciation for that year is $1,000 [$8,000 × 25% (Chapter 5, Exhibit 5.8) × 0.5]. Sawyer's negative AMT adjustment for year 3, reflecting the additional depreciation for AMT purposes, is $407 ($593 regular income tax depreciation − $1,000 AMT depreciation).

In computing gain (or loss) as a result of the sale, the adjusted basis in the asset is different for regular income tax and AMT purposes because of depreciation. The adjusted basis for each purpose is determined as follows.

	Regular Income Tax	AMT
Cost	$ 8,000	$ 8,000
Less: Depreciation for prior tax years (see Example 19)	(6,222)	(5,000)
Depreciation for year 3	(593)	(1,000)
Adjusted basis	$ 1,185	$ 2,000

continued

[42] § 56(a)(6).

Having determined the adjusted basis, the recognized gain for regular tax and AMT purposes is calculated as follows.

	Regular Income Tax	AMT
Amount realized	$12,500	$12,500
Adjusted basis	(1,185)	(2,000)
Recognized gain	$11,315	$10,500

Because the regular income tax gain is greater than the AMT gain on the sale of the asset, Sawyer has a negative AMT adjustment of $815 ($11,315 regular income tax gain − $10,500 AMT gain). Note that this negative adjustment offsets the prior and current-year adjustments for depreciation.

Completed Contract Method of Accounting

For a long-term contract, taxpayers are required to use the percentage of completion method for AMT purposes.[43] However, in limited circumstances, taxpayers can use the completed contract method for regular income tax purposes. Thus, where the percentage of completion method is not used for regular tax purposes, a taxpayer recognizes a different amount of income for regular income tax purposes than for AMT purposes. The resulting AMT adjustment is equal to the difference between income reported under the percentage of completion method and the amount reported using the completed contract method. The adjustment can be either positive or negative depending on the amount of income recognized under the different methods.

Similar to some of the other adjustments discussed previously, a taxpayer can avoid an AMT adjustment on long-term contracts by using the percentage of completion method for regular income tax purposes rather than the completed contract method.

Incentive Stock Options

Like other compensatory options, **incentive stock options (ISOs)** are granted by employers to motivate employees to work harder to increase the value of the company. In return, employees should benefit from the increased compensation that a higher stock price brings. However, the exercise of an ISO is one of the more common triggers of an AMT liability.

At the time an ISO is granted, the option typically has a zero value. As a result, no gross income is recognized at the date of grant for regular tax purposes, and no adjustment is required for AMT purposes. If the value of the stock increases during the option period, the employee can obtain shares at a favorable price by exercising the option. For regular tax purposes, the exercise of an ISO does not increase taxable income.[44] However, for AMT purposes, the excess of the fair market value of the stock over the exercise price (the *spread* or the *bargain element*) is treated as an adjustment in the taxable year in which the option is exercised.[45]

Example 21

In January 2022, Manuel exercised an ISO that had been granted by his employer, Gold Corporation, in March 2018. Manuel acquired 1,000 shares of Gold stock for the exercise price of $20 per share. The fair market value of the stock at the date of exercise was $50 per share. The transaction does not affect regular taxable income in either 2018 or 2022. For AMT purposes, Manuel records a positive adjustment of $30,000 ($50,000 fair market value − $20,000 exercise price) for 2022.

As a result of this adjustment, the regular income tax basis of the stock acquired through the exercise of ISOs is different from the AMT basis. The regular income tax basis of the stock is equal to its cost, the exercise price of the option, whereas the AMT basis is equal to the fair market value of the stock on the date the option is exercised. Consequently, the amount of any gain or loss upon disposition of the stock likely will differ for regular income tax and AMT purposes.

[43] § 56(a)(3).

[44] § 421(a).

[45] § 56(b)(3).

Example 22

Assume the same facts as in the previous example, and assume that Manuel sells the stock acquired with the option for $60,000 in December 2023. His gain for regular income tax purposes is $40,000 ($60,000 amount realized − $20,000 regular income tax basis). For AMT purposes, the gain is $10,000 ($60,000 amount realized − $50,000 AMT basis). Therefore, Manuel will make a negative $30,000 adjustment in computing AMT in 2023.

Because the gain on sale was $30,000 larger for regular tax purposes ($40,000 regular income tax gain − $10,000 AMT gain), a negative adjustment of $30,000 is required to reflect the $10,000 AMT gain. Note that this $30,000 negative adjustment upon disposition offsets the $30,000 positive adjustment made in the year of exercise.

An employee may be restricted as to when he or she can dispose of stock acquired with an ISO. In other words, the stock acquired with the option may not be freely transferable until some specified period has passed. If there were some restriction, then the employee would not make the AMT adjustment until the stock was freely transferable.

Example 23

In January 2021, Manuel exercised an ISO that had been granted by his employer, Gold Corporation, in March 2018. Manuel acquired 1,000 shares of Gold stock for the exercise price of $20 per share, when the fair market value of the stock was $50 per share. The stock became freely transferable in February 2022, when the fair market value was $55 per share. For AMT purposes, Manuel will make a positive adjustment of $30,000 ($50,000 fair market value − $20,000 exercise price) in 2022. The option contract does not affect regular taxable income in any tax year.

If the taxpayer exercises the ISO and disposes of the stock in the same tax year (a disqualifying disposition), compensation income is reported for regular tax purposes, which means that an AMT adjustment is not required for that option exercise.

Alternative Tax Net Operating Loss Deduction

In computing taxable income, taxpayers can deduct net operating losses (NOLs) created in prior years. While an NOL deduction also is allowed for AMT purposes, the regular income tax NOL must be modified to compute AMTI correctly.

The starting point in computing the **alternative tax NOL deduction (ATNOLD)** is the NOL computed for regular income tax purposes. The regular income tax NOL is modified for AMT adjustments and tax preferences to arrive at the ATNOLD. In other words, the adjustments made in calculating AMTI are also made to the regular tax NOL amount; preferences that increase the regular tax NOL amount also increase the ATNOLD. As a result, the regular tax NOL and ATNOLD will not be the same.[46]

Example 24

In 2022, Bianca incurred a regular tax NOL of $400,000. In 2021, Bianca incurred mine exploration and development expenditures of $100,000; no additional expenditures were incurred in 2022. For AMT purposes, in 2022, Bianca will expense (make a negative AMT adjustment of) $10,000 related to the 2021 expenditures. Bianca's deductions also include tax preferences of $80,000. Her ATNOLD carryforward to 2023 is $330,000 ($400,000 regular income tax NOL − $80,000 tax preferences deducted in computing the NOL + $10,000 mine exploration and development costs adjustment).

In Example 24, if the regular income tax NOL was allowed in full for AMT purposes, the $80,000 of tax preference items would have the effect of reducing AMTI in the year (or years) the 2022 NOL was utilized. Such a result is contradictory to the purpose of the AMT.

[46] § 56(a)(4).

Finally, in keeping with the goal of ensuring that taxpayers with economic income pay some minimum amount of tax, a ceiling exists on the amount of the ATNOLD that can be deducted. The deduction is limited to 90 percent of AMTI (before the ATNOLD) in the year to which the NOL is carried forward.[47]

Assume the same facts as in the previous example, and that Bianca's AMTI (before the ATNOLD) in 2023 is $190,000. Therefore, of the $330,000 ATNOLD carryforward from 2022, only $171,000 ($190,000 × 90%) can be used in recalculating the 2023 AMT. The unused $159,000 of 2022 ATNOLD will next be carried forward to 2024 for use in recalculating that year's AMT.

In general, the regular tax NOL carryover provisions apply for purposes of the AMT. For instance, NOLs generated after 2020 are carried forward indefinitely (refer to text Section 7-6a).[48] A taxpayer who has an ATNOLD carryforward is considered to have utilized that ATNOLD in the calculation of the carryforward year's AMTI even if the taxpayer is not subject to the AMT in that carryover year. This can result in the loss of an ATNOLD even when the taxpayer does not have an AMT liability.

Emily's ATNOLD for 2023 (carried forward from 2022) is $10,000. AMTI in 2023, before considering the ATNOLD, is $25,000. If Emily's regular income tax liability exceeds her TMT, the AMT does not apply. Nevertheless, Emily's ATNOLD of $10,000 is "used up" in 2023 and is not available for carryover to a later year.

The Standard Deduction

For regular tax purposes, taxpayers may reduce their AGI by the greater of the standard deduction or itemized deductions. However, the standard deduction is an AMT adjustment.[49] Therefore, for AMT purposes, taxpayers may only reduce their AGI by itemized deductions. Further, taxpayers who do not itemize for regular tax purposes are not allowed to do so for AMT purposes.[50]

Itemized Deductions

Most of the itemized deductions that are allowed for regular income tax purposes are allowed for AMT purposes. As discussed below, for AMT purposes, the itemized deductions for certain taxes as well as interest expense require adjustment.

Taxes Any state and local sales, income, or property taxes deducted by an individual taxpayer in the calculation of regular taxable income are not allowed as a deduction in computing AMTI.[51] Thus, a positive AMT adjustment equal to the amount of such taxes deducted (up to $10,000) is required.

Also remember that under the tax benefit rule, a tax refund is included in regular taxable income to the extent the taxpayer obtained a tax benefit by deducting the tax in a prior year. If the taxpayer's gross income includes the recovery of any tax deducted as an itemized deduction for regular income tax purposes, a negative AMT adjustment in the amount of the recovery is allowed for AMTI purposes.[52] For example, state income taxes can be deducted for regular income tax purposes but cannot be deducted in computing AMTI. Because of this, any refund of such taxes from a prior year that would be included in the calculation of regular taxable income is not included in AMTI.

[47] § 56(d)(1)(A)(i)(II).
[48] § 172(b)(1).
[49] § 56(b)(1)(E).
[50] SCA 200103073.
[51] § 56(b)(1)(A).
[52] § 56(b)(1)(C).

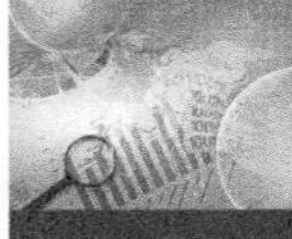

Tax Planning Strategies

Control the Timing of Preferences and Adjustments

Framework Focus: Tax Rate

Strategy: Control the Character of Income and Deductions.

If preference and adjustment amounts cannot be avoided, the timing of these amounts may help to mitigate AMT liabilities.

- The AMT exemption often keeps items of tax preference from being subject to the AMT. To use the AMT exemption effectively, taxpayers should attempt to manage the timing of preference items.
- In a year that a taxpayer expects to be subject to the AMT, real estate or fourth-quarter estimated state tax payments should be paid in the following year. Any current-year benefit received from the regular income tax deduction for these amounts will be offset by the AMT adjustment made.

Example 27

Asma, age 35, is a resident of Minnesota. In 2021, her Federal taxable income included an itemized deduction of $4,200 for Minnesota income taxes. In February 2022, Asma received a Federal income tax refund of $5,800 and a Minnesota income tax refund of $600.

In 2022, Asma makes a negative AMT adjustment of $600 for the state tax refund. The $600 refund is included in 2022 regular taxable income because the deduction for state taxes reduced her prior year Federal income tax liability. However, the $600 refund is excluded from her 2022 AMTI because the deduction for state taxes was not allowed for AMT purposes.

Asma's Federal income tax refund does not create an AMT adjustment, because Federal income taxes never are deducted in the calculation of regular taxable income or AMTI.

Interest in General Generally, the deductibility of interest for regular tax and AMT are similar. However, there are two situations in which an AMT adjustment may arise, one with respect to housing interest and the other related to investment interest. The AMT adjustments for these amounts are discussed below.

Housing Interest For regular tax purposes, a taxpayer may deduct interest on acquisition indebtedness on up to two homes (see further discussion in text Section 10-4c). This is generally true for AMT purposes as well. However, while almost any dwelling that serves as a residence and is used by the taxpayer for personal purposes will qualify as a second residence for regular tax purposes,[53] the deduction for a second residence for AMT purposes is limited to houses, apartments, condominiums, and mobile homes.[54] Therefore, a taxpayer deducting interest on a second residence that is not a house, an apartment, a condominium, or a mobile home (e.g., a houseboat) will have an AMT adjustment.

Investment Interest Investment interest is deductible for regular income tax purposes and for AMT purposes to the extent of qualified net investment income. However, because the categorization and treatment of interest may differ for regular tax and AMT purposes, an adjustment may be required if the amount of investment interest deductible for regular income tax purposes differs from the amount deductible for AMT purposes. For example, as discussed in text Section 17-4c, the interest on private activity bonds usually is a tax preference for AMT purposes. Such interest will increase the net investment income for AMT purposes and, therefore, potentially increase the amount of deductible investment interest expense.

Digging Deeper 3

Discussions of other AMT adjustments can be found on this book's companion website: www.cengage.com

[53] § 1.163-10T(p)(3)(ii).

[54] § 56(b)(1)(C)(i) and (e).

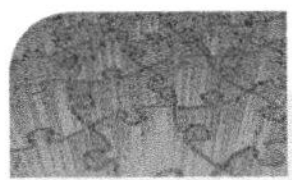

Concept Summary 17.2

Summary of Common AMT Adjustment Provisions

1. Most adjustments reflect *timing differences* between regular taxable income and AMTI and can, therefore, be either positive or negative.
2. Although *depreciation* adjustments are generally required, no adjustment is required for any asset eligible for *bonus depreciation*. When a depreciation adjustment is required, a corresponding adjustment must be made if and when the taxpayer disposes of the asset.
3. The adjustment for the standard deduction *enters the AMT calculation indirectly* by adjusting the taxable income amount that begins the AMTI computation.
4. With the exception of taxes and certain interest, most itemized deductions do not trigger adjustments.
5. Apart from adjustments related to itemized deductions, some adjustments *can be avoided* if the taxpayer adopts the same tax treatment for regular tax purposes as is required for AMT purposes.

17-4c AMT Preferences

LO.6

Identify the preferences that are included in calculating AMTI.

Unlike most adjustments, which can be positive or negative, AMT **preferences** always are positive. In other words, preferences are always added back to regular taxable income in the calculation of AMTI.

Percentage Depletion

Congress enacted the percentage depletion rules to provide taxpayers with incentives to invest in the development of certain natural resources. Percentage depletion is computed by multiplying a rate specified in the Code by the gross income from the property (see text Section 5-9b).[55] The rate is based on the type of resource involved. Generally, the basis of the property is reduced by the amount of depletion taken until the basis reaches zero. However, because percentage depletion is based on gross income rather than the investment in the property, taxpayers are allowed to continue taking percentage depletion deductions even after the basis of the property reaches zero. Thus, over the life of the property, depletion deductions may greatly exceed the cost of the property.

The percentage depletion preference is equal to the excess of the regular income tax deduction for percentage depletion over the adjusted basis of the property at the end of the taxable year.[56] Note that the end-of-year basis is determined without regard to the depletion deduction for the taxable year. This preference is calculated separately for each mineral property owned by the taxpayer.[57] As a result, a taxpayer cannot use basis in one property to reduce the preference for excess depletion on another property.

Kim owns a mineral property that qualifies for a 22% depletion rate. The basis of the property at the beginning of the year, prior to any current-year depletion deduction, is $10,000. Gross income from the property for the year is $100,000. For regular income tax purposes, Kim's percentage depletion deduction (assume that the deduction is not limited by taxable income from the property) is $22,000. For AMT purposes, Kim has a tax preference of $12,000 ($22,000 – $10,000).

[55] § 613(a).

[56] § 57(a)(1). The preference does not include percentage depletion on oil and gas wells of independent producers or royalty owners, as defined in § 613A(c).

[57] § 614(a).

Intangible Drilling Costs

In computing regular taxable income, taxpayers can deduct certain intangible drilling and development costs in the year incurred, although such costs are normally capital in nature. The deduction is allowed for costs incurred in connection with oil and gas wells and geothermal wells.

For AMT purposes, a portion of the excess IDC (the amount that is immediately deducted over what would be deducted if the costs were capitalized and amortized over 10 years) is a preference item.[58] The IDC preference is computed separately for oil and gas wells and geothermal wells. The excess IDC preference is computed as follows.

IDC expensed in the year incurred
Minus: Deduction if IDC were capitalized and amortized over 10 years
Equals: Excess of IDC expense over amortization
Minus: 65% of net oil and gas or geothermal income
Equals: Preference amount

Ben incurred IDC of $50,000 during the year and elected to expense that amount for regular tax purposes. His net oil and gas income for the year was $60,000. Ben has no income from geothermal wells. Ben's preference for IDC is $6,000 [($50,000 IDC − $5,000 amortization) − (65% × $60,000 income)].

A taxpayer can avoid the preference for IDC by electing to write off the expenditures over a 10-year period for regular income tax purposes.

Interest on Private Activity Bonds

Like interest income earned on other municipal bonds, income from private activity bonds is not included in regular taxable income, and expenses related to carrying such bonds are not deductible for regular income tax purposes. However, interest on private activity bonds is considered a preference in computing AMTI. As a result, expenses incurred in carrying the bonds are offset against the interest income in computing the preference amount.[59] Interest on private activity bonds issued in 2009 and 2010 is not treated as a preference.

In general, **private activity bonds** are bonds issued by states or municipalities but more than 10 percent of the proceeds are for private business use.[60] For example, a state or local government seeking to attract jobs to a particular region might issue a bond the proceeds of which are used to construct a factory that is leased to a private business at a favorable rate. Such a municipal bond would be a private activity bond.

The majority of tax-exempt bonds issued by states and municipalities are not classified as private activity bonds. Therefore, the interest income from such bonds does not regularly create a preference for AMT purposes.

In the current year, Danae earned $8,300 of interest income, comprised of the following amounts.

10-year Treasury bond (issued in 2016)	$4,000
10-year municipal bond (issued in 2017)	2,500
10-year private activity bond (issued in 2019)	1,800

All of the bonds were purchased on their issuance date. Danae's preference for interest is $1,800, the interest on the private activity bond. Treasury bond interest is included in both regular taxable income and AMTI; the interest from the non-private activity municipal bond is not included in either regular taxable income or AMTI.

[58] § 57(a)(2). Independent oil and gas producers are exempt from this preference item.

[59] § 57(a)(5).

[60] § 141.

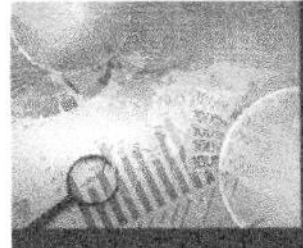

Tax Planning Strategies **Avoiding Preferences and Adjustments**

Framework Focus: Tax Rate

Strategy: Control the Character of Income and Deductions.

One strategy to managing AMT liabilities is to avoid preference and adjustment amounts where possible.

- A taxpayer who expects to be subject to the AMT should more closely consider investing in private activity bonds. Any AMT triggered by interest on private activity bonds reduces the yield on an investment in such bonds.
- A taxpayer could be better off taking itemized deductions even when those deductions are less than the standard deduction if the itemized deductions do not require AMT adjustments. For example, a taxpayer with itemized deductions comprised of charitable contributions (that were less than the standard deduction) would not make an AMT adjustment for such contributions, but would be required to make an adjustment for the standard deduction, which could potentially put the taxpayer into AMT.
- Neither property taxes nor real estate taxes are deductible for AMT if they are categorized as itemized deductions. However, taxes deductible as a part of business operations or rental activities are allowed for AMT purposes. Therefore, a taxpayer who could qualify for a home-office deduction would be able to deduct a portion of his or her home's real estate taxes as business expenses rather than as an itemized deduction.

Exclusion for Certain Small Business Stock

Gain on the sale of certain small business stock that is owned for more than five years is excluded from gross income for regular tax purposes.[61] If the stock was acquired prior to 2010, 7 percent of the amount excluded is a preference item. An exclusion for stock acquired after 2009 does not create a preference item.[62]

17-4d Illustration of the AMT Computation

LO.7 **Compute the AMT.**

The computation of the AMT is illustrated in the following example.

Example 31

Molly Seims, single and age 56, resides in Houston, Texas. Molly, recorded taxable income for 2022 as follows.

Salary		$292,000
Interest received on corporate bonds		18,000
Adjusted gross income		$310,000
Less itemized deductions:		
Medical expenses (do not exceed 7.5% of AGI)	$ -0-	
State income taxes	9,500	
Interest[a]		
Home mortgage (for qualified housing)	20,000*	
Investment interest	6,300*	
Charitable contributions (cash)	15,000*	
Casualty loss ($48,000 − 10% of $310,000 AGI)[b]	17,000*	(67,800)
Taxable income		$242,200

[a]In this illustration, all interest is deductible in computing AMTI. Qualified housing interest is deductible without adjustment. Investment interest ($6,300) is deductible to the extent of net investment income included in AMTI.

[b]The casualty loss is the result of flooding that occurred in a Federally declared disaster area. Per § 165(h)(A), such losses are deductible subject to the $100 floor and the 10%-of-AGI limit. The $48,000 loss amount is after the $100 floor.

continued

[61]§ 1202(a)(4). Different percentages of the realized gain are excludable for stock purchased prior to this date.

[62]§§ 57(a)(7) and 1202(a)(4)(C).

Deductions marked with an asterisk are allowed for AMT purposes. However, an adjustment is required for state income taxes.

In addition, Molly earned $40,000 of interest income on private activity bonds issued in 2017. She also exercised ISOs in 2022. The option spread (the difference between the exercise price and the fair market value on the date of exercise) was $35,000. Molly's regular tax liability in 2022 is $58,523. AMTI is computed as follows.

Taxable income	$242,200
Plus: Adjustments	
State income taxes	9,500
Incentive stock options	35,000
Plus: Preference (interest on private activity bonds)	40,000
Equals: AMTI	$326,700
Minus: AMT exemption	(75,900)
Equals: Minimum tax base	$250,800
TMT [($206,100 × 26%) + ($44,700 × 28%)]	$ 66,102
Minus: Regular tax liability	(58,523)
Equals: AMT	$ 7,579

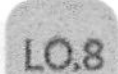

LO.8

Apply the AMT credit in the alternative minimum tax structure.

17-4e AMT Credit

As was illustrated in several of the examples in this chapter, timing differences that give rise to AMT adjustments eventually reverse. However, because a taxpayer always pays the higher of the regular tax and the AMT, the reversal may not result in a lower tax liability if the taxpayer must pay the regular tax in the year of reversal. To provide equity for taxpayers, a tax credit is created in a year in which a taxpayer pays AMT as a result of these timing differences.[63] The credit may be carried forward and used to offset a taxpayer's future regular tax liability.

This credit, known as the **alternative minimum tax credit**, is generally created only for the portion of the AMT liability that results from timing differences.[64] A credit is neither created nor increased by most permanent differences between the regular income tax liability and the AMT. For example, no AMT credit is created by the following:

- The standard deduction.
- Itemized deductions not allowable for AMT purposes, including state and local taxes and certain interest expense.
- Excess percentage depletion.
- Tax-exempt interest on private activity bonds.
- The exclusion of gain on the sale of small business stock.

Patrick, who is single, reports zero taxable income for 2022. He has positive AMT adjustments of $600,000 and a preference item of $300,000 for a gain on the sale of small business stock. Because of the amount of his AMTI, the exemption is phased out completely and his AMT base is $900,000. Patrick's TMT is $247,878 [($206,100 × 26%) + ($693,900 × 28%)].

To determine the amount of AMT credit to carry over, the AMT must be recomputed to reflect only the effect of timing differences. The AMT credit is equal to the difference between the total AMT and the AMT that would have been due considering only the permanent differences.

[63] § 53.

[64] S. Rep. No. 99–313 (PL 99–514), p. 536.

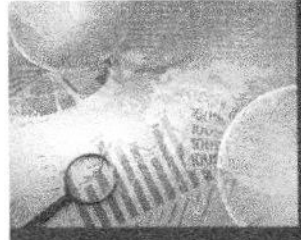

Tax Planning Strategies **Other AMT Planning Strategies**

Framework Focus: Tax Rate

Strategy: Control the Character of Income and Deductions.

A potential AMT liability can be reduced by decreasing adjusted gross income (AGI). For example, certain contributions to qualified retirement savings plans are excluded from gross income, reducing AGI. Where a taxpayer participates in a § 401(k), § 457(b) plan, or SIMPLE IRA plan, contributions to the plan would reduce AGI, which is beneficial for both regular tax and AMT purposes as well as for retirement planning.

Although the lower tax rates for long-term capital gains apply for both regular tax and AMT purposes, such long-term capital gains increase AGI and AMTI, and these income items could reduce the amount of the AMT exemption available to a taxpayer. In a year for which a taxpayer expects to be subject to the AMT, the taxpayer should evaluate how the recognition of long-term capital gains affects AMTI and consider, where possible, whether the recognition of such gains should be deferred to a future year.

Assume the same facts as in the previous example. If there had been no positive timing adjustments for the year, Patrick's AMT base would have been $224,100 ($300,000 AMTI − $75,900 exemption) and his TMT would have been $58,626 [($206,100 × 26%) + ($18,000 × 28%)]. Patrick may carry over to 2023 and subsequent years an AMT credit of $189,252 ($247,878 actual TMT − $58,626 TMT unrelated to timing differences).

An AMT credit can be utilized only in a year in which the taxpayer is not subject to the AMT. In addition, as demonstrated in the following example, the amount of the credit that can be used is equal to the excess of the taxpayer's regular tax liability over their tentative minimum tax liability. Finally, while the AMT credit cannot be carried back, the credit is carried forward indefinitely.

Cho holds a $11,600 AMT credit from 2016. In 2022, prior to consideration of the AMT credit, Cho's regular tax liability is $60,000 and her tentative minimum tax is $54,000. In this situation, Cho can use $6,000 of the AMT credit from 2016 to reduce her 2022 regular tax liability. Thus, Cho's tax liability in 2022 is $54,000. The remaining $5,600 AMT credit is carried forward to future tax years.

A discussion of the relation of the foreign tax credit and the AMT can be found on this book's companion website: www.cengage.com

Concept Summary 17.3

Summary of AMT Preference Provisions

1. Preferences are *always* positive in amount. A preference reflects a permanent difference between the regular tax and the AMT treatment of an amount.
2. With the exception of the IDC preference, preferences *cannot be avoided* by adopting the same tax treatment for regular tax and AMT purposes. In general, preferences can be avoided only by avoiding the activity that causes the preference, which may not be economically rational.
3. On occasion, Congress changes the tax code to stimulate economic activity. To the extent that an AMT preference could hinder this economic goal, the *preference also may be modified* (e.g., private activity bond interest, small business stock gain).

Concept Summary 17.4

AMT Adjustments and Preferences

Adjustments	**Positive**	**Negative**	**Both***
Adjusted gain or loss on property dispositions			X
Alternative tax NOL deduction (ATNOLD)			X
Completed contract method			X
Depreciation of personal property			X
Depreciation of real property (placed in service before 1999)			X
Incentive stock options	X**		
Itemized deductions:			
Private activity bond interest that is AMT investment interest		X	
Property tax on personalty	X		
Property tax on realty	X		
Investment interest deductible for AMTI but not for regular taxable income		X	
Qualified residence interest that is not qualified housing interest for AMTI	X		
State income taxes	X		
Tax benefit rule for state income tax refund		X	
Research and experimental expenditures			X
Standard deduction	X		
Preferences			
Intangible drilling costs	X		
Percentage depletion in excess of adjusted basis	X		
Private activity bond interest income	X***		

*Timing differences.
**While the adjustment is positive, the AMT basis for the stock acquired is increased by the amount of the positive adjustment.
***Interest on private activity bonds issued after 2008 and before 2011 is not treated as a tax preference.

Refocus on The Big Picture

Dealing with Tax Credits and the AMT

Tax credits are used by the Federal government to promote certain social and economic objectives. Credits are dollar-for-dollar reductions in tax liability. While tax credits may have strict qualification requirements, taking advantage of available credits may significantly reduce a business's tax liability. Progress Corporation qualifies for a 20 percent tax credit for rehabilitating a certified historic building (see Example 4). In addition, Progress hires workers from economically disadvantaged groups, so it qualifies for the work opportunity tax credit (see Example 5).

The company also qualifies for the credit for employer-provided child care, equal to 25 percent of qualified child care expenses (see Example 11). Mike and his CPA might also want to explore taking advantage of the disabled access credit, which is designed to encourage small businesses to make their facilities accessible to disabled individuals.

What If?

Mike has heard horror stories about the alternative minimum tax (AMT) and is concerned about its potential impact. Is Mike's concern warranted?

The AMT is not applicable to corporations. Therefore, Mike should not have concerns with it. The AMT for individual taxpayers is still in existence, but as long as Progress Corporation remains a C corporation, its operations will not generate an AMT liability. If Progress Corporation should make an S election in the future, the items that flow through to Mike could potentially impact the likelihood that he is subject to the individual AMT.

Suggested Readings

Yair Holtzman, "U.S. Research and Development Tax Credit," *CPA Journal*, October 2017.

Thomas Horan and Margaret Horan, "Strategies for Reducing the Alternative Minimum Tax Liability," *The CPA Journal*, March 2013.

Kreig D. Mitchell, "The R&D Tax Credit for Start-Up Companies," *Practical Tax Strategies*, February 2012.

Jeanne Sahadi, "Why You Probably Won't Have to Pay the AMT Again," **money.cnn.com/2018/01/18/pf/taxes/2018-amt-exemption-increase/index.html**, January 18, 2018.

Kris Siolka, "A Closer Look at AMT: Common Adjustments and Preferences," *Taxpro Monthly*, July 2014.

S. Wayne Swilley, "Long-Term Contracts and AMT," *Journal of Accountancy*, December 2017.

Key Terms

Adjustments, 17-16
Alternative minimum tax (AMT), 17-13
Alternative minimum tax credit, 17-26
Alternative minimum taxable income (AMTI), 17-14
Alternative tax NOL deduction (ATNOLD), 17-20
Credit for employer-provided child care, 17-9
Credit for employer-provided family and medical leave, 17-11
Credit for small employer pension plan startup costs, 17-9
Disabled access credit, 17-8
Energy credits, 17-8
Exemption amount, 17-15
Foreign tax credit (FTC), 17-13
General business credit, 17-2
Incentive stock options (ISOs), 17-19
Preferences, 17-23
Private activity bonds, 17-24
Rehabilitation expenditures credit, 17-4
Research activities credit, 17-6
Tax credits, 17-2
Work opportunity tax credit, 17-5

Computational Exercises

1. **LO.2** Carlson's (a sole proprietor) general business credit for the current year is $84,000. His net income tax is $190,000, tentative minimum tax is $175,000, and net regular tax liability is $185,000. He has no other tax credits. Determine the amount of Carlson's general business credit for the year.

2. **LO.2** Emily spent $135,000 to rehabilitate a certified historic building (adjusted basis of $90,000) that originally had been placed in service in 1935. What is Emily's rehabilitation expenditures tax credit?

3. **LO.2** During 2022, Lincoln Company hires seven individuals who are certified to be members of a qualifying targeted group. Each employee works in excess of 600 hours and is paid wages of $7,500 during the year. Determine the amount of Lincoln's work opportunity credit.

4. **LO.2** Alison incurs the following research expenditures.

In-house wages	$60,000
In-house supplies	5,000
Payment to ABC, Inc., for research	80,000

   a. Determine the amount of qualified research expenditures.
   b. Assuming that the base amount is $50,000, determine Alison's incremental research activities credit.

5. **LO.3** In March 2022, Serengeti exercised an ISO that had been granted by his employer, Thunder Corporation, in December 2019. Serengeti acquired 5,000 shares of Thunder stock for the exercise price of $65 per share. The fair market value of the stock at the date of exercise was $90 per share.
   What is Serengeti's 2019 AMT adjustment related to the ISO? What is the 2022 adjustment?

6. **LO.5** Brennen sold a machine used in his sole proprietorship for $180,000. The machine was purchased eight years ago for $340,000. It did not qualify for bonus depreciation when it was initially purchased. Depreciation up to the date of the sale for regular income tax purposes was $210,000 and $190,000 for AMT purposes.
   What, if any, AMT adjustment arises as a result of the sale of the machine?

7. **LO.5** Pineview Company, a single member LLC, placed in service on June 1, 2022 a $5,000 asset. The asset has a three-year MACRS class life and is ineligible for § 179 expensing and bonus depreciation. Complete the table below by providing the AMT adjustment, and indicate whether the adjustment increases or decreases taxable income.

Year	Tax Deduction	AMT Deduction	AMT Adjustment	Increases or Decreases
2022	$1,667	$1,250	________	________
2023	2,222	1,875	________	________
2024	740	1,250	________	________
2025	371	625	________	________

8. **LO.6** Dimitri owns a gold mine that qualifies for a 15% percentage depletion rate. The basis of the property at the beginning of the year, prior to any current-year depletion deduction, is $21,000. Gross income from the property for the year is $200,000, and taxable income before depletion is $65,000.
   What is Dimitri's AMT depletion preference?

Problems

9. **LO.2** Adelyn has a tentative general business credit of $42,000 for the current year. Her net regular tax liability before the general business credit is $107,000, and her tentative minimum tax is $88,000. Compute Adelyn's allowable general business credit for the year.

10. **LO.2** Oak Corporation holds the following general business credit carryovers.

2018	$ 5,000
2019	15,000
2020	6,000
2021	19,000
Total carryovers	$45,000

If the general business credit generated by activities during 2022 equals $36,000 and the total credit allowed during the current year is $60,000 (based on tax liability), what amounts of the current general business credit and carryovers are utilized against the 2022 income tax liability? What is the amount of the unused credit carried forward to 2023?

11. **LO.2** In January 2021, Iris Corporation purchased and placed in service a certified historic structure building that houses retail businesses. The cost was \$300,000, of which \$25,000 applied to the land. In modernizing the facility, Iris Corporation incurred \$312,000 of renovation costs of the type that qualify for the rehabilitation credit. These improvements were placed in service in October 2022.
    a. Compute Iris Corporation's rehabilitation tax credit for 2022.
    b. Calculate the cost recovery deductions for the building and the renovation costs for 2022.

12. **LO.2** In the current year, Paul Chaing (4522 Fargo Street, Geneva, IL 60134) acquires a qualifying historic structure for \$350,000 (excluding the cost of the land) and plans to substantially rehabilitate the structure. He is planning to spend either \$320,000 or \$380,000 on rehabilitation expenditures.

    Communications
    Critical Thinking
    Decision Making
    Planning

    Write a letter to Paul and a memo for the tax files explaining, for the two alternative expenditures, (1) the computation that determines the rehabilitation expenditures tax credit available to Paul, (2) the effect of the credit on Paul's adjusted basis in the property, and (3) the cash-flow differences as a result of the tax consequences related to his expenditure choice.

13. **LO.2** The tax credit for rehabilitation expenditures is available to help offset the costs related to substantially rehabilitating certain buildings. The credit is calculated on the rehabilitation expenditures incurred and not on the acquisition cost of the building itself.

    Ethics and Equity

    You are a developer who buys, sells, and does construction work on real estate in the inner city of your metropolitan area. A potential customer approaches you about acquiring one of your buildings that easily could qualify for the 20% rehabilitation credit on historic structures. The stated sales price of the structure is \$100,000 (based on appraisals ranging from \$80,000 to \$120,000), and the rehabilitation expenditures, if the job is done correctly, would be about \$150,000.

    Your business has been slow recently due to the sluggish real estate market in your area, and the potential customer makes the following proposal: if you reduce the sales price of the building to \$75,000, he will pay you \$175,000 to perform the rehabilitation work. Although the buyer's total expenditures would be the same, he would benefit from this approach by obtaining a larger tax credit (\$25,000 increased rehabilitation costs × 20% = \$5,000).

    It has been a long time since you have sold any of your real estate. How will you respond?

14. **LO.2** Green Corporation hires six individuals on January 4, 2022, all of whom qualify for the work opportunity credit. Three of these individuals receive wages of \$8,500 during 2022, and each individual works more than 400 hours during the year. The other three individuals each work 300 hours and receive wages of \$5,000 during the year.
    a. Calculate the amount of Green's work opportunity credit for 2022.
    b. If Green pays total wages of \$140,000 to its employees during the year, how much of this amount is deductible in 2022 assuming that the work opportunity credit is taken?

15. **LO.2** Tom, a calendar year taxpayer, informs you that during the year, he incurs expenditures of \$40,000 that qualify for the incremental research activities credit. In addition, it is determined that his base amount for the year is \$32,800.

    Decision Making

    a. Determine Tom's incremental research activities credit for the year.
    b. Tom is in the 24% tax bracket. Determine which approach to the research expenditures and the research activities credit (other than capitalization and subsequent amortization) would provide the greater tax benefit to Tom.

Communications

16. **LO.2** Ahmed Zinna (16 Southside Drive, Charlotte, NC 28204), one of your clients, owns two retail establishments in downtown Charlotte and has come to you seeking advice concerning the tax consequences of complying with the Americans with Disabilities Act. He understands that he needs to install various features at his stores (e.g., ramps, doorways, and restrooms that are handicapped-accessible) to make them more accessible to disabled individuals. He asks whether any tax credits will be available to help offset the cost of the necessary changes. He estimates the cost of the planned changes to his facilities as follows.

Location	Projected Cost
Calvin Street	$22,000
Stowe Avenue	8,500

He reminds you that the Calvin Street store was constructed in 2004, while the Stowe Avenue store is in a building that was constructed in 1947. Ahmed operates his business as a sole proprietorship and has approximately eight employees at each location. Write a letter to Ahmed in which you summarize your conclusions concerning the tax consequences of the proposed capital improvements.

17. **LO.2** Blue Sky, Inc., a U.S. corporation, is a manufacturing concern that sells most of its products in the United States. It also conducts some business in the European Union through various branches. During the current year, Blue Sky reports taxable income of $700,000, of which $500,000 is U.S.-sourced and $200,000 is foreign-sourced. Foreign income taxes paid amounted to $38,000. Blue Sky's U.S. income tax liability is $147,000. What is its U.S. income tax liability net of the allowable foreign tax credit?

18. **LO.4** Use the following data to calculate Chiara's AMT base in 2022. Chiara will itemize deductions and will file as a single taxpayer.

Taxable income	$248,000
Positive AMT adjustments	73,000
Negative AMT adjustments	25,000
AMT Preferences	30,000

19. **LO.6** Falcon has a sole proprietorship that owns a silver mine that she purchased several years ago for $925,000. The adjusted basis at the beginning of the year is $400,000. For the year, Falcon deducts depletion of $700,000 (greater of cost depletion of $290,000 or percentage depletion of $700,000) for regular income tax purposes.
    a. Calculate Falcon's AMT preference.
    b. Calculate Falcon's adjusted basis for regular income tax purposes.
    c. Calculate Falcon's adjusted basis for AMT purposes.

Communications
Decision Making
Planning

20. **LO.5** In March 2022, Helen Carlon acquired used equipment for her business at a cost of $300,000. The equipment is five-year property for regular tax depreciation purposes.
    a. If Helen depreciates the equipment using the method that will produce the greatest deduction for 2022 for regular income tax purposes, what is the amount of the AMT adjustment?
    b. Draft an e-mail to Helen regarding the choice of depreciation methods. Helen's e-mail address is HCarlon@WestFederal.com

21. **LO.5** David is the sole proprietor of a real estate construction business. He uses the completed contract method on a particular contract that requires 16 months to complete. The contract is for $500,000, with estimated costs of $300,000. At the

end of 2021, $180,000 of costs had been incurred. The contract is completed in 2022, with the total cost being $295,000. Determine the AMT adjustments for 2021 and 2022.

22. **LO.5** Allie, who was an accounting major in college, is the owner of a medium-size construction limited liability company. She prepares the company's tax return each year. Due to reporting a home construction contract using the completed contract method, the corporation is subject to the AMT in 2022. Allie files her 2022 tax return in early February 2023. Her total tax liability is $58,000 ($53,000 regular income tax liability + $5,000 AMT). Assume that Allie is in the 37% tax bracket. Ethics and Equity

In early March, Allie reads an article on minimizing income taxes. Based on this article, she decides that it would be beneficial for the company to report the home construction contract using the percentage of completion method on its 2022 return. Although this will increase her 2022 income tax liability, it will minimize the total income tax liability over the two-year construction period. Therefore, Allie files an amended return on March 14, 2023. Evaluate Allie's actions from both a tax avoidance and an ethical perspective.

23. **LO.5** Buford sells an apartment building for $720,000. His adjusted basis is $500,000 for regular income tax purposes and $550,000 for AMT purposes. Calculate Buford's:

a. Gain for regular income tax purposes.
b. Gain for AMT purposes.
c. AMT adjustment, if any.

24. **LO.5** Lilia is going to be subject to the AMT in 2022. She owns an investment building and is considering disposing of it and investing in other realty. Based on an appraisal of the building's value, the realized gain would be $85,000. Issue ID

Two individuals, Ed and Abby, have indicated an interest in buying the building. Ed has offered to purchase the building from Lilia with a December 29, 2022 closing date. Ed wants to close the transaction in 2022 because he will receive certain beneficial tax consequences only if the transaction is closed prior to 2023. Abby has offered to purchase the building with a January 2, 2023 closing date.

The adjusted basis of the building is $95,000 greater for AMT purposes than for the regular income tax. Lilia expects to be in the 37% regular income tax bracket.

What are the relevant Federal income tax issues that Lilia faces in making her decision?

25. **LO.5** Flicker, a single member LLC, acquired a passive activity this year. Gross income from operations of the activity was $160,000. Operating expenses, not including depreciation, were $122,000. Regular income tax depreciation of $49,750 was computed under MACRS. AMT depreciation, computed using the ADS, was $41,000. Compute Flicker's passive activity loss deduction and passive activity loss suspended for regular income tax purposes. Then determine the same amounts for AMT purposes.

26. **LO.5** Wolfgang, who is age 33, records AGI of $125,000. He incurs the following itemized deductions for 2022.

Medical expenses [$11,875 − (7.5% × $125,000)]	$ 2,500
State income taxes	4,200
Charitable contributions	5,000
Home mortgage interest on his personal residence	6,000
	$17,700

a. Calculate Wolfgang's itemized deductions for AMT purposes.
b. What is the total amount of his AMT adjustments from these items?

27. **LO.6** Walter, who is single, owns a personal residence in the city. He also owns a cabin near a ski resort in the mountains. He uses the cabin as a vacation home. In the current year, he borrowed $60,000 on a home equity loan and used the proceeds to reduce credit card obligations and other debt. During the year, he paid the following amounts of interest.

On his personal residence	$16,000
On the cabin	7,000
On the home equity loan	2,500
On credit card obligations	1,500
On the purchase of an SUV	1,350

What amount, if any, must Walter recognize as an AMT adjustment concerning these items?

28. **LO.4, 5, 6** Determine whether each of the following transactions is a preference (P), is an adjustment (A), or is not applicable (NA) for purposes of the AMT.
    a. Depletion in excess of basis.
    b. Bargain element of incentive stock option on exercise date.
    c. Charitable contributions of cash.
    d. State income taxes.
    e. Untaxed appreciation on property donated to charity.
    f. 2% miscellaneous itemized deductions.

29. **LO.7** Gabriel, age 40, and Emma, age 33, are married with two dependents. They recorded AGI of $250,000 in 2022 that included net investment income of $3,000 and gambling winnings of $2,500.

    The couple incurred the following expenses during the year (all of which resulted in itemized deductions for regular income tax purposes).

Medical expenses (before 7.5%-of-AGI floor)	$12,000
State income taxes	5,800
Real estate tax	9,100
Interest on personal residence	18,600
Interest on home equity loan (proceeds were used to remodel the couple's kitchen)	9,800
Investment interest expense	4,500
Charitable contribution (cash)	14,200

    a. What is Gabriel and Emma's AMT adjustment for itemized deductions in 2022? Is it positive or negative?
    b. Gabriel and Emma also earned interest of $5,000 on private activity bonds that were issued in 2017. They borrowed money to buy these bonds and paid interest of $3,900 on the loan. Determine the effect on AMTI.

30. **LO.7** Anh is single, has no dependents, and itemizes deductions. In the current year for regular tax purposes, she records $60,000 of income and $105,000 of deductions and losses, primarily from business activities. Included in the losses are $30,000 of AMT preferences. Given this information, what are Anh's regular tax and alternative tax NOL amounts?

31. **LO.7** Included in Alice's regular taxable income and in her AMT base is a $300,000 capital gain on the sale of stock she owned for three years. Alice is in the 20% tax bracket for net capital gains for regular income tax purposes.
    a. What rate should Alice use in calculating her tentative AMT?
    b. What is Alice's AMT adjustment?

32. **LO.6,7** In the current year, Dylan earned interest from the following investments.

Investment	Interest Income
10-year municipal bond (issued in 2009)	$1,300
10-year private activity bond (issued in 2010)	1,600
10-year Treasury bond (issued in 2015)	2,000
10-year private activity bond (issued in 2021)	900
Savings account	1,100

Dylan purchased all of the bonds on their issuance date. In addition, Dylan borrowed funds with which to purchase the 2010 private activity bond and incurred interest expense of $350 on that loan in the current year.

a. How much interest income will Dylan recognize for regular tax purposes in the current year?

b. What is her current-year AMT preference or adjustment for interest?

33. **LO.7** Jane and Robert Brown are married and have eight children, all of whom are considered dependents for tax purposes. Robert earns $250,000 working as a senior manager in a public accounting firm, and Jane earns $78,000 as a second-grade teacher. Given their large family, they live in a frugal manner. The Browns maintain a large garden and fruit trees from which they get most of their produce, and the children take family and consumer science classes so that they can help make the family's clothing and make household repairs.

The Browns record no gross income other than their salaries (all of their investment income is earned from qualified retirement savings), and their itemized deductions are less than the standard deduction. In addition, they incur no additional adjustments or preferences for AMT purposes.

a. What is the couple's 2022 regular tax liability?

b. What is the couple's 2022 AMT?

c. Express the calculation of the couple's AMT for 2022 as an Excel formula. Place any parameter that could change annually in a separate cell, and incorporate the cell references into the formula.

34. **LO.7** Pat is 40, is single, and has no dependents. She received a salary of $390,000 in 2022. She earned interest income of $11,000, dividend income of $15,000, gambling winnings of $14,000, and interest income from private activity bonds (issued in 2018) of $40,000. The dividends are not qualified dividends. The following additional information is relevant. Compute Pat's tentative minimum tax for 2022.

State income taxes	$ 8,100
Real estate taxes	4,000
Mortgage interest on residence	13,100
Investment interest expense	3,800
Gambling losses	5,100

35. **LO.7** Renee and Sanjeev Patel, who are married, reported taxable income of $1,008,000 for 2022. They incurred positive AMT adjustments of $75,000 and tax preference items of $67,500. The couple itemizes their deductions.

a. Compute the Patels' AMTI for 2022.

b. Compute their tentative minimum tax for 2022.

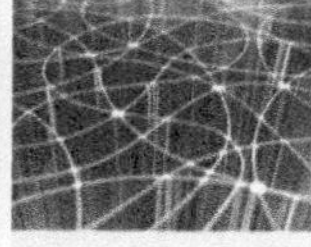

Bridge Discipline

1. Balm, Inc., has a general business credit for 2022 of $90,000. Balm's regular income tax liability before credits is $140,000, and its tentative AMT is $132,000.
   Calculate the amount of general business credit Balm can use in 2022, and calculate its general business credit carryback and carryforward, if any.
2. Cooper Partnership, a calendar year partnership, made qualifying rehabilitation expenditures to a building that it has used in its business for eight years. These improvements were placed in service on January 5, 2017. The amount of the rehabilitation expenditures credit was $40,000. For qualifying property placed in service before 2018, 100% of the credit was taken in the year the expenses were incurred. If the building was not held for five years, 20% of the credit was recaptured for each year remaining in the five-year window.
   Cooper is negotiating to sell the building in either December 2021 or January 2022. The sales price will be $600,000, and the recognized gain will be $100,000. Provide support for the CFO's position that Cooper should delay the sale until 2022.
3. For many years, Saul's sole proprietorship and his related Form 1040 have had a number of AMT tax preferences and AMT adjustments. He has made the AMT calculation each year, but the calculated amount always has been $0. Saul's regular taxable income and the AMT adjustments and preferences for 2022 are the same as for last year. Yet, he must pay AMT this year. Explain how this could happen.

Research Problems

Note: Solutions to the Research Problems can be prepared by using the Thomson Reuters Checkpoint™ online tax research database, which accompanies this textbook. Solutions can also be prepared by using research materials found in a typical tax library.

Research Problem 1. During a recent Sunday afternoon excursion, Miriam, an admirer of early twentieth-century architecture, discovers a 1920s-era house in the countryside outside Mobile, Alabama. She wants not only to purchase and renovate the house but also to move the structure into Mobile so that her community can enjoy its architectural features.

Being aware of the availability of the tax credit for rehabilitation expenditures, she wants to maximize her use of the provision, if it is available in this case, once the renovation work begins in Mobile. However, Miriam informs you that she will pursue the purchase, relocation, and renovation of the house only if the tax credit is available.

Comment on Miriam's decision and on whether any renovation expenditures incurred will qualify for the tax credit for rehabilitation expenditures.

Partial list of research aids:
George S. Nalle III v. Comm., 72 AFTR 2d 93–5705, 997 F.2d 1134, 93–2 USTC ¶50,468 (CA–5, 1993).

Communications

Research Problem 2. Your ophthalmologist, Dr. Hunter Francis (55 Wheatland Drive, Hampton, CT 06247), has been very pleased with the growth of his practice in the 15 years he has been in business. This growth has resulted, at least in part, because he has aggressively marketed his services and tried to accommodate clients with various needs.

This year Dr. Francis purchased a sophisticated piece of equipment that enables him to diagnose persons with mental handicaps, hearing impairments, and physical disabilities without having to go through a series of questions. In addition, he can treat his patients who are not disabled more accurately and efficiently by using this equipment.

Since purchasing the machine this year for $9,500, Dr. Francis has used it on many occasions. Unfortunately, he has not been able to attract any patients with disabilities even though previously he referred such people to other ophthalmologists who owned the necessary equipment. Therefore, the primary purpose for acquiring the equipment (i.e., to attract patients with disabilities) has not been realized, but he has put it to good use in treating other patients. Write a letter to Dr. Francis explaining whether he may claim the disabled access credit for this acquisition.

Research Problem 3. Teal Company, a single member LLC, owns two warehouses that were placed in service before 1987. This year accelerated depreciation on Warehouse A is $36,000 (straight-line depreciation would have been $30,000). On Warehouse B, accelerated depreciation was $16,000 (straight-line depreciation would have been $20,000). What is the amount of Teal's AMT tax preference for excess depreciation?

Use internet tax resources to address the following questions. Look for reliable websites and blogs of the IRS and other government agencies, media outlets, businesses, tax professionals, academics, think tanks, and political outlets.

Research Problem 4. The foreign tax credit is especially valuable when a U.S. business earns income in a country whose income tax rates exceed those of the United States. List five countries whose tax rates on business income exceed those of the United States and five where the corresponding U.S. rates are higher.

Communications
Data Analytics

Research Problem 5. Use *IRS Tax Statistics* (**irs.gov/statistics/soi-tax-stats-individual-income-tax-returns**) to determine how many individual income tax returns reported an AMT liability from 2014 to 2019. What percentage of returns filed in this time period report an AMT liability? What percentage of tax revenues collected in that same period does the AMT comprise?

Summarize your findings in a series of graphs to share with your classmates. Use the information gathered to discuss whether the tax revenues collected from the AMT justify the additional compliance costs imposed on taxpayers.

Becker CPA Review Questions

Becker

1. Anthony entered into a long-term construction contract in year 3. The total profit of the contract is $80,000 and does not change over the life of the contract. The contract will be completed in year 5. The contract is 20% and 70% complete at the end of years 3 and 4, respectively. What is the alternative minimum tax adjustment required in year 4?

   a. $16,000
   b. $40,000
   c. $56,000
   d. $80,000

2. How is the alternative minimum tax credit applied in the calculation of the tentative minimum tax (TMT)?

   a. It is carried forward indefinitely and applied to regular tax only.
   b. It is carried back five years and applied to regular tax only.
   c. It is carried forward indefinitely and can be applied to regular tax or AMT.
   d. It is carried forward five years and applied to regular tax only.

3. Carol reports taxable income of $48,000. Included in that calculation are the following items.

Real estate taxes on her home	$2,000
Mortgage interest on acquisition indebtedness	1,200
Charitable contribution	550

Carol also had excluded municipal bond interest income of $8,000, $3,000 of which was deemed to be private activity bond interest. What are Carol's total alternative minimum tax (AMT) adjustments?

a. $1,200
b. $2,000
c. $3,000
d. $6,750

4. Which of the following statements is most correct?
    a. Tax preference items for the alternative minimum tax are always added back to regular taxable income.
    b. Itemized deductions that are added back to regular taxable income for the alternative minimum tax are preference items.
    c. Tax preference items for the alternative minimum tax can be an increase or decrease to regular taxable income.
    d. All taxpayers are able to deduct the full exemption in the calculation of the alternative minimum tax.

5. Betty is age 34 and has AGI of $50,000. The following items may qualify as itemized deductions for Betty:

Qualified medical expenses (before 7.5% of AGI floor)	$6,000
Real estate tax	1,200
State income tax	800
Charitable contributions	600
Mortgage interest on acquisition indebtedness	2,000
Home equity interest on a loan used to improve the home	300

What is the itemized deduction add-back for the AMT?

a. $2,000
b. $2,800
c. $3,800
d. $8,800

6. Betty is age 34 and has AGI of $50,000. The following items may qualify as itemized deductions for Betty:

Qualified medical expenses (before percentage of AGI floor)	$3,000
Real estate tax	1,200
State income tax	800
Charitable contributions	600
Mortgage interest on acquisition indebtedness	2,000
Home equity interest on a loan used to improve the home	300

What are the itemized deductions allowed for the AMT?

a. $2,500
b. $2,900
c. $3,400
d. $3,700

7. Betty is age 34 and has AGI of $50,000 and regular taxable income of $35,000. The following items may qualify as itemized deductions for Betty:

Qualified medical expenses (before percentage of AGI floor)	$3,000
Real estate tax	1,200
State income tax	800
Charitable contributions	600
Mortgage interest on acquisition indebtedness	2,000
Home equity interest on a loan used to improve the home	300

What is the alternative minimum taxable income (AMTI)?

a. $35,000
b. $37,500
c. $37,000
d. $52,800

Chapter 18

Comparative Forms of Doing Business

Learning Objectives: *After completing Chapter 18, you should be able to:*

- **LO.1** Identify the principal legal and tax forms in which a business may be conducted.
- **LO.2** Contrast the conduit and entity approaches to legal organizational forms.
- **LO.3** Apply nontax factors in making the choice among alternative organizational forms.
- **LO.4** Identify the influence of the conduit and entity perspectives on the tax treatment of an entity's operations for the entity and its owners.
- **LO.5** Identify techniques for avoiding double taxation.
- **LO.6** Analyze the effects of the disposition of a business on the owners and the entity for each organizational form.

Chapter Outline

Tax Talk *[My firm] had a rule—at least it seemed to be a rule—that everybody that came had to spend at least a year working on taxes. The general rationale for the rule as I could understand it was that taxes were so important to everything that you do, whatever the kind of case you are handling, you have to know something about the tax consequences of things.* —Charles A. Horsky

The Big Picture

Choosing a Business Form and Other Investments

Bill and George are going to start a new business and have come to you for advice on the most appropriate organizational form for the business. They have narrowed the choice to a C corporation, an S corporation, or an LLC, but they would like you to advise them as to the primary advantages and disadvantages of each. They have an adequate amount in savings to finance the business initially. Limited liability is a significant concern as is limiting the amount of taxes paid. Bill and George anticipate that the company will lose money in the first two years of operation. After that, however, they expect to earn $200,000 in before-tax profit and distribute any after-tax profit to the owners. Bill and George are both single, and both are subject to a 24 percent marginal tax rate.

George also is considering investing $10,000 in an existing business organized as a limited partnership. Bill earlier had acquired a 30 percent interest in a boutique retail coffee franchise outlet. Bill now is considering selling this investment, which has experienced rapid appreciation, and needs to know the adjusted basis of his ownership interest.

Read the chapter and formulate your response.

A variety of factors, both tax and nontax, can affect the choice of the legal form in which a business is initially conducted. Further, the form that is most appropriate at one point in the life of a business and its owners may not remain the best choice as the circumstances faced by the business and its owners evolve.

This chapter provides the basis for comparing and contrasting the tax consequences of several business decisions across different types of tax and legal business forms. Understanding the comparative tax consequences of those decisions will help business owners and advisers better manage the tax costs of the business throughout its life, starting with the initial choice of the business's legal form.

LO.1

Identify the principal legal and tax forms in which a business may be conducted.

18-1 Alternative Organizational Forms in Which Businesses May Be Conducted

The principal legal forms in which a business may be conducted are the sole proprietorship, partnership, limited liability company (LLC), and corporation. The specific legal attributes of each of these organizational forms, including their relations to their owners and non-owners, are determined by the laws of the state in which they are organized.

LO.2

Contrast the conduit and entity approaches to legal organizational forms.

State law generally uses one of two perspectives when defining the rights and responsibilities of a business entity: the **conduit perspective** or the **entity perspective**. In its simplest form, the conduit, or aggregate, perspective treats the business as simply an aggregation of its owners joined together in an agency relationship. Under the strictest interpretation of the conduit perspective, the business has no existence separate from its owners. Conversely, the entity perspective considers the business as separate and distinct from its owners, with its own rights and responsibilities.

The rights and responsibilities afforded to corporations consistently reflect the entity perspective. A corporation is recognized as a separate legal entity with the following characteristics.

- *Continuity of life.* A corporation's existence does not depend on the life of its owners. A corporation continues to exist even if its shareholders die or sell their stock.
- *Centralized management.* All management responsibilities of a corporation lie in its board of directors. The board then appoints officers to carry out the corporation's business. Shareholders vote for board members but have no other ability to participate directly in the management of the corporation or its business.
- *Free transferability of interests.* Shares of stock in a corporation are freely transferable without the need of the corporation's or other shareholders' approval.
- *Limited liability.* Corporations have the right to contract directly with other parties and are responsible for their own liabilities. A shareholder's liability for the debts of the corporation is limited to the amount paid for their stock.

The perspective from which partnerships is viewed is less consistent. In many respects, partnerships reflect the conduit perspective. For example, general partners have the right to participate directly in the management of a partnership as well as to bind the partnership to contracts. It follows then that general partners are liable for the debts arising from the partnership's activities and contractual obligations. Furthermore, a significant change in ownership may result in the dissolution of the partnership. However, partnerships also reflect the entity perspective in several respects. For example, a partnership's income is determined separately from that of its owners.

Different types of partnerships are afforded even more characteristics consistent with the entity perspective. For example, limited partners in a **limited partnership (LP)** are treated much like shareholders in a corporation, with no ability to participate in the management of the partnership and their liability limited to their investment in the entity. However, limited partnerships must have at least one general partner. A **limited liability partnership (LLP)** provides all partners protection from partnership liabilities, but only those liabilities arising from acts of negligence, fraud, or malpractice committed by other partners. Like general partners in a general partnership, partners in an LLP continue to be liable for the contractual liabilities of the partnership.

Exhibit 18.1 **The Legal Forms in Which Businesses Are Conducted**

The following chart illustrates the number and proportion of 2018 Federal income tax returns filed for each legal form in which businesses were conducted. Included as partnerships are general and limited partnerships as well as limited liability companies taxed as partnerships.

Source: Pie chart created from data provided at Joint Committee on Taxation, *Overview of the Federal Tax System as in Effect for 2021*, April 15, 2021 (JCX-18-21), p. 38. **jct.gov/publications/2021/jcx-18-21/**.

Similar to shareholders of a corporation, all members of a **limited liability company (LLC)** are shielded from all of the entity's liabilities. However, although LLCs provide the same liability protection of a corporation, they typically lack one or more other corporate characteristics (e.g., centralized management, free transferability of interest, or continuity of life). The combination and extent of these other characteristics afforded LLCs differ depending on the state in which the LLC is organized.

See Exhibit 18.1 for a breakdown of the relative number of business conducted in each of these organizational forms.

18-2 Nontax Factors Affecting the Choice of Business Form

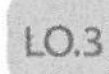
LO.3

Apply nontax factors in making the choice among alternative organizational forms.

Of course, taxes are only one of many factors to consider when making a business decision and often not the most important one. Above all, any business decision must make economic sense. Although the economics of most business decisions are impacted by taxes, often influencing how a business and its owners achieve their goals, tax savings alone are not sufficient to support a business or investment decision.

The Big Picture

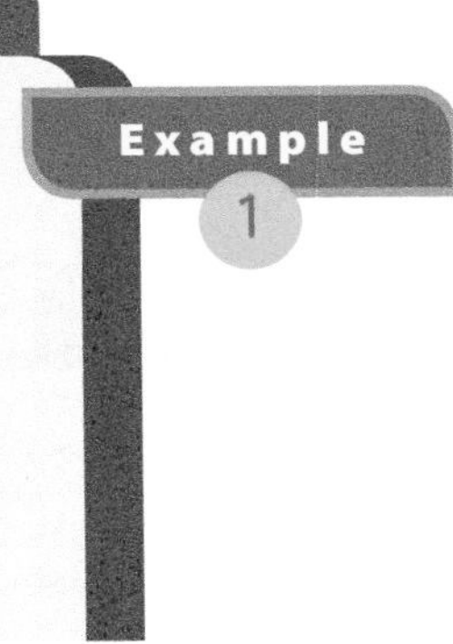

Return to the facts of *The Big Picture* on p. 18-1. George is considering investing $10,000 in a business organized as a limited partnership. The partnership is expected to generate losses for two years before generating any profits. George projects that he will be able to deduct his share of the losses up to his $10,000 capital contribution within the next two years. Because George's marginal tax rate is 24%, the investment will produce tax savings of $2,400 ($10,000 × 24%), increasing the after-tax return available from the investment.

However, there is a substantial risk that George will never recover any of his original investment. If this occurs, his negative cash flow from the investment in the limited partnership is $7,600 ($10,000 − $2,400). The tax savings cannot make up for the loss of the investment itself. George must decide whether the investment makes economic sense.

The importance of both tax and nontax factors extends to the choice of the legal form in which to conduct the business. Although the choice of organizational form can significantly impact the after-tax return available from a business venture, other factors may be just as, or more, important. Some of those factors are discussed briefly next.

Tax Fact The Relative Popularity of Flow-Through Entities

	Tax Returns Filed (millions)				
Business Form	**1980**	**1990**	**2000**	**2010**	**2018**
Sole proprietorship	12.3	17.1	20.0	24.9	28.9
Partnership	1.4	1.6	2.1	3.2	4.0
C corporation	2.2	2.1	2.2	1.7	1.6
S corporation	0.5	1.6	2.9	4.1	4.9

The increase in the popularity of LLCs has led to a notable increase in the number of partnership returns filed since 1980. However, despite the tax and nontax advantages offered by LLCs, the number of S corporation returns has increased proportionately more than has the number of partnership returns over the same period.

Source: Joint Committee on Taxation, *Overview of the Federal Tax System as in Effect for 2021, April 15, 2021* (JCX-18-21). **jct.gov/publications/2021/jcx-18-21/**.

18-2a Limited Liability

Perhaps the most important nontax factor affecting a business owner's choice of organizational form is his or her personal exposure to the liabilities of the business. As a separate legal entity, distinct from its shareholders, a corporation is liable under state law for its own debts. A shareholder cannot be held responsible for the debts or actions of the corporation. Therefore, a shareholder's personal liability resulting from investing in a corporation is limited to their investment. This protection from personal liability is perhaps the most valued nontax advantage of the corporate form.

Ed, Fran, and Gabriella each invest $25,000 for all of the stock of Brown Corporation. Brown borrows an additional $100,000 to finance its operations. Brown later becomes the defendant in a personal injury suit resulting from an accident involving one of its delivery trucks. The court awards a judgment of $2,500,000 to the plaintiff. The award exceeds Brown's insurance coverage by $1,500,000. Even though the judgment may result in Brown's bankruptcy, the shareholders have no personal liability for the unpaid corporate debts.

It should be noted that limited liability may not be available to the shareholders of all corporations. For example, many states do not limit the liability of certain professionals (e.g., accountants, attorneys, architects, and physicians) who incorporate their practices. Furthermore, even when state law provides for limited liability, the shareholders of small corporations may be forced, in effect, to forgo this benefit. For example, a corporation may be unable to obtain external financing (e.g., a bank loan) at reasonable interest rates unless the shareholders personally guarantee the loan.

Conversely, the debts of a sole proprietorship are the debts of the proprietor. Similarly, each partner in a general partnership is personally liable for the debts of the partnership. However, as discussed earlier, certain partnerships may offer their owners liability protection. For example, a limited partnership provides limited liability, but only to its limited partners. Like shareholders in a corporation, a limited partner's liability is limited to the amount of the partner's investment in the entity. However, limited partnerships are generally required to have at least one general partner potentially liable for partnership debts.

HIJ is a limited partnership. Hazel, the general partner, invests $250,000 in HIJ. Iris and Jane, the limited partners, each invest $50,000. Although the potential loss for Iris and Jane is limited to the $50,000 each has invested, Hazel's liability for any debts HIJ incurs is unlimited.

Digging Deeper 1

One possible way to limit the liability of a general partner is discussed on this book's companion website: www.cengage.com

Like a corporation, an LLC provides liability protection to all of its owners. This protection, coupled with the ability to be taxed as a partnership, is the most frequently cited benefit of an LLC. However, as discussed earlier, other potentially desirable corporate characteristics

Tax Fact Revenue Relevance of Corporate versus Individual Taxpayers

Federal income taxes (FIT) provide over half of the Federal budget receipts. As indicated in the table to the right, the portion provided by individual taxpayers (which includes the effect of flow-through entities) is expected to far exceed that provided by corporate taxpayers in the near future.

	2021–2025
% of budget receipts from FIT	55%
% of FIT from individual taxpayers	88%
% of FIT from corporate taxpayers	12%

Source: Federal Budget of the United States. **cbo.gov/publication/56542**.

often are missing from LLCs (e.g., under state law, an LLC may lack unlimited life or the transferability of ownership interests may be limited). Limited liability partnerships (LLPs) also provide liability protection to all of their owners, but only for liabilities arising from the negligence or wrongdoing (i.e., "torts") of the other owners. This makes LLPs a popular organizational form for professional service firms (e.g., accountants, architects, attorneys). However, partners in an LLP are not protected from the entity's contractual liabilities.

18-2b Other Factors

Other nontax factors may be significant in selecting an organizational form. For example, in addition to limited liability, the corporation generally is characterized by unlimited life (i.e., the corporation's existence is unaffected by a change in its ownership), separation of ownership and management, and the free transferability of interests. One or more of these characteristics is usually absent in other business forms.

18-2c Capital Formation

The combination of liability exposure with other nontax factors may significantly affect a venture's ability to raise capital. For example, a sole proprietorship offers the proprietor no protection against the venture's liabilities and limits its available capital to that which can be provided, or raised, by the proprietor. A partnership has a greater opportunity to raise funds through the pooling of owner resources. However, general partners remain subject to any liabilities generated by the business, making it relatively difficult to attract additional investors.

Example 4

Adam and Beth form a general partnership, AB, to build and manage an apartment building. Adam contributes cash of $200,000 and Beth contributes land (FMV $200,000; adjusted basis $60,000) on which the apartment building will be constructed. The building will cost $1,000,000.

The partnership is considering borrowing $800,000 to construct the building. Adam and Beth would each be legally responsible for the repayment of the loan as well as for other liabilities the venture generates. Alternatively, Adam and Beth are considering borrowing only $200,000 and seeking additional partners to finance the remaining cost of the building. However, new partners may be concerned about being responsible for the loan as well as other debts of the venture that may arise. Adam and Beth are also concerned about sharing management rights and responsibilities with additional general partners.

A limited partnership offers greater potential to raise capital than does a general partnership because a limited partnership can secure funds from investors (i.e., limited partners) without exposing them to the liabilities related to the venture or involving them in the management of the business.

Carol and Dave form a limited partnership, CD. Carol contributes cash of $200,000, and Dave contributes land with an adjusted basis of $60,000 and a fair market value of $200,000. The partnership is going to construct a shopping center at a cost of $5,000,000. Included in this cost is $800,000 for land adjacent to that contributed by Dave. Thirty limited partnership interests are sold for $100,000 each to raise $3,000,000. CD then borrows another $2,000,000 from a third party.

continued

Limited partners may find this an attractive investment because, like shareholders in a corporation, they have unlimited ability to benefit from the success of the venture while being liable only for the $100,000 they invest. Even if CD is unable to repay the loan, the limited partners will not be required to make additional contributions to the partnership or to personally pay off the loan. As general partners, Carol and Dave remain liable for repayment of the third-party loan as well as any other debts incurred by CD. However, they are not liable for the $3,000,000 of financing provided by the limited partners.

Of the different business entities, the corporate form offers the greatest ease and potential for obtaining owner financing, because it can offer investors a combination of liability protection and liquidity that other business forms cannot. The ultimate examples of this are the large public companies that are listed on the stock exchanges.

18-3 The Tax Consequences of Organizational Form Choice

The same organizational forms discussed earlier are recognized for Federal income tax purposes as well, with the tax treatment of a business and its activities generally determined by the legal form in which the business is conducted. However, four major exceptions exist. First, the Check-the-box Regulations (see text Section 12-1e) provide for most unincorporated business entities to be either disregarded or treated as partnerships for tax purposes depending on the number of owners. For example, an LLC with only one owner is a disregarded entity for tax purposes, treated as a sole proprietorship if the owner is an individual or as a division of a corporate owner. An LLC with more than one owner is taxed as a partnership.

Second, the same Regulations allow most unincorporated entities to *elect* to be treated as corporations for Federal income tax purposes.[1] Therefore, an entity may be taxed as a corporation even though it is not organized as such under state law. Third, a corporation may elect to be treated as an S corporation for tax purposes.[2] The income of an S corporation is taxed similarly to that of a partnership. However, the designation has no effect on the corporation for state law purposes: it is relevant only for tax purposes.

The final exception applies to **publicly traded partnerships**. Recall that limited partners have similar liability protection as shareholders in a corporation. This provides limited partnerships much the same ability to raise capital as corporations. In some instances, limited partnerships have registered their interests on established securities exchanges so that they may be publicly traded. Generally, publicly traded partnerships are treated as corporations for tax purposes. However, an important exception allows limited partnerships who derive nearly all of their revenues from investments and natural resources to be treated as partnerships even if their partnership interests are publicly traded.[3]

LO.4

Identify the influence of the conduit and entity perspectives on the tax treatment of an entity's operations on the entity and its owners

Chapters 12–15 each covered the basics regarding the taxation of businesses conducted in a particular organizational form. This section reviews many of the ideas covered in those chapters as they relate to the owners' initial choice of organizational form, comparing and contrasting the tax consequences of that choice on common business transactions and activities as well as on transactions and transfers between the entity and its owners. The goal is to facilitate taxpayers' and tax advisers' analyses of the optimal organizational form in which to conduct a particular business activity, taking into account the characteristics and goals of both the business and its owners.

[1] Reg. §§ 301.7701–1 through –4, and –6.

[2] §§ 1361 and 1362. See Chapter 15.

[3] § 7704.

18-3a The Taxation of Business Operations

As discussed earlier, the view of the corporation as an entity separate from its owners leads to it also being considered a separate taxable entity, legally responsible for the income tax on the income it earns. As the corporation's shareholders are taxed on this income when it is distributed, the income generated by a corporation is subject to double taxation before it is available for use by shareholders. This potential for double taxation frequently is cited as the major disadvantage of the corporate form. However, as discussed below, several features of the tax law itself, as well as actions the corporation and its shareholders can take, can mitigate or eliminate the burden of double taxation.

Conversely, sole proprietorships and partnerships, including LLCs, are not considered taxpayers separate and distinct from their owners and, therefore, are not subject to the income tax. Rather, the owners of these entities are directly and immediately responsible for any tax on the income these entities generate. These entities are commonly referred to as "flow-through" entities, since their income flows through to their owners for tax purposes. Therefore, the income generated by proprietorships and partnerships is taxed only once before it is available for use by owners, escaping double taxation. Further, the income, gains, losses, etc., generated by sole proprietorships and partnerships retain their character when recognized by the entity's owners. This can be beneficial (e.g., capital gains recognized by the entity may receive preferential treatment) or disadvantageous (e.g., preference items generated by the entity may trigger the AMT) for a partner in a partnership relative to a shareholder of a corporation. Finally, as discussed further below, the conduit perspective also eliminates the owner's ability to defer the recognition of this income.

S corporations provide an opportunity for certain corporations and their shareholders to avoid double taxation while retaining the nontax benefits of corporate status. However, as discussed in text Section 15-2a, the tax law limits the number and type of shareholders a corporation may have and still be eligible for S status.

Even if the double taxation of corporate income might be mitigated, the tax cost of operating as a corporation is exacerbated by the fact that the owners of businesses conducted as sole proprietorships, partnerships, and S corporations are often eligible for the qualified business income (QBI) deduction.[4] Individuals, estates, and trusts are eligible for a deduction of up to 20 percent of the domestic business income flowing through to them from most businesses that are not organized as C corporations. As discussed in text Section 11-4d, several limitations based on the type of business and the taxpayer's income may limit this deduction.

Sarah, a married taxpayer, owns a car wash. The business generates $200,000 of income annually before considering $50,000 of compensation paid to Sarah. Sarah has a marginal tax rate of 24%. If Sarah incorporated the business, it would generate a total of $200,000 of taxable income annually, $150,000 taxable to the corporation and $50,000 to Sarah, with a combined tax liability of $43,500 [(150,000 × 21% = $31,500) + ($50,000 × 24% = $12,000)]. If the corporation immediately distributed its $118,500 of after-tax income ($150,000 taxable income less the $31,500 corporate tax paid) to Sarah, the total combined Federal income tax would increase by $17,775 ($118,500 × 15%) to $61,275.

Assume instead that Sarah chose to run her business as an S corporation. Her taxable income from the business after the QBI deduction would be $170,000 [$50,000 + 0.8($200,000 − $50,000)], resulting in a tax liability of $40,800 ($170,000 × 24%) and a Federal income tax savings of at least $2,700 and as much as $20,475.

[4] § 199A.

18-3b The Ability to Specially Allocate Income among Owners

Business entities may have several reasons to attribute certain income and expenses to specific owners. For example, they may have the desire to:

- Share profits and losses in a proportion different from that of their capital contributions (e.g., based on relative contributions to the generation of those profits or losses).
- Share profits and losses differently from year to year.
- Allocate a built-in gain or loss on contributed property to the contributing owner.

Partnerships and LLCs may allocate taxable income, gains, losses, etc., among their owners in any way they desire as long as the economic consequences follow that same allocation (i.e., as long as the allocation has a *substantial economic effect*). In fact, a special allocation generally is required when a partnership sells property originally contributed by a partner if the property had a built-in gain or loss at the time of the contribution.

Conversely, the right of shareholders to corporate income is legally determined by their stock ownership. Corporations and their shareholders may be able to achieve results similar to those produced with special allocations by making payments to owners (e.g., salary payments, lease rental payments, and interest payments) and by using different classes of stock (e.g., preferred and common). However, C corporations cannot directly allocate taxable income, gains, losses, etc., among their owners, as partnerships and LLCs can.

Although the income generated by S corporations generally is taxed in a manner similar to that generated by partnerships, S corporations still are corporations with the owners' right to income determined by their stock ownership. Therefore, special allocations of income are not permitted for S corporations, though, like C corporations, S corporations may be able to achieve similar results by making deductible payments to shareholders.

Digging Deeper 2

Limitations on the ability of S corporations to indirectly allocate income using deductible payments to shareholders is discussed on this book's companion website: www.cengage.com

Example 7

Khalid contributes land with an adjusted basis of $10,000 and a fair market value of $50,000 for a 50% ownership interest in Maple Company. At the same time, Tracy contributes cash of $50,000 for the remaining 50% ownership interest. Because Maple is unable to obtain the desired zoning for the property, it subsequently sells the land for $50,000.

Khalid has a realized gain of $40,000 ($50,000 − $10,000) and a recognized gain of $0 resulting from the contribution. His basis in his ownership interest in Maple is $10,000, and Maple takes a basis in the land of $10,000. Maple realizes and recognizes a gain of $40,000 ($50,000 − $10,000) when it sells the land.

If Maple is a corporation, the appreciation of the land attributable to the time it was owned by Khalid becomes part of the corporation's taxable income, the resulting tax is paid by the corporation, and the tax burden is indirectly shared equally by both shareholders. There is no way by which the corporation can allocate the recognized gain, and the related tax burden, directly to Khalid.

If Maple is a partnership, the entire $40,000 recognized gain on the sale is allocated to Khalid regardless of his profits or equity interest. Note that although S corporations are taxed similarly to partnerships, the S corporation provisions do not allow special allocations. If the entity were an S corporation, Khalid and Tracy would each include $20,000 of the recognized gain in their taxable income.

18-3c The Tax Treatment of Capital Contributions

Because of the conduit approach generally applied to partnerships, § 721 generally provides that no gain or loss is recognized when a partner contributes property to a partnership in exchange for a partnership interest. Code § 721 applies to contributions associated with the formation of the partnership as well as all subsequent contributions. As a result, the partnership takes a carryover basis in the contributed property, and the partners have a carryover basis in their partnership interests.[5]

Because of the entity approach applied to corporations, the transfer of property to a corporation in exchange for its stock is more likely to be a taxable event than is a transfer of property from a partner to a partnership. Although shareholders can avoid immediate recognition of gain on the contribution of appreciated property to a corporation under § 351, deferral under that provision requires the contributing shareholders to be in control of the corporation after the contribution. The control requirement increases the likelihood of gain recognition, especially on contributions made after the corporation's initial formation. When no gain or loss must be recognized, both the corporate property and the shareholders' stock take a carryover basis.[6]

18-3d The Basis of an Ownership Interest

As alluded to above, because the contribution of property to a partnership or an LLC in exchange for an ownership interest is not a taxable event under § 721, the owner's initial basis for the ownership interest carries over from the contributed property, thereby preserving any realized gain or loss for future recognition. The same is true of contributions to C and S corporations if the control requirement of § 351 is satisfied. If the control requirement is not satisfied and any realized gain or loss on a contribution of property to a corporation is recognized by the shareholder, the investor's initial stock basis is equal to the fair market value of the contributed property.

The impact of an entity's activities on an owner's adjusted basis in that entity will also differ across entities. For a partnership or an LLC, because the owner immediately recognizes his or her allocable share of the income, gains, losses, etc., of the entity, those items also affect the owner's basis in the entity interest. Likewise, the owner's basis is increased by the owner's share of the amount by which the entity's liabilities increase and is decreased by the owner's share of the amount by which the entity's liabilities decrease. Accordingly, the owner's basis in the ownership interest changes annually.[7] Conversely, because the income of a shareholder in a C corporation is unaffected by the corporation's operations, the shareholder's basis in his or her stock is not affected by corporate income, gain, loss, etc. Similarly, because the shareholder of a C corporation is not responsible for any of the corporation's liabilities, those liabilities have no effect on the basis of the shareholder's stock.

The treatment of an S corporation shareholder falls between that of the partner and the C corporation shareholder. Because the shareholder immediately recognizes the income, gains, losses, etc., of an S corporation, an S corporation shareholder's stock basis is affected by the owner's share of those items. However, because S corporation shareholders are not responsible for the corporation's liabilities, the shareholder's stock basis is not affected by the corporation's liabilities.

The Big Picture

Example 8

Return to the facts of *The Big Picture* on p. 18-1. Bill contributed cash of $100,000 to an entity for a 30% ownership interest in the franchise. Assume that the entity's profits for the year are $90,000 and that its liabilities increased by $30,000 during the taxable year.

Bill's basis in his ownership interest in the entity at the end of the period would depend on the entity's organizational form as follows.

	C Corporation	S Corporation	Partnership/LLC
Original investment	$100,000	$100,000	$100,000
Share of profits		27,000	27,000
Share of increase in liabilities			9,000
Basis in ownership interest	$100,000	$127,000	$136,000

[5]Refer to the pertinent discussion in text Section 14-2.

[6]Refer to the pertinent discussion in text Section 12-2.

[7]§§ 705 and 752.

18-3e The Application of the At-Risk and Passive Activity Loss Rules

The at-risk and passive activity loss rules prevent certain taxpayers from recognizing losses that might otherwise be available to them. The at-risk rules prevent affected taxpayers from recognizing losses for which they are not at a risk of economic loss. The passive activity loss rules generally allow affected taxpayers to recognize losses from passive activities only to offset income from passive activities.

The at-risk and passive activity loss rules apply to both individuals and closely held C corporations. The passive activity loss rules apply to personal service corporations as well. Although neither set of rules applies to flow-through entities directly, the rules are especially relevant to the individual owners of these entities who may not be at risk for all of the losses that may pass through to them from the entity or who may not actively participate in the entity's activities. For a detailed discussion of the at-risk and passive loss rules, see text Sections 6-6 and 6-7, respectively.

The at-risk rules are particularly relevant to partners who may have nonrecourse debt included in the basis of their partnership interest (see discussion in text Section 14-3e). Note that in spite of partners being able to include nonrecourse debt in the basis of their partnership interest, the at-risk rules will prevent such partners from being able to recognize any more losses than if the entity had been organized as an S corporation.

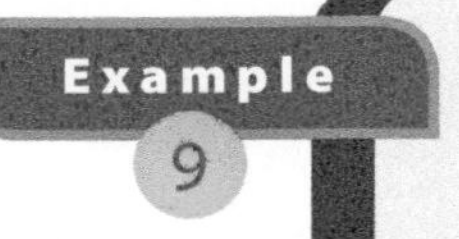

Wyatt is the general partner and Ira and Vera are the limited partners in the WIV limited partnership. Wyatt contributes land with an adjusted basis of $40,000 and a fair market value of $50,000 for his partnership interest, and Ira and Vera each contribute cash of $100,000 for their partnership interests. They agree to share profits and losses in proportion to their capital contributions.

To finance construction of an apartment building, the partnership obtains $600,000 of nonrecourse debt (not qualified nonrecourse financing; see text Section 14-3e), pledging the land and building as collateral on the loan. Each partner's basis in the partnership interest is computed as follows.

	Wyatt	Ira	Vera
Contribution	$ 40,000	$100,000	$100,000
Share of nonrecourse debt	200,000	200,000	200,000
Basis	$240,000	$300,000	$300,000

Without the at-risk rules, Ira and Vera could recognize losses up to $300,000 each even though they invested only $100,000 and have no personal liability for the nonrecourse debt. However, the at-risk rules limit loss recognition to the at-risk basis, which is $100,000 each for Ira and Vera.

The at-risk rules also affect the general partner. Because Wyatt is not at risk for the nonrecourse debt, his at-risk basis is $40,000.

If, instead, the entity were an S corporation and Wyatt received 20% of the stock and Ira and Vera each received 40%, the basis for their stock would be computed as follows.

	Wyatt	Ira	Vera
Contribution	$40,000	$100,000	$100,000
Share of nonrecourse debt	–0–	–0–	–0–
Basis	$40,000	$100,000	$100,000

Notice that the at-risk rules prevent any nonrecourse debt included in basis of a partner's interest from increasing the ability to recognize losses over what would be available if the owners had organized as an S corporation. Whether WIV had organized as a partnership or an S corporation, Wyatt would be able only to recognize losses up to $40,000, and Ira and Vera would only be able to recognize losses up to $100,000.

If the debt were recourse debt, however, it would be included in the at-risk basis of Wyatt's partnership interest, allowing him to recognize losses up to $640,000 ($40,000 contribution + $600,000 partnership recourse debt). It would not, however, affect the basis of his stock if WIV had organized as an S corporation.

However, as partnership recourse debt may also be included in a partner's basis in the partnership interest, organizing as a partnership rather than as an S corporation may allow business owners to recognize more losses that may be generated by a pass-through entity. Of course, this will expose the owners to a greater risk of economic loss as well. Recall that an important exception to the at-risk rules allows taxpayers, including partners in partnerships, to be considered at-risk for qualified nonrecourse debt. This allows taxpayers to recognize losses from real estate activities even though they may not be at risk.

The passive activity loss rules generally allow individuals and personal service corporations to recognize losses from passive activities only to offset income from passive activities. The passive activity losses of a closely held corporation, however, can be used to offset active income.

Neither the at-risk nor the passive activity loss rules apply to C corporations that are not closely held. A closely held corporation is one in which five or fewer individuals own more than 50 percent of the value of its outstanding stock. Therefore, C corporations that are not closely held can recognize losses for which they may not be at risk as well as from activities in which they do not materially participate.

As noted above, the passive activity loss rules also apply to personal service corporations. A corporation is classified as a *personal service corporation* if the following requirements are satisfied.[8]

- The principal activity of the corporation is the performance of personal services.
- The services are substantially performed by owner-employees.
- Owner-employees own more than 10 percent in value of the stock of the corporation.

Because the conduit concept applies to partnerships, S corporations, and limited liability entities, passive activity income and losses are separately stated at the entity level and are passed through to the owners with their passive character maintained.

18-3f The Tax Treatment of Distributions

The application of the conduit perspective to partnerships, including LLCs, results in distributions being generally tax-free. The distribution triggers no gain or loss for the partnership, and the owners treat it as a recovery of capital. The application of the entity perspective to corporations produces the opposite result. Distributions of appreciated property by a C corporation are taxed immediately to the corporation, and the owners generally recognize any distribution as a taxable dividend to the extent of the corporation's earnings and profits.

A combination entity/conduit approach applies to noncash distributions from S corporations. The entity perspective generally applicable to corporations leads to the recognition of gain by the corporation for any appreciation attributable to the distributed property.[9] However, despite the distribution itself representing a recovery of capital to the shareholder, the conduit concept leads to any gain recognized by the corporation being taxable at the shareholder level.

Tan, an S corporation, is equally owned by Leif and Matt. Tan distributes two parcels of land to Leif and Matt. Tan has a basis of $10,000 for each parcel. Each parcel has a fair market value of $15,000. The distribution results in a $10,000 ($30,000 − $20,000) recognized gain for Tan. Leif and Matt each include $5,000 of the gain in their taxable incomes.

[8] §§ 469(j)(2) and 269A.

[9] § 311(b).

18-3g Other Taxes

The choice of organizational form will have state and local as well as Federal income tax consequences. Although the state tax consequences often are similar to the Federal results, this may not always be the case.

The S corporation provides a good illustration of this point. Not all states recognize the Federal S election. Therefore, although the income, gains, losses, etc., from S corporations and partnerships may affect their owners' Federal taxable incomes and tax liabilities similarly, the same may not be true with respect to their state taxable income and tax liability. Rather, the items recognized by S corporations may be taxable directly to the corporation with no change in its owners' state taxable incomes or tax liabilities until distributed.

Income taxes are not the only taxes affected by the choice of organizational form. For example, the taxes imposed by the Federal Insurance Contributions Act (i.e., FICA) are assessed on most earned income of individuals, including that of business owners. FICA taxes include assessments to fund Social Security and Medicare and are imposed on individuals at rates of 6.2% and 1.45% of earned income, respectively. Employers typically withhold these taxes from employees' wages. Employers are also responsible for matching the amounts paid by employees, resulting in taxes equal to 15.3% of the employee's earned income. However, the Social Security tax is imposed on only the first $147,000 of wages in 2022.[10]

Business owners who organize as sole proprietorships are required to pay both the employer's and employee's share of the tax in the form of the self-employment tax. Since the proprietor has no "wages," the tax is imposed on his or her self-employment income, generally the income earned by the business, subject to the same limitations. A general partner in a partnership is treated similarly, with the partner's share of the partnership's aggregate income subject to the tax.

However, other organizational forms may offer their owners an opportunity to reduce their FICA taxes. For example, although the wages paid to a shareholder of an S corporation are subject to FICA tax, a shareholder's share of the corporation's aggregate income is not.

Wayne and Irving are starting a new business venture. Each will own one-half of the company. Wayne will be paid $50,000 annually to provide personal services to the venture. Irving is solely an investor. It is estimated that after the $50,000 paid to Wayne, the venture will generate $80,000 of income. That income will be reinvested in the venture for the foreseeable future. The income subject to FICA taxes will be:

	Wayne	Irving
If organized as a general partnership	$50,000 + 0.5($80,000) = $90,000	$40,000
If organized as a C corporation	$50,000	$0
If organized as an S corporation	$50,000	$0

As this table suggests, shareholders of an S corporation have an incentive not to receive wages from the corporation. The IRS, therefore, may be interested in whether an S corporation pays adequate compensation to its owners.[11]

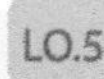

Identify techniques for avoiding double taxation.

18-4 Minimizing Double Taxation

As explained earlier, only income earned in the corporate form is potentially subject to double taxation. In spite of this potential tax cost, nontax factors may nonetheless make the corporate form the preferred choice in which to conduct a business. Regardless, when initially choosing the form in which to organize a business or

[10]This amount is indexed annually.

[11]This issue has been the subject of a series of court cases brought by the Treasury.

considering how best to distribute corporate earnings, it is important to realize that two features of the tax law help mitigate the double taxation of income earned by corporations. First, corporate income is subject to a flat tax rate of 21 percent, much lower than the top rate that individuals can face. Second, the lower tax rates that apply to dividends (i.e., 0%/15%/20%) reduce the burden of double taxation on all qualified dividends. Together, these lower rates prevent the effective tax rate on income earned by corporations from exceeding approximately 37% [1 – (1 – 0.21)(1 – 0.20)], the top marginal rate that individuals face.

For some individual taxpayers, the double taxation of corporate income can result in an effective tax rate higher than income earned in other organizational forms. For instance, an individual with a marginal tax rate of 24 percent would incur an effective rate of approximately 33 percent [1 – (1 – 0.21)(1 – 0.15)] on income earned through a corporation. To achieve a lower effective tax rate on business income, individuals might operate as a sole proprietorship or partnership (or LLC). However, as discussed earlier, profits earned in a sole proprietorship or partnership may also be subject to the 15.3 percent self-employment tax. Several planning techniques available for further reducing or eliminating the impact of double taxation are discussed next.

18-4a Making Deductible Distributions

The double taxation of corporate income typically is triggered by the payment of dividends by the corporation to its shareholders. As distributions of corporate income, dividends are taxable to shareholders but are not deductible by the corporation. However, if distributions can be made to shareholders in their capacity other than as shareholders, the distributions may be deductible by the corporation. Although the payment may increase the rate at which the distribution is taxed at the individual shareholder level (e.g., from 20 to 37 percent for a shareholder in the top marginal bracket), it will save 21 percent tax at the corporate level. Again, a deductible compensation payment may also trigger the self-employment tax, eliminating the tax benefit of reclassifying the payment. Common examples of such deductible distributions include:

- Salary payments to shareholder-employees.
- Lease or rental payments to shareholder-lessors.
- Interest payments to shareholder-creditors.

Recognizing the potential for abuse, the IRS scrutinizes these types of distributions carefully. For example, all deductible payments made to shareholders may be evaluated for *reasonableness*.[12] In addition, shareholder loans that lack a sufficient number of the characteristics usually associated with debt may be reclassified as equity.[13] The recharacterization of shareholder debt as equity can have especially negative consequences for the shareholder because the repayment of the "debt" itself, as well as the related "interest," will be treated as a taxable dividend rather than a recovery of capital.

Using Deductible Distributions to Avoid Double Taxation

Example 12

Imani owns all the stock of Green Corporation and is the chief executive officer. Green's taxable income before salary payments to Imani is as follows.

Year 1	Year 2	Year 3
$80,000	$50,000	$250,000

continued

[12] § 162(a)(1). *Mayson Manufacturing Co. v. Comm.*, 49–2 USTC ¶9467, 38 AFTR 1028, 178 F.2d 115 (CA–6); *Harolds Club v. Comm.*, 65–1 USTC ¶9198, 15 AFTR 2d 241, 340 F.2d 861 (CA–9).

[13] § 385; Rev.Rul. 83–98; *Bauer v. Comm.*, 84–2 USTC ¶9996, 55 AFTR 2d 85–433, 748 F.2d 1365 (CA–9).

Each year, Imani receives a monthly salary of $3,000. In December of each year, Imani reviews the operations for the year and determines the year-end bonus she is to receive. Imani's yearly bonuses are as follows.

Year 1	Year 2	Year 3
$44,000	$14,000	$214,000

The apparent purpose of Green's bonus program is to reduce the corporate taxable income to zero and thereby avoid double taxation. Assuming that Imani's marginal tax rate was 24%, the total tax on the year 3 income distributed as a bonus would be $51,360 ($214,000 × 0.24).

However, the IRS would likely find the bonus to be unreasonable compensation and, therefore, nondeductible by the corporation. Rather, the distribution would be considered a constructive dividend. In this case, the total tax on the income distributed as a dividend would be $70,299 {[$214,000 × 0.21] + [214,000 × (1 − 0.21) × 0.15]}.

Tom and Margo are each in the 24% marginal tax bracket. Each contributes $20,000 to TM Corporation in return for all of its stock. In addition, they each lend $80,000 to TM, evidenced by notes payable by the corporation to Tom and Margo.

The notes require the corporation to make interest payments of $6,400 each year to both Tom and Margo. Although the annual interest payments are taxable to Tom and Margo, they are deductible by the corporation, escaping double taxation. The total income tax due on the interest payments to Tom and Margo will be $3,072 ($6,400 × 2 × 24%). At the time of repayment in 10 years, neither Tom nor Margo recognizes gross income from the repayment of the notes; the $80,000 amount realized is equal to the basis for the note of $80,000.

If the notes lack sufficient characteristics typically associated with debt (e.g., they lack a reasonable interest rate or penalty for failure to make timely payments) and the IRS succeeded in reclassifying them as equity, Tom and Margo still would recognize annual gross income of $6,400, but the amount would be reclassified as dividend income. Although the dividends may be taxable to Tom and Margo at a lower rate than would be interest income, the tax due on the dividend nonetheless would trigger double taxation because the distribution no longer would be deductible by the corporation. This increases the total income tax due on the income distributed to Tom and Margo to $4,608 [($6,400 × 2 × 21%) + ($6,400 × 2 × 15%)]. To make matters worse, the repayment of the notes in 10 years would no longer qualify as a recovery of capital, resulting in additional dividend income for Tom and Margo.

Note, however, that characterizing a distribution to a shareholder as a deductible expense may not always result in a reduction in taxes. Given the lower tax rate that corporations face and the rate reduction available to individuals for qualified dividends, the double taxation of corporate income may actually reduce overall taxes.

Return to the facts of Example 12. Assume that Imani's marginal tax rate was 35% rather than 24%. The total tax due on the year 3 income distributed as a bonus would increase to $74,900 ($214,000 × 0.35). A portion of the bonus may also be subject to FICA taxes. However, if the income were distributed as a dividend, the total tax would remain $70,299 {[$214,000 × 0.21] + [214,000 × (1 − 0.21) × 0.15]}. In this case, the lower tax rates on corporate income and dividends relative to Imani's marginal tax rate on her ordinary income result in the dividend triggering less overall tax, despite subjecting the distributed income to double taxation.

Bridge Discipline Bridge to Economics

Corporations such as Coca-Cola, IBM, Microsoft, Walmart, and ExxonMobil are major players not only in their industries but also in the world economy, attracting much attention from policymakers. Policymakers also take great interest in small businesses that cumulatively play a major role in the economy.

In recognition of the important role of small businesses and the competitive disadvantages that often result from their size, Congress has provided small businesses with tax benefits that are not available to larger business entities. Included among such benefits are the following.

- § 179—immediate expensing for tangible personal property.
- § 1045—deferral of gain for qualified small business stock.
- § 1202—partial exclusion of gain for certain small business stock.
- § 1244—ordinary loss treatment on the sale of certain small business stock.

Each of these provisions defines *small* differently. Sometimes, however, the term *small* may be interpreted inappropriately by taxpayers. The classic example is the small business corporation of Subchapter S. Although many assume that S corporations must be "small," some S corporations hold billions of dollars of assets. They are "small" chiefly in the sense that the number of shareholders cannot exceed 100 unrelated shareholders.

18-4b Deferring Distributions

Double taxation is not triggered until the corporation makes (actual or deemed) distributions to shareholders. Deferring distributions to shareholders can postpone the second layer of taxation on corporate earnings, reducing the net present value of the tax.

Further tax savings are available if the distributions are delayed until a shareholder's death. Note that any earnings retained by the corporation will increase the value of its stock. Under the basis step-up rule, the basis of the stock for the shareholder's beneficiaries will be its fair market value, including the value due to the undistributed income, at the date of the shareholder's death. The increased basis will allow the beneficiaries to dispose of the stock without recognizing any gain, with the undistributed earnings totally escaping income tax at the individual level. However, the penalty taxes on corporate accumulations may limit the benefit of this planning strategy (see text Section 13-8).

An example of the deleterious effects of the accumulated earnings tax can be found on this book's companion website: www.cengage.com

3 Digging Deeper

18-4c Making Return-of-Capital Distributions

Double taxation also can be avoided if a corporate distribution can qualify as a recovery of capital rather than as a dividend. Distributions treated as a repayment of shareholder debt (discussed above) or made when the corporation has no earnings and profits (E & P) (see discussion in text Section 13-2) qualify as recoveries of capital. The stock redemption and liquidation provisions offer another opportunity to avoid dividend treatment. Under these rules, a distribution may be treated as a sale of the shareholder's stock. Although any gain on such a sale would be taxed at the same rate as would a dividend, the amount of the distribution representing a recovery of capital would escape current income taxation altogether. Further, a final distribution that is less than the shareholder's basis in the stock triggers recognition of a capital loss.[14]

[14]See §§ 302(a) and 331(a) and text Section 13-7.

18-4d Electing S Corporation Status

Making an S election generally eliminates double taxation.[15] However, as discussed in Chapter 15, several factors should be considered when making this election.

- Given the corporation's plans regarding distributions and the shareholders' individual tax rates, is double taxation problematic?
- Are all of the shareholders willing to consent to the election?
- Can the qualification requirements for S status be satisfied both at the time of the election and in the future?
- For what period will the conditions that make the election beneficial continue to prevail?

Emerald Corporation commenced business in January 2021. The two shareholders, Diego and Jaime, are both in the 28% combined state and Federal income tax bracket. The following operating results are projected for the first five years of operations.

2021	2022	2023	2024	2025
($50,000)	$400,000	$600,000	$800,000	$1,000,000

The corporation plans to expand rapidly. Therefore, no distributions to shareholders are anticipated. In addition, beginning in 2022, preferred stock will be offered to a substantial number of investors to help finance the expansion. This will make Emerald ineligible for S status.

If the S corporation election is made for 2021, the $50,000 loss can be passed through to Diego and Jaime. Even if the S election is either revoked or involuntarily terminated at the beginning of 2022 as a result of the issuance of the preferred stock, the loss passed through to Diego and Jaime in 2021 will produce an immediate tax savings of $14,000 ($50,000 × 28%) for the shareholders.

If the S corporation election is not made for 2021, the $50,000 loss can be carried forward to reduce Emerald's 2022 corporate taxable income by $50,000, producing a tax savings of only $10,500 ($50,000 × 21%) for Emerald Corporation.

Should the S corporation election be made for just the one-year period? It appears so. Given the higher tax rates that Diego and Jaime face relative to the corporation, the S election will save $3,500 ($14,000 − $10,500) in taxes. Further, assuming an after-tax rate of return to the shareholders of 3%, the accelerated deduction available from the election is worth an additional $315 ($10,500 × 3%).

Analyze the effects of the disposition of a business on the owners and the entity for each organizational form.

18-5 The Tax Consequences of Disposing of a Business

The prior two sections discussed the choice of a business venture's organizational form and the tax consequences of that choice. At some point, the owner or owners of a business may wish to dispose of that business, perhaps to move on to another venture or to get out of business entirely. The tax consequences of the disposition could also differ significantly across organizational forms and, ideally, should be considered when the form is being chosen.

A key factor in evaluating the tax consequences of a business disposition is whether the disposition is viewed as the sale of an ownership interest in the business or as a sale of the underlying assets used in the business. Generally, the tax consequences are more favorable to the seller if the transaction is treated as a sale of the ownership interest. Conversely, the purchaser will prefer that the transaction be treated as a purchase of the individual assets because this results in a higher basis in those assets. This difference in the preferences of the parties may influence the price paid by the seller.

[15]Recall the text Section 15-4 discussions of the taxes on an S corporation's built-in gains, LIFO recapture, and investment income. These taxes ensure that income earned before a corporation elects S corporation status remains subject to double taxation in certain circumstances.

18-5a Sole Proprietorships

Because a sole proprietorship is not recognized as an entity separate and distinct from its owner, the sale of a sole proprietorship is always treated as the sale of the business's individual assets. Thus, gains and losses must be calculated separately for each with the tax treatment dependent on the nature and holding period of the individual assets. Ordinary income property such as inventory will result in ordinary gains and losses. Code § 1231 property such as land, buildings, and machinery used in the business will produce § 1231 gains and losses (subject to depreciation recapture under §§ 1245 and 1250). Capital assets such as investment land and stocks qualify for capital gain or loss treatment.

In addition to amounts received for the business's identifiable assets, the seller may receive an additional amount for an agreement not to compete with the business after the sale or for goodwill. Any amount received for a covenant not to compete is treated by the seller as ordinary income. If the amount realized exceeds the sum of the fair market value of the identifiable assets and any covenant not to compete, the excess is treated as goodwill. Payments for goodwill generate capital gain for the seller. Both goodwill and covenants are amortized by the purchaser over a 15-year statutory period.[16]

16

Ethan, who is in the 32% tax bracket, is considering selling his sole proprietorship to Tuan for $600,000. The identifiable assets are as follows.

	Adjusted Basis	Fair Market Value
Inventory	$ 20,000	$ 25,000
Accounts receivable	40,000	40,000
Machinery and equipment*	125,000	150,000
Buildings	175,000	250,000
Land	40,000	100,000
	$400,000	$565,000

*Potential § 1245 recapture of $50,000.

The tentative sale agreement calls for the payments to be classified as follows.

	Gain (Loss)	Ordinary Income	§ 1231 Gain	Capital Gain
Inventory	$ 5,000	$ 5,000		
Accounts receivable	–0–			
Machinery and equipment	25,000	25,000		
Buildings	75,000		$ 75,000	
Land	60,000		60,000	
Goodwill	35,000			$35,000
	$200,000	$30,000	$135,000	$35,000

If the sale is structured this way, Ethan will recognize the $35,000 received for goodwill as a capital gain. Tuan would prefer the amount be paid for a covenant not to compete. Though the tax treatment will be the same for her, she would prefer not to worry about Ethan starting a competing business. However, this would require Ethan to recognize the payment as ordinary income. Ethan may insist on a higher selling price to compensate him for the increased taxes that would result from the change in the terms of the agreement.

[16] § 197.

18-5b Partnerships and Limited Liability Companies

The disposition of a partnership or an LLC can be structured as the sale of assets or as the sale of an ownership interest. If the transaction takes the form of an asset sale, it is treated the same as it would be for a sole proprietorship (described previously), with the tax consequences flowing through to the entity's owners.

The sale of an ownership interest in a partnership or an LLC generally is treated as the sale of a capital asset. Therefore, structuring a transaction as a sale of an ownership interest may be preferable to structuring it as a sale of the partnership assets. However, this benefit is severely curtailed by the need to recognize gain related to appreciation of many of the partnership's ordinary income-producing assets as ordinary gain, even on the sale of an ownership interest.[17]

From a buyer's perspective, the tax consequences are not affected by the form of the transaction when the purchaser acquires all of the interests in a partnership. If the transaction is an asset purchase, the basis for the assets equals the amount paid. If a buyer intends to continue to operate as an LLC or a partnership, the assets can be contributed to the entity tax-free with the owner's basis in the entity interest equal to the purchase price for the assets. Likewise, if all ownership interests are purchased, the partnership is deemed to have terminated and distributed the assets to the former partners who are then deemed to have sold the assets to the purchaser. The purchaser's basis in the assets is again their purchase price and the purchaser's holding period for the assets begins on the day immediately following the purchase.[18]

A problem may arise when a taxpayer purchases a partnership or LLC interest (rather than the entire business) from another owner. In such a case, the amount paid for the interest may not be equal to the new owner's share of the entity's basis in its assets. Put another way, the basis of the assets inside the entity may not reflect the amount paid for them by the new owner. To help mitigate this problem, the entity may make an election to adjust its basis in its assets to reflect the amount paid by the new owner. This basis adjustment is allocable entirely to the new owner, ensuring that the new owner can recover the (indirect) cost of the underlying assets.

Roz buys a one-third interest in the RST Partnership for $50,000. All of the entity's assets are depreciable, and their basis to the partnership (i.e., their inside basis) is $90,000. Roz's basis in her partnership interest (i.e., her outside basis) is $50,000. However, her share of the basis of the partnership's assets (i.e., her share of the inside basis) is only $30,000. If a § 754 election is in effect, the partnership can step up the basis of its depreciable assets by $20,000, the difference between Roz's outside basis and Roz's share of the inside basis amounts [$50,000 − (1/3 × $90,000)]. All of the "new" asset basis is allocated to Roz.

Such an election, once made, is binding on the entity and applies to all subsequent exchanges of ownership interests. Therefore, although it may benefit a purchaser if the entity's assets have appreciated prior to the acquisition date, creating a positive basis adjustment for the new owner, it may be detrimental to a future purchaser if assets are depreciated at the time of acquisition, resulting in a negative basis adjustment for the new owner.[19]

18-5c C Corporations

The sale of a business held by a C corporation can be structured as either an asset sale or a stock sale. The stock sale has the dual advantage to the seller of being less complex both as a legal transaction and as a tax transaction. It also has the advantage of providing a way to avoid double taxation since the only gain recognized is on the sale of the stock by the shareholder. Finally, any gain or loss on the sale of the stock is treated as a capital gain or loss to the shareholder.

Jane and Zina each own 50% of the stock of Purple Corporation. They have owned the business for 10 years. Jane's basis in her stock is $40,000, and Zina's basis in her stock is $60,000. They agree to sell the stock to Rex for $300,000. Jane recognizes a long-term capital gain of $110,000 ($150,000 − $40,000), and Zina recognizes a long-term capital gain of $90,000 ($150,000 − $60,000). Rex takes a basis in his stock of $300,000. Purple recognizes no gain or loss, and its basis in its assets does not change as a result of the stock sale.

[17] § 751.

[18] § 708(b)(1), *Edwin E. McCauslen*, 45 T.C. 588 (1966), and Rev.Rul. 99–6.

[19] §§ 743 and 754.

Conversely, the purchaser will prefer that the transaction be structured as a sale of the individual assets, assuming that those assets have a fair market value in excess of their basis to the corporation. This allows the purchaser to increase the basis of the assets to their fair market value.

Returning to the previous example, assume that Purple's assets have a fair market value of $300,000 but an adjusted basis to Purple of $100,000. If the transaction is structured as an asset sale rather than a stock sale, Rex will take a basis of $300,000 in his acquired assets. However, Purple will recognize a gain of $200,000 ($300,000 − $100,000) in addition to the gain recognized by Jane and Zina on the liquidation of Purple.

18-5d S Corporations

Because the S corporation is a corporation under state law, it is subject to the provisions for a C corporation discussed in the prior section. An asset sale at the corporate level or a liquidating distribution of assets followed by a sale of the assets by the shareholders produces gain or loss recognition at the corporate level. However, under the conduit concept applicable to the S corporation, the recognized gain or loss is passed through to the shareholders. Therefore, double taxation is avoided directly on a stock sale (because only the shareholder is involved) and indirectly on an asset sale (because the gain or loss is passed through directly to the shareholders).[20] However, an asset sale still is more likely to generate ordinary income than is a sale of S corporation stock.

Concept Summary 18.1 reviews the tax consequences of business dispositions.

Concept Summary 18.1

Tax Treatment of Disposition of a Business

Form of Entity	Form of Transaction	Tax Consequences: Seller	Tax Consequences: Buyer
Sole proprietorship	Sale of individual assets.	Gain or loss is calculated separately for the individual assets. Classification as capital or ordinary depends on the nature and holding period of the individual assets. If amount realized exceeds the fair market value of the identifiable assets, the excess is allocated to goodwill (except to the extent identified with a covenant not to compete), producing a capital gain.	Basis for individual assets is the allocated cost. The buyer is neutral regarding the classification of any amount paid over the fair market value of the identifiable assets, because both goodwill and noncompete covenants are amortized over a 15-year statutory period.
	Sale of the business.	Treated as a sale of the individual assets (as above).	Treated as a purchase of the individual assets (as above).
Partnership and limited liability company	Sale of individual assets.	Treatment is the same as for the sole proprietorship.	Treatment is the same as for the sole proprietorship. If the intent is to operate in partnership form, the assets can be contributed to a partnership under § 721.
	Sale of ownership interest.	Entity interest is treated as the sale of a capital asset [subject to ordinary income potential for any gain attributable to ordinary income-producing ("hot") assets].	Basis for new owner's ownership interest is the cost. The new entity's basis for the assets is also the pertinent cost (i.e., contributed to the entity under § 721) because the original entity will have terminated.

continued

[20]Double taxation might seem to be avoided by making an S corporation election prior to the liquidation of a C corporation, but the built-in gains tax eliminates this opportunity; taxation occurs at the corporate level, and double taxation results. See text Section 15-4a.

Tax Treatment of Disposition of a Business—(Continued)

		Tax Consequences	
Form of Entity	**Form of Transaction**	**Seller**	**Buyer**
C corporation	Sale of corporate assets by corporation (i.e., corporation sells assets, pays debts, and makes liquidating distribution to the shareholders).	Double taxation occurs. Corporation is taxed on the sale of the assets with the gain or loss determination and the classification as capital or ordinary treated the same as for the sole proprietorship. Shareholders calculate gain or loss as the difference between the stock basis and the amount received from the corporation in the liquidating distribution. Capital gain or loss usually results, because stock typically is a capital asset.	Basis for individual assets is the allocated cost. If the intent is to operate in corporate form, the assets can be contributed to a corporation in a tax-deferred manner under § 351.
	Sale of corporate assets by the shareholders (i.e., corporation pays debts and makes liquidating distribution to the shareholders).	Double taxation occurs. At the time of the liquidating distribution to the shareholders, the corporation is taxed as if it had sold the assets. Shareholders calculate gain or loss as the difference between the stock basis and the fair market value of the assets received from the corporation in the liquidating distribution. Capital gain or loss usually results, because stock typically is a capital asset.	Same as corporate asset sale.
	Sale of corporate stock.	Double taxation is avoided. Because the corporation is not a party to the transaction, there are no tax consequences at the corporate level. Shareholders calculate gain or loss as the difference between the stock basis and the amount received for the stock. Capital gain or loss usually results, because stock typically is a capital asset.	Basis for the stock is its cost. The basis for the corporate assets is not affected by the stock purchase.
S corporation	Sale of corporate assets by corporation.	Recognition occurs at the corporate level on the sale of the assets, with the gain or loss determination and the classification as capital or ordinary treated the same as for the sole proprietorship. Conduit concept applicable to the S corporation results in the recognized amount being taxed at the shareholder level. Double taxation associated with the asset sale is avoided because any gain or loss on the sale is recognized directly by the shareholders, increasing or decreasing their basis in the stock. Shareholders calculate gain or loss as the difference between the stock basis and the amount received from the corporation in the liquidating distribution. Capital gain or loss usually results, because stock typically is a capital asset.	Basis for individual assets is the allocated cost. If the intent is to operate in corporate form (i.e., as an S corporation), the assets can be contributed to a corporation in a tax-deferred manner under § 351.

continued

Tax Treatment of Disposition of a Business—(Continued)

		Tax Consequences	
Form of Entity	**Form of Transaction**	**Seller**	**Buyer**
S corporation *(continued)*	Sale of corporate assets by the shareholders.	At the time of the liquidating distribution to the shareholders, recognition occurs at the corporation level as if the corporation had sold the assets. The resulting tax consequences for the shareholders and the corporation are the same as for the sale of corporate assets by the S corporation.	Same as corporate asset sale by the S corporation.
	Sale of corporate stock.	Same as the treatment for the sale of stock of a C corporation.	Same as the treatment for the purchase of stock of a C corporation.

18-6 The Tax Consequences of Converting to Another Business Form

As the business owners' tax and nontax goals change, they may decide to change the organizational form in which the business is conducted. Such a change may have significant tax consequences for the entity as well as the owners. This section discusses the tax consequences of converting from each organizational form in which a business may be conducted to alternate forms that may be available. The tax issues that must typically be addressed are the following:

- Does the conversion result in the recognition of gain or loss?
- What is the basis of the owners' interests in the new entity?
- What is the basis of the assets held by the new entity?

18-6a Sole Proprietorship

Converting a sole proprietorship into another entity form can be achieved without any recognition of gain or loss at the entity or owner level. This result occurs regardless of the choice of the new entity form.

Given the conduit approach taken for sole proprietorships, the liquidation of a proprietorship triggers no immediate income tax consequences. If the proprietorship converts into a partnership or an LLC, the owner's basis in the ownership interest carries over from the contributed property.[21] Similarly, if the proprietorship converts into a corporation, the shareholder's basis for the stock received carries over from the shareholder's basis in the contributed property.[22] After a conversion, the entity takes a carryover basis for its assets.[23] As discussed below, a newly formed corporation then may elect S status if the owner desires.

18-6b Partnership or LLC

A partnership or an LLC can be converted into a corporation. The corporation may then elect S status if the owners desire, with no immediate income tax consequences.

[21] § 722.

[22] § 358(a).

[23] §§ 362(a) and 723.

The owners can transfer their interests to the corporation in exchange for the stock of the entity. Because the transfer likely satisfies the § 351 requirements, any realized gain or loss is not recognized.[24] If, however, the control requirement is not satisfied, the realized gain or loss is recognized by the owners.[25]

Assuming that the § 351 requirements for nonrecognition are satisfied:

- The basis of the stock to the shareholders is a carryover basis.[26]
- The basis of the assets to the corporation is a carryover basis.[27]

18-6c C Corporation

A C corporation can be converted into any of the following entity forms.

- Sole proprietorship.
- Partnership or LLC.
- S corporation.

Converting to an S corporation merely requires the election of S status by the entity.[28] As discussed in text Section 15-2, the S election can be made only if all shareholders consent to the election and if the S corporation qualification requirements are satisfied.[29] These qualification requirements become maintenance requirements that must be met to retain the S election.

The election of S status has no immediate income tax consequences for the corporation or its shareholders. No gains or losses are recognized, and the bases of the shareholders' stock and the corporation's assets all are unchanged. However, an S corporation's prior status as a C corporation may trigger a corporate-level tax on the subsequent recognition of built-in gains related to assets the corporation held at the time it converted.

Conversely, a corporation must be liquidated in order to convert it to a sole proprietorship, a partnership, or an LLC. As discussed above, the liquidation will trigger gain or loss at the corporate level on the distribution of the assets held by the corporation,[30] as well as the recognition of gain or loss at the shareholder level related to the stock deemed to be sold back to the corporation.[31] The former shareholders of the corporation then have a basis in the distributed assets equal to their fair market value.[32]

After liquidation, the C corporation's former shareholders contribute the assets to the new entity. The tax consequences of the contributions to the owners and to the entity are the same as those discussed earlier.

18-7 Overall Comparison of Business Forms

Concept Summary 18.2 provides an issue-by-issue comparison of the tax consequences of the choice among the most common forms of doing business.

[24] § 351(a).
[25] §§ 351(a) and 368(c).
[26] § 358(a).
[27] § 362(a).
[28] § 1362(a).
[29] §§ 1361 and 1362(a)(2).
[30] § 336(a).
[31] § 331(a).
[32] § 334(a).

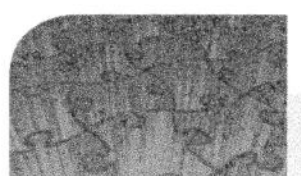

Concept Summary 18.2

Tax Attributes and Consequences of Different Organizational Forms of Doing Business

	Sole Proprietorship	Partnership/Limited Liability Company	S Corporation	C Corporation
Restrictions on type or number of owners	One owner. The owner must be an individual.	Must have at least two owners.	Only individuals, estates, certain trusts, and certain tax-exempt entities can be owners. Maximum number of shareholders limited to 100.*	None, except some states require a minimum of two shareholders.
Incidence of tax	Income and deductions are included in the proprietor's taxable income, reported on Schedule C of the individual's Form 1040. A separate Schedule C is prepared for each business.	Entity not subject to Federal income tax. Owners in their separate capacity subject to tax on their distributive share of income. Entity files Form 1065.	Except for certain built-in gains and passive investment income when earnings and profits are present from C corporation tax years, entity not subject to Federal income tax. S corporation files Form 1120S. Shareholders are subject to tax on income attributable to their stock ownership.	Income subject to double taxation. Entity subject to tax, and shareholder subject to tax on any corporate dividends received. Corporation files Form 1120.
Highest tax rate (before additional Medicare taxes)	37% at individual level.	37% at owner level.	37% at shareholder level.	21% at corporate level; 20%/15%/0% on qualified dividends at shareholder level.
Qualified business income deduction (§ 199A)	Available.	Available. Eligible partners (noncorporate) need data from the entity to compute the deduction amount.	Available. Eligible shareholders need data from the entity to compute the deduction amount.	Deduction not available to C corporations.
Contribution of property to the entity	Not a taxable transaction.	Generally not a taxable transaction.	Taxable transaction unless the § 351 requirements are satisfied.	Taxable transaction unless the § 351 requirements are satisfied.
Choice of tax year	Same tax year as owner.	Selection generally restricted to coincide with tax year of owners.	Generally restricted to a calendar year.	Unrestricted selection allowed at time of filing first tax return.
Timing of taxation	Based on owner's tax year.	Owners report their share of income in their tax year within which the entity's tax year ends. Owners in their separate capacities are subject to payment of estimated taxes.	Shareholders report their shares of income in their tax year within which the corporation's tax year ends. Shareholders may be subject to payment of estimated taxes.	Corporation subject to tax at close of its tax year. May be subject to payment of estimated taxes. Dividends are subject to tax at the shareholder level in the tax year received.

* Spouses and family members can be treated as one shareholder.

continued

Tax Attributes and Consequences of Different Organizational Forms of Doing Business—(Continued)

	Sole Proprietorship	Partnership/Limited Liability Company	S Corporation	C Corporation
Basis for allocating income/losses to owners	Not applicable (only one owner).	Profit and loss sharing agreement. Cash basis items of cash basis entities are allocated on a daily basis. Other entity items are allocated after considering varying interests of owners. Special allocations are available if they have substantial economic effect.	Pro rata share based on stock ownership. Shareholder's pro rata share is determined on a daily basis according to the number of shares of stock held on each day of the corporation's tax year. Special allocations are not available.	Not applicable.
Character of income/losses taxed to owners	Retains source characteristics.	Conduit—retains source characteristics.	Conduit—retains source characteristics.	All source characteristics are lost when income is distributed to owners.
Limitation on losses deductible by owners	Investment in business assets plus prior income.	Owner's investment plus share of liabilities and prior income.	Shareholder's investment plus loans made by shareholder to corporation and owner's share of prior income.	Not applicable.
Subject to at-risk rules?	Yes, at the owner level. Indefinite carryover of excess loss.	Yes, at the owner level. Indefinite carryover of excess loss.	Yes, at the shareholder level. Indefinite carryover of excess loss.	Yes, for closely held corporations. Indefinite carryover of excess loss.
Subject to passive activity loss rules?	Yes, at the owner level. Indefinite carryover of excess loss.	Yes, at the owner level. Indefinite carryover of excess loss.	Yes, at the shareholder level. Indefinite carryover of excess loss.	Yes, for closely held corporations and personal service corporations. Indefinite carryover of excess loss.
Subject to limitation on excess business losses [§ 461(l)]?	Yes, at the owner level.	Yes, at the owner level (unless partner is a corporation).	Yes, at the shareholder level.	No. Limitation does not apply to corporate taxpayers.
Nonliquidating distributions to owners	Not taxable.	Not taxable unless money received exceeds recipient owner's basis in entity interest. Existence of § 751 assets may cause recognition of ordinary income.	Generally not taxable unless the distribution exceeds the shareholder's AAA or stock basis. Existence of accumulated earnings and profits could cause some distributions to be dividends.	Taxable in year of receipt to extent of earnings and profits or if exceeds basis in stock. Corporation may be subject to penalty tax on unreasonable accumulations.
Net capital gains (before additional Medicare taxes)	Taxed at owner level at potentially reduced rates.	Conduit—owners must account for their respective shares. Taxed at owner level.	Conduit, with certain exceptions (a possible penalty tax)—shareholders must account for their respective shares. Tax treatment determined at shareholder level.	Taxed at corporate rate of 21%. No other benefits.

continued

Tax Attributes and Consequences of Different Organizational Forms of Doing Business—(Continued)

	Sole Proprietorship	Partnership/Limited Liability Company	S Corporation	C Corporation
Net capital losses	Only $3,000 of capital losses can be offset each tax year against ordinary income. Indefinite carryover.	Conduit—owners must account for their respective shares. Tax treatment determined at owner level.	Conduit—shareholders must account for their respective shares. Tax treatment determined at shareholder level.	Carried back three years and carried forward five years. Deductible only to offset other entity capital gains.
§ 1231 gains and losses	Taxable or deductible at owner level. Five-year lookback rule for § 1231 losses.	Conduit—owners must account for their respective shares. Tax treatment determined at owner level.	Conduit—shareholders must account for their respective shares. Tax treatment determined at shareholder level.	Taxable or deductible at corporate level only. Five-year lookback rule for § 1231 losses.
Deduction for fringe benefits to owners	None.	None unless included in a guaranteed payment.	None unless a 2% or less shareholder.	Available within antidiscrimination rules.
Foreign tax credits	Available at owner level.	Conduit—tax payments passed through to owners.	Generally conduit—tax payments passed through to shareholders.	Available at corporate level only.
§ 1244 treatment of loss on sale of interest	Not applicable.	Not applicable.	Available.	Available.
Basis treatment of entity liabilities	Not applicable.	Includible in interest basis.	Not includible in stock basis.	Not includible in stock basis.
Effect of liquidation/ redemption/ reorganization on basis of entity assets	Not applicable.	Usually carried over from entity to owner.	Taxable step-up to fair market value.	Taxable step-up to fair market value.
Sale of ownership interest	Treated as the sale of individual assets. Classification of recognized gain or loss depends on the nature of the individual assets.	Treated as the sale of an entity interest. Recognized gain or loss is classified as capital, although appreciated inventory and receivables are subject to ordinary income treatment.	Treated as the sale of corporate stock. Recognized gain is classified as capital gain. Recognized loss is classified as capital loss, subject to ordinary loss treatment under § 1244.	Treated as the sale of corporate stock. Recognized gain is classified as capital gain. Noncorporate taxpayers are able to defer (§ 1045) or exclude (§ 1202) gains related to stock of certain small businesses. Recognized loss is classified as capital loss, though noncorporate taxpayers may be able to classify losses related to stock of certain small businesses as ordinary (§ 1244).
Distribution of appreciated property	Not taxable.	No recognition at the entity level.	Gain recognition at the corporate level to the extent of the appreciation. Conduit—amount of recognized gain is passed through to shareholders.	Taxable at the corporate level to the extent of any realized appreciation.

continued

Tax Attributes and Consequences of Different Organizational Forms of Doing Business—(Continued)

	Sole Proprietorship	Partnership/Limited Liability Company	S Corporation	C Corporation
Splitting of income among family members	Not applicable (only one owner). Spouses running a business together can elect "qualified joint venture" status where earnings are split and identical Schedules Cs are filed for each spouse rather than a partnership return [§ 761(f)].	IRS will not recognize a family member as an owner unless certain requirements are met.	IRS can make adjustments to reflect adequate compensation for services.	Other than unreasonable compensation, IRS generally cannot make adjustments to reflect adequate compensation for services and capital.
Organizational and startup costs	Startup expenditures are eligible for $5,000 limited expensing (subject to phaseout) with any balance amortized over 180 months.	Organizational and startup expenditures each are eligible for $5,000 limited expensing (subject to phaseout) with any balance amortized over 180 months.	Same as partnership.	Same as partnership.
Charitable contributions	Various limitations apply at owner level.	Conduit—owners are subject to deduction limitations in their own capacities.	Conduit—shareholders are subject to deduction limitations in their own capacities.	Limited to 10% of taxable income before certain deductions.
Alternative minimum tax	Applies at owner level. AMT rates are 26% and 28%.	Applies at the owner level rather than at the entity level. AMT preferences and adjustments are passed through from the entity to the owners.	Applies at the shareholder level rather than at the corporate level. AMT preferences and adjustments are passed through from the S corporation to the shareholders.	C corporations are not subject to AMT.

Refocus on The Big Picture

Choosing a Business Form and Other Investments

Navistock/Shutterstock.com

Conducting their business as a C corporation, an S corporation, or an LLC would meet Bill and George's objectives of providing limited liability. From a tax perspective, both the S corporation and the LLC would allow the early-year losses to be passed through to the owners. This cannot be achieved with a C corporation, in which the losses are trapped until future years when the company is profitable. Once the entity turns profitable, the tax consequences are as follows.

- As a C corporation, the entity would pay income tax of $42,000 on taxable earnings of $200,000. If the remaining after-tax earnings of $158,000 are distributed equally to Bill and George (each owner would receive a taxable dividend of $79,000), each shareholder pays an additional income tax of $11,850 ($79,000 × 15%). The combined entity/owner tax liability is $65,700, resulting in after-tax cash flows of $134,300.

continued

- If the entity is operated as an S corporation or an LLC, no tax is paid at the entity level. Assume that Bill and George also claim a qualified business income deduction equal to 20 percent of their share of the entity income, resulting in net income of $80,000 for each individual. The income will be taxed as ordinary income at the owner level, resulting in each owner paying $19,200 ($80,000 × 24%) income tax. The combined entity/owner tax liability is $38,400, resulting in after-tax cash flows of $161,600.

It appears that either the S corporation or the LLC meets Bill and George's objectives of having limited liability and minimizing tax liability. The LLC form offers an additional advantage in that an LLC need not satisfy the numerous statutory qualification requirements to elect and maintain S corporation status. However, based on the facts in this situation, it is unlikely that satisfying the requirements would create any difficulty for Bill and George. Further, an LLC might result in a portion of any gains recognized when the business is sold or liquidated being characterized as ordinary.

The results of George's investing in a limited partnership appear in Example 1. Athough beneficial tax results are expected to occur, George needs to be aware of the economic risk of losing his $10,000 investment.

For Bill, the recognized gain on the sale of his investment in the retail coffee franchise outlet is dependent on that entity's form. If the franchise were a pass-through entity, the recognized gain would be different than if the entity were a C corporation: entity profits increase the owner's interest basis in a pass-through entity, whereas entity profits have no effect on a shareholder's basis in C corporation stock.

What If?

Assume that the $200,000 of anticipated business profits could be paid to Bill and George as reasonable salaries. This would allow the owners to escape double taxation, even if organized as a C corporation. However, given the income and self-employment taxes due on the compensation, the total tax liability would nonetheless increase to $78,600 [$200,000 × (0.24 + 0.153)]. Note that wages are not eligible for the qualified business income deduction.

Assume instead that Bill and George decide to expand the business and reinvest the annual $200,000 before-tax earnings instead of paying out dividends to the owners. If the business is organized as a C corporation, it can accumulate the earnings and avoid the additional tax that would have been paid by Bill and George when the company made taxable dividend distributions. Although the entity-level tax of $42,000 still must be paid, after-tax cash flows increase to $158,000. Although the S corporation or LLC with after-tax cash flows of $161,600 still would be preferred in this situation, the double tax problem of the C corporation can be reduced with effective planning.

Suggested Readings

Stewart Karlinsky and Hughlene Burton, "Dis-Incorporation of the American Business Model," *ATA Journal of Legal Tax Research*, Spring 2016.

Roger A. McEowen, "Form C Corporation—The New Vogue in Business Structure?" *Law Professors Blog*, February 26, 2018.

Ruth Simon, "Pass-Through Businesses Are Rethinking Their Status," *Wall Street Journal*, February 22, 2018.

Michael A. Yuhas and Richard Harris, "The Retiring LLC Member: Sale Versus Liquidation," *Journal of Taxation*, January 2016.

Key Terms

Conduit perspective, 18-2
Entity perspective, 18-2
Limited liability company (LLC), 18-3
Limited liability partnership (LLP), 18-2
Limited partnership (LP), 18-2
Publicly traded partnership, 18-6

Computational Exercises

1. **LO.4** Roscoe contributes a personal use asset, adjusted basis $15,000 and fair market value $28,000, to a new business in which he is an owner. Determine Roscoe's recognized gain on the transfer and the basis of the asset to the business if the new operation is a:
   a. Sole proprietorship.
   b. Partnership in which Roscoe holds a 10% interest.
   c. Corporation in which Roscoe holds a 25% interest and all shareholders contribute assets for stock in the transaction.

2. **LO.4** Mira and Lemma are equal owners of a business entity. Each contributed $25,000 cash to the business. Then the entity acquired a $100,000 loan from a bank. This year operating profits totaled $30,000. Determine Lemma's basis in her interest at the end of the tax year assuming that the entity is:
   a. A partnership.
   b. A C corporation.
   c. An S corporation.

3. **LO.4** Carlota and Dave formed an S corporation; Carlota owns 75% of the outstanding shares, and Dave owns the rest. When the entity's AAA balance is $1,000,000, it distributes an asset to each shareholder; the basis of each asset to the corporation is $45,000. Carlota's asset is worth $90,000, and Dave's is worth $50,000.
   a. How much gain, if any, does the the corporation recognize as a result of the distribution?
   b. By how much, if any, does the distribution increase Dave's gross income?
   c. By how much, if any, does the distribution increase Carlota's gross income?

Problems

4. **LO.2, 3** Sea Green Enterprises reports the following assets and liabilities on its balance sheet.

	Net Book Value	Fair Market Value
Assets	$600,000	$925,000
Liabilities	200,000	200,000

Sea Green just lost a product liability suit with damages of $10,000,000 being awarded to the plaintiff. Although Sea Green will appeal the judgment, legal counsel indicates that the judgment is highly unlikely to be overturned by the appellate court. The product liability insurance carried by Sea Green includes a payout ceiling of $6,000,000. For how much of the judgment is the entity and its owners liable if Sea Green is:
   a. A sole proprietorship?
   b. A general partnership?
   c. An LLC?
   d. A C corporation?
   e. An S corporation?

5. **LO.2, 3** With which of the two perspectives to business forms, conduit or entity, is each of the following most consistent?
   a. Limited liability for the entity's owners.
   b. Unlimited life for the entity.
   c. The ability of owners to participate directly in the management of the entity.
   d. The ability of owners to transfer assets to the entity without recognizing gain or loss.
   e. The payment of a wage from the entity to an owner who provides services to the entity.
   f. The inclusion of entity debt in the basis of an owner's interest in the entity.

6. **LO.3, 4** Amy and Jeff Barnes will operate their florist shop as a partnership or as an S corporation. After paying salaries of $45,000 to each of the owners, the shop's annual earnings are projected to be about $60,000. The earnings are to be invested in the growth of the business. Write a letter to Amy and Jeff, advising them of which of the two entity forms they should select. Their mailing address is 5700 Richmond Highway, Alexandria, VA 22301.

   Communications
   Decision Making
   Planning

7. **LO.1,2, 3** Gerald is an entrepreneur who likes to be actively involved in his business ventures. He is going to invest $500,000 in a business that he projects will produce a tax loss of approximately $125,000 per year in the short run. However, Gerald is confident that once consumers become aware of the new product being sold by the business and the quality of the service it provides, the business will generate a profit of at least $200,000 per year. Gerald generates substantial other income (from both business ventures and investment activities) each year. Advise Gerald on the business form he should select for the short run. He will be the sole owner of the business.

   Decision Making

8. **LO.1,2, 3, 4** Mr. and Mrs. Chang, married filing jointly, will establish a manufacturing business. The couple anticipates that the business will be profitable immediately due to a patent that Mrs. Chang holds; profits for the first year will be about $300,000 and will increase at a rate of about 20% per year for the foreseeable future. Advise the Changs as to the form of business entity they should select. The Changs are in the 37% Federal income tax bracket.

   Decision Making
   Planning

9. **LO.4** Plum Corporation will begin operations on January 1. Earnings for the next five years are projected to be relatively stable at about $80,000 per year. The shareholders of Plum are in the 32% tax bracket. Evaluate whether Plum should operate as a C corporation or as an S corporation given the following assumptions.

   Decision Making
   Planning

   a. Plum will reinvest its after-tax earnings in the growth of the company.
   b. Plum will distribute its after-tax earnings each year to its shareholders.

10. **LO.4** Owl is a closely held corporation owned by eight shareholders (each owns 12.5% of the stock). Its taxable income for the most recent year was $6,250,000.
    a. Calculate Owl's Federal income tax liability if it is a C corporation.
    b. Explain Owl's Federal tax calculation if it is an S corporation.
    c. How would your answers in parts (a) and (b) change if Owl was not closely held (e.g., 5,000 shareholders with no shareholder owning more than 2% of the stock)?

11. **LO.4** Using the legend provided, indicate which form of business entity each of the following characteristics describes. Some of the characteristics may apply to more than one form of business entity.

Legend
P = Applies to partnership and LLC
S = Applies to S corporation
C = Applies to C corporation

a. Basis for an ownership interest is increased by an investment by the owner.
b. Basis for an ownership interest is decreased by a distribution to the owner.
c. Basis for an ownership interest is increased by entity profits.
d. Basis for an ownership interest is decreased by entity losses.
e. Basis for an ownership interest is increased as the entity's liabilities increase.
f. Basis for an ownership interest is decreased as the entity's liabilities decrease.

Decision Making

12. **LO.4** Phillip and Evans form a business entity. Each contributes the following property.

	Phillip	Evans
Cash	$600,000	
Land		$600,000*

*Fair market value. Evans's adjusted basis is $200,000.

Three months later, the entity sells the land for $652,000 because of unexpected zoning problems. The proceeds are to be applied toward the purchase of another parcel of land to be used for real estate development. Determine the Federal income tax consequences to the entity and to the owners upon both the formation and the later sale of the land. Perform your analysis assuming that the entity is:

a. A partnership.
b. An S corporation.
c. A C corporation.

13. **LO.4** Amy, Becky, and Chau form a business entity with each contributing the following.

	Adjusted Basis	Fair Market Value
Amy: Cash	$100,000	$100,000
Becky: Land	60,000	120,000
Chau: Services		50,000

Their ownership percentages will be as follows.

Amy	40%
Becky	40%
Chau	20%

Becky's land has a $20,000 mortgage that is assumed by the entity. Chau is an attorney who receives her ownership interest in exchange for legal services performed to organize the entity. Determine the recognized gain to the owners, the basis for their ownership interests, and the entity's basis for its assets if the entity is organized as:

a. A partnership.
b. A C corporation.
c. An S corporation.

14. **LO.4** Emmy contributes $40,000 to MeldCo in exchange for a 30% ownership interest. During the first year of operations, MeldCo earns a profit of $200,000. At the end of that year, MeldCo holds liabilities of $75,000. Calculate Emmy's basis for her ownership interest if the entity is:
    a. A C corporation.
    b. An S corporation.
    c. A partnership.

15. **LO.4, 6** For many years, Sophie has owned and operated several apartment buildings. In 2015 upon the advice of her attorney, Sophie transferred the apartment buildings to a newly created corporation. Her main reason for incorporating the business was to achieve the legal protection of limited liability. Ethics and Equity

    Every year since 2015 Sophie has prepared and filed a Form 1120 for the corporation. No corporate income tax has been paid because, after the deduction of various expenses (including Sophie's "management fee"), the corporation reports zero taxable income.

    This year Sophie decides that filing Form 1120 is a waste of time and serves no useful purpose. Instead, she plans to report all of the financial activities of the apartment business on her own individual Form 1040.

    Comment on the propriety of what Sophie plans to do.

16. **LO.4** The Coffee Company engages in the following transactions during the taxable year.
    - Sells stock held for three years as an investment for $30,000 (adjusted basis of $20,000).
    - Sells land used in the business for $65,000. The land has been used as a parking lot and originally cost $40,000.
    - Receives tax-exempt interest on municipal bonds of $5,000.
    - Receives dividends on IBM stock of $80,000.

    Describe the tax consequences of these transactions for the entity and its owners if the entity is organized as:
    a. A partnership.
    b. A C corporation.
    c. An S corporation.
    d. An LLC.

17. **LO.4** Swift Corporation agreed to redeem some of the shares of two of its shareholders. It distributed land (basis $55,000 and fair market value $120,000) to Sam in exchange for part of his stock. Sam's basis in the redeemed stock was $25,000. Swift also distributed $240,000 cash to Allison in exchange for part of her stock. Allison's basis in the redeemed stock was $40,000. As a result of the redemptions, Sam's interest in the corporation declined from 20% to 15%, and Allison's interest declined from 70% to 60%.

    Determine the tax consequences to Swift, Sam, and Allison if Swift is:
    a. A C corporation.
    b. An S corporation.

18. LO.4 Indigo, Inc., a closely held C corporation, incurs the following income and losses.

Active income	$325,000
Portfolio income	49,000
Passive activity loss	333,000

a. Calculate Indigo's taxable income.

b. Would the answer in part (a) change if the passive loss was $320,000 rather than $333,000? Explain.

19. LO.4 Rosa contributes $50,000 to FlipCo in exchange for a 10% ownership interest. Rosa materially participates in FlipCo's business.

FlipCo incurs a loss of $900,000 for the current tax year. Entity liabilities at the end of the year are $700,000. Of this amount, $150,000 is for recourse debt, and $550,000 is for nonrecourse debt.

a. Assume that FlipCo is a partnership. How much of Rosa's share of the loss can she deduct for the year on her individual tax return? What is Rosa's basis for her partnership interest at the end of the year?

b. Assume that FlipCo is a C corporation. How much of Rosa's share of the loss can she deduct for the year on her individual tax return? What is Rosa's basis for her stock at the end of the year?

20. LO.4 Bishop contributes undeveloped land to a business entity in January for a 40% ownership interest. Bishop's basis for the land is $140,000, and the fair market value is $600,000. The business entity was formed three years ago by Petula and Rene, who have equal ownership. The entity is successful in getting the land rezoned from agricultural to residential use, but the owners decide to sell the land so that the entity can invest in another project.

In August, the land is sold for $650,000. Determine the tax consequences of the sale of the undeveloped land for the business entity and the three owners if the entity is organized as:

a. A C corporation.

b. An S corporation.

c. A partnership.

d. An LLC.

21. LO.4 Jo and Velma are equal owners of JV Company. Jo invests $500,000 cash in the venture. Velma contributes land and a building (basis to her of $125,000, fair market value of $500,000). The entity then borrows $250,000 cash using recourse financing and $100,000 using nonrecourse financing.

a. Determine each owner's basis in her ownership interest and her amount at risk assuming that the venture is a general partnership.

b. Determine each owner's basis in her ownership interest and her amount at risk assuming that the venture is an S corporation.

22. LO.4 Megan owns 55% and Vern owns 45% of a business entity. The owners would like to share profits (55% for Megan and 45% for Vern) and losses (80% for Vern and 20% for Megan) differently if possible. Determine the tax consequences for the entity and its owners if the entity has a tax loss of $160,000 and is organized as:

a. A partnership.

b. A C corporation.

c. An S corporation.

23. **LO.4** Abby Morales is a general partner in High Success Partnership that provides executive coaching services. She works about 20 hours per week providing coaching and related services for the partnership business activities. A portion of her Schedule K–1 for 2021 is shown below. What is the missing figure for box 14, Self-employment earnings (loss)?

651121

☐ Final K-1 ☐ Amended K-1 OMB No. 1545-0123

Schedule K-1 (Form 1065) **2021**
Department of the Treasury
Internal Revenue Service

For calendar year 2021, or tax year
beginning 1 / 1 / 2021 ending 12 / 31 / 2021

Partner's Share of Income, Deductions, Credits, etc. ▶ **See back of form and separate instructions.**

Part I Information About the Partnership

A Partnership's employer identification number
12-3456789

B Partnership's name, address, city, state, and ZIP code
High Success I Partnership
123 Main Street
Las Vegas, NV 89104

C IRS center where partnership filed return ▶ Ogden

D ☐ Check if this is a publicly traded partnership (PTP)

Part II Information About the Partner

E Partner's SSN or TIN (Do not use TIN of a disregarded entity. See instructions.)
XXX-XX-1234

F Name, address, city, state, and ZIP code for partner entered in E. See instructions.
Abby Morales
1542 Meridian Avenue
Las Vegas, NV 89110

G ☒ General partner or LLC member-manager ☐ Limited partner or other LLC member

Part III Partner's Share of Current Year Income, Deductions, Credits, and Other Items

Box	Item	Amount	Box	Item
1	Ordinary business income (loss)	56,897	14	Self-employment earnings (loss)
2	Net rental real estate income (loss)			
3	Other net rental income (loss)		15	Credits
4a	Guaranteed payments for services	30,000		
4b	Guaranteed payments for capital	1,000	16	Schedule K-3 is attached if checked . . . . ▶ ☐
4c	Total guaranteed payments	31,000	17	Alternative minimum tax (AMT) items
5	Interest income	72		
6a	Ordinary dividends	0		
6b	Qualified dividends	0	18	Tax-exempt income and nondeductible expenses
6c	Dividend equivalents	0		
7	Royalties	0		
8	Net short-term capital gain (loss)	0	19	Distributions
9a	Net long-term capital gain (loss)	0		

24. **LO.5** Heron Corporation has been in operation for 10 years. Since Heron's creation, all of its stock has been owned by Andy, who initially invested $200,000 in the corporation. Heron has been successful far beyond Andy's expectations, and the current fair market value of the stock is $10,000,000. While Andy has been paid a salary of $200,000 per year by the corporation, all of Heron's earnings have been reinvested in the growth of the corporation.

Digging Deeper
Ethics and Equity

Heron currently is being audited by the IRS. One of the issues raised by the IRS agent is the possibility of the assessment of the accumulated earnings tax. Andy is not concerned about this issue because he believes Heron can easily justify the accumulations based on its past rapid expansion by opening new outlets. The expansion program is fully documented in the minutes of Heron's board of directors. Andy has provided this information to the IRS agent.

Two years ago, Andy decided that he would curtail any further expansion into new markets by Heron. In his opinion, further expansion would exceed his ability to manage the corporation effectively. Because the tax year under audit is three years in the past, Andy sees no reason to provide the IRS agent with this information.

Heron will continue its policy of no dividend payments into the foreseeable future. Andy believes that if the accumulated earnings issue is satisfactorily resolved on this audit, it probably will not be raised again on any subsequent audits. Thus, double taxation in the form of the tax on dividends at the shareholder level or the accumulated earnings tax at the corporate level can be avoided.

What is Heron's responsibility to disclose to the IRS agent the expected change in its growth strategy? Are Andy's beliefs regarding future accumulated earnings tax issues realistic? Explain.

Critical Thinking

25. **LO.5** Turtle, a C corporation, reports taxable income of $200,000 before paying salaries to the two equal shareholder-employees, Britney and Alan. Turtle follows a policy of distributing all after-tax earnings to the shareholders.

    a. Determine the tax consequences for Turtle, Britney, and Alan if the corporation pays salaries as follows. Britney and Alan are both single with approximately $250,000 of taxable income before considering any payments from Turtle.

Option 1		**Option 2**	
Britney	$50,000	Britney	$100,000
Alan	50,000	Alan	100,000

    b. Which option would you recommend? Explain.

26. **LO.5** Parrott, Inc., a C corporation, is owned by Alfonso (60%) and Deanna (40%). Alfonso is the president, and Deanna is the vice president for sales. Parrott, Alfonso, and Deanna are cash basis taxpayers. Parrott encounters working capital difficulties, so Alfonso loans the corporation $810,000, and Deanna loans the corporation $540,000. Each loan uses a 5% note that is due in five years with interest payable annually. Determine the tax consequences to Parrott, Alfonso, and Deanna if:

    a. The notes are classified as debt.
    b. The notes are classified as equity.

Communications
Decision Making

27. **LO.5** Laurie Gladin owns land and a building that she has been using in her sole proprietorship. She is going to incorporate her sole proprietorship as a C corporation. Laurie must decide whether to contribute the land and building to the corporation or to lease them to the corporation. The net income of the sole proprietorship for the past five years has averaged $250,000. Advise Laurie on the tax consequences. Summarize your analysis in a memo for the tax research file.

Decision Making
Planning

28. **LO.5** Marci and Jennifer each own 50% of the stock of Lavender, a C corporation. After each of them is paid a "reasonable" salary of $125,000, the taxable income of Lavender is normally around $600,000. The corporation is about to purchase a $2,000,000 shopping mall ($1,500,000 allocated to the building and $500,000 allocated to the land). The mall will be rented to tenants at a net rent income (i.e., includes rental commissions, depreciation, etc.) of $500,000 annually. Marci and Jennifer will contribute $1,000,000 each to the corporation to provide the cash required for the acquisition.

    Lavender's CPA has suggested that Marci and Jennifer purchase the shopping mall as individuals and lease it to Lavender for a fair rental of $300,000. Both Marci and Jennifer are in the 32% tax bracket.

    Determine whether the shopping mall should be acquired by Lavender, or by Marci and Jennifer, in accordance with their CPA's recommendation.

Decision Making
Planning

29. **LO.5** Since Garnet Corporation was formed five years ago, its stock has been held as follows: 525 shares by Frank and 175 shares by Grace. Their basis in the stock is $350,000 for Frank and $150,000 for Grace. As part of a stock redemption, Garnet redeems 125 of Frank's shares for $175,000 and 125 of Grace's shares for $175,000.

    a. What are the tax consequences of the stock redemption to Frank and Grace?
    b. How would the tax consequences to Frank and Grace be different if, instead of the redemption, they each sell 125 shares to Chuck (an unrelated party)?
    c. What factors should influence their decision on whether to redeem or sell the 250 shares of stock?

Critical Thinking

30. **LO.5** Oscar created Lavender Corporation four years ago. The C corporation has paid Oscar as president a salary of $200,000 each year. Annual earnings after taxes approximate $700,000 each year. Lavender has not paid any dividends, nor does it intend to do so in the future. Instead, Oscar wants his heirs to receive the stock with a step-up in stock basis when he dies. Identify the relevant tax issues.

31. **LO.5** Clay Corporation has been an S corporation since its incorporation 10 years ago. During the first three years of operations, it incurred total losses of $250,000. Since then, Clay has generated earnings of approximately $180,000 each year. None of the earnings have been distributed to the three equal shareholders, Claire, Lynn, and Tomás, because the corporation has been in an expansion mode. — Decision Making, Planning

At the beginning of this year, Claire sells her stock to Nell for $400,000. Nell has reservations about the utility of the S election. Therefore, Lynn, Tomás, and Nell are discussing whether the election should be continued. They expect the earnings to remain at approximately $180,000 each year. However, because they perceive that the company's expansion period is over and Clay has adequate working capital, they may start distributing the earnings to the shareholders. All of the shareholders are in the 32% tax bracket.

Advise the three shareholders as to whether Clay's S election should be maintained.

32. **LO.6** Emily and Frida are negotiating with George to purchase the business he operates as Pelican, Inc. The assets of Pelican, Inc., a C corporation, are recorded as follows.

Asset	Basis	FMV
Cash	$ 20,000	$ 20,000
Accounts receivable	50,000	50,000
Inventory	100,000	110,000
Furniture and fixtures	150,000	170,000*
Building	200,000	250,000**
Land	40,000	150,000

*Potential depreciation recapture is $45,000.
**The straight-line method was used to depreciate the building. Accumulated depreciation is $340,000.

George's basis for the Pelican stock is $560,000. George is subject to a 32% marginal tax rate.

a. Emily and Frida purchase the *stock* of Pelican from George for $908,000. Determine the tax consequences to Emily, Frida, Pelican, and George.
b. Emily and Frida purchase the *assets* from Pelican for $908,000. Determine the tax consequences to Emily, Frida, Pelican, and George.
c. The purchase price is $550,000 because the fair market value of the building is $150,000 and the fair market value of the land is $50,000. No amount is assigned to goodwill. Emily and Frida purchase the *stock* of Pelican from George. Determine the tax consequences to Emily, Frida, Pelican, and George.

33. **LO.6** Linda is the owner of a sole proprietorship. The entity has the following assets. — Decision Making, Planning

Asset	Basis	FMV
Cash	$10,000	$10,000
Accounts receivable	–0–	25,000
Office furniture and fixtures*	15,000	17,000
Building**	75,000	90,000
Land	60,000	80,000

*Potential depreciation recapture is $5,000.
**The straight-line method has been used to depreciate the building.

Linda sells the business for $260,000 to Juan.

a. Determine the tax consequences to Linda, including the classification of any recognized gain or loss.
b. Determine the tax consequences to Juan.
c. Advise Juan on how the purchase agreement could be modified to produce more beneficial tax consequences for him. *Hint*: Consider the use of a covenant not to compete.

Critical Thinking
Planning

34. **LO.6** Gabriela and Harry own the GH Partnership. They have conducted the business as a partnership for 10 years. The bases for their partnership interests are as follows.

Gabriela	Harry
$100,000	$150,000

GH Partnership holds the following assets.

Asset	Basis	FMV
Cash	$ 10,000	$ 10,000
Accounts receivable	30,000	28,000
Inventory	25,000	26,000
Building*	100,000	150,000
Land	250,000	400,000

*The straight-line method has been used to depreciate the building. Accumulated depreciation is $70,000.

Gabriela and Harry sell their partnership interests to Keith and Liang for $307,000 each.

a. Determine the tax consequences of the sale to Gabriela, Harry, and GH Partnership.

b. From a tax perspective, should it matter to Keith and Liang whether they purchase Gabriela and Harry's partnership interests or the partnership assets from GH Partnership? Explain.

Decision Making

35. **LO.6** Hector and Walt are purchasing the Copper Partnership from Jan and Gail for $700,000; Hector and Walt will be equal partners. During the negotiations, Jan and Gail succeeded in having the transaction structured as the purchase of the partnership rather than as a purchase of the individual assets. The adjusted basis of the individual assets of Copper is $580,000.

a. What are Hector's and Walt's bases for their partnership interests (i.e., outside bases)?

b. What is Copper's adjusted basis for its assets after the transaction? Would an optional adjustment-to-basis election be helpful? Why or why not?

Critical Thinking

36. **LO.6** Vladimir owns all of the stock of Ruby Corporation. The fair market value of the stock (and Ruby's assets) is about four times Vladimir's adjusted basis for the stock. Vladimir is negotiating with an investor group for the sale of the corporation. Identify the relevant tax issues for Vladimir.

Communications
Decision Making
Planning

37. **LO.6** Miguel Allred is going to purchase either the stock or the assets of Jewel Corporation. All of the Jewel stock is owned by Charley. Miguel and Charley agree that Jewel is worth $700,000. The tax basis for Jewel's assets is $500,000.

Write a letter to Miguel, advising him on whether he should negotiate to purchase the stock or the assets. Prepare a memo for the tax research file on this matter. Miguel's address is 100 Aspen Green, Chattanooga, TN 37403.

38. **LO.2, 3, 4, 5, 6** Using the legend provided, indicate which form of business entity each of the following characteristics describes. Some of the characteristics may apply to more than one form of business entity.

Legend
SP = Applies to sole proprietorship
P = Applies to general partnership
L = Applies to LLC
S = Applies to S corporation
C = Applies to C corporation
N = Applies to none

a. Has limited liability.
b. Greatest ability to raise capital.
c. Subject to double taxation.
d. Limit on types and number of shareholders.
e. Has unlimited liability.
f. Sale of the business can be subject to double taxation.
g. Contribution of property to the entity in exchange for an ownership interest can result in the nonrecognition of realized gain.
h. Profits and losses affect the basis for an ownership interest.
i. Entity liabilities affect the basis for an ownership interest.
j. Distributions of earnings are taxed as dividend income to the owners.
k. Total invested capital cannot exceed $1,000,000.
l. AAA is an account that relates to this entity.

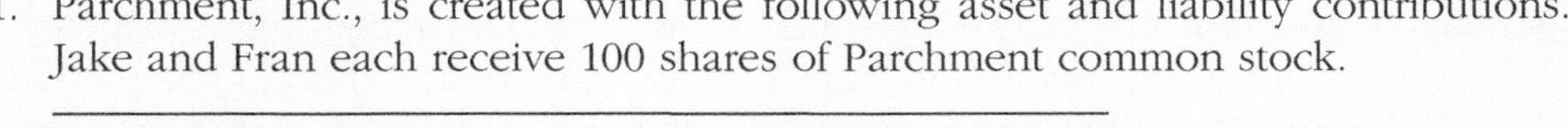
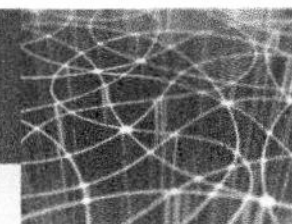

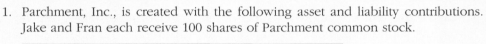

Bridge Discipline

1. Parchment, Inc., is created with the following asset and liability contributions. Jake and Fran each receive 100 shares of Parchment common stock.

Shareholder	Assets	Basis	Fair Market Value
Jake	Cash	$100,000	$100,000
Fran	Land	40,000	120,000*

*The land is subject to a mortgage of $20,000 that Parchment assumes.

a. Prepare a financial accounting balance sheet for Parchment. Does financial accounting take a conduit or entity perspective to the formation of a business venture?
b. Prepare a tax balance sheet for Parchment. Does the tax law take a conduit or entity perspective to the formation of a business venture?
c. Assume that Parchment sells the land for $150,000 ($130,000 cash plus the assumption of the related mortgage) four months after Parchment was created. Discuss the effect of the sale on the financial accounting statements and the related income tax computations.

2. Assume that Parchment in (1) elects S corporation status at the time of its creation. Respond to parts (a), (b), and (c).

3. Assume that Parchment in (1) is a general partnership rather than a corporation. Respond to parts (a), (b), and (c). Would your answer change if Parchment were an LLC that "checked the box" to be taxed as a partnership? Explain.

Research Problems

Note: Solutions to the Research Problems can be prepared by using the Thomson Reuters Checkpoint™ online tax research database, which accompanies this textbook. Solutions can also be prepared by using research materials found in a typical tax library.

Communications
Decision Making
Planning

Research Problem 1. The Turnaround LLC was formed several years ago. It incurred losses for several years, reducing many of its members' bases in their interests to zero. However, the business recently obtained some promising contracts, and there is an expectation of profits in the coming years.

Turnaround then admitted several new members, each making capital contributions for their interests. The new owners anticipate that it will be necessary to reinvest any profits back into the business for some time. Since there no longer will be losses to pass through and any double taxation of profits will be delayed for some time, the owners of Turnaround are considering converting the business to a C corporation.

The business controls the following assets. There is no § 754 election in effect.

	Fair Market Value	Adjusted Basis
Cash	$ 500,000	$500,000
PP&E	500,000	500,000
Customer contracts	1,000,000	–0–

The original owners of Turnaround now hold a 50% capital and profits interest. They have come to you for advice regarding the potential tax consequences of the conversion for them as well as for the new corporation.

Partial list of research aids:
Rev.Rul. 70–239, 1970–1 C.B. 74.
Rev.Rul. 84–111, 1984–2 C.B. 88.
Rev.Rul. 2004–59, 2004–24 I.R.B. 1050.
Treas. Reg. § 301.7701–3(g)(i).

Research Problem 2. Crane is a partner in the Cardinal Partnership. A dispute arose with the partnership regarding Crane's share of current earnings. The partnership contends that the amount is $75,000, but Crane believes his share is $100,000.

Crane ceased being a partner on November 1. As a result of the dispute, the partnership distributed only $75,000 to Crane. It placed the disputed $25,000 in escrow. However, Crane's Schedule K–1 from the partnership included the full $100,000. Crane believes that the K–1 should include only the $75,000 that is not in dispute. Is Crane correct? Explain.

Use internet tax resources to address the following questions. Look for reliable websites and blogs of the IRS and other government agencies, media outlets, businesses, tax professionals, academics, think tanks, and political outlets.

Communications

Research Problem 3. Find a blog posting or discussion thread with comments from tax professionals about Federal income tax consequences that occur when a business converts from an LLC to an S corporation or when a C corporation converts to a pass-through entity. Summarize the comments and suggestions that you find in these discussions in a one-page memo to your instructor.

Communications
Critical Thinking

Research Problem 4. The Tax Cuts and Jobs Act (TCJA) of 2017 made changes in how business entities are taxed. Find an article written by a tax practitioner that discusses how the TCJA of 2017 changed choice of entity considerations. In a paper you send to your instructor, summarize the article, and explain how the changes are relevant to (a) a retail clothing business and (b) a CPA firm.

Appendix A

Tax Formulas, Tax Rate Schedules, and Tables

(The 2022 Individual Income Tax Tables and the 2022 Individual Optional Sales Tax Tables can be accessed at the IRS website when released: **irs.gov**)

Tax Formula for Individuals

Income (broadly defined)	$xx,xxx
Less: Exclusions	(x,xxx)
Gross income	$xx,xxx
Less: Deductions *for* adjusted gross income	(x,xxx)
Adjusted gross income	$xx,xxx
Less: The greater of— Total itemized deductions *or* standard deduction	(x,xxx)
Less: Personal and dependency exemptions*	(x,xxx)
Deduction for qualified business income**	(x,xxx)
Taxable income	$xx,xxx
Tax on taxable income	$ x,xxx
Less: Tax credits (including Federal income tax withheld and prepaid)	(xxx)
Tax due (or refund)	$ xxx

*Exemption deductions are not allowed from 2018 through 2025.
**Only applies from 2018 through 2025.

Note: For 2021, individuals using the standard deduction may also subtract *from* adjusted gross income, cash charitable contributions of up to $300 ($600 if married, filing jointly).

Basic Standard Deduction Amounts

Filing Status	2021	2022
Single	$12,550	$12,950
Married, filing jointly	25,100	25,900
Surviving spouse	25,100	25,900
Head of household	18,800	19,400
Married, filing separately	12,550	12,950

Amount of Each Additional Standard Deduction

Filing Status	2021	2022
Single	$1,700	$1,750
Married, filing jointly	1,350	1,400
Surviving spouse	1,350	1,400
Head of household	1,700	1,750
Married, filing separately	1,350	1,400

Personal and Dependency Exemption

2021	2022
$4,300	$4,400

Note: Exemption deductions have been suspended from 2018 through 2025. However, the personal and dependency exemption amount is used for other purposes (including determining whether a "qualifying relative" is a taxpayer's dependent).

2021 Tax Rate Schedules

Single—Schedule X

If taxable income is: Over—	But not over—	The tax is:	of the amount over—
$ 0	$ 9,950	.........10%	$ 0
9,950	40,525	$ 995.00 + 12%	9,950
40,525	86,375	4,664.00 + 22%	40,525
86,375	164,925	14,751.00 + 24%	86,375
164,925	209,425	33,603.00 + 32%	164,925
209,425	523,600	47,843.00 + 35%	209,425
523,600	....	157,804.25 + 37%	523,600

Head of household—Schedule Z

If taxable income is: Over—	But not over—	The tax is:	of the amount over—
$ 0	$ 14,200	.........10%	$ 0
14,200	54,200	$ 1,420.00 + 12%	14,200
54,200	86,350	6,220.00 + 22%	54,200
86,350	164,900	13,293.00 + 24%	86,350
164,900	209,400	32,145.00 + 32%	164,900
209,400	523,600	46,385.00 + 35%	209,400
523,600	....	156,355.00 + 37%	523,600

Married filing jointly or Qualifying widow(er)—Schedule Y–1

If taxable income is: Over—	But not over—	The tax is:	of the amount over—
$ 0	$ 19,900	.........10%	$ 0
19,900	81,050	$ 1,990.00 + 12%	19,900
81,050	172,750	9,328.00 + 22%	81,050
172,750	329,850	29,502.00 + 24%	172,750
329,850	418,850	67,206.00 + 32%	329,850
418,850	628,300	95,686.00 + 35%	418,850
628,300	....	168,993.50 + 37%	628,300

Married filing separately—Schedule Y–2

If taxable income is: Over—	But not over—	The tax is:	of the amount over—
$ 0	$ 9,950	.........10%	$ 0
9,950	40,525	$ 995.00 + 12%	9,950
40,525	86,375	4,664.00 + 22%	40,525
86,375	164,925	14,751.00 + 24%	86,375
164,925	209,425	33,603.00 + 32%	164,925
209,425	314,150	47,843.00 + 35%	209,425
314,150	....	84,496.75 + 37%	314,150

2022 Tax Rate Schedules

Single—Schedule X

If taxable income is: Over—	But not over—	The tax is:	of the amount over—
$ 0	$ 10,275	.........10%	$ 0
10,275	41,775	$ 1,027.50 + 12%	10,275
41,775	89,075	4,807.50 + 22%	41,775
89,075	170,050	15,213.50 + 24%	89,075
170,050	215,950	34,647.50 + 32%	170,050
215,950	539,900	49,335.50 + 35%	215,950
539,900	....	162,718.00 + 37%	539,900

Head of household—Schedule Z

If taxable income is: Over—	But not over—	The tax is:	of the amount over—
$ 0	$ 14,650	.........10%	$ 0
14,650	55,900	$ 1,465.00 + 12%	14,650
55,900	89,050	6,415.00 + 22%	55,900
89,050	170,050	13,708.00 + 24%	89,050
170,050	215,950	33,148.00 + 32%	170,050
215,950	539,900	47,836.00 + 35%	215,950
539,900	....	161,218.50 + 37%	539,900

Married filing jointly or Qualifying widow(er)—Schedule Y–1

If taxable income is: Over—	But not over—	The tax is:	of the amount over—
$ 0	$ 20,550	.........10%	$ 0
20,550	83,550	$ 2,055.00 + 12%	20,550
83,550	178,150	9,615.00 + 22%	83,550
178,150	340,100	30,427.00 + 24%	178,150
340,100	431,900	69,295.00 + 32%	340,100
431,900	647,850	98,671.00 + 35%	431,900
647,850	....	174,253.50 + 37%	647,850

Married filing separately—Schedule Y–2

If taxable income is: Over—	But not over—	The tax is:	of the amount over—
$ 0	$ 10,275	.........10%	$ 0
10,275	41,775	$ 1,027.50 + 12%	10,275
41,775	89,075	4,807.50 + 22%	41,775
89,075	170,050	15,213.50 + 24%	89,075
170,050	215,950	34,647.50 + 32%	170,050
215,950	323,925	49,335.50 + 35%	215,950
323,925	....	87,126.75 + 37%	323,925

2021 Tax Table

See the instructions for line 16 to see if you must use the Tax Table below to figure your tax.

Example. Mr. and Mrs. Brown are filing a joint return. Their taxable income on Form 1040, line 15, is $25,300. First, they find the $25,300-25,350 taxable income line. Next, they find the column for married filing jointly and read down the column. The amount shown where the taxable income line and filing status column meet is $2,641. This is the tax amount they should enter in the entry space on Form 1040, line 16.

Sample Table

At Least	But Less Than	Single	Married filing jointly*	Married filing sepa-rately	Head of a house-hold
		Your tax is—			
25,200	**25,250**	2,828	2,629	2,828	2,743
25,250	**25,300**	2,834	2,635	2,834	2,749
25,300	**25,350**	2,840	(2,641)	2,840	2,755
25,350	**25,400**	2,846	2,647	2,846	2,761

If line 15 (taxable income) is—		And you are—			
At least	But less than	Single	Married filing jointly *	Married filing sepa-rately	Head of a house-hold
		Your tax is—			
0	5	0	0	0	0
5	15	1	1	1	1
15	25	2	2	2	2
25	50	4	4	4	4
50	75	6	6	6	6
75	100	9	9	9	9
100	125	11	11	11	11
125	150	14	14	14	14
150	175	16	16	16	16
175	200	19	19	19	19
200	225	21	21	21	21
225	250	24	24	24	24
250	275	26	26	26	26
275	300	29	29	29	29
300	325	31	31	31	31
325	350	34	34	34	34
350	375	36	36	36	36
375	400	39	39	39	39
400	425	41	41	41	41
425	450	44	44	44	44
450	475	46	46	46	46
475	500	49	49	49	49
500	525	51	51	51	51
525	550	54	54	54	54
550	575	56	56	56	56
575	600	59	59	59	59
600	625	61	61	61	61
625	650	64	64	64	64
650	675	66	66	66	66
675	700	69	69	69	69
700	725	71	71	71	71
725	750	74	74	74	74
750	775	76	76	76	76
775	800	79	79	79	79
800	825	81	81	81	81
825	850	84	84	84	84
850	875	86	86	86	86
875	900	89	89	89	89
900	925	91	91	91	91
925	950	94	94	94	94
950	975	96	96	96	96
975	1,000	99	99	99	99

If line 15 (taxable income) is—		And you are—			
At least	But less than	Single	Married filing jointly *	Married filing sepa-rately	Head of a house-hold
		Your tax is—			
1,000					
1,000	1,025	101	101	101	101
1,025	1,050	104	104	104	104
1,050	1,075	106	106	106	106
1,075	1,100	109	109	109	109
1,100	1,125	111	111	111	111
1,125	1,150	114	114	114	114
1,150	1,175	116	116	116	116
1,175	1,200	119	119	119	119
1,200	1,225	121	121	121	121
1,225	1,250	124	124	124	124
1,250	1,275	126	126	126	126
1,275	1,300	129	129	129	129
1,300	1,325	131	131	131	131
1,325	1,350	134	134	134	134
1,350	1,375	136	136	136	136
1,375	1,400	139	139	139	139
1,400	1,425	141	141	141	141
1,425	1,450	144	144	144	144
1,450	1,475	146	146	146	146
1,475	1,500	149	149	149	149
1,500	1,525	151	151	151	151
1,525	1,550	154	154	154	154
1,550	1,575	156	156	156	156
1,575	1,600	159	159	159	159
1,600	1,625	161	161	161	161
1,625	1,650	164	164	164	164
1,650	1,675	166	166	166	166
1,675	1,700	169	169	169	169
1,700	1,725	171	171	171	171
1,725	1,750	174	174	174	174
1,750	1,775	176	176	176	176
1,775	1,800	179	179	179	179
1,800	1,825	181	181	181	181
1,825	1,850	184	184	184	184
1,850	1,875	186	186	186	186
1,875	1,900	189	189	189	189
1,900	1,925	191	191	191	191
1,925	1,950	194	194	194	194
1,950	1,975	196	196	196	196
1,975	2,000	199	199	199	199

If line 15 (taxable income) is—		And you are—			
At least	But less than	Single	Married filing jointly *	Married filing sepa-rately	Head of a house-hold
		Your tax is—			
2,000					
2,000	2,025	201	201	201	201
2,025	2,050	204	204	204	204
2,050	2,075	206	206	206	206
2,075	2,100	209	209	209	209
2,100	2,125	211	211	211	211
2,125	2,150	214	214	214	214
2,150	2,175	216	216	216	216
2,175	2,200	219	219	219	219
2,200	2,225	221	221	221	221
2,225	2,250	224	224	224	224
2,250	2,275	226	226	226	226
2,275	2,300	229	229	229	229
2,300	2,325	231	231	231	231
2,325	2,350	234	234	234	234
2,350	2,375	236	236	236	236
2,375	2,400	239	239	239	239
2,400	2,425	241	241	241	241
2,425	2,450	244	244	244	244
2,450	2,475	246	246	246	246
2,475	2,500	249	249	249	249
2,500	2,525	251	251	251	251
2,525	2,550	254	254	254	254
2,550	2,575	256	256	256	256
2,575	2,600	259	259	259	259
2,600	2,625	261	261	261	261
2,625	2,650	264	264	264	264
2,650	2,675	266	266	266	266
2,675	2,700	269	269	269	269
2,700	2,725	271	271	271	271
2,725	2,750	274	274	274	274
2,750	2,775	276	276	276	276
2,775	2,800	279	279	279	279
2,800	2,825	281	281	281	281
2,825	2,850	284	284	284	284
2,850	2,875	286	286	286	286
2,875	2,900	289	289	289	289
2,900	2,925	291	291	291	291
2,925	2,950	294	294	294	294
2,950	2,975	296	296	296	296
2,975	3,000	299	299	299	299

(Continued)

* This column must also be used by a qualifying widow(er).

2021 Tax Table — *Continued*

If line 15 (taxable income) is—		And you are—			
At least	But less than	Single	Married filing jointly *	Married filing sepa-rately	Head of a house-hold
		Your tax is—			
3,000					
3,000	3,050	303	303	303	303
3,050	3,100	308	308	308	308
3,100	3,150	313	313	313	313
3,150	3,200	318	318	318	318
3,200	3,250	323	323	323	323
3,250	3,300	328	328	328	328
3,300	3,350	333	333	333	333
3,350	3,400	338	338	338	338
3,400	3,450	343	343	343	343
3,450	3,500	348	348	348	348
3,500	3,550	353	353	353	353
3,550	3,600	358	358	358	358
3,600	3,650	363	363	363	363
3,650	3,700	368	368	368	368
3,700	3,750	373	373	373	373
3,750	3,800	378	378	378	378
3,800	3,850	383	383	383	383
3,850	3,900	388	388	388	388
3,900	3,950	393	393	393	393
3,950	4,000	398	398	398	398
4,000					
4,000	4,050	403	403	403	403
4,050	4,100	408	408	408	408
4,100	4,150	413	413	413	413
4,150	4,200	418	418	418	418
4,200	4,250	423	423	423	423
4,250	4,300	428	428	428	428
4,300	4,350	433	433	433	433
4,350	4,400	438	438	438	438
4,400	4,450	443	443	443	443
4,450	4,500	448	448	448	448
4,500	4,550	453	453	453	453
4,550	4,600	458	458	458	458
4,600	4,650	463	463	463	463
4,650	4,700	468	468	468	468
4,700	4,750	473	473	473	473
4,750	4,800	478	478	478	478
4,800	4,850	483	483	483	483
4,850	4,900	488	488	488	488
4,900	4,950	493	493	493	493
4,950	5,000	498	498	498	498
5,000					
5,000	5,050	503	503	503	503
5,050	5,100	508	508	508	508
5,100	5,150	513	513	513	513
5,150	5,200	518	518	518	518
5,200	5,250	523	523	523	523
5,250	5,300	528	528	528	528
5,300	5,350	533	533	533	533
5,350	5,400	538	538	538	538
5,400	5,450	543	543	543	543
5,450	5,500	548	548	548	548
5,500	5,550	553	553	553	553
5,550	5,600	558	558	558	558
5,600	5,650	563	563	563	563
5,650	5,700	568	568	568	568
5,700	5,750	573	573	573	573
5,750	5,800	578	578	578	578
5,800	5,850	583	583	583	583
5,850	5,900	588	588	588	588
5,900	5,950	593	593	593	593
5,950	6,000	598	598	598	598

If line 15 (taxable income) is—		And you are—			
At least	But less than	Single	Married filing jointly *	Married filing sepa-rately	Head of a house-hold
		Your tax is—			
6,000					
6,000	6,050	603	603	603	603
6,050	6,100	608	608	608	608
6,100	6,150	613	613	613	613
6,150	6,200	618	618	618	618
6,200	6,250	623	623	623	623
6,250	6,300	628	628	628	628
6,300	6,350	633	633	633	633
6,350	6,400	638	638	638	638
6,400	6,450	643	643	643	643
6,450	6,500	648	648	648	648
6,500	6,550	653	653	653	653
6,550	6,600	658	658	658	658
6,600	6,650	663	663	663	663
6,650	6,700	668	668	668	668
6,700	6,750	673	673	673	673
6,750	6,800	678	678	678	678
6,800	6,850	683	683	683	683
6,850	6,900	688	688	688	688
6,900	6,950	693	693	693	693
6,950	7,000	698	698	698	698
7,000					
7,000	7,050	703	703	703	703
7,050	7,100	708	708	708	708
7,100	7,150	713	713	713	713
7,150	7,200	718	718	718	718
7,200	7,250	723	723	723	723
7,250	7,300	728	728	728	728
7,300	7,350	733	733	733	733
7,350	7,400	738	738	738	738
7,400	7,450	743	743	743	743
7,450	7,500	748	748	748	748
7,500	7,550	753	753	753	753
7,550	7,600	758	758	758	758
7,600	7,650	763	763	763	763
7,650	7,700	768	768	768	768
7,700	7,750	773	773	773	773
7,750	7,800	778	778	778	778
7,800	7,850	783	783	783	783
7,850	7,900	788	788	788	788
7,900	7,950	793	793	793	793
7,950	8,000	798	798	798	798
8,000					
8,000	8,050	803	803	803	803
8,050	8,100	808	808	808	808
8,100	8,150	813	813	813	813
8,150	8,200	818	818	818	818
8,200	8,250	823	823	823	823
8,250	8,300	828	828	828	828
8,300	8,350	833	833	833	833
8,350	8,400	838	838	838	838
8,400	8,450	843	843	843	843
8,450	8,500	848	848	848	848
8,500	8,550	853	853	853	853
8,550	8,600	858	858	858	858
8,600	8,650	863	863	863	863
8,650	8,700	868	868	868	868
8,700	8,750	873	873	873	873
8,750	8,800	878	878	878	878
8,800	8,850	883	883	883	883
8,850	8,900	888	888	888	888
8,900	8,950	893	893	893	893
8,950	9,000	898	898	898	898

If line 15 (taxable income) is—		And you are—			
At least	But less than	Single	Married filing jointly *	Married filing sepa-rately	Head of a house-hold
		Your tax is—			
9,000					
9,000	9,050	903	903	903	903
9,050	9,100	908	908	908	908
9,100	9,150	913	913	913	913
9,150	9,200	918	918	918	918
9,200	9,250	923	923	923	923
9,250	9,300	928	928	928	928
9,300	9,350	933	933	933	933
9,350	9,400	938	938	938	938
9,400	9,450	943	943	943	943
9,450	9,500	948	948	948	948
9,500	9,550	953	953	953	953
9,550	9,600	958	958	958	958
9,600	9,650	963	963	963	963
9,650	9,700	968	968	968	968
9,700	9,750	973	973	973	973
9,750	9,800	978	978	978	978
9,800	9,850	983	983	983	983
9,850	9,900	988	988	988	988
9,900	9,950	993	993	993	993
9,950	10,000	998	998	998	998
10,000					
10,000	10,050	1,004	1,003	1,004	1,003
10,050	10,100	1,010	1,008	1,010	1,008
10,100	10,150	1,016	1,013	1,016	1,013
10,150	10,200	1,022	1,018	1,022	1,018
10,200	10,250	1,028	1,023	1,028	1,023
10,250	10,300	1,034	1,028	1,034	1,028
10,300	10,350	1,040	1,033	1,040	1,033
10,350	10,400	1,046	1,038	1,046	1,038
10,400	10,450	1,052	1,043	1,052	1,043
10,450	10,500	1,058	1,048	1,058	1,048
10,500	10,550	1,064	1,053	1,064	1,053
10,550	10,600	1,070	1,058	1,070	1,058
10,600	10,650	1,076	1,063	1,076	1,063
10,650	10,700	1,082	1,068	1,082	1,068
10,700	10,750	1,088	1,073	1,088	1,073
10,750	10,800	1,094	1,078	1,094	1,078
10,800	10,850	1,100	1,083	1,100	1,083
10,850	10,900	1,106	1,088	1,106	1,088
10,900	10,950	1,112	1,093	1,112	1,093
10,950	11,000	1,118	1,098	1,118	1,098
11,000					
11,000	11,050	1,124	1,103	1,124	1,103
11,050	11,100	1,130	1,108	1,130	1,108
11,100	11,150	1,136	1,113	1,136	1,113
11,150	11,200	1,142	1,118	1,142	1,118
11,200	11,250	1,148	1,123	1,148	1,123
11,250	11,300	1,154	1,128	1,154	1,128
11,300	11,350	1,160	1,133	1,160	1,133
11,350	11,400	1,166	1,138	1,166	1,138
11,400	11,450	1,172	1,143	1,172	1,143
11,450	11,500	1,178	1,148	1,178	1,148
11,500	11,550	1,184	1,153	1,184	1,153
11,550	11,600	1,190	1,158	1,190	1,158
11,600	11,650	1,196	1,163	1,196	1,163
11,650	11,700	1,202	1,168	1,202	1,168
11,700	11,750	1,208	1,173	1,208	1,173
11,750	11,800	1,214	1,178	1,214	1,178
11,800	11,850	1,220	1,183	1,220	1,183
11,850	11,900	1,226	1,188	1,226	1,188
11,900	11,950	1,232	1,193	1,232	1,193
11,950	12,000	1,238	1,198	1,238	1,198

(Continued)

* This column must also be used by a qualifying widow(er).

2021 Tax Table — *Continued*

If line 15 (taxable income) is—		And you are—			
At least	But less than	Single	Married filing jointly *	Married filing separately	Head of a household
		Your tax is—			
12,000					
12,000	12,050	1,244	1,203	1,244	1,203
12,050	12,100	1,250	1,208	1,250	1,208
12,100	12,150	1,256	1,213	1,256	1,213
12,150	12,200	1,262	1,218	1,262	1,218
12,200	12,250	1,268	1,223	1,268	1,223
12,250	12,300	1,274	1,228	1,274	1,228
12,300	12,350	1,280	1,233	1,280	1,233
12,350	12,400	1,286	1,238	1,286	1,238
12,400	12,450	1,292	1,243	1,292	1,243
12,450	12,500	1,298	1,248	1,298	1,248
12,500	12,550	1,304	1,253	1,304	1,253
12,550	12,600	1,310	1,258	1,310	1,258
12,600	12,650	1,316	1,263	1,316	1,263
12,650	12,700	1,322	1,268	1,322	1,268
12,700	12,750	1,328	1,273	1,328	1,273
12,750	12,800	1,334	1,278	1,334	1,278
12,800	12,850	1,340	1,283	1,340	1,283
12,850	12,900	1,346	1,288	1,346	1,288
12,900	12,950	1,352	1,293	1,352	1,293
12,950	13,000	1,358	1,298	1,358	1,298
13,000					
13,000	13,050	1,364	1,303	1,364	1,303
13,050	13,100	1,370	1,308	1,370	1,308
13,100	13,150	1,376	1,313	1,376	1,313
13,150	13,200	1,382	1,318	1,382	1,318
13,200	13,250	1,388	1,323	1,388	1,323
13,250	13,300	1,394	1,328	1,394	1,328
13,300	13,350	1,400	1,333	1,400	1,333
13,350	13,400	1,406	1,338	1,406	1,338
13,400	13,450	1,412	1,343	1,412	1,343
13,450	13,500	1,418	1,348	1,418	1,348
13,500	13,550	1,424	1,353	1,424	1,353
13,550	13,600	1,430	1,358	1,430	1,358
13,600	13,650	1,436	1,363	1,436	1,363
13,650	13,700	1,442	1,368	1,442	1,368
13,700	13,750	1,448	1,373	1,448	1,373
13,750	13,800	1,454	1,378	1,454	1,378
13,800	13,850	1,460	1,383	1,460	1,383
13,850	13,900	1,466	1,388	1,466	1,388
13,900	13,950	1,472	1,393	1,472	1,393
13,950	14,000	1,478	1,398	1,478	1,398
14,000					
14,000	14,050	1,484	1,403	1,484	1,403
14,050	14,100	1,490	1,408	1,490	1,408
14,100	14,150	1,496	1,413	1,496	1,413
14,150	14,200	1,502	1,418	1,502	1,418
14,200	14,250	1,508	1,423	1,508	1,423
14,250	14,300	1,514	1,428	1,514	1,429
14,300	14,350	1,520	1,433	1,520	1,435
14,350	14,400	1,526	1,438	1,526	1,441
14,400	14,450	1,532	1,443	1,532	1,447
14,450	14,500	1,538	1,448	1,538	1,453
14,500	14,550	1,544	1,453	1,544	1,459
14,550	14,600	1,550	1,458	1,550	1,465
14,600	14,650	1,556	1,463	1,556	1,471
14,650	14,700	1,562	1,468	1,562	1,477
14,700	14,750	1,568	1,473	1,568	1,483
14,750	14,800	1,574	1,478	1,574	1,489
14,800	14,850	1,580	1,483	1,580	1,495
14,850	14,900	1,586	1,488	1,586	1,501
14,900	14,950	1,592	1,493	1,592	1,507
14,950	15,000	1,598	1,498	1,598	1,513
15,000					
15,000	15,050	1,604	1,503	1,604	1,519
15,050	15,100	1,610	1,508	1,610	1,525
15,100	15,150	1,616	1,513	1,616	1,531
15,150	15,200	1,622	1,518	1,622	1,537
15,200	15,250	1,628	1,523	1,628	1,543
15,250	15,300	1,634	1,528	1,634	1,549
15,300	15,350	1,640	1,533	1,640	1,555
15,350	15,400	1,646	1,538	1,646	1,561
15,400	15,450	1,652	1,543	1,652	1,567
15,450	15,500	1,658	1,548	1,658	1,573
15,500	15,550	1,664	1,553	1,664	1,579
15,550	15,600	1,670	1,558	1,670	1,585
15,600	15,650	1,676	1,563	1,676	1,591
15,650	15,700	1,682	1,568	1,682	1,597
15,700	15,750	1,688	1,573	1,688	1,603
15,750	15,800	1,694	1,578	1,694	1,609
15,800	15,850	1,700	1,583	1,700	1,615
15,850	15,900	1,706	1,588	1,706	1,621
15,900	15,950	1,712	1,593	1,712	1,627
15,950	16,000	1,718	1,598	1,718	1,633
16,000					
16,000	16,050	1,724	1,603	1,724	1,639
16,050	16,100	1,730	1,608	1,730	1,645
16,100	16,150	1,736	1,613	1,736	1,651
16,150	16,200	1,742	1,618	1,742	1,657
16,200	16,250	1,748	1,623	1,748	1,663
16,250	16,300	1,754	1,628	1,754	1,669
16,300	16,350	1,760	1,633	1,760	1,675
16,350	16,400	1,766	1,638	1,766	1,681
16,400	16,450	1,772	1,643	1,772	1,687
16,450	16,500	1,778	1,648	1,778	1,693
16,500	16,550	1,784	1,653	1,784	1,699
16,550	16,600	1,790	1,658	1,790	1,705
16,600	16,650	1,796	1,663	1,796	1,711
16,650	16,700	1,802	1,668	1,802	1,717
16,700	16,750	1,808	1,673	1,808	1,723
16,750	16,800	1,814	1,678	1,814	1,729
16,800	16,850	1,820	1,683	1,820	1,735
16,850	16,900	1,826	1,688	1,826	1,741
16,900	16,950	1,832	1,693	1,832	1,747
16,950	17,000	1,838	1,698	1,838	1,753
17,000					
17,000	17,050	1,844	1,703	1,844	1,759
17,050	17,100	1,850	1,708	1,850	1,765
17,100	17,150	1,856	1,713	1,856	1,771
17,150	17,200	1,862	1,718	1,862	1,777
17,200	17,250	1,868	1,723	1,868	1,783
17,250	17,300	1,874	1,728	1,874	1,789
17,300	17,350	1,880	1,733	1,880	1,795
17,350	17,400	1,886	1,738	1,886	1,801
17,400	17,450	1,892	1,743	1,892	1,807
17,450	17,500	1,898	1,748	1,898	1,813
17,500	17,550	1,904	1,753	1,904	1,819
17,550	17,600	1,910	1,758	1,910	1,825
17,600	17,650	1,916	1,763	1,916	1,831
17,650	17,700	1,922	1,768	1,922	1,837
17,700	17,750	1,928	1,773	1,928	1,843
17,750	17,800	1,934	1,778	1,934	1,849
17,800	17,850	1,940	1,783	1,940	1,855
17,850	17,900	1,946	1,788	1,946	1,861
17,900	17,950	1,952	1,793	1,952	1,867
17,950	18,000	1,958	1,798	1,958	1,873
18,000					
18,000	18,050	1,964	1,803	1,964	1,879
18,050	18,100	1,970	1,808	1,970	1,885
18,100	18,150	1,976	1,813	1,976	1,891
18,150	18,200	1,982	1,818	1,982	1,897
18,200	18,250	1,988	1,823	1,988	1,903
18,250	18,300	1,994	1,828	1,994	1,909
18,300	18,350	2,000	1,833	2,000	1,915
18,350	18,400	2,006	1,838	2,006	1,921
18,400	18,450	2,012	1,843	2,012	1,927
18,450	18,500	2,018	1,848	2,018	1,933
18,500	18,550	2,024	1,853	2,024	1,939
18,550	18,600	2,030	1,858	2,030	1,945
18,600	18,650	2,036	1,863	2,036	1,951
18,650	18,700	2,042	1,868	2,042	1,957
18,700	18,750	2,048	1,873	2,048	1,963
18,750	18,800	2,054	1,878	2,054	1,969
18,800	18,850	2,060	1,883	2,060	1,975
18,850	18,900	2,066	1,888	2,066	1,981
18,900	18,950	2,072	1,893	2,072	1,987
18,950	19,000	2,078	1,898	2,078	1,993
19,000					
19,000	19,050	2,084	1,903	2,084	1,999
19,050	19,100	2,090	1,908	2,090	2,005
19,100	19,150	2,096	1,913	2,096	2,011
19,150	19,200	2,102	1,918	2,102	2,017
19,200	19,250	2,108	1,923	2,108	2,023
19,250	19,300	2,114	1,928	2,114	2,029
19,300	19,350	2,120	1,933	2,120	2,035
19,350	19,400	2,126	1,938	2,126	2,041
19,400	19,450	2,132	1,943	2,132	2,047
19,450	19,500	2,138	1,948	2,138	2,053
19,500	19,550	2,144	1,953	2,144	2,059
19,550	19,600	2,150	1,958	2,150	2,065
19,600	19,650	2,156	1,963	2,156	2,071
19,650	19,700	2,162	1,968	2,162	2,077
19,700	19,750	2,168	1,973	2,168	2,083
19,750	19,800	2,174	1,978	2,174	2,089
19,800	19,850	2,180	1,983	2,180	2,095
19,850	19,900	2,186	1,988	2,186	2,101
19,900	19,950	2,192	1,993	2,192	2,107
19,950	20,000	2,198	1,999	2,198	2,113
20,000					
20,000	20,050	2,204	2,005	2,204	2,119
20,050	20,100	2,210	2,011	2,210	2,125
20,100	20,150	2,216	2,017	2,216	2,131
20,150	20,200	2,222	2,023	2,222	2,137
20,200	20,250	2,228	2,029	2,228	2,143
20,250	20,300	2,234	2,035	2,234	2,149
20,300	20,350	2,240	2,041	2,240	2,155
20,350	20,400	2,246	2,047	2,246	2,161
20,400	20,450	2,252	2,053	2,252	2,167
20,450	20,500	2,258	2,059	2,258	2,173
20,500	20,550	2,264	2,065	2,264	2,179
20,550	20,600	2,270	2,071	2,270	2,185
20,600	20,650	2,276	2,077	2,276	2,191
20,650	20,700	2,282	2,083	2,282	2,197
20,700	20,750	2,288	2,089	2,288	2,203
20,750	20,800	2,294	2,095	2,294	2,209
20,800	20,850	2,300	2,101	2,300	2,215
20,850	20,900	2,306	2,107	2,306	2,221
20,900	20,950	2,312	2,113	2,312	2,227
20,950	21,000	2,318	2,119	2,318	2,233

(Continued)

* This column must also be used by a qualifying widow(er).

2021 Tax Table — *Continued*

If line 15 (taxable income) is—		And you are—			
At least	But less than	Single	Married filing jointly *	Married filing separately	Head of a household
		Your tax is—			
21,000					
21,000	21,050	2,324	2,125	2,324	2,239
21,050	21,100	2,330	2,131	2,330	2,245
21,100	21,150	2,336	2,137	2,336	2,251
21,150	21,200	2,342	2,143	2,342	2,257
21,200	21,250	2,348	2,149	2,348	2,263
21,250	21,300	2,354	2,155	2,354	2,269
21,300	21,350	2,360	2,161	2,360	2,275
21,350	21,400	2,366	2,167	2,366	2,281
21,400	21,450	2,372	2,173	2,372	2,287
21,450	21,500	2,378	2,179	2,378	2,293
21,500	21,550	2,384	2,185	2,384	2,299
21,550	21,600	2,390	2,191	2,390	2,305
21,600	21,650	2,396	2,197	2,396	2,311
21,650	21,700	2,402	2,203	2,402	2,317
21,700	21,750	2,408	2,209	2,408	2,323
21,750	21,800	2,414	2,215	2,414	2,329
21,800	21,850	2,420	2,221	2,420	2,335
21,850	21,900	2,426	2,227	2,426	2,341
21,900	21,950	2,432	2,233	2,432	2,347
21,950	22,000	2,438	2,239	2,438	2,353
22,000					
22,000	22,050	2,444	2,245	2,444	2,359
22,050	22,100	2,450	2,251	2,450	2,365
22,100	22,150	2,456	2,257	2,456	2,371
22,150	22,200	2,462	2,263	2,462	2,377
22,200	22,250	2,468	2,269	2,468	2,383
22,250	22,300	2,474	2,275	2,474	2,389
22,300	22,350	2,480	2,281	2,480	2,395
22,350	22,400	2,486	2,287	2,486	2,401
22,400	22,450	2,492	2,293	2,492	2,407
22,450	22,500	2,498	2,299	2,498	2,413
22,500	22,550	2,504	2,305	2,504	2,419
22,550	22,600	2,510	2,311	2,510	2,425
22,600	22,650	2,516	2,317	2,516	2,431
22,650	22,700	2,522	2,323	2,522	2,437
22,700	22,750	2,528	2,329	2,528	2,443
22,750	22,800	2,534	2,335	2,534	2,449
22,800	22,850	2,540	2,341	2,540	2,455
22,850	22,900	2,546	2,347	2,546	2,461
22,900	22,950	2,552	2,353	2,552	2,467
22,950	23,000	2,558	2,359	2,558	2,473
23,000					
23,000	23,050	2,564	2,365	2,564	2,479
23,050	23,100	2,570	2,371	2,570	2,485
23,100	23,150	2,576	2,377	2,576	2,491
23,150	23,200	2,582	2,383	2,582	2,497
23,200	23,250	2,588	2,389	2,588	2,503
23,250	23,300	2,594	2,395	2,594	2,509
23,300	23,350	2,600	2,401	2,600	2,515
23,350	23,400	2,606	2,407	2,606	2,521
23,400	23,450	2,612	2,413	2,612	2,527
23,450	23,500	2,618	2,419	2,618	2,533
23,500	23,550	2,624	2,425	2,624	2,539
23,550	23,600	2,630	2,431	2,630	2,545
23,600	23,650	2,636	2,437	2,636	2,551
23,650	23,700	2,642	2,443	2,642	2,557
23,700	23,750	2,648	2,449	2,648	2,563
23,750	23,800	2,654	2,455	2,654	2,569
23,800	23,850	2,660	2,461	2,660	2,575
23,850	23,900	2,666	2,467	2,666	2,581
23,900	23,950	2,672	2,473	2,672	2,587
23,950	24,000	2,678	2,479	2,678	2,593

If line 15 (taxable income) is—		And you are—			
At least	But less than	Single	Married filing jointly *	Married filing separately	Head of a household
		Your tax is—			
24,000					
24,000	24,050	2,684	2,485	2,684	2,599
24,050	24,100	2,690	2,491	2,690	2,605
24,100	24,150	2,696	2,497	2,696	2,611
24,150	24,200	2,702	2,503	2,702	2,617
24,200	24,250	2,708	2,509	2,708	2,623
24,250	24,300	2,714	2,515	2,714	2,629
24,300	24,350	2,720	2,521	2,720	2,635
24,350	24,400	2,726	2,527	2,726	2,641
24,400	24,450	2,732	2,533	2,732	2,647
24,450	24,500	2,738	2,539	2,738	2,653
24,500	24,550	2,744	2,545	2,744	2,659
24,550	24,600	2,750	2,551	2,750	2,665
24,600	24,650	2,756	2,557	2,756	2,671
24,650	24,700	2,762	2,563	2,762	2,677
24,700	24,750	2,768	2,569	2,768	2,683
24,750	24,800	2,774	2,575	2,774	2,689
24,800	24,850	2,780	2,581	2,780	2,695
24,850	24,900	2,786	2,587	2,786	2,701
24,900	24,950	2,792	2,593	2,792	2,707
24,950	25,000	2,798	2,599	2,798	2,713
25,000					
25,000	25,050	2,804	2,605	2,804	2,719
25,050	25,100	2,810	2,611	2,810	2,725
25,100	25,150	2,816	2,617	2,816	2,731
25,150	25,200	2,822	2,623	2,822	2,737
25,200	25,250	2,828	2,629	2,828	2,743
25,250	25,300	2,834	2,635	2,834	2,749
25,300	25,350	2,840	2,641	2,840	2,755
25,350	25,400	2,846	2,647	2,846	2,761
25,400	25,450	2,852	2,653	2,852	2,767
25,450	25,500	2,858	2,659	2,858	2,773
25,500	25,550	2,864	2,665	2,864	2,779
25,550	25,600	2,870	2,671	2,870	2,785
25,600	25,650	2,876	2,677	2,876	2,791
25,650	25,700	2,882	2,683	2,882	2,797
25,700	25,750	2,888	2,689	2,888	2,803
25,750	25,800	2,894	2,695	2,894	2,809
25,800	25,850	2,900	2,701	2,900	2,815
25,850	25,900	2,906	2,707	2,906	2,821
25,900	25,950	2,912	2,713	2,912	2,827
25,950	26,000	2,918	2,719	2,918	2,833
26,000					
26,000	26,050	2,924	2,725	2,924	2,839
26,050	26,100	2,930	2,731	2,930	2,845
26,100	26,150	2,936	2,737	2,936	2,851
26,150	26,200	2,942	2,743	2,942	2,857
26,200	26,250	2,948	2,749	2,948	2,863
26,250	26,300	2,954	2,755	2,954	2,869
26,300	26,350	2,960	2,761	2,960	2,875
26,350	26,400	2,966	2,767	2,966	2,881
26,400	26,450	2,972	2,773	2,972	2,887
26,450	26,500	2,978	2,779	2,978	2,893
26,500	26,550	2,984	2,785	2,984	2,899
26,550	26,600	2,990	2,791	2,990	2,905
26,600	26,650	2,996	2,797	2,996	2,911
26,650	26,700	3,002	2,803	3,002	2,917
26,700	26,750	3,008	2,809	3,008	2,923
26,750	26,800	3,014	2,815	3,014	2,929
26,800	26,850	3,020	2,821	3,020	2,935
26,850	26,900	3,026	2,827	3,026	2,941
26,900	26,950	3,032	2,833	3,032	2,947
26,950	27,000	3,038	2,839	3,038	2,953

If line 15 (taxable income) is—		And you are—			
At least	But less than	Single	Married filing jointly *	Married filing separately	Head of a household
		Your tax is—			
27,000					
27,000	27,050	3,044	2,845	3,044	2,959
27,050	27,100	3,050	2,851	3,050	2,965
27,100	27,150	3,056	2,857	3,056	2,971
27,150	27,200	3,062	2,863	3,062	2,977
27,200	27,250	3,068	2,869	3,068	2,983
27,250	27,300	3,074	2,875	3,074	2,989
27,300	27,350	3,080	2,881	3,080	2,995
27,350	27,400	3,086	2,887	3,086	3,001
27,400	27,450	3,092	2,893	3,092	3,007
27,450	27,500	3,098	2,899	3,098	3,013
27,500	27,550	3,104	2,905	3,104	3,019
27,550	27,600	3,110	2,911	3,110	3,025
27,600	27,650	3,116	2,917	3,116	3,031
27,650	27,700	3,122	2,923	3,122	3,037
27,700	27,750	3,128	2,929	3,128	3,043
27,750	27,800	3,134	2,935	3,134	3,049
27,800	27,850	3,140	2,941	3,140	3,055
27,850	27,900	3,146	2,947	3,146	3,061
27,900	27,950	3,152	2,953	3,152	3,067
27,950	28,000	3,158	2,959	3,158	3,073
28,000					
28,000	28,050	3,164	2,965	3,164	3,079
28,050	28,100	3,170	2,971	3,170	3,085
28,100	28,150	3,176	2,977	3,176	3,091
28,150	28,200	3,182	2,983	3,182	3,097
28,200	28,250	3,188	2,989	3,188	3,103
28,250	28,300	3,194	2,995	3,194	3,109
28,300	28,350	3,200	3,001	3,200	3,115
28,350	28,400	3,206	3,007	3,206	3,121
28,400	28,450	3,212	3,013	3,212	3,127
28,450	28,500	3,218	3,019	3,218	3,133
28,500	28,550	3,224	3,025	3,224	3,139
28,550	28,600	3,230	3,031	3,230	3,145
28,600	28,650	3,236	3,037	3,236	3,151
28,650	28,700	3,242	3,043	3,242	3,157
28,700	28,750	3,248	3,049	3,248	3,163
28,750	28,800	3,254	3,055	3,254	3,169
28,800	28,850	3,260	3,061	3,260	3,175
28,850	28,900	3,266	3,067	3,266	3,181
28,900	28,950	3,272	3,073	3,272	3,187
28,950	29,000	3,278	3,079	3,278	3,193
29,000					
29,000	29,050	3,284	3,085	3,284	3,199
29,050	29,100	3,290	3,091	3,290	3,205
29,100	29,150	3,296	3,097	3,296	3,211
29,150	29,200	3,302	3,103	3,302	3,217
29,200	29,250	3,308	3,109	3,308	3,223
29,250	29,300	3,314	3,115	3,314	3,229
29,300	29,350	3,320	3,121	3,320	3,235
29,350	29,400	3,326	3,127	3,326	3,241
29,400	29,450	3,332	3,133	3,332	3,247
29,450	29,500	3,338	3,139	3,338	3,253
29,500	29,550	3,344	3,145	3,344	3,259
29,550	29,600	3,350	3,151	3,350	3,265
29,600	29,650	3,356	3,157	3,356	3,271
29,650	29,700	3,362	3,163	3,362	3,277
29,700	29,750	3,368	3,169	3,368	3,283
29,750	29,800	3,374	3,175	3,374	3,289
29,800	29,850	3,380	3,181	3,380	3,295
29,850	29,900	3,386	3,187	3,386	3,301
29,900	29,950	3,392	3,193	3,392	3,307
29,950	30,000	3,398	3,199	3,398	3,313

(Continued)

* This column must also be used by a qualifying widow(er).

2021 Tax Table — *Continued*

If line 15 (taxable income) is— / And you are— / Your tax is—

30,000

At least	But less than	Single	Married filing jointly *	Married filing separately	Head of a household
30,000	30,050	3,404	3,205	3,404	3,319
30,050	30,100	3,410	3,211	3,410	3,325
30,100	30,150	3,416	3,217	3,416	3,331
30,150	30,200	3,422	3,223	3,422	3,337
30,200	30,250	3,428	3,229	3,428	3,343
30,250	30,300	3,434	3,235	3,434	3,349
30,300	30,350	3,440	3,241	3,440	3,355
30,350	30,400	3,446	3,247	3,446	3,361
30,400	30,450	3,452	3,253	3,452	3,367
30,450	30,500	3,458	3,259	3,458	3,373
30,500	30,550	3,464	3,265	3,464	3,379
30,550	30,600	3,470	3,271	3,470	3,385
30,600	30,650	3,476	3,277	3,476	3,391
30,650	30,700	3,482	3,283	3,482	3,397
30,700	30,750	3,488	3,289	3,488	3,403
30,750	30,800	3,494	3,295	3,494	3,409
30,800	30,850	3,500	3,301	3,500	3,415
30,850	30,900	3,506	3,307	3,506	3,421
30,900	30,950	3,512	3,313	3,512	3,427
30,950	31,000	3,518	3,319	3,518	3,433

31,000

At least	But less than	Single	Married filing jointly *	Married filing separately	Head of a household
31,000	31,050	3,524	3,325	3,524	3,439
31,050	31,100	3,530	3,331	3,530	3,445
31,100	31,150	3,536	3,337	3,536	3,451
31,150	31,200	3,542	3,343	3,542	3,457
31,200	31,250	3,548	3,349	3,548	3,463
31,250	31,300	3,554	3,355	3,554	3,469
31,300	31,350	3,560	3,361	3,560	3,475
31,350	31,400	3,566	3,367	3,566	3,481
31,400	31,450	3,572	3,373	3,572	3,487
31,450	31,500	3,578	3,379	3,578	3,493
31,500	31,550	3,584	3,385	3,584	3,499
31,550	31,600	3,590	3,391	3,590	3,505
31,600	31,650	3,596	3,397	3,596	3,511
31,650	31,700	3,602	3,403	3,602	3,517
31,700	31,750	3,608	3,409	3,608	3,523
31,750	31,800	3,614	3,415	3,614	3,529
31,800	31,850	3,620	3,421	3,620	3,535
31,850	31,900	3,626	3,427	3,626	3,541
31,900	31,950	3,632	3,433	3,632	3,547
31,950	32,000	3,638	3,439	3,638	3,553

32,000

At least	But less than	Single	Married filing jointly *	Married filing separately	Head of a household
32,000	32,050	3,644	3,445	3,644	3,559
32,050	32,100	3,650	3,451	3,650	3,565
32,100	32,150	3,656	3,457	3,656	3,571
32,150	32,200	3,662	3,463	3,662	3,577
32,200	32,250	3,668	3,469	3,668	3,583
32,250	32,300	3,674	3,475	3,674	3,589
32,300	32,350	3,680	3,481	3,680	3,595
32,350	32,400	3,686	3,487	3,686	3,601
32,400	32,450	3,692	3,493	3,692	3,607
32,450	32,500	3,698	3,499	3,698	3,613
32,500	32,550	3,704	3,505	3,704	3,619
32,550	32,600	3,710	3,511	3,710	3,625
32,600	32,650	3,716	3,517	3,716	3,631
32,650	32,700	3,722	3,523	3,722	3,637
32,700	32,750	3,728	3,529	3,728	3,643
32,750	32,800	3,734	3,535	3,734	3,649
32,800	32,850	3,740	3,541	3,740	3,655
32,850	32,900	3,746	3,547	3,746	3,661
32,900	32,950	3,752	3,553	3,752	3,667
32,950	33,000	3,758	3,559	3,758	3,673

33,000

At least	But less than	Single	Married filing jointly *	Married filing separately	Head of a household
33,000	33,050	3,764	3,565	3,764	3,679
33,050	33,100	3,770	3,571	3,770	3,685
33,100	33,150	3,776	3,577	3,776	3,691
33,150	33,200	3,782	3,583	3,782	3,697
33,200	33,250	3,788	3,589	3,788	3,703
33,250	33,300	3,794	3,595	3,794	3,709
33,300	33,350	3,800	3,601	3,800	3,715
33,350	33,400	3,806	3,607	3,806	3,721
33,400	33,450	3,812	3,613	3,812	3,727
33,450	33,500	3,818	3,619	3,818	3,733
33,500	33,550	3,824	3,625	3,824	3,739
33,550	33,600	3,830	3,631	3,830	3,745
33,600	33,650	3,836	3,637	3,836	3,751
33,650	33,700	3,842	3,643	3,842	3,757
33,700	33,750	3,848	3,649	3,848	3,763
33,750	33,800	3,854	3,655	3,854	3,769
33,800	33,850	3,860	3,661	3,860	3,775
33,850	33,900	3,866	3,667	3,866	3,781
33,900	33,950	3,872	3,673	3,872	3,787
33,950	34,000	3,878	3,679	3,878	3,793

34,000

At least	But less than	Single	Married filing jointly *	Married filing separately	Head of a household
34,000	34,050	3,884	3,685	3,884	3,799
34,050	34,100	3,890	3,691	3,890	3,805
34,100	34,150	3,896	3,697	3,896	3,811
34,150	34,200	3,902	3,703	3,902	3,817
34,200	34,250	3,908	3,709	3,908	3,823
34,250	34,300	3,914	3,715	3,914	3,829
34,300	34,350	3,920	3,721	3,920	3,835
34,350	34,400	3,926	3,727	3,926	3,841
34,400	34,450	3,932	3,733	3,932	3,847
34,450	34,500	3,938	3,739	3,938	3,853
34,500	34,550	3,944	3,745	3,944	3,859
34,550	34,600	3,950	3,751	3,950	3,865
34,600	34,650	3,956	3,757	3,956	3,871
34,650	34,700	3,962	3,763	3,962	3,877
34,700	34,750	3,968	3,769	3,968	3,883
34,750	34,800	3,974	3,775	3,974	3,889
34,800	34,850	3,980	3,781	3,980	3,895
34,850	34,900	3,986	3,787	3,986	3,901
34,900	34,950	3,992	3,793	3,992	3,907
34,950	35,000	3,998	3,799	3,998	3,913

35,000

At least	But less than	Single	Married filing jointly *	Married filing separately	Head of a household
35,000	35,050	4,004	3,805	4,004	3,919
35,050	35,100	4,010	3,811	4,010	3,925
35,100	35,150	4,016	3,817	4,016	3,931
35,150	35,200	4,022	3,823	4,022	3,937
35,200	35,250	4,028	3,829	4,028	3,943
35,250	35,300	4,034	3,835	4,034	3,949
35,300	35,350	4,040	3,841	4,040	3,955
35,350	35,400	4,046	3,847	4,046	3,961
35,400	35,450	4,052	3,853	4,052	3,967
35,450	35,500	4,058	3,859	4,058	3,973
35,500	35,550	4,064	3,865	4,064	3,979
35,550	35,600	4,070	3,871	4,070	3,985
35,600	35,650	4,076	3,877	4,076	3,991
35,650	35,700	4,082	3,883	4,082	3,997
35,700	35,750	4,088	3,889	4,088	4,003
35,750	35,800	4,094	3,895	4,094	4,009
35,800	35,850	4,100	3,901	4,100	4,015
35,850	35,900	4,106	3,907	4,106	4,021
35,900	35,950	4,112	3,913	4,112	4,027
35,950	36,000	4,118	3,919	4,118	4,033

36,000

At least	But less than	Single	Married filing jointly *	Married filing separately	Head of a household
36,000	36,050	4,124	3,925	4,124	4,039
36,050	36,100	4,130	3,931	4,130	4,045
36,100	36,150	4,136	3,937	4,136	4,051
36,150	36,200	4,142	3,943	4,142	4,057
36,200	36,250	4,148	3,949	4,148	4,063
36,250	36,300	4,154	3,955	4,154	4,069
36,300	36,350	4,160	3,961	4,160	4,075
36,350	36,400	4,166	3,967	4,166	4,081
36,400	36,450	4,172	3,973	4,172	4,087
36,450	36,500	4,178	3,979	4,178	4,093
36,500	36,550	4,184	3,985	4,184	4,099
36,550	36,600	4,190	3,991	4,190	4,105
36,600	36,650	4,196	3,997	4,196	4,111
36,650	36,700	4,202	4,003	4,202	4,117
36,700	36,750	4,208	4,009	4,208	4,123
36,750	36,800	4,214	4,015	4,214	4,129
36,800	36,850	4,220	4,021	4,220	4,135
36,850	36,900	4,226	4,027	4,226	4,141
36,900	36,950	4,232	4,033	4,232	4,147
36,950	37,000	4,238	4,039	4,238	4,153

37,000

At least	But less than	Single	Married filing jointly *	Married filing separately	Head of a household
37,000	37,050	4,244	4,045	4,244	4,159
37,050	37,100	4,250	4,051	4,250	4,165
37,100	37,150	4,256	4,057	4,256	4,171
37,150	37,200	4,262	4,063	4,262	4,177
37,200	37,250	4,268	4,069	4,268	4,183
37,250	37,300	4,274	4,075	4,274	4,189
37,300	37,350	4,280	4,081	4,280	4,195
37,350	37,400	4,286	4,087	4,286	4,201
37,400	37,450	4,292	4,093	4,292	4,207
37,450	37,500	4,298	4,099	4,298	4,213
37,500	37,550	4,304	4,105	4,304	4,219
37,550	37,600	4,310	4,111	4,310	4,225
37,600	37,650	4,316	4,117	4,316	4,231
37,650	37,700	4,322	4,123	4,322	4,237
37,700	37,750	4,328	4,129	4,328	4,243
37,750	37,800	4,334	4,135	4,334	4,249
37,800	37,850	4,340	4,141	4,340	4,255
37,850	37,900	4,346	4,147	4,346	4,261
37,900	37,950	4,352	4,153	4,352	4,267
37,950	38,000	4,358	4,159	4,358	4,273

38,000

At least	But less than	Single	Married filing jointly *	Married filing separately	Head of a household
38,000	38,050	4,364	4,165	4,364	4,279
38,050	38,100	4,370	4,171	4,370	4,285
38,100	38,150	4,376	4,177	4,376	4,291
38,150	38,200	4,382	4,183	4,382	4,297
38,200	38,250	4,388	4,189	4,388	4,303
38,250	38,300	4,394	4,195	4,394	4,309
38,300	38,350	4,400	4,201	4,400	4,315
38,350	38,400	4,406	4,207	4,406	4,321
38,400	38,450	4,412	4,213	4,412	4,327
38,450	38,500	4,418	4,219	4,418	4,333
38,500	38,550	4,424	4,225	4,424	4,339
38,550	38,600	4,430	4,231	4,430	4,345
38,600	38,650	4,436	4,237	4,436	4,351
38,650	38,700	4,442	4,243	4,442	4,357
38,700	38,750	4,448	4,249	4,448	4,363
38,750	38,800	4,454	4,255	4,454	4,369
38,800	38,850	4,460	4,261	4,460	4,375
38,850	38,900	4,466	4,267	4,466	4,381
38,900	38,950	4,472	4,273	4,472	4,387
38,950	39,000	4,478	4,279	4,478	4,393

(Continued)

* This column must also be used by a qualifying widow(er).

2021 Tax Table — *Continued*

39,000

If line 15 (taxable income) is— At least	But less than	And you are— Single	Married filing jointly *	Married filing separately	Head of a household
		Your tax is—			
39,000	39,050	4,484	4,285	4,484	4,399
39,050	39,100	4,490	4,291	4,490	4,405
39,100	39,150	4,496	4,297	4,496	4,411
39,150	39,200	4,502	4,303	4,502	4,417
39,200	39,250	4,508	4,309	4,508	4,423
39,250	39,300	4,514	4,315	4,514	4,429
39,300	39,350	4,520	4,321	4,520	4,435
39,350	39,400	4,526	4,327	4,526	4,441
39,400	39,450	4,532	4,333	4,532	4,447
39,450	39,500	4,538	4,339	4,538	4,453
39,500	39,550	4,544	4,345	4,544	4,459
39,550	39,600	4,550	4,351	4,550	4,465
39,600	39,650	4,556	4,357	4,556	4,471
39,650	39,700	4,562	4,363	4,562	4,477
39,700	39,750	4,568	4,369	4,568	4,483
39,750	39,800	4,574	4,375	4,574	4,489
39,800	39,850	4,580	4,381	4,580	4,495
39,850	39,900	4,586	4,387	4,586	4,501
39,900	39,950	4,592	4,393	4,592	4,507
39,950	40,000	4,598	4,399	4,598	4,513

40,000

At least	But less than	Single	Married filing jointly *	Married filing separately	Head of a household
40,000	40,050	4,604	4,405	4,604	4,519
40,050	40,100	4,610	4,411	4,610	4,525
40,100	40,150	4,616	4,417	4,616	4,531
40,150	40,200	4,622	4,423	4,622	4,537
40,200	40,250	4,628	4,429	4,628	4,543
40,250	40,300	4,634	4,435	4,634	4,549
40,300	40,350	4,640	4,441	4,640	4,555
40,350	40,400	4,646	4,447	4,646	4,561
40,400	40,450	4,652	4,453	4,652	4,567
40,450	40,500	4,658	4,459	4,658	4,573
40,500	40,550	4,664	4,465	4,664	4,579
40,550	40,600	4,675	4,471	4,675	4,585
40,600	40,650	4,686	4,477	4,686	4,591
40,650	40,700	4,697	4,483	4,697	4,597
40,700	40,750	4,708	4,489	4,708	4,603
40,750	40,800	4,719	4,495	4,719	4,609
40,800	40,850	4,730	4,501	4,730	4,615
40,850	40,900	4,741	4,507	4,741	4,621
40,900	40,950	4,752	4,513	4,752	4,627
40,950	41,000	4,763	4,519	4,763	4,633

41,000

At least	But less than	Single	Married filing jointly *	Married filing separately	Head of a household
41,000	41,050	4,774	4,525	4,774	4,639
41,050	41,100	4,785	4,531	4,785	4,645
41,100	41,150	4,796	4,537	4,796	4,651
41,150	41,200	4,807	4,543	4,807	4,657
41,200	41,250	4,818	4,549	4,818	4,663
41,250	41,300	4,829	4,555	4,829	4,669
41,300	41,350	4,840	4,561	4,840	4,675
41,350	41,400	4,851	4,567	4,851	4,681
41,400	41,450	4,862	4,573	4,862	4,687
41,450	41,500	4,873	4,579	4,873	4,693
41,500	41,550	4,884	4,585	4,884	4,699
41,550	41,600	4,895	4,591	4,895	4,705
41,600	41,650	4,906	4,597	4,906	4,711
41,650	41,700	4,917	4,603	4,917	4,717
41,700	41,750	4,928	4,609	4,928	4,723
41,750	41,800	4,939	4,615	4,939	4,729
41,800	41,850	4,950	4,621	4,950	4,735
41,850	41,900	4,961	4,627	4,961	4,741
41,900	41,950	4,972	4,633	4,972	4,747
41,950	42,000	4,983	4,639	4,983	4,753

42,000

At least	But less than	Single	Married filing jointly *	Married filing separately	Head of a household
42,000	42,050	4,994	4,645	4,994	4,759
42,050	42,100	5,005	4,651	5,005	4,765
42,100	42,150	5,016	4,657	5,016	4,771
42,150	42,200	5,027	4,663	5,027	4,777
42,200	42,250	5,038	4,669	5,038	4,783
42,250	42,300	5,049	4,675	5,049	4,789
42,300	42,350	5,060	4,681	5,060	4,795
42,350	42,400	5,071	4,687	5,071	4,801
42,400	42,450	5,082	4,693	5,082	4,807
42,450	42,500	5,093	4,699	5,093	4,813
42,500	42,550	5,104	4,705	5,104	4,819
42,550	42,600	5,115	4,711	5,115	4,825
42,600	42,650	5,126	4,717	5,126	4,831
42,650	42,700	5,137	4,723	5,137	4,837
42,700	42,750	5,148	4,729	5,148	4,843
42,750	42,800	5,159	4,735	5,159	4,849
42,800	42,850	5,170	4,741	5,170	4,855
42,850	42,900	5,181	4,747	5,181	4,861
42,900	42,950	5,192	4,753	5,192	4,867
42,950	43,000	5,203	4,759	5,203	4,873

43,000

At least	But less than	Single	Married filing jointly *	Married filing separately	Head of a household
43,000	43,050	5,214	4,765	5,214	4,879
43,050	43,100	5,225	4,771	5,225	4,885
43,100	43,150	5,236	4,777	5,236	4,891
43,150	43,200	5,247	4,783	5,247	4,897
43,200	43,250	5,258	4,789	5,258	4,903
43,250	43,300	5,269	4,795	5,269	4,909
43,300	43,350	5,280	4,801	5,280	4,915
43,350	43,400	5,291	4,807	5,291	4,921
43,400	43,450	5,302	4,813	5,302	4,927
43,450	43,500	5,313	4,819	5,313	4,933
43,500	43,550	5,324	4,825	5,324	4,939
43,550	43,600	5,335	4,831	5,335	4,945
43,600	43,650	5,346	4,837	5,346	4,951
43,650	43,700	5,357	4,843	5,357	4,957
43,700	43,750	5,368	4,849	5,368	4,963
43,750	43,800	5,379	4,855	5,379	4,969
43,800	43,850	5,390	4,861	5,390	4,975
43,850	43,900	5,401	4,867	5,401	4,981
43,900	43,950	5,412	4,873	5,412	4,987
43,950	44,000	5,423	4,879	5,423	4,993

44,000

At least	But less than	Single	Married filing jointly *	Married filing separately	Head of a household
44,000	44,050	5,434	4,885	5,434	4,999
44,050	44,100	5,445	4,891	5,445	5,005
44,100	44,150	5,456	4,897	5,456	5,011
44,150	44,200	5,467	4,903	5,467	5,017
44,200	44,250	5,478	4,909	5,478	5,023
44,250	44,300	5,489	4,915	5,489	5,029
44,300	44,350	5,500	4,921	5,500	5,035
44,350	44,400	5,511	4,927	5,511	5,041
44,400	44,450	5,522	4,933	5,522	5,047
44,450	44,500	5,533	4,939	5,533	5,053
44,500	44,550	5,544	4,945	5,544	5,059
44,550	44,600	5,555	4,951	5,555	5,065
44,600	44,650	5,566	4,957	5,566	5,071
44,650	44,700	5,577	4,963	5,577	5,077
44,700	44,750	5,588	4,969	5,588	5,083
44,750	44,800	5,599	4,975	5,599	5,089
44,800	44,850	5,610	4,981	5,610	5,095
44,850	44,900	5,621	4,987	5,621	5,101
44,900	44,950	5,632	4,993	5,632	5,107
44,950	45,000	5,643	4,999	5,643	5,113

45,000

At least	But less than	Single	Married filing jointly *	Married filing separately	Head of a household
45,000	45,050	5,654	5,005	5,654	5,119
45,050	45,100	5,665	5,011	5,665	5,125
45,100	45,150	5,676	5,017	5,676	5,131
45,150	45,200	5,687	5,023	5,687	5,137
45,200	45,250	5,698	5,029	5,698	5,143
45,250	45,300	5,709	5,035	5,709	5,149
45,300	45,350	5,720	5,041	5,720	5,155
45,350	45,400	5,731	5,047	5,731	5,161
45,400	45,450	5,742	5,053	5,742	5,167
45,450	45,500	5,753	5,059	5,753	5,173
45,500	45,550	5,764	5,065	5,764	5,179
45,550	45,600	5,775	5,071	5,775	5,185
45,600	45,650	5,786	5,077	5,786	5,191
45,650	45,700	5,797	5,083	5,797	5,197
45,700	45,750	5,808	5,089	5,808	5,203
45,750	45,800	5,819	5,095	5,819	5,209
45,800	45,850	5,830	5,101	5,830	5,215
45,850	45,900	5,841	5,107	5,841	5,221
45,900	45,950	5,852	5,113	5,852	5,227
45,950	46,000	5,863	5,119	5,863	5,233

46,000

At least	But less than	Single	Married filing jointly *	Married filing separately	Head of a household
46,000	46,050	5,874	5,125	5,874	5,239
46,050	46,100	5,885	5,131	5,885	5,245
46,100	46,150	5,896	5,137	5,896	5,251
46,150	46,200	5,907	5,143	5,907	5,257
46,200	46,250	5,918	5,149	5,918	5,263
46,250	46,300	5,929	5,155	5,929	5,269
46,300	46,350	5,940	5,161	5,940	5,275
46,350	46,400	5,951	5,167	5,951	5,281
46,400	46,450	5,962	5,173	5,962	5,287
46,450	46,500	5,973	5,179	5,973	5,293
46,500	46,550	5,984	5,185	5,984	5,299
46,550	46,600	5,995	5,191	5,995	5,305
46,600	46,650	6,006	5,197	6,006	5,311
46,650	46,700	6,017	5,203	6,017	5,317
46,700	46,750	6,028	5,209	6,028	5,323
46,750	46,800	6,039	5,215	6,039	5,329
46,800	46,850	6,050	5,221	6,050	5,335
46,850	46,900	6,061	5,227	6,061	5,341
46,900	46,950	6,072	5,233	6,072	5,347
46,950	47,000	6,083	5,239	6,083	5,353

47,000

At least	But less than	Single	Married filing jointly *	Married filing separately	Head of a household
47,000	47,050	6,094	5,245	6,094	5,359
47,050	47,100	6,105	5,251	6,105	5,365
47,100	47,150	6,116	5,257	6,116	5,371
47,150	47,200	6,127	5,263	6,127	5,377
47,200	47,250	6,138	5,269	6,138	5,383
47,250	47,300	6,149	5,275	6,149	5,389
47,300	47,350	6,160	5,281	6,160	5,395
47,350	47,400	6,171	5,287	6,171	5,401
47,400	47,450	6,182	5,293	6,182	5,407
47,450	47,500	6,193	5,299	6,193	5,413
47,500	47,550	6,204	5,305	6,204	5,419
47,550	47,600	6,215	5,311	6,215	5,425
47,600	47,650	6,226	5,317	6,226	5,431
47,650	47,700	6,237	5,323	6,237	5,437
47,700	47,750	6,248	5,329	6,248	5,443
47,750	47,800	6,259	5,335	6,259	5,449
47,800	47,850	6,270	5,341	6,270	5,455
47,850	47,900	6,281	5,347	6,281	5,461
47,900	47,950	6,292	5,353	6,292	5,467
47,950	48,000	6,303	5,359	6,303	5,473

(Continued)

* This column must also be used by a qualifying widow(er).

2021 Tax Table — *Continued*

If line 15 (taxable income) is—		And you are—			
At least	But less than	Single	Married filing jointly *	Married filing sepa-rately	Head of a house-hold
		Your tax is—			
48,000					
48,000	48,050	6,314	5,365	6,314	5,479
48,050	48,100	6,325	5,371	6,325	5,485
48,100	48,150	6,336	5,377	6,336	5,491
48,150	48,200	6,347	5,383	6,347	5,497
48,200	48,250	6,358	5,389	6,358	5,503
48,250	48,300	6,369	5,395	6,369	5,509
48,300	48,350	6,380	5,401	6,380	5,515
48,350	48,400	6,391	5,407	6,391	5,521
48,400	48,450	6,402	5,413	6,402	5,527
48,450	48,500	6,413	5,419	6,413	5,533
48,500	48,550	6,424	5,425	6,424	5,539
48,550	48,600	6,435	5,431	6,435	5,545
48,600	48,650	6,446	5,437	6,446	5,551
48,650	48,700	6,457	5,443	6,457	5,557
48,700	48,750	6,468	5,449	6,468	5,563
48,750	48,800	6,479	5,455	6,479	5,569
48,800	48,850	6,490	5,461	6,490	5,575
48,850	48,900	6,501	5,467	6,501	5,581
48,900	48,950	6,512	5,473	6,512	5,587
48,950	49,000	6,523	5,479	6,523	5,593
49,000					
49,000	49,050	6,534	5,485	6,534	5,599
49,050	49,100	6,545	5,491	6,545	5,605
49,100	49,150	6,556	5,497	6,556	5,611
49,150	49,200	6,567	5,503	6,567	5,617
49,200	49,250	6,578	5,509	6,578	5,623
49,250	49,300	6,589	5,515	6,589	5,629
49,300	49,350	6,600	5,521	6,600	5,635
49,350	49,400	6,611	5,527	6,611	5,641
49,400	49,450	6,622	5,533	6,622	5,647
49,450	49,500	6,633	5,539	6,633	5,653
49,500	49,550	6,644	5,545	6,644	5,659
49,550	49,600	6,655	5,551	6,655	5,665
49,600	49,650	6,666	5,557	6,666	5,671
49,650	49,700	6,677	5,563	6,677	5,677
49,700	49,750	6,688	5,569	6,688	5,683
49,750	49,800	6,699	5,575	6,699	5,689
49,800	49,850	6,710	5,581	6,710	5,695
49,850	49,900	6,721	5,587	6,721	5,701
49,900	49,950	6,732	5,593	6,732	5,707
49,950	50,000	6,743	5,599	6,743	5,713
50,000					
50,000	50,050	6,754	5,605	6,754	5,719
50,050	50,100	6,765	5,611	6,765	5,725
50,100	50,150	6,776	5,617	6,776	5,731
50,150	50,200	6,787	5,623	6,787	5,737
50,200	50,250	6,798	5,629	6,798	5,743
50,250	50,300	6,809	5,635	6,809	5,749
50,300	50,350	6,820	5,641	6,820	5,755
50,350	50,400	6,831	5,647	6,831	5,761
50,400	50,450	6,842	5,653	6,842	5,767
50,450	50,500	6,853	5,659	6,853	5,773
50,500	50,550	6,864	5,665	6,864	5,779
50,550	50,600	6,875	5,671	6,875	5,785
50,600	50,650	6,886	5,677	6,886	5,791
50,650	50,700	6,897	5,683	6,897	5,797
50,700	50,750	6,908	5,689	6,908	5,803
50,750	50,800	6,919	5,695	6,919	5,809
50,800	50,850	6,930	5,701	6,930	5,815
50,850	50,900	6,941	5,707	6,941	5,821
50,900	50,950	6,952	5,713	6,952	5,827
50,950	51,000	6,963	5,719	6,963	5,833

If line 15 (taxable income) is—		And you are—			
At least	But less than	Single	Married filing jointly *	Married filing sepa-rately	Head of a house-hold
		Your tax is—			
51,000					
51,000	51,050	6,974	5,725	6,974	5,839
51,050	51,100	6,985	5,731	6,985	5,845
51,100	51,150	6,996	5,737	6,996	5,851
51,150	51,200	7,007	5,743	7,007	5,857
51,200	51,250	7,018	5,749	7,018	5,863
51,250	51,300	7,029	5,755	7,029	5,869
51,300	51,350	7,040	5,761	7,040	5,875
51,350	51,400	7,051	5,767	7,051	5,881
51,400	51,450	7,062	5,773	7,062	5,887
51,450	51,500	7,073	5,779	7,073	5,893
51,500	51,550	7,084	5,785	7,084	5,899
51,550	51,600	7,095	5,791	7,095	5,905
51,600	51,650	7,106	5,797	7,106	5,911
51,650	51,700	7,117	5,803	7,117	5,917
51,700	51,750	7,128	5,809	7,128	5,923
51,750	51,800	7,139	5,815	7,139	5,929
51,800	51,850	7,150	5,821	7,150	5,935
51,850	51,900	7,161	5,827	7,161	5,941
51,900	51,950	7,172	5,833	7,172	5,947
51,950	52,000	7,183	5,839	7,183	5,953
52,000					
52,000	52,050	7,194	5,845	7,194	5,959
52,050	52,100	7,205	5,851	7,205	5,965
52,100	52,150	7,216	5,857	7,216	5,971
52,150	52,200	7,227	5,863	7,227	5,977
52,200	52,250	7,238	5,869	7,238	5,983
52,250	52,300	7,249	5,875	7,249	5,989
52,300	52,350	7,260	5,881	7,260	5,995
52,350	52,400	7,271	5,887	7,271	6,001
52,400	52,450	7,282	5,893	7,282	6,007
52,450	52,500	7,293	5,899	7,293	6,013
52,500	52,550	7,304	5,905	7,304	6,019
52,550	52,600	7,315	5,911	7,315	6,025
52,600	52,650	7,326	5,917	7,326	6,031
52,650	52,700	7,337	5,923	7,337	6,037
52,700	52,750	7,348	5,929	7,348	6,043
52,750	52,800	7,359	5,935	7,359	6,049
52,800	52,850	7,370	5,941	7,370	6,055
52,850	52,900	7,381	5,947	7,381	6,061
52,900	52,950	7,392	5,953	7,392	6,067
52,950	53,000	7,403	5,959	7,403	6,073
53,000					
53,000	53,050	7,414	5,965	7,414	6,079
53,050	53,100	7,425	5,971	7,425	6,085
53,100	53,150	7,436	5,977	7,436	6,091
53,150	53,200	7,447	5,983	7,447	6,097
53,200	53,250	7,458	5,989	7,458	6,103
53,250	53,300	7,469	5,995	7,469	6,109
53,300	53,350	7,480	6,001	7,480	6,115
53,350	53,400	7,491	6,007	7,491	6,121
53,400	53,450	7,502	6,013	7,502	6,127
53,450	53,500	7,513	6,019	7,513	6,133
53,500	53,550	7,524	6,025	7,524	6,139
53,550	53,600	7,535	6,031	7,535	6,145
53,600	53,650	7,546	6,037	7,546	6,151
53,650	53,700	7,557	6,043	7,557	6,157
53,700	53,750	7,568	6,049	7,568	6,163
53,750	53,800	7,579	6,055	7,579	6,169
53,800	53,850	7,590	6,061	7,590	6,175
53,850	53,900	7,601	6,067	7,601	6,181
53,900	53,950	7,612	6,073	7,612	6,187
53,950	54,000	7,623	6,079	7,623	6,193

If line 15 (taxable income) is—		And you are—			
At least	But less than	Single	Married filing jointly *	Married filing sepa-rately	Head of a house-hold
		Your tax is—			
54,000					
54,000	54,050	7,634	6,085	7,634	6,199
54,050	54,100	7,645	6,091	7,645	6,205
54,100	54,150	7,656	6,097	7,656	6,211
54,150	54,200	7,667	6,103	7,667	6,217
54,200	54,250	7,678	6,109	7,678	6,226
54,250	54,300	7,689	6,115	7,689	6,237
54,300	54,350	7,700	6,121	7,700	6,248
54,350	54,400	7,711	6,127	7,711	6,259
54,400	54,450	7,722	6,133	7,722	6,270
54,450	54,500	7,733	6,139	7,733	6,281
54,500	54,550	7,744	6,145	7,744	6,292
54,550	54,600	7,755	6,151	7,755	6,303
54,600	54,650	7,766	6,157	7,766	6,314
54,650	54,700	7,777	6,163	7,777	6,325
54,700	54,750	7,788	6,169	7,788	6,336
54,750	54,800	7,799	6,175	7,799	6,347
54,800	54,850	7,810	6,181	7,810	6,358
54,850	54,900	7,821	6,187	7,821	6,369
54,900	54,950	7,832	6,193	7,832	6,380
54,950	55,000	7,843	6,199	7,843	6,391
55,000					
55,000	55,050	7,854	6,205	7,854	6,402
55,050	55,100	7,865	6,211	7,865	6,413
55,100	55,150	7,876	6,217	7,876	6,424
55,150	55,200	7,887	6,223	7,887	6,435
55,200	55,250	7,898	6,229	7,898	6,446
55,250	55,300	7,909	6,235	7,909	6,457
55,300	55,350	7,920	6,241	7,920	6,468
55,350	55,400	7,931	6,247	7,931	6,479
55,400	55,450	7,942	6,253	7,942	6,490
55,450	55,500	7,953	6,259	7,953	6,501
55,500	55,550	7,964	6,265	7,964	6,512
55,550	55,600	7,975	6,271	7,975	6,523
55,600	55,650	7,986	6,277	7,986	6,534
55,650	55,700	7,997	6,283	7,997	6,545
55,700	55,750	8,008	6,289	8,008	6,556
55,750	55,800	8,019	6,295	8,019	6,567
55,800	55,850	8,030	6,301	8,030	6,578
55,850	55,900	8,041	6,307	8,041	6,589
55,900	55,950	8,052	6,313	8,052	6,600
55,950	56,000	8,063	6,319	8,063	6,611
56,000					
56,000	56,050	8,074	6,325	8,074	6,622
56,050	56,100	8,085	6,331	8,085	6,633
56,100	56,150	8,096	6,337	8,096	6,644
56,150	56,200	8,107	6,343	8,107	6,655
56,200	56,250	8,118	6,349	8,118	6,666
56,250	56,300	8,129	6,355	8,129	6,677
56,300	56,350	8,140	6,361	8,140	6,688
56,350	56,400	8,151	6,367	8,151	6,699
56,400	56,450	8,162	6,373	8,162	6,710
56,450	56,500	8,173	6,379	8,173	6,721
56,500	56,550	8,184	6,385	8,184	6,732
56,550	56,600	8,195	6,391	8,195	6,743
56,600	56,650	8,206	6,397	8,206	6,754
56,650	56,700	8,217	6,403	8,217	6,765
56,700	56,750	8,228	6,409	8,228	6,776
56,750	56,800	8,239	6,415	8,239	6,787
56,800	56,850	8,250	6,421	8,250	6,798
56,850	56,900	8,261	6,427	8,261	6,809
56,900	56,950	8,272	6,433	8,272	6,820
56,950	57,000	8,283	6,439	8,283	6,831

(Continued)

* This column must also be used by a qualifying widow(er).

2021 Tax Table — *Continued*

If line 15 (taxable income) is—		And you are—			
At least	But less than	Single	Married filing jointly *	Married filing sepa-rately	Head of a house-hold
		Your tax is—			
57,000					
57,000	57,050	8,294	6,445	8,294	6,842
57,050	57,100	8,305	6,451	8,305	6,853
57,100	57,150	8,316	6,457	8,316	6,864
57,150	57,200	8,327	6,463	8,327	6,875
57,200	57,250	8,338	6,469	8,338	6,886
57,250	57,300	8,349	6,475	8,349	6,897
57,300	57,350	8,360	6,481	8,360	6,908
57,350	57,400	8,371	6,487	8,371	6,919
57,400	57,450	8,382	6,493	8,382	6,930
57,450	57,500	8,393	6,499	8,393	6,941
57,500	57,550	8,404	6,505	8,404	6,952
57,550	57,600	8,415	6,511	8,415	6,963
57,600	57,650	8,426	6,517	8,426	6,974
57,650	57,700	8,437	6,523	8,437	6,985
57,700	57,750	8,448	6,529	8,448	6,996
57,750	57,800	8,459	6,535	8,459	7,007
57,800	57,850	8,470	6,541	8,470	7,018
57,850	57,900	8,481	6,547	8,481	7,029
57,900	57,950	8,492	6,553	8,492	7,040
57,950	58,000	8,503	6,559	8,503	7,051
58,000					
58,000	58,050	8,514	6,565	8,514	7,062
58,050	58,100	8,525	6,571	8,525	7,073
58,100	58,150	8,536	6,577	8,536	7,084
58,150	58,200	8,547	6,583	8,547	7,095
58,200	58,250	8,558	6,589	8,558	7,106
58,250	58,300	8,569	6,595	8,569	7,117
58,300	58,350	8,580	6,601	8,580	7,128
58,350	58,400	8,591	6,607	8,591	7,139
58,400	58,450	8,602	6,613	8,602	7,150
58,450	58,500	8,613	6,619	8,613	7,161
58,500	58,550	8,624	6,625	8,624	7,172
58,550	58,600	8,635	6,631	8,635	7,183
58,600	58,650	8,646	6,637	8,646	7,194
58,650	58,700	8,657	6,643	8,657	7,205
58,700	58,750	8,668	6,649	8,668	7,216
58,750	58,800	8,679	6,655	8,679	7,227
58,800	58,850	8,690	6,661	8,690	7,238
58,850	58,900	8,701	6,667	8,701	7,249
58,900	58,950	8,712	6,673	8,712	7,260
58,950	59,000	8,723	6,679	8,723	7,271
59,000					
59,000	59,050	8,734	6,685	8,734	7,282
59,050	59,100	8,745	6,691	8,745	7,293
59,100	59,150	8,756	6,697	8,756	7,304
59,150	59,200	8,767	6,703	8,767	7,315
59,200	59,250	8,778	6,709	8,778	7,326
59,250	59,300	8,789	6,715	8,789	7,337
59,300	59,350	8,800	6,721	8,800	7,348
59,350	59,400	8,811	6,727	8,811	7,359
59,400	59,450	8,822	6,733	8,822	7,370
59,450	59,500	8,833	6,739	8,833	7,381
59,500	59,550	8,844	6,745	8,844	7,392
59,550	59,600	8,855	6,751	8,855	7,403
59,600	59,650	8,866	6,757	8,866	7,414
59,650	59,700	8,877	6,763	8,877	7,425
59,700	59,750	8,888	6,769	8,888	7,436
59,750	59,800	8,899	6,775	8,899	7,447
59,800	59,850	8,910	6,781	8,910	7,458
59,850	59,900	8,921	6,787	8,921	7,469
59,900	59,950	8,932	6,793	8,932	7,480
59,950	60,000	8,943	6,799	8,943	7,491

If line 15 (taxable income) is—		And you are—			
At least	But less than	Single	Married filing jointly *	Married filing sepa-rately	Head of a house-hold
		Your tax is—			
60,000					
60,000	60,050	8,954	6,805	8,954	7,502
60,050	60,100	8,965	6,811	8,965	7,513
60,100	60,150	8,976	6,817	8,976	7,524
60,150	60,200	8,987	6,823	8,987	7,535
60,200	60,250	8,998	6,829	8,998	7,546
60,250	60,300	9,009	6,835	9,009	7,557
60,300	60,350	9,020	6,841	9,020	7,568
60,350	60,400	9,031	6,847	9,031	7,579
60,400	60,450	9,042	6,853	9,042	7,590
60,450	60,500	9,053	6,859	9,053	7,601
60,500	60,550	9,064	6,865	9,064	7,612
60,550	60,600	9,075	6,871	9,075	7,623
60,600	60,650	9,086	6,877	9,086	7,634
60,650	60,700	9,097	6,883	9,097	7,645
60,700	60,750	9,108	6,889	9,108	7,656
60,750	60,800	9,119	6,895	9,119	7,667
60,800	60,850	9,130	6,901	9,130	7,678
60,850	60,900	9,141	6,907	9,141	7,689
60,900	60,950	9,152	6,913	9,152	7,700
60,950	61,000	9,163	6,919	9,163	7,711
61,000					
61,000	61,050	9,174	6,925	9,174	7,722
61,050	61,100	9,185	6,931	9,185	7,733
61,100	61,150	9,196	6,937	9,196	7,744
61,150	61,200	9,207	6,943	9,207	7,755
61,200	61,250	9,218	6,949	9,218	7,766
61,250	61,300	9,229	6,955	9,229	7,777
61,300	61,350	9,240	6,961	9,240	7,788
61,350	61,400	9,251	6,967	9,251	7,799
61,400	61,450	9,262	6,973	9,262	7,810
61,450	61,500	9,273	6,979	9,273	7,821
61,500	61,550	9,284	6,985	9,284	7,832
61,550	61,600	9,295	6,991	9,295	7,843
61,600	61,650	9,306	6,997	9,306	7,854
61,650	61,700	9,317	7,003	9,317	7,865
61,700	61,750	9,328	7,009	9,328	7,876
61,750	61,800	9,339	7,015	9,339	7,887
61,800	61,850	9,350	7,021	9,350	7,898
61,850	61,900	9,361	7,027	9,361	7,909
61,900	61,950	9,372	7,033	9,372	7,920
61,950	62,000	9,383	7,039	9,383	7,931
62,000					
62,000	62,050	9,394	7,045	9,394	7,942
62,050	62,100	9,405	7,051	9,405	7,953
62,100	62,150	9,416	7,057	9,416	7,964
62,150	62,200	9,427	7,063	9,427	7,975
62,200	62,250	9,438	7,069	9,438	7,986
62,250	62,300	9,449	7,075	9,449	7,997
62,300	62,350	9,460	7,081	9,460	8,008
62,350	62,400	9,471	7,087	9,471	8,019
62,400	62,450	9,482	7,093	9,482	8,030
62,450	62,500	9,493	7,099	9,493	8,041
62,500	62,550	9,504	7,105	9,504	8,052
62,550	62,600	9,515	7,111	9,515	8,063
62,600	62,650	9,526	7,117	9,526	8,074
62,650	62,700	9,537	7,123	9,537	8,085
62,700	62,750	9,548	7,129	9,548	8,096
62,750	62,800	9,559	7,135	9,559	8,107
62,800	62,850	9,570	7,141	9,570	8,118
62,850	62,900	9,581	7,147	9,581	8,129
62,900	62,950	9,592	7,153	9,592	8,140
62,950	63,000	9,603	7,159	9,603	8,151

If line 15 (taxable income) is—		And you are—			
At least	But less than	Single	Married filing jointly *	Married filing sepa-rately	Head of a house-hold
		Your tax is—			
63,000					
63,000	63,050	9,614	7,165	9,614	8,162
63,050	63,100	9,625	7,171	9,625	8,173
63,100	63,150	9,636	7,177	9,636	8,184
63,150	63,200	9,647	7,183	9,647	8,195
63,200	63,250	9,658	7,189	9,658	8,206
63,250	63,300	9,669	7,195	9,669	8,217
63,300	63,350	9,680	7,201	9,680	8,228
63,350	63,400	9,691	7,207	9,691	8,239
63,400	63,450	9,702	7,213	9,702	8,250
63,450	63,500	9,713	7,219	9,713	8,261
63,500	63,550	9,724	7,225	9,724	8,272
63,550	63,600	9,735	7,231	9,735	8,283
63,600	63,650	9,746	7,237	9,746	8,294
63,650	63,700	9,757	7,243	9,757	8,305
63,700	63,750	9,768	7,249	9,768	8,316
63,750	63,800	9,779	7,255	9,779	8,327
63,800	63,850	9,790	7,261	9,790	8,338
63,850	63,900	9,801	7,267	9,801	8,349
63,900	63,950	9,812	7,273	9,812	8,360
63,950	64,000	9,823	7,279	9,823	8,371
64,000					
64,000	64,050	9,834	7,285	9,834	8,382
64,050	64,100	9,845	7,291	9,845	8,393
64,100	64,150	9,856	7,297	9,856	8,404
64,150	64,200	9,867	7,303	9,867	8,415
64,200	64,250	9,878	7,309	9,878	8,426
64,250	64,300	9,889	7,315	9,889	8,437
64,300	64,350	9,900	7,321	9,900	8,448
64,350	64,400	9,911	7,327	9,911	8,459
64,400	64,450	9,922	7,333	9,922	8,470
64,450	64,500	9,933	7,339	9,933	8,481
64,500	64,550	9,944	7,345	9,944	8,492
64,550	64,600	9,955	7,351	9,955	8,503
64,600	64,650	9,966	7,357	9,966	8,514
64,650	64,700	9,977	7,363	9,977	8,525
64,700	64,750	9,988	7,369	9,988	8,536
64,750	64,800	9,999	7,375	9,999	8,547
64,800	64,850	10,010	7,381	10,010	8,558
64,850	64,900	10,021	7,387	10,021	8,569
64,900	64,950	10,032	7,393	10,032	8,580
64,950	65,000	10,043	7,399	10,043	8,591
65,000					
65,000	65,050	10,054	7,405	10,054	8,602
65,050	65,100	10,065	7,411	10,065	8,613
65,100	65,150	10,076	7,417	10,076	8,624
65,150	65,200	10,087	7,423	10,087	8,635
65,200	65,250	10,098	7,429	10,098	8,646
65,250	65,300	10,109	7,435	10,109	8,657
65,300	65,350	10,120	7,441	10,120	8,668
65,350	65,400	10,131	7,447	10,131	8,679
65,400	65,450	10,142	7,453	10,142	8,690
65,450	65,500	10,153	7,459	10,153	8,701
65,500	65,550	10,164	7,465	10,164	8,712
65,550	65,600	10,175	7,471	10,175	8,723
65,600	65,650	10,186	7,477	10,186	8,734
65,650	65,700	10,197	7,483	10,197	8,745
65,700	65,750	10,208	7,489	10,208	8,756
65,750	65,800	10,219	7,495	10,219	8,767
65,800	65,850	10,230	7,501	10,230	8,778
65,850	65,900	10,241	7,507	10,241	8,789
65,900	65,950	10,252	7,513	10,252	8,800
65,950	66,000	10,263	7,519	10,263	8,811

(Continued)

* This column must also be used by a qualifying widow(er).

2021 Tax Table — *Continued*

If line 15 (taxable income) is—		And you are—			
At least	But less than	Single	Married filing jointly *	Married filing separately	Head of a household
		Your tax is—			
66,000					
66,000	66,050	10,274	7,525	10,274	8,822
66,050	66,100	10,285	7,531	10,285	8,833
66,100	66,150	10,296	7,537	10,296	8,844
66,150	66,200	10,307	7,543	10,307	8,855
66,200	66,250	10,318	7,549	10,318	8,866
66,250	66,300	10,329	7,555	10,329	8,877
66,300	66,350	10,340	7,561	10,340	8,888
66,350	66,400	10,351	7,567	10,351	8,899
66,400	66,450	10,362	7,573	10,362	8,910
66,450	66,500	10,373	7,579	10,373	8,921
66,500	66,550	10,384	7,585	10,384	8,932
66,550	66,600	10,395	7,591	10,395	8,943
66,600	66,650	10,406	7,597	10,406	8,954
66,650	66,700	10,417	7,603	10,417	8,965
66,700	66,750	10,428	7,609	10,428	8,976
66,750	66,800	10,439	7,615	10,439	8,987
66,800	66,850	10,450	7,621	10,450	8,998
66,850	66,900	10,461	7,627	10,461	9,009
66,900	66,950	10,472	7,633	10,472	9,020
66,950	67,000	10,483	7,639	10,483	9,031
67,000					
67,000	67,050	10,494	7,645	10,494	9,042
67,050	67,100	10,505	7,651	10,505	9,053
67,100	67,150	10,516	7,657	10,516	9,064
67,150	67,200	10,527	7,663	10,527	9,075
67,200	67,250	10,538	7,669	10,538	9,086
67,250	67,300	10,549	7,675	10,549	9,097
67,300	67,350	10,560	7,681	10,560	9,108
67,350	67,400	10,571	7,687	10,571	9,119
67,400	67,450	10,582	7,693	10,582	9,130
67,450	67,500	10,593	7,699	10,593	9,141
67,500	67,550	10,604	7,705	10,604	9,152
67,550	67,600	10,615	7,711	10,615	9,163
67,600	67,650	10,626	7,717	10,626	9,174
67,650	67,700	10,637	7,723	10,637	9,185
67,700	67,750	10,648	7,729	10,648	9,196
67,750	67,800	10,659	7,735	10,659	9,207
67,800	67,850	10,670	7,741	10,670	9,218
67,850	67,900	10,681	7,747	10,681	9,229
67,900	67,950	10,692	7,753	10,692	9,240
67,950	68,000	10,703	7,759	10,703	9,251
68,000					
68,000	68,050	10,714	7,765	10,714	9,262
68,050	68,100	10,725	7,771	10,725	9,273
68,100	68,150	10,736	7,777	10,736	9,284
68,150	68,200	10,747	7,783	10,747	9,295
68,200	68,250	10,758	7,789	10,758	9,306
68,250	68,300	10,769	7,795	10,769	9,317
68,300	68,350	10,780	7,801	10,780	9,328
68,350	68,400	10,791	7,807	10,791	9,339
68,400	68,450	10,802	7,813	10,802	9,350
68,450	68,500	10,813	7,819	10,813	9,361
68,500	68,550	10,824	7,825	10,824	9,372
68,550	68,600	10,835	7,831	10,835	9,383
68,600	68,650	10,846	7,837	10,846	9,394
68,650	68,700	10,857	7,843	10,857	9,405
68,700	68,750	10,868	7,849	10,868	9,416
68,750	68,800	10,879	7,855	10,879	9,427
68,800	68,850	10,890	7,861	10,890	9,438
68,850	68,900	10,901	7,867	10,901	9,449
68,900	68,950	10,912	7,873	10,912	9,460
68,950	69,000	10,923	7,879	10,923	9,471

If line 15 (taxable income) is—		And you are—			
At least	But less than	Single	Married filing jointly *	Married filing separately	Head of a household
		Your tax is—			
69,000					
69,000	69,050	10,934	7,885	10,934	9,482
69,050	69,100	10,945	7,891	10,945	9,493
69,100	69,150	10,956	7,897	10,956	9,504
69,150	69,200	10,967	7,903	10,967	9,515
69,200	69,250	10,978	7,909	10,978	9,526
69,250	69,300	10,989	7,915	10,989	9,537
69,300	69,350	11,000	7,921	11,000	9,548
69,350	69,400	11,011	7,927	11,011	9,559
69,400	69,450	11,022	7,933	11,022	9,570
69,450	69,500	11,033	7,939	11,033	9,581
69,500	69,550	11,044	7,945	11,044	9,592
69,550	69,600	11,055	7,951	11,055	9,603
69,600	69,650	11,066	7,957	11,066	9,614
69,650	69,700	11,077	7,963	11,077	9,625
69,700	69,750	11,088	7,969	11,088	9,636
69,750	69,800	11,099	7,975	11,099	9,647
69,800	69,850	11,110	7,981	11,110	9,658
69,850	69,900	11,121	7,987	11,121	9,669
69,900	69,950	11,132	7,993	11,132	9,680
69,950	70,000	11,143	7,999	11,143	9,691
70,000					
70,000	70,050	11,154	8,005	11,154	9,702
70,050	70,100	11,165	8,011	11,165	9,713
70,100	70,150	11,176	8,017	11,176	9,724
70,150	70,200	11,187	8,023	11,187	9,735
70,200	70,250	11,198	8,029	11,198	9,746
70,250	70,300	11,209	8,035	11,209	9,757
70,300	70,350	11,220	8,041	11,220	9,768
70,350	70,400	11,231	8,047	11,231	9,779
70,400	70,450	11,242	8,053	11,242	9,790
70,450	70,500	11,253	8,059	11,253	9,801
70,500	70,550	11,264	8,065	11,264	9,812
70,550	70,600	11,275	8,071	11,275	9,823
70,600	70,650	11,286	8,077	11,286	9,834
70,650	70,700	11,297	8,083	11,297	9,845
70,700	70,750	11,308	8,089	11,308	9,856
70,750	70,800	11,319	8,095	11,319	9,867
70,800	70,850	11,330	8,101	11,330	9,878
70,850	70,900	11,341	8,107	11,341	9,889
70,900	70,950	11,352	8,113	11,352	9,900
70,950	71,000	11,363	8,119	11,363	9,911
71,000					
71,000	71,050	11,374	8,125	11,374	9,922
71,050	71,100	11,385	8,131	11,385	9,933
71,100	71,150	11,396	8,137	11,396	9,944
71,150	71,200	11,407	8,143	11,407	9,955
71,200	71,250	11,418	8,149	11,418	9,966
71,250	71,300	11,429	8,155	11,429	9,977
71,300	71,350	11,440	8,161	11,440	9,988
71,350	71,400	11,451	8,167	11,451	9,999
71,400	71,450	11,462	8,173	11,462	10,010
71,450	71,500	11,473	8,179	11,473	10,021
71,500	71,550	11,484	8,185	11,484	10,032
71,550	71,600	11,495	8,191	11,495	10,043
71,600	71,650	11,506	8,197	11,506	10,054
71,650	71,700	11,517	8,203	11,517	10,065
71,700	71,750	11,528	8,209	11,528	10,076
71,750	71,800	11,539	8,215	11,539	10,087
71,800	71,850	11,550	8,221	11,550	10,098
71,850	71,900	11,561	8,227	11,561	10,109
71,900	71,950	11,572	8,233	11,572	10,120
71,950	72,000	11,583	8,239	11,583	10,131

If line 15 (taxable income) is—		And you are—			
At least	But less than	Single	Married filing jointly *	Married filing separately	Head of a household
		Your tax is—			
72,000					
72,000	72,050	11,594	8,245	11,594	10,142
72,050	72,100	11,605	8,251	11,605	10,153
72,100	72,150	11,616	8,257	11,616	10,164
72,150	72,200	11,627	8,263	11,627	10,175
72,200	72,250	11,638	8,269	11,638	10,186
72,250	72,300	11,649	8,275	11,649	10,197
72,300	72,350	11,660	8,281	11,660	10,208
72,350	72,400	11,671	8,287	11,671	10,219
72,400	72,450	11,682	8,293	11,682	10,230
72,450	72,500	11,693	8,299	11,693	10,241
72,500	72,550	11,704	8,305	11,704	10,252
72,550	72,600	11,715	8,311	11,715	10,263
72,600	72,650	11,726	8,317	11,726	10,274
72,650	72,700	11,737	8,323	11,737	10,285
72,700	72,750	11,748	8,329	11,748	10,296
72,750	72,800	11,759	8,335	11,759	10,307
72,800	72,850	11,770	8,341	11,770	10,318
72,850	72,900	11,781	8,347	11,781	10,329
72,900	72,950	11,792	8,353	11,792	10,340
72,950	73,000	11,803	8,359	11,803	10,351
73,000					
73,000	73,050	11,814	8,365	11,814	10,362
73,050	73,100	11,825	8,371	11,825	10,373
73,100	73,150	11,836	8,377	11,836	10,384
73,150	73,200	11,847	8,383	11,847	10,395
73,200	73,250	11,858	8,389	11,858	10,406
73,250	73,300	11,869	8,395	11,869	10,417
73,300	73,350	11,880	8,401	11,880	10,428
73,350	73,400	11,891	8,407	11,891	10,439
73,400	73,450	11,902	8,413	11,902	10,450
73,450	73,500	11,913	8,419	11,913	10,461
73,500	73,550	11,924	8,425	11,924	10,472
73,550	73,600	11,935	8,431	11,935	10,483
73,600	73,650	11,946	8,437	11,946	10,494
73,650	73,700	11,957	8,443	11,957	10,505
73,700	73,750	11,968	8,449	11,968	10,516
73,750	73,800	11,979	8,455	11,979	10,527
73,800	73,850	11,990	8,461	11,990	10,538
73,850	73,900	12,001	8,467	12,001	10,549
73,900	73,950	12,012	8,473	12,012	10,560
73,950	74,000	12,023	8,479	12,023	10,571
74,000					
74,000	74,050	12,034	8,485	12,034	10,582
74,050	74,100	12,045	8,491	12,045	10,593
74,100	74,150	12,056	8,497	12,056	10,604
74,150	74,200	12,067	8,503	12,067	10,615
74,200	74,250	12,078	8,509	12,078	10,626
74,250	74,300	12,089	8,515	12,089	10,637
74,300	74,350	12,100	8,521	12,100	10,648
74,350	74,400	12,111	8,527	12,111	10,659
74,400	74,450	12,122	8,533	12,122	10,670
74,450	74,500	12,133	8,539	12,133	10,681
74,500	74,550	12,144	8,545	12,144	10,692
74,550	74,600	12,155	8,551	12,155	10,703
74,600	74,650	12,166	8,557	12,166	10,714
74,650	74,700	12,177	8,563	12,177	10,725
74,700	74,750	12,188	8,569	12,188	10,736
74,750	74,800	12,199	8,575	12,199	10,747
74,800	74,850	12,210	8,581	12,210	10,758
74,850	74,900	12,221	8,587	12,221	10,769
74,900	74,950	12,232	8,593	12,232	10,780
74,950	75,000	12,243	8,599	12,243	10,791

(Continued)

* This column must also be used by a qualifying widow(er).

2021 Tax Table — *Continued*

If line 15 (taxable income) is—		And you are—			
At least	But less than	Single	Married filing jointly *	Married filing separately	Head of a household
		Your tax is—			
75,000					
75,000	75,050	12,254	8,605	12,254	10,802
75,050	75,100	12,265	8,611	12,265	10,813
75,100	75,150	12,276	8,617	12,276	10,824
75,150	75,200	12,287	8,623	12,287	10,835
75,200	75,250	12,298	8,629	12,298	10,846
75,250	75,300	12,309	8,635	12,309	10,857
75,300	75,350	12,320	8,641	12,320	10,868
75,350	75,400	12,331	8,647	12,331	10,879
75,400	75,450	12,342	8,653	12,342	10,890
75,450	75,500	12,353	8,659	12,353	10,901
75,500	75,550	12,364	8,665	12,364	10,912
75,550	75,600	12,375	8,671	12,375	10,923
75,600	75,650	12,386	8,677	12,386	10,934
75,650	75,700	12,397	8,683	12,397	10,945
75,700	75,750	12,408	8,689	12,408	10,956
75,750	75,800	12,419	8,695	12,419	10,967
75,800	75,850	12,430	8,701	12,430	10,978
75,850	75,900	12,441	8,707	12,441	10,989
75,900	75,950	12,452	8,713	12,452	11,000
75,950	76,000	12,463	8,719	12,463	11,011
76,000					
76,000	76,050	12,474	8,725	12,474	11,022
76,050	76,100	12,485	8,731	12,485	11,033
76,100	76,150	12,496	8,737	12,496	11,044
76,150	76,200	12,507	8,743	12,507	11,055
76,200	76,250	12,518	8,749	12,518	11,066
76,250	76,300	12,529	8,755	12,529	11,077
76,300	76,350	12,540	8,761	12,540	11,088
76,350	76,400	12,551	8,767	12,551	11,099
76,400	76,450	12,562	8,773	12,562	11,110
76,450	76,500	12,573	8,779	12,573	11,121
76,500	76,550	12,584	8,785	12,584	11,132
76,550	76,600	12,595	8,791	12,595	11,143
76,600	76,650	12,606	8,797	12,606	11,154
76,650	76,700	12,617	8,803	12,617	11,165
76,700	76,750	12,628	8,809	12,628	11,176
76,750	76,800	12,639	8,815	12,639	11,187
76,800	76,850	12,650	8,821	12,650	11,198
76,850	76,900	12,661	8,827	12,661	11,209
76,900	76,950	12,672	8,833	12,672	11,220
76,950	77,000	12,683	8,839	12,683	11,231
77,000					
77,000	77,050	12,694	8,845	12,694	11,242
77,050	77,100	12,705	8,851	12,705	11,253
77,100	77,150	12,716	8,857	12,716	11,264
77,150	77,200	12,727	8,863	12,727	11,275
77,200	77,250	12,738	8,869	12,738	11,286
77,250	77,300	12,749	8,875	12,749	11,297
77,300	77,350	12,760	8,881	12,760	11,308
77,350	77,400	12,771	8,887	12,771	11,319
77,400	77,450	12,782	8,893	12,782	11,330
77,450	77,500	12,793	8,899	12,793	11,341
77,500	77,550	12,804	8,905	12,804	11,352
77,550	77,600	12,815	8,911	12,815	11,363
77,600	77,650	12,826	8,917	12,826	11,374
77,650	77,700	12,837	8,923	12,837	11,385
77,700	77,750	12,848	8,929	12,848	11,396
77,750	77,800	12,859	8,935	12,859	11,407
77,800	77,850	12,870	8,941	12,870	11,418
77,850	77,900	12,881	8,947	12,881	11,429
77,900	77,950	12,892	8,953	12,892	11,440
77,950	78,000	12,903	8,959	12,903	11,451

If line 15 (taxable income) is—		And you are—			
At least	But less than	Single	Married filing jointly *	Married filing separately	Head of a household
		Your tax is—			
78,000					
78,000	78,050	12,914	8,965	12,914	11,462
78,050	78,100	12,925	8,971	12,925	11,473
78,100	78,150	12,936	8,977	12,936	11,484
78,150	78,200	12,947	8,983	12,947	11,495
78,200	78,250	12,958	8,989	12,958	11,506
78,250	78,300	12,969	8,995	12,969	11,517
78,300	78,350	12,980	9,001	12,980	11,528
78,350	78,400	12,991	9,007	12,991	11,539
78,400	78,450	13,002	9,013	13,002	11,550
78,450	78,500	13,013	9,019	13,013	11,561
78,500	78,550	13,024	9,025	13,024	11,572
78,550	78,600	13,035	9,031	13,035	11,583
78,600	78,650	13,046	9,037	13,046	11,594
78,650	78,700	13,057	9,043	13,057	11,605
78,700	78,750	13,068	9,049	13,068	11,616
78,750	78,800	13,079	9,055	13,079	11,627
78,800	78,850	13,090	9,061	13,090	11,638
78,850	78,900	13,101	9,067	13,101	11,649
78,900	78,950	13,112	9,073	13,112	11,660
78,950	79,000	13,123	9,079	13,123	11,671
79,000					
79,000	79,050	13,134	9,085	13,134	11,682
79,050	79,100	13,145	9,091	13,145	11,693
79,100	79,150	13,156	9,097	13,156	11,704
79,150	79,200	13,167	9,103	13,167	11,715
79,200	79,250	13,178	9,109	13,178	11,726
79,250	79,300	13,189	9,115	13,189	11,737
79,300	79,350	13,200	9,121	13,200	11,748
79,350	79,400	13,211	9,127	13,211	11,759
79,400	79,450	13,222	9,133	13,222	11,770
79,450	79,500	13,233	9,139	13,233	11,781
79,500	79,550	13,244	9,145	13,244	11,792
79,550	79,600	13,255	9,151	13,255	11,803
79,600	79,650	13,266	9,157	13,266	11,814
79,650	79,700	13,277	9,163	13,277	11,825
79,700	79,750	13,288	9,169	13,288	11,836
79,750	79,800	13,299	9,175	13,299	11,847
79,800	79,850	13,310	9,181	13,310	11,858
79,850	79,900	13,321	9,187	13,321	11,869
79,900	79,950	13,332	9,193	13,332	11,880
79,950	80,000	13,343	9,199	13,343	11,891
80,000					
80,000	80,050	13,354	9,205	13,354	11,902
80,050	80,100	13,365	9,211	13,365	11,913
80,100	80,150	13,376	9,217	13,376	11,924
80,150	80,200	13,387	9,223	13,387	11,935
80,200	80,250	13,398	9,229	13,398	11,946
80,250	80,300	13,409	9,235	13,409	11,957
80,300	80,350	13,420	9,241	13,420	11,968
80,350	80,400	13,431	9,247	13,431	11,979
80,400	80,450	13,442	9,253	13,442	11,990
80,450	80,500	13,453	9,259	13,453	12,001
80,500	80,550	13,464	9,265	13,464	12,012
80,550	80,600	13,475	9,271	13,475	12,023
80,600	80,650	13,486	9,277	13,486	12,034
80,650	80,700	13,497	9,283	13,497	12,045
80,700	80,750	13,508	9,289	13,508	12,056
80,750	80,800	13,519	9,295	13,519	12,067
80,800	80,850	13,530	9,301	13,530	12,078
80,850	80,900	13,541	9,307	13,541	12,089
80,900	80,950	13,552	9,313	13,552	12,100
80,950	81,000	13,563	9,319	13,563	12,111

If line 15 (taxable income) is—		And you are—			
At least	But less than	Single	Married filing jointly *	Married filing separately	Head of a household
		Your tax is—			
81,000					
81,000	81,050	13,574	9,325	13,574	12,122
81,050	81,100	13,585	9,334	13,585	12,133
81,100	81,150	13,596	9,345	13,596	12,144
81,150	81,200	13,607	9,356	13,607	12,155
81,200	81,250	13,618	9,367	13,618	12,166
81,250	81,300	13,629	9,378	13,629	12,177
81,300	81,350	13,640	9,389	13,640	12,188
81,350	81,400	13,651	9,400	13,651	12,199
81,400	81,450	13,662	9,411	13,662	12,210
81,450	81,500	13,673	9,422	13,673	12,221
81,500	81,550	13,684	9,433	13,684	12,232
81,550	81,600	13,695	9,444	13,695	12,243
81,600	81,650	13,706	9,455	13,706	12,254
81,650	81,700	13,717	9,466	13,717	12,265
81,700	81,750	13,728	9,477	13,728	12,276
81,750	81,800	13,739	9,488	13,739	12,287
81,800	81,850	13,750	9,499	13,750	12,298
81,850	81,900	13,761	9,510	13,761	12,309
81,900	81,950	13,772	9,521	13,772	12,320
81,950	82,000	13,783	9,532	13,783	12,331
82,000					
82,000	82,050	13,794	9,543	13,794	12,342
82,050	82,100	13,805	9,554	13,805	12,353
82,100	82,150	13,816	9,565	13,816	12,364
82,150	82,200	13,827	9,576	13,827	12,375
82,200	82,250	13,838	9,587	13,838	12,386
82,250	82,300	13,849	9,598	13,849	12,397
82,300	82,350	13,860	9,609	13,860	12,408
82,350	82,400	13,871	9,620	13,871	12,419
82,400	82,450	13,882	9,631	13,882	12,430
82,450	82,500	13,893	9,642	13,893	12,441
82,500	82,550	13,904	9,653	13,904	12,452
82,550	82,600	13,915	9,664	13,915	12,463
82,600	82,650	13,926	9,675	13,926	12,474
82,650	82,700	13,937	9,686	13,937	12,485
82,700	82,750	13,948	9,697	13,948	12,496
82,750	82,800	13,959	9,708	13,959	12,507
82,800	82,850	13,970	9,719	13,970	12,518
82,850	82,900	13,981	9,730	13,981	12,529
82,900	82,950	13,992	9,741	13,992	12,540
82,950	83,000	14,003	9,752	14,003	12,551
83,000					
83,000	83,050	14,014	9,763	14,014	12,562
83,050	83,100	14,025	9,774	14,025	12,573
83,100	83,150	14,036	9,785	14,036	12,584
83,150	83,200	14,047	9,796	14,047	12,595
83,200	83,250	14,058	9,807	14,058	12,606
83,250	83,300	14,069	9,818	14,069	12,617
83,300	83,350	14,080	9,829	14,080	12,628
83,350	83,400	14,091	9,840	14,091	12,639
83,400	83,450	14,102	9,851	14,102	12,650
83,450	83,500	14,113	9,862	14,113	12,661
83,500	83,550	14,124	9,873	14,124	12,672
83,550	83,600	14,135	9,884	14,135	12,683
83,600	83,650	14,146	9,895	14,146	12,694
83,650	83,700	14,157	9,906	14,157	12,705
83,700	83,750	14,168	9,917	14,168	12,716
83,750	83,800	14,179	9,928	14,179	12,727
83,800	83,850	14,190	9,939	14,190	12,738
83,850	83,900	14,201	9,950	14,201	12,749
83,900	83,950	14,212	9,961	14,212	12,760
83,950	84,000	14,223	9,972	14,223	12,771

(Continued)

* This column must also be used by a qualifying widow(er).

2021 Tax Table — *Continued*

If line 15 (taxable income) is—		And you are—			
At least	But less than	Single	Married filing jointly *	Married filing sepa-rately	Head of a house-hold
		Your tax is—			
84,000					
84,000	84,050	14,234	9,983	14,234	12,782
84,050	84,100	14,245	9,994	14,245	12,793
84,100	84,150	14,256	10,005	14,256	12,804
84,150	84,200	14,267	10,016	14,267	12,815
84,200	84,250	14,278	10,027	14,278	12,826
84,250	84,300	14,289	10,038	14,289	12,837
84,300	84,350	14,300	10,049	14,300	12,848
84,350	84,400	14,311	10,060	14,311	12,859
84,400	84,450	14,322	10,071	14,322	12,870
84,450	84,500	14,333	10,082	14,333	12,881
84,500	84,550	14,344	10,093	14,344	12,892
84,550	84,600	14,355	10,104	14,355	12,903
84,600	84,650	14,366	10,115	14,366	12,914
84,650	84,700	14,377	10,126	14,377	12,925
84,700	84,750	14,388	10,137	14,388	12,936
84,750	84,800	14,399	10,148	14,399	12,947
84,800	84,850	14,410	10,159	14,410	12,958
84,850	84,900	14,421	10,170	14,421	12,969
84,900	84,950	14,432	10,181	14,432	12,980
84,950	85,000	14,443	10,192	14,443	12,991
85,000					
85,000	85,050	14,454	10,203	14,454	13,002
85,050	85,100	14,465	10,214	14,465	13,013
85,100	85,150	14,476	10,225	14,476	13,024
85,150	85,200	14,487	10,236	14,487	13,035
85,200	85,250	14,498	10,247	14,498	13,046
85,250	85,300	14,509	10,258	14,509	13,057
85,300	85,350	14,520	10,269	14,520	13,068
85,350	85,400	14,531	10,280	14,531	13,079
85,400	85,450	14,542	10,291	14,542	13,090
85,450	85,500	14,553	10,302	14,553	13,101
85,500	85,550	14,564	10,313	14,564	13,112
85,550	85,600	14,575	10,324	14,575	13,123
85,600	85,650	14,586	10,335	14,586	13,134
85,650	85,700	14,597	10,346	14,597	13,145
85,700	85,750	14,608	10,357	14,608	13,156
85,750	85,800	14,619	10,368	14,619	13,167
85,800	85,850	14,630	10,379	14,630	13,178
85,850	85,900	14,641	10,390	14,641	13,189
85,900	85,950	14,652	10,401	14,652	13,200
85,950	86,000	14,663	10,412	14,663	13,211
86,000					
86,000	86,050	14,674	10,423	14,674	13,222
86,050	86,100	14,685	10,434	14,685	13,233
86,100	86,150	14,696	10,445	14,696	13,244
86,150	86,200	14,707	10,456	14,707	13,255
86,200	86,250	14,718	10,467	14,718	13,266
86,250	86,300	14,729	10,478	14,729	13,277
86,300	86,350	14,740	10,489	14,740	13,288
86,350	86,400	14,751	10,500	14,751	13,299
86,400	86,450	14,763	10,511	14,763	13,311
86,450	86,500	14,775	10,522	14,775	13,323
86,500	86,550	14,787	10,533	14,787	13,335
86,550	86,600	14,799	10,544	14,799	13,347
86,600	86,650	14,811	10,555	14,811	13,359
86,650	86,700	14,823	10,566	14,823	13,371
86,700	86,750	14,835	10,577	14,835	13,383
86,750	86,800	14,847	10,588	14,847	13,395
86,800	86,850	14,859	10,599	14,859	13,407
86,850	86,900	14,871	10,610	14,871	13,419
86,900	86,950	14,883	10,621	14,883	13,431
86,950	87,000	14,895	10,632	14,895	13,443

If line 15 (taxable income) is—		And you are—			
At least	But less than	Single	Married filing jointly *	Married filing sepa-rately	Head of a house-hold
		Your tax is—			
87,000					
87,000	87,050	14,907	10,643	14,907	13,455
87,050	87,100	14,919	10,654	14,919	13,467
87,100	87,150	14,931	10,665	14,931	13,479
87,150	87,200	14,943	10,676	14,943	13,491
87,200	87,250	14,955	10,687	14,955	13,503
87,250	87,300	14,967	10,698	14,967	13,515
87,300	87,350	14,979	10,709	14,979	13,527
87,350	87,400	14,991	10,720	14,991	13,539
87,400	87,450	15,003	10,731	15,003	13,551
87,450	87,500	15,015	10,742	15,015	13,563
87,500	87,550	15,027	10,753	15,027	13,575
87,550	87,600	15,039	10,764	15,039	13,587
87,600	87,650	15,051	10,775	15,051	13,599
87,650	87,700	15,063	10,786	15,063	13,611
87,700	87,750	15,075	10,797	15,075	13,623
87,750	87,800	15,087	10,808	15,087	13,635
87,800	87,850	15,099	10,819	15,099	13,647
87,850	87,900	15,111	10,830	15,111	13,659
87,900	87,950	15,123	10,841	15,123	13,671
87,950	88,000	15,135	10,852	15,135	13,683
88,000					
88,000	88,050	15,147	10,863	15,147	13,695
88,050	88,100	15,159	10,874	15,159	13,707
88,100	88,150	15,171	10,885	15,171	13,719
88,150	88,200	15,183	10,896	15,183	13,731
88,200	88,250	15,195	10,907	15,195	13,743
88,250	88,300	15,207	10,918	15,207	13,755
88,300	88,350	15,219	10,929	15,219	13,767
88,350	88,400	15,231	10,940	15,231	13,779
88,400	88,450	15,243	10,951	15,243	13,791
88,450	88,500	15,255	10,962	15,255	13,803
88,500	88,550	15,267	10,973	15,267	13,815
88,550	88,600	15,279	10,984	15,279	13,827
88,600	88,650	15,291	10,995	15,291	13,839
88,650	88,700	15,303	11,006	15,303	13,851
88,700	88,750	15,315	11,017	15,315	13,863
88,750	88,800	15,327	11,028	15,327	13,875
88,800	88,850	15,339	11,039	15,339	13,887
88,850	88,900	15,351	11,050	15,351	13,899
88,900	88,950	15,363	11,061	15,363	13,911
88,950	89,000	15,375	11,072	15,375	13,923
89,000					
89,000	89,050	15,387	11,083	15,387	13,935
89,050	89,100	15,399	11,094	15,399	13,947
89,100	89,150	15,411	11,105	15,411	13,959
89,150	89,200	15,423	11,116	15,423	13,971
89,200	89,250	15,435	11,127	15,435	13,983
89,250	89,300	15,447	11,138	15,447	13,995
89,300	89,350	15,459	11,149	15,459	14,007
89,350	89,400	15,471	11,160	15,471	14,019
89,400	89,450	15,483	11,171	15,483	14,031
89,450	89,500	15,495	11,182	15,495	14,043
89,500	89,550	15,507	11,193	15,507	14,055
89,550	89,600	15,519	11,204	15,519	14,067
89,600	89,650	15,531	11,215	15,531	14,079
89,650	89,700	15,543	11,226	15,543	14,091
89,700	89,750	15,555	11,237	15,555	14,103
89,750	89,800	15,567	11,248	15,567	14,115
89,800	89,850	15,579	11,259	15,579	14,127
89,850	89,900	15,591	11,270	15,591	14,139
89,900	89,950	15,603	11,281	15,603	14,151
89,950	90,000	15,615	11,292	15,615	14,163

If line 15 (taxable income) is—		And you are—			
At least	But less than	Single	Married filing jointly *	Married filing sepa-rately	Head of a house-hold
		Your tax is—			
90,000					
90,000	90,050	15,627	11,303	15,627	14,175
90,050	90,100	15,639	11,314	15,639	14,187
90,100	90,150	15,651	11,325	15,651	14,199
90,150	90,200	15,663	11,336	15,663	14,211
90,200	90,250	15,675	11,347	15,675	14,223
90,250	90,300	15,687	11,358	15,687	14,235
90,300	90,350	15,699	11,369	15,699	14,247
90,350	90,400	15,711	11,380	15,711	14,259
90,400	90,450	15,723	11,391	15,723	14,271
90,450	90,500	15,735	11,402	15,735	14,283
90,500	90,550	15,747	11,413	15,747	14,295
90,550	90,600	15,759	11,424	15,759	14,307
90,600	90,650	15,771	11,435	15,771	14,319
90,650	90,700	15,783	11,446	15,783	14,331
90,700	90,750	15,795	11,457	15,795	14,343
90,750	90,800	15,807	11,468	15,807	14,355
90,800	90,850	15,819	11,479	15,819	14,367
90,850	90,900	15,831	11,490	15,831	14,379
90,900	90,950	15,843	11,501	15,843	14,391
90,950	91,000	15,855	11,512	15,855	14,403
91,000					
91,000	91,050	15,867	11,523	15,867	14,415
91,050	91,100	15,879	11,534	15,879	14,427
91,100	91,150	15,891	11,545	15,891	14,439
91,150	91,200	15,903	11,556	15,903	14,451
91,200	91,250	15,915	11,567	15,915	14,463
91,250	91,300	15,927	11,578	15,927	14,475
91,300	91,350	15,939	11,589	15,939	14,487
91,350	91,400	15,951	11,600	15,951	14,499
91,400	91,450	15,963	11,611	15,963	14,511
91,450	91,500	15,975	11,622	15,975	14,523
91,500	91,550	15,987	11,633	15,987	14,535
91,550	91,600	15,999	11,644	15,999	14,547
91,600	91,650	16,011	11,655	16,011	14,559
91,650	91,700	16,023	11,666	16,023	14,571
91,700	91,750	16,035	11,677	16,035	14,583
91,750	91,800	16,047	11,688	16,047	14,595
91,800	91,850	16,059	11,699	16,059	14,607
91,850	91,900	16,071	11,710	16,071	14,619
91,900	91,950	16,083	11,721	16,083	14,631
91,950	92,000	16,095	11,732	16,095	14,643
92,000					
92,000	92,050	16,107	11,743	16,107	14,655
92,050	92,100	16,119	11,754	16,119	14,667
92,100	92,150	16,131	11,765	16,131	14,679
92,150	92,200	16,143	11,776	16,143	14,691
92,200	92,250	16,155	11,787	16,155	14,703
92,250	92,300	16,167	11,798	16,167	14,715
92,300	92,350	16,179	11,809	16,179	14,727
92,350	92,400	16,191	11,820	16,191	14,739
92,400	92,450	16,203	11,831	16,203	14,751
92,450	92,500	16,215	11,842	16,215	14,763
92,500	92,550	16,227	11,853	16,227	14,775
92,550	92,600	16,239	11,864	16,239	14,787
92,600	92,650	16,251	11,875	16,251	14,799
92,650	92,700	16,263	11,886	16,263	14,811
92,700	92,750	16,275	11,897	16,275	14,823
92,750	92,800	16,287	11,908	16,287	14,835
92,800	92,850	16,299	11,919	16,299	14,847
92,850	92,900	16,311	11,930	16,311	14,859
92,900	92,950	16,323	11,941	16,323	14,871
92,950	93,000	16,335	11,952	16,335	14,883

(Continued)

* This column must also be used by a qualifying widow(er).

2021 Tax Table — *Continued*

If line 15 (taxable income) is—		And you are—			
At least	But less than	Single	Married filing jointly *	Married filing sepa-rately	Head of a house-hold
		Your tax is—			
93,000					
93,000	**93,050**	16,347	11,963	16,347	14,895
93,050	**93,100**	16,359	11,974	16,359	14,907
93,100	**93,150**	16,371	11,985	16,371	14,919
93,150	**93,200**	16,383	11,996	16,383	14,931
93,200	**93,250**	16,395	12,007	16,395	14,943
93,250	**93,300**	16,407	12,018	16,407	14,955
93,300	**93,350**	16,419	12,029	16,419	14,967
93,350	**93,400**	16,431	12,040	16,431	14,979
93,400	**93,450**	16,443	12,051	16,443	14,991
93,450	**93,500**	16,455	12,062	16,455	15,003
93,500	**93,550**	16,467	12,073	16,467	15,015
93,550	**93,600**	16,479	12,084	16,479	15,027
93,600	**93,650**	16,491	12,095	16,491	15,039
93,650	**93,700**	16,503	12,106	16,503	15,051
93,700	**93,750**	16,515	12,117	16,515	15,063
93,750	**93,800**	16,527	12,128	16,527	15,075
93,800	**93,850**	16,539	12,139	16,539	15,087
93,850	**93,900**	16,551	12,150	16,551	15,099
93,900	**93,950**	16,563	12,161	16,563	15,111
93,950	**94,000**	16,575	12,172	16,575	15,123
94,000					
94,000	**94,050**	16,587	12,183	16,587	15,135
94,050	**94,100**	16,599	12,194	16,599	15,147
94,100	**94,150**	16,611	12,205	16,611	15,159
94,150	**94,200**	16,623	12,216	16,623	15,171
94,200	**94,250**	16,635	12,227	16,635	15,183
94,250	**94,300**	16,647	12,238	16,647	15,195
94,300	**94,350**	16,659	12,249	16,659	15,207
94,350	**94,400**	16,671	12,260	16,671	15,219
94,400	**94,450**	16,683	12,271	16,683	15,231
94,450	**94,500**	16,695	12,282	16,695	15,243
94,500	**94,550**	16,707	12,293	16,707	15,255
94,550	**94,600**	16,719	12,304	16,719	15,267
94,600	**94,650**	16,731	12,315	16,731	15,279
94,650	**94,700**	16,743	12,326	16,743	15,291
94,700	**94,750**	16,755	12,337	16,755	15,303
94,750	**94,800**	16,767	12,348	16,767	15,315
94,800	**94,850**	16,779	12,359	16,779	15,327
94,850	**94,900**	16,791	12,370	16,791	15,339
94,900	**94,950**	16,803	12,381	16,803	15,351
94,950	**95,000**	16,815	12,392	16,815	15,363
95,000					
95,000	**95,050**	16,827	12,403	16,827	15,375
95,050	**95,100**	16,839	12,414	16,839	15,387
95,100	**95,150**	16,851	12,425	16,851	15,399
95,150	**95,200**	16,863	12,436	16,863	15,411
95,200	**95,250**	16,875	12,447	16,875	15,423
95,250	**95,300**	16,887	12,458	16,887	15,435
95,300	**95,350**	16,899	12,469	16,899	15,447
95,350	**95,400**	16,911	12,480	16,911	15,459
95,400	**95,450**	16,923	12,491	16,923	15,471
95,450	**95,500**	16,935	12,502	16,935	15,483
95,500	**95,550**	16,947	12,513	16,947	15,495
95,550	**95,600**	16,959	12,524	16,959	15,507
95,600	**95,650**	16,971	12,535	16,971	15,519
95,650	**95,700**	16,983	12,546	16,983	15,531
95,700	**95,750**	16,995	12,557	16,995	15,543
95,750	**95,800**	17,007	12,568	17,007	15,555
95,800	**95,850**	17,019	12,579	17,019	15,567
95,850	**95,900**	17,031	12,590	17,031	15,579
95,900	**95,950**	17,043	12,601	17,043	15,591
95,950	**96,000**	17,055	12,612	17,055	15,603

If line 15 (taxable income) is—		And you are—			
At least	But less than	Single	Married filing jointly *	Married filing sepa-rately	Head of a house-hold
		Your tax is—			
96,000					
96,000	**96,050**	17,067	12,623	17,067	15,615
96,050	**96,100**	17,079	12,634	17,079	15,627
96,100	**96,150**	17,091	12,645	17,091	15,639
96,150	**96,200**	17,103	12,656	17,103	15,651
96,200	**96,250**	17,115	12,667	17,115	15,663
96,250	**96,300**	17,127	12,678	17,127	15,675
96,300	**96,350**	17,139	12,689	17,139	15,687
96,350	**96,400**	17,151	12,700	17,151	15,699
96,400	**96,450**	17,163	12,711	17,163	15,711
96,450	**96,500**	17,175	12,722	17,175	15,723
96,500	**96,550**	17,187	12,733	17,187	15,735
96,550	**96,600**	17,199	12,744	17,199	15,747
96,600	**96,650**	17,211	12,755	17,211	15,759
96,650	**96,700**	17,223	12,766	17,223	15,771
96,700	**96,750**	17,235	12,777	17,235	15,783
96,750	**96,800**	17,247	12,788	17,247	15,795
96,800	**96,850**	17,259	12,799	17,259	15,807
96,850	**96,900**	17,271	12,810	17,271	15,819
96,900	**96,950**	17,283	12,821	17,283	15,831
96,950	**97,000**	17,295	12,832	17,295	15,843
97,000					
97,000	**97,050**	17,307	12,843	17,307	15,855
97,050	**97,100**	17,319	12,854	17,319	15,867
97,100	**97,150**	17,331	12,865	17,331	15,879
97,150	**97,200**	17,343	12,876	17,343	15,891
97,200	**97,250**	17,355	12,887	17,355	15,903
97,250	**97,300**	17,367	12,898	17,367	15,915
97,300	**97,350**	17,379	12,909	17,379	15,927
97,350	**97,400**	17,391	12,920	17,391	15,939
97,400	**97,450**	17,403	12,931	17,403	15,951
97,450	**97,500**	17,415	12,942	17,415	15,963
97,500	**97,550**	17,427	12,953	17,427	15,975
97,550	**97,600**	17,439	12,964	17,439	15,987
97,600	**97,650**	17,451	12,975	17,451	15,999
97,650	**97,700**	17,463	12,986	17,463	16,011
97,700	**97,750**	17,475	12,997	17,475	16,023
97,750	**97,800**	17,487	13,008	17,487	16,035
97,800	**97,850**	17,499	13,019	17,499	16,047
97,850	**97,900**	17,511	13,030	17,511	16,059
97,900	**97,950**	17,523	13,041	17,523	16,071
97,950	**98,000**	17,535	13,052	17,535	16,083
98,000					
98,000	**98,050**	17,547	13,063	17,547	16,095
98,050	**98,100**	17,559	13,074	17,559	16,107
98,100	**98,150**	17,571	13,085	17,571	16,119
98,150	**98,200**	17,583	13,096	17,583	16,131
98,200	**98,250**	17,595	13,107	17,595	16,143
98,250	**98,300**	17,607	13,118	17,607	16,155
98,300	**98,350**	17,619	13,129	17,619	16,167
98,350	**98,400**	17,631	13,140	17,631	16,179
98,400	**98,450**	17,643	13,151	17,643	16,191
98,450	**98,500**	17,655	13,162	17,655	16,203
98,500	**98,550**	17,667	13,173	17,667	16,215
98,550	**98,600**	17,679	13,184	17,679	16,227
98,600	**98,650**	17,691	13,195	17,691	16,239
98,650	**98,700**	17,703	13,206	17,703	16,251
98,700	**98,750**	17,715	13,217	17,715	16,263
98,750	**98,800**	17,727	13,228	17,727	16,275
98,800	**98,850**	17,739	13,239	17,739	16,287
98,850	**98,900**	17,751	13,250	17,751	16,299
98,900	**98,950**	17,763	13,261	17,763	16,311
98,950	**99,000**	17,775	13,272	17,775	16,323

If line 15 (taxable income) is—		And you are—			
At least	But less than	Single	Married filing jointly *	Married filing sepa-rately	Head of a house-hold
		Your tax is—			
99,000					
99,000	**99,050**	17,787	13,283	17,787	16,335
99,050	**99,100**	17,799	13,294	17,799	16,347
99,100	**99,150**	17,811	13,305	17,811	16,359
99,150	**99,200**	17,823	13,316	17,823	16,371
99,200	**99,250**	17,835	13,327	17,835	16,383
99,250	**99,300**	17,847	13,338	17,847	16,395
99,300	**99,350**	17,859	13,349	17,859	16,407
99,350	**99,400**	17,871	13,360	17,871	16,419
99,400	**99,450**	17,883	13,371	17,883	16,431
99,450	**99,500**	17,895	13,382	17,895	16,443
99,500	**99,550**	17,907	13,393	17,907	16,455
99,550	**99,600**	17,919	13,404	17,919	16,467
99,600	**99,650**	17,931	13,415	17,931	16,479
99,650	**99,700**	17,943	13,426	17,943	16,491
99,700	**99,750**	17,955	13,437	17,955	16,503
99,750	**99,800**	17,967	13,448	17,967	16,515
99,800	**99,850**	17,979	13,459	17,979	16,527
99,850	**99,900**	17,991	13,470	17,991	16,539
99,900	**99,950**	18,003	13,481	18,003	16,551
99,950	**100,000**	18,015	13,492	18,015	16,563

$100,000
or over
use the Tax
Computation
Worksheet

* This column must also be used by a qualifying widow(er).

2021 Optional Sales Tax Tables

When Used

The election to deduct state and local general sales taxes requires that the taxpayer give up any deduction for state and local income taxes. Whether this is advisable or not depends on a comparison of the amounts involved. In making the choice, however, the outcome could be influenced by the additional sales tax incurred due to certain "big ticket" purchases that were made. For example, a taxpayer who chose to deduct state and local income taxes for 2020 might well prefer the sales tax deduction in 2021 if a new boat was purchased or home improvements were made during the year. To make the sales tax election, the taxpayer must enter the amount on Schedule A, line 5a, and check the related box.

If the sales tax election is made, the amount of the deduction can be determined by use of the *actual expense method* or *the optional sales tax tables* issued by the IRS. The actual expense method can be used only when the taxpayer has actual receipts to support the deduction claimed. In the absence of receipts (the usual case with most taxpayers), the optional sales tax tables must be used. Sales taxes related to the purchase of items used in a taxpayer's trade or business are determined separately, with this amount deducted on Schedule C (Form 1040).

Adjustments Necessary

The optional sales tax tables are based on a number of assumptions that require adjustments to be made. As the starting point for the use of the tables is AGI, nontaxable receipts have not been included. Examples of receipts that should be added include: tax-exempt interest, veterans' benefits, nontaxable combat pay, public assistance payments, workers' compensation, nontaxable Social Security, and other retirement benefits. They do not include any large nontaxable items that are not likely to be spent. For example, a $100,000 inheritance should not be added if it was invested in a certificate of deposit.

The tables represent the sales tax on the average (and recurring) expenditures based on level of income by family size and do not include exceptional purchases. Therefore, add to the table amount any sales taxes on major purchases (such as motor vehicles, aircraft, boats, and home building materials, etc.).

When the optional sales tax tables are used, special adjustments may be needed when a taxpayer has lived in more than one taxing jurisdiction (e.g., state, county, city) during the year. The adjustments involve apportionment of taxes based on days involved and are illustrated in Instructions for Schedule A (Form 1040), pages A-3 to A-7.

Local Sales Taxes

Local sales taxes (i.e., those imposed by counties, cities, transit authorities) may or may not require a separate determination. In those states where they are not imposed, no further computations are necessary. This is also the case where the local taxes are uniform and are incorporated into the state sales tax table. In other situations, another step is necessary to arrive at the optional sales tax table deduction. Depending on where the taxpayer lives, one of two procedures needs to be used. In one procedure, the local sales tax is determined by using the **state table** amount—see Example 1 and the related worksheet. In the other procedure, special **local tables** issued by the IRS for specified state and local jurisdictions are modified (if necessary) and used—see Example 2 and the related worksheet.

IRS Sales Tax Deduction Calculator

The IRS has created an online Sales Tax Deduction Calculator to assist taxpayers in making this calculation (**apps.irs.gov/app/stdc/**). The calculator includes the ability to make adjustments for large purchases and includes a local sales tax calculation.

Use Illustrated

Example 1 The Archers file a joint return for 2021 reflecting AGI of $88,000 and have three dependents. They have tax-exempt interest of $3,000, and during the year they incurred sales tax of $1,650 on the purchase of an automobile for their dependent teenage son. They live in Bellaire, Texas, where the general sales tax rates are 6.25% for state and 2% for local. Since the IRS *has not issued* optional local sales tax tables for Texas, use the Worksheet below to arrive at the Archers' general sales tax deduction of $3,035.

Sales Tax Deduction Worksheet
(To be used when *no* IRS Optional Local Sales Tax Table Available)

Adjusted Gross Income (AGI) as listed on line 11 of Form 1040		$88,000
Add nontaxable items		3,000
Table income to be used for purposes of line 1 below		$91,000
1. Use table income to determine table amount—go to state of residence and find applicable range of table income and family size column for *state* sales tax		$ 1,049
2a. Enter local general sales tax rate	2.00	
2b. Enter state general sales tax rate	6.25	
2c. Divide 2a by 2b	0.32	
2d. Multiply line 1 by line 2c for the local sales tax		336
3. Enter general sales tax on large purchases		1,650
4. Deduction for general sales tax (add lines 1 + 2d + 3) and report on line 5a of Schedule A of Form 1040		$ 3,035

Example 2 The Hardys file a joint return for 2021, reporting AGI of $42,000 and have two dependents. They received $30,000 in nontaxable pension benefits. Although the Hardys do not keep sales tax receipts, they can prove that they paid $1,185 in sales tax on the purchase of a new boat in 2021. The Hardys are residents of Georgia and live in a jurisdiction that imposes a 2% local sales tax. Since the IRS *has issued* optional local sales tax tables for Georgia, use the Worksheet below to arrive at the Hardys' general sales tax deduction of $2,121.

Sales Tax Deduction Worksheet
(To be used for Alaska, Arizona, Arkansas, Colorado, Georgia, Illinois, Louisiana, Mississippi, Missouri, New York, North Carolina, South Carolina, Tennessee, Utah, and Virginia)

Adjusted Gross Income (AGI) as listed on line 11 of Form 1040		$42,000
Add nontaxable income		30,000
Table income to be used for purposes of line 1 below		$72,000
1. Use the table income to determine *state* sales tax amount—go to table for state of residence and find applicable income range and family size column		$ 530
2a. Enter local general sales tax rate	2.0	
2b. Enter IRS *local* sales tax table amount (based on a 1% tax rate)	$203	
2c. Multiply line 2b by 2a for the local sales tax		406
3. Enter general sales tax on large purchases		1,185
4. Deduction for general sales tax (add lines 1 + 2c + 3) and report on line 5a of Schedule A of Form 1040		$ 2,121

Assume that the Hardys live in Lawrenceville, GA 30045. Use the IRS Sales Tax Deduction Calculator to confirm the calculated amount (**apps.irs.gov/app/stdc/**).

2021 Optional State Sales Tax Tables

Alabama — 1 — 4.0000%

Income: At least	Income: But less than	Family Size 1	2	3	4	5	Over 5
$0	$20,000	252	294	323	345	363	389
$20,000	$30,000	360	421	461	493	519	555
$30,000	$40,000	415	485	531	567	597	639
$40,000	$50,000	461	538	590	630	663	710
$50,000	$60,000	502	586	642	685	721	772
$60,000	$70,000	538	628	688	735	773	827
$70,000	$80,000	571	666	730	780	821	878
$80,000	$90,000	601	702	769	821	864	925
$90,000	$100,000	630	735	805	860	905	968
$100,000	$120,000	667	778	853	911	958	1025
$120,000	$140,000	716	835	915	976	1028	1099
$140,000	$160,000	760	887	971	1037	1091	1167
$160,000	$180,000	801	934	1023	1092	1149	1229
$180,000	$200,000	839	978	1072	1144	1204	1288
$200,000	$225,000	878	1024	1122	1198	1260	1348
$225,000	$250,000	920	1073	1176	1255	1320	1412
$250,000	$275,000	960	1119	1226	1308	1376	1472
$275,000	$300,000	997	1162	1273	1359	1430	1529
$300,000	or more	1213	1414	1549	1653	1739	1859

Arizona — 2 — 5.6000%

Income: At least	Income: But less than	Family Size 1	2	3	4	5	Over 5
$0	$20,000	246	280	302	319	332	352
$20,000	$30,000	363	413	445	470	491	519
$30,000	$40,000	423	481	519	548	572	605
$40,000	$50,000	475	540	582	615	641	678
$50,000	$60,000	520	591	638	674	703	744
$60,000	$70,000	561	638	688	727	758	802
$70,000	$80,000	599	681	734	775	809	856
$80,000	$90,000	634	720	777	820	856	906
$90,000	$100,000	666	757	817	863	900	952
$100,000	$120,000	709	806	870	919	959	1014
$120,000	$140,000	765	870	939	991	1034	1094
$140,000	$160,000	817	929	1002	1058	1104	1168
$160,000	$180,000	865	983	1061	1120	1169	1236
$180,000	$200,000	910	1034	1116	1178	1229	1300
$200,000	$225,000	956	1087	1173	1238	1292	1367
$225,000	$250,000	1006	1143	1234	1303	1359	1438
$250,000	$275,000	1052	1196	1291	1363	1423	1505
$275,000	$300,000	1097	1247	1346	1421	1483	1568
$300,000	or more	1358	1544	1666	1759	1835	1941

Arkansas — 2 — 6.5000%

Income: At least	Income: But less than	Family Size 1	2	3	4	5	Over 5
$0	$20,000	283	318	341	358	372	391
$20,000	$30,000	433	488	523	549	571	600
$30,000	$40,000	513	578	620	651	677	712
$40,000	$50,000	582	656	704	739	768	808
$50,000	$60,000	645	726	779	819	851	895
$60,000	$70,000	701	790	848	891	926	975
$70,000	$80,000	754	849	911	958	996	1048
$80,000	$90,000	802	905	971	1020	1061	1116
$90,000	$100,000	849	957	1027	1079	1122	1181
$100,000	$120,000	910	1027	1102	1158	1204	1267
$120,000	$140,000	991	1118	1199	1261	1311	1380
$140,000	$160,000	1066	1203	1291	1358	1412	1486
$160,000	$180,000	1136	1282	1376	1447	1505	1584
$180,000	$200,000	1202	1357	1456	1532	1593	1677
$200,000	$225,000	1271	1435	1541	1620	1685	1774
$225,000	$250,000	1346	1519	1631	1716	1784	1879
$250,000	$275,000	1416	1599	1717	1806	1878	1977
$275,000	$300,000	1484	1675	1799	1892	1968	2072
$300,000	or more	1887	2132	2290	2409	2506	2640

California — 3 — 7.2500%

Income: At least	Income: But less than	Family Size 1	2	3	4	5	Over 5
$0	$20,000	314	356	384	405	422	446
$20,000	$30,000	458	520	560	591	616	651
$30,000	$40,000	532	603	650	686	715	755
$40,000	$50,000	595	674	726	766	799	844
$50,000	$60,000	650	737	794	837	873	922
$60,000	$70,000	700	793	855	901	940	993
$70,000	$80,000	745	845	910	960	1001	1057
$80,000	$90,000	787	892	961	1014	1057	1117
$90,000	$100,000	827	937	1009	1064	1110	1172
$100,000	$120,000	879	996	1073	1131	1179	1246
$120,000	$140,000	946	1072	1155	1218	1270	1341
$140,000	$160,000	1008	1143	1231	1298	1353	1429
$160,000	$180,000	1065	1207	1300	1371	1429	1510
$180,000	$200,000	1119	1268	1366	1440	1501	1586
$200,000	$225,000	1174	1331	1433	1512	1576	1665
$225,000	$250,000	1234	1398	1506	1588	1655	1749
$250,000	$275,000	1289	1461	1574	1660	1730	1827
$275,000	$300,000	1342	1521	1638	1728	1801	1902
$300,000	or more	1652	1871	2015	2125	2215	2340

Colorado — 2 — 2.9000%

Income: At least	Income: But less than	Family Size 1	2	3	4	5	Over 5
$0	$20,000	127	138	144	150	154	159
$20,000	$30,000	191	208	218	226	232	241
$30,000	$40,000	225	245	257	266	273	283
$40,000	$50,000	254	276	290	301	309	320
$50,000	$60,000	280	305	320	331	341	353
$60,000	$70,000	304	330	347	359	369	383
$70,000	$80,000	325	354	372	385	396	410
$80,000	$90,000	346	376	395	409	420	435
$90,000	$100,000	364	396	416	431	443	459
$100,000	$120,000	390	424	445	461	474	491
$120,000	$140,000	422	459	483	500	514	532
$140,000	$160,000	453	493	517	536	551	571
$160,000	$180,000	481	523	550	569	585	606
$180,000	$200,000	508	552	580	601	617	640
$200,000	$225,000	535	582	612	634	651	675
$225,000	$250,000	565	614	646	669	687	713
$250,000	$275,000	593	645	678	702	721	748
$275,000	$300,000	619	674	708	733	754	782
$300,000	or more	777	846	889	921	946	981

Connecticut — 4 — 6.3500%

Income: At least	Income: But less than	Family Size 1	2	3	4	5	Over 5
$0	$20,000	218	237	248	257	264	273
$20,000	$30,000	337	366	384	397	408	423
$30,000	$40,000	401	435	457	473	486	503
$40,000	$50,000	457	496	521	539	553	573
$50,000	$60,000	508	551	578	598	614	636
$60,000	$70,000	554	601	631	653	670	694
$70,000	$80,000	597	648	680	703	722	747
$80,000	$90,000	637	691	725	750	771	798
$90,000	$100,000	675	733	769	795	817	845
$100,000	$120,000	726	788	827	855	878	909
$120,000	$140,000	793	861	903	934	959	993
$140,000	$160,000	856	929	974	1008	1035	1072
$160,000	$180,000	914	992	1041	1077	1106	1145
$180,000	$200,000	970	1053	1104	1142	1173	1214
$200,000	$225,000	1028	1116	1171	1211	1244	1287
$225,000	$250,000	1091	1184	1242	1285	1320	1366
$250,000	$275,000	1151	1249	1310	1356	1392	1441
$275,000	$300,000	1209	1312	1376	1423	1461	1513
$300,000	or more	1555	1688	1770	1831	1880	1946

District of Columbia — 4 — 6.0000%

Income: At least	Income: But less than	Family Size 1	2	3	4	5	Over 5
$0	$20,000	196	210	218	224	229	235
$20,000	$30,000	310	331	344	353	361	371
$30,000	$40,000	371	396	412	424	433	445
$40,000	$50,000	425	454	472	485	496	510
$50,000	$60,000	473	506	526	541	553	569
$60,000	$70,000	518	553	576	592	605	622
$70,000	$80,000	559	598	622	639	653	672
$80,000	$90,000	598	639	665	684	699	719
$90,000	$100,000	634	679	706	726	742	763
$100,000	$120,000	684	731	761	783	800	823
$120,000	$140,000	749	801	833	857	876	901
$140,000	$160,000	810	866	901	927	947	975
$160,000	$180,000	866	927	964	992	1014	1043
$180,000	$200,000	920	985	1025	1054	1077	1109
$200,000	$225,000	977	1046	1088	1119	1144	1177
$225,000	$250,000	1038	1111	1156	1189	1216	1251
$250,000	$275,000	1096	1173	1221	1256	1284	1322
$275,000	$300,000	1152	1233	1284	1320	1350	1389
$300,000	or more	1490	1595	1660	1708	1746	1798

Florida — 1 — 6.0000%

Income: At least	Income: But less than	Family Size 1	2	3	4	5	Over 5
$0	$20,000	265	301	325	343	357	378
$20,000	$30,000	394	448	483	510	532	563
$30,000	$40,000	460	524	565	597	623	659
$40,000	$50,000	517	589	635	671	700	741
$50,000	$60,000	568	646	698	737	769	814
$60,000	$70,000	614	698	754	796	831	879
$70,000	$80,000	656	746	806	851	888	940
$80,000	$90,000	694	791	854	902	941	996
$90,000	$100,000	731	832	898	949	991	1048
$100,000	$120,000	779	887	958	1012	1057	1118
$120,000	$140,000	842	959	1036	1094	1142	1208
$140,000	$160,000	900	1025	1107	1170	1221	1292
$160,000	$180,000	954	1087	1174	1240	1294	1370
$180,000	$200,000	1005	1144	1236	1306	1363	1443
$200,000	$225,000	1057	1204	1301	1374	1435	1518
$225,000	$250,000	1113	1268	1370	1448	1511	1599
$250,000	$275,000	1166	1329	1435	1517	1583	1676
$275,000	$300,000	1216	1386	1497	1582	1652	1748
$300,000	or more	1513	1724	1863	1969	2056	2176

Georgia — 2 — 4.0000%

Income: At least	Income: But less than	Family Size 1	2	3	4	5	Over 5
$0	$20,000	172	187	196	203	209	216
$20,000	$30,000	261	284	298	309	317	329
$30,000	$40,000	308	335	352	364	375	388
$40,000	$50,000	348	379	398	412	424	439
$50,000	$60,000	384	418	439	455	468	485
$60,000	$70,000	417	453	477	494	508	526
$70,000	$80,000	447	486	511	530	544	565
$80,000	$90,000	475	517	543	563	579	600
$90,000	$100,000	501	545	573	594	611	634
$100,000	$120,000	536	584	614	636	654	678
$120,000	$140,000	582	633	666	690	710	736
$140,000	$160,000	624	680	715	741	762	790
$160,000	$180,000	664	723	760	787	810	840
$180,000	$200,000	701	763	802	832	855	887
$200,000	$225,000	739	805	847	878	902	936
$225,000	$250,000	781	851	895	927	953	989
$250,000	$275,000	820	893	939	974	1001	1039
$275,000	$300,000	858	934	982	1018	1047	1086
$300,000	or more	1079	1176	1237	1282	1318	1368

Hawaii — 1,6 — 4.0000%

Income: At least	Income: But less than	Family Size 1	2	3	4	5	Over 5
$0	$20,000	275	312	336	355	370	390
$20,000	$30,000	412	468	505	532	555	586
$30,000	$40,000	483	549	592	625	652	688
$40,000	$50,000	544	619	668	705	735	776
$50,000	$60,000	599	682	735	776	809	855
$60,000	$70,000	649	738	796	840	876	925
$70,000	$80,000	694	790	852	899	938	991
$80,000	$90,000	736	838	904	954	995	1051
$90,000	$100,000	776	883	953	1006	1049	1108
$100,000	$120,000	829	943	1018	1074	1120	1184
$120,000	$140,000	897	1022	1102	1164	1214	1282
$140,000	$160,000	961	1095	1181	1247	1300	1374
$160,000	$180,000	1020	1162	1254	1323	1380	1458
$180,000	$200,000	1076	1225	1322	1396	1456	1538
$200,000	$225,000	1134	1291	1393	1471	1534	1621
$225,000	$250,000	1196	1362	1470	1552	1618	1710
$250,000	$275,000	1254	1428	1542	1628	1698	1794
$275,000	$300,000	1310	1492	1610	1700	1773	1874
$300,000	or more	1639	1868	2016	2129	2221	2347

Idaho — 1 — 6.0000%

Income: At least	Income: But less than	Family Size 1	2	3	4	5	Over 5
$0	$20,000	379	455	507	548	582	630
$20,000	$30,000	537	643	716	774	822	890
$30,000	$40,000	615	737	821	887	942	1020
$40,000	$50,000	682	817	909	982	1043	1129
$50,000	$60,000	740	886	986	1065	1131	1225
$60,000	$70,000	792	948	1055	1139	1210	1310
$70,000	$80,000	839	1004	1118	1207	1282	1387
$80,000	$90,000	883	1056	1176	1269	1348	1459
$90,000	$100,000	923	1105	1229	1327	1409	1525
$100,000	$120,000	977	1169	1300	1404	1490	1613
$120,000	$140,000	1046	1251	1391	1502	1594	1725
$140,000	$160,000	1109	1326	1475	1592	1690	1828
$160,000	$180,000	1167	1395	1551	1674	1777	1923
$180,000	$200,000	1221	1459	1623	1751	1859	2011
$200,000	$225,000	1277	1526	1697	1831	1943	2102
$225,000	$250,000	1336	1596	1775	1916	2033	2199
$250,000	$275,000	1391	1662	1848	1995	2117	2290
$275,000	$300,000	1444	1725	1918	2069	2196	2376
$300,000	or more	1749	2088	2320	2503	2656	2872

Illinois — 2 — 6.2500%

Income: At least	Income: But less than	Family Size 1	2	3	4	5	Over 5
$0	$20,000	273	313	340	361	378	402
$20,000	$30,000	402	461	501	531	556	591
$30,000	$40,000	469	537	583	618	647	688
$40,000	$50,000	525	602	653	693	725	771
$50,000	$60,000	575	659	715	759	794	844
$60,000	$70,000	620	711	771	818	856	910
$70,000	$80,000	661	758	822	872	913	970
$80,000	$90,000	700	802	870	922	966	1026
$90,000	$100,000	735	843	914	969	1015	1079
$100,000	$120,000	783	897	973	1032	1080	1148
$120,000	$140,000	844	967	1049	1113	1165	1238
$140,000	$160,000	901	1032	1120	1187	1243	1321
$160,000	$180,000	953	1092	1185	1256	1315	1397
$180,000	$200,000	1002	1148	1246	1321	1383	1469
$200,000	$225,000	1053	1207	1309	1388	1453	1544
$225,000	$250,000	1108	1269	1376	1459	1528	1623
$250,000	$275,000	1159	1327	1440	1527	1598	1698
$275,000	$300,000	1207	1383	1500	1591	1665	1769
$300,000	or more	1493	1710	1854	1966	2058	2186

Income		Family Size						Family Size						Family Size					
At least	But less than	1	2	3	4	5	Over 5	1	2	3	4	5	Over 5	1	2	3	4	5	Over 5
		Indiana			4		7.0000%	**Iowa**			1		6.0000%	**Kansas**			1		6.5000%
$0	$20,000	318	365	396	420	439	466	270	301	322	337	350	366	423	515	579	630	672	732
$20,000	$30,000	462	531	576	611	639	678	410	459	490	514	533	559	588	716	804	874	933	1017
$30,000	$40,000	535	615	668	708	741	787	484	542	579	607	630	661	669	815	916	995	1062	1157
$40,000	$50,000	598	687	746	791	828	879	549	614	656	688	714	749	737	897	1008	1096	1170	1274
$50,000	$60,000	653	751	815	864	905	961	606	679	726	761	789	828	796	969	1090	1184	1264	1377
$60,000	$70,000	702	808	877	930	973	1034	658	737	788	826	857	899	848	1033	1161	1262	1347	1468
$70,000	$80,000	747	860	934	990	1036	1101	707	792	846	887	920	966	896	1091	1227	1333	1423	1550
$80,000	$90,000	789	908	986	1046	1095	1163	752	842	900	944	979	1028	940	1145	1287	1398	1492	1626
$90,000	$100,000	828	953	1035	1098	1149	1220	794	890	951	997	1035	1086	980	1194	1342	1459	1557	1696
$100,000	$120,000	880	1013	1100	1167	1221	1297	851	953	1019	1069	1109	1164	1034	1259	1415	1538	1642	1789
$120,000	$140,000	947	1090	1184	1256	1314	1396	925	1036	1108	1162	1206	1265	1102	1342	1509	1640	1750	1907
$140,000	$160,000	1008	1161	1261	1338	1401	1488	994	1114	1191	1249	1296	1360	1165	1419	1595	1733	1850	2015
$160,000	$180,000	1065	1226	1332	1413	1480	1572	1057	1186	1268	1330	1380	1448	1222	1488	1673	1818	1940	2114
$180,000	$200,000	1118	1288	1399	1484	1554	1651	1118	1254	1341	1406	1459	1531	1275	1553	1746	1897	2025	2206
$200,000	$225,000	1174	1351	1468	1558	1631	1733	1181	1325	1417	1486	1542	1618	1330	1620	1821	1979	2112	2301
$225,000	$250,000	1232	1419	1542	1636	1713	1820	1249	1401	1498	1571	1631	1712	1388	1691	1900	2066	2204	2402
$250,000	$275,000	1288	1483	1611	1710	1790	1902	1313	1473	1575	1652	1715	1800	1442	1757	1974	2146	2290	2495
$275,000	$300,000	1340	1543	1677	1780	1863	1980	1375	1542	1649	1730	1795	1885	1493	1819	2045	2222	2372	2584
$300,000	or more	1647	1897	2062	2189	2292	2435	1741	1954	2090	2193	2276	2389	1788	2178	2448	2661	2840	3094

Income																			
		Kentucky			4		6.0000%	**Louisiana**			2		4.4500%	**Maine**			4		5.5000%
$0	$20,000	251	274	288	298	307	318	201	228	245	259	270	285	210	237	256	270	281	297
$20,000	$30,000	395	430	453	470	483	502	297	337	363	383	399	421	303	343	369	390	406	429
$30,000	$40,000	472	515	542	562	578	601	347	393	424	447	465	492	351	397	427	450	469	496
$40,000	$50,000	539	589	620	643	662	687	389	441	475	501	522	552	391	442	476	502	523	553
$50,000	$60,000	600	655	690	716	737	765	427	484	521	550	573	605	426	482	519	548	571	603
$60,000	$70,000	656	716	754	782	805	836	460	522	563	593	618	653	458	518	558	588	613	647
$70,000	$80,000	707	772	814	844	869	902	491	557	601	633	660	697	487	551	593	625	652	688
$80,000	$90,000	755	825	869	902	928	964	520	590	636	670	699	738	514	582	626	660	688	726
$90,000	$100,000	801	875	922	957	985	1023	547	621	669	705	735	777	539	610	656	692	721	761
$100,000	$120,000	862	942	993	1030	1060	1101	583	661	712	751	783	827	572	647	697	734	765	808
$120,000	$140,000	942	1030	1085	1126	1159	1204	629	714	769	811	846	893	615	696	749	789	822	868
$140,000	$160,000	1018	1112	1172	1217	1252	1301	672	762	821	867	903	954	655	740	797	840	875	924
$160,000	$180,000	1087	1189	1253	1300	1339	1391	711	807	870	917	956	1010	691	781	840	886	923	975
$180,000	$200,000	1154	1262	1330	1380	1421	1476	748	849	915	965	1006	1063	725	819	882	929	968	1022
$200,000	$225,000	1223	1338	1410	1464	1507	1566	787	893	962	1015	1058	1118	760	859	924	974	1015	1072
$225,000	$250,000	1298	1420	1497	1554	1600	1662	828	940	1013	1068	1114	1177	797	901	970	1022	1065	1124
$250,000	$275,000	1369	1498	1579	1639	1688	1754	867	984	1060	1118	1166	1232	832	941	1013	1067	1112	1174
$275,000	$300,000	1438	1572	1658	1721	1772	1841	904	1026	1105	1166	1216	1285	866	979	1053	1110	1156	1221
$300,000	or more	1847	2022	2132	2214	2280	2369	1120	1271	1371	1446	1508	1593	1060	1198	1289	1358	1415	1494

Income																			
		Maryland			4		6.0000%	**Massachusetts**			4		6.2500%	**Michigan**			4		6.0000%
$0	$20,000	245	284	310	330	347	370	241	271	291	306	319	336	253	287	309	326	339	359
$20,000	$30,000	355	411	448	477	501	535	349	393	422	443	461	486	374	424	457	482	502	531
$30,000	$40,000	411	475	518	552	579	618	404	455	488	513	533	562	436	495	533	562	586	619
$40,000	$50,000	459	530	578	615	646	689	451	507	544	572	595	626	489	555	598	631	658	695
$50,000	$60,000	500	578	630	671	704	751	492	553	594	624	649	683	537	609	656	692	721	762
$60,000	$70,000	538	621	677	720	756	807	529	595	638	671	697	734	579	657	708	747	778	822
$70,000	$80,000	572	660	720	766	804	858	563	633	678	713	742	781	618	701	755	797	831	878
$80,000	$90,000	604	697	759	808	848	905	594	668	716	753	783	824	654	742	800	843	879	929
$90,000	$100,000	633	731	796	847	890	949	623	700	751	789	821	864	688	780	841	887	925	977
$100,000	$120,000	672	776	845	899	944	1007	661	744	797	838	871	917	733	831	896	945	985	1041
$120,000	$140,000	723	834	909	966	1015	1082	711	799	857	901	937	986	791	897	967	1020	1064	1124
$140,000	$160,000	769	887	967	1028	1079	1151	757	851	912	959	997	1049	845	958	1033	1090	1136	1200
$160,000	$180,000	812	936	1020	1085	1139	1214	799	898	963	1012	1052	1107	895	1015	1093	1154	1203	1271
$180,000	$200,000	852	982	1070	1138	1195	1274	839	942	1010	1062	1104	1162	941	1068	1150	1214	1266	1337
$200,000	$225,000	893	1030	1122	1194	1253	1336	879	988	1059	1113	1157	1218	990	1123	1210	1276	1331	1406
$225,000	$250,000	938	1081	1178	1252	1314	1401	923	1037	1112	1168	1215	1279	1042	1181	1273	1343	1400	1480
$250,000	$275,000	979	1129	1229	1307	1372	1463	964	1083	1161	1220	1268	1335	1090	1237	1333	1406	1466	1549
$275,000	$300,000	1018	1174	1279	1360	1427	1521	1003	1127	1207	1269	1319	1389	1137	1289	1389	1466	1528	1615
$300,000	or more	1248	1438	1566	1665	1747	1862	1229	1381	1480	1555	1616	1701	1409	1598	1722	1817	1894	2002

Income																			
		Minnesota			1		6.8750%	**Mississippi**			2		7.0000%	**Missouri**			2		4.2250%
$0	$20,000	259	283	298	309	318	330	462	556	620	671	713	772	195	226	246	262	275	293
$20,000	$30,000	402	439	462	480	493	512	650	782	872	943	1002	1086	287	332	362	385	404	431
$30,000	$40,000	479	523	551	571	588	610	743	894	998	1079	1146	1242	334	386	421	448	470	501
$40,000	$50,000	546	597	628	652	670	696	821	988	1103	1192	1267	1373	374	432	471	502	527	562
$50,000	$60,000	607	663	698	724	745	773	890	1071	1195	1292	1373	1488	409	473	516	549	577	615
$60,000	$70,000	662	723	761	790	813	843	951	1145	1277	1381	1468	1590	441	510	556	592	622	663
$70,000	$80,000	713	779	821	851	876	909	1006	1211	1352	1462	1553	1683	470	544	593	631	663	706
$80,000	$90,000	762	832	876	909	935	970	1057	1273	1420	1536	1632	1768	497	575	627	668	701	747
$90,000	$100,000	807	881	928	963	991	1028	1105	1330	1484	1605	1706	1848	523	604	659	701	736	785
$100,000	$120,000	868	948	998	1036	1065	1106	1167	1405	1568	1696	1802	1953	556	643	701	746	784	835
$120,000	$140,000	948	1035	1090	1131	1164	1208	1247	1502	1676	1812	1926	2087	600	693	756	805	845	901
$140,000	$160,000	1023	1117	1177	1221	1256	1304	1321	1591	1775	1919	2040	2211	640	740	807	859	901	961
$160,000	$180,000	1092	1193	1257	1304	1341	1392	1388	1671	1865	2017	2144	2323	677	782	853	908	953	1016
$180,000	$200,000	1159	1266	1333	1383	1423	1477	1451	1747	1950	2109	2241	2428	711	823	897	955	1002	1068
$200,000	$225,000	1228	1342	1413	1466	1508	1566	1515	1825	2037	2203	2341	2537	747	864	942	1003	1053	1122
$225,000	$250,000	1303	1424	1499	1555	1600	1661	1584	1908	2129	2303	2448	2652	786	909	991	1054	1107	1180
$250,000	$275,000	1374	1501	1581	1640	1688	1752	1648	1985	2216	2396	2547	2760	822	950	1036	1103	1158	1234
$275,000	$300,000	1442	1576	1660	1722	1771	1839	1709	2059	2298	2485	2641	2862	856	990	1080	1149	1206	1286
$300,000	or more	1852	2024	2132	2212	2276	2363	2060	2482	2770	2996	3185	3451	1057	1223	1333	1419	1489	1588

Income		Family Size						Family Size						Family Size					
At least	But less than	1	2	3	4	5	Over 5	1	2	3	4	5	Over 5	1	2	3	4	5	Over 5
		Nebraska			1		5.5000%	Nevada			5		6.8500%	New Jersey			4		6.6250%
$0	$20,000	256	291	314	332	346	366	295	334	360	380	396	418	246	264	276	285	292	301
$20,000	$30,000	376	428	462	488	509	538	433	491	529	558	581	614	388	418	437	451	462	477
$30,000	$40,000	438	499	538	569	593	627	504	572	616	649	677	715	465	501	524	540	554	572
$40,000	$50,000	490	559	603	637	665	703	565	640	690	727	758	801	532	574	600	619	634	655
$50,000	$60,000	537	612	661	698	729	771	619	701	755	796	830	877	593	640	669	690	708	731
$60,000	$70,000	579	660	713	753	786	831	667	756	814	858	895	945	649	700	732	756	774	800
$70,000	$80,000	617	704	760	803	838	887	711	806	868	915	954	1007	701	756	791	816	836	864
$80,000	$90,000	653	745	805	850	887	938	752	852	918	968	1009	1065	750	809	846	873	895	924
$90,000	$100,000	686	783	846	894	933	986	790	895	964	1017	1060	1120	796	859	898	927	950	981
$100,000	$120,000	730	833	901	951	993	1051	841	953	1026	1082	1128	1191	858	926	968	999	1024	1058
$120,000	$140,000	788	899	971	1027	1071	1133	907	1027	1106	1167	1216	1284	939	1013	1060	1094	1122	1159
$140,000	$160,000	841	960	1037	1096	1144	1210	967	1096	1180	1245	1298	1371	1015	1096	1146	1183	1213	1253
$160,000	$180,000	890	1016	1098	1160	1211	1281	1023	1159	1249	1317	1372	1450	1086	1173	1227	1267	1298	1341
$180,000	$200,000	936	1068	1155	1220	1274	1348	1076	1219	1313	1384	1443	1524	1154	1246	1303	1346	1380	1425
$200,000	$225,000	983	1123	1214	1283	1339	1417	1130	1280	1379	1454	1516	1601	1225	1323	1384	1429	1465	1513
$225,000	$250,000	1034	1181	1277	1349	1409	1491	1188	1346	1450	1529	1594	1684	1302	1406	1471	1519	1557	1608
$250,000	$275,000	1082	1236	1336	1412	1474	1560	1243	1408	1517	1599	1667	1761	1374	1484	1553	1604	1644	1699
$275,000	$300,000	1128	1288	1393	1472	1537	1626	1295	1467	1580	1666	1737	1835	1444	1560	1632	1685	1728	1786
$300,000	or more	1396	1595	1725	1823	1904	2015	1599	1812	1952	2058	2145	2266	1866	2016	2110	2179	2235	2309
Income		New Mexico			1		5.1250%	New York			2		4.0000%	North Carolina			2		4.7500%
$0	$20,000	260	285	301	313	322	335	151	156	159	162	164	166	248	290	319	341	359	385
$20,000	$30,000	400	438	462	480	495	514	243	252	257	261	264	268	358	419	460	492	519	556
$30,000	$40,000	474	519	548	569	586	610	294	305	311	315	319	323	414	485	532	569	600	643
$40,000	$50,000	538	590	622	647	666	693	340	351	358	363	367	373	461	540	593	635	669	717
$50,000	$60,000	595	653	689	716	738	767	381	394	402	407	412	418	503	589	647	692	729	782
$60,000	$70,000	648	710	750	779	803	834	419	433	441	448	453	459	541	633	695	744	784	840
$70,000	$80,000	696	764	806	837	863	897	454	469	479	485	491	498	575	673	739	791	833	893
$80,000	$90,000	742	813	858	892	919	955	487	504	514	521	527	534	606	710	780	834	879	942
$90,000	$100,000	784	860	908	943	972	1010	519	537	547	555	561	569	636	745	818	875	922	988
$100,000	$120,000	841	923	974	1012	1043	1084	562	581	592	600	607	615	675	790	868	928	978	1048
$120,000	$140,000	916	1005	1060	1102	1135	1180	618	639	651	660	667	677	725	849	933	997	1051	1126
$140,000	$160,000	986	1081	1141	1186	1222	1270	671	694	707	717	725	735	772	903	992	1061	1118	1198
$160,000	$180,000	1050	1152	1216	1264	1302	1354	721	745	760	770	778	789	814	953	1047	1120	1180	1264
$180,000	$200,000	1112	1219	1287	1338	1378	1433	769	794	810	821	830	841	854	1000	1098	1175	1238	1326
$200,000	$225,000	1176	1290	1361	1415	1457	1515	819	846	862	874	884	896	895	1048	1151	1231	1298	1391
$225,000	$250,000	1245	1365	1441	1498	1543	1604	873	902	919	932	942	955	939	1100	1208	1292	1361	1459
$250,000	$275,000	1310	1437	1517	1576	1624	1688	925	955	974	987	998	1012	981	1148	1261	1349	1421	1523
$275,000	$300,000	1372	1505	1589	1651	1701	1769	975	1007	1026	1040	1051	1066	1020	1194	1311	1402	1478	1584
$300,000	or more	1746	1915	2022	2101	2164	2251	1279	1321	1346	1364	1378	1397	1248	1461	1605	1716	1809	1938
Income		North Dakota			1		5.0000%	Ohio			1		5.7500%	Oklahoma			1		4.5000%
$0	$20,000	216	249	271	288	303	323	246	271	287	299	309	322	281	336	374	404	430	465
$20,000	$30,000	314	362	395	420	440	469	379	418	443	462	477	497	399	477	531	573	609	659
$30,000	$40,000	364	420	458	486	510	544	450	496	526	548	566	591	458	548	609	658	699	756
$40,000	$50,000	407	469	511	543	570	607	511	564	598	623	644	672	508	607	675	729	774	838
$50,000	$60,000	445	513	558	594	623	664	566	625	663	691	714	745	552	659	733	792	840	910
$60,000	$70,000	479	552	601	638	670	714	616	681	722	752	777	811	591	706	785	847	900	973
$70,000	$80,000	510	587	639	680	713	760	663	732	776	809	836	872	627	748	832	898	953	1032
$80,000	$90,000	538	620	675	718	753	802	706	780	827	862	891	929	659	787	876	945	1003	1085
$90,000	$100,000	565	651	709	753	790	842	747	825	875	912	942	983	690	824	916	988	1049	1135
$100,000	$120,000	600	692	753	800	840	894	801	885	939	979	1011	1055	730	872	969	1046	1110	1201
$120,000	$140,000	646	744	810	861	903	962	872	964	1022	1066	1102	1150	782	934	1038	1120	1188	1285
$140,000	$160,000	689	793	863	917	962	1025	939	1038	1101	1148	1186	1238	830	990	1101	1188	1260	1363
$160,000	$180,000	727	838	912	969	1016	1083	1000	1106	1173	1223	1264	1319	874	1042	1158	1250	1326	1434
$180,000	$200,000	764	880	957	1017	1067	1137	1059	1171	1242	1295	1338	1397	915	1091	1212	1308	1388	1501
$200,000	$225,000	802	923	1004	1068	1120	1193	1120	1238	1314	1370	1416	1478	957	1141	1268	1368	1451	1569
$225,000	$250,000	842	969	1055	1121	1176	1253	1185	1311	1391	1451	1499	1565	1002	1195	1327	1431	1519	1642
$250,000	$275,000	880	1013	1102	1171	1228	1309	1247	1379	1464	1527	1578	1647	1044	1245	1383	1491	1582	1711
$275,000	$300,000	916	1054	1147	1219	1278	1362	1306	1445	1534	1600	1653	1726	1084	1292	1435	1548	1642	1775
$300,000	or more	1126	1295	1409	1498	1571	1673	1661	1838	1951	2035	2104	2197	1315	1566	1739	1875	1989	2150
Income		Pennsylvania			1		6.0000%	Rhode Island			4		7.0000%	South Carolina			2		6.0000%
$0	$20,000	211	229	241	249	255	265	293	335	362	382	399	422	274	314	340	359	375	398
$20,000	$30,000	329	358	375	389	399	413	419	479	518	548	572	605	396	453	491	519	543	575
$30,000	$40,000	393	426	448	463	476	493	483	552	597	631	659	697	457	524	567	600	627	665
$40,000	$50,000	448	486	511	529	543	563	537	613	663	701	732	775	510	584	632	669	699	741
$50,000	$60,000	497	540	568	588	604	626	584	667	722	763	797	844	556	637	690	730	763	809
$60,000	$70,000	542	590	619	641	659	683	626	716	774	818	855	905	597	684	741	784	820	869
$70,000	$80,000	584	635	667	691	710	736	665	760	822	869	908	961	635	727	788	834	872	924
$80,000	$90,000	624	678	713	738	758	786	700	800	866	915	956	1012	670	767	831	880	920	975
$90,000	$100,000	661	719	755	782	804	833	733	838	907	959	1002	1060	702	804	871	923	964	1022
$100,000	$120,000	710	773	812	841	864	896	777	888	961	1016	1061	1124	745	854	925	979	1024	1085
$120,000	$140,000	776	844	887	919	944	979	834	953	1031	1090	1139	1206	800	917	994	1052	1100	1166
$140,000	$160,000	837	910	957	991	1019	1056	886	1012	1095	1158	1210	1281	852	976	1058	1120	1171	1241
$160,000	$180,000	893	972	1022	1058	1088	1128	933	1067	1154	1220	1275	1350	898	1030	1116	1182	1235	1310
$180,000	$200,000	947	1031	1083	1123	1154	1196	978	1118	1209	1279	1336	1415	943	1080	1171	1240	1296	1374
$200,000	$225,000	1003	1092	1148	1190	1223	1268	1024	1170	1266	1339	1399	1482	988	1133	1228	1300	1359	1441
$225,000	$250,000	1064	1158	1218	1262	1297	1345	1073	1226	1327	1404	1466	1553	1037	1189	1288	1364	1426	1512
$250,000	$275,000	1121	1221	1284	1330	1368	1418	1118	1279	1384	1464	1529	1619	1082	1241	1345	1424	1489	1578
$275,000	$300,000	1177	1281	1347	1396	1435	1488	1162	1329	1438	1521	1589	1683	1125	1290	1399	1481	1548	1642
$300,000	or more	1508	1643	1728	1791	1841	1910	1415	1618	1751	1853	1935	2050	1377	1580	1712	1814	1896	2011

Income At least	Income But less than	South Dakota 1 (4.5000%) Family Size 1	2	3	4	5	Over 5
$0	$20,000	291	338	370	394	414	442
$20,000	$30,000	430	501	548	584	614	655
$30,000	$40,000	501	584	640	682	717	766
$40,000	$50,000	563	656	718	766	805	860
$50,000	$60,000	617	720	788	840	883	944
$60,000	$70,000	666	777	851	907	954	1019
$70,000	$80,000	711	830	908	969	1019	1088
$80,000	$90,000	753	878	962	1026	1079	1152
$90,000	$100,000	792	924	1012	1079	1135	1212
$100,000	$120,000	844	985	1078	1150	1210	1292
$120,000	$140,000	911	1063	1165	1243	1307	1396
$140,000	$160,000	973	1136	1245	1328	1397	1492
$160,000	$180,000	1031	1204	1318	1407	1479	1581
$180,000	$200,000	1085	1267	1388	1481	1557	1664
$200,000	$225,000	1141	1333	1460	1558	1638	1751
$225,000	$250,000	1201	1403	1537	1640	1725	1843
$250,000	$275,000	1257	1469	1609	1717	1806	1930
$275,000	$300,000	1311	1532	1678	1791	1884	2013
$300,000	or more	1628	1902	2085	2225	2341	2502

Income At least	Income But less than	Tennessee 2 (7.0000%) Family Size 1	2	3	4	5	Over 5
$0	$20,000	389	458	504	540	570	612
$20,000	$30,000	561	660	727	780	823	884
$30,000	$40,000	649	763	841	901	951	1021
$40,000	$50,000	723	850	936	1004	1059	1137
$50,000	$60,000	788	927	1021	1094	1155	1240
$60,000	$70,000	846	996	1097	1175	1240	1332
$70,000	$80,000	900	1058	1166	1249	1318	1416
$80,000	$90,000	949	1116	1229	1317	1390	1493
$90,000	$100,000	995	1170	1289	1381	1458	1565
$100,000	$120,000	1056	1242	1368	1465	1547	1661
$120,000	$140,000	1134	1334	1469	1574	1661	1784
$140,000	$160,000	1206	1419	1563	1674	1767	1897
$160,000	$180,000	1273	1497	1648	1766	1864	2002
$180,000	$200,000	1335	1570	1729	1852	1955	2099
$200,000	$225,000	1399	1646	1812	1942	2049	2200
$225,000	$250,000	1468	1726	1901	2037	2149	2308
$250,000	$275,000	1532	1802	1984	2126	2243	2409
$275,000	$300,000	1593	1873	2063	2210	2333	2505
$300,000	or more	1948	2291	2523	2703	2852	3063

Income At least	Income But less than	Texas 1 (6.2500%) Family Size 1	2	3	4	5	Over 5
$0	$20,000	268	301	321	337	349	367
$20,000	$30,000	410	460	492	516	535	562
$30,000	$40,000	486	545	582	611	634	666
$40,000	$50,000	551	618	661	693	720	756
$50,000	$60,000	609	684	732	768	797	837
$60,000	$70,000	663	744	796	835	867	910
$70,000	$80,000	712	799	855	897	931	978
$80,000	$90,000	758	851	911	956	992	1042
$90,000	$100,000	801	900	963	1010	1049	1102
$100,000	$120,000	859	965	1033	1084	1125	1182
$120,000	$140,000	935	1050	1124	1180	1225	1287
$140,000	$160,000	1006	1130	1210	1270	1318	1385
$160,000	$180,000	1071	1204	1289	1353	1405	1476
$180,000	$200,000	1134	1274	1364	1432	1487	1562
$200,000	$225,000	1199	1347	1442	1514	1572	1652
$225,000	$250,000	1269	1426	1527	1603	1664	1749
$250,000	$275,000	1335	1500	1607	1687	1752	1841
$275,000	$300,000	1398	1572	1683	1767	1835	1929
$300,000	or more	1777	1999	2141	2248	2335	2454

Income At least	Income But less than	Utah 2 (4.8500%) Family Size 1	2	3	4	5	Over 5
$0	$20,000	271	318	349	373	394	422
$20,000	$30,000	393	460	506	541	570	611
$30,000	$40,000	454	532	585	626	660	707
$40,000	$50,000	507	594	652	698	736	788
$50,000	$60,000	553	648	712	762	803	860
$60,000	$70,000	594	696	765	818	863	925
$70,000	$80,000	632	741	814	871	918	983
$80,000	$90,000	667	782	859	919	968	1038
$90,000	$100,000	700	820	901	964	1016	1089
$100,000	$120,000	743	870	956	1023	1078	1156
$120,000	$140,000	798	936	1028	1100	1159	1242
$140,000	$160,000	850	996	1094	1171	1234	1322
$160,000	$180,000	897	1051	1155	1235	1302	1396
$180,000	$200,000	941	1103	1212	1296	1366	1464
$200,000	$225,000	987	1157	1271	1359	1433	1536
$225,000	$250,000	1036	1214	1334	1427	1504	1612
$250,000	$275,000	1082	1267	1393	1490	1570	1683
$275,000	$300,000	1125	1318	1449	1550	1633	1751
$300,000	or more	1379	1615	1775	1899	2001	2145

Income At least	Income But less than	Vermont 1 (6.0000%) Family Size 1	2	3	4	5	Over 5
$0	$20,000	203	222	234	243	250	260
$20,000	$30,000	290	318	335	348	359	373
$30,000	$40,000	334	366	387	401	413	430
$40,000	$50,000	372	407	430	446	460	478
$50,000	$60,000	405	443	468	486	500	520
$60,000	$70,000	434	476	502	521	537	558
$70,000	$80,000	461	505	533	553	570	592
$80,000	$90,000	486	532	561	583	601	624
$90,000	$100,000	509	557	588	611	629	654
$100,000	$120,000	539	591	623	648	667	693
$120,000	$140,000	579	634	669	695	716	744
$140,000	$160,000	615	674	711	738	760	790
$160,000	$180,000	648	710	749	778	801	833
$180,000	$200,000	679	744	785	815	840	873
$200,000	$225,000	711	779	822	854	880	914
$225,000	$250,000	745	817	862	895	922	958
$250,000	$275,000	777	852	899	934	962	1000
$275,000	$300,000	808	885	934	970	999	1039
$300,000	or more	984	1079	1138	1183	1218	1266

Income At least	Income But less than	Virginia 2 (4.3000%) Family Size 1	2	3	4	5	Over 5
$0	$20,000	199	232	254	271	285	305
$20,000	$30,000	290	338	371	396	416	446
$30,000	$40,000	337	393	430	459	483	517
$40,000	$50,000	377	439	481	513	540	578
$50,000	$60,000	412	480	526	561	591	632
$60,000	$70,000	444	517	566	604	636	680
$70,000	$80,000	472	550	603	644	677	725
$80,000	$90,000	499	582	637	680	716	766
$90,000	$100,000	524	611	669	714	751	804
$100,000	$120,000	557	649	711	759	799	855
$120,000	$140,000	600	699	766	817	860	920
$140,000	$160,000	640	745	816	871	917	981
$160,000	$180,000	676	787	862	921	969	1036
$180,000	$200,000	710	827	906	967	1018	1089
$200,000	$225,000	746	868	951	1015	1068	1143
$225,000	$250,000	783	912	999	1066	1122	1200
$250,000	$275,000	819	954	1044	1115	1173	1255
$275,000	$300,000	853	993	1087	1160	1221	1306
$300,000	or more	1050	1222	1338	1428	1503	1608

Income At least	Income But less than	Washington 1 (6.5000%) Family Size 1	2	3	4	5	Over 5
$0	$20,000	281	313	334	349	362	379
$20,000	$30,000	433	483	515	540	559	586
$30,000	$40,000	514	573	612	641	664	697
$40,000	$50,000	584	652	696	729	756	792
$50,000	$60,000	647	723	771	808	838	879
$60,000	$70,000	704	787	840	880	912	957
$70,000	$80,000	757	846	903	946	981	1029
$80,000	$90,000	806	901	962	1008	1046	1097
$90,000	$100,000	853	953	1018	1067	1106	1161
$100,000	$120,000	915	1023	1093	1145	1188	1246
$120,000	$140,000	996	1114	1190	1247	1294	1357
$140,000	$160,000	1072	1199	1281	1343	1393	1462
$160,000	$180,000	1143	1278	1366	1431	1485	1558
$180,000	$200,000	1210	1353	1446	1515	1572	1650
$200,000	$225,000	1279	1431	1529	1603	1663	1745
$225,000	$250,000	1354	1515	1619	1698	1761	1848
$250,000	$275,000	1425	1595	1704	1787	1854	1946
$275,000	$300,000	1493	1671	1786	1872	1942	2039
$300,000	or more	1898	2125	2272	2383	2473	2596

Income At least	Income But less than	West Virginia 1 (6.0000%) Family Size 1	2	3	4	5	Over 5
$0	$20,000	250	278	297	310	321	337
$20,000	$30,000	391	437	466	487	505	529
$30,000	$40,000	468	522	557	583	604	633
$40,000	$50,000	535	598	637	667	692	725
$50,000	$60,000	596	666	710	744	771	808
$60,000	$70,000	652	728	777	813	843	883
$70,000	$80,000	703	786	839	878	910	954
$80,000	$90,000	752	840	897	939	973	1020
$90,000	$100,000	798	892	952	997	1033	1083
$100,000	$120,000	859	961	1025	1074	1113	1167
$120,000	$140,000	941	1052	1123	1176	1219	1278
$140,000	$160,000	1017	1137	1214	1272	1318	1382
$160,000	$180,000	1088	1217	1299	1361	1411	1479
$180,000	$200,000	1156	1292	1380	1446	1499	1572
$200,000	$225,000	1227	1372	1465	1535	1592	1669
$225,000	$250,000	1303	1458	1557	1631	1692	1774
$250,000	$275,000	1376	1540	1644	1723	1787	1874
$275,000	$300,000	1446	1618	1728	1811	1878	1969
$300,000	or more	1870	2093	2236	2343	2430	2549

Income At least	Income But less than	Wisconsin 1 (5.0000%) Family Size 1	2	3	4	5	Over 5
$0	$20,000	218	243	260	272	281	295
$20,000	$30,000	334	372	397	416	431	451
$30,000	$40,000	395	441	470	492	510	534
$40,000	$50,000	448	500	533	559	579	607
$50,000	$60,000	495	553	590	618	641	672
$60,000	$70,000	538	602	642	672	697	730
$70,000	$80,000	578	646	690	722	749	785
$80,000	$90,000	616	688	734	769	797	836
$90,000	$100,000	651	727	776	813	843	884
$100,000	$120,000	698	780	833	872	904	948
$120,000	$140,000	759	849	906	949	984	1032
$140,000	$160,000	817	913	975	1021	1059	1110
$160,000	$180,000	870	973	1038	1088	1128	1183
$180,000	$200,000	920	1029	1099	1151	1193	1251
$200,000	$225,000	973	1088	1162	1217	1262	1323
$225,000	$250,000	1030	1152	1230	1288	1336	1401
$250,000	$275,000	1083	1212	1294	1356	1406	1474
$275,000	$300,000	1134	1269	1355	1420	1472	1544
$300,000	or more	1441	1612	1722	1805	1872	1963

Income At least	Income But less than	Wyoming 1 (4.0000%) Family Size 1	2	3	4	5	Over 5
$0	$20,000	181	197	207	215	221	229
$20,000	$30,000	273	298	313	324	334	346
$30,000	$40,000	321	350	368	382	393	407
$40,000	$50,000	363	395	416	431	444	460
$50,000	$60,000	400	436	459	475	489	507
$60,000	$70,000	433	472	497	515	530	550
$70,000	$80,000	464	506	532	552	568	589
$80,000	$90,000	493	537	565	586	603	626
$90,000	$100,000	520	567	596	618	636	660
$100,000	$120,000	555	606	637	661	680	705
$120,000	$140,000	602	657	691	717	737	765
$140,000	$160,000	645	704	741	768	790	820
$160,000	$180,000	686	748	787	816	839	871
$180,000	$200,000	723	789	830	861	886	919
$200,000	$225,000	763	832	876	908	934	970
$225,000	$250,000	805	878	924	959	986	1023
$250,000	$275,000	845	922	970	1006	1035	1074
$275,000	$300,000	883	963	1014	1051	1082	1123
$300,000	or more	1107	1209	1272	1320	1358	1409

Note: Residents of **Alaska** do not have a state sales tax, but should follow the instructions on the next page to determine their local sales tax amount.

1. Use the Ratio Method to determine your local sales tax deduction. Your state sales tax rate is provided next to the state name.
2. Follow the instructions on the next page to determine your local sales tax deduction.
3. The California table includes the 1.25% uniform local sales tax rate in addition to the 6.00% state sales tax rate for a total of 7.25%. Some California localities impose a larger local sales tax. Taxpayers who reside in those jurisdictions should use the Ratio Method to determine their local sales tax deduction. The denominator of the correct ratio is 7.25%, and the numerator is the total sales tax rate minus 7.25%.
4. This state does not have a local general sales tax, so the amount in the state table is the only amount to be deducted.
5. The Nevada table includes the 2.25% uniform local sales tax rate in addition to the 4.60% state sales tax rate for a total of 6.85%. Some Nevada localities impose a larger local sales tax. Taxpayers who reside in those jurisdictions should use the Ratio Method to determine their local sales tax deduction. The denominator of the correct ratio is 6.85%, and the numerator is the total sales tax rate minus 6.85%.
6. The 4.0% rate for Hawaii is actually an excise tax but is treated as a sales tax for purpose of this deduction.

Which Optional Local Sales Tax Table Should I Use?

IF you live in the state of...	AND you live in...	THEN use Local Table...
Alaska	Juneau, Kenai, Ketchikan, Kodiak, Sitka, Wasilla or any locality that imposes a local sales tax	C
Arizona	Mesa, Phoenix, Tucson	A
	Chandler, Gilbert, Glendale, Peoria, Scottsdale, Tempe, Yuma or any other locality that imposes a local sales tax	B
Arkansas	Any locality that imposes a local sales tax	C
Colorado	Adams County, Arapahoe County, Aurora, Boulder County, Centennial, Colorado Springs, Denver City, El Paso County, Larimer County, Pueblo City, Pueblo County or any other locality that imposes a local sales tax	A
	Arvada, Boulder, Fort Collins, Greeley, Jefferson County, Lakewood, Longmont, Thornton or Westminster	B
Georgia	Dekalb County (excluding Atlanta)	B
	Any locality that imposes a local sales tax	C
Illinois	Arlington Heights, Bloomington, Champaign, Chicago, Cicero, Decatur, Evanston, Palatine, Peoria, Schaumburg, Skokie, Springfield or any other locality that imposes a local sales tax	A
	Aurora, Elgin, Joliet, Waukegan	B
Louisiana	East Baton Rouge Parish, Jefferson Parish	B
	Ascension Parish, Bossier Parish, Caddo Parish, Calcasieu Parish, Iberia Parish, Lafayette Parish, Lafourche Parish, Livingston Parish, Orleans Parish, Ouachita Parish, Rapides Parish, St. Bernard Parish, St. Landry Parish, St Tammany Parish, Tangipahoa Parish, Terrebonne Parish or any other locality that imposes a local sales tax	C
Mississippi	City of Jackson only	A
	City of Tupelo only	C
Missouri	Any locality that imposes a local sales tax	C
New York	Counties: Chautauqua, Chenango, Columbia, Delaware, Greene, Hamilton, Tioga Cities: New York, Norwich (Chenango County)	A
	Counties: Albany, Allegany, Broome, Cattaraugus, Cayuga, Chemung, Clinton, Cortland, Dutchess, Erie, Essex, Franklin, Fulton, Genesee, Herkimer, Jefferson, Lewis, Livingston, Madison, Monroe, Montgomery, Nassau, Niagara, Oneida, Onondaga, Ontario, Orange, Orleans, Oswego, Otsego, Putnam, Rensselaer, Rockland, St. Lawrence, Saratoga, Schenectady, Schoharie, Schuyler, Seneca, Steuben, Suffolk, Sullivan, Tompkins, Ulster, Warren, Washington, Wayne, Westchester, Wyoming or Yate Cities: Auburn, Glens Falls, Gloversville, Ithaca, Johnstown, Mount Vernon, New Rochelle, Olean, Oneida (Madison County), Oswego, Rome, Salamanca, Saratoga Springs, Utica, White Plains, Yonkers	B
	Any other locality that imposes a local sales tax	D*
North Carolina	Any locality that imposes a local sales tax	A
South Carolina	Aiken County, Anderson County, Greenwood County, Horry County, Lexington County, Myrtle Beach, Newberry County, Orangeburg County, Spartanburg County and York County	A
	Allendale County, Bamberg County, Barnwell County, Calhoun County, Charleston County, Cherokee County, Chester County, Chesterfield County, Colleton County, Darlington County, Dillon County, Edgefield County, Florence County, Hampton County, Jasper County, Kershaw County, Lancaster County, Laurens County, Lee County, Marion County, Marlboro County, McCormick County, Saluda County, Sumter County and Williamsburg County	B
	Abbeville County, Beaufort County, Berkeley County, Clarendon County, Dorchester County, Fairfield County, Pickens County, Richland County, Union County or any other locality that imposes a local sales tax	C
Tennessee	Any locality that imposes a local sales tax	C
Utah	Any locality that imposes a local sales tax	A
Virginia	Any locality that imposes a local sales tax	B

*** Note: Local Table D is just 25% of the NY State table.**

2021 Optional Local Sales Tax Tables

Income		Family Size						Family Size					
		1	2	3	4	5	Over 5	1	2	3	4	5	Over 5
At least	But less than	Local Table A						Local Table B					
$0	$20,000	42	45	48	49	50	52	53	61	65	69	72	76
20,000	30,000	64	69	72	75	76	79	78	89	96	101	106	112
30,000	40,000	75	81	85	88	90	93	90	103	111	118	123	130
40,000	50,000	85	92	96	99	102	105	101	115	125	132	138	146
50,000	60,000	94	101	106	110	113	116	111	126	136	144	151	159
60,000	70,000	102	110	115	119	122	126	119	136	147	155	162	172
70,000	80,000	109	118	123	128	131	135	127	145	157	165	173	183
80,000	90,000	116	125	131	136	139	144	134	153	165	175	183	193
90,000	100,000	122	132	138	143	147	152	141	161	174	184	192	203
100,000	120,000	131	141	148	153	157	162	150	171	185	195	204	216
120,000	140,000	142	154	161	166	170	176	161	184	199	211	220	233
140,000	160,000	152	165	173	178	183	189	172	196	212	225	234	248
160,000	180,000	162	175	183	189	194	201	182	208	225	237	248	262
180,000	200,000	171	185	194	200	205	212	191	218	236	249	260	276
200,000	225,000	180	195	204	211	217	224	201	229	248	262	274	290
225,000	250,000	190	206	216	223	229	237	211	241	260	275	288	304
250,000	275,000	200	216	227	234	240	248	221	252	272	288	301	318
275,000	300,000	209	226	237	245	251	260	230	262	284	300	313	331
300,000	or more	263	285	298	308	316	327	283	323	350	370	386	409

Income		Family Size						Family Size					
		1	2	3	4	5	Over 5	1	2	3	4	5	Over 5
At least	But less than	Local Table C						Local Table D					
$0	$20,000	65	75	82	87	91	97	38	39	40	41	41	42
20,000	30,000	94	109	118	126	132	140	61	63	64	65	66	67
30,000	40,000	109	126	137	146	153	163	74	76	78	79	80	81
40,000	50,000	122	141	153	163	171	182	85	88	90	91	92	93
50,000	60,000	133	154	167	178	186	198	95	99	101	102	103	105
60,000	70,000	143	165	180	191	200	213	105	108	110	112	113	115
70,000	80,000	152	176	192	203	213	227	114	117	120	121	123	125
80,000	90,000	161	186	202	215	225	240	122	126	129	130	132	134
90,000	100,000	169	195	212	225	236	251	130	134	137	139	140	142
100,000	120,000	179	207	225	239	251	267	141	145	148	150	152	154
120,000	140,000	193	223	242	258	270	287	155	160	163	165	167	169
140,000	160,000	205	237	258	274	288	306	168	174	177	179	181	184
160,000	180,000	217	250	273	290	304	323	180	186	190	193	195	197
180,000	200,000	228	263	286	304	319	339	192	199	203	205	208	210
200,000	225,000	239	276	300	319	335	356	205	212	216	219	221	224
225,000	250,000	251	290	315	335	351	374	218	226	230	233	236	239
250,000	275,000	262	302	329	350	367	390	231	239	244	247	250	253
275,000	300,000	272	315	343	364	382	406	244	252	257	260	263	267
300,000	or more	334	386	421	447	469	499	320	330	337	341	345	349

Tax Formula for Corporations

Income *(from whatever source)*.	$ xxx,xxx
Less: Exclusions from gross income.	− xx,xxx
Gross Income.	$ xxx,xxx
Less: Deductions.	− xx,xxx
Taxable Income.	$ xxx,xxx
Applicable tax rates.	× xx%
Gross Tax.	$ xx,xxx
Less: Tax credits and prepayments.	− x,xxx
Tax Due *(or refund)*.	$ xx,xxx

Income Tax Rates—C Corporations, 2018 and After

For all taxable income levels, the tax rate is 21%.

Income Tax Rates—Estates and Trusts

Tax Year 2021

Taxable Income		The Tax Is:	
Over—	**But not Over—**		**Of the Amount Over—**
$ 0	$ 2,650	10%	$ 0
2,650	9,550	$ 265.00 + 24%	2,650
9,550	13,050	1,921.00 + 35%	9,550
13,050	....	3,146.00 + 37%	13,050

Tax Year 2022

Taxable Income		The Tax Is:	
Over—	**But not Over—**		**Of the Amount Over—**
$ 0	$ 2,750	10%	$ 0
2,750	9,850	$ 275.00 + 24%	2,750
9,850	13,450	1,979.00 + 35%	9,850
13,450	....	3,239.00 + 37%	13,450

Unified Transfer Tax Rates

For Gifts Made and for Deaths After 2012

If the Amount with Respect to Which the Tentative Tax to Be Computed Is:	The Tentative Tax Is:
Not over $10,000	18 percent of such amount.
Over $10,000 but not over $20,000	$1,800, plus 20 percent of the excess of such amount over $10,000.
Over $20,000 but not over $40,000	$3,800, plus 22 percent of the excess of such amount over $20,000.
Over $40,000 but not over $60,000	$8,200, plus 24 percent of the excess of such amount over $40,000.
Over $60,000 but not over $80,000	$13,000, plus 26 percent of the excess of such amount over $60,000.
Over $80,000 but not over $100,000	$18,200, plus 28 percent of the excess of such amount over $80,000.
Over $100,000 but not over $150,000	$23,800, plus 30 percent of the excess of such amount over $100,000.
Over $150,000 but not over $250,000	$38,800, plus 32 percent of the excess of such amount over $150,000.
Over $250,000 but not over $500,000	$70,800, plus 34 percent of the excess of such amount over $250,000.
Over $500,000 but not over $750,000	$155,800, plus 37 percent of the excess of such amount over $500,000.
Over $750,000 but not over $1,000,000	$248,300, plus 39 percent of the excess of such amount over $750,000.
Over $1,000,000	$345,800, plus 40 percent of the excess of such amount over $1,000,000.

Valuation Tables, Excerpts

Table S: Single Life Remainder Factors Interest Rate

AGE	4.2%	4.4%	4.6%	4.8%	5.0%	5.2%	5.4%	5.6%
0	.06083	.05483	.04959	.04501	.04101	.03749	.03441	.03170
1	.05668	.05049	.04507	.04034	.03618	.03254	.02934	.02652
2	.05858	.05222	.04665	.04178	.03750	.03373	.03042	.02750
3	.06072	.05420	.04848	.04346	.03904	.03516	.03173	.02871
4	.06303	.05634	.05046	.04530	.04075	.03674	.03319	.03006
5	.06547	.05861	.05258	.04726	.04258	.03844	.03478	.03153
6	.06805	.06102	.05482	.04935	.04453	.04026	.03647	.03312
7	.07074	.06353	.05717	.05155	.04658	.04217	.03826	.03479
8	.07356	.06617	.05964	.05386	.04875	.04421	.04017	.03658
9	.07651	.06895	.06225	.05631	.05105	.04637	.04220	.03849
10	.07960	.07185	.06499	.05889	.05347	.04865	.04435	.04052
11	.08283	.07490	.06786	.06160	.05603	.05106	.04663	.04267
12	.08620	.07808	.07087	.06444	.05871	.05360	.04903	.04494
13	.08967	.08137	.07397	.06738	.06149	.05623	.05152	.04729
14	.09321	.08472	.07715	.07038	.06433	.05892	.05406	.04971
15	.09680	.08812	.08036	.07342	.06721	.06164	.05664	.05214
16	.10041	.09154	.08360	.07649	.07011	.06438	.05923	.05459
17	.10409	.09502	.08689	.07960	.07305	.06716	.06185	.05707
18	.10782	.09855	.09024	.08276	.07604	.06998	.06452	.05959
19	.11164	.10217	.09366	.08600	.07910	.07288	.06726	.06218
20	.11559	.10592	.09721	.08937	.08228	.07589	.07010	.06487
21	.11965	.10977	.10087	.09283	.08557	.07900	.07305	.06765
22	.12383	.11376	.10465	.09642	.08897	.08223	.07610	.07055
23	.12817	.11789	.10859	.10016	.09252	.08559	.07930	.07358
24	.13270	.12221	.11270	.10408	.09625	.08914	.08267	.07678
25	.13744	.12674	.11703	.10821	.10019	.09289	.08625	.08018
26	.14239	.13149	.12158	.11256	.10435	.09686	.09003	.08380
27	.14758	.13647	.12636	.11714	.10873	.10106	.09405	.08764
28	.15300	.14169	.13137	.12195	.11335	.10549	.09829	.09171
29	.15864	.14712	.13660	.12698	.11819	.11013	.10275	.09598
30	.16448	.15275	.14203	.13222	.12323	.11498	.10742	.10047
31	.17053	.15861	.14769	.13768	.12849	.12006	.11230	.10517
32	.17680	.16468	.15357	.14336	.13398	.12535	.11741	.11009
33	.18330	.17099	.15968	.14927	.13970	.13088	.12275	.11525
34	.19000	.17750	.16599	.15539	.14562	.13661	.12829	.12061

continued

Valuation Tables, Excerpts

Table S: Single Life Remainder Factors Interest Rate

AGE	4.2%	4.4%	4.6%	4.8%	5.0%	5.2%	5.4%	5.6%
35	.19692	.18423	.17253	.16174	.15178	.14258	.13408	.12621
36	.20407	.19119	.17931	.16833	.15818	.14879	.14009	.13204
37	.21144	.19838	.18631	.17515	.16481	.15523	.14635	.13811
38	.21904	.20582	.19357	.18222	.17170	.16193	.15287	.14444
39	.22687	.21348	.20105	.18952	.17882	.16887	.15962	.15102
40	.23493	.22137	.20878	.19707	.18619	.17606	.16663	.15784
41	.24322	.22950	.21674	.20487	.19381	.18350	.17390	.16493
42	.25173	.23786	.22494	.21290	.20168	.19120	.18141	.17227
43	.26049	.24648	.23342	.22122	.20982	.19918	.18922	.17990
44	.26950	.25535	.24214	.22979	.21824	.20742	.19730	.18781
45	.27874	.26447	.25112	.23862	.22692	.21595	.20566	.19600
46	.28824	.27385	.26038	.24774	.23589	.22476	.21431	.20450
47	.29798	.28349	.26989	.25712	.24513	.23386	.22326	.21328
48	.30797	.29338	.27967	.26678	.25466	.24325	.23250	.22238
49	.31822	.30355	.28974	.27674	.26449	.25294	.24206	.23179
50	.32876	.31401	.30011	.28701	.27465	.26298	.25196	.24156
51	.33958	.32477	.31079	.29759	.28513	.27335	.26221	.25168
52	.35068	.33582	.32178	.30851	.29595	.28407	.27282	.26216
53	.36206	.34717	.33308	.31974	.30710	.29513	.28378	.27301
54	.37371	.35880	.34467	.33127	.31857	.30651	.29507	.28420
55	.38559	.37067	.35652	.34308	.33032	.31820	.30668	.29572
56	.39765	.38275	.36859	.35512	.34232	.33014	.31855	.30751
57	.40990	.39502	.38086	.36739	.35455	.34233	.33068	.31957
58	.42231	.40747	.39333	.37985	.36700	.35474	.34304	.33188
59	.43490	.42011	.40600	.39253	.37968	.36740	.35567	.34446
60	.44768	.43296	.41890	.40546	.39261	.38033	.36858	.35733
61	.46064	.44600	.43200	.41860	.40578	.39351	.38175	.37048
62	.47373	.45920	.44527	.43194	.41915	.40690	.39514	.38387
63	.48696	.47253	.45870	.44544	.43271	.42049	.40876	.39749
64	.50030	.48601	.47229	.45911	.44645	.43428	.42258	.41133
65	.51377	.49963	.48603	.47295	.46037	.44827	.43662	.42540
66	.52750	.51352	.50007	.48711	.47464	.46262	.45103	.43987
67	.54144	.52765	.51436	.50154	.48919	.47727	.46578	.45468
68	.55554	.54196	.52885	.51619	.50398	.49218	.48079	.46978
69	.56976	.55640	.54349	.53102	.51896	.50731	.49603	.48513

Valuation Tables, Excerpts

Table B: Term Certain Remainder Factors Interest Rate

YEARS	4.2%	4.4%	4.6%	4.8%	5.0%	5.2%	5.4%	5.6%
1	.959693	.957854	.956023	.954198	.952381	.950570	.948767	.946970
2	.921010	.917485	.913980	.910495	.907029	.903584	.900158	.896752
3	.883887	.878817	.873786	.868793	.863838	.858920	.854040	.849197
4	.848260	.841779	.835359	.829001	.822702	.816464	.810285	.804163
5	.814069	.806302	.798623	.791031	.783526	.776106	.768771	.761518
6	.781257	.772320	.763501	.754801	.746215	.737744	.729384	.721135
7	.749766	.739770	.729925	.720230	.710681	.701277	.692015	.682893
8	.719545	.708592	.697825	.687242	.676839	.666613	.656561	.646679
9	.690543	.678728	.667137	.655765	.644609	.633663	.622923	.612385
10	.662709	.650122	.637798	.625730	.613913	.602341	.591009	.579910
11	.635997	.622722	.609750	.597071	.584679	.572568	.560729	.549157
12	.610362	.596477	.582935	.569724	.556837	.544266	.532001	.520035
13	.585760	.571339	.557299	.543630	.530321	.517363	.504745	.492458
14	.562150	.547259	.532790	.518731	.505068	.491790	.478885	.466343
15	.539491	.524195	.509360	.494972	.481017	.467481	.454350	.441612
16	.517746	.502102	.486960	.472302	.458112	.444374	.431072	.418194
17	.496877	.480941	.465545	.450670	.436297	.422408	.408987	.396017
18	.476849	.460671	.445071	.430028	.415521	.401529	.388033	.375016
19	.457629	.441256	.425498	.410332	.395734	.381681	.368153	.355129
20	.439183	.422659	.406786	.391538	.376889	.362815	.349291	.336296
21	.421481	.404846	.388897	.373605	.358942	.344881	.331396	.318462
22	.404492	.387783	.371794	.356494	.341850	.327834	.314417	.301574
23	.388188	.371440	.355444	.340166	.325571	.311629	.298309	.285581
24	.372542	.355785	.339813	.324586	.310068	.296225	.283025	.270437
25	.357526	.340791	.324869	.309719	.295303	.281583	.268525	.256096
26	.343115	.326428	.310582	.295533	.281241	.267664	.254768	.242515
27	.329285	.312670	.296923	.281998	.267848	.254434	.241715	.229654
28	.316012	.299493	.283866	.269082	.255094	.241857	.229331	.217475
29	.303275	.286870	.271382	.256757	.242946	.229902	.217582	.205943
30	.291051	.274780	.259447	.244997	.231377	.218538	.206434	.195021
31	.279319	.263199	.248038	.233776	.220359	.207736	.195858	.184679
32	.268061	.252106	.237130	.223069	.209866	.197468	.185823	.174886
33	.257256	.241481	.226702	.212852	.199873	.187707	.176303	.165612
34	.246887	.231304	.216732	.203103	.190355	.178429	.167270	.156829
35	.236935	.221556	.207201	.193801	.181290	.169609	.158701	.148512

AMT Formula for Individuals

Taxable income (increased by any standard deduction taken)
Plus or minus: Adjustments
Plus: Preferences
Equals: Alternative minimum taxable income (AMTI)
Minus: Exemption
Equals: Alternative minimum tax (AMT) base
Multiplied by: 26% or 28% rate
Equals: Tentative minimum tax before foreign tax credit
Minus: AMT foreign tax credit
Equals: Tentative minimum tax (TMT)
Minus: Regular tax liability (less any foreign tax credit)
Equals: AMT (if TMT > regular tax liability)

2021 AMT Exemption and Phaseout for Individuals

		Phaseout	
Filing Status	**Exemption**	**Begins at**	**Ends at**
Married, filing jointly	$114,600	$1,047,200	$1,505,600
Single or Head of household	73,600	523,600	818,000
Married, filing separately	57,300	523,600	752,800

2022 AMT Exemption and Phaseout for Individuals

		Phaseout	
Filing Status	**Exemption**	**Begins at**	**Ends at**
Married, filing jointly	$118,100	$1,079,800	$1,552,200
Single or Head of household	75,900	539,900	843,500
Married, filing separately	59,050	539,900	776,100

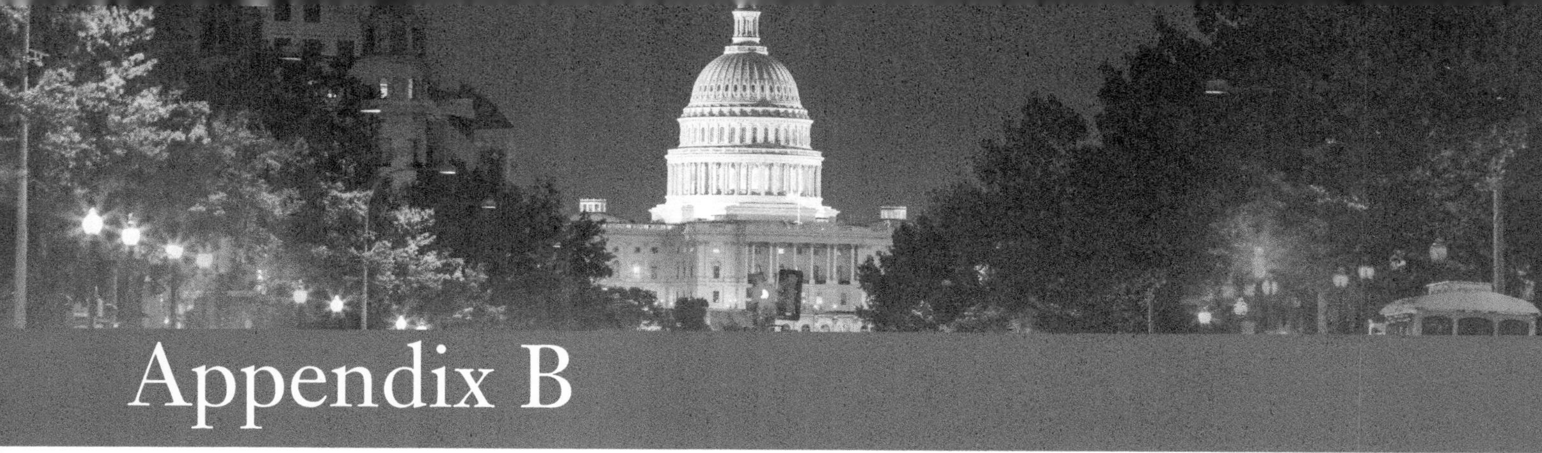

Appendix B

Tax Forms

The IRS tax forms mentioned in this text can be found at the IRS website at **irs.gov/forms-instructions**. In addition to reviewing and using the IRS tax forms in your study of taxation, also consider reviewing the comparable forms from the tax agency in your state (usually called the Department of Revenue). A list of state tax agency links is available at **aicpa.org/research/externallinks/taxesstatesdepartmentsofrevenue.html**. This can help you see some of the differences between Federal and state income tax rules, as well as similarities.

Form **1040** Department of the Treasury—Internal Revenue Service (99)
U.S. Individual Income Tax Return **2021** OMB No. 1545-0074 IRS Use Only—Do not write or staple in this space.

Filing Status ☐ Single ☐ Married filing jointly ☐ Married filing separately (MFS) ☐ Head of household (HOH) ☐ Qualifying widow(er) (QW)
Check only one box.
If you checked the MFS box, enter the name of your spouse. If you checked the HOH or QW box, enter the child's name if the qualifying person is a child but not your dependent ▶

Your first name and middle initial	Last name			**Your social security number**
If joint return, spouse's first name and middle initial	Last name			**Spouse's social security number**
Home address (number and street). If you have a P.O. box, see instructions.			Apt. no.	**Presidential Election Campaign** Check here if you, or your spouse if filing jointly, want $3 to go to this fund. Checking a box below will not change your tax or refund. ☐ **You** ☐ **Spouse**
City, town, or post office. If you have a foreign address, also complete spaces below.		State	ZIP code	
Foreign country name	Foreign province/state/county		Foreign postal code	

At any time during 2021, did you receive, sell, exchange, or otherwise dispose of any financial interest in any virtual currency? ☐ **Yes** ☐ **No**

Standard Deduction **Someone can claim:** ☐ You as a dependent ☐ Your spouse as a dependent
☐ Spouse itemizes on a separate return or you were a dual-status alien

Age/Blindness **You:** ☐ Were born before January 2, 1957 ☐ Are blind **Spouse:** ☐ Was born before January 2, 1957 ☐ Is blind

Dependents (see instructions):
If more than four dependents, see instructions and check here ▶ ☐

(1) First name Last name	**(2)** Social security number	**(3)** Relationship to you	**(4)** ✔ if qualifies for (see instructions): Child tax credit	Credit for other dependents
			☐	☐
			☐	☐
			☐	☐
			☐	☐

Attach Sch. B if required.

1	Wages, salaries, tips, etc. Attach Form(s) W-2			1	
2a	Tax-exempt interest	2a	**b** Taxable interest	2b	
3a	Qualified dividends	3a	**b** Ordinary dividends	3b	
4a	IRA distributions	4a	**b** Taxable amount	4b	
5a	Pensions and annuities	5a	**b** Taxable amount	5b	
6a	Social security benefits	6a	**b** Taxable amount	6b	
7	Capital gain or (loss). Attach Schedule D if required. If not required, check here ▶ ☐			7	
8	Other income from Schedule 1, line 10			8	
9	Add lines 1, 2b, 3b, 4b, 5b, 6b, 7, and 8. This is your **total income** ▶			9	
10	Adjustments to income from Schedule 1, line 26			10	
11	Subtract line 10 from line 9. This is your **adjusted gross income** ▶			11	
12a	**Standard deduction or itemized deductions** (from Schedule A)	12a			
b	Charitable contributions if you take the standard deduction (see instructions)	12b			
c	Add lines 12a and 12b			12c	
13	Qualified business income deduction from Form 8995 or Form 8995-A			13	
14	Add lines 12c and 13			14	
15	**Taxable income.** Subtract line 14 from line 11. If zero or less, enter -0-			15	

Standard Deduction for—
- Single or Married filing separately, $12,550
- Married filing jointly or Qualifying widow(er), $25,100
- Head of household, $18,800
- If you checked any box under *Standard Deduction,* see instructions.

For Disclosure, Privacy Act, and Paperwork Reduction Act Notice, see separate instructions. Cat. No. 11320B Form **1040** (2021)

Form 1040 (2021) Page **2**

16	**Tax** (see instructions). Check if any from Form(s): **1** ☐ 8814 **2** ☐ 4972 **3** ☐ ________		16	
17	Amount from Schedule 2, line 3		17	
18	Add lines 16 and 17		18	
19	Nonrefundable child tax credit or credit for other dependents from Schedule 8812		19	
20	Amount from Schedule 3, line 8		20	
21	Add lines 19 and 20		21	
22	Subtract line 21 from line 18. If zero or less, enter -0-		22	
23	Other taxes, including self-employment tax, from Schedule 2, line 21		23	
24	Add lines 22 and 23. This is your **total tax** ▶		24	
25	Federal income tax withheld from:			
a	Form(s) W-2	25a		
b	Form(s) 1099	25b		
c	Other forms (see instructions)	25c		
d	Add lines 25a through 25c		25d	
26	2021 estimated tax payments and amount applied from 2020 return		26	
27a	Earned income credit (EIC)	27a		
	Check here if you were born after January 1, 1998, and before January 2, 2004, and you satisfy all the other requirements for taxpayers who are at least age 18, to claim the EIC. See instructions ▶ ☐			
b	Nontaxable combat pay election — 27b			
c	Prior year (2019) earned income — 27c			
28	Refundable child tax credit or additional child tax credit from Schedule 8812	28		
29	American opportunity credit from Form 8863, line 8	29		
30	Recovery rebate credit. See instructions	30		
31	Amount from Schedule 3, line 15	31		
32	Add lines 27a and 28 through 31. These are your **total other payments and refundable credits** ▶		32	
33	Add lines 25d, 26, and 32. These are your **total payments** ▶		33	

If you have a qualifying child, attach Sch. EIC.

Refund

Direct deposit? See instructions.

34	If line 33 is more than line 24, subtract line 24 from line 33. This is the amount you **overpaid**		34	
35a	Amount of line 34 you want **refunded to you.** If Form 8888 is attached, check here ▶ ☐		35a	
▶b	Routing number ▶ **c** Type: ☐ Checking ☐ Savings			
▶d	Account number			
36	Amount of line 34 you want **applied to your 2022 estimated tax** ▶	36		

Amount You Owe

37	**Amount you owe.** Subtract line 33 from line 24. For details on how to pay, see instructions ▶		37	
38	Estimated tax penalty (see instructions) ▶	38		

Third Party Designee

Do you want to allow another person to discuss this return with the IRS? See instructions ▶ ☐ **Yes.** Complete below. ☐ **No**

Designee's name ▶ | Phone no. ▶ | Personal identification number (PIN) ▶

Sign Here

Under penalties of perjury, I declare that I have examined this return and accompanying schedules and statements, and to the best of my knowledge and belief, they are true, correct, and complete. Declaration of preparer (other than taxpayer) is based on all information of which preparer has any knowledge.

Joint return? See instructions. Keep a copy for your records.

Your signature	Date	Your occupation	If the IRS sent you an Identity Protection PIN, enter it here (see inst.) ▶
Spouse's signature. If a joint return, **both** must sign.	Date	Spouse's occupation	If the IRS sent your spouse an Identity Protection PIN, enter it here (see inst.) ▶
Phone no.	Email address		

Paid Preparer Use Only

Preparer's name	Preparer's signature	Date	PTIN	Check if: ☐ Self-employed
Firm's name ▶				Phone no.
Firm's address ▶				Firm's EIN ▶

Go to *www.irs.gov/Form1040* for instructions and the latest information. Form **1040** (2021)

SCHEDULE 1 (Form 1040)

Department of the Treasury Internal Revenue Service

Additional Income and Adjustments to Income

▶ Attach to Form 1040, 1040-SR, or 1040-NR.

▶ Go to *www.irs.gov/Form1040* for instructions and the latest information.

OMB No. 1545-0074

2021

Attachment Sequence No. 01

Name(s) shown on Form 1040, 1040-SR, or 1040-NR	**Your social security number**

Part I Additional Income

1	Taxable refunds, credits, or offsets of state and local income taxes			1	
2a	Alimony received			2a	
b	Date of original divorce or separation agreement (see instructions) ▶ ______				
3	Business income or (loss). Attach Schedule C			3	
4	Other gains or (losses). Attach Form 4797			4	
5	Rental real estate, royalties, partnerships, S corporations, trusts, etc. Attach Schedule E			5	
6	Farm income or (loss). Attach Schedule F			6	
7	Unemployment compensation			7	
8	Other income:				
a	Net operating loss	8a	( )		
b	Gambling income	8b			
c	Cancellation of debt	8c			
d	Foreign earned income exclusion from Form 2555	8d	( )		
e	Taxable Health Savings Account distribution	8e			
f	Alaska Permanent Fund dividends	8f			
g	Jury duty pay	8g			
h	Prizes and awards	8h			
i	Activity not engaged in for profit income	8i			
j	Stock options	8j			
k	Income from the rental of personal property if you engaged in the rental for profit but were not in the business of renting such property	8k			
l	Olympic and Paralympic medals and USOC prize money (see instructions)	8l			
m	Section 951(a) inclusion (see instructions)	8m			
n	Section 951A(a) inclusion (see instructions)	8n			
o	Section 461(l) excess business loss adjustment	8o			
p	Taxable distributions from an ABLE account (see instructions)	8p			
z	Other income. List type and amount ▶ ______	8z			
9	Total other income. Add lines 8a through 8z			9	
10	Combine lines 1 through 7 and 9. Enter here and on Form 1040, 1040-SR, or 1040-NR, line 8			10	

Part II Adjustments to Income

11	Educator expenses	11	
12	Certain business expenses of reservists, performing artists, and fee-basis government officials. Attach Form 2106	12	
13	Health savings account deduction. Attach Form 8889	13	
14	Moving expenses for members of the Armed Forces. Attach Form 3903	14	
15	Deductible part of self-employment tax. Attach Schedule SE	15	
16	Self-employed SEP, SIMPLE, and qualified plans	16	
17	Self-employed health insurance deduction	17	
18	Penalty on early withdrawal of savings	18	
19a	Alimony paid	19a	
b	Recipient's SSN ▶		
c	Date of original divorce or separation agreement (see instructions) ▶		
20	IRA deduction	20	
21	Student loan interest deduction	21	
22	Reserved for future use	22	
23	Archer MSA deduction	23	
24	Other adjustments:		
a	Jury duty pay (see instructions) — 24a		
b	Deductible expenses related to income reported on line 8k from the rental of personal property engaged in for profit — 24b		
c	Nontaxable amount of the value of Olympic and Paralympic medals and USOC prize money reported on line 8l — 24c		
d	Reforestation amortization and expenses — 24d		
e	Repayment of supplemental unemployment benefits under the Trade Act of 1974 — 24e		
f	Contributions to section 501(c)(18)(D) pension plans — 24f		
g	Contributions by certain chaplains to section 403(b) plans — 24g		
h	Attorney fees and court costs for actions involving certain unlawful discrimination claims (see instructions) — 24h		
i	Attorney fees and court costs you paid in connection with an award from the IRS for information you provided that helped the IRS detect tax law violations — 24i		
j	Housing deduction from Form 2555 — 24j		
k	Excess deductions of section 67(e) expenses from Schedule K-1 (Form 1041) — 24k		
z	Other adjustments. List type and amount ▶ — 24z		
25	Total other adjustments. Add lines 24a through 24z	25	
26	Add lines 11 through 23 and 25. These are your **adjustments to income.** Enter here and on Form 1040 or 1040-SR, line 10, or Form 1040-NR, line 10a	26	

SCHEDULE 2 (Form 1040) Department of the Treasury Internal Revenue Service	**Additional Taxes** ▶ Attach to Form 1040, 1040-SR, or 1040-NR. ▶ Go to *www.irs.gov/Form1040* for instructions and the latest information.	OMB No. 1545-0074 2021 Attachment Sequence No. 02
Name(s) shown on Form 1040, 1040-SR, or 1040-NR		Your social security number

Part I Tax

1	Alternative minimum tax. Attach Form 6251			1	
2	Excess advance premium tax credit repayment. Attach Form 8962			2	
3	Add lines 1 and 2. Enter here and on Form 1040, 1040-SR, or 1040-NR, line 17			3	

Part II Other Taxes

4	Self-employment tax. Attach Schedule SE			4	
5	Social security and Medicare tax on unreported tip income. Attach Form 4137	5			
6	Uncollected social security and Medicare tax on wages. Attach Form 8919	6			
7	Total additional social security and Medicare tax. Add lines 5 and 6			7	
8	Additional tax on IRAs or other tax-favored accounts. Attach Form 5329 if required			8	
9	Household employment taxes. Attach Schedule H			9	
10	Repayment of first-time homebuyer credit. Attach Form 5405 if required			10	
11	Additional Medicare Tax. Attach Form 8959			11	
12	Net investment income tax. Attach Form 8960			12	
13	Uncollected social security and Medicare or RRTA tax on tips or group-term life insurance from Form W-2, box 12			13	
14	Interest on tax due on installment income from the sale of certain residential lots and timeshares			14	
15	Interest on the deferred tax on gain from certain installment sales with a sales price over $150,000			15	
16	Recapture of low-income housing credit. Attach Form 8611			16	

(continued on page 2)

Schedule 2 (Form 1040) 2021 Page **2**

Part II Other Taxes *(continued)*

17	Other additional taxes:			
a	Recapture of other credits. List type, form number, and amount ▶ ______	17a		
b	Recapture of federal mortgage subsidy. If you sold your home in 2021, see instructions	17b		
c	Additional tax on HSA distributions. Attach Form 8889	17c		
d	Additional tax on an HSA because you didn't remain an eligible individual. Attach Form 8889	17d		
e	Additional tax on Archer MSA distributions. Attach Form 8853 .	17e		
f	Additional tax on Medicare Advantage MSA distributions. Attach Form 8853	17f		
g	Recapture of a charitable contribution deduction related to a fractional interest in tangible personal property	17g		
h	Income you received from a nonqualified deferred compensation plan that fails to meet the requirements of section 409A . . .	17h		
i	Compensation you received from a nonqualified deferred compensation plan described in section 457A	17i		
j	Section 72(m)(5) excess benefits tax	17j		
k	Golden parachute payments	17k		
l	Tax on accumulation distribution of trusts	17l		
m	Excise tax on insider stock compensation from an expatriated corporation	17m		
n	Look-back interest under section 167(g) or 460(b) from Form 8697 or 8866	17n		
o	Tax on non-effectively connected income for any part of the year you were a nonresident alien from Form 1040-NR	17o		
p	Any interest from Form 8621, line 16f, relating to distributions from, and dispositions of, stock of a section 1291 fund	17p		
q	Any interest from Form 8621, line 24	17q		
z	Any other taxes. List type and amount ▶ ______	17z		
18	Total additional taxes. Add lines 17a through 17z			18
19	Additional tax from Schedule 8812			19
20	Section 965 net tax liability installment from Form 965-A . . .	20		
21	Add lines 4, 7 through 16, 18, and 19. These are your **total other taxes.** Enter here and on Form 1040 or 1040-SR, line 23, or Form 1040-NR, line 23b			21

Schedule 2 (Form 1040) 2021

SCHEDULE 3 (Form 1040)

Department of the Treasury Internal Revenue Service

Additional Credits and Payments

► Attach to Form 1040, 1040-SR, or 1040-NR.
► Go to *www.irs.gov/Form1040* for instructions and the latest information.

OMB No. 1545-0074
2021
Attachment Sequence No. 03

Name(s) shown on Form 1040, 1040-SR, or 1040-NR	Your social security number

Part I Nonrefundable Credits

1	Foreign tax credit. Attach Form 1116 if required			1	
2	Credit for child and dependent care expenses from Form 2441, line 11. Attach Form 2441			2	
3	Education credits from Form 8863, line 19			3	
4	Retirement savings contributions credit. Attach Form 8880			4	
5	Residential energy credits. Attach Form 5695			5	
6	Other nonrefundable credits:				
a	General business credit. Attach Form 3800	6a			
b	Credit for prior year minimum tax. Attach Form 8801	6b			
c	Adoption credit. Attach Form 8839	6c			
d	Credit for the elderly or disabled. Attach Schedule R	6d			
e	Alternative motor vehicle credit. Attach Form 8910	6e			
f	Qualified plug-in motor vehicle credit. Attach Form 8936	6f			
g	Mortgage interest credit. Attach Form 8396	6g			
h	District of Columbia first-time homebuyer credit. Attach Form 8859	6h			
i	Qualified electric vehicle credit. Attach Form 8834	6i			
j	Alternative fuel vehicle refueling property credit. Attach Form 8911	6j			
k	Credit to holders of tax credit bonds. Attach Form 8912	6k			
l	Amount on Form 8978, line 14. See instructions	6l			
z	Other nonrefundable credits. List type and amount ► ______	6z			
7	Total other nonrefundable credits. Add lines 6a through 6z			7	
8	Add lines 1 through 5 and 7. Enter here and on Form 1040, 1040-SR, or 1040-NR, line 20			8	

(continued on page 2)

Schedule 3 (Form 1040) 2021 Page **2**

Part II Other Payments and Refundable Credits

9	Net premium tax credit. Attach Form 8962			**9**	
10	Amount paid with request for extension to file (see instructions)			**10**	
11	Excess social security and tier 1 RRTA tax withheld			**11**	
12	Credit for federal tax on fuels. Attach Form 4136			**12**	
13	Other payments or refundable credits:				
a	Form 2439	**13a**			
b	Qualified sick and family leave credits from Schedule(s) H and Form(s) 7202 for leave taken before April 1, 2021	**13b**			
c	Health coverage tax credit from Form 8885	**13c**			
d	Credit for repayment of amounts included in income from earlier years	**13d**			
e	Reserved for future use	**13e**			
f	Deferred amount of net 965 tax liability (see instructions)	**13f**			
g	Credit for child and dependent care expenses from Form 2441, line 10. Attach Form 2441	**13g**			
h	Qualified sick and family leave credits from Schedule(s) H and Form(s) 7202 for leave taken after March 31, 2021	**13h**			
z	Other payments or refundable credits. List type and amount ▶	**13z**			
14	Total other payments or refundable credits. Add lines 13a through 13z			**14**	
15	Add lines 9 through 12 and 14. Enter here and on Form 1040, 1040-SR, or 1040-NR, line 31			**15**	

Schedule 3 (Form 1040) 2021

SCHEDULE A (Form 1040)

Department of the Treasury
Internal Revenue Service (99)

Itemized Deductions

▶ Go to *www.irs.gov/ScheduleA* for instructions and the latest information.
▶ Attach to Form 1040 or 1040-SR.
Caution: If you are claiming a net qualified disaster loss on Form 4684, see the instructions for line 16.

OMB No. 1545-0074
2021
Attachment Sequence No. 07

Name(s) shown on Form 1040 or 1040-SR | **Your social security number**

Medical and Dental Expenses		**Caution:** Do not include expenses reimbursed or paid by others.				
	1	Medical and dental expenses (see instructions)	1			
	2	Enter amount from Form 1040 or 1040-SR, line 11 | 2 |				
	3	Multiply line 2 by 7.5% (0.075)	3			
	4	Subtract line 3 from line 1. If line 3 is more than line 1, enter -0-			4	
Taxes You Paid	5	State and local taxes.				
	a	State and local income taxes or general sales taxes. You may include either income taxes or general sales taxes on line 5a, but not both. If you elect to include general sales taxes instead of income taxes, check this box ▶ ☐	5a			
	b	State and local real estate taxes (see instructions)	5b			
	c	State and local personal property taxes	5c			
	d	Add lines 5a through 5c	5d			
	e	Enter the smaller of line 5d or $10,000 ($5,000 if married filing separately)	5e			
	6	Other taxes. List type and amount ▶	6			
	7	Add lines 5e and 6			7	
Interest You Paid Caution: Your mortgage interest deduction may be limited (see instructions).	8	Home mortgage interest and points. If you didn't use all of your home mortgage loan(s) to buy, build, or improve your home, see instructions and check this box ▶ ☐				
	a	Home mortgage interest and points reported to you on Form 1098. See instructions if limited	8a			
	b	Home mortgage interest not reported to you on Form 1098. See instructions if limited. If paid to the person from whom you bought the home, see instructions and show that person's name, identifying no., and address ▶	8b			
	c	Points not reported to you on Form 1098. See instructions for special rules	8c			
	d	Mortgage insurance premiums (see instructions)	8d			
	e	Add lines 8a through 8d	8e			
	9	Investment interest. Attach Form 4952 if required. See instructions	9			
	10	Add lines 8e and 9			10	
Gifts to Charity Caution: If you made a gift and got a benefit for it, see instructions.	11	Gifts by cash or check. If you made any gift of $250 or more, see instructions	11			
	12	Other than by cash or check. If you made any gift of $250 or more, see instructions. You **must** attach Form 8283 if over $500	12			
	13	Carryover from prior year	13			
	14	Add lines 11 through 13			14	
Casualty and Theft Losses	15	Casualty and theft loss(es) from a federally declared disaster (other than net qualified disaster losses). Attach Form 4684 and enter the amount from line 18 of that form. See instructions			15	
Other Itemized Deductions	16	Other—from list in instructions. List type and amount ▶			16	
Total Itemized Deductions	17	Add the amounts in the far right column for lines 4 through 16. Also, enter this amount on Form 1040 or 1040-SR, line 12a			17	
	18	If you elect to itemize deductions even though they are less than your standard deduction, check this box ▶ ☐				

For Paperwork Reduction Act Notice, see the Instructions for Forms 1040 and 1040-SR. Cat. No. 17145C **Schedule A (Form 1040) 2021**

SCHEDULE C (Form 1040)

Department of the Treasury Internal Revenue Service (99)

Profit or Loss From Business

(Sole Proprietorship)

▶ Go to *www.irs.gov/ScheduleC* for instructions and the latest information.

▶ Attach to Form 1040, 1040-SR, 1040-NR, or 1041; partnerships must generally file Form 1065.

OMB No. 1545-0074

2021

Attachment Sequence No. **09**

Name of proprietor | **Social security number (SSN)**

A Principal business or profession, including product or service (see instructions) | **B Enter code from instructions** ▶

C Business name. If no separate business name, leave blank. | **D Employer ID number (EIN)** (see instr.)

E Business address (including suite or room no.) ▶

City, town or post office, state, and ZIP code

F Accounting method: **(1)** ☐ Cash **(2)** ☐ Accrual **(3)** ☐ Other (specify) ▶

G Did you "materially participate" in the operation of this business during 2021? If "No," see instructions for limit on losses . ☐ **Yes** ☐ **No**

H If you started or acquired this business during 2021, check here . . . ▶ ☐

I Did you make any payments in 2021 that would require you to file Form(s) 1099? See instructions . . . ☐ **Yes** ☐ **No**

J If "Yes," did you or will you file required Form(s) 1099? . . . ☐ **Yes** ☐ **No**

Part I Income

1	Gross receipts or sales. See instructions for line 1 and check the box if this income was reported to you on Form W-2 and the "Statutory employee" box on that form was checked . . . ▶ ☐	1	
2	Returns and allowances . . .	2	
3	Subtract line 2 from line 1 . . .	3	
4	Cost of goods sold (from line 42) . . .	4	
5	**Gross profit.** Subtract line 4 from line 3 . . .	5	
6	Other income, including federal and state gasoline or fuel tax credit or refund (see instructions) . . .	6	
7	**Gross income.** Add lines 5 and 6 . . . ▶	7	

Part II Expenses. Enter expenses for business use of your home **only** on line 30.

8	Advertising . . .	8		18	Office expense (see instructions) .	18	
9	Car and truck expenses (see instructions) . . .	9		19	Pension and profit-sharing plans .	19	
10	Commissions and fees .	10		20	Rent or lease (see instructions):		
11	Contract labor (see instructions)	11		a	Vehicles, machinery, and equipment	20a	
12	Depletion . . .	12		b	Other business property . . .	20b	
13	Depreciation and section 179 expense deduction (not included in Part III) (see instructions) . . .	13		21	Repairs and maintenance . . .	21	
				22	Supplies (not included in Part III) .	22	
				23	Taxes and licenses . . .	23	
				24	Travel and meals:		
14	Employee benefit programs (other than on line 19) .	14		a	Travel . . .	24a	
15	Insurance (other than health)	15		b	Deductible meals (see instructions) . . .	24b	
16	Interest (see instructions):			25	Utilities . . .	25	
a	Mortgage (paid to banks, etc.)	16a		26	Wages (less employment credits)	26	
b	Other . . .	16b		27a	Other expenses (from line 48) . .	27a	
17	Legal and professional services	17		b	**Reserved for future use** . . .	27b	

28	**Total expenses** before expenses for business use of home. Add lines 8 through 27a . . . ▶	28	
29	Tentative profit or (loss). Subtract line 28 from line 7 . . .	29	
30	Expenses for business use of your home. Do not report these expenses elsewhere. Attach Form 8829 unless using the simplified method. See instructions. **Simplified method filers only:** Enter the total square footage of (a) your home: ______ and (b) the part of your home used for business: ______ . Use the Simplified Method Worksheet in the instructions to figure the amount to enter on line 30 . . .	30	
31	**Net profit or (loss).** Subtract line 30 from line 29. • If a profit, enter on both **Schedule 1 (Form 1040), line 3,** and on **Schedule SE, line 2.** (If you checked the box on line 1, see instructions). Estates and trusts, enter on **Form 1041, line 3.** • If a loss, you **must** go to line 32.	31	

32 If you have a loss, check the box that describes your investment in this activity. See instructions.

• If you checked 32a, enter the loss on both **Schedule 1 (Form 1040), line 3,** and on **Schedule SE, line 2.** (If you checked the box on line 1, see the line 31 instructions.) Estates and trusts, enter on **Form 1041, line 3.**

• If you checked 32b, you **must** attach **Form 6198.** Your loss may be limited.

32a ☐ All investment is at risk.

32b ☐ Some investment is not at risk.

For Paperwork Reduction Act Notice, see the separate instructions. Cat. No. 11334P **Schedule C (Form 1040) 2021**

Schedule C (Form 1040) 2021 Page 2

Part III **Cost of Goods Sold** (see instructions)

33 Method(s) used to value closing inventory: **a** ☐ Cost **b** ☐ Lower of cost or market **c** ☐ Other (attach explanation)

34 Was there any change in determining quantities, costs, or valuations between opening and closing inventory? If "Yes," attach explanation . . . ☐ **Yes** ☐ **No**

35	Inventory at beginning of year. If different from last year's closing inventory, attach explanation . . .	35	
36	Purchases less cost of items withdrawn for personal use . . .	36	
37	Cost of labor. Do not include any amounts paid to yourself . . .	37	
38	Materials and supplies . . .	38	
39	Other costs . . .	39	
40	Add lines 35 through 39 . . .	40	
41	Inventory at end of year . . .	41	
42	**Cost of goods sold.** Subtract line 41 from line 40. Enter the result here and on line 4 . . .	42	

Part IV **Information on Your Vehicle.** Complete this part **only** if you are claiming car or truck expenses on line 9 and are not required to file Form 4562 for this business. See the instructions for line 13 to find out if you must file Form 4562.

43 When did you place your vehicle in service for business purposes? (month/day/year) ▶ ___ / ___ / ___

44 Of the total number of miles you drove your vehicle during 2021, enter the number of miles you used your vehicle for:

a Business ________ **b** Commuting (see instructions) ________ **c** Other ________

45 Was your vehicle available for personal use during off-duty hours? . . . ☐ **Yes** ☐ **No**

46 Do you (or your spouse) have another vehicle available for personal use?. . . ☐ **Yes** ☐ **No**

47a Do you have evidence to support your deduction? . . . ☐ **Yes** ☐ **No**

b If "Yes," is the evidence written? . . . ☐ **Yes** ☐ **No**

Part V **Other Expenses.** List below business expenses not included on lines 8–26 or line 30.

48 Total other expenses. Enter here and on line 27a . . .	48	

Schedule C (Form 1040) 2021

SCHEDULE D (Form 1040)

Department of the Treasury Internal Revenue Service (99)

Capital Gains and Losses

► Attach to Form 1040, 1040-SR, or 1040-NR.
► Go to *www.irs.gov/ScheduleD* for instructions and the latest information.
► Use Form 8949 to list your transactions for lines 1b, 2, 3, 8b, 9, and 10.

OMB No. 1545-0074

2021

Attachment Sequence No. 12

Name(s) shown on return | Your social security number

Did you dispose of any investment(s) in a qualified opportunity fund during the tax year? ☐ Yes ☐ No
If "Yes," attach Form 8949 and see its instructions for additional requirements for reporting your gain or loss.

Part I Short-Term Capital Gains and Losses—Generally Assets Held One Year or Less (see instructions)

See instructions for how to figure the amounts to enter on the lines below. This form may be easier to complete if you round off cents to whole dollars.	(d) Proceeds (sales price)	(e) Cost (or other basis)	(g) Adjustments to gain or loss from Form(s) 8949, Part I, line 2, column (g)	(h) Gain or (loss) Subtract column (e) from column (d) and combine the result with column (g)
1a Totals for all short-term transactions reported on Form 1099-B for which basis was reported to the IRS and for which you have no adjustments (see instructions). However, if you choose to report all these transactions on Form 8949, leave this line blank and go to line 1b .				
1b Totals for all transactions reported on Form(s) 8949 with **Box A** checked				
2 Totals for all transactions reported on Form(s) 8949 with **Box B** checked				
3 Totals for all transactions reported on Form(s) 8949 with **Box C** checked				

4 Short-term gain from Form 6252 and short-term gain or (loss) from Forms 4684, 6781, and 8824 . .	4	
5 Net short-term gain or (loss) from partnerships, S corporations, estates, and trusts from Schedule(s) K-1	5	
6 Short-term capital loss carryover. Enter the amount, if any, from line 8 of your **Capital Loss Carryover Worksheet** in the instructions	6	( )
7 **Net short-term capital gain or (loss).** Combine lines 1a through 6 in column (h). If you have any long-term capital gains or losses, go to Part II below. Otherwise, go to Part III on the back	7	

Part II Long-Term Capital Gains and Losses—Generally Assets Held More Than One Year (see instructions)

See instructions for how to figure the amounts to enter on the lines below. This form may be easier to complete if you round off cents to whole dollars.	(d) Proceeds (sales price)	(e) Cost (or other basis)	(g) Adjustments to gain or loss from Form(s) 8949, Part II, line 2, column (g)	(h) Gain or (loss) Subtract column (e) from column (d) and combine the result with column (g)
8a Totals for all long-term transactions reported on Form 1099-B for which basis was reported to the IRS and for which you have no adjustments (see instructions). However, if you choose to report all these transactions on Form 8949, leave this line blank and go to line 8b .				
8b Totals for all transactions reported on Form(s) 8949 with **Box D** checked				
9 Totals for all transactions reported on Form(s) 8949 with **Box E** checked				
10 Totals for all transactions reported on Form(s) 8949 with **Box F** checked.				

11 Gain from Form 4797, Part I; long-term gain from Forms 2439 and 6252; and long-term gain or (loss) from Forms 4684, 6781, and 8824	11	
12 Net long-term gain or (loss) from partnerships, S corporations, estates, and trusts from Schedule(s) K-1	12	
13 Capital gain distributions. See the instructions	13	
14 Long-term capital loss carryover. Enter the amount, if any, from line 13 of your **Capital Loss Carryover Worksheet** in the instructions	14	( )
15 **Net long-term capital gain or (loss).** Combine lines 8a through 14 in column (h). Then, go to Part III on the back	15	

For Paperwork Reduction Act Notice, see your tax return instructions. Cat. No. 11338H **Schedule D (Form 1040) 2021**

Part III Summary

16	Combine lines 7 and 15 and enter the result	**16**	
	• If line 16 is a **gain,** enter the amount from line 16 on Form 1040, 1040-SR, or 1040-NR, line 7. Then, go to line 17 below. • If line 16 is a **loss,** skip lines 17 through 20 below. Then, go to line 21. Also be sure to complete line 22. • If line 16 is **zero,** skip lines 17 through 21 below and enter -0- on Form 1040, 1040-SR, or 1040-NR, line 7. Then, go to line 22.		
17	Are lines 15 and 16 **both** gains? ☐ **Yes.** Go to line 18. ☐ **No.** Skip lines 18 through 21, and go to line 22.		
18	If you are required to complete the **28% Rate Gain Worksheet** (see instructions), enter the amount, if any, from line 7 of that worksheet . . . . ▶	**18**	
19	If you are required to complete the **Unrecaptured Section 1250 Gain Worksheet** (see instructions), enter the amount, if any, from line 18 of that worksheet . . . . ▶	**19**	
20	Are lines 18 and 19 both zero or blank and are you not filing Form 4952? ☐ **Yes.** Complete the **Qualified Dividends and Capital Gain Tax Worksheet** in the instructions for Forms 1040 and 1040-SR, line 16. **Don't** complete lines 21 and 22 below. ☐ **No.** Complete the **Schedule D Tax Worksheet** in the instructions. **Don't** complete lines 21 and 22 below.		
21	If line 16 is a loss, enter here and on Form 1040, 1040-SR, or 1040-NR, line 7, the **smaller** of: • The loss on line 16; or • ($3,000), or if married filing separately, ($1,500)	**21**	( )
	Note: When figuring which amount is smaller, treat both amounts as positive numbers.		
22	Do you have qualified dividends on Form 1040, 1040-SR, or 1040-NR, line 3a? ☐ **Yes.** Complete the **Qualified Dividends and Capital Gain Tax Worksheet** in the instructions for Forms 1040 and 1040-SR, line 16. ☐ **No.** Complete the rest of Form 1040, 1040-SR, or 1040-NR.		

Form **1065**

Department of the Treasury
Internal Revenue Service

U.S. Return of Partnership Income

For calendar year 2021, or tax year beginning ________, 2021, ending ________, 20____.

▶ Go to *www.irs.gov/Form1065* for instructions and the latest information.

OMB No. 1545-0123

2021

A Principal business activity	Type or Print	Name of partnership	**D** Employer identification number
B Principal product or service		Number, street, and room or suite no. If a P.O. box, see instructions.	**E** Date business started
C Business code number		City or town, state or province, country, and ZIP or foreign postal code	**F** Total assets (see instructions) $

G Check applicable boxes: **(1)** ☐ Initial return **(2)** ☐ Final return **(3)** ☐ Name change **(4)** ☐ Address change **(5)** ☐ Amended return

H Check accounting method: **(1)** ☐ Cash **(2)** ☐ Accrual **(3)** ☐ Other (specify) ▶ ________

I Number of Schedules K-1. Attach one for each person who was a partner at any time during the tax year ▶ ________

J Check if Schedules C and M-3 are attached . . . ▶ ☐

K Check if partnership: **(1)** ☐ Aggregated activities for section 465 at-risk purposes **(2)** ☐ Grouped activities for section 469 passive activity purposes

Caution: Include **only** trade or business income and expenses on lines 1a through 22 below. See instructions for more information.

Income	1a	Gross receipts or sales	1a			
	b	Returns and allowances	1b			
	c	Balance. Subtract line 1b from line 1a			1c	
	2	Cost of goods sold (attach Form 1125-A)			2	
	3	Gross profit. Subtract line 2 from line 1c			3	
	4	Ordinary income (loss) from other partnerships, estates, and trusts (attach statement)			4	
	5	Net farm profit (loss) (attach Schedule F (Form 1040))			5	
	6	Net gain (loss) from Form 4797, Part II, line 17 (attach Form 4797)			6	
	7	Other income (loss) (attach statement)			7	
	8	**Total income (loss).** Combine lines 3 through 7			8	
Deductions (see instructions for limitations)	9	Salaries and wages (other than to partners) (less employment credits)			9	
	10	Guaranteed payments to partners			10	
	11	Repairs and maintenance			11	
	12	Bad debts			12	
	13	Rent			13	
	14	Taxes and licenses			14	
	15	Interest (see instructions)			15	
	16a	Depreciation (if required, attach Form 4562)	16a			
	b	Less depreciation reported on Form 1125-A and elsewhere on return	16b		16c	
	17	Depletion **(Do not deduct oil and gas depletion.)**			17	
	18	Retirement plans, etc.			18	
	19	Employee benefit programs			19	
	20	Other deductions (attach statement)			20	
	21	**Total deductions.** Add the amounts shown in the far right column for lines 9 through 20			21	
	22	**Ordinary business income (loss).** Subtract line 21 from line 8			22	
Tax and Payment	23	Interest due under the look-back method—completed long-term contracts (attach Form 8697)			23	
	24	Interest due under the look-back method—income forecast method (attach Form 8866)			24	
	25	BBA AAR imputed underpayment (see instructions)			25	
	26	Other taxes (see instructions)			26	
	27	**Total balance due.** Add lines 23 through 26			27	
	28	Payment (see instructions)			28	
	29	**Amount owed.** If line 28 is smaller than line 27, enter amount owed			29	
	30	**Overpayment.** If line 28 is larger than line 27, enter overpayment			30	

Sign Here

Under penalties of perjury, I declare that I have examined this return, including accompanying schedules and statements, and to the best of my knowledge and belief, it is true, correct, and complete. Declaration of preparer (other than partner or limited liability company member) is based on all information of which preparer has any knowledge.

▶ Signature of partner or limited liability company member ▶ Date

May the IRS discuss this return with the preparer shown below? See instructions. ☐ **Yes** ☐ **No**

Paid Preparer Use Only

Print/Type preparer's name	Preparer's signature	Date	Check ☐ if self-employed	PTIN
Firm's name ▶			Firm's EIN ▶	
Firm's address ▶			Phone no.	

Form 1065 (2021) Page 2

Schedule B Other Information

		Yes	No
1	What type of entity is filing this return? Check the applicable box: a ☐ Domestic general partnership b ☐ Domestic limited partnership c ☐ Domestic limited liability company d ☐ Domestic limited liability partnership e ☐ Foreign partnership f ☐ Other ▶		
2	At the end of the tax year:		
a	Did any foreign or domestic corporation, partnership (including any entity treated as a partnership), trust, or tax-exempt organization, or any foreign government own, directly or indirectly, an interest of 50% or more in the profit, loss, or capital of the partnership? For rules of constructive ownership, see instructions. If "Yes," attach Schedule B-1, Information on Partners Owning 50% or More of the Partnership		
b	Did any individual or estate own, directly or indirectly, an interest of 50% or more in the profit, loss, or capital of the partnership? For rules of constructive ownership, see instructions. If "Yes," attach Schedule B-1, Information on Partners Owning 50% or More of the Partnership		
3	At the end of the tax year, did the partnership:		
a	Own directly 20% or more, or own, directly or indirectly, 50% or more of the total voting power of all classes of stock entitled to vote of any foreign or domestic corporation? For rules of constructive ownership, see instructions. If "Yes," complete (i) through (iv) below		

(i) Name of Corporation	(ii) Employer Identification Number (if any)	(iii) Country of Incorporation	(iv) Percentage Owned in Voting Stock

		Yes	No
b	Own directly an interest of 20% or more, or own, directly or indirectly, an interest of 50% or more in the profit, loss, or capital in any foreign or domestic partnership (including an entity treated as a partnership) or in the beneficial interest of a trust? For rules of constructive ownership, see instructions. If "Yes," complete (i) through (v) below . .		

(i) Name of Entity	(ii) Employer Identification Number (if any)	(iii) Type of Entity	(iv) Country of Organization	(v) Maximum Percentage Owned in Profit, Loss, or Capital

		Yes	No
4	Does the partnership satisfy **all four** of the following conditions?		
a	The partnership's total receipts for the tax year were less than $250,000.		
b	The partnership's total assets at the end of the tax year were less than $1 million.		
c	Schedules K-1 are filed with the return and furnished to the partners on or before the due date (including extensions) for the partnership return.		
d	The partnership is not filing and is not required to file Schedule M-3 . . . . If "Yes," the partnership is not required to complete Schedules L, M-1, and M-2; item F on page 1 of Form 1065; or item L on Schedule K-1.		
5	Is this partnership a publicly traded partnership, as defined in section 469(k)(2)?		
6	During the tax year, did the partnership have any debt that was canceled, was forgiven, or had the terms modified so as to reduce the principal amount of the debt?		
7	Has this partnership filed, or is it required to file, Form 8918, Material Advisor Disclosure Statement, to provide information on any reportable transaction?		
8	At any time during calendar year 2021, did the partnership have an interest in or a signature or other authority over a financial account in a foreign country (such as a bank account, securities account, or other financial account)? See instructions for exceptions and filing requirements for FinCEN Form 114, Report of Foreign Bank and Financial Accounts (FBAR). If "Yes," enter the name of the foreign country ▶		
9	At any time during the tax year, did the partnership receive a distribution from, or was it the grantor of, or transferor to, a foreign trust? If "Yes," the partnership may have to file Form 3520, Annual Return To Report Transactions With Foreign Trusts and Receipt of Certain Foreign Gifts. See instructions		
10a	Is the partnership making, or had it previously made (and not revoked), a section 754 election? . . . . See instructions for details regarding a section 754 election.		
b	Did the partnership make for this tax year an optional basis adjustment under section 743(b) or 734(b)? If "Yes," attach a statement showing the computation and allocation of the basis adjustment. See instructions		

Form 1065 (2021) Page **3**

Schedule B **Other Information** *(continued)*

		Yes	No
c	Is the partnership required to adjust the basis of partnership assets under section 743(b) or 734(b) because of a substantial built-in loss (as defined under section 743(d)) or substantial basis reduction (as defined under section 734(d))? If "Yes," attach a statement showing the computation and allocation of the basis adjustment. See instructions		
11	Check this box if, during the current or prior tax year, the partnership distributed any property received in a like-kind exchange or contributed such property to another entity (other than disregarded entities wholly owned by the partnership throughout the tax year) . . . ▶ ☐		
12	At any time during the tax year, did the partnership distribute to any partner a tenancy-in-common or other undivided interest in partnership property? . . .		
13	If the partnership is required to file Form 8858, Information Return of U.S. Persons With Respect To Foreign Disregarded Entities (FDEs) and Foreign Branches (FBs), enter the number of Forms 8858 attached. See instructions . . . ▶		
14	Does the partnership have any foreign partners? If "Yes," enter the number of Forms 8805, Foreign Partner's Information Statement of Section 1446 Withholding Tax, filed for this partnership . . . ▶		
15	Enter the number of Forms 8865, Return of U.S. Persons With Respect to Certain Foreign Partnerships, attached to this return . . . ▶		
16a	Did you make any payments in 2021 that would require you to file Form(s) 1099? See instructions . . .		
b	If "Yes," did you or will you file required Form(s) 1099? . . .		
17	Enter the number of Forms 5471, Information Return of U.S. Persons With Respect To Certain Foreign Corporations, attached to this return . . . ▶		
18	Enter the number of partners that are foreign governments under section 892 . . . ▶		
19	During the partnership's tax year, did the partnership make any payments that would require it to file Forms 1042 and 1042-S under chapter 3 (sections 1441 through 1464) or chapter 4 (sections 1471 through 1474)? . . .		
20	Was the partnership a specified domestic entity required to file Form 8938 for the tax year? See the Instructions for Form 8938		
21	Is the partnership a section 721(c) partnership, as defined in Regulations section 1.721(c)-1(b)(14)? . . .		
22	During the tax year, did the partnership pay or accrue any interest or royalty for which one or more partners are not allowed a deduction under section 267A? See instructions . . . If "Yes," enter the total amount of the disallowed deductions . . . ▶ $		
23	Did the partnership have an election under section 163(j) for any real property trade or business or any farming business in effect during the tax year? See instructions . . .		
24	Does the partnership satisfy one or more of the following? See instructions . . . **a** The partnership owns a pass-through entity with current, or prior year carryover, excess business interest expense. **b** The partnership's aggregate average annual gross receipts (determined under section 448(c)) for the 3 tax years preceding the current tax year are more than $26 million and the partnership has business interest. **c** The partnership is a tax shelter (see instructions) and the partnership has business interest expense. If "Yes" to any, complete and attach Form 8990.		
25	Is the partnership attaching Form 8996 to certify as a Qualified Opportunity Fund? . . . If "Yes," enter the amount from Form 8996, line 15 . . . ▶ $		
26	Enter the number of foreign partners subject to section 864(c)(8) as a result of transferring all or a portion of an interest in the partnership or of receiving a distribution from the partnership . . . ▶ ________ Complete Schedule K-3 (Form 1065), Part XIII, for each foreign partner subject to section 864(c)(8) on a transfer or distribution.		
27	At any time during the tax year, were there any transfers between the partnership and its partners subject to the disclosure requirements of Regulations section 1.707-8? . . .		
28	Since December 22, 2017, did a foreign corporation directly or indirectly acquire substantially all of the properties constituting a trade or business of your partnership, and was the ownership percentage (by vote or value) for purposes of section 7874 greater than 50% (for example, the partners held more than 50% of the stock of the foreign corporation)? If "Yes," list the ownership percentage by vote and by value. See instructions. Percentage: By Vote By Value		
29	Is the partnership electing out of the centralized partnership audit regime under section 6221(b)? See instructions. If "Yes," the partnership must complete Schedule B-2 (Form 1065). Enter the total from Schedule B-2, Part III, line 3 ▶ ________ If "No," complete Designation of Partnership Representative below.		

Designation of Partnership Representative (see instructions)

Enter below the information for the partnership representative (PR) for the tax year covered by this return.

Name of PR ▶

U.S. address of PR ▶	U.S. phone number of PR ▶

If the PR is an entity, name of the designated individual for the PR ▶

U.S. address of designated individual ▶	U.S. phone number of designated individual ▶

Form **1065** (2021)

Form 1065 (2021) Page 4

Schedule K **Partners' Distributive Share Items**

Section	Line	Description	Box	Total amount
Income (Loss)	1	Ordinary business income (loss) (page 1, line 22)	1	
	2	Net rental real estate income (loss) (attach Form 8825)	2	
	3a	Other gross rental income (loss) . . . 3a		
	b	Expenses from other rental activities (attach statement) . . . 3b		
	c	Other net rental income (loss). Subtract line 3b from line 3a	3c	
	4	Guaranteed payments: **a** Services 4a ___ **b** Capital 4b ___		
		c Total. Add lines 4a and 4b	4c	
	5	Interest income	5	
	6	Dividends and dividend equivalents: **a** Ordinary dividends	6a	
		b Qualified dividends 6b ___ **c** Dividend equivalents 6c ___		
	7	Royalties	7	
	8	Net short-term capital gain (loss) (attach Schedule D (Form 1065))	8	
	9a	Net long-term capital gain (loss) (attach Schedule D (Form 1065))	9a	
	b	Collectibles (28%) gain (loss) . . . 9b		
	c	Unrecaptured section 1250 gain (attach statement) . . . 9c		
	10	Net section 1231 gain (loss) (attach Form 4797)	10	
	11	Other income (loss) (see instructions) Type ▶	11	
Deductions	12	Section 179 deduction (attach Form 4562)	12	
	13a	Contributions	13a	
	b	Investment interest expense	13b	
	c	Section 59(e)(2) expenditures: **(1)** Type ▶ ___ **(2)** Amount ▶	13c(2)	
	d	Other deductions (see instructions) Type ▶	13d	
Self-Employment	14a	Net earnings (loss) from self-employment	14a	
	b	Gross farming or fishing income	14b	
	c	Gross nonfarm income	14c	
Credits	15a	Low-income housing credit (section 42(j)(5))	15a	
	b	Low-income housing credit (other)	15b	
	c	Qualified rehabilitation expenditures (rental real estate) (attach Form 3468, if applicable)	15c	
	d	Other rental real estate credits (see instructions) Type ▶ ___	15d	
	e	Other rental credits (see instructions) Type ▶ ___	15e	
	f	Other credits (see instructions) Type ▶	15f	
International Transactions	16	Attach Schedule K-2 (Form 1065), Partners' Distributive Share Items-International, and check this box to indicate that you are reporting items of international tax relevance . . . ☐		
Alternative Minimum Tax (AMT) Items	17a	Post-1986 depreciation adjustment	17a	
	b	Adjusted gain or loss	17b	
	c	Depletion (other than oil and gas)	17c	
	d	Oil, gas, and geothermal properties—gross income	17d	
	e	Oil, gas, and geothermal properties—deductions	17e	
	f	Other AMT items (attach statement)	17f	
Other Information	18a	Tax-exempt interest income	18a	
	b	Other tax-exempt income	18b	
	c	Nondeductible expenses	18c	
	19a	Distributions of cash and marketable securities	19a	
	b	Distributions of other property	19b	
	20a	Investment income	20a	
	b	Investment expenses	20b	
	c	Other items and amounts (attach statement)		
	21	Total foreign taxes paid or accrued	21	

Form **1065** (2021)

Analysis of Net Income (Loss)

1	Net income (loss). Combine Schedule K, lines 1 through 11. From the result, subtract the sum of Schedule K, lines 12 through 13d, and 21					1	
2	Analysis by partner type:	(i) Corporate	(ii) Individual (active)	(iii) Individual (passive)	(iv) Partnership	(v) Exempt Organization	(vi) Nominee/Other
a	General partners						
b	Limited partners						

Schedule L Balance Sheets per Books

		Beginning of tax year		End of tax year	
	Assets	(a)	(b)	(c)	(d)
1	Cash				
2a	Trade notes and accounts receivable				
b	Less allowance for bad debts				
3	Inventories				
4	U.S. government obligations				
5	Tax-exempt securities				
6	Other current assets (attach statement)				
7a	Loans to partners (or persons related to partners)				
b	Mortgage and real estate loans				
8	Other investments (attach statement)				
9a	Buildings and other depreciable assets				
b	Less accumulated depreciation				
10a	Depletable assets				
b	Less accumulated depletion				
11	Land (net of any amortization)				
12a	Intangible assets (amortizable only)				
b	Less accumulated amortization				
13	Other assets (attach statement)				
14	Total assets				
	Liabilities and Capital				
15	Accounts payable				
16	Mortgages, notes, bonds payable in less than 1 year				
17	Other current liabilities (attach statement)				
18	All nonrecourse loans				
19a	Loans from partners (or persons related to partners)				
b	Mortgages, notes, bonds payable in 1 year or more				
20	Other liabilities (attach statement)				
21	Partners' capital accounts				
22	Total liabilities and capital				

Schedule M-1 Reconciliation of Income (Loss) per Books With Income (Loss) per Return

Note: The partnership may be required to file Schedule M-3. See instructions.

1	Net income (loss) per books		6	Income recorded on books this year not included on Schedule K, lines 1 through 11 (itemize):	
2	Income included on Schedule K, lines 1, 2, 3c, 5, 6a, 7, 8, 9a, 10, and 11, not recorded on books this year (itemize):		a	Tax-exempt interest $	
3	Guaranteed payments (other than health insurance)		7	Deductions included on Schedule K, lines 1 through 13d, and 21, not charged against book income this year (itemize):	
4	Expenses recorded on books this year not included on Schedule K, lines 1 through 13d, and 21 (itemize):		a	Depreciation $	
a	Depreciation $		8	Add lines 6 and 7	
b	Travel and entertainment $		9	Income (loss) (Analysis of Net Income (Loss), line 1). Subtract line 8 from line 5	
5	Add lines 1 through 4				

Schedule M-2 Analysis of Partners' Capital Accounts

1	Balance at beginning of year		6	Distributions: **a** Cash	
2	Capital contributed: **a** Cash			**b** Property	
	b Property		7	Other decreases (itemize):	
3	Net income (loss) (see instructions)				
4	Other increases (itemize):		8	Add lines 6 and 7	
5	Add lines 1 through 4		9	Balance at end of year. Subtract line 8 from line 5	

651121

☐ Final K-1 ☐ Amended K-1 OMB No. 1545-0123

Schedule K-1 (Form 1065) **2021**

Department of the Treasury
Internal Revenue Service

For calendar year 2021, or tax year

beginning / / 2021 ending / /

Partner's Share of Income, Deductions, Credits, etc.

► See back of form and separate instructions.

Part I Information About the Partnership

A Partnership's employer identification number

B Partnership's name, address, city, state, and ZIP code

C IRS center where partnership filed return ►

D ☐ Check if this is a publicly traded partnership (PTP)

Part II Information About the Partner

E Partner's SSN or TIN (Do not use TIN of a disregarded entity. See instructions.)

F Name, address, city, state, and ZIP code for partner entered in E. See instructions.

G ☐ General partner or LLC member-manager ☐ Limited partner or other LLC member

H1 ☐ Domestic partner ☐ Foreign partner

H2 ☐ If the partner is a disregarded entity (DE), enter the partner's:

TIN ______ Name ______

I1 What type of entity is this partner? ______

I2 If this partner is a retirement plan (IRA/SEP/Keogh/etc.), check here ► ☐

J Partner's share of profit, loss, and capital (see instructions):

	Beginning	Ending
Profit	%	%
Loss	%	%
Capital	%	%

Check if decrease is due to sale or exchange of partnership interest . ► ☐

K Partner's share of liabilities:

	Beginning	Ending
Nonrecourse . .	$	$
Qualified nonrecourse financing . . .	$	$
Recourse . . .	$	$

Check this box if Item K includes liability amounts from lower tier partnerships ► ☐

L **Partner's Capital Account Analysis**

Beginning capital account . . . $ ______

Capital contributed during the year . . $ ______

Current year net income (loss) . . . $ ______

Other increase (decrease) (attach explanation) $ ______

Withdrawals and distributions . . . $ (______)

Ending capital account . . . . $ ______

M Did the partner contribute property with a built-in gain (loss)?

☐ **Yes** ☐ **No** If "Yes," attach statement. See instructions.

N **Partner's Share of Net Unrecognized Section 704(c) Gain or (Loss)**

Beginning . . . . $ ______

Ending . . . . $ ______

Part III Partner's Share of Current Year Income, Deductions, Credits, and Other Items

1	Ordinary business income (loss)	14	Self-employment earnings (loss)
2	Net rental real estate income (loss)		
3	Other net rental income (loss)	15	Credits
4a	Guaranteed payments for services		
4b	Guaranteed payments for capital	16	Schedule K-3 is attached if checked . . . . ► ☐
4c	Total guaranteed payments	17	Alternative minimum tax (AMT) items
5	Interest income		
6a	Ordinary dividends		
6b	Qualified dividends	18	Tax-exempt income and nondeductible expenses
6c	Dividend equivalents		
7	Royalties		
8	Net short-term capital gain (loss)	19	Distributions
9a	Net long-term capital gain (loss)		
9b	Collectibles (28%) gain (loss)	20	Other information
9c	Unrecaptured section 1250 gain		
10	Net section 1231 gain (loss)		
11	Other income (loss)		
12	Section 179 deduction	21	Foreign taxes paid or accrued
13	Other deductions		

22 ☐ More than one activity for at-risk purposes*

23 ☐ More than one activity for passive activity purposes*

*See attached statement for additional information.

For IRS Use Only

For Paperwork Reduction Act Notice, see the Instructions for Form 1065. www.irs.gov/Form1065 Cat. No. 11394R **Schedule K-1 (Form 1065) 2021**

Form **1120**
Department of the Treasury
Internal Revenue Service

U.S. Corporation Income Tax Return

For calendar year 2021 or tax year beginning ________, 2021, ending ________, 20 ____

▶ Go to *www.irs.gov/Form1120* for instructions and the latest information.

OMB No. 1545-0123

2021

A Check if:
1a Consolidated return (attach Form 851) ☐
b Life/nonlife consolidated return ☐
2 Personal holding co. (attach Sch. PH) ☐
3 Personal service corp. (see instructions) ☐
4 Schedule M-3 attached ☐

TYPE OR PRINT
Name
Number, street, and room or suite no. If a P.O. box, see instructions.
City or town, state or province, country, and ZIP or foreign postal code

B Employer identification number
C Date incorporated
D Total assets (see instructions) $

E Check if: (1) ☐ Initial return (2) ☐ Final return (3) ☐ Name change (4) ☐ Address change

Income

Line	Description			Line	Amount
1a	Gross receipts or sales	1a			
b	Returns and allowances	1b			
c	Balance. Subtract line 1b from line 1a			1c	
2	Cost of goods sold (attach Form 1125-A)			2	
3	Gross profit. Subtract line 2 from line 1c			3	
4	Dividends and inclusions (Schedule C, line 23)			4	
5	Interest			5	
6	Gross rents			6	
7	Gross royalties			7	
8	Capital gain net income (attach Schedule D (Form 1120))			8	
9	Net gain or (loss) from Form 4797, Part II, line 17 (attach Form 4797)			9	
10	Other income (see instructions—attach statement)			10	
11	**Total income.** Add lines 3 through 10 ▶			11	

Deductions (See instructions for limitations on deductions.)

Line	Description			Line	Amount
12	Compensation of officers (see instructions—attach Form 1125-E) ▶			12	
13	Salaries and wages (less employment credits)			13	
14	Repairs and maintenance			14	
15	Bad debts			15	
16	Rents			16	
17	Taxes and licenses			17	
18	Interest (see instructions)			18	
19	Charitable contributions			19	
20	Depreciation from Form 4562 not claimed on Form 1125-A or elsewhere on return (attach Form 4562)			20	
21	Depletion			21	
22	Advertising			22	
23	Pension, profit-sharing, etc., plans			23	
24	Employee benefit programs			24	
25	Reserved for future use			25	
26	Other deductions (attach statement)			26	
27	**Total deductions.** Add lines 12 through 26 ▶			27	
28	Taxable income before net operating loss deduction and special deductions. Subtract line 27 from line 11.			28	
29a	Net operating loss deduction (see instructions)	29a			
b	Special deductions (Schedule C, line 24)	29b			
c	Add lines 29a and 29b			29c	

Tax, Refundable Credits, and Payments

Line	Description			Line	Amount
30	**Taxable income.** Subtract line 29c from line 28. See instructions			30	
31	Total tax (Schedule J, Part I, line 11)			31	
32	Reserved for future use			32	
33	Total payments and credits (Schedule J, Part III, line 23)			33	
34	Estimated tax penalty. See instructions. Check if Form 2220 is attached ▶ ☐			34	
35	**Amount owed.** If line 33 is smaller than the total of lines 31 and 34, enter amount owed			35	
36	**Overpayment.** If line 33 is larger than the total of lines 31 and 34, enter amount overpaid			36	
37	Enter amount from line 36 you want: **Credited to 2022 estimated tax ▶**		**Refunded ▶**	37	

Sign Here

Under penalties of perjury, I declare that I have examined this return, including accompanying schedules and statements, and to the best of my knowledge and belief, it is true, correct, and complete. Declaration of preparer (other than taxpayer) is based on all information of which preparer has any knowledge.

Signature of officer | Date | Title

May the IRS discuss this return with the preparer shown below? See instructions. ☐ **Yes** ☐ **No**

Paid Preparer Use Only

Print/Type preparer's name	Preparer's signature	Date	Check ☐ if self-employed	PTIN
Firm's name ▶			Firm's EIN ▶	
Firm's address ▶			Phone no.	

Form 1120 (2021) Page 2

Schedule C **Dividends, Inclusions, and Special Deductions** (see instructions)	**(a)** Dividends and inclusions	**(b)** %	**(c)** Special deductions **(a)** × **(b)**
1 Dividends from less-than-20%-owned domestic corporations (other than debt-financed stock)		50	
2 Dividends from 20%-or-more-owned domestic corporations (other than debt-financed stock)		65	
3 Dividends on certain debt-financed stock of domestic and foreign corporations		See instructions	
4 Dividends on certain preferred stock of less-than-20%-owned public utilities		23.3	
5 Dividends on certain preferred stock of 20%-or-more-owned public utilities		26.7	
6 Dividends from less-than-20%-owned foreign corporations and certain FSCs		50	
7 Dividends from 20%-or-more-owned foreign corporations and certain FSCs		65	
8 Dividends from wholly owned foreign subsidiaries		100	
9 **Subtotal.** Add lines 1 through 8. See instructions for limitations		See instructions	
10 Dividends from domestic corporations received by a small business investment company operating under the Small Business Investment Act of 1958		100	
11 Dividends from affiliated group members		100	
12 Dividends from certain FSCs		100	
13 Foreign-source portion of dividends received from a specified 10%-owned foreign corporation (excluding hybrid dividends) (see instructions)		100	
14 Dividends from foreign corporations not included on line 3, 6, 7, 8, 11, 12, or 13 (including any hybrid dividends)			
15 Reserved for future use			
16a Subpart F inclusions derived from the sale by a controlled foreign corporation (CFC) of the stock of a lower-tier foreign corporation treated as a dividend (attach Form(s) 5471) (see instructions)		100	
b Subpart F inclusions derived from hybrid dividends of tiered corporations (attach Form(s) 5471) (see instructions)			
c Other inclusions from CFCs under subpart F not included on line 16a, 16b, or 17 (attach Form(s) 5471) (see instructions)			
17 Global Intangible Low-Taxed Income (GILTI) (attach Form(s) 5471 and Form 8992)			
18 Gross-up for foreign taxes deemed paid			
19 IC-DISC and former DISC dividends not included on line 1, 2, or 3			
20 Other dividends			
21 Deduction for dividends paid on certain preferred stock of public utilities			
22 Section 250 deduction (attach Form 8993)			
23 **Total dividends and inclusions.** Add column (a), lines 9 through 20. Enter here and on page 1, line 4			
24 **Total special deductions.** Add column (c), lines 9 through 22. Enter here and on page 1, line 29b			

Form **1120** (2021)

Form 1120 (2021) Page **3**

Schedule J Tax Computation and Payment (see instructions)

Part I—Tax Computation

1	Check if the corporation is a member of a controlled group (attach Schedule O (Form 1120)). See instructions ▶ ☐				
2	Income tax. See instructions			2	
3	Base erosion minimum tax amount (attach Form 8991)			3	
4	Add lines 2 and 3			4	
5a	Foreign tax credit (attach Form 1118)	5a			
b	Credit from Form 8834 (see instructions)	5b			
c	General business credit (attach Form 3800)	5c			
d	Credit for prior year minimum tax (attach Form 8827)	5d			
e	Bond credits from Form 8912	5e			
6	**Total credits.** Add lines 5a through 5e			6	
7	Subtract line 6 from line 4			7	
8	Personal holding company tax (attach Schedule PH (Form 1120))			8	
9a	Recapture of investment credit (attach Form 4255)	9a			
b	Recapture of low-income housing credit (attach Form 8611)	9b			
c	Interest due under the look-back method—completed long-term contracts (attach Form 8697)	9c			
d	Interest due under the look-back method—income forecast method (attach Form 8866)	9d			
e	Alternative tax on qualifying shipping activities (attach Form 8902)	9e			
f	Interest/tax due under section 453A(c) and/or section 453(l)	9f			
g	Other (see instructions—attach statement)	9g			
10	**Total.** Add lines 9a through 9g			10	
11	**Total tax.** Add lines 7, 8, and 10. Enter here and on page 1, line 31			11	

Part II—Reserved For Future Use

12	Reserved for future use	12	

Part III—Payments and Refundable Credits

13	2020 overpayment credited to 2021			13	
14	2021 estimated tax payments			14	
15	2021 refund applied for on Form 4466			15	( )
16	Combine lines 13, 14, and 15			16	
17	Tax deposited with Form 7004			17	
18	Withholding (see instructions)			18	
19	**Total payments.** Add lines 16, 17, and 18			19	
20	Refundable credits from:				
a	Form 2439	20a			
b	Form 4136	20b			
c	Reserved for future use	20c			
d	Other (attach statement—see instructions)	20d			
21	**Total credits.** Add lines 20a through 20d			21	
22	Reserved for future use			22	
23	**Total payments and credits.** Add lines 19 and 21. Enter here and on page 1, line 33			23	

Form 1120 (2021) Page 4

Schedule K Other Information (see instructions)

		Yes	No
1	Check accounting method: a ☐ Cash b ☐ Accrual c ☐ Other (specify) ▶		
2	See the instructions and enter the:		
a	Business activity code no. ▶		
b	Business activity ▶		
c	Product or service ▶		
3	Is the corporation a subsidiary in an affiliated group or a parent–subsidiary controlled group? . . . . If "Yes," enter name and EIN of the parent corporation ▶		
4	At the end of the tax year:		
a	Did any foreign or domestic corporation, partnership (including any entity treated as a partnership), trust, or tax-exempt organization own directly 20% or more, or own, directly or indirectly, 50% or more of the total voting power of all classes of the corporation's stock entitled to vote? If "Yes," complete Part I of Schedule G (Form 1120) (attach Schedule G)		
b	Did any individual or estate own directly 20% or more, or own, directly or indirectly, 50% or more of the total voting power of all classes of the corporation's stock entitled to vote? If "Yes," complete Part II of Schedule G (Form 1120) (attach Schedule G) .		
5	At the end of the tax year, did the corporation:		
a	Own directly 20% or more, or own, directly or indirectly, 50% or more of the total voting power of all classes of stock entitled to vote of any foreign or domestic corporation not included on **Form 851,** Affiliations Schedule? For rules of constructive ownership, see instructions. If "Yes," complete (i) through (iv) below.		

(i) Name of Corporation	**(ii)** Employer Identification Number (if any)	**(iii)** Country of Incorporation	**(iv)** Percentage Owned in Voting Stock

		Yes	No
b	Own directly an interest of 20% or more, or own, directly or indirectly, an interest of 50% or more in any foreign or domestic partnership (including an entity treated as a partnership) or in the beneficial interest of a trust? For rules of constructive ownership, see instructions. If "Yes," complete (i) through (iv) below.		

(i) Name of Entity	**(ii)** Employer Identification Number (if any)	**(iii)** Country of Organization	**(iv)** Maximum Percentage Owned in Profit, Loss, or Capital

		Yes	No
6	During this tax year, did the corporation pay dividends (other than stock dividends and distributions in exchange for stock) in excess of the corporation's current and accumulated earnings and profits? See sections 301 and 316 . . . . If "Yes," file **Form 5452,** Corporate Report of Nondividend Distributions. See the instructions for Form 5452. If this is a consolidated return, answer here for the parent corporation and on Form 851 for each subsidiary.		
7	At any time during the tax year, did one foreign person own, directly or indirectly, at least 25% of the total voting power of all classes of the corporation's stock entitled to vote or at least 25% of the total value of all classes of the corporation's stock? . For rules of attribution, see section 318. If "Yes," enter: **(a)** Percentage owned ▶ ________ and **(b)** Owner's country ▶ ________ **(c)** The corporation may have to file **Form 5472,** Information Return of a 25% Foreign-Owned U.S. Corporation or a Foreign Corporation Engaged in a U.S. Trade or Business. Enter the number of Forms 5472 attached ▶ ________		
8	Check this box if the corporation issued publicly offered debt instruments with original issue discount . . . . ▶ ☐ If checked, the corporation may have to file **Form 8281,** Information Return for Publicly Offered Original Issue Discount Instruments.		
9	Enter the amount of tax-exempt interest received or accrued during the tax year ▶ $ ________		
10	Enter the number of shareholders at the end of the tax year (if 100 or fewer) ▶ ________		
11	If the corporation has an NOL for the tax year and is electing to forego the carryback period, check here (see instructions) ▶ ☐ If the corporation is filing a consolidated return, the statement required by Regulations section 1.1502-21(b)(3) must be attached or the election will not be valid.		
12	Enter the available NOL carryover from prior tax years (do not reduce it by any deduction reported on page 1, line 29a.) . . . . ▶ $		

Form **1120** (2021)

Schedule K Other Information *(continued from page 4)*

		Yes	No
13	Are the corporation's total receipts (page 1, line 1a, plus lines 4 through 10) for the tax year **and** its total assets at the end of the tax year less than $250,000?		
	If "Yes," the corporation is not required to complete Schedules L, M-1, and M-2. Instead, enter the total amount of cash distributions and the book value of property distributions (other than cash) made during the tax year ▶ $		
14	Is the corporation required to file Schedule UTP (Form 1120), Uncertain Tax Position Statement? See instructions		
	If "Yes," complete and attach Schedule UTP.		
15a	Did the corporation make any payments in 2021 that would require it to file Form(s) 1099?		
b	If "Yes," did or will the corporation file required Form(s) 1099?		
16	During this tax year, did the corporation have an 80%-or-more change in ownership, including a change due to redemption of its own stock?		
17	During or subsequent to this tax year, but before the filing of this return, did the corporation dispose of more than 65% (by value) of its assets in a taxable, non-taxable, or tax deferred transaction?		
18	Did the corporation receive assets in a section 351 transfer in which any of the transferred assets had a fair market basis or fair market value of more than $1 million?		
19	During the corporation's tax year, did the corporation make any payments that would require it to file Forms 1042 and 1042-S under chapter 3 (sections 1441 through 1464) or chapter 4 (sections 1471 through 1474) of the Code?		
20	Is the corporation operating on a cooperative basis?		
21	During the tax year, did the corporation pay or accrue any interest or royalty for which the deduction is not allowed under section 267A? See instructions		
	If "Yes," enter the total amount of the disallowed deductions ▶ $		
22	Does the corporation have gross receipts of at least $500 million in any of the 3 preceding tax years? (See sections 59A(e)(2) and (3))		
	If "Yes," complete and attach Form 8991.		
23	Did the corporation have an election under section 163(j) for any real property trade or business or any farming business in effect during the tax year? See instructions		
24	Does the corporation satisfy one or more of the following? See instructions		
a	The corporation owns a pass-through entity with current, or prior year carryover, excess business interest expense.		
b	The corporation's aggregate average annual gross receipts (determined under section 448(c)) for the 3 tax years preceding the current tax year are more than $26 million and the corporation has business interest expense.		
c	The corporation is a tax shelter and the corporation has business interest expense.		
	If "Yes," complete and attach Form 8990.		
25	Is the corporation attaching Form 8996 to certify as a Qualified Opportunity Fund?		
	If "Yes," enter amount from Form 8996, line 15 ▶ $		
26	Since December 22, 2017, did a foreign corporation directly or indirectly acquire substantially all of the properties held directly or indirectly by the corporation, and was the ownership percentage (by vote or value) for purposes of section 7874 greater than 50% (for example, the shareholders held more than 50% of the stock of the foreign corporation)? If "Yes," list the ownership percentage by vote and by value. See instructions		
	Percentage: By Vote By Value		

Form 1120 (2021) Page 6

Schedule L **Balance Sheets per Books**

Assets		Beginning of tax year (a)	(b)	End of tax year (c)	(d)
1	Cash				
2a	Trade notes and accounts receivable				
b	Less allowance for bad debts	( )		( )	
3	Inventories				
4	U.S. government obligations				
5	Tax-exempt securities (see instructions)				
6	Other current assets (attach statement)				
7	Loans to shareholders				
8	Mortgage and real estate loans				
9	Other investments (attach statement)				
10a	Buildings and other depreciable assets				
b	Less accumulated depreciation	( )		( )	
11a	Depletable assets				
b	Less accumulated depletion	( )		( )	
12	Land (net of any amortization)				
13a	Intangible assets (amortizable only)				
b	Less accumulated amortization	( )		( )	
14	Other assets (attach statement)				
15	Total assets				
	Liabilities and Shareholders' Equity				
16	Accounts payable				
17	Mortgages, notes, bonds payable in less than 1 year				
18	Other current liabilities (attach statement)				
19	Loans from shareholders				
20	Mortgages, notes, bonds payable in 1 year or more				
21	Other liabilities (attach statement)				
22	Capital stock: **a** Preferred stock				
	b Common stock				
23	Additional paid-in capital				
24	Retained earnings—Appropriated (attach statement)				
25	Retained earnings—Unappropriated				
26	Adjustments to shareholders' equity (attach statement)				
27	Less cost of treasury stock		( )		( )
28	Total liabilities and shareholders' equity				

Schedule M-1 **Reconciliation of Income (Loss) per Books With Income per Return**

Note: The corporation may be required to file Schedule M-3. See instructions.

1	Net income (loss) per books		7	Income recorded on books this year not included on this return (itemize): Tax-exempt interest $	
2	Federal income tax per books				
3	Excess of capital losses over capital gains				
4	Income subject to tax not recorded on books this year (itemize):		8	Deductions on this return not charged against book income this year (itemize):	
5	Expenses recorded on books this year not deducted on this return (itemize):		a	Depreciation $	
a	Depreciation $		b	Charitable contributions $	
b	Charitable contributions $				
c	Travel and entertainment $		9	Add lines 7 and 8	
6	Add lines 1 through 5		10	Income (page 1, line 28)—line 6 less line 9	

Schedule M-2 **Analysis of Unappropriated Retained Earnings per Books (Schedule L, Line 25)**

1	Balance at beginning of year		5	Distributions: **a** Cash	
2	Net income (loss) per books			**b** Stock	
3	Other increases (itemize):			**c** Property	
			6	Other decreases (itemize):	
			7	Add lines 5 and 6	
4	Add lines 1, 2, and 3		8	Balance at end of year (line 4 less line 7)	

Form **1120** (2021)

Form **1120-S**

Department of the Treasury
Internal Revenue Service

U.S. Income Tax Return for an S Corporation

▶ **Do not file this form unless the corporation has filed or is attaching Form 2553 to elect to be an S corporation.**
▶ **Go to *www.irs.gov/Form1120S* for instructions and the latest information.**

OMB No. 1545-0123

2021

For calendar year 2021 or tax year beginning , 2021, ending , 20

A S election effective date	TYPE OR PRINT	Name	**D Employer identification number**
B Business activity code number (see instructions)		Number, street, and room or suite no. If a P.O. box, see instructions.	**E** Date incorporated
C Check if Sch. M-3 attached ☐		City or town, state or province, country, and ZIP or foreign postal code	**F** Total assets (see instructions) $

G Is the corporation electing to be an S corporation beginning with this tax year? See instructions. ☐ Yes ☐ No

H Check if: **(1)** ☐ Final return **(2)** ☐ Name change **(3)** ☐ Address change **(4)** ☐ Amended return **(5)** ☐ S election termination

I Enter the number of shareholders who were shareholders during any part of the tax year . . . . ▶

J Check if corporation: **(1)** ☐ Aggregated activities for section 465 at-risk purposes **(2)** ☐ Grouped activities for section 469 passive activity purposes

Caution: Include **only** trade or business income and expenses on lines 1a through 21. See the instructions for more information.

Income	1a	Gross receipts or sales	1a			
	b	Returns and allowances	1b			
	c	Balance. Subtract line 1b from line 1a			1c	
	2	Cost of goods sold (attach Form 1125-A)			2	
	3	Gross profit. Subtract line 2 from line 1c			3	
	4	Net gain (loss) from Form 4797, line 17 (attach Form 4797)			4	
	5	Other income (loss) (see instructions—attach statement)			5	
	6	**Total income (loss).** Add lines 3 through 5 ▶			6	
Deductions (see instructions for limitations)	7	Compensation of officers (see instructions—attach Form 1125-E)			7	
	8	Salaries and wages (less employment credits)			8	
	9	Repairs and maintenance			9	
	10	Bad debts			10	
	11	Rents			11	
	12	Taxes and licenses			12	
	13	Interest (see instructions)			13	
	14	Depreciation not claimed on Form 1125-A or elsewhere on return (attach Form 4562)			14	
	15	Depletion **(Do not deduct oil and gas depletion.)**			15	
	16	Advertising			16	
	17	Pension, profit-sharing, etc., plans			17	
	18	Employee benefit programs			18	
	19	Other deductions (attach statement)			19	
	20	**Total deductions.** Add lines 7 through 19 ▶			20	
	21	**Ordinary business income (loss).** Subtract line 20 from line 6			21	
Tax and Payments	22a	Excess net passive income or LIFO recapture tax (see instructions)	22a			
	b	Tax from Schedule D (Form 1120-S)	22b			
	c	Add lines 22a and 22b (see instructions for additional taxes)			22c	
	23a	2021 estimated tax payments and 2020 overpayment credited to 2021	23a			
	b	Tax deposited with Form 7004	23b			
	c	Credit for federal tax paid on fuels (attach Form 4136)	23c			
	d	Add lines 23a through 23c			23d	
	24	Estimated tax penalty (see instructions). Check if Form 2220 is attached ▶ ☐			24	
	25	**Amount owed.** If line 23d is smaller than the total of lines 22c and 24, enter amount owed			25	
	26	**Overpayment.** If line 23d is larger than the total of lines 22c and 24, enter amount overpaid			26	
	27	Enter amount from line 26: **Credited to 2022 estimated tax ▶** **Refunded ▶**			27	

Sign Here

Under penalties of perjury, I declare that I have examined this return, including accompanying schedules and statements, and to the best of my knowledge and belief, it is true, correct, and complete. Declaration of preparer (other than taxpayer) is based on all information of which preparer has any knowledge.

▶ Signature of officer | Date | ▶ Title

May the IRS discuss this return with the preparer shown below? See instructions. ☐ Yes ☐ No

Paid Preparer Use Only

Print/Type preparer's name	Preparer's signature	Date	Check ☐ if self-employed	PTIN
Firm's name ▶			Firm's EIN ▶	
Firm's address ▶			Phone no.	

For Paperwork Reduction Act Notice, see separate instructions. Cat. No. 11510H Form **1120-S** (2021)

Form 1120-S (2021) Page 2

Schedule B Other Information (see instructions)

		Yes	No
1	Check accounting method: a ☐ Cash b ☐ Accrual c ☐ Other (specify) ▶		
2	See the instructions and enter the: a Business activity ▶ b Product or service ▶		
3	At any time during the tax year, was any shareholder of the corporation a disregarded entity, a trust, an estate, or a nominee or similar person? If "Yes," attach Schedule B-1, Information on Certain Shareholders of an S Corporation		
4	At the end of the tax year, did the corporation:		
a	Own directly 20% or more, or own, directly or indirectly, 50% or more of the total stock issued and outstanding of any foreign or domestic corporation? For rules of constructive ownership, see instructions. If "Yes," complete (i) through (v) below		

(i) Name of Corporation	**(ii)** Employer Identification Number (if any)	**(iii)** Country of Incorporation	**(iv)** Percentage of Stock Owned	**(v)** If Percentage in (iv) Is 100%, Enter the Date (if applicable) a Qualified Subchapter S Subsidiary Election Was Made

		Yes	No
b	Own directly an interest of 20% or more, or own, directly or indirectly, an interest of 50% or more in the profit, loss, or capital in any foreign or domestic partnership (including an entity treated as a partnership) or in the beneficial interest of a trust? For rules of constructive ownership, see instructions. If "Yes," complete (i) through (v) below		

(i) Name of Entity	**(ii)** Employer Identification Number (if any)	**(iii)** Type of Entity	**(iv)** Country of Organization	**(v)** Maximum Percentage Owned in Profit, Loss, or Capital

		Yes	No
5a	At the end of the tax year, did the corporation have any outstanding shares of restricted stock? If "Yes," complete lines (i) and (ii) below. **(i)** Total shares of restricted stock ▶ **(ii)** Total shares of non-restricted stock ▶		
b	At the end of the tax year, did the corporation have any outstanding stock options, warrants, or similar instruments? If "Yes," complete lines (i) and (ii) below. **(i)** Total shares of stock outstanding at the end of the tax year ▶ **(ii)** Total shares of stock outstanding if all instruments were executed ▶		
6	Has this corporation filed, or is it required to file, **Form 8918,** Material Advisor Disclosure Statement, to provide information on any reportable transaction?		
7	Check this box if the corporation issued publicly offered debt instruments with original issue discount ▶ ☐ If checked, the corporation may have to file **Form 8281,** Information Return for Publicly Offered Original Issue Discount Instruments.		
8	If the corporation **(a)** was a C corporation before it elected to be an S corporation **or** the corporation acquired an asset with a basis determined by reference to the basis of the asset (or the basis of any other property) in the hands of a C corporation, **and (b)** has net unrealized built-in gain in excess of the net recognized built-in gain from prior years, enter the net unrealized built-in gain reduced by net recognized built-in gain from prior years. See instructions ▶ $		
9	Did the corporation have an election under section 163(j) for any real property trade or business or any farming business in effect during the tax year? See instructions		
10	Does the corporation satisfy one or more of the following? See instructions		
a	The corporation owns a pass-through entity with current, or prior year carryover, excess business interest expense.		
b	The corporation's aggregate average annual gross receipts (determined under section 448(c)) for the 3 tax years preceding the current tax year are more than $26 million and the corporation has business interest expense.		
c	The corporation is a tax shelter and the corporation has business interest expense. If "Yes," complete and attach Form 8990.		
11	Does the corporation satisfy **both** of the following conditions?		
a	The corporation's total receipts (see instructions) for the tax year were less than $250,000.		
b	The corporation's total assets at the end of the tax year were less than $250,000. If "Yes," the corporation is not required to complete Schedules L and M-1.		

Form 1120-S (2021) Page **3**

Schedule B **Other Information** (see instructions) *(continued)*

		Yes	No
12	During the tax year, did the corporation have any non-shareholder debt that was canceled, was forgiven, or had the terms modified so as to reduce the principal amount of the debt?		
	If "Yes," enter the amount of principal reduction ▶ $		
13	During the tax year, was a qualified subchapter S subsidiary election terminated or revoked? If "Yes," see instructions		
14a	Did the corporation make any payments in 2021 that would require it to file Form(s) 1099?		
b	If "Yes," did the corporation file or will it file required Form(s) 1099?		
15	Is the corporation attaching Form 8996 to certify as a Qualified Opportunity Fund?		
	If "Yes," enter the amount from Form 8996, line 15 ▶ $		

Schedule K **Shareholders' Pro Rata Share Items**

						Total amount
Income (Loss)	1	Ordinary business income (loss) (page 1, line 21)			1	
	2	Net rental real estate income (loss) (attach Form 8825)			2	
	3a	Other gross rental income (loss)	3a			
	b	Expenses from other rental activities (attach statement)	3b			
	c	Other net rental income (loss). Subtract line 3b from line 3a			3c	
	4	Interest income			4	
	5	Dividends: **a** Ordinary dividends			5a	
		b Qualified dividends	5b			
	6	Royalties			6	
	7	Net short-term capital gain (loss) (attach Schedule D (Form 1120-S))			7	
	8a	Net long-term capital gain (loss) (attach Schedule D (Form 1120-S))			8a	
	b	Collectibles (28%) gain (loss)	8b			
	c	Unrecaptured section 1250 gain (attach statement)	8c			
	9	Net section 1231 gain (loss) (attach Form 4797)			9	
	10	Other income (loss) (see instructions) Type ▶			10	
Deductions	11	Section 179 deduction (attach Form 4562)			11	
	12a	Charitable contributions			12a	
	b	Investment interest expense			12b	
	c	Section 59(e)(2) expenditures Type ▶			12c	
	d	Other deductions (see instructions) Type ▶			12d	
Credits	13a	Low-income housing credit (section 42(j)(5))			13a	
	b	Low-income housing credit (other)			13b	
	c	Qualified rehabilitation expenditures (rental real estate) (attach Form 3468, if applicable)			13c	
	d	Other rental real estate credits (see instructions) Type ▶			13d	
	e	Other rental credits (see instructions) Type ▶			13e	
	f	Biofuel producer credit (attach Form 6478)			13f	
	g	Other credits (see instructions) Type ▶			13g	
International Transactions	14	Attach Schedule K-2 (Form 1120-S), Shareholders' Pro Rata Share Items—International, and check this box to indicate you are reporting items of international tax relevance ▶ ☐				
Alternative Minimum Tax (AMT) Items	15a	Post-1986 depreciation adjustment			15a	
	b	Adjusted gain or loss			15b	
	c	Depletion (other than oil and gas)			15c	
	d	Oil, gas, and geothermal properties—gross income			15d	
	e	Oil, gas, and geothermal properties—deductions			15e	
	f	Other AMT items (attach statement)			15f	
Items Affecting Shareholder Basis	16a	Tax-exempt interest income			16a	
	b	Other tax-exempt income			16b	
	c	Nondeductible expenses			16c	
	d	Distributions (attach statement if required) (see instructions)			16d	
	e	Repayment of loans from shareholders			16e	
	f	Foreign taxes paid or accrued			16f	

Form **1120-S** (2021)

Schedule K		Shareholders' Pro Rata Share Items *(continued)*		Total amount
Other Information	17a	Investment income	17a	
	b	Investment expenses	17b	
	c	Dividend distributions paid from accumulated earnings and profits	17c	
	d	Other items and amounts (attach statement)		
Recon-ciliation	18	**Income (loss) reconciliation.** Combine the amounts on lines 1 through 10 in the far right column. From the result, subtract the sum of the amounts on lines 11 through 12d and 16f	18	

Schedule L Balance Sheets per Books		Beginning of tax year		End of tax year	
	Assets	(a)	(b)	(c)	(d)
1	Cash				
2a	Trade notes and accounts receivable				
b	Less allowance for bad debts	( )		( )	
3	Inventories				
4	U.S. government obligations				
5	Tax-exempt securities (see instructions)				
6	Other current assets (attach statement)				
7	Loans to shareholders				
8	Mortgage and real estate loans				
9	Other investments (attach statement)				
10a	Buildings and other depreciable assets				
b	Less accumulated depreciation	( )		( )	
11a	Depletable assets				
b	Less accumulated depletion	( )		( )	
12	Land (net of any amortization)				
13a	Intangible assets (amortizable only)				
b	Less accumulated amortization	( )		( )	
14	Other assets (attach statement)				
15	Total assets				
	Liabilities and Shareholders' Equity				
16	Accounts payable				
17	Mortgages, notes, bonds payable in less than 1 year				
18	Other current liabilities (attach statement)				
19	Loans from shareholders				
20	Mortgages, notes, bonds payable in 1 year or more				
21	Other liabilities (attach statement)				
22	Capital stock				
23	Additional paid-in capital				
24	Retained earnings				
25	Adjustments to shareholders' equity (attach statement)				
26	Less cost of treasury stock		( )		( )
27	Total liabilities and shareholders' equity				

Schedule M-1 Reconciliation of Income (Loss) per Books With Income (Loss) per Return

Note: The corporation may be required to file Schedule M-3. See instructions.

1	Net income (loss) per books		5	Income recorded on books this year not included on Schedule K, lines 1 through 10 (itemize):	
2	Income included on Schedule K, lines 1, 2, 3c, 4, 5a, 6, 7, 8a, 9, and 10, not recorded on books this year (itemize) ______________		a	Tax-exempt interest $ ______________	
3	Expenses recorded on books this year not included on Schedule K, lines 1 through 12 and 16f (itemize):		6	Deductions included on Schedule K, lines 1 through 12 and 16f, not charged against book income this year (itemize):	
a	Depreciation $ ______________		a	Depreciation $ ______________	
b	Travel and entertainment $ ______________		7	Add lines 5 and 6	
4	Add lines 1 through 3		8	Income (loss) (Schedule K, line 18). Subtract line 7 from line 4	

Schedule M-2 Analysis of Accumulated Adjustments Account, Shareholders' Undistributed Taxable Income Previously Taxed, Accumulated Earnings and Profits, and Other Adjustments Account

(see instructions)

		(a) Accumulated adjustments account	**(b)** Shareholders' undistributed taxable income previously taxed	**(c)** Accumulated earnings and profits	**(d)** Other adjustments account
1	Balance at beginning of tax year				
2	Ordinary income from page 1, line 21 . . .				
3	Other additions				
4	Loss from page 1, line 21	( )			
5	Other reductions	( )			( )
6	Combine lines 1 through 5				
7	Distributions				
8	Balance at end of tax year. Subtract line 7 from line 6				

671121

☐ Final K-1 ☐ Amended K-1 OMB No. 1545-0123

Schedule K-1 (Form 1120-S) 2021

Department of the Treasury
Internal Revenue Service

For calendar year 2021, or tax year

beginning / / 2021 ending / /

Shareholder's Share of Income, Deductions, Credits, etc.

▶ See separate instructions.

Part I Information About the Corporation

A Corporation's employer identification number

B Corporation's name, address, city, state, and ZIP code

C IRS Center where corporation filed return

D Corporation's total number of shares
Beginning of tax year . . . . . . ________
End of tax year . . . . ________

Part II Information About the Shareholder

E Shareholder's identifying number

F Shareholder's name, address, city, state, and ZIP code

G Current year allocation percentage . . . ________ %

H Shareholder's number of shares
Beginning of tax year . . . . . . ________
End of tax year . . . . ________

I Loans from shareholder
Beginning of tax year . . . . . . $ ________
End of tax year . . . . $ ________

For IRS Use Only

Part III Shareholder's Share of Current Year Income, Deductions, Credits, and Other Items

1	Ordinary business income (loss)	13	Credits
2	Net rental real estate income (loss)		
3	Other net rental income (loss)		
4	Interest income		
5a	Ordinary dividends		
5b	Qualified dividends	14	Schedule K-3 is attached if checked . . . . ▶ ☐
6	Royalties	15	Alternative minimum tax (AMT) items
7	Net short-term capital gain (loss)		
8a	Net long-term capital gain (loss)		
8b	Collectibles (28%) gain (loss)		
8c	Unrecaptured section 1250 gain		
9	Net section 1231 gain (loss)	16	Items affecting shareholder basis
10	Other income (loss)		
		17	Other information
11	Section 179 deduction		
12	Other deductions		

18 ☐ More than one activity for at-risk purposes*
19 ☐ More than one activity for passive activity purposes*

* See attached statement for additional information.

Form **4562**

Department of the Treasury
Internal Revenue Service (99)

Depreciation and Amortization
(Including Information on Listed Property)
▶ Attach to your tax return.
▶ Go to *www.irs.gov/Form4562* for instructions and the latest information.

OMB No. 1545-0172
2021
Attachment Sequence No. **179**

Name(s) shown on return	Business or activity to which this form relates	Identifying number

Part I Election To Expense Certain Property Under Section 179
Note: If you have any listed property, complete Part V before you complete Part I.

1	Maximum amount (see instructions)	1	
2	Total cost of section 179 property placed in service (see instructions)	2	
3	Threshold cost of section 179 property before reduction in limitation (see instructions)	3	
4	Reduction in limitation. Subtract line 3 from line 2. If zero or less, enter -0-	4	
5	Dollar limitation for tax year. Subtract line 4 from line 1. If zero or less, enter -0-. If married filing separately, see instructions	5	

6 (a) Description of property	(b) Cost (business use only)	(c) Elected cost
7 Listed property. Enter the amount from line 29	7	

8	Total elected cost of section 179 property. Add amounts in column (c), lines 6 and 7	8	
9	Tentative deduction. Enter the **smaller** of line 5 or line 8	9	
10	Carryover of disallowed deduction from line 13 of your 2020 Form 4562	10	
11	Business income limitation. Enter the smaller of business income (not less than zero) or line 5. See instructions	11	
12	Section 179 expense deduction. Add lines 9 and 10, but don't enter more than line 11	12	
13	Carryover of disallowed deduction to 2022. Add lines 9 and 10, less line 12 ▶ 13		

Note: Don't use Part II or Part III below for listed property. Instead, use Part V.

Part II Special Depreciation Allowance and Other Depreciation (Don't include listed property. See instructions.)

14	Special depreciation allowance for qualified property (other than listed property) placed in service during the tax year. See instructions	14	
15	Property subject to section 168(f)(1) election	15	
16	Other depreciation (including ACRS)	16	

Part III MACRS Depreciation (Don't include listed property. See instructions.)

Section A

17	MACRS deductions for assets placed in service in tax years beginning before 2021	17	
18	If you are electing to group any assets placed in service during the tax year into one or more general asset accounts, check here ▶ ☐		

Section B—Assets Placed in Service During 2021 Tax Year Using the General Depreciation System

(a) Classification of property	(b) Month and year placed in service	(c) Basis for depreciation (business/investment use only—see instructions)	(d) Recovery period	(e) Convention	(f) Method	(g) Depreciation deduction
19a 3-year property						
b 5-year property						
c 7-year property						
d 10-year property						
e 15-year property						
f 20-year property						
g 25-year property			25 yrs.		S/L	
h Residential rental			27.5 yrs.	MM	S/L	
property			27.5 yrs.	MM	S/L	
i Nonresidential real			39 yrs.	MM	S/L	
property				MM	S/L	

Section C—Assets Placed in Service During 2021 Tax Year Using the Alternative Depreciation System

(a) Classification of property	(b)	(c)	(d)	(e)	(f)	(g)
20a Class life					S/L	
b 12-year			12 yrs.		S/L	
c 30-year			30 yrs.	MM	S/L	
d 40-year			40 yrs.	MM	S/L	

Part IV Summary (See instructions.)

21	Listed property. Enter amount from line 28	21	
22	**Total.** Add amounts from line 12, lines 14 through 17, lines 19 and 20 in column (g), and line 21. Enter here and on the appropriate lines of your return. Partnerships and S corporations—see instructions	22	
23	For assets shown above and placed in service during the current year, enter the portion of the basis attributable to section 263A costs ▶ 23		

Form 4562 (2021) Page 2

Part V **Listed Property** (Include automobiles, certain other vehicles, certain aircraft, and property used for entertainment, recreation, or amusement.)

Note: For any vehicle for which you are using the standard mileage rate or deducting lease expense, complete **only** 24a, 24b, columns (a) through (c) of Section A, all of Section B, and Section C if applicable.

Section A—Depreciation and Other Information (Caution: See the instructions for limits for passenger automobiles.**)**

24a Do you have evidence to support the business/investment use claimed? ☐ **Yes** ☐ **No** | **24b** If "Yes," is the evidence written? ☐ **Yes** ☐ **No**

(a) Type of property (list vehicles first)	(b) Date placed in service	(c) Business/ investment use percentage	(d) Cost or other basis	(e) Basis for depreciation (business/investment use only)	(f) Recovery period	(g) Method/ Convention	(h) Depreciation deduction	(i) Elected section 179 cost
25 Special depreciation allowance for qualified listed property placed in service during the tax year and used more than 50% in a qualified business use. See instructions .						25		
26 Property used more than 50% in a qualified business use:								
		%						
		%						
		%						
27 Property used 50% or less in a qualified business use:								
		%				S/L –		
		%				S/L –		
		%				S/L –		
28 Add amounts in column (h), lines 25 through 27. Enter here and on line 21, page 1 .						28		
29 Add amounts in column (i), line 26. Enter here and on line 7, page 1							29	

Section B—Information on Use of Vehicles

Complete this section for vehicles used by a sole proprietor, partner, or other "more than 5% owner," or related person. If you provided vehicles to your employees, first answer the questions in Section C to see if you meet an exception to completing this section for those vehicles.

	(a) Vehicle 1		(b) Vehicle 2		(c) Vehicle 3		(d) Vehicle 4		(e) Vehicle 5		(f) Vehicle 6	
30 Total business/investment miles driven during the year (**don't** include commuting miles) .												
31 Total commuting miles driven during the year												
32 Total other personal (noncommuting) miles driven												
33 Total miles driven during the year. Add lines 30 through 32												
	Yes	**No**	**Yes**	**No**	**Yes**	**No**	**Yes**	**No**	**Yes**	**No**	**Yes**	**No**
34 Was the vehicle available for personal use during off-duty hours?												
35 Was the vehicle used primarily by a more than 5% owner or related person? . .												
36 Is another vehicle available for personal use?												

Section C—Questions for Employers Who Provide Vehicles for Use by Their Employees

Answer these questions to determine if you meet an exception to completing Section B for vehicles used by employees who **aren't** more than 5% owners or related persons. See instructions.

	Yes	**No**
37 Do you maintain a written policy statement that prohibits all personal use of vehicles, including commuting, by your employees?		
38 Do you maintain a written policy statement that prohibits personal use of vehicles, except commuting, by your employees? See the instructions for vehicles used by corporate officers, directors, or 1% or more owners . .		
39 Do you treat all use of vehicles by employees as personal use?		
40 Do you provide more than five vehicles to your employees, obtain information from your employees about the use of the vehicles, and retain the information received?		
41 Do you meet the requirements concerning qualified automobile demonstration use? See instructions.		
Note: If your answer to 37, 38, 39, 40, or 41 is "Yes," don't complete Section B for the covered vehicles.		

Part VI **Amortization**

(a) Description of costs	(b) Date amortization begins	(c) Amortizable amount	(d) Code section	(e) Amortization period or percentage	(f) Amortization for this year
42 Amortization of costs that begins during your 2021 tax year (see instructions):					
43 Amortization of costs that began before your 2021 tax year				43	
44 **Total.** Add amounts in column (f). See the instructions for where to report				44	

Form **4562** (2021)

Form **4797**

Department of the Treasury
Internal Revenue Service

Sales of Business Property

(Also Involuntary Conversions and Recapture Amounts Under Sections 179 and 280F(b)(2))

▶ **Attach to your tax return.**

▶ **Go to *www.irs.gov/Form4797* for instructions and the latest information.**

OMB No. 1545-0184

2021

Attachment Sequence No. **27**

Name(s) shown on return | **Identifying number**

1a	Enter the gross proceeds from sales or exchanges reported to you for 2021 on Form(s) 1099-B or 1099-S (or substitute statement) that you are including on line 2, 10, or 20. See instructions	**1a**	
b	Enter the total amount of gain that you are including on lines 2, 10, and 24 due to the partial dispositions of MACRS assets	**1b**	
c	Enter the total amount of loss that you are including on lines 2 and 10 due to the partial dispositions of MACRS assets	**1c**	

Part I Sales or Exchanges of Property Used in a Trade or Business and Involuntary Conversions From Other Than Casualty or Theft—Most Property Held More Than 1 Year (see instructions)

2 (a) Description of property	(b) Date acquired (mo., day, yr.)	(c) Date sold (mo., day, yr.)	(d) Gross sales price	(e) Depreciation allowed or allowable since acquisition	(f) Cost or other basis, plus improvements and expense of sale	(g) Gain or (loss) Subtract (f) from the sum of (d) and (e)

3	Gain, if any, from Form 4684, line 39	**3**	
4	Section 1231 gain from installment sales from Form 6252, line 26 or 37	**4**	
5	Section 1231 gain or (loss) from like-kind exchanges from Form 8824	**5**	
6	Gain, if any, from line 32, from other than casualty or theft	**6**	
7	Combine lines 2 through 6. Enter the gain or (loss) here and on the appropriate line as follows	**7**	
	Partnerships and S corporations. Report the gain or (loss) following the instructions for Form 1065, Schedule K, line 10, or Form 1120-S, Schedule K, line 9. Skip lines 8, 9, 11, and 12 below. **Individuals, partners, S corporation shareholders, and all others.** If line 7 is zero or a loss, enter the amount from line 7 on line 11 below and skip lines 8 and 9. If line 7 is a gain and you didn't have any prior year section 1231 losses, or they were recaptured in an earlier year, enter the gain from line 7 as a long-term capital gain on the Schedule D filed with your return and skip lines 8, 9, 11, and 12 below.		
8	Nonrecaptured net section 1231 losses from prior years. See instructions	**8**	
9	Subtract line 8 from line 7. If zero or less, enter -0-. If line 9 is zero, enter the gain from line 7 on line 12 below. If line 9 is more than zero, enter the amount from line 8 on line 12 below and enter the gain from line 9 as a long-term capital gain on the Schedule D filed with your return. See instructions	**9**	

Part II Ordinary Gains and Losses (see instructions)

10 Ordinary gains and losses not included on lines 11 through 16 (include property held 1 year or less):

11	Loss, if any, from line 7	**11**	( )
12	Gain, if any, from line 7 or amount from line 8, if applicable	**12**	
13	Gain, if any, from line 31	**13**	
14	Net gain or (loss) from Form 4684, lines 31 and 38a	**14**	
15	Ordinary gain from installment sales from Form 6252, line 25 or 36	**15**	
16	Ordinary gain or (loss) from like-kind exchanges from Form 8824	**16**	
17	Combine lines 10 through 16	**17**	
18	For all except individual returns, enter the amount from line 17 on the appropriate line of your return and skip lines a and b below. For individual returns, complete lines a and b below.		
a	If the loss on line 11 includes a loss from Form 4684, line 35, column (b)(ii), enter that part of the loss here. Enter the loss from income-producing property on Schedule A (Form 1040), line 16. (Do not include any loss on property used as an employee.) Identify as from "Form 4797, line 18a." See instructions	**18a**	
b	Redetermine the gain or (loss) on line 17 excluding the loss, if any, on line 18a. Enter here and on Schedule 1 (Form 1040), Part I, line 4	**18b**	

For Paperwork Reduction Act Notice, see separate instructions. Cat. No. 13086I Form **4797** (2021)

Form 4797 (2021) Page 2

Part III **Gain From Disposition of Property Under Sections 1245, 1250, 1252, 1254, and 1255** (see instructions)

19	(a) Description of section 1245, 1250, 1252, 1254, or 1255 property:	(b) Date acquired (mo., day, yr.)	(c) Date sold (mo., day, yr.)
A			
B			
C			
D			

	These columns relate to the properties on lines 19A through 19D. ▶		Property A	Property B	Property C	Property D
20	Gross sales price (**Note:** *See line 1a before completing.*)	20				
21	Cost or other basis plus expense of sale	21				
22	Depreciation (or depletion) allowed or allowable	22				
23	Adjusted basis. Subtract line 22 from line 21	23				
24	Total gain. Subtract line 23 from line 20	24				
25	**If section 1245 property:**					
a	Depreciation allowed or allowable from line 22	25a				
b	Enter the **smaller** of line 24 or 25a	25b				
26	**If section 1250 property:** If straight line depreciation was used, enter -0- on line 26g, except for a corporation subject to section 291.					
a	Additional depreciation after 1975. See instructions	26a				
b	Applicable percentage multiplied by the **smaller** of line 24 or line 26a. See instructions	26b				
c	Subtract line 26a from line 24. If residential rental property **or** line 24 isn't more than line 26a, skip lines 26d and 26e	26c				
d	Additional depreciation after 1969 and before 1976	26d				
e	Enter the **smaller** of line 26c or 26d	26e				
f	Section 291 amount (corporations only)	26f				
g	Add lines 26b, 26e, and 26f	26g				
27	**If section 1252 property:** Skip this section if you didn't dispose of farmland or if this form is being completed for a partnership.					
a	Soil, water, and land clearing expenses	27a				
b	Line 27a multiplied by applicable percentage. See instructions	27b				
c	Enter the **smaller** of line 24 or 27b	27c				
28	**If section 1254 property:**					
a	Intangible drilling and development costs, expenditures for development of mines and other natural deposits, mining exploration costs, and depletion. See instructions	28a				
b	Enter the **smaller** of line 24 or 28a	28b				
29	**If section 1255 property:**					
a	Applicable percentage of payments excluded from income under section 126. See instructions	29a				
b	Enter the **smaller** of line 24 or 29a. See instructions	29b				

Summary of Part III Gains. Complete property columns A through D through line 29b before going to line 30.

30	Total gains for all properties. Add property columns A through D, line 24	30	
31	Add property columns A through D, lines 25b, 26g, 27c, 28b, and 29b. Enter here and on line 13	31	
32	Subtract line 31 from line 30. Enter the portion from casualty or theft on Form 4684, line 33. Enter the portion from other than casualty or theft on Form 4797, line 6	32	

Part IV **Recapture Amounts Under Sections 179 and 280F(b)(2) When Business Use Drops to 50% or Less** (see instructions)

			(a) Section 179	(b) Section 280F(b)(2)
33	Section 179 expense deduction or depreciation allowable in prior years	33		
34	Recomputed depreciation. See instructions	34		
35	Recapture amount. Subtract line 34 from line 33. See the instructions for where to report	35		

Form **6251**

Department of the Treasury
Internal Revenue Service (99)

Alternative Minimum Tax—Individuals

► Go to *www.irs.gov/Form6251* for instructions and the latest information.
► Attach to Form 1040, 1040-SR, or 1040-NR.

OMB No. 1545-0074
2021
Attachment Sequence No. 32

Name(s) shown on Form 1040, 1040-SR, or 1040-NR | Your social security number

Part I Alternative Minimum Taxable Income (See instructions for how to complete each line.)

1	Enter the amount from Form 1040 or 1040-SR, line 15, if more than zero. If Form 1040 or 1040-SR, line 15, is zero, subtract line 14 of Form 1040 or 1040-SR from line 11 of Form 1040 or 1040-SR and enter the result here. (If less than zero, enter as a negative amount.)	1	
2a	If filing Schedule A (Form 1040), enter the taxes from Schedule A, line 7; otherwise, enter the amount from Form 1040 or 1040-SR, line 12a	2a	
b	Tax refund from Schedule 1 (Form 1040), line 1 or line 8z	2b	( )
c	Investment interest expense (difference between regular tax and AMT)	2c	
d	Depletion (difference between regular tax and AMT)	2d	
e	Net operating loss deduction from Schedule 1 (Form 1040), line 8a. Enter as a positive amount	2e	
f	Alternative tax net operating loss deduction	2f	( )
g	Interest from specified private activity bonds exempt from the regular tax	2g	
h	Qualified small business stock, see instructions	2h	
i	Exercise of incentive stock options (excess of AMT income over regular tax income)	2i	
j	Estates and trusts (amount from Schedule K-1 (Form 1041), box 12, code A)	2j	
k	Disposition of property (difference between AMT and regular tax gain or loss)	2k	
l	Depreciation on assets placed in service after 1986 (difference between regular tax and AMT)	2l	
m	Passive activities (difference between AMT and regular tax income or loss)	2m	
n	Loss limitations (difference between AMT and regular tax income or loss)	2n	
o	Circulation costs (difference between regular tax and AMT)	2o	
p	Long-term contracts (difference between AMT and regular tax income)	2p	
q	Mining costs (difference between regular tax and AMT)	2q	
r	Research and experimental costs (difference between regular tax and AMT)	2r	
s	Income from certain installment sales before January 1, 1987	2s	( )
t	Intangible drilling costs preference	2t	
3	Other adjustments, including income-based related adjustments	3	
4	**Alternative minimum taxable income.** Combine lines 1 through 3. (If married filing separately and line 4 is more than $752,800, see instructions.)	4	

Part II Alternative Minimum Tax (AMT)

5 Exemption.

IF your filing status is . . .	AND line 4 is not over . . .	THEN enter on line 5 . . .
Single or head of household	$ 523,600	$ 73,600
Married filing jointly or qualifying widow(er)	1,047,200	114,600
Married filing separately	523,600	57,300

If line 4 is **over** the amount shown above for your filing status, see instructions. . . . **5**

6	Subtract line 5 from line 4. If more than zero, go to line 7. If zero or less, enter -0- here and on lines 7, 9, and 11, and go to line 10	6	
7	• If you are filing Form 2555, see instructions for the amount to enter. • If you reported capital gain distributions directly on Form 1040 or 1040-SR, line 7; you reported qualified dividends on Form 1040 or 1040-SR, line 3a; **or** you had a gain on both lines 15 and 16 of Schedule D (Form 1040) (as refigured for the AMT, if necessary), complete Part III on the back and enter the amount from line 40 here. • **All others:** If line 6 is $199,900 or less ($99,950 or less if married filing separately), multiply line 6 by 26% (0.26). Otherwise, multiply line 6 by 28% (0.28) and subtract $3,998 ($1,999 if married filing separately) from the result.	7	
8	Alternative minimum tax foreign tax credit (see instructions)	8	
9	Tentative minimum tax. Subtract line 8 from line 7	9	
10	Add Form 1040 or 1040-SR, line 16 (minus any tax from Form 4972), and Schedule 2 (Form 1040), line 2. Subtract from the result Schedule 3 (Form 1040), line 1 and any negative amount reported on Form 8978, line 14 (treated as a positive number). If zero or less, enter -0-. If you used Schedule J to figure your tax on Form 1040 or 1040-SR, line 16, refigure that tax without using Schedule J before completing this line. See instructions	10	
11	**AMT.** Subtract line 10 from line 9. If zero or less, enter -0-. Enter here and on Schedule 2 (Form 1040), line 1	11	

Part III **Tax Computation Using Maximum Capital Gains Rates**

Complete Part III only if you are required to do so by line 7 or by the Foreign Earned Income Tax Worksheet in the instructions.

12	Enter the amount from Form 6251, line 6. If you are filing Form 2555, enter the amount from line 3 of the worksheet in the instructions for line 7	12	
13	Enter the amount from line 4 of the Qualified Dividends and Capital Gain Tax Worksheet in the Instructions for Form 1040 or the amount from line 13 of the Schedule D Tax Worksheet in the Instructions for Schedule D (Form 1040), whichever applies (as refigured for the AMT, if necessary). See instructions. If you are filing Form 2555, see instructions for the amount to enter	13	
14	Enter the amount from Schedule D (Form 1040), line 19 (as refigured for the AMT, if necessary). See instructions. If you are filing Form 2555, see instructions for the amount to enter	14	
15	If you did not complete a Schedule D Tax Worksheet for the regular tax or the AMT, enter the amount from line 13. Otherwise, add lines 13 and 14, and enter the **smaller** of that result or the amount from line 10 of the Schedule D Tax Worksheet (as refigured for the AMT, if necessary). If you are filing Form 2555, see instructions for the amount to enter	15	
16	Enter the **smaller** of line 12 or line 15	16	
17	Subtract line 16 from line 12	17	
18	If line 17 is $199,900 or less ($99,950 or less if married filing separately), multiply line 17 by 26% (0.26). Otherwise, multiply line 17 by 28% (0.28) and subtract $3,998 ($1,999 if married filing separately) from the result ▶	18	
19	Enter: • $80,800 if married filing jointly or qualifying widow(er), • $40,400 if single or married filing separately, or • $54,100 if head of household.	19	
20	Enter the amount from line 5 of the Qualified Dividends and Capital Gain Tax Worksheet or the amount from line 14 of the Schedule D Tax Worksheet, whichever applies (as figured for the regular tax). If you did not complete either worksheet for the regular tax, enter the amount from Form 1040 or 1040-SR, line 15; if zero or less, enter -0-. If you are filing Form 2555, see instructions for the amount to enter	20	
21	Subtract line 20 from line 19. If zero or less, enter -0-	21	
22	Enter the **smaller** of line 12 or line 13	22	
23	Enter the **smaller** of line 21 or line 22. This amount is taxed at 0%	23	
24	Subtract line 23 from line 22	24	
25	Enter: • $445,850 if single, • $250,800 if married filing separately, • $501,600 if married filing jointly or qualifying widow(er), or • $473,750 if head of household.	25	
26	Enter the amount from line 21	26	
27	Enter the amount from line 5 of the Qualified Dividends and Capital Gain Tax Worksheet or the amount from line 21 of the Schedule D Tax Worksheet, whichever applies (as figured for the regular tax). If you did not complete either worksheet for the regular tax, enter the amount from Form 1040 or 1040-SR, line 15; if zero or less, enter -0-. If you are filing Form 2555, see instructions for the amount to enter	27	
28	Add line 26 and line 27	28	
29	Subtract line 28 from line 25. If zero or less, enter -0-	29	
30	Enter the smaller of line 24 or line 29	30	
31	Multiply line 30 by 15% (0.15) ▶	31	
32	Add lines 23 and 30	32	
	If lines 32 and 12 are the same, skip lines 33 through 37 and go to line 38. Otherwise, go to line 33.		
33	Subtract line 32 from line 22	33	
34	Multiply line 33 by 20% (0.20) ▶	34	
	If line 14 is zero or blank, skip lines 35 through 37 and go to line 38. Otherwise, go to line 35.		
35	Add lines 17, 32, and 33	35	
36	Subtract line 35 from line 12	36	
37	Multiply line 36 by 25% (0.25) ▶	37	
38	Add lines 18, 31, 34, and 37	38	
39	If line 12 is $199,900 or less ($99,950 or less if married filing separately), multiply line 12 by 26% (0.26). Otherwise, multiply line 12 by 28% (0.28) and subtract $3,998 ($1,999 if married filing separately) from the result	39	
40	Enter the **smaller** of line 38 or line 39 here and on line 7. If you are filing Form 2555, do not enter this amount on line 7. Instead, enter it on line 4 of the worksheet in the instructions for line 7	40	

Form **8949** | Department of the Treasury Internal Revenue Service

Sales and Other Dispositions of Capital Assets

► Go to *www.irs.gov/Form8949* for instructions and the latest information.

► File with your Schedule D to list your transactions for lines 1b, 2, 3, 8b, 9, and 10 of Schedule D.

OMB No. 1545-0074 | 2021 | Attachment Sequence No. **12A**

Name(s) shown on return | **Social security number or taxpayer identification number**

Before you check Box A, B, or C below, see whether you received any Form(s) 1099-B or substitute statement(s) from your broker. A substitute statement will have the same information as Form 1099-B. Either will show whether your basis (usually your cost) was reported to the IRS by your broker and may even tell you which box to check.

Part I **Short-Term.** Transactions involving capital assets you held 1 year or less are generally short-term (see instructions). For long-term transactions, see page 2.

Note: You may aggregate all short-term transactions reported on Form(s) 1099-B showing basis was reported to the IRS and for which no adjustments or codes are required. Enter the totals directly on Schedule D, line 1a; you aren't required to report these transactions on Form 8949 (see instructions).

You *must* check Box A, B, *or* C below. Check only one box. If more than one box applies for your short-term transactions, complete a separate Form 8949, page 1, for each applicable box. If you have more short-term transactions than will fit on this page for one or more of the boxes, complete as many forms with the same box checked as you need.

☐ **(A)** Short-term transactions reported on Form(s) 1099-B showing basis was reported to the IRS (see **Note** above)

☐ **(B)** Short-term transactions reported on Form(s) 1099-B showing basis **wasn't** reported to the IRS

☐ **(C)** Short-term transactions not reported to you on Form 1099-B

1 (a) Description of property (Example: 100 sh. XYZ Co.)	(b) Date acquired (Mo., day, yr.)	(c) Date sold or disposed of (Mo., day, yr.)	(d) Proceeds (sales price) (see instructions)	(e) Cost or other basis. See the **Note** below and see *Column (e)* in the separate instructions	**Adjustment, if any, to gain or loss.** If you enter an amount in column (g), enter a code in column (f). **See the separate instructions.** (f) Code(s) from instructions	(g) Amount of adjustment	(h) **Gain or (loss).** Subtract column (e) from column (d) and combine the result with column (g)
2 Totals. Add the amounts in columns (d), (e), (g), and (h) (subtract negative amounts). Enter each total here and include on your Schedule D, **line 1b** (if **Box A** above is checked), **line 2** (if **Box B** above is checked), or **line 3** (if **Box C** above is checked) ►							

Note: If you checked Box A above but the basis reported to the IRS was incorrect, enter in column (e) the basis as reported to the IRS, and enter an adjustment in column (g) to correct the basis. See *Column (g)* in the separate instructions for how to figure the amount of the adjustment.

Form 8949 (2021) Attachment Sequence No. **12A** Page **2**

Name(s) shown on return. Name and SSN or taxpayer identification no. not required if shown on other side	**Social security number or taxpayer identification number**

Before you check Box D, E, or F below, see whether you received any Form(s) 1099-B or substitute statement(s) from your broker. A substitute statement will have the same information as Form 1099-B. Either will show whether your basis (usually your cost) was reported to the IRS by your broker and may even tell you which box to check.

Part II **Long-Term.** Transactions involving capital assets you held more than 1 year are generally long-term (see instructions). For short-term transactions, see page 1.

Note: You may aggregate all long-term transactions reported on Form(s) 1099-B showing basis was reported to the IRS and for which no adjustments or codes are required. Enter the totals directly on Schedule D, line 8a; you aren't required to report these transactions on Form 8949 (see instructions).

You *must* check Box D, E, *or* F below. Check only one box. If more than one box applies for your long-term transactions, complete a separate Form 8949, page 2, for each applicable box. If you have more long-term transactions than will fit on this page for one or more of the boxes, complete as many forms with the same box checked as you need.

☐ **(D)** Long-term transactions reported on Form(s) 1099-B showing basis was reported to the IRS (see **Note** above)

☐ **(E)** Long-term transactions reported on Form(s) 1099-B showing basis **wasn't** reported to the IRS

☐ **(F)** Long-term transactions not reported to you on Form 1099-B

1 (a) Description of property (Example: 100 sh. XYZ Co.)	(b) Date acquired (Mo., day, yr.)	(c) Date sold or disposed of (Mo., day, yr.)	(d) Proceeds (sales price) (see instructions)	(e) Cost or other basis. See the **Note** below and see *Column (e)* in the separate instructions	**Adjustment, if any, to gain or loss.** If you enter an amount in column (g), enter a code in column (f). **See the separate instructions.** (f) Code(s) from instructions	(g) Amount of adjustment	(h) **Gain or (loss).** Subtract column (e) from column (d) and combine the result with column (g)
2 Totals. Add the amounts in columns (d), (e), (g), and (h) (subtract negative amounts). Enter each total here and include on your Schedule D, **line 8b** (if **Box D** above is checked), **line 9** (if **Box E** above is checked), or **line 10** (if **Box F** above is checked) ▶							

Note: If you checked Box D above but the basis reported to the IRS was incorrect, enter in column (e) the basis as reported to the IRS, and enter an adjustment in column (g) to correct the basis. See *Column (g)* in the separate instructions for how to figure the amount of the adjustment.

Form **8959**

Department of the Treasury
Internal Revenue Service

Additional Medicare Tax

► If any line does not apply to you, leave it blank. See separate instructions.
► Attach to Form 1040, 1040-SR, 1040-NR, 1040-PR, or 1040-SS.
► Go to *www.irs.gov/Form8959* for instructions and the latest information.

OMB No. 1545-0074

2021

Attachment Sequence No. **71**

Name(s) shown on return | **Your social security number**

Part I Additional Medicare Tax on Medicare Wages

1	Medicare wages and tips from Form W-2, box 5. If you have more than one Form W-2, enter the total of the amounts from box 5	1	
2	Unreported tips from Form 4137, line 6	2	
3	Wages from Form 8919, line 6	3	
4	Add lines 1 through 3	4	
5	Enter the following amount for your filing status: Married filing jointly . . . $250,000 Married filing separately . . . $125,000 Single, Head of household, or Qualifying widow(er) . . . $200,000	5	
6	Subtract line 5 from line 4. If zero or less, enter -0-	6	
7	Additional Medicare Tax on Medicare wages. Multiply line 6 by 0.9% (0.009). Enter here and go to Part II	7	

Part II Additional Medicare Tax on Self-Employment Income

8	Self-employment income from Schedule SE (Form 1040), Part I, line 6. If you had a loss, enter -0- (Form 1040-PR or 1040-SS filers, see instructions.)	8	
9	Enter the following amount for your filing status: Married filing jointly . . . $250,000 Married filing separately . . . $125,000 Single, Head of household, or Qualifying widow(er) . . . $200,000	9	
10	Enter the amount from line 4	10	
11	Subtract line 10 from line 9. If zero or less, enter -0-	11	
12	Subtract line 11 from line 8. If zero or less, enter -0-	12	
13	Additional Medicare Tax on self-employment income. Multiply line 12 by 0.9% (0.009). Enter here and go to Part III	13	

Part III Additional Medicare Tax on Railroad Retirement Tax Act (RRTA) Compensation

14	Railroad retirement (RRTA) compensation and tips from Form(s) W-2, box 14 (see instructions)	14	
15	Enter the following amount for your filing status: Married filing jointly . . . $250,000 Married filing separately . . . $125,000 Single, Head of household, or Qualifying widow(er) . . . $200,000	15	
16	Subtract line 15 from line 14. If zero or less, enter -0-	16	
17	Additional Medicare Tax on railroad retirement (RRTA) compensation. Multiply line 16 by 0.9% (0.009). Enter here and go to Part IV	17	

Part IV Total Additional Medicare Tax

18	Add lines 7, 13, and 17. Also include this amount on Schedule 2 (Form 1040), line 11 (Form 1040-PR or 1040-SS filers, see instructions), and go to Part V	18	

Part V Withholding Reconciliation

19	Medicare tax withheld from Form W-2, box 6. If you have more than one Form W-2, enter the total of the amounts from box 6	19	
20	Enter the amount from line 1	20	
21	Multiply line 20 by 1.45% (0.0145). This is your regular Medicare tax withholding on Medicare wages	21	
22	Subtract line 21 from line 19. If zero or less, enter -0-. This is your Additional Medicare Tax withholding on Medicare wages	22	
23	Additional Medicare Tax withholding on railroad retirement (RRTA) compensation from Form W-2, box 14 (see instructions)	23	
24	**Total Additional Medicare Tax withholding.** Add lines 22 and 23. Also include this amount with federal income tax withholding on Form 1040, 1040-SR, or 1040-NR, line 25c (Form 1040-PR or 1040-SS filers, see instructions)	24	

For Paperwork Reduction Act Notice, see your tax return instructions. Cat. No. 59475X Form **8959** (2021)

Form **8960**

Department of the Treasury
Internal Revenue Service (99)

Net Investment Income Tax—Individuals, Estates, and Trusts

▶ Attach to your tax return.
▶ Go to *www.irs.gov/Form8960* for instructions and the latest information.

OMB No. 1545-2227
2021
Attachment Sequence No. 72

Name(s) shown on your tax return | Your social security number or EIN

Part I Investment Income

☐ Section 6013(g) election (see instructions)
☐ Section 6013(h) election (see instructions)
☐ Regulations section 1.1411-10(g) election (see instructions)

1	Taxable interest (see instructions)			1	
2	Ordinary dividends (see instructions)			2	
3	Annuities (see instructions)			3	
4a	Rental real estate, royalties, partnerships, S corporations, trusts, etc. (see instructions)	4a			
b	Adjustment for net income or loss derived in the ordinary course of a non-section 1411 trade or business (see instructions)	4b			
c	Combine lines 4a and 4b			4c	
5a	Net gain or loss from disposition of property (see instructions)	5a			
b	Net gain or loss from disposition of property that is not subject to net investment income tax (see instructions)	5b			
c	Adjustment from disposition of partnership interest or S corporation stock (see instructions)	5c			
d	Combine lines 5a through 5c			5d	
6	Adjustments to investment income for certain CFCs and PFICs (see instructions)			6	
7	Other modifications to investment income (see instructions)			7	
8	Total investment income. Combine lines 1, 2, 3, 4c, 5d, 6, and 7			8	

Part II Investment Expenses Allocable to Investment Income and Modifications

9a	Investment interest expenses (see instructions)	9a			
b	State, local, and foreign income tax (see instructions)	9b			
c	Miscellaneous investment expenses (see instructions)	9c			
d	Add lines 9a, 9b, and 9c			9d	
10	Additional modifications (see instructions)			10	
11	Total deductions and modifications. Add lines 9d and 10			11	

Part III Tax Computation

12	Net investment income. Subtract Part II, line 11, from Part I, line 8. Individuals, complete lines 13–17. Estates and trusts, complete lines 18a–21. If zero or less, enter -0-			12	
	Individuals:				
13	Modified adjusted gross income (see instructions)	13			
14	Threshold based on filing status (see instructions)	14			
15	Subtract line 14 from line 13. If zero or less, enter -0-	15			
16	Enter the smaller of line 12 or line 15			16	
17	Net investment income tax for individuals. Multiply line 16 by 3.8% (0.038). **Enter here and include on your tax return** (see instructions)			17	
	Estates and Trusts:				
18a	Net investment income (line 12 above)	18a			
b	Deductions for distributions of net investment income and deductions under section 642(c) (see instructions)	18b			
c	Undistributed net investment income. Subtract line 18b from line 18a (see instructions). If zero or less, enter -0-	18c			
19a	Adjusted gross income (see instructions)	19a			
b	Highest tax bracket for estates and trusts for the year (see instructions)	19b			
c	Subtract line 19b from line 19a. If zero or less, enter -0-	19c			
20	Enter the smaller of line 18c or line 19c			20	
21	Net investment income tax for estates and trusts. Multiply line 20 by 3.8% (0.038). **Enter here and include on your tax return** (see instructions)			21	

For Paperwork Reduction Act Notice, see your tax return instructions. Cat. No. 59474M Form **8960** (2021)

Form **8995**

Department of the Treasury
Internal Revenue Service

Qualified Business Income Deduction Simplified Computation

► Attach to your tax return.

► Go to *www.irs.gov/Form8995* for instructions and the latest information.

OMB No. 1545-2294

2021

Attachment Sequence No. **55**

Name(s) shown on return | **Your taxpayer identification number**

Note. *You can claim the qualified business income deduction* ***only*** *if you have qualified business income from a qualified trade or business, real estate investment trust dividends, publicly traded partnership income, or a domestic production activities deduction passed through from an agricultural or horticultural cooperative. See instructions.*
Use this form if your taxable income, before your qualified business income deduction, is at or below $164,900 ($164,925 if married filing separately; $329,800 if married filing jointly), and you aren't a patron of an agricultural or horticultural cooperative.

1	**(a)** Trade, business, or aggregation name	**(b)** Taxpayer identification number	**(c)** Qualified business income or (loss)
i			
ii			
iii			
iv			
v			

2	Total qualified business income or (loss). Combine lines 1i through 1v, column (c)	2			
3	Qualified business net (loss) carryforward from the prior year	3	( )		
4	Total qualified business income. Combine lines 2 and 3. If zero or less, enter -0-	4			
5	Qualified business income component. Multiply line 4 by 20% (0.20)			5	
6	Qualified REIT dividends and publicly traded partnership (PTP) income or (loss) (see instructions)	6			
7	Qualified REIT dividends and qualified PTP (loss) carryforward from the prior year	7	( )		
8	Total qualified REIT dividends and PTP income. Combine lines 6 and 7. If zero or less, enter -0-	8			
9	REIT and PTP component. Multiply line 8 by 20% (0.20)			9	
10	Qualified business income deduction before the income limitation. Add lines 5 and 9			10	
11	Taxable income before qualified business income deduction (see instructions)	11			
12	Net capital gain (see instructions)	12			
13	Subtract line 12 from line 11. If zero or less, enter -0-	13			
14	Income limitation. Multiply line 13 by 20% (0.20)			14	
15	Qualified business income deduction. Enter the smaller of line 10 or line 14. Also enter this amount on the applicable line of your return (see instructions) ►			15	
16	Total qualified business (loss) carryforward. Combine lines 2 and 3. If greater than zero, enter -0-			16	( )
17	Total qualified REIT dividends and PTP (loss) carryforward. Combine lines 6 and 7. If greater than zero, enter -0-			17	( )

For Privacy Act and Paperwork Reduction Act Notice, see instructions. Cat. No. 37806C Form **8995** (2021)

Appendix C

Glossary

The key terms in this glossary have been defined to reflect their conventional use in the field of taxation. The definitions may therefore be incomplete for other purposes.

A

AAA bypass election. In the context of a distribution by an S corporation, an election made by the entity to designate that the distribution is first from accumulated earnings and profits (AEP) and only then from the accumulated adjustments account (AAA). § 1368(e)(3).

Abandoned spouse. The abandoned spouse provision enables a married taxpayer with a dependent child whose spouse did not live in the taxpayer's home during the last six months of the tax year to file as a head of household rather than as married filing separately. §§ 2(b) and 7703(b).

Accelerated cost recovery system (ACRS). A method in which the cost of tangible property is recovered (depreciated) over a prescribed period of time. This depreciation approach disregards salvage value, imposes a period of cost recovery that depends upon the classification of the asset into one of various recovery periods, and prescribes the applicable percentage of cost that can be deducted each year. A modified system is currently the default cost recovery method; it is referred to as MACRS. § 168.

Accelerated death benefits. The amount received from a life insurance policy by the insured who is terminally ill or chronically ill. Any realized gain may be excluded from the gross income of the insured if the policy is surrendered to the insurer or is sold to a licensed viatical settlement provider. § 101(g).

Acceleration rule. Treatment of an intercompany transaction on a consolidated return, when a sold asset leaves the group.

Accident and health benefits. Employee fringe benefits provided by employers through the payment of health and accident insurance premiums or the establishment of employer-funded medical reimbursement plans. Employers generally are entitled to a deduction for such payments, whereas employees generally exclude such fringe benefits from gross income. §§ 105 and 106.

Accident and health insurance benefits. See *accident and health benefits*.

Accountable plan. A type of expense reimbursement plan that requires an employee to render an adequate accounting to the employer and return any excess reimbursement or allowance. If the expense qualifies, it will be treated as a deduction *for* AGI. §§ 62(a)(2)(A) and (c).

Accounting income. The accountant's concept of income is generally based upon the realization principle. Financial accounting income may differ from taxable income (e.g., accelerated depreciation might be used for Federal income tax and straight-line depreciation for financial accounting purposes). Differences are included in a reconciliation of taxable and accounting income on Schedule M–1 or Schedule M–3 of Form 1120 for corporations.

Accounting method. The method under which income and expenses are determined for tax purposes. Important accounting methods include the cash basis and the accrual basis. Special methods are available for the reporting of gain on installment sales, recognition of income on construction projects (the completed contract and percentage of completion methods), and the valuation of inventories (last-in, first-out and first-in, first-out). Accounting methods deal with the timing of *when* income and deductions are reported. §§ 446–474.

Accounting period. The period of time, usually a year, used by a taxpayer for the determination of tax liability. Unless a fiscal year is chosen, taxpayers must determine and pay their income tax liability by using the calendar year (January 1 through December 31) as the period of measurement. An example of a fiscal year is July 1 through June 30. A change in accounting period (e.g., from a calendar year to a fiscal year) generally requires the consent of the IRS. Usually, taxpayers are free to select either an initial calendar or a fiscal year without the consent of the IRS. §§ 441–444.

Accrual method. A method of accounting that recognizes expenses as incurred and income as earned. In contrast to the cash basis of accounting, expenses need not be paid to be deductible, nor need income be received to be taxable. § 446(c)(2).

Accumulated adjustments account (AAA). An account that aggregates an S corporation's post-1982 income, loss, and deductions for the tax year (including nontaxable income and nondeductible losses and expenses). After the year-end income and expense adjustments are made, the account is reduced by distributions made during the tax year.

Accumulated E & P. Net undistributed tax-basis earnings of a corporation aggregated from March 1, 1913, to the end of the prior tax year. Used to determine the amount of dividend income associated with a distribution to shareholders. § 316 and Reg. § 1.316–2.

Accumulated earnings tax. A special 20 percent tax imposed on C corporations that accumulate (rather than distribute) their earnings beyond the reasonable needs of the business. The accumulated earnings tax and related interest are imposed on accumulated taxable income in addition to the corporate income tax. §§ 531–537.

Accuracy-related penalties. Major civil taxpayer penalties relating to the accuracy of tax return data, including misstatements stemming from taxpayer negligence and improper valuation of income and deductions, are coordinated under this umbrella term. The penalty usually equals 20 percent of the understated tax liability. § 6662.

Acquiescence. Agreement by the IRS on the results reached in certain judicial decisions; sometimes abbreviated *Acq.* or *A.*

Acquisition indebtedness. Debt incurred in acquiring, constructing, or substantially improving a qualified residence of the taxpayer. The interest on such loans is deductible as qualified residence interest. However, interest on such debt is deductible only on the portion of the indebtedness that does not exceed $750,000 ($1,000,000 for debt incurred before December 15, 2017). § 163(h)(3).

Active income. Wages, salary, commissions, bonuses, profits from a trade or business in which the taxpayer is a material participant, gain on the sale or other disposition of assets used in an active trade or business, and income from intangible property if the taxpayer's personal efforts significantly contributed to the creation of the property. The passive activity loss rules require classification of income and losses into three categories with active income being one of them.

Ad valorem taxes. A tax imposed on the value of property. The most common ad valorem tax is that imposed by states, counties, and cities on real estate. Ad valorem taxes can be imposed on personal property as well.

Additional first-year depreciation. In general, this provision provides for an additional cost recovery deduction of 100 percent for qualified property acquired and placed in service after September 27, 2017, and before January 1, 2027. (The bonus depreciation percentage is reduced by 20 percent for each tax year after 2022.) Qualified property includes most types of new and used property other than buildings. The taxpayer can elect to forgo this bonus depreciation. Different rules applied between 2008 and September 28, 2017. § 168(k).

Adjusted basis. The cost or other basis of property reduced by depreciation allowed or allowable and increased by capital improvements. Other special adjustments are provided in § 1016 and the related Regulations.

Adjusted gross estate. Used in determining eligibility for deferred payments of Federal estate tax. The gross estate less the sum allowable as deductions under § 2053 (expenses, indebtedness, and taxes) and § 2054 (casualty and theft losses during the administration of the estate). § 6166(b)(6).

Adjustments. In calculating AMTI, certain amounts (i.e., adjustments) are added to or deducted from the taxable income starting point of the AMTI calculation. These adjustments generally reflect timing differences. § 56.

Adoption expenses credit. A provision intended to assist taxpayers who incur nonrecurring costs directly associated with the adoption process, such as legal costs, social service review costs, and transportation costs. Up to $14,890 of costs incurred to adopt an eligible child qualify for the credit (unique rules apply when adopting a special needs child). A taxpayer may claim the credit in the year qualifying expenses are paid or incurred if the expenses are paid during or after the year in which the adoption is finalized. For qualifying expenses paid or incurred in a tax year prior to the year the adoption is finalized, the credit must be claimed in the tax year following the tax year during which the expenses are paid or incurred. § 23.

Affiliated group. A parent-subsidiary group of corporations that is eligible to elect to file on a consolidated basis. Eighty percent ownership of the voting power and value of all of the corporations must be achieved every day of the tax year, and an identifiable parent corporation must exist (i.e., it must own at least 80 percent of another group member without applying attribution rules). § 1504(a).

Aggregate (or conduit) concept. A perspective that regards a venture as an aggregation of its owners joined together in an agency relationship rather than as a separate entity. For tax purposes, this results in the income of the venture being taxable directly to its owners. For example, partnership income and expense, capital gains and losses, tax credits, etc., pass through the partnership (a conduit) and are subject to taxation at the partner level. Also, in an S corporation, certain items pass through and are reported on the returns of the shareholders. See also *entity concept.*

Alimony and separate maintenance payments. Alimony deductions result from the payment of a legal obligation arising from the termination of a marital relationship. Payments designated as alimony generally are included in the gross income of the recipient and are deductible *for* AGI by the payor. For divorce or separation instruments executed after December 31, 2018, alimony is neither gross income for the recipient nor deductible by the payor. § 71.

Alimony recapture. The amount of alimony that previously has been included in the gross income of the recipient and deducted by the payor that now is deducted by the recipient and included in the gross income of the payor as the result of front-loading. Alimony recapture is applicable for divorce or separation agreements executed before 2019. § 71(f).

All events test. As applied to the recognition of income, the all events test requires that income of an accrual basis taxpayer be recognized when (1) all events have occurred that fix the taxpayer's right to receive the income and (2) the amount can be determined with reasonable accuracy. Under § 451(b), an accrual method taxpayer must include amounts in income no later than for financial reporting purposes (other than for special rules such as the installment method). As applied to the recognition of expenses, the all events test prevents the recognition of a deduction by an accrual basis taxpayer until all the events have occurred that fix the taxpayer's related obligation. This can be contrasted with GAAP under which a fixed or legal obligation is not required before an expense is recognized. Reg. §§ 1.446–1(c)(1)(ii) and 1.461–1(a)(2).

Allocate. The assignment of income for various tax purposes. A multistate corporation's nonbusiness income usually is allocated to the state where the nonbusiness assets are located; it is not apportioned with the rest of the entity's income. The income and expense items of an estate or a trust are allocated between income and corpus components. Specific items of income, expense, gain, loss, and credit can be allocated to specific partners if a substantial economic nontax purpose for the allocation is established.

Alternate valuation date. Property passing from a decedent by death may be valued for estate tax purposes as of the date of death or the alternate valuation date. The alternate valuation date is six months after the date of death or the date the property is disposed of by the estate, whichever comes first. To use the alternate valuation date, the executor or administrator of the estate must make an affirmative election. The election applies to all of the estate's assets. Election of the alternate valuation date is not available unless it decreases the amount of the gross estate and reduces the estate tax liability. § 2032.

Alternative depreciation system (ADS). A cost recovery system in which the cost or other initial basis of an asset is recovered using the straight-line method over recovery periods similar to those used in MACRS. The alternative system must be used in certain instances and can be elected in other instances. § 168(g).

Alternative minimum tax (AMT). The AMT is a surtax, calculated as a percentage of alternative minimum taxable income (AMTI). AMTI generally starts with the taxpayer's taxable income, prior to any standard deduction taken. To this amount, the taxpayer (1) adds designated preference items (e.g., tax-exempt interest income on private activity bonds), (2) makes other specified adjustments (e.g., to reflect a slower cost recovery method), (3) adjusts certain AMT itemized deductions (e.g., interest incurred on housing), and (4) subtracts an exemption amount. The taxpayer must pay the greater of the resulting AMT or the regular income tax (reduced by all allowable tax credits). The AMT applies to individuals, trusts, and estates; the AMT does not apply to C corporations after 2017. AMT preferences and adjustments are assigned to partners, LLC members, and S corporation shareholders. §§ 55–59.

Alternative minimum tax credit. AMT liability can result from timing differences that give rise to positive adjustments in calculating AMTI. To provide equity for the taxpayer when these timing differences reverse, the regular tax liability may be reduced by a tax credit for a prior year's minimum tax liability attributable to timing differences. § 53.

Alternative minimum taxable income (AMTI). The base (prior to deducting the exemption amount) for computing a taxpayer's alternative minimum tax. This consists of the taxable income for the year modified for AMT adjustments and AMT preferences. § 55(b)(2).

Alternative tax. An option that is allowed in computing the tax on net capital gain. For noncorporate taxpayers, the rate is usually 15 percent (but is 25 percent for unrecaptured § 1250 gain and 28 percent for collectibles). However, the alternative tax rate is 0 percent (rather than 15 percent) for lower-income taxpayers (e.g., taxable income of $83,350 or less for married persons filing jointly). Certain high-income taxpayers (e.g., taxable income of more than $517,200 for married persons filing jointly) have an alternative tax rate of 20 percent. § 1(h).

Alternative tax NOL deduction (ATNOLD). In calculating the AMT, the taxpayer is allowed to deduct NOL carryovers following the regular tax NOL carryover provisions. The AMT NOL amount is referred to as the ATNOLD. The regular income tax NOL is modified for AMT adjustments and preferences to produce the ATNOLD. § 56(d).

American Opportunity credit. This credit applies for qualifying expenses for the first four years of postsecondary education. Qualified expenses include tuition and related expenses and books and other course materials. Room and board are ineligible for the credit. The maximum credit available per student is $2,500 (100 percent of the first $2,000 of qualified expenses and 25 percent of the next $2,000 of qualified expenses). Eligible students include the taxpayer, taxpayer's spouse, and taxpayer's dependents. To qualify for the credit, a student must take at least one-half of the full-time course load for at least one academic term at a qualifying educational institution. The credit is phased out for higher-income taxpayers. § 25A.

Amortization. The tax deduction for the cost or other basis of an intangible asset over the asset's estimated useful life. Examples of amortizable intangibles include patents, copyrights, and leasehold interests. Most purchased intangible assets (e.g., goodwill) can be amortized for income tax purposes over a 15-year period. § 197.

Amount realized. The amount received by a taxpayer upon the sale or exchange of property. Amount realized is the sum of the cash and the fair market value of any property or services received by the taxpayer plus any related debt assumed by the buyer. Determining the amount realized is the starting point for arriving at realized gain or loss. § 1001(b).

Annual exclusion. In computing the taxable gifts for the year, each donor excludes the first $16,000 (for 2022) of a gift to each donee. Usually, the annual exclusion is not available for gifts of future interests. § 2503(b).

Annuity. A fixed sum of money payable to a person at specified times for a specified period of time or for life. If the party making the payment (i.e., the obligor) is regularly engaged in this type of business (e.g., an insurance company), the arrangement is classified as a commercial annuity. A so-called private annuity involves an obligor that is not regularly engaged in selling annuities (e.g., a charity or family member).

Apportion. The assignment of the business income of a multistate corporation to specific states for income taxation. Usually, the apportionment procedure accounts for the property, payroll, and sales activity levels of the various states, and a proportionate assignment of the entity's total income is made using a statutory apportionment formula. Most states exclude nonbusiness income from the apportionment procedure; they allocate nonbusiness income to the states where the nonbusiness assets are located.

Appreciated inventory. In partnership taxation, appreciated inventory is a hot asset, and a partner's share of its ordinary income potential must be allocated to that partner. If a partner sells an interest in the partnership, ordinary income is recognized to the extent of the partner's share of the partnership's inventory and unrealized receivables. The definition of "inventory" here is broad enough to include any accounts receivable, including unrealized receivables. See also *substantially appreciated inventory*. § 751.

Arm's length. See *arm's length price*.

Arm's length price. The standard under which unrelated parties would determine an exchange price for a transaction. Suppose, for example, Cardinal Corporation sells property to its sole shareholder for $10,000. In testing whether the $10,000 is an "arm's length" price, one would ascertain the price that would have been negotiated between the corporation and an unrelated party in a bargained exchange.

ASC 740. Under Generally Accepted Accounting Principles, the rules for the financial reporting of the tax expense of an enterprise. Permanent differences affect the enterprise's effective tax rate. Temporary differences create a deferred tax asset or a deferred tax liability on the balance sheet.

ASC 740-10. An interpretation by the Financial Accounting Standards Board. When an uncertain tax return position exists, this interpretation is used to determine the financial reporting treatment, if any, for the taxpayer. If it is more likely than not (i.e., a greater than 50 percent probability) that the uncertain return position will be sustained (e.g., by the courts) on its technical merits, it must be reported on the financial statements. The amount to be reported then is computed based on the probabilities of the outcome of the technical review and the amounts at which the dispute would be resolved. If the more-likely-than-not test is failed, no current financial disclosure of the results of the return position is required.

Asset Depreciation Range (ADR) system. A system of estimated useful lives for categories of tangible assets prescribed by the IRS. The system provides a range for each category that extends from 20 percent above to 20 percent below the guideline class lives prescribed by the IRS.

Asset use test. In the context of a corporate reorganization, a means by which to determine if the continuity of business enterprise requirement is met. The acquiring corporation must continue to use the target entity's assets in the acquiror's business going forward; if this is not the case, the requirement is failed.

Assignment of income. A taxpayer attempts to avoid the recognition of income by assigning to another the property that generates the income. Such a procedure will not avoid income recognition by the taxpayer making the assignment if the income was earned at the point of the transfer. In this case, the income is taxed to the person who earns it.

At-risk limitation. Generally, a taxpayer can deduct losses related to a trade or business, S corporation, partnership, or investment asset only to the extent of the at-risk amount. The taxpayer has an amount at risk in a business or investment venture to the extent that personal assets have been subjected to the risks of the business. Typically, the taxpayer's at-risk amount includes (1) the amount of money or other property that the investor contributed to the venture for the investment, (2) the amount of any of the entity's liabilities for which the taxpayer personally is liable and that relate to the investment, and (3) an allocable share of nonrecourse debts incurred by the venture from third parties in arm's length transactions for real estate investments. § 465.

Attribution. Under certain circumstances, the tax law applies attribution (constructive ownership) rules to assign to one taxpayer the ownership interest of another taxpayer. If, for example, the stock of Gold Corporation is held 60 percent by Marsha and 40 percent by Sidney, Marsha may be deemed to own 100 percent of Gold Corporation if Marsha and Sidney are mother and child. In that case, the stock owned by Sidney is attributed to Marsha. Stated differently, Marsha has a 60 percent direct and a 40 percent indirect interest in Gold Corporation. It can also be said that Marsha is the constructive owner of Sidney's interest.

Automatic mileage method. Automobile expenses are generally deductible only to the extent the automobile is used in business or for the production of income. Personal commuting expenses are not deductible. The taxpayer may deduct actual expenses (including depreciation and insurance), or the standard (automatic) mileage rate may be used (58.5 cents per mile for 2022 and 56 cents per mile for 2021). Automobile expenses incurred for medical purposes are deductible to the extent of actual out-of-pocket expenses or at the rate of 18 cents per mile for 2022 and 16 cents per mile for 2021. For charitable activities, the rate is 14 cents per mile.

Average tax rate. The average tax rate is equal to the tax liability divided by taxable income. This rate can be useful in comparing taxpayers or a taxpayer's changed tax picture from one year to another.

B

Bad debt. A deduction is permitted if a business account receivable subsequently becomes partially or completely worthless, providing the income arising from the debt previously was included in income. Available methods are the specific charge-off method and the reserve method. However, except for certain financial institutions, TRA of 1986 repealed the use of the reserve method for 1987 and thereafter. If the reserve method is used, partially or totally worthless accounts are charged to the reserve. A nonbusiness bad debt deduction is allowed as a short-term capital loss if the loan did not arise in connection with the creditor's trade or business activities. Loans between related parties (family members) generally are classified as nonbusiness. § 166.

Balance sheet approach. The process under ASC 740 (SFAS 109) by which an entity's deferred tax expense or deferred tax benefit is determined as a result of the reporting period's changes in the balance sheet's deferred tax asset and deferred tax liability accounts.

Base Erosion and Anti-Abuse Tax (BEAT). A 10 percent minimum tax designed to prevent multinational corporations from shifting profits out of the United States to a foreign subsidiary located in a low-tax jurisdiction. § 59A.

Basis in partnership interest. The acquisition cost of the partner's ownership interest in the partnership. Includes purchase price and associated debt acquired from other partners and in the course of the entity's trade or business.

Benchmarking. The tax professional's use of two or more entities' effective tax rates and deferred tax balance sheet accounts. Used chiefly to compare the effectiveness of the entities' tax planning techniques and to suggest future tax-motivated courses of action.

Blockage rule. A factor to be considered in valuing a large block of corporate stock. Application of this rule generally justifies a discount in the asset's fair market value, because the disposition of a large amount of stock at any one time may depress the value of the shares in the marketplace.

Boot. Cash or property of a type not included in the definition of a tax-deferred exchange. The receipt of boot causes an otherwise tax-deferred transfer to become immediately taxable to the extent of the lesser of the fair market value of the boot or the realized gain on the transfer. For example, see transfers to controlled corporations under § 351(b), reorganizations under § 368, and like-kind exchanges under § 1031(b).

Built-in gains tax. A penalty tax designed to discourage a shift of the incidence of taxation on unrealized gains from a C corporation to its shareholders, via an S election. Under this provision, any recognized gain during the first five years of S status generates a corporate-level tax on a base not to exceed the aggregate untaxed built-in gains brought into the S corporation upon its election from C corporation taxable years. § 1374.

Built-in loss property. Property contributed to a corporation under § 351 or as a contribution to capital that has a basis in excess of its fair market value. An adjustment is necessary to step down the basis of the property to its fair market value. The adjustment prevents the corporation and the contributing shareholder from obtaining a double tax benefit. The corporation allocates the adjustment proportionately among the assets with the built-in loss. As an alternative to the corporate adjustment, the shareholder may elect to reduce the basis in the stock. § 362(e).

Business bad debt. A tax deduction allowed for obligations obtained in connection with a trade or business that have become either partially or completely worthless. In contrast to nonbusiness bad debts, business bad debts are deductible as business expenses. § 166.

Business purpose. A justifiable business reason for carrying out a transaction. Mere tax avoidance is not an acceptable business purpose. The presence of a business purpose is crucial in the area of corporate reorganizations and certain liquidations.

Buy-sell agreement. An arrangement, particularly appropriate in the case of a closely held corporation or a partnership, whereby the surviving owners (shareholders or partners) or the entity agrees to purchase the interest of a withdrawing owner. The buy-sell agreement provides for an orderly disposition of an interest in a business and may aid in setting the value of the interest for estate tax purposes.

Bypass amount. The amount that can be transferred by gift or at death free of any unified transfer tax. For 2022, the bypass amount is $12,060,000 for estate tax and $12,060,000 for gift tax.

Bypass election. In the context of a distribution by an S corporation, an election made by the entity to designate that the distribution is first from accumulated earnings and profits and only then from the accumulated adjustments account (AAA). § 1368(e)(3).

C

C corporation. A separate taxable entity subject to the rules of Subchapter C of the Code. This business form may create a double taxation effect relative to its shareholders. The entity is subject to the regular corporate tax and a number of penalty taxes at the Federal level.

Cafeteria plan. An employee benefit plan under which an employee is allowed to select from among a variety of employer-provided fringe benefits. Some of the benefits may be taxable, and some may be statutory nontaxable benefits (e.g., health and accident insurance and group term life insurance). The employee is taxed only on the taxable benefits selected. A cafeteria benefit plan is also referred to as a flexible benefit plan. § 125.

Capital account. The financial accounting analog of a partner's tax basis in the entity.

Capital account maintenance. Under the § 704(b) Regulations, partnership allocations will be respected only if capital accounts are maintained in accordance with those regulations. These so-called "§ 704(b) book capital accounts" are properly maintained if they reflect the partner's contributions and distributions of cash; increases and decreases for the fair market value of contributed/distributed property; and adjustments for the partner's share of income, gains, losses, and deductions. Certain other adjustments are also required. See also *economic effect test* and *Section 704(b) book capital accounts*.

Capital asset. Broadly speaking, all assets are capital except those specifically excluded from that definition by the Code. Major categories of noncapital assets include property held for resale in the normal course of business (inventory), trade accounts and notes receivable, and depreciable property and real estate used in a trade or business (§ 1231 assets). § 1221.

Capital contribution. Various means by which a shareholder makes additional funds available to the corporation (placed at the risk of the business), sometimes without the receipt of additional stock. If no stock is received, the contributions are added to the basis of the shareholder's existing stock investment and do not generate gross income to the corporation. § 118.

Capital gain property. Property contributed to a charitable organization that, if sold rather than contributed, would have resulted in long-term capital gain to the donor. § 170(e).

Capital gains. The gain from the sale or exchange of a capital asset.

Capital interest. Usually, the percentage of the entity's net assets that a partner would receive on liquidation. Typically determined by the partner's capital sharing ratio.

Capital losses. The loss from the sale or exchange of a capital asset.

Capital sharing ratio. A partner's percentage ownership of the entity's capital.

Carbon tax. A tax on fossil fuels to help reduce greenhouse gas emissions.

Carried interest. A "partnership interest held in connection with performance of services," as defined under § 1061. Long-term capital gains from such an interest are reclassified as short-term capital gains (with potential ordinary income treatment) unless the underlying asset that triggered the gain had more than a three-year holding period. This provision only applies to income and gains arising from managing portfolio investments on behalf of third-party investors, including publicly traded securities, commodities, certain real estate, or options to buy/sell such assets. Section 1061 was enacted in the TCJA of 2017 in an effort to curtail an industry practice that resulted in fund managers receiving partnership profits interests in exchange for services: these "profits partners" received long-term capital gain allocations from the fund, rather than ordinary income for the services provided in managing the fund's assets. In addition to § 1061, the IRS has, from time to time, announced that it might issue regulations (under its general "anti-abuse" authority) to expand the scope of the carried interest rules.

Cash balance plan. A hybrid form of pension plan similar in some aspects to a defined benefit plan. Such a plan is funded by the employer, and the employer bears the investment risks and rewards. But like defined contribution plans, a cash balance plan establishes allocations to individual employee accounts, and the payout for an employee depends on investment performance.

Cash method. See *cash receipts method.*

Cash receipts method. A method of accounting that reflects deductions as paid and income as received in any one tax year. However, deductions for prepaid expenses that benefit more than one tax year (e.g., prepaid rent and prepaid interest) usually are spread over the period benefited rather than deducted in the year paid. § 446(c)(1).

Casualty loss. A casualty is defined as "the complete or partial destruction of property resulting from an identifiable event of a sudden, unexpected, or unusual nature" (e.g., floods, storms, fires, auto accidents). Individuals may deduct a casualty loss only if the loss is incurred in a trade or business or in a transaction entered into for profit or arises from fire, storm, shipwreck, or other casualty or from theft. Individuals usually deduct personal casualty losses as itemized deductions subject to a $100 nondeductible amount and to an annual floor equal to 10 percent of adjusted gross income that applies after the $100 per casualty floor has been applied. Special rules are provided for the netting of certain casualty gains and losses. For tax years beginning after 2017 (and before 2026), personal casualty losses are limited to those sustained in an area designated as a disaster area by the President of the United States. §§ 165(c)(3) and (h).

Charitable contribution. Contributions made to qualified nonprofit organizations. Taxpayers, regardless of their accounting method, are generally allowed to deduct (subject to various restrictions and limitations) contributions in the year of payment. Accrual basis corporations may accrue contributions at year-end if payment is properly authorized before the end of the year and payment is made within three and one-half months after the end of the year. § 170.

Check-the-box Regulations. By using the check-the-box rules prudently, an entity can select the most attractive tax results offered by the Code, without being bound by legal forms. By default, an unincorporated entity with more than one owner is taxed as a partnership; an unincorporated entity with one owner is a disregarded entity, taxed as a sole proprietorship or corporate division. No action is necessary by the taxpayer if the legal form or default status is desired. Form 8832 is used to "check a box" and change the tax status. Not available if the entity is incorporated under state law.

Child tax credit. A tax credit based solely on the number of qualifying children under age 17. The maximum credit available is $2,000 per qualifying child. (In addition, a $500 nonrefundable credit is available for qualifying dependents other than qualifying children.) A qualifying child must be claimed as a dependent on a parent's tax return and have a Social Security number to qualify for the credit. Taxpayers who qualify for the child tax credit may also qualify for a supplemental credit. The supplemental credit is treated as a component of the earned income credit and is therefore refundable. The credit is phased out for higher-income taxpayers. (Different rules applied for 2021.) § 24. See also *dependent tax credit.*

Circuit Court of Appeals. Any of 13 Federal courts that consider tax matters appealed from the U.S. Tax Court, a U.S. District Court, or the U.S. Court of Federal Claims. Appeal from a U.S. Court of Appeals is to the U.S. Supreme Court by Certiorari.

Circular 230. A portion of the Federal tax Regulations that describes the levels of conduct at which a tax preparer must operate. Circular 230 dictates, for instance, that a tax preparer may not charge an unconscionable fee or delay the execution of a tax audit with inappropriate delays. Circular 230 requires that there be a reasonable basis for a tax return position and that no frivolous returns be filed.

Citator. A tax research resource that presents the judicial history of a court case and traces the subsequent references to the case. When these references include the citating cases' evaluations of the cited case's precedents, the research can obtain some measure of the efficacy and reliability of the original holding.

Claim of right doctrine. A judicially imposed doctrine applicable to both cash and accrual basis taxpayers that holds that an amount is includible in income upon actual or constructive receipt if the taxpayer has an unrestricted claim to the payment. For the tax treatment of amounts repaid when previously included in income under the claim of right doctrine, see § 1341.

Closely held C corporation. A regular corporation (i.e., the S election is not in effect) for which more than 50 percent of the value of its outstanding stock is owned, directly or indirectly, by five or fewer individuals at any time during the tax year. The term is relevant in identifying C corporations that are subject to the passive activity loss provisions. § 469.

Closely held corporation. A corporation where stock ownership is not widely dispersed. Rather, a few shareholders are in control of corporate policy and are in a position to benefit personally from that policy.

Closing agreement. In a tax dispute, the parties sign a closing agreement to spell out the terms under which the matters are settled. The agreement is binding on both the Service and the taxpayer. § 7121.

Collectibles. A special type of capital asset, the gain from which is taxed at a maximum rate of 28 percent if the holding period is more than one year. Examples include art, rugs, antiques, gems, metals, stamps, some coins and bullion, and alcoholic beverages held for investment. §§ 1(h)(5) and 408(m).

Combined return. In multistate taxation, a group of unitary corporations may elect or be required to file an income tax return that includes operating results for all of the affiliates, not just those with nexus in the state. Thus, apportionment data are reported for the group's worldwide or waters'-edge operations.

Community property. Arizona, California, Idaho, Louisiana, Nevada, New Mexico, Texas, Washington, and Wisconsin have community property systems. Alaska residents can elect community property status for assets. The rest of the states are common law property jurisdictions. The difference between common law and community property systems centers around the property rights possessed by married persons. In a common law system, each spouse owns whatever he or she earns. Under a community property system, one-half of the earnings of each spouse is considered owned by the other spouse. Assume, for example, that Jeff and Alice are husband and wife and that their only income is the

$50,000 annual salary Jeff receives. If they live in New York (a common law state), the $50,000 salary belongs to Jeff. If, however, they live in Texas (a community property state), the $50,000 salary is owned one-half each by Jeff and Alice.

Compensatory damages. Damages received or paid by the taxpayer can be classified as compensatory damages or as punitive damages. Compensatory damages are paid to compensate one for harm caused by another. Compensatory damages received on account of physical injuries are excludible from the recipient's gross income. § 104(a)(2).

Complete termination redemption. Sale or exchange treatment is available relative to this type of redemption. The shareholder must retire all of his or her outstanding shares in the corporation (ignoring family attribution rules) and cannot hold an interest, other than that of a creditor, for the 10 years following the redemption. § 302(b)(3).

Completed contract method. A method of reporting gain or loss on certain long-term contracts. Under this method of accounting, all gross income and expenses are recognized in the tax year in which the contract is completed. Reg. § 1.451–3.

Complex trust. Not a simple trust. Such trusts may have charitable beneficiaries, accumulate income, and distribute corpus. §§ 661–663.

Composite return. In multistate taxation, an S corporation may be allowed to file a single income tax return that assigns pass-through items to resident and nonresident shareholders. The composite or "block" return allows the entity to remit any tax that is attributable to the nonresident shareholders.

Conduit concept. A perspective taken toward a venture that regards the venture as an aggregation of its owners joined together in an agency relationship rather than as a separate entity. For tax purposes, this results in the income of the venture being taxable directly to its owners. For example, items of income and expense, capital gains and losses, tax credits, etc., realized by a partnership pass through the partnership (a conduit) and are subject to taxation at the partner level. Also, in an S corporation, certain items pass through and are reported on the returns of the shareholders.

Conduit perspective. See *conduit concept*.

Consolidated returns. A procedure whereby certain affiliated corporations may file a single return, combine the tax transactions of each corporation, and arrive at a single income tax liability for the group. The election to file a consolidated return usually is binding on future years. §§ 1501–1505 and related Regulations.

Consolidation. The combination of two or more corporations into a newly created corporation. Thus, Black Corporation and White Corporation combine to form Gray Corporation. A consolidation may qualify as a nontaxable reorganization if certain conditions are satisfied. §§ 354 and 368(a)(1)(A).

Constructive dividends. A taxable benefit derived by a shareholder from his or her corporation that is not actually initiated by the board of directors as a dividend. Examples include unreasonable compensation, excessive rent payments, bargain purchases of corporate property, and shareholder use of corporate property. Constructive dividends generally are found in closely held corporations.

Constructive liquidation scenario. The means by which recourse debt is shared among partners in basis determination.

Constructive receipt. If income is unqualifiedly available although not physically in the taxpayer's possession, it still is subject to the income tax. An example is accrued interest on a savings account. Under the constructive receipt concept, the interest is taxed to a depositor in the year available, rather than the year actually withdrawn. The fact that the depositor uses the cash basis of accounting for tax purposes is irrelevant. See Reg. § 1.451–2.

Continuity of business enterprise. In a tax-favored reorganization, the acquiring corporation must continue the historic business of the target or use a significant portion of the target's assets in the new business.

Continuity of interest. In a tax-favored reorganization, a shareholder or corporation that has substantially the same investment after an exchange as before should not be taxed on the transaction. Specifically, the target shareholders must acquire an equity interest in the acquiring corporation equal in value to at least 40 percent of all the outstanding stock of the target entity.

Control. Holding a specified level of stock ownership in a corporation. For § 351, the new shareholder(s) must hold at least 80 percent of the total combined voting power of all voting classes of stock and at least 80 percent of the shares of all nonvoting classes. Other tax provisions require different levels of control to bring about desired effects, such as 50 or 100 percent.

Controlled foreign corporation (CFC). A non-U.S. corporation in which more than 50 percent of the total combined voting power of all classes of stock entitled to vote or the total value of the stock of the corporation is owned by U.S. shareholders on any day during the taxable year of the foreign corporation. For purposes of this definition, a U.S. shareholder is any U.S. person who owns, or is considered to own, 10 percent or more of the total combined voting power of all classes of voting stock of the foreign corporation. Stock owned directly, indirectly, and constructively is used in this measure. See *U.S. shareholder*. §§ 951–965.

Controlled group. Controlled groups include parent-subsidiary groups, brother-sister groups, combined groups, and certain insurance companies. Controlled groups are required to share certain elements of tax calculations (e.g., $250,000 accumulated earnings credit) or tax credits (e.g., research credit). §§ 1561 and 1563.

Corporate liquidation. Occurs when a corporation distributes its net assets to its shareholders and ceases to be a going concern. Generally, a shareholder recognizes capital gain or loss upon the liquidation of the entity, regardless of the corporation's balance in its earnings and profits account. The liquidating corporation recognizes gain and loss on assets that it sells during the liquidation period and on assets that it distributes to shareholders in kind.

Corpus. The body or principal of a trust. Suppose, for example, Grant transfers an apartment building into a trust, income payable to Ruth for life, remainder to Shawn upon Ruth's death. Corpus of the trust is the apartment building.

Correspondence audit. An audit conducted by the IRS by the U.S. mail. Typically, the IRS writes to the taxpayer requesting the verification of a particular deduction or exemption. The remittance of copies of records or other support is requested of the taxpayer.

Cost depletion. Depletion that is calculated based on the adjusted basis of the asset. The adjusted basis is divided by the expected recoverable units to determine the depletion per unit. The depletion per unit is multiplied by the units sold during the tax year to calculate cost depletion. §§ 611 and 612.

Cost recovery. The system by which taxpayers are allowed to recover their investment in an asset by reducing their taxable income by the asset's cost or initial basis. Cost recovery methods include MACRS, § 179 expense, additional first-year deprecation, amortization, and depletion. §§ 168, 179, and 611.

Court of original jurisdiction. The Federal courts are divided into courts of original jurisdiction and appellate courts. A dispute between a taxpayer and the IRS is first considered by a court of original jurisdiction (i.e., a trial court). The four Federal courts of original jurisdiction are the U.S. Tax Court, the U.S. District Court, the U.S. Court of Federal Claims, and the Small Cases Division of the U.S. Tax Court.

Coverdell education savings account (§ 530 plan). Coverdell education savings account exempts from tax the earnings on amounts placed in a qualified account for the education expenses of a named beneficiary. Contributions are limited to $2,000 per year per beneficiary, and the proceeds can be withdrawn without tax provided the funds are used to pay qualified educational expenses for primary, secondary, or higher education. (There is an annual $10,000 per student limitation on distributions for tuition expenses for primary and secondary education.) Qualified educational expenses also include certain homeschooling expenses. The account is named for the late Senator Paul Coverdell (R-GA), who sponsored the legislation in Congress. § 530.

Credit for certain retirement plan contributions. A nonrefundable credit is available based on eligible contributions of up to $2,000 to certain qualified retirement plans, such as traditional and Roth IRAs and § 401(k) plans. The benefit provided by this credit is in addition to any deduction or exclusion that otherwise is available resulting from the qualifying contribution. The amount of the credit depends on the taxpayer's AGI and filing status. § 25B.

Credit for child and dependent care expenses. A nonrefundable tax credit ranging from 20 percent to 35 percent of employment-related expenses (child and dependent care expenses) for amounts of up to $6,000 is available to individuals who are employed (or deemed to be employed) and maintain a household for a dependent child under age 13, disabled spouse, or disabled dependent. (Different rules applied for 2021.) § 21.

Credit for employer-provided child care. A nonrefundable credit is available to employers who provide child care facilities to their employees during normal working hours. The credit, limited to $150,000, is comprised of two components. The portion of the credit for qualified child care expenses is equal to 25 percent of these expenses, while the portion of the credit for qualified child care resource and referral services is equal to 10 percent of these expenses. Any qualifying expenses otherwise deductible by the taxpayer must be reduced by the amount of the credit. In addition, the taxpayer's basis for any property used for qualifying purposes is reduced by the amount of the credit. § 45F.

Credit for employer-provided family and medical leave. A nonrefundable credit is available to employers who pay wages to employees while they are on family and medical leave. The credit is equal to 12.5 percent of wages paid to qualifying employees (limited to 12 weeks per employee per year). Employers must pay a minimum of 50 percent of the wages normally paid; if wages paid during the leave *exceed* 50 percent of normal wages, the credit is increased by 0.25 percent for each percentage point above 50 percent to a maximum of 25 percent of wages paid. The credit does not apply to wages paid in taxable years beginning after 2025. § 45S.

Credit for small employer pension plan startup costs. A nonrefundable credit available to small businesses based on administrative costs associated with establishing and maintaining certain qualified plans. While such qualifying costs generally are deductible as ordinary and necessary business expenses, the availability of the credit is intended to lower the costs of starting a qualified retirement program and therefore encourage qualifying businesses to establish retirement plans for their employees. The credit is available for eligible employers at the rate of 50 percent of qualified startup costs. The maximum credit is $500 (based on a maximum $1,000 of qualifying expenses). § 45E.

Crop insurance proceeds. The proceeds received when an insured crop is destroyed. Section 451(f) permits the farmer to defer reporting the income from the insurance proceeds until the tax year following the taxable year of the destruction.

Crop method. A method of accounting for agricultural crops that are planted in one year but harvested in a subsequent year. Under this method, the costs of raising the crop are accumulated as inventory and are deducted when the income from the crop is realized.

Cross-purchase buy-sell agreement. Under this arrangement, the surviving owners of the business agree to buy out the withdrawing owner. Assume, for example, Ron and Sara are equal shareholders in Tip Corporation. Under a cross-purchase buy-sell agreement, Ron and Sara would contract to purchase the other's interest, should that person decide to withdraw from the business.

Current distribution. A payment made by a partnership to a partner when the partnership's legal existence does not cease thereafter. The partner usually assigns a basis in the distributed property that is equal to the lesser of the partner's basis in the partnership interest (substituted basis) or the basis of the distributed asset to the partnership (carryover basis). The partner first assigns basis to any cash that he or she receives in the distribution. A cash distribution in excess of the partner's basis triggers a gain. The partner's remaining basis, if any, is assigned to the noncash assets according to their relative bases to the partnership.

Current E & P. Net tax-basis earnings of a corporation aggregated during the current tax year. A corporate distribution is deemed to be first from the entity's current earnings and profits and then from accumulated earnings and profits. Shareholders recognize dividend income to the extent of the earnings and profits of the corporation. A dividend results to the extent of current earnings and profits, even if there is a larger negative balance in accumulated earnings and profits.

Current tax expense. Under ASC 740 (SFAS 109), the book tax expense that relates to the current reporting period's net income and is actually payable (or creditable) to the appropriate governmental agencies for the current period. Also known as "cash tax" or "tax payable."

D

***De minimis* fringe.** Benefits provided to employees that are too insignificant to warrant the time and effort required to account for the benefits received by each employee and the value of those benefits. Such amounts are excludible from the employee's gross income. § 132.

***De minimis* fringe benefits.** See *de minimis fringe*.

Death benefits. A payment made by an employer to the beneficiary or beneficiaries of a deceased employee on account of the death of the employee.

Debt-financed income. Included in computations of the unrelated business income of an exempt organization, the gross income generated from debt-financed property.

Deceased spouse's unused exclusion (DSUE). In computing the Federal estate tax, the decedent uses the exclusion amount to shelter an amount of the gross estate from taxation. When the first spouse to die fails to use a portion of his/her exclusion amount, the unused portion is "portable" and becomes available to the surviving spouse. The surviving spouse can use the DSUE only of his/her last spouse to predecease. § 2010(c)(4).

Deduction for qualified business income. A deduction allowed for noncorporate taxpayers based on the qualified business income of a qualified trade or business. In general, the deduction is limited to the lesser of 20 percent of qualified business income, or 20 percent of taxable income before the qualified business income deduction less any net capital gain. There are *three limitations* on the deduction—an overall limitation (based on modified taxable income), another that applies to high-income taxpayers, and a third that applies to certain types of services businesses. § 199A.

Deductions *for* adjusted gross income. The Federal income tax is not imposed upon gross income. Rather, it is imposed upon taxable income. Congressionally identified deductions for individual taxpayers are subtracted either from gross income to arrive at adjusted gross income or from adjusted gross income to arrive at the tax base, taxable income.

Deductions *from* adjusted gross income. See *deductions for adjusted gross income*.

Deductions in respect of a decedent. Deductions accrued at the moment of death but not recognizable on the final income tax return of a decedent because of the method of accounting used. Such items are allowed as deductions on the estate tax return and on the income tax return of the estate (Form 1041) or the heir (Form 1040). An example of a deduction in respect of a decedent is interest expense accrued to the date of death by a cash basis debtor.

Deferred compensation. Compensation that will be taxed when received or upon the removal of certain restrictions on receipt and not when earned. Contributions by an employer to a qualified pension or profit sharing plan on behalf of an employee are an example. The contributions will not be taxed to the employee until the funds are made available or distributed to the employee (e.g., upon retirement).

Deferred tax asset. Under ASC 740, an asset recorded on the balance sheet to reflect the future tax benefits related to a transaction or activity which has already been reflected in the financial statements. A deferred tax asset is often the result of the deferral of a deduction or the acceleration of income for tax purposes relative to Generally Accepted Accounting Principles.

Deferred tax benefit. Under ASC 740, a reduction in the book tax expense that relates to the current reporting period's net income but will not be realized until a future reporting period. Creates or adds to the entity's deferred tax asset balance sheet account. For instance, the carryforward of a net operating loss is a deferred tax benefit.

Deferred tax expense. Under ASC 740, a book tax expense that relates to the current reporting period's net income but will not be realized until a future reporting period. Creates or adds to the entity's deferred tax liability balance sheet account. For instance, a deferred tax expense is created when tax depreciation deductions for the period are "accelerated" and exceed the corresponding book depreciation expense.

Deferred tax liability. Under ASC 740, a liability recorded on the balance sheet to reflect the future tax costs of a transaction or activity which has already been reflected in the financial statements. A deferred tax liability is often the result of the deferral of the recognition of income or the acceleration of a deduction for tax purposes relative to Generally Accepted Accounting Principles.

Defined benefit plan. Qualified plans can be dichotomized into defined benefit plans and defined contribution plans. Under a defined benefit plan, a formula defines the benefits employees are to receive. The formula usually includes years of service, employee compensation, and some stated percentage. The employer must make annual contributions based on actuarial computations that will be sufficient to pay the vested retirement benefits.

Defined contribution pension plan. Qualified plans can be dichotomized into defined benefit plans and defined contribution plans. Under a defined contribution plan, a separate account is maintained for each covered employee. The employee's benefits under the plan are based solely on (1) the amount contributed and (2) income from the fund that accrues to the employee's account. The plan defines the amount the employer is required to contribute (e.g., a flat dollar amount, an amount based on a special formula, or an amount equal to a certain percentage of compensation).

Dependency exemptions. See *personal and dependency exemptions*.

Dependent tax credit. For 2018 through 2025, the TCJA of 2017 replaced the dependency exemption with a $500 nonrefundable credit. This credit can be claimed for dependents who are not a qualifying child or under the age of 17. The dependent must be a citizen or resident of the United States. § 24(h).

Depletion. The process by which the cost or other basis of a natural resource (e.g., an oil or gas interest) is recovered upon extraction and sale of the resource. The two ways to determine the depletion allowance are the cost and percentage (or statutory) methods. Under cost depletion, each unit of production sold is assigned a portion of the cost or other basis of the interest. This is determined by dividing the cost or other basis by the total units expected to be recovered. Under percentage (or statutory) depletion, the tax law provides a special percentage factor for different types of minerals and other natural resources. This percentage is multiplied by the gross income from the interest to arrive at the depletion allowance. §§ 611–613A.

Depreciation. The system by which a taxpayer allocates for financial reporting purposes the cost of an asset to periods benefited by the asset.

Determination letter. Upon the request of a taxpayer, the IRS will comment on the tax status of a completed transaction. Determination letters frequently are used to determine whether a retirement or profit sharing plan qualifies under the Code and to determine the tax-exempt status of certain nonprofit organizations.

Disabled access credit. A tax credit designed to encourage small businesses to make their facilities more accessible to disabled individuals. The credit is equal to 50 percent of the eligible expenditures that exceed $250 but do not exceed $10,250. Thus, the maximum amount for the credit is $5,000. The adjusted basis for depreciation is reduced by the amount of the credit. To qualify, the facility must have been placed in service before November 6, 1990. § 44.

Disaster area losses. A casualty sustained in an area designated as a disaster area by the President of the United States. In such an event, the disaster loss may be treated as having occurred in the taxable year immediately preceding the year in which the disaster actually occurred. Thus, immediate tax benefits are provided to victims of a disaster. § 165(i).

Disclaimer. Rejections, refusals, or renunciations of claims, powers, or property. Section 2518 sets forth the conditions required to avoid gift tax consequences as the result of a disclaimer.

Disguised sale. When a partner contributes property to the entity and soon thereafter receives a distribution from the partnership, the transactions are collapsed and the distribution is seen as a purchase of the asset by the partnership. § 707(a)(2)(B).

Disproportionate distribution. A distribution from a partnership to one or more of its partners in which at least one partner's interest in partnership hot assets is increased or decreased. For example, a distribution of cash to one partner and hot assets to another changes both partners' interest in hot assets and is disproportionate. The intent of the disproportionate distribution rules is to ensure that each partner eventually recognizes his or her proportionate share of partnership ordinary income.

Disproportionate redemption. Sale or exchange treatment is available relative to this type of redemption. After the exchange, the shareholder owns less than 80 percent of his or her pre-redemption interest in the corporation and only a minority interest in the entity. § 302(b)(2).

Disregarded entity. The Federal income tax treatment of business income usually follows the legal form of the taxpayer (i.e., an individual's sole proprietorship is reported on the Form 1040); a C corporation's taxable income is computed on Form 1120. The check-the-box Regulations are used if the unincorporated taxpayer wants to use a different tax regime. Under these rules, a disregarded entity is taxed as an individual or a corporate division; other tax regimes are not available. For instance, a one-member limited liability company is a disregarded entity.

Distributable net income (DNI). The measure that determines the nature and amount of the distributions from estates and trusts that the beneficiaries must include in income. DNI also limits the amount that estates and trusts can claim as a deduction for such distributions. § 643(a).

Distributive share. In partnership or S corporation taxation, the distributive share is the amount of income, gain, deduction, loss, or credit allocated to a given partner or shareholder. The distributive share is the amount reported on a given line of the owner's Schedule K–1. For example, a partner's distributive share of ordinary income is the amount of income shown on that partner's Schedule K–1, Part III, line 1. For S corporations, the distributive share must be determined based on the shareholder's ownership percentage. For partnerships, the distributive share is generally determined in accordance with the partnership agreement. For both types of entities, amounts can be prorated if the ownership interest is transferred during the tax year.

Dividend. A nondeductible distribution to the shareholders of a corporation. A dividend constitutes gross income to the recipient if it is paid from the current or accumulated earnings and profits of the corporation. § 316.

Dividends received deduction. A deduction allowed a shareholder that is a corporation for dividends received from a domestic corporation. The deduction usually is 50 percent of the dividends received, but it could be 65 or 100 percent depending upon the ownership percentage held by the recipient corporation. §§ 243–246.

Divisive reorganization. A "Type D" spin-off, split-off, or split-up reorganization in which the original corporation divides its active business (in existence for at least five years) assets among two or more corporations. The stock received by the original corporation shareholders must be at least 80 percent of the other corporations.

Dock sales. A purchaser uses its owned or rented vehicles to take possession of the product at the seller's shipping dock. In most states, the sale is apportioned to the operating state of the purchaser, rather than the seller. See also *apportion* and *sales factor*.

Dollar-value LIFO. An inventory technique that focuses on the dollars invested in the inventory rather than the particular items on hand each period. Each inventory item is assigned to a pool. A pool is a collection of similar items and is treated as a separate inventory. At the end of the period, each pool is valued in terms of prices at the time LIFO was adopted (base period prices), whether or not the particular items were actually on hand in the year LIFO was adopted, to compare with current prices to determine if there has been an increase or decrease in inventories.

E

Earned income credit. A tax credit designed to provide assistance to certain low-income individuals who generally have a qualifying child. This is a refundable credit. To receive the most beneficial treatment, the taxpayer must have qualifying children. However, it is possible to qualify for the credit without having a child. See the text chapter on credits for the computation procedure required in order to determine the amount of the credit allowed. § 32.

Earnings and profits (E & P). Measures the economic capacity of a corporation to make a distribution to shareholders that is not a return of capital. Such a distribution results in dividend income to the shareholders to the extent of the corporation's current and accumulated earnings and profits.

Economic effect test. Requirements that must be met before a special allocation may be used by a partnership. The premise behind the test is that each partner who receives an allocation of income or loss from a partnership bears the economic benefit or burden of the allocation.

Economic income. The change in the taxpayer's net worth, as measured in terms of market values, plus the value of the assets the taxpayer consumed during the year. Because of the impracticality of this income model, it is not used for tax purposes.

Economic performance test. One of the requirements that must be satisfied for an accrual basis taxpayer to deduct an expense. Economic performance occurs when property or services are provided to the taxpayer, or in the case in which the taxpayer is required to provide property or services, whenever the property or services are actually provided by the taxpayer.

Education expenses. Taxpayers may deduct education expenses that are incurred either (1) to maintain or improve existing job-related skills or (2) to meet the express requirements of the employer or the requirements imposed by law to retain employment status. The expenses are not deductible if the education is required to meet the minimum educational standards for the taxpayer's job or if the education qualifies the individual for a new trade or business. The TCJA of 2017 suspended the deduction of unreimbursed employee trade or business expenses for tax years after 2017 (and through 2025). Reg. § 1.162–5.

Educational savings bonds. U.S. Series EE bonds whose proceeds are used for qualified higher educational expenses for the taxpayer, the taxpayer's spouse, or a dependent. The interest may be excluded from gross income, provided the taxpayer's adjusted gross income does not exceed certain amounts. § 135.

Effective tax rate. The financial statements for an entity include several footnotes, one of which reconciles the expected (statutory) income tax rate (e.g., 21 percent for a C corporation) with the effective tax rate. The effective tax rate is equal to taxes paid (often the tax liability) divided by the taxpayer's ability to pay (some income measure, like adjusted gross income or disposable income). For financial reporting purposes, effective tax rate generally refers to total tax expense as a percentage of pretax book income. The reconciliation often is done in dollar and/or percentage terms.

Effectively connected income. Income of a nonresident alien or foreign corporation that is attributable to the operation of a U.S. trade or business under either the asset use or the business activities test.

E-file. The electronic filing of a tax return. The filing is either direct or indirect. In direct filing, the taxpayer goes online using a computer and tax return preparation software. Indirect filing occurs when a taxpayer utilizes an authorized IRS e-file provider. The provider often is the *tax preparer*.

E-filing. See *e-file*.

Employment taxes. Taxes that an employer must pay on account of its employees. Employment taxes include FICA (Federal Insurance Contributions Act) and FUTA (Federal Unemployment Tax Act) taxes. Employment taxes are paid to the IRS in addition to income tax withholdings at specified intervals. Such taxes can be levied on the employees, the employer, or both.

Energy credits. See *energy tax credits*.

Energy tax credits. Various tax credits are available to those who invest in certain energy property. The purpose of the credit is to create incentives for conservation and to develop alternative energy sources.

Enrolled agents (EAs). A tax practitioner who has gained admission to practice before the IRS by passing an IRS examination and maintaining a required level of continuing professional education.

Entity accounting income. Entity accounting income is not identical to the taxable income of a trust or estate, nor is it determined in the same manner as the entity's financial accounting income would be. The trust document or will determines whether certain income, expenses, gains, or losses are allocated to the corpus of the entity or to the entity's income beneficiaries. Only the items that are allocated to the income beneficiaries are included in entity accounting income.

Entity buy-sell agreement. An arrangement whereby the entity is to purchase a withdrawing owner's interest. When the entity is a corporation, the agreement generally involves a stock redemption on the part of the withdrawing shareholder. See also *buy-sell agreement* and *cross-purchase buy-sell agreement*.

Entity concept. A perspective that regards a venture as an entity separate and distinct from its owners. For tax purposes, this results in the venture being directly responsible for the tax on the income it generates. The entity perspective taken toward C corporations results in the double taxation of income distributed to the corporation's owners.

Entity perspective. See *entity concept*.

Estate tax. A tax imposed on the right to transfer property by death. Thus, an estate tax is levied on the decedent's estate and not on the heir receiving the property. § 2001.

Estimated tax. The amount of tax (including alternative minimum tax and self-employment tax) a taxpayer expects to owe for the year after subtracting tax credits and income tax withheld. The estimated tax must be paid in installments at designated intervals (e.g., for a calendar year individual taxpayer, by April 15, June 15, September 15, and January 15 of the following year).

Excess business loss. The excess of aggregate deductions of the taxpayer attributable to trades or businesses of the taxpayer over the sum of aggregate gross income or gain of the taxpayer plus a threshold amount. In 2022, the threshold amount is $270,000 ($540,000 in the case of a married taxpayer filing a joint return). The threshold amount is adjusted for inflation each year. This loss limitation applies to taxpayers other than C corporations and applies after the passive activity loss limitation of § 469. § 461(l).

Excess lobbying expenditures. An excise tax is applied on otherwise tax-exempt organizations with respect to the excess of total lobbying expenditures over grass roots lobbying expenditures for the year.

Excess loss account. When a subsidiary has generated more historical losses than its parent has invested in the entity, the parent's basis in the subsidiary is zero, and the parent records additional losses in an excess loss account. This treatment allows the parent to continue to deduct losses of the subsidiary, even where no basis reduction is possible, while avoiding the need to show a negative stock basis on various financial records. If the subsidiary stock is sold while an excess loss account exists, capital gain income usually is recognized to the extent of the balance in the account.

Excise taxes. A tax on the manufacture, sale, or use of goods; on the carrying on of an occupation or activity; or on the transfer of property. Thus, the Federal estate and gift taxes are, theoretically, excise taxes.

Exclusion amount. The value of assets that is exempt from transfer tax due to the credit allowed for gifts or transfers by death. For gifts and deaths in 2022, the exclusion amount is $12,060,000. An exclusion amount unused by a deceased spouse may be used by the surviving spouse. See also *exemption equivalent amount.*

Exempt organizations. An organization that is either partially or completely exempt from Federal income taxation. § 501.

Exemption amount. An amount deducted from alternative minimum taxable income (AMTI) to determine the alternative minimum tax base. The exemption amount is adjusted for inflation and is phased out when AMTI exceeds specified threshold amounts. § 55(d).

Exemption equivalent. The maximum value of assets that can be transferred to another party without incurring any Federal gift or estate tax. See also *exemption equivalent amount.*

Exemption equivalent amount. The nontaxable amount (in 2022, $12,060,000 for gift tax and estate tax) that is the equivalent of the unified transfer tax credit allowed.

F

Fair market value. The amount at which property would change hands between a willing buyer and a willing seller, neither being under any compulsion to buy or to sell and both having reasonable knowledge of the relevant facts. Reg. §§ 1.1001–1(a) and 20.2031–1(b).

Farm price method. A method of accounting for agricultural crops. The inventory of crops is valued at its market price less the estimated cost of disposition (e.g., freight and selling expense).

Feeder organization. An entity that carries on a trade or business for the benefit of an exempt organization. However, such a relationship does not result in the feeder organization itself being tax-exempt. § 502.

FICA tax. An abbreviation that stands for Federal Insurance Contributions Act, commonly referred to as the Social Security tax. The FICA tax is comprised of the Social Security tax (old age, survivors, and disability insurance) and the Medicare tax (hospital insurance) and is imposed on both employers and employees. The employer is responsible for withholding from the employee's wages the Social Security tax at a rate of 6.2 percent on a maximum wage base and the Medicare tax at a rate of 1.45 percent (no maximum wage base). The maximum Social Security wage base for 2022 is $147,000 and for 2021 is $142,800.

Fiduciary. One who holds a legal obligation to act on another's behalf. A *trustee* and an *executor* take fiduciary relationships relative to the *grantor* and the *decedent,* respectively. The fiduciary is assigned specific duties by the principal party (e.g., to file tax returns, manage assets, satisfy debt and other obligations, and to make investment decisions). The fiduciary often possesses specialized knowledge and experience. A fiduciary must avoid conflicts of interest in which the principal's goals are compromised in some way.

Field audit. An audit conducted by the IRS on the business premises of the taxpayer or in the office of the tax practitioner representing the taxpayer.

Filing status. Individual taxpayers are placed in one of five filing statuses each year (single, married filing jointly, married filing separately, surviving spouse, or head of household). Marital status and household support are key determinants. Filing status is used to determine the taxpayer's filing requirements, standard deduction, eligibility for certain deductions and credits, and tax liability.

Final Regulations. The U.S. Treasury Department Regulations (abbreviated Reg.) represent the position of the IRS as to how the Internal Revenue Code is to be interpreted. Their purpose is to provide taxpayers and IRS personnel with rules of general and specific application to the various provisions of the tax law. Regulations are published in the *Federal Register* and in all tax services.

Financial Accounting Standards Board (FASB). See *Generally Accepted Accounting Principles (GAAP).*

Financial transaction tax. A tax imposed on some type of financial transaction, such as stock sales.

Fiscal year. A 12-month period ending on the last day of a month other than December. In certain circumstances, a taxpayer is permitted to elect a fiscal year instead of being required to use a calendar year.

Flat tax. A form of consumption tax designed to alleviate the regressivity of a value added tax (VAT). It is imposed on individuals and businesses at the same single (flat) rate.

Flexible spending plans. An employee benefit plan that allows the employee to take a reduction in salary in exchange for the employer paying benefits that can be provided by the employer without the employee being required to recognize income (e.g., medical and child care benefits). Contributions to a flexible spending plan are limited to $2,850 for 2022. § 125(i).

Flow-through entity. The entity is a tax reporter rather than a taxpayer. The owners are subject to tax. Examples are partnerships, S corporations, and limited liability companies.

Foreign-Derived Intangible Income (FDII). Income earned from sales by U.S. corporations to foreign customers from intangible assets held in the United States. § 250(b).

Foreign earned income exclusion. The Code allows exclusions for earned income generated outside the United States to alleviate any tax base and rate disparities among countries. In addition, the exclusion is allowed for housing expenditures incurred by the taxpayer's employer with respect to the non-U.S. assignment, and self-employed individuals can deduct foreign housing expenses incurred in a trade or business. The exclusion is limited to $112,000 per year for 2022 ($108,700 in 2021). § 911.

Foreign Investment in Real Property Tax Act (FIRPTA). Under the Foreign Investment in Real Property Tax Act, gains or losses realized by nonresident aliens and non-U.S. corporations on the disposition of U.S. real estate create U.S.-source income and are subject to U.S. income tax.

Foreign tax credit (FTC). A U.S. citizen or resident who incurs or pays income taxes to a foreign country on income subject to U.S. tax may be able to claim some of these taxes as a credit against the U.S. income tax. §§ 27 and 901–905.

Franchise. An agreement that gives the transferee the right to distribute, sell, or provide goods, services, or facilities within a specified area. The cost of obtaining a franchise may be amortized over a statutory period of 15 years. In general, the franchisor's gain on the sale of franchise rights is an ordinary gain because the franchisor retains a significant power, right, or continuing interest in the subject of the franchise. §§ 197 and 1253.

Franchise tax. A tax levied on the right to do business in a state as a corporation. Although income considerations may come into play, the tax usually is based on the capitalization of the corporation.

Fraud. Tax fraud falls into two categories: civil and criminal. Under civil fraud, the IRS may impose as a penalty an amount equal to as much as 75 percent of the underpayment [§ 6651(f)]. Fines and/or imprisonment are prescribed for conviction of various types of criminal tax fraud (§§ 7201–7207). Both civil and criminal fraud involve a specific intent on the part of the taxpayer to evade the tax; mere negligence is not enough. Criminal fraud requires the additional element of willfulness (i.e., done deliberately and with evil purpose). In practice, it becomes difficult to distinguish between the degree of intent necessary to support criminal, rather than civil, fraud. In either situation, the IRS has the burden of proof to show the taxpayer committed fraud.

Fringe benefits. Compensation or other benefit received by an employee that is not in the form of cash. Some fringe benefits (e.g., accident and health plans, group term life insurance) may be excluded from the employee's gross income and therefore are not subject to the Federal income tax.

Fruit and tree metaphor. The courts have held that an individual who earns income from property or services cannot assign that income to another. For example, a father cannot assign his earnings from commissions to his child and escape income tax on those amounts.

Functional currency. The currency of the economic environment in which the taxpayer carries on most of its activities and in which the taxpayer transacts most of its business.

FUTA tax. An employment tax levied on employers. Jointly administered by the Federal and state governments, the tax provides funding for unemployment benefits. FUTA applies at a rate of 6.0 percent on the first $7,000 of covered wages paid during the year for each employee. The Federal government allows a credit for FUTA paid (or allowed under a merit rating system) to the state. The credit cannot exceed 5.4 percent of the covered wages. §§ 3301–3311.

Future interest. An interest that will come into being at some future time. It is distinguished from a present interest, which already exists. Assume that Dan transfers securities to a newly created trust. Under the terms of the trust instrument, income from the securities is to be paid each year to Wilma for her life, with the securities passing to Sam upon Wilma's death. Wilma has a present interest in the trust because she is entitled to current income distributions. Sam has a future interest because he must wait for Wilma's death to benefit from the trust. The annual exclusion of $16,000 (in 2022) is not allowed for a gift of a future interest. § 2503(b).

G

General business credit. The summation of various nonrefundable business credits, including the tax credit for rehabilitation expenditures, business energy credit, work opportunity credit, research activities credit, low-income housing credit, and disabled access credit. The amount of general business credit that can be used to reduce the tax liability is limited to the taxpayer's net income tax reduced by the greater of (1) the tentative minimum tax or (2) 25 percent of the net regular tax liability that exceeds $25,000. Unused general business credits can be carried back one year and forward 20 years. § 38.

General partners. A partner who is fully liable in an individual capacity for the debts owed by the partnership to third parties. A general partner's liability is not limited to the investment in the partnership. See also *limited partners.*

General partnership (GP). A partnership that is owned by general partners (only). Creditors of a general partnership can collect amounts owed them from both the partnership assets and the assets of the partners individually.

Generally Accepted Accounting Principles (GAAP). Guidelines relating to how to construct the financial statements of enterprises doing business in the United States. Promulgated chiefly by the Financial Accounting Standards Board (FASB).

Gift tax. A tax imposed on the transfer of property by gift. The tax is imposed upon the donor of a gift and is based on the fair market value of the property on the date of the gift. § 2501.

Global Intangible Low-Taxed Income (GILTI). Income earned by a controlled foreign corporation on intellectual property or intangibles, the tax on which being designed to limit the shifting of intangible assets to countries with tax rates below the U.S. corporate rate. § 951A.

Golden parachute payments. A severance payment to employees that meets the following requirements: (1) the payment is contingent on a change of ownership of a corporation through a stock or asset acquisition and (2) the aggregate present value of the payment equals or exceeds three times the employee's average annual compensation. To the extent the severance payment meets these conditions, a deduction is disallowed to the employer for the excess of the payment over a statutory base amount (a five-year average of compensation if the taxpayer was an employee for the entire five-year period). In addition, a 20 percent excise tax is imposed on the employee who receives the excess severance pay. §§ 280G and 4999.

Goodwill. The reputation and other unidentifiable intangible assets of a company. For accounting purposes, goodwill has no basis unless it is purchased. In the purchase of a business, goodwill generally is the difference between the purchase price and the fair market value of the assets acquired. The intangible asset goodwill can be amortized for tax purposes over a 15-year period. § 197 and Reg. § 1.167(a)–3.

Grantor. A transferor of property. The creator of a trust is usually referred to as the grantor of the entity.

Grantor trust. A trust under which the grantor retains control over the income or corpus (or both) to such an extent that he or she is treated as the owner of the property and its income for income tax purposes. Income from a grantor trust is taxable to the grantor and not to the beneficiary who receives it. §§ 671–679.

Grass roots expenditures. Exempt organizations are prohibited from engaging in political activities, but spending incurred to influence the opinions of the general public relative to specific legislation is permitted by the law.

Gross estate. The property owned or previously transferred by a decedent that is subject to the Federal estate tax. The gross estate can be distinguished from the probate estate, which is property actually subject to administration by the administrator or executor of an estate. §§ 2031–2046.

Gross income. Income subject to the Federal income tax. Gross income does not include all economic income. That is, certain exclusions are allowed (e.g., interest on municipal bonds). For a manufacturing or merchandising business, gross income usually means gross profit (gross sales or gross receipts less cost of goods sold). § 61 and Reg. § 1.61–3(a).

Group term life insurance. Life insurance coverage provided by an employer for a group of employees. Such insurance is renewable on a year-to-year basis, and typically no cash surrender value is built up. The premiums paid by the employer on the insurance are not taxed to the employees on coverage of up to $50,000 per person. § 79 and Reg. § 1.79–1(b).

Guaranteed payments. Payments made by a partnership to a partner for services rendered or for the use of capital to the extent the payments are determined without regard to the income of the partnership. The payments are treated as though they were made to a nonpartner and thus are deducted by the entity. On the partnership's Schedule K and the partners' Schedules K–1, guaranteed payments are distinguished between those payments for use of the partners' capital and those paid for services provided by the partners to the partnership. The partners report the amounts as ordinary income based on the timing and amounts reported on their respective Schedules K–1. In addition to being subject to the income tax, a guaranteed payment might be subject to self-employment tax (guaranteed payment for services) or net investment income tax (guaranteed payment for capital). Guaranteed payments are not eligible for the qualified business income deduction. § 707(c).

H

Half-year convention. A cost recovery convention that assumes that property is placed in service at mid-year and thus provides for a half-year's cost recovery for that year. § 168(d).

Head of household. An unmarried individual who maintains a household for another and satisfies certain conditions set forth in § 2(b). This status enables the taxpayer to use a set of income tax rates that are lower than those applicable to other unmarried individuals but higher than those applicable to surviving spouses and married persons filing a joint return.

Health Savings Account (HSA). A medical savings account created in legislation enacted in December 2003 that is designed to replace and expand Archer Medical Savings Accounts. § 223.

Highly compensated employee. The employee group is generally divided into two categories for fringe benefit (including pension and profit sharing plans) purposes. These are (1) highly compensated employees and (2) non-highly compensated employees. For most fringe benefits, if the fringe benefit plan discriminates in favor of highly compensated employees, it will not be a qualified plan with respect, at a minimum, to the highly compensated employees.

Historic business test. In a corporate reorganization, a means by which to determine if the continuity of business enterprise requirement is met. The acquiring corporation must continue to operate the target entity's existing business(es) going forward; if this is not the case, the requirement is failed.

Hobby losses. Losses from an activity not engaged in for profit. The Code restricts the amount of losses that an individual can deduct for hobby activities so that these transactions cannot be used to offset income from other sources. The TCJA of 2017 suspended the deduction of hobby expenses for tax years after 2017 (and through 2025). § 183.

Holding period. The period of time during which property has been held for income tax purposes. The holding period is significant in determining whether gain or loss from the sale or exchange of a capital asset is long or short term. § 1223.

Home equity loans. Loans that utilize the personal residence of the taxpayer as security. The interest on such loans is deductible as qualified residence interest. However, interest is deductible only on the portion of the loan that does not exceed the lesser of (1) the fair market value of the residence, reduced by the acquisition indebtedness, or (2) $100,000 ($50,000 for married persons filing separate returns). A major benefit of a home equity loan is that there are no tracing rules regarding the use of the loan proceeds. The TCJA of 2017 suspended the deduction of interest on home equity indebtedness for tax years after 2017 (and through 2025). § 163(h)(3).

Hot assets. Unrealized receivables and substantially appreciated inventory under § 751. [For a sale of a partnership interest, "inventory" (as defined) need not be appreciated.] When hot assets are present, the sale of a partnership interest or the disproportionate distribution of the assets can cause ordinary income to be recognized.

Hybrid method. A combination of the accrual and cash methods of accounting. That is, the taxpayer may account for some items of income on the accrual method (e.g., sales and cost of goods sold) and other items (e.g., interest income) on the cash method.

I

Imputed interest. For certain long-term sales of property, under §§ 483 and 1274 the IRS can convert some of the gain from the sale into interest income if the contract does not provide for a minimum rate of interest to be paid by the purchaser. The seller recognizes less long-term capital gain and more ordinary income (interest income). Imputed interest rules also apply on certain below-market loans under § 7872.

Inbound taxation. U.S. tax effects when a non-U.S. person begins an investment or business activity in the United States.

Incentive stock options (ISOs). A type of stock option that receives favorable tax treatment. If various qualification requirements can be satisfied, stock option grants do not create taxable income for the recipient. However, the spread (the excess of the fair market value at the date of exercise over the option price) is an adjustment item for purposes of the alternative minimum tax (AMT). The gain on disposition of the stock resulting from the exercise of the stock option will be classified as long-term capital gain if certain holding period requirements are met (the employee must not dispose of the stock within two years after the option is granted or within one year after acquiring the stock). § 422.

Income. For tax purposes, an increase in wealth that has been realized.

Income in respect of a decedent (IRD). Income earned by a decedent at the time of death but not reportable on the final income tax return because of the method of accounting that appropriately is utilized. Such income is included in the gross estate and is taxed to the eventual recipient (either the estate or heirs). The recipient is, however, allowed an income tax deduction for the estate tax attributable to the income. § 691.

Income tax provision. Under ASC 740, a synonym for the book tax expense of an entity for the financial reporting period. Following the "matching principle," all book tax expense that relates to the net income for the reporting period is reported on that period's financial statements, including not only the current tax expense but also any deferred tax expense and deferred tax benefit.

Income tax treaties. See *tax treaties*.

Independent contractor. A self-employed person as distinguished from one who is employed as an employee.

Indexation. A procedure whereby adjustments are made by the IRS to key tax components (e.g., standard deduction, tax brackets, personal and dependency exemptions) to reflect inflation. The adjustments usually are made annually and are based on the change in the consumer price index.

Individual Retirement Accounts (IRAs). A type of retirement plan to which an individual with earned income can contribute a statutory maximum of $6,000 ($7,000 if age 50 or above) in 2022. IRAs can be classified as traditional IRAs or Roth IRAs. With a traditional IRA, an individual can contribute and deduct a maximum of $6,000 ($7,000 if age 50 or above) per tax year in 2022. The deduction is a deduction *for* AGI. However, if the individual is an active participant in another qualified retirement plan, the deduction is phased out proportionally between certain AGI ranges (note that the phaseout limits the amount of the deduction and not the amount of the contribution). With a Roth IRA, an individual can contribute a maximum of $6,000 ($7,000 if age 50 or above) per tax year in 2022. No deduction is permitted. However, if a five-year holding period requirement is satisfied and if the distribution is a qualified distribution, the taxpayer can make tax-free withdrawals from a Roth IRA. The maximum annual contribution is phased out proportionally between certain AGI ranges. §§ 219 and 408A.

Inheritance tax. A tax imposed on the right to receive property from a decedent. Thus, theoretically, an inheritance tax is imposed on the heir. The Federal estate tax is imposed on the estate.

Inside basis. A partnership's basis in the assets it owns.

Installment method. A method of accounting enabling certain taxpayers to spread the recognition of gain on the sale of property over the collection period. Under this procedure, the seller arrives at the gain to be recognized by computing the gross profit percentage from the sale (the gain divided by the contract price) and applying it to each payment received. § 453.

Intangible drilling and development costs (IDCs). Taxpayers may elect to expense or capitalize (subject to amortization) intangible drilling and development costs. However, ordinary income recapture provisions apply to oil and gas properties on a sale or other disposition if the expense method is elected. §§ 263(c) and 1254(a).

Intercompany transaction. A sale or exchange of goods or services between members of an *affiliated group* that files a *consolidated return*. Generally, the results of the transaction are recorded by both affiliates under general Federal income tax rules, but certain gains, losses, income, or deductions may be deferred until a later tax year.

Intermediate sanctions. The IRS can assess excise taxes on disqualified persons and organization management associated with so-called public charities engaging in excess benefit transactions. An excess benefit transaction is one in which a disqualified person engages in a non-fair market value transaction with the exempt organization or receives unreasonable compensation. Prior to the enactment of intermediate sanctions, the only option available to the IRS was to revoke the organization's exempt status.

International Accounting Standards Board (IASB). The body that promulgates International Financial Reporting Standards (IFRS). Based in London, representing accounting standard setting bodies in over 100 countries, the IASB develops accounting standards that can serve as the basis for harmonizing conflicting reporting standards among nations.

International Financial Reporting Standards (IFRS). Produced by the International Accounting Standards Board (IASB), guidelines developed since 2001 as to revenue recognition, accounting for business combinations, and a conceptual framework for financial reporting. IFRS provisions are designed so that they can be used by all entities, regardless of where they are based or conduct business. IFRS have gained widespread acceptance throughout the world, and the SEC is considering how to require U.S. entities to use IFRS in addition to, or in lieu of, the accounting rules of the Financial Accounting Standards Board.

Interpretive Regulations. A Regulation issued by the Treasury Department that purports to explain the meaning of a particular Code Section. An interpretive Regulation is given less deference than a legislative Regulation.

Inventory. Under § 1221(a)(1), a taxpayer's stock in trade or property held for resale. For partnership tax purposes, inventory is defined in § 751(d) as inventory (per the above definition) or any partnership asset other than capital or § 1231 assets. See also *appreciated inventory.*

Investment income. Consisting of virtually the same elements as portfolio income, a measure by which to justify a deduction for interest on investment indebtedness.

Investment interest. Payment for the use of funds used to acquire assets that produce investment income. The deduction for investment interest is limited to net investment income for the tax year.

Investor loss. Losses on stock and securities. If stocks and bonds are capital assets in the hands of the holder, a capital loss materializes as of the last day of the taxable year in which the stocks or bonds become worthless. Under certain circumstances involving stocks and bonds of affiliated corporations, an ordinary loss is permitted upon worthlessness.

Involuntary conversion. The loss or destruction of property through theft, casualty, or condemnation. Gain realized on an involuntary conversion can, at the taxpayer's election, be deferred for Federal income tax purposes if the owner reinvests the proceeds within a prescribed period of time in property that is similar or related in service or use. § 1033.

Itemized deductions. Personal expenditures allowed by the Code as deductions from adjusted gross income. Examples include certain medical expenses, interest on home mortgages, state income taxes, and charitable contributions. Itemized deductions are reported on Schedule A of Form 1040.

J

Joint tenants. Two or more persons having undivided ownership of property with the right of survivorship. Right of survivorship gives the surviving owner full ownership of the property. Suppose Bob and Tami are joint tenants of a tract of land. Upon Bob's death, Tami becomes the sole owner of the property. For the estate tax consequences upon the death of a joint tenant, see § 2040.

K

Keogh plans. Retirement plans available to self-employed taxpayers. They are also referred to as H.R. 10 plans. Under such plans, a taxpayer may deduct each year up to 100 percent of net earnings from self-employment or $61,000 for 2022, whichever is less. If the plan is a profit sharing plan, the percentage is 25 percent.

Kiddie tax. Passive income, such as interest and dividends, that is recognized by a child under age 19 (or under age 24 if a full-time student) is taxed according to the brackets applicable to the child's parent(s), generally to the extent the income exceeds $2,300 for 2022. The additional tax is assessed regardless of the source of the income or the income's underlying property. § 1(g).

L

Least aggregate deferral method. An algorithm set forth in the Regulations to determine the tax year for a partnership or limited liability entity with owners whose tax years differ. The tax year selected is the one that produces the least aggregate deferral of income for the owners.

Least aggregate deferral rule. See *least aggregate deferral method.*

Legislative Regulations. Some Code Sections give the Secretary of the Treasury or his delegate the authority to prescribe Regulations to carry out the details of administration or to otherwise complete the operating rules. Regulations issued pursuant to this type of authority truly possess the force and effect of law. In effect, Congress is almost delegating its legislative powers to the Treasury Department.

Lessee. One who rents property from another. In the case of real estate, the lessee is also known as the tenant.

Lessor. One who rents property to another. In the case of real estate, the lessor is also known as the landlord.

Letter ruling. The written response of the IRS to a taxpayer's request for interpretation of the revenue laws with respect to a proposed transaction (e.g., concerning the tax-free status of a reorganization). Not to be relied on as precedent by other than the party who requested the ruling.

Liabilities in excess of basis. On the contribution of capital to a corporation, an investor recognizes gain on the exchange to the extent contributed assets carry liabilities with a face amount in excess of the tax basis of the contributed assets. This rule keeps the investor from holding the investment asset received with a negative basis. § 357(c).

Life insurance proceeds. A specified sum (the face value or maturity value of the policy) paid to the designated beneficiary of the policy by the life insurance company upon the death of the insured.

Lifetime learning credit. A tax credit for qualifying expenses for taxpayers pursuing education beyond the first two years of postsecondary education. Individuals who are completing their last two years of undergraduate studies, pursuing graduate or professional degrees, or otherwise seeking new job skills or maintaining existing job skills are all eligible for the credit. Eligible individuals include the taxpayer, taxpayer's spouse, and taxpayer's dependents. The maximum credit is 20 percent of the first $10,000 of qualifying expenses and is computed per taxpayer. The credit is phased out for higher-income taxpayers. § 25A.

Like-kind exchanges. An exchange of real property held for productive use in a trade or business or for investment for other investment or trade or business real property. Unless non-like-kind property (boot) is received, the exchange is fully tax-deferred. § 1031.

Limited liability company (LLC). A legal entity in which all owners are protected from the entity's debts but which may lack other characteristics of a corporation (i.e., centralized management, unlimited life, free transferability of interests). LLCs generally are treated as partnerships (or disregarded entities if they have only one owner) for tax purposes.

Limited liability partnership (LLP). A legal entity allowed by many of the states, where a general partnership registers with the state as an LLP. All partners are at risk with respect to any liabilities arising from their own malpractice or torts or those of their subordinates. However, all partners are protected from any liabilities resulting from the malpractice or torts of other partners.

Limited partners. A partner whose liability to third-party creditors of the partnership is limited to the amounts invested in the partnership. See also *general partners* and *limited partnership (LP)*.

Limited partnership (LP). A partnership in which some of the partners are limited partners. At least one of the partners in a limited partnership must be a general partner.

Liquidating distribution. A distribution by a partnership that is in complete liquidation of the partnership trade or business activities or in complete liquidation of a partner's interest in the partnership. A liquidating distribution is generally a tax-deferred transaction if it is proportionate with respect to the partnership's hot assets. In a proportionate liquidating distribution, the partnership recognizes no gain or loss. The partner only recognizes gain if the distributed cash (and cash equivalents, such as debt relief or certain marketable securities) exceeds the partner's basis in the partnership. The partner recognizes a loss if *only* cash and hot assets are distributed and their combined inside (partnership) basis is less than the partner's basis in the partnership interest. In any case where no gain or loss is recognized, the partner's basis in the partnership interest is fully assigned to the basis of the assets received in the distribution.

Listed property. Property that includes (1) any passenger automobile; (2) any other property used as a means of transportation; (3) any property of a type generally used for purposes of entertainment, recreation, or amusement; and (4) any other property of a type specified in the Regulations. If listed property is predominantly used for business, the taxpayer is allowed to use the statutory percentage method of cost recovery. Otherwise, the straight-line cost recovery method must be used. § 280F.

Lobbying expenditures. An expenditure made for the purpose of influencing legislation. Such payments can result in the loss of the exempt status of, and the imposition of Federal income tax on, an exempt organization. Lobby expenditures are not deductible. § 162(e).

Long-term care insurance. Insurance that helps pay the cost of care when the insured is unable to care for himself or herself. Such insurance is generally thought of as insurance against the cost of an aged person entering a nursing home. The employer can provide the insurance, and the premiums may be excluded from the employee's gross income. § 7702B.

Long-term contract. A building, installation, construction, or manufacturing contract that is entered into but not completed within the same tax year. A manufacturing contract is a long-term contract only if the contract is to manufacture (1) a unique item not normally carried in finished goods inventory or (2) items that normally require more than 12 calendar months to complete. The two available methods to account for long-term contracts are the percentage of completion method and the completed contract method. The completed contract method can be used only in limited circumstances. § 460.

Long-term nonpersonal use capital assets. Includes investment property with a long-term holding period. Such property disposed of by casualty or theft may receive § 1231 treatment.

Long-term tax-exempt rate. Used in deriving the yearly limitation on net operating loss and other tax benefits that carry over from the target to the acquiring when there is a more than 50-percentage-point ownership change (by value). The highest of the Federal long-term interest rates in effect for any of the last three months. § 382.

Lower of cost or market (replacement cost). An elective inventory method, whereby the taxpayer may value inventories at the lower of the taxpayer's actual cost or the current replacement cost of the goods. This method cannot be used in conjunction with the LIFO inventory method.

Low-income housing credit. Beneficial treatment to owners of low-income housing is provided in the form of a tax credit. The calculated credit is claimed in the year the building is placed in service and in the following nine years. § 42.

Lump-sum distribution. Payment of the entire amount due at one time rather than in installments. Such distributions often occur from qualified pension or profit sharing plans upon the retirement or death of a covered employee. The recipient of a lump-sum distribution may recognize both long-term capital gain and ordinary income upon the receipt of the distribution. The ordinary income portion may be subject to a special 10-year income averaging provision. § 402(e).

M

Majority interest partners. Partners who have more than a 50 percent interest in partnership profits and capital, counting only those partners who have the same taxable year. The term is of significance in determining the appropriate taxable year of a partnership. § 706(b).

Marginal tax rate. The tax rate applicable to the next dollar of income (if describing an income tax).

Marital deduction. A deduction allowed against the taxable estate or taxable gifts upon the transfer of property from one spouse to another.

Marriage penalty. The additional tax liability that results for a married couple when compared with what their tax liability would be if they were not married and filed separate returns.

Matching rule. Treatment of an intercompany transaction on a consolidated return, when a sold asset remains within the group.

Material participation. If an individual taxpayer materially participates in a nonrental trade or business activity, any loss from that activity is treated as an active loss that can be offset against active income. Material participation is achieved by meeting any one of seven tests provided in the Regulations. § 469(h).

Meaningful reduction test. A decrease in the shareholder's voting control. Used to determine whether a stock redemption qualifies for sale or exchange treatment.

Medical expenses. Medical expenses of an individual, a spouse, and dependents are allowed as an itemized deduction to the extent such amounts (less insurance reimbursements) exceed 7.5 percent of adjusted gross income. § 213.

Merger. The absorption of one corporation by another with the corporation being absorbed losing its legal identity. Flow Corporation is merged into Jobs Corporation, and the shareholders of Flow receive stock in Jobs in exchange for their stock in Flow. After the merger, Flow ceases to exist as a separate legal entity. If a merger meets certain conditions, it is not currently taxable to the parties involved. § 368(a)(1).

Mid-month convention. A cost recovery convention that assumes that property is placed in service in the middle of the month that it is actually placed in service. § 168(d).

Mid-quarter convention. A cost recovery convention that assumes that property placed in service during the year is placed in service at the middle of the quarter in which it is actually placed in service. The mid-quarter convention applies if more than 40 percent of the value of property (other than eligible real estate) is placed in service during the last quarter of the year. § 168(d).

Miscellaneous itemized deductions. A special category of itemized deductions that includes expenses such as professional dues, tax return preparation fees, job-hunting costs, unreimbursed employee business expenses, and certain investment expenses. Such expenses are deductible only to the extent they exceed 2 percent of adjusted gross income. The TCJA of 2017 suspended the deduction for these items for tax years after 2017 (and through 2025). § 67.

Modified accelerated cost recovery system (MACRS). A method in which the cost of tangible property is recovered over a prescribed period of time. Enacted by the Economic Recovery Tax Act (ERTA) of 1981 and substantially modified by the Tax Reform Act (TRA) of 1986, the method disregards salvage value, imposes a period of cost recovery that depends upon the classification of the asset into one of various recovery periods, and prescribes the applicable percentage of cost that can be deducted each year. § 168.

Multiple support agreement. To qualify for a dependency exemption, the support test must be satisfied. This requires that over 50 percent of the support of the potential dependent be provided by the taxpayer. Where no one person provides more than 50 percent of the support, a multiple support agreement enables a taxpayer to still qualify for the dependency exemption. Any person who contributed more than 10 percent of the support is entitled to claim the exemption if each person in the group who contributed more than 10 percent files a written consent (Form 2120). Each person who is a party to the multiple support agreement must meet all of the other requirements for claiming the dependency exemption. § 152(c).

Multistate Tax Commission (MTC). A regulatory body of the states that develops operating rules and regulations for the implementation of the UDITPA and other provisions that assign the total taxable income of a multistate corporation to specific states.

N

National sales tax. Intended as a replacement for the current Federal income tax. Unlike a value added tax (VAT), which is levied on the manufacturer, it would be imposed on the consumer upon the final sale of goods and services. To reduce regressivity, individuals would receive a rebate to offset a portion of the tax.

Negligence. Failure to exercise the reasonable or ordinary degree of care of a prudent person in a situation that results in harm or damage to another. A penalty is assessed on taxpayers who exhibit negligence or intentional disregard of rules and Regulations with respect to the underpayment of certain taxes. § 6662(c).

Net capital gain (NCG). The excess of the net long-term capital gain for the tax year over the net short-term capital loss. The net capital gain of an individual taxpayer is eligible for the alternative tax. § 1222(11).

Net capital loss (NCL). The excess of the losses from sales or exchanges of capital assets over the gains from sales or exchanges of such assets. Up to $3,000 per year of the net capital loss may be deductible by noncorporate taxpayers against ordinary income. The excess net capital loss carries over to future tax years. For corporate taxpayers, the net capital loss cannot be offset against ordinary income, but it can be carried back three years and forward five years to offset net capital gains. §§ 1211, 1212, and 1221(10).

Net Deemed Tangible Income Return (NDTIR). The excess of 10 percent of a controlled foreign corporation shareholder's qualified business asset investment over the amount of interest expense considered in determining net tested income of such corporation. § 951A(b)(2).

Net investment income. The excess of investment income over investment expenses. Investment expenses are those deductible expenses directly connected with the production of investment income. Investment expenses do not include investment interest. The deduction for investment interest for the tax year is limited to net investment income. § 163(d).

Net operating loss (NOL). To mitigate the effect of the annual accounting period concept, § 172 allows taxpayers to use an excess loss of one year as a deduction for certain past or future years. For NOLs incurred after 2020, an indefinite carryforward period applies, and such NOLs are subject to an 80 percent of taxable income limitation in any carryforward year. (Different carryover rules apply for NOLs incurred before 2021, and there is no limitation on an NOL deduction in such years.)

Nexus. The degree of activity that must be present before a taxing jurisdiction has the right to impose a tax on an out-of-state entity. The rules for income tax nexus are not the same as for sales tax nexus.

Ninety-day (90-day) letter. This notice is sent to a taxpayer upon request, upon the expiration of the 30-day letter, or upon exhaustion by the taxpayer of his or her administrative remedies before the IRS. The notice gives the taxpayer

90 days in which to file a petition with the U.S. Tax Court. If a petition is not filed, the IRS will demand payment of the assessed deficiency. §§ 6211–6216.

No-additional-cost service. Services the employer may provide the employee at no additional cost to the employer. Generally, the benefit is the ability to utilize the employer's excess capacity (e.g., vacant seats on an airliner). Such amounts are excludible from the recipient's gross income. § 132(b).

Nonaccountable plan. An expense reimbursement plan that does not have an accountability feature. The result is that employee expenses are not deductible.

Nonacquiescence. Disagreement by the IRS on the result reached in certain judicial decisions. *Nonacq.* or *NA.*

Nonbusiness bad debt. A bad debt loss that is not incurred in connection with a creditor's trade or business. The loss is classified as a short-term capital loss and is allowed only in the year the debt becomes entirely worthless. In addition to family loans, many investor losses are nonbusiness bad debts. § 166(d).

Nonqualified deferred compensation (NQDC). Compensation arrangements that are frequently offered to executives. Such plans may include stock options or annuities upon separation, for example. Often, an executive may defer the recognition of taxable income. The employer, however, does not receive a tax deduction until the employee is required to include the compensation in income. § 409A.

Nonqualified stock option (NQSO). A type of stock option that does not satisfy the statutory requirements of an incentive stock option. If the NQSO has a readily ascertainable fair market value (e.g., the option is traded on an established exchange), the value of the option must be included in the employee's gross income at the date of the grant. Otherwise, the employee does not recognize income at the grant date. Instead, ordinary income is recognized in the year of exercise of the option.

Nonrecourse debt. Debt secured by the property that it is used to purchase. The purchaser of the property is not personally liable for the debt upon default. Rather, the creditor's recourse is to repossess the related property. Nonrecourse debt generally does not increase the purchaser's at-risk amount.

Nonrefundable credits. A credit that is not paid if it exceeds the taxpayer's tax liability. Some nonrefundable credits qualify for carryback and carryover treatment.

Nonresident alien (NRA). An individual who is neither a citizen nor a resident of the United States. Citizenship is determined under the immigration and naturalization laws of the United States. Residency is determined under § 7701(b) of the Internal Revenue Code.

Nontaxable exchange. A transaction in which realized gains or losses are not recognized. The recognition of gain or loss is postponed (deferred) until the property received in the nontaxable exchange is subsequently disposed of in a taxable transaction. Examples are § 1031 like-kind exchanges and § 1033 involuntary conversions.

Not essentially equivalent redemption. Sale or exchange treatment is given to this type of redemption. Although various safe-harbor tests are failed, the nature of the redemption is such that dividend treatment is avoided, because it represents a meaningful reduction in the shareholder's interest in the corporation. § 302(b)(1).

Notices. A Notice is issued by the National Office of the IRS as official guidance when such information is needed before the time it takes to issue a Final Regulation. Such guidance is typically transitional until final guidance is issued. A Notice is published in an *Internal Revenue Bulletin* (I.R.B.).

Occupational fee. A tax imposed on various trades or businesses. A license fee that enables a taxpayer to engage in a particular occupation.

Occupational taxes. See *occupational fee.*

Offer in compromise. A settlement agreement offered by the IRS in a tax dispute, especially where there is doubt as to the collectibility of the full deficiency. Offers in compromise can include installment payment schedules as well as reductions in the tax and penalties owed by the taxpayer. § 7122.

Office audit. An audit conducted by the IRS in the agent's office.

Office in the home expenses. Employment and business-related expenses attributable to the use of a residence (e.g., den or office) are allowed only if the portion of the residence is exclusively used on a regular basis as a principal place of business of the taxpayer or as a place of business that is used by patients, clients, or customers. In computing the office in the home expenses, a taxpayer can use either the regular method or simplified method. As a general rule, the regular method requires more effort and recordkeeping but results in a larger deduction. Office in home expenses incurred by an employee are not deductible for tax years after 2017 (and through 2025). § 280A.

Operating agreement. The governing document of a limited liability company. This document is similar in structure, function, and purpose to a partnership agreement.

Optional adjustment election. See *Section 754 election.*

Options. The sale or exchange of an option to buy or sell property results in capital gain or loss if the property is a capital asset. Generally, the closing of an option transaction results in short-term capital gain or loss to the writer of the call and the purchaser of the call option. § 1234.

Ordinary and necessary. Two tests for the deductibility of expenses incurred or paid in connection with a trade or business; for the production or collection of income; for the management, conservation, or maintenance of property held for the production of income; or in connection with the determination, collection, or refund of any tax. An expense is ordinary if it is common and accepted in the general industry or type of activity in which the taxpayer is engaged. An expense is necessary if it is appropriate and helpful in furthering the taxpayer's business or income-producing activity. §§ 162(a) and 212.

Ordinary income property. Property contributed to a charitable organization that, if sold rather than contributed, would have resulted in other than long-term capital gain to the donor (i.e., ordinary income property and short-term capital gain property). Examples are inventory and capital assets held for less than the long-term holding period. A contribution of ordinary income property must generally be valued at its fair market value less the gain, if any, that would have been realized if sold. § 170(e).

Organizational expenditures. Expenditures related to the creation of a corporation or partnership. Common organizational expenditures include legal and accounting fees and state incorporation payments. Organizational expenditures exclude those incurred to obtain capital (underwriting fees) or assets (subject to cost recovery). Such expenditures incurred by the end of the entity's first year are eligible for a $5,000 limited expensing (subject to phaseout) and an amortization of the balance over 180 months. §§ 248 and 709(b).

Original issue discount (OID). The difference between the issue price of a debt obligation (e.g., a corporate bond) and the maturity value of the obligation when the issue price is less than the maturity value. OID represents interest and must be amortized over the life of the debt obligation using the effective interest method. The difference is not considered to be original issue discount for tax purposes when it is less than one-fourth of 1 percent of the redemption price at maturity multiplied by the number of years to maturity. §§ 1272 and 1273(a)(3).

Other adjustments account (OAA). Used in the context of a distribution from an S corporation. The net accumulation of the entity's exempt income (e.g., municipal bond interest), net of related nondeductible expenses. See § 1368(e)(1)(A).

Other property. In a corporate reorganization, any property in the exchange that is not stock or securities, such as cash or land. This amount constitutes boot. This treatment is similar to that in a like-kind exchange.

Outbound taxation. U.S. tax effects when a U.S. person begins an investment or business activity outside the United States.

Outside basis. A partner's basis in his or her partnership interest.

Ownership change. An event that triggers a § 382 limitation for the acquiring corporation.

P

Partial liquidation. A stock redemption where noncorporate shareholders are permitted sale or exchange treatment. In certain cases, an active business must have existed for at least five years. Only a portion of the outstanding stock in the entity is retired. §§ 302(b)(4) and (e).

Partnership. For income tax purposes, a partnership includes a syndicate, group, pool, or joint venture as well as ordinary partnerships. In an ordinary partnership, two or more parties combine capital and/or services to carry on a business for profit as co-owners. § 7701(a)(2).

Partnership agreement. The governing document of a partnership. A partnership agreement should describe the rights and obligations of the partners; the allocation of entity income, deductions, and cash flows; initial and future capital contribution requirements; conditions for terminating the partnership; and other matters.

Passive activity loss. Any loss from (1) activities in which the taxpayer does not materially participate or (2) rental activities (subject to certain exceptions). Net passive activity losses cannot be used to offset income from nonpassive activity sources. Rather, they are suspended until the taxpayer either generates net passive activity income (and a deduction of such losses is allowed) or disposes of the underlying property (at which time the loss deductions are allowed in full). One relief provision allows landlords who actively participate in the rental activities to deduct up to $25,000 of passive activity losses annually. However, a phaseout of the $25,000 amount commences when the landlord's AGI exceeds $100,000. Another relief provision applies for material participation in a real estate trade or business. § 469.

Passive investment company. A means by which a multistate corporation can reduce the overall effective tax rate by isolating investment income in a low- or no-tax state.

Passive investment income (PII). Gross receipts from royalties, certain rents, dividends, interest, annuities, and gains from the sale or exchange of stock and securities. When earnings and profits (E & P) also exist, if the passive investment income of an S corporation exceeds 25 percent of the corporation's gross receipts for three consecutive years, S status is lost.

Pass-through entities. A form of business structure for which the income and other tax items are attributed directly to the owners and generally no separate tax is levied upon the entity itself. Examples include sole proprietorships, partnerships, and S corporations. Also referred to as a flow-through entity.

Patent. An intangible asset that may be amortized over a statutory 15-year period as a § 197 intangible. The sale of a patent usually results in favorable long-term capital gain treatment. §§ 197 and 1235.

Payroll factor. The proportion of a multistate corporation's total payroll that is traceable to a specific state. Used in determining the taxable income that is to be apportioned to that state.

Pension plan. A type of deferred compensation arrangement that provides for systematic payments of definitely determinable retirement benefits to employees who meet the requirements set forth in the plan.

Percentage depletion. Depletion based on a statutory percentage applied to the gross income from the property. The taxpayer deducts the greater of cost depletion or percentage depletion. § 613.

Percentage of completion method. A method of reporting gain or loss on certain long-term contracts. Under this method of accounting, the gross contract price is included in income as the contract is completed. Reg. § 1.451–3.

Permanent differences. Under ASC 740, tax-related items that appear in the entity's financial statements or its tax return but not both. For instance, interest income from a municipal bond is a permanent book-tax difference.

Permanent establishment (PE). A level of business activity, as defined under an income tax treaty, that subjects the taxpayer to taxation in a country other than that in which the taxpayer is based. Often evidenced by the presence of a plant, an office, or other fixed place of business. Inventory storage and temporary activities do not rise to the level of a PE. PE is the treaty's equivalent to nexus.

Personal and dependency exemptions. The tax law provides an exemption for each individual taxpayer and an additional exemption for the taxpayer's spouse if a joint return is filed. An individual may also claim a dependency exemption for each dependent, provided certain tests are met. The TCJA of 2017 suspended the deduction for exemptions for tax years after 2017 (and through 2025).

Personal exemptions. See *personal and dependency exemptions.*

Personal holding company (PHC) tax. A penalty tax imposed on certain closely held corporations with excessive investment income. Assessed at a 20 percent tax rate on personal holding company income, reduced by dividends paid and other adjustments. § 541.

Personal residence. If a residence has been owned and used by the taxpayer as the principal residence for at least two years during the five-year period ending on the date of sale, up to $250,000 of realized gain is excluded from gross income. For a married couple filing a joint return, the $250,000 is increased to $500,000 if either spouse satisfies the ownership requirement and both spouses satisfy the use requirement. § 121.

Personal service corporation (PSC). A corporation whose principal activity is the performance of personal services (e.g., health, law, engineering, architecture, accounting, actuarial science, performing arts, or consulting) and where such services are substantially performed by the employee-owners. § 269A(b).

Personalty. All property that is not attached to real estate (realty) and is movable. Examples of personalty are machinery, automobiles, clothing, household furnishings, and personal effects.

Points. Loan origination fees that may be deductible as interest by a buyer of property. A seller of property who pays points reduces the selling price by the amount of the points paid for the buyer. While the seller is not permitted to deduct this amount as interest, the buyer may do so.

Portfolio income. Income from interest, dividends, rentals, royalties, capital gains, or other investment sources. Net passive activity losses cannot be used to offset net portfolio income.

Precedents. A previously decided court decision that is recognized as authority for the disposition of future decisions.

Precontribution gain or loss. Partnerships allow for a variety of special allocations of gain or loss among the partners, but gain or loss that is "built in" on an asset contributed to the partnership is assigned specifically to the contributing partner. § 704(c)(1)(A).

Preferences. In calculating alternative minimum taxable income (AMTI), preference items are added to the taxable income starting point of the AMT calculation. AMT preferences are amounts allowed in the calculation of regular taxable income but not allowed in the calculation of AMTI. For instance, interest income from certain state and local bonds (i.e., private activity bonds) is an AMT preference item. § 57.

Preferred stock bailout. A process where a shareholder used the issuance and sale, or later redemption, of a preferred stock dividend to obtain long-term capital gains, without any loss of voting control over the corporation. In effect, the shareholder received corporate profits without suffering the consequences of dividend income treatment. This procedure led Congress to enact § 306, which, if applicable, converts the prior long-term capital gain on the sale or redemption of the tainted stock to dividend income.

Premium Tax Credit (PTC). A tax credit that is refundable and available in advance of filing a return for the year. The PTC serves to reduce the cost of health coverage obtained on the Marketplace (Exchange). A PTC is available to individuals who purchase coverage on the Exchange and have household income equal to or greater than 100 percent of the Federal poverty line (FPL) and no greater than 400 percent of the FPL. Also, an individual must not have been able to obtain affordable coverage from his or her employer. If obtained in advance, the PTC is given to the insurance provider to lower the monthly premium cost to the individual. The PTC is reconciled on Form 8962 (Premium Tax Credit) filed with Form 1040 or 1040-A (not Form 1040-EZ). Individuals who obtain insurance through the Marketplace receive Form 1095-A (Health Insurance Marketplace Statement) by January 31 of the following year. This form provides information necessary to claim or reconcile the PTC, including the monthly cost of premiums and the amount of PTC received in advance each month. § 36B.

Preparer Tax Identification Number (PTIN). This number is required for individuals who are compensated for preparing or assisting in the preparation of all or substantially all of most Federal tax returns. The number must be renewed annually and reported along with the preparer's signature on the tax return to avoid imposition of a penalty. §§ 6109 and 6695.

Principal partner. A partner with a 5 percent or greater interest in partnership capital or profits. § 706(b)(3).

Private activity bonds. Interest on state and local bonds is excludible from gross income. Certain such bonds are labeled private activity bonds. Although the interest on such bonds is excludible for regular tax purposes, it is treated as a tax preference in calculating the AMT. §§ 57(a)(5) and 103.

Private foundations. An exempt organization that is subject to additional statutory restrictions on its activities and on contributions made to it, because it is not sufficiently supported by the public. Excise taxes may be levied on certain prohibited transactions, and the Code places more stringent restrictions on the deductibility of contributions to private foundations. § 509.

Probate costs. The costs incurred in administering a decedent's estate.

Probate estate. The property of a decedent that is subject to administration by the executor or administrator of an estate.

Procedural Regulations. A Regulation issued by the Treasury Department that is a housekeeping-type instruction indicating information that taxpayers should provide the IRS as well as information about the internal management and conduct of the IRS itself.

Profit and loss sharing ratios. Specified in the partnership agreement and used to determine each partner's allocation of ordinary taxable income and separately stated items. Profits and losses can be shared in different ratios. The ratios can be changed by amending the partnership agreement or by using a special allocation. § 704(a).

Profit sharing plan. A deferred compensation plan established and maintained by an employer to provide for employee participation in the company's profits. Contributions are paid from the employer's current or accumulated profits to a trustee. Separate accounts are maintained for each participant employee. The plan must provide a definite, predetermined formula for allocating the contributions among the participants. It also must include a definite, predetermined formula for distributing the accumulated funds after a fixed number of years, on the attainment of a stated age, or on the occurrence of certain events such as illness, layoff, or retirement.

Profits (loss) interest. The extent of a partner's entitlement to an allocation of the partnership's operating results. This interest is measured by the profit and loss sharing ratios.

Property. Assets defined in the broadest legal sense. Property includes the unrealized receivables of a cash basis taxpayer, but not services rendered. § 351.

Property dividend. Generally treated in the same manner as a cash distribution, measured by the fair market value of the property on the date of distribution. Distribution of appreciated property causes the distributing C or S corporation to recognize gain. The distributing corporation does not recognize loss on property that has depreciated in value. §§ 311 and 1371(a).

Property factor. The proportion of a multistate corporation's total property that is traceable to a specific state. Used in determining the taxable income that is to be apportioned to that state.

Proportionate distribution. A distribution in which the partners' interests in hot assets does not change. This can happen, for instance, when no hot assets are distributed (e.g., a proportionate cash distribution) or when each partner in a partnership receives a pro rata share of hot assets being distributed. For example, a distribution of $10,000 of hot assets equally to two 50 percent partners is a proportionate distribution.

Proposed Regulations. A Regulation issued by the Treasury Department in proposed, rather than final, form. The interval between the proposal of a Regulation and its finalization permits taxpayers and other interested parties to comment on the propriety of the proposal.

Proprietorship. A business entity for which there is a single owner. The net profit of the entity is reported on the owner's Federal income tax return (Schedule C of Form 1040).

Public Law 86–272. A congressional limit on the ability of the state to force a multistate corporation to assign taxable income to that state. Under P.L. 86–272, where orders for tangible personal property are both filled and delivered outside the state, the entity must establish more than the mere solicitation of such orders before any income can be apportioned to the state.

Publicly traded partnership. A partnership the interests in which are traded on an established securities market or are readily tradable on a secondary market. Publicly traded partnerships are generally treated as corporations for tax purposes unless substantially all of their income is passive or is derived in connection with any mineral or natural resource or certain fuels. § 7704.

Punitive damages. Damages received or paid by the taxpayer can be classified as compensatory damages or as punitive damages. Punitive damages are those awarded to punish the defendant for gross negligence or the intentional infliction of harm. Such damages are includible in gross income. § 104(a)(2).

Q

QBI deduction. See *deduction for qualified business income.*

Qualified ABLE program. A state program that allows funds to be set aside for the benefit of an individual who became disabled or blind before age 26. Cash may be put into the fund annually up to the annual gift tax exclusion amount. Distributions to the designated beneficiary are not taxable provided they do not exceed qualified disability expenses for the year. § 529A.

Qualified business income (QBI). For purposes of the qualified business income deduction, it is the ordinary income less ordinary deductions a taxpayer earns from a qualified trade or business conducted in the United States by the taxpayer. Includes the distributive share of these amounts from each partnership or S corporation interest held by the taxpayer. Does not include certain types of investment income (e.g., capital gains or losses and dividends), "reasonable compensation" paid to a taxpayer with respect to any qualified trade or business, or guaranteed payments made to a partner for services rendered. § 199A(c).

Qualified business income deduction (QBID). See *deduction for qualified business income.*

Qualified business unit (QBU). A subsidiary, branch, or other business entity that conducts business using a currency other than the U.S. dollar.

Qualified dividend income (QDI). See *qualified dividends.*

Qualified dividends. Distributions made by domestic (and certain non-U.S.) corporations to noncorporate shareholders that are subject to tax at the same rates as those applicable to net long-term capital gains (i.e., 0 percent, 15 percent, or 20 percent). The 20 percent rate applies to certain high-income taxpayers. The dividend must be paid out of earnings and profits, and the shareholders must meet certain holding period requirements as to the stock. §§ 1(h)(1) and (11).

Qualified employee discount. Discounts offered employees on merchandise or services that the employer ordinarily sells or provides to customers. The discounts must be generally available to all employees. In the case of property, the discount cannot exceed the employer's gross profit (the sales price cannot be less than the employer's cost). In the case of services, the discounts cannot exceed 20 percent of the normal sales price. § 132(c).

Qualified improvement property. Any improvement to an interior portion of nonresidential real property made after the property is placed in service, including leasehold improvements. § 168(e)(6).

Qualified joint venture. At the election of the taxpayers, certain joint ventures between spouses can avoid partnership classification. Known as a qualified joint venture, the spouses generally report their share of the business activities from the venture as sole proprietors (using two Schedule C forms). This would be reported on Schedule E if the venture relates to a rental property. § 761(f).

Qualified nonrecourse financing. Debt issued on realty by a bank, retirement plan, or governmental agency. Included in the at-risk amount by the investor. In a partnership tax return, the partners' shares of qualified nonrecourse financing are reported on their Schedules K–1. § 465(b)(6).

Qualified real property business indebtedness. Indebtedness that was incurred or assumed by the taxpayer in connection with real property used in a trade or business and is secured by such real property. The taxpayer must not be a C corporation. For qualified real property business indebtedness, the taxpayer may elect to exclude some or all of the income realized from cancellation of debt on qualified real property. If the election is made, the basis of the property must be reduced by the amount excluded. The amount excluded cannot be greater than the excess of the principal amount of the outstanding debt over the fair market value (net of any other debt outstanding on the property) of the property securing the debt. § 108(c).

Qualified residence interest. A term relevant in determining the amount of interest expense the individual taxpayer may deduct as an itemized deduction for what otherwise would be disallowed as a component of personal interest (consumer interest). Qualified residence interest consists of interest paid on qualified residences (principal residence and one other residence) of the taxpayer. Debt that qualifies as qualified residence interest is limited to $1,000,000 of debt to acquire, construct, or substantially improve qualified residences (acquisition indebtedness). For acquisition indebtedness incurred after December 15, 2017, the limit is reduced to $750,000. § 163(h)(3).

Qualified small business corporation. For purposes of computing an exclusion upon the sale of *qualified small business stock*, a C corporation that has aggregate gross assets not exceeding $50 million and that is conducting an active trade or business. § 1202.

Qualified small business stock. Stock in a qualified small business corporation, purchased as part of an original issue after August 10, 1993. The shareholder may exclude from gross income 100 (or 50 or 75) percent of the realized gain on the sale of the stock if he or she held the stock for more than five years. The exclusion percentage depends on when the stock was acquired. § 1202.

Qualified terminable interest property (QTIP). Generally, the marital deduction (for gift and estate tax purposes) is not available if the interest transferred will terminate upon the death of the transferee spouse and pass to someone else. Thus, if Jim (the husband) places property in trust, life estate to Mary (the wife), and remainder to their children upon Mary's death, this is a terminable interest that will not provide Jim (or Jim's estate) with a marital deduction. If, however, the transfer in trust is treated as qualified terminable interest property (the QTIP election is made), the terminable interest restriction is waived and the marital deduction becomes available. In exchange for this deduction, the surviving spouse's gross estate must include the value of the QTIP election assets, even though he or she has no control over the ultimate disposition of the asset. Terminable interest property qualifies for this election if the donee (or heir) is the only beneficiary of the asset during his or her lifetime and receives income distributions relative to the property at least annually. For gifts, the donor spouse is the one who makes the QTIP election. For property transferred by death, the executor of the estate of the deceased spouse makes the election. §§ 2056(b)(7) and 2523(f).

Qualified trade or business. Used in determining the deduction for qualified business income (§ 199A). In general, it includes any trade or business other than providing services as an employee. In addition, a "specified services trade or business" is not a qualified trade or business. § 199A(d)(1)(B).

Qualified transportation fringes. Transportation benefits provided by the employer to the employee. If these benefits are reimbursed by the employer, they are excludible from gross income by the employee, but not deductible by the employer after 2017. Such benefits include (1) transportation in a commuter highway vehicle between the employee's residence and the place of employment, (2) a transit pass, and (3) qualified parking. Qualified transportation fringes are excludible from the employee's gross income to the extent categories (1) and (2) above do not exceed $280 per month in 2022 and category (3) does not exceed $280 per month in 2022. These amounts are indexed annually for inflation. § 132(f).

Qualified tuition program (§ 529 plan). A program that allows college tuition to be prepaid for a beneficiary. When amounts in the plan are used, nothing is included in gross income provided they are used for qualified higher education expenses. § 529.

Qualifying child. An individual who, as to the taxpayer, satisfies the relationship, abode, and age tests. To be claimed as a dependent, such individual must also meet the citizenship and joint return tests and not be self-supporting. §§ 152(a)(1) and (c).

Qualifying relative. An individual who, as to the taxpayer, satisfies the relationship, gross income, support, citizenship, and joint return tests. Such an individual can be claimed as a dependent of the taxpayer. §§ 152(a)(2) and (d).

R

Rate reconciliation. Under Generally Accepted Accounting Principles, a footnote to the financial statements often includes a table that accounts for differences in the statutory income tax rate that applies to the entity (e.g., 21 percent) and the higher or lower effective tax rate that the entity realized for the reporting period. The rate reconciliation includes only permanent differences between the book tax expense and the entity's income tax provision. The rate reconciliation table often is expressed in dollar and/or percentage terms.

Realized gain. See *realized gain or loss*.

Realized gain or loss. The difference between the amount realized upon the sale or other disposition of property and the adjusted basis of the property. § 1001.

Realized loss. See *realized gain or loss*.

Realty. Real estate.

Reasonable cause. Relief from taxpayer and preparer penalties often is allowed where reasonable cause is found for the taxpayer's actions. For example, reasonable cause for the late filing of a tax return might be a flood that damaged the taxpayer's record-keeping systems and made a timely completion of the return difficult.

Reasonable needs of the business. A means of avoiding the penalty tax on an unreasonable accumulation of earnings.

In determining the base for this tax (accumulated taxable income), § 535 allows a deduction for "such part of earnings and profits for the taxable year as are retained for the reasonable needs of the business." § 537.

Reasonableness. See *reasonableness requirement.*

Reasonableness requirement. The Code includes a reasonableness requirement with respect to the deduction of salaries and other compensation for services. The courts have expanded this requirement to all business expenses, ruling that an expense must be reasonable in order to be ordinary and necessary. What constitutes reasonableness is a question of fact. If an expense is unreasonable, the amount that is classified as unreasonable is not allowed as a deduction. The question of reasonableness generally arises with respect to closely held corporations where there is no separation of ownership and management. § 162(a)(1).

Recapitalization. A "Type E" reorganization, constituting a major change in the character and amount of outstanding equity of a corporation. Tax-free exchanges are stock for stock, bonds for bonds, and bonds for stock. For example, common stock exchanged for preferred stock can qualify as a tax-free "Type E" reorganization.

Recognized gain. See *recognized gain or loss.*

Recognized gain or loss. The portion of realized gain or loss subject to income taxation.

Recognized loss. See *recognized gain or loss.*

Recourse debt. Debt for which the lender may both foreclose on the property and assess a guarantor for any payments due under the loan. A lender also may make a claim against the assets of any general partner in a partnership to which debt is issued, without regard to whether the partner has guaranteed the debt.

Recovery of capital doctrine. When a taxable sale or exchange occurs, the seller may be permitted to recover his or her investment (or other adjusted basis) in the property before gain or loss is recognized.

Redemption to pay death taxes. Sale or exchange treatment is available relative to this type of stock redemption, to the extent of the proceeds up to the total amount paid by the estate or heir for estate/inheritance taxes and administration expenses. The stock value must exceed 35 percent of the value of the decedent's adjusted gross estate. In meeting this test, shareholdings in corporations where the decedent held at least 20 percent of the outstanding shares are combined. § 303.

Refundable credits. A credit that is paid to the taxpayer even if the amount of the credit (or credits) exceeds the taxpayer's tax liability.

Regular corporations. See *C corporation.*

Rehabilitation expenditures credit. A credit that is based on expenditures incurred to rehabilitate industrial and commercial buildings and certified historic structures. The credit is intended to discourage businesses from moving from older, economically distressed areas to newer locations and to encourage the preservation of historic structures. § 47.

Related party. Various Code Sections define related parties and often include a variety of persons within this (usually detrimental) category. Generally, related parties are accorded different tax treatment from that applicable to other taxpayers who enter into similar transactions. For instance, realized losses that are generated between related parties are not recognized in the year of the loss. However, these deferred losses can be used to offset recognized gains that occur upon the subsequent sale of the asset to a nonrelated party. Other uses of a related-party definition include the conversion of gain upon the sale of a depreciable asset into all ordinary income (§ 1239) and the identification of constructive ownership of stock relative to corporate distributions, redemptions, liquidations, reorganizations, and compensation.

Related-party transactions. The tax law places restrictions upon the recognition of gains and losses between related parties because of the potential for abuse. For example, restrictions are placed on the deduction of losses from the sale or exchange of property between related parties. In addition, under certain circumstances, related-party gains that would otherwise be classified as capital gain are classified as ordinary income. §§ 267, 707(b), and 1239.

Rental activity. Any activity where payments are received principally for the use of tangible property is a rental activity. Temporary Regulations provide that in certain circumstances, activities involving rentals of real and personal property are not to be treated as rental activities. The Temporary Regulations list six exceptions.

Reorganization. Any corporate restructuring, including when one corporation acquires another, a single corporation divides into two or more entities, a corporation makes a substantial change in its capital structure, a corporation undertakes a change in its legal name or domicile, or a corporation goes through a bankruptcy proceeding and continues to exist. The exchange of stock and other securities in a corporate reorganization can be effected favorably for tax purposes if certain statutory requirements are followed strictly. Tax consequences include the nonrecognition of any gain that is realized by the shareholders except to the extent of boot received. § 368.

Report of Foreign Bank and Financial Accounts (FBAR). FinCEN Form 114, Report of Foreign Bank and Financial Accounts (FBAR), must be filed by individuals and some businesses if they have foreign bank, brokerage, or similar accounts where at any time during the calendar year the aggregate balance exceeds $10,000. The form is filed electronically with the U.S. Department of the Treasury and is due by April 15 with an automatic extension to October 15. Significant penalties apply for failure to file the FBAR. The form is not attached to the income tax return (it is separately filed), but any interest earned by the foreign accounts is generally included in the account holder's U.S. taxable income.

Required taxable year. A partnership or limited liability company must use a required tax year as its tax accounting period, or one of three allowable alternative tax year-ends. If there is a common tax year used by owners holding a majority of the entity's capital or profits interests or if the same year-end is used by all "principal partners" (partners who hold 5 percent or more of the capital or profits interests), then that tax year-end is used by the entity. If neither of the first tests results in an allowable year-end (e.g., because there is no majority partner or because the principal partners do not have the same tax year), then the partnership uses the least aggregate deferral method to determine its tax year. § 706.

Research activities credit. A tax credit whose purpose is to encourage research and development. It consists of three components: the incremental research activities credit, the basic research credit, and the energy credit. The incremental research activities credit is equal to 20 percent of the excess qualified research expenditures over the base amount. The basic research credit is equal to 20 percent of the excess of basic research payments over the base amount. § 41.

Research and experimental expenditures. Costs incurred to develop a product or process for which there exists uncertainty regarding its viability. The Code provides three alternatives for the tax treatment of research and experimentation expenditures. They may be expensed in the year paid or incurred, deferred subject to amortization, or capitalized. If the taxpayer does not elect to expense such costs or to defer them subject to amortization (over 60 months), the expenditures must be capitalized. § 174. In general, research and experimentation expenditures paid or incurred after 2021 must be capitalized and amortized over a five-year period. Some of these expenditures may also qualify the taxpayer for the credit for increasing research activities. § 41.

Reserve method. A method of accounting whereby an allowance is permitted for estimated uncollectible accounts. Actual write-offs are charged to the reserve, and recoveries of amounts previously written off are credited to the reserve. The Code permits only certain financial institutions to use the reserve method. § 166.

Residential rental real estate. Buildings for which at least 80 percent of the gross rents are from dwelling units (e.g., an apartment building). This type of building is distinguished from nonresidential (commercial or industrial) buildings in applying the recapture of depreciation provisions. The term also is relevant in distinguishing between buildings that are eligible for a 27.5-year life versus a 39-year life for MACRS purposes. Generally, residential buildings receive preferential treatment. § 168(e)(2)(A).

Revenue Agent's Report (RAR). A Revenue Agent's Report (RAR) reflects any adjustments made by the agent as a result of an audit of the taxpayer. The RAR is mailed to the taxpayer along with the 30-day letter, which outlines the appellate procedures available to the taxpayer.

Revenue neutrality. A description that characterizes tax legislation when it neither increases nor decreases the total revenue collected by the taxing jurisdiction. Thus, any tax revenue losses are offset by tax revenue gains.

Revenue Procedures. A matter of procedural importance to both taxpayers and the IRS concerning the administration of the tax laws is issued as a Revenue Procedure (abbreviated Rev.Proc.). A Revenue Procedure is published in an *Internal Revenue Bulletin* (I.R.B.).

Revenue Rulings. A Revenue Ruling (abbreviated Rev.Rul.) is issued by the National Office of the IRS to express an official interpretation of the tax law as applied to specific transactions. It is more limited in application than a Regulation. A Revenue Ruling is published in an *Internal Revenue Bulletin* (I.R.B.).

Reversionary interest. The trust property that reverts to the grantor after the expiration of an intervening income interest. Assume that Phil places real estate in trust with income to Junior for 11 years and that upon the expiration of this term, the property returns to Phil. Under these circumstances, Phil holds a reversionary interest in the property. A reversionary interest is the same as a remainder interest, except that, in the latter case, the property passes to someone other than the original owner (e.g., the grantor of a trust) upon the expiration of the intervening interest.

Roth IRA. See *Individual Retirement Accounts (IRAs)*.

S

S corporation. The designation for a corporation that elects to be taxed similarly to a partnership. See also *Subchapter S*.

Sale or exchange. A requirement for the recognition of capital gain or loss. Generally, the seller of property must receive money or relief from debt to have sold the property. An exchange involves the transfer of property for other property. Thus, collection of a debt is neither a sale nor an exchange. The term *sale or exchange* is not defined by the Code.

Sales factor. The proportion of a multistate corporation's total sales that is traceable to a specific state. Used in determining the taxable income that is to be apportioned to that state.

Sales tax. A state- or local-level tax on the retail sale of specified property. Generally, the purchaser pays the tax, but the seller collects it, as an agent for the government. Various taxing jurisdictions allow exemptions for purchases of specific items, including certain food, services, and manufacturing equipment. If the purchaser and seller are in different states, a use tax usually applies.

Salvage value. The estimated amount a taxpayer will receive upon the disposition of an asset used in the taxpayer's trade or business. Salvage value is relevant in calculating depreciation under § 167, but is not relevant in calculating cost recovery under § 168.

Schedule K–1. A tax information form prepared for each partner in a partnership, each shareholder of an S corporation, and some beneficiaries of certain trusts. The Schedule K–1 reports the owner's share of the entity's ordinary income or loss from operations as well as the owner's share of separately stated items, along with any other information the partner, shareholder, or beneficiary needs to prepare the return.

Schedule M–1. On the Form 1120, a reconciliation of book net income with Federal taxable income. Accounts for temporary and permanent differences in the two computations, such as depreciation differences, exempt income, and nondeductible items. On Forms 1120S and 1065, the Schedule M–1 reconciles book income with the owners' aggregate taxable income.

Schedule M–3. An *expanded* reconciliation of book net income with Federal taxable income (see *Schedule M–1*). Required of C and S corporations and partnerships/LLCs with total assets of $10 million or more.

Scholarship. Scholarships are generally excluded from the gross income of the recipient unless the payments are a disguised form of compensation for services rendered. However, the Code imposes restrictions on the exclusion. The recipient must be a degree candidate. The excluded amount is limited to amounts used for tuition, fees, books, supplies, and equipment required for courses of instruction. Amounts received for room and board are not eligible for the exclusion. § 117.

Section 121 exclusion. If a residence has been owned and used by the taxpayer as the principal residence for at least two years during the five-year period ending on the date of sale, up to $250,000 of realized gain is excluded from gross income. For a married couple filing a joint return, the $250,000 is increased to $500,000 if either spouse satisfies the ownership requirement and both spouses satisfy the use requirement.

Section 179 expensing. The ability to deduct the cost of qualified property in the year the property is placed in service rather than over the asset's useful life or cost recovery period. The annual ceiling on the deduction is $1,080,000 in 2022 ($1,050,000 in 2021). However, the deduction is reduced dollar for dollar when § 179 property placed in service during the taxable year exceeds $2,700,000 ($2,620,000 in 2021). In addition, the amount expensed under § 179 cannot exceed the aggregate amount of taxable income derived from the conduct of any trade or business by the taxpayer.

Section 179 expensing election. See *Section 179 expensing*.

Section 338 election. When a corporation acquires at least 80 percent of a subsidiary within a 12-month period, it can elect to treat the acquisition of such stock as an asset purchase. The acquiring corporation's basis in the subsidiary's assets then is the cost of the stock. The subsidiary is deemed to have sold its assets for an amount equal to the grossed-up basis in its stock.

Section 382 limitation. When one corporation acquires another, the acquiring corporation's ability to use the loss and credit carryovers of the target may be limited by this anti-abuse provision. For instance, the maximum NOL deduction available to the acquiring is the value of the target when acquired times the long-term tax-exempt interest rate on that date.

Section 401(k) plan. A cash or deferred arrangement plan that allows participants to elect to receive up to $20,500 ($27,000 if age 50 or above) in 2022 in cash (taxed currently) or to have a contribution made on their behalf to a qualified retirement plan (excludible from gross income). The plan may be in the form of a salary reduction agreement between the participant and the employer.

Section 704(b) book capital accounts. Capital accounts calculated as described under Reg. § 1.704–1(b)(2)(iv). All partnerships must maintain § 704(b) book capital accounts for the partners with the intent that final liquidating distributions are in accordance with these capital account balances. Partnership allocations will not be accepted unless they are properly reflected in the partners' § 704(b) book capital accounts. These capital accounts are a hybrid of book and tax accounting methods. They reflect contributions and distributions of property at their fair market values, but the capital accounts are otherwise generally increased by the partnership's tax-basis income and decreased by tax-basis deductions (as reported on the partner's Schedule K–1). Liabilities are only reflected in these capital accounts to the extent the partnership assumes a partner's liability [reduces that partner's § 704(b) book capital account] or a partner assumes a partnership liability [increases that partner's § 704(b) book capital account]. See also *capital account maintenance* and *economic effect test*.

Section 754 election. An election that may be made by a partnership to adjust the basis of partnership assets to reflect a purchasing partner's outside basis in interest or to reflect a gain, loss, or basis adjustment of a partner receiving a distribution from a partnership. The intent of the election is to maintain the equivalence between outside and inside bases for the purchasing partner (in the case of a sale of a partnership interest) or the remaining partners in the partnership (in the case of a distribution that changes the balance of inside and outside bases). Once the election is made, the partnership must make basis adjustments for all future transactions, unless the IRS consents to revoke the election.

Section 1231 gains and losses. If the combined gains and losses from the taxable dispositions of § 1231 assets plus the net gain from business involuntary conversions (of both § 1231 assets and long-term capital assets) result in a gain, the gains and losses are treated as long-term capital gains and losses. In arriving at § 1231 gains, however, the depreciation recapture provisions (e.g., § 1245) are applied first to produce ordinary income. If the net result of the combination is a loss, the gains and losses from § 1231 assets are treated as ordinary gains and losses. § 1231(a).

Section 1231 lookback. For gain to be classified as § 1231 gain, the gain must survive the § 1231 lookback. To the extent of nonrecaptured § 1231 losses for the five prior tax years, the gain is classified as ordinary income. § 1231(c).

Section 1231 property. Depreciable assets and real estate used in trade or business and held for the required long-term holding period. § 1231(b).

Section 1244 stock. Stock issued under § 1244 by qualifying small business corporations. If § 1244 stock becomes worthless, the shareholders may claim an ordinary loss rather than the usual capital loss, within statutory limitations.

Section 1245 property. Property that is subject to the recapture of depreciation under § 1245. For a definition of § 1245 property, see § 1245(a)(3).

Section 1245 recapture. Upon a taxable disposition of § 1245 property, all depreciation claimed on the property is recaptured as ordinary income (but not to exceed any recognized gain from the disposition).

Section 1250 property. Real estate that is subject to the recapture of depreciation under § 1250. For a definition of § 1250 property, see § 1250(c).

Section 1250 recapture. Upon a taxable disposition of § 1250 property, accelerated depreciation or cost recovery claimed on the property may be recaptured as ordinary income.

Securities. Stock, debt, and other financial assets. To the extent securities other than the stock of the transferee corporation are received in a § 351 exchange, the new shareholder recognizes a gain. For purposes of corporate reorganizations, securities are generally debt with terms longer than 10 years. To the extent stock and securities are transferred in a corporate reorganization under § 368, no gain or loss is recognized.

Self-employment tax. A tax of 12.4 percent is levied on individuals with net earnings from self-employment (up to $147,000 in 2022) to provide Social Security benefits (i.e., the old age, survivors, and disability insurance portion) for such individuals. In addition, a tax of 2.9 percent is levied on individuals with net earnings from self-employment (with no statutory ceiling) to provide Medicare benefits (i.e., the hospital insurance portion) for such individuals. If a self-employed individual also receives wages from an employer that are subject to FICA, the self-employment tax will be reduced. A partial deduction is allowed in calculating the self-employment tax. Individuals with net earnings of $400 or more from self-employment are subject to this tax. §§ 1401 and 1402.

Separate foreign tax credit income categories. The foreign tax credit of a taxpayer is computed for each of several types of income sources, as specified by the Code to limit the results of tax planning. FTC income "baskets" include general and passive. The FTC for the year is the sum of the credits as computed within all of the taxpayer's separate FTC baskets used for the tax year.

Separate return limitation year (SRLY). A series of rules limits the amount of an acquired corporation's net operating loss carryforwards that can be used by the acquiror. Generally, a consolidated return can include the acquiree's net operating loss carryforward only to the extent of the lesser of the subsidiary's (1) current-year or (2) cumulative positive contribution to consolidated taxable income.

Separately stated items. Any item of a partnership or an S corporation that might be taxed differently to any two owners of the entity. These amounts are not included in the ordinary income of the entity, but are instead reported separately to the owners; tax consequences are determined at the owner level.

Severance taxes. A tax imposed upon the extraction of natural resources.

Short period. See *short taxable year.*

Short sale. A sale that occurs when a taxpayer sells borrowed property (usually stock) and repays the lender with substantially identical property either held on the date of the short sale or purchased after the sale. No gain or loss is recognized until the short sale is closed, and such gain or loss is generally short term. § 1233.

Short taxable year. A tax year that is less than 12 months. A short taxable year may occur in the initial reporting period, in the final tax year, or when the taxpayer changes tax years. Special income tax computations may be required.

Significant participation activity. Seven tests determine whether an individual has achieved material participation in an activity, one of which is based on more than 500 hours of participation in significant participation activities. A significant participation activity is one in which the individual's participation exceeds 100 hours during the year. Temp.Reg. § 1.469–5T.

Simple trust. Trusts that are not complex trusts. Such trusts may not have a charitable beneficiary, accumulate income, or distribute corpus.

Simplified employee pension (SEP) plans. An employer may make contributions to an employee's IRA in amounts not exceeding the lesser of 15 percent of compensation or $61,000 ($67,500 if age 50 or above) per individual in 2022. These employer-sponsored simplified employee pensions are permitted only if the contributions are nondiscriminatory and are made on behalf of all employees who have attained age 21 and have worked for the employer during at least three of the five preceding calendar years. § 219(b).

Small business corporation. A corporation that satisfies the definition of § 1361(b), § 1244(c), or both. Satisfaction of § 1361(b) permits an S election, and satisfaction of § 1244 enables the shareholders of the corporation to claim an ordinary loss on the worthlessness of stock.

Small business stock (§ 1244 stock). See *Section 1244 stock.*

Small Cases Division. A division within the U.S. Tax Court where jurisdiction is limited to claims of $50,000 or less. There is no appeal from this court.

Solicitation of orders. A level of activity brought about by the taxpayer within a specific state. Under Public Law 86–272, certain types of solicitation activities do not create nexus with the state. Exceeding mere solicitation, though, creates nexus.

Special allocation. Any amount for which an agreement exists among the partners of a partnership outlining the method used for spreading the item among the partners.

Special use value. Permits the executor of an estate to value, for estate tax purposes, real estate used in a farming activity or in connection with a closely held business at its current use value rather than at its most suitable or optimal use value. Under this option, a farm is valued for farming purposes even though, for example, the property might have a higher potential value as a shopping center. For the executor of an estate to elect special use valuation, the conditions of § 2032A must be satisfied.

Specific charge-off method. A method of accounting for bad debts in which a deduction is permitted only when an account becomes partially or completely worthless.

Specified service trade or business. For purposes of the deduction for qualified business income, a specified service trade or business includes those involving the performance of services in certain fields, including health, law, accounting, actuarial science, performing arts, consulting, athletics, financial services, and brokerage services; services consisting of investing and investment management, trading or dealing in securities, partnership interests, or commodities; and any trade or business where the business's principal asset is the reputation of one or more of its employees or owners. § 199A(d)(2).

Spin-off. A type of reorganization where, for example, Apple Corporation transfers some assets to Core Corporation in exchange for Core stock representing control. Apple then distributes the Core stock to its shareholders.

Split-off. A type of reorganization where, for example, Apple Corporation transfers some assets to Core Corporation in exchange for Core stock representing control. Apple then distributes the Core stock to its shareholders in exchange for some of their Apple stock. Not all shareholders need to exchange stock.

Split-up. A type of reorganization where, for example, Firefly Corporation transfers some assets to Fire Corporation and the remainder to Fly Corporation. In return, Firefly receives enough Fire and Fly stock representing control of each corporation. Firefly then distributes the Fire and Fly stock to its shareholders in return for all of their Firefly stock. Firefly then liquidates, and its shareholders now have control of Fire and Fly.

Sprinkling trust. When a trustee has the discretion to either distribute or accumulate the entity accounting income of the trust and to distribute it among the trust's income beneficiaries in varying magnitudes. The trustee can "sprinkle" the income of the trust.

Standard deduction. The individual taxpayer can either itemize deductions or take the standard deduction. The amount of the standard deduction depends on the taxpayer's filing status (single, head of household, married filing jointly, surviving spouse, or married filing separately). For 2022, the amount of the standard deduction ranges from $12,950 (for single) to $25,900 (for married, filing jointly). Additional standard deductions of either $1,400 (for married taxpayers) or $1,750 (for single taxpayers) are available if the taxpayer is blind or age 65 or over. Limitations exist on the amount of the standard deduction of a taxpayer who is another taxpayer's dependent. The standard deduction amounts are adjusted for inflation each year. § 63(c).

Startup expenditures. Expenditures paid or incurred prior to the beginning of the business that would have been deductible as an ordinary and necessary business expense if business operations had begun. Examples of such expenditures include advertising; salaries and wages; travel and other expenses incurred in lining up prospective distributors, suppliers, or customers; and salaries and fees to executives, consultants, and professional service providers. A taxpayer will immediately expense the first $5,000 (subject to phaseout) of startup expenditures and amortize the balance over a period of 180 months, unless the taxpayer elects not to do so. § 195.

Statute of limitations. Provisions of the law that specify the maximum period of time in which action may be taken concerning a past event. Code §§ 6501–6504 contain the limitation periods applicable to the IRS for additional assessments, and §§ 6511–6515 relate to refund claims by taxpayers.

Statutory employees. Statutory employees are considered self-employed independent contractors for purposes of reporting income and expenses on their tax returns. Generally, a statutory employee must meet three tests:

- It is understood from a service contract that the services will be performed by the person.
- The person does not have a substantial investment in facilities (other than transportation used to perform the services).
- The services involve a continuing relationship with the person for whom they are performed.

For further information on statutory employees, see Circular E, *Employer's Tax Guide* (IRS Publication 15).

Statutory tax rate. The statutory tax rate is the tax rate (or rates) specified in the law. For example, § 11 provides that the income tax rate for corporations is 21 percent.

Step down. See *step-down in basis.*

Step transaction. Disregarding one or more transactions to arrive at the final result. Assume, for example, Beta Corporation creates Alpha Corporation by transferring assets desired by Beta's sole shareholder, Carl. Carl then causes Alpha to liquidate to obtain the assets. Under these circumstances, the IRS may contend that the creation and liquidation of Alpha be disregarded. What really happened was a dividend distribution from Beta to Carl.

Step up. See *step-up in basis.*

Step-down in basis. A reduction in the tax basis of property. See also *step-up in basis.*

Step-up in basis. An increase in the income tax basis of property. In an estate context, a step-up in basis occurs when a decedent dies owning appreciated property. Because the estate or heir acquires a basis in the property equal to the property's fair market value on the date of death (or alternate valuation date if available and elected), any appreciation is not subject to the income tax. Thus, a step-up in basis is the result, with no immediate income tax consequences. In the partnership context, a step-up arises when a § 754 election is in effect and when one of several transactions arises: (1) a partner purchases a partnership interest for an amount that exceeds the partner's share of the partnership's inside basis, (2) the partner recognizes a gain on a distribution of cash from the partnership, or (3) a partner takes a basis in a distributed asset that is less than the partnership's basis in that asset. In the opposite situations (e.g., loss recognition or where a partner takes a basis in a distributed asset that exceeds the partnership's basis in that asset), a step-down can arise. See also *step-down in basis.*

Stock bonus plan. A type of deferred compensation plan in which the employer establishes and maintains the plan and contributes employer stock to the plan for the benefit of employees. The contributions need not be dependent on the employer's profits. Any benefits of the plan are distributable in the form of employer stock, except that distributable fractional shares may be paid in cash.

Stock dividend. Not taxable if pro rata distributions of stock or stock rights on common stock. Section 305 governs the taxability of stock dividends and sets out five exceptions to the general rule that stock dividends are nontaxable.

Stock option. The right to purchase a stated number of shares of stock from a corporation at a certain price within a specified period of time. §§ 421 and 422.

Stock redemption. A corporation buys back its own stock from a specified shareholder. Typically, the corporation recognizes any realized gain on the noncash assets that it uses to effect a redemption, and the shareholder obtains a capital gain or loss upon receipt of the purchase price.

Stock rights. Assets that convey to the holder the power to purchase corporate stock at a specified price, often for a limited period of time. Stock rights received may be taxed as a distribution of earnings and profits. After the right is exercised, the basis of the acquired share includes the investor's purchase price or gross income, if any, to obtain the right. Disposition of the right also can be taxable.

Subchapter S. Sections 1361–1379 of the Internal Revenue Code. An elective provision permitting certain small business corporations (§ 1361) and their shareholders (§ 1362) to elect to be treated for income tax purposes in accordance with the operating rules of §§ 1363–1379. S corporations usually avoid the corporate income tax, and corporate losses can be claimed by the shareholders.

Subpart F income. Certain types of income earned by a controlled foreign corporation that are included in U.S. gross income by U.S. shareholders of such an entity as they are generated, not when they are repatriated. See § 951.

Substance over form. A standard used when one must ascertain the true reality of what has occurred. Suppose, for example, a father sells stock to his daughter for $1,000. If the stock is really worth $50,000 at the time of the transfer, the substance of the transaction is probably a gift to her of $49,000.

Substantial authority. Taxpayer and tax preparer understatement penalties are waived where substantial authority existed for the disputed position taken on the return.

Substantial basis reduction. Arises when the partnership makes a liquidating distribution to a partner (under § 736) and the distributee partner recognizes a loss (or has a basis increase for the distributed assets) of at least $250,000. (The second situation would arise when the basis of the assets the liquidated partner receives must be stepped up to absorb all remaining partnership interest basis.) If there is a substantial basis reduction, the partnership is required to make a downward adjustment to the basis of its assets, even if the partnership does not have a § 754 election in effect. This adjustment is treated as a § 754 adjustment related to a distribution and so is allocated to the basis of all remaining partnership assets (except for cash). See also *substantial built-in loss* and *§ 754 election*.

Substantial built-in loss. Arises when a partner sells a partnership interest (under § 741) and the selling partner recognizes a loss on the sale of at least $250,000. In addition, a substantial built-in loss arises if the selling partner would be allocated more than a $250,000 loss if all partnership assets were sold (after considering special allocations). If there is a substantial built-in loss, the partnership is required to make a downward adjustment in the basis of its assets, even if the partnership does not have a § 754 election in effect. This adjustment is treated as a § 754 adjustment related to a sale of a partnership interest and so is allocated to the purchasing partner. See also *substantial basis reduction* and *§ 754 election*.

Substantially appreciated inventory. In partnership taxation, for purposes of the regular distribution rules and distributions under § 736, a distribution of inventory is only treated as a hot asset if it is substantially appreciated, meaning the fair market value of the inventory exceeds 120 percent of its basis. See *appreciated inventory*.

Sunset provision. A provision attached to new tax legislation that will cause such legislation to expire at a specified date. Sunset provisions are attached to tax cut bills for long-term budgetary reasons to make their effect temporary. Once the sunset provision comes into play, the tax cut is rescinded and former law is reinstated. An example of a sunset provision is contained in the Tax Relief Reconciliation Act of 2001 that related to the estate tax. After the estate tax was phased out in 2010, a sunset provision called for the reinstatement of the estate tax as of January 1, 2011.

Surviving spouse. When a husband or wife predeceases the other spouse, the survivor is known as a surviving spouse. Under certain conditions, a surviving spouse may be entitled to use the income tax rates in § 1(a) (those applicable to married persons filing a joint return) for the two years after the year of death of his or her spouse. § 2(a).

Syndication costs. Incurred in promoting and marketing partnership interests for sale to investors. Examples include legal and accounting fees, printing costs for prospectus and placement documents, and state registration fees. These items are capitalized by the partnership as incurred, with no amortization thereof allowed.

T

Tax avoidance. The minimization of one's tax liability by taking advantage of legally available tax planning opportunities. Tax avoidance can be contrasted with tax evasion, which entails the reduction of tax liability by illegal means.

Tax basis capital account. Capital accounts calculated using the tax rules by which the Form 1065 income, expenses, gains, and losses are reported. Beginning in tax year 2020, all partnerships must report partners' capital on Schedules K–1 using the tax method. These capital accounts reflect contributions and distributions of property at their tax (generally carryover) basis. Capital accounts are otherwise generally increased by the partnership's tax-basis income and decreased by tax-basis deductions. Liabilities are not included in the partners' tax basis capital accounts. See also *§ 704(b) book capital accounts*.

Tax benefit rule. A provision that limits the recognition of income from the recovery of an expense or a loss properly deducted in a prior tax year to the amount of the deduction that generated a tax saving. Assume that last year Gary had medical expenses of $4,000 and adjusted gross income of $30,000. Because of the AGI limitation, Gary could deduct only $1,000 of these expenses [$4,000 − (10% × $30,000)]. If this year Gary is reimbursed in full by his insurance company for the $4,000 of expenses, the tax benefit rule limits the amount of income from the reimbursement to $1,000 (the amount previously deducted with a tax saving).

Tax credits. Amounts that directly reduce a taxpayer's tax liability. The tax benefit received from a tax credit is not dependent on the taxpayer's marginal tax rate, whereas the benefit of a tax deduction or exclusion is dependent on the taxpayer's tax bracket.

Tax evasion. The reduction of taxes by the use of subterfuge or fraud or other nonlegal means. For example, a cash basis taxpayer tries to increase his or her charitable contribution deduction by prepaying next year's church pledge with a pre-dated check issued in the following year.

Tax haven. A country in which either locally sourced income or residents of the country are subject to a low rate of taxation.

Tax preparer. One who prepares tax returns for compensation. A tax preparer must register with the IRS and receive a special ID number to practice before the IRS and represent taxpayers before the agency in tax audit actions. The conduct of a tax preparer is regulated under Circular 230. Tax preparers also are subject to penalties for inappropriate conduct when working in the tax profession.

Tax Rate Schedules. Rate schedules that are used by upper-income taxpayers and those not permitted to use the tax table. Separate rate schedules are provided for married individuals filing jointly, heads of households, single taxpayers, estates and trusts, and married individuals filing separate returns. § 1.

Tax research. The method used to determine the best available solution to a situation that possesses tax consequences. Both tax and nontax factors are considered.

Tax shelters. The typical tax shelter generated large losses in the early years of the activity. Investors would offset these losses against other types of income and therefore avoid paying income taxes on this income. These tax shelter investments could then be sold after a few years and produce capital gain income, which is taxed at a lower rate compared to ordinary income. The passive activity loss rules and the at-risk rules now limit tax shelter deductions.

Tax Table. A table that is provided for taxpayers with less than $100,000 of taxable income. Separate columns are provided for single taxpayers, married taxpayers filing jointly, heads of households, and married taxpayers filing separately. § 3.

Tax treaties. An agreement between the U.S. Department of State and another country designed to alleviate double taxation of income and asset transfers, and to share administrative information useful to tax agencies in both countries. The United States has income tax treaties with almost 70 countries and transfer tax treaties with about 20.

Taxable estate. The taxable estate is the gross estate of a decedent reduced by the deductions allowed by §§ 2053–2057 (e.g., administration expenses, marital and charitable deductions). The taxable estate is subject to the unified transfer tax at death. § 2051.

Taxable gift. The amount of a gift that is subject to the unified transfer tax. Thus, a taxable gift has been adjusted by the annual exclusion and other appropriate deductions (e.g., marital and charitable). § 2053.

Taxable year. The annual period over which income is measured for income tax purposes. Most individuals use a calendar year, but many businesses use a fiscal year based on the natural business year. Certain entities, including S corporations, have a required taxable year. §§ 441, 706, and 1378.

Technical Advice Memoranda (TAM). TAMs are issued by the IRS in response to questions raised by IRS field personnel during audits. They deal with completed rather than proposed transactions and are often requested for questions related to exempt organizations and employee plans.

Temporary differences. Under ASC 740 (SFAS 109), tax-related items that appear in the entity's financial statements and its tax return, but in different time periods. For instance, doubtful accounts receivable often create a temporary book-tax difference, as a bad debt reserve is used to compute an expense for financial reporting purposes, but a bad debt often is deductible only under the specific write-off rule for tax purposes, and the difference observed for the current period creates a temporary difference.

Temporary Regulations. A Regulation issued by the Treasury Department in temporary form. When speed is critical, the Treasury Department issues Temporary Regulations that take effect immediately. These Regulations have the same authoritative value as Final Regulations and may be cited as precedent for three years. Temporary Regulations are also issued as proposed Regulations.

Tenants by the entirety. Essentially, a joint tenancy between husband and wife.

Tenants in common. A form of ownership where each tenant (owner) holds an undivided interest in property. Unlike a joint tenancy or a tenancy by the entirety, the interest of a tenant in common does not terminate upon that individual's death (there is no right of survivorship). Assume that Tim and Cindy acquire real estate as equal tenants in common. Upon Tim's death, his one-half interest in the property passes to his estate or heirs, not automatically to Cindy.

Terminable interests. An interest in property that terminates upon the death of the holder or upon the occurrence of some other specified event. The transfer of a terminable interest by one spouse to the other may not qualify for the marital deduction. §§ 2056(b) and 2523(b).

Theft losses. A loss from larceny, embezzlement, or robbery. It does not include misplacement of items.

Thin capitalization. When debt owed by a corporation to the shareholders becomes too large in relation to the corporation's capital structure (i.e., stock and shareholder equity), the IRS may contend that the corporation is thinly capitalized. In effect, some or all of the debt is reclassified as equity. The immediate result is to disallow any interest deduction to the corporation on the reclassified debt. To the extent of the corporation's earnings and profits, interest payments and loan repayments on the reclassified debt are treated as dividends to the shareholders.

Thirty-day (30-day) letter. A letter that accompanies an RAR (Revenue Agent's Report) issued as a result of an IRS audit of a taxpayer (or the rejection of a taxpayer's claim for refund). The letter outlines the taxpayer's appeal procedure before the IRS. If the taxpayer does not request any such procedures within the 30-day period, the IRS issues a statutory notice of deficiency (the 90-day letter).

Throwback rule. If there is no income tax in the state to which a sale otherwise would be apportioned, the sale essentially is exempt from state income tax, even though the seller is domiciled in a state that levies an income tax. Nonetheless, if the seller's state has adopted a throwback rule, the sale is attributed to the seller's state and the transaction is subjected to a state-level tax.

Traditional IRA. See *Individual Retirement Accounts (IRAs)*.

Transfer pricing. The process of setting internal prices for transfers of goods and services among related taxpayers. For example, what price should be used when Subsidiary purchases management services from Parent? The IRS can adjust transfer prices when it can show that the taxpayers were attempting to avoid tax by, for example, shifting losses, deductions, or credits from low-tax to high-tax entities or jurisdictions.

Transportation expenses. Expenses that include the cost of transporting the self-employed taxpayer (or employee) from one place to another in the course of business when the taxpayer is not in travel status. For tax years beginning after 2017 and before 2026, only reimbursed transportation expenses are deductible by employees. Commuting expenses are not deductible.

Travel expenses. Expenses that include meals (generally subject to a 50 percent disallowance) and lodging and transportation expenses while away from home in the pursuit of a trade or business (including that of an employee). For tax years beginning after 2017 and before 2026, only reimbursed travel expenses are deductible by employees.

Treaty shopping. An international investor attempts to use the favorable aspects of a tax treaty to his or her advantage, often elevating the form of the transaction over its substance (e.g., by establishing only a nominal presence in the country offering the favorable treaty terms).

Twelve-month (12-month) rule for prepaid expenses. Taxpayers who use the cash method are required to use the accrual method for deducting certain prepaid expenses (i.e., must capitalize the item and can deduct only when used). If a prepayment will not be consumed or expire by the end of the tax year following the year of payment, the prepayment must be capitalized and prorated over the benefit period. Conversely, if the prepayment will be consumed by the end of the tax year following the year of payment, it can be expensed when paid. To obtain the current deduction under the one-year rule, the payment must be a required payment rather than a voluntary payment.

U

UDITPA. The Uniform Division of Income for Tax Purposes Act has been adopted in some form by many of the states. The Act develops criteria by which the total taxable income of a multistate corporation can be assigned to specific states.

Unclaimed property. A U.S. state may have the right to acquire property that has been made available to an individual or legal entity for a fixed period of time, where the claimant has not taken possession of the property after a notice period. Examples of such property that a state could acquire are an uncashed payroll check or an unused gift card.

Unearned income. Income received but not yet earned. Normally, such income is taxed when received, even for accrual basis taxpayers.

Unified transfer tax. Rates applicable to transfers by gift and death made after 1976. § 2001(c).

Unified transfer tax credit. A credit allowed against any unified transfer tax. §§ 2010 and 2505.

Uniform capitalization (UNICAP) rules. Under § 263A, the Regulations provide a set of rules that all taxpayers (regardless of the particular industry) can use to determine the items of cost (and means of allocating those costs) that must be capitalized with respect to the production of tangible property. Small businesses, defined as those with average annual gross receipts in the prior three-year period of $27 million or less, that are not a tax shelter, are not required to use the UNICAP rules.

Unitary approach. See *unitary theory*.

Unitary theory. Sales, property, and payroll of related corporations are combined for nexus and apportionment purposes, and the worldwide income of the unitary entity is apportioned to the state. Subsidiaries and other affiliated corporations found to be part of the corporation's unitary business (because they are subject to overlapping ownership, operation, or management) are included in the apportionment procedure. This approach can be limited if a waters'-edge election is in effect.

Unit-livestock-price method. A method of accounting for the cost of livestock. The livestock are valued using a standard cost of raising an animal with the characteristics of the animals on hand to the same age as those animals.

Unrealized receivables. Amounts earned by a cash basis taxpayer but not yet received. Because of the method of accounting used by the taxpayer, these amounts have a zero income tax basis. When unrealized receivables are distributed to a partner, they generally convert a transaction from nontaxable to taxable or an otherwise capital gain to ordinary income (i.e., as a "hot asset").

Unreasonable compensation. A deduction is allowed for "reasonable" salaries or other compensation for personal services actually rendered. The issue of unreasonable compensation usually is limited to closely held corporations, where the motivation is to pay out profits in some form that is deductible to the corporation. To the extent compensation is "excessive" ("unreasonable"), the distribution could be treated as a dividend, such that no deduction is allowed.

Unreasonable position. A tax preparer penalty is assessed regarding the understatement of a client's tax liability due to a tax return position that is found to be too aggressive. The penalty is avoided if there is substantial authority for the position or if the position is disclosed adequately on the tax return. The penalty equals the greater of $1,000 or one-half of the tax preparer's fee that is traceable to the aggressive position.

Unrecaptured § 1250 gain. Gain from the sale of depreciable real estate held more than one year. The gain is equal to or less than the depreciation taken on such property and is reduced by § 1245 and § 1250 gain. § 1(h)(6).

Unrelated business income (UBI). Income recognized by an exempt organization that is generated from activities not related to the exempt purpose of the entity. For instance, the gift shop located in a hospital may generate unrelated business income. §§ 511 and 512.

Unrelated business income tax (UBIT). Levied on the unrelated business income of an exempt organization.

U.S. Court of Federal Claims. A trial court (court of original jurisdiction) that decides litigation involving Federal tax matters. Appeal from this court is to the Court of Appeals for the Federal Circuit.

U.S. District Court. A trial court for purposes of litigating Federal tax matters. This court allows a jury trial.

U.S. shareholder. For purposes of classification of an entity as a controlled foreign corporation, a U.S. person who owns, or is considered to own, 10 percent or more of the total combined voting power of all classes of voting stock of a foreign corporation. Stock owned directly, indirectly, and constructively is counted for this purpose. § 951(b).

U.S. Supreme Court. The highest appellate court or the court of last resort in the Federal court system and in most states. Only a small number of tax decisions of the U.S. Courts of Appeal are reviewed by the U.S. Supreme Court under its certiorari procedure. The Supreme Court usually grants certiorari to resolve a conflict among the Courts of Appeal (e.g., two or more appellate courts have assumed opposing positions on a particular issue) or when the tax issue is extremely important (e.g., due to the size of the revenue loss to the Federal government).

U.S. Tax Court. One of four trial courts of original jurisdiction that decides litigation involving Federal income, death, or gift taxes. The only trial court where the taxpayer must not first pay the deficiency assessed by the IRS. The Tax Court does not have jurisdiction over a case unless a statutory notice of deficiency (90-day letter) has been issued by the IRS and the taxpayer files the petition for hearing within the time prescribed.

U.S. trade or business. A set of activities that is carried on in a regular, continuous, and substantial manner. A non-U.S. taxpayer is subject to U.S. tax on the taxable income that is effectively connected with a U.S. trade or business.

Use tax. A use tax is designed to complement the sales tax. The use tax has two purposes: to prevent consumers from evading sales tax by purchasing goods outside the state for in-state use, and to provide an equitable taxing environment between in-state and out-of-state retailers. Purchasers of taxable goods or services who were not charged sales tax because the seller did not have *nexus* with the purchaser's state may owe use tax on the purchase.

V

Vacation homes. The Code places restrictions upon taxpayers who rent their residences or vacation homes for part of the tax year. The restrictions may result in a scaling down of expense deductions for the taxpayers. § 280A.

Valuation allowance. Under ASC 740 (SFAS 109), a tax-related item is reported for book purposes only when it is more likely than not that the item actually will be realized. When the "more likely than not" test is failed, a contra-asset account is created to offset some or all of the related deferred tax asset. For instance, if the entity projects that it will not be able to use all of its net operating loss carryforward due to a lack of future taxable income, a valuation allowance is created to reduce the net deferred tax asset that corresponds to the carryforward. If income projections later change and it appears that the carryforward will be used, the valuation allowance is reversed or "released." Creation of a valuation allowance usually increases the current tax expense and thereby reduces current book income, and its release often increases book income in the later reporting period.

Value added tax (VAT). A national sales tax that taxes the increment in value as goods move through the production process. A VAT is much used in the majority of countries but has not yet been incorporated as part of the U.S. Federal tax structure.

Vesting requirements. A qualified deferred compensation arrangement must satisfy a vesting requirement. Under this provision, an employee's right to accrued plan benefits derived from employer contributions must be nonforfeitable in accordance with one of two vesting time period schedules (or two required alternate vesting schedules for certain employer matching contributions).

Voluntary revocation. The owners of a majority of shares in an S corporation elect to terminate the S status of the entity as of a specified date. The day on which the revocation is effective is the first day of the C corporation's tax year.

W

W–2 Wages/Capital Investment Limit. A limitation on the deduction for qualified business income that caps the deduction at the greater of (1) 50 percent of the wages paid by a qualified trade or business or (2) 25 percent of the wages paid by the qualified trade or business plus 2.5 percent of the taxpayer's share of the unadjusted basis of property used in the business that has not been fully depreciated prior to the close of the taxable year. § 199A(b)(2)(B).

Wash sale. A loss from the sale of stock or securities that is disallowed because the taxpayer, within 30 days before or after the sale, has acquired stock or securities substantially identical to those sold. § 1091.

Waters' edge. A limitation on the worldwide scope of the unitary theory. If a corporate waters'-edge election is in effect, the state can consider in the apportionment procedure only the activities that occur within the boundaries of the United States.

Waters'-edge election. See *waters' edge*.

Wherewithal to pay. This concept recognizes the inequity of taxing a transaction when the taxpayer lacks the means with which to pay the tax. Under it, there is a correlation between the imposition of the tax and the ability to pay the tax. It is particularly suited to situations in which the taxpayer's economic position has not changed significantly as a result of the transaction.

Whistleblower Program. An IRS initiative that offers special rewards to informants who provide evidence regarding tax evasion activities of businesses or high-income individuals. More than $2 million of tax, interest, and penalty must be at stake. The reward can reach 30 percent of the tax recovery that is attributable to the whistleblower's information.

Work opportunity tax credit. Employers are allowed a tax credit equal to 40 percent of the first $6,000 of wages (per eligible employee) for the first year of employment. Eligible employees include certain hard-to-employ individuals (e.g., qualified ex-felons, high-risk youth, food stamp recipients, and veterans). The employer's deduction for wages is reduced by the amount of the credit taken. For qualified summer youth employees, the 40 percent rate is applied to the first $3,000 of qualified wages. The credit does not apply to any amount paid to an individual who begins work for the employer after 2025. §§ 51 and 52.

Working condition fringes. A type of fringe benefit received by the employee that is excludible from the employee's gross income. It consists of property or services provided (paid or reimbursed) by the employer for which the employee could take a tax deduction if the employee had paid for them. § 132(d).

Worthless securities. A loss (usually capital) is allowed for a security that becomes worthless during the year. The loss is deemed to have occurred on the last day of the year. Special rules apply to securities of affiliated companies and small business stock. § 165.

Writ of Certiorari. Appeal from a U.S. Court of Appeals to the U.S. Supreme Court is by Writ of Certiorari. The Supreme Court need not accept the appeal and usually does not (*cert. den.*) unless a conflict exists among the lower courts that must be resolved or a constitutional issue is involved.

Appendix D

Table of Code Sections Cited

Appendix E

Present Value and Future Value Tables

Present Value of $1

N/R	1%	2%	3%	4%	5%	6%	7%	8%	9%	10%	11%	12%
1	0.9901	0.9804	0.9709	0.9615	0.9524	0.9434	0.9346	0.9259	0.9174	0.9091	0.9009	0.8929
2	0.9803	0.9612	0.9426	0.9246	0.9070	0.8900	0.8734	0.8573	0.8417	0.8264	0.8116	0.7972
3	0.9706	0.9423	0.9151	0.8890	0.8638	0.8396	0.8163	0.7938	0.7722	0.7513	0.7312	0.7118
4	0.9610	0.9238	0.8885	0.8548	0.8227	0.7921	0.7629	0.7350	0.7084	0.6830	0.6587	0.6355
5	0.9515	0.9057	0.8626	0.8219	0.7835	0.7473	0.7130	0.6806	0.6499	0.6209	0.5935	0.5674
6	0.9420	0.8880	0.8375	0.7903	0.7462	0.7050	0.6663	0.6302	0.5963	0.5645	0.5346	0.5066
7	0.9327	0.8706	0.8131	0.7599	0.7107	0.6651	0.6227	0.5835	0.5470	0.5132	0.4817	0.4523
8	0.9235	0.8535	0.7894	0.7307	0.6768	0.6274	0.5820	0.5403	0.5019	0.4665	0.4339	0.4039
9	0.9143	0.8368	0.7664	0.7026	0.6446	0.5919	0.5439	0.5002	0.4604	0.4241	0.3909	0.3606
10	0.9053	0.8203	0.7441	0.6756	0.6139	0.5584	0.5083	0.4632	0.4224	0.3855	0.3522	0.3220
11	0.8963	0.8043	0.7224	0.6496	0.5847	0.5268	0.4751	0.4289	0.3875	0.3505	0.3173	0.2875
12	0.8874	0.7885	0.7014	0.6246	0.5568	0.4970	0.4440	0.3971	0.3555	0.3186	0.2858	0.2567
13	0.8787	0.7730	0.6810	0.6006	0.5303	0.4688	0.4150	0.3677	0.3262	0.2897	0.2575	0.2292
14	0.8700	0.7579	0.6611	0.5775	0.5051	0.4423	0.3878	0.3405	0.2992	0.2633	0.2320	0.2046
15	0.8613	0.7430	0.6419	0.5553	0.4810	0.4173	0.3624	0.3152	0.2745	0.2394	0.2090	0.1827
16	0.8528	0.7284	0.6232	0.5339	0.4581	0.3936	0.3387	0.2919	0.2519	0.2176	0.1883	0.1631
17	0.8444	0.7142	0.6050	0.5134	0.4363	0.3714	0.3166	0.2703	0.2311	0.1978	0.1696	0.1456
18	0.8360	0.7002	0.5874	0.4936	0.4155	0.3503	0.2959	0.2502	0.2120	0.1799	0.1528	0.1300
19	0.8277	0.6864	0.5703	0.4746	0.3957	0.3305	0.2765	0.2317	0.1945	0.1635	0.1377	0.1161
20	0.8195	0.6730	0.5537	0.4564	0.3769	0.3118	0.2584	0.2145	0.1784	0.1486	0.1240	0.1037

Present Value of an Ordinary Annuity of $1

N/R	1%	2%	3%	4%	5%	6%	7%	8%	9%	10%	11%	12%
1	0.9901	0.9804	0.9709	0.9615	0.9524	0.9434	0.9346	0.9259	0.9174	0.9091	0.9009	0.8929
2	1.9704	1.9416	1.9135	1.8861	1.8594	1.8334	1.8080	1.7833	1.7591	1.7355	1.7125	1.6901
3	2.9410	2.8839	2.8286	2.7751	2.7232	2.6730	2.6243	2.5771	2.5313	2.4869	2.4437	2.4018
4	3.9020	3.8077	3.7171	3.6299	3.5460	3.4651	3.3872	3.3121	3.2397	3.1699	3.1024	3.0373
5	4.8534	4.7135	4.5797	4.4518	4.3295	4.2124	4.1002	3.9927	3.8897	3.7908	3.6959	3.6048
6	5.7955	5.6014	5.4172	5.2421	5.0757	4.9173	4.7665	4.6229	4.4859	4.3553	4.2305	4.1114
7	6.7282	6.4720	6.2303	6.0021	5.7864	5.5824	5.3893	5.2064	5.0330	4.8684	4.7122	4.5638
8	7.6517	7.3255	7.0197	6.7327	6.4632	6.2098	5.9713	5.7466	5.5348	5.3349	5.1461	4.9676
9	8.5660	8.1622	7.7861	7.4353	7.1078	6.8017	6.5152	6.2469	5.9952	5.7590	5.5370	5.3282
10	9.4713	8.9826	8.5302	8.1109	7.7217	7.3601	7.0236	6.7101	6.4177	6.1446	5.8892	5.6502
11	10.3676	9.7868	9.2526	8.7605	8.3064	7.8869	7.4987	7.1390	6.8052	6.4951	6.2065	5.9377
12	11.2551	10.5753	9.9540	9.3851	8.8633	8.3838	7.9427	7.5361	7.1607	6.8137	6.4924	6.1944
13	12.1337	11.3484	10.6350	9.9856	9.3936	8.8527	8.3577	7.9038	7.4869	7.1034	6.7499	6.4235
14	13.0037	12.1062	11.2961	10.5631	9.8986	9.2950	8.7455	8.2442	7.7862	7.3667	6.9819	6.6282
15	13.8651	12.8493	11.9379	11.1184	10.3797	9.7122	9.1079	8.5595	8.0607	7.6061	7.1909	6.8109
16	14.7179	13.5777	12.5611	11.6523	10.8378	10.1059	9.4466	8.8514	8.3126	7.8237	7.3792	6.9740
17	15.5623	14.2919	13.1661	12.1657	11.2741	10.4773	9.7632	9.1216	8.5436	8.0216	7.5488	7.1196
18	16.3983	14.9920	13.7535	12.6593	11.6896	10.8276	10.0591	9.3719	8.7556	8.2014	7.7016	7.2497
19	17.2260	15.6785	14.3238	13.1339	12.0853	11.1581	10.3356	9.6036	8.9501	8.3649	7.8393	7.3658
20	18.0456	16.3514	14.8775	13.5903	12.4622	11.4699	10.5940	9.8181	9.1285	8.5136	7.9633	7.4694

Future Value of $1

N/R	1%	2%	3%	4%	5%	6%	7%	8%	9%	10%	11%	12%
1	1.0100	1.0200	1.0300	1.0400	1.0500	1.0600	1.0700	1.0800	1.0900	1.1000	1.1100	1.1200
2	1.0201	1.0404	1.0609	1.0816	1.1025	1.1236	1.1449	1.1664	1.1881	1.2100	1.2321	1.2544
3	1.0303	1.0612	1.0927	1.1249	1.1576	1.1910	1.2250	1.2597	1.2950	1.3310	1.3676	1.4049
4	1.0406	1.0824	1.1255	1.1699	1.2155	1.2625	1.3108	1.3605	1.4116	1.4641	1.5181	1.5735
5	1.0510	1.1041	1.1593	1.2167	1.2763	1.3382	1.4026	1.4693	1.5386	1.6105	1.6851	1.7623
6	1.0615	1.1262	1.1941	1.2653	1.3401	1.4185	1.5007	1.5869	1.6771	1.7716	1.8704	1.9738
7	1.0721	1.1487	1.2299	1.3159	1.4071	1.5036	1.6058	1.7138	1.8280	1.9487	2.0762	2.2107
8	1.0829	1.1717	1.2668	1.3686	1.4775	1.5938	1.7182	1.8509	1.9926	2.1436	2.3045	2.4760
9	1.0937	1.1951	1.3048	1.4233	1.5513	1.6895	1.8385	1.9990	2.1719	2.3579	2.5580	2.7731
10	1.1046	1.2190	1.3439	1.4802	1.6289	1.7908	1.9672	2.1589	2.3674	2.5937	2.8394	3.1058
11	1.1157	1.2434	1.3842	1.5395	1.7103	1.8983	2.1049	2.3316	2.5804	2.8531	3.1518	3.4785
12	1.1268	1.2682	1.4258	1.6010	1.7959	2.0122	2.2522	2.5182	2.8127	3.1384	3.4985	3.8960
13	1.1381	1.2936	1.4685	1.6651	1.8856	2.1329	2.4098	2.7196	3.0658	3.4523	3.8833	4.3635
14	1.1495	1.3195	1.5126	1.7317	1.9799	2.2609	2.5785	2.9372	3.3417	3.7975	4.3104	4.8871
15	1.1610	1.3459	1.5580	1.8009	2.0789	2.3966	2.7590	3.1722	3.6425	4.1772	4.7846	5.4736
16	1.1726	1.3728	1.6047	1.8730	2.1829	2.5404	2.9522	3.4259	3.9703	4.5950	5.3109	6.1304
17	1.1843	1.4002	1.6528	1.9479	2.2920	2.6928	3.1588	3.7000	4.3276	5.0545	5.8951	6.8660
18	1.1961	1.4282	1.7024	2.0258	2.4066	2.8543	3.3799	3.9960	4.7171	5.5599	6.5436	7.6900
19	1.2081	1.4568	1.7535	2.1068	2.5270	3.0256	3.6165	4.3157	5.1417	6.1159	7.2633	8.6128
20	1.2202	1.4859	1.8061	2.1911	2.6533	3.2071	3.8697	4.6610	5.6044	6.7275	8.0623	9.6463

Future Value of an Ordinary Annuity of $1

N/R	1%	2%	3%	4%	5%	6%	7%	8%	9%	10%	11%	12%
1	1.0000	1.0000	1.0000	1.0000	1.0000	1.0000	1.0000	1.0000	1.0000	1.0000	1.0000	1.0000
2	2.0100	2.0200	2.0300	2.0400	2.0500	2.0600	2.0700	2.0800	2.0900	2.1000	2.1100	2.1200
3	3.0301	3.0604	3.0909	3.1216	3.1525	3.1836	3.2149	3.2464	3.2781	3.3100	3.3421	3.3744
4	4.0604	4.1216	4.1836	4.2465	4.3101	4.3746	4.4399	4.5061	4.5731	4.6410	4.7097	4.7793
5	5.1010	5.2040	5.3091	5.4163	5.5256	5.6371	5.7507	5.8666	5.9847	6.1051	6.2278	6.3528
6	6.1520	6.3081	6.4684	6.6330	6.8019	6.9753	7.1533	7.3359	7.5233	7.7156	7.9129	8.1152
7	7.2135	7.4343	7.6625	7.8983	8.1420	8.3938	8.6540	8.9228	9.2004	9.4872	9.7833	10.0890
8	8.2857	8.5830	8.8923	9.2142	9.5491	9.8975	10.2598	10.6366	11.0285	11.4359	11.8594	12.2997
9	9.3685	9.7546	10.1591	10.5828	11.0266	11.4913	11.9780	12.4876	13.0210	13.5795	14.1640	14.7757
10	10.4622	10.9497	11.4639	12.0061	12.5779	13.1808	13.8164	14.4866	15.1929	15.9374	16.7220	17.5487
11	11.5668	12.1687	12.8078	13.4864	14.2068	14.9716	15.7836	16.6455	17.5603	18.5312	19.5614	20.6546
12	12.6825	13.4121	14.1920	15.0258	15.9171	16.8699	17.8885	18.9771	20.1407	21.3843	22.7132	24.1331
13	13.8093	14.6803	15.6178	16.6268	17.7130	18.8821	20.1406	21.4953	22.9534	24.5227	26.2116	28.0291
14	14.9474	15.9739	17.0863	18.2919	19.5986	21.0151	22.5505	24.2149	26.0192	27.9750	30.0949	32.3926
15	16.0969	17.2934	18.5989	20.0236	21.5786	23.2760	25.1290	27.1521	29.3609	31.7725	34.4054	37.2797
16	17.2579	18.6393	20.1569	21.8245	23.6575	25.6725	27.8881	30.3243	33.0034	35.9497	39.1899	42.7533
17	18.4304	20.0121	21.7616	23.6975	25.8404	28.2129	30.8402	33.7502	36.9737	40.5447	44.5008	48.8837
18	19.6147	21.4123	23.4144	25.6454	28.1324	30.9057	33.9990	37.4502	41.3013	45.5992	50.3959	55.7497
19	20.8109	22.8406	25.1169	27.6712	30.5390	33.7600	37.3790	41.4463	46.0185	51.1591	56.9395	63.4397
20	22.0190	24.2974	26.8704	29.7781	33.0660	36.7856	40.9955	45.7620	51.1601	57.2750	64.2028	72.0524

Index

A

B

C

D

E

F

G

H

I

J

M

N

O

P

Q

R

S

T

U

V

W

Y

AMT Formula for Individuals

Taxable income (increased by any standard deduction taken)
Plus or minus: Adjustments
Plus: Preferences
Equals: Alternative minimum taxable income (AMTI)
Minus: Exemption
Equals: Alternative minimum tax (AMT) base
Multiplied by: 26% or 28% rate
Equals: Tentative minimum tax before foreign tax credit
Minus: AMT foreign tax credit
Equals: Tentative minimum tax (TMT)
Minus: Regular tax liability (less any foreign tax credit)
Equals: AMT (if TMT > regular tax liability)

2021 AMT Exemption and Phaseout for Individuals

		Phaseout	
Filing Status	**Exemption**	**Begins at**	**Ends at**
Married, filing jointly	$114,600	$1,047,200	$1,505,600
Single or Head of household	73,600	523,600	818,000
Married, filing separately	57,300	523,600	752,800

2022 AMT Exemption and Phaseout for Individuals

		Phaseout	
Filing Status	**Exemption**	**Begins at**	**Ends at**
Married, filing jointly	$118,100	$1,079,800	$1,552,200
Single or Head of household	75,900	539,900	843,500
Married, filing separately	59,050	539,900	776,100